SKETCHES

OF

PROMINENT TENNESSEANS.

SKETCHES

OF

PROMINENT TENNESSEANS.

CONTAINING

BIOGRAPHIES AND RECORDS OF MANY OF THE FAMILIES WHO HAVE
ATTAINED PROMINENCE IN TENNESSEE.

COMPILED AND EDITED BY

HON. WILLIAM S. SPEER.

Originally published: Nashville, 1888
Reprinted: Genealogical Publishing Co., Inc.
Baltimore, 2003
Library of Congress Catalogue Card Number 2002114472
International Standard Book Number 0-8063-1715-9
Made in the United States of America

INDEX TO SKETCHES.

PROMINENT TENNESSEANS.

GEN. WILLIAM G. HARDING.

NASHVILLE.

GEN. WILLIAM G. HARDING, the eminent agriculturist and breeder of thoroughbred stock, was born September 15, 1808, in a log cabin, still standing on his present celebrated and magnificent Belle Meade estate, six miles from the city of Nashville. He grew up on that place when the Indians were plentiful in its neighborhood, and it has been his home ever since, except during the six years he engaged in cotton planting on his Stone's river farm. Said he, "I am to the manner born," and alluding to his birthplace he said, "I am a log cabin man." And, indeed, he is a splendid illustration of the virtue of the staying power as a factor of success. He is one of the few men whose personal records appear in this volume, who are now living where they were born, and such men are, as a rule, eminent examples of success in life.

Gen. Harding was educated at the "old field schools" until he was fourteen years old, when he went to the Cumberland College (predecessor of the University of Nashville), under Prof. Philip Lindsley, and there studied two years, displaying the characteristic which foreshadowed his manhood, resolution. He then said to his father, "I want to go off in search of an education, for I cannot get one here, surrounded, as I am, by clever chums, who do not study and will not permit me to study." His father, immersed in a large business, could give neither time nor thought to his son's request, and not comprehending why he could not get an education nearer home, reluctantly yielded to his request, gave him funds, and told him to go to any school he might select. He visited Yale, Harvard, and Princeton, inspecting their methods, and at last found that system, order and studiousness which he was seeking at the American Military Academy, at Middletown, Connecticut, under Capt. Alden Partridge, then having two hundred and fifty students. He had no acquaintances there, and did not want to find any. The absence of acquaintances was to his liking, for those he wanted to form slowly and with proper care. After four years'

stay, he graduated with the highest honors, having attained the first position in the corps of cadets. He returned home, to the great gratification of his father and mother, bringing with him as his guest old Capt. Partridge, this being the latter's first visit to any of the Southern States. Shortly after their arrival they paid a visit to the "Hero of the Hermitage," a man whom Capt. Partridge resembled in many respects. Andrew J. Donelson, the private secretary of President Jackson, was a cadet at West Point when Capt. Partridge was superintendent, prior to his organizing the Military Academy at Middletown. The course of instruction at this institution combining, as it did, the strict systems and accurate methods of military science, was also coupled with literary advantages and interspersed with the thoroughly practical, and consisted of marches over New York, Pennsylvania and Maryland, laying out roads, perfecting engineering plans, drawing canal locks, building of bridges, acqueducts, etc., and was of immense advantage to the young student who, at the age of sixteen, had the audacity to inspect for himself the merits of the oldest and most famous educational institutions of the country.

In attendance at the military academy with young Harding were ex-Gov. Harry Seymour, of Connecticut; ex-Gov. Horatio Seymour, of New York; Iturbide, son of the Emperor of Mexico; Col. M. H. Sandford, of New York; ex-Gov. Hoge, of North Carolina, and many others equally distinguished in the military and civil service of the nation. The only certificate of graduation ever given to Capt. Partridge's own handwriting was to young Harding, and closed with the following words: "I hereby recommend Wm. G. Harding as a scholar, a gentleman and a soldier."

At the age of twenty Gen. Harding married Miss Selene McNairy, the history of whose family is elsewhere given, and commenced life on a tract of six hundred acres and with forty-five dollars in money. There he early displayed those traits of energy, close application to business, and systematic and economical methods which have guided him to eminent success as an agriculturist and breeder of fine stock, and given him a rank among the most distinguished farmers and stockmen in the United States. Remaining on his patrimonial inheritance on Stone's river, engaged in cotton growing, until 1839, he took possession of the Belle Meade estate, then comprising about fourteen hundred acres of land and one hundred and twenty-five slaves of all ages, and here he has resided till the present time, constantly giving his personal attention to his plantation, and adding adjoining acres to the estate, to make room for the increase of his negroes. He was opposed, as his father before him had been, to purchasing slaves, and also opposed to trusting his slaves to the charge of an overseer. Consequently he would never invest in a cotton or sugar plantation, but kept his slaves under his immediate supervision, a course generally thought to be a less profitable method of working slave labor, but by him considered the more humane. During the civil war his slaves remained faithful to him, and a goodly number remain with him at this writing. He cares for them in sickness and in health as formerly. They are a contented, happy set; well fed; well clothed; fat, sleek and merry. An incident is told illustrative of their affection and the delight with which they welcomed their old master's return home in 1862, after he had been confined as a political prisoner at Mackinaw. A number of them met the vehicle in which he was riding a mile from home, took him out of the carriage and carried him, with great exultation, on their shoulders. On arriving at the front yard he wanted to go immediately to see his wife, but they said, " No; old master, you must go first to see Bob " (Bob Green, the faithful groom of the thoroughbred stock, who had been shot by the Federals on account of his faithfulness to his master's interest in his absence), where he was carried, and afterwards returned to his family.

Thus, ever since 1839, he has resided on his farm, Belle Meade, conducting, on the most extensive scale, farming operations and the breeding of blooded stock, and the management of labor with intelligent direction, order and rare good judgment. Particularly has he adhered with great persistence to the rearing of the thoroughbred horse, bringing to bear learning and research, and backing these with great outlay of funds in his breeding and development; and, although he has oftentimes seen his noble products below the price of mules, he has continued to persevere in this branch of animal industry, clinging with tenacity of purpose to his first love, until now, in his declining years, he enjoys the proud satisfaction of knowing that his blood-horse stock has a reputation for excellence second to none in either the old world or the new. This fact is attested by the representatives of the French government in their report on the horses of America to their

government. Such is the result of firm resolution, integrity, fair dealing, and a calm, cool judgment. The time was when he chased foxes, having only an old-fashioned " bit " to his name, but he held to that as a nest egg, and rode without a girth to his saddle until he had a few lambs old enough for sale, when he gave the "bit" to his wife to buy bluings with, and helped the butchers drive the lambs to Nashville.

A commendable pride of character has ever been Gen. Harding's guiding star; but he was never proud in the worldly sense of looking down on any body. He esteems men in every condition of life for their cleverness and goodness of heart and integrity, rather than for great intellect without those noble traits. He is given to large, discriminating charity, of which he has been his own dispenser, never trusting to committees. He is ever ready to assist the industrious of both sexes, but never gives to the drone. He is noted for his generous and elegant hospitality, and at his palatial residence he has entertained nearly every man of prominence that lives in or has visited this section of the United States.

Gen. William H. Jackson, his son-in-law, who has lived with him now sixteen years, says of Gen. Harding: " In his course of conduct and bearing towards his fellow-men he has fulfilled literally the golden rule, more so than any man I have seen, either in or out of the church. As illustrating the difference, I have known him, at a public auction of his colts, to direct the auctioneer to knock the colt off when he had reached a certain price, remarking that that was price enough for any yearling colt; and, again, when a young man, representing a city firm, offered him one dollar and fifty cents per bushel for his wheat, he remarked, ' Young man, I am afraid you are not a judge of wheat after inspecting it. This wheat is not of sufficiently good quality for that price, and you may have it for one dollar and twenty-five cents,' a beautiful commentary upon the grasping, sordid times in which we live. This action on Gen. Harding's part was but natural, when we consider the early associations of his life. He grew up in an age when confidence between man and man was almost universal, the note or bond never required; when good and neighborly feeling was the rule; when neighbor helped neighbor to shuck his corn, roll logs, clear new ground and raise his cabin; when the incarceration of a single prisoner in the log jail at Nashville produced a great ripple of excitement in the public mind, and integrity and fair dealing were the rule with scarcely an exception. He attained the age of fifty years before he believed there was a man in the world who would look him in the face and tell him a lie—a beautiful confidence in his fellow-man, illustrative of the purity and simplicity of his own life. I believe he would suffer death rather than sacrifice a friend or betray a trust confided to him."

All who read the foregoing estimate of Gen. Harding's character by one fully competent to speak, will recognize it as a true picture of a truly noble Tennessean. Such integrity of life could not help producing like effect on those surrounding him. During the war his negroes buried a barrel of solid silverware that had been awarded him at fairs as premiums, and when the danger was over unearthed the treasure and brought it home, every piece of it.

Gen. Harding has lived as he was born, a "dyed in the wool" Democrat of the Old Hickory school. When Tennessee seceded he was appointed a member of the State Military Board, which expended five million dollars in the equipment of the Tennessee soldiery of all arms for the Confederate service. He had no other connection with the war, having been taken prisoner in April, 1862, and released on his parole of honor, which he observed most sacredly until the end of the war. His title came from being elected brigadier-general of militia, about 1838.

Though a leading turfman forty years or more, enjoying the confidence, esteem and high regard of every man of his acquaintance who ever dealt in thoroughbred horses, yet he has been absolutely free from any of the vices attendant upon the race course. He has never wagered a cent on any race, but has at all times taken a broad view of the high and important mission of the thoroughbred horse, which is to improve all of the equine race; and believes that his chief mission is not, as many suppose, to contribute to the amusement and pleasure of the public on the race-course, but subscribing to the idea that without the theater the world would never have known those distinguished delineators of human character in all its phases, so without the race-course—the theater of action and competition of the thoroughbred horse—the intelligent breeders of this animal would never have discovered the most valuable strains of blood to propagate.

Gen. Harding has also been an advanced thinker as an agriculturist, keeping pace with the latest improvements in farming machinery and the most valuable modes for the recuperation and culture of the soil. Occupying through life prominent positions in the different bureaus of agriculture of the State, he has at all times taken an active interest in all measures tending to build up Tennessee. He was the first farmer who ever shipped grain from Tennessee to the Charleston market; the first to ship a load of hay to New Orleans; the first to suggest the idea of building the Nashville & Chattanooga Railroad, opposing the expenditure of our money for the building of roads leading North, believing that we should connect with our natural markets of the South, and let the North expend her own money in reaching our southern connections.

Gen. Harding's father was John Harding, a native of Virginia, who came to Tennessee in 1805, with his father's family, consisting of two daughters (Sallie, who married a Mr. Page, and Patsey, who married

Matthew Johnson), and four sons, besides himself, Giles, William, Thomas, and David Morris, who all became excellent farmers, and were a hardy pioneer race, who did the first clearing in their respective localities, and were noted for their hospitality and fondness for field sports. They were all men of the strictest integrity, truth-tellers, and fair in their dealings, but firm in contending for their rights.

John Harding married in Davidson county, November, 1806, Miss Susannah Shute, daughter of John Shute, a farmer from the vicinity of Carlisle, Pennsylvania, and of German extraction. To this marriage were born Amanda (who married Frank McGavock), William Giles (subject of this sketch), and Elizabeth (who married Joseph Clay). Gen. Harding's father died in September, 1865, at the age of 87; his mother died September 12, 1845, at the age of 60. From a brief biographical sketch of John Harding in the *History of Davidson County*, it appears that he was a warm friend of education, a member of the Christian Church, a prosperous farmer and stock raiser, a large land and slaveholder, and a man of energy, industry and versatility of talents. He purchased the Belle Meade place and built the log cabin in which his distinguished son, the subject of this sketch, was born. No man in this country ever made for himself so high a reputation as a hard and constant worker. Gen. Harding relates of his father that he was the only man, as the imported horse "Priam" was the only horse, whom he never saw resting, alternately, on either leg. No one ever saw him in any position except standing erect or sitting erect. On this remark being repeated to the late venerable Dr. W. K. Bowling, he quietly replied: "Gen. Harding might have said he never saw his father standing on one foot or two, for he was always going." He never took a rocking chair or lounge up to the age of seventy. He was a tall man, six feet high, and of very gentle presence, mild in expression, careful of speech, never going above the mark in assertion. His motto was, "If you had tried a little harder, don't you think you could have got a little further?" He was possessed of indomitable will, and had an iron constitution. At the age of seventy, at one end of a cross-cut saw and the best negro man of two hundred and fifty pounds that he owned at the other, he would go through the toughest tree of five feet in diameter without stopping to blow. At the age of seventy, having cleared up three farms in Tennessee and one in Louisiana, he proceeded to Arkansas with eight hands, and at that advanced age, cleared and put in successful operation a magnificent cotton plantation, near Plum Point Bend, which he gave to his grandson, John McGavock, and for which he was offered and refused one hundred and fifty thousand dollars in gold. In 1860 he returned to Nashville, and lived in his city home, bewildered in his old age by the war. He could never be made to understand how people could take things which did not belong to them. He devoted his old age to the Christian Church, of which he was an honored member, and for many years was its prominent support. His name, wherever known, was the synonym of honorable and upright conduct. Such was John Harding, a factor in the early development of Middle Tennessee, and of more than one of its leading industries. He left his sturdy, vigorous personality impressed upon the memories of thousands of his survivors, and is therefore a Tennessee historic character, more important than hundreds of noisy politicians, his contemporaries, who died and left neither sign nor name. The mother of Gen. Harding was likewise a person of strong character, a lady of marked individuality, exceptionally kind and benevolent, and of proverbial candor. It is reported of her that she would not, out of mere formal courtesy, invite any one to visit her whom she did not want to see again, so great was her devotion to truth. It is easy to see that these virtues of the old family back of Gen. Harding, formed in him a character which is but a reproduction of their own.

Gen. Harding first married in Nashville, November 17, 1829, Miss Selene McNairy, daughter of Nathaniel McNairy, and niece of Dr. Boyd McNairy and Judge John McNairy, of a prominent North Carolina family of Scotch origin. The county of McNairy in Tennessee was named for Judge McNairy. Mrs. Harding's sister, Amanda, is now the widow of James Porter, a merchant of prominence at Nashville, and is a lady remarkable as a business woman and manager of finance. Her youngest sister, Kittie, married John Kirkman, now president of the American National Bank of Nashville. Her mother was Catharine Hobson, of a Virginia family, sister of Nicholas Hobson, noted for his sterling integrity and success as a banker; a man who enjoyed the unlimited confidence of the community; a man of simplicity of character, truthfulness, and kindness of heart. Mrs. Harding was educated at the old Nashville Female Academy, and was a lady of domestic and economical habits, and a member of the Christian Church. She died in 1836, at the age of twenty-four, having borne two children: (1). John, a graduate of the North Carolina University at Chapel Hill; married first Miss Sophia Merritt, daughter of Embry Merritt, of Lawrenceville, Virginia. She died a few years after marriage, leaving one child, Sophia Harding, now the wife of Granville S. Johnson, and mother of two children, William Harding and Morgiana. John Harding next married Mrs. Philip Owen, nee Margaret Murphy, of Mississippi, who bore him three children—Selene McNairy, William Giles, and John. Selene McNairy Harding is now the wife of Prof. Charles P. Curd, of Washington University, St. Louis, author of several educational text-books, and a brilliant man of great promise. They have one child, Hayden T. William Giles married Miss Bessie Caruthers, of Nashville. (2). Nathaniel Mc-

Nairy, Gen. Harding's second son, died at the age of ten years, his death being caused by a fall from a horse.

Gen. Harding's second marriage, which occurred at Franklin, Tennessee, January 2, 1840, was with Miss Elizabeth Irwin McGavock, daughter of Randal McGavock, a large landowner and farmer of Williamson county, and a large holder of city property in Nashville, and the first county clerk of Davidson county. The McGavocks are of Scotch-Irish descent, and are numerous in Williamson and Davidson counties, and in Virginia. Her youngest brother, Col. John McGavock, one of the most prominent citizens of Williamson, is a highly educated gentleman, thoroughly posted in the careers of the public men and measures of the government, and having been the private secretary of Hon. Felix Grundy while at Washington, he is regarded as a typical gentleman of the school of those days. Her mother's sister was the wife of Felix Grundy, and was the lady to whom Washington society deferred in all matters of taste, etiquette and court manners. Mrs. Harding's brother, James R. McGavock, was a fine farmer in Williamson county, possessed of a noble, generous heart, given to large charity and overflowing hospitality; of great sympathy for the struggling masses, the soul of honor, and a general favorite and standard man in his county. He married his first cousin, Miss Louisa Chenault, of Missouri, a lady of sterling qualities, similar to those of her husband, and their sons and daughters are notable likewise for their liberality and hospitality. Mary Cloyd McGavock, Mrs. Harding's sister, married J. B. Southall, a nephew of Gov. Branch, of Florida, and lived in princely style at their house, "Rosemont," three miles from Nashville. Her striking characteristics were a strong will-power, a very highly cultivated intellect, and the highest order of Christian virtues. She gave her only son, Randal McGavock Southall, to the Confederacy, saying, "My son, you are all I have to give to the Southern cause," and placing her hand on his head, added, "Go, with my blessing." Mrs. Harding's mother was Miss Sarah Dougherty Rogers, daughter of John Rogers and Margaret M. Dougherty. Her father was a descendant of John Rogers, the Protestant martyr.

By his marriage with Miss McGavock, Gen. Harding has two children: (1). Selene, born April 5, 1846, at Belle Meade, where her father and her own children were born. She was educated at the Nashville Female Academy under Rev. C. D. Elliott until the war broke out, when she was sent to Philadelphia, where she studied a year in Madame Masse's private French school. She married December 15, 1868, Gen. William H. Jackson, a planter of West Tennessee, whose sketch appears elsewhere in this volume, and has three children, Eunice, William Harding and Selene Harding. (2). Mary Elizabeth, born February 5, 1850, at Belle Meade, educated at Nashville, under Rev. Philip Fall; married Judge Howell E. Jackson, present United

States Senator from Tennessee, and has three children, Bessie, Louise, and Harding Alexander. See Judge Jackson's sketch elsewhere in this volume.

Thus surrounded by his children and his grandchildren, and living upon the goodly inheritance bequeathed him by his father, Gen. Harding has wisely made himself his own executor, and disposed of his large estate among his heirs to their entire satisfaction, and is passing the evening of his life in happiness unalloyed, undisturbed by the cares of business or distress of mind caused by the bad conduct of any of his descendants, and is free from the petulance and little foibles and weaknesses so often attendant upon old age.

His life is gradually passing out smoothly, serenely and quietly, with the consciousness of years well and usefully spent, without a wrong inflicted on his fellowman.

Gen. Harding professed religion under the preaching of Rev. Sam. Jones, in May, 1885, and immediately thereafter connected himself with the Christian church in Nashville, being received into the same by Rev. R. Linn Cave, its pastor.

HON. JAMES W. DEADERICK.

JONESBOROUGH.

THE present Chief Justice of the Supreme Court of Tennessee was born in Jonesborough, Washington county, on the 25th of November, 1812. He is the youngest child of David Deaderick, a native of Winchester, Virginia, who died in 1823, at the age of sixty-five. Judge Deaderick's father was a soldier of the Revolution, and paymaster of a Virginia regiment which served in that war. He moved to Jonesborough at an early day after the close of the war for independence, and was president of the branch of the first bank of the State of Tennessee located in that town. He also at one time represented Washington county in the General Assembly of the State. He was a warm personal friend of Gen. Jackson, who, when Circuit Judge in East Tennessee, made his home at Mr. Deaderick's house. He was one of the most intelligent men of his day; but was chiefly noted for his unswerving integrity in all the relations of life. So marked was this characteristic that no higher praise could be bestowed upon a person than to say, " He is as honest a man as David Deaderick," and this saying as to him passed into a proverb throughout the region in which he lived. During most of his life he was engaged in mercantile pursuits, and a common saying among his patrons was: " We can get as much for our money from him by sending a child as by going ourselves." He was possessed of a vast fund of information, was very fond of reading, and made it a point to give all his children the benefit of the best schools accessible in those early days.

Judge Deaderick's paternal grandfather and grandmother were Germans, who settled in Winchester, Virginia. They retained the German form of the family name, Deitrich—master-key—which has been anglicized into Deaderick by their descendants. Besides the father of Judge Deaderick, this worthy couple had other children, one of whom, Michael Deaderick, settled in Nashville at an early day, as a merchant, and was also president of the old State Bank of Tennessee about 1810. Deaderick street in Nashville was so called in his honor. Another son, Thomas Deaderick, was also among the early settlers of Nashville and one of the pioneer merchants of that city, as was a younger brother, John Deaderick, who was engaged in business with his brothers, but who died quite young. Judge Deaderick's only paternal aunt was the wife of David Murrell, of Lynchburg, Virginia. Of her children, one is a physician of that city, one a tobacco merchant, and another, John Murrell, was at one time a millionaire cotton merchant in New Orleans. The mother of Judge Deaderick, Margaret Anderson, was a native of Delaware, daughter of a Mr. Anderson of a German family. She had six brothers in the Revolutionary army, all of whom were officers. Her oldest brother, Joseph Anderson, was the first United States Senator from Tennessee, and also one of the first federal judges in the State. He was for many years, and up to a short time before his death, Comptroller of the Treasury at Washington, where he died. Another brother, William Anderson, was a Congressman from the State of Delaware. Inslee Anderson, another of the brothers, was killed in one of the battles of the Revolution. Dr. Thomas Anderson, of Tullahoma, Tennessee, is a son of Judge Joseph Anderson, mentioned above. Judge Deaderick's maternal grandmother was an Inslee. His mother died at Jonesborough in 1856, at the advanced age of eighty-five. She was a lady of fine literary tastes, of extensive reading, and possessed a remarkable store of information upon a great variety of subjects. She was by nature kind, affectionate and generous, and a working member of the Presbyterian church. It was truthfully said of her, " No better woman ever lived than she."

In his youth Judge Deaderick enjoyed excellent educational advantages. After a course of primary training at home, he entered East Tennessee College at

Knoxville (now the University of Tennessee), and afterwards Centre College, at Danville, Kentucky, then under the presidency of John C. Young. While at Danville, be became engaged to his wife, and married her before completing his college course, being at the time under twenty years of age. Soon after his marriage he settled at Cheek's Cross-roads, in Jefferson (now Hamblen) county, where he commenced merchandising in 1833, on a limited capital, carrying on a farm at the same time. Generous and confiding, without business experience or knowledge of men, and fond of good living and the manly sports of the day, he soon ran through his moderate patrimony, most of it going to pay security debts for friends for whom he had endorsed. In 1841 he left Cheek's Cross-roads and went to Iowa, under an appointment from President Tyler as Indian agent for the Pottawattomies. He remained there only some six or eight months, when he returned to Jonesborough and commenced the study of law, Judge Luckey lending him books and giving him some instruction. He was admitted to the bar in 1844, at Jonesborough, by Judge Luckey and Chancellor Thomas L. Williams, Judge L. remarking, when he presented himself to be examined for license, "You need no examination." He opened an office at Jonesborough and practiced in that circuit with reasonable success until the close of the civil war. Having been a sympathizer with the South in that unfortunate struggle, he was, after its close, subjected to much trouble and annoyance from the "truly loyal" people of that section, to avoid which he removed, in the spring of 1866, to Bristol, on the Tennessee and Virginia line, where he remained for about a year, when he removed to Knoxville, remaining there until he was elected one of the judges of the Supreme Court in 1870, under the present Constitution of the State, which was adopted in that year. Since his elevation to the Supreme bench he has made his home at Jonesborough.

In the division of parties which prevailed from the time of his majority till the disruption of the old Whig organization, some years prior to the civil war, Judge Deaderick was an ardent follower of the great Harry of the West. After the war he allied himself with the Democratic party, but having been on the bench for most of the time, has taken no active part in politics.

He has frequently occupied public stations, and always with honor to himself and advantage to those whom he served. From 1833 to 1841 he was postmaster at Cheek's Cross-roads, and in the last-named year was agent for the Pottawattomie tribe of Indians. In 1851–52, he was chosen Senator in the General Assembly from the district composed of the counties of Washington, Sullivan, Carter and Johnson. At that session he served as chairman of the committee on internal improvements. This was the session of the Legislature at which the internal improvement act, known as the "omnibus bill," was

passed, which loaned the credit of the State to several railroad companies. The bonds issued under this act and subsequent enactments are the obligations that have entered so largely into the politics and legislation of the State since the war. Judge Deaderick advocated and voted for all the internal improvement measures adopted at that session. In 1860 he was elector on the Bell and Everett ticket for the first congressional district. As before stated, he was elected to the Supreme bench in 1870, and re-elected in 1878. In 1875, upon the death of Chief Justice A. O. P. Nicholson, he was chosen Chief Justice by his associates on the bench, and unanimously re-elected in 1878.

Judge Deaderick is a member of the Presbyterian church—the church of his mother—as are also his wife and all their children. He has never allied himself to but one secret society, the Odd-Fellows, which order he joined in 1845.

He was married at Danville, Kentucky, November 8, 1832, to Miss Adeline McDowell, daughter of Dr. Ephraim McDowell, known in his day as "the great surgeon of Kentucky." Dr. McD. was a Virginian by birth. He studied his profession in Edinburgh, Scotland, and is too well and widely known to need further mention here. He died in 1829, at the age of sixty. Judge Deaderick and his estimable wife, who still survives to bless him in his old age, celebrated their golden wedding in Jonesborough on the 8th of November, 1882. Mrs. Deaderick's mother, Sarah Shelby, the first white female born in Kentucky, was the daughter of Gov. Isaac Shelby. Her death took place at Danville, in that State, where she had always resided, at the age of sixty-five. She was a member of the Protestant Episcopal church, "the corner-stone of that church in Danville," a woman of vigorous mind, highly cultivated, of fine presence, and prided herself greatly on her domestic qualifications. Her mother, Susan Hart, of North Carolina, was the daughter of Nathaniel Hart, of that State. Her brother, Nat. Hart, was a prosperous farmer at Versailles, Kentucky. The Harts were all wealthy men, gentlemen of elegant leisure. Mrs. Deaderick's only surviving sister, Catharine, married Judge D.'s cousin, Addison A. Anderson, who represented Jefferson county in the Tennessee Legislature in 1848–49. He died in 1883, in Monroe county, Missouri, where his widow now resides. Mrs. Deaderick was educated at Danville and Lexington, Kentucky, and is a lady of most admirable traits of character, a wise and safe counselor, and a helpmate in every sense to her distinguished husband. Even in her old age she is always busy, believing, as she says, it is a sin to be idle.

To Judge Deaderick and his worthy wife have been born ten children, as follows: (1). Arthur, a farmer in Washington county; married Miss Addie Walker, of New Market, daughter of James Walker, a farmer of that place, and has six children, viz.: James William, McDowell, Lizzie, Lula, Charles and Monroe. (2).

Shelby, who was killed in the battle of Chicamauga, September 21, 1863, leaving one child, a son, John Wallace; his widow, Louisa Brown Deaderick, is a daughter of Maj. Byrd Brown, of Washington county. (3). Anna Mary, widow of William D. VanDyke, formerly a prominent lawyer of Chattanooga, who died in 1883, leaving four children, Annie, Thomas Nixon, Fannie and Carey. (4). James G., a lawyer, now residing in California, engaged in fruit culture, who married Miss Lizzie Sayers, of Virginia, and has two children, Ella and Howe. (5). D. Frank, a commission merchant, and at this writing mayor of Quincy, Illinois, who married Miss Nannie Haynes, daughter of Col. J. G. Haynes, of Washington county, by whom he has seven children, viz.: Mary, Fannie, Nannie, Frank, Lavinia, Carrie and Fred. (6). Wallace, a merchant and lawyer of Greeneville, Tennessee, who married Miss Sarah Hardin, daughter of Chief Justice Mordecai Hardin, of Kentucky, and has two children, Sallie and Mary. (7). Alfred Shelby, a lawyer, living at Jonesborough; married Miss Carter Luster, daughter of Rev. Mr. Luster, of Fincastle, Virginia; has four children, Kate, Lucy, Addie and James. (8). Louis, a farmer in Washington county; married Miss Nannie Bayless, daughter of Byrd Bayless, a farmer of that county; has two children, Addie and Byrd. (9). Charles, a merchant at Hamilton, Missouri; married Miss Sue Anderson, daughter of Addison A. Anderson, previously mentioned; has one child, Pauline. (10). Addie McDowell, a graduate of Dr. Ward's Seminary, Nashville; unmarried.

Judge Deaderick owes his success in life chiefly to a firm adherence to the principles of honesty instilled into him by his father, and to a faithful discharge of every duty devolved upon him in the various stations he has been called to occupy. His steady persistence in this course through his whole life has made him troops of friends, and secured the unbounded confidence of the people of his State, who have elevated him to the highest judicial position in their power to bestow. Naturally one of the most modest and diffident of men, he never put himself forward—never seemed to know the value of himself; but the people, quick to discern true worth and ever ready to appreciate and reward the exercise of noble qualities and high purposes, have singled him out and crowned him with the enviable distinction of their approval. When about to enter upon the practice of the law, he was somewhat despondent, in view of the rather unpromising prospect which presented itself to him in the profession. At this time he was much strengthened in his purpose by the late Judge T. A. R. Nelson, who remarked to him: "It seems to me you look discouraged; but I know enough of the law and enough of you to feel sure that if you will persevere you will succeed." Taking courage from these words, he went forward and has achieved a measure of success attained by but few men in the profession. It must have been peculiarly gratifying to the generous and noble-hearted Nelson to find, in after years, the young lawyer whom he had thus encouraged in his early struggles, occupying a seat on the Supreme bench with himself.

HON. NEILL S. BROWN.

NASHVILLE.

THE life of this gentleman may be considered as coeval with the history of Middle Tennessee. His father came to Giles county in 1809, and he was born the next year. There is a wonderful unity of type in these early pioneers of Tennessee, who settled in its central valley during the first decade of the nineteenth century, and impressed their best qualities on their descendants, who are now the leading families of the State. They came from the Carolinas or Virginia, where they were known to be of Scotch or Scotch-Irish descent; they were Presbyterians of the old school; plain, industrious farmers, who brought a moderate supply of the world's goods with them, and with it their frugal, simple habits and well-directed industry. Discipline was strict in their families, and a plain English education was usually attainable by the young; an education, however, which was largely interspersed with work on the farm; in truth, it was generally the

half session system of six months' schooling and six months' work on the farm; an arrangement contemplated with high disdain by those trained on the modern high pressure system, but which gave our Websters to the North, our Clays to the West, and our Wrights and Browns, Friersons, Coopers and Flemings, and a host of other great men, to Tennessee.

In such a community Neill S. Brown manfully struggled on his way from obscurity to distinction. His surroundings were depressing and discouraging to youthful ambition beyond what was common, even in that modest settlement. The limitations of his home must have amounted to actual poverty; for, whether from deficiency of means or from the need of his labor on the farm, his education did not commence until his seventeenth year. Most minds would have been crushed and deadened under such depressing circumstances; not so the indomitable spirit of Neill S. Brown. He was only stimulated to the more heroic efforts to raise himself above the humiliating level in which he found himself. From the little known about his boyhood, he seems to have been thoughtful beyond his years; not unsocial, but evidently possessed of the aspirations that come in more mature life. He was, even then, seeking to break through the close environment that hemmed him in. When, at length, in his seventeenth year, he did commence his school education, it was by his own savings, the scanty earnings of his previous labor; and, when these were exhausted, he taught school himself to acquire means for further instruction.

In 1831 he entered what was called the Manual Labor Academy in Maury county, and studied there two sessions, after which he taught school in Giles county for a short time.

In 1833 he commenced the study of law with Chancellor Bramlett at Pulaski, and was admitted to the bar at the close of 1834, at Pulaski, by Judges Bramlett and Stuart. He now opened an office at Pulaski, at which place, with some interruptions, he practiced law till 1847. The first interruption was a trip he made to Texas, in 1835, to test the probability of doing a lucrative practice there; but not meeting with encouragement, he returned to Tennessee the same year. In 1836 he enlisted in Armstrong's brigade for the Seminole war in Florida. He was in the battle on the Withlacoochee, October 13, 1836. He went out as a private and was promoted to be sergeant-major of his regiment, the First Tennessee.

His political life now commences, for before his return from Florida he was nominated by the Whig party candidate for presidential elector on the ticket of the Hon. Hugh L. White. In that and in the two successive presidential elections, he took the stump for the Whig candidates in the same capacity, viz.: in 1840, for Gen. Harrison, and in 1844, for Henry Clay.

In 1837 he was elected a member of the State Legislature, wherein he served for a session, the youngest member in it.

In 1847 he was elected Governor of Tennessee, served one term and has since resided in Nashville. He was the youngest man ever elected to the gubernatorial office. When it is taken into consideration that he went to school for the first time in his seventeenth year, and in only twenty more years had so impressed the people of Tennessee with his merits and abilities as to receive at their hands the highest office they were capable of bestowing, the career of Gov. Brown may be considered unique in the records of political life. The chief faculty by which this eminence was attained was his matchless power of addressing crowds of men. Sprung himself from the very heart of the people, he knew what was in that mighty heart, and could count its every throb, and his speeches were those of a man speaking from his own experience to those whose experience had been the same. The college trained orator

cannot meet such a man before the populace without defeat, whatever he may do in the Senate and at the bar.

In 1850 he was commissioned by President Taylor as minister to Russia, in which capacity he resided in that country three years.

In 1853 he was elected to the State Legislature as member for Davidson county, and, when the Assembly met, was elected by it Speaker of the House of Representatives.

In 1856 he was again in his element as a popular orator, being placed on the electoral ticket for the State at large in the interest of Mr. Fillmore, this time canvassing the whole State, and acquiring universal reputation as an eloquent and powerful champion of Whig principles.

In 1870 he was member for Davidson county of the most important constitutional convention ever summoned in Tennessee, that convention whose duty it was to modify the institutions of the State so as to adapt them to the vast organic changes which had been brought about by the abolition of slavery and the results of the recent civil war.

This was the last political position held by Gov. Brown; but he has once since then come forward from the dignified and peaceful retirement which he had chosen. In 1880, when the last struggle of parties came on in relation to the State debt question, the venerable Governor was induced to step on the platform again and put in one more plea for the credit and honor of the State. He was at once recognized as the old man eloquent, pleading with impaired physical powers, but with undiminished fire, the cause of righteous dealing, and though that plea was unavailing, it will be remembered in the coming years, when the present generation of politicians has passed away, and a future race of Tennesseans may haply be induced to reconsider calmly a question decided in the heat of party animosity.

In politics Gov. Brown has been a life-long Whig, at least so long as the Whig party had an organized existence, but since the war has acted with what is now styled the Democratic party. He has, however, abstained for some time from party conflicts, preferring to give his valuable support to those measures which are advocated not on party lines. Among these the foremost is that of popular education. Among self-educated men no better test of their magnanimity can be found than that of observing how they look upon education. One class delights in disparaging every better educated man than themselves as a pedant and dreamer; this is not the magnanimous class. Another, on remembering the disadvantages which clogged their own early career, are only inspired by it to vow that no meritorious young man of the future shall be shackled and impeded at the threshold of life as they have been; and to this class belongs Neill S. Brown, the most zealous and active promoter of public education in the Tennessee of the present.

The father of Gov. Brown was Duncan Brown, a native of Robertson county, North Carolina, who married and emigrated to Giles county, Tennessee, in 1809, where in 1810, he became father of the future Governor. It will be gathered from what has already been said, that he was a poor man. He was a farmer, and, from the time when the Whig party was first organized a Whig, and to the day of his death. He was a man of strong intellect, but of moderate educational advantages. He seems to have been a man of poetical turn, as both his sons were, though none of the three are known to have published any poetry. It is the testimony of one who knew him that the old gentleman was better looking than either of his sons, which is saying much, for both of them have been very fine looking men. His father (grandfather to the Governor), was Angus Brown, born in Scotland and settled in Robertson county, North Carolina, about the middle of the last century. There he lived and died a farmer. He served a short campaign in the Revolutionary war under Gen. Marion. He lived to be about seventy years of age.

All these people have been plain farmers, in moderate circumstances, Presbyterians of the old school, and respected in their days as fair dealing, upright citizens.

Gov. Brown married at Nashville, December 26, 1839, Miss Mary Ann Trimble, daughter of Judge James Trimble, of that city, deceased, a man of position and influence, of a Virginia family. Her mother, Letitia Clark, was born in East Tennessee, daughter of Norris Clark, a merchant and farmer from Virginia. Mrs. Brown's brother, Hon. John Trimble, was several times a member of the Legislature, and once district attorney-general. He was a noted leader of the Union party in the days of secession. Her sister, Louisa, died wife of John Reid, a prominent lawyer at Nashville. Her sister, Eliza, married A. V. S. Lindsley, a lawyer at Nashville, son of Dr. Philip Lindsley. Her sister, Susan, married Col. W. B. A. Ramsey, of Knoxville, Secretary of State of Tennessee; both now dead. Mrs. Brown is a lady of taste and intellect, of pleasing, amiable manners, religious, and endowed with the tact and native politeness which are beautifully manifested in the practice of a genial and elegant hospitality.

By this marriage Gov. Brown has had eight children: (1). James Trimble, born at Pulaski, February 25, 1842, a lawyer; married Miss Jennie F. Nichol, sister of Dr. William L. Nichol, of Nashville; died May 31, 1878; he was a soldier in the Confederate service; left three children, William Lytle, Elizabeth and Trimble. (2). George Tully, born at Pulaski, December, 1843; a lawyer at Nashville; married Miss Lou. Ezell, daughter of P. H. Ezell, of Pulaski. (3). Neill S., born at Pulaski, February 1, 1846; now reading clerk in the House of Representatives at Washington; married Miss Susan Walton, daughter of Col. W. B. Walton, of

Davidson county; has two children, Neill and Walton; served in the Confederate army four years. (4). Duncan, born at Nashville, August 4, 1848; died July 8, 1879; clerk of the Davidson County Court at the time of his death. (5.). Susan Louisa, born at Nashville, November 5, 1850; not married. (6). Henry A., born at Nashville, May 7, 1854; was express agent on the Atchison, Topeka & Santa Fe railroad, and was killed at Albuquerque, March 27, 1881; unmarried. (7). Mary Letitia, born at Nashville, June 27, 1856; wife of Capt. Vinet Donelson, a merchant at Nashville. (8). John C., born at Nashville, December 28, 1858; United States mail agent; unmarried.

The career of Gov. Brown is confidently offered as a most instructive lesson to such young men as, feeling themselves possessed of the ability to rise above the ordinary level of humanity, find themselves impeded and shackled by straitened circumstances. The advantages of the Governor's youth were limited to a pure, simple and frugal home, with religious training and a necessity for constant industry; its disadvantages were the absence of educational facilities, straitened finance, and distance from center of population. No young man who is now complaining of his obstacles to self-elevation will find, on reading the above sketch, that they were greater than those which stood in the way of Gov. Brown, who practiced no arts but those of self-denial, industry and perseverance; and yet, twenty years after he commenced his education on the slenderest of means, he was Governor of the State, and three years after that was ambassador in one of the greatest courts in Europe.

How was it done? This question was put to the Governor by the editor, and his answer shall be given in his own words. He points out his first advantage as being "the manner in which I was raised by my parents, who were strict diciplinarians, instilling correct morals." He goes on to say of himself: "I had a native ambition to rise from obscurity and make myself useful in the world; to shine and be distinguished. A pains-taking father and mother inculcated moral and religious principles, without which no success is worth anything. My poverty pushed me on. I started life on nothing, was as poor as any man in Tennessee who ever became at all known."

So after all there were no methods beyond taking hold of whatever there was to do and doing it with all his might, observing, the while, those principles of strict morality in which he had been trained. That is your method, young man; it never failed, and there is no other.

Gov. Brown is six feet two inches in height, a little bowed at seventy-five years of age; perfectly accessible, his manners those of a man who, being at ease himself, puts all who approach him at ease and conciliates their confidence; manners which have given him acceptance in the courts of great monarchs, and which make the

2

plainest farmer feel at home with him. Such, and such only, are the manners of a finished gentleman.

In one respect Gov. Brown does not commend his own example to young men—that of rushing into politics before establishing themselves in their profession or calling in life, so as to be independent of results. Party success is so fluctuating a thing, he says, that it is not sufficiently reliable for a man to make it his main dependence in life. He is far from being a rich man him-self, and believes he would be much better off if he had given his undivided attention to his profession as a lawyer during those early years when he was on the stump. The truth is, there are only two results that can accrue from a premature entry into political life : an old age of honorable poverty, or an unscrupulous scramble for the spoils of office, regardless of political principle, which is now the curse of American politics.

HON. ARCHIBALD WRIGHT.

MEMPHIS.

ARCHIBALD WRIGHT was born in Maury county, Tennessee, November 28, 1809, the son of John Wright and Nancy Wright, nee McIntyre. John Wright was son of Duncan Wright, of Scotland, of whom we learn nothing but his longevity; he died a centenarian. He must have migrated some time in the eigtheenth century, as John was born in Cumberland county, North Carolina, and emigrated to Tennessee in 1809, where he settled first in Maury county and afterwards in Giles county, having purchased property on Big Creek. He inherited his father's privilege of longevity, having died recently at very little short of one hundred years of age.

Nancy McIntyre was born in Chatham county, North Carolina, where she was married to John Wright above named. She was known as a lady of great stature and remarkable energy of character, devoting herself to the laborious duties of a farmer's wife in the early days of Tennessee, and to the care and training of her children. She died at the age of fifty, and is buried at Mount Pleasant, Maury county, Tennessee.

A cousin of the Judge is mentioned, a lawyer in Mississippi named Daniel B. Wright, invincible as a pleader before a jury. He at one time represented Mississippi in Congress, and was severely wounded in the service of the Confederate States.

Judge Wright's early training was that which has produced the best men of our nation, that of a well-raised farmer's son, attending a good English country school part of the year and doing farm work the rest. His teacher was a Mr. Chadduck, living first in the neighborhood of Big Creek, afterward at Mount Pleasant, Maury county, who seems to have acquired considerable reputation as a teacher, and his opinion of young Wright is evinced by his making him his assistant teacher. At what age we are not informed, he was sent to the academy at Pulaski, by the advice of Judge Bramlett. This institution was at the time in the hands of William W. Potter and G. W. McGhee, both prominent educators, the latter a graduate of West Point. He here made some proficiency in Latin, algebra and geometry; but the basis of his intellectual character in after life is believed to have been the sound English education he received from Mr. Chadduck. He became in youth a good practical surveyor under the instruction of Peter Swanson. He was much devoted to the manly sports favored by the country youth of those days, and being of a powerful frame and healthy constitution, must have been a prominent sportsman among his comrades. Such was his boyhood, laying up for him a fund of health and strength, together with a practical acquaintance with the affairs of life.

In the years intermediate between his school days and his professional training, he became himself a school teacher, according to the primitive customs of those days. The first year he took a three months' school on the old condition of boarding around with the parents of his pupils. This was in Maury county, near his birthplace. The second year it was a nine months' school near Mount Pleasant, where he had himself been educated by Mr. Chadduck. He humorously summed up the profits of his teaching as follows : First year, one bridle, one pair of martingales and five dollars in cash ; second year, forty-five dollars in cash.

At the age of nineteen, while looking around for a new location as teacher, he accidentally heard an eminent lawyer named Craighead deliver a masterly speech in a slander case at Columbia. This finally decided him to adopt the bar as his professional career, and he thenceforth lived and died in its practice. He studied in the office of Judge Bramlett at Pulaski, and afterwards obtained his license at Nashville from Judge Thomas Stewart, of Franklin, and Robert White, of Nashville, the latter being then on the Supreme bench of the State. He commenced practice in Pulaski, and we have it on his own statement that he made twenty-five hundred dollars by his first year's practice, a handsome income in those days, even for a lawyer in established practice.

It cannot be said that Archibald Wright was a man

of extensive learning when he entered on the profession of law. His books had been few, but those thoroughly mastered. The chief elements of his success were a keen insight into character and motive, an impressive earnestness of manner, a great facility in the expression of his ideas, combined with a power of commending them to the judgment of other men. It has been remarked that, while his judgments from the bench were characterized by an extreme terseness and concentration of thought and language, his pleadings at the bar were diffusive and exhaustive, omitting nothing which could have any possible bearing upon the case in hand; and it should be added that if he commenced with a moderate amount of book lore, his subsequent studies must have been extensive, as his legal opinions evince a very copious acquaintance with previous cases bearing upon the issues before him.

In 1835–36 he served as a volunteer in the Seminole war, under Gen. Armstrong, and in company with many other noted Tennesseans, among them Terry H. Cahal, Dr. Cheairs, Gen. William Trousdale and Gov. Neill S. Brown. He and Brown were at the same time presidential electors on opposite sides, Wright on the Van Buren ticket (Democrat), and Brown on that of Hugh L. White (Whig). They returned from the army to vote, just before the close of the war and, with it, of their military careers.

He married, in 1837, Miss Mary Elizabeth Eldridge, daughter of Dr. Elisha Eldridge, a physician of eminence and a Methodist preacher, a native of New Hampshire, of whom more will be stated at the close of this chapter.

In 1847 he was nominated and elected to the State Legislature from Giles county, and served his term therein, during which he held the important position of chairman of the judiciary committee. After this he never held political office, and indeed frequently expressed himself averse to the routine of party politics with a great distaste for the machinery of partisan warfare, including caucuses and conventions, which he believed to act rather as an impediment than as an aid to the advancement of public interests.

His professional practice continued to increase from the day he entered upon it, and he invested the profits of it in real estate, and engaged in 1844 largely in cotton planting, his plantation being upon the Tombigbee river, in Lowndes county, Mississippi; he also had property in Tunica county in the same State, and at one time worked as many as a hundred negroes. At the outbreak of the war, his whole property was valued at two hundred and eighty thousand dollars. While, however, he was at one time a wealthy man, his wealth had but two sources, industry intelligently directed and its proceeds judiciously invested. He never shaved notes or speculated, or resorted to even doubtful methods of becoming suddenly rich.

In 1858 he was appointed to the Supreme bench of

Tennessee by Gov. Isham G. Harris to fill a vacancy, and was elected to the same position before taking his seat, which he did at Knoxville in September of the same year, his associates being Robert L. Caruthers and Robert J. McKinney. All three occupied the Supreme bench until the war. Judge Wright's term legally expired in 1866, but he was arbitrarily displaced by Gov. Brownlow in 1865, and Alvin Hawkins appointed in his place.

Towards the close of his life, Judge Wright once more entered the political arena to take part in the last desperate struggle of the State credit party, being delegate to the convention which nominated Mr. Fussell for Governor in 1882, and again as a candidate for the State Senate in the same year. In both he was defeated, as was anticipated from the first. His candidacy must be looked upon rather as a protest than as a practical candidature for office.

The wife of Judge Archibald Wright was, as has been already stated, the daughter of a New Hampshire gentleman, a physician and Methodist minister, named Elisha Eldridge, who died in 1833. On the mother's side she was descended from the noble Irish family of Dillon, a member of which emigrated towards the close of the last century, became a large landowner, and was grandfather of the lady in question. She was educated in Pulaski, Tennessee, and is a prominent and active member of the Methodist church. Four of the children of this lady by Judge Wright are living, as follows: (1). Luke E. Wright, educated at the University of Mississippi; a fine scholar and accomplished gentleman, whose reputation at the bar as a close reasoner, a well qualified lawyer, and an eloquent advocate already promises to raise him to the level of his father's high position. He married Miss Kate Semmes, daughter of the celebrated Admiral, and by her he is the father of four children, Eldridge, Anna, Luke E., junior, and Semmes. (2). Mary, educated by the widow of Gen. Leonidas Polk, at Columbia, Tennessee, and married to William C. Fowlkes, a law partner of Judge Wright, of high military and legal reputation. (3). Lizzie, educated at Memphis. (4). Kate, educated at Poughkeepsie, New York. A second son of Judge Wright, named Elisha Eldridge, distinguished himself at the University of North Carolina at Chapel Hill, taking the first honors of his year, and receiving from the hands of President Buchanan a copy of Hawkes' History of North Carolina, as a prize for composition. He was killed at the head of his company at the battle of Murfreesborough.

Judge Wright was a director of the Planters Bank at Pulaski, and afterwards of the Planters Bank at Memphis, and throughout his career was always looked upon as a fit person for offices of trust and responsibility. He was of commanding stature and powerful frame, distinguished for physical and moral courage, and both honored and feared for his unflinching condemnation of meanness and dishonesty. His manner was such as to repel indiscriminate familiarity but to attract the friendship of the noble and the good. He belonged to a past generation, the best of whose qualities are now at a discount, being eclipsed by the more superficial element of popularity. It will be well for Tennessee when her chosen leaders shall be men stamped with the same high qualities that gave to Judge Wright the powerful and extensive influence he exercised when alive.

The opinions and decrees given from the Supreme bench of Tennessee by Judge Wright, can be found in the Reports of Sneed and Head, and the two first volumes of Coldwell.

HON. WILLIAM F. COOPER.

NASHVILLE.

THE maternal ancestors of this gentleman were members of the same colony, originally Scotch-Irish, which migrated from South Carolina to Tennessee quite at the commencement of the present century, and settled in Maury county in 1805, as is stated more in detail in the memoir of Chancellor S. D. Frierson, given in another part of this work. He and Chancellor W. S. Fleming are related to the late chancellor and to one another.

Franklin, in Williamson county, is the place of Judge Cooper's birth, which took place March 11, 1820, and in infancy he was carried to the permanent residence of the clan, as it may be called, in Maury county. His father was a man of education and literary tastes, and gave him the best education attainable in those days. He attended school until he was fourteen years old and then entered the class of 1834 at Yale College, graduating there in 1838. This class comprised the names of many men afterwards prominent in life; among them are the following, the first three of whom were members of Congress: (1). Joseph B. Varnum, member of Congress from New York, many years in the New York Legislature. (2). Richard S. Donnel, member of Congress from North Carolina. (3). William P. Lynde, of Milwaukee, member of Congress from Wisconsin. (4). William S. Fleming, chancellor of the Columbia district. (5). J. Knox Walker, private secretary to President Polk. (6). Benjamin S. Edwards, of Springfield, Illinois, many years a judge in that State. (7). Francis P. Blair, a general in the Federal army during the late war, and candidate for vice-president on the ticket with Gov. Seymour, of New York.

After the completion of his academical course, law was not Mr. Cooper's first love, but a brief flirtation with medicine preceded his courtship of the profession to which he was finally wedded. He studied medicine two years at Columbia with Dr. Hayes of that city, and took one course of lectures in the medical department of the University of Pennsylvania, when he discovered that law rather than medicine was his true vocation. He then studied law with S. D. Frierson, afterwards the celebrated chancellor, and, on admission to the bar, became his partner. His admission to the bar was in March, 1841, Judges Anderson and Dillahunty participating in that ceremony.

His partnership with his preceptor, Mr. Frierson, lasted four years, and in 1845 he moved to Nashville, where he has since resided. Here he became a partner with A. O. P. Nicholson, afterwards Chief Justice of the State (elected to that office 1870, died 1876). This second partnership lasted only one year, and he practiced alone until 1851, when he became partner of the Hon. Andrew Ewing, and practiced with him ten years.

In 1861 he was elected one of the judges of the Supreme Court of the State, but the war causing the closing of the courts, and Judge Cooper being strongly southern in his sympathies, William G. Brownlow, as military governor, interdicted him from the exercise of his office.

Returning to the bar, he formed a partnership successively with Judge Robert L. Caruthers and with his brother, Henry Cooper. This latter gentleman was elected United States Senator in 1870. After two years practicing alone he was again removed from the bar by his appointment as chancellor of the Seventh, or Nashville, district, by Gov. John C. Brown. He was soon after elected to the same post by the people, and held it till 1878, when he was elected to the Supreme bench for eight years, defeating in this election Judge John L. T. Sneed, who had beaten him in 1853, when both of them were candidates for the office of attorney-general.

While nearly all his family connections were Whigs before the war, and have been and still are Presbyterians, he has always been a Democrat, and has never joined any religious organization. Neither is he a member of any secret society; he is eminently an independent thinker, and not willing to be bound in his thoughts by any organization, religious, political or social.

Judge Cooper has been successful in life in a financial point of view, his property before the war amounting to over one hundred thousand dollars in value. He attributes his success in this respect to constant and close attention to business, and always living within his means. These two observances are in truth the condition of all success in life, the exceptions being so rare and accidental that they form no guide for men's conduct. The judge was never married.

In stating the ancestry and family connections of William F. Cooper, Samuel D. Frierson and W. S. Fleming separately, many repetitions must inevitably occur, for the members of that Maury county colony, several times alluded to in this volume, intermarried so frequently with one another that the relations of one are the relations of all. His maternal grandfather was one of the original members of the colony, which owned sixteen sections of land (over ten thousand acres), with the Presbyterian church in the middle, the first building put up on it, and the school-house close by. [See the memoir on another page of S. D. Frierson]. His father, Matthew D. Cooper, was born in 1793, in Chester district, South Carolina. He was one of the earliest graduates of Cumberland College, at Nashville, since known as the University of Nashville, in the same class with the Hon. John Bell, once United States Senator, and Judge W. B. Turley, of the Supreme Court. He married in Maury county, was cashier of the bank at Franklin, and afterwards engaged in mercantile business in that town in partnership with Dr. William G. Dickenson. In 1822 he moved to Columbia, engaged in the mercantile business till 1827, when he became a commission merchant in New Orleans. This business he kept up for thirty-five years, but continued to make his home in Maury county, where, until 1867, he was a successful farmer. He died December 18, 1878, at Columbia. He was a lieutenant and acting captain under Jackson in the Creek war. He was a man of energetic character, well educated and of literary tastes. His whole property at the commencement of the war vested in negroes, land and merchandise, was probably not worth less than one hundred thousand dollars, all the proceeds of his own exertions. His credit stood high as a business man. From 1840 to 1862 he was president of the Columbia branch of the Union Bank. His wife, mother of Judge Cooper, was a daughter of William Frierson, the acknowledged head of the Frierson clan, repeatedly mentioned as settling in Maury county in 1805, and was first cousin to the mother of Chancellor S. D. Frierson. She died in 1833, at Columbia, leaving four children, viz.: (1). William F., the subject of this sketch. (2). Edmund, a graduate of Jackson College at Columbia, now a lawyer at Shelbyville. He was for several years a member of the State Legislature, both before and since the war, and assistant secretary of the treasury under President Johnson. (3). Henry, graduated at Jackson College, Columbia; for many years practiced law in partnership with his brother Edmund, at Shelbyville; appointed circuit judge by Gov. Brownlow, and held the office three or four years, and afterwards became a professor in the law school at Lebanon;

in 1869 he moved to Nashville, and practiced law there in partnership with his brother, William F. ; in 1869 and 1870 he represented Davidson county in the State Legislature, and during that session was elected United States Senator, and served as such for six years; in 1878 he settled at Columbia, returning to the practice of the law. He was killed near Culiacan, Mexico, on February 4, 1884, while returning from a silver mine in the mountains. (4). Mary Agnes, Judge Cooper's only full sister; graduated from the Columbia Female Institute, and married Richard S. Sansom, a lawyer, who died at Georgetown, Texas, where his sister still resides. He was for several years a member of the Texas Legislature ; he left five children : Edmund, who died at Columbia when twenty years old, Cevantha, Richard, Mary and William. Judge Cooper's half brothers and sisters are: (1). Duncan B., who represented Maury and Williamson counties in the Legislature of 1881–82. (2). Addison, a lawyer, clerk in a government office at Washington. (3, 4, 5). Martha Ann, Alice and Emma all graduated at the Columbia Female Institute, and are living in that city unmarried. (6). Eloise graduated at the same school, and married A. W. Stockell, a lawyer and editor at Columbia, but now connected with the American newspaper, and residing at Nashville. (7). Fannie, died the wife of George Milner, leaving three children.

Judge Cooper's remoter paternal ancestors migrated from Tyrone county, in the north of Ireland, considerably before the Revolutionary war. They were of Scotch-Irish derivation. Among them we find a great grandfather who died in South Carolina at the age of one hundred and nine years, originally an Irish weaver, but in this country a farmer. The Judge's grandfather, by trade a blacksmith, was a captain in Sumner's brigade during the Revolutionary war. He was a very handsome man, and made a runaway match with a Miss Hamilton, daughter of a rich Philadelphia merchant, who had a branch establishment at Mobile. She was a lady highly educated and of great energy of character. She educated her own children, and in 1803, after her husband's death, conveyed them all in a carryall to Nashville, and settled in Davidson county, near the old town of Haysborough, where she lived for several years. She died in Mississippi at the age of ninety-three. She gave birth to and raised twelve children, of whom Matthew D., the Judge's father, was the youngest. The great number of her distinguished descendants is a confirmation of the general belief that intellectual qualities generally descend in the female line. Judge Cooper's mother was also descended from Scotch-Irish ancestors who emigrated from the north of Ireland.

During the war the Judge spent several years traveling in Europe, chiefly in England, Scotland and Switzerland, visiting also the cities of Rome, Naples, Paris, Berlin, Vienna, Trieste and Venice. He has published three volumes of reports of cases decided in his own chancellor's court, and has edited the standard edition of Tennessee Reports from the earliest decisions up to the reorganization of the Supreme Court in 1865. In the winter of 1851–52 he edited temporarily the Nashville *Union*.

In 1849–50 he was made a director of the Nashville and Northwestern railroad, and served in this capacity from the commencement to the completion of the line, and was very active in advancing the road to a successful issue. He was also a director of the Bank of Tennessee in 1853–54–55.

Judge Cooper is of short stature, compactly built, weighing one hundred and thirty pounds; has brown eyes, and a large round head. His motions are quick. He is easy of access, and a most entertaining conversationalist.

His position on the Supreme bench and in society, and his great array of distinguished family connections, together with his undeniably exceptional talents, constitute him, beyond dispute, one among the most prominent men in Tennessee.

JUDGE THOMAS H. COLDWELL.

SHELBYVILLE.

THOMAS H. COLDWELL was born in Shelbyville, Bedford county, Tennessee, August 29, 1822. His father, John Campbell Coldwell, was born January 8, 1791, in Hawkins county, East Tennessee, and removed with his father, Ballard Coldwell, and family to Bedford county, January 1, 1808. John Campbell Coldwell served two campaigns under Gen. Jackson—one against the Creek Indians, in which he participated in the battle at Horse Shoe; and the other against the British, in which he participated in the decisive battle at New Orleans, January 8, 1815. On his return from this campaign he settled in Shelbyville, and was a merchant there from 1818 to 1843, when he retired to his farm, where he died July 17, 1867.

Thomas H. Coldwell's mother was Jane Northcott, born in Fleming county, Kentucky, the daughter of Rev. Benjamin Northcott. Thomas was the eldest of four children, two boys and two girls. He was educated at Dixon Academy, Shelbyville, and studied law with Irwin J. Frierson, Esq. He was licensed to practice in January, 1844, remained in practice at Shelbyville, where he is still one of the leading and most active members of the bar.

He married first Mary J. Hodge, at Murfreesboro, November 24, 1844. After her death he married Sarah E. Gosling, in Cincinnati, May 6, 1851. After her death he married Mrs. Mary H. Bosworth, in Shelbyville, September 20, 1854, and after her death, he married his present wife, Carrie Hopkins, in Cincinnati, November 11, 1875.

For many years of his life Thomas H. Coldwell was an active and zealous worker in the Sons of Temperance organization, and was elected Grand Worthy Patriarch for the State of Tennessee in 1851. He was a decided and unflinching Union man throughout the late war and unwavering in his adherence to the government. In 1864 he was commissioned by Gov. Andrew Johnson chancellor of the Fourth Chancery Division of Tennessee, but held the office only a short time, when he resigned. In October, 1865, he was commissioned

Attorney-General of the State and Reporter of the Supreme Court, and in May, 1867, was elected by the people to the office without opposition. While serving in this capacity he reported seven volumes of the decisions of the Supreme Court of Tennessee, and considers this the most pleasant part of his professional career. While attorney-general he entered a *nolle prosequi* in all cases that came to the Supreme Court where persons were indicted for treason against the State—a class of indictments which grew out of the late civil war, the disposal of which, in this summary manner, brought about an era of good feeling, and won for Judge Coldwell the earnest gratitude of many of his fellow-citizens. In 1868 he was the Grant and Colfax elector for the Fifth Congressional District of Tennessee.

From 1865 to 1871 he served as one of the directors of the Nashville and Chattanooga railroad. He was a lay member of the General Conference of the Methodist Episcopal church at its session held at Brooklyn, New York, in 1873, and while there was the author of the resolution sending fraternal delegates from the Methodist Episcopal church to the Methodist Episcopal church, South—he being one of the most earnest advocates of the measure. He has always been a zealous worker in his church, giving most liberally to all of its enterprises, and has always been an active Sunday-school man. Few things seem to give him more pleasure than to watch the young people as they develop into noble man and womanhood.

During 1871–72 he was president of Bedford county Agricultural Society, and his earnest efforts contributed much to the success which has attended the society, even up to the present time. In 1869 he induced the county court of Bedford county to rebuild the court-house, which had been destroyed during the occupation of the town by Gen. Bragg's army. The court appointed him chairman of the building committee, and Shelbyville now has one of the most beautiful, durable and convenient court-houses in the State. He was president of the Shelbyville Savings Bank three years, and has been one of its directors from its organization up to the present time.

Judge Coldwell, from the organization of the Central Tennessee College at Nashville, has been a member of its board of directors a great deal of the time, also president of the board of trustees, and is at present its vice-president and acting president. This is one of the institutions for the education of the colored people, for which Nashville is so famous, and is under the patronage of the Methodist Episcopal church. Judge Coldwell is a fearless advocate of the education and Christianization of the negro, his theory being, "Give them a fair and even chance in life, and if there is anything in them, they will succeed; if not, they must seek the level of other inefficients."

He is now the president of the board of common school directors of the seventh civil district of Bedford county, which includes the town of Shelbyville. He had served almost twelve years as director, and proved himself one of the most enthusiastic friends of the common schools. His term of office having expired, at an election held in his native town in August, 1884, it was found that of the three hundred and forty-two votes cast for school director, Judge Coldwell received every one—a fact which he regarded as one of the handsomest compliments of his life.

In 1871 Gov. DeWitt C. Senter recommended Judge Coldwell to President Grant as a suitable person to be appoited commissioner for the State of Tennessee to the Centennial Exposition at Philadelphia in 1876. He received his commission and served until 1877, was on many of the important committees and was elected first vice-president of the commission, being one of the most active participants in the measures that made the exhibition so great a success.

Judge Coldwell has two children, Gen. Ernest Coldwell, the child of his third wife, and who is now twenty-seven years of age, and his partner in the practice of the law; and Carrie (" Sunshine ") Coldwell, now seven years of age, the child of his present wife.

Gen. Ernest Coldwell was born at Shelbyville, November 12, 1858, and was educated at Shelbyville, at Athens, Tennessee, and at Carbondale, Illinois. After reading law in his father's office two years he was licensed by Judges Robert Cantrell and Peter Turney. In September, 1882, he was appointed special revenue collector under A. M. Hughes, jr. He was secretary of the Middle Tennessee and Bedford county Sunday-school Associations while a law student. In November, 1884, he was elected Representative from Bedford county to the Forty-fourth General Assembly of Tennessee, overcoming a Democratic majority of six hundred by two hundred and twenty-six majority. For a pronounced Republican, the son of an outspoken Republican, this was a handsome testimonial of public confidence. He is a director of the Bedford county Agricultural Society, a director in the Bedford county Stock Breeders' Society, and register for a time, and was a director and treasurer of the Eakin Library Society, and is a member of the library committee. Ernest Coldwell was appointed May 21, 1881, on Gov. Alvin Hawkins' staff with the rank of brigadier-general. He is six feet three inches in height, and of handsome, graceful carriage. His mother, nee Mary Henderson, was a lady versatile in her accomplishments and of marked firmness of character. She, was born in New York, raised in Ohio, and died in Tennessee in 1874, fifty-three years old, leaving, by her first marriage to a Mr. Bosworth, two children : Helen, now wife of Rev. M. M. Callen, Saint Joseph, Michigan, and Frances, who married S. Tower, Greeneville, Michigan.

HENRY CRAFT.

MEMPHIS.

IN studying the careers of eminent men, it is sometimes an instructive method to bring out their distinctive characters into higher relief by the force of contrast, and it is proposed to apply this method to the sketches of two men, each successful in the path marked out for himself, but by opposite methods and in virtue of mental characteristics as sharply contrasted as if the two men belonged to different races of the human species.

Let the reader then study in connection with the sketch now presented to him that given on another page of Col. Leonidas C. Houk. He will thus find, in abrupt contrast, one man always eager to match

himself against other men, the other pursuing his own course in self-chosen seclusion ; the one always seeking a conspicuous position in the eyes of the world, the other instinctively shrinking from publicity ; the one always aggressive, the other with scarcely combativeness enough in his nature to assume the defensive. Nor is the contrast made with the purpose of exalting the one type as superior to the other ; both have their place in the economy of society, and it is a matter of thankfulness that all men are not made according to the same type, but differently constituted so as to meet one or other of the varied requirements of the social system.

It has been said of Henry Craft that he might have

risen to the highest public honors of his profession but for his retiring disposition; but let not this be read as if it pronounced his life a failure; the position he has attained without entering the arena of competition for public office is probably exactly that which he would have chosen for himself in preference to such as are attained by the promiscuous suffrages of the public, namely, the recognition of himself by those capable of judging as indisputably without a rival in legal attainments, while a still smaller circle are attracted by a personal knowledge of his sterling moral qualities, and so consolidated into a circle of trusted and trusting friends. It is better, after all, to have it asked why one is not in high public office, than, being there, to hear men say, " How on earth came he, of all men, to be there?"

Henry Craft was born April 8, 1823, at Milledgeville, in Baldwin county, Georgia, at that time the capital of the State. Both his parents were true Christians, and it has been the characteristic of most of his relations on both sides that they were and are devout members of the Church. Whether from hereditary bias, or through early training, Judge Craft resembles the rest of the family in this respect.

When he was ten years old his family removed to Macon, Georgia, which was his home till he was sixteen years of age; but he received the chief part of his education at Oglethorpe University, Milledgeville, which he left in his senior year in 1839, when he settled in Holly Springs, Mississippi, where he devoted himself to business pursuits.

In 1847–48 he attended the law school at Princeton, New Jersey, and was admitted to the bar in 1848, by Chancellor Henry Dickinson, at Holly Springs, at which place he forthwith commenced the practice of law; here he practiced in partnership with Mr. J. W. C. Watson, who had been his preceptor, and took him into partnership before he had completed his studies or received his license.

In 1858 he finally removed to Memphis, where he has practiced ever since. While in practice there, he was offered a professorship in the law department of the Cumberland University at Lebanon, and a partnership with a law firm at New York, which was doing a very extensive practice; both of these offers, however, he declined, preferring the steady pursuit of his profession at Memphis. He has several times sat as judge in special cases, but never either sought or accepted permanent official position.

The only case of much public interest in which he has been engaged was the celebrated 100-3 case, in which the constitutionality of the act of the Legislature of 1881 was tried, by which the settlement of the State debt was intended. In this case a great array of legal talent was employed, comprising the names of Judge Campbell, Gov. Marks, Ed. Baxter, Thomas H. Malone, R. McPhail Smith, John J. Vertrees, A. S.

Champion, George Gantt, William M. Smith, N. N. Cox, Spl. Hill and D. M. Bright.

Much of his success in legal practice is attributable to his early business training, giving him a knowledge of accounts and book-keeping. His method in law cases is first to ascertain the exact point upon which a case hinges, and then to bring all the evidence and law to bear upon that point, comparatively disregarding side issues; aiming at an objective point rather than firing at random: a practice indeed applicable to all pursuits in life where concentration insures success, while diffusion of efforts entails almost certain failure. Judge Craft never appeared in the criminal courts, his practice having been confined almost exclusively to chancery cases.

In 1862 he went with the Confederate army on the staff of Gen. James R. Chalmers, and was present at the battle of Shiloh, but retired from the service with an honorable discharge on account of broken health, caused by exposure in camp at Corinth.

In politics the Judge was a Whig down to the war, but since that has voted with the Democrats, but has little of the partisan in his nature; he has never taken an active part in politics, either by canvassing, making speeches or attending conventions; he has never held office, or been a candidate for it. He is a member of no secret society, all his interest and associations outside of his profession being concentrated on religious and general literature. He is a member of the Cumberland Presbyterian church, and an elder in the congregation at Memphis. His is a settled mind, not disposed to go off into new issues, but to live consistently in the practice of those principles which were implanted in his mind in early life. He has no ambition beyond that involved in his profession, and the welfare of his family. Finally, his aspirations are not confined to the present state of existence, but all that he does, and all that happens to him, is regarded by him mainly as bearing upon the higher existence beyond the grave; for that future he looks upon the present life as a probation and a prepartory training.

He derives his title of judge, by which he is usually addressed, from his appointment in 1877 as commissioner of arbitration in aid of the Supreme Court.

The Crafts are by origin a Welsh family, who have lived for two hundred years as farmers on the eastern shore of Maryland.

Hugh Craft, father of the Judge, was born in 1799, at Vienna, on the eastern shore of Maryland, but moved, in 1814, to the State of Georgia. He was partially educated at Athens, Georgia, looking to medicine as a profession, but soon devoted himself to merchandise, re-receiving his training in that occupation from his uncle, David Stanford, at Augusta, Georgia. With that gentlemen as partner, he then entered into business at Milledgeville, and lived there a successful merchant for twelve years, when he went to Macon, where he also was a successful merchant till the panic of 1837, when he failed, and removed to Holly Springs, Mississippi. Here he was a land agent till 1860, and died in 1867. He was a strict Presbyterian of the old school, devoted to church work, and especially to that of the Sunday-school.

Judge Craft married in Nashville, November 5, 1856, Miss Ella D. Boddie, daughter of Elijah Boddie, of Sumner county, Tennessee, formerly a prominent Democratic leader in that county, frequently in the Legislature, a soldier in Jackson's army at New Orleans. The Boddies are a well-known North Carolina family, well represented in Nashville and in Sumner county. Mrs. Craft's brother, Charles E. Boddie, is a farmer in Sumner county. Her sister, Elizabeth B., widow of William R. Elliston, resides in Nashville; her sister Maria is the wife of Carrington Mason, once of Holly Springs, Mississippi, now an insurance agent at Memphis, and another sister, Mary, is the wife of Rufus K. Cage, Esq., of Houston, Texas. Her mother, Maria Elliott, was of an old Sumner county family, originally from North Carolina. Her uncle, Col. George Elliott, was with Gen. Jackson at New Orleans, and a noted stock raiser and turfman of Sumner county. Mrs. Craft was educated at the old Nashville Female Academy, under Dr. Elliott, and is noted for her retiring disposition, her domestic tastes and habits, and her intense religious devotion.

By his marriage with this lady, Judge Craft has had six children: (1). Alfred Douglas, born 1858, now deceased. (2). Mary F., born 1861. (3). Henry, born 1866; a young man who promises to honor the name which he inherits. (4). Charles Kortrecht, born in 1868; now deceased. (5). Paul, born 1870. (6). Hugh, born 1874.

Judge Craft had one full sister, Martha C., widow of James Fort, now deceased. By his father's second marriage were born five others: (1). Carrie, wife of Dr. Richard Venable., now deceased. (2). Addison, now of Holly Springs, Mississippi. (3). Heber, now living in McComb, Mississippi. (4). Stella, widow of J. B. Hill, now at Holly Springs, Mississippi. (5). Helen, wife of Prof. Anderson, at Holly Springs, Mississippi.

Judge Craft's maternal grandfather, John Pitts, moved to Hancock county, Georgia, in 1815. He and all his family were zealous Methodists. It was in Hancock that Hugh Craft married his daughter, Mary E. Pitts, of which marriage Judge Craft was the offspring. This lady was born in 1799, and educated at Chapel Hill, North Carolina. She was an eminently devoted Methodist, and died in 1826. The Pitts family have all been farmers and Methodists, and Judge Craft himself was baptized by Mr., afterwards Bishop, Capers. None of them have been professional men except the Rev. Epaminondas Pitts, a Methodist preacher of some distinction in Texas, nor any of them politicians except Peyton T. Pitts, brother of Mrs. Hugh Craft, who, at one time, represented Jones county in the Georgia Legislature.

The whole of Judge Craft's kindred, on both sides, have been religious people, not seeking conspicuous position, but making it their chief aim to keep their consciences void of offense before God and man, and to bring up their children in the fear and admonition of the Lord.

Judge Craft is an accomplished and elegant scholar; his extensive reading has been so thoroughly digested and assimilated as to have become an intrinsic element in his intellect, manifested not by a pedantic frequency of quotation, but by a richness of thought which pours a flood of illustration upon any subject he undertakes to elucidate; thus his oratory derives light from his well-stored intellect, and warmth from his intense moral and religious instincts. It differs from the impetuous declamation of the stump orator as a deep, clear, placid stream differs from the mountain torrent; the latter bears down all opposing forces, carrying away trees and rocks before it; the former fertilizes the fields it visits, and bears the freighted fleets of commerce on its bosom. His speech on the Sunday law is a case in point, wherein he contended that "whatever the origin of Sunday, whether divine or human, wise or unwise, it is, as to America, a law of the Anglo-Saxon people." Whatever the subject, he exhausts its capabilities while enchaining the attention of his hearers by the beauty and translucent clearness of his rhetoric. He will long be known in Tennessee as a good man, a lawyer of consummate ability, and a polished, Christian gentleman.

HON. SAMUEL DAVIES FRIERSON.

COLUMBIA.

PERHAPS no community contributed more to the honor and well-being of Tennessee during the first half of the present century than Maury county. She gave to the bench and bar a Frierson, a Wright, a Cooper and a Fleming; to the Church the two eminent prelates, Bishops Otey and Polk; to the navy and to science a Maury; to the arms of her country a Pillow, a Brown and a Polk; to the capital of the United States another Polk as President. Some of the men who gave lustre to this community will now be passed

3

briefly in review, and as a central figure we will present the memoir of Chancellor Samuel Davies Frierson.

The father of this eminent jurist emigrated from the district of Williamsburgh, South Carolina, in 1805, with a colony of Friersons, Coopers, Flemings, Armstrongs and Wilsons, settling first in Williamson county, and afterwards in Maury county in 1807. This colony was quite unlike the heterogeneous assemblies of restless adventurers who generally settle in new countries; on the contrary, it consisted of families who had associated together in their old Carolina homes, and worshipped together in the old Presbyterian church, whose minister accompanied them in their expedition to the western lands in which they proposed to establish new hearths and altars for themselves and their children.

Samuel D. Frierson, the subject of this memoir, was less than two years old when his father first brought him from South Carolina to Tennessee, so that he knew no country but that of his adoption, his native State having no place in his memory. Of his boyhood life we have no knowledge, and can only conjecture what it was from our slight acquaintance with his father's history and character. Samuel Frierson, then, father of the Chancellor, was born in Williamsburgh district, South Carolina, December 15, 1765, and married Sarah Wilson, of the same district, March 29, 1787. He was a plain farmer and slaveholder, and seems to have been chiefly noted as a strict and pious member of the Presbyterian church, of which he was a ruling elder and the chief director of its affairs, and of the school established in connection with it. It is recorded of him that he always doffed his hat on entering the church yard, and never resumed it until, worship being over, he again passed the gate and found himself in the open road. He became father of seven children, one of whom, William Vincent, became a Presbyterian minister of note in Mississippi. He died suddenly, as his son did after him, being stricken with paralysis while at the communion table. The date of his death is July 9, 1815.

We can imagine then the life of sober industry and godly restraint lived by young Frierson in the frugal farm house of the new settlement, subject to the austere discipline of the church school, with the minister for his teacher, and his father for superintendent; probably as wholesome a training for a boy of vigorous intellect and healthy constitution as could well be adopted, always bearing in mind that the exceptive restraint of the home and school could always be alternated with the unbounded freedom of the yet uncleared forests around. He was born July 27, 1803, and was the youngest child save one. He graduated at Transylvania University, Lexington, Kentucky, and studied law in Columbia, Tennessee. In the practice of his profession he was successively the partner of James K. Polk, William P. Martin, A. O. P. Nicholson, William F. Cooper and L. D. Myers, thus including two members of the Supreme bench of the State and a President of the United States.

He was raised to the bench A. D., 1854, by Gov. William B. Campbell, who appointed him to fill the unexpired term of Terry H. Cahal, at the expiration of which he was twice elected by the people, retaining it for twelve years, to the day of his death, which occurred suddenly, like that of his father. He had suffered a paralytic stroke of the left side in 1863, but after a short time continued to hold his courts with entire satisfaction to the bar. He had been holding court in Pulaski, and on March 11, 1866, took supper with a few friends at the residence of Gov. John C. Brown, whence he repaired to his hotel, had a second stroke while disrobing for bed, and died that night.

Chancellor Frierson was not a member of any church. His ancestry and his immediate family were Presbyterians, and doubtless his preferences were for that denomination, although he had a life-long friendship for Bishop James Hervey Otey, of the diocese of Tennessee, whose legal adviser he was to the day of his death.

Politically he was a Whig, and was presidential elector on the Clay ticket in 1844. Since the war the political arena has been a conflict from which the bench was to him a welcome harbor of refuge.

His practice in law was of a nature that is generally remunerative, and with judicious economy enabled him to accumulate a considerable fortune. He was the legal adviser of the wealthiest people in the county, and for a long time acted as attorney for the Columbia branch of the Union Bank. He began life with a moderate inheritance, and accumulated his property by the practice of his profession. His economy did not prevent him, however, from exercising a liberal hospitality, equally removed from penurious meanness and from extravagant ostentation. The highly intelligent and refined society of Columbia was nowhere more thoroughly at home than in his elegant residence.

Immediately after his death a meeting of the bar at Pulaski was called, the proceedings of which we now quote, as an indication of the respect entertained for him by his brothers in the profession. It was followed by similar meetings in all the towns within his district, at all of which his death was deplored as an irreparable loss to the profession and to the people.

Many distinguished members of his family and kindred survived him, some of them succeeding him in his high position, but all recognizing it as their proudest distinction that they were of kin to the great Columbia chancellor.

Proceedings of a meeting of the Bar at Pulaski, Tennessee, held immediately after the death of the Hon. Chancellor, Samuel Davies Frierson, for the purpose of doing honor to his memory:

The bar of Pulaski met this day to unite with the members of the profession throughout Tennessee in paying a tribute of respect to the memory of that able jurist, upright judge and good man, who died while holding court in our midst.

It was with the most painful feelings and profound sensation that the tidings reached us early on Sunday morning that Chancellor Frierson was dead. We all 'elt that we had lost a warmhearted and dear friend and an impartial and equitable judge, and that his loss at this critical juncture was a great public calamity. For twelve years he was chancellor of this division, and, during all the time that he presided over our courts, not an unkind word was ever uttered by any member of the profession respecting the court. Patiently and courteously he listened to every argument, and as calmly and clearly he delivered his opinions and decrees; inspiring all with the settled conviction that, in coming to his conclusions, he was influenced by the single determination to administer the law and do justice. Among the many distinguished judges who have adorned the bench in Tennessee, none have left, or will leave, a more pure and unsullied reputation than the Hon. Samuel D. Frierson.

Such was the man whose loss we deplore. On this occasion it becomes us to mourn, and we feel that, in paying the highest honors to his memory, we are but giving utterance to the feelings of every member of the bar, by whom the recollection of the virtues of our deceased chancellor will be long cherished.

In order that we may place in an enduring form, to last as long as the records shall be preserved, this expression of our sentiments and tribute of respect for the memory of the deceased, it is directed that some member of the bar, at the next term of the chancery, circuit and county courts, present a copy of these proceedings and accompanying resolutions, signed by the chairman and secretary of the meeting, and ask that the same may be entered on their records.

Resolved, That in the death of the chancellor, the State of Tennessee has been deprived of the services of a model judge, the profession of one of its ablest and most distinguished jurists, and the people of the bright example of an honest and good man.

Resolved, That we tender to the widow and child of the lamented dead our deepest sympathy, and that a copy of these proceedings be respectfully furnished them.

Resolved, That a copy of these proceedings be published in the Pulaski *Citizen*.

Messrs. McCallum, Jones and Brown were appointed to present the entire proceedings of the bar to the chancery, circuit and county courts.

Mr. Whitson, Maj. Richardson, Maj. Jones and Gen. Brown addressed the bar relative to the public and private character of the deceased chancellor, whereupon the meeting adjourned.

JAMES McCALLUM, *Chairman.*

NATHAN ADAMS, *Secretary.*

Chancellor W. S. Fleming, who aided in the compilation of this memoir, says, in reference to the above proceedings: "What could be said of this excellent man more gratifying to his posterity, more complimentary to the profession in which he was a shining light, or more honorable to the bench which he adorned by his learning, his impartiality and his unquestioned integrity?"

*   *   *   *   *   *   *

As the hereditary transmission of both bodily and mental characteristics is a settled conviction with the author of these memoirs, and as we are now concerned with a family which has given many illustrious men to Tennessee, we will give some details of its lineage.

Of Samuel Frierson, sr., the father of the Chancellor, some account has already been given. He married Sarah Wilson in 1787, who was a member of that Wilson family which emigrated from South Carolina at the same time with her husband.

The wife of the Chancellor was Miss Mary McCottery Mayes, another emigrant from Williamsburgh district, South Carolina. She was born August 12, 1805, and married October 5, 1826. Her father was Samuel Mayes, a prominent physician, a Revolutionary soldier who fought at the battle of King's mountain. He was of Scotch-Irish descent, and emigrated to Tennessee at the same time with the Armstrongs and Flemings.

There was a Capt. William Frierson, who also fought at King's mountain, and was a common ancestor of the Friersons, Flemings and Coopers. Dr. Mayes died at the age of ninety, and his son, Scott Mayes, was still living, at the age of ninety-one years, at the time these memoirs were compiled.

Mrs. Frierson died six years after her husband, December 23, 1872. She had six children, only one of whom survived her, Lucius Frierson. A daughter, Salina Jane was married October 19, 1848, to John A. Mc-Ewen, now deceased, a lawyer of Nashville, and once mayor of that city. They had a son, Samuel D. F. Mc-Ewen, born July 10, 1850; educated at Yale College, now a merchant at Columbia. He married Miss Maggie Phillips, daughter of Charles Phillips, planter and commission merchant of New Orleans, and has two children, Margaret and Lucia. Lucius Frierson, surviving son of the Chancellor, was born April 1, 1840, at Columbia; graduated at Chapel Hill, North Carolina, in 1859; was clerk two years in the Columbia branch of the Union Bank; afterwards engaged in merchandise for some years; May 17, 1870, he married Miss Kate, daughter of John F. Morgan, a merchant of Columbia, whose father, Calvin Morgan, was a pioneer merchant of Knoxville. John F. Morgan was related to Gen. John Morgan and Samuel D. Morgan, of Nashville. Mrs. Lucius Frierson's mother was a Miss Louisa Porter, daughter of William Porter, a merchant of Nashville, and afterwards a large farmer of Maury county. He and his brother James were Catholic refugees from Ireland. William settled at Carthage, afterwards at Nashville, and James settled in Louisiana, where he became judge and the father of James Porter, United States Senator from Louisiana. Mrs. Lucius Frierson was educated in the Columbia Female Institute. Her maternal grandmother, wife of the above-named William Porter, is still living at the age of ninety-one.

Lucius Frierson, by his marriage with Miss Morgan, has four children: (1). John Morgan Frierson, born June 23, 1871. (2). Samuel Davies Frierson, born August 27, 1873. (3). Lucius Frierson, jr., born March 8, 1875. (4). Louisa Porter Frierson, born January 26, 1878.

Lucius Frierson became a Mason in 1868, in Roche Lodge, No. 195, and is now Eminent Commander of DeMolay Commandery, No. 3, at Columbia, and has for years been connected with the banking interests of Columbia.

COL. ROBERT I-O-H-NSTONE CHESTER.

JACKSON.

COL. ROBERT I. CHESTER, a gentleman remarkable for his great age and distinguished for his high character, the extreme cordiality of his Chesterfieldian manners, his chivalric faith in woman, and love for choice society, was born in Carlisle, Cumberland county, Pennsylvania, July 31, 1793. His boyhood, till the age of twenty-three, was spent in Jonesborough, East Tennessee, his father having moved to that place in December, 1796. His education was limited to the old field schools and very little of that, but mostly under the tutorship of John Harris, of Jonesborough. He was a clerk in David Deaderick's store there when James W. Deaderick, present Chief Justice of Tennessee, was born.

He volunteered in the place of his uncle, Judge John Kennedy, who was drafted in the war of 1812, and served at Mobile as quartermaster of Col. Samuel Bayliss' Third Tennessee regiment. Mustered into service October 14, 1814, at Knoxville, to join Gen. Jackson at New Orleans. Two regiments, the Third and Fourth, commenced building boats at Washington, Rhea county, in which they were to descend the Tennessee and Mississippi rivers, but the order being countermanded, the regiments were marched overland to Mobile, where they were stationed until peace was declared, in March, 1815.

In July, 1816, young Chester formed a partnership for merchandising at Carthage, Tennessee, with his uncle, Col. Robert Allen, member of Congress, under the firm name of Robert I. Chester & Co., and prospered until 1819, when he engaged largely in the tobacco business and lost a fortune. In 1822 the Legislature made him surveyor of Smith county, and he was engaged in the land warrant business, which brought him to Jackson, where he has lived ever since, except a brief interval, and where his children were all born. From 1824 to 1830 he merchandised at Jackson; was postmaster from 1825 to 1833, resigning to build a steam mill on Reelfoot lake, Obion county, which proved a disastrous venture.

In 1835, with his two brothers-in-law, Dr. William E. Butler and Gen. Samuel J. Hayes, he went to Texas, settled on the Brazos below Waco, planted crops on three plantations, but on the proclamation of Santa Anna, who had invaded the country, and after destroying the Alamo, promised to free the negroes if they would join him, Col. Chester and his companions left that section with their forty negro men. Gen. Sam. Houston having commissioned him colonel, and authorized him to raise a regiment for the Texas revolution, he left Texas, and had already appointed the officers of his regiment, when Gen. Houston's victory at the battle

of San Jacinto put an end to the necessity of sending troops to that quarter.

Having lost by these several removals nearly everything he possessed, Col. Chester returned to Jackson May 1, 1836; was reappointed postmaster and deputy register for the Western district, which latter gave him favorable opportunities to enter and speculate in lands. He has been engaged more or less in the land business ever since, and has issued some five thousand grants. He did most of this work at night, assisted by his wife, she reading to him and he writing until late hours—for both were noted for their industry and energy. Being the owner of several negro men that were good brickmasons and plasterers, he built the Presbyterian church and Female Institute at Jackson, and soon recovered in fortune.

In 1837 President VanBuren appointed Col. Chester United States marshal for the Western district of Tennessee, in which position he remained under various administrations sixteen years, up to 1861, with three years interval under Gen. Taylor's administration. During all his career as marshal he never carried about him a deadly weapon, and never had trouble in the discharge of the duties of his office. He has always maintained an irreproachable character in office. His high standing in this respect is amply attested in letters, still in his possession, from Judge Catron, President Polk and Gen. Jackson. After the war of 1812 he was associated with Gen. Jackson as much as a young man could be, and afterwards married his niece, youngest daughter of Robert Hayes. He began life a poor boy; made a great deal of money, but also paid a great deal of it for security and for the support of his political party. His reputation over the State is sufficient evidence of the integrity of his life and his business transactions. The three talismanic words that account for his success are, hard work, economy and uprightness. Whatever embarrassments he labored under were the result of securities, not his own debts. When the civil war began it found him and his two sons in possession of three fine cotton farms, one hundred and eighty-six slaves, fifty mules, and all the appliances of cotton farming, all of which were lost except the land. From 1841 to 1851 he practiced law; also in 1860–61.

In 1870 Robert B. Hurt and William W. Gates, prominent Whigs of that day, solicited him to run for legislative floater, to fill out the unexpired term of Mr. Roach, deceased, the district being composed of the counties of Madison, Gibson, Carroll and Henderson, and promised to elect him without his going out to canvass. Col. Chester was elected, and re-elected for the following term. When in the Legislature in

1871–72 he went with the members of that body to visit Mrs. ex-President Polk, who was a schoolmate of his first wife. Col. Chester, then an octogenarian, offered this toast, raising his glass and addressing Mrs. Polk: "I hope, madam, you will live to be one hundred years old, and that I may live to see you die." "Yes," quickly responded the venerable lady, "you always wanted something good for yourself ever since I knew you." One reason for his longevity is his temperate habits. Though never abstemious, he was never intoxicated, and never used tobacco. Among the souvenirs and collections of a long life Col. Chester has a cane made from wood from the old American ship "Ironsides," originally presented to President Polk, and by his widow presented to Col. Chester. But the most interesting of the Colonel's treasures is his fine memory stored with historical reminiscences of the statesmen and distinguished characters he has known, and the wars, the changes and times that have gone over him. What a bonanza of interesting incident he would prove to an enterprising short-hand reporter.

Col. Chester has all his life long been a Democrat, and active in politics, contributing to every presidential campaign and voting for every Democratic nominee, from President Madison down to President Cleveland. In recognition of these veteran services he was chosen by the Tennessee electors, in 1884, messenger to carry to Washington the electoral vote of the State for Cleveland and Hendricks. After delivering the vote, he went to Albany to see Mr. Cleveland. Not being a card man, he sent into the office of Gov. Cleveland his name on a slip of paper. Mr. Cleveland soon came into the hall and said, "I need no introduction to you; I am glad to see you, Col. Chester." After about half an hour's conversation, Mr. Cleveland presented Col. Chester his photograph, which is highly appreciated.

Col. Chester is the oldest living Freemason in the United States, having been made a member of Carthage Benevolent Lodge No. 14, in May, 1817. He is also a Knight Templar. He has filled the offices of Grand High Priest of the Grand Chapter and Thrice Illustrious Grand Master of the Grand Council of the State of Tennessee. He is also an elder in the Presbyterian church, which he joined in 1868.

He married first near Jackson, January 20, 1825, Miss Elizabeth Hayes, daughter of Col. Robert Hayes, who was the first United States marshal for West Tennessee. Gen. Jackson and Col. Hayes both marrying Donelsons, Mrs. Chester was niece of Mrs. Gen. Jackson. Her mother, nee Jane Donelson, was a daughter of Col. John Donelson, of Virginia, one of the first settlers in Davidson county, Tennessee. Mrs. Chester died in November, 1841, at the age of thirty-eight. She was a beautiful woman, very much admired; a Christian, and a domestic lady with the rarest graces of female character about her. By this marriage Col. Chester had seven children: (1). Mary Jane, died De-

cember 1, 1846, the wife of Mr. George W. Bond, a lawyer, leaving an infant son, Chester George Bond, now a prominent man and able lawyer at Jackson—"a man," says his grandfather, "of as much probity and honor as any man that ever lived on earth;" he married Miss Kate Royster, of North Carolina, and has two children, Aphia Chester and Chester. His father, Mr. George W. Bond, died in 1851. (2). John, born May 18, 1827; graduated at the West Tennessee College under Mr. McKinney; graduated also at the Jefferson Medical College, Philadelphia; was appointed lieutenant and fought with gallantry all through the Mexican war; married Miss Aphia Taylor, in 1848, by whom he had several children, all of whom died but one, Aphia, now wife of Richard Bostick, in mercantile life in St. Louis; he proved himself a worthy son of a noble sire, being not only a distinguished physician, but was eminent commander of the Knights Templar of Jackson, which he helped to organize. (3). Robert Hayes, born April 29, 1829; graduated at Jackson, and is now a successful farmer in Madison county; married Miss Mary Long, and has three children, William Long, Robert I., jr., and Dolly Vernon, all married. (4). Martha Butler, born June 3, 1832; married Dr. L. L. Battle, now in Shelby county, Tennessee; died April 1, 1872, leaving five children, William P., Jane Royster, Mary Ormand, Belle and Martha. (5). William Butler, born August 10, 1834; graduated at Jackson; is a farmer in Madison county; married Miss Laura O'Connor, and has four children, Ann O'Connor, John, O'Connor and William. (6). Andrew Jackson, called "the king Chester," born May 29, 1836, died October 8, 1856, unmarried, in his twentieth year; a gallant boy, remarkable for his manly form and bearing. (7). Samuel Hayes, born February 24, 1840; graduated at Jackson, and also as an M. D. at Baltimore, where he remained two years studying in a hospital; is now practicing medicine at Jackson; married Miss Ella Ragland, daughter of Senator F. B. Ragland, and has two children, Mamie and Elizabeth.

Col. Chester next married, in Shelby county, Tennessee, January 22, 1855, Mrs. Jane P. Donelson, nee Royster, daughter of David Royster, of Goochland county, Virginia. Her mother, Elizabeth Samson, was sister of Dick Samson, one of the largest farmers in the "Old Dominion." Mrs. Chester was born April 10, 1812, and educated in Goochland county. When Col. Chester married her she had one child, Linnie, who died in Shelby county, the wife of Col. James M. Crews, one of Forrest's great men, leaving at her death a daughter, Linnie Donelson Crews, born October 3, 1865, now under the maternal grandfather's roof. Mrs. Chester's brother, Frank W. Royster, is a prominent real estate agent at Memphis. Her maternal grandmother was a Curd, of Goochland county, Virginia. Her paternal grandmother was a Watkins, of Virginia.

The grandfather of Col. Robert I-o-h-nstone Chester

was a Welshman, born in Limerick, Ireland, He came to Pennsylvania, and was quartermaster in the Pennsylvania line in the Revolutionary war; after the war a United States revenue officer. He married Elizabeth Patterson, of Latark, near Carlisle, Pennsylvania. He had four children: (1). Dr. William Patterson Chester, who moved in 1793 to Jonesborough, Tennessee; his wife was Miss Mary Adams; died a very old man (ninety) at Jonesborough. John Blair, a member of Congress of some distinction, married his daughter Mary. (2). John, father of the subject of this sketch, was raised a coppersmith; married Mary Greer, in Carlisle, Pennsylvania. She was the daughter of Samuel and Rebecca Greer. Samuel Greer was born in Dublin, Ireland, and was in the Revolutionary war. John Chester moved to Jonesborough, Tennessee, in 1796; became a farmer and trader; died in 1832, in Hawkins county, Tennessee; settled the place known as Bowling Green, near Jonesborough; was a man of great energy, self-sustaining and successful; of good common sense, without the finish of an education. (3). Richard, a silversmith; married in McColasterstown, Pennsylvania, to a Dutch woman and died childless. (4). Mary, married an Irishman named William Connell, a merchant at Huntingdon, Pennsylvania, and raised a large family. Col. Chester's paternal grandmother, Elizabeth Patterson, lived with her daughter Mary, at Huntingdon, after the death of her husband. Her two sons, William and John, being in Tennessee, she rode horseback by herself seven hundred miles to see them when she was fifty-five years old, and returned, after a few months, in the same way. She died at Jonesborough in 1810. It will thus be seen that the Chester family on both sides are long lived.

All of Col. Chester's sons, John, Robert, William B. and Samuel, and his grandson, G. Bond, were in the Confederate army, and fought through the war. John commanded the Fifty-first Tennessee regiment, and was in most of the hard-fought contests of the war in the West. In one charge at Perryville he lost one hundred and sixty men killed and wounded, and had his horse killed and hat shot through at Murfreesborough. At the battle of Chickamauga Gen. Bragg put him into the medical corps, saying, "I can make generals, but I can't make doctors." After the Chickamauga fight he and Col. John F. House and Gen. Pope Walker were the judges of the corps court for the Army of Tennessee, and he held that position until the close of the war. William B. Chester was marshal to that court.

The Chesters and the Greers were in the Revolution, and in every war since—a fearlessly brave people.

Dr. John Chester, the second child and oldest son of Col. Chester, to whom brief reference is made in the above family record, was a man of most amiable traits of character, high and noble deeds, whose life was so full of good and useful actions as to deserve more than a mere passing notice in this sketch. He died at Jackson, on June 4, 1877, of small-pox, which disease he contracted in performing a charitable operation on a poor woman. He was a successful physician and skillful surgeon, and was at all times as ready to obey the calls of those whom he knew could never pay his fees, as of those upon whom fortune had showered her gifts. An intimate personal friend, the editor of the Jackson *Whig and Tribune*, writing on the occasion of his death, said of him: "There was a *suaviter in modo* in his style and an electricity in his pleasant face and cheerful, witty words which, it is proverbial, were sunlight in the chamber of the sick, and thrilled the suffering frame of the patient with something like the glow of health as soon as he entered the sick-room; and for many years up to the close of his career, he did a very large and lucrative practice." His death threw the whole city into mourning, and the entire community poured out its grief at the loss of one of its noblest citizens. The business houses were closed and draped in mourning, and the people, with one accord, assembled to commemorate the virtues of the distinguised dead. At this meeting there was a large attendance of ladies, who felt that in the death of Dr. Chester almost every family in the city had been bereaved. The meeting was presided over by Gen. Alexander W. Campbell, who appointed the following gentlemen as a committee to give formal expression to the feelings of the community on the sad occurrence, viz.: B. A. Enloe, chairman, R. W. Haynes, Thomas S. Vincent, Rev. E. McNair and J. L. H. Tomlin. The committee submitted the following report:

The large assembly that is here to-day portrays, in a manner more potent than language can express, the heavy affliction that has fallen upon this community. The sad whispering of every heart is, that "Dr. John Chester is dead;" the noble man, the sincere friend, the disinterested philanthropist, the pure Christian, is no more. Having embalmed himself in all hearts by his unselfish and pre-eminent life of usefulness, no words that we can now employ could add anything to the universal sense of our great loss. His character was so complete and well rounded in every relation of life, that the moment we touch it or attempt to express our appreciation of what he was, we are burdened with a sense of our inability to tell what is keenly felt by all, and is far more vividly spoken by the dark pall which hangs over us to-day. "Mark the perfect man, and behold the upright, the end of that man is peace." Dr. John Chester was born in the city of Jackson, May 18, 1827; was educated in West Tennessee College, where he received his first honorary degree. As soon as he graduated he promptly responded to the call of his country, then engaged in war with Mexico. Having served his country with distinguished gallantry, he returned to his home, and soon after commenced the chosen profession of his life. In the late war he was again found in the ranks of the soldier. The testimony of those who knew him well, and who were with him in the conflict, is that a braver heart never throbbed upon the battle field than his. While a gentle and affectionate companion in social life, he rose to the dignity of a born commander; with the gentle submission and reverence of a son, he combined the prudence and wisdom of a father; as a citizen he was ever a patriot; as a physician, he manifested the highest skill in his noble profession, to which he died a martyr; and by the magic inspiration of his faultless manner he encouraged, comforted and blessed his patients, and demonstrated his own greatness and the influence of a great mind and character.

Resolved, That in the death of Dr. John Chester suffering humanity has lost a noble benefactor, whose ear was ever open to the call of distress as his hand was willing to tender relief; society one of its brightest members; the medical profession one of its noblest and most devoted exponents; the church a true and tried member, whose life was a living witness to the beauty of Christian charity; the State a self-sacrificing and disinterested patriot; the world a man whose character justified the declaration that "an honest man is the noblest work of God."

Resolved, That we, the citizens of Jackson and Madison county, in mass meeting assembled, do, with one voice, give this expression of our sense of the loss we have sustained in the death of a citizen so eminent and useful in all the walks of life, and we beg leave to tender to his bereaved family our profoundest sympathies in this hour of their deep distress, and to join our prayers with theirs that the love of a merciful Father may bring the consolation of the Christian's hope to heal the stricken hearts of his family and friends.

The preamble and resolutions were adopted by a rising vote, every person in the vast assembly, many of whom were in tears, voting in the affirmative. Eloquent and heartfelt tributes to the memory of Dr. Chester were also adopted by all the Masonic bodies of Jackson, the Ancient Order United Workmen and the Knights of Honor, of all which he was an active and zealous member.

HON. JACOB THOMPSON.

MEMPHIS.

THIS gentleman, like a great many prominent Tennesseans, was born in North Carolina. His father seems to have combined the business of a tannery and harness factory with agriculture on a considerable scale. The subject of this sketch was born in Caswell county, North Carolina, May 10, 1810, and was one of eight children, six male and two female. His education up to fourteen years of age was obtained in the common schools of the county, and then he was placed at the Bingham Academy in Orange county, at that time quite a renowned school. After a preparation here of three years, he was entered at the University of North Carolina, where he graduated in 1831. The graduating class of that year consisted of thirteen students, nearly all of whom became distinguished in after life. Among them were Chancellor Calvin M. Jones, of Tennessee, Judge James Grant, of Iowa, the Rev. W. W. Speare and Dr. Steadman of the Episcopal and Presbyterian churches respectively, the latter of whom died at Memphis, and Prof. Hooper, now of the University of North Carolina. That he had acquired the good opinion of the faculty was proved by his appointment as tutor in the University on the day of his graduation. This office he held for eighteen months, when he left the University and entered the law office of Judge Dick, of Greensborough, North Carolina, as a law student. In 1834 he obtained his first license, and his second in 1835. The former authorized him to practice in the lower courts of the State and the latter in the higher.

The same year (1835) he emigrated to Pontotoc, Mississippi, where he commenced practicing, and continued to do so successfully till 1839, when he was elected to Congress for the Northern District of Mississippi. He served uninterruptedly in Congress for twelve years, but in 1851 was beaten by Mr. B. D. Nabors, a Whig clergyman. It was during this canvass that Mr. Thompson made one of his characteristic humorous speeches. He commenced, "Gentlemen, I have now been your Representative in Congress for twelve years and understand all the routine of business there, and have sustained all the impressions which the life in Washington City is capable of making upon a man's character and morals. Now, if you send Mr. Nabors there, you will spoil a good preacher and make a very poor Congressman, and I confidently predict that if you do send him there he will never preach again. I know the influence that society at the capital has upon new men." Nabors was elected and the prediction was verified—he never preached again.

To go back a few years, when Polk was elected President, in 1844, Gov. Brown of Mississippi appointed Mr. Thompson United States Senator to fill some unexpired term and sent the appointment to the Secretary of State, Robert J. Walker. For some unexplained reason Mr. Walker failed to communicate the appointment to Mr. Thompson, which is the more remarkable, as it was through the earnest solicitation of Mr. Thompson that Walker was admitted to the cabinet. On his return to Mississippi he was unanimously renominated by his party for Congress, and, when Gov. Brown insisted upon his accepting his appointment as Senator, he declined, inasmuch as he had accepted the nomination, and was elected that fall to Congress by the largest majority ever given to a congressional candidate in the State. Early in 1857 he was appointed Secretary of the Interior in Mr. Buchanan's cabinet, entered upon the duties of the office in March of that year, and made a peculiarly favorable impression by his manner of conducting the business of the office. No recommendation made by him to Congress ever failed of being promptly acted upon.

In 1861, after the agitation of secession had commenced, an event occurred productive of much scandal at the time, and which was made the pretext of much

groundless obloquy against Mr. Thompson in after
years. A clerk in the office of the Interior Department,
it would appear, allowed eight hundred and seventy
thousand dollars of the Indian trust funds to be transferred to the office of the Secretary of War, taking the
acceptance of that officer for the amount. Strange to
say, this transaction was reported to Congress the same
day that Mr. Thompson first heard of it. Of course, it
excited much comment and discussion, and a committee
of Congress was appointed to investigate the whole
affair. The clerk was prosecuted, and the congressional
committee, after a rigid investigation, reported that
Secretary Thompson was clear of all complicity in the
affair. But those were days of intense and bitter personal animosities, and the most injurious charges were
constantly alleged against him, nor have his political
enemies even yet foregone the indulgence of those
malicious innuendoes for which this unfortunate affair
has furnished the basis.

Mr. Thompson continued in the performance of his
official duties as Secretary till the secession of Mississippi, when he resigned his office and gave in his adhesion to the Southern Confederacy. He became a volunteer aide on Gen. Beauregard's staff, but did not
remain long enough with the army to leave any important
military record. He was appointed lieutenant-colonel
of Ballantine's regiment, and had a horse shot under
him in an engagement at Water Valley. Immediately
after this Gen. Pemberton appointed him inspector-
general of his corps. He held that position until the
surrender of Vicksburg, when he returned to his home
at Oxford, Mississippi, and was elected to the Confederate Legislature. While a member, President Davis
summoned him by telegraph to Richmond, whence he
despatched him on an important mission.

Information had been received that a large number
of influential men in the Northwest were desirous of
forming a peace party, and wished for confidential communication with influential Confederates to ascertain
what terms of peace would be accepted. Always desirous of a peaceful solution of the existing troubles,
the President made it the duty of Mr. Thompson to
communicate with these gentlemen and ascertain whether
any understanding could be arrived at. This mission
was very reluctantly accepted by Mr. Thompson, but
believing that nothing which promised an honorable
termination to the war ought to be neglected, he started
for Canada. He had to run the blockade at Wilmington,
whence he sailed to Bermuda, and thence to Halifax,
Nova Scotia. Here and at other points in British
America he entered into communication with the "Sons
of Liberty."

It is not known, and probably will never be known
now, what were the precise purposes of this organization,
or what negotiations with them were attempted by Mr.
Thompson or authorized by the Confederate government,
and, for this very reason, conjectural scandal has long

been busy with the reputation of Jacob Thompson, and
has not even ceased its attacks since his death. Slanders
which can neither be proved nor disproved are long
lived and die hard. On the one hand, negotiations with
the disaffected in the enemy's country have always been
considered legitimate during war, subject always to the
risk of prosecution for treason on the part of the disaffected, and execution as spies on that of the emissaries,
if captured within the enemy's territory. On the other
hand such negotiations, though justifiable and necessary,
are in their nature distasteful to high minded gentlemen,
and, as has been seen, Mr. Thompson entered on them
reluctantly and gladly relinquished them. One purpose
contemplated was the care of Confederate prisoners
who had escaped from the military prisons in the North
and their conveyance to the South, and it has been
alleged that the arrangement contemplated aid to them
in escaping, but this purpose, if it was ever seriously
entertained, was soon abandoned through the natural
indisposition of the Sons of Liberty to commit themselves by overt acts which would lead to their arrest
and indictment by the Federal authorities. It is not
deemed necessary to refute the sensational fictions of
the northern press about schemes to import rags infected
with yellow fever and small-pox, to burn northern
cities, and other monstrosities, though these are still
occasionally reproduced for electioneering purposes,
and will still probably "revisit the glimpses of the
moon" from time to time. There is no limit in fact to
the number of iniquities that were attributed to Mr.
Thompson and the Confederate government in connection with this mission by the Federal papers during
the war, and the lower class of Republican organs have
kept them up to the present day: meantime, through
fear of compromising his northern correspondents, Mr.
Thompson's lips have been closed, and are now closed
in death. Silence, therefore, is imposed on this editor
also.

Having carried out what was practicable in his mission, and ascertained the impracticability of the rest,
Mr. Thompson reported accordingly and requested to
be recalled, which was done, but he resided until the
close of the war in Toronto.

On his way home he was detained at Portland, Maine.
Secretary Stanton immediately issued an order for his
arrest. As soon as this was known to the President he
directed that the order should be withdrawn, stating
that he preferred that Mr. Thompson should be permitted to escape if he desired to do so. It was withdrawn
but afterwards renewed, and Mr. Lincoln, on the very
day on which he was assassinated, orally directed
that the order should be a second time withdrawn.
Mr. Thompson had served in Congress with Mr. Lincoln,
and there was a kindly feeling between them, as the
following transaction shows; the date of it is not given,
but it must have been shortly before the surrender at
Appomattox. While Mr. Thompson was in Canada

Mr. Emmons, the district-attorney for Michigan, was directed to look after the cases under investigation in the Canadian courts in which the United States government was interested While he was in Canada for that purpose, he was requested by Mr. Lincoln to see Mr. Thompson in person and inform him that Mr. Lincoln desired a private interview with him, and wished him to come to Washington for that purpose, promising the amplest protection should he consent: he did consent, and upon his arrival at Washington, the President directed him to apply to Mr. Seward for letters of protection. Mr. Seward objected, and while the President and Secretary were discussing the subject, Mr. Thompson left Washington and made his way back to Canada without the letters.

After the surrender at Appomattox, he went to Mississippi for Mrs. Thompson and took her to Europe, where he remained two years, visiting Palestine, Egypt and other places of historical interest.

Among themany annoyances heaped upon him by the officials at Washington was the absurd charge got up by Messrs. Holt and Stanton and, at their instance, made the subject of a proclamation by President Johnson, that he had been an accomplice in the assassination of President Lincoln. This charge was so utterly absurd and groundless that after a short time it was withdrawn by a second proclamation.

After the rancor of political vindictiveness abated he returned to the United States and settled himself at Memphis, where he chiefly occupied his time in collecting the relics of his dilapidated fortune. He also devoted himself with great zeal to the affairs of the Episcopal church, of which he was a member, regularly attending both its State and general conventions. He died at Memphis on March 24, 1885, in the seventy-fifth year of his age.

At the time he was visited by the editor of this work, the impression conveyed was that he was a man of affairs, of culture and refinement, and in his careful but easy politeness and attention to his visitors a typical southern gentleman. His height was five feet eleven inches; his form somewhat attenuated and a little bowed with age.

As a speaker his oratory was eager and earnest, as well as closely argumentative, sparing in the use of ornamental diction, and, perhaps for that reason, always practically effective.

He became a Master Mason in 1842, but for twenty years previous to his death had not attended a lodge. He was a member of the Episcopal church, a director

4

in railroad, bank and insurance companies, and prominent in other offices of trust.

He commenced life on two thousand dollars and a body servant, two horses and a good law library, and before the war was worth a million and a half of dollars.

Mr. Thompson's father was Nicholas Thompson, a native of Orange county, North Carolina. He was moderately well educated and of industrious, thrifty habits. His trade was that of a saddler, to which he added a tannery, and he was the proprietor of two farms, and generally successful and prosperous in business. He had six sons and two daughters, and it seems to have been a laudable object of his ambition to give his sons a better education than he had received himself.

In 1838 Jacob Thompson married Miss Catharine Anne, daughter of Col. John P. Jones, a Mississippian of wealth, whose property was eventually inherited by his daughter. Her mother was a daughter of Col. Whately, an eminent Georgian, member of the Legislature of his State. An anecdote is told illustrative of his bravery. A squad of men was sent by the Federal government to arrest and remove him from the Cherokee country, where he had settled. He came out in front of his house, leveled his gun on the commanding officer and commanded him, on pain of instant death, to give the order to ground arms. The officer hesitated, but finally complied. He then marched the men away from their arms, had them collected and delivered to military headquarters. He was no more molested. The Jones family were men of property and intelligence but without political ambition. The paternal grandfather of Mrs. Thompson was a Revolutionary soldier of the Virginia militia, and lost a leg at the battle of Guilford Court-house. He died in the receipt of a government pension. She had three paternal uncles, settled as planters in North Alabama and Mississippi, Weldon, Richard and William Jones. Her brother, Thomas L. Jones, died in the Mexican war. Mrs. Thompson is a lady of great personal attractions. She acquired social distinction in Washington City. Her prominent trait was cheerfulness combined with thoughtful consideration.

By his marriage with this lady, Mr. Thompson had one son, Tazewell Macon, who graduated at the University of Mississippi, and afterwards devoted himself to agricultural pursuits. He married Miss Sallie Fox, who was educated at Washington. He died at the age of thirty-seven years, leaving two children, (1), Katie J., graduated at Fairmount, Tennessee. (2). Mary Anne, now at school at Fairmount.

MAJ. JOHN W. CHILDRESS.

MURFREESBOROUGH.

MAJ. JOHN W. CHILDRESS, for many years a leading and highly respected citizen of Murfreesborough, was born in Sumner county, Tennessee, June 1, 1807. His father was Joel Childress, who came to Tennessee from North Carolina at an early day, and engaged in merchandising at Fox Camp Spring, then a noted place, remaining there until the sale of lots at the present site of Murfreesborough, when he went there and built the first house in Murfreesborough. He was made first postmaster at Murfreesborough, and held the appointment until his death, in 1819, The mother of Maj. Childress was Miss Elizabeth Whitsitt, daughter of John Whitsitt, also a native of North Carolina, who came to Sumner county among the pioneers and located there before the Indian troubles of the frontier were settled. He was associated with the Browns, Haskells, and Blackmores, families so well known in Tennessee.

Maj. Childress was the youngest of a family of two girls and two boys. One of his sisters married President James K. Polk, and the other Dr. Wm. R. Rucker, of Murfreesborough. His brother, Anderson Childress, was a lawyer of ability at Murfreesborough.

Maj. Childress began his education under Samuel P. Black, of Rutherford county, a noted teacher in his day, and continued it under Rev. Robert Henderson, for a long time a Presbyterian minister at Murfreesborough. In 1822 he entered the University of North Carolina, at Chapel Hill, and remained there more than two years, when he graduated. He returned to Tennessee, and began the study of law at Columbia · in the office of his brother-in-law, Hon. James K. Polk, and remained under his instruction until the following year, when Mr. Polk was elected to Congress. He then went into the office of his brother, Anderson Childress, at Murfreesborough. At the age of nineteen he was admitted to the bar by Judge Thomas Stuart, one of the ablest judges that ever presided on the Murfreesborough circuit. Young Childress then settled in Greene county, Alabama, and began the practice of law with fair prospects of success, but in a few months was compelled to leave that section on account of ill health, being threatened with consumption, and once more returning to Tennessee he went to work on a farm, and followed the business of farming all his life, with the firm conviction that farming is the greatest and best of professions.

In 1855, Andrew Johnson, then Governor of Tennessee, appointed him a director of the Bank of Tennessee, at Nashville, the largest banking institution in the State, and he served a term of four years. During this period Hon. Cave Johnson was president of the bank

and James Morton cashier, and the institution was in a more flourishing condition than ever before. Of the fifteen directors who served during that time but two are now living—Hon. Michael Burns, of Nashville, and Col. John McGavock, of Franklin. When the Planters' Bank of Nashville established a branch at Murfreesborough, Maj. Childress, at the request of Mr. Dempsey Weaver, cashier of the parent bank, became president of the branch, and filled that position with great credit and ability until the branch was withdrawn during the war. After the war, when the Murfreesborough Savings Bank was organized, he was made one of its directors and served as such until the bank was merged into the First National Bank of Murfreesborough. He then served as a director of that bank until the death of its president, Mr. Kimbrough, a year or two later, when he was made president, and remained so until 1881, when he resigned on account of increasing age, and was succeeded by Mr. E. L. Jordan, whose sketch appears elsewhere in this volume. During all his banking career, covering a period of some twelve or fourteen years, Maj. Childress never owed a dollar to any bank with which he was connected, and in every case the position came to him unsought. He was also twice appointed a director of the Nashville, Chattanooga & St. Louis Railroad, serving in that capacity about thirteen years in all, and in both instances the position came to him without previous solicitation.

Maj. Childress was raised a Democrat, and lived a Democrat all his life, casting his first vote for Andrew Jackson in 1828. He never held a political office, never was a candidate or office-seeker, but always took a lively interest in politics through principle, patriotism, and on account of his friends. In 1848 he was a delegate to the National Democratic convention, at Baltimore, which nominated Gen. Lewis Cass for President.

Maj. Childress married twice: first, in June, 1831, near Murfreesborough, to Miss Sarah Williams, daughter of Mr. Elisha Williams, a wealthy farmer in Rutherford county. Mrs. Childress's mother was a daughter of Mr. Philip Philips, of Pennsylvania, a large land speculator in Tennessee. By this marriage there were six children: (1). Mary, wife of Col. James M. Avent, a prominent lawyer of Murfreesborough, and mother of four children. (2). James K. Polk Childress, who married the daughter of Dr. Ben. W. Avent, and died in 1862, at the age of twenty-four. (3). Elisha, who entered the Confederate service in the famous Second Tennessee regiment, commanded by Col. Wm. B. Bate, and died in 1862, just after the battle of Shiloh. (4). John W., jr., now a successful lawyer at Nashville, and junior partner of the firm of Colyar, Marks & Childress; married Miss Mary Lyon, daughter of Rev. Dr. James A. Lyon, an eminent Presbyterian minister of Washington county, Tennessee, for thirty years stationed at Columbus, Mississippi, and for ten years professor in the University of Mississippi, at Oxford; by this marriage there are three children. At the beginning of the war he was a cadet at the Western Military Institute, at Nashville, and left there to enter the Confederate army; was given a commission as drill sergeant by Gen. Albert Sidney Johnston, and joined the command the day before the battle of Fort Donelson, where he was captured, being at the time not sixteen years of age. On being exchanged he was made adjutant of his regiment, with the rank of lieutenant, and held that rank until the battle of Bentonville, when he was made captain. On the several occasions during the war when his regiment was consolidated with other regiments he, though always the junior adjutant, was every time appointed adjutant of the new regiment. Capt. Childress since the war was for several terms chairman of the State Democratic Executive Committee of Tennessee, and filled the place with signal ability. (5). Bettie, now the wife of Ex-Gov. John C. Brown, and noted as one of the most elegant and highly cultivated ladies in the State; is the mother of four children. (6). Joseph, who joined the Confederate army near the close of the war at the age of fifteen; after the war marrried Mollie, the daughter of Hon. Edwin A. Keeble, of Murfreesborough, at one time Speaker of the lower house of the Tennessee Legislature, and also a member of the Confederate Congress. Joseph died a few years after marriage, leaving three children.

The first Mrs. Childress died in 1851, and in October, 1852, Maj. Childress was married to Miss Mary Philips, daughter of Judge Joseph Philips, of Rutherford county, uncle of the first Mrs. Childress. Judge Philips was a captain of artillery in the war of 1812, and at the close of that war settled in Illinois, and was made the first Secretary of the Territory of Illinois, and was afterwards made Judge of the Supreme Court. He was

first married in Illinois to Miss Morrison, and after her death came to Tennessee and married again. Several years later he was made president of the People's Bank, at Nashville, and filled that position several years. He died in Rutherford county. in 1857, at the age of seventy-three.

By his second marriage Maj. Childress was the father of six children: (1). William, a farmer of Rutherford county; married Miss Inez Wade, daughter of Levi Wade, Esq., and has three children. (2). Horace, also a farmer in Rutherford county; married to Miss Shelley Maney, daughter of Maj. Louis M. Maney, of Murfreesborough, and granddaughter of Ex-Gov. Newton Cannon; has two children. (3). Eloise, wife of Edgar P. Smith, Esq., an able lawyer, who at one time was assistant attorney-general of the Murfreesborough district; has one child. (4). Annie, aged eighteen years. (5). Eugene, aged fifteen years. (6). Saline, aged eleven years.

Maj. Childress came of Presbyterian stock, and his wives have both been members of that church; but he was never connected with any church organization.

Maj. Childress began his life with but little of this world's goods, but by steady industry, energy, and close attention to business he worked his way to the front. He always dealt on a cash basis, never going in debt, especially after the late war. Previous to the war he had amassed a handsome property, and was one of the largest land and slave owners in Rutherford county. He remained at home when the war began, but being harassed by the Federals he went South with his family, and on returning after peace was declared, found every thing swept away except his lands. But the same indomitable energy that characterized the struggles of his earlier manhood was brought to bear on his shattered fortunes.

Maj. Childress died at Murfreesborough, October 6, 1884, since this volume was begun, universally regretted, and followed to his grave by an immense concourse of his fellow-citizens, who now cherish the memory of his upright life and sterling integrity.

GEN. ALEXANDER W. CAMPBELL.

JACKSON.

THE subject of this sketch was born in the city of Nashville, June 4, 1828, being descended, on his paternal side, from a member of the colony, bearing the family name, which emigrated from Scotland and the north of Ireland, in 1825, settling first in Lancaster county, Pennsylvania, but removing after a few years to Amelia county, Virignia. His great grandfather, with others of the same colony, afterwards moved from Amelia county to western Virginia, and settled in the

territory now embraced in Washington and Wythe counties. His grandfather, Maj. William Campbell, was born in Wythe county, and his grandmother, Miss Anne Campbell (a distant relative), was born in Washington county, where they were married. Soon after their marriage they removed to Lexington, Kentucky, where Gen. Campbell's father was born, in 1799. Maj. William Campbell was a cousin of Col. Arthur Campbell, and his wife a niece of Gen. William Campbell, who fell in the Revolutionary battle of Eutaw Springs. Maj. William Campbell was at one time one of the largest pioneer merchants west of the Alleghanies, his business connections extending from the falls of the Ohio to New Orleans, and embracing every important business point on the Ohio and Mississippi rivers. The business disasters growing out of the great financial crisis of 1817 so impaired his fortunes that he retired from commercial pursuits and accepted the position of superintendent of the mineral lands of the Northwest, tendered him by Gen. Jackson, who was his intimate personal and political friend, his headquarters being fixed at Galena, Illinois. While residing here the Black Hawk war broke out, and he was elected to command a battalion of volunteers from the State of Illinois. While the father of our subject was a youth Maj. William Campbell moved from Lexington to the Green river country, in Kentucky, and made his home in Greeneville, where he established the first bank in that part of the State, of which he made his son, then only nineteen years old, the cashier. After a considerable period of most acceptable service in his father's bank, the father of Gen. Campbell, who had received a good preparatory education at Hopkinsville, Kentucky, entered Dickinson college, Pennsylvania, from which he was graduated in 1825. In the meantime, Maj. Campbell had moved to Nashville, to which place his son returned upon leaving college, and studied and commenced the practice of law, being associated, both in the study and practice of his profession, with such subsequently distinguished men as Bailey Peyton, Henry A. Wise, Dixon Allen, Thomas Washington and Francis B. Fogg. In 1827 he was married to Miss Jane E. Porter, daughter of Alexander Porter, one of the pioneer merchants of Nashville. Before he had well established himself in his profession, in which his talents and excellent training promised a brilliant career, the Union bank was chartered, and there being in those days so few who had any experience in the banking business, he was offered and accepted the position of cashier of the branch of the new bank at Jackson, in West Tennessee, to which point he proceeded and opened the bank on the first day of July, 1833, his young family following in the succeeding November. He continued in charge of the affairs of the bank for sixteen years, until 1849, when he retired and devoted himself to his planting interest, dealing largely also in wild lands in West Tennessee. He died on his plantation, near Jackson, in June, 1874. He had one brother and one sister. The former, Robert C. Campbell, lived for many years at Ashport, Tennessee, engaged in planting, where he raised a large family of children, and from which place he removed to Paducah, Kentucky, just previous to the civil war. He died while on a visit to a daughter in Texas, in 187–. His sister, Cynthia Ann, married first Dr. Samuel R. Campbell, who lived but a short time. She then married Lieutenant George W.

McGehee, of Georgia, a graduate of West Point, who died at an early age. She afterwards married Mr. John Siddall, of Illinois, who died of yellow fever in New Orleans, in 1853. She is still living with her only child, John O. McGehee, in Concrete, Texas.

The maternal grandfather of Gen. Campbell, Alexander Porter, was born in Ireland, and first settled at Jonesborough, in East Tennessee, where he married Miss Susan Massengill. While living at Jonesborough, the Irish rebellion of 1798 broke out, and his eldest brother, Rev. James Porter, a Presbyterian minister, one time professor of chemistry in the University of Dublin, became involved in the troubles of the country, which determined him to return to his native island to look after the welfare of his relatives. His brother James was tried on a charge of treason, convicted and executed. His younger brothers, Robert and William, succeeded in making their escape from the country, and came to America with him. He afterwards brought over two sisters and two nephews, Alexander and James, sons of his brother James. His brother Robert died unmarried. His brother William first lived at Carthage, in Smith county, from which place he removed to Maury county, where he died, leaving three children, Louisa, Mary and William. Louisa married John Morgan, and Mary married Samuel Mayes, merchants of Columbia. William Porter, jr., died during the civil war, leaving a widow and several children in Columbia. Alexander and James Porter, sons of Rev. James Porter, both read law while living with the grandfather of Gen. Campbell, in Nashville, and after the acquisition of the territory of Louisiana by the United States, removed there and commenced the practice of their profession. Upon the organization of the State government of Louisiana, Alexander was appointed one of the judges of the Supreme Court, and his brother James was made Attorney-General. They both engaged in sugar planting and acquired large estates. Alexander Porter represented the State of Louisiana in the Senate of the United States, and was an intimate friend of Henry Clay. His only child, a daughter, married Mr. Alston, a son of Gov. Alston, of South Carolina. Both died young, leaving no children. The widow of James Porter, and two daughters, are now living in Attakapas, Louisiana. Alexander Porter's sister, Rebecca, married Mr. Allison, who left, surviving her, Maj. Alexander Allison and Mr. Andrew Allison, of Nashville, and Dr. Robert Allison, of Lebanon.

Gen. Campbell's maternal grandfather, Alexander Porter, and his wife, Susan Massengill, had seven children, to-wit: James A. Porter, Matilda Porter (who married Robert W. Green), Penelope Porter (who married James Woods), Jane Eliza (who married John W. Campbell, his father), Alexander M. Porter, William Porter, and Robert M. Porter. James A. Porter first married Miss Sally Ann Murphy, of Louisiana, by whom he had one child, Capt. Alexander J. Porter, now living in Nashville. His second wife, Miss Amanda McNairy, is also living in that city. Mrs. Matilda Green died in 1831, in Decatur, Alabama, and left four children, Susan, Jane, Alexander P., Robert W., and Matilda P., all of whom are dead except the last, who married James W. Armstrong, and now resides in Abilene, Texas. Jane Eliza, the mother of Gen. Campbell, died in December, 1849, leaving ten children, viz.: Alexander W., Susan Ann, Ann Matilda, Penelope Porter, Jane Eliza, Cynthia Roberta, Mary Madeline, John James, Robert Porter, and Allison Woods. Ann Matilda died single; Penelope Porter, who married Col. Robert Sterling, died in 1872, leaving two children, Jane P. and Carrie M; John James was killed at the battle of Shiloh when nineteen years old; Robert and Allison died in 1850, of cholera, in Nashville; Jane Eliza married Dr. Preston B. Scott, of Louisville, Kentucky, where she now resides; the others live in Jackson, with the exception of Mary, whose home is in Washington City.

The subject of this sketch received his primary and collegiate training at the Jackson Male Academy and West Tennessee College, and his professional education in the law department of Cumberland University, at Lebanon. Before entering the law school he had pursued his legal studies for more than a year under the late Judge A. W. O. Totten.

On January 13, 1852, he married, at Lebanon, Miss Ann Dixon Allen, a native of Nashville, daughter and only child of Dixon Allen, a lawyer, who had greatly distinguished himself, and gave promise of a most brilliant career, but who died at the early age of twenty-six years. Mrs. Campbell's grandfather, Col. Robert Allen, a wealthy merchant of Carthage, was for several terms a member of Congress from his district. Her mother was a daughter of George W. Gibbs, who settled at Sparta, Tennessee, at a very early day, and removed to Nashville about 1812, where he was distinguished as a land holder and as a land lawyer, standing at the head of his profession in that department. Gen. Gibbs' father was a native of Germany, who came to America in early life, and settled in East Tennessee as a farmer. Mrs. Campbell is a niece of Joseph W. Allen, a retired banker of Nashville. Her mother first married Judge William L. Brown, of Nashville, one of the leading lawyers of the State. She afterwards became the wife of Dixon Allen, and after his death married the father of Gen. Campbell. Mrs. Campbell received her education at the Jackson Female Institute, and the Columbia Female Institute, having graduated at both of these schools. She is a lady of finished education, fine literary taste, and possesses an extensive knowledge of books. Her acquirements in this respect are so thorough and accurate as to enable her to serve as a ready reference for her husband when he wishes to recur to a forgotten historical fact or a classical quotation. She is noted for her devotion to the duties of religion, being ever foremost in all the charities of her church and city. She is a member of the Episcopal church, as are also her husband and the younger members of the family.

In 1852, soon after completing his law course, Gen. Campbell opened an office in Jackson, and entered upon the practice of his profession. In 1855, he formed a partnership with the late T. P. Scurlock, which continued until the breaking out of the civil war. He was appointed United States district attorney for the Western district of Tennessee, in 1854, by President Pierce, and reappointed in 1857, by President Buchanan. He resigned the position in 1860, after six years of acceptable service.

Gen. Campbell's record during the civil war is a most creditable one. Having always been a Democrat of the Jeffersonian school, and believing that the political doctrines and constitutional interpretations taught by the immortal author of the Declaration of Independence and his great contemporary, Mr. Madison, to be the true theory of our government, and the correct exposition of the relations between the Federal government and the States, he did not hesitate for a moment upon which side he should take his stand when the war between the sections was inaugurated. On the first call for volunteers to repel the proposed invasion of the South, he enrolled himself as a private in the Independent Guards, a company raised at Jackson, which afterwards became a part of the Sixth Tennessee regiment. Before this regiment was mustered into service, however, he was appointed by Gov. Harris Assistant Inspector General in the provisional army of Tennessee, and was engaged for some time in mustering in and organizing the West Tennessee troops. In June, 1861, he was assigned to duty on Gen. Cheatham's staff, and remained on staff duty until October of the same year, when he was elected colonel of the Thirty-third Tennessee regiment. The first battle in which he was engaged was that of Shiloh, fought on the 6th and 7th of April, 1862, where his regiment distinguished itself for gallantry, being the last that fought in the battle, and the last to leave the field. At this battle Gen. Campbell was shot through the left arm, just below the shoulder, by a minnie ball, but did not leave the field. Later on in the fight he was wounded in the right foot, and had his horse killed under him. He was at the head of his regiment at the battle of Perryville, fought on the 10th and 11th of October, 1863, where he was slightly wounded in the thigh. At the battle of Murfreesborough, he was attached to the staff of Gen. Polk, and served as Assistant Inspector General. After that battle, at the request of Gov. Harris, he was placed in charge of the conscript bureau of a portion of Middle Tennessee, with headquarters at Fayetteville, where he continued until July, 1863, when Gen. Bragg evacuated that territory and fell back towards Chattanooga. He was then sent to West Tennessee by Gen. Bragg to collect up and organize the desultory cavalry in that portion of the State. While engaged in this service he was captured near Lexington, Henderson county, in August, 1863, and sent as a prisoner to Johnson's Island in September following. He remained at Johnson's Island until September 16, 1864, one year to a day, when he was taken with others to City Point and exchanged. While a prisoner at Johnson's Island, the authorities at Richmond, not having been informed of his capture, promoted him to the rank of Brigadier General. After his exchange was declared, he was assigned to duty as commander of one of Gen. Forrest's brigades, and served in that command until the surrender of Gen. Forrest's troops at Gainesville, Alabama, May 5, 1865.

This brief record of the part taken by Gen. Campbell in the war between the States needs no comment. It tells the simple story of a brave man trying to do his duty, and who had made up his mind to die, if necessary, in its accomplishment. It is doubtful if any man is prepared for the battle of life, either in peace or war, in any business or profession, until he has first answered to himself affirmatively the question: "Can you die if duty calls in the line of your profession or calling?" This question answered in the affirmative, all the troubles incident to the battle of life are easily surmounted.

The war over, Gen. Campbell returned to his home at Jackson, and took up the practice of his profession in partnership with Judge A. W. O. Totten, the partnership continuing until the death of the latter, in June, 1867. He continued the practice alone until 1870, when he associated with himself H. W. McCorry, formerly a law student under him, and practiced with him until 1875, when he formed a partnership with Hon. Howell E. Jackson, with whom he practiced until Judge Jackson's election to the United States Senate, in 1881. After this he was for a short time in partnership with John L. Brown, but since April, 1883, he has practiced alone. During his professional career he has been engaged as counsel in a number of important banking, railroad and criminal cases of some celebrity in the State, but as these things go without saying, it is deemed unnecessary to make special mention of them here. Although he has enjoyed a large and lucrative practice,

he has not grown rich, but is in comfortable circumstances. Being most liberal and generous by nature, he never set himself to the accumulation of wealth, but always used his income freely. Besides being charged with almost the entire support of two or three families, he has paid twenty thousand dollars of his father's debts. His motto through life has been: "Be honest; do your duty, and let the consequences take care of themselves."

Gen. Campbell has always possessed in a marked degree the esteem and confidence of the community in which he has spent his life. Jackson has been his home ever since his father moved there from Nashville, in 1833, when he was five years old. He was mayor of the city in 1856; was president of the Bank of Madison from June, 1866, to February, 1881; was a director in the Mobile and Ohio railroad company from 1868 to to 1872; and is a director in the Jackson Gas-light company. In 1868, in New York, and in 1876, at St. Louis, he was a delegate from Tennessee to the National Democratic convention. In 1870, he was a delegate from Madison county to the State constitutional convention, and served on the judiciary committee of that body, of which the late Chief Justice Nicholson was chairman. He has on several occasions served as special judge on the Supreme bench of the State.

Gen. Campbell is a man of spare build, with keen black eyes and a face and forehead thickly corrugated with the lines of thought. His mind is one of great power, capable of intense concentration, and while possessed of the keenest sensibilities, he has about him that air of self-possession and collectedness that Virgil expressed in the words,

"Librata suis ponderibus."

By his marriage with Miss Allen have been born six children: (1). Dixon Allen; died in infancy. (2). Louisa Jane; educated at Jackson Female Institute; married Dr. Samuel B. Carey, of Union City, Tennessee; burned to death in 1877, by her clothing accidentally taking fire. (3). Anne Allen; educated at Jackson; married W. R. McIntosh, a merchant and general southern freight agent of the Chesapeake and Ohio railroad company; has one child, Campbell. (4). John W.; born June 2, 1866. (5). Katharine Fenner. (6). Alexander W.

HON. ARCHELAUS M. HUGHES.

COLUMBIA.

A MONG the many distinguished lawyers who made the bar of Columbia famous during the middle of the present century, no reputation was more brilliant than that of A. M. Hughes.

He was born in Stokes county, North Carolina, November 21, 1811. His father having moved to Maury

county in 1828, the son, then seventeen years of age, accompanied him, and that county has been his home ever since. He was principally educated at the Patrick Henry Academy, Henry county, Virginia, where he studied two years.

After leaving school he engaged in teaching at Cedar

Springs, then in Maury county, but which is now included in the newer county of Marshall, and was afterwards employed as clerk in the firm of Frierson & Stratton for four years. He then became the partner of Gardner Frierson in mercantile business. This partnership lasted six years, from 1836 to 1842, but did not prove successful.

He had been privately studying law in his leisure hours, even while engaged in business, having evidently looked forward to that as his ultimate profession. And here the editor would call attention to the fact that almost all our lawyers who have attained pre-eminence in their profession have, in their early years, engaged in general business as merchants, bankers' clerks, book-keepers, or in other occupations which gave them practical acquaintance with the routine of business transactions, a knowledge which could not fail to be useful in a profession which brings men in constant contact with business in all its forms.

He now devoted his entire time and attention to the study of law in the office of Madison S. Frierson, and was admitted to the bar about 1846–47, at the age of thirty-five, by Judge Dillahunty. He commenced practice at Columbia, which has been his residence ever since, and where he still occasionally takes part in the conduct of important cases.

In 1847 he was elected attorney-general for Columbia judicial circuit, and re-elected in 1853. A year and a half after this the constitution was changed, and he was thrown out of office, but was re-elected in 1860, holding the office altogether for thirteen years. He was elected judge of the same court in 1866, and presided therein till 1870, when the adoption of the revised constitution of that year again remanded him to private practice. From 1873 till 1877 he was United States district attorney under appointment from President Grant.

He was a Whig before the war, and was never a candidate for political office except in 1861, when he was elected as a Union delegate to the constitutional convention by the counties of Maury and Williamson; but the convention never met, being voted down by the people.

Since the war Judge Hughes has been a Republican, and has attended nearly all the State conventions of his party, and received many ballots for nomination as Republican candidate for governor in the convention of 1881. He attended as an alternate the convention at Cincinnati which nominated Mr. Hayes for president.

Educated by Methodist parents, he joined the Presbyterian church about 1848, all his associations from the time that he first went to Columbia having been Presbyterians.

He became a Mason at Columbia about 1837–38, and is a Knight Templar. He has been three several times Grand Master of the State of Tennessee, and is the oldest grand master in it. He has been twice Grand High Priest of the State of Tennessee. He belongs to no other secret associations.

In the practice of his profession Judge Hughes has been financially successful, having built up a handsome fortune by his own unaided exertions; he has given his children a fine education, which he considers the best fortune he could give them.

His methods in the conduct of life, as pursued by himself and enjoined upon his children, are strict veracity and the avoidance of dissipation. He never made anything by speculation or by any other means than the practice of his profession. The highest fee he ever received was fifteen hundred dollars. The best part of his life has been spent before juries, either as prosecuting attorney or in private practice. While attorney-general he did his best to convict the guilty, but never used his influence to persecute anybody, believing it to be as much his duty to let the innocent go free as to convict the guilty. In one instance a female, indicted on a criminal charge, was, as he thought, insufficiently defended, and believing her innocent, instead of continuing the prosecution, he addressed the court in favor of her discharge, which was granted by Judge Dillahunty with a high compliment to the attorney general.

Judge Hughes has been twice married, the two ladies being first cousins.

His first marriage was in Bedford county, Tennessee, in 1836; the lady was Miss Sarah G., daughter of Thomas B. Moseley, a successful farmer of a Virginia family. Her mother was Rebecca Martin, daughter of Capt. Matt. Martin, now deceased. The first Mrs. Hughes' grandmother was sister of Rachel Clay, and own cousin of Henry Clay, of Kentucky.

By his first marriage, Judge Hughes has had two children: (1). Rebecca, who died in her thirteenth year. (2.) Sarah, graduated at the Columbia Female Institute, and is still living.

The first Mrs. Hughes died in 1843, leaving behind her an enviable reputation as possessing a character of high moral elevation and all the accomplishments of a finished lady.

His second marriage took place in Bedford county, December 14, 1844, the lady being Miss Mattie B., daughter of Col. John L. Neill, who was in the war of 1812, captured December 23, and a prisoner till after the battle of New Orleans in 1815. Her mother and the mother of the first Mrs. Hughes were sisters, both being daughters of Capt. Matt. Martin, mentioned above.

By his second marriage the Judge has five children living: (1). A. M. Hughes, jr.; educated at Sidney, Ohio; is a lawyer by profession, and resides at Columbia. (2). William Neill Hughes, educated at Earlham, Indiana; is a lieutenant in the Thirteenth infantry, United States army, appointed from civil life. (3). Edmond D. Hughes, educated at the University of

Tennessee, Knoxville; late deputy collector of internal revenue for Middle Tennessee. (4). James White Hughes, graduate of the University of Tennessee; now in the engineer's department of the Atchison, Topeka and Santa Fe railroad. (5). Alice, graduated from the Columbia Female Institute, and now living. The present Mrs. Hughes is a Presbyterian, a lady of great force of character, a model housekeeper, noted for her liberality and charity to the poor.

The foundation of the American branch of the Hughes family was the settlement of three brothers of the name near Richmond, Virginia, about the middle of the eighteenth century. It is believed that all the Hugheses in the southern States are their descendants. One of these is Judge Hughes of the Federal court in Virginia.

Judge Hughes' brothers are: (1). Samuel Hughes, half brother, of Surrey county, North Carolina, father of Powell Hughes, a United States marshal in Virginia. (2). John F. Hughes, a presiding elder in the Methodist Episcopal church, of which he has been a member since boyhood. (3). William H. Hughes, a Methodist preacher since twenty years old.

The father of Judge Hughes was William Hughes, a native of Virginia; the family are of Welsh descent, remarkable for their longevity, as the following table will show:

NAME.	RELATIONSHIP.	Age at Death.
Mary Dalton	Paternal grandmother	97
—— Dalton	Paternal great aunt	95
—— Dalton	Paternal great aunt	95
William Hughes	Father	87
Nancy Stoval	Paternal aunt	70
Mrs. Fulkerson	Paternal aunt	98
Sallie Martin	Aunt, still alive at ninety..	
Matilda Dillard	Aunt	86
John Hughes	Uncle	88
Madison R. Hughes	Uncle	84
Archelaus Hughes	Uncle, over	80
Samuel M. Hughes	Uncle	70
Reuben Hughes	Uncle	70

GEN. E. KIRBY SMITH.

SEWANEE.

THE University of the South, at Sewanee, on the Cumberland plateau of Tennessee, is now the peaceful home of the military chieftain whose name stands at the head of this section. The visitor, who seeks with interest there the retired veteran of a life-long military service, naturally looks for the curt and peremptory speech, the erect figure and formal gait accepted as the characteristic expression of the retired military officer. No contrast could be greater than that of the reality with this fancied sketch. What we see when we visit his cottage home is a jovial middle-aged country gentleman who, at first sight, seems to have no object in life but that of making the world pleasant to himself and his neighbors. Even this second impression, however, will meet with further correction upon further acquaintance, for beneath that genial exterior, lies a stern sense of duty and a profound religious conviction, the characteristics of a man who, throughout his life, has done and suffered much for what he believed to be the cause of right and truth. But the character of such a man cannot be described in a paragraph; it has to be ascertained by a study of his life.

Edmund Kirby Smith was born at St. Augustine, Florida, in May, 1824. His father had been an officer in the United States army, but had retired, become a lawyer, and was appointed judge of the Federal courts in the Florida territory, which office he was filling at the time of our hero's birth. He lived at his birth-place till he was ten years old, when, his father having been sent to Congress from Florida, he was sent to the famous Hallowell school, at Alexandria, Virginia. Here he studied for six years, when, obtaining an appointment at West Point, he completed his course there and graduated in the class of 1845, with Fitz-John Porter, C. P. Stone, W. F. Smith, B. E. Bee, Gordon Granger, D. B. Sacket, and many other officers subsequently distinguished in both armies.

The record of his military achievements in two great wars and an Indian campaign cannot be given here; they are spread on the page of history wherever the triumphs and calamities of the Mexican and civil wars are recorded for the instruction, the example and the warning of future generations. He received his first commission as brevet second lieutenant, fifth United States infantry in July 1, 1845, and brevet second lieutenant seventh infantry, August 22, 1846. He soon got his "baptism of fire" in the Mexican war, for we find him breveted first lieutenant April 18, 1847, for gallant and meritorious conduct, in the battle of Cerro Gordo, Mexico, and captain on August 20, 1847, for gallant and meritorious conduct. The war being closed, however, it soon appeared that the military authorities had discerned in him intellectual qualities beyond those which attach to mere gallantry in the field, for he was ordered to West Point, October 23, 1849, to assume the post of acting assistant professor of mathematics in the National

Military Academy; and when, after the Mexican war, it became necessary to survey the new frontier established by the results of that war, in 1855, he acted as botanist to the military commission detailed for that purpose. Botany, entomology and conchology have been and are still his favorite studies. The professorship he held for three years. In 1855, he was appointed captain in the second cavalry, and with this command was constantly engaged in frontier warfare from this time till the outbreak of the civil war. Like many of the best soldiers of the Confederate army, he was opposed to secession until it was a *fait accompli*, but then offered his sword and his life for the defense of the new government. His offer was gladly accepted, and his promotion rapid, as is testified by the following list of his commissions : (1.) Colonel of cavalry at the first organization of the Confederate government and army at Montgomery, 1861. (2.) Brigadier-general, June 17, 1861. (3.) Major-general, October 10, 1861. (4.) Lieutenant-general, October 9, 1862. (5.) Full-general, February 19, 1864. He held important commands successively in Virginia, Tennessee, Kentucky, and the trans-Mississippi department; in the first he was present at the first battle of Manassas; in the two last fields of operation he was largely left to his own discretion, and conducted masterly campaigns in both of them.

For his brilliant victory at Richmond, Kentucky, the Confederate Congress, on February 17, 1864, voted him a resolution of thanks, styling the action " the only really decisive battle of the war."

This expression points to the fact that his merits as a commander consist not so much in winning pitched battles, as in so disposing his troops, both before and after the fight, as not only to obtain victory but to secure substantial advantages to his government as its fruits. In his trans-Mississippi campaigns he had to create the resources with which he operated. He organized not only his military command but the civil government. Even his financial resources were raised by means of the State Legislature, which he inaugurated, basing its operations upon the cotton at the disposal of the government. The Texas Legislature twice voted him resolutions of thanks for services in that State. It can not be doubted that the department administered by him was left in a better condition for future prosperity than any other which had been the seat of active warfare.

When the end came, and the surrender at Appomattox proclaimed disarmament to the forces of the South which still kept the field, and while it was still uncertain whether criminal charges would not be preferred against the leading officers of the Southern army, Gen. Smith found it necessary to leave the United States for a time. He first surrendered his army to Gen. Canby, May 26, 1865, and bade farewell to his devoted soldiers in a solemn and touching address from which we extract the following peroration : " Your

present duty is plain ; return to your families, resume the occupations of peace, yield obedience to the laws, labor to restore order. Strive, both by counsel and example, to give security to both life and liberty, and may God in his mercy direct you aright and heal the wounds of our distracted country." His own life during the last twenty years has been a beautiful and impressive realization of this counsel.

After doing all in his power for his army, he went through Mexico to Cuba, and after two months, finding that it was safe to return, sailed for New York and thence repaired to Lynchburg, Virginia, where he rejoined his family and then moved to Louisville, Kentucky.

Here he assisted in organizing the Atlantic and Pacific Telegraph company, and became its president, which office he filled till that concern was absorbed by the Western Union company.

In 1867, he became president of the Western Military Academy, Henry county, Kentucky, and held the office for two years, when bad luck again followed him ; the buildings were burned down and he was again without employment. But his talents and great administrative ability were well known and he became chancellor of the University of Nashville.

After six years' honorable service in this capacity, he was invited to take the chair of mathematics in the University of the South, at Sewanee, Tennessee, in the duties of which he has been occupied to the present day, idolized by his pupils and commanding the respectful esteem and sympathy of the whole South, for whose cause he gave his splendid talents, his powerful influence and four of the best years of his life.

The military experience of Gen. Smith is in many respects unique. In constant military service for twenty years, holding commands in Mexico, on the Texas frontier, in Virginia, in Kentucky, in the States west of the Mississippi, he never knew defeat. In the Mexican war he was present at every battle, both in Scott's and Taylor's line, except that of Buena Vista, when he was engaged in the siege of Vera Cruz. He was never taken prisoner, and his command never retreated before the enemy; he was never in an unsuccessful engagement, either as subaltern or as in chief command.

Every expedition he organized was successful, and he organized the brilliant raids of Morgan, Forrest and others. It was he who commissioned Forrest as brigadier-general when organizing the expedition from his department which, dashing into Tennessee under Forrest, captured the entire brigade, infantry and cavalry, of Crittenden at Murfreesborough, one of the most brilliant *coups* of the war.

He had thirteen relatives and connections in the Mexican war ; all his people for generations back have been soldiers; all his nephews are graduates of West Point, as he is himself, and as was his brother, Ephraim Kirby Smith, who fell in 1847, at Molino del Rey. One

5

of his nephews, named after him, E. Kirby Smith, fell at Corinth in the Federal army.

He was twice wounded, first by an Indian's arrow, at the decisive Indian battle in the big bend of Arkansas river, near Fort Atkinson; the missile passed entirely through the body, coming out at his hip. He was a young man at that time, and certainly a healthy one, for his wound healed in the saddle during a ride of four hundred miles. His second wound was in the Confederate army, in the first battle of Manassas; the ball entering at the right shoulder and escaping under the left shoulder-blade. This wound confined him for several months.

Of his bravery no one need speak, for no man could have passed through all the achievements and endured all the hardships which he has encountered without courage of the very finest temper. But his courage has been tested in other ways than on the field of battle. Many men have " sought the bubble reputation in the cannon's mouth " who would shrink appalled from an encounter with the pestilence; through the former the excitement of the fray sustains a man, the latter has to be encountered in cold blood at the bidding of holy charity. Such commands have been obeyed by Gen. Smith with the same punctilious completeness as he rendered to orders from headquarters. He nursed sick soldiers for many months of an epidemic of yellow fever at Fort Brown, Texas, and performed similar services in several other epidemics, both of cholera and yellow fever, taking both diseases himself.

But even the courage which faces the terrors of war and pestilence gives way, in our estimation, before that moral heroism which sustains a truly great man under the crushing trials of disaster and defeat. When the final collapse of the Southern Confederacy at length arrived, two men above all others stood out as shining examples of the sublime dignity with which a brave man submits to inevitably adversity. They were Gens. Lee and Kirby Smith. They had not been beaten. Gen. Lee was but once even repulsed in an assault, and Gen. Smith never turned his back where the enemy kept the field. They simply relinquished the field when the nation could no longer furnish them the resources for keeping it. The nation had gladly given them its manhood and its treasure, its toil and blood, and continued to give them till there was no more to give, and then the end came. It was not that our generals or our soldiers were defeated, but that the nation was exhausted. And how then did these two great men act? Not as many smaller heroes did; they did not stand forward as martyrs and cry out to their people: "See what we have done and suffered for you; what are you going to do for us? Give us emolument and honor; make us your governors and representatives, your judges and senators," and then subside into a state of querulous bitterness because their transcendent services had not been better acknowledged. Not so they. They looked upon all they had done as in the line of duty; the nation had done its duty and suffered, and so had they, and things were even; then, as duty had been their guiding principle throughout, they looked around to see what duties were still in their power? The South was laboring to reinstate its educational system, and there was their opportunity; they could teach mathematics, and they proffered their services as they had proffered their swords before, and one of them, at Washington-Lee University, has died at his post, amid the tears of a nation; the other is still quietly and cheerfully rendering the same services in the University at Sewanee, and no one has heard either of them repine. They lived as if it were a matter of course that, as their services were no longer called for in the army, they should render them wherever they were needed. Two men whose military operations have been in men's mouths through two hemispheres, quietly teaching youths algebra and the calculus, and thinking the one occupation as well becoming them as the other. Disaster cannot humiliate such men as these.

It remains that we give something of the lineage and progeny of our hero. Of his father we have already said something; his name was Joseph E. Smith, a colonel in the United States army, afterwards lawyer, judge and congressional representative of the Florida territory. He died at St. Augustine, 1846, at the age of seventy-six. He is represented as a man of immense physical powers, six feet two inches high and muscular, of great mental abilities, of strong will and positive character. His grandfather, Col. Elnathan Smith, of Connecticut, was a wealthy farmer in that State, prominent in politics, and an officer in the Revolutionary army. He married Chloe Lee, daughter of Gen. Isaac Lee, of Connecticut, and died at New Britain, Connecticut, very nearly ninety years of age.

Gen. Smith's mother, nee Frances Kirby, was born in Lichfield, Connecticut, daughter of Gen. Ephraim Kirby, also a native of that State, a prominent officer in the Revolutionary army. He was appointed by President Jefferson on the commission for the purchase of Louisiana; and was subsequently appointed first United States judge of the Mississippi territory, and died at Fort Stoddard, Alabama; his tomb on the Alabama river is to this day called "the patriot's grave." The Kirbys were a prominent family among the early settlers of Connecticut; the old farm houses at Lichfield and New Britain are among the oldest houses in the State.

Gen. Smith's maternal grandmother was Ruth Marvin, daughter of Reynold Marvin, of Lyme, Connecticut, of the same family with Bishop Marvin. Ruth was a noted character; she helped to mould bullets out of the old leaden statue of King George at the commencement of the Revolutionary war.

The two Seymours, governors of New York and Connecticut, are relatives of Gen. Smith; so also was Bishop Francis L. Hawkes, one of the most eloquent divines produced by this country, and especially noted as an impressive reader of the Protestant Episcopal liturgy. He was a lawyer in North Carolina before his ordination, and author of a well-known history of that State.

Gen. Smith's mother was a remarkable woman, highly educated and accomplished; she was educated at Bethlehem, Pennsylvania, was a member of the Episcopal church, as were all Gen. Smith's relatives on both sides. She kept up with the literatures and politics of the day to the day of her death. Her energy of character was astonishing; when the first Federal gunboat arrived at St. Augustine, she went out and urged the citizens to fight, and offered to command them, though eighty years old. When she found that they would not fight, she, with her own hands, helped to cut down the flagstaff, then went to her room and locked herself in. Refusing to take the oath, she was imprisoned by the Federal authorities. Even in death she manifested her extraordinary energy of will; having protested during life that she would never go to bed to die, she finally expired in a sitting posture in her ninety-fourth year. She left two children, the general and his sister, Frances Marvin, who died in 1881, widow of Col. L. B. Webster, of the United States artillery.

Gen. Smith married at Lynchburg, in 1861, Miss Cassie Selden, born at Lynchburg, Virginia, daughter of Samuel L. Selden, a lineal descendant of the learned English lawyer of that name. Her mother was a Miss Hare, daughter of a wealthy tobacco manufacturer in Virginia.

Mrs. Smith was educated at the Catholic college, Georgetown, District of Columbia; is a member of the Episcopal church, much esteemed in society, and the careful and conscientious mother of a very large family.

Their children are as follows: Caroline Selden, born at Lynchburg, Virginia, October 5, 1862; Frances Kirby, born at Hampstead, Texas, July 7, 1864; Edmund Kirby, born at Louisville, Kentucky, August 28, 1866; Lydia, born at Louisville, Kentucky, April 4, 1868; Rowena Selden, born at New Castle, Kentucky, October 2, 1870; Elizabeth Chaplin, born at Nashville, Tennessee, January 2, 1872; Reynold Marvin, born at Nashville, Tennessee, June 14, 1874; William Selden, born at Sewanee, Tennessee, February 27, 1876; Josephine, born at Sewanee, Tennessee, October 11, 1878; Joseph Lee, born at Sewanee, Tennessee, April 16, 1882; Ephraim Kirby, born at Sewanee, Tennessee, August 30, 1884. Gen. Smith (as all his ancestors were) is a member of the Protestant Episcopal church, and has served as vestryman, senior warden, lay reader and Sunday-school superintendent in a great number of churches in that communion. He is a Mason and Knight Templar.

In politics he is a Democrat; was opposed to secession, but, when it was accomplished, was the first to offer his sword to the service of the South, and the last to lay it down. He was the first Confederate officer to enter Virginia, being sent thither by the government at Montgomery to select depots and to muster in troops. Among the first of those were the Tennessee regiments of Turney, Bate and Maney.

Enough has been stated to show that he was a soldier by inheritance, has always been a correct, conservative man, with no bad habits, always full of life and always in the lead. He began life on no capital, has supported his mother almost since boyhood, and having been devoted to military life, has never gone into mercantile business.

GOV. JAMES DAVIS PORTER.

NASHVILLE.

IT has been said of Gov. Porter that a promise from him is equivalent to its fulfillment, and that a statement from him is a guarantee of its truth, his natural courage rendering him incapable of dissimulation or evasion. He has a calm, judicial mind, and his speeches and written articles are clear, concise and pointed. As a governor he won the praise of being laborious, decisive, prompt and frank. He owes his prominence to no sort of arts. He is incapable of performing those acts of simulation by which some men rise to distinction. His genuine politeness and courtesy are not the results of study or art, but arise from his natural instincts, to render unto others that which he feels he has a right to claim for himself. His mind is more characterized by strength than brilliancy. He is quick to perceive the

right; yet he rarely acts without first giving the subject mature thought, and when he does come to a conclusion he can not be driven from it, or persuaded to abandon it merely to please others. Not that he is stubborn, for on minor matters of difference, no man is more ready to yield for the sake of harmony or courtesy. As a lawyer and a judge, he was painstaking and careful, and whether in advising a client or in rendering an opinion, he was cautious not to mislead and anxious to be precisely right. His information is varied and more uniformly correct than that of most men; but he does not like to dwell on abstract or hypothetical questions, while the practical, concerning either the present or future, attracts his earnest attention. He has no pretentions to the politician. The character of his mind and his habits of thought forbid this. His views of public questions are based on his belief as to their probable effects on the country, and not how they are likely to affect his personal ambition. It is not meant to say that he is not ambitious, but that his ambition is of a kind which prompts him rather to desire permanent approval than temporary success. His character for truth, candor, honesty and integrity, was made by strict attention to details in business, both public and private. He is a man of decided opinions, and his moral and personal courage both unite in making him a formidable advocate or adversary. No man in Tennessee possesses to a higher degree the confidence and respect of the intelligence of the country, and even those who have felt called on honestly to join issue with him, award to him the virtues of sincerity, honesty and courage in his advocacy of opposing views. A clearer estimate of him as a man and a statesman may be gathered from his messages to the Legislature, and the measures passed on his recommendation, some of which are imperishable monuments to his memory, and entitle him to the gratitude of this and coming generations. In his inaugural address, January 18, 1875, he submitted the following subjects of State policy in language characteristic of the philanthropist and builder: "A great political revolution in public sentiment has begun, and is in progress in Tennessee and in the other States of the Union. What influence for good or for evil it is to have on the country remains to be seen; but our duty is a plain one—to avoid the errors that have brought disaster to the best interests of the country. Foremost among them is that spirit of party which has gained such an ascendency over the minds of men as has caused them to substitute party for country, and make them seek party approbation rather than the approval and prosperity of the country. The people of Tennessee will count him a public benefactor who will direct the popular energies to useful pursuits—to a diversification of labor—to the encouragement of immigration—the opening of mines—the improvement of agriculture—the erection of school-houses, and especially is the great body of our people anxious for an utter oblivion of all local jealousies and animosities, and for the encouragement and perpetuation of a spirit of brotherhood among the people of all the States of the Union.

"Thanking the people of Tennessee for the distinction they have conferred upon me, I will labor to repay this generous confidence by taking 'care that the laws are faithfully executed,' and by maintaining the jurisdiction and rights of the State; and 'this is the point to which the vigilance of the people should be chiefly directed. Their highest interest is at home; their palladium is their own State government. They ought to know that they can look nowhere else with perfect. assurance of safety and protection. Let them maintain their local government, not only in its rights, but in its

dignity and influence. It is vain to hope that the principles of our government can be preserved, or that anything can prevent it from running into the absolutism of consolidation, if we suffer the rights of the States to be filched away, and their dignity and influence lost through our carelessness or neglect.'"

In his message to the Thirty-ninth General Assembly he recommended such legislation as would afford the benefits of the public schools to every child in the State. On the subject of immigration he said: "I recommend that you indicate, in some form, the desire of our people to encourage the honest immigrant without regard to his nationality, religion or politics." He recommended that the Federal Congress be urged to improve the Mississippi, Tennessee and Cumberland rivers; and he urged the Legislature to appeal to the federal Congress to place the names of Mexican veterans upon the pension rolls of the government.

During his administrations the public expenditures were largely reduced. In his message he said: "The current expenses of the State government for the past two years amount to $1,044,414.00, or to the sum of $522,207.00 per annum; this statement shows a reduction of the current expense account in ten years that must be full of encouragement to the tax-payer. Further large reductions can be made by the adoption of certain changes recommended in this message and in the able report of the comptroller. The current expense account for the years 1868–69 amounted to $1,943,663.54; for the years 1870–71 it was $1,519,088.00; for 1873–74 it was $1,324,934.00; for 1875–76 it was $1,278,908.00."

The appropriation bill passed upon his recommendation by the Fortieth General Assembly was the first compliance with the constitutional provision that no money shall be drawn from the treasury but in consequence of appropriations made by law; and he earnestly recommended "a strict adherence to this precedent, not alone as a constitutional duty of maintaining legislative authority and responsibility, but as the only method of securing certainty and economy in administration."

The State Board of Health, a beneficent measure of more than State importance, was created upon his recommendation, at the suggestion of Dr. J. D. Plunket, who was his adviser on that subject. [See Dr. Plunket's biography elsewhere in this volume.] The State Normal College was established under his administration, as was also the Bureau of Agriculture, Statistics and Mines. Fish culture was adopted upon his recommendation. Humanity in the conduct of the State prison he urged in this language: "The prison has no sewerage, no adequate hospital arrangement; it is in the way of the improvement of the city of Nashville, and the absence of sewers makes it, at certain seasons of the year, dangerous to the general health. In my message to the Thirty-ninth General Assembly, I urged its removal. The reasons for it are more potent now, and I earnestly repeat the recommendation, and suggest its removal to some point below the city on the west side of the river, where the State can secure isolation and perfect ventilation and sewerage, without the expenditure of any considerable amount of money; the rental derived from the labor of the convicts should be appropriated to the purchase of another site, and for the construction of a new prison. In six years, the term of the present lease, it will amount to four hundred and twenty-three thousand dollars. With this sum a prison can be constructed creditable to the humanity and character of the State. The necessity for separate accommodations for female and juvenile convicts is great and growing, and in the construction of a new prison provision can be made for this class of offenders. Upon the discharge of a convict, the lessees furnish him with a suit of clothes and transportation to the place of his conviction. I recommend that he be furnished by the State with a few dollars in money for his subsistence from the prison to his home."

His exercise of the veto power evinces the conservative cast of his character. He vetoed the bill taxing the losing party with the jury fees in civil suits, the bill for reducing the salaries of judges, and the bill abolishing the office of county superintendent of schools.

The editor is not competent to discuss the political issues involved in the State debt question, but is of the opinion that Gov. Porter's highest honor lies in the unequivocal position he took on that subject. The evasion of the payment of debts, public or private, by bankrupt laws, repudiation acts or other subterfuges, was never popular in America, and never will be. The man or the State whose commercial honor is not sustained by the prompt payment of one hundred cents on the dollar, principal and interest, will be spotted and shunned, and come to the bad in the long run. Gov. Porter's recommendation to the Legislature has a high moral business tone in it that all men, not professional politicians, must applaud and commend to their children as the true measure of manhood and of statesmanship. He said: "The settlement of this debt is paramount to all questions of legislation that can engage the attention of the General Assembly; it involves the honor and good name of the State, the credit and honor of every one of its citizens; it is a liability that was voluntarily contracted, and whether it was wisely created or not, can not now be a question. I hold, and have always believed, that in the light of moral and legal duty, as a question of commercial honor and of State pride, the best settlement of the debt of Tennessee would be to pay the entire debt according to the terms of the contract."

James Davis Porter was born at Paris, Tennessee, December 7th, 1828. He is descended from John, the first American Porter, born in 1590, at Kenilworth, Warwickshire, England, and in Wraxhall Abbey, the ancient home of the family, where many of their num-

ber are buried. John Porter, his wife Rose, and their children sailed from England in the ship Anna, arriving at Dorchester Quays, May 30, 1627.

His ancestor, John Porter, who came to America in 1627, was not a Puritan, and did not leave the old country to escape any sort of persecution, but to improve his fortune. His descendants are very numerous. Many of them were soldiers of the Revolutionary war, among them a great-uncle of Gov. Porter, Gen. Peter B. Porter of the war of 1812, afterwards a member of the cabinet of John Quincy Adams. The admirals of the United States Navy are his descendants. John Porter and Rose, his wife, had nine children, who lived to rear families. Their eldest son, John, born in 1618, was nine years old when his parents emigrated to America. He married Mary Stanley, daughter of Thomas Stanley, of Hartford, Connecticut. They had twelve children. Their fourth son, Samuel, was born March 5, 1664. He settled in Chester county, Pennsylvania; married and reared a large family. His son William, born in 1695, owned and lived upon his father's homestead. He died on the 3rd of May, 1749, leaving several sons. The youngest was William, born in 1729, who emigrated to Adams county, Pennsylvania, and married Sarah Percel, of Delaware. He died in 1802. His wife survived for several years. They were buried at Tom's creek Presbyterian church. They had six sons and four daughters. William, the youngest son, married Hannah Kennedy, the paternal grandmother of Gov. Porter. She was the daughter of Thomas Kennedy, who was born in Chester county, Pennsylvania, and settled, in May, 1791, on a farm on the Ohio river, upon which the city of Covington now stands. His wife, Diana Davis, was the daughter of James Davis, from whom Gov. Porter derives his name. The Thomas Kennedy above named was the only son of his father, for whom he was named. The latter was from the north of Ireland, and was one of the pioneers of Chester county, Pennsylvania. He settled on Brandywine creek, and was buried in the church-yard of Brandywine church. William Porter, the paternal grandfather of Gov. Porter, after his marriage, settled first in Franklin county, Kentucky, from which place he removed, in 1822, to Henry county, Tennessee, where he lived until his death, in 1833. His wife died in 1820. They had six sons and four daughters. Their second son, Thomas Kennedy Porter, the father of Gov. James D. Porter, was born February 19, 1801. He was educated by Kean O'Hara, at Frankfort, Kentucky, a distinguished teacher (father of Col. Theodore O'Hara), studied medicine and was graduated at Transylvania University, 1822. He settled at Paris, Tennessee, in 1823, and was a leading citizen of that place up to his death, in February, 1848. He was married February, 1824, to Geraldine Horton, of Davidson county, Tennessee, who survived him for four years. She was the youngest daughter of Josiah Horton, who settled in

Davidson county, Tennessee, in 1795, and died in 1828. He was a man of education and character, and was the son of Richard Horton, and his wife, Elizabeth Harrison, born in Delaware county, Pennsylvania. He settled in New Hanover county, North Carolina, where he married Nancy White, daughter of Joseph White. His wife survived him until 1842. Josiah Horton was a descendant—the fifth generation—from Barnabas Horton, who came over in the ship Swallow, in 1633-38. He was the son of Joseph Horton, of Mousely, Leicestershire, England, where the name has been known to the remotest period of any authentic records. Barabas Horton and his wife, Mary, with two children, landed at Hampton Quays; went to New Haven in 1640, and settled on the east end of Long Island, now Southold, Suffolk county, New York. The house built by him was the first frame dwelling erected on the east end of Long Island, and was standing and occupied in 1875. Six generations, all bearing the Horton name, lived and died in this house.

Gov. Porter was the third son, and third child of his parents. The eldest, Dr. Jno. H. Porter, resides in Henry county, where he has always been a leading citizen. The second son was killed in infancy by the accidental discharge of a gun in the hands of his nurse. The fourth child, a daughter, died in infancy. The fifth was Catherine, who married Rev. E. C. Trimble, a distinguished minister of the Presbyterian church, by whom she had a son and two daughters. She died in 1862. The sixth child was Thomas Kennedy Porter. He commanded with great distinction Porter's battery at the battle of Fort Donelson, where he was dangerously wounded; was again wounded at the combat at Hoover's Gap; commanded the artillery of Buckner's corps at the battle of Chickamauga; afterwards was ordered to the Confederate steamer Florida as her executive officer, and was captured with her at the port of Bahia, Brazil, in October, 1864. He died in 1869. The seventh child was Geraldine, wife of Dixon G. Fowler, of Paducah, Kentucky. She died in 1874, leaving three daughters. The eighth child was William H. Porter. He was a cadet in the Confederate States army, doing duty as *aid-de-camp* on the staff of Gen. T. H. Bell, and was killed at the battle of Tishomingo creek, in 1864, at the age of twenty. The youngest child, Anna, died just as she reached womanhood.

Gov. Porter was educated by David Cochrane, a distinguished teacher, an alumnus of Belfast, Ireland, and for many years principal of the academy at Paris. At sixteen he entered the junior class in the University of Nashville, then under the presidency of Dr. Philip Lindsley, and was graduated two years thereafter (in the class of 1846). He was in poor health for many years after that date. He studied law in the office of Gen. John H. Dunlap in his native town, and at the law school at Lebanon, Tennessee, and commenced the practice in 1851. He was married in June of that year, to Susannah, eldest daughter and eldest child of his legal preceptor. Soon thereafter he settled on a farm near Paris, where he has always resided, except when absent in the public service. His married life has been a happy one, and would have been still happier if he had at all times heeded the counsel of Mrs. Porter. His professional life was a successful one, and it was her wish and that of her honored father, that he should not turn away from it for the vanities of public life.

He was elected in 1859 a representative in the Legislature of Tennessee, from the counties of Carroll, Gibson, Madison and Henry, and was an active participant in the memorable proceedings of the extra session of 1861, through which Tennessee dissolved her relations with the federal government. He was the author of the " Porter resolutions," passed January, 1861, which pledged Tennessee to co-operate with the South in case of war between the States. In advocating their adoption he stated that he hoped there would be a peaceful solution of pending difficulties, but if there should be war between the sections, Tennesseans must be united; there must be no division at home. He wanted to avoid local divisions and animosities; and did not want to see what afterwards occurred, the confiscation of the property of Tennesseans by Tennesseans, the disfranchisement of her own people through the agency of their neighbors. These resolutions attracted the attention of the entire country. They were almost unanimously adopted by the Legislature of Tennessee, and were adopted in several other States of the South.

When hostilities were about to commence he spent several weeks with Gen. Pillow, whose headquarters were at Memphis, as his adjutant-general, and assisted him in organizing the provisional army of Tennessee. He then joined Gen. Cheatham and was with him as his chief of staff during the four years of the war, and was paroled with him in May, 1865, at the surrender of the army of Tennessee.

He resumed the practice of his profession in the fall of 1865, and was actively engaged in it until 1870, when a convention was called to provide a new constitution for Tennessee. He was unanimously elected by the people a delegate to this convention from his native county, was a member of the judiciary committee, and participated actively in the formation of the present constitution. He was the author of the first section of the schedule, by the adoption of which all offices in the State were vacated. In advocating this measure on the floor of the convention, he avowed that it was not meant as a measure of retaliation or as a means of punishment for Union men, but was done to enable all the people of the State to have a voice in the selection of their rulers and agents. As full justification for the proposed measured, it need only be stated that at the time three-fourths of the white people of the State were disfranchised, and the small minority of voters had filled every place, from constable up.

In the summer of 1870 he was elected by a very large majority judge of the twelfth judicial circuit of Tennessee, composed of the counties of Henry, Benton, Carroll, Weakley, Obion and Lake, for the term of eight years. After filling this position most acceptably for nearly four years, he resigned the judgeship in February, 1874, and in August following received the nomination for governor of the State, at the hands of the State convention of the Democratic party, over ex-Senator Bailey and others. He was opposed by the Hon. Horace Maynard, the Republican candidate, and made a joint canvass of the State with him. He was elected by a majority of forty-seven thousand, and two years thereafter was re-nominated without opposition, and re-elected by a majority of over fifty thousand. His last term as governor closed in January, 1879.

At the State Democractic convention of 1880 he was elected a delegate for the State at large to the National convention of the party at Cincinnati, and was made chairman of the Tennessee delegation. At this convention he zealously advocated the nomination of Senator Bayard, of Delaware, for the presidency.

In July, 1880, he was elected president of the Nashville, Chattanooga & St. Louis railway company, and was annually re-elected until 1884, when he voluntarily retired from the position. The following extract from the Nashville *American*, written in reference to Gov. Porter's election as president of the leading railroad company of Tennessee, truthfully reflects the public sentiment in regard to the new position he had been called to fill: "The selection of Gov. Porter for the position of president of the Chattanooga railroad is one which promises well for the road and for the State. While he will have to acquire, in a great measure, the special knowledge necessary, yet his clear and rapid comprehension and ready business grasp of any subject he takes hold of, will place him at the head of the profession in a very brief time. The field is the highest that can tempt the ambition of any man. There is no politics comparable to the position of a railroad president. With the exception of a position on the Supreme bench, there is none under the government equal to the presidency of a great railroad system, especially to a man of Gov. Porter's splendid qualifications for the position, insuring him occupation at the topmost round of the profession. We had expected that he might be needed in the politics of the State, but this is the higher field by far, and in its permanency and the power it confers, overtops all the political positions, while it is a field in which a man can be of equal, of far greater service to his State, than in the temporary occupation of any political office. Indeed, it is in such fields and out of politics, that our young men are to find the true field for ambition hereafter, and we should like to see Gov. Porter, after having enjoyed the highest

honors the State can confer, set the example of seeking higher honors in the direction of the industrial progress of the State and of the South."

His *alma-mater*, the University of Nashville, years ago, conferred upon Gov. Porter the degree of LL. D. He is also a trustee of the University, and a member of the board of trustees of the Peabody educational fund, which is charged with the management of the munificent bequest of George Peabody for the education of the children of the South. He is Vice-President of the Tennessee Historical Society for West Tennessee, a director in the First National Bank of Nashville, a director in the Equitable Fire Insurance company, of Nashville, and also in the Tennessee Coal, Iron and Railroad company, and president of the Hermitage Club, of Nashville.

Gov. Porter married in Paris, Tennessee, June 17,· 1851, Miss Susannah Dunlap, daughter of Gen. John H. Dunlap, a native of Knox county. He was a lawyer by profession. He was a volunteer in the Florida (Seminole) war, under his brother, Richard G. Dunlap, who was a captain, and afterwards brigadier-general, in that service, and was subsequently a member of the cabinet of President Lamar, of Texas, and minister from that republic to the United States. Gen. John H. Dunlap died in December, 1874, at the age of seventy-three. He enjoyed great professional success and amassed a large fortune, the result of his energy and excellent judgment in business. He was for many years the law partner of Gov. Porter, the association terminating in 1870, when the latter went upon the bench. Mrs. Porter's grandfather, Hugh Dunlap, was a native of Londonderry, Ireland, who came to America when a young man, and settled at Knoxville, Tennessee, where he married his wife, Susannah Gilliam, and raised a large family of children of his own, besides adopting and raising seven or eight others, children of deceased relatives of his own and his wife and their friends. He removed from Knox county to Roane, where some of his younger children were born. When the tide of emigration set in towards West Tennessee he followed some of his children there in 1826. Several of his sons had preceded him to his new home in 1823 and 1824. He died in 1846. Of Mrs. Porter's uncles who have distinguished the name was Judge William C. Dunlap, who was frequently a member of the Tennessee Legislature, twice a member of Congress, and for eight years judge of the Memphis circuit court. Hugh W. Dunlap, a twin brother of William C. Dunlap, was a member of the General Assembly of the State, attorney-general of the old ninth judicial circuit, a lieutenant-colonel in the Mexican war, and long a leading lawyer in Madison parish, Louisiana, where he died in 1848. Another uncle, James T. Dunlap, was several times a member of both the Senate and House of Representatives of the Tennessee Legislature, presidential elector for the ninth congressional district on the Buchanan ticket, and for six years comptroller of the State treasury. Mrs. Porter's grandmother, Susannah Gilliam, wife of Hugh Dunlap, was the daughter of Devereux Gilliam, whose wife was a descendant of the third generation from John Ellis, who settled at Tuckahoe, in the county of Henrico, Virginia, in 1683, a planter and leading man, the founder of one of the largest and most respectable families of the South. Mrs. Porter was educated at the Nashville Female Academy under the direction of Drs. Lapsley and Elliott, and possesses in an em.- nent degree all the virtues that go to make up the good daughter, wife, mother, mistress and neighbor. The love her children bear her amounts to a sublime devotion on their part.

Financially Gov. Porter, though never making an effort to accumulate a fortune, has always been in comfortable circumstances. He is quite liberal in his disposition, and cheerfully divides his means with those dependent upon him.

He practiced law from 1851 to 1870, except during the period of the civil war; from August, 1870, to February, 1874, he was circuit court judge, resigning the bench to enter the gubernatorial canvass of that year; inaugurated governor of the State January 15, 1875, continuing in this office until January 15, 1879; from July 1, 1880, to September, 1884, president of the Nashville, Chattanooga and St. Louis railway company.

In March, 1885, a few days after the inauguration of President Cleveland, Gov. Porter was requested by the Hon. Thomas F. Bayard, the newly appointed Secretary of State, to visit Washington, and on repairing thither was asked by the Secretary if he would accept the position of Assistant Secretary of State, to which he replied that he would consider the proposition until the following morning, and then advise him of his decision. At the hour named, he announced to the Secretary his willingness to accept the office so unexpectedly tendered, and together they called on the President, who expressed his pleasure at the appointment. He sent Gov. Porter's name to the Senate at once, and the nomination was immediately confirmed by that body unanimously. The high compliment conveyed in his appointment to the position he now so worthily and acceptably occupies is greatly enhanced by the consideration that it was conferred without solicitation or suggestion on his part, he not having been an applicant for this or any other place under the administration of Mr. Cleveland.

Gov. Porter's methods of life have been, First—to attend to his own business. Second—while a lawyer, to master all cases put into his hands, and to go into the court-house after the fullest preparation, a course which has always enabled him to compete with any opponent. Third—never to live beyond his income. In this his wife has heartily seconded him, and it has always been a rule with them never to buy anything until able to pay for it. It is probable that Gov. Porter has paid less interest on personal obligations than any man in the State. He never had any controversies or litigation with his neighbors, and has kept clients out of court when possible. His Latin motto, which came from his maternal ancestors, is "*Quod vult valde vult*"—what he wills he wills cordially and without stint; or, what he does he does well.

When a young man Gov. Porter was a Whig, and as such was elected a member of the Legislature in 1859, the first official position he ever held. He was a member of the State convention of 1860, that nominated Mr. Bell for President. He never held a civil office, except the one he now fills, that he did not derive directly from the people, and has never been defeated before the people for any place he has aspired to.

Gov. Porter has four children, viz.: (1). Susannah Dunlap, educated at the private school of Miss Fanny O'Bryan, Nashville; the wife of Dr. W. G. Bibb, who resides at Nashville. (2). Charles D., educated at Lexington, Kentucky; studied law at Cumberland University, Lebanon, Tennessee, where he graduated in 1876; resides at Nashville, where he is practicing his profession. (3). Dudley, educated at the public schools of Nashville, Montgomery Bell Academy Nashville, and at Cecilian College, near Elizabethtown, Kentucky. (4). Thomas Kennedy, now at school.

HON. J. W. CLAPP.

MEMPHIS.

HON. J. W. CLAPP, the able and distinguished lawyer of Memphis, was born in Abingdon, Washington county, Virginia, September 24, 1814, and received his education at Abingdon Academy and at Hampden Sidney College, Virginia, where he graduated in 1835, and where he was the classmate of Judge Asa Dickinson, of Virginia. Having determined at an early age to become a lawyer, as soon as he left college he began to read law at Abingdon, in the office of J. W. C. Watson, now Judge Watson, of Holly Springs, Mississippi, and was admitted to the bar at Abingdon in 1839. He practiced law at Abingdon until 1841, when he removed to Holly Springs, Mississippi, and remained until 1866, when he went to Memphis, where he still resides.

Mr. Clapp was raised a Henry Clay Whig, but on the disruption of parties in Mississippi in 1850 the Whig and Democratic parties were broken up and new political organizations, called the Union and State's Rights parties, were formed. He joined the latter, and took an active part in politics for several years. In 1856 he was elected to the Mississippi Legislature for a term of two years, and took part in the formation of the code of Mississippi. In 1860 he was made an elector for the State on the Breckinridge ticket, and bore an active part in the memorable campaign which followed. In 1861 he was elected a member of the State convention of Mississippi which passed the ordinance of secession, and being on the side of State's Rights he voted for that ordinance. In 1861 he was elected to the Confederate Congress, received his commission as a member of that body November 25, and served a term of two years. At the request of Mr. Memminger, Secretary of the Treasury of the Confederate States, he took charge of the Confederate cotton in Mississippi, part of Alabama, and part of Louisiana. It was his business to preserve this cotton from destruction and pillage, and to convert it as far as possible into sterling exchange, which he was to forward to Richmond, and into army supplies, which he turned over to Gen. Richard Taylor's army. He held this position until the surrender of the Confederate armies, and then turned over the cotton and every thing in his hands to the Federal authorities, represented by Gen. Canby, at New Orleans. Gen. Canby very kindly insisted that he should retain the office, fixing his own salary and choosing his own agents, but the offer was respectfully declined.

Previous to the war Judge Clapp had an income of about ten thousand dollars per annum, and owned a large plantation and numerous slaves, but when the war closed every thing had been swept away except the land. He resolved to leave Mississippi, and accordingly went to Memphis in June, 1866, and resumed the practice of law. He tried to keep out of politics, but in 1876 was made a Tilden elector, and took part in the campaign, making a number of able speeches for the party. In 1878, during his absence from home, he was nominated for the State Senate and elected for a term of two years. He took an active part in the reorganization of the government of the city of Memphis, and also in the State debt controversy, in which he was one of the leaders of the State credit Democracy. While in the Senate he was made chairman of the committee on Federal relations.

Mr. Clapp was made a Master Mason at Abingdon, Virginia, in 1836, but after leaving Virginia never connected himself with any lodge. He joined the Presbyterian church at Holly Springs, Mississippi, in 1843, and was afterwards made an elder in that Church. After moving to Memphis he connected himself with the Second Presbyterian church of that place, and was made an elder, in which capacity he has served up to

the present time. He is liberal in his religious views and charitable towards other denominations. One cardinal principle with which he started in life was to keep out of debt. To this he has adhered, and it would not take half an hour to settle all the debts he owes in the world. He has always made it a conscientious duty to do well whatever he undertook, and a point to be always punctual, holding that while he has a right to his own time he ought not to needlessly waste that of others. He has led a busy life, and has amassed a comfortable estate, and now owns valuable lands in Mississippi and Arkansas, as well as choice property in Memphis.

Mr. Clapp's father was Dr. Earl B. Clapp, a physician of large practice and a surgeon of fine reputation. He was descended from a family of Northern stock which came to Virginia at an early day. He died in Washington county, Virginia, at an advanced age. The family moved away to Tennessee, Missouri, and other States, and there now remain only his brother's children and a few other relatives at Abingdon.

The mother of Judge Clapp was Miss Elizabeth Craig, daughter of Capt. Robert Craig, a gentleman of Scotch-Irish descent, who came to America, settled in Pennsylvania, and subsequently removed to Washington county, Virginia, where he died at a very venerable age.

Mr. Clapp was married at Holly Springs, in May, 1843, to Miss Evelina D. Lucas, daughter of Col. P. W. Lucas, who originally came from Fauquier county, Virginia, went to Tennessee, and settled first at Hartsville, and removed thence to Memphis, where he was the law partner of Frederick P. Stanton, brother of Secretary Stanton, of Lincoln's cabinet. In 1839 he went to Holly Springs, where he was very successful as a lawyer, and owned large interests in government lands. He died at Memphis in 1870. Mrs. Clapp's mother was a Miss Donoho, of Tennessee. By this marriage there are eight living children: (1). Clementine L., born in 1844; now the wife of H. A. McCrosky, of Memphis, and the mother of four children. (2). E. W. Clapp, born in 1848; married Miss Lucy M. Jones, of Memphis; has two children. (3). W. L. Clapp, born in 1850; now one of the partners of his father in the law firm of Clapp & Beard; married Miss Lamira M. Parker, and has four children. (4). J. W. Clapp, jr., born in 1852; now a partner in the firm of Clapp & Taylor, of Memphis; married Miss Ellen B. Kennedy, daughter of Hon. D. N. Kennedy, a banker of Clarksville, Tennessee; has one child. (5). Eva Walton Clapp, born in 1854; now the wife of Dr. A. M. West, son of Gen. A. M. West, of Mississippi; has three children, and is now living at Memphis. (6). Charles T. Clapp, born in 1856; now a merchant at Brookhaven, Mississippi; married Miss Alice D. Powell, of Mississippi, and has three children. (7). Leura L. Clapp, born in 1858; now wife of Dr. Jno. I. Taylor, of Jackson, Tennessee; has one child. (8). Miss Ola B. Clapp, born in 1866.

6

HON. WILLIAM STUART FLEMING.

COLUMBIA.

THIS gentleman is a descendant of the South Carolina colony of Flemings, Friersons, Armstrongs, Coopers, etc., who settled in Maury county, Tennessee, very early in the present century. As this colony has been already spoken of in the sketches of Judges Frierson and Cooper, the reader is referred to those papers for a further account of it.

He was born April 23, 1816, in Maury county, Tennessee, son of Thomas Frierson Fleming, a noted teacher of his day. He acquired the rudiments of his education from his father, but his preparation for college was derived from a Mr. John Borland, principal of a high school in New York, who for two years taught the classical languages to a few pupils in Tennessee. He obtained further preparation in mathematics from William H. Russel, New Haven, Connecticut, in 1835. Finally he entered the sophomore class of Yale College in September, 1835. William F. Cooper, whose memoir is given in another place, was his classmate at Yale, and when the two young men after graduation were on their way home a serious and nearly fatal accident happened to Fleming. His legs were severely crushed between the steamboat and the wall of a lock. The resulting injury came near necessitating amputation, and confined him to his room for two months.

Like most young men of that day, after graduation he applied himself to teaching, a class of young gentlemen of Maury county becoming his pupils; but this did not last long. He married in 1839, and commenced the study of law under Chancellor S. D. Frierson, his mother's cousin, whose memoir is given in this book.

He was called to the bar in the winter of 1841-2, and licensed to practice by the Hon. Edmund Dillahunty, circuit court judge, and Chancellor Lunsford M. Bramlett. He lived in the country at that time, seven miles from Columbia, but opened an office in that city, and for five years rode into town every day, except Sunday, and returned at night, scarcely ever failing on account of weather. During the early years of his practice he was city attorney for Columbia. During this period also he formed a partnership with Madison S. Frierson, a relative, of considerable reputation as a lawyer, though not a fine speaker. In 1847 he bought a residence in Columbia, and has resided in or near that city ever since.

During the stirring political times from 1840 to 1848 Mr. Fleming took an active part in the contests of the day, frequently taking the stump in the interest of the Whig presidential candidates, especially Clay and Taylor.

After the death of his first wife, in 1849, Fleming fell into intemperate habits, but in 1853 broke loose from them abruptly and totally. He relapsed for a short time during the war, but soon broke off again, and has practiced total abstinence down to the present day.

His law practice was extensive and lucrative from the beginning, and he devoted himself to it industriously till the outbreak of the civil war closed our courts of law. His practice was not renewed until peace gave the welcome order, "*Cedant arma togæ.*"

His second marriage took place January 12, 1854, the lady being a Frierson, daughter of J. W. S. Frierson, M.D., of Columbia. She only lived till 1858, but gave birth to three children, all of whom died in infancy or early youth.

His third marriage took place about 1860, the lady being Mrs. Ruth A. Booker, a widow. [A further account will be given of these three ladies presently.]

About the time of this third marriage he moved to a very handsome residence about a mile from town. The house was large and commodious, and the site beautiful, and he filled it with every thing that can make home attractive to a family of intellect and culture. Here he lived until the time of Hood's invasion of Tennessee in the latter days of the civil war, when it fell into the hands of the Federal army. It was then set on fire and completely destroyed, with all its contents, including furniture, carriages, probably the most complete miscellaneous library in the county, manuscripts, addresses (written and printed), with innumerable other valuable and to him invaluable possessions, the whole loss amounting to twenty-two thousand dollars. Added to this loss was that of fifty slaves emancipated and a large number of horses and mules impressed into service and never paid for. His whole loss, including the suspension of work on his farm, cannot have been less than a hundred thousand dollars.

At the outbreak of the war his convictions and sympathies were all with the South, and it became a question to be anxiously and thoughtfully considered whether he ought to enter the Confederate army. He had a wife, recently married, two unmarried daughters, and one son, who had just completed his sixteenth year. The question was solved purely on considerations of duty. The family must be protected, and for this the son was too young, but he could do service in the army. He went and the father took charge of the home. The son did good service as a soldier, as will be seen when we come to make separate mention of him. The father, as has been seen, suffered untold tribulations and indignities at home.

After the war there was necessarily a struggle to reinstate himself and his family in the competency they had lost, the details of which we are unable to give. As soon as the State was emancipated from the control of the carpet-bag government—viz., in 1870—he was, by a very large majority, elected chancellor of the eighth chancery district of Tennessee. In 1878 he was re-elected for a second term of eight years, his competitors being Judge T. W. Turley, of Franklin, and Capt. Lester, of Giles county. The eighth chancery district includes the four important counties of Maury, Giles, Williamson and Marshall.

The well-known literary culture of Judge Fleming has caused him to be frequently called upon for public addresses, the most important of which was his centennial address, of 1876, which is published in his history of the early settlement of Maury county. He was in 1853 editor of a literary paper, and soon after that of a political journal, entitled the Columbia *Mirror*, the files of which were among the losses occasioned by the burning of his residence. His decisions in chancery are in high esteem, both with bench and bar, and have generally been confirmed when referred to higher courts.

Judge Fleming has long been a member of the Presbyterian church, in which he and all his relatives were educated, and for twenty years has served as a ruling elder in the First Presbyterian church of Columbia.

He became an Odd Fellow in 1843, in which order he has passed all the chairs and taken all the degrees.

The family of Judge Fleming migrated from Scotland to the north of Ireland at a period not stated, and thence to Williamsburg district, South Carolina in 1732.

John Fleming, great-great-grandfather of the judge, was at this latter date the representative of the family. He married a lady named Witherspoon, also of Scotch descent, and the fruit of that marriage was James Fleming, who came over with his father from Ireland when a boy. He married three times, his first wife being a Stuart, of Scotch descent, who became the mother of Judge Fleming's grandfather, to be presently mentioned. By his second wife he had a family, some of whom seem to have emigrated to Georgia, in which State his son, William B., and his grandson, William O. Fleming, became judges of the superior court.

James Fleming, son of the above and grandfather of the subject of this memoir, married Mary Frierson, and by her had a son, Thomas Frierson Fleming, father of Judge Fleming. He, with his widowed mother and three younger brothers, moved to Williamson county, Tennessee, in 1805, and in 1807 to Maury county. Here they settled, having purchased a portion of the grant of twenty-five thousand acres received by the Revolutionary general, Nathaniel Green, in consideration of his military services. Their settlement was seven miles west of Columbia, still occupied by the family. One of the brothers, uncle to Judge Fleming, was Maj. John D. Fleming, who, with his elder brother Thomas, followed Jackson in all his wars, participating in most of

his battles, including that of the Horse Shoe. The major died at the age of ninety years and six months, in 1883. He was a man well-known in his county for honesty, integrity, and hospitality. The third brother, William Stuart Fleming, died at the age of twenty-one, a student of promise. The fourth, James S., a gentleman of fine culture, yet survives in the possession of all his faculties, in the eighty-ninth year of his age.

To return to Thomas Frierson Fleming: His wife, mother of the Judge, was Margaret E., daughter of James Armstrong, one of Marion's Revolutionary soldiers, and Agnes Frierson, only sister of William Frierson, the grandfather of Judge W. F. Cooper, whose memoir is given in another place. T. F. Fleming himself was a farmer and teacher of repute, and died at the age of fifty. He was one of the few men who combined deep religious convictions with a genial and even jovial temperament, which rendered him a delightful companion to all who knew him. He loved his jokes and loved his books, a spare built man, with blue eyes, aquiline nose, and great physical activity and vitality. He was for many years an elder in the Presbyterian Church.

The first wife of Judge Fleming was Miss Frances McClellan Stephenson, married September 5, 1839. She was a grandniece of the Rev. James White Stephenson, a character of great interest in the annals of the colony. He was the Presbyterian minister who preached for twenty years to the colonists in South Carolina before their emigration, then emigrated with them to Maury county, Tennessee, and was for twenty years longer their faithful and beloved minister in their new home. He was the schoolmate and intimate friend of General Jackson in the Waxhaws, who often visited him at his home in Maury county. The reverend gentleman was second husband to Mrs. James Fleming, *nee* Frierson, grandmother of the Judge. His nephew, Mrs. Fleming's father emigrated from the Waxhaws, in Lancaster district, South Carolina, to Maury county with his father, where he was extensively engaged in farming.

By his first marriage the Judge had six children, three of whom died in infancy. The surviving children are: (1). Mary White, who married A. N. Dobbin, a farmer near Columbia, and has three children: Fannie Belle, William S., and Florence F. (2). Florence, who married Col. D. B. Cooper, half-brother of Judge Wm. F. Cooper, and died August, 1870, leaving three children: Florence, Flavel F., and Matthew D. (3). Thomas Frierson Fleming, born about 1845. This is the son who represented the family in the Confederate army, which he entered in his sixteenth year. He went out in the Forty-eighth Tennessee, was captured at Fort Donelson, taken as prisoner to Camp Douglass, at Chicago, where he was confined seven months. He was then exchanged, and taken to Port Hudson, Louisiana, and afterward joined Forrest's cavalry brigade, in which he served to the end of the war. He was in every battle in which his command was engaged. He married Miss Lily Baird, and has one child, a daughter, Miss Julia B.

Judge Fleming's first wife died April 30, 1849, at the age of twenty-eight.

His second marriage (Columbia, January 12, 1854) was with Miss Mary Witherspoon Frierson, second daughter of Dr. J. W. S. Frierson, of Columbia. There are no surviving children of this marriage. She died November 8, 1858.

His third marriage was with Mrs. Ruth A. Booker, in 1860. She was the widow of Albert Booker and daughter of Alexander Johnson, a farmer, for many years chairman of the Maury county court. Her mother was Mary Ballanfant, daughter of John Ballanfant, a Frenchman, who came to America with La Fayette at the time of the Revolutionary war, in which he served, and married a Virginia lady named Yeomans.

Three children were born of Judge Fleming's third marriage, of whom only one survives, William Stuart, born in 1861, a lawyer, who on January 1, 1884, married Miss Anna May Williams, of East Carrol parish, Louisiana.

The third Mrs. Fleming had by her former marriage one child, named Susan G., a lady of great intellectual endowments, who was married in 1869 to Col. J. W. Dunnington, now deceased. He was a lieutenant in the United States navy, but resigned at the outbreak of the war, came South and entered the Confederate service. He became brigadier-general, and was sent to France on a private mission for the Confederate government. After this he commanded the flag-ship in Admiral Semmes' fleet in James river. When the fall of Richmond was imminent he superintended the blowing up of the Confederate fleet, and surrendered with Lee at Appomattox. He left no children. Mrs. Dunnington, his widow, now resides with her step-father, Judge Fleming.

Strict adherence to the truth seems to be the prominent feature in Judge Fleming's character. Whether we listen to the observations of his friends when questioned about him, or to his own statements as to what he considers the most direct road to success in life, absolute truthfulness seems to be the one impression his life has made upon his friends and acquaintances, and absolute truthfulness appears to have been the principle he has kept his eye upon as the guiding star in the voyage of life. Where this principle is made the basis of a man's character it means much more than mere abstinence from verbal falsehood. It means that hatred of false pretense and duplicity of character, that frank openness of soul that makes a man scorn the vulgar arts by which men strive to assume a specious appearance of qualities they do not possess, makes him moreover rigidly avoid any secret baseness which, if committed, might tempt him into dissembling and hypocrisy. Nor are such men, as is often supposed, at the mercy of deceitful and designing people. There is something in the clear and steady gaze of a perfectly truthful man which rebukes and awes the incipient prevarication, and scares away the lie e'er it has passed the lips of the deceiver, and if he should muster courage enough to utter his lie, after all he does it with a shrinking of the eye and a stammering of speech which detects the falsehood when spoken by the lips, but which the countenance and manner fail to endorse. There is no element so unfavorable to falsehood and duplicity as the cloudless atmosphere of a perfectly truthful intellect.

A gentleman, himself a thoroughly reliable witness, said to the author of these sketches: "He is one of the men who never say a thing they do not mean. Truth being the bed-rock of his character it is very easy to account for the eminence he has attained in his profession and his standing in the State."

He himself, when interrogated as to the methods by which he had attained success in life, said: "In boyhood I had instilled into me by my father a very strict regard for truth, hence I have endeavored to make my word as good as my bond and to be true to my promises."

The life of his early boyhood was admirably adapted to the formation of such a character. At our first glance we find him living the healthy life of a country school-boy, sometimes riding to mill and doing other light services at his father's farm, at other times a diligent scholar at his father's school, and again joining in the rough and manly sports of the forest, hunting coons, opossums, rabbits, foxes, but strictly observing the Sabbath and submitting to the firm but loving discipline of his father. All this was well adapted to building up a character in which health and strength were the endowment of his mind and body. Such health and strength entail moral and physical courage, and courage is the very basis of veracity—a courage which enables and inspires man to face the truth and all its consequences rather than seek the coward's refuge in a lie.

Judge Fleming said to the author of these sketches: "In the early years of my professional career I was exceedingly fond of controversies before juries, but at a later period I acquired a fondness for equity, and since I have been on the bench I have spared neither time nor labor in the prosecution of that department of law. Indeed, I have been a harder student on the bench than at any other period of my life."

The bar of Columbia, at the time that Judge Fleming was called to a participation in its transactions, was an arena such as to appal the weak but to inspire the strong. To demonstrate this it only needs that the names of some who occupied it be given. There might be seen and heard Chancellors Cahal and Frierson, Chief-justice Nicholson, General Pillow, Russell Houston, Judge Baxter, James K. Polk, James H. Thomas, and Judge William P. Martin, and among these, giants as they were, Judge Fleming also developed a giant's strength, tempering, however, its force with wisdom and rectitude.

The character of this noble specimen of the great lawyer has been dwelt on the more in detail because it is feared that such characters are becoming rare, either at the bar or on the bench, and it has seemed well that succeeding generations may know what sort of men their predecessors have been, and by what training their characters have been molded.

Judge McLemore says of him: "Judge Fleming is a charming man in conversation, is one of the ripest scholars and among the ablest chancellors in the State."

COL. JAMES H. HOLMAN.

FAYETTEVILLE.

JAMES H. HOLMAN was born in Lincoln county, Tennessee, March 7, 1836, the son of Elder James W. Holman, a minister of the Primitive Baptist Church, a native of the same county, born in 1812. Elder Holman was a tax-collector of Lincoln county twice, a justice of the peace for some twelve years, a large farmer, and one of the most successful men in the county. He is still living at Fayetteville, a man of rather rigid and exacting character, but kind-hearted, public-spirited, and punctual to every engagement of his life.

The grandfather of Col. Holman was Elder Hardy Holman, also a Primitive Baptist preacher. He was a native of Kentucky, born near Frankfort, and was one of the first settlers of Lincoln county, Tennessee. He was also a surveyor, and assisted in laying out the town of Fayetteville about 1811. He also became an extensive farmer and large slave owner. He married Miss Betsy Wilson in Kentucky, and raised a large family of children. One of his daughters, Nancy, married Gen. William Moore, of Lincoln county, an officer in the war of 1812 under Gen. Jackson, several times a member of the Tennessee Legislature, and famous as "the mill-dam candidate." Another daughter, Martha W., married Maj. James S. Holman, a distant relative, who figured prominently in Texas politics from 1853 to 1867, when he died. Elder Hardy Holman's other sons were Willis H. Holman, who died in 1857, aged forty, and Daniel Holman, who died at the age of twenty.

The Holmans are of Swiss descent. One branch of the family came from Great Britain before the American Revolution and settled in Virginia, and from this family the Tennessee Holmans are descended, the great-grandfather of Col. Holman having come from Virginia to Kentucky, and thence to Lincoln county, Tennessee.

Col. Holman's mother, Jane Flack, was born in Lincoln county, Tennessee, in 1810, daughter of Thomas Flack, from Guilford Court-house, North Carolina, and one of the first settlers of Lincoln county. Her mother, Susan Dougherty, was also a native of Guilford Court-house, and married her husband there; emigrated first to Davidson county, Tennessee, about 1800, and settled in Lincoln county, on Mulberry creek, about 1806 or 1807. The great-grandfather, Thomas Flack's father, came from Ireland about 1755 or 1760. Wm. Dougherty, a prominent lawyer of Georgia, and Judge Charles Dougherty, of the same State, and Judge Robert Dougherty, of Tuskegee, Alabama, circuit judge for about fifteen years previous to the breaking out of the war, were all nephews of Col. Holman's grandmother Flack, she having been a Dougherty.

Col. Holman's mother, now living at Fayetteville at the age of seventy-three, has been the mother of five sons and three daughters: (1). Col. D. W. Holman,* a colonel in the Confederate service, a prominent lawyer at Fayetteville, partner of the subject of this sketch. (2). Dr. Thos. P. Holman, a physician and farmer near Fayetteville. (3). James H. Holman, subject of this sketch. (4). Robert F. Holman, who died on the battle-field of Shiloh, of malarial fever, April 6, 1862. (5). Rufus M. Holman, who died August 8, 1884; was a soldier in the Confederate army and a successful farmer. (6). Laura Jane Holman, died in 1855, ten years old. (7). Susan W. Holman, now wife of Dr. Wm. A. Milhows, Pulaski, Tennessee. (8). Virginia P. Holman, now wife of Capt. John D. Tolley, Lynchburg, Tennessee.

Col. James H. Holman, after receiving a common school education, entered Union University, at Murfreesborough, under Rev. Dr. Jos. Eaton, and studied there until February 27, 1857, when he was commissioned by President Pierce as second lieutenant in the First United States Infantry, his commission being signed by Hon. Jefferson Davis, then secretary of war. He was assigned to duty in Texas, under Gen. David E. Twiggs, and served on the frontier until January 1, 1861, when he obtained a furlough to visit the States, during which time he also came home. Before the expiration of his furlough he proceeded to Washington City. While there Fort Sumter was bombarded. Mr. Lincoln called for troops to suppress the rebellion. The furloughs of all officers were revoked, and they were required to report for duty. Lieut. Holman was required to report in Washington. By personal appeal to Gen.

* Since the foregoing was put in type Col. D. W. Holman, one of the noblest men that ever lived, died September 22, 1885, aged fifty-three years.—EDITOR.

Scott, then commanding the army, he obtained another short furlough, during which time he dropped his resignation in the Washington post-office, and crossing the Potomac river to Alexandria, proceeded down the river on the Virginia side. Virginia had passed the ordinance of secession the day previous, April 17, 1861. Being in United States uniform, he was arrested by the people and detained until he explained the situation in a little speech, when they gave him three cheers, and he proceeded southward. Immediately after resigning at Washington City he was commissioned first lieutenant in the Confederate regulars by the authorities at Montgomery. On reaching Tennessee he found that a regiment, Turney's First Tennessee, was being organized, and Holman was at once elected lieutenant-colonel of it. He served with Turney's regiment from May 1, 1861, to May 1, 1862; was in the campaign of Gen. Jos. E. Johnson in the Valley of Virginia; reached Manassas July 21, 1861, just as the rout of the Federal troops had taken place, and moved next with Gen. Johnson to the Peninsula, at which time his year of service with the First Tennessee regiment expired.

He was then assigned to duty with Gen. E. Kirby Smith, who was then commanding the department of East Tennessee, and served with that army in the East Tennessee and Kentucky campaigns through the year 1862. He was next ordered to Gen. Bragg's army as instructor of tactics. He is said to have drilled more men than any other man in the Confederacy.

About July 1, 1863, he was assigned to duty as inspector-general of cavalry with Gen. Joseph Wheeler, a position which he filled but a short time, when he was promoted and assigned to duty with Gen. Wheeler with the rank of colonel in the provisional army, and was ordered on an expedition into Tennessee in August, 1863. On the retreat of Bragg's army a large number of soldiers and small commands were cut off and left north of the Tennessee river, and Col. Holman was sent to collect them, with such other volunteer troops as he could get, into provisional commands, and operate with them until further instructions. On September 23, 1863, in a fight near Winchester with infantry and cavalry, he was captured by the disabling of his horse, and was slightly wounded himself. He was taken to Decherd, where the Federal commander professed to have received orders that Col. Holman should be tried by a drum-head court-martial and shot. Afterwards he professed to have gotten a commutation of that sentence, and orders to turn the prisoner over to Andrew Johnson, military governor at Nashville, as Holman was a Tennessean. Johnson directed the officers to give the prisoner choice of the rope or the oath of allegiance to the United States government. Col. Holman facetiously remarked to the officer, Gen. Payne, that he "would try the rope for a day or two, and if he couldn't stand it he would give him an answer as to whether he would take the oath or not." He finally told the Federal officers

that he was a prisoner of war in the hands of the United States, and claimed treatment as such, remarking that whoever treated him differently would certainly be held responsible, having said which he declined to further talk. He was then sent to Nashville, and carried to the governor's head-quarters. A staff officer of the governor waited on him, and stated that he "would be permitted to see Gov. Johnson next morning." Col. Holman replied that he did not know any man named Johnson who was then governor of Tennessee, but if such a man wanted to see him he would doubtless find him at the penitentiary. The governor did not call, but one of his staff officers remarked that the governor had said that "Holman could go to h—l."

After being detained in Nashville penitentiary three weeks he was sent to Camp Chase, Ohio, where he remained three weeks, and was transferred to Johnson's Island, where he remained until October, 1864, when he was put upon the sick exchange list and sent through to Richmond, being paroled until January 1, 1865. At the expiration of his parole Col. Holman was assigned to duty with Gen. E. Kirby Smith, commanding the trans-Mississippi department, and attached to the army of Gen. J. B. Magruder, of the department of Texas. He remained on duty in that department until the terms of surrender were agreed upon by Gens. Kirby Smith and Canby. Not being certain what would be the policy of the United States government towards officers who had resigned from the United States army at the beginning of the war, he declined to surrender, and resolved to go to Mexico until he could ascertain what that policy would be. Accordingly he moved to the western border of Texas, and remained there until he became satisfied that the government would not deal rigorously with him, and then returned to Houston, Texas, and surrendered to Gen. Canby, July 18, 1865, gave his parole, and received papers that were an assurance of protection, and returned to his father's house, in Lincoln county, Tennessee, his entire baggage consisting of the clothing he had on, a haversack, and a dirty shirt.

Soon after reaching home he commenced reading law. On November 23, 1865, he was married to Miss Elizabeth C. Kimbrough, second daughter of Rev. Bradley Kimbrough. After marriage his wife, like the noble woman she is, proposed to teach school to make money enough to support them until he could get into the practice of law. By the aid of such a helpmate Col. Holman succeeded, and in 1867, at the March term of the Lincoln county circuit court he was sworn in as a practicing attorney. He then formed a partnership with his brother, Col. D. W. Holman, who had been in practice for some time before the war. In August, 1870, Col. Holman was elected attorney-general of the sixth judicial circuit of Tennessee, which office he filled until October, 1877, when he tendered his resignation to Gov. James D. Porter, in order to give more time to civil practice, in which he has been actively engaged ever since.

After being elected attorney-general he was indicted in the United States circuit court for the middle district of Tennessee for holding office contrary to the fourteenth amendment to the constitution of the United States. At the same time *quo warranto* proceedings were instituted in that court to remove him from the office. He was arrested and gave bonds for his appearance before the court, when a demurrer was filed, both to the indictment and *quo warranto*. Judge Trigg, presiding, sustained the demurrer, and discharged Col. Holman from further attendance on that court. The United States district attorney appealed the case to the United States supreme court, where it is understood the decision of the district judge was affirmed, though no report of the case has ever been made.

In 1878 Col. Holman was appointed by Gov. Porter a commissioner for Tennessee to the International Exhibition at Paris. He attended the exhibition, and while in Europe he and Mrs. Holman visited the principal places of interest in Great Britain, France, Switzerland, Italy, Austria and Germany.

In politics Col. Holman is a Democrat, as were his paternal ancestors. His grandfather and people on his mother's side were Whigs. In 1880 he was a "State credit" candidate for Congress, but was defeated by Hon. Richard Warner.

Col. Holman became a Mason in 1866, and is at present a member of the council. Religiously he is inclined towards the Primitive Baptists, but is very liberal in his opinions, and belongs to no church. Mrs. Holman is a member of the Missionary Baptist Church, graduated in 1860 at Mary Sharp College, Winchester, Tennessee, and taught school some three years after her marriage.

Col. Holman began life without property, and resolved never to go in debt; never to spend money until he had made it; never to contract an obligation until he knew he could certainly meet it; to trust nothing to luck; to go without his supper before he would ask credit for it; to keep out of all speculations unless he was able to lose the amount of money he invested; never to go security unless he could pay the liability of his principal; to comply with every monetary obligation on the very day promised; to deny himself none of the necessities of life.

He never brings a law-suit for a client who does not first make out his case by his own statement and proof that he is able to bring forward. He always accepts the statement of his client as *prima facie* true as to the facts, but gives the client no control in the conduct of his controversy. When he sees that a client is about to lose his cause, or that he is likely to make nothing by litigation, he immediately so informs him, and if he refuses to take advice in that emergency the client is requested to employ other counsel; Holman retires from the case. He brings no law-suit, either civil or criminal, for a client whose sole object is to annoy and vex his antagonist, and will not be a party to his ill-will towards an adversary. He always aids a young lawyer, and has a reputation for never giving up the cause of his client so long as he thinks he is right. There is hardly any sacrifice he will not make for a meritorious cause. He throws his whole nature into his suits, and assumes them as his own.

Col. Holman's law library is one of the finest in the State, and financially he is on a good footing, one of the few lawyers who are good financial successes.

GEN. WASHINGTON CURRAN WHITTHORNE.

COLUMBIA.

THIS gentleman is of mingled Irish and American extraction; his father, William J. Whitthorne, named him after the two great objects of his admiration in his native and adopted country, whose names he now bears.

He was born April 19, 1825, near Petersburg, in Lincoln county; thence he removed with his parents to Farmington, Bedford county, and received an average country school education there, working at his father's trade when not in school. In his fourteenth year he was sent to an academy at Arrington, in Williamson county, where he studied eighteen months, and thence to the Campbell Academy in Lebanon, which was the nucleus of the now well-known Cumberland University.

After studying there two sessions, he entered the University of Nashville, then under Dr. Philip Lindsley, and after a session and a half there matriculated at the East Tennessee University, at Knoxville, under President Joseph Esterbrook. Here he graduated after a two years' course.

His father had by this time removed to a house near Nashville, and from college he made a visit of three months there, and then went to study law under Messrs. Polk and Thomas, the former gentleman being James K. Polk, afterwards President of the United States. Here he studied until 1845, when he was called to the bar, after examination by Chancellor Cahal and Judge Dillahunty. This, it will be remembered, was the year in which his preceptor, Mr. Polk, attained the presidential chair. The new President immediately constituted Mr. Whitthorne one of his most highly favored *proteges*. He had evidently recognized in him exceptional abilities while the young man was studying under his guidance. He first appointed him to a clerkship in the Sixth Auditor's office, whence he was soon transferred to the Post-office Department proper, and thence to the Fourth Auditor's office. Always acting under Mr. Polk's advice, his plan was, as soon as he had saved money enough to commence the practice of his profession, to resign his office. This he did the first day of 1848, when Mr. Polk sent him as a bearer of dispatches to the City of Mexico. He was instructed on his arrival there to inquire into the causes of Gen. Scott's misunderstanding with Gens. Worth and Pillow. As soon as he had reported at Washington, after the fulfillment of his instructions, he returned to Tennessee, and, on the fourth of the ensuing July, married Miss Jane Campbell, and settled down to the practice of his profession in Columbia.

In 1852 the presidential contest between Gens. Scott (Whig) and Pierce (Democrat), called him to the political arena.

In 1853 he was a candidate for representative in the Tennessee General Assembly of that year, the district being composed of the counties of Maury, Williamson and Lewis, which, at that time, was thoroughly Whig. His opponent, William E. Erwin, defeated him by a reduced majority. This never happened again in an election before the people.

In 1855 and 1857 he was elected to the State Senate, and in 1859 was elected to the House of Representatives from the district in which he had been beaten in 1853. His opponent in this contest was Fayette McConnico, the eloquent grandson of a very eloquent Baptist orator, Elder Garner McConnico. In this Legislature he was elected Speaker of the House. It was occupied with the most momentous questions that ever came before the Legislature of Tennessee, for all the principles were discussed and acted upon which ultimately became the subjects of contention between the union and secession parties; the vehemence and pertinacity with which this contest was carried on by both sides, rendered the speaker's chair something very different from a bed of roses.

On the secession of the State, before Tennessee had united herself with the government of the Confederate States, and while she stood apart as a separate and distinct sovereignty, viz.: during the summer of 1861, Gen. Whitthorne was appointed by Gov. Harris assistant adjutant-general of the provisional army of Tennessee, with rank of lieutenant-colonel, and was on duty in Nashville aiding in the military organization of the State, until the first call for volunteers was completed, when Tennessee united herself to the Southern Confederacy, and her army was transferred to the control of that government. Upon this, Gen. Whitthorne accompanied Gen. Anderson's brigade to western Virginia as its adjutant. In November, 1861, Gov. Harris urged very strongly his acceptance of the office of adjutant-general of the State. At this time Albert Sidney Johnston was organizing the defenses of Kentucky, and requested Gov. Harris to select for him a man who knew how to organize a volunteer force. Gov. Harris sent for Gen. Whitthorne, endorsed by Gen. Lee himself, who became acquainted with Gen. Whitthorne in western Virginia, and pronounced him the best adjutant that he had ever found serving in a volunteer force.

At the time when active campaigns commenced, he, with his leader, Gov. Isham G. Harris, followed the fortunes of Gen. Albert Sidney Johnston's army, Gen. Whitthorne serving as volunteer aid on the staff successively of Gens. Hardee, Anderson, Marcus J. Wright and others. In western Virginia he had been at the attack on Cheat mountain, and experienced the realities of war at Nashville, Murfreesborough, Mumfordsville, Chattanooga and Chickamauga. At this last battle he was the only mounted officer in Gen. Wright's command who escaped without a wound to himself or his horse, and that though he was within forty feet of Carnes' battery at a time when all its horses were cut down. Gen. Whitthorne is no vulgar braggart, and when questioned as to his sensations on that occasion by the editor, said, with a laugh, that he never heard a shell burst or a bullet whistle past him that he did not involuntarily button his coat and try to contract himself to narrower dimensions. The truth is, that bravery and bravado are two things that have nothing in common. The test of bravery is, not to be insensible to fear, but to do one's duty steadily and thoroughly in spite of it.

At the close of the war Gen. Whitthorne was held as a prisoner of war under parole at Columbia. This was in fact a friendly durance on the part of President Johnson, who kept him in that way, subject to military law, so as to shield him from a civil indictment before the Federal court, and, in 1865, made it one of his first official acts to pardon him. Andrew Johnson was, in fact, personally friendly to the General. On the other hand, this course was more acceptable to Gen. Whitthorne than that of temporary exile, embraced by many of the prominent Confederate officers; he knew the laws, manners, customs and habits of the American people, and especially those of Tennessee, and preferred living among them on any terms rather than to wait in foreign and uncongenial countries the possible opportunity for a general pardon.

He had now to begin the world again, and resumed with energy the practice of his profession.

The congressional district in which he lived then consisted of the counties of Maury, Lawrence, Wayne, Hardin, Lewis, Perry, Decatur, Hickman, Humphreys, Stewart and Montgomery. The people of this district elected him in 1870 to the Forty-second Congress, and he was re-elected at every recurring biennial election till the close of the Forty-seventh Congress; but the State was redistricted between his first and second terms of service, so that the counties he thenceforward represented were those of Maury, Williamson, Giles, Lawrence, Wayne, Lewis and Hickman. During the greater part of his service in Congress he was chairman of the committee on naval affairs. The information and familiarity with the methods of the Navy Department which he thus acquired became of inestimable value to him when that committee was charged to investigate the immense frauds which had been practiced for years in that department.

Next to naval affairs, the topic which has engrossed most of his attention has been that of the foreign affairs of the nation, and especially its relations with Mexico.

Since his retirement from Congress he has given his attention exclusively to his private affairs.

From early youth he has always been more keenly interested in political affairs than in all other subjects, and his many friends in Tennessee have never acquiesced in his permanent seclusion from the business of the nation.

Gen. Whitthorne became a Mason as soon as eligible; was made a Master Mason in National Lodge, No. 12, at Washington, in 1846, by Gen. James Shields, W. M. He was made a Royal Arch Mason in Columbia, Tennessee, in 1850; a Knight Templar in 1870, and has served as W. M. of Columbia Lodge, No. 31, and held some Chapter offices. He joined the Knights of Pythias in 1870.

He was an alternate delegate to the Charleston Democratic convention in 1860. He was nominated to that convention through the influence of Andrew Johnson, and represented there the leading views of that statesman.

He was elector for the State at large in 1860, on the Breckinridge electoral ticket, and made a thorough canvass of the State, meeting on the stump such men as N. G. Taylor, John S. Brien, Henry S. Foote, John L. Hopkins, Harvey M. Watterson, J. Knox Walker and Reese Brabson.

Gen. Whitthorne is not a member of any church organization. Mrs. Whitthorne is a member of the Episcopal church.

The family of Gen. Whitthorne are generally supposed to have migrated into Ireland during the sixteenth or seventeenth century, from near the border line between England and Scotland. His father, William J. Whitthorne, lost his father while he was yet an infant, and came to Richmond, Virginia, with one of his maternal uncles while very young, and when in his fourteenth year was apprenticed to the saddler's trade in Orange county, North Carolina. Upon reaching his majority, he settled at Carthage, in Tennessee, where

he worked at his trade with Mr. John Rains and Robert I. Chester, who were fellow-journeymen with him. Gen. Whitthorne's father died in 1875, at the age of seventy-eight years. He was a man of great firmness, energy and exactitude of character, the latter quality being manifested in the form of punctuality and a noticeable neatness of person. He was a member of the Presbyterian church, though educated as a Catholic.

Gen. Whitthorne's mother was Eliza J. Wisener, who was remarkable for energy, industry and common sense. She was of mingled Welch and German descent; her grandparents were in our Revolutionary war, and her father, Martin Wisener, was in the war of 1812. Her brother, William H. Wisener, of Shelbyville, a lawyer, was a prominent politician in the ranks of the Whig and Republican parties. He was several times in the State Legislature, and once speaker of the House of Representatives; he was also a candidate for governor of the State, but was not elected.

Gen. Whitthorne's deceased brothers were: (1). James Whitthorne, died at home of disease contracted while serving in the Mexican war. (2). DeWitt Clinton Whitthorne, killed in Nicaragua in 1851 or 1852, while serving as a lieutenant in Gen. Walker's filibusters. (3). Dr. G. M. Whitthorne, died recently in Fayette county, Tennessee. (4). Dr. A. J. Whitthorne, died at Pulaski from the effects of wounds received in the civil war. His living brothers are: (1). Samuel H. Whitthorne, who removed some eight or ten years ago to Benton, Arkansas; lawyer, politician and editor; has shown ability in all three capacities. (2). W. J. Whitthorne, Columbia; held the position of circuit court clerk there for eight years; an active and efficient officer. (3). Bromfield R. Whitthorne, cashier of the National Bank of Shelbyville. Gen. Whitthorne has one sister, Miss Felicia Whitthorne, who resides with her brother Bromfield.

Gen. Whitthorne married in Columbia, Tennessee, July 4, 1848, Miss Jane Campbell, a native of Columbia, daughter of Col. Robert Campbell, a planter of a North Carolina family. Her mother was Elizabeth Polk, daughter of John Polk. Both her parents, who were cousins, were related to President Polk, who, as well as Robert Campbell, was a grandson of Ezekiel Polk. Mrs. Whitthorne graduated at the Columbia Female Institute; she still preserves much of the beauty for which she was noted when a young lady. She is remarkable for energy and industry, as well as for her dignity and urbanity in her social relations.

Gen. and Mrs. Whitthorne have had ten children in all, four of whom they lost within ten days by the dreaded children's epidemic, diphtheria. They have left to them three sons and three daughters: (1). Campbell W., now occupied with some mining property near Batesville, Arkansas. (2). Lily, married to Charles P.

Cecil, a farmer and stock raiser near Danville, Kentucky; they have three children, Charles P., Janie and Sarah. (3). Ella, married to Alexander Harvey, a manufacturer residing in Baltimore; they have one child, Janie. (4). The single daughter, Mary, attending Mount Vernon Institute, Baltimore. (5). Washington C., jr., and (6), Harry, attending Center College, Danville, Kentucky.

The earliest principle Gen. Whitthorne adopted for his conduct in life was to live within his income. He says that he has had many ups and downs in life, and that his circumstances have uniformly been prosperous or adverse according as he adhered to that rule or departed from it. In any undertaking, whether it was a lawsuit, a speech in Congress, or committee work, or a stump speech, he was always successful, provided he had previously made himself thoroughly familiar with all the details of the matter in hand; on the other hand, whenever he has failed to do this, he has met with embarrassment and uncertainty in the result. In all cases it has been essential to success to give his undivided attention to the business before him.

The revising editor ventures on the opinion that an important element in this gentleman's political success has been fidelity to party leaders. In the earlier stages of his career he received valuable aid from President Polk and Andrew Johnson, and these services he repaid by devotion to the interests of his party chiefs. The writer is aware that such conduct is in the present day esteemed inconsistent with originality and independence of spirit, but he always suspects that independence which leads a young man to disdain the guidance of more experienced statesmen to arise much more from self-conceit than originality of intellect.

Gen. Whitthorne is five feet eight inches high; weighs one hundred and sixty-three pounds, has gray eyes and hair, with features of a type partly Grecian, partly Irish; his manners are graceful and easy, and may be pronounced those of the typical lawyer and congressman.

HON. RODERICK RANDOM BUTLER.

MOUNTAIN CITY.

THIS gentleman, like his political associate, Mr. Houck, is one of the self-made men of East Tennessee. He was born in Wytheville, Virginia, April 8, 1830. His father died while he was an infant, and he was raised in his mother's family till he was thirteen years old, when he was apprenticed to a tailor, John W. Haney, of Newbern, Virginia, with whom he served an apprenticeship of six years, and then emigrated to Johnson county, Tennessee, where he now lives. He states that he arrived there with a bundle of clothing tied up in a handkerchief, on his back, and seventy-five cents in his pocket. He commenced working at his trade at Taylorsville, the county seat of Johnson, which has recently adopted the more romantic name of Mountain City. Here he worked till he was twenty-one years old, when he commenced studying law with Carrick W. Nelson. He was called to the bar in November, 1853, being licensed by Chancellor Thomas L. Williams and Judge Seth Luckey. He was at once taken into partnership by his preceptor, C. W. Nelson, with whom he practiced in Johnson and Carter counties from 1853 to 1861.

When the war broke out, he took the Union side and was commissioned by Gen. Burnside to raise a regiment of infantry. Col. Miller was at the same time similarly engaged, and when each had partially succeeded their respective contingents were consolidated into a single regiment, of which Miller became colonel, and Butler lieutenant-colonel. He resigned at Nashville, in 1864, on account of impaired health. Prior to actual hostilities he was several times arrested by the Confederate authorities, and tried for treason at Knoxville, but acquitted.

Prior to the war he had attained the following positions: (1). Elected major of first battalion of Tennessee militia, about 1850, before he was of age. (2). Appointed brigade inspector on Gen. James T. Carter's staff. (3). Elected judge of the county court in 1855, and held the office two years. (4). Elected to the Legislature from Johnson county, and served in the session of 1859–60. (5). Re-elected and served in the session of 1861–62, and was one of the sixteen who voted against the military organization and the other measures which resulted in the secession of the State. As soon as the war was over and the Legislature re-established, he was elected (6) State Senator from the counties of Johnson, Sullivan, Washington and Carter, and served in the session of 1865–66. During that session he was appointed by Gov. Brownlow (7) judge of the first judicial circuit, comprising the counties of Sullivan, Washington, Johnson, Carter, Greene, Hawkins and Hancock. This post he held till (8) he was elected to Congress, in 1867, from the first congressional district, comprising the counties of Johnson, Carter, Sullivan, Washington, Greene, Hawkins, Hancock, Grainger, Cocke, Jefferson and Sevier. (9). Elected to the four ensuing Congresses, serving eight years. Throughout this period he acted steadily with the Republican party, and served on many important committees, those on Indian affairs, elections, education, labor, and the revision of the laws; he was the youngest member on the last-named committee, and was also chairman of the committee on military affairs. (10).

In 1878 he was again elected to the State Legislature from Johnson and Carter counties, and served in the sessions of that year and 1879. He was re-elected in 1880, 1881, 1883, and (11) in 1884 he was elected floterial representative from the district composed of the counties of Johnson, Carter, Sullivan, Washington, Greene and Unicoi.

In all he has served fourteen years in the State Legislature and eight in Congress. He was successively delegate to the national Republican conventions which nominated Lincoln, Grant, Hayes and Garfield, though he was prevented attending the latter by ill health. He was a Whig before the war, and as such was appointed postmaster of Taylorsville, and held the office for four years. When not serving in Congress or in the State Legislature he practices law, being a member of several law firms, such as Butler & McDowell, in Bristol; Butler & Donelly, in Mountain City; and Butler & Emmert, at Erwin, in Unicoi county.

Judge Butler is a man made for popularity, and has been recognized since his first entrance into public life as a political leader of consummate ability, second only in East Tennessee to Andrew Johnson, whose origin and early start in life present a remarkable parallel with his antecedents. In his own county there was but one vote cast against him in each of two elections. He has a commanding presence, being six feet high, with a weight of two hundred pounds; upright in attitude and jovial in bearing, always ready to express his views and able to defend them; knowing the people and known of them. In political work he is indefatigable, never resting while there is an end to be accomplished to which he can contribute his efforts. In the State Legislature, while his influence is supreme with his own party, there is no man with whom his political antagonists are so ready to discuss points of common interest, and he enters into such discussions with an engaging frankness that disarms political animosity. He drinks no whiskey, uses no tobacco, sleeps barely six hours, and is never idle when awake. His rule of life may be expressed in his own words: "Never desert a friend or pander to an enemy; especially never desert an old friend for a new one—rivet your friends to you and let your enemies go."

Judge Butler said to the editor, "If my time were to go over, I would attend to my profession and nothing else; I would never go into politics; there is no money in it, it is a dog's life; the politician is a pack-horse for everybody, has to go everybody's security and neglect one's private affairs."

To all which this editor is profoundly skeptical, firmly believing that, if the time were to go over, if R. R. Butler were again only twenty years old, and a political opening were visible, he would jump in, even as young ducks take to the water; yes, though he knew all he does now; if he knew, as he does know, that politics involves much loss and but little profit; if he knew that he should meet with treacherous friends and unscrupulous enemies; if he knew, as he well knows, that the politician's merits are constantly nibbled at by detractors and his errors proclaimed from the house-top, he would still be a politician and nothing but a politician. The strife of parties is the only element in which his faculties can find their field of action, the storm of political agitation, the only atmosphere in which he can breathe. R. R. Butler is a politician by nature and *Naturam expellas furca tamen usque recurret.*

Judge Butler married in Johnson county, Tennessee, January 7, 1849, Miss Emmeline Donelly, daughter of Richard Donelly, an old-style Virginian gentleman who emigrated from Albemarle county, Virginia; noted in his day as a splendid horseman. His father emigrated from Dublin to Albemarle county, Virginia, and settled there; he was a soldier in the war of 1812.

Mrs. Butler's mother, Rebecca Doran, was a daughter of Maj. Alexander Doran, a large farmer of Washington county, Virginia. He, too, was a soldier of 1812. He served as a member of the Tennessee Legislature from Carter county, the first representative of that part of the county which lies east of the mountains. He was brigade inspector under Gen. Taylor.

By his marriage with Miss Donelly, Judge Butler has seven sons and two daughters: (1). Richard H., has been county court clerk; is a farmer and merchant at Mountain City. (2). James G., married a Miss Grayson, and is a physician of high reputation. (3). Geo. O., now in Oregon sheep farming. (4). William R., a prominent physician; married a Miss Grayson. (5). Samuel S. D. G., a farmer in Johnson county; married a Miss Kiser. (6). John Bell, sheep farming in Oregon, with his brother George. (7). Edward East, reading law. (8). Virginia, wife of James H. Church, a lawyer at Mountain City. (9). Bessie, wife of W. R. Keys, a teacher and proprietor of the *Tennessee Tomahawk.*

Judge Butler's father, George Butler, was born in Maryland, raised and married in Virginia, and died in Wytheville, Virginia, in 1829, at the age of forty. He was a school teacher, a graduate of a German college; tall and handsome; an independent man of decisive character. He was the only man in his county who voted for Adams against Jackson for the presidency, he being sheriff of the county at the time.

The grandfather of Judge Butler, the Rev. John George Butler, of Cumberland, Maryland, was a minister of the Lutheran church. A grandson of his, the Rev. Dr. Butler, is known as pastor of the Memorial Lutheran church at Washington City, which was "dedicated to Almighty God for the preservation of the union of the United States." The Butlers are a German family, of which United States Senator Butler, of South Carolina, is a member; another branch of the family emigrated to Ohio.

Judge Butler's mother, was of Scotch-Irish origin, born in Tyrone county, Ireland, near Newton Stewart, daughter of Dr. Samuel Leitch, of Edinborough. Her mother, Rebecca Hay, of Tyrone county, Ireland, died at Wytheville, Virginia, 1847, leaving two children, Nancy, mother of Judge Butler, and Rebecca.

Judge Butler's mother died in 1859, leaving four children, George, Gustavus, Oliver and Roderick Random, all of whom are now dead except the last named, subject of this sketch. He has succeeded by hard work and indomitable resolution; has given his children a good education and trained them to work for their living. By industry and economy he has accumulated a respectable fortune in spite of the loss of fifteen thousand dollars security debts. Without disregarding public opinion, he has never yielded his leading opinions, policy or principles to it; he accepts flattery for what it is worth and laughs detraction out of countenance.

He became a Master Mason at Taylorsville, in 1852.

He has good health and great constitutional vigor, and promises to be a man of influence in political affairs for many years.

A prominent lawyer of East Tennessee writes to the editor as follows: "I have known Judge Butler intimately ever since the war. He went on the bench in 1865, and presided with dignity and impartiality. Afterwards he was four times elected to Congress. As a lawyer, he stands at the head of the profession; as an advocate, he is superior; as a man, he is noble and generous, faithful to his duties, true to his friends, and liberal to his enemies; as a politician, he is shrewd and cunning, and most generally carries his point. Socially, he has few, if any, superiors. He is now, as he has been ever since I have known him—twenty years—a consistent but firm, unflinching Republican, and a strong advocate for temperance in all its forms. He is a member of no church, yet attends church services more regularly than many professed Christians. In manners and in social life, he is an exceptionably pleasant gentleman, and a man who commands the respect of all with whom he comes in contact.

HON. HENRY J. LIVINGSTON.

BROWNSVILLE.

THE immediate ancestry of Hon. Henry J. Livingston were of South Carolina stock. His father, Thomas Price Livingston, was born on James Island, in front of Charleston, South Carolina, March 29, 1807. He was a cotton planter and slaveholder; a class-leader and steward in the Methodist church; a man of uncompromising integrity and a strong advocate of the South during the war. He removed to Tennessee in 1847, locating first in Henry county, and in 1848 settled in Haywood county, where he died, April 19, 1875.

Judge Livingston's mother was Rachel Livingston nee Shuler. The Shuler family are of German extraction and one among the oldest German families in the Palmetto State. Her father was Daniel Shuler, and her mother, Catharine Rhodes, also of South Carolina. Mrs. Livingston was born in Orangeburg district, South Carolina, December 21, 1800; was married there; and died in Haywood county, Tennessee, June 17, 1853. She was an excellent and most pious Christian woman.

By this marriage there were six children: (1). James L., now a farmer in Haywood county, Tennessee. (2). Henry J., subject of this sketch. (3). Lawrence W., who was a Confederate soldier under Gen. Price, and was killed in Arkansas. (4). Adaline A., now

the wife of J. N. Carlton, a farmer in Haywood county. (5). Thomas O., deceased. (6). Caroline E., wife of W. C. McConico, a farmer in Haywood county.

Henry J. Livingston was born in Orangeburg district, South Carolina, February 20, 1834. He was brought up to work on his father's farm, picked cotton and plowed corn there until 1847, when his father removed to Tennessee, and the young man continued the same occupation, gaining in health, muscle and industry, as he grew in years. His literary education was obtained at the best schools in Brownsville, and included a fair knowledge of Latin, Greek and mathematics, with a especial fondness for the latter and subsequently for the study of law, as early as his twentieth year. He began reading law January 1, 1856, under Gen. L. M. Campbell, of Brownsville, and after eight months' active and studious preparation, entered the middle class in the Law Department of the Cumberland University at Lebanon, Tennessee. He remained at Lebanon from September, 1856 to June, 1857, at which time he graduated under Profs. Nathan Green, Sr., Nathan Green, Jr., Abram Caruthers, and President Robert L. Caruthers. After graduating he was licensed by Chancellor B. L. Ridley and Judges Robert L. Caruthers. Robert J. McKinney and William R. Harris, of the Supreme bench. He began practice at Brownsville, in

November, 1857, and practiced there up to the war, and also, after the war, until he went on the bench— thus evincing the possession of staying power which must be reckoned always as a factor of success. During nearly all this time he was a partner of Attorney-General Benjamin J. Lea, the firm being Lea & Livingston.

In August, 1872, Gov. John C. Brown appointed the Hon. Henry J. Livingston chancellor of the tenth chancery division of the State of Tennessee, comprising the counties of Hardeman, Lauderdale, Fayette, Madison, Tipton and Haywood, and under this commission he served two years at a salary of two thousand five hundred dollars per annum. He has since been twice elected to the same place: first, in 1874, to fill out the unexpired term of Judge James Fentress, who had resigned; and, secondly, in 1878, for a term of eight years, which expires September, 1886.

Judge Livingston also served with credit and bravery as a Confederate soldier. He entered the army in May, 1861, at Jackson, Tennessee, as a private in the "Haywood Rangers," a cavalry company, commanded by Capt. R. W. Haywood, and served in that company until the close of the war. This company formed a part of the Seventh Tennessee cavalry regiment, Forrest's command. Livingston was made a lieutenant soon after joining the company, and remained a lieutenant therein until its surrender at Gainesville, Alabama, May 10, 1865, after seeing service in Tennessee, Missouri, Kentucky, Mississippi and Alabama, and in all the various battles where Forrest led. He commanded his regiment in the fight at Wyatt, on the Tallahatchie river, in Mississippi. He was taken prisoner November 8, 1862, at Lamar, Mississippi, and exchanged at Vicksburg, December 3, 1862. At Columbia, Tennessee, November 25, 1864, in the fight when Hood was moving upon Nashville, he was wounded in the left shoulder by a minnie ball, and in every engagement in which he participated he bore himself with the gallantry of a good soldier.

In politics Judge Livingston is regarded as an unwavering Democrat. He was a Democrat in childhood, a Breckinridge Democrat when the war came on, and since the war a regular, straight party man, voting the square ticket. In the Democratic State convention of 1872, which nominated John C. Brown for governor, Judge Livingston opposed the nomination of Greeley for president. In that convention he was with Hon. John M. Fleming, of Knoxville; Hon. D. M. Key, of Chattanooga; Gen. William A. Quarles, Hon. T. B. Ivie, Col. M. C. Gallaway and others, placed on the committee on platform, and advocated a square Democrat as the national nominee of the party. Messrs. Quarles, Ivie and Livingston opposed the majority of the committee and presented a minority report, Judge Livingston making an able speech on it, but the minority report was voted down. Since that time he

has attended no State convention; but he has many times since been congratulated by men who opposed him in that convention for the firm stand he took against the Greeley nomination. He has never believed in shams or half-way measures.

Judge Livingston has never belonged to any order or secret society of any kind. In religion, he is a Methodist, having joined that church in 1873. He was raised in a Methodist family, and always had a reverence for religion, being fully persuaded of its propriety and necessity, and never once doubted the truth of Christianity.

Judge Livingston married, at Stanton, Haywood county, Tennessee, November 28, 1872, Miss Tempe J. Somervell, who was born at White Sulphur Springs, North Carolina, November 10, 1850. Mrs. Livingston's father was Joseph Brehon Somervell, a large planter, of firm character and unquestioned integrity, the son of James Somervell, a lawyer of ability and note in North Carolina. James Somervell was the son of John Somervell, who was the son of John Somervell, son of James Somervell, of Kennox, the last being a lineal descendant of Walter Somervell, who came from Normandy with William, the Conquerer, about 1066. Her mother, nee Mary Eliza Jones, was the daughter of William Duke Jones, a prominent citizen of North Carolina. William Duke Jones was a direct descendant of the famous "grandmother Cook," the first white woman that ever crossed Roanoke river. Among "grandmother Cook's" descendants in Tenessee are Judge Carthell, of Trenton, Hon. John H. Freeman, and Judge Thomas J. Freeman, the latter of the Supreme Court of the State. Mrs. Livingston graduated at the Memphis Conference Female Institute under Dr. Amos W. Jones. She is also a member of the Methodist church, and is beloved as a most excellent Christian lady. Among other accomplishments, she is a fine musician, and, indeed, is one of those intelligent, dignified and practical women, all devotion, who make the world bright and man's life a delight.

Four children have blessed this happy marriage: (1). Mary Somervell, born August 31, 1873. (2). Henry J., born January 2, 1875. (3). Rosa Gibson, born May 9, 1877. (4). Genevieve, born September 20, 1881.

In speaking of his happy family, Judge Livingston once said: "If our children do not prove of unbending integrity, firm and unyielding, it will not have been the fault of their grandparents." And then, for example, he stated that Mr. Somervell, his wife's father, held a receipt from a Federal quartermaster for four thousand five hundred dollars' worth of property—mules, wheat, bacon, flour, etc., taken from him for military uses, and after the war he might have recovered on that voucher, if he had only consented to swear to his unionism and loyalty during the war, or permitted his neighbors to swear for him; but this he refused to do on moral grounds, and this, although in straightened circumstances as a result of the war, and notwithstanding his being repeatedly urged thereto by his friends and neighbors, and not having actively participated in the war. Another example: Judge Livingston's father, in 1862, when the Federals had taken Fort Pillow and Memphis, and the Confederates were burning cotton to prevent its falling into the hands of the Federals, burnt his own cotton, fifty bales, to be on a footing with his neighbors, whose cotton the Confederates had burnt, he understanding this to be the policy of the Confederate government. This illustrates the high-toned character of the man, and shows he was influenced by principle, even when it was apparently against his present interest. Of such sterling material were the parents of Chancellor Livingston and his lovely wife.

Judge Livingston's life has been a peculiarly happy one. Not only was his boyhood joyous, but his manhood seems to have been pleasant all the way. His vigorous and stalwart constitution is without doubt the result of his industrious activity while but a lad on his father's plantation; and in his youth and manhood he never indulged in the many vices to which young men are too often addicted. To this day he has never taken a pint of liquor, except medicinally; nor smoked a pipe or cigar, or used tobacco in any form; and something singular in his history, he has not in thirty years drank coffee or tasted hog meat. More than that, he has not in all his life sworn an oath or uttered a profane word, and all this including his four years of service in the army, and in spite of such demoralizing influences. Such has been the clean, honorable record of the boy and the man. How suggestive his career to mothers who have sons to raise in the way of success! And to what extent is it not true, that a sound and strong physique and good health are the basis of good morals, good sense and good thinking power? His early academic studies, in the midst of professional duties, have been supplemented by a wide range of miscellaneous reading, and his very large and well selected private library well indicates both his natural and cultivated fondness for literature in many directions. Thus he proves a pet theory of the writer that a judge on the bench should be like Adam Clark's Methodist preacher; "he should know everything," and not be merely learned in the law.

His business methods also challenge admiration. Beginning life on but a small inheritance, when the war closed he had nothing. He now owns a comfortable property, and can afford his family a good living. He never goes security; never had a note protested. Fidelity in business, punctuality in all engagements, and attending with promptness and without procrastination to all matters entrusted to him; these are some of his leading characteristics. His policy is to keep out of debt, pay as he goes, and to act honorably with all men under all circumstances.

As a judge, he closes his courts with clean dockets, never adjourning as long as there is anything necessary to be done. His rule is to *try cases* and not have his courts stigmatized with the old taunt, "once in chancery, always in chancery." Such a chancellor is a jewel to the commonwealth.

HON. WILLIAM CULLOM.

CLINTON.

FOR sixty years in public life, associated with the great men of the most brilliant days of the Republic, the name of Gen. William Cullom has long been honored and beloved in Tennessee. He was born June 4, 1810, in Elk Spring Valley, near Monticello, Wayne county, Kentucky, the son of William Cullom, a moderate farmer, who for a time was tax-assessor of his county. But the father's chief characteristic was his religion, which with him was everything. He believed in praying without ceasing, and in every thing giving thanks. He moved to Overton county, Tennessee, where his two sons, Alvin and Edward N., and two daughters, Mrs. Elizabeth McHenry and Mrs. Lucinda Hart, were living at the time, and there he died in 1838, at the age of seventy-four. He was fifty-six years a Methodist class-leader, a very stern man, inflexible in his religious and political principles. In politics he was a Henry Clay Whig. His brother, Edward N. Cullom, who served several terms in the Kentucky Legislature, moved to Illinois and was a member of the convention that framed the original constitution of that State. He was a plain man, a farmer, but of strong native talent.

The grandfather of Gen. William Cullom was George Cullom, a Marylander, a tobacco farmer, who died in the Valley of Virginia, near what is now known as Bull Run. The family are of Scotch origin, of the Clan McCullom, and the family name constantly recurs in Scotch history. By intermarriage there is a dash of Welsh blood in the family.

Gen. Cullom's mother, Elizabeth Northcraft, was born in Maryland, near Washington City, and was a first cousin of her husband. She was a devout Methodist lady, popular with everybody on account of her high order of talent and boundless charities. Her children, sons and daughters, were all talented. They derived the dash that was in them from her. She had the *suaviter in modo ;* the father transmitted to the children the stamina, the stern inflexibility of principle and rugged manhood that characterized them all. She died in her ninety-fourth year, the mother of eleven children: (1). Tillman, who ran away from home when fifteen years old and fought under Gen. Harrison in the Northwestern war of 1812. (2). Edward N., mentioned above as having moved to Illinois. (3). Richard N., father of Hon. Shelby M. Cullom, ex-Speaker of the Illinois Legislature, ex-Governor, and now United States Senator from that State. (4). Alvin, one of the first lawyers of Middle Tennessee. He was twice a Democratic member of Congress from Tennessee, and settled in Overton county, where he died. (5). Vertinder F., became a paralytic and died unmarried. (6). James N., the only boy of the family that never figured in public life. He married a Miss Totten, sister of Hon. A. W. O. Totten, of the Tennessee Supreme bench, and of Hons. B. C. Totten and James Totten, circuit judges. (7). Susan, married Alfred Phillips, moved to Illinois, and died there. She is said to have been one of the brightest women in the United States in her day. (8). Permelia, died the widow of Rev. Wm. Brown, a Methodist minister, noted for his extreme devoutness. (9). Elizabeth, also a talented lady, died of consumption, the wife of Dr. Spencer McHenry. (10). William, subject of this sketch. (11). Lucinda, wife of John Hart, present clerk of the county court of Overton county. She is the only surviving member of the family except Gen. Cullom.

Gen. Cullom was raised in Wayne county, Kentucky, where he cast his maiden vote, and soon after came to Overton county, Tennessee, and was sworn in as deputy sheriff, which office he filled with high credit two years, meanwhile reading law. He then went to Lexington, Kentucky, and took a thorough course in the law department of Transylvania University, graduated, returned home, and was the first lawyer licensed by Judge Abram Caruthers and Judge Reese, of the Supreme Court of Tennessee. He began practice at Gainesborough, Jackson county, Tennessee, and his success as a young lawyer was most remarkable. He went right up, though a strange Kentucky boy. In 1839, he married and settled at Carthage, and he had hardly got his house there well warmed before the Whig party nominated him for the State Senate against Maj. David Burford, a man of great wealth, and highly and extensively connected. Gen. Cullom overcame a Democratic majority of six hundred, and beat his opponent three hundred votes. In 1845, he was again elected to the State Senate, doubling his majority in a district strongly Democratic, and dominated by the personal influence of Gen. Jackson, beating his opponent eighty-one votes in the Hermitage precinct.

In 1835 he had been elected attorney-general of the sixth judicial circuit, beating Judge John S. Brien,

father of Gen. W. G. Brien, a position which he held six years, just prior to his first election to the Senate.

In 1851 he was elected as a Whig to Congress from the Nashville district, over Hon. J. B. Southall, and two years afterwards he beat Judge E. L. Gardenhire for the same position. During his career in Congress he had as much influence in that body as many older members, and made golden opinions by his opposition to the Kansas-Nebraska bill. Extracts from his speeches, especially the one against the Kossuth mania, have been published in the school books as specimens of American oratory. Standing six feet three inches in height, of handsome presence, courtly manners, and fine address, he was one of the conspicuous figures in Congress. For his opposition to the Kansas-Nebraska bill he was defeated in his next candidacy for Congress, but his political friends in that body espoused his cause and elected him clerk of the next House of Representatives. When he was elected to this position, he had in his trunk letters from at least two-thirds of the members of Congress promising him that position or any other in their gift, though he had never intimated a wish for favors of that kind.

Gen. Cullom was presidential elector on the Taylor ticket, in 1848, and took an active part in the campaigns for Clay, Harrison, Taylor and Scott, and canvassed the State at various times. He was a delegate at large to the national Whig convention at Philadelphia that nominated Gen. Scott for the presidency. In that convention he voted fifty-four times for Fillmore. He was a personal friend of Henry Clay, and was the only man, except Gov. James C. Jones, that was present when Mr. Clay died, he being one of the privileged few who had access to his room at all hours. In politics, since the expiration of the Whig party, he has been a Democrat, "as there was nowhere else to go."

In 1845 he was chairman of the Tennessee delegation to the commercial convention at Memphis, at which John C. Calhoun presided. In the civil conflict of 1861-65 he advised against the dismemberment of the States and made speeches for the Union, but finally acquiesced in what was forced upon the State. When Tennessee went out he went with the South—went in his heart with the southern soldiers—but remained at home and never fired a gun on either side. He has several times been special circuit judge and chancellor. He belongs to no secret society, and in his religious inclinations is a Methodist, but is not a member of any communion.

In November, 1872, Gov. John C. Brown appointed him attorney-general of the sixteenth judicial circuit, and to the same position he was elected in 1874, by the people, in a district having one thousand seven hundred Republican majority. While prosecuting attorney, in all some twelve years, it is said he has had more men convicted and hung than any man in the State. He has long enjoyed the reputation of being one of the foremost criminal lawyers in the State, as the records of every court where he has practiced abundantly show. He made probably the largest fortune any lawyer in Tennessee ever made simply by practice. He began life without an inheritance, and with an education limited to what he learned by going to school on rainy days and when he could not work. His early practice was too large to admit of his becoming profoundly read in the books, but his gift of speech, his flow of eloquence, his keen insight into human nature, his observation of men and the run of events daily transpiring, and withal an ambition to succeed and shine, characteristic of his mother and all of his family, made him one of the most popular and powerful advocates at the bar of Tennessee.

Gen. Cullom married first in Kentucky, September 26, 1839, Miss Virginia Ingram, sister of W. P. Ingram, a banker at Columbia. By this marriage he has five children: (1). Marietta, wife of John Allen, now in Arkansas, who was a delegate from Smith county to the Tennessee constitutional convention of 1870, son of Robert Allen, who was eight years a member of Congress from Tennessee, and a member of the State constitutional convention of 1834. (2). Virginia, wife of Thomas Goodall; has two children. (3). Cornelius Perry, a standard farmer in Smith county, Tennessee.

(4). Ella, wife of Rev. Dr. Booth, a Methodist minister in Giles county, Tennessee. (5). Leslie, a lawyer at Columbia, Tennessee.

By his second marriage, which occurred in White county, Tennessee, with Miss Mary Griffith, Gen. Cullom has eight children: (1). Minnie, wife of Rufus Kincaid, a merchant at Clinton, Tennessee; has two children, Perry and Ed. McCarthy. (2). Florence, wife of John Baxter, a railroad engineer. (3). Clara. (4). Albert Sidney Johnson. (5). William. (6). Ella. (7). Rosa May. (8). Cora Henderson.

With as great an amount of energy as any one man can have, with a heart overflowing with kindness, with a clear judgment of men and property, one of the best of financiers, a most companionable gentleman; with extraordinary natural talents, hardy in debate and courteous in conduct; with an inherited mercurial temperament, Gen. William Cullom's success in life—professional, official and financial—has been almost phenomenal. He is prompt to pay and slow to go in debt. His personal friends are numerous and warm. It is said of him among his neighbors at Clinton, he never harmed a human being. Brilliant record! Grand, noble old man! The State has honored him, but not more than he has honored the State.

JOHN W. MADDIN, A.M., M.D.

NASHVILLE.

DR. JOHN W. MADDIN was born in Columbia Tennessee, August 28, 1834, and spent his boyhood from the age of five to twelve in Huntsville, Alabama, and from twelve to fifteen in Louisville, Kentucky, attending literary schools in both places. At the age of fifteen he entered Lagrange College, Alabama, where also his brothers, Dr. Thomas L. Maddin and Prof. Ferdinand P. Maddin, were educated. After three and a half years' study at that then noted institution he graduated as an A. B. in 1854, and two years afterwards as A. M., taking the first honor of his class of twenty-eight, and having the distinction of delivering the valedictory. Immediately after graduation he was offered a position in the college at which he graduated, and subsequently was solicited by Dr. Wadsworth, president of the University of Nashville, to accept the chair of ancient languages in that school. Among his fellow-graduates were William Price, of Florence, Alabama; Samuel Young, of Aberdeen, Mississippi; Dr. Benjamin Weir, of Columbus, Mississippi; and James Hutchison, of South Alabama. Most of his class mates fell in the Confederate service. After graduation he entered upon the study of medicine with his

brother-in-law, Dr. Frank Steger, a distinguished practitioner of Madison county, Alabama, who is now practicing at the advanced age of seventy. Subsequently he pursued his studies with Dr. T. L. Maddin, at Nashville, Tennessee. Dr. Maddin attended medical lectures in the medical department of the University of Nashville, and took his degree of M.D. in the spring of 1856, under Profs. Paul F. Eve, Thomas R. Jennings, W. K. Bowling, John M. Watson, C. K. Winston, A. H. Buchanan, John B. Lindsley and Robert M. Porter.

From 1856 to 1862, Dr. Maddin practiced medicine in Waco, Texas. In February, 1862, he entered the Confederate army as surgeon of the post at Lagrange College, Alabama, where he had graduated. Subsequently he was assigned to duty in the general hospital at Corinth, Mississippi, pending the battle of Shiloh, and afterwards was placed in charge of a special hospital for the wounded at Corinth. He was next ordered on duty as surgeon of the Thirty-fifth Alabama regiment at the first bombardment of Vicksburg, where he remained in service with his command until it was ordered to Baton Rouge, Louisiana, where he established the first field hospital at the battle there. In

August, 1862, he was transferred by Gen. Breckinridge to the trans-Mississippi department, and ordered to report for duty to Gen. E. Kirby Smith, at Shreveport, Louisiana. Here he was assigned to duty as surgeon of the Thirtieth Texas cavalry, and subsequently was made medical purveyor in the trans-Mississippi department, with Gen. Henry E. McCullough's division of the army, headquarters at Bonham, Texas, at which place he was on duty at the close of the war.

Immediately after the close of the war, Dr. Maddin removed his family, in 1866, from Texas to Nashville, Tennessee, and began the practice of medicine in partnership with his brother, Dr. Thomas L. Maddin, one of the foremost physicians and surgeons of the South, a full biography of whom appears elsewhere in these pages. Dr. Maddin has remained in Nashville without change since his first location, and it is probable no two men in this period of time have done more professional labor in all the branches of medicine than these two brothers.

Dr. Maddin was married, September 25, 1856, to Miss Annie Downs, daughter of Maj. W. W. Downs, for many years an extensive merchant and planter at Leighton, Alabama, a man of high standing and great public spirit, who infused himself into every public enterprise in Alabama, and in his subsequent home in Texas. Maj. Downs attained large wealth and influence before the war, and moved to Waco, Texas, in 1856. Great numbers of persons who were seeking homes in Texas about that time visited him for counsel and advice as to locating in that distant State. He built a Methodist church and a female college at Waco, and made a present of the college to that city, together with an entire square of ground in the heart of the city. With the exception of Mrs. Maddin, all of Maj. Downs' connections are still residing at Waco, represented in all departments of trade and business, people of influence and position. Mrs. Maddin's mother, *nee* Henrietta Sparks, of a leading Georgia family, is still living at Waco, at the age of seventy-six.

By his marriage with Miss Downs, Dr. Maddin has five children: (1). Ida Belle Maddin, born at Waco; graduated from Ward's Seminary, Nashville, and finished her education at Mrs. Sylvanus Read's school, New York city; married, in 1878, to William J. Bass, son of Dr. John Bass, and grandson of Hon. John M. Bass, of Nashville. His grandmother was a daughter of the Hon. Felix Grundy. (2). Percy D. Maddin, born at Waco, in 1861; began his education in the first grade at the high school, Nashville, went through all its grades and graduated in 1878; next entered Vanderbilt University, remaining three years, taking a university course and the degree of Bachelor of Science; next graduated from the Vanderbilt University law school, under President Thomas H. Malone and Profs. Ed. Baxter and William B. Reese; is a finished scholar, and, for

a man of his age, a lawyer of fine merit and promise. (3). John W. Maddin, Jr., M.D., born at Waco; educated in the Nashville high school and at Vanderbilt University, and in 1884 graduated M. D. from the medical department of the University of Nashville and Vanderbilt University, under Profs. W. T. Briggs, Thomas L. Maddin, Thomas Menees, Thomas A. Atchison, John H. Callender, Van S. Lindsley, W. L. Nichol, Charles S, Briggs and Orville Menees. Dr. J. W. Maddin, jr., has received careful clinical instruction from his uncle and father. He is now assistant lecturer to the chair of obstetrics in the University in which he graduated. He has fine professional promise. (4). Annie Maddin, born at Waco; educated in the high school of Nashville, and finished her course of study at the Nashville College for Young Ladies, conducted by Rev. Dr. George W. F. Price. (5). Louise Lea Maddin, born at Nashville, now a little girl of eight years, a pupil of Dr. Price's Nashville College for Young Ladies.

Dr. Maddin's family is a Methodist family. Politically, the doctor has always been a Democrat, but has never held civil office. Financially, he is in comfortable circumstances, the income from his practice always being very satisfactory. Raised in a family of extremely limited means and early taught the lessons of frugality, he began life on no inheritance except as good an education as could be afforded in that day in this country, and the legacy of a family character and family name honored all over the land. When asked how he had succeeded in life, Dr. Maddin replied: "I have made my profession the exclusive business of my life; I have endeavored to prepare myself thoroughly for my work; I have been kept busy in it, and it has amply compensated me." As an illustration of the retiring nature of Dr. Maddin, it may be mentioned that at the outbreak of the cholera epidemic in Nashville, in 1873, Hon. Thomas A. Kercheval, mayor of the city, selected and appointed Dr. Maddin as the health officer of the city, but he declined it because he preferred the private walks of his profession to public position.

Dr. Maddin has been an active member of all city, county and State medical organizations with which he has been associated. He is a member of the American Medical Association. He has contributed a number of scientific papers to these organizations, and always participates, with much pleasure, in the discussions of medical subjects before these societies.

Dr. Maddin has the air, the tone of voice, the manners of a modest, retiring man of dignity and clearness of character, and carefulness, accuracy and promptness in business. He seems a combination of the rigid principles of his father and the tenderness of his mother.

For a more detailed account of the life of Dr. Maddin's parents, see the sketch of Dr. Thomas L. Maddin in this volume.

8

HON. BEDFORD M. ESTES.

MEMPHIS.

THE subject of this sketch appears in these pages as a representative lawyer, and a representative Presbyterian gentleman, and is commonly described as steady, formal, polite and accomplished, and by general consent is a man of spotless integrity and splendid moral character.

Bedford M. Estes was born in Haywood county, Tennessee, October 10, 1832, and grew up in Brownsville—was educated, read law and admitted to the bar there. He attended the University of Nashville two years, and then entered the Louisville, Kentucky, Law School, where he graduated under Profs. Pirtle, Loughborough and Bullock. He obtained license to practice law at nineteen, having selected the law for a profession in his eighteenth year, up to which time he was full of life, indulging in all sorts of merriment and mischief, but abstaining from vice and dissipation, and thenceforward concentrating his powers on his chosen profession. At the age of twenty-one he went to Memphis, where he has lived ever since, except during the Federal occupation of the city during the war, and has steadily practiced law there, first in partnership with Judge Howell E. Jackson, now United States senator from Tennessee, next with Judge Ellett, and now with H. C. Warinner, Esq.

In the memorable Tennessee Legislature of 1861–62 Mr. Estes represented Shelby county in the House of Representatives, and was a member of the several committees on banking, ways and means, finance and judiciary. In 1862 he was appointed by President Jefferson Davis Confederate States district attorney for West Tennessee, but owing to Federal occupation was prevented from discharging the duties of his office.

In May, 1878, Mr. Estes was appointed by Gov. James D. Porter and commissioned as a member of the court of arbitration for West Tennessee, and with Judge L. D. McKissick and Judge Henry Craft, held court at Jackson, and disposed of many of the causes pending in the Supreme court of Tennessee, thereby aiding in relieving the crowded docket of that court. In 1882 Mr. Estes was elected president of the Bar Association of Tennessee, and held this office the constitutional term of one year, or until the meeting of the Association at Bon Aqua Springs, in July, 1883. Mr. Estes is also a member of the general council of the Bar Association of America.

Mr. Estes married, first, May, 1854, Miss Sarah Jane Johnston, daughter of James Johnston, a leading farmer of Madison county, Tennessee. Her mother was a Miss Alston, daughter of Philip Alston, of the same county. Mrs. Estes was educated at Trenton, Tennessee, and was remarkable for the beauty of her person, the grace of her manners and the gentlene and purity of her character. She died in 1867, at th early age of thirty-two, leaving six children: (1 Bedford M. Estes, jr., who died in 1873. (2). Mollie Estes; graduated at the Augusta Female Seminar Staunton, Virginia; is a superior musician, and ha much merit as a literary writer. (3). Emma A. Este graduated from Mrs. Pegram's school, Baltimore, an married James G. Snedecor, a planter in Florida. (4 Sarah Jane Estes; educated at Augusta Female Sem nary, Staunton, Virginia; married James C. Bell, Memphis. (5). Ione Estes; spent two years at August Female Seminary, Staunton, Virginia; graduated Sayre Female Institute, Lexington, Kentucky. (6 Kate Estes, now at Sayre Female Institute, Lexingto Kentucky.

Mr. Estes next married, at Memphis, Miss Lizz Guion, daughter of H. L. Guion, Esq., decease of that city. Her mother was a Miss McMillan daughter of Rev. Murdock McMillan, of a North Car olina family, a distinguished Presbyterian divine, wh preached the first Presbyterian sermon in Memphi Mrs. Estes was educated at Walnut Hill, Rev. D Bullock's school, near Lexington, Kentucky, and als at the Nashville Female Academy, under Rev. Dr. C D. Elliott. By this marriage Mr. Estes has fiv children: Lizzie, Henry Witherspoon, Morgan, Blanch and Flora Estes.

Mr. Estes is an elder in the Presbyterian churc and has been from his twenty-seventh year. Mr Estes and all of their children old enough are member of the same communion. Mr. Estes was a prim mover in the establishment of the Lauderdale stree Presbyterian church, Memphis, secured the contribu tions for the purchase of the lot and erection of th church building and had it dedicated without debt on it

In 1861 the Presbyterian church of the Unite States was divided, and the churches of the souther States formed a separate General Assembly called th General Assembly of the Presbyterian church of th Confederate States. After the close of the war, th name of the assembly was changed to the Genera Assembly of the Presbyterian church in the Unite States. The church has since maintained its separat organizations. During the war and shortly thereafte the northern church had made deliverances of th bitterest sort against the southern church. Som unsuccessful efforts were made to restore "fraterna relations" between the churches, and in 1874 eac church appointed commissioners to meet and arrang plans for the establishment of fraternal relations. Th southern church appointed Rev. Dr. William Brow of Virginia, Rev. Dr. B. M. Palmer, of New Orleans, Rev. Dr. Farris, of Missouri, Chancellor Ingles, of Baltimore, and Mr. B. M. Estes, of Memphis, its commissioners. These commissioners met the commissioners of the northern church in Baltimore in 1875, and spent about a week in negotiations. The conference did not succeed in re-establishing fraternal relations at that time, but the terms proposed by the southern commissioners were subsequently, in substance, accepted, and good fellowship was restored.

Mr. Estes, as a lawyer, has occupied for twenty years a very prominent position at the Memphis bar, and has extended his reputation during that period throughout Tennessee, Mississippi and Arkansas. Early after the close of the civil war he entered upon one of the largest and most lucrative practices in the southwest, and was engaged in the heaviest and most important cases in his section of the country. He has held his position at the bar in the midst of a bar at Memphis noted for its learning and ability, and all the time ranked as one of its very ablest members.

The distinguishing traits of Mr. Estes as a lawyer are his critical analyses and thorough mastery of his cases. No amount of labor is spared by him to reach the fundamental principles underlying his cases, and a perfect comprehension of the facts upon which the lawsuit is based. When these are ascertained, he applies to them a clear, vigorous and comprehensive intellect, thoroughly trained in the science of the law.

Mr. Estes has been a very successful lawyer, and stands in the southwest as he deserves to—among the foremost men in the profession of the law.

Mr. Estes has also made a business success of his life. He began on a patrimony of a few thousand dollars, and is now among the solid men of Memphis, not only financially, but so regarded for his high character and stern integrity. He is a stockholder in the Bank of Commerce, and in the Hernando Insurance company and other corporations, besides owning valuable real estate in the city. Faithful and unremitting attention to business, close application to his profession, conscientious discharge of duty, and promptitude in meeting all engagements, pecuniary or otherwise—these are some of the marked characteristics of this man of sterling worth. In court he presents his cases tersely, with directness, and in as few words as possible. When a young man he was frequently a speaker on holiday occasions, but he never wasted language or beat around his subject, for he has always been noted as a man of moral force and earnestness, and devoid of trifling. He was a Whig until the breaking out of the war, but since the war has acted with the Democrats, without taking any prominent part, abstaining from politics on account of true devotion to his profession.

The Estes family is of French descent. Mr. Estes' father, Capt. Joel Estes, was a native of Bedford county, Virginia, and a farmer. He moved to Haywood county, Tennessee, at an early day, and was a candidate for Congress against the celebrated Davy Crockett. He was a man of great industry and probity, and was very successful in business. He died in 1833. Mr. Estes' mother was Miss Mary L. Wilson, a native of Baltimore, daughter of William Wilson, who died in Tipton county, Tennessee. Her mother was a Miss Lee, of Maryland. Mrs. Estes died in Memphis in 1871, aged seventy-two years. Mr. Estes' maternal uncle, Dr. Paca Wilson, is now a prominent physician at Brownsville, Tennessee, and his paternal uncles, residents of Virginia and Kentucky, were all men of splendid character, but without prominence in public life.

Mr. Estes is a man of positive character. If he has any enemies, as men of his decided stamp are almost certain to have, they are not among his professional brethren, or numbered with those who know him well. He himself is morally and religiously unbending.

JOHN HILL CALLENDER, M.D.

NASHVILLE.

JOHN HILL CALLENDER was born near Nashville, Davidson county, Tennessee, November 28, 1832. His father was Thomas Callender, born in Philadelphia, Pennsylvania, in 1796, and removed to Nashville in 1817, where he resided until his death in 1851. His occupation was that of tobacconist and merchant. He was an alderman of the city several terms, and a member of the county court. His religious faith was Presbyterian. He was the only son of James Thompson Callender, a native of Scotland, who came to America as a political exile in 1792, on account of the publica-tion of radically democratic opinions in a work entitled *The Political History of Great Britain*. Shortly after, he attracted the attention of Thomas Jefferson, and became a political writer in the interest of the views of that statesman, and a severe critic of some of the measures of Washington's administration, and particularly that of the elder Adams. He was a strenuous opponent of the Federal party of that day in its principles of government and its measures, and was master of a trenchant style in controversy, which rendered him quite obnoxious to its leaders. During the years of

John Adams' administration he published in Philadelphia *The Political Register*, a review of current political events. In 1798 he published a brochure entitled *The Prospect Before Us*—a caustic arraignment of President Adams and denunciation of the Alien and Sedition Act. He was then residing in Richmond, Virginia. Being an alien by birth, he was indicted for this publication under the provisions of the law he had denounced, for defamation of the President, and was the first of the few convictions had under it. He was defended by William Wirt and George Hay, and for his illegal and tyrannical rulings in the trial, Justice Chase of the United States Supreme Court, was afterwards impeached. James Thompson Callender afterwards founded the Richmond *Recorder*—the predecessor of the Richmond *Enquirer*, afterwards and for many years a newspaper of great power. He died in that city in 1806.

The mother of John H. Callender was Miss Mary Sangster, born in Fairfax county, Virginia, January 10, 1805. She was the daughter of John Sangster, a farmer, who moved to Davidson county in 1820. In 1835 he removed to West Tennessee, where he died in 1855. Her religious faith was Presbyterian. She died September 15, 1847.

John H. Callender attended the best classical schools at Nashville, until his seventeenth year, when he entered the University of Nashville and remained there until its suspension in October, 1850—the termination of his collegiate junior year. In 1851 he entered the law office of Nicholson & Houston, Nashville, and soon after the law department of the University of Louisville. The illness of his father followed by his death, recalled him in a short time, and his legal studies were suspended and finally abandoned. In 1852 he visited St. Louis, and was employed in the house of Woods, Christy & Co., one of the largest at that time in the West. In 1853 he returned to Nashville and commenced the study of medicine, taking his degree in the medical department of the University of Pennsylvania in 1855. December, 1855, he became joint proprietor and editor of the Nashville *Patriot*, and so remained until 1858. In that year he was made professor of materia medica and therapeutics in the Shelby Medical College, Nashville, Tennessee, and filled that position until the suspension of exercises caused by the civil war in 1861. The same year he was appointed surgeon to the Eleventh Tennessee regiment, in command of Gen. Zollicoffer and then in service in eastern Kentucky, which position he resigned in February, 1862.

After the close of hostilities he, in December, 1865, became editorially connected with the Nashville *Union and American*, and retained that position until 1869. He was a delegate from the State at large to the Union National Convention in 1860 which nominated Bell and Everett, and also to the Democratic convention in 1868 which nominated Seymour and Blair.

During 1868 he was made professor of materia medica and therapeutics in the medical department of the University of Nashville. In 1870 he was appointed medical superintendent of the Tennessee Hospital for the Insane, which position he yet holds. The same year he was transferred to the chair of diseases of the brain and nervous system in the medical department of the University of Nashville, and in 1880 was transferred to the chair of physiology and psychology in the medical departments of the University of Nashville and Vanderbilt University. In 1876 he was a delegate from the Tennessee Medical Society to the International Medical Congress at Philadelphia. In 1881 he was made president of the Association of Medical Superintendents of American Institutions for the Insane, and is the youngest man and the only man from the South ever honored with that position. He was one of the witnesses summoned to give expert testimony in the celebrated trial of Charles J. Guiteau on the question of his sanity, and after a laborious investigation pronounced him not insane, though leaving home with a different impression.

It will thus be seen that Dr. Callender has led a varied, busy and successful life. He has never been a schemer or of a mere speculative turn, but original and independent, maintaining his own views. Carefully trained in the classics, a cormorant, both as student and reader, of boundless memory and wonderful power of analysis—as a writer, he is graceful, fluent and exhaustive, and figured conspicuously and brilliantly as a political leader, having few equals in the South. Born and reared in Nashville, his sympathies readily blend with the social, scientific or political interests of the State, and being of an ardent nature, intensely individual and positive in his opinions and character, he is as prompt as incisive in the expression of his own convictions. It was this bent of his mind rather than a love for party or party conflict that prompted his acceptance of the editorship of the leading newspaper of the State. As a mere boy he placed himself at the head of the Whig party of Tennessee, and by his terse and vigorous style as a political editor and his great sagacity in moulding events, he proved himself worthy to follow the footsteps of his distinguished grandfather.

As a teacher he is thorough, classic in style, and purely didactic in manner. As an essayist on many literary and scientific subjects he has few, if any, equals in Tennessee. In his specialty as an alienist he has received from his associates many marks of distinguished honor, and in the management of the institution over which he presides, he is ranked as something original, managing it in a different manner and with success equal to the best in the land.

"There," said Dr. Thomas A. Atchison, pointing to Dr. Callender, "is the typical man of our faculty. A man of high culture and fine literary tastes; he never trusts himself before his class without due preparation.

He composes rapidly and brilliantly, and speaks from notes from which he reads elegantly, as if speaking impromptu. He is one of the brainiest men in the State, and is a light in medical literature. He has a logical, analytical mind, an elegant presence and easy manners."

Dr. Thomas L. Maddin furnishes the following high but just estimate of Dr. Callender's character: " He is of liberal education and broad scholarship. His tastes run after classical literature. There is no trash about him. He has cultivated his profession with care, industry and success. His tastes run more particularly toward medicine, and in cultivating it for its science and literature. As a professor, he is profound in his teaching, fluent in his discourse, clear in his demonstrations, and always commands a pre-eminent position in the esteem of his students and his colleagues in the faculty. At times he is eloquent in his diction and conception of his subject. As a man, he is of unblemished integrity, of broad views and general cultivation, standing high in public estimation for his ability and familiarity, not only with his profession, but with the politics of the times. He has a ready command of his resources, both as a speaker and a writer. In fact he is a man of high order of intellectuality, assisted by a most extraordinary and remarkably retentive memory; but he does not excel simply in memory, but in his conception of what he undertakes to learn."

Dr. Daniel F. Wright, of Clarksville, writes the following to the editor: "You request me to give you my impressions of the professional and personal character of Dr. John H. Callender. You could not set me a more grateful task; in executing it I will confine myself, as in such cases should always be done, to what I have known of him by personal observation. I was first made acquainted with Dr. Callender when I became his colleague in the Shelby Medical College, Nashville, he holding the chair of materia medica and therapeutics, and I that of physiology and pathology. I have a lively recollection of his lectures, which had for their main subject the mode of the action of remedies in the human system. In treating this subject, he manifested a profound acquaintance for so young a man with the subjects of pathology and therapeutics, and applied that knowledge with an originality of thought still more remarkable. At the dissolution of the college by the events of the war, I lost sight of the Doctor for a long time; on his becoming superintendent of the Insane Asylum, however, I had frequent business intercourse with him in the way of recommending patients to the asylum. This led to my paying frequent visits there, and enabled me to observe the combined intelligence and humanity with which he alleviated the sufferings of his unfortuate patients.

"Added to all this, Dr. Callender's personal character, based upon principles of the strictest integrity, unites with a dignity and geniality of manner only combined in the person of a finished gentleman. I appreciate him as a faithful and reliable friend and as a delightful companion.

"Of Dr. Callender's standing in his profession, and of his eminence in the special department of it to which he is devoted, it is superfluous for me to speak. He is *facile princeps* in Tennessee as an authority in cases of insanity and diseases of the nervous system, and among alienists of the United States, whose really recognized experts may be counted on the fingers, he is a peer among the proudest."

In personal appearance Dr. Callendar is tall, portly and stately, with the air of a student rather than of a master of his profession. Before lecturing, he is accustomed to pace the floor of the private office, meditating, as if preparing himself for the ordeal of appearing before an audience where every eye is a scalpel. But his lectures are plain, practical and direct, setting forth the facts in his subject rather than making efforts at oratory. Yet, although didactic, his lectures have a fine literary finish, and are delivered in scholarly style.

Dr. Callender is not a communicant of any church, although his religious training was Presbyterian. It is understood that he holds liberal views on religious topics, but is not to be classed among the agnostics. In politics he was raised a Henry Clay Whig, and stood for the Union until compelled to go the other way. Since the war his political affiliations have been with the Democratic party.

Dr. Callender married at Nashville, Tennessee, February 24, 1858, Miss Della Jefferson Ford, daughter of Dr. John Pryor Ford, of that city. Dr. Ford was born in Cumberland county, Virginia, in 1810, and removed to Nashville from Huntsville, Alabama, in 1842, and was a leading practioner and teacher of medicine until his death in 1865—being professor of obstetrics and diseases of women and children from 1858 to 1862. His wife, Ann Smith Jefferson, was born also in Cumberland county, Virginia, and was collaterally related to Thomas Jefferson, of Monticello. Mrs. Callender is a great grand-niece of President Jefferson, and a niece of Gen. John R. Jefferson, of Seguin, Texas. Her religious connection is Protestant Episcopal.

By his marriage with Miss Ford, Dr. Callender has but one child—a daughter—Annie Mary Callender, born August 5, 1864, and a graduate of the Nashville College for Young Ladies.

HON. JOHN NETHERLAND.

ROGERSVILLE.

HON. JOHN NETHERLAND, who still lives at his home in Rogersville, was born September 20 1808, in Powhatan county, Virginia. His parents removed to Tennessee while he was yet an infant, settling at Kingsport, in Sullivan county, in 1811. They were thus among the primitive settlers who gave character to the civilization of the eastern portion of our State. Of a family of eleven children, of whom he was the youngest, he is now the sole survivor. His early facilities were fortunate in his day. He was sent when quite young as a pupil to the venerated Dr. Samuel Doak, who was pioneer with the famous Dr. Coffin in education in Tennessee. Completing his academic course at the early age of fourteen, he further prosecuted his studies at home, in the nature of a review under the tutelage of Mr. Henry Hoss, a scholar of much celebrity.

In 1828 he entered upon the study of law in the office or under the instruction of Judge Samuel Powell, of Rogersville. He was licensed to practice in August, 1829. In 1830, catching the feeling for a western movement, he left Blountville and took up his home in Franklin, Williamson county, for the practice of his profession. His residence in Franklin was brief, extending only about two years. The sickness and death of his father called him back to Kingsport.

At an early age he manifested an interest in the political affairs of the State and nation, and also a capacity for public service. In 1833, when he was but twenty-five years of age, he was elected to the State Senate from the district comprising the counties of Hawkins, Sullivan and Carter. On a month's notice, he canvassed the extended district in horseback style, and was elected by a majority of more than three hundred votes. As a State Senator he took a very high stand for a young man. One of the leading measures before the Legislature, which some philanthropic people have always considered harsh, was the bill extending the law over and finally resulting in the removal of the few remaining Indians from our State. Against this measure he protested in an able and eloquent speech, which was extensively circulated in pamphlet form. The bill passed, but that speech of young Netherland will remain of record as a testimonial, not only of his regard for constitutional rights, but of his decent respect for the feelings of humanity.

The State convention of 1834 to revise the State constitution, inserted a provision in the constitution, as is well known, fixing the minimum age of State senators at thirty years. This gave a temporary pause to our subject's political prospects as to State offices. However, in 1835 he was elected as representative from Sullivan county in the Legislature, and it was while serving in this capacity that a test was presented which developed John Netherland's independence of thought and character. The famous resolution was pending in the United States Senate, known as the "expunging resolution," intended to strike from the journals of the Senate the vote of censure previously passed upon Gen. Jackson, then president of the United States. A resolution was introduced into the Tennessee Legislature instructing the senators from Tennessee to vote for the expunging resolution. A primary convention of the people of Sullivan county passed a resolution instructing him to vote for this resolution. Believing that the record of the United States Senate was designed to be a record of truth, and that mutilation was not to be tolerated, Mr. Netherland, in one of the most creditable acts of his life, surrendered his commission as representative of his county and returned to private life.

John Netherland is not a man who has had "an itching palm." Public office has occasionally come to him, but almost invariably without his seeking. Back in the times when old parties were breaking up—when Jackson men and White men and Bell men were taking their stand on new issues, John Netherland, true to his instincts, became a pronounced Whig. (Of course this biography is reciting facts, not proposing to propagate political ideas.)

In 1837 Mr. Netherland removed to Rogersville and opened his law office. Two years afterwards he married Miss Susan McKinney, daughter of the late John A. McKinney, and has ever since resided in Rogersville. Of the six children born to them only two are living, to-wit: Eliza, the wife of Judge Carrick W. Heiskell, of Memphis, and Margaret, the wife of Mr. Joseph C. Stamps, who, with his family, now occupies the family mansion at Rogersville.

Back in the old days of Whiggery and Democracy, Mr. Netherland was often called into service. In the days of 1839–40–41, when Polk was defeating Cannon and James C. Jones was coming upon the political scene, there was a demand for local politicians of character and influence. Polk had defeated Cannon and carried the Legislature. The next year the Whigs determined to secure the State. Hawkins county was a recognized battle-ground. Mr. Netherland was pressed into the service as a candidate for representative, and although Gov. Polk had carried the county by six hundred and twenty-five majority, Mr. Netherland was only defeated by the scant majority of one hundred votes.

It should have been stated that in 1836 Mr. Netherland was elector for Judge Hugh Lawson White for ie presidency. Twelve years later, in 1848, he was lector for the State at large for Taylor and Fillmore, is associate on the ticket being James C. Jones. he ticket was successful in the State, as in the Union, y a handsome majority. In this contest Mr. Netherand's chief competitor was Judge William T. Brown, f Memphis, though he had several discussions with lon. Aaron V. Brown, who was on the Cass electoral cket.

In 1851 Mr. Netherland was elected representative om Hawkins county, and served his county most onorably.

In 1859 the Whig or "Opposition" party, with but ttle prospect of success in the State, demanded a andidate, and Mr. Netherland, being unanimously ominated by one of the most creditable conventions ver assembled in Nashville, accepted the nomination, nd was of course defeated. But few of the intelligent en of his party had expected any other result, nor had Ir. Netherland himself.

Upon the breaking out of the civil war Mr. Netherand's convictions led him to adhere to the cause of the Jnion. Indeed, while the question was yet an open ne, his outspoken and eloquent opposition to the ecession movement, in co-operation with Andrew ohnson, Thomas A. R. Nelson and other popular aders of like opinions, did much to develop and conrm that devoted feeling with which a majority of the eople of East Tennessee clung to the Union throughut the war. After the conclusion of peace, however, lthough he had keenly felt, in person and property, he consequences of his own personal position throughut the struggle, he became at once the champion of oleration and forgiveness. He approved the main eatures of President Johnson's administration, and nce that period, though still cherishing with knightly ffection his "old Whig love," he has given his sympaiies and support to the Democratic party.

In 1870 Mr. Netherland was chosen a member of the onvention to revise the State constitution of Tennesee. His services in that body were conspicuous for heir conservative character.

Mr. Netherland never held nor seriously sought any osition in the Federal government. A foreign mission as tendered to him by President Johnson, but he reoectfully declined it.

The later years of Mr. Netherland's life, until misortune in the shape of a serious bodily affliction rostrated him, were devoted to his profession of the aw. In the brief space allowed to this biographer ill justice can scarcely be done to such a representative 'ennessean as Hon. John Netherland. It is not solely a lawyer that he has made his distinguished reputaion, although in his profession he has long commanded he very front rank as an advocate at the bar. Few awyers in East Tennessee who have ever encountered im will not concede that he is one of the most suc-

cessful advocates that ever made an appeal to an East Tennessee jury.

But, as we have intimated, it is not as a lawyer or politician that Mr. Netherland's character best appears. It is not too much to say that there is no man in all the State who has better and more charming command of a social circle than John Netherland. A political rival, who afterwards became his devoted friend, once derisively styled him "the tall and stately Netherland." The appellation has often been repeated in kindness by his friends. The designation was universally recognized as a most apt one. For while Mr. Netherland—being but little above six feet—is, of course, not of remarkable height, yet, when in vigorous health, he had a certain stateliness of bearing that rendered the description of "tall" peculiarly appropriate. Indeed, in his prime, he was a man of remarkable personal figure, one calculated to attract attention on any promenade or in any throng. In addition, he had, in a marked degree, what may be called strength of physiognomy. His face was most striking and impressive, severe as wrath itself when indignation or other strong feeling moved him, and yet, as his mood changed, softening into a countenance that attracted by its pleasantness. These characteristics were specially noticeable in his efforts at the bar, and contributed much to his wonderful power over a jury. He could effect as much by a look and a nod, as any man the writer ever saw. It was often remarked by those, who had seen both men, that in many respects he was suggestive of Gen. Jackson. He was fond of polite society in which he was ever a favorite. His manners were always courtly. Gentility is a part of his nature.

None hold, or ever held, Mr. Netherland in higher esteem than his brethren of the bar. With him professional courtesy was ever a cardinal virtue, and a breach of professional honor was abhorrent to his nature. Besides, his splendid social qualities, enlivening always the otherwise tedious hours of a slow dragging court-term, or the long dreary ride around the circuit, as in the olden time, made him a favorite companion always among his associate lawyers, to whom his inimitably-told and continually-flowing stories were as food and drink along the way. In the traditions of the East Tennessee bar the "anecdotes" of John Netherland will live through generations.

The sum of his personal afflictions has been heavy. The loss of children—one a lovely daughter, under most shocking accidental circumstances; the other, an only son, bearing his name, a noble, generous and gifted young lawyer, full of promise that he would worthily wear his father's name—these, added to a most severe personal injury, which has made him a permanent cripple, would seem to have been enough to break the spirit of a man of seventy-seven. Yet, while this biography is being prepared, there is not a brighter spirit than John Netherland's, nor is there a parlor in

Tennessee in which the visitor is greeted with a more genial entertainment. His fund of anecdote and wit, from which his conversation was always most piquantly and enjoyably enriched, remains still unexhausted. His memory of the events of his own life and of his very extensive reading, remains undimmed, and his old friends and neighbors find no greater social pleasure than in "dropping in" and listening to the real music of his charming discourse. Throughout his life he has been a most "neighborly" man, having sacrificed most of his hard earned fortune in the interest of friends. Of course his lengthened span of life is now measured and has not much further extent. But his record is secure. He will leave to his descendants a rich legacy in the memory that he lived and died an honest man.

GEN. JOHN M. D. MITCHELL.

LIVINGSTON.

THE subject of this sketch, a nephew of Hon. W. W. Goodpasture, was born in Jackson (now Clay) county, Tennessee, April 12, 1851, the son of Dennis Mitchell. His mother, Margaret Goodpasture, was the daughter of John Goodpasture and wife, Margery, nee Bryan.

Mr. Mitchell was educated in the schools and academy of Overton county, and was himself superintendent of public instruction in that county some two years. His administration of this trust passed with most favorable criticism. After reading law one year with his uncle, Hon. W. W. Goodpasture, he entered the law department of Cumberland University, Lebanon, from which he graduated in 1876, his diploma bearing the honored names of Hons. Robert L. Caruthers, Nathan Green, jr., and other distinguished members of that faculty. In 1876, Gen. William Cullom having resigned the office of attorney-general of the sixteenth judicial circuit, for the purpose of running for Congress in the Knoxville district, Gov. James D. Porter commissioned Mr. Mitchell to fill the vacancy. At the November, 1876, term of the circuit court of Anderson county, Tennessee, Judge D. K. Young presiding, Mr. Mitchell appeared for the first time, both as a lawyer and attorney-general, without any practice as a lawyer or experience in courts. He was somewhat awkward, being unfamiliar with court proceedings, and with nothing to recommend him but honesty of purpose, the ability to succeed, and an unconquerable will to know and do his duty. By constant application, assisted most cordially by his admiring friend, Judge Young, the rough ashlar soon became the polished marble. In a remarkably short period in his official career, he developed into a power that was felt in all the counties of the circuit. In the prosecution of his official duties he was brought into contact with such experienced and distinguished lawyers as Gen. William Cullom, of Clinton, Col. W. A. Henderson, the silver-tongued orator, Col. Henry R. Gibson and Maj. L. A. Gratz, of Knoxville, and ex-Congressman and ex-Judge John P.

Murray, of Gainesborough, and proved himself on all occasions a man among men.

At the general election of 1878 he was a candidate for election before the people of the circuit, and made the race against two gentlemen of acknowledged ability, and by reason of the satisfactory manner in which he discharged his duties under Gov. Porter's appointment, he was triumphantly elected. Up to this time he had developed into an efficient prosecutor, and was a terror to wrong-doers. He was admired most for stating his propositions of law clearly and in the fewest possible words, limiting his speeches to about ten minutes, riveting the facts upon the minds of his jurymen, and in an unusually large number of cases securing convictions.

But the main characteristics of Gen. Mitchell as a prosecutor were, that he knew his cases, knew the facts, and would never let his grand juries make mistakes. He was as careful that the innocent should not be falsely accused as that the guilty should be convicted. He stood like a wall of fire around the innocent, but against the guilty he proceeded as with a two edged sword. In a short notice of his death, written by Judge Young, occur these words: "The power of the man consisted not in education and culture, but in the force of native intellect, and the confidence the people had in his integrity."

As a friend he was genial and companionable. They loved him most who knew him best. His morals were good. It is said he never swore an oath. Shortly before his death he professed religion, was baptized and received into the Cumberland Presbyterian church. He never married. His father having died when the son was only four months old, he was raised by his widowed mother, and was a self-made man.

His mother, Mrs. Margaret Mitchell, is still living at Livingston, Tennessee, with her other son, Isaiah W. Mitchell, a prosperous farmer. The subject of this sketch died June 18, 1884, aged thirty-three years two months and six days, and was buried at Good Hope church, near Livingston.

At the first court held in the judicial circuit of which he was attorney-general, at Wartburg, Morgan county, Tennessee, after his death, a memorial meeting of the bar and people was convened in the court-house, the first Monday in July, 1884, which adopted resolutions highly complimentary and heart-felt, which demonstrate his standing as a representative lawyer and representative Tennessean. He died in the prime of life, and it is still said in judicial and legal circles, his circuit will scarcely ever see his equal as a prosecutor. Judge Young, under whom he practiced during his entire official term, said of him: "He was the most efficient prosecutor I have known during my entire life as a lawyer or as a judge."

ROBERT FRANK EVANS, M. D.

SHELBYVILLE.

DR. ROBERT FRANK EVANS was born August 24, 1821, in Caroline county, Virginia, and removed to Bedford county, Tennessee, in 1832, with his father, David S. Evans. His mother was Judith Bowlware, and was a worthy representative of that grand old family. There was a large family, but Robert was the only son. His father engaged in farming until 1837, when he took charge of the leading hotel at Shelbyville, the house, which still stands, "The Evans House," having been built by him. The son was partly educated in Virginia and partly at the Dixon Academy, Shelbyville, and in 1843 commenced the study of medicine with Dr. G. W. Fogleman, who, at that time, was doing a large and lucrative practice. In the autumn of 1845 he went to Louisville, Kentucky, going through the country in a buggy, and attended the medical department of the University of Louisville, and listened to the lectures of such eminent medical educators as Profs. Gross, Drake, Cobb, Miller, Caldwell and others. Returning home, he pursued his studies until the following autumn, when he went to Philadelphia, and entered the medical department of the University of Pennsylvania, where he had the benefit of the teachings of Profs. Horner, Gibson, Wood, Hare, Chapman, Jackson and Meigs, who, at that day, were regarded as great lights in the profession. Receiving his degree and diploma in April, 1847, Dr. Evans returned to Shelbyville, and practiced his profession there until the spring of 1851, when a party of friends—four other young men beside himself—went to California, being attracted by the wonderful stories of that wonderful country, Dr. Evans also feeling the necessity of some change to repair the ill health he had fallen into from too much confinement and application.

The party left home in April, 1851, and went to New Orleans on the steamboat "America," and from New Orleans to Chagres on a sailing vessel. Hiring a native and a mule to transfer baggage, they walked across the isthmus of Darien to Panama, where they had to wait two weeks for an opportunity to get to the land of gold. Finally they secured passage on board a French ship, which getting out of provisions and water, and meeting with severe storms, had to put into the Sandwich Islands, and they spent ten days at Honolulu. They landed at San Francisco, August 12, 1851. Striking out for the mines, they were soon in the rough and rugged mining region of that time. The kind of life they led—working with pick and shovel and rocker, sleeping on the ground in the open air, and having only a very plain diet—soon restored Dr. Evans' health and strength, and when the keen relish of the new life had worn off, he returned to his home and resumed the practice of medicine in the summer of 1852. He has continued steadily at practice ever since, leading the life incident to the calling—going at all times, in all kinds of weather, trying to help the afflicted and distressed, and do some good for his fellow-man.

Dr. Evans has been a Mason for many years, and presided as Master of Shelbyville Benevolent Lodge, No. 122, for six or seven years, and as High Priest of Tannehill Chapter, No. 40, Royal Arch Masons about the same length of time; was created a Knight Templar in Nashville Commandery, No. 1, in 1859, and retains his membership in all the branches of Masonry at the present time, and has ever tried to live up to the elevated standard taught by this noble order.

Dr. Evans was an early advocate of county medical societies, and upon the organization of the Bedford county society, served as secretary and president for several terms. He is also a member of the Shelbyville Board of Health, and has been since its organization in 1879. He became a member of the State medical society of Tennessee many years since, has been a regular attendant upon its annual meetings, and is a contributor to its literature, as well as to the medical press. At the State society meeting in Memphis, in 1878, he was elected president, and served as such for the year (re-election not being allowed under the rules). As president, he had the good and interest of the society at heart, and desired that it might go on doing good, benefitting the profession and the people of the State. His medical reputation is with the people of his own and adjoining counties, where he is content to leave it

9

until the Great Physician summons him to rest from his labors.

In a financial sense Dr. Evans is in excellent circumstances, owning a good property, and being a director of the Shelbyville National Bank.

Dr. Evans married Miss Julia E. Greer, February 14, 1856, and there were two children born to them, a daughter and a son. The mother died in October, 1859, and in the following summer both children went to join her in the blessed country where there is no sickness or death.

He married a second time, December 24, 1867, Mrs. Mary Coldwell Fite, maiden name Mary Summers Coldwell, widow of Jacob C. Fite, who had two children, both living: (1). Dr. Campbell Coldwell Fite, who studied medicine with Dr. Evans, and practiced in partnership with him nearly six years, until h● moved to Nashville, in 1883, to practice there, havin● been elected secretary and executive officer of the Stat● Board of Health. (2). Jennie Nixon Fite, who marrie● Surgeon A. M. Moore, of the United States navy. Ther● are two children by the present marriage, Stella an● Mary Frank Evans.

Dr. Evans has always been noted for his quiet an● peaceful methods of life, has the respect of his entir● acquaintance, and is held up as an example of what man should be in all the relations of life. He is ● member of the Protestant Episcopal church, and ha● been for years senior warden of the church at Shelby● ville. Christianity with him is not a theory, but a fact● Only those who know him intimately know his greates● virtues.

P. H. McBRIDE, M.D.

NOAH.

DR. P. H. McBRIDE, Noah, Tennessee, was born December 27, 1825, at Beech Grove, Coffee county, Tennessee. His boyhood days were spent on the farm and in attending the county schools of that place. He early manifested a desire to study medicine, but not having the means to do so, apprenticed himself to a blacksmith, and at the end of two years, having mastered his trade, began business for himself. In 1846 he enlisted in Capt. L. D. Newman's company for the Mexican war, and was elected second sergeant. He served twelve months, the term of his enlistment, and, on account of sickness, was honorably discharged at New Orleans, Louisiana, in May, 1847. After returning home he finished his education in the winter of 1847-48, at Manchester Academy, Manchester, Tennessee. From 1848 to 1851 he was a farmer and blacksmith, dividing his time between the two occupations. From 1851 to 1861 he added to his tasks the study of medicine, making it a rule to read until twelve o'clock at night, and catching a preceptor whenever he could. When the war between the States broke out he volunteered in Col. John H. Savage's Sixteenth Tennessee regiment, and served for twelve months as color-bearer of that gallant command. In 1862 he was commissioned by Hon. Judah P. Benjamin, Secretary of War for the Confederate States, to enlist a company of mounted men, to be selected from the Sixteenth Tennessee. Mounting and equipping his men, he attached his command to Col. Starnes' regiment at Chattanooga, in 1862. His command was then made the advance guard of Gen. E. Kirby Smith's army in the Kentucky campaign, and participated with credit in the sanguinary battle of Richmond, Kentucky. After returning from this campaign, he was attached to Gen. Forrest's comman● until October, 1864, during which period he was in a● the numerous battles, skirmishes and raids of Forrest' cavalry. His company was considered one of the ver● best in the Confederacy, and was among the last t● surrender. Owing to great exposure and the awfu● fatigue of the campaigns through which he passed, Dr● McBride's health again broke down, and in October 1864, he was ordered to the hospital indefinitely, bein● unfit for duty. In the November following, being abl● to travel, he returned home, where he remained th● rest of the war.

After the war, his property all gone, he again took t● his trade, at which he continued until 1868. when h● moved to Noah Fork on Duck river, where he no● lives, and where he began the practice of medicine● Quite a number of old and successful practitioners liv● in his neighborhood, but by closely applying himself● Dr. McBride has gained a good practice, and has● especially, the treatment of nearly all the chronic case● around him. More than this, he has built up a goo● name, as an honorable, straightforward man, correct i● all his dealings, and is a citizen of first-class standin● and great popularity.

As a politician Dr. McBride is known as a Democrat● staunch and true. In 1870 he was a candidate for th● State Senate, having as his competitor Hon. Georg● McKnight and Col. J. H. Hughes. Dr. McBrid● received a large majority in his county and every vot● in his civil district. In 1882 he made a short canvass fo● representative, but as there were so many candidates i● the field, he withdrew before the election, so as not t● defeat the party ticket. Again, in 1884, he was a can●

didate for the Senate from his district, and was elected by a handsome majority, the full Democratic vote. He served with ability and influence in the Tennessee Legislature of 1885, and made many additional friends by his firm and unflinching stand on all vital questions.

His faith has always been in the Methodist church, of which organization he has been a member for forty years. His family is also of the same faith, except one son. He has always been a careful, prudent, economical man, though of a liberal and hospitable nature. He forms his plans with deliberation and caution, and then concentrates his whole mind to accomplish them.

Dr. McBride married, August 17, 1848, Miss Elizabeth S. Emerson, daughter of Gen. Hiram S. Emerson. She is a woman of many good traits, religious in her nature, and a model wife and mother. Five children have been born to them, four sons and one daughter: (1). William H. McBride, born at Manchester, Tennessee; now merchandising at Noah, Tennessee; married Miss Ella Farrar, who died in January, 1884,

leaving two children, Eugene and Arthur. (2). Thomas M. McBride, born May 9, 1850; now farming at Noah. (3). P. H. McBride, born January 24, 1855; now a merchant at Morrison Station, Warren county, Tennessee; married, March 4, 1885, Miss Mary Lee Keel, daughter of J. W. Keel. (4). B. H. McBride, born in 1858; now a farmer at Noah. (5). Mary C. McBride, born July 2, 1862.

The McBride family are of Scotch-Irish descent. Dr. McBride's great-grandfather was Dr. Daniel McBride, of Dublin, Ireland. His son, John McBride, came from Ireland, lived a while in Virginia, and then emigrated to Tennessee, and was one of the first settlers of Bedford county. His son, William McBride, father of Dr. P. H. McBride, was born December 28, 1791, at Lynchburg, Virginia. William McBride was a farmer of good property, and for many years was a magistrate and chairman of the county court of Bedford county. From 1851 to 1855 he was revenue collector of Coffee county. He was married, in Bedford county, to Miss Millie Conwell, daughter of John Conwell, who served the whole of the Revolutionary war as a private.

HON. ROBERT McFARLAND.

MORRISTOWN.

HON. ROBERT McFARLAND, at present one of the Supreme Judges of Tennessee, was born in Jefferson county, Tennessee, April 15, 1832. He is the son of Col. Robert McFarland, a native of the same county, who in early life was a lieutenant in the regular United States army, serving during the war of 1812 at Lundy's Lane, Fort Erie, and other notable engagements. Soon after the war he resigned, and returned to his native county, married, and settled down as a private citizen, following the occupation of a tanner. He was colonel of militia, and for many years a justice of the peace. He died in Kentucky in August, 1844, while on his return from Missouri, at the age of fifty-five years. He was a man of the highest personal integrity, and commanded universal respect wherever he was known. One of his great purposes in life was to give his children all the educational advantages within his reach. He was in religion a Presbyterian and in politics a Whig. His father was also known as Col. Robert McFarland, and was a native of Virginia, but removed to Tennessee at an early day; was the first sheriff of Jefferson county; was a noted Indian fighter in the early settlement of the county; a man of vigorous character, and prominent in his county during his life. His death occurred about 1838. The McFarland family originally came from the highlands of Scotland. Judge McFarland's mother was born in Jefferson

county, Tennessee, the daughter of James Scott, a Scotch-Irish Presbyterian, who, with his wife, emigrated from Ireland and settled in Jefferson county at an early day, where he spent the remainder of his life, an ardent Presbyterian elder. His daughter, the mother of Judge McFarland, was a woman of most excellent character, of quick mind and remarkable energy, and was loved and respected by every one. She was also a Presbyterian. Her death occurred in February, 1866, at the age of sixty-six.

The brothers and sisters of Judge McFarland, in the order of their ages, are as follows: (1). Isaac B. McFarland, a half-brother, of Brenham, Texas, who for many years has been judge of the district court in that State. (2). William McFarland, who, for a short time, was judge of the second Tennessee circuit by appointment of Gov. D. W. C. Senter; represented the first Tennessee district in Congress from 1874 to 1876, and is still a prominent and leading citizen, and resides at Morristown. (3). Mrs. H. M. Barton, the wife of Judge R. M. Barton, now of Chattanooga. (4). Mrs. Jones, who died many years ago, the wife of Thomas M. Jones. (5). Mrs. M. C. Smith, the wife of Rev. W. H. Smith. (6). Mrs. Emma Kidwell, the wife of R. J. Kidwell. (7). Robert McFarland, subject of this sketch. (8). Mary A. McFarland, the youngest, who died in 1876, the wife of Wm. H. Turley.

There was nothing in the boyhood of Judge McFarland to attract attention. He was regarded as a rather dreary, listless boy. An eccentric Irishman once made a remark about him that afforded infinite amusement to his brothers and sisters. Said the Irishman, "Robert, poor boy, will never be wise." He attended the common schools of the county, where he acquired such knowledge and instruction as could not well be avoided; afterwards attended Tusculum College for a short time, and also a high school at Greeneville, but his school education was very incomplete. At the age of nineteen he began the study of law with his brother-in-law, Judge Barton, at Greeneville, making his house his home. He does not remember, however, that the selection of the law as his profession was ever determined upon by himself; his brother and brother-in-law merely determined to make a lawyer of him, *nolens volens*, and he simply acquiesced. He gratefully acknowledges his obligations to them, and in fact to the entire family, for their assistance and encouragement. He resided several years at Greeneville, at the home of Judge Barton, and to the assistance received from him and Mrs. Barton he attributes the greater part of whatever success he met with in after life.

He was licensed in 1854 by Judge McKinney, of the Supreme Court, and Chancellor Lucky, and began practice in the counties of Greene, Jefferson, and others adjoining, his partner in Greeneville being Col. Robert Johnson, son of the late President Andrew Johnson, and in the other counties he formed partnerships with his preceptor, Judge Barton, and the late Montgomery Thornburgh.

On May 17, 1859, he married Miss Jennie Baker, a daughter of H. B. Baker, a merchant of Greeneville. They shortly after took up their residence at Dandridge, Jefferson county, but their home was soon broken up by the war, Judge McFarland volunteering in the Confederate army in the latter part of 1861. He became major of Col. Bradford's regiment, Thirty-first Tennessee infantry, afterwards mounted, and in that capacity served to the end of the war, participating in the Kentucky campaign, the defense of Vicksburg, with Gen. Jubal Early in his raid on Washington City in 1864, and in many cavalry engagements.

After the war he returned to his native county, where, however, it was very difficult to remain, owing to prejudices engendered by the war, and the mob spirit prevailing against returned Confederate soldiers. He did remain, however, being countenanced and sustained by a few personal friends on the Union side, and he especially acknowledges the generous and manly treatment he received from Col. J. M. Thoruburgh, of the Federal army, who, though an antagonist in arms, was a warm personal friend. He also mentions others to whom he is under like obligations. He resumed the practice of the law in the same counties, in partnership with R. M. McKee, Esq., of Greeneville, and Col.

Thornburgh in the other counties. In 1869–70 he was on two or three occasions appointed special judge of the Supreme Court by Gov. Senter. On the resignation of Hon. Thos. A. R. Nelson, he was appointed by Gov. John C. Brown, December 11, 1871, to fill the vacancy on the Supreme bench. In August following he was elected to the office, defeating Col. J. B. Cooke, an able and popular lawyer of Chattanooga. At the general election in August, 1878, he was again elected for the term expiring September 1, 1886.

The elements of success in Judge McFarland's character, or such as his friends attribute to him, are few and simple, but they have enabled him to overcome many obstacles. In the first place he has steady, well-formed moral habits, and is noted for his perfect honesty. He has succeeded in impressing those with whom he has come in contact with his faultless candor and high sense of fairness. In the next place, the selection of the law as his profession was, in the light of after developments, very fortunate. He thinks it doubtful if he would have met with even moderate success in any other calling, but, as was said of him by the late Chief Justice Nicholson, "He is a born lawyer."

He possesses an almost intuitive perception of legal principles and the faculty of practically applying them. He is not a systematic student, nor very industrious, except when actively engaged in the management of causes, or on the bench, when he works with earnestness and vigor. At the bar he was not an orator or an advocate, but was regarded as a close, zealous, intense, and logical legal debater. In social life he is rather diffident and retiring, but in the management of causes he has sufficient self-confidence to enable him to act with promptness and decision. He is not of a popular turn, and mixes poorly with the general public, but he is apt to make fast friends of the few with whom he is intimately associated. In all his conduct there is an absence of any effort at display, a contempt for sham and pretense. As a judge he is laborious and careful. His mind is well-balanced and eminently judicial in its character. He has few, if any hobbies, and is as free from improper influences as a judge well can be. If his judgment is ever disturbed, it is by his sympathy for the poor and oppressed, for notwithstanding his calm and quiet exterior, he has the gentlest emotions and tenderest sympathies. The controlling motive of his actions is a sense of duty, a love of justice and the right.

Judge McFarland has been most happy in his domestic relations. His wife is in every sense a congenial spirit—gentle, quiet, affectionate, and faithfully devoted to her husband and family. They have three children, Misses Anna and Emma, educated at Ward's Seminary, Nashville, and Henry, a youth of seventeen, who says he is destined for the law. Judge McFarland and his wife are Presbyterians, and he is in politics a Democrat, and a Royal Arch Mason. He is five feet, ten inches in height, and of very light, slender build. For the past two years he has been severely afflicted with rheumatism, but rarely misses his post of duty.

Judge Robert McFarland died at his home in Morristown, on the morning of the 2d of October, 1884, surrounded by his wife and children, his brother and one of his sisters, and a few other friends, apparently in possession of his faculties almost to the moment of dissolution. He had been laboring under an attack of rheumatism for nearly two years, and had visited Hot Springs, Arkansas, and spent part of the previous winter in Florida, in the hope of obtaining relief, but without success. The remedies administered to arrest the disease seriously affected his stomach, and at last, his lungs becoming involved, death ensued. No man ever displayed more patience, or more resignation to his fate. He was long confined to his room, and saw but few persons, except such of his personal friends as called upon him; yet he was ever cheerful, and often, in his way, indulged in pleasantry with those who called to see him.

He was a quiet, unobtrusive, retiring man, distant and diffident in his intercourse with the world, and not formed for popularity with the masses; yet so well was he known and appreciated by the people, that he had the unbounded confidence and esteem of all parties. Dying in the midst of the people with whom he was born and reared, he died without an enemy. If there is a man in the limits of the State who ever doubted his honesty and integrity, we have never heard of him. His brethren of the bar throughout the State have testified as to their appreciation of his character as a man, and as to his ability as a lawyer and a judge.

From the tribute to his memory, adopted by the Supreme court bar of East Tennessee, shortly after his death, we copy the following just estimate of the character of Judge McFarland:

Considered, as man or judge, the simplicity and purity of his character is a delightful object of contemplation. His sentiments were lofty and noble, his demeanor modest and unassuming, even to diffidence. He was kind, liberal and generous, slow to promise, scrupulously faithful in performance; grateful for personal favors, and never forgetful of obligation. Though lacking in effusive affection, there was unswerving fidelity in his friendship. Strong in convictions of right, he was singularly free from bigotry and fanaticism. Courteous and polite in his association, he had many friends; but his confidence and intimacy were reserved for a few. He met cordially men of all classes, but commanded respect for his office from all by the quiet dignity of his character and unpretentious purity of his life. He was no politician, and no one ever suspected him of favor or policy in his judicial office. He was religious without display or pretense, charitable without boast or ostentation, tenacious of truth and consecrated to duty. Free from arrogance, vanity or self-seeking, he devoted his life to the study and exposition of the law, and was ever strong to execute justice and maintain truth. For this he always possessed, in a remarkable degree, the trust of the people and the implicit confidence of the bar.

He was a born lawyer—a judge by nature. He had a logical mind, patient of investigation and trained by reflection rather than much reading. He was singularly free from bias or prejudice, and if as a judge he was not famed for erudition, he fully compensated for its absence by an accurate discrimination, sound judgment and rare practical wisdom. In clearness of vision and perspicuity of statement he was pre-eminent, unrivaled. None ever had occasion to distrust his knowledge of the case, or doubt the meaning of his opinion.

His disposition and habit was, if possible, to solve doubt and determine cases by the application of fundamental principles of law to the facts. In this he resembled the great Chief Justice Marshall; and like Marshall, too, his judicial style was dry and unadorned, void of simile and metaphor and rhetoric. No one will ever seek his opinions for beauty of style or wealth of illustration. But he never failed to be clear and convincing; and though his opinions may not abound in citation of cases to support them, one feels at the conclusion the same serene satisfaction experienced in finishing a geometrical demonstration or a logical syllogism.

His sense of justice was strong, his love of right profound; but above all towered his reverence for law. He could never consent to permit hard cases to make bad law.

In a marked degree, too, he had the judicial temperament, and a singular freedom from the pride of opinion. He weighed and balanced all arguments with an eye single to the law and its requirements. If he had prejudice, he conquered it; if preconception of the law, he suspended it, and listened patiently to adverse views; if he had erred, he was open to correction, and readily recalled an erroneous opinion.

No impertinent suggestion, no extraneous consideration, ever seemed to divert his mind from the matter to be decided. So entirely judicial was he, so devoted to the solution of the legal problems before him, that nothing ever seemed to interrupt his steady and even progress to a conclusion; this was reached only after a painstaking investigation and impartial consideration of all the material facts in the case before him. His personality never obtrusive, was lost, or rather absorbed, in legal reflection; so that when he announced his decision, it seemed to the bar not so much the opinion of the court, as the logical, solemn and inevitable judgment of the law.

In correctness of decision, the highest test of a supreme judge, he had no superior. He was not as learned a lawyer as Reese, nor as exact and precise as McKinney, but in clearness of perception, soundness of judgment and correctness of decision, he rivaled either. The country can boast of a Story, a Kent and a Marshall; East Tennessee has had her Reese, her McKinney and her McFarland.

The judicial record of Judge McFarland's eleven years' continuous service on the Supreme bench of Tennessee is contained in the Reports from 3 Heiskell to 10 Lea, inclusive, and is as free from error as any in the annals of the judicial history of the State.

EDMUND W. COLE.

NASHVILLE.

THE distinguished subject of this biographical sketch was born in Giles county, Tennessee, July 19, 1827. His grandparents on both sides were prominent people of Virginia, and the male members of the family were participants and officers in the Revolutionary war. His father and mother, Willis W. and Johanna J. Cole, were both Virginians, who went first from that State to Kentucky, and afterwards came to Tennessee. His father died when he was three months old, leaving his mother with six sons and three daughters, and extremely limited means. Four brothers and one sister have died, and of the survivors only one brother and one sister remain. The brother, Robert A. Cole, now in his seventy-fifth year, is living in Nashville. He was at one time marshal of Nashville, and held position in the internal revenue office many years. One sister, Mrs. Rebecca W. Blow, of Giles county, died at the advanced age of seventy-five, and the surviving sister, Mrs. Martha Ann Elizabeth Simpson, widow of William F. Simpson, is still living in Giles county, Tennessee. Raised a farmer's boy, Edmund Cole worked on his mother's place until eighteen, and had only the ordinary country school facilities during that time, which consisted of a few months in each year "after the crop was laid by." In 1845, at the age of eighteen, he came to Nashville. Without any acquaintances in the city, he had to rely on his own resources. He commenced his career as clerk in a clothing store, at a small salary. Everybody seeing that the young man was bent on success, he had tempting offers from other houses, but stood to the contract with his employer until the year was out. The next year he went into a book store on an increased salary, followed by two more years as clerk in a boot and shoe house. By close application to business and the interest of his employers he advanced rapidly in position and salary, never being out of employment, and all the time utilizing every spare hour in educating himself for the important and responsible positions he was destined to fill in after life. His mother, who was a very pious, good Methodist woman, of remarkable mind and settled, solid habits, gave to Edmund the best moral culture, and particularly taught him that moral character is the basis of all true success. Hence, following the advice of his good old mother, he very soon after reaching Nashville joined the Methodist church, of which he has been a member thirty-nine years, and is now president of the board of trustees of McKendree church. She advised him also to have decided opinions of his own on all subjects, but always to respect the opinions and rights of others. Once when an editor asked Mr. Cole the secret of his success in life, he replied, "By being faithful to my employers and studying their interests." In early life

he made up his mind that he would never have business difficulties and litigations, hence, in all his life he has never been sued individually. Making it a rule to always look ahead and have fair understandings with men at the beginning of transactions, he never went into a business engagement or enterprise without first asking himself, "Will this be just and fair to everybody? Will my action in the premises do more good than harm?" And believing that a man must have a moral idea in his head and reverence for a superintending Providence, he has made it a rule of conduct to be remarkably particular and exact in everything he does. Instead of going out "sky-larking" of nights with the town boys, young Cole went to his room and read and studied to improve himself. The result was that he never danced a step, never was intoxicated, and never gambled.

In 1849 Edmund Cole was made book-keeper in the Nashville post-office, where he remained two years, and filled the place with such credit that in 1851 he was elected general book-keeper of the Nashville and Chattanooga railroad, which laborious position he filled with great satisfaction to the company until December, 1857, when he was elected superintendent of the road—a splendid advance in twelve years for a friendless but resolute boy! This latter office he held until the war between the States broke out. Fort Donelson fell, Nashville was evacuated, and Mr. Cole, having identified himself with the fortunes of the Confederacy, sent his family south. After the war they returned to Tennessee, but finding politics and society much changed, he went to Augusta, Georgia, in the summer of 1865. In the fall of that year he was elected general superintendent of the Georgia Railroad and Banking Company, which position he resigned in May, 1875. In August, 1868, he was elected president of the Nashville and Chattanooga railroad, which position he held without opposition for twelve consecutive years. His success in the management of the affairs of this company was something phenomenal; he added millions to the value of its capital stock. During his administration the Nashville and Northwestern, McMinnville and Manchester, Winchester and Alabama, and Tennessee Pacific railroads were added to the main line.

Mr. Cole was the first to conceive the idea of a grand trunk line, under one management, from the West to the Atlantic seaboard, believing such a line with a trans-Atlantic line of steamers practicable. With this idea, he went to work in 1879, forming his combinations by purchasing the St. Louis and Southeastern railroad, from St. Louis to Evansville, Indiana, having previously purchased the Owens-

orough and Nashville, and putting under contract
the unfinished portion between Evansville and Nashville. He next, with the aid of his own and his friends'
tock, bought for his company a controlling interest in
the Western and Atlantic railroad, from Chattanooga
to Atlanta; afterwards contracting for his company to
ease the Central railroad of Georgia, together with all
ts branches and leased lines, about one thousand miles,
with its splendid steamship line. He then had control
of two thousand miles of road; but, having flanked his
rival, the Louisville and Nashville railroad company,
in the West and in the South, that company bought in
New York city, in January, 1880, a majority of the
stock in the Nashville, Chattanooga and St. Louis
railway, and Mr. Cole resigned.

He was for twelve years vice-president, and one of the
lessees of the State road of Georgia since 1871, and still
holds the latter relation to that road. On May 27, 1880,
he was elected president of the East Tennessee, Virginia
and Georgia railroad company, having control also of the
Memphis and Charleston railroad. While president of
the East Tennessee, Virginia and Georgia railroad, he
formed in New York the syndicate with Mr. George I.
Seney and others, by which he extended the line of his
road to Meridian, Mississippi, and to Brunswick on the
Atlantic, and by extending the Knoxville branch to
the State line of Kentucky, and by contracts with the
Kentucky Central and the Louisville and Nashville,
secured connections from the West to the Atlantic, via
Knoxville and Atlanta. Having large private interests
requiring his personal attention, and desiring some
recreation after many years of close attention to business, he resigned the presidency of the East Tennessee,
Virginia and Georgia railroad in May, 1882.

Since then Mr. Cole has contributed largely to the
prosperity of Nashville by the erection of several large
business blocks. The one on the corner of Union and
Cherry streets, the Cole building, is considered the
handsomest in the South. In the room at the corner
of this building, fitted up with all modern improvements and almost without regard to cost, Mr. Cole
inaugurated and opened to public favor, September 1,
1883, "The American National Bank," with a capital
of six hundred thousand dollars. The rush to
subscribe for stock in his bank was unprecedented
in the history of banking in Nashville. He took the
presidency himself, and after managing this financial
institution for about six months, with the assistance of
his able cashier, he established its credit so high that
he was enabled to consolidate with it the Third National
Bank of Nashville, an old and prosperous bank, well
established in the confidence of the public. This permitted him to withdraw from the details of banking,
which are not particularly tasteful to him. He was
mainly instrumental in reorganizing the American
National Bank after its consolidation, with a capital of
one million dollars, and electing John Kirkman presi-

dent, John M. Lea and Edgar Jones vice-presidents,
and A. W. Harris cashier, accepting himself the place
of chairman of the executive committee. Under this
strong organization this bank has become one of the
most important financial institutions in the South.

In the basement story below the American National
Bank, a story absolutely fire-proof, with tiled flooring,
elegantly fitted up offices and coupon rooms, and an
enormous burglar and fire-proof vault for the public,
containing eight hundred safes or apartments for private
use, Mr. Cole inaugurated the Safe Deposit, Trust and
Banking company, which is destined to be a blessing
not only to Nashville but to the surrounding country.
Nothing, however, seems too much for his indomitable
will and energy to accomplish. His powers of combination are wonderful, and while not neglecting the
minutest detail, his mind seems to grasp readily and
with ease and to put together aggregates in harmonious
relations that would stagger and confuse most minds.

Mr. Cole's *personnel* is very striking. He is fifty-eight
years old, of tall, commanding figure, weighs two hundred and twenty-five pounds, is remarkably well preserved; his manner is grave and polished. He has
almost magnetic influence over men, which is partly
accounted for by the justness and liberality of his
opinions and actions. As an illustration of this may
be mentioned his opposition to extreme railroad legislation by the Tennessee Legislature of 1882–83. Contrary
to the advice of friends, he stood up against such
legislation, and in a most elaborate and exhaustive
speech, at the grand opera house in Nashville, on February 27, 1883, against the measures of the bill then
pending in the Legislature, drew public attention to
the matter; and what was known as the caucus railroad
commission bill, with plenary powers, was superseded
by one only advisory in terms.

Mr. Cole has been pecuniarily a very successful man.
He is by long odds the largest owner of city property in
Nashville, besides having extensive real estate interests
elsewhere. At the same time he has been a liberal and
public-spirited citizen; there is scarcely one public
enterprise, educational, religious or charitable, in the
city built in his time to which he has not been a contributor. In politics he is a Democrat, in religion, as
before said, a Methodist, but he is broad-minded, and
never finds fault with others about either their political
or religious views. He is an active and influential
member of the State Board of Health and of the
Tennessee Historical Society, is a Mason, and a patron
of literature, music and the fine arts. His home,
Terrace Place, in Nashville, is noted for its elegant
hospitality, and fully illustrates within the motto, *Salve*,
over its entrance. It has recently been remodeled and
improved, and is now, beyond doubt, one of the handsomest and most truly palatial places in the South.

Mr. Cole has been twice married. First, to Miss
Louise McGavock Lytle, daughter of Archibald Lytle,

Esq., one of the most prominent citizens of Williamson county, and of an old and distinguished Tennessee family. Mrs. Louise M. Cole died in 1869, leaving five children: (1). Elizabeth Johanna, born February 16, 1852, in Williamson county, at her maternal grandfather's; graduated at Ward's Seminary, in 1872, and married S. Walker Edwards, a native of Davidson county, and stepson of Col. A. W. Putnam. His mother was a sister of Chief Justice A. O. P. Nicholson, of the Supreme court of Tennessee. Mr. Edwards has for thirteen years been general agent at Nashville for the East Tennessee, Virginia and Georgia Air Line railroad. They have one child, a daughter, Anna Walker. (2). Addie, born September 21, 1854, at Nashville; graduated from the Wesleyan Female College, at Macon, Georgia; married L. F. Benson, a wholesale merchant at Nashville, and has one child, a son, Edmund. (3). Randall Anderson, born in Augusta, Georgia, February 4, 1866; educated at schools in Nashville and Mount St. Mary's College, and destined for a business man. By a most distressing railroad accident, this promising young man lost his life. As a memorial Mr. Cole bought and presented to the State of Tennessee the handsome property known as the Randall Cole Industrial School, situated near the Murfreesborough turnpike, about one and a half miles from Nashville. (4). Louise Lytle, born November 24, 1867, in Augusta, Georgia; attended Mrs. Sylvester Read's school, New York city; graduated at the Academy of the Visitation, Georgetown, District of Columbia. (5). Henry Lytle, born July 17, 1869.

Mr. Cole was married to Miss Anna V. Russell, of Augusta, Georgia, December 24, 1872, and has one child, Whiteford Russell, born at Nashville, on January 14, 1874. Miss Russell was called "the pride of Georgia,"

and was considered the most beautiful and brilliant woman in the State. Her classic beauty, intellectual culture, rare dignity and grace of manner have excited universal admiration, both in this country and in Europe. Those who know Mrs. Cole well say she is possessed of great patience and fortitude. A pen picture of her, drawn by a correspondent from the Greenbrier White Sulphur Springs, says: "She is a magnificent looking woman, with powdered hair, fair complexion and eyes soft, with a sheer dreamery of gray tinting. She sat surrounded, and was as quiet in manner and as serene in power as a picture from a master."

A recently published sketch of Mr. Cole says: "We risk nothing when we affirm that he is one of the marked men of this age—of the active, stirring times in which we live. The make-up of his head, its broad base and crowning elevation, designate him at once as no ordinary man. Its whole exterior indicates an enormous brain power, and thoroughly poised. He is no dreamer—no wild, incoherent enthusiast. Deliberation, careful and judicious thought, stamp his brow, while his movements, so steady and uniform, unfold the real character of the man. Breadth of comprehension and a vigorous, determined will are his great resources in traversing the field of destiny into which his qualifications have thrown him. Not, perhaps, so quick to act as some of his peers, yet as sure and certain when he does act. His standpoint is that of reason, of facts. He seems to adopt the inductive system in reaching conclusions. He ascends from parts to the whole, leaving nothing in his rear to interfere with his investigations and their results. Nor has he reached his zenith. There are yet further conquests in store for him."

MAJ. BYRON G. McDOWELL.

BRISTOL.

THE subject of this sketch, Maj. Byron G. McDowell, now an attorney of the firm of Butler & McDowell, Bristol, Tennessee, was born in Macon county, North Carolina, June 22, 1837, and grew up there; raised a farmer's boy until the age of twenty. He then attended Sand Hill College, North Carolina, three years, after which he went to Athens, Georgia, and engaged in mercantile business, first as salesman, then as book-keeper for the firm of Pitner, England & Freeman, and remained there from the fall of 1860 until the war broke out, when he joined the Southern army as a private in Company B, Thirty-ninth North Carolina infantry, Col. David Coleman cammanding, and served in North Carolina, Tennessee, and Kentucky, participating in the battle of Newbern, in the winter of

1862. The regiment was then transferred to the Army of Tennessee under Gen. E. Kirby Smith. In the meantime McDowell had been promoted to the quartermastership of the Thirty-ninth regiment. The regiment was stationed at Cumberland Gap. It next went with Gens. Bragg and Kirby Smith on the Kentucky campaign to Perryville, and engaged in the terrible and bloody fight at that place. On the return of the troops from Kentucky to Tennessee he was promoted to major of the Sixty-second North Carolina regiment. A few months before the war closed Col. R. G. A. Lowe, of the Sixty-second, resigned on account of ill-health, and Major McDowell was promoted to the lieutenant-colonelcy of the regiment, and remained in that position until the surrender, and though entitled to be called "colonel," is best known by his rank as major. He participated in all the battles of the East Tennessee campaign, and was wounded March 20, 1864, in an engagement on the French Broad river, by a minnie ball through the wrist, the scar of which he will bear till "the last enemy" subdues him. He was taken prisoner by Gen. Samuel Carter, now an uncle by marriage, on his first raid into East Tennessee in the spring of 1862, but was paroled the same day and exchanged about a month subsequently.

An interesting piece of history is connected with the Sixty-second regiment. While at Cumberland Gap, on September 13, 1863, the regiment was surrendered by Gen. Frazier, and the men thought needlessly so. They were satisfied they had been sold out, and that a surrender was unnecessary. Maj. McDowell and all the regiment able to travel, together with a large portion of the Thirty-seventh Virginia regiment, determined that they would not be surrendered, that they would come out of Cumberland Gap, and they did come out, though surrounded by a large force of Federals. They cut their way through in the night, and escaped with about eight hundred men unhurt, not a man being touched. They returned to East Tennessee and united themselves with the army under Gen. Samuel Jones, afterwards under Gen. Breckinridge.

During the war, January 27, 1863, Maj. McDowell was captured the second time, this time by Miss Margaret Rhea, daughter of Col. James D. Rhea. The affair occurred at Union Depot (then Zollicoffer), Sullivan county, Tennessee, and it is needless to say the gallant Major gallantly surrendered, has never asked for a parole, would not accept one if tendered, but remains a willing prisoner.

The war over, Maj. McDowell settled with his wife at Union Depot, read law under Col. N. M. Taylor and Judge R. R. Butler (whose sketches appear elsewhere in this volume), and was admitted to the bar in March, 1866, by Judge R. R. Butler and Judge Sam Milligan, of the Supreme bench. He began practice in Sullivan county, and has been engaged continuously in practice till now in the counties of Sullivan, Washington, and Carter, and in the Supreme and Federal courts at Knoxville. In the fall of 1879 he formed a partnership with Judge R. R. Butler, which continues to the present time.

In politics Maj. McDowell is an hereditary Democrat, his family having been Democrats from "a time beyond which the memory of man runneth not to the contrary," but though a working member with his political party he has never held or sought civil office. As a delegate he has frequently attended the State Democratic conventions, and has frequently spoken in political campaigns. In 1866 he was made an Entered Apprentice Mason at Bristol, but has never taken the higher degrees. In 1874–75 he edited the Sullivan *Landmark*, published at Union Depot. In religion he first attached

himself to the Methodist church, in 1852, but in 1880 he joined the Presbyterian church at Bristol. For twenty years he has been a Sunday-school teacher, and for four years was a Sunday-school superintendent.

The McDowell family is of Scotch-Irish origin. The advent of the family into this country was previous to the Revolution. Many of them participated in the war for independence, some of them were at King's Mountain, and some figured in the war of 1812. At the battle of King's Mountain, according to the "History of the Heroes of King's Mountain," John and Charles McDowell both commanded forces. They were not generals in fact, but two of the commanders having faltered as the battle was progressing, John and Charles McDowell assumed command and went forward, and so were complimented with the title of general. Maj. McDowell is a descendant of the fifth remove from Gen. John McDowell. Another McDowell, a kinsman of Maj. McDowell, was a member of Congress from Maryland.

The grandfather of Maj. McDowell was John McDowell, a farmer and politician, born in McDowell county, North Carolina (the county receiving its name as a compliment to other members of the family); married at Pleasant Gardens, in the same county, and there lived and died. He was a member of the North Carolina Legislature, and occupied various civil positions. He was a Baptist. His son, Rev. John McDowell, father of the subject of this biography, was born in Haywood county, North Carolina, in 1804; was a merchant in early life, and originally a Baptist, but dissolved his connection with that Church on account of disagreement with its doctrine of immersion. He then attached himself to the Methodist church, in which he preached until his death, September 11, 1883. He was an active worker in the church, of limited education, but of wonderful originality; a very zealous man in any thing he undertook, and exceptionally devoted to the work of the ministry, and of good business qualities, mostly acquired by experience. He was county surveyor of Macon and Haywood counties, North Carolina, for forty years. He had few enemies; was a man of even temperament, and always had a kind word for everybody, irrespective of their positions in life. He taught his children at an early age to respect the Sabbath and the Church, which resulted in their early connection with the church of his choice. He died a triumphant death, making a profound religious impression upon those who witnessed his departure. He left six children living: (1). William R., who married Elizabeth Gibbs, and is living, a farmer near the old homestead. (2). Nancy E.; unmarried, and living on the old homestead. (3). Sarah T., wife of Joseph Brendle, a farmer in Haywood county, North Carolina; has one child, John. (4). Caroline, wife of William McClure, a farmer in Macon county, North Carolina, living near the old homestead. (5). Byron G., subject of this sketch. (6). Athan L., a farmer on

10

the old homestead; married Caroline Russell, daughter of James Russell; has four children, Ara, Adaline, Emma and Elizabeth.

Two of Maj. McDowell's brothers died—Leander at the age of twenty-three, and John at the age of six. Two of his sisters are also dead—Nancy at the age of ten, and Maria, who died the wife of John McClure, leaving five children, Elizabeth, Martha, Mary, Daniel, and Jerome, all married. Elizabeth married a Dryman, Martha married John Vanhook, Mary married a Norton, John married a Norton.

Maj. McDowell s mother, *nee* Elizabeth Morrow, was born in Haywood county, North Carolina, daughter of William Morrow, a farmer, her mother being Elizabeth Medford, of a well-known "old North State" family, living on Pigeon river, Haywood county. She was a Methodist, and is spoken of gratefully by the son for her faithfulness and self-sacrificing devotion to her children, and her constant and consistent Christian life. She died June 11, 1876, at the age of sixty-seven.

Maj. McDowell's wife was born in Sullivan county, Tennessee, December 30, 1840, daughter of Col. James D. Rhea, a farmer, a native of Sullivan county, and a man of large property. He has four children living: (1). Margaret, wife of Maj. McDowell. (2). Sarah, wife of Matthew Rhea. (3). James T.; married Fannie Rhea, a distant relative, in Fayette county, Tennessee, where he now lives, a farmer. (4). Elizabeth, wife of B. W. Norvell, a merchant at Union Depot, Sullivan county, Tennessee.

Three of Mrs. McDowell's sisters are dead: (1). Matilda; died the wife of W. G. Rutledge; (2). Elizabeth; died unmarried, and (3). May; died the wife of E. A. McClellan, leaving six children, Samuel D., James, John, Rhea, Edward and Elizabeth.

Mrs. McDowell's mother, Elizabeth Carter, was daughter of Alfred M. Carter, of Carter county, Tennessee (the county being named for the family). He was a prominent man of that section, of large wealth and extensive influence. Mrs. McDowell is a niece of David W. Carter, now of Bristol, and of Landon Carter, who lost his life about the close of the war by the wreck of a vessel at sea. Her grandfather, Alfred M. Carter, was twice married—first, to a Miss Duffield, who became the mother of David, Landon and Elizabeth Carter. The children of his second wife are Samuel P. Carter, now an admiral in the United States navy; James P. T. Carter, deceased, and Rev. W. B. Carter, of Elizabethtown, Carter county, Tennessee. Mrs. McDowell is also connected with the well-known Taylor family of East Tennessee, and, being a Rhea, is related to one of the largest and most interesting families in that region. She was educated at Rogersville and Blountville, belongs to the Presbyterian church, and is beloved for her domestic virtues and her uniform Christian life.

Six children have been born of this marriage: (1). James R. McDowell, born November 27, 1863; graduated at King College, in 1880; now a book-keeper in Knoxville. (2). Ella Irene McDowell, born September 8, 1866. (3). Elizabeth J. McDowell, born August 12, 1868. (4). Albert S. McDowell, born September 12, 1870. (5). Mary Eva McDowell, born December 13, 1875. (6). Margaret Rhea McDowell, born June 19, 1880.

Maj. McDowell began life without property, and what he now owns he made by industry, economy, close application, and a faithful keeping of every trust committed to his hands, a record of which his posterity will be more justly proud than of the estate he may transmit to them. In boyhood his habits were sober, steady and quiet. He never but once in his life, and then when a very small boy, was under the influence of whiskey.

GOV. ALBERT S. MARKS.

WINCHESTER.

THIS gentleman was born in Daviess county, Kentucky, October 16, 1836. His father was a farmer, and both his parents, as well as his grandparents, were pious and zealous Methodists. He grew up on his father's farm, receiving an academical education there till the age of fourteen, when his father died. After this event he continued working on the farm. He got about five months' additional schooling in his seventeenth year, and beyond this is a self-educated man. He has always been a great reader, and during the interval between his school days and his professional career, his literary appetite seems to have been omnivorous, but with a special taste for fiction, history, biography, and the classical authors of Greece and Rome, partly in the original and partly in translations. His early preference was for the law as a profession, and this was probably intensified when, at a school exhibition, he had made a creditable oratorical effort and received the congratulations of his friends, who recommended that profession as best suited to his talents. He lived, however, at the farm and worked regularly upon it till his nineteenth year, when he removed to Winchester, Tennessee, and commenced the study of law in the office of Colyar & Frizzell, the senior member of which, the Hon. A. S. Colyar, was a blood relative. After studying with these gentlemen for two years he was dmitted to the bar in the fall of 1858, and commenced ractice in partnership with them. In January, 1861, Ir. Frizzell retired from the firm, and Colyar & Marks racticed together. The next month Marks was put orward as the Union candidate for the constitutional onvention, the Hon. Peter Turney being opposed to im as the secession candidate. Marks had hitherto een identified with the Breckinridge wing of the Democratic party. The two men had been intimate personal riends, and, though diametrically opposed in politics, ade the canvass together, boarding, lodging and riding ogether throughout the contest. It is well known that Iarks was defeated and the State seceded. War having broken out in consequence, the two friends ran a ngulary parallel course. Both became commanders f regiments, both were severely wounded, and both ere at the same time confined to their beds and treated or their wounds at Winchester. To complete the arallel, both lost exactly the same number of men by he casualties of war.

Judge Marks entered the Confederate service as aptain of Company E, Seventeenth Tennessee regient of infantry. This regiment was included in Gen. ollicoffer's command, and was in all his engagements o the date of his death, at the disastrous battle of ishing Creek. In the affair at Rock Castle, out of leven thousand men only eleven were killed, and six f these were members of Marks' company. The reason f this was that that part of the hill attacked which as opposite to Marks' command, was alone accessible, hile the troops on either side of it were unable to scend, so that the brunt of the battle was encountered y that one company. After the defeat and death of ollicoffer, the regiment was transferred to the comand of Gen. Bushrod Johnson, of Hardee's corps, nd participated in the engagements around Corinth, here Marks became major, May, 1862, and in the June ollowing assumed the command of the regiment as olonel. This was when the army was reorganized, and he Seventeenth Tennessee formed part of Buckner's ommand during the Kentucky campaign of 1862. In his campaign he was appointed by Gen. Buckner to he honor of receiving the surrender of the Federal roops which were defeated at Mumfordsville, in September, 1862.

On the return of Buckner's command to Tennessee, en. Buckner himself was ordered to take charge of he department of Alabama, with Mobile as his headuarters. His division was transferred to the command f Gen. Pat. Cleburne, and with it, of course, Marks' egiment. In this command the regiment was present t the battle of Murfreesborough, December 31, 1862, nd there Col. Marks received a very severe wound in is right leg from a canister-shot, which necessitated mputation below the knee. To the editor of these ketches, on being asked the cause of his lameness, he nswered "through trifling with the Union." At the

same time his compatriots recognize in the missing limb the evidence that he did his duty in defense of the southern country and people. The Seventeenth regiment in that battle captured three batteries and lost two hundred and forty-six men, killed and wounded, and upon the recommendation of Gen. Cleburne, President Davis placed its colonel's name upon the roll of honor. This terminated the military career of Col. Marks.

After the close of the war he practiced law for two years in partnership with his former partner, A. S. Colyar; then Mr. Colyar moved to Nashville, in 1866. His partners then were Capt. J. B. Fitzpatrick and Capt. T. D. Gregory, with whom he practiced until 1870. At this latter date he was elected chancellor of the fourth chancery division of Tennessee, to which office he was re-elected at the expiration of his first term, 1878. He gained great credit while on the bench by the energy with which he pushed forward the business which had accumulated through the proverbially dilatory proceedings of that court, but, though re-elected, he did not serve through a second term. The year of his re-election, 1878, he was nominated as the Democratic candidate for governor of the State, and elected to that office in the November of that year. He served for two years, but declined to allow his name to go before the next Democratic convention for re-election. The division in the Democratic party, occasioned by the State debt question, had already manifested itself during the election of 1878, and he was satisfied that, in 1880, he could not, if nominated, obtain the united Democratic vote, and would therefore be very probably defeated. Judge Marks was the last governor of Tennessee who received the united vote of the Democratic party.

He resumed the practice of law in Franklin and the adjoining counties until 1883, when he rejoined his relative and former partner, A. S. Colyar, at Nashville, where was established the firm now known as Colyar, Marks & Childress.

In politics Gov. Marks is a Democrat by inheritance, as well as by conviction. Prior to their settlement in Tennessee, his family were Virginians, who lived near the seat of Thomas Jefferson, and followed the political fortunes of that gentleman throughout, and when the old Republican party separated into Whigs and Democrats they gave in their permanent adhesion to the latter party.

Gov. Marks married, April 29, 1863, Miss Novella Davis, a native of Wilson county, Tennessee. He had been engaged to this lady before he lost his leg, and and when he recovered, mutilated in body and broken in fortune, he honorably offered to release her from her engagement. The same offer was made to many southern ladies during and after our civil war, and this editor knows of no single instance in which one of them availed herself of her lover's permission. Certainly Miss Davis was one of the last persons who could be expected to do so, and she gladly claimed the fulfillment of the engagement, devoting herself thenceforward with redoubled affection to the happiness of her wounded lover. Any intelligent person enjoying the privilege of an introduction to Mrs. Marks, at once discovers that he has formed the acquaintance of a superior woman; superior, that is, intellectually, morally and in person. She in fact combines the elements of a perfect lady; noble in person, elevated in mental qualities, a fine scholar, and brilliant in conversation, the ornament of society, and still domestic and practical in the management of her home, she seems nowhere out of place, but, whatever she undertakes, accomplishes it as thoroughly as if that alone had been the occupation of her life. It is said that when her husband was chancellor, and necessarily absent from home a good deal, she managed the farm with the skill and energy of a first rate practical farmer. On the other hand, that her intellect and culture were made available in training the minds of her children is manifested by the high position they took as scholars when sent to school. It is believed that her cultivated intellect stimulated that of her husband, and that her towering ambition kindled his to its highest efforts. This estimate of the wife of Gov. Marks justifies the editor, as he thinks, in giving her a distinguished place among the eminent Tennesseans, whose memoirs are included in this collection.

[The revising editor also, having himself been admitted to the honor of a brief acquaintance with this lady, cannot refrain from adding his testimony to the nobility of her character and the fascination of her conversation. He recognizes in her a perfect type of the grandeur with which the southern ladies rose to the emergencies of the war and its consequences, and, without ceasing to be refined and cultivated ladies, showed themselves self-sacrificing and practical women in coping with the adversity entailed on all by that terrible calamity.]

By his marriage with this lady, Gov. Marks has two sons : (1). Arthur Handly, born at LaGrange, Georgia, March 8, 1864; a scholar of high standing at the University of the South, Sewanee. (2). Albert Davis, born at Winchester, Tennessee, September 1, 1867; now finishing his education at the Winchester Normal College.

Mrs. Marks is a member of the Cumberland Presbyterian church. Her father was the Hon. John R. Davis, of Wilson county, Tennessee, a member of the General Assembly of 1859–60, and 1861–62; a planter and a major in the Confederate States army; of a family originally from North Carolina. His father was Thomas Davis, one of the early settlers of Wilson county. Mrs. Marks' mother was Caroline Hunter, a native of Wilson county, and also of a North Carolina family.

Gov. Marks' father, Elisha S. Marks. was a native of Loudon county, Virginia, but emigrated in early life with his father to Daviess county, Kentucky. The father died there at the age of thirty-one years. Elisha succeeded to his patrimony and lived long on the farm in Daviess county, his mother living with him. Both inherited a comfortable fortune, but made no effort to increase it. No member of the family has ever been insolvent. He married Elizabeth Lashbrook, whose mother was a Miss Colyar, sister of the father of A. S. Colyar. Gov. Marks' grandmother was a member of the Daniel family, of Virginia. His mother died in Daviess county, Kentucky, in 1859, leaving five daughters and two sons, all now deceased except the governor's sister, Margaret, widow of Capt. J. B. Fitzpatrick, and Elizabeth, wife of Mr. Robert Handly, of Winchester, and Gov. Marks' brother, Dr. Edward C. Marks, who is practicing medicine at Tracy City, Tennessee. His father's and grandfather's families were all pious and devoted Methodists. The following letter from a venerable Methodist minister will show the estimation in which they were held by the ministers and members of that church:

RUSSELLVILLE, KY., August 21, 1878.

Hon. A. S. Marks:

DEAR SIR—I was greatly delighted to see from the papers that you were nominated by the late Democratic convention of your State as candidate for the office of governor, and I write to congratulate you upon this honorable distinction.

In 1812 I was appointed as preacher on the Owensborough circuit, in this State, where I remained two years. Your father's house was one of my preaching places, and also one of my best homes. Your grandmother, your father's mother, who resided with him, was a devoted Methodist, of the old type, and one of the most pious persons I ever knew. She seemed very much to me as my own mother. I was then a young man, and her counsels and advice were a great blessing to me. Your father and mother were my devoted friends. They were distinguished for that warm hospitality, especially towards Methodist preachers, for which Kentucky has always been distinguished, more eminently, however, in that day, than in the present. You were then a small boy, I would think, eight or ten years of age—the oldest of the children, as I recollect. You were the favorite of your grandmother, who had the settled conviction that you might become a Methodist preacher, the highest distinction, in her estimation, to which you could attain. You were a great favorite of mine, and you became very much attached to me. You, like little boys generally, were very fond of a horse, and nearly always when I would arrive, you would ride my horse to water, and to the stable. I made it a rule to wait on myself as much as I was allowed. But when I would go to the stable to get my horse, you were along to aid me, and do the riding. I look back on those days of nearly forty years ago, with great pleasure, mingled with sadness.

Your sainted grandmother has long ago entered into her heavenly rest; so also your father and mother. Your father was a man of more than ordinary natural endowments and a high-toned, honorable gentleman. Your mother was a model of all the virtues that make up the true woman. She was amiable and sprightly and remarkable for her personal beauty. Your maternal grandmother, Lashbrook, was distinguished for her fine sense and excellent character. She was a devoted Christian, and a Methodist. Her house was one of my best homes. She died while I was on the circuit, and I preached her funeral to a very large congregation.

You will, I am sure, bear with me in thus writing to you. My friendships have always been very strong, especially those formed in early life, and I feel an interest in the children of my early friends almost as strong as if they were my kindred by ties of blood. When, at Nashville, in 1873, I spent some days with Col.

Colyar, a relation of yours, who gave me your history in Tennessee. I had the pleasure also of seeing two of your sisters, who
called on me.
I failed (strangely) to inquire if you were a professor of religion,
and a member of the church. I would be happy to know if such
be the case; for, permit me to say, that whatever distinction a
man may gain among men, his life is a terrible failure if he has
failed to live a religious life, and thus prepare for a better and
higher state. Yours truly,
N. H. LEE.

Questioned as to the methods observed by him in
attaining success in life, Judge Marks answered: " I
feel that labor and temperance have been the means of
my success. My course has been a strange one in one
respect—I have never had to wait. Ever since I have
been at the bar I have been fully occupied. I have
always tried to perform the duties that lay nearest to
me."

RICHARD B. MAURY, M.D.

MEMPHIS.

RICHARD B. MAURY was born in Georgetown,
D. C., February 5, 1834, but his father moving
first to Norfolk, a few weeks after he was born, and subsequently to Fredericksburg, Virginia, he grew up at the
latter place. He early manifested a desire to study
medicine, and when but a lad of seven years, having
heard a lecture by a Chinese missionary, he came home
and, with boyish enthusiasm, announced to his mother
that he intended to become a physician and go to China.
He had the advantage of a careful training by one of
the most faithful of mothers, a most refined and conscientious woman; and after leaving her hands all his
school-boy days were spent under the instruction of
Thomas H. Hanson, who for twenty-five years was the
prominent teacher in Fredericksburg. He then entered
the University of Virginia, of which he is an *alumnus*,
having graduated from several of the literary schools of
that institution. The next four years he taught school
in Petersburg and Fredericksburg, at a salary of about
six hundred dollars per annum. He then re-entered
the University of Virginia, and in 1857 graduated
thence in medicine, under Profs. James L. Cabell, John
S. Davis, S. S. Maupin and Henry Howard. He
next went to New York, and, after standing a competitive examination, was appointed as interne to Belle
Vue hospital, and while holding that appointment took
the degree of M.D. in the University of New York—a
second medical graduation. At the close of his hospital career, being threatened with disease of the lungs,
he decided to go to Mississippi. Soon after, the war
broke out and Dr. Maury entered the Confederate army
as surgeon of the Twenty-eighth Mississippi cavalry,
and after one year of service in the field was transferred
to hospital duty and served the Confederacy until
the close of the war, in charge of hospitals at Brookhaven and Lauderdale Springs, Mississippi, and at
Greenville, Alabama.
The war over, he moved to Memphis, in 1867, where
he has resided ever since, devoted exclusively to
his profession. In 1869 he was elected professor of
physiology, and in 1870 professor of the practice of

medicine, in the Memphis Medical College. He however took an active interest in public education, and on
account of his eminent fitness, was elected and served
two years as president of the Memphis board of education. Dr. Maury has contributed frequently to medical
journals, among the most important of his papers being
"Topical Medication in the Treatment of Chronic
Dysentery," and various articles on gynecological
subjects. In 1885 he was elected professor of Gynecology in the Memphis Hospital Medical College.
Dr. Maury is a valued member of the Tennessee State
and Shelby county medical societies, and a Fellow of the
American Gynecological Society. For the past ten years
he has devoted himself especially to the diseases of
women, much of his work being surgical, in which he has
built up an honorable and enviable reputation. A physician's life, even though he may be studious and have
at his command a vast amount of brain, skill and
experience, is necessarily uneventful and quiet, so far
as the outside world may know. The very nature of his
studies and of his practice is private, unsuited for general publication, and hence his name does not make
half the noise in the world that an ordinary politician
does with one-half the mental ability. For this reason
the writer takes especial pride in recording the lives of
these medical gentlemen whose actions are "at once a
service and a sacrifice" for the welfare of their fellow-
men.
Dr. Maury married, first in Port Gibson, Mississippi,
Miss Jane S. Ellett, born in that town, June 14, 1840.
Mrs. Maury was the daughter of Hon. Henry T. Ellett,
a distinguished lawyer, now of Memphis, formerly on
the Supreme bench of Mississippi, and a member of
Congress from that State. Her mother, Rebecca C.
Seeley, was a daughter of Gov. Seeley, of New Jersey.
Mrs. Maury was educated at Natchez, Mississippi. She
died in Memphis, April 10, 1875, leaving six children:
(1). Richard B., born March 25, 1862, in Port Gibson;
educated in Virginia; now on a cattle ranch in Texas.
(2). Kate Ellett, born August 27, 1864, in Greenville;
graduated at Miss Higby's high school, Memphis. (3).

Henry Ellett, born August 19, 1866, in Port Gibson.
(4). John Metcalfe, born July 25, 1868, in Memphis.
(5). Ellen, born August 27, 1870, and died January 5,
1871. (6). Joseph Ellett, born November 11, 1871, in
Memphis.

Dr. Maury's second marriage, which occurred at
Memphis, October 10, 1876, was with Miss Jennie B.
Poston, daughter of Hon. William K. Poston, a prominent lawyer of Memphis. He was a member of the
Tennessee Legislature from Shelby county during
Brownlow's administration, and resigned to prevent a
quorum and in order to defeat the passage of the bill
disfranchising ex-Confederates. He was re-elected by
his fellow-citizens of Shelby county, but was refused
his seat by Brownlow. Mr. Poston was born in Clarksville, Tennessee, of a family originally from Virginia,
and of Scotch-English descent. His father, Hon. John
H. Poston, was also a member of the Tennessee Legislature, and once represented Montgomery county.

Mrs. Maury has six brothers and five sisters living. Of the brothers, David H., William K., and
Frank P. Poston are leading lawyers in Memphis; J.
B. Poston is a merchant at Dallas, Texas; G. S. Poston,
a merchant at Como, Mississippi; and John H. Poston,
a merchant at Memphis. The oldest sister, Mary, is
the wife of Wiley J. Littlejohn, a distinguished insur-
ance man at Chicago; Kate, is the wife of W. E. Mc-
Gehee, a planter in Panola county, Mississippi, and
Misses Annie, Maggie and Josie Poston are living in
Memphis. Mrs. Maury's mother, Miss Mary Park, a
Kentuckian by birth, was the daughter of David Park
and Jane Barron, of Virginia, both of Irish extraction.
David Park was at one time a prominent merchant at
Nashville, and afterwards at Memphis. Mrs. Maury
graduated from the State Female College at Memphis.

By his marriage with Miss Poston, Dr. Maury has
three children: (1). William Poston, born July 21,
1877. (2). Robert Mitchell, born December 15, 1878.
(3). Jennie June, born January 24, 1881. They have
also an adopted son, Charles A., son of Dr. Maury's
deceased brother, Rev. Magruder Maury.

Dr. Maury and wife are both members of the Protestant Episcopal church, he being a vestryman of
Calvary church, Memphis. He became a Mason in
1865, at Greenville, Alabama. In politics he votes
the Democratic ticket. Financially and professionally,
Dr. Maury has proven a success by steady, faithful,
persevering labor in one channel, looking neither to the
right nor to the left for the greener grass which may
grow on either side.

The family history of the Maurys is so exceedingly
interesting that more extended notice is due them. The
family is of French Huguenot extraction, descended
from John de LaFontaine, born in Maine, near the
borders of Normandy, A. D. 1500. The ancestral line,
ascending from Dr. Richard B. Maury, subject of this
sketch, is as follows: 1. Richard B. Maury and his

wife, Ellen Magruder. 2. Fontaine Maury and h[?]
wife, Betsy Brooke. 3. Rev. James Maury, rector o[?]
Frederickville parish, Virginia, and his wife, Mar[?]
Walker. 4. Matthew Maury, born in Dublin, in 171[?]
emigrated to Virginia in 1718. His wife was Mary An[?]
Fontaine, born in Taunton, England, in 1690 (?). Sh[?]
was the daughter of Rev. James Fontaine and A. I[?]
Boureicault. This James Fontaine was the direct an[?]
cester of the Fontaine and Maury families of Virgini[?]
He was the son of the Rev. James Fontaine, pastor o[?]
Vaux and Royan, France. This latter James Fontain[?]
was the son of James Fontaine and grandson o[?]
John de LaFontaine, who was born A. D. 150[?]
and martyred A. D. 1563. John de LaFontaine hel[?]
a commission in the household of Francis I. In th[?]
tenth or twelfth year of that monarch's reign he en[?]
tered his service, and conducted himself with suc[?]
uniform honor and uprightness that he retained hi[?]
command, not only to the end of the reign of Francis I
but during the reigns of Henry II. and Francis II., an[?]
until the second year of Charles IX., when he resigned
He was a leading representative and staunch supporte[?]
of protestantism in France, and died for his piety an[?]
zeal for the pure worship of God. Henry IV. said o[?]
James de LaFontaine that he was the handsomest ma[?]
in his kingdom. For a fuller account of these distin[?]
guished ancestors of distinguished American familie[?]
the readers of this volume are referred to the "Histor[?]
of a Huguenot Family," by Henry Fontaine and An[?]
Maury, 512 pp., 1853.

Dr. Maury's father, Richard B. Maury, was a nativ[?]
of Spottsylvania county, Virginia, born January 2[?]
1794, the son of Fontaine Maury and Betsy Brooke. H[?]
was the private secretary of President Monroe, an[?]
afterwards first clerk in the Navy Department for [?]
number of years. He was a nephew of James Maury
who was the first consul Gen. Washington sent to Liv[?]
erpool, and who continued to be the American consu[?]
there until he was turned out of office for being a Whi[?]
by Gen. Jackson. Dr. Maury's father was a soldier i[?]
the war of 1812. He died at Fredericksburg, Virginia
in 1840, at the age of forty-six. He was one of th[?]
most popular men in Fredericksburg, where he spen[?]
his last days, and was in birth, education and manner[?]
a high-toned Virginia gentleman of the old school.

The celebrated Lieutenant M. F. Maury, of th[?]
United States Navy, author of Physical Geography of th[?]
Seas, and other widely-known scientific works, was Dr[?]
Maury's second cousin, and his guardian after hi[?]
father's death. He almost took the place of a fathe[?]
to him in his boyhood, and proved his kind friend an[?]
adviser.

Dr. Maury's mother was Miss Ellen Magruder, bor[?]
in Upper Marlboro, Maryland, in 1798. Her father wa[?]
James A. Magruder, a well-known merchant of George[?]
town, D. C., engaged very largely in shipments o[?]
tobacco from this country to England. He was a pris[?]

oner of war in 1812, on board a British ship with Charles Francis Key, when the latter wrote the "Star Spangled Banner." He married Miss Millicent Beans, a member of an old Maryland family. Dr. Maury's mother was a woman of very strong character, of great refinement and culture, of most remarkable piety, a thorough Bible scholar, a believer in prayer, and one whose prayers availed much. She died, near Danville, Kentucky, September 12, 1879, leaving three children:

(1). Richard B. Maury, subject of this sketch. (2). Magruder Maury, who was an *alumnus* of the University of Virginia, and died in April, 1877, an Episcopal clergyman at Philadelphia. He left three children, Charles A. (adopted by Dr. Maury), Lida and Anne Page. (3). Thompson B. Maury, an *alumnus* of the University of Virginia; well known as a writer and lecturer on meteorology; now residing in New York.

JAMES BENJAMIN COWAN, M.D.

TULLAHOMA.

JAMES BENJAMIN COWAN, one of the most prominent surgeons and physicians in Tennessee, was born in Fayetteville, Tennessee, September 15, 1831. His grandfather, Maj. James Cowan, was a soldier in the Seminole and Creek wars; was with Jackson in 1812, and held a commission from the United States government for a number of years as commander of what was known as "Regulators," engaged in keeping Indians off the frontier of Tennessee. He was a farmer, originally from Virginia, and came to Blount county, Tennessee. At the age of fifteen he was captured by the Cherokee Indians, kept prisoner a year, but managed to escape. At the same time of his capture his mother, *nee* Mary Walker, was also captured and carried to the northern lakes, kept a prisoner seven years, when she also made her escape. The Cowans are of Scotch-Irish descent. They emigrated to Ireland at an early day amid the difficulties in Scotland. They were Presbyterians, settled in Londonderry, Ireland, and from Londonderry emigrated to Virginia, before the Revolution, and are now scattered west and south. Dr. Cowan's father, Samuel Montgomery Cowan, was born in Blount county, Tennessee, March 10, 1801, and moved with his father to Franklin county, Tennessee, in 1806, when that country was a wilderness, his father being the second man that moved into that county. At the death of his father, in 1815, he found that the support of the family devolved upon his exertions. He went to work upon the little farm left by his father and did support and take care of his widowed mother, four sisters and one brother, all younger than himself. At eighteen he determined to educate himself, worked upon the farm, continued to support the family, and began a private course of study, and ultimately succeeded in acquiring a finished and classical education. In 1822 he entered the ministry of the Cumberland Presbyterian church, and became one of the most distinguished men of that denomination, both as a scholar and popular pulpit orator, and followed his vocation until age and declining health forced him to resign his

mantle to others. Probably no man of his age was more popular or better known in Tennessee and adjoining States. He married, July 20, 1830, Miss Nancy Coker Clements, of Fayetteville, Tennessee, daughter of Maj. Benjamin Clements. She was born December 6, 1811. Her parents emigrated from South Carolina to Lincoln county, Tennessee, in the spring of 1811. Her mother, Sarah Brazil, was a daughter of Joel Brazil, of South Carolina. Her paternal grandfather, Maj. Reuben Clements, was of French Huguenot origin. Maj. Clements made an immense fortune surveying government lands in Alabama, Mississippi and Florida. He made the first coast survey of Florida, in connection with his oldest son, Gen. Jesse B. Clements, who afterwards served as United States marshal under Presidents Polk, Pierce and Buchanan, and died in 1877, in Edgefield, Tennessee. Dr. Cowan's mother is a most remarkable lady, universally beloved for her purity of life, her good influence in society and her high Christian character. She has but one child, James Benjamin Cowan, subject of this sketch.

In 1842 Dr. Cowan's father removed from Fayetteville to Horn Lake, DeSoto county, Mississippi, and remained there on his plantation and in Memphis until 1851, when he returned to Fayetteville. Here it was that the young man Cowan began reading medicine, under the eminent Drs. William and Moses Bonner, which he continued eighteen months. He then entered, in 1852, the University Medical College of New York city, and graduated in March, 1855, under Profs. Valentine Mott, John W. Draper, Martin Paine, Alford C. Post, Gunning S. Bedford, William VanBuren, J. T. Metcalfe and Chancellor James Ferris. In the same year he graduated as an M.D. from Aylett's Institute of Medicine, and from the faculty of the University Medical College of New York city he received a certificate of honor, in addition to his diploma. The reason of his lengthened medical course was that he spent eighteen months in taking a full course of clinical instruction in the New York city hospitals. Thus exceptionally equipped for his profession, he practiced two years at Meridianville, Madison county, Alabama, and next practiced at Memphis, and out on his plantation near that city, until the war broke out, when he went to Pensacola, Florida, with the first troops that volunteered from Mississippi for the Confederate army. On March 27, 1861, he was commissioned acting assistant surgeon, and assigned to duty with the Ninth Mississippi regiment, Col. Chalmers commanding, then at Pensacola.

The latter part of November, 1861, he accepted a commission as surgeon in charge of Forrest's cavalry battalion, then at Hopkinsville, Kentucky. In June, 1862, he was appointed chief surgeon of cavalry, and assigned to personal duty with Brig.-Gen. N. B. Forrest, then organizing his brigade in East Tennessee, and remained on the staff of that cavalry chieftain until the close of the war. In January, 1865, he was promoted to medical director of Lieut.-Gen. Forrest's cavalry corps, and surrendered as such at Gainesville, Alabama, May 12, 1865. For a more detailed war record of Dr. Cowan, the reader is referred to Dr. J. Berrien Lindsley's Military Annals of Tennessee. He has the reputation among medical men of having performed more capital operations than almost any man in the service.

After the war, finding himself prostrated in fortune and his family refugeeing at Marion, Alabama, he joined them at that place. The September following, having collected sufficient means to pay his way to Memphis, he returned to that city, where by the assistance of friends, he was enabled to open an office and resume the practice of his profession. The following fall he found himself enabled to return to Marion and move his family to Memphis, where he remained until the terrible cholera epidemic in 1866, when he was seized with that dreadful disease himself, and upon recovering from it found his general health utterly broken down. He then moved his family to Franklin county, Tennessee, and after several months' recuperation, resumed the practice of medicine. In 1870 he received an invitation from friends at Selma, Alabama, to locate there. He found, after remaining there two years, that his family was completely at the mercy of the malarial influences of that low latitude, and that he would either have to take them back to the mountains or bury them. Therefore, in 1873, he abandoned his lucrative practice at Selma and brought his family to Tullahoma, where they rapidly regained health. In 1877 he opened an office in Nashville, at the solicitation of his friends, and remained there seven months, until he saw a practice rapidly growing up around him with most encouraging prospects for the future. These brilliant prospects he laid down and returned to Tullahoma for the purpose of nursing and taking care of his invalid father, which he did with exemplary filial devotion, until his death, May 5, 1881, in his eighty-

first year. Since then Dr. Cowan has continued to reside at Tullahoma, enjoying a large practice, and devoting his leisure to scientific researches.

Dr. Cowan was married at Huntsville, Alabama, October 20, 1857, to Miss Lucy C. Robinson, who was born in Madison county, Alabama, October 5, 1833, daughter of James B. Robinson, a cotton planter and large slaveholder. Her mother, Frances Otey Robinson, now living with the daughter at Tullahoma, in her seventy-sixth year, is a cousin of Bishop Otey. She was born in Bedford county, Virginia, May 19, 1810, daughter of Capt. Walter Otey, an officer in the war of 1812, and a prominent planter. Her mother, Mary Walton, was born in Roanoke county, Virginia, daughter of William Walton, who married a Miss Leftwich. Mrs. Cowan's paternal grandfather, Littleberry Robinson, was a native of Russell county, Virginia; a merchant in Virginia, but a planter in Alabama. He died in Madison county, Alabama. Mrs. Cowan was educated at Huntsville; is a member of the Cumberland Presbyterian church, as are also most of her family. She is a lady of culture and accomplishments, the pride of her parents, a devout Christian, and has nobly filled her station in life. During the war she underwent all the privations of separation from her husband, and of refugeeing, without a murmur.

By his marriage with Miss Robinson Dr. Cowan has seven children: (1). James M., born September 3, 1858; now in the insurance business at Cincinnati; is a Knight Templar, and is noted for his piety, steady habits and fine talents. (2). Mary Lou Coker, born October 19, 1859; graduated at the Cumberland Female College, McMinnville, and is now a member of the faculty of Tullahoma Female Seminary. (3). Otey Clements, born August 18, 1861. (4). Lilly Forrest, born November 1, 1863; married Robert Johnson November 20, 1883. (5). Presley Strange, born May 9, 1867. (6). Minnie Horton, born April 1, 1869. (7). Fannie Robinson, born January 27, 1871.

In 1851 Dr. Cowan was made a Mason in Fayetteville, Tennessee, and took the Chapter and Council degrees in 1854; the former at Columbus, Mississippi, and the latter at Verona, Mississippi. He was made an Odd Fellow in 1855, at Huntsville, Alabama. He is also a member of the Knights of Honor, Knights of Pythias, and of the Independent Order of Red Men, and in all of these orders is a past officer. In politics he is a Democrat, holding his faith as an inheritance from his grandfathers down, but has never held office, being wedded to his profession as a science. His motto in life has been to do right, act honorably with all men, and let principle be the foundation of all his actions, with thoroughness in qualification for every duty. He is, when occasion calls forth his animation, among the most earnest and impressive orators of the State. Social and convivial in his temperament, he is liberal to a fault, impulsive, quick to resent an insult or an injury, and has always been a stickler for the ethics of his profession, preferring an honorable position among his professional brethren to the emoluments or esteem of the world. He is always ready to lend a helping hand to young men in the profession, to lift them up and advance them to higher planes.

He is six feet high, weighs two hundred pounds, and is in physique a fine specimen of Tennessee manhood.

JUDGE JOHN WOODS.

MURFREESBOROUGH.

THIS gentleman, who has served the people of Rutherford county in one capacity and another nearly all of his life, and is now one of its oldest, best known and respected citizens, was born near Murfreesborough, September 11, 1807. He is the son of Thomas Woods, who came to Tennessee from Orange county, North Carolina, in 1807. In 1827 he went to Hickman, Kentucky, and there remained until his death, in 1838. He was a well educated, well-to-do gentleman and quiet citizen. He was the father of eleven children, of whom Judge John Woods, subject of this sketch, was the second born. Judge Woods' grandfather was John Woods, a native of Pennsylvania, who moved when young to North Carolina, and was in the employ of the colonies during the American Revolution, and three of his sons were in the American army.

Judge Woods' paternal grandmother was Miss Mebane, daughter of William Mebane, of North Carolina, a man of prominence in his time, who took an active and leading part in the affairs of the country during the Revolution. This family, distinguished in North Carolina in those days, is mentioned with much favor in "*Wheeler's Historical Sketches of North Carolina.*"

The mother of Judge Woods was Miss Susan Baldridge, daughter of a gentleman of Irish descent, who emigrated to North Carolina and married Miss Jane White, the daughter of Stephen White, near Chapel Hill, North Carolina.

Judge Woods was brought up as a farmer's boy, and educated in the old field schools of Rutherford county. At the age of twenty he was elected to his first office, that of constable, and served four years. He then went into merchandising and continued at that business until 1836, when he returned to farming, and continued at it until 1840. In the latter year he was elected register of Rutherford county and re-elected in 1844, serving two terms, until 1848. He was then elected clerk of the county court of Rutherford county and served two terms of four years each, when he returned to farming and was so engaged at the beginning of the war. In 1859 his fellow-citizens urged upon him the candidacy for member of the lower house of the Legislature, for which he was elected by a handsome majority, and served two years during the stormy period just preceding the civil war. After this he returned to his home and remained upon his farm until the close of hostilities. Upon the reorganization of the State, in 1866, he was commissioned a magistrate, and in the following year was made chairman of the county court, and has held the position by re-elections up to the present time.

Judge Woods has always been a Jeffersonian Democrat, and cast his first vote for Gen. Jackson in 1828, since which time he has always voted with the Democrats. He has been a delegate to several Democratic State conventions, both before and since the war, and is justly regarded as " one of the old wheel-horses of Democracy."

In 1828 he was made major of the Forty-fifth regiment of Tennessee militia, and received his commission from Gen. Sam Houston, then governor of Tennessee. He, however, did not enter the late war, owing to age and physical disabilities.

Judge Woods was married to Miss Mary F. Jarratt, October 30, 1833. She is a daughter of Thomas Jarratt, of Goochland county, Virginia, who came to Tennessee in 1806. Her mother was Miss Susan Thompson, who was also of a Virginia family of good standing. Judge and Mrs. Woods have no children, but have shown true parental affection by taking into their family and bringing up with care and tenderness several children of their relatives. Judge Woods comes from a Presbyterian family, but has never connected himself with any church, being broad in his religious views and not willing to be bound to any one denomination. His wife's family were originally Presbyterians, but on coming to Tennessee became Methodists.

Judge Woods began life a poor, hard-working farmer's boy, and had but few early advantages; but, by industry and close application to business, always taking a firm hold on whatever came to hand, and endeavoring to accomplish it and fill his obligations, he worked himself up to a position of respec' and influence. Previous to the war he had amassed a very considerable property, but suffered from the long protracted and destructive struggle. He still, however, possesses a comfortable competency. He was a director in the branch of the Planters Bank at Murfreesborough, and in the Murfreesborough Savings Bank, and a member of the directory board of the First National Bank of Murfreesborough. Always a liberal man, willing to help others, he has spent much of his fortune in this way, but can look back now in a serene old age and feel thankful that he has been the cause of happiness to many others.

HON. JOSEPH BUCKNER KILLEBREW, A.M., Ph.D.

NASHVILLE.

JOSEPH BUCKNER KILLEBREW was born in Montgomery county, Tennessee, May 29, 1831, son of Bryan Whitfield and Elizabeth Smith Killebrew.

The Killebrews of America are of English stock, and the name was originally Killegrew. The paternal great-grandfather of the subject of this sketch lived in Duplin county, North Carolina, while his maternal grandfather was from Halifax county, Virginia, half-brother of John Sims, a near neighbor of John Randolph of Roanoake. His maternal grandmother was Judith Pleasants, of the Pleasants of Virginia, a family distinguished for literary attainments and culture. His paternal grandmother, Mary Whitfield, was one of twenty-nine children, most of whom lived to maturity. Her father's family removed, about 1720, from England to Bertie county, North Carolina. Her father owned almost a principality on the Neuse, and at his death was able to leave ten thousand dollars to each of his many children. He was a near relative to Rev. George Whitefield. The descendants of Mr. Whitfield are scattered all over the South, and are generally men of mark and influence. His paternal grandfather, Buckner Killebrew, came from North Carolina and settled in Montgomery county, Tennessee, in 1796. He was a man of wealth and noted for his generous hospitality. His father, Bryan Whitfield Killebrew, was born April 1, 1805, and reared in Montgomery county, Tennessee, and educated in such schools as the country then afforded. He was a great reader and a fine natural mathematician, a farmer in good circumstances, owner of many slaves, free from vices, great or small; of amiable temperament, and genuinely hospitable, he was exceedingly popular, winning the affections of all men and inspiring confidence and regard. He married, in 1829, Elizabeth Ligon, daughter of Mathew Ligon, the son of a Revolutionary soldier. The issue of this marriage was Joseph Buckner Killebrew, the subject of this present sketch, and Mathew Ligon Killebrew, a farmer of Robertson county.

In 1835 his father removed to Stewart county, Tennessee, but, his mother dying in 1836, he was sent back to Montgomery county in the following year, where he attended school for six years under his maternal uncle, Joseph P. Ligon, an excellent man and a good classical scholar. In 1843 he returned to Stewart and worked there on his father's farm till 1848. While there, during the school months, he walked six miles daily to attend a neighborhood school, kept by a Mr. Myrtle who taught him grammar and arithmetic. In 1846 he went to live with an aunt, (Mrs. Lettice M. Fortson, to whose care his mother had commended him on her death-bed, and who always encouraged him in his studies), not going to school, but reading much of biography, history and other literature. In 1848 Mr. C. F. Uhlrich, a graduate of Bethany college, Virginia, taught school at Lafayette, Kentucky. At his school Mr. Killebrew made the acquaintance of geometry and algebra, taking a full course of mathematics in the years 1848 and 1849. His interest in mathematics was such that at one time he owned some forty algebras, which he ransacked for difficult problems. He would even take conic sections to the "new-ground" and study problems while burning brush. He left school in 1849, and the death of his father in 1850 devolved upon him the care of the farm for that year. In 1851, having at his disposal the limited sum of one hundred and twenty dollars, he entered Franklin college, near Nashville, then under the presidency of Tolbert Fanning. He remained there for one year, gaining such reputation in mathematics that, although a freshman, he was often called to take charge of the mathematical classes in the absence of the professor in charge of that branch. He began a classical course while at Franklin, but, compelled by want of means to leave college, he returned to Clarksville, unable to see his way forward. While there he met, one morning in a barber shop, an old gentleman, who, on hearing his name, said to him: "You are the man I am looking for; I have a school near Clarksville; if you will teach mathematics under me, I will teach you the languages." This gentleman was John D. Tyler, one of the most celebrated classical scholars and teachers in Tennessee. Mr. Killebrew accepted the proposition, remaining with Mr. Tyler for two years, and taking a very complete preparatory course in Latin and Greek.

In 1854 he was anxious to take a regular college course, but he was utterly without means, until the way was again opened before him. Mr. George S. Wimberly, a gentleman of fortune, and a warm friend and near neighbor of Mr. Tyler, had heard of young Killebrew and his studious habits and laudable ambitions. Meeting him one day he said to him: "I hear that you have completed in two years a course which ordinarily requires four years. You may select any college in the United States and I will advance the money to pay your expenses during a full course, simply taking your notes, to be paid when you get into business." The generous offer was accepted. After studying the catalogues and histories of a number of colleges, he selected Chapel Hill, North Carolina, being chiefly determined thereto by the fact that it seemed to have been the *alma mater* of most of the prominent men of the South. In January, 1854, he stood his examination and entered the sophomore class, half advanced, only

is deficiency in modern languages barring his way to
he junior. Here, as at Franklin, he was noted for his
bility in mathematics. He graduated in 1856 with the
rst distinction, and was elected to the tutorship in
athematics, but declined. During his term at Chapel
ill he was editor of the college paper, the *North
arolina University Magazine*. While under his
ditorial supervision, it took very high rank as a college
eriodical, publishing, among other able and valuable
rticles, a series of papers by Gov. Swain, the presi-
ent of the university, and others, bearing upon the
arly history of North Carolina. While at the univer-
ty an incident occurred which serves to show his
emarkable mathematical gift. One of his earliest
chievements was to draw from Dr. Phillips a caustic
riticism by deducing a conclusion in fluxions not
iven by the author. This the learned professor pro-
ounced wrong, but on further hearing complimented
ery highly as an original demonstration, which pro-
ured him to be pointed out by his fellow-students as
the fellow who rushed old Phillips." With all of his
athematical capacity and decided love for that branch
f learning, an important key to his intellectual char-
cteristics and to his future success is found in the fact
at he was so well able to master the languages,
espite early neglect of that branch, that he was
lected to deliver the Latin salutatory on commence-
ent day.

Returning to Clarksville, he read law with Robb &
ailey until October, 1857, when he began practicing.
hile engaged in his law studies he managed, by his
wn exertions and with some assistance from his aunt,
rs. Lettice M. Fortson, to pay off the notes given to
r. Wimberly for his expenses at Chapel Hill. During
e first two months of his practice he made five
undred dollars.

On the third day of December, 1857, he married the
aughter of Mr. George S. Wimberly, Mary Catharine,
ho had just completed her education under Dr. Elliott
the old Nashville Academy. To his marriage Mr.
illebrew owes much of his success in life. In his
ife he found a companion of extraordinary kindness,
ood sense and firmness of character, inspiring affection
the highest degree, while managing her household
nd family affairs with discretion, vigor and ability.

On Mr. Wimberly's death, in 1857, Mr. Killebrew
ttled on his plantation, conducting it with great suc-
ess until 1871; and during that time more than doub-
ng its acreage and improving it handsomely. He was
aring this period one of three commissioners appointed
y the county court to organize a system of public
hools for Montgomery county. In January, 1871, he
nnected himself with the *Union and American*, of
ashville, as agricultural editor, and labored assidu-
sly in that position for twenty-one months, his articles
eing copied all over the South, and embodying in
dvance of realization that progressive thought which

is now just reaching practical realization throughout
the South. In October, 1872, Gov. John C. Brown,
Mr. A. Cox, Gen. W. G. Harding and others subscribed
twenty thousand dollars for the organization of an
agricultural paper, to be called the *Rural Sun*, and
unanimously elected Mr. Killebrew editor-in-chief,
with Prof. J. M. Safford and Prof. Hunter Nicholson
as assistants, and Mrs. L. Virginia French as literary
editor. The *Rural Sun* was the best agricultural
paper ever published in the South, and contained more
original matter of superior quality than any other
journal of its kind. While engaged in this work he
also devoted himself to pressing upon the Legislature
and to have organized a bureau of agriculture, statistics
and mines.

In 1872 he was appointed general agent of the
Peabody education fund for Tennessee and assistant
State superintendent of public instruction, the State
treasurer being *ex officio* superintendent. In this
capacity he canvassed much of the State in the interest
of public schools at a time when political complications,
education of the negro and the poverty of a people
impoverished by war, rendered the task anything but
popular or pleasant to one less devoted to the public
good. Dr. Sears, in his report to the trustees of the
Peabody fund for 1873, says: " A highly intelligent and
influential gentleman (Mr. Killebrew) was appointed
agent of the association, and on the 22d of January he
was made assistant superintendent of public instruction, which circumstance is of itself sufficient evidence
of the wisdom of the course pursued. On the 14th of
March he made a most valuable report, which was published by authority for the purpose of circulation
within the State. The views presented in it are of the
most elevated character; and the facts brought to light
are well adapted to awaken the people from their
lethargy. He maintains that education has become
absolutely indispensable to the material prosperity of
every community; that 'the system as it at present exists
is utterly devoid of vitality, and the want of unity in
aim and action throughout the State can best be reme-
died by the appointment of a State superintendent.'
' Less than thirty counties,' he informs us, ' have levied
a tax for school purposes; and in the remainder, no
action has been taken by the county courts.' In appealing to an honorable sentiment of pride, he says: ' It is
a painful distinction to a State whose sons heretofore
have been distinguished for their valor, and whose
daughters have been noted for their accomplishments,
to be classed second in illiteracy.' "

During 1872 and part of 1873 Mr. Killebrew was
editor of the *Rural Sun*, agent of the Peabody fund,
commissioner of agriculture and secretary of the National Agricultural Association; any one of which positions afforded work enough for any man of ordinary
working capacity. Not merely occupying but thoroughly filling every position entrusted to his care, his

health gave way and he was compelled to cease from all work save that of commissioner of agriculture, while he sought rest and recovery.

He returned to Nashville in January, 1874, and between that time and July fourth, with some assistance, prepared the "Resources of Tennessee," a volume of twelve hundred pages, a most thorough and comprehensive treatment of all that which must be the foundation of future material wealth, of all the connections of the wonderful resources of Tennessee with the rest of the world, and of the way to make them available. It is complete in general and in detail, leaving but little ever to be added, and at best hereafter merely the filling up here and there of outlines thoroughly sketched. It was widely read in Tennessee and served the most important office of making Tennesseans know their own State and its value. It was for Tennessee the means to realizing the first step to immediate material and subsequent intellectual and moral greatness based on it, the first step toward "know thyself." It was thoroughly circulated and sought for in all parts of the northern United States, and by far more widely in demand and more generally read in Europe than any work of its kind, and especially in England and Germany.

Prof. Huxley, in an address in Nashville on September 7, 1876, said : " I am indebted to a most admirable work, of which a copy has been presented to me—a report of the resources of Tennessee—which, in my judgment, does infinite credit to the State which paid for it, and to the persons who put it together—which I do not profess to have read, yet out of which I have contrived to pick the sort of information I want of the structure of this region where we now stand."

Mr. James C. Bayles, of the *Iron Age*, of New York, said in a speech at Chattanooga: "To Col. Killebrew the world is indebted for a fuller and more explicit exposition of the natural resources of Tennessee than, so far as I know, has been presented of any other State. I can only wish that the wisdom and liberality of your people in securing the services of so competent an officer, and in placing at his command the means of giving currency to the results of his investigations, would excite the people of every State in the Union to a genuine emulation, fruitful of like results." This work is still in great demand. In 1876, in connection with Prof. J. M. Safford, Mr. Killebrew published the Geology of Tennessee, which is now used as a text-book in the public schools of the State.

In 1878 he received from his *alma mater*, Chapel Hill, the degree of Ph. D., as a special acknowledgement of superior merit, since, to merit this degree, is usually added the condition of three years' residence after graduation.

From 1872 to 1881 he remained commissioner of agriculture, statistics and mines, publishing about thirty volumes and pamphlets on almost every subject pertaining to the natural resources and existing and desirable industries of the State. These include brochures on grasses; sheep husbandry; wheat; tobacco; the oil region of Tennessee, besides several on the mineral interests of the State, in the aggregate about ten thousand pages. He also prepared several maps, showing the iron, coal and other mineral regions, and a large geographical map of the State, which is now a standard authority.

During Mr. Killebrew's term of office as commissioner of agriculture, he traveled in the North, and especially in New England, delivering lectures on the South as a field for immigration. These attracted wide attention and received high encomiums from many who least sympathized with the object, while they have borne already much good fruit.

In 1880 he was appointed by Gen. Francis A. Walker, superintendent of census, as special agent to report on the culture and curing of tobacco; and traveled in all the tobacco growing regions of the United States, the result being the publication of a 4to volume by the government which has been received with great favor by the trade, the tobacco growing industry and the press.

In June, 1881, while preparations were being made for the grand southern cotton and world's exposition at Atlanta, Georgia, the management of that enterprise, without solicitation on his part, tendered Mr. Killebrew the position of chief of the department of minerals and woods. With his characteristic promptness and energy, he at once set to work to organize the department committed to his charge, and although the time was far too short to accomplish the great work in hand, he succeeded in bringing together the largest collection of specimens of the mineral and forest wealth of the southern States ever shown at one place and at one time. His department was one of the most attractive, as it certainly was the most important, at that great exhibition of the resources and natural wealth of the South; and his management of it reflected the highest credit upon his judgment, intelligence and skill, and won for him the highest encomiums of the thousands of visitors to that great exposition.

Upon the coming in of a Republican administration, in 1881, another gentleman was appointed agricultural commissioner, and Mr. Killebrew found time to devote himself to his private interests, which had somewhat suffered from neglect. He has been reasonably prosperous, doing more for himself in one year than in ten of office holding. He is now engaged in iron and coal mining in Tennessee and Alabama, and is interested in a large silver mine in Mexico, whither he made two journeys during 1883, one requiring a horseback journey of six hundred miles.

He is now engaged in journalism, being the editor and general manager of the weekly issue of the Nashville *American*, and his articles are more generally copied in northern papers than those in any other journal. He is also a contributor to many other newspapers and magazines.

As the result of his happy union with Miss Wimberly, Mr. Killebrew has an interesting family of children, four sons and two daughters, one daughter having died in infancy. They are all fine specimens of physical, moral and intellectual manhood and womanhood. He divides his time between his business and his home upon his farm, where he, when at home, or his wife and children in his absence, dispenses genuine, plain, old-fashioned hospitality, entertaining usually a houseful of young guests from all parts of the South during the summer months.

Mr. Killebrew's success in life, both as a severe practical laborer, with keen judgment in private affairs, and as an enthusiastic and devoted worker for the public weal, is due to a rare combination of faculties. To his practical mathematical talent was added in a high degree the indispensable faculty of imagination under control of a strong will and of the practical side of his mental character. Notwithstanding a mathematical bent which seldom goes, when so strongly developed as in his case, with the linguistic faculty, he was not only rapidly successful in the acquisition of ancient and modern languages, but also in the practical use of his own tongue. Few have excelled him in a clear, simple and exceedingly pure English style in writing and speaking, in orderly arrangement, in the use of the logical powers, or in graphic description, and what is popularly called " word painting." With a mind well stored to a rare degree with facts and statistics, versed in the economical, industrial and general history of his own country, all illuminated by a broad knowledge of human progress in other lands, he has always been able to present, in attractive and popular form, the dry industrial, productive and practical economical problems, school questions, and descriptions of resources with a view to practical development, and, indeed, whatever he has undertaken to present to the public.

From 1865 to 1870, with a mind well stored, coming from the study of law and from practical and skillful management of business under the slave system, thoroughly understanding the old economical and industrial conditions, he was one of the first to understand and to adapt himself to the changed conditions. The faculty of imagination, the power to look ahead, and the habit of looking ahead, found him level with the times. It was because, with the practical quality which held him successfully close to business, imagination, so well reined in as not to lead him beyond bounds or into vagaries, had led him to look ahead and thus, with progressive thought, he was abreast the times. With cash payment of wages, and kindness and forbearance with firmness, he was one of the first to reach the best results with the new labor, and also one of the first to set out for the public the conditions of success under the changed system.

During that same period, 1865 to 1870, while attending successfully to private business, he was addressing farmers' clubs, writing for local papers, writing and publishing pamphlets on the resources of his native county, often at his own expense, and always replete with pregnant fact and apt theory ; and thus, with practical economical thought, stimulating the public to progressive development. That he was neither generally understood nor appreciated at that time, is true. He was abreast the times and too far ahead of the public to be generally kept in sight. He was widely enough appreciated to obtain at once, on branching out into a larger field, a firm and enduring footing. His own practical success was not to be gainsaid. That it was the plain, practical, plodding success of a man guided by judgment, and not speculative nor attained by chance in a wild pursuit of theory, was very clear ; still, many of his neighbors pronounced him a dreamer as to his public theories. The public has advanced to where he stood as to public schools and material progress, to see that he was as accurate in pointing out the multitudinous lines of progress for the people of Tennessee, as in pursuing with plain judgment his own private business. One of the most striking facts in his character and life has been the ability to confine himself to his own chosen ground, and at the same time, with rare insight and unerring foresight, to see far ahead for the public, without being tempted to embrace for himself everything he saw. Thus he perceived with a rare gift of practical imagination the true lines of progress for his people, and contented himself with using his own progressive thought for himself within a narrow practical field, branching out in private business only as he saw his way clear before him.

His views, as they are embodied in his speeches, addresses and pamphlets, written before 1870, and after, in the columns of the *Union and American* and *Rural Sun*, in the "Resources of Tennessee," and in his numerous speeches, addresses and thirty-odd pamphlets, have been for Tennessee, the New South and the changed conditions, what the views of that eminently wise and far-seeing sage, DeBow, were for the Old South, with this difference : That DeBow was never able to see that slavery (and slavery alone) vitiated all his far-reaching dreams; while Mr. Killebrew saw clearly the true, practical and inevitable lines of progress, which the South is now pursuing, with his own State in the lead. His correct views, unlike those of DeBow, were marred by no obstacle to their realization, save the always present difficulty of moving fossilism forward. To the accomplishment of that end no man in the South has contributed more.

He has been successful in private business. Rarely gifted with imagination, lifting him above the narrow, practical, routine plodding of every day, to see also beyond to-day, and to survey the entire field, he has been an enthusiastic and devoted philanthropist and public servant. In him, however, imagination was what it has been in every progressive public teacher who has given the world a shove forward, not the inclination to dream dreams, or to pursue theory and vagaries, but imagination controlled by will, reined in by judgment, seeing clearly the well defined lines of practical progress for many men, while, as one man, he has pursued his own path with almost unerring practical sagacity.

Holding office, when office holding lay bent with his own tastes and thought, he has steadily refused to enter politics, to accept political station or to engage in party strife, although often besought to do so, when political office seemed to lie within easy grasp. And here it may be well to mention, that in this era, when the highest private standard is so seldom carried rigidly into public life, the writer of this sketch has been in position to know, and all who have served with or under him will attest, that his accounts of personal expenditures were a marvel of scrupulous exactness down to the very cent This was not a matter of pride or of boast, for it was never alluded to, so far as is known; it was a matter of character practically working itself out in small affairs as in great ones.

Such men leave their annals illustrated by few stirring events. The field of thought and the task human advancement and of natural progress, afford ■ themes for battle scenes. Their storm and stress peri is truly a time of uneventful strife, but it is strife that cushioned field of thought whence no stroke lance resounds from the helm of antagonist to re-ec in the far times. When the struggle against darkne is over, arduous as may have been the labor, stubbo and hard the conflict, there is left but the fact th there was darkness, that there is light, and that the are those who lighted and bore torches. They leave well filled cemeteries as warriors do; they have er bodied themselves in no enduring and recorded enac ments as statesmen have done; they have linked ther selves with none of those stirring events which me call dramatic and make the themes of song and speecl but they have made light the dark places; they ha builded in the field of all of human progress, a fie broader than that of warrior or statesman; they ha builded strongly and firmly in the only enduring fabric that of human progress, human labor and hum thought. In this field of human endeavor, Josep Buckner Killebrew has builded his own monument i Tennessee, and for the lasting advantage of the peop of Tennessee.

HON. LEONIDAS CAMPBELL HOUK.

KNOXVILLE.

IN sketching the careers of prominent men, it has always been the purpose of the editor to demonstrate the methods by which they achieved their prominence. With this view we have been giving brief memoirs of grave and learned judges, pious and reverend divines, gallant soldiers and skilled physicians. Our present problem of study is the successful progress in life of a noted political leader who, commencing from an humble origin and attaining high honor and commanding influence, must have studied and practiced well the arts which command success—arts which may well be scrutinized with interest by those who propose to themselves a similar career.

Leonidas Campbell Houk was the son of a working cabinet-maker, and himself worked at the same trade for a livelihood, while he was qualifying himself for a self-taught education for the higher sphere in which he now moves. He was born in Sevier county, Tennessee, June 8, 1836. His father died when he was less than three years old, and his mother married again four years afterwards. The family moved, and he with it, first to Knox county and afterwards to Louisville, in Blount county, where he learned the cabinet trade. He began working at this craft at fifteen, and at about

eighteen returned to Sevier county, where he followe his trade till he married. Three months covers th whole time that he went to school, his education bein acquired by his own unaided efforts while working his trade, and driving an ox-cart while work was du Let no man despise such an education; it is a scho whose graduates are men like Leonidas Houk an Andrew Johnson. He has himself described the cab net shop in which, after working hours, he worked st harder at his books than he had with his saws ar chisels, lighted only by the flames of pine-knots collecte by himself in the roads. His reading, as soon as he cou read a book at all, was directed to the study of law. Th preference he seems to have inherited from his fathe who, though not professionally a lawyer, was muc consulted by his neighbors and frequently wrote ot contracts and other law papers for them. Perhaj among the boy's scanty library were some old elementar law-books which had been so used by his father. Suc a life he lived till his marriage.

He now devoted himself in earnest to the law as profession, and was called to the bar October 13, 185 his license being signed by Chancellor T. Nixon Var Dyke and Circuit Judge E. L. Gardenhire. He con menced the practice of law at Clinton, in Anderson county, Tennessee, where he resided thirteen years, doing a lucrative practice from the first. His first effort in politics was as sub-elector on the Bell-Everett ticket in 1860, and after the election of Lincoln he attended as a member the Union convention at Greeneville, Tennessee, in 1861.

His political career was now interrupted by the war. He entered the Federal army August 9, 1861, enlisting as a private in Company H, First Tennessee infantry, Col. R. K. Byrd, and served in Kentucky, West Virginia and Tennessee. He took part in the battle of Mill Springs and in the skirmishing that resulted in the capture of Cumberland Gap (Gen. G. W. Morgan's campaign). After this he was placed in charge of the line of transportation communicating with headquarters at London, Kentucky, where, August 17, 1862, a severe engagement took place, in which he commanded.

After this battle he went to Cumberland Gap, thence with Morgan to Ohio, to West Virginia, and thence to Nashville. He was in the first two days' skirmishing in the battle of Stone's river, and afterwards took part in what is known as the Dog creek expedition, in pursuit of Wheeler. After the battle of Murfreesborough and some subsequent skirmishes, he was taken sick at Carthage, Tennessee, and resigned. His first commission was as lieutenant and quartermaster in the First Tennessee regiment. He served on Gen. Thomas' staff at the battle of Fishing Creek, and was immediately afterwards promoted to the colonelcy of the Third Tennessee infantry. He served as colonel from February 3, 1862, to the day of his resignation, April 5, 1863. He did his duty as a good soldier, without making any pretensions to military science.

He attended, in 1865, the Republican convention or mass meeting, called by Andrew Johnson, Gov. Brownlow, Mr. Maynard and others, at Nashville. The purpose of this meeting was to consider the plan of reconstruction drawn up by these gentlemen and submitted by them to the convention. Mr. Houk opposed this measure, especially the disfranchising clause, and favored a regularly elected constitutional convention. His proposition was defeated by a majority of eighteen, and Johnson's measure was carried. Had Mr. Houk's counsel been acted upon, he believes that Tennessee would have been Republican at this day. He was elector on the Lincoln and Johnson ticket in 1864.

In 1866 he became judge of the Seventeenth judicial circuit of Tennessee, comprising the counties of Anderson, Campbell, Cumberland, Fentress, Morgan and Scott. He held this office for four years, when, finding its salary too small to support his family, he went to Knoxville in March, 1870, and practiced law there till 1878.

In 1868 he was a delegate from the State at large to the national Republican convention which nominated Gen. Grant for president.

In 1872 he represented Knox and Anderson counties in the State Legislature, serving as chairman of the finance, ways and means committee. He introduced and conducted through the House the measure on which was based the State school law; he was the Republican nominee for speaker of the House.

From 1871 to 1873, he was a special commissioner under the southern claims commission.

In 1878 he was elected to the Fortieth Congress with a majority of two thousand four hundred and fifty. In 1880 re-elected with a majority of eight thousand and seventeen. In 1882 re-elected, majority five thousand seven hundred and fourteen. His district is one of eight giving the largest Republican majorities in the United States. In 1884 he was again re-elected, with a majority of ten thousand three hundred and eighty-two.

He served in Congress as chairman of the war claims committee, and acquired much popularity with his people for the zeal and effectiveness with which he advanced their interests. In 1884 he was also a delegate to the State convention which nominated Frank Reid for governor, and to the national convention which nominated Blaine and Logan. He was in favor of the nomination of Arthur, but returned a zealous promoter of the Blaine ticket.

Mr. Houk is a member of no secret society except the Knights of Pythias. He is a member and trustee of the Methodist Episcopal church at Knoxville.

Judge Houk possesses in an eminent degree the qualities which combine to make a successful party leader. Aggressive and self-assertive, the atmosphere of political strife is the element in which he breathes most freely. He himself, when asked to state the leading principle of his life, answered that it was never to inflict a wrong and never to submit to one without resenting it. Risen from a position in which he earned his daily bread by his daily manual labor, he knows the million who still occupy that position; he knows their wants and wishes, their likings and animosities, and knowing this can always address them with effect, can always excite their attention, conciliate their confidence and warm their sympathies. Always ready to converse with men of every grade, his conversation is genial and jovial, full of humor and repartee and adapted to every collocutor. Let him on the other hand meet with an antagonist, and he never rests till he has demolished him beyond all possibility of future opposition.

The way in which he got his education makes it needless to say that he did not spend his time in frivolous amusements. He describes a day in his sixteenth year, when lying on the root of a tree reading, he for the first time sketched out a definite course of life for himself. He determined that "he was as good as anybody, that he had as many rights in the world as anybody, that he would do no man an intentional wrong, or if he did he would repair it, and that no man should do him a wrong without his resenting it, and that he would improve every advantage."

From his earliest years he was fond of politics, and attended public speakings, and felt inspired to obtain the power to mould the policy of his country.

His first reading was the Bible and Brownlow's Knoxville Whig, to both of which he frequently refers in his speeches. His speeches, like his conversation, abound with anecdote and incident, told with gay good humor ; but the body of them consists of a close chain of reasoning drawn less from the closet than from a close and keen observation of current events. They are the efforts of a well informed man, earnestly desirous of impressing his ideas upon his hearers. His judgments from the bench were clear and intelligent, and generally impartial, but the bar is more congenial to a man of his temperament than the bench, and the political arena more so than either. The Republicans of East Tennessee have had no such leader since the deaths of Brownlow and Andrew Johnson.

Judge Houk's first wife was Miss Elizabeth M. Smith, whom he married in Knox county, Tennessee, February 28, 1858. Her father was Barnet Smith, of North Carolina, her mother a Walker, also of North Carolina. By this marriage he had eight children, two of whom died in early childhood. The remaining six are as follows : (1). John C., born February 26, 1860 ; already esteemed as an adroit party manager, and one of the most popular young men in Knoxville, where he practices law with success. (2). Lincoln C., born December 18, 1863 ; a law student and a political speaker at Knoxville. (3). William C., born February 2, 1869. (4). Ellsworth C., born May 18, 1871. (5). Annie, born January 15, 1874. (6). Edmond Spence, born June 19, 1879.

The first Mrs. Houk died exactly a month after the birth of this last child, at the age of about forty-two. She was a member of the Methodist Episcopal church, a woman of extraordinary good sense, and, as a mother, exceptionally devoted.

He married his next wife in Baltimore, Maryland, December 20, 1880. She was Miss Mary Belle Von-Rosen, born in Canada and educated in the island of Jersey, in the British channel. Her father was an Austrian, and her mother an English lady. Her parents were married by the father of the celebrated Mrs. Langtry, and she was educated in the same school with that lady. Her mother died when she was two years old. Her father still lives at Jacobsville, Maryland, engaged in farming ; he is also a skillful architect. The judge has one child by his second marriage, Susie, born October 6, 1882.

The present Mrs. Houk is a member of the Episcopal church. She is a highly educated and accomplished lady, speaks, reads and writes French, German and Latin. She was raised by her grandmother, Mrs. Goldie, in affluent circumstances, and prior to her marriage, spent her life, after her school days, in travel. After her marriage, however, she devoted herself to her duties as mother of her husband's first family, whose love she earned and received by sedulous and maternal care. She spends her winters with her husband in Washington, where her social tact and high breeding render her the ornament and delight of society. Her education and accomplishments, though brilliant, are not superficial, but thorough and exact.

The Houks are a German family, the name being originally spelt Haugeh. The grandfather, John Adam Haugeh, was born in Germany, emigrated to Pennsylvania, afterwards to Botetourt county, Virginia, and finally settled in East Tennessee, in that portion now Sevier county. He raised a large family, two boys, named John and Martin, and four girls, three of whom, Sally, Polly and Elizabeth, married three brothers named Hicks, and the fourth a Mr. Hunt. The old gentleman was a thrifty German farmer, one of the pioneers who settled Sevier county.

The father, John Houk, was born in Virginia, and moved to Tennessee with his father when a small boy. Too young to work, he was sent out about the settlement to watch for Indians, and warn the settlers if they approached. He died October 28, 1839, aged seventy, his son, the subject of this sketch, being then less than three years old. He was a man of sense and information, better educated than the average settlers with whom he lived ; had some knowledge of law and frequently wrote deeds, etc., for his neighbors. He was a farmer and cabinet-maker ; he served two campaigns under Jackson ; was captain in the war of 1812–14, and was at the battle of the Horseshoe. After he returned home he was elected major of militia ; he took a prominent part in the politics of the day, but was never a candidate for office ; a Jackson man in the first campaign, he was afterwards a supporter of Hugh Lawson White and a Whig to the end.

Judge Houk's mother was a South Carolina lady, daughter of Thomas Gibson, who died in South Carolina ; her mother moved with her to Sevier county, where she married Maj. John Houk. She was a person of good natural sense, but of little education ; he was a man of books, though he had but slight school advantages. Mrs. Houk, mother of the judge, was a Methodist, originally a Lutheran. She died, in 1867, at the age of fifty-eight, leaving two children, viz.: Leonidas, the subject of this paper, and, by her marriage with James Ray, a son also named James Ray, an eminent criminal lawyer, late of Jacksborough, Tennessee. He is now dead.

DANIEL T. BOYNTON, M. D.

KNOXVILLE.

DANIEL T. BOYNTON was born in Athens, Maine, February 8, 1837; the son of Joshua Boynton, a native of that State, a farmer and cattle dealer, who moved to Elyria, Ohio, in the fall of 1837. Joshua Boynton was known as a man of iron-clad integrity, of proverbial fidelity in friendship, a member of the Congregational church, a Whig, and afterwards a Republican. He died in March, 1881, at the age of seventy-one.

The grandfather of Dr. Boynton was Capt. Joshua Boynton, a sea captain, who crossed the Atlantic in his sailing vessel sixty-two times, and was one of five brothers, all ship commanders, born in Newburyport, Massachusetts, where the family settled in 1637. The Georgia Boyntons are a branch of the same family, and the name is numerous in several other States. Capt. Joshua Boynton married a Miss Delano, of a New England seafaring family. The original ancestor was of Irish stock, and took his name from the celebrated river Boyne. Among the more distinguished members of the family are, Hon. W. W. Boynton, formerly chief justice of the Supreme court of Ohio, (Dr. Boynton's cousin), and Gov. Boynton, ex-speaker of the Georgia Senate, and the successor of Hon. Alexander H. Stephens as governor of that State.

Dr. Boynton's mother, Parmela Emerson, was a daughter of Daniel R. Emerson, who was born in 1774, at Haverhill, Massachusetts. He was a farmer and miller, and a religious and industrious man. He died in Elyria, Ohio, in 1846. Mrs. Boynton's mother was a Miss Carter, of an old New England family. Mrs. Boynton died at Elyria in 1849, at the age of thirty-seven, having borne nine children.

Dr. Boynton's family were a religious people, much given to talking religion and quoting Scripture, especially on Sunday afternoons. In this respect they were typical of the New England families of fifty years ago. It is said his mother substantially knew the Bible from Genesis to Revelation, and was famous as the "story-teller" of the family, often repeating the tales of the Arabian Nights Entertainments, stories of travel, etc., for the entertainment of children, but the Bible was the literature of the family.

Dr. Boynton grew up at Elyria, working on the farm, and when not at school, traveling with his father with stock from New York to northern Wisconsin. He early acquired a taste for literature, especially for biography and history, and became a studious reader of Shakspeare. At the age of fifteen he made up his mind to become a physician, and read and studied somewhat with a view to that purpose. His literary education consisted of a wide range of English literature, history and the classics

generally. He entered, August 1, 1860, the medical office of Dr. Jamine Strong, at Elyria, Ohio; matriculated in the medical department of the Western Reserve University, Cleveland, Ohio, October 7, 1860; attended the fall and winter courses of 1860–61, 1861–62 and 1862–63, graduating in the class of February, 1863. He immediately entered the United States army as first assistant surgeon of the One Hundred and Fourth Ohio volunteer infantry, Twenty-third army corps, and was promoted to surgeon of that regiment in January, 1865. He served in Kentucky under Gen. Burnside the summer of 1863; in the East Tennessee expedition, fall of 1863; Lamar House hospital, Knoxville, in the winter of 1863–64, and throughout the Atlanta campaign on the operating staff of the Twenty-third army corps; was with Gen. Thomas in Middle Tennessee, the fall and winter of 1864–65, in the Twenty-third army corps, commanded by Gen. Schofield, including the battles of Franklin and Nashville. After the battle of Nashville, which virtually terminated the armed struggle in the southwest, he was transferred *via* Cincinnati and Washington, and by ocean transport to North Carolina, and rejoined Gen. Sherman's army at Goldsboro in March, 1865.

After the war, he went to New York city and took the fall and winter course of 1866–67, in Bellevue College Hospital, under Profs. James R. Woods, Willard Parker, Austin Flint, sr., Frank Hamilton, Doremus Taylor, Elliott, Fordyce Barker and Alonzo Clark, taking also a course in microscopy under Prof. Austin Flint, jr. He returned to Knoxville, Tennessee, married in January, 1866, located and has practiced there almost continually since. His natural taste runs toward surgery, but he has done a general and leading practice.

He served as adjutant-general of Tennessee and private secretary to Gov. Brownlow from October, 1867, to March, 1869. He was United States pension agent at Knoxville from April, 1869, to July, 1883, and disbursed some fifty million dollars among seventeen thousand pensioners in the southern States. He also practiced his profession meantime. He is ranked among the prominent surgeons of Knoxville.

Dr. Boynton married at Knoxville, January 17, 1866, Mrs. Sue Sawyers, who was born in Elizabethton, Carter county, Tennessee, July, 1837, the eldest daughter of the famous editor, preacher, Whig politician, governor and United States senator, William G. Brownlow. Her mother was Eliza Ann O'Brien, daughter of John O'Brien, of Pennsylvania, of Irish descent. Mrs. Boynton was educated at Knoxville, and is characterized by fidelity as a wife and daughter, and devotion as a mother, adopting her father's religious and political

12

principles and his moral courage and heroism. She is a vivacious lady, and exceedingly popular with her acquaintances. By his marriage with Mrs. Sawyers Dr. Boynton has four children, all born at Knoxville : (1). Lucille Boynton, born October 30, 1866; educated at the Academy of the Visitation, Georgetown, District of Columbia. (2). Ilia Boynton, born October 25, 1868; educated at same school. (3). Emerson Boynton, born May 6, 1872. (4). Edmee Boynton, born April 22, 1876.

By her first husband, Dr. James E. Sawyers, Mrs. Boynton has a daughter, Lillie, who married, December 21, 1883, Rev. Samuel Long, of the Methodist Episcopal church, South, at Okolona, Mississippi, where they now reside.

Dr. Boynton is a Master Mason, a member of the East Tennessee Medical Society, and in politics is Republican. His success in life has come of his application to business and study, by becoming qualified for a surgeon and physician, recognizing pathology as the basis of all treatment, and treating every case on its own merits, shaping his course to meet as many indications as careful diagnoses bring to his knowledge.

NATHANIEL WILSON BAPTIST.

COVINGTON.

THIS gentleman was born in Mecklenburg county, Virginia, October 10, 1846. The names of his ancestors are closely interwoven with the history of that county; more than one of them held the office of county court clerk there. The office in fact was never held by any one outside of that family from the first organization of the county in colonial times, till 1856, when the father of N. W. Baptist resigned, and the office, for the first time, passed out of the family.

The subject of this sketch was the son of Richard B. and Mary L. Baptist, who had only one other child, Mary Winifred Baptist. He attended school in the preparatory department of Randolph Macon College, Virginia, till he was fourteen years old, where he acquired the reputation of a lively, mischievous, intelligent boy, popular with his school-fellows, and at the same time successful in his studies, and of good standing in his class. At this time (early in 1861), Virginia became the seat of civil war, and his father placed him under the training and instruction of Ralph H. Graves, of Granville, North Carolina. School restraints were impossible for spirited school-boys in those stirring times and as early as May 27, 1863, he was to be found in the ranks of company A, First Virginia infantry, Walker's brigade, he being then a little over sixteen years old. In February, 1864, he was transferred to the Eighteenth Virginia regiment, Hunton's brigade, and before he was of the military age, May 1, 1864, was elected second lieutenant. He was present at the battles of Stanton River, Burgess' Mills, Hatcher s Run, Sailor's Creek and Slash Cottage. He was never wounded, never in hospital, and never unable for duty a day. He was taken prisoner at Sailor's Creek and carried to Point Lookout, Maryland, where he remained till August 24, when he was discharged and sent home.

With the establishment of peace, the young man's desires for the completion of his education revived, but alas, were frustrated for want of means. He did enter at Randolph Macon College, but after a few months study there, found it necessary to seek the means of subsistence. He began at the foot of the ladder, and was employed as porter in the grocery house of H. G. Thomas. Seeing no prospect of promotion from this humiliating position, he returned, after a few months to Mecklenburg county, and secured the office of deputy sheriff in the same court in which his father and other progenitors had served as county court clerk. After a few months' service in this office, he entered the law office of Thomas F. Goode, and remained there as clerk and student about eighteen months. He here acquired that familiarity with the procedure of the law courts and those habits of strict attention to business which qualified him for success in future life. Seeking a field for the exertion of these faculties, he found himself, in 1869, in Memphis, with but little money and no friend to promote his advancement. Deficient in means to sustain him in that rather expensive city, he put out and drifted to Mason Station, in Tipton county, Tennessee. Here he found employment for two years in the grocery house of R. F. Maclin & Co., and then became a partner in a drug and grocery establishment under the style of Reid & Baptist. This was his business till 1875.

He now took the first step in official life, for which his previous training had so well qualified him, being elected mayor and justice of the peace. The next year he became chairman and financial agent of the county court, in which office he inaugurated important financial reforms. He was re-elected in 1877. In 1878 he was elected clerk of the county court, and removed to Covington, the county seat of Tipton. In 1882 he at length attained the object he had been aiming at from his boyhood by being admitted to the bar, on examination before Judge Thomas J. Flippin and Chancellor Henry J. Livingston. He already ranks among the foremost members of the Covington bar.

He is a Democrat in politics, and a member of the Presbyterian church, in which he has been for several years a ruling elder. He is a Mason, Knight of Honor, a Master Workman, and a member of the Knights and Ladies of Honor.

He married on the 18th of January, 1871, Miss Belle H. Boyd, whose father, Col. Frank W. Boyd, was for years a member of the Virginia State Legislature. They lived in Mecklenburg county, Virginia, the native county of Mr. Baptist himself. Her mother was Miss Isabella Townes, daughter of Col. Townes, a wealthy citizen of Mecklenburg county, of which he was for many years sheriff. He was also a member of the Virginia Legislature, both before and after the war. Mrs. Baptist is a lady of attractive and dignified presence, modest, gentle, amiable and hospitable, much beloved by her husband's friends and her own. She is a sincere and devout member of the Presbyterian church. They have four children, namely: Frank Boyd and Richard Bannister, Belle T. and Mary L.

Thus, with a modest home, cheered by the presence of a loving wife and affectionate children, and well furnished with books and other appliances of intellectual recreation, he has always at hand a tranquil and happy retreat from the wearing toils of his profession.

His ancestors, on the paternal side, were French Huguenots, and in the early records of the Mecklenburg county court, the name is spelt with the French termination "Baptiste." His mother's ancestors were of Scotch-Irish descent. On both sides members of the courts and Legislature of Virginia are found at frequent intervals.

HON. MICHAEL BURNS.

NASHVILLE.

THIS gentleman came to Tennessee in 1836, a foreigner by birth, belonging to the working class of society, and has here made a fine fortune and a still finer reputation as a man of integrity and impulsive kindness and generosity. He began as a saddler, and has been successively a leather merchant, president of two railroads, president of a bank, and State senator.

Michael Burns was born in county Sligo, Ireland, March, 1813. His father, Patrick Burns, and his mother, Catharine Clark, were both natives of Ireland. His father was in good circumstances, and held some of the most important offices in the county Sligo, and in point of integrity none stood higher. His mother's relatives held positions of great responsibility. He was only nine years old when his father died and fifteen at the death of his mother. He went to school in the old country seven years, and became a fair English scholar. At an early age he was apprenticed to the saddler's trade in Sligo; emigrated to Quebec, Canada, in July, 1831 (then eighteen years of age), and shortly after went to Montreal. From there he went to New York city, and thence to Nashville, in 1836. Remaining in Nashville one year, he went to the old town of Jefferson, Rutherford county, spending two years at his business. In 1839 he returned to Nashville, and permanently located, engaging in the saddlery, saddlery hardware and leather business until the civil war broke out.

In his physical make and his mental characteristics and manners, Mr. Burns is a typical "fine old Irish gentleman," of broad, strong build, outspoken and downright in his utterances, companionable, humorous, and sunny in his disposition. He has a broad, comprehensive mind, is a fine talker and a good writer, and generally succeeds in impressing his views upon his hearers without wrangling; talks plain, to the point, and with sincerity. A man of lofty integrity, wanting always and only to do right, he is always independent. It used to be a common saying about Nashville that "Gov. Andy Johnson had as much confidence in Mike Burns as in any other man."

November 29, 1853, Mr. Burns was elected director of the Nashville and Northwestern railroad, and vice-president October 27, 1861. In 1864 he was elected president, serving until August 10, 1868. He was also president of the Nashville and Chattanooga railroad—two different roads, but having offices filled by men who were connected with both. He was re-elected three times to these positions.

From 1853 to 1859 he was a director of the Bank of Tennessee, and from 1859 to 1865 a director of the Union Bank of Tennessee. In 1870 he was elected president of the First National Bank of Nashville. Since 1878 he has been a director in the Third National and American National Banks of Nashville, and for some twenty years has also been a director of the Nashville Commercial Insurance Company.

In addition to the offices he has held in connection with Tennessee railroads and banks, Mr. Burns was also elected State senator from Davidson county in 1882. During his term in the senate he was chairman of the committee on banking and a member of the ways and means committee. In the senate he manifested that independence and open expression of his sentiments that has characterized him as a private citizen through life. He has also been most favorably mentioned as a proper man to fill the high office of governor of Tennessee.

Mr. Burns had a large influence in shaping the course of the Federal administration in matters pertaining to Tennessee. He was on intimate and friendly relations with Andrew Johnson when he was governor and afterwards when he became president, and was particularly admired by President Lincoln, who once gave him an interview of four hours when crowds were waiting to see him.

There was a battery of artillery in the Confederate army called after him—the Burns' Artillery—but he was never an active rebel, though he harmonized with the State in the rebellion, his family and property all being here, and though it was not his wish that the State should go into rebellion, yet when it seceded he gave his aid in that direction. As soon as the Federal army arrived he showed them a great deal of friendship, both officers and men, and singular to say he had the confidence of the authorities on both sides. It was the respect that broad good sense and manliness command from all men.

The following letter, besides showing the intimate relations existing between Mr. Burns and Gov. Johnson, also has an historic value:

STATE OF TENNESSEE, EXECUTIVE DEPARTMENT,
NASHVILLE, TENN., January 21, 1864.

DEAR SIR:—I have the pleasure of commending to your consideration my old friend, Michael Burns, of the city of Nashville. Mr. Burns is a gentleman of high standing in the city, and rare business qualifications. He is the president of the Nashville and Chattanooga and the Northwestern railroads, and by his energy, skill, and capital has contributed largely to the successful progress of the latter road, which, as you are advised, is now in running order to the Tennessee river. The government owes him much for his hearty co-operation with the Secretary of War and others in constructing this great military and commercial enterprise, by which we soon can be relieved from the exacting extortions of the Louisville and Nashville road, and all the troops and munitions of war can be transported over a much shorter, cheaper, and more secure and, at all seasons, certain line, to this point. Mr. Burns visits Washington on important business, which he will lay before you, and any assistance or kindness you may be pleased to give him will be heartily appreciated and conferred upon an esteemed friend and worthy gentleman. I have the honor to be, with great regard, your obedient servant,   ANDREW JOHNSON.

ABRAHAM LINCOLN,
    President of the United States.

[ENDORSED.] Hon. Secretary of War, please see and hear the bearer, Mr. Burns.   A. LINCOLN.
August 3, 1864.

Andrew Johnson and Mr. Burns were intimate personal friends for thirty years, and time seemed to increase their mutual appreciation.

It is needless to say that Mr. Burns is, by virtue of his Irish blood, and by associations this side of the water, a life-long Democrat. During the war, though a Union man, the State having seceded, he, being a foreigner, acquiesced and went with it, believing he had no right to go against the majority. Naturally enough he co-operated with the Confederacy. The war and results perplexed him greatly.

During the war Mr. Burns busied himself in relieving the poor, getting prisoners released, executions stayed, and in procuring pardons for prisoners.

The following, in his own words, is illustrative of the man: "Whilst in Washington, in 1864, I called upon President Lincoln, when I was promptly admitted to his office, and he appeared glad to see me. I had called on him previously on railroad business. Whilst we were in conversation, a young man entered the office, and the President said to him, 'I sent for you to ask what knowledge you have of the prisoners who are to be executed to-morrow, having been sentenced by a court-martial for desertion.' The young man answered that he knew the sergeant, who was a native of Rhode Island; that the prisoner had sent for and given him a last message for his mother and sister, with whom he was acquainted; had shed tears and deplored his fate. The President said that, under a decision of a court-martial, they were to be executed next day, telling me of the circumstances of their desertion. I asked him to permit me to say a few words in extenuation of their crime. He asked for my reasons why the sentence should not be enforced, when I said that it appeared that one of them was a sergeant in the regular army, the others were privates; their regiments were stationed in Washington, and that they got one thousand dollars each to go as substitutes for men who were drafted to serve in the army; that this appeared a very large sum to these men, and that the sergeant sent the money to his mother and sister, who were needy, and went to the front to fight the rebels, where he could serve his country best; gave up his rank in the army and his ease in Washington; and for his filial act the great government of the United States desires to kill him. Had they gone over to the enemy I would not say a word in their defense. Mr. Lincoln said, with animation, that he would pardon them, they should not die, and expressed pleasure at my presence—in the natural kindness of his heart seeming glad of a reason for exercising clemency. Other matters came up where life and death were in the balance, and in every instance my suggestions were adopted. A better man I never knew. After a four hours' visit I left, but was urgently pressed to call whenever in Washington, but alas, I never saw him again."

Mr. Burns never took the oath of allegiance to either government, but was loyal to the "powers that be," whether Federal or Confederate. His policy during the war seems to have been to take care of his railroads, in which he was very successful. During this presidency of the Nashville and Chattanooga and Northwestern railroads he was sorely pressed in 1866 by the officers of the government to pay in part for the material he purchased for the road from the quartermaster's department, but by an appeal to President Johnson the payment was postponed until a settlement could be made, or time given the road to earn the money. In

May, 1865, after Johnson became president, he got an order from him to bring out cotton, and secured about one thousand two hundred and fifty-four bales belonging to the road; sold some in Boston, depositing the money in a New York bank to pay interest on the road's indebtedness. The balance he sold in Liverpool, depositing the money in the Bank of the Republic, New York, to pay coupons due there, all monies going to build the unfinished road and to pay its indebtedness. His judgment and management gave him a place on the roll of honor which few men can boast.

An investigation by a committee of the State senate in 1870–71 resulted in a long report to the senate, showing, what his whole previous life in all relations, public and private, had already shown, that Mr. Burns is an honest, square man. The senate committee in this report says (see House Journal Appendix, 1870–71, page 821, *et seq.*): "At the time said road was turned over to Mr. Burns, in September, 1865, of the ninety-two miles west of the Tennessee river only about fifty had ever been constructed, and that had not been operated for years. The iron had been torn up by the United States authorities and removed for about thirty miles of the route. The embankment had washed, cuts caved in, and cross-ties rotted, as well as all bridges and trestles of every kind, and that part which was left had grown up in wild growth, so that it was as costly and difficult to rebuild that portion of the road which had been built as that which had never been touched. The committee here beg leave to call attention to the economical manner in which Mr. Burns, as president of said company, husbanded the small means at his disposal for the construction of said ninety-eight miles of road, to which must be added the immense bridge over the Tennessee river, and the committee deem it but just to Mr. Burns also to commend the dispatch with which said herculean task was accomplished. Ninety-three miles of railroad built in eighteen months, with the bridge over the Tennessee river, is a feat, the like of which is not often performed in building roads, and is not only in happy contrast with the tardy progress made by his predecessors and others who have undertaken the construction of railroads; it also compares favorably with the rapidity with which the great Pacific was built."

Mr. Burns was married in Nashville, March 14, 1842, to Miss Margaret Gilliam, who was born in Ireland, daughter of William Gilliam, a queensware merchant, who was lost in the Arctic ocean in 1856. Her mother was a Donnelly, also a native of Ireland. To his wife Mr. Burns attributes in a large degree his financial success, as he never did any good until he got married. After his marriage he managed to save one hundred and fourteen dollars, with which he began business and laid the foundation of his handsome fortune. His partner in all of his successes, the sharer of his struggles and the true helpmate of his life, departed this life after a brief illness, in Nashville September 1, 1885. She was a member of the Methodist church at the time of her marriage, while Mr. Burns is a Roman Catholic, but she joined the Catholic church in 1844.

When the writer asked Mr. Burns how much he is now worth he replied, "Well, I am not in debt." When questioned as to what methods he had employed in succeeding, he answered: "I never made a promise unless I intended to fulfill it, and did fulfill it. I never failed in business, and was never sued for a debt of my own. Always ambitious to stand in the front rank among men, my credit in Nashville was above that of many men worth more than myself. When other men were frolicking around having a good time I was attending to business. I kept my own books for a number of years, and did my own correspondence. My motto in business has always been, Honesty. I never sold an article to a man for good unless it was good, or if the purchaser found it was not so I made it good. I did the heaviest business in my line that had ever been done in Nashville. I never kept a poor man out of his money. I had fairly good habits in youth; never abused my system; read every thing that came in my way. Among my companions I was popular, and was something of a guide to them. I always felt that to meet great men as my equals and to control them was my right. I have been well treated by great and good men, and through life never paid less than one hundred cents on the dollar."

THOMAS L. MADDIN, M.D.

NASHVILLE.

THIS gentleman, whose name will descend in the medical history of Tennessee, stands eminent among the prominent members of the medical profession.

Dr. Maddin, as co-editor of the *Monthly Record of Medicine and Surgery* at Nashville, from 1857 to 1861; as professor and lecturer in Shelby Medical college, Nashville, Tennessee; as one of the most successful surgeons in the South, having performed exceptionally difficult and delicate surgical operations; by the number of years, between 1857 and 1885, that he has occupied various professorships in the Nashville medical schools, and as a successful private practitioner, ranks high in the noblest of all professions. As a teacher, his style is full, accurate and clear; as a professor, he is a sound and reliable exponent of advanced medical science, while his learning and skill as a diagnostician are recognized by his professional brethren wherever his name is known.

Though of gentle and sympathetic nature, he is self-possessed, unembarrassed, and self-reliant in medical or surgical emergencies, and proceeds alike with equanimity, celerity and dexterity. No physician's life better illustrates the saying of Dr. Menees, that "the practice of medicine is a pleasure, a service and a sacrifice," than that of Dr. Maddin, who, when a call is made, has no respect to weather, his own peril, or the pecuniary or social position of the patient.

But what writer, not a physician, can know or assign to his proper medical rank the physician and surgeon? From the very nature of the profession his lectures can be attended only by medical students, and can not be reported. So of a physician's practice; it is all private and of a nature too delicate to be discussed. His skill, the result of a life of study, can only be judged by the results of his practice; in testimony of which but few professional men can claim a more hearty endorsement of the community in which he lives, of the profession of which he is a member, and a larger and more grateful clientage than Dr. Maddin. As a citizen he is liberal and progressive in matters of public interest.

Thomas L. Maddin was born in Columbia, Tennessee, September 4, 1826. In 1845 he graduated A. B. from Lagrange college, Alabama, and in March, 1849, took his medical degree from the medical department of the University of Louisville, under Profs. Gross, Drake, Caldwell (a connecting link between ancient and modern medicine), Cobb, Yandell and Miller. After receiving his diploma he practiced four years in Limestone county, Alabama, in partnership with his former preceptor, Dr. Jonathan McDonald, a man of very high professional claims, and of preeminent ability in the practical duties, both of physician and surgeon. In April, 1853, Dr. Maddin settled in Nashville. From 1856 to 1858 he was professor of anatomy, and from 1858 to 1861, professor of surgery in Shelby Medical College, Nashville. From 1869 to 1873 he was professor of the institutes of medicine in the University of Nashville, and from 1873, professor of the institutes and practice of medicine and clinical medicine in the same institution, and also from that date (1873), professor of the same branch in the medical department of Vanderbilt University, both of which positions he still fills (1885). From 1873 he has also been president of the faculty of the medical department of the University of Nashville and Vanderbilt University.

Dr. Maddin is a member of the Nashville Medical Society; the Tennessee State Medical Society, of which he has served as president; the American Association; the American Medical Association; and in 1876 was a Tennessee delegate to the International Medical College at Philadelphia.

In the first year of the late war, during the occupation of Nashville by the Confederate States army, he had the management of a large hospital in the city. The wounded of both armies sent from the battle of Fort Donelson, and a large number of Confederate sick were left in his care when Gen. Johnston retreated to Shiloh, and were surrendered by him on the occupation by the Federal army.

From the beginning of the late war for six or seven years, educational enterprises were in a state of chaos at Nashville, as it was the Federal military base of the "Army of the Cumberland." For several years after peace was declared it was necessary to enforce a military despotism to prevent anarchy. Dr. Maddin remained in the city, and though from nativity, education and socially, in sympathy and fellowship with the people of the South, yet, politically, he was loyal to the integrity of the Union. But the interpretation of those in authority admitted no conditions of divided loyalty; demanding not only that of the head but also of the heart. Yet he demeaned himself with the good judgment to command the respect and professional confidence of the medical staff and officers stationed in the city, who availed themselves liberally of his medical skill, both for themselves and their families. He was thus enabled to be of service to many citizens, who were resting under the censure of disloyalty, and justly, for there were but few families not represented in the Confederate States army. On one occasion, while attending upon the wife of a major-general, stationed at Nashville, for typhoid fever, some eight or ten staff officers were awaiting in the parlor to hear the report of the Doctor. When he announced the patient much improved, the party received the report with much satisfaction; and this led to many social pleasantries. The doctor laid a complaint in his own behalf before them: "that the officers in command at Nashville did not recognize his social, professional and personal merits." They inquired, one and all, "How so? Don't we send for you when we are sick? and we do not remember to have been remiss in polite consideration." "Not that," he responded, "for on that score you extend more than I merit; but it is this, that I am about the only citizen of Nashville you have not honored with a place among the convicts in the penitentiary; for you have made it the post of honor with our best citizens." They responded with much pleasantness: "Doctor, don't give yourself discomfort on that score; we have not overlooked you, for you would have been there too, but we have use for you professionally." This incident illustrates his good sense, prudence and judgment; for although he was classed by them with the South, yet he commanded their confidence and respect.

Whether his reputation be best based on the learning displayed in his lectures, on the success of his practice as a private physician, or on his skill as a surgeon, it is hard for the writer to determine, but the fact is easily stated that he has devoted his best energies to the study and practice of medicine, and consecrated the activities of a busy life to his profession with a loyalty alike creditable to himself and to science. He has successfully performed most of the capital surgical operations, among them ovariotomy; ligation of the external iliac, femoral, hypogastric and circumflex ilii, all in the same operation for traumatic aneurism of the external iliac; ligation of the left subclavian artery, also for traumatic aneurism. This operation was, under the circumstances, deemed impracticable by able and experienced surgeons in consultation. The patient was a distinguished officer of the First Tennessee Confederate regiment. On a second consultation with Dr. Frank H. Hamilton, of New York, who was serving in high official rank on the medical staff of the Federal army, and then on duty at Nashville, who, in common with other able counselors, agreed that, though a forlorn hope, the operation gave the only chance for the patient's life, tendered his valuable assistance to Dr. Maddin in executing the work. Some of Dr. Maddin's other difficult though alike successful operations were: hip joint amputation in a child about two years old; removal of superior maxillary and palate bones, etc.

On his paternal side Dr. Maddin is of Irish extraction. His grandfather, Maddin, was an Irish patriot, and was compelled to leave that country as a refugee on account of his loyalty to his native land. He settled in Philadelphia and died there.

Dr. Maddin's father was Rev. Thomas Maddin, D.D., a clergyman of the Methodist Episcopal church, South, and for upwards of sixty years an itinerant preacher. He was stationed in Nashville, Tennessee, as early as 1817, and organized the first church Sunday-school in that city. He repeatedly represented his conference in the General Conference of the church. From his personal character he was not only esteemed but sincerely loved by all with whom he had ministerial, social and personal relations. He was a firm, stern, uncompromising man on all questions where right was concerned, yet gentle and kind, and of a most lovable nature. His native modesty and sensitiveness of character were such that he was always shocked at unrefined or profane language used in his presence, and would turn away from the company of that kind. He was not only a very distinguished divine, but ranked among the foremost, both in council and in pulpit, as one of the highest dignitaries of his church. A natural born orator, he did much to popularize and advance Methodism in Kentucky, Tennessee and Alabama. He was also a Mason of high rank, and for a time was Grand Lecturer of the Grand Lodge of Tennessee. He died in Nashville in 1874, at the age of seventy-six.

Dr. Maddin's mother's maiden name was Miss Sarah Moore, a native of Kentucky, of an old Maryland family. Her father was a farmer near Louisville, Kentucky. She was devoted to her family and her domestic duties, and her life was characterized by great gentleness and purity, traits which her children seem to have largely inherited. It is said of her that she was never heard to speak a harsh word. Her children obeyed her, not through fear, but because they loved, honored and revered her, which made it always their pleasure to shape their conduct in accordance with her teachings and her wishes. Her's was that sort of family discipline that made the children feel punished if they offended or disobeyed her. She died at her home near Huntsville, Alabama, in 1864, at the age of sixty-four, having been the mother of eight children: (1). Mary Maddin, wife of Dr. F. E. H. Steger, near Huntsville, Alabama. She has four children; Capt. Thomas M. Steger, a prominent lawyer at Nashville: Dr. Robert W. Steger, a successful physician, now living in Chicago; Mrs. James Jackson, of North Alabama, and Miss Alice Steger. (2). Dr. Thomas L. Maddin, subject of this sketch. (3). Prof. Ferdinand P. Maddin, a very successful educator, first at Athens, Alabama, then at Columbia, Tennessee, and last at Waco, Texas, where he has lived since 1857. He was for many years president of Waco College. He married Miss Mattie Malone, daughter of Thomas Hill Malone, a planter of Limestone county, Alabama. He has four children: Dr. Stith Maddin, of Waco; Thomas Maddin; Miss Josie Maddin and Miss Pearl Maddin. (4). Dr. John W. Maddin, an eminent physician of Nashville, whose biographical sketch appears elsewhere in this volume. (5). Margaret F. Maddin, now the widow of Andrew J. Connally. She has one child, Miss Ammie Connally. These two constitute Dr. Thomas L. Maddin's family, and make their home with him. Dr. Maddin has never married.

Though not a politician, Dr. Maddin is an hereditary Democrat. The only Whig vote he ever cast was for Hon. Gustavus A. Henry, for Governor of Tennessee, because the views of his opponent, Andrew Johnson, were something too agrarian to suit the doctor's political ideas.

Dr. Maddin has not only made a name among the leading physicians and surgeons of the South, but he has been comfortably successful financially. He began business life without inheritance, and has often been heard to say, of his youth and early manhood, it was the highest pride of his life to be self-sustaining. His note has never gone to protest. He has lost some money by endorsing for friends, but has made it a cardinal feature of his financial operations never to go in debt beyond his ability to check upon the bank. His success has come from his devotion to his profession and an ambition to qualify himself in the highest sense for its administration, loving it as a science and for the blessings it puts in his power to bestow upon his fellow men;

therefore he has practiced not altogether for pecuniary profit, but from a spirit of humanity and professional pride. He has never used tobacco, nor been a drinker of intoxicating spirits. Governed by the instructions of his good parents, the warp of his early education in Christianity has controlled his life. He has been a member of the Methodist church from early childhood, and believes it the duty of every one to identify themselves with some Christian institution, yet he is known to be liberal in reference to opinions and creeds, and very charitable in his judgment of men's motives and actions. His moral creed is to keep a conscience void of offense.

He had a liberal college education; his preference was the law, but his father wanted to make a preacher of him, so they compromised on medicine; the study of which, as a science, opens up to a man the noblest conceptions of nature, of his God and of his own destiny.

Dr. Maddin is five feet ten inches high, weighs one hundred and fifteen pounds, has fine silky hair and beard, a face unwrinkled and a form unstooped by the weight of years, though he is a man of the most delicate organization and of the finest sensibilities, as his splendid portrait, itself a study, shows at a glance. It is the very picture of health and amiability.

HON. JAMES CROGHAN HARREL.

ELBA.

THE peaceful, uneventful life of a planter, a country gentleman and a magistrate, who lives a life of dignity and usefulness in the place of his birth, may not present salient points of interest to stimulate the attention of strangers, but is apt to exemplify qualities (as in the present instance) more beneficial to society than the achievements of the military hero, or the intrigues of the political aspirant.

James C. Harrel was born near the little town of Elba, in Fayette county, October 5, 1839, where he still resides, honored and beloved by a community which could not have been uninformed if any stain had fallen upon his character, for he has been subject to their observation from childhood to the present day. The son of a planter, he adopted agriculture as the occupation of his choice, though qualified by education and intellect for any of the professions which attract the adhesion of ambitious youth.

From the age of six to thirteen he attended the country schools of his neighborhood, after which he was sent to Somerville, the county seat, thence to LaGrange College, and finally to Semple Broaddus College, Mississippi, which he left in 1859, during his junior year, returned home, devoted himself to farming, and married. Omitting the period of his service in the army, farming has been his leading occupation ever since.

He entered the Confederate States army in 1863, as first lieutenant in company C, Ballantine's regiment, and served with it in Mississippi, Alabama, Georgia and Tennessee, participating in the battles of Holly Springs (under Van Dorn), Jackson, the Georgia campaign from Dalton to Atlanta, and with Hood from the time of evacuation at Lovejoy, through the battles of Murfreesborough, Franklin and Nashville. He was surrendered at Selma, Alabama, under Gen. Frank Armstrong, in April, 1865.

Returning home after the war, he found himself stripped of everything except his land, of which, however, he resumed the cultivation under all the disadvantages which attended southern agriculture after our civil conflict.

In 1867 he established a store at Rossville, but moved his business, in 1870, to Elba, and still lives on the old homestead, and cultivates the old plantation.

Mr. Harrel has been a Democrat from his youth upward, and adheres tenaciously to the old party, taking an active interest in elections, but seeking none of the spoils of party warfare. He was elected a magistrate in 1876, and still holds the office. In 1884 he was elected to the State Legislature, a striking proof of the estimation in which he is held in Fayette county, which generally votes Republican by fifteen hundred majority. On taking his seat, he was placed on the committees on public schools, railroads, penitentiary, agriculture, public roads, labor, tippling and tippling-houses. He is a thorough business member, never absent from his post, active in business, without making speeches about it.

He is a Royal Arch Mason, a Knight of Honor, and a member of the Ancient Order United Workmen. He has been a member of the Christian church since 1874, though originally a Baptist.

His moral character is stainless. He was an obedient boy to his parents; was never drunk in his life; never bet a nickel on anything; was never in a house of ill-fame, but has lived consistently the life to which he was trained by his Christian parents.

Mr. Harrel's father, Ira Harrel, was born in Nash county, North Carolina, in 1802; he settled in Fayette county early in life, when that part of Tennessee was a wilderness. He, as well as his two sons, were all magistrates in their respective counties. He died October 20, 1856, leaving six children, namely: (1). Mattie A., widow of J. M. Williams. (2). James C., subject of this sketch. (3). Callie D., wife of Virginius H. Swift, a farmer. (4). Lucy A., wife of J. H. Mitchell, a farmer. (5). William R.; married Jennie Buchanan, of Williamson county, Tennessee; farmer, lawyer and magistrate of Collierville, Shelby county. (6). Ida T., died wife of Dr. John Buchanan, of Collierville, Tennessee, leaving a daughter, Blanche.

Mr. Harrel's mother was Temperance Barnes, born in Nash county, North Carolina, died October 13, 1879. She was a successful business manager during her widowhood, and a good mother.

Mr. Harrel married near Elba, Fayette county, Tennessee, March 17, 1859. His wife was Miss Fannie Mitchell (a schoolmate), born April 20, 1843, daughter of Thomas H. Mitchell, a planter, who died in the infancy of his daughter. Her mother, Elizabeth Newsom, was married by Mr. Mitchell in her North Carolina home. Mrs. Harrel is their only surviving child.

By his marriage with this lady Mr. Harrel became father of eleven children, ten of whom are still alive.

The survivors are: (1). William Clarence, born May 5, 1861; graduated at a commercial school, Atlanta, Georgia; married, November 19, 1884, Miss Florence Canada, a schoolmate, following herein his father's example; she was a daughter of the Rev. J. B. Canada, a Baptist clergyman. (2). James Elton, born August 1, 1864; graduated at a Memphis commercial school; he and his brother William constitute the firm of Harrel Brothers, druggists, Collierville, Tennessee. (3). John Lindsley, born February 7, 1866; engaged in farming. (4). Effie Celestine, born July 4, 1869, studying at Bellevue College. (5). Earl Herbert, born August 4, 1871. (6). Walter Ovid, born December 31, 1874. (7). Twins, Bessie May and Jesse June, born November 7, 1876; Bessie died July 23, 1877. (8). Susie Matthews, born June 23, 1878. (9). Frank T.; born December 13, 1880. (10). Cora Peck, born January 9, 1883. "Blessed is he that has his quiver full of them."

Mrs. Harrel has lived, since her marriage, a life of wise and devoted affection for this extensive family. The Harrels are of Irish descent.

CAPT. SAMUEL RANKIN LATTA.

DYERSBURG.

THE name Latta is Welsh, but the family came to America from Ireland. Capt. Samuel Rankin Latta's grandfather, John Latta, was born in Ireland, married a Miss Rankin there, and settled in eastern Pennsylvania, in the latter part of the last century. He was a millwright, and was killed in building a mill in western Pennsylvania. He left two children, John and Mary, the latter dying very young. John Latta became the father of the subject of this sketch. He was born in Lancaster county, Pennsylvania, in 1798, and was a saddler by trade, and noted for his industry, economy, sobriety and intelligence, and for being devoutly religious. He died in Dyersburg, Tennessee, at the age of seventy-six, leaving three surviving children, John G., William B. and Samuel R. John G. Latta has for fifteen years been postmaster at Newton, Massachusetts. William B. Latta died at Dyersburg, unmarried. Another son, James M. Latta, died in 1857. He married in Pennsylvania, and left two children, Lucy, now wife of John G. Seat, of Dyersburg, and Samuel J., now in mercantile life at Memphis.

Capt. Latta's mother, who died at Dyersburg in 1870, at the age of eighty-one, was born near Harrisburg, Pennsylvania, the daughter of John Gilchrist, a planter and slaveholder in Dauphin county, Pennsylvania. He was a lieutenant in the Revolutionary war. He married a Miss Berryhill, of Dauphin county. Capt. Latta's

mother was remarkable for her domestic economy and industry, and was animated with an ambition to raise her children respectably.

Samuel Rankin Latta was born December 2, 1827, in New Alexandria, Westmoreland county, Pennsylvania, but his father having moved to Blairsville, Indiana county, Pennsylvania, in 1837, the son went to the common schools and to academy there until the age of seventeen, when the father, no longer able to send him to school, allowed him to do for himself. In boyhood he did but little work, except at the age of fourteen, when he worked one year in his father's saddler's shop. When he started to the academy, which he attended three years, his ambition was to become a lawyer, but his hopes were deferred for a number of years. At the age of seventeen he taught school in Westmoreland county, Pennsylvania—taught school in winter and went to school himself in summer. He taught three years in Pennsylvania and three years, 1851-52-53, at Dyersburg, Tennessee. He, however, previous to coming to Dyersburg, attended Washington College, Washington, Pennsylvania, and also Jefferson College, Pennsylvania, from which latter institution he graduated in 1850, under President Brown. He made the money himself on which he was educated. When he started out in life at the age of twenty-three, he had, besides his education, a stout heart and a firm resolution, and

13

just forty-five cents in money. After graduating he came south looking for a situation as a school-teacher, because teaching paid better south than in the north. He came to Dyersburg by accident. He had taken passage on an Ohio river boat for Memphis, intending to go to Mississippi, when a fellow-passenger told him of a vacant situation at Dyersburg. He came to that town from Hickman, Kentucky, on foot, carrying a big carpet-bag, on which account Capt. Latta often laughs now, and calls himself an original carpet-bagger. He soon got a good situation, and soon after married and settled, and is still living in the house he first occupied, one-half mile out from the town.

He began studying law in Dyersburg in his twenty-fifth year, under his present partner, Col. T. E. Richardson, and was licensed by Chancellor John W. Harris and Judge John Read. He has continued in practice in Dyersburg from the date of his admission to the bar till the present, some thirty-five years, practicing in all the courts of the State and in all branches of the profession, but prefers chancery practice. A peculiarity of Col. Latta's methods is that he dissuades men from litigation, and he has probably broken up more lawsuits than most lawyers. Before juries and judges he relies on the merits of his cases, seldom indulges in long speeches, and has always got along pleasantly with both bench and bar.

In May, 1861, he took a company, "The Dyer Grays," of which he was captain, into the Confederate service, and joined Col. John V. Wright's (afterwards Col. A. J. Vaughn's) Thirteenth Tennessee infantry regiment. He fought at the battles of Belmont and Shiloh, and left the army after the latter engagement on account of domestic affliction which compelled his attendance at home.

Capt. Latta was raised by Presbyterian parents, and, indeed, his ancestors on both sides were orthodox Presbyterians for two hundred years. He joined the church in 1858, and for the last twenty-five years has been a ruling elder; served as lay delegate to the General Assembly at Knoxville in 1878, and several times in synods and presbyteries. He was also at one time continuously for fifteen years a Sunday-school superintendent.

Capt. Latta is a Democrat, recently a "sky-blue" Democrat, and in favor of paying dollar for dollar the State's indebtedness. It was doubtless the tenacity with which he has held to this principle that prevented his nomination and election to Congress, his friends having pressed his name before conventions several times.

In 1852 Capt. Latta was made a Master Mason in Hess Lodge No. 93, Dyersburg, and has taken the Chapter degrees. and filled all the offices in both Lodge and Chapter. He joined the Odd-Fellows in 1851, and passed all the chairs of both Lodge and Encampment. He became a Knight of Honor in 1881.

In 1870 he was appointed a director in the Mississippi River railroad.

In h's profession and general business he has been quite successful. He owns real estate in Dyersburg and several unimproved tracts in Dyer county. Paying close attention to his business and by trading some, he has, however, been on principle opposed to accumulating a big fortune for his children, believing that i is better to turn out a child with a good education and let him go and manage for himself. "If I had began life with a fortune," he once said, "I do not believe I should have been any account. Boys who are pushed out and forced to rely on themselves, make better citizens, and as a rule, make the most money." He has been all his life a very liberal donator to charitable enterprises, and his reputation in this line costs him a great deal annually. At no time in his life has he even been wild or dissipated. In managing his business he has frequently gone in debt, mostly for lands, but has always paid promptly, and was never sued on his own debt.

Capt. Latta married at Eaton, Gibson county, Tennessee, December 9, 1852, Miss Mary Grainger Guthrie a native of Greene county, East Tennessee, the daughter of John Guthrie, a Scotchman, and an iron manufacturer in East Tennessee at an early day. Her mother was Miss Minerva Wear, of East Tennessee. Mrs. Latta graduated in 1851 at the Columbia Female Institue Columbia, Tennessee, under Rector Smith, and is a lady who has the happy faculty of making everybody her friend; is of a most amiable disposition, loved especially by the young people, popular with all her associates, and a lady of strong will and fine intellect. Losing her parents at an early age, she was raised among strangers, and like her husband, had to make her way in the world. She taught a school one session before and one session after her marriage.

By his marriage with Miss Guthrie Capt. Latta has six children: (1). John G. Latta, born June 21, 1857 educated at Newton, Massachusetts, and at Poughkeepsie, New York, and by private teachers at home, and is now clerking in the Merchants National Bank, Little Rock, Arkansas. He married Miss Lee Poland, at Marshall, Texas, and has one child, a daughter, Leslie (2). Kate Latta, born October 17, 1859; educated at home by private teachers; married Prof. T. C. Gordon a native of Louisiana, and has three children, Mary Winfield Osceola and Sadie. (3). Sarah K. Latta, born February 12, 1862; educated by private teachers at home attended Mary Sharpe College, Winchester, Tennessee one year. (4). Mary Eleanor ("Nellie") Latta, born March 9, 1864; educated by private teachers at home (5). Frank Wallace Latta, born July 4, 1866: educated at Southwestern University, Clarksville, Tennessee. (6) Samuel Grainger Latta, born August 5, 1871.

Capt. Latta is a tall man with a flowing silvery beard and has the air of one who has seen the world and has little ambition for its honors. In manner, he is outspoken, pointed and emphatic. In all his dealings he is candid to a fault. His chief happiness is in his wife and in his children, whom he has happily succeeded in raising with credit. Moral and great families make great States, and he is the most patriotic citizen who bequeaths to his State intelligent, industrious and obedient children, of high moral tone, too proud to stoop to mean or little things, or to dishonorable practices or crooked methods.

JOHN WESLEY ELDER.

TRENTON.

JOHN WESLEY ELDER, the well-known Trenton banker and business man, was born in Rutherford county, Tennessee, June 4, 1819. His education was acquired mostly in the counting-room. When only eleven years old he became a clerk in the store of Niles & Elder, at Murfreesburough, his brother, James Elder, being the junior member of the firm. He remained with them four years, and then went to Trenton, Gibson county, Tennessee, in December, 1834, spending a few months with some relatives, then entered as clerk in a store at the village of Shady Grove, near where Milan now stands. Here he clerked eight months at ten dollars per month, one half of which he saved. From Shady Grove he returned to Trenton and took employment at two hundred dollars a year, under his brother, Benjamin Elder, one of the earliest merchants of West Tennessee. While doing business for him, he received in 1836 an invitation from a Rutherford county friend to go to Jacksonville, Alabama, and clerk for four hundred dollars per year. He accepted, and went by way of Florence, Tuscumbia, Decatur and Gunter's Landing, walking from the latter place to Jacksonville, a distance of sixty miles over the mountains. He remained at Jacksonville until the latter part of 1838, when he went traveling to Mobile and New Orleans, and finally back to Trenton with about six hundred dollars than he had made and saved—a very good start for a boy just turned nineteen years of age.

On January 1, 1840, he went into partnership with his brother, Benjamin, and these two did business together as merchants some twenty years, with good success. In 1852 he was elected a director of the branch Bank of Tennessee, at Trenton, and in 1854 was elected president of the same institution, but resigned during the course of the year. When the war broke out Mr. Elder was in possession of a very handsome property, the fruits of his exemplary industry and economy.

However, the happiest event of Mr. Elder's life occurred in June, 1841, when, at Jacksonville, Alabama, he married Miss Martha G. Houston. It was a true-love match, and the newly married young people began their life-long honeymoon by riding on horseback from Jacksonville to Trenton, a distance of two hundred and sixty-five miles, which they accomplished in seven days, it being before the era of railroads—even buggies being almost unknown in that section, and when it was difficult to find houses at which to spend the nights. Miss Houston was a daughter of Maj. Matthew McClung Houston, native of Blount county, East Tennessee, and kin to the Houston, Gillespie and McClung families of that section. Her great-grandfather and the grandfather of the celebrated Gen. Sam. Houston were brothers. Her mother, Mary Gillespie, was the daughter of Esq. John Gillespie, of Blount county, Tennessee.

Mrs. Elder died at Trenton July 23, 1879, and now (together with her father and mother, Maj. M. M. Houston, and wife), lies buried in the cemetery at Trenton. Mrs. Elder's only brother, James M. Houston, is a very reputable merchant, now head of the house of Houston, West & Co., St. Louis. Mrs. Elder was educated at Jacksonville, Alabama, and was a lady of very graceful person, and exceptionally excellent as a Christian, wife, mother, friend and neighbor. Her judgment was almost unerring, and to her husband she proved a wise counselor, a helpmate, indeed, and all that a good woman with a good head and a good heart could be.

Ten children were born unto them, six of whom are living and four dead. The latter were: (1). Henry Houston Elder, born August 17, 1842; died May 8, 1854. (2). Mary Eloise Elder, born May 29, 1850; died April 23, 1854. (3). Sallie May Elder, born November 4, 1854; married Alexander B. White, of Paris, Tennessee, October 19, 1881; died September 12, 1882. (4). Robert Elder, died in infancy.

The children now living are as follows: (1). Leander Melville Elder, born July 16, 1847; graduated at Andrew College, Trenton; and then spent three years at the University of Virginia; now practicing law at Chattanooga; married, in 1876, Miss Mollie E. Saffarans, of Memphis, and has three children, Blanche, Irene and George. (2). Irene Amelia Elder; graduated in Trenton under the tuition of Prof. William K. Jones, now president of Martin College, Pulaski; married in 1872 Dr. Thomas J. Hoppel, who was educated at the Southern University, Greensborough, Alabama, and graduated in medicine at Bellevue Hospital Medical

College, New York; has two children living, Tom and Horace. (3). Mattie Louise Elder; graduated at Jackson, Tennessee, under Dr. J. E. Bright; married Robert F. Ross, a hardware merchant at Trenton, and has one child, Albert. (4). Lucie Belle Elder; graduated at Clarksville, Tennessee, in 1879. (5). Gracie Elder; completed her education at Pulaski under Prof. William K. Jones. (6). Albert Sidney Elder, born January 14, 1862; educated at Trenton, and since 1881 has been in the banking business with his father.

The Elder family is from Virginia, but originally came from England. Mr. Elder's father, William Elder, came from Dinwiddie county, Virginia, to Rutherford county, Tennessee, about 1810, and lived a farmer. He was a soldier in the war of 1812. In 1837, he moved to Gibson county, Tennessee, and died there in 1851, at the good old age of eighty-five years. He was a passionate man, of florid complexion, high-strung temperament, and remarkable for integrity of character, for his word was his bond.

Mr. Elder's mother, nee Miss Mary Towler, was the daughter of Benjamin and Martha Towler, of Charles City county, Virginia, near Richmond. Benjamin Towler was a soldier in the Revolutionary war.

Mrs. Elder was a lady of remarkable patience; a most inflexible Christian, of great strength and fortitude of character, yet of a singularly calm and sweet disposition; deliberate and philosophic in her views of life. She was a great lover of Christian literature, and always had in her house her religious papers and periodicals. She died in January, 1865, at her son's house in Trenton, leaving six children, only four of whom are now living: (1). Benjamin Elder, now eighty-one years old, living on his farm one mile from Trenton. (2). James Elder, the prominent banker at Memphis, whose portrait and sketch appear elsewhere in this volume, and which should be read in connection with this biography. (3). Monroe B. Elder, now a farmer and stock raiser, four and a half miles from Trenton. (4). John Wesley Elder, subject of this sketch.

When the late war came on Mr. John W. Elder, who although as has been seen, was a quiet, successful business man, considered it his patriotic duty to volunteer in defense of the Confederate cause. He enlisted as a member of Col. Hill's Forty-seventh Tennessee regiment, and at the bloody battle of Shiloh, in April, 1862, was badly wounded by a minnie ball, which made a permanent indentation in his head, deep as an acorn cup.

After the war, having lost four years of time, as well as his negroes and most of his other property, he went to Cincinnati, in September, 1865, to try and retrieve his fortunes. He did business for Duncan, Ford & Co., wholesale grocers, three months in 1865, and all of 1866, on a salary, at first, of two hundred dollars per month, which was raised to five thousand dollars a year. On January 1, 1867, he was admitted as a member of the firm, which conducted business under the style of Duncan, Ford & Elder, remaining in that firm in the wholesale grocery business until December 31, 1878. He then returned to Trenton, and organized the Gibson county Bank, of which institution he was elected president, and has continued in that position ever since. He is also a director in the Trenton Cotton Seed Oil Mills, and in the Trenton Cotton Factory Company.

In politics Mr. Elder is a Democrat, and cast his first vote for James K. Polk for governor of Tennessee.

He belongs to the Methodist church, which he joined in 1833, and has served as class-leader, steward, Sunday-school superintendent, and lay delegate to annual conferences. He was one year lay delegate to the conference at Paducah. He is the only living member of the official board of Trenton station, organized in 1839. Something in his history of which he is very proud, is the fact that he has been superintendent of the Sunday-school thirty-three years. Very early in life he became identified with his church; his parents were pious, and he has from boyhood tried to walk worthily of the Christian character, and to square his life by the Word of God, which teaches one to be both fervent in spirit and diligent in business. It may be said, he was born industrious; there is not a drop of lazy blood in his system, for he loves work, loves to be honest, and to deal on principles of square justice and equity. As a business man he has sought to inform himself through all channels accessible to him, and has kept wide awake, as the presence on his table of such works as "*Hunt's Merchants' Magazine*," "*The Bankers' Magazine*," and other such eminent authorities amply testify. His character and his methods furnish a shining example to the young business men of Tennessee.

COL. JAMES L. GAINES.

NASHVILLE.

COL. GAINES was born in Knoxville, December 3, 1836, but in his thirteenth year moved with his father to Buncombe county, North Carolina, where, as in Knoxville, he did business as a merchant. He was educated at the University of North Carolina, at Chapel Hill, and graduated there in 1859. His college course completed, he studied law for a year under Judge Bailey, at Black Mountain, North Carolina, and obtained license from Chief Justice Pearson, of the Supreme Court of that State; he never, however, practiced law in his life. He moved the same year to St. Charles, Missouri, and became professor of mathematics in the college of that name, but in 1861 returned to North Carolina and entered the Confederate army, his father furnishing him a horse and equipments, and hurrying him off, "lest," as he said, " he should be too late for the fight" (the first battle of Manassas); he was too late, but participated in every other in which his command was engaged. He commenced service in the first North Carolina cavalry as a private, under the command of Col. Robert Ransom, brother of the present United States Senator from North Carolina, and was promoted sergeant, lieutenant, adjutant of his regiment, then adjutant of the North Carolina cavalry brigade, afterwards colonel of the second North Carolina cavalry, and was recommended by W. H. F. Lee for a brigadier's commission, too late for the recommendation to be acted on, the calamity of Appomattox intervening. He was at first in Wade Hampton's division, afterwards in that of W. H. F. Lee, but always in the great cavalry corps of J. E. B. Stewart, under whose command he participated in the retreat from Centreville, the battles around Richmond, the fight at Brandy Station, in the first Maryland campaign, the Pennsyvania campaign, including Gettysburg, and all the subsequent great battles, including Fredericksburg, Chancellorsville, and the campaign around Richmond and Petersburg. At the battle of Five Forks he was wounded in the elbow-joint, and amputation became necessary. This occurred only ten days before the surrender at Appomattox; at which he was present, having traveled thither in an ambulance.

To anticipate matters a little, on arriving home he presented himself with an empty sleeve to the lady to whom he was engaged, offering to release her on account of his mutilation and his poverty. She refused to be released and a marriage soon followed.

As soon as he was able to travel, Col. Gaines returned to St. Louis, covered with the honors of war, but stripped of every thing else. The marriage above alluded to took place. The lady was Miss Belle Porter, a native of St. Mary's, Ohio, only daughter of Erastus Porter, a wealthy retired merchant of that place. The marriage took place November 22, 1865; Mr. Porter died four years after.

After his marriage Col. Gaines moved to New York and engaged in the wholesale grocery business, the style of the firm being Harris, Gaines & Co. The firm established a branch concern in Savannah, Georgia, and Col. Gaines went to that city to manage the business there.

In 1869 he moved to Knoxville and engaged in the shoe trade in partnership with his brother, Ambrose

Gaines, and was so occupied till elected comptroller of the State treasury, when he removed to Nashville. He was first elected to this office by the Legislature of Tennessee, in 1875, and re-elected in 1877 and 1879, serving in all six years, under Govs. James D. Porter and Albert S. Marks.

Since his first election as comptroller he has resided in Nashville, and is now of the firm of Duncan & Gaines, brokers, miners and coal merchants.

The grandfather of Col. Gaines was Ambrose Gaines, originally from Culpepper Court-house, Virginia, settled in Sullivan county, Tennessee, and became successful as a pioneer and farmer there. He was of the same family with Gen. Edmond Pendleton Gaines. Matthew Gaines, his son, was the father of Col. Gaines, the subject of this sketch. He was born in Sullivan county, Tennessee, but was living in Knoxville when Col. Gaines was born. Some years afterwards, he moved to Buncombe county, North Carolina, where he was long engaged in business. He is now living with his son in his seventy-ninth year. He is a member of the Methodist church, of which he has been trustee and steward. He is also a Royal Arch Mason, and a Democrat.

Col. Gaines' mother was a Miss Margaret Luttrel, a native of Knox county, Tennessee, daughter of James C. Luttrel, a large farmer and slaveholder. She is now living in Nashville with Col. Gaines, in her sixty-eighth year. Her mother was Martha Armstrong, of the East Tennessee family of Armstrongs. Col. Gaines' maternal uncle, James C. Luttrel, was comptroller of the treasury of Tennessee in 1855-6-7.

Mrs. Gaines, wife of the colonel, was educated at St. Charles, and at St Louis, Missouri. She is a member of the Episcopal church, and is noted for her beauty and her remarkably youthful appearance. They have had three children : (1). Ambrose Porter, born in New York, November 6, 1866 ; now a student at Nashville. (2). Lillian, born in Savannah, Georgia, December 17, 1868, died at Nashville, April, 1876. (3). James L., born in the Maxwell House, Nashville, September, 1878.

Col. Gaines is a member and vestryman of the Protestant Episcopal church, a Master Mason, a member of the Royal Arcanum, and of the Knights of Honor. In politics he is a Democrat, but not an active partisan. Requested to state his methods of life he answered : " I have always tried to do my duty in whatever position I have been placed."

He is six feet high, of slender frame, weighs one hundred and forty-eight pounds, without his arm, has a long head, clear face and high forehead. To this editor he appears an exceptionally modest and retiring man, content to do his duty and take his share of the world's work.

THOMAS LIPSCOMB, M.D.

SHELBYVILLE.

THIS gentleman was born in Louisa county, Virginia, July 22, 1808. He was brought up on a farm to do all sorts of work, such as coopering, house building and stocking plows, as well as farm work proper. He was not a college man, but received his education in the common schools of Virginia. In 1826 he left the "Old Dominion," and moved with his father to Tennessee, settling first in Franklin county. In 1829 he began the study of medicine with Dr. Robert Turner at Winchester. In the fall of 1830 he attended medical lectures at the University of Pennsylvania, at Philadelphia, and remained there about five months. This trip he had to make across the country, traveling about six hundred and fifty miles each way on horseback. Being determined to make his way, and not possessing the means to go on with his course, he returned to Tennessee and began practice, at the same time continuing his studies. A few months after he removed to Shelbyville, Bedford county, Tennessee, where he has ever since remained, having been in the practice of medicine over fifty-four years, long enough to see the people who first settled in the town pass away and a new generation take their places; long enough to see men whom he attended at birth grow up to be grandfathers, and to attend at the birth of their grandchildren. The first night after his arrival at Shelbyville, he was called to visit the daughter of a prominent merchant, and he at once began a successful practice which continued to flourish. He has practiced there through three epidemics of cholera —1833, 1866 and 1873. Meanwhile, he has paid considerable attention to surgery as well as medicine, and at the advanced age of seventy-three performed successfully the difficult operation of ovariotomy. He has also operated a number of times for strangulated hernia, and performed numerous amputations of thighs, arms and legs; has exsected many tumors, large and small, including the mammary glands, and used the trephine very often. In all his surgical operations Dr. Lipscomb has been very successful.

Dr. Lipscomb has also been the author of numerous valuable artices on professional topics in the *Louisville Medical Journal* and the *Nashville Medical Journal.* In 1840 he had the honorary degree of Doctor of Medicine conferred upon him by the University of Louisville, and some years ago received the same degree from the Tennessee Medical College. He has been a member of the American Medical Association for many years; is a member, and has served as president, of the Bedford County Medical Society; also as president of the State Medical Society of Tennessee. Of the latter body he is the oldest living member, having been present at its sec-

ond meeting in Nashville in 1831, and has been a member continuously since that remote time. Dr. James Roane was then president of the society, and some of those who attended were Drs. Felix Robertson, Samuel Hogg, Boyd McNairy, James Newman, John H. Waters, John Shelby, Higgenbotham, Wallace Estill and John Lawrence. Dr. Lipscomb has always labored earnestly for the success of this honorable body, and has done much to keep it together.

Dr. Lipscomb was president of the branch Bank of Tennessee at Shelbyville for several years previous to the late war. In 1854 he purchased a farm near Shelbyville and engaged in farming as well as the practice of medicine. After the war he became vice-president of the Bedford County Agricultural Society, was afterwards made president and served three years. The past thirteen years he has been a director of the Nashville, Chattanooga & St. Louis railroad, has also filled the position of director in the Shelbyville Savings Bank several years, and for many years has been president of the board of trustees of the Shelbyville Female Institute. He was one of the founders of the Victor flouring mills, and, together with his sons, now owns and controls them.

Several years prior to the war he was postmaster at Shelbyville, serving two years. He has been a member of the Presbyterian church upwards of fifty years, and has been three times elected an elder, but never consented to serve until about three years ago, when he was elected for the third time.

Politically, Dr. Lipscomb has always voted with the Democrats, to whose party he was won by Andrew Jackson during the nullification struggles. However, he has never taken any very active part in politics.

The Lipscomb family is of English descent, Dr. Thomas Lipscomb's great-grandfather being an Englishman. He had only two sons, Thomas and John, Thomas being the grandfather of the subject of this sketch. He lived in Spottsylvania county, Virginia, and was a farmer. William Lipscomb, the father of Dr. Thomas Lipscomb, was born and raised on his father's farm in Virginia, and followed the profession of his ancestors. He married Miss Ann Day Cook, of Louisa county, Virginia, and removed to that county, where he lived an honest, industrious farmer, rearing a family of ten children—five daughters and five sons, all sober, steady men, and all the sons dead except the subject of this sketch—training them in all the virtues and precepts that help to form the character of good men and women. As before stated, he removed with his family from Virginia to Middle Tennessee in 1826.

Dr. Lipscomb's brother, Dr. Dabney M. Lipscomb,

hough two years his senior, read medicine with him, moved first to Mississippi and then to Tarrant county, Texas, where he died, April 5th, 1885. Though he never received a classical education, he determined to read the Scriptures in the language in which they were written, and after he began the practice of his profession, mastered Greek, Latin and Hebrew without a teacher. The mother of Dr. Lipscomb was Miss Ann Day Cook, daughter of Rev. William Cook, a Baptist minister in Louisa county, Virginia.

Dr. Lipscomb has been twice married : First, on May 22, 1832, to Miss Rebecca Stevenson, of Straban, Ireland, who came to the United States in 1830. This union was blessed with ten children, all of whom lived to adult age: (1). Mary Ann, married John Davidson, and is now dead (2). Harriet E., who married her cousin, Walter S. Lipscomb, and died leaving two children, now in Waco, Texas. (3). Sarah J., married to U. E. Peacock, (4). Virginia, who married William C. Little, and is now a widow with two children. (5). Agnes, wife of Henry C. Whiteside, of Shelbyville. (6). William E., who was a soldier in Forrest's command, and was killed during Hood's Tennessee campaign. (7). James S., now married to Miss Lula Allison, of Williamson county. (8). Emma F., wife of Evander Shep-

hard. (9). Thomas C., married to Miss Laura A. Banks, of Columbia, Missouri. (10). Fannie Stevenson.

Mrs. Lipscomb died December 6, 1880, and on October 26, 1882, Dr. Lipscomb married Miss Mary A. Cowan, of Shelbyville, a lady of Irish descent, and related to the Cowan and Eakin families of Nashville. The success of Dr. Lipscomb in life is largely due to his early training and to the instruction he received, by precept and example, from prudent and careful parents. Reared in a plain and frugal manner, he was taught to believe that work is a good thing, economy a virtue, and extravagance an evil. When he was attending school he always had to work on Saturdays and in the evenings after school. While at Philadelphia he was thrown with young men who frequented the theaters and other places of amusement, but he had gone there to study, and the only time he ever went sight-seeing was on Christmas-day, when he visited Peel's museum, and spent twenty-five cents. At night he would read over in the text-books everything that had been lectured upon that day. He has always been a hardworker and close student; yet, at the same time, has, with faithfulness and honesty, discharged all duties devolving upon him.

HON. FLETCHER R. BURRUS.

MURFREESBOROUGH.

THIS gentleman was born, September 16, 1844, in Rutherford county, Tennessee, and has always lived in that county. The Burrus family are of Scotch-Irish origin. His great grandfather Burrus emigrated to America and settled in Amherst county, Virginia, in the early part of the eighteenth century, and was a large planter and slaveholder. His grandfather, Joseph Burrus, was born in Amherst county, Virginia, in 1765, and at the age of fifteen enlisted as a volunteer in the American Revolution, and participated as a private soldier at the surrender of Lord Cornwallis at Yorktown. He was several times a member of the House of Burgesses of the State of Virginia. He removed to Rutherford county, Tennessee, in 1805, and, upon the advice of Gen. Jackson, purchased lands on Stones river, and remained upon his plantation until his death, in 1821. He left a large family of sons and daughters who have intermarried with prominent families in Tennessee and other States, and his descendants are numerous, several of whom have figured with credit and ability in the political history of the southern States. He was a man of very positive convictions, of the highest order of morality, and of cultivated tastes.

Judge Burrus' second son was Lafayette Burrus,

father of Judge Fletcher R. Burrus, the subject of this sketch. Lafayette Burrus married, when quite young, Miss Eliza Ready, daughter of Charles Ready, sr., who settled in Rutherford county, in 1802, and died at Readyville, in 1859, aged ninety years. Charles Ready's wife was Miss Palmer, of a Maryland family. One of his sons, Col. Charles Ready, was, prior to the war, a leading lawyer in Tennessee, and served three terms in the lower house of Congress, and one of his daughters, Miss Nancy Ready, married Joshua Haskell and became the mother of Gen. William T. Haskell, one of the most gifted and brilliant orators this country has ever produced. Capt. W. C. J. Burrus, an uncle to Fletcher R. Burrus, was a prominent political man in Tennessee and served several terms in the Legislature, and an aunt on the same side was the first wife of Gov. Aaron V. Brown. The Burrus and Ready families have been for a long time prominently known in Tennessee. [For additional matters of interest connected with the family of Fletcher R. Burrus' mother, the reader is directed to the sketches of Gen. J. B. Palmer, Hon. W. H. Williamson, and Hon. A. B. Martin.] Lafayette Burrus was born in Amherst county, Virginia, November 21, 1797, and died in Rutherford county, Tennessee,

November 7, 1854. His wife, Eliza Ready, was born at Readyville, January 31, 1805, and died at Readyville, March 7, 1875.

Thirteen children were born to the parents of Fletcher R. Burrus, six of whom are living: (1). Elizabeth M., wife of George W. House, Murfreesborough, Tennessee. (2). Dr. W. L. Burrus, Murfreesborough, Tennessee. (3). Lucien B. Burrus, a planter in Arkansas. (4). Cassandra A., wife of James M. Alexander, Rutherford county, Tennessee. (5). Fletcher R. Burrus, subject of this sketch. (6). Lafayette Burrus, jr., Rutherford county, Tennessee. The children not living are: (1). Dr. Joseph C. Burrus, who was an eminent young physician at Napoleon, Arkansas. (2). Lucy Burrus, who died the wife of P. D. McCulloch. (3). Miss Martha A. Burrus, a young lady remarkable for the beauty of her person, who died just after attaining her position as a member of society. (4). Ophelia Maria Burrus, who died the wife of Gen. Joseph B. Palmer, whose sketch see elsewhere in this volume. (5). Robert A. Burrus, who followed mercantile pursuits with success, and died in Memphis, Tennessee, in 1879. (6). Francis Marion Burrus, who died before attaining his majority, a youth of much vigor and sprightliness. (7). Sophia Emma, who died the wife of F. H. Lytle, a lady of great beauty and possessed of qualities that made her a favorite social attraction.

The Burrus family have ever been an intelligent, cultivated people, the parents sparing no means to educate their children. It has been often remarked that the entire family were fine-looking, not a member of it having an ungainly feature. Another striking trait of the family is that they are very modest and retiring in their disposition, and are prompted only by a sense of duty to respond to the demands of society, to the end that they should not unworthily be considered as negative citizens.

Judge Fletcher R. Burrus was brought up on his father's farm, and was kept in the common schools of Murfreesborough and vicinity until the age of fifteen. In 1861 he entered the Western Military Institute as a cadet, and remained there until the following fall, when he left the military college to enter the Confederate army. He repaired to Bowling Green, Kentucky, where he was at once commissioned drill-master with the rank of first lieutenant, by Gen. Albert Sidney Johnston, after a rigid examination by the general himself. He continued in that position until the office ceased to exist, when he enlisted as a private in Company C, Eighteenth Tennessee infantry regiment, commanded by that magnificent soldier and officer, Col. Joseph B. Palmer. He was soon made sergeant-major and adjutant of the regiment, and afterwards was made inspector-general of the brigade—participating in all the battles in which his regiment and brigade were engaged from the battle of Murfreesborough, Tennessee, to Bentonville, North Carolina. He was wounded

seriously, but not dangerously, in the battle of Murfreesborough. He was in the battles of Murfreesborough, Chickamauga, Dalton, Resaca, Adairville, New Hope church, Kennesaw mountain, Powder Spring road and the skirmishing contests up to the gates of Atlanta, by which time, being but a slender boy, his health gave way completely, and still, against his protest, the brigade commander, Gen. John C. Brown, ordered him to the rear for the purpose of regaining his health, which consumed about four weeks' time, and covered the entire period of his absence from duty during the whole war. Upon his return to the army at Jonesborough, Georgia, the army was immediately ordered to get ready for the campaign known as the Hood raid, and he participated in all the conflicts of that campaign and retired with the army upon the defeat of Hood's enterprise. He then accompanied the army of Tennessee in its transfer to the Carolinas, participating in the various engagements of his command, winding up with the battle of Bentonville, and surrendered at Greensborough and received his parole there. He then returned to his home in Rutherford county, where he has since resided.

He had always intended to follow the law as a profession, and so after remaining at home with his mother two years to repair the ravages of war on her splendid farm, he entered the law department of Cumberland University, at Lebanon, in 1868. Having read law privately prior to his college course, he was enabled to graduate in June, 1868, taking the degree of L.B. under Profs. Nathan Green, Robert L. Caruthers and Henry Cooper. He commenced practice at Murfreesborough, in July, 1868, in partnership with his uncle, Hon. Charles Ready, a partnership which lasted until Col. Ready's death, in June, 1879. In September following he associated with him in practice Mr. Andrew J. Woods, the firm continuing to this day, Burrus & Woods.

During 1880–81 he was appointed by Gov. Marks to preside as special chancellor in the fourth chancery division of the State.

In politics Judge Burrus is a life-long Democrat, hereditarily and by conviction, and has generally taken a comparatively active part in the various campaigns, making speeches in Rutherford and adjoining counties.

In 1882 he was elected to the Tennessee House of Representatives from his county, and served during the session of 1883. He was chairman of the committee on rules, and was tendered the chairmanship of the judiciary committee, but declined it. He was chairman of the legislative caucus that agreed upon the bill for the settlement of the bonded indebtedness of the State.

He has filled the office of president of the board of aldermen of Murfreesborough for several consecutive terms. He was a commissioner to the Southern Cotton Planters' convention at Vicksburg, in 1883, having himself a planting interest in Phillips county, Arkansas, where he owns, with other parties, a plantation of seven or eight hundred acres.

Judge Burrus is a Mason and a Knight Templar; has taken the thirty-second degree, Scottish Rite, and has filled the offices of Master, Master of the different vails and Royal Arch Captain. He is also a Knight of Pythias, and a member of the Knights of Honor, and of the Ancient Order of United Workmen. In religion he is a member of the Methodist Episcopal church, South, and has the honor of being a teacher in the Sunday-school of his own church. He has been the attorney and a director in the Stones River National Bank from its organization, in 1871.

Judge Burrus married in Pulaski, Tennessee, May 30, 1871, Miss Hattie E. Pointer, a native of that place, daughter of John H. and Martha A. Pointer. Her father was a planter in Giles county, in which he attained very considerable success. The Pointers are of Virginia descent, and are numerous in Giles and Maury counties, standing socially and financially prominent, and noted for their public spirit. Mrs. Burrus is noted for her beauty and accomplishments. She was educated under Mrs. Nathan Adams, a celebrated private teacher at Pulaski, and subsequently went to St. Cecilia's

Academy, at Nashville, and leaving, completed her education at the Columbia Female Institute, Maury county, where she graduated in 1868. She is a lady of culture and intellect, of graceful manners, but utterly unostentatious. Her charities are numerous, and the purity of her Christian character has caused her to be universally respected and beloved.

Judge Burrus is one among the few men of financial success who began life on an inheritance. From his father's estate he received about five thousnd dollars, and he has been fortunate in his business enterprises, devoting the greater part of his time and energies to the law, a work in which he takes great pleasure, without inclination to change the channel of his aspirations. He also inherited habits of industry, and since he came to years of discretion and chose his course of action, his fundamental idea and controlling principle has been that of integrity, and that no man is really entitled to success who has any other motive and method as a prompter and a guide. Judge Burrus states that he never told a mischievous lie or made a willful misrepresentatation of facts in his life. His family has always held that a man who will lie will steal. In their estimate of human character veracity is the chiefest element.

WILLIAM T. BRIGGS, M.D.

NASHVILLE.

OF the distinguished surgeon whose name heads this biography, the late Dr. William K. Bowling, than whom there is no more competent authority, said: "Dr. Briggs ranks high among the first surgeons of the continent. He has had extraordinary success in all the capital operations of surgery, and has performed operations that no other man ever did perform successfully. Endowed by nature with inflexible determination of purpose and unflinching energy, he has from the beginning shown such celerity and dexterity in his operations, or what I may denominate deftness in manipulations, that he is simply unparalleled."

From other sources, chiefly "Physicians and Surgeons of the United States," edition of 1878, is gathered mention of some of Dr. Briggs' most notable successful cases, to-wit: Ligation of the internal carotid artery for traumatic aneurism, 1871; removal of both entire upper jaws for gunshot-shot injury, 1863; removal of lower jaw for gun-shot wound, 1863; hip-joint amputation for elephantiasis arabum, leg weighing eighty pounds, 1875.

Some of Dr. Briggs' more important publications are as follows: "History of Surgery in Middle Tennessee;"

"Tetanus treated by Chloroform," *Nashville Journal of Medicine and Surgery*, 1851; "Enchondromatous Tumors of the Hand, Forearm and Arm;" "Successful Amputation at the Shoulder Joint," *Ibid*, 1871; "Traumatic Aneurism of the Internal Carotid, the Result of a Puncture, Ligation of the Common Carotid and then of the Internal at the Seat of Injury," *Ibid*, 1871; "Death from Chloroform," *Ibid;* "Escape of Cathater into the Bladder during its use for the Relief of Retention," *Ibid*, 1871; "Unilocular Ovarian Tumor—Operation—Recovery," *Ibid*, October, 1871; "Dislocation of the Radius and Ulna backwards in a patient two and a half years old," *Ibid*, 1871; "Multilocular Ovarian Tumor—Tapped more than fifty times; Extensive Parietal, Intestinal and Vesical Adhesion; Incision eight inches long; weight of tumor eighty-five pounds, Recovery," *Ibid*, May, 1872; "Trephining in Epilepsy," *Ibid*, 1869; "Dugas' Pathognomonic Symptom in Dislocation at Shoulder Joint," *Ibid*, 1875; "The Trephine, its Uses in Injuries of the Head," *Ibid*, 1876. The Antiseptic Treatment of Wounds after Operations and Injuries, a paper read before the Surgical Association in 1881—pamphlet. The Surgical Treatment of Epilepsy,

14

read before the American Surgical Association, June 1, 1884—pamphlet.

From Dr. Briggs himself the writer learned that he has performed the operation of lithotomy one hundred and fifty-two times by the media-bilateral method, with but six deaths; of trephining seventy-three times with only five deaths; removed over one hundred ovarian tumors and ligated all the principal arteries. One knows not whether to admire more the dexterity of his operations or the audacious celerity with which they are performed.

One of his published addresses, delivered before the McDowell Medical Society of Kentucky, November 4, 1874, is a masterpiece of occasional oratory, rich with gems from almost every field of science and literature, and showing a breadth of culture belonging only to a finished scholar.

In early life his inclinations were to medicine, and he chose the profession because he liked it, and to it he has devoted his energies, day and night, ever since. His work is at once a labor of love and a professional and personal pride. On the subject of honorable, high-toned, regular medical practice, he is enthusiastic, perhaps "fanatical" is the more appropriate term, and this not more for the honor of the profession than from pure benevolence and love of relieving human suffering. He commenced the study at the age of seventeen, and has ignored all things else from that day to this, refusing alike civil office and medical commissions during the war, though attending the hospitals—Federal and Confederate alike, for humanity's sake.

Dr. Briggs is of large physique, has blue eyes, corrugated forehead, and is the picture of roseate health. When standing, he has the appearance of inclining forward, as if giving attention; when walking, of stretching forward in pursuit. The rapidity of his mental combinations are marvelous. At a glance he comprehends the situation, and in a moment his measures are determined upon. In their execution he is in a perpetual hurry. He is a medical storm. He talks and goes and works in a hurry; but his is the practiced eye and unerring hand of a surgeon absolute master of his business. He seems to love the activities of his calling more as a mode of self-assertion than for the inflow of revenue to his office. It is not vanity, nor self-importance in the man, but an anxiety to do the work assigned him, to act well his part as a member of the human family. No man does it with more alacrity, as if labor were its own reward. One duty done and he is eager for the next. In these respects he and his partner, the celebrated Dr. John M. Watson, were as much alike as twin brothers. No two men were ever more fitted for a medical partnership. When Dr. Watson in his last illness was informed by Dr. Briggs that his case was hopeless, he replied, " I am not afraid to die, but I would rather live in order to work." In that single utterance is the characteristic sentiment of both men. With them the value of life is measured by its opportunities for work in the most benevolent, self-sacrificing and noble of all callings. No more inviting field for surgical operations can be found in all the south than Nashville—a great geographical, railroad, commercial and educational center, and it is from this field that Fame has gathered up the name of Briggs and sent it back to Europe, whence the family originated, with an undimmed and added luster.

Dr. Briggs was born at Bowling Green, Kentucky, December 4, 1828, received his literary education at the same place; graduated in medicine from the Transylvania University, at Lexington, Kentucky, when not yet twenty-one; practiced with his father three years at Bowling Green; married in 1850, and upon his election to the position of Demonstrator of Anatomy in the medical department of the University of Nashville, removed to that city in 1852, where he has resided ever since. Soon after his settlement at Nashville, he formed a partnership in the practice of medicine with the illustrious Dr. John M. Watson, professor of obstetrics in the university; an Old Baptist divine; author of a volume entitled " The Old Baptist Test," the profoundest theological treatise Tennessee has ever produced. This partnership, with slight interruptions, lasted, under the name of Watson & Briggs, up to Dr. Watson's death in 1866.

In 1856 Dr. Briggs was made adjunct professor of anatomy with Dr. Thomas R. Jennings, professor of anatomy in the University of Nashville. The war suspended the operations of the university until 1865, when he took the chair of surgical anatomy and physiology, vacated by the death of Prof. A. H. Buchanan, which he held until he was transferred in 1866 to the chair made vacant by the death of Dr. Watson—the chair of obstetrics and diseases of women and children. In 1868 he succeeded Dr. Paul F. Eve, sr., as professor of surgery in the same university, which Dr. Eve had resigned. This latter position Dr. Briggs continues to hold in the consolidated medical departments of the University of Nashville and Vanderbilt University. The chair of surgery in medical schools of four different cites have been tendered to him. He has so far, however, refused to sever his connection with his first love, the medical department of the University of Nashville.

Dr. Briggs is a member and ex-vice-president of the American Medical Association, and in 1881, was one of its delegates to the International Medical Congress at London, England. He was one of the founders of the American Surgical Association, and its president in 1885. In September, 1885, he was chosen president of the section of general surgery in the International Medical Congress to be held in Washington in September, 1887. In his younger days he made the tour of Europe, visiting its most celebrated hospitals. Dr. Briggs has always been a patient student. He has to-day probably the largest medical and surgical library in the South, comprising more than four thousand volumes, and is a man of careful and profound research, following the best methods, and improving upon them as necessity and occasion suggest.

In his youth Dr. Briggs imbibed the Whig political principles, and it will go without saying that he still retains the proclivities and antipathies of the grand old Henry Clay party, and that during the war he was, of course, a southern man.

His financial success has been highly satisfactory, though out of the impulsive generosity of his nature he at times stood security, and had to "smart for it."

In 1850 he became a Master Mason at Bowling Green, Kentucky. In religion he is orthodox, though not a communicant. His wife is a Presbyterian, an excellent mother, and to her his two oldest sons, Drs. Charles and Waldo Briggs, owe their success in life. She had the management of them.

Dr. Briggs married in Bowling Green, Kentucky, May 25, 1850, Miss Annie E. Stubbins, a native of that town, the daughter of Mr. Samuel Stubbins. Her mother was a Miss Garrison. By this marriage four children have been born: (1). Dr. Charles S. Briggs, the prominent young surgeon, who is now professor of surgical anatomy and operative surgery in medical department of the University of Nashville and Vanderbilt University, a full biography of whom appears elsewhere in this volume. (2). Dr. Waldo Briggs, born in Bowling Green, Kentucky, July 2, 1854; graduated in medicine from the University of Nashville and Vanderbilt University in 1876; settled in St. Louis in 1877 as a practitioner of surgery. He was professor of surgical anatomy and operative surgery in the College of Physicians and Surgeons, in St. Louis, and is largely engaged in the practice of surgery. (3). Virginia Lee ("Dovie") Briggs, born in Nashville, February 11, 1862; educated in Nashville and at Baltimore, and is highly accomplished in every sense of the word. (4). Samuel S. Briggs, born in Nashville, June 8, 1868; now a student in Nashville, and probably destined for medical life.

Dr. Briggs' father, John M. Briggs, M.D., was a native of Nelson county, Kentucky, born April 9, 1798, and died April —, 1882. He was the son of a farmer, native of the same county, of Scotch descent. With his father's family he moved to Bowling Green, Kentucky, and there worked on a farm in summer, going to school in winter, until twenty-one years of age, when he studied medicine under Dr. Beauchamp, and graduated from the medical department of the Transylvania University, and returned to Bowling Green, where he practiced medicine and surgery sixty years. Such were the father and grandfather of three generations of learned physicians. When twenty-four years of age, Dr. John M. Briggs married Miss Harriet Morehead, the beautiful sister of Gov. Charles S. Morehead, of Kentucky. "This estimable lady," says Dr. Bowling in his "Life of John M. Briggs," "with

much of the mental force and sweetness of manner that made her illustrious brother the idol of his people, was the mother of W. T. Briggs, M.D., of the University of Nashville and Vanderbilt University, who has earned for himself a national and European reputation, imperishable, because it rests upon not what he has taught or said, but upon what he has actually done." Dr. Briggs' father was a Baptist; dressed elegantly, and was a fine specimen of the *suaviter in modo* of the old regime. His wife died in 1881, after sixty years of happy wedded life.

The eldest son of Dr. John M. Briggs, Charles M. Briggs, graduated at the University of Nashville, and settled as a lawyer at Louisville, Kentucky, and died there in 1875.

The writer has before him a volume of three hundred and sixty-five pages, giving geneological tables of "The Briggs Family," from A.D., 1273, with nine ways of spelling the name, originally "Bridge," the coats of arms of the various branches of the family, etc. But the subject of this sketch, his father and his sons, are constructing a span of the "Bridge" at the Tennessee end of the line more immediately interesting. There is much in blood, in race, in family, but these are secondary matters in the presence of a grand character which a descendant has built up for himself, and which reflects more luster upon the family name than it derives from it.

Dr. Briggs is an extraordinary man, viewed from any light, but perhaps appears to best advantage as a lecturer before his auditory of medical students. In twenty years he has never lost an hour, but has been on hand at the first tap of the bell, and he is very severe in reprimanding students who come late. Himself a strict temperance man, both as regards whisky and tobacco—as physicians, of all men, ought to be—he lectures his classes at least once every winter on the subject of temperance.

The writer attended one of his eleven o'clock lectures —the subject was treatment of hemorrhage from wounds —and understood the entire discourse, so plain does he make everything. The Doctor afterwards remarked that when his youngest son was but fourteen years old, he sometimes made him attend a lecture and afterwards asked him if he comprehended it. This is but one of his means of making himself lucid, and a good way of ascertaining whether he was properly handling the momentous subjects, on a correct knowledge of which by his classes the lives of thousands must depend. As a lecturer he never lacks for words, nor recalls a word to substitute a better, nor uses synonyms, nor repeats himself. When on general principles his delivery is rapid, his gesticulations forcible and aptly illustrative. He uses no notes, changes his position as if restless to hurry on to the nicer points of the topic, and what the young gentlemen most appreciate as the most delicate of all compliments, he looks a little absorbed, as if speaking to an audience of critics and handling a subject that only a master may dare to touch. His style is intensely earnest, as if to arouse the students to the fearful importance of the subject. His familiar allusions to the names of medical men of the past, their methods, inventions and modes of treatment, impress one with a sort of feeling that he is in the presence of a man who has lived and conversed with the illustrious surgeons of all ages, and made himself an expert in all their proceedings. He is familiar with the minutæ of every subject, and his language and gesture and practical illustration are a steady stream of pellucid thought, language necessarily technical, but otherwise clear to a common mind. He lectures as if he had never practiced, he practices as if he never talks. Fastening his eye upon a single individual in the center of the class, he never diverts his look in any other direction. This is a grave fault in a public speaker, but it is characteristic of the man. It is the necessity of his nature to concentrate all the parts and faculties of soul and body on one subject at a time. He is all concentration, and this unquestionably is the key to the mystery of his marvelous learning and unexampled success. As a lecturer, as a practical surgeon, he is a man of exhaustless resources and quick at invention to illustrate or apply at the urgent moment. He speaks with a face radiant with gladness, because he knows that he knows what he is talking about, and that through his students he is distributing his knowledge over the whole South, and transmitting himself to distant ages as a benefactor. A most honorable feature of his lectures is that he gives due honor to the men to whom he refers, and credit to those from whom he quotes. All the lines of his face come to a point. He is power focalized, condensed and solidified. Yet he is not hostile to innovation. On the nicer work of a surgeon his speech is slow and measured, to enable his class to comprehend the dangerous intricacies of the operation and description, reminding one of a great steamer going slow over shoals. The writer listened delighted and with bewildered interest to the learned Doctor, and could detect but one mistake in the lecture—the reference to Dr. Gross as "the greatest surgeon in the world." The compliment would be just with the added words—"outside of Nashville."

JOSEPH MOTTLEY ANDERSON, M.D.

LEBANON.

THIS gentleman, "native here, and to the manner born," appears in these pages not only as a representative Tennessean, but as one of the best representatives of Wilson county, where he has lived from his birth, now seventy years, distinguished as a physician and as a Mason. He has served twice, 1866 and 1867, as Grand Master of Tennessee; has taken all the degrees of the York, and eighteen degrees of the Scottish Rite, and conferred more degrees in Masonry than any other man in Tennessee. He served one year as Grand High Priest, one year as Thrice Illustrious Grand Master of the Grand Council, one year as Deputy Grand Commander, and served as Eminent Commander the same year; has held the offices of Junior and Senior Grand Warden, Deputy Grand Master, Deputy Grand Commander, and also served as Grand Commander the same year. He was made a Mason in Lebanon Lodge No. 98, in 1842, and has presided in all the offices of the Lodge, Chapter, Council and Commandery at Lebanon, and is also Grand Representative of the Grand Lodges of New Brunswick and New Hampshire near the Grand Lodge of Tennessee.

He commenced studying medicine in 1833, in the office of Doctors John Ray and Miles McCorkle; attended medical lectures in 1835-36-37, at Pennsylvania University, Philadelphia, and graduated in 1837, under Profs. Gibson, Horner, Chapman, Hare, Dewees, Samuel Jackson and Wood, and has been doing a fine practice at Lebanon ever since. Dr. Anderson is eminent as an obstetrician. He has made that branch of his profession a specialty, and has done a larger obstetrical practice than any physician in the State—in one instance including three generations of the same family. Before the war he had accumulated a handsome fortune, aggregating seventy-five thousand dollars, all of which he lost but ten thousand dollars by the war, but has since grown independent and is now in easy circumstances.

Prior to the war Dr. Anderson was a Whig, but since the close of hostilities has been a Democrat. Though not in the service himself, he had fourteen representatives in the Confederate army—two sons and twelve cousins.

Dr. Anderson married in Wilson county, Tennessee, September 24, 1835, Miss Mary D. Sypert, a native of that county, daughter of Lawrence Sypert, a farmer, living near Lebanon, originally from North Carolina. Her mother was Miss Mary Lambeth, also from the "Old North State." Mrs. Anderson was educated at Lebanon, and is remarkable for her fine common sense, her talents and her culture. She is a member of the Christian church, while the Doctor, himself, belongs to the Baptist church, of which he is a deacon.

By his marriage with Miss Sypert, Dr. Anderson has

had twelve children, only three of whom are now living: (1). Joseph B. Anderson; educated at Lebanon; served in the Confederate army four years, in Col. Starnes' cavalry regiment; was with Gen. Forrest in the seven days' and nights' pursuit and capture of Streight; was at the battle of Chickamauga and other noted engagements, and was wounded by the loss of a forefinger. After the war he married Miss Annie Betty, of Smith county, and now has eight children: Joseph, Mary, Kay, Edwin, Annie, Eugene, Samuel and James. He is now a large farmer in Smith county, near Gordonsville. (2). Samuel M. Anderson, now a druggist at Lebanon; educated at Lebanon and Knoxville; married Miss Clara Alexander, daughter of Dr. Alexander of Dixon Springs, Smith county, Tennessee. (3). Kate Anderson, graduated with the highest distinction at Cumberland University in 1882.

Four of Dr. Anderson's children died in infancy. His daughter, Emma, died the wife of William David Lumpkin, of Memphis, leaving three children, daughters, Emma, Mary and Anna Lumpkin, all of whom are living with Dr. Anderson at Lebanon. Misses Emma and Mary Lumpkin are graduates of Cumberland University, and Miss Anna Lumpkin is now a student in that institution.

Dr. Anderson's daughter, Eugenia, died May 20, 1876, the wife of Henry Clay Brown, leaving two children, Eugenia and Marie Brown, both now living with their grandfather at Lebanon.

His daughter Ida died unmarried, in September, 1876, and his daughter Mary died the day after. Dr. Anderson's first child, Edwin P. Anderson, graduated from the Jefferson Medical College, Philadelphia, and died, unmarried, in Texas, twenty-two years old.

Dr. Anderson's father, Patrick Anderson, a native of Virginia, came to Wilson county with his father, and there married Miss Fanny Chandler; engaged in merchandising in Lebanon, and died of consumption, thirty-two years old, leaving two children: Thompson Anderson, now an extensive wholesale dry goods merchant at Nashville, and Dr. Joseph M. Anderson, subject of this article.

Dr. Anderson's grandfather, Francis Anderson, was also a Virginian by birth, and after coming to Tennessee was a merchant and farmer at Lebanon. His wife was a Miss Mottley, aunt of Benjamin T. Mottley, who, in his day, was one of the most conspicuous men in Wilson county, having represented the county several terms in the Legislature, both as senator and representative. No man was ever more highly respected and beloved by his constituents and the people of his county. The Anderson family originally are of English and Welsh stock.

Dr. Anderson's uncle, Gen. Paulding Anderson, of Wilson county, served many terms in the Tennessee Legislature, and was one of the most prominent men of his county. His son, Col. Paulding Anderson, served in the Confedrate army with conspicuous gallantry and distinction, as did also his brothers, Capt. Monroe Anderson and Rufus and Richard Anderson.

By energy and industry and by staying at one place and pursuing faithfully one line of business, Dr. Anderson has risen to eminence in his profession and to distinction over the State. He is remarkable for the enthusiasm and devotion he has shown for his selected practice. There never was a night so inclement, so dark or so stormy, that he would not go at the call of a patient. As brave as Julius Cæsar, he is the soul of honor, of generous hospitality, and kind in his nature, yet he is also impulsive in his intercourse with men, and firm and faithful in his defense of friends.

GEN. RUFUS POLK NEELY.

BOLIVAR.

GEN. RUFUS POLK NEELY, of Bolivar, now in his seventy-seventh year, having been one of the early settlers and now the oldest citizen of Hardeman county, is a sort of encyclopedia of its social, political and business history, and on account of his fine sense, his humor, wit, and ready repartee, as well as his high character and connection with the railroad and other leading interests of Tennessee, stands prominent among the representative men of the State, while his military record is enrolled among the annals of the nation.

The Neely family is of Irish blood, and has a most interesting history, numbering, as it does, among its members some of the most distinguished and worthy people of Tennessee. Gen. Neely's grandfather was born of Irish parentage in Virginia, settled in Middle Tennessee, in Maury county, and moved to Franklin county, Alabama, near Tuscumbia, where he died at an advanced age, leaving five sons and four daughters: (1). Samuel Neely, who died in his one hundredth year in Franklin county, Alabama. (2). George Neely. (3). James Neely. (4). Pallas Neely. (5). Charles Neely, father of the subject of this sketch. (6). Sophia Neely, who married first Maj. Leonard of the United States army; and secondly, Col. Ezekiel Polk, grandfather of James K. Polk, tenth president of the United States.

(7). Catharine Neely, who married Dr. Stephen Doxy. (8). Rhoda Neely, who married first Col. Frazer, first sheriff of Franklin county, Alabama; and secondly, Dr. Stout. (9). Jane Neely, who married Thomas J. Frierson, of Maury county, Tennessee.

The children of Gen. Neely's aunt, Sophia Neely Polk, are: (1). Eugenia, widow of Alexander Nelson, who died at Bolivar. She is now living at Corinth, Mississippi. (2). Col. Charles Perry Polk, now living at Corinth, Mississippi. (3). Benigna, who married William H. Wood, of Memphis. (4). Gen. Edwin Polk, who was speaker of the Tennessee Senate at the time of his death, in 1850. His widow, *nee* Miss Octavia Jones, daughter of Gen. Calvin Jones, of North Carolina, is now living at Bolivar, and has one daughter, Octavia, wife of T. F. Brooks, of St. Louis.

Capt. Charles Neely, father of Gen. R. P. Neely, was born in Botetort county, Virginia, and was an officer under Gen. Jackson through all his campaigns. He married Miss Louisa, daughter of Col. Ezekiel Polk, in Maury county, Tennessee. His occupation was that of a farmer, but having entered the army soon after his marriage, he engaged but little in the business until after the war of 1815, when he settled in Franklin county, Alabama, near Tuscumbia, where he died in 1820, thirty-three years of age, leaving four children: (1). Rufus P. Neely, subject of this sketch. (2). Mary C. Neely, now the widow of William W. Atwood, Austin, Texas. She has three children living: Mary Josephine, wife of Major Durst, Austin, Texas; Adelie, wife of Mr. Palm, near Austin; and Octavia, who married Prof. Bittle, of Roanoke College, Virginia. The only son of Mrs. Atwood (Rufus) died in hospital in the Confederate service after being wounded and taken prisoner. (3). Adelie C. Neely, who is now living without children, the widow, first of James G. Bell, of Sussex county, Virginia; secondly, of Thomas Chambliss, of Memphis, Tennessee; and lastly of Col. John Pope, the famous cotton planter of Memphis, and author of articles on the subject of cotton cultivation. (4). Col. James Jackson Neely, who is now a leading physician at Bolivar. He was a colonel commanding a brigade (Richardson's) in the Confederate service. He married Miss Fannie Stephens, daughter of Rev. Dr. Stephens, an Episcopal minister at Columbia and Bolivar, and sister of Judge William H. Stephens, now of Los Angeles, California.

On the maternal side also Gen. Neely is of Irish descent. His mother, Miss Louisa Polk, who, as before said, was a daughter of Col. Ezekiel Polk, whose father was William Polk, of Mecklenburg county, North Carolina, and whose mother was a Miss Wilson, of the same State—both families of Irish origin and both of high standing in the early days of the "Old North State." Col. Ezekiel Polk died at Bolivar, in August, 1824.

Gen. Neely's maternal uncles were: (1). William Polk, born in North Carolina, lived in Maury county moved to Hardeman county, Tennessee, and then move to Walnut Bend, Arkansas, where he died, a large cotton planter. (2). Maj. Sam Polk, father of James K Polk, president of the United States. (3). Thoma Polk, of Robertson county, Tennessee. Gen. Neely's maternal aunts were: (1). Mary Polk, who marrie Capt. Thomas Jones Hardeman, for whom Hardeman county is named. He was a captain in the war of 1815 was taken prisoner by the British and whipped over the head with a sabre for refusing to give information as to Jackson's position when Packenham attacked the Americans at New Orleans. (2). Clarissa Polk, who married Capt. Thomas McNeal, of Bolivar. Her son Maj. Ezekiel Polk McNeal, now living at Bolivar, is among the most prominent planters and capitalists of Tennessee. His individual sketch appears elsewhere in this volume. (3). Matilda Polk, who married John Campbell, of Maury county, Tennessee.

Gen. Rufus Polk Neely was born in Maury county Tennessee, November 26, 1808. He grew up there until nine years of age, and went to school on Carter's creek. In 1817 his father moved to Franklin county, Alabama, and died there in 1821, when, with his widowed mother, Rufus returned to Maury county In 1823 he moved to Hardeman county with his uncle Hardeman and McNeal, and has lived there ever since being partly raised by his grandfather, Col. Ezekiel Polk. Like most men of mark, Gen. Neely's early education was limited. He attended Burrus Academy a Russellville, Alabama, under the celebrated Dr. Cartwright, and afterwards went to school in Maury county Tennessee.

He began his business career as a clerk in a dry goods establishment in 1825, selling goods to the earliest settlers of Hardeman county and to the Indians. A soon as the county was organized, he was made register of deeds before he was of age, and had to wait until he attained his majority to be sworn in. He held tha office until 1833, when he was elected county cour clerk, and served in all, as clerk and deputy clerk thirty-two years. Meantime he was in various other positions. In August, 1839, he was elected to the Legislature and served in the session of 1840. In 1842 he was appointed a commissioner to clean ou and pay for the improvement of the Big Hatchie river to fit it for navigation. In 1842 he went to farming, a which he was quite successful. After this he returned to his old office of county clerk. His elections were by the court up to 1832–33, and by the people after 1836.

Gen. Neely has seen considerable military life, having been connected with the war of 1836, between Mexico and Texas, the Mexican war and the late war between the States. In 1836 he was elected brigadier-general of the Twenty-second Tennessee militia brigade, covering the counties of Shelby, Fayette, Hardeman and Mc Nairy. Under the proclamation of Gov. Cannon i

1836, he raised troops to aid Gen. Edmond P. Gaines and Gen. Sam Houston, then struggling for Texas independence on the Sabine. Gen. Neely organized a regiment at Jackson, Tennessee, and was elected its colonel, but the troops were disbanded by the governor, at the instance of President Jackson, as the United States were then at peace with Mexico. After being mustered out of service he came home, but kept the company he took from Bolivar organized until Gen. Scott called for troops to remove the Cherokee and Creek Indians. With his company he reported to Gen. Scott at Fort Cass (Cherokee Nation), and served in getting the Indians west of the Mississippi river until 1838, after which he was quiet till 1846, when he aided in raising a company for the Mexican war. Although he mustered part of the troops into service at Memphis, he did not himself go into active service in Mexico. The second Monday in May of every year the survivors of his old company have a reunion and dine with Gen. Neely at his hospitable home. There are but ten of the members of the company now living.

In 1855-6-7 he was engaged in building and operating the Mississippi Central and Tennessee railroad, now a part of the great Illinois Central system. He operated the road as president from 1856 until the war broke out, and has been connected with the road from the first shovel of dirt (which he himself threw) until now, either as secretary, superintendent, president or receiver.

In 1861, after a visit to Montgomery, Alabama, in company with Jefferson Davis, to be present at the inauguration of President Davis and Vice-President Alexander H. Stephens, he returned home and in company with Hon. Milton Brown, went to Nashville to confer with Gov. Harris and Gen. Zollicoffer on the subjects of secession, independence of the South, raising of troops, etc. Gen. Neely at once set about raising a regiment for the Confederate service. He went out as captain of the "Pillow Guards" of Hardeman county, which company became a part of the Fourth Tennessee infantry regiment, and at the organization of the regiment at Germantown, Tennessee, Gen. Neely was enthusiastically elected colonel, and under him that gallant regiment acquired its celebrity. With Col. John V. Wright's Thirteenth Tennessee and Col. Knox Walker's Second Tennessee regiments, Gen. Neely went with his command from Memphis to Randolph. After fortifying that place he was ordered to Fort Pillow, and it was he who struck the first lick there. He remained there until relieved by Gen. Leonidas Polk, who ordered him to Island No. 10, but before he got there Gen. Pillow ordered him into Missouri in connection with the regiments of Col. John V. Wright and Gen. Preston Smith. He took his command to Bentonville and then back to New Madrid, and up the Mississippi river to Hickman and Columbus. Late in the battle of Belmont, Missouri, Gen. Neely commanded

his regiment (Fourth Tennessee), and the Twelfth Louisiana regiment.

At the battle of Shiloh Gen. Neely was conspicuous for his bravery and efficiency. He went into the fight at the head of his beloved Fourth Tennessee and captured a Federal battery. The second day he also commanded the remnant of Tappan's Arkansas regiment, which had been cut to pieces at Belmont. The orders came thick and fast, several additional regiments were assigned to his command, and in the afternoon he was ordered to take Polk's battery off the field, which he did under cover of the unerring rifles of the Fourth Tennessee.

Not only at Shiloh but again at Perryville, the Fourth Tennessee distinguished itself, under command of Gen. Strahl, Gen. Neely being confined in prison at Alton, Illinois. The regiment went out from Memphis with one thousand and sixty-three men; was reduced by loss and detail at Shiloh to five hundred and odd. Gens. Polk and Pillow both had great faith in the regiment, and it was generally placed where it would get hurt. At the close of the war the regiment surrendered with eighty-two men.

In the latter part of 1862, Gen. Neely was captured by the Federals and kept a prisoner at Alton, Illinois, until released by special order from Gen. Grant. He returned home on parole to remain within the Federal lines until exchanged, but was rearrested shortly after and returned to the Alton prison in the winter of 1862-3. He was sent from Alton to Camp Chase, Ohio, in May, 1863, to prevent him from persuading Confederate prisoners against taking the oath of allegiance. From Camp Chase he was sent to City Point, Virginia, and exchanged in the fall of 1863. He reported at Richmond and was commissioned to gather up the troops said to be behind the Federal lines in Tennessee and unable to get out. He was engaged in that sort of work until the close of the war, and surrendered at Bolivar in 1865.

Gen. Neely lost two sons in the war, William and Charles Rufus. Another of his sons, Dr. James Neely, went out to the war when under fifteen years of age, and came through unharmed.

Since the war Gen. Neely has been prominently identified with the railroad interests of Tennessee; as receiver and resident director for Tennessee, and also as director in the M. & T.; as president of the M. & K. (now M. & N.); and as director in the Canton, Aberdeen and Nashville, and the Yazoo Valley railroads.

Gen. Neely is a Democrat, as all of his family connections have been, and in State politics he is known as a "sky-blue." He and ex-Gov. James D. Porter were delegates at large from Tennessee to the national Democratic convention which nominated Gen. Winfield S. Hancock for president in 1880. He has also been a member of the press, having owned several newspapers at Bolivar—the *Bolivar Democrat*, the *Bolivar Palla-*

dium, and had an interest in the *Bolivar Bulletin*. He was made a Master Mason at Bolivar, in 1832, and has several times served as Worshipful Master. His mother having been a Presbyterian, he has followed in her footsteps; his wife and all his children are Presbyterians; he attends that church, contributes to it and in his faith is orthodox, according to the Presbyterian standard.

Gen. Neely was married to Miss Elizabeth Lea, at Bolivar, Tennessee, May 18, 1829, he being only twenty years of age and his bride sixteen. Mrs. Neely is a daughter of John Lea, a native of Delaware, a merchant and a man of literary and scientific ability, having published several valuable treatises on the subject of cholera. Her mother's maiden name was Catharine McClement, also of a Delaware family. Hon. John M. Clayton, United States Senator from Delaware, is Mrs. Neely's cousin. Isaac Lea, of Carey & Lea, the well-known Philadelphia book publishers, is her paternal uncle. Mrs. Neely was born in Philadelphia, educated at Cincinnati, and is in all respects an intelligent, superior Christian woman, excelling in the different and delicate arts of hospitality; even tempered, public-spirited; a woman of wonderful go-ahead activeness, never undertaking anything she does not accomplish. She is now seventy-one years old, but young-looking and active for her advanced years. Their golden wedding was celebrated in 1879, at which their children, grandchildren and great-grandchildren were present.

General and Mrs. Neely have had ten children born unto them: (1). William Henry Neely, who went to California in 1850, and never returned. He was killed near El Paso, in 1861, on his way to join the Confederate army. (2). Harriet McClement Neely, who died the wife of John A. Jarrett, a merchant at Bolivar. (3). Mary Bell Neely, first the wife of Col. J. H. Unthank, a lawyer of Memphis, Tennessee, by whom she has two children: Lizzie, wife of Charles A. Miller, a lawyer at Bolivar, and at one time a member of the Tennessee Legislature; he is a son of Judge Austin Miller; and Sallie, who first married Walter Calhoun, a

conductor on the railroad at Canton, Mississippi, now dead; at present she is the wife of R. L. Walker, a claim agent of the Illinois Central railroad, at Bolivar, by whom she has one child, Nellie. (4). Louisa Neely, now the widow of Dr. A. A. Coleman, who died of yellow fever in 1878; she had five children, John R. and Fannie now living. (5). Kate Neely, wife of Thomas Collins, a farmer and educator at Bolivar; has four children, Linda, Kathleen, Neely and William. (6). Elizabeth Neely, who died the wife of Hon. Francis Fentress, an eminent lawyer at Bolivar, leaving three children, Elizabeth, Frank and Louise. (7). Dr. James J. Neely, graduated at Oxford, Mississippi, and at Bellevue Medical College, New York, now practicing at Bolivar. He married Julia, daughter of Judge Thomas R. Smith, of Memphis, and has three children, Rufus, Thomas and Frank. (8). Fannie Neely, wife of Austin Miller, a lawyer and farmer at Bolivar; has one child, Bessie. (9). Prudence Neely. (10). Lillie Neely, who died in childhood.

Such is the interesting record of this honorable and prominent family—a record of which the venerable patriarch may well look back upon with affection and pride.

Gen. Neely began life owning only a little tract of land which he let the celebrated Davy Crockett, his agent, live upon several years. In his busy career he has made several fortunes, has always been successful at money making, but has also lost much by insurance companies, by fires, war, and by going security. He did business for good men when he was young, was economical, did not stray off into wildness and dissipation, but applied himself diligently to whatever he undertook. He has never been ambitious to be merely a millionaire, but in accumulating property has had in view the laudable object of leaving his family comfortable, and above all, to leave them a good name. His services have been generously appreciated, and his fortune has come to him through salaries and fees and enhancement of stocks and properties, won on fair terms, honestly, without joining syndicates or resorting to wild speculation—a fortune gained honestly and a name that will never bring the blush of shame to the cheeks of his offspring.

EDWARD L. JORDAN.

MURFREESBOROUGH.

THIS gentleman was born in Williamson county, near Triune, July 23, 1817, youngest son of Archer Jordan, a native of Lunenburg county, Virginia. Archer Jordan was the eldest son of William Jordan, also a native of Lunenburg county, Virginia, who, at the early age of eighteen years, became a soldier of the Revolution. Archer Jordan, the father of the

subject of this sketch, was the oldest son of William Jordan, who had nine brothers, all of whom succeeded well in life, with one exception, and made good estates and raised large families.

Mr. Jordan's mother was Elizabeth Walker, daughter of Thomas Walker, a farmer of good family and a native of Lunenburg county, Virginia. Her mother was a Miss Jeffries, of the family so well known in Virginia until the present time. She was married to Archer Jordan, father of the subject of this sketch, in 1794, and went with his father's family to Lexington, Kentucky, where they remained one year and then moved to Davidson county, Tennessee, and settled in the Maxwell neighborhood. It is mentioned as an interesting incident of their trip to Tennessee, that they crossed the Cumberland river on the ice with all their goods. After remaining in the Maxwell neighborhood four years, they bought land near Triune, in Williamson county, and settled there permanently, and there died, leaving twelve surviving children, all of whom married and achieved fair success in life. Of these twelve children, five are now living, the oldest of whom, Mrs. Ralston, of Ralston's station, Nashville, Chattanooga and St. Louis railroad, is eighty-five years of age, and the next, Dr. Clem. Jordan, is eighty-four, while the youngest, the subject of this sketch, is sixty-eight.

Edward L. Jordan was brought up on a farm until the death of his father, which took place in 1835. His opportunity for education was but moderate, being confined to the old field schools, for he never went to a college or an academy. In 1836 he entered the store of Thomas F. Perkins & Co., at Triune, as a clerk, and remained with them until January, 1839, when, in connection with Col. William P. Cannon, son of the late Gov. Newton Cannon, he bought out the firm. They continued together for three years, and then Cannon married and left the business, which was carried on by Mr. Jordan until 1844, at which time he sold the stock of goods. He then retired from merchandising and bought the old homestead of Hon. Meredith P. Gentry, in Williamson county, where he lived until 1851, when he settled at Murfreesborough, where he still resides, following merchandising as well as farming, until the war.

Immediately after the war Mr. Jordan organized the Murfreesborough Savings Bank, and was its president up to the time it was merged into the First National Bank of Murfreesborough. Some years later he was made president of the last named institution, which position he still holds.

Before the war Mr. Jordan was a Whig, and during the war was a staunch Union man, though he did much to aid the soldiers of the Confederacy, spending his money for their relief. Since the war he has never identified himself with any political party, always voting for his friends, rather than for party. He has, however, been a strong State credit man. At the early age of twenty-one he was made a magistrate at Triune, but since that time has never held any political office and has never been an active politician.

Mr. Jordan has been three times married: First, at the age of twenty-three, to Miss Martha Fletcher, daughter of Monford Fletcher, of Rutherford county, and a man of considerable prominence there, being sheriff of the county for several years. One of her uncles, James Fletcher, was for many years clerk and master of the chancery court of Rutherford county, and her grandfather, John Fletcher, was chairman of the county court of Rutherford county for a long time. By this marriage Mr. Jordan had six children, three of whom are now living.

After the death of his first wife, he was married to Mrs. Jane Cook, daughter of James Caruthers, of Franklin, Tennessee. By this marriage there were no children. The second Mrs. Jordan died in 1858, and in the latter part of 1859 Mr. Jordan was married to his third wife, Mrs. Mildred Williams, daughter of Dr. George Hopson, of Port Royal, Montgomery county, Tennessee. She was brought up in Montgomery county and went to Murfreesborough after the death of her first husband to educate her three children. By this last marriage there have been two children, the elder, a daughter, is now wife of Rev. E. A. Taylor, pastor of the First Baptist church at Knoxville. The youngest child, a son, twenty-one years of age, is connected with the railroad office at Murfreesborough. Mr. Jordan has five children now living, besides the three of his last wife by her former marriage, and there are twenty-eight grandchildren.

Mr. Jordan's ancestors were members of the Baptist church far back in the family history, and he himself has been a member of that church for nearly thirty years, and is now well known as one of the leading Baptists of his county. His three wives have all been members of the Baptist church.

Mr. Jordan began life a poor boy with the idea that a man should be industrious, attentive to business, and always correct. By carrying out these principles, and adhering to the determination to keep out of debt, he has achieved success in life and accumulated a handsome property.

HON. FRANK T. REID.

NASHVILLE.

THIS distinguished gentleman, a native Tennessean and one of its best representatives, sprang into prominent notice in the spring of 1884, as the nominee of the Republican State convention for governor of Tennessee. In the ensuing campaign he amply fulfilled his promise, made in the speech accepting the nomination, to carry the party banner placed in his hands to victory or honorable defeat, having reduced the Democratic majority from more than twenty-seven thousand to a little over six thousand. In his speeches during the canvass his political principles were clearly and boldly enunciated. He was in the habit of stating that his father and all his family being Whigs, he, as a boy, came under that influence; that he never drew a Democratic breath in his life; and that, following the doctrines of the old Whigs to their logical conclusion, he cast his first presidential vote in 1872 for Gen. Grant, and had been a Republican ever since, advocating a protective tariff; the Blair educational bill; internal improvements by the general government; the payment of every dollar of the State debt; a free ballot and a fair count; opposing a State railroad commission; and denouncing the system of leasing out the labor of convicts as an iniquitous abomination.

Judge Reid was born in Williamson county, Tennessee, March 9, 1845, at his uncle's, Dr. Frank T. Reid, for whom he was named, but grew up in Nashville, where he has resided ever since, except the war episode in his life, and twelve months' travel in Europe.

In 1862 he joined company F, Starnes' cavalry regiment, but was transferred, just before the battle of Chickamauga, in the fall of 1863, to Capt. John W. Morton's battery, and served in Tennessee, Georgia, Mississippi and Alabama till the close of the war, having taken part in all the battles and skirmishes in which Forrest's command was engaged, from the battle of Thompson's Station to the end. When transferred from Starnes' regiment he was promoted to first sergeant of the battery.

His father, John Reid, was born in Williamson county, Tennessee, in 1816, at the home of his grandfather, Abram Maury (after whom Maury county was named), one of the early settlers of the State. He was a lawyer—having been State senator, and occasionally having acted as special chancellor. He died at Nashville, August 11, 1885.

Judge Reid's grandfather, Maj. John Reid, who married Miss Elizabeth, daughter of Abram Maury, above mentioned, was born in Bedford county, Virginia, in 1784. He received a classical education, read law, and in 1807 removed to Tennessee, first settling at Jefferson, in Rutherford county; but on his marriage, in 1809, he changed his residence to Franklin, in Williamson county, where he was engaged in the successful practice of his profession when the war of 1812 began.

Judge Reid married in Nashville, June 4, 1872, Miss Josephine Woods, who was born at her father's, on High street, in that city, May 25, 1852, daughter of Robert F. Woods, a merchant, formerly a sugar planter of Louisiana, of an old family of early settlers in Davidson county, from Virginia. Her mother, Marina Cheatham, was a daughter of Gen. George Cheatham, a stock-raiser in Robertson county. The Cheathams of Tennessee are all of the same family, and originally from North Carolina. Mrs. Reid was educated at Nashville, and is a member of the Episcopal church.

By his marriage with Miss Woods, Judge Reid has three children: (1). Nina, born February 23, 1877. (2). Louisa Trimble, born November 12, 1881. (3). John, born February 5, 1885.

He began the study of law in 1866, under his father, Judge John Reid; was admitted to the bar in 1867, licensed by Judges Frazier and Cooper. His first partner was Neill S. Brown, jr., 1868–1872, after which he became partner with his father.

He inherited from his mother a quick, mobile and emotional nature, combined with very great gentleness, exquisite sensitiveness, and the nicest sense of honor. He is a man who revels in the luxuries of learning and æsthetics, lives in a world of ideas, and if a man's library may be taken as an index of his tastes, he is, by this test, fond of poetry, works of imagination, tales and essays, rather than of metaphysics and kindred subjects. For his literary taste and cast of mind he is more deeply indebted to Mr. Carlyle than to any other writer. It is probable that from him he imbibed that hatred of sham, boldness of utterance, and keenness of satire that characterize him as a stump speaker. It is noteworthy that in his speeches he makes few quotations, either from prose or poetry, but delivers his own thoughts in his own language. Hence, his public addresses are novel in conception, fresh in make-up, genuine in purpose, and presented in forcible style, strengthening the strong, fixing the wavering, and attracting an enthusiastic following.

Judge Reid never had a collegiate education. When young he attended primary schools, and was a year or more in the military college or University of Nashville, but at the age of sixteen he joined the Confederate army, which closed his scholastic career. His information is due, not to the school-master, but to his efforts to educate himself, and especially after the death of his mother in 1849 (when he was only four years old), to the rearing he had under the care of his maternal aunt, Mrs. Gov. Neill S. Brown, and to his association with the best people in Davidson county. At the age of twenty-four (1869), he made a trip to Europe, and spent twelve months traveling over the continent "to see the world."

In August, 1878, he was elected circuit court judge of the eighth judicial district, term expiring September 1, 1886, and his decisions on the bench have been given under a high sense of the moral responsibility of a judge to mete out exact justice, according to the law and facts in the case. Like Chancellor Kent, he makes himself certain of the facts, and the real point in the controversy. Any judge with a clear head pursuing this course will have little difficulty in deciding a cause, for once the real facts are clearly established, the answer is at his elbow. The same rule applies to the bar; for if a lawyer once gets thorough knowledge of the facts of a case, he will readily discover the point of merit upon which it rests, and can then easily turn to his library for authorities, should they be needed, to fortify his conclusions. But Judge Reid has very little sympathy for that class of the profession who have run mad after authorities—after the letter of the law rather than its spirit—for case and precedent lawyers, and he himself never decides a case unless he is clearly satisfied in his own mind what the right decision is.

Judge Reid's gubernatorial canvass of the State in 1884 made Republicanism respectable in Tennessee, won for himself friends all over the State in both political parties, and fully sustained the reputation of Tennessee stump oratory. His style of oratory was earnest without vehemence, logical but not cold, and his delivery was stamped with the sincerity of conviction. The editor has heard but one opinion of Judge Reid as a speaker, and that is, that he ranks among the most finished orators of the State, an accomplished gentleman, a man of letters, a thinker, an original investigator, always speaking the thought that is within him, and loyal to his own convictions. The editor heard him three times, and noted that he never lacked for a word; was elaborate without prolixity or repetition; that his diction was scholarly and chaste; that he enthused his audience without resort to anecdotes unbecoming the dignity of a statesman, and that his tastes are very different from those of the ordinary politician. Though a candidate for high office, yet, during the heated and bitter canvass, no reproach or stigma or suspicion of taint was urged against his character.

His opening address as the Republican candidate for governor abounds in passages of remarkable force and brilliance. A few are selected:

"It was from under the roof of that honored and eloquent old Whig leader, ex-Gov. Neill S. Brown, where the greater part of my life had been passed, that, a sixteen year old boy, I left to join the ranks of the Southern army. * * * Because I enlisted in that army did that commit me, for the balance of my life, to the support of the political doctrines of John C. Calhoun? Was it loyalty to the doctrines of nullification, State sovereignty and the constitutional right of secession that led those of us who were bred in the school of Henry Clay to enlist under the Confederate flag? What was it that did lead us? It was the wild enthusiasm of that wonderful hour that preceded the uprolling of the curtain which disclosed the terrible four years' tragedy of a nation's struggle for life; when the air throbbed with the fierce beat of drums, and was rent with the martial cries of war-intoxicated men."

* * * * * * *

"The impartial student of history now sees that for twenty years and more before the breaking out of the war, this country was rushing with awful velocity upon ruin and death. It was shooting Niagara. The storm of war purified the foul pestilence-breeding atmosphere that was sowing in our political system the seeds of corruption and death. Unwittingly we fought against ourselves, and God saved us from our own madness. The stars in their courses fought against Sisera."

* * * * * * *

"A boy, I fought in the ranks, under the Confederate flag, bare-footed in the depth of winter, and in rags; and because, upon my restoration to American citizenship, a grown man, my matured reason said to me that it was vastly better for the best interests of mankind that that flag had gone down in defeat, albeit covered with glory; that the Republican party was the true exponent and representative of the principles that had triumphed, and which we who had appealed to the sword were in honor bound to accept, and which the God of Battles had declared should mould the future historical development of the country; because I refused to live among the tombs and wear crape for the dead, believing it to be my duty to "live in the living present," forsooth, I am denounced as a renegade, an apostate, a traitor!"

After referring to the oppressive measures of the Republican party during the period of reconstruction, he said:

"At any rate, when in 1869 I left this country, and for a twelvemonth traveled through the countries of the old world; when I saw the condition of the masses of the people there and the character of the governments under which they groaned; when I saw tyrants and aristocrats with their heels on the necks of my brothers—manhood abased and our common humanity dishonored—and then saw in their seaports and towns the starry flag of the American republic, floating proudly and loftily among their emblazoned ensigns as though it felt the spirit of God and freedom consecrating its folds, proclaiming 'to the king on his throne, to the slave on his knee,' the equality and brotherhood of all men, as Christ proclaimed it, and died to sanctify it with his blood; proclaiming 'the rank is but the guinea's stamp, the man's the gold for a' that,' I confess my heart leaped with a feeling for which I can find no expression in words in the proud consciousness of American citizenship."

Discussing the national idea of the Republican party, and contrasting it with the Democratic doctrine, he said:

"Mr. Tilden embodied the Democratic doctrine when he defined the Union as 'a federative agency.' What do the survivors, on that side, think of this Democratic definition? What do those think of it who, when the tocsin of war sounded like an alarm bell in the night, and the cry rang out from the capital, 'Arm, citizens, the country is in danger?' rushed forth by thousands from their shops and farms to follow the great flag of the Union ' down to the fields of glory?' Again I catch a glimpse of that awful vision. Again the earth trembles under the shock of struggling armies, and the air is wild with affright from the mad roar of the cannon and the fierce scream of the shell. Amid the storm of battle that rages above the clouds on Lookout mountain the life-blood ebbs from the heart of the color-bearer of Tattersall's regiment, and away yonder on the western prairies, as the sun sinks below the horizon, a little curly-headed girl plays with her doll, all unconscious that her father, who, but a year before, had trotted her on his knee, is lying on the yellow leaves with the picture of home and wife and children rising up before him out of the gathering mists and gloom of death. Oh! how the thought must comfort and strengthen him in that dark hour, that he yielded up his life in defense of—'the federative agency.' Ah! it is a cruel slander. He knows, if Mr. Tilden does not, that he is dying for his country; that the Nation may live; that the great American republic, the mighty defender of the rights of man, whose mission is to Christianize the world, may not pass away from earth; may not be whelmed

> 'In that great ocean of Oblivion
> Where already, in numbers numberless,
> The graves of buried empires heave like passing waves.'

It is that thought that lights up his poor wounded face with a glad smile, and gives him strength to whisper his last words on earth into the ear of the dark, tender-eyed Angel of Death who stoops over him: 'Yes, it is sweet to die for one's country.'

"It was restored love of country, love of the Union, that led me into the ranks of the Republican party."

The literary productions of Judge Reid would of themselves make a charming volume. Space can be given only to a few passages in prose and in verse, for he writes both with equal facility and elegance:

"Does it not cause in us, at times, a fearful feeling to reflect that we can never be children again; no more, through all eternity, return to that quiet time when we lay on a loving mother's bosom, or prattled at her knee?"

* * * * * * *

"The great aim of our life should be, to aggregate together and to fuse into a whole all our particles of spiritual intelligence and strength. Mere vague, dreamy, spiritual aspirations are nothing, except in so far as they indicate spiritual capabilities. We appear in that other world the same identical spirits we were in this. If we were to lose our identity, we would not be ourselves. The real spirit of anything is a portion of the universal Spirit, or God. If particles of spirit can grow and develop themselves into higher forms, would it not follow that the Universal Spirit is constantly growing and developing into higher forms of spiritual being, and consequently not all perfect?"

* * * * * * *

> "Fair flowers emanations are
> Of Beauty's spirit everywhere;
> In sun and moon, and stars and sky,
> In streams and lakes, and mountains high.
> Spirit that lurks each form within,
> Evolving life from death and sin.
> Life and love, the lily and rose—
> Each to dark earth its beauty owes.
> Of the oyster is born the pearl,
> And high heaven of our low world.
> Spirit of beauty in everything,
> Always changing and fashioning—
> Gradually, slowly fitting its shell,
> In which higher forms of life shall dwell."

* * * * * * *

"Man's mission is to earn his bread—natural and spiritual bread—by the sweat of his brow and brain. This city-dotted globe was once but a waste-tangled wilderness, and two human beings stood herein with only fig-tree coverings; and see the change wrought by their sons and daughters—by those of them that have worked! We are born children of order, and enemies of disorder. The carpenter makes smooth plank of rough, gnarled timber; the sculptor transforms flinty rocks into symmetrical, life-looking bodies; the mechanic converts mountain ore into useful implements and machines. Thus are we engaged in bringing about that 'far-off, Divine event, to which the whole creation moves.' If all men would but work, how much longer would we have to journey on through the Desert; if all these innumerable yawning idlers, waiting for God to mend matters, would but help him to mend them? Work is man's mission, his highest act of worship—'its litany and psalmody the noble acts and true heart utterance of all the valiant of the sons of men; its choir music the ancient winds and oceans, and deep-toned, inarticulate, but most speaking, voices of Destiny and History, supernal ever as of old.'"

* * * * * * *

"What an Aceldama this world is! I sometimes wonder if it must not vex the ear of Heaven, the countless sighs and groans and shrieks that human hearts and lips pour out upon the empty air! If all that have escaped since time began could but be volumed forth in one great cry that should go forth to search the universe for God, the fearful sound would crack the very globe itself. Or if each scene of human suffering, since first the pitiless sky vaulted this charnel-house, the earth, could be transferred, life-size, upon a canvas wide and high as heaven; and power of vision granted us to grasp each smallest object, what a picture would be unrolled to mortal eyes. God sees it thus: and yet there are who say He is an angry and a jealous God."

* * * * * * *

"Thank God, some days the sky looks down upon me with a face as noble and serene as any Spartan mother's, and all the air is full of music, and the fall of feet upon the pavement sounds like the tramp of armies marching onward."

* * * * * * *

"One who has left behind him the 'dreams of his youth;' who has squandered his inheritance in carnal company and riot, or attained the end of his ambition in having secured great wealth, or fame, only to realize the desolate cry 'all is vanity!' passes along the street, of a calm Sabbath morning, and hears the voices of children singing an old, long-forgotten hymn, which he himself sang when a child, telling of a beautiful land beyond the valley of the dark Shadow, where all tears will be wiped away, and the father will again feel the little arms of the child he buried so many weary years before around his neck, can it be that that within him which forces the tears into his eyes will bear no other fruit or blossoms than those which fade and wither or turn to ashes on the lip?"

* * * * * * *

"A hot July day. The long, white, dusty macadamized turnpike, steaming. A drove of sheep panting, with tongues out, and with tender, appealing eyes. Little lambs, footsore, and limping by the side of mothers powerless to help (the unspeakable anguish in those supplicating eyes!), driven by human beings, made in the likeness of God, with heavy whips in their hands; and down in the town a red-faced butcher, with a sharp knife, waiting to draw it across their tender throats! But how would the world exist without spring lamb and green peas?"

* * * * * * *

"Some years ago I was in Naples. In front of the hotel, and lying along the sea, was a garden and public promenade. Here, in the cool of the evening, a fine band of music would play for hours, and the *elite* and fashion display themselves. It was a rare pleasure, after returning from the day's ramble, to secure a good seat on the side nearest the bay, and listen to the music and the long ripple and splash of the waves on the clear white sand at one's feet; to watch the gaily-dressed, animated crowds, lovely ladies leaning on the arms of handsome gentlemen, and beautiful little boys and girls running hoops, or engaged in some other childish sport, while the hum of the wonderful and busy city in the distance came subdued and softened on the evening air. In the soft, mellow twilight, what a weird feeling would creep into one's breast while sitting here looking out upon the great sheet of water, undulating, rising and falling like a mighty carpet by gusts of wind underneath, carrying on its bosom white-winged sailing vessels, fishermen's smacks and ocean steamers ; at the great dark fire-mountain opposite, which one knew, and could not but recall, had in the past thrilled and horrified so many human beings with its terrible vomitings forth of fire and red-hot stones and ashes. One could see the people of Pompeii and Herculaneum fleeing, horror-struck, in all directions, in the great darkness, preter-naturally lit up at times with huge flames and bursts of fire."

* * * * * * *

"The day I visited Mount Vesuvius was wonderfully clear and bright. A few white, fleecy clouds drifted across the sky, which only seemed a short distance overhead, and extraordinarily pure and blue. All the ground we had come over lay immediately beneath us, and could be distinctly viewed ; the huge, upturned, crested rocks; the serpentine windings of mighty streams of petrified lava, and vast fields of dust and ashes. Far off to the left, stretching for miles in a semi-circular form along the beautiful bay, lay Naples, its house-tops and cupolas and spires glittering under a brilliant mid-day sun. Hundreds of sailing crafts lazily floated on the blue waves, and steamers, leaving long lines of black smoke in their track, were coming and going. On the side nearest the sea could be seen charming villas, surrounded by the most picturesque fairy scenery; here standing out on jutting promontories, at whose base the great waves lashed themselves into angry foam, and here, half hid in deep gorges, whose sides were covered with orange and lemon trees laden with golden fruit, the white rock turnpike leading from Castellemmare to Sorrento could be caught glimpses of, now and then breaking from some deep ravine and winding like a silver thread along the sea-coast, up steep declivities, to where some iron or stone light-house stood lonely, looking out upon the sea, or where an old time-worn ruin spoke of long forgotten sieges and battles."

* * * * * * *

> "Hark! that heavy, pompous tread
> Tells of one well cloth'd and fed.
> Here comes one whose cold heart ne'er
> To the eye can force a tear.
> Ragged children round him weep.
> ' Feed my sheep, oh feed my sheep!'
> But he counts his rich gains o'er,
> Robs and cheats to swell the store,
> And grinds the faces of God's poor,
> Lives respected, and will die
> In the odor of sanctity."

* * * * * * *

ON THE DEATH OF A CHILD.

> In a darkened room a mother kneels
> By the side of a trundle-bed,
> Where a little child with folded hands
> And closed eyes lies dead.
>
> Outside, the glare of the blinding sun,
> And the noises of the street,
> Shrill cries, and the rattle of vehicles,
> And the patter of children's feet.
>
> His torn straw hat hangs up on a peg,
> And his well worn suit of gray,
> That his mother will brush, with breaking heart,
> And fold and lay away.
>
> And dear grandchildren, in far-off years,
> Will gather around her knee,
> Their little dead uncle's suit of clothes,
> Faded and worn, to see.

They will lay him out in the parlor below,
  On a sofa old and rare,
Where his father and mother used to sit
  In the days of courtship fair.

They will lay him out in his Sunday clothes,
  And smooth down his curly hair,
While his own dear look sleeps sweet on his face
  That will never be seen elsewhere.

His father will come and gaze on the face
  And small form hid under flowers,
And see himself before he was changed
  By the cruel, remorseless hours.

He will sit by the side of the corpse so still,
  A soft, white hand in his own,
And the fearful cry in his heart, " O where,
  Where has my little child gone !

Out into the Night that hugs this earth
  In dark and vast embrace,
He's had to go alone, so small, so weak!
  O God, shall I ever again see his face?

My darling, why will you not open your eyes?
  Where has your merry laugh fled?
Will I never again feel your arms 'round my neck?
  Your little hands pressed to my head !

All the hours of last night I lay wide awake,
  And you were not there by my side;
I turned to throw my arm over you, Charley,
  For I had forgot you had died.

I felt so weary, and sin-stain'd and sad,
  My eyes were too hot for tears;
And I could not kiss your pure brow and lips
  To banish my doubts and fears.

These barren days where art thou, Lord Christ?
  Why not the awful secret tell?
Did God, in truth, forsake thee in thy need !
  Or cans't thou say 'All, all is well?'"

Through stained glass, into the quiet church,
  Steal the soften'd rays of the sun,
And a woman's voice, like an angel's, sings
  " O God, thy will be done !"

The white robed priest in the chancel kneels,
  And the people follow in prayer,
And a sob breaks out from a young girl's heart
  That thrills the listening air;
And the face of the child through the coffin's lid
  Smiles softly sweet and fair.

The years are powerless to change it now,
  To stamp it with the frown of care,
Or with the cold and crafty business look,
  Or bloated drunkard's stare.

From the cool and solemn and mellow'd gloom
  To the noise and dust of the street,
Under the fierce, vulgar stare of the sun
  Comes the dead, 'midst the tramp of feet.

Out on the street, in front of saloons,
  Red-nosed mortals stand
And gaze at the hearse and coffin inside,
  And the cortege long and grand.

Out on the street a ragged girl
  From a perfumed tempter flies,

While hunger and woe fiercely look out
  Through her tear-stain'd, frighten'd eyes.

Out on the street a reveller reels,
  Who was once a stainless man,
The dreams of his youth forever fled
  Or changed to nightmares wan.

A broker stops on his way down town,
  And toys with his fob and chain.
What thinks he of death ? Bah! he's practical,
  And thinks of cotton and grain.

The heartless streets are left behind, and out
  The long white turnpike creeps
The slow procession; the mourners talk and laugh,
  The poor sad mother weeps.

Here where the tall grass waves, and evergreens
  Stand hush'd and solemn round,
Under a sky serene and unconcern'd
  A pit dug in the ground.

And to the spoken words of prayer that break
  The silence how profound !
The grate of spades and heavy thud of clods
  The only answering sound.

And now the hackmen crack their whips and race :
  Each tries to be the winner ;
The family friends are in great haste
  To get back home to dinner.

The pall of night falls down ; the hot, foul stench
  From gutters and alleys rise ;
And cool and pure and still the gravestones stand
  Under the awful skies.

Oh, choking heart, in yon gas-lighted room,
  See here this peaceful grave ;
Upon it shines the light of all the stars—
  Be patient and be brave.

Under their wings the birds have hid their heads :
  The flowers have gone to sleep;
The infinite serenity that's here
  Bids thee no longer weep.

But for the storm the rainbow would not arch
  The smiling, lately frowning, sky ;
But for the strife and wounds would not be felt
  The joy and calm of victory.

Heard in this solemn city of the dead,
  Under the midnight sky,
Even the loud voices of the day proclaim
  Man's immortality.

These extracts doubtless reveal to the reader th
man's real character and nature better than could an
words of ours.

Judge Reid's father was John Reid, an eminent mem
ber of the Nashville bar, whose character is well de
scribed in an obituary notice, from the pen of a life
long friend, that appeared in *The American*, Augus
18, 1885, and from which we make this extract: "A
steadfast man was John Reid. Wherever he stood, o
sat or walked, honor and strength were by his side—
legacy to his fellow-men priceless as the stars. 'A ma
is already of consequence in the world when it is know

that we may implicitly rely upon him.' That crown of honor John Reid won and wore. Fidelity was his life-long badge. His veracity was absolute. He hated a lie. The inner life of this quiet, unobtrusive, strong man was known only to the few. He lived in his reserves. He was equal to every strife, within and without. Popular applause was not one of his conquests. His conquests were within. John Reid was of a mould that unfitted him for the frivolous pastimes of life and what the world calls happiness. Nature withheld from him qualities that disqualify for the serious conditions of life. Long ago, we have reason to believe, this silent, meditative man, as we saw him on the street, entered into what Carlyle calls the 'sanctuary of sorrows,' where only the thoughtful enter, and where 'no religion,' says Goethe, 'that grounds itself on fear is regarded.' By the simple tenor of his life he won the public regard without the asking. He was singularly free from self-seeking. He shunned notoriety with the modesty of a woman. He was faithful to his trusts, and made the cause of his client his own. If he was impulsive, and overstepped the boundary of decorous debate, the ready reparation was at hand."

Judge Reid's grandfather was Maj. John Reid, the aid-de-camp of Gen. Jackson. He died January 18, 1816, in his thirty-second year. Gen. Jackson, in the following letter to his brother, written in 1842, bears this testimony to his character:

HERMITAGE, 24th August, 1842.

Nathan Reid, Esq.:

MY DEAR SIR—Your letter of the 1st inst. has been this day received, and found me greatly debilitated; so much so, that I can scarcely wield the pen. But I hasten to acknowledge it, fearful from increasing debility that I may hereafter be unable; and justice to my deceased friend requires that I should speak of him as his services merit. Maj. John Reid acted as my aid-de-camp in the Creek war, and was with me as such in the defense of New Orleans, and on all occasions displayed the calm courage of the true soldier. If I had strength it would give me great pleasure to give a detailed account of his important services. Suffice it to say that in all the engagements I had with the enemy he was everywhere, where duty or danger called; and upon all and every occasion performed his duty well. He was a man of high literary acquirements—of most punctilious honor, and had he lived was calculated to become one of the brightest ornaments of our country. I viewed him as one of the best belle-lettre scholars of his age, and I would with great pleasure here rehearse all his merits as an officer and civilian, if I had strength to do so. To close, I can only add that on every occasion in the field his acts met with my full approbation.

With assurances of regard, etc., I am, etc.,

ANDREW JACKSON.

P. S.—Maj. John Reid had my confidence as much as any man that ever lived. A. J.

He was brevetted by President Madison "for gallantry at the siege of New Orleans."

His father, Nathan Reid, Judge Reid's great grandfather, was a Revolutionary veteran, and fought eight years in that struggle. He was one of the eighty selected by Gen. Wayne to assist him in storming Stony Point.

The Reids are a mixture of French and English blood, and connect with the Fontaines, Maurys, Perkinses, DeGraffenreids, and is one of the most extensive families in the country, one of the most illustrious of whom was Lieut. Matthew Fontaine Maury.

Judge Reid's mother, Miss Margaret Louisa Trimble, was born in Davidson county, Tennessee, in 1820, daughter of Judge James Trimble, judge of Davidson county circuit court. Her mother was Miss Letitia Clark, a sister of James P. Clark, former clerk of the Supreme Court of this State.

Judge Reid being descended, on his mother's side, from the Trimbles, renders appropriate some mention of his maternal uncle, John Trimble, who was born February 2, 1812, in Roane county, Tennessee, and died February 23, 1884, at his home, "National Hill," Nashville. He was one of the most original thinkers and remarkable men Tennessee has ever produced. Judge E. H. East, at the bar meeting after Judge Trimble's death, said: " Mr. Trimble has filled many official positions—district attorney for the State, member of the General Assembly of the State during several sessions, district attorney for the United States, and member of Congress from this district. As a lawyer, none were more earnest and vigorous, or held his client and cause in greater sympathy. For thirty years he ranked with the foremost of our profession in the State, and was a participant in all the great lawsuits of the day. In whatever sphere he was called to act he was felt and heard. He was pronounced and readily defined; no prudence, no compromise, and thoroughly independent. Mr. Trimble was original in everything, and yielded to decisions and precedents only to the extent that they convinced his judgment. He was capable of great thought, and kept on thinking to the last. He divided mankind into two classes—the natural man and the spiritual man—and measured and appreciated them according to spiritual development. He declined to know men after the flesh. The haughty, the supercilious, the shams and the demagogues he detested, and ordinary vocabulary failing, he would coin a word or a sentence of contempt for such. His faith in the ultimate triumph of truth was complete and sublime. He believed that God ruled the world, and in His own all-wise and mysterious way was doing the best for our weak, short-sighted and death-doomed race. He believed that nations, governments and men were all His instrumentalities, and His moral agencies; therefore these were sacred in his eyes. Mr. Trimble had an absolute confidence in God, and thus armed, he looked things fairly in the face. He never dodged, never retreated behind a great man, a great name, custom or institution, and to this confidence he added the highest reverence and devotion. These high moral qualities wrought out as high a man as Tennessee has produced in these long years."

HON. WILLIAM Y. ELLIOTT.

MURFREESBOROUGH.

THIS gentleman, one of the leading citizens of Murfreesborough, was born in Rutherford county, Tennessee, November 2, 1827. His father, James Elliott, was a native of North Carolina, and came to Tennessee about the year 1810, engaged in farming and was also extensively employed in constructing bridges, building mills, and in other useful enterprises in the then newly settled country. He was a successful business man in all his undertakings. He served as a soldier in the United States army in the war of 1812. He was the oldest of four brothers, sons of William Elliott, who died in North Carolina a short time before the family came to Tennessee, the father having previously visited this State and located lands, to these his widow came with her family of four girls and four boys.

William Y. Elliott's mother's maiden name was Adaline Bowman. She was the daughter of Samuel Bowman, who came to Rutherford county, Tennessee, from North Carolina about 1806, and settled in the vicinity of what afterwards became the celebrated battlefield of Stones river, where the family acquired possession of a large landed estate. Samuel Bowman was a major in the war of the American Revolution and took part in the battle of King's Mountain. The family was of old orthodox Presbyterian stock, and is now well-known in the church, both in North Carolina and Tennessee.

Mr. Elliott's parents were in comfortable circumstances, and kept him at the best common schools of his day, most of the time up to his eighteenth year. He then began business life as a dry goods clerk at Murfreesborough, and subsequently became a partner in the firm of Jordan & Elliott, remaining in the dry goods business during the progress of hostilities.

In early life Mr. Elliott was an ardent Whig, but became a Republican when that party was organized in Tennessee. During the war he was a strong Union man; since the war he has been a consistent Republican. He was a delegate to four Republican national conventions—Chicago in 1868; Philadelphia in 1872; Cincinnati in 1876, and Chicago in 1880. In 1865 he was elected to the lower house of the Tennessee Legislature and served two years, after which he was elected to the State Senate and served a term of two years in that body. While in the Legislature he was made

chairman of the committee on ways and means, a position in which his fine business qualifications were ably shown.

From 1868 to 1870 Mr. Elliott was a director of the Murfreesborough Savings Bank, and also served one year in the same capacity in the First National Bank of Murfreesborough. He was also a director in the First National Bank of Nashville for five years, declining a re-election in 1873 because of his appointment as United States pension agent at Nashville. This latter position he held more than four years, at the expiration of which time, the agency having been consolidated with the Knoxville agency, he went out of office. Since that time he has not held public position of any kind, devoting himself exclusively to his private interests.

Mr. Elliott was made a Master Mason in Mt. Moriah Lodge No. 18, at Murfreesborough, June 12, 1850; Royal Arch Mason in Pythagoras Chapter No. 23, Murfreesborough, October 15, 1852, and a Knight Templar in Nashville Commandery No. 1, Nashville, 1859.

Mr. Elliott was married October 13, 1870, at McMinnville, Tennessee, to Miss Margaret G. Johnston, daughter of James W. Johnston, a paymaster in the United States army during the late war, originally a lawyer at New Castle, Pennsylvania, who settled in Tennessee at the close of the war, and being made a register in bankruptcy, held that position until 1872. His father, Rev. Robert Johnston, was a Presbyterian minister and a pioneer in Western Pennsylvania; of Scotch-Irish descent, and a man of strong character, being distinguished among the ministers of his day. Mrs. Elliott's family, on her mother's side, were also of Scotch descent, her mother being Miss Esther Loughry, daughter of John Loughry, a native of "Auld Scotia."

Mr. and Mrs. Elliott have four children, all sons: (1). William Y. Elliott, jr., now fourteen years old. (2). James Johnston Elliott, aged twelve years. (3). Edward G. Elliott, aged ten years. (4). Harry W. Elliott, the youngest.

Mr. and Mrs. Elliott are both Presbyterians, he having been a communicant of that church since 1843.

Mr. Elliott's life presents a pleasing illustration of a self-made and successful business man; one whose good fortune has come to him as the legitimate reward of constant integrity and purpose.

COL. ROBERT F. LOONEY.

MEMPHIS.

A distinguished gentleman of Memphis who has known Col. Robert F. Looney long and intimately, gives this high, but just, estimate of his character: "Col. Looney, though in business a pushing man, is noted among his acquaintances for his modesty. He is a man of great suavity of manner, who is certain to ingratiate himself into the favor of all whom he meets. He is of exceeding gentleness of nature, yet bold and decisive; a man whose heart is ever moved by the appeals of the oppressed or distressed ; a man who loves his family, his friends, his country and his church. He is a very constant churchman, and never fails to attend service twice every Sunday when there is a church to be reached. As an orator, there are but few, if any, in the State who excel him; a speaker of fine imaginative powers, while classical and finished in his style, he yet possesses that gift of eloquence that influences the multitude and exercises a magic-like power over the masses, enthusing an audience of thousands by the torrent of his eloquent logic in a single address. His is the art of firing the popular heart. In his family relations, he may well be termed the youngest member. He is the one man of my knowledge who has not a black sheep in his flock or a skeleton in his closet. He has five daughters and three sons, all of whom are now grown, and neither of whom have in any way violated the mandates and examples of Christian parents. He is by nature endowed with an intellect and a physique that give him prominence as a man of mark in any company. In business relations he is quick of conception, bold and venturesome, and when he sustains losses he sleeps well over them, and troubles neither himself, his family or his friends with his failures, while, on the other hand, everybody enjoys his successes. He is a man of great enthusiasm in whatever he undertakes. His differences of opinion in business, in politics, or in the other relations of life, occasion no severances of friendship. He may oppose you ever so bitterly on a matter of principle, yet his heart will ever be open to you, and his latch string hangs on the outside always. He is peculiarly adapted to large enterprises. His powers of persuasion, together with his earnestness of conviction, often enlist the co-operation of large bodies of influential men. He was the first inaugurator and organizer in this section of the immense mining corporations now operating in Mexico, out of which he has realized large sums."

Robert F. Looney was born in Maury county, Tennessee, August 5, 1824, and grew up there, going to school in that county until the age of twenty. He then commenced reading law under Hon. Edmund Dillahunty, (who had married his sister, Miss Sarah G.

Looney). He was admitted to the bar in 1845 by Judge Dillahunty and Chancellor Terry H. Cahal, and at once began practice at the Columbia bar. In the spring of 1847 he moved to Memphis, but went back to Columbia, married and settled there, practicing at Columbia from the fall of 1847 to the summer of 1852, very successfully, making a good deal of money. In 1852 he moved back to Memphis and, omitting the hiatus of the war, practiced law there until 1870. Since 1870 he has been engaged in a thousand things, the recital of which would fill a book.

In 1861 he went into the Confederate army as captain of a company, was elected colonel of the Thirty-eighth Tennessee regiment, and commanded it two years in the Tennessee and Georgia campaigns. He was at the battle of Shiloh, where he won great distinction, as also at the battles of Farmington, Corinth, and other noted engagements. He surrendered at Oxford, Mississippi, in 1865.

Col. Looney has never held a civil office in his life. In politics he was a Henry Clay Whig before the war, opposed secession, and made about the last Union speech that was ever made in Memphis before the commencement of hostilities. He also spoke in various other places in West Tennessee against secession and for the Union, but after the State seceded he went with her and cast his lot with her. Since the war he has acted with the Democratic party, one of the most zealous of its members, and highly valued for his great organizing and executive ability. He was a delegate to the Chicago National Democratic convention, in 1884, which nominated Cleveland and Hendricks, and at which convention Col. Looney was made the member of the National Democratic executive committee from Tennessee.

Col. Looney is a public-spirited citizen in its highest sense, and proves his faith by his works, subscribing liberally to enterprises to improve the city of Memphis, to advance its school facilities, and to church benefactions. He is a member of the Presbyterian church, as are also the other members of his family. He joined the Odd-Fellows when a young man, but has never become a member of any other secret order.

Col. Looney's ancestors are of Irish origin. His great grandfather, David Looney, emigrated from Ireland and located in Maryland, and afterwards in Virginia, long before the Revolutionary war. His son, David Looney, grandfather of Col. Looney, was a colonel in the American army, a native of Virginia ; afterwards removed to Tennessee ; was a member of the convention that framed the first constitution of Tennessee, and was often a member of the Legislature from Sullivan county. He was a wealthy farmer, and left a large landed estate

16

and negroes to his children. He married Miss Mary McClellan, a sister of the father of Col. Abe McClellan, formerly a member of Congress from East Tennessee. Judges Robert L. Caruthers and Abram L. Caruthers were nephews of Col. Looney's father. Hon. Robert L. Caruthers' father married Col. Looney's paternal aunt.

Col. Looney's father, Abram Looney, was a native of Sullivan county, East Tennessee. At an early day he moved to Maury county. He was an educated man, of fine literary attainments; a very successful merchant and farmer; a Whig; a Presbyterian, and a man who stood high for his character and splendid sense. He died in 1841, at the age of sixty-five.

The mother of Col. Looney, whose maiden name was Elizabeth Gammon, was born in Sullivan county, Tennessee, the daughter of Hon. Richard Gammon, who came from London, England, settled first in Baltimore, and came to Sullivan county, Tennessee, while it was yet a part of North Carolina. His father, George Gammon, lived and died in London. Richard Gammon was a very successful merchant in Sullivan county, and left a large estate to his children. He also was a member of the first Tennessee constitutional convention, and several times a member of the Tennessee Legislature. He is said to have been a most excellent man, morally, and it is furthermore related of him that he could not be induced to say anything harsh of anyone, not even the worst characters. On one occasion, when pressed to give his opinion of a noted gambler, he replied, " Well, I never saw him when he was not well dressed." Col. Looney's maternal grandmother was Sarah Gamble, a daughter of Samuel Gamble, of Maryland, of a Presbyterian family originally from the north of Ireland.

Col. Looney's mother was a devout Presbyterian, and a woman remarkable for her charities—kind to everybody, beloved by everyone, and, like her husband, enjoyed the confidence and esteem of all who knew her. They were both the soul of honor and honesty. She died in 1838 at the age of fifty-five, the mother of twelve children, six sons and six daughters, to-wit: (1). Mary Looney, who married Matthew Rhea, of Sullivan county, and died at the age of eighty. (2). Sarah G. Looney, wife of Judge Dillahunty. (3). David Looney, first a merchant, then a lawyer at Memphis. (4). Richard G. Looney, a merchant; died young. (5). Jane Looney, died the widow of P. W. Porter, of Memphis. (6). Eliza Looney, died the wife of Dr. A. F. Bracken, of Somerville, Tennessee. (7). Anise Looney, died fifteen years old. (8). George G. Looney, died young. (9). Abram M. Looney, colonel in the Confederate army; now a prominent lawyer at Columbia, and State senator from Maury county in the Tennessee Legislature, session of 1884-5. (10). Joseph W. Looney, a farmer; died young. (11). Robert Fain Looney, subject of this sketch. (12). Adelaide Looney, died in infancy. Of

these Robert F. and Abram M. Looney are the only survivors.

Col. Looney married in Maury county, Tennessee, November 2, 1847, Miss Louisa M. Crofford, daughter of Col. James T. Crofford, a very successful planter. He came of a very distinguished family of South Carolina and Georgia, of which Hon. William H. Crawford, of Georgia, was a member. He was a soldier with Gen. Jackson in all his battles, including New Orleans. Mrs. Looney's mother was Miss Jane B. Porter, daughter of William Porter, one of the early settlers of Middle Tennessee, and belonged to a prominent Pennsylvania family. Mrs. Looney's paternal grandmother was a Craighead, sister to the celebrated Presbyterian preacher, Rev. Dr. Craighead. Mrs. Looney graduated from the Columbia Female Institute, Columbia, Tennessee. She is a highly cultivated lady, a fine writer, and one of the most scholarly women in Tennessee. Nine children were born of this marriage—three sons and six daughters. The sons: Robert F. Looney, who is in mercantile life in Memphis; Thomas C. Looney, a young lawyer, and Abram Looney, as yet a school-boy. The daughters: Sarah Elizabeth, who died young; Janie C., who is now the wife of Hon. L. L. Lewis, of Virginia, and Mary, Louisa, Sallie and Bettie.

Col. Looney is a man of splendid and striking personal appearance. He stands six feet two inches high, weighs two hundred and twenty pounds, and not only has the look of the typical southerner, but impresses one as being a strong man in every way, with a sound mind in a sound body. And although he is the son of a family of wealth and distinction, he began life on nothing, his father having failed about the time the son attained his majority. To-day he owns valuable real estate and stocks in Memphis, owns property in New Mexico, and has an interest in extensive silver mines in Mexico. He has been a very active man all his life, has failed often, has had many successes and many reverses, but has always "lit on his feet," and never stopped paying. He spends his money like a man that makes it easy. He has made a good deal by speculating in coal and iron lands, and has dealt largely in real estate at times. Having large faith in mankind he was never a close collector, consequently has lost heavily by bad debts and by going security, and has made and lost money in almost every way. He never drank liquor in his life, not even wine, except medicinally; has never gambled, never bet on anything. His success has come of energy, activity, enterprise, clear-headedness, boldness and as the legitimate fruit of strong intellectual ability.

He is a man of great will power and remarkable evenness of temper; hospitable, genial and companionable. While adapted to, and engaged in, the varied pursuits of life, he observes all the demands and usages of religion. Youthful and impulsive in all his habits, his attentions and indulgences to his family are without stint or limit, so far as his purse can buy, and of his large family of children, physically and mentally perfect, it is a happy reflection to him to know not one of them has ever given him a pang. He is never out of humor, and this is remarkable in one so exceedingly quick of action and thought, yet there is nothing sluggish about him—nothing petulant, foolish or eccentric. Not only is he gifted with exceptional oratorical powers, but his soul is full of poetry, and both his forensic style and conversational manner are at once florid, classical and logical, with great magnetic power in literary composition. Unselfish in his nature, he concedes to every one the right to think and act for himself. Original and audacious in his operations, he has conceived and carried forward more gigantic projects, perhaps, than any man in Tennessee. He handles men like chessmen on the board, with dash and brilliancy and venturesome spirit, but with the consummate grace and cool confidence of a master of the art.

CAPT. JOHN POMFRET LONG.

CHATTANOOGA.

CAPT. JOHN POMFRET LONG, of Chattanooga, was born at Knoxville, Tennessee, November 25, 1807. His father was William Long, a native of Mecklenburg county, North Carolina, born February 19, 1775, settled at Knoxville in 1797, married Miss Jane Bennett in 1805, resided at Knoxville until 1813, when he removed to Washington, Rhea county, Tennessee, and staid there until November, 1836, when he removed to Chattanooga, where he died November 1, 1844. He was a house-carpenter by trade. In the latter part of his life he was an elder in the Presbyterian church. He was plain William Long, but was so uniformly upright that it came to be a saying "As honest as Billy Long." He was one of the first settlers of Chattanooga, and assisted in organizing the Presbyterian church there in 1840.

Capt. Long's grandfather, John Long, was born in county Antrim, Ireland, settled in Mecklenburg county, North Carolina, participated in the Revolutionary war, married Miss Elizabeth Shields, of Mecklenburg county, and was drowned in 1799, while returning in the night from a Masonic lodge meeting. He came alone to America, leaving only a maiden sister in Ireland. During the Revolution, in Charlotte, North Carolina, some tories were captured, from whom information was obtained that an attack was to be made on "Post Ninety-six," one hundred miles distant from Charlotte. The Whigs posted two couriers on horseback, taking different routes, to notify the garrison at "Post Ninety-six." John Long proposed to carry the information on foot, started at sunrise and at sundown delivered his dispatches at Ninety-six, and put the garrison on their guard—a remarkable record, showing the patriotism of the man, the spirit of those times, and the pluck that is in the blood of the Longs.

Capt. Long's mother, Miss Jane Bennett, was the daughter of Maj. Peter Bennett, a native of Virginia, who married Miss Elizabeth Pomfret, daughter of John Pomfret, of King William county, Virginia. Maj. Bennett was in the Revolutionary war, at the close of which he served as sheriff of Granville county, North Carolina. He died in 1822, in Knox county, Tennessee, where he had settled in 1802, a farmer. Capt. Long's maternal great grandfather, John Pomfret, came from England, settled in King William county, Virginia, married a Miss Hunt, and died in Granville county, North Carolina, in 1802, at the age of eighty-four.

Capt. Long's mother was born in Granville county, North Carolina, January 26, 1781, and moved with her father to Knox county, Tennessee, in 1802. She was a Presbyterian. She died at Chattanooga, December 10, 1859, leaving three children: (1). Mary Long, now the widow of John A. Hooke, an attorney-at-law, who died at Chattanooga in 1865. She has five children, James, William, Robert, Jane and Elizabeth. (2). James Shields Long, a physician; married Jane Caldwell, of Monroe county, Georgia; died in 1866, leaving two children, Mary and Virginia. (3). John Pomfret Long, subject of this sketch. The latter grew up at Washington, Rhea county, Tennessee; finished his schooling at Knoxville when fourteen years old; engaged next in a tannery for three years; next clerked three years for Col. Thomas McCallie, a merchant at Washington, then opened a store on his own account at that place, and from there moved to Ross' Landing (now Chattanooga), reaching there April 18, 1836. Here he opened a general store, which he continued, with varying success, until 1860. He was then elected city recorder of Chattanooga, and filled the position three years, until the city was evacuated by the Confederates. Prior to the evacuation, in 1862, he was appointed provost-marshal of Chattanooga by Gen. McCown, and served in that capacity several months.

A few days after the battle of Chickamauga his house was torn down and his effects destroyed. He having gone south in the meantime, leaving his family in Chattanooga, they subsequently rejoined him at Griffin, Georgia, where they remained until the close of the war. Capt. Long then returned to find himself without home or property, and a family to support. He began business as a real estate agent and fortune favored him, for he soon was very successful. In 1868 he applied to Judges Trewhitt and Adams, at Chattanooga, for a law license, which was granted. His practice has been principally in the chancery court, where his knowledge of the land and titles in Chattanooga has been of great value to him. Notwithstanding his losses by war and going security, he has accumulated a nice property, mostly in real estate.

When he first came to Ross' Landing—then a mere ferry and steamboat landing in an Indian country—he found no post-office and no post-roads. He made application to the post-office department for a post-office, which was granted, and he was appointed postmaster, without compensation. The name of the post-office was changed to Chattanooga in 1838. Capt. Long held the postmastership until 1844, when he had to give way for one of the friends of President James K. Polk.

In 1832 he cast his first vote for Gen. Jackson; his next was for Hugh L. White, and thenceforward he voted the Whig ticket from Harrison to Bell, since which time he has been a Democrat. He attended the Whig State convention at Murfreesborough in 1841, when Jones was nominated for governor against Polk. In February, 1861, he voted against secession, but when President Lincoln ordered out troops, he voted for secession. He was always a States' rights man, as was his father before him. He has, however, never been so warm a partisan as to vote the party ticket unless he liked the men; always considered it a duty to vote, but equally a duty to scratch objectionable names from the ticket.

In 1845 he was elected to take his father's place as an elder in the Presbyterian church, which he had joined in 1843. He was a commissioner of the town of Chattanooga when the land was subject to entry, and the occupants were entitled to preference of entry. The three commissioners, Aaron M. Rawlings, George W. Williams and Capt. Long, entered the quarter-section, sold the lots, and made titles to the purchasers April 20, 1839, which was the day on which the town of Chattanooga had its birth. Capt. Long's staying power is illustrated in the fact that he has never yet seen the Mississippi river, and of the large cities only a few.

Capt. Long was married to Miss Eliza Smith, November 6, 1834, at Smith's Cross-roads (now Dayton), Rhea county, Tennessee. Mrs. Long was born January 25, 1813, at Washington, Rhea county, Tennessee. Her father was William Smith, a native of Massachusetts, who came to Knox county in 1808; was a school-teacher, and had for one of his pupils Dr. J. G. M. Ramsey, the historian, who said of him, "He was one of the best common school teachers I ever saw." Mrs. Long's mother was Elizabeth Cozby, daughter of Dr. James Cozby, a man noted in the early history of East Tennessee as a physician and an Indian fighter. (See Ramsey's

History of Tennessee). Mrs. Long's brother, Dr. Milo Smith, was an able physician, and for several terms mayor of Chattanooga, where he died in 1868. Mrs. Long was educated at Knoxville; made a profession of religion and joined the church in 1843, the same day her husband made profession and joined. She has been an invalid the greater part of her married life, but is beloved for her sweetness of temper. She is fond of the company of young folks; has an unconquerable will-power that has carried her through all her troubles; is notably cheerful and pleasant, and, for one of her age, remarkably active, especially when "upon hospitable cares intent." To this union there were eleven children—all born in Chattanooga. Five of these died in infancy and childhood. The others are: (1). William Pomfret Long, died nineteen years old. (2). Elizabeth Jane Long, died sixteen years old. (3). James Cozby Long, born December 2, 1844; educated in the Naval Academy at Annapolis; resigned and joined the Confederate navy in 1861, attaching himself to the fleet along the coast of North Carolina. He was in the fight at Roanoke Island, the second in command of the *Curlew*, Capt. Hunter. He was then transferred to the *Merrimac*, as midshipman, and was in the famous naval fights in Hampton Roads, and remained with his ship until she was burnt. He was then transferred to Drury's Bluff, and finally to Plymouth, North Carolina, and was on board the iron-clad *Plymouth* when she was blown up by the United States navy. He next served under Capt. Moffit on a blockade runner. After the war he went into civil engineering, and had charge of the government works at Muscle shoals for a while. He is now a manufacturer of iron paint at Birmingham, Alabama. He married at Elyton, Alabama, November 20, 1872, Miss Frances Walker, and has four children, William Walker, John Pomfret, James Cozby and Mary. (4). John Pomfret Long, jr., born March 4, 1847; joined Col. Walker's Nineteenth Tennessee regiment in May, 1864, at Dalton, Georgia; participated in all the fights from there to Atlanta, and on July 22, 1864, was disabled by a shell taking his foot off; died March 1, 1880, unmarried. (5). Milo Smith Long, born May 10, 1850; graduated in medicine at Nashville, and is now in Dakota. (6). Marcus Bearden Long, born January 27, 1854; now a civil engineer, and was for a while engaged as engineer in Mexico on the Atchison, Topeka and Santa Fe railroad; unmarried.

One of the aims of Capt. Long's life has been to give his children something to start upon and to help them attain a standing in society, and he believes that every man ought to have a home and a family, and next, that he has duties to perform as a citizen. He has desired wealth, and has been sometimes up and sometimes down, but has always made it a rule to pay his debts. With one exception he has always made a profit on whatever he has sold. He never swore an oath in his life, and was brought up to regard the Sabbath. He has never been dissipated, though not always strictly temperate. He is a self-assertive man, and of quick temper. Being the oldest citizen of Chattanooga, he is often resorted to as an oracle on matters pertaining to the history of persons, families and property in that now important city. He has been a public-spirited man all along, and is uniformly spoken of as the best representative man of the city where he located when it was simply a river landing, and surrounded by the Cherokees. It was very appropriate that in 1881 he was selected to write the historical sketch of Chattanooga, on the occasion of representatives of the North and the South meeting at that city to shake hands over the bloody chasm. His article, printed in the Chattanooga *Times* in September, 1881, is full of valuable history—local, personal and general.

REV. JAMES HOLMES, D.D., AND PROF. GEORGE D. HOLMES.

(FATHER AND SON.)

COVINGTON.

THE Rev. James Holmes, well-known as a missionary and preacher, as well as a successful educator, was ordained to the ministry in 1846. He was the son of Abraham Holmes, of Carlisle, Pennsylvania, in which place he was born in 1801. He attended Princeton College one or two years, and afterwards graduated at Dickinson College, Carlisle. After this he entered the theological department at Princeton, but, on account of failing health, never completed his theological course there. He now became a lay missionary to the Chickasaw Indians in North Mississippi, and among them taught and preached from 1825 to 1833.

When the Chickasaws were removed west, Mr. Holmes removed to Tipton county, Tennessee, where, in 1834, he established the Mountain Academy, in which he taught for fifteen years. This establishment was attended by a large number of pupils from Tennessee, Arkansas, Mississippi, Louisiana, and other surrounding States.

In 1849 he was appointed president of the West Tennessee College, at Jackson, and after filling this office with credit for eight years, returned to the Tipton county, Tennessee, and being elected principal of the Tipton Female Seminary. Here he taught till 1868, when he retired from active professional life, and devoted himself to ministrations of religion and humanity, visiting the afflicted and bereaved, and administering the solace of religion to all who would receive it from him. Thus employed, he died, February 4, 1873, leaving behind him a name blessed by innumerable survivors who had received from him either the privileges of a Christian education, or the consolation of Christian sympathy in affliction. Many ministers of the gospel are now doing good service in pulpits throughout the southwestern States who owe their first religious impressions to the early training and teachings of this man of God. Those who remember his conversation, at once genial and sympathetic, unanimously agree in the testimony that no one was ever intimately associated with him without being the better for it.

Dr. Holmes married Sarah A. Van Wagenen, who was born at Newark, New Jersey, in 1801. She was the daughter of Peter Van Wagenen and Sarah Plume. The Van Wagenens were of Dutch extraction. She is still living with her daughter, Mrs. Hall, of Covington, her mind still active and vigorous, and occupied, as it has been all her life, with all matters of a religious character. Dr. Holmes was, by this lady, father of seven children, as follows: (1). Emma, widow of Rev. D. H. Cummins, founder and for many years pastor of the Covington Presbyterian church. (2). Sarah, wife of Dr. W. M. Hall, of Covington. (3). Prof. George D. Holmes, subject of the ensuing sketch. (4). Mary A., wife of Rev. L. McNeely. (5). William B., merchant at Danville, Kentucky. (6). James P., bookkeeper in a bank and insurance agent at Bonham, Texas. (7). Anna W., widow of Capt. T. F. Patterson, of Memphis.

Abraham Holmes, the father of Dr. Holmes, was one of the eleven children of Andrew Holmes, of Pennsylvania. This Andrew was the son of an emigrant from the north of Ireland, who may be considered the founder of the family in America.

PROF. GEORGE D. HOLMES was third child and eldest son of the above. He was born in Marshall county, Mississippi, while his father was pursuing his missionary labors in that State, November 13, 1831. He was brought to Tipton county when two years old, and grew up there.

He received his preparatory education in his father's school, and in 1846 entered Princeton College, New Jersey, where he graduated in 1849. After graduation, he had charge, for eight years, of the preparatory department of West Tennessee College, at Jackson.

In 1857 he settled at Covington, in Tipton county, and taught school there from 1857 to 1868, being associated with his father in the conduct of the Tipton

Female Seminary. In 1868, his father retiring, as related in the former sketch, Prof. Holmes was elected to his present position as principal of that institution.

Prof. Holmes is a Royal Arch Mason, Knight of Honor, an elder in the Presbyterian church, and in politics a Democrat.

He married first, in Jackson, Tennessee, January 24, 1854, Miss Mary E. Pyles, a native of Henderson county, Tennessee. She was the daughter of Addison Pyles, a merchant and planter, of a South Carolina family. Her mother was Martha Crenshaw, also a South Carolina lady. She was educated at Jackson, was a member of the Presbyterian church, and died in 1862, at the age of thirty-one. By this marriage Prof. Holmes became the father of three children: (1). Mattie A., born in 1856; died in infancy. (2). James Addison, born July 20, 1859; educated at the School for the Blind, Nashville; now living with his father. (3). George Walter, born July 9, 1861; graduate of the Baptist University, Jackson, Tennessee; afterward a merchant at Newbern, Tennessee, in partnership with George Jarman, son of Prof. Jarman, of Jackson, and now in business in Kansas City, Missouri.

Prof. Holmes married secondly at Covington, January 18, 1866, Miss Sallie E. Munford, daughter of Col. R. H. Munford, for a long time county court clerk and register of Tipton county. He settled at Randolph, in that county, in 1828, and engaged in trade there, and in 1840 moved to Covington, where he died March 10, 1884, leaving behind him a reputation for the strictest integrity His son, Dr. M. Munford, has, for over ten years, been editor and proprietor of the Kansas City *Times*. Another son, Richard D. Munford, is teller in the Southern Bank of Georgia, at Savannah. His daughter, Ermine, is the widow of Col. John Gracey Hall, of Covington.

The mother of the second Mrs. Holmes was Sarah D., daughter of D. L. Morrison, who died at Covington in 1873, at the age of sixty.

Mrs. Holmes was educated in the Tipton Female Seminary, partly by Prof. Holmes himself. She is a member of the Presbyterian church, and is noted for her energy and for the womanly virtues that endear home to husband and children. By his second marriage, Prof. Holmes has two children: (1). Embry M., born July 27, 1867; now at school in Kansas City, Missouri. (2). Anna Van, born October 14, 1872; died August 31, 1880.

Prof. Holmes attributes his success in life to the methods and principles he inherited from his father, which may be summed up in the simple words, " a conscientious discharge of duty from day to day."

COL. A. J. BROWN.

JONESBOROUGH.

THIS gentleman is a native of the oldest town and of the first county in the State, and grew up, was educated and lived there all his life, having been born in Jonesborough, Tennessee, December 16, 1834. His father being a very poor man, the son passed a rugged boyhood, driving first a two and then a six horse team over the rough mountain roads, hauling produce and iron to Knoxville and Wytheville, Virginia, and merchandise from those places back to Jonesborough and other places in East Tennessee. He was inured from childhood to farm work, plowing, chopping wood, and to do anything as a day laborer. He had no idle, playful childhood, nor joyous, careless boyhood, nor by any means was he a goody-goody sort of boy. Yet he has never to this day tasted liquor, nor been in any way dissipated.

His education was obtained in the old field schools, ten months at Jonesborough Academy, one year at Taylor's Mount, Carter county, and one year at Washington College. While in the latter school he worked for his board, went in debt for his clothes and tuition, which he paid after he went to the bar. He read law under Chief Justice James W. Deaderick, teaching school to support himself while studying law, and reading almost exclusively at night. He was admitted to the bar at Jonesborough, in 1858, by Judge John C. Gaut and Chancellor Seth J. W. Luckey, and practiced his profession at Jonesborough until the war came up. He then, in company with Col. S. K. N. Patton, commenced raising the Tenth East Tennessee cavalry, and in February, 1864, this inchoate regiment was consolidated with the Eighth Tennessee cavalry at Nashville, Patton being made colonel and Brown lieutenant-colonel. The regiment saw service in Tennessee, North Carolina, Virginia and South Carolina. Col. Brown participated in the battles of Greeneville, Bull's Gap, Morristown, Tennessee, and Salisbury and Morganton, North Carolina, and in almost numberless skirmishes. From March 22 to May 1, 1864, Col. Brown commanded the regiment, Eighth Tennessee, in the last raid of the war, from Knoxville through East Tennessee, into North Carolina and Virginia, as far as Christiansburg, Virginia, and returned to North Carolina, and commanded it at the battles of Salisbury and

Morganton. At the close of the war, in May, 1865, he resigned from the army and resumed the practice of law.

Before the war Col. Brown was a Whig, and since the war has been a leading Republican. He was the mayor of Jonesborough in 1861–2, and again after the war. In 1860 he was sub-elector on the Bell and Everett ticket, and in 1876 was sub-elector on the Hayes and Wheeler ticket. In 1882, and again in 1884, he was a delegate to the State Republican convention at Nashville. At the latter he was nominated elector for the State at large, but ordered his name withdrawn. In 1880 he was elected State senator from the counties of Johnson, Carter, Unicoi, Washington and Greene, receiving the largest majority ever given to a senator from that district. In the Senate he took a very prominent and leading part, was chairman of several important committees and recognized as one of the ablest debaters in that body. As a public speaker he had already won a name among the most eloquent of the gifted sons of East Tennessee, but he showed himself an unexceptionally strong man while in the Senate. In a speech called out by a senator who had repeatedly charged that lawyers legislated in their own interest rather than in that of their constituents, Col. Brown replied, substantially, in the following powerful language: "Not on account of what has been said, nor yet on accouut of who said it, but from the manner in which it was said and the persons to whom it was addressed, I notice the remarks of the senator who has just taken his seat. He has seen fit to indulge in a tirade against lawyers as a class. I would say to the senator, it is not the lawyers against whom the people are to be warned, or taught to fear, but it is the arrant demagogue who, by some strange concatenation of human events and by feeding the passions and prejudices of the people, has crept into place and power. I would say to the senator, if he will but read the history of his own country, and not only of his country, but of the world, he will find that every important step that has been taken to advance civil and religious liberty was proposed by lawyers; that they have been the peculiar and steadfast guardians of the rights of man throughout all time; that the forms of every government that has had for its object the perpetuation of civil and religious liberty are the handiwork of lawyers; that they have been as true and steadfast friends of civilization and progress as any other class of men the world has ever known; that by their painstaking and love of order and liberty, they did as much as any other class in untangling the tangled web of governments, of bringing light out of chaos, and order out of confusion, in almost every nation. And that when the Savior of mankind was on earth, forsaken by His kindred and His friends, and denied by His disciples, it was a lawyer who asked for His body and furnished it a tomb for burial."

Col. Brown joined the Methodist church at Jones

borough, in 1856, remaining a member of that communion till 1868, when he transferred his membership to the Presbyterian church; at the same time his wife became a member of the latter church. He is now a ruling elder, has attended presbytery and synod as a delegate, and was a lay delegate to the General Assembly at Madison, Wisconsin, May, 1880.

He became a Mason in Rhea Lodge No. 47, Jonesborough, and is a Knight of Honor, and a member of the Grand Army of the Republic.

Col. Brown married at Jonesborough, September 25, 1862, Miss Agnes M. Wilds, youngest daughter of John A. Wilds, a merchant of that place. Her mother was Caroline Boreing, a native of Washington county. Mrs. Brown was educated at Jonesborough, is of a happy, genial disposition, and noted for devotion to her family and kindness to the poor.

Ten children have been the fruits of their marriage : Carrie Rebecca, Cora May, Clarence Granville, Lillie Baker, Andrew Jackson, Paul Cowan, Horace, Walter Hubert, Agnes Wilds, Edgar Odom.

Col. Brown's father was Enoch Brown, born in Washington county, Tennessee, May 10, 1810. He was a laboring man and ran teams hauling goods and produce up to a short time before the war began. He then sold out his teams, enlisted in the United States army as a private, and was made second-lieutenant of Company I, Eighth Tennessee cavalry. He was in all the battles and skirmishes of the regiment, and was mustered out with his regiment in 1865. After the war he settled down on the farm on which he was born and remained there till his death, September 15, 1878, having been the father of three children : (1). Mary E. Brown, wife of Matthew Carter, now a produce merchant at Sweetwater, Tennessee; has six children, Edgar Vernon Carter, a lawyer at Atlanta, Georgia; Robert L. Carter, who assists his father in business at Sweetwater ; Andrew Paul Carter, a commission merchant of the firm of McGaughey & Carter, Atlanta, Georgia; Walter Carter, clerk for McGaughey & Carter; Fred and Mary Carter. (2). Andrew Jackson Brown, subject of this sketch. (3). Maria Agnes Brown, wife of Robert L. Gillespie; has seven children, Marmora Lake Gillespie, wife of J. D. Self, Telford, Tennessee; Mary Gillespie, wife of Melvin Wells, Washington county ; Ann Gillespie, Sarah Sims Gillespie, Charles Gillespie, Robert and Maria Gillespie, twins.

The grandfather of Col. Brown was Abraham Brown, born in North Carolina, of German parentage, and moved from Tennessee to Illinois, where he died.

Col. Brown's mother, nee Ann Rebecca McMahon, was born in Baltimore, of Scotch descent on her father's side and English on that of her mother. She was twice married: first, to Isaac George, by whom she had three children, Elizabeth, James and Seraphina. The first two are dead. Seraphina George is now the wife of David Barnes, of Washington county, and has five children, Elizabeth, wife of James Grisham; Byron, Andrew J., Ann and Ulysses Grant Barnes.

Col. Brown's mother died February 5, 1855. She was a Methodist, and a woman of strong native intellect, which had been developed by a good education; industrious and domestic in her habits, and devoted to her children. The foundation of the son's success was laid when a boy around his mother's knee. She was his guide and teacher, and knowing the disadvantages under which her son must be reared, she early inspired him with an ambition to improve himself and avail himself of every opportunity for improvement. He was raised to habits of industry and economy. When on the road wagoning he carried his books with him and read them by the camp fires at night, or while his horses were feeding at noon. He embraced every opportunity he found for the education and cultivation of his mind. While teaching school in the country he

walked thirteen miles to recite his law lessons to Judge Deaderick. His rule of life has been to accomplish and encompass all he could by habits of sobriety and industry. Too poor to buy candles while at school in Carter county, he gathered pine-knots and studied by the light of their fitful and flickering blaze. To-day he is a man of strong intellect, of eloquent oratorical ability, of wide and remarkable legal attainments, unostentatious in his manners, modest almost to diffidence, yet a man of power, willing and competent to freely discuss all subjects, except himself. His is but the history of nearly all the men of success whose lives are written in this volume. Indeed, it seems to be a law of success, that no man shall become prominent in Tennessee and worthy to be enrolled among "Prominent Tennesseans," unless he begins at the bottom and works his way up, with courage in himself and fidelity to his duties.

HON. WILLIAM WALLACE McDOWELL.

MEMPHIS.

CHANCELLOR WILLIAM WALLACE Mc-DOWELL was born in Gibson county, Tennessee, June 26, 1835, and grew up there on a farm, receiving his education at Andrew College, Trenton, Tennessee. He entered the law department of Cumberland University at Lebanon, Tennessee, in 1857, and graduated in the summer of 1858, after which he read law one year longer at Trenton, with Judge T. J. Freeman, now of the Supreme bench of Tennessee, and in 1860 began to practice with him.

He has always been a Democrat; in 1860 belonged to the Douglass' wing of the party, and opposed secession, but went with his State after it seceded, and entered the Confederate service May 13, 1861, receiving a commission as first lieutenant in the Twelfth regiment Tennessee infantry. At the battle of Belmont, November, 1861, he received a severe wound from a bullet, which he still carries in his body. At Shiloh, in April, 1862, he was again wounded, and shortly after this battle was made captain of his company. Fearing to remain in the infantry service on account of his old wounds, about one month after the Shiloh fight he got permission from the Confederate war department to raise a company of cavalry. The company was composed of Tennessee and Mississippi volunteers, and he being made its captain, became connected with Col. Balentine's regiment of Gen. William H. Jackson's division, and operated during the war in Mississippi, Alabama, Georgia and Tennessee. During a portion of this time his command was connected with the cavalry of Gen.

Forrest, with whom he surrendered at Gainesville, Alabama, May 13, 1865, just four years from the date he entered the service.

The war over, he returned to Tennessee and edited the *Trenton Gazette* for one year, when he resumed the practice of law in partnership with Samuel Brewer, since distinguished as a minister of the Methodist church. In January, 1868, he removed to Memphis and became the law partner of Col. George Gantt, with whom he continued in partnership for about e'ght years. In 1871 he was elected county attorney for Shelby county, and was re-elected to that office for five successive years, at the end of which he declined re-election. He was appointed chancellor by Gov. James D. Porter, and held the office under this appointment until August, 1880, when he was elected by the people, receiving a majority of four thousand five hundred votes over J. E. Bigelow—one thousand two hundred votes more than any candidate on the ticket, except Judge Horrigan, who was nominated by both Democrats and Republicans. This office he still fills.

In 1872 Judge McDowell was district elector on the Greeley ticket. He has never been a candidate for any office, other than those he has held.

He became a Master Mason at Trenton in 1867, and a Royal Arch Mason at Memphis in 1881; is a member of the Knights of Honor, and of the Ancient Order of United Workmen. He became a member of the Cumberland Presbyterian church at Memphis, in 1884.

The ancestors of Judge McDowell, the McDowells and Irwins, emigrated from Ireland to Lancaster county, Pennsylvania, some time prior to 1750. From there his great-grandfather, who was born in 1743, moved to Mecklenburg county, North Carolina, where his son, John McDowell, was born March 18, 1775, and his grandson, John D. McDowell, the father of the judge, was born January 10, 1810, and moved to Gibson county, Tennessee, in 1832. The judge's great-grandfather, Robert Irwin, also emigrated from Pennsylvania to Mecklenburg, North Carolina.

Judge McDowell's father, John D. McDowell, was a farmer by occupation and a zealous member of the Presbyterian church, and though he never held any civil office, except justice of the peace, was a man of prominence and influence in his county. The family is of Irish descent, and is the same family to which the late Major-General Irwin McDowell, of the United States army, and Gov. McDowell, of the famous Virginia orator, belong. His brother, Hon. John H. McDowell, of Union City, Tennessee, represented Obion county in the Legislature of 1882-3, and was State senator from his district in the Tennessee Legislature for 1885-6, and is the author of the celebrated " gambling bill " passed by those bodies. His other brother, Samuel Irwin McDowell, is a prominent citizen and Democrat of Memphis, Tennessee, and is now clerk and master of the chancery court of Shelby county, to which position he was appointed in November, 1884, upon the recommendation of two-thirds of the bar of that county. He also has three sisters, Mrs. C. F. H. Harrison, Jennie S. Mitchum and Loura A. McNeilly, the last two of whom are widows.

Judge McDowell's mother, nee Miss Nancy H. Irwin, was the daughter of William Irwin, of Mecklenburg county, North Carolina, and grand-daughter of Gen. Robert Irwin, of Revolutionary fame, one of the signers of the Mecklenburg Declaration of Independence, who moved from Pennsylvania to that county.

Judge McDowell was married, March 27, 1867, to Miss Anna Jones, daughter of Thomas Jones, of Memphis, and grand-daughter of Rev. John W. Jones, a Methodist minister of Gibson county. She is also a cousin of Judge T. J. Freeman, of the Tennessee Supreme Court, and of Judge Carthell, of Trenton. Her mother was Miss Mary Kimball, of Maury county, Tennessee.

Mrs. McDowell died December 11, 1882, the mother of four children : (1). Eulalia E. McDowell, born November 11, 1868. (2). John O. McDowell, born August 11, 1873. (3). W. W. McDowell, jr., born January 10, 1875. (4). Annie L. McDowell, born December 11, 1877 ; died May 8, 1884.

On the 14th of October, 1885, he married Mrs. Lizzie A. Freeman, widow of E. T. Freeman. She was born June 26, 1853, and has one daughter, Edna A. Freeman, who was born June 11, 1877. Mrs. McDowell is

the daughter of Capt. Joseph Lenow, who is and has been one of the most liberal, progressive and enterprising citizens of Memphis, Tennessee, for a third of a century, and is known as the founder of Elmwood cemetery. He was born December 24, 1813, in Southampton county, Virginia.

Judge McDowell has always led a strictly moral and sober life. He never gambled, was never intoxicated, and never swore an oath. He has been a hard worker, and has always had a large practice. He is fond of activity, and indulges in hunting as a relaxation from the labors of his profession.

One of the leading members of the Memphis bar says : " Judge McDowell has made a reputation for being a conscientious, painstaking judge, who thoroughly investigates all cases submitted to his decision, and has the confidence of the entire community."

Another says : " When made chancellor he had not had much experience in equity practice, but, to the surprise of the bar, he exhibited from the first a high order of capacity for the duties of the position. He is gifted with a power of rapid comprehension, and a tenacity of memory quite unusual. These enable him to fix his attention upon the presentation of a case, to grasp and group the facts, and to clearly perceive the questions to be decided. His knowledge of men, derived from actual mingling with them, has greatly aided him to understand the under-currents of feeling and motive that influence human action, and thus to ascertain the real equities which legal contrivances involve. His mind is of the judicial order. No trace of partisanship or partiality can be found in his judgments. He listens patiently to argument, which for him tends to elucidation, but the quickness of his perception leads him to discourage much of detailed discussion, which might be acceptable and helpful to a slower mind. Mere technicalities do not stand high in his favor; nor does he plod willingly through the misty analogies of decided cases, by which lawyers are prone to seek support for their positions. He looks much more to the reasons and principles than to the number of decisions, and much more to the fundamental right as between the parties than the precedents that may seem to correspond in general form and feature with the case in hand. He discriminates well, and in his discrimination lies his strength as a judge. He is no innovator, and always recognizes as settled, at least for him, whatever our own Supreme Court has so declared. Appeals from his decisions, and reversals on appeal, are as infrequent as in the case of any chancellor in the State. His great administrative capacity and tact in the dispatch of business, enable him to keep well in hand a very heavy docket, and also enable him, while performing immense labor, to husband, in some measure, his physical resources. He is yet a young man. He grows as a judge by his judicial labor. His memory lets go no principle or method which he has learned to be of value. On or

17

off the bench, therefore, he will always be a well-grounded lawyer, learned in the reasons rather than in the names of cases, and skilled in jurisprudence as something meant to regulate the developments of busy life rather than as a code of rules or a system of abstractions."

HON. G. W. SMITHEAL.

COVINGTON.

MR. SMITHEAL was born at Covington, Tennessee, August 23d, 1835, and has made his home in his native town ever since. He was educated there by Prof. James Byars, a fine English and classical scholar, recognized as their teacher by many of the leading men of Tipton county. Under this eminent teacher he acquired a knowledge of Greek, Latin and mathematics, and then, at the age of eighteen, commenced the study of law in the office of Bate & Morrison. Here he studied two years, acting part of the time as deputy clerk of the chancery court through the appointment of Judge W. M. Smith, now of Memphis. He was licensed to practice law in 1859 by Chancellor Smith and Judge John C. Humphreys, and has been engaged in his profession ever since with good success from the first.

At the commencement of the civil war, he entered the Confederate States army as a volunteer, enlisting as private in Company I, Capt. J. G. Hall, of the Fifty-first Tennessee regiment, in Gen. Daniel S. Donelson's brigade, Cheatham's division. He remained in the same command throughout the war, and was soon promoted to the rank of first lieutenant and adjutant of the regiment. He served with his command in Tennessee, Mississippi and Georgia, and participated in the battles of Shiloh, Murfreesborough, Chickamauga, Missionary Ridge, and all the battles of the Georgia campaign from Dalton to Atlanta. From Atlanta he was sent on the sick list to hospital at Columbus, Georgia, where he remained on post duty till Wilson's raid, when he surrendered as prisoner; was paroled at Macon, Georgia. He was elected major of his regiment in 1862, but declined the rank.

He returned home July 3d, 1865, and formed a law partnersip with Col. H. R. Bate, which has continued to the present day. This firm has been engaged in all the important cases which have for twenty years arisen in the courts of Tipton and the neighboring counties.

In politics, he cast his first vote for Millard Fillmore, and in the election of 1860 voted for Bell and Everett; but, since the war, has acted with the Democratic party. He several times declined to become a candidate for the Legislature. In 1874 he was a candidate before the nominating convention at Humboldt for Congress, but failed to receive the nomination by one vote. In 1876 he was district presidential elector on the Tilden ticket. In 1880 he supported the Wilson wing of the Democratic party against John V. Wright for governor, and was a candidate for the Legislature on that ticket, but was defeated. In 1882 he was again a candidate, and in the State convention of that year made persevering efforts to harmonize the divided party; he was nominated and elected with the united support of both wings of the party—but the party was not harmonized. In the Legislature he was chairman of the committee on public roads and a member of several other important commitees.

He has served as alderman of Covington for ten years.

In religion he professes the creed of his ancestors—that of the Presbyterian church.

Mr. T. Smitheal, the father of G. W. Smitheal, was born in Rowan county, State of North Carolina, the son of John L. Smitheal, of that county. He continued to reside in North Carolina until he became of age, and then migrated to Tipton county, Tennessee, in the year 1832, being among the first settlers of the county. In 1833 he was married to Miss Caroline Young, daughter of Robert and Sarah Young. Mr. T. Smitheal died in 1875, in the seventieth year of his age, a deacon in the Presbyterian church, a consistent and pious member of that communion. He was a strict but kind parent, and a faithful and trusted man in all the relations of life.

Mr. G. W. Smitheal's mother, Caroline Smitheal, *nee* Young, was born in Hawkins county, Tennessee, in the year 1808. She moved with her parents, Robert and Sarah Young, to Tipton county in the latter part of the year 1831, and was married in 1833 to Mr. T. Smitheal, and became the mother of four children: (1). Green W., the subject of this sketch. (2). William T., a merchant, Navasota, Texas. (3). Narcissa C., wife of William Hamilton, merchant, Covington, Tennessee. (4) Bettie T., now living unmarried with her sister, Mrs. Hamilton.

Mr. G. W. Smitheal married, first in Covington, Tennessee, Miss Florence Strother Menefee, daughter of Dr. B. S. Menefee, of that place, originally from Virginia, and a family distinguished for its refinement and culture. By this marriage Mr. Smitheal had one child, Elizabeth Maud, who died in childhood in 1874. The mother herself died the year following.

Mr. Smitheal married next in Memphis, January 27, 1880, Miss Susan Dalton Jackson, daughter of Capt.

Shepherd Jackson, who fell at Corinth in the early part of the war. Mrs. Jackson was Miss Mary Harris, a native of Fayette county, Tennessee, a lady of great energy and kindness of heart, particularly noted for her hospitality. Mrs. Smitheal was educated in a Catholic school at Memphis and is a member of the Episcopal church, a lady of intelligence, refinement and culture. By this marriage Mr. Smitheal has three children, Mary Shepherd, Florence Jackson and G. W. Smitheal, jr.

He has been a sober, self-contained man, who has lived within his income, and through close attention to business has been successful in life, his object being to make a safe and honest living, preferring a quiet domestic life to public position. He is self-made; was unable

through restricted means to go to college, but as a student of law, manifested a degree of industry and talent which induced his precepter, Mr. Bate, to offer him a partnership at the close of the civil war.

He is a high-toned, moral gentleman, and his influence, always exerted on the side of right, is good and salutary.* His word or simple statement is taken among those who know him as an ample guarantee for truth. He has natural rhetorical gifts which constitute him a fine speaker, powerful especially before a jury; for this reason he has been largely employed in criminal cases. As a friend, a neighbor, a church member and a man, he commands the high esteem of all who associate with him.

CHARLES S. BRIGGS, A.M., M.D.

NASHVILLE.

THIS eminent young surgeon, son of the illustrious surgeon, Dr. W. T. Briggs, whose biography appears in another place in this book, was born in Bowling Green, Kentucky, March 29, 1851. He was educated in Nashville and took the degree of A.M. in the regular course from the literary department of the University of Nashville, in 1873. Accustomed from his early boyhood to think of becoming a physician and surgeon, the whole bent of his mind was trained in that direction. Even his classical course was studied with that end in view. This, of course, his father enthusiastically endorsed and encouraged, and although the history of the Briggs family has been given elsewhere in this volume, the subject of this sketch has risen to such prominence as a practitioner, medical professor and editor, it is due to him to have special mention made.

Immediately after graduating from the literary department, young Briggs began the study of medicine, and particularly surgery, under his father, and graduated in 1875 as an M.D. from the medical department of the University of Nashville and Vanderbilt University. In 1875 he was attached to the clinical staff of Prof. S. D. Gross at Philadelphia, and worked with him for six months, devoting himself while there to surgery, pathology, microscopy and hospital work. During his stay at Philadelphia, Dr. Briggs was elected demonstrator of anatomy of his alma mater, and returned to Nashville and began work in that position in the autumn of 1875. In this he was engaged three years. In 1878, in addition to that position, he was elected adjunct professor of anatomy and held that place one year. On account of sickness he resigned the demonstratorship in 1880 and soon after was tendered the adjunct professorship of surgery, in which chair he lectured three years on genito-urinary surgery. In 1883 he was elected to the

position he now holds—professor of surgical anatomy and operative surgery in the University of Nashville and Vanderbilt University.

In 1876 Dr. Charles S. Briggs was associated with Dr. W. L. Nichol as editor of the Nashville Journal of Medicine and Surgery, an able periodical, founded by Dr. W. K. Bowling. In this position Dr. Briggs succeeded his father, and soon after, Dr. Nichol retiring, he became the sole editor. Dr. Briggs is a member of the State, county and city medical societies, and has contributed many valuable articles to those organizations, in addition to the able work he has done on his journal. He is also a member of the American Association for the Advancement of Science, and at its session at Nashville, 1878, took an active part in the microscopical department.

Dr. Briggs has risen rapidly in his profession, and has already performed most of the major operations in surgery; among them, amputations of the shoulder joint, ovariotomy, lithotomy, trephining, ligation of the principal vessels, removal of the upper jaw (twice), excision of the elbow joint, and amputation of all the limbs. Having had the advantage of the instruction, and of witnessing, assisting in, and studying the methods of two of the leading surgeons of this country, his father and Dr. Gross, it is not a matter of astonishment that he is so early in life prominent in the line of his inherited and chosen profession. Dr. Briggs' private practice is large and rapidly increasing, his collections now amounting to about five thousand dollars per annum. Financially he is in easy circumstances.

When young he was a leader in athletic, boyish sports. Now he is a well-rounded man of large proportions, standing five feet eleven inches high, and weighs two hundred pounds. His remarkable grandfather,

Dr. John M. Briggs, of Bowling Green, Kentucky, to whom chiefly this distinguished family owes its standing in the medical world, while in his eightieth year, said to the subject of this sketch, then a mere lad, " Charles, I want you to live in such a way that when you are eighty years old, as I am, you may say of yourself what I can say of myself, that I cannot recall a single instance of my life of which I am ashamed." That advice followed out will ultimately ennoble any family.

Dr. Briggs married in Louisville, Kentucky, April 26, 1876, Miss Carrie Carter, a native of that city, educated at Science Hill Academy, Shelbyville, Kentucky, and at the Louisville Female High School. Her father is a member of the large wholesale dry goods firm of Carter Bros. & Co., Louisville. Her mother, *nee* Miss Binnie Carter, is a relative of the Toombs family of Georgia, and remarkable for her charities and purity of life. By his marriage with Miss Carter Dr. Briggs has three children : (1). Elsie. (2). Binnie. (3). William T., jr.

Dr. Briggs is spoken of as one of the best educated men of his age in Nashville, and is a student in every sense, but makes his learning subserve the one purpose of his life, to excel in his profession. He is a strong man, of broad, comprehensive mind, and emphasizes whatever he undertakes. He has a concentrated look, with a chin and general physique indicating energy, push, self-poise and boldness—qualities essential in a surgeon. His future is brilliant.

HON. WILLIAM M. BRADFORD.

CHATTANOOGA.

THIS distinguished jurist, now chancellor of the Third chancery division of Tennessee, was born in McMinn county (now Polk), Tennessee, February 14, 1827. He is the son of Col. Henry Bradford, and was the youngest of ten children, nine sons and one daughter. His father, Col. Henry Bradford, was born in Burke county, North Carolina, December 24, 1776, moved to Jefferson county, Tennessee, in 1796, and married, in 1799, Miss Rachel McFarland, of the family of one of the late judges of the Supreme Court of Tennessee, Hon. Robert McFarland. She died in 1852, aged sixty-seven years. Her ancestors were from Scotland, but no detailed history of the family has been preserved. Col. Henry Bradford was an excellent gunsmith, and made the gun that Davy Crockett called his " Long Bess." He was also a justice of the peace, and performed the marriage ceremony for Davy Crockett. He was an elector on the Madison ticket in 1812; and represented Jefferson county in the Tennessee Legislature from 1811 to 1821. He removed to Polk county in 1821, and died there May 10, 1871, at the advanced age of ninety-five years. He was a man of extraordinary energy and decision of character, and, for his times, of superior intelligence. His father was Joseph Bennett Bradford, of Fauquier county, Virginia, who died in Caldwell county, North Carolina, in 1830, also aged ninety-five years. Joseph Bennett Bradford's father was John Bradford, of Fauquier county, Virginia, who, according to the tradition of the family, was a great-grandson of Gov. William Bradford, of " Mayflower " fame.

Gen. Alexander B. Bradford, who was a colonel in the Florida war, and a major in Col. Jefferson Davis' regiment in the Mexican war, was a double-cousin of Judge Bradford. There was a Maj. Henry Bradford in the Revolutionary war in Harry Lee's brigade, who distinguished himself. He was a cousin of Judge Bradford's father. Many of his descendants—the Nichol, Cowden, Fall and Foster families, of Nashville, are members of the Bradford family. There are also families of Bradfords at Huntsville, Alabama, who are descendants of Judge Bradford's father's half-brother, William Bradford, who had four sons, Joseph, Morgan, Larkin and Fielding Bradford, who settled at Huntsville, Alabama.

The early life of Judge Bradford was spent in the healthy and salubrious mountain atmosphere of Polk county, Tennessee. Here he grew up, developing tastes and habits in the direction of attaining the best education that could be obtained in the rural districts in which he lived. He attended an excellent school, from 1840 to 1844, at " Forest Hill," Athens, Tennessee, under the supervision of Charles P. Samuel, a fine scholar and educator. At the age of seventeen he was elected county surveyor of Polk county; at eighteen was appointed postmaster at Columbus, Tennessee, and the same year began the study of law under the late Judge Charles F. Keith. He obtained license to practice his profession at the age of twenty, from Judges Thomas L. Williams and R. M. Anderson, and also was married the same year to Miss E. K. Inman at Dandridge, Tennessee. He located at Dandridge, and the next year, being but twenty-one years old, was elected a justice of the peace. At twenty-four he was appointed clerk and master of the chancery court at Dandridge, and held that position from 1851 to 1859. During this period he was also a merchant for five years, but never lost sight of his legal profession, studying and practicing continually.

In 1859 he was nominated by a Whig convention for

the State senate; resigned his clerkship and was elected senator from Jefferson, Hawkins and Hancock counties, without opposition. At the close of the memorable sessions of the Legislature, 1859–60, he volunteered in the Confederate army, and in February, 1862, was elected colonel of the Thirty-first Tennessee mounted infantry, and served as colonel of the regiment, having been re-elected, until the close of the war. He participated in many battles and skirmishes, and bore himself with gallantry at the siege of Vicksburg, and in the battles of Morristown, Tennessee, Ball's Gap and Marion, Virginia, Champion Hills, Mississippi, and others.

At the termination of the war, in 1865, Col. Bradford removed to Athens, Tennessee, and engaged in the practice of law, as partner with the able Col. A. Blizard, and so continued until August 19, 1875. On this last date the Hon. D. M. Key, chancellor of the Third chancery division of Tennessee, having been appointed to the United States Senate, Gov. James D. Porter appointed Col. Bradford to fill the place hitherto occupied by Judge Key. In August, 1876, Judge Bradford was elected by the people, Hon. D. C. Trewhitt being his competitor. In August, 1878, he was re-elected for the full term of eight years, Hon. P. B. Mayfield being his competitor. He is now presiding chancellor at Chattanooga, having removed to that city in 1880.

Judge Bradford married Miss Elizabeth K. Inman, September 23, 1846, at Dandridge, Tennessee. She was the daughter of Shadrach and Sarah Inman. Her mother's family was named Henderson. Mrs. Bradford is a lady of remarkably fine sense, modest deportment, fine appearance, and of great purity of character. She is never elated in prosperity; and under trials of adversity she never manifests trouble to those who surround her in the family circle. She and Judge Bradford are both members of the Presbyterian church, South, at Chattanooga. When Judge Bradford started in life a married man he had no capital. When the war broke out he had accumulated about twenty-five thousand dollars in negroes and personalty. The misfortunes which befell him at the close of the war left him penniless. He began life anew with less than nothing, for he owed security debts, which have all been paid in full, and he is now in comfortable circumstances. He never promised a dollar that he did not pay it at the hour when demanded. Such fortune as he has accumulated since the war he has presented to his noble wife, for her Christian forbearance and fortitude in rearing their children during that trying and eventful period.

By his marriage with Miss Inman Judge Bradford has five children living of eleven born, six having died in infancy or early childhood. Those surviving are : (1). May Bradford, born in Jefferson county, there educated, and now under the paternal roof. (2). Linda

Bradford, born in Jefferson county; educated at Sullin's Institute, Athens, Tennessee; married, in 1879, Dr. O. E. Rose, of Athens, nephew of Gov. William G. Brownlow; now practicing medicine at Chattanooga; they have two children, Gus Bradford and Elizabeth. (3). Henry Bradford, born in Jefferson county, November 27, 1855; educated at the University at Athens, Tennessee; began life at sixteen as a merchant's clerk; has made a remarkable success, and is now with the firm of Whitfield, Powers & Co., New York city. (4). Elizabeth Tipton Bradford, born in Jefferson county; educated also at Athens; married in 1877, John H. Cleage, a furniture merchant at Chattanooga, and has two children, William and Elizabeth. (5). Augusta Franklin Bradford, born in Jefferson county, and educated at Chattanooga.

Judge Bradford is a Mason, the only secret society to which he belongs, and joined the Lodge at Dandridge, in 1850, served three years as Worshipful Master, and took the Chapter degrees in 1874, at Athens, Tennessee. Before the war a Whig, since the war he has been an undeviating, consistent and conscientious Democrat. He was never drunk in his life, and in all things is strictly a temperate man. As a lawyer he is chiefly noted for his rigid discipline, brevity of argument and briefs, and avoidance of long-winded, tedious and prolix pleadings and practice. As a chancellor he tries to model his court after the same style. His success in life is attributable to an indomitable energy, together with an honest resolution to deal honestly with all men, under all circumstances, and fairness and impartiality mark his course in every emergency and in every station.

Few men are so fond of telling a good anecdote, of giving a good hearty hand-shake, or who enjoy social life and good neighborhood so well as Judge Bradford. In this respect he is a type of the Tennessee gentleman of the old *regime*. With dignity of character he unites great plainness and directness of address, and is noted for his impulsive hospitality and liberality. A finished gentleman and prominent among the eminent jurists of Tennessee, he is equally distinguished for those fine social qualities called "flow of soul" that give every man who meets him a cheerful opinion of himself and of human nature. A man of consummate grace of manner and adaptability, he is so deferentially respectful as to divert his company's attention away from himself into an introspection of themselves. With all classes of people, school-girls promenading on the streets, shopmen, stalwart farmers, literati, professional men of all sorts, and mechanics, he seems equally at home, and has the enviable faculty of appearing to take infinite pains to make everybody feel at home with him. His father trained him and his brothers to do all manner of mechanical work needed on a farm, and when a mere boy Judge Bradford could make a horseshoe and nail it on.

HON. GEORGE W. MARTIN.

MARTIN.

GEORGE W. MARTIN was born in Weakley county, Tennessee, October 16, 1839. William Martin, his father, was born in Halifax county, Virginia, January 30, 1806, and died in Weakley county, Tennessee, January 17, 1859. His ancestors were among the first settlers of Virginia, but claim no lineage from titled royalty, but with pride they refer to a long line of descendants, each one handing down to the other an untarnished reputation. He was reared on a farm, and received, for that day, a good education in the schools of the county. He married while quite young, against the wishes of her parents, Sarah Glass, of Halifax county, Virginia. Soon after his marriage his wife's parents moved from Virginia to Weakley county, Tennessee, and in 1832 he followed, and settled six miles northeast of Dresden, Weakley county. When he settled in Weakley county, he had about half a dozen slaves, a few hundred dollars in money, a wagon and team, and household furniture for a small family. His family having been tobacco farmers in Virginia for several generations, and as he had been reared on a tobacco plantation himself, he very naturally brought with him tobacco seed to Tennessee, and to him belongs the honor of planting the first tobacco ever raised in Weakley county. From the beginning he made a specialty of tobacco culture, and made a great success of it, and continued up to his death to be the largest tobacco raiser in his county. He not only cultivated tobacco largely, but for many years he bought largely and shipped it on his own flatboats down the Obion and Mississippi rivers to New Orleans. In 1839 he moved from his farm northeast of Dresden to a large tract of fine woodland nine miles west of Dresden, on the well-known stage road leading from Nashville to Hickman, Kentucky. Here, upon this magnificent landed domain, the life and sphere of William Martin at once began to broaden and widen, and from 1839 to 1859, the latter the year of his death, no man ever led a more active life. Everything he undertook prospered, and he grew rich rapidly. Though he was only fifty-three years old when he died, he was worth a quarter of a million dollars. He was never a candidate for office, and never held any. His life was purely the life of a business man, and in that line he had but few equals. No man of the county ever had more friends, and no one ever did more to deserve them. His faults, whatever they were, injured no one but himself, and no one was more outspoken for the right than he, and no one more positive against the wrong. He was a Whig in politics, and always took a lively interest in behalf of Whig candidates. He was thoroughly alive to all public enterprises, and took an active part in behalf of the Nashville and Northwestern railroad, and subscribed liberally to help build the road through the county. He was a man of individuality, strong will-power, decision of character, and arrived at definite conclusions quickly. When he once set out to perform a certain thing, no obstacle seemed to deter him. He was genial and sunny, fond of fun, and never morose. His house was on a public highway, and it was always open to the traveler, let him be friend or stranger, free of charge.

Sarah Martin, *nee* Glass, mother of George W. Martin, and wife of William Martin, was born in Halifax county, Virginia, July 26, 1810. Her father, Dudley Glass, was a man of considerable means, and gave his daughter a fine education, and was displeased when she married, as he preferred her remaining single a few years longer. She was a lady of commanding appearance, rather tall and graceful. She was never stout, and therefore did not live to be very old. She died in Weakley county, Tennessee, July 29, 1853. Several of her brothers were men of prominence and distinction. Thomas Glass is one of the most successful and prominent planters of Weakley county. John Glass, of Trenton, Tennessee, was one of the most cultivated and accomplished gentlemen of the State. Presley T. Glass, of Ripley, Tennessee, has been a member of the General Assembly of the State of Tennessee, and a member of the United States Congress, and was a prominent member of each body. He is a gentleman of large information, and is now, and has been all his life, a close student. But few gentlemen of the State are so thoroughly acquainted with the history of Tennessee. He is a gentleman of great modesty, and claims less for himself than is conceded to him by others.

George W. Martin was born and reared on a farm nine miles west of Dresden. He was the fifth child, having four brothers and sisters older and four younger than himself. He was kept constantly at school in the neighborhood from eight years old until fourteen—most of the time walking three miles. At school he was idle and full of mischief, and the rod was used on him with great freedom. Whenever a strange noise or an unknown prank took place in the school-room and the offender was not known to the teacher, it was generally fastened upon George. The teacher to whom he went the greatest length of time, did him the credit of saying in after years that he would always confess and tell the truth when called upon for information, although he knew it would in many cases cost him a whipping. During the entire time of going to school in the neighborhood books were distasteful to him, and he looked forward with great pleasure to the time when his school days would be over. His father believed thoroughly in the beneficial results of industry, and he never allowed his children to grow up in idleness, but always found something for them to do during vacation, and George was taught all kinds of farm work. At this time he made much better progress at the plow-handles than he did in the school-room. When he was about fifteen years of age, he was sent to the Male Academy of Dresden, Weakley county, and boarded with the family of Maj. Alfred Gardner. Here he studied better, and began to feel the importance of an education, and was popular with his teachers. After going to the academy in Dresden for one year, he was sent to Bethel College, at McLemoresville, Tennessee, at that time one of the most flourishing schools in the State. Here he found about three hundred young men from all parts of the South; a well-selected library of several thousand books, a well-filled laboratory, and a corps of competent teachers. Here a total change took place in George. He joined one of the literary societies, took a great interest in the debates, and at once began to read books. His taste first led in the direction of light biography, then to history. The first ten months he read over twenty-five volumes of biography and history outside of a full course of studies. He has been fond of books and a great reader since this period. After remaining at Bethel College for two years, he went to Union University, at Murfreesborough, Tennessee—took a full English course, and studied Latin, French and German; belonged to the Calliopean society, and was elected to deliver the commencement address for that society.

In a few months after leaving Union University, he joined the Ninth Tennessee regiment, and in May, 1861, was mustered into the *service of the State of Tennessee* for twelve months, at Jackson, Tennessee. His regiment was at Columbus, Kentucky, the day the battle of Belmont was fought, but was held in reserve, and did not cross the river. When the battle of Shiloh was fought, G. W. Martin was in the hospital in Mississippi. His term in the service of the State of Tennessee expired in May, 1862, and he did not enlist in the Confederate service. He went to his home in Weakley county, and remained there for a few months, but soon found he could not live there in peace, and resolved to leave the country until the war was over. He left New York for Europe early in 1863, and remained there until about the close of the war. He visited all of the leading countries of Europe, and remained long enough in each to become well acquainted with the manners and customs of the people. After an extended trip of more than a year, he went to Paris and took rooms in the Latin quarter, near the university, and convenient to the library of St. Genevieve. He made this his head-quarters for about ten months, and when not engaged in short excursions in and around the city, he was in the library, reading up the history of each country he had visited. Here he met George Alfred Townsend (Gath), and for several months they roomed together.

He learned to speak the French and German languages fairly well, but could not speak either so as to be understood when he first entered the country, though he had studied each at college.

He returned to New York a few months before the war closed, and remained there until it did close, when he went to his old home in Weakley county. He found all the live stock of all kinds gone, the farm in a dilapidated condition, the labor system thoroughly demoralized. He remained on the farm for two years, but was not satisfied with the results. He rented the farm and erected a saw mill at Gardner station, Weakley county, Tennessee, and operated it for one year with fine results and sold it.

In 1869 he erected a large grist mill, steam cotton gin and wool-carding machinery at Gardner station. He operated this machinery with great success until 1873, then sold it.

The Mississippi Central railroad was extended from Jackson, Tennessee, to Cairo, Illinois, in the year 1873, and it crossed the Nashville, Chattanooga and St. Louis railway on his land, near his father's old homestead. He laid off the town of Martin at the junction of the two roads in May, 1873, and at once erected a large saw mill, flouring mill, steam cotton gin, and built a large hotel, together with many other buildings of less note. In ten years from the time the town of Martin was laid out it had a population of fifteen hundred inhabitants, three white and two colored churches, a fine academy with two hundred pupils, a large planing mill, a number of fine brick business houses, and many handsome private residences. George W. Martin contributed largely in building up the town, and always took an active part in all public enterprises.

From 1868 to 1880, his life was one of *great activity*, and he made money very rapidly. He made no business mistakes.

On the 23d of May, 1878, he married Miss Mattie Williams, daughter of D. P. Williams, of Haywood county, Tennessee. Miss Williams was the grand-daughter of Rev. Thomas Joyner, of North Mississippi. Her father came from Mecklenburg county, Virginia, and settled in Haywood county, Tennessee, in 1826.

Mr. Martin took a bridal tour to Europe, and spent the remainder of the year 1878 in an extended tour, visiting the great universal exposition of Paris, and all the principal European cities.

Mr. Martin has always taken a prominent part in politics, and is a Democrat. He was elected to the lower house of the Thirty-eighth General Assembly of the State of Tennessee, for the years 1873-74. He advocated the public school system in his county when it was unpopular, and aided in passing a law allowing counties to levy a tax for school purposes, and that law is the basis of the present school system of the State. He introduced, in 1873, the first bill ever introduced in the Tennessee Legislature on the subject of State regulation and control of railroads. The bill did not pass that session, but the principle was adopted by all parties in a few years. He was elected to the State Senate for the years 1877–78, from the counties of Henry, Weakley, Obion and Lake. During that session the adjustment of the State debt was the most important question. He was elected by the Senate as one of the commissioners whose duty it was to go to New York and ascertain from the creditors of the State upon what terms the State debt could be settled. A proposition was made to settle the debt at sixty cents on the dollar, the new bonds of the State issued in place of the old ones to have interest-bearing coupons that were to be made receivable for all State taxes. He opposed the proposition upon the ground that the Legislature could not make coupons receivable for taxes, and the Supreme court of the State afterwards sustained that position. He held that precedent justified the State in making a proposition of adjustment to the creditors, and acting upon that principle, he introduced in the Senate a bill to settle the debt at fifty cents on the dollar, and the new bonds to bear four per cent. per annum for five years, five per cent. for five years, and six per cent. for ten years, at which time they were due. The bill passed the Senate, but failed in the House. It was opposed by many of the most prominent men of Tennessee upon the ground that the State could accept propositions to settle the debt with honor, but could not make propositions to scale the debt without dishonor. A few years after the State debt was permanently settled upon the principle that the State had a right to make propositions. In 1880 the great split in the Democratic party took place in regard to the State debt. The State credit wing was led by John V. Wright, and the low tax wing by S. F. Wilson. We have had nothing in the State to equal the excitement of that year since the commencement of the civil war. It was generally conceded that Weakley county was a low tax county, and the low tax candidate and his friends claimed that he would carry the county by fifteen hundred or two thousand majority. When the State credit Democrats met in convention to nominate a candidate for the lower house of the Legislature, they found several candidates before them, but it was not believed that either of them could be elected. Mr. Martin was unanimously nominated against his protest, and, very much against his wishes, persuaded to accept the nomination. After the most exciting race ever made in the county, he was elected by six hundred and fifty-two majority. During this session, what was known as the one hundred-and-three bill passed. It provided that the entire debt of the State should be settled dollar for dollar, with three per cent. interest, the coupons to be made receivable for all State taxes. Mr. Martin voted against it.

He was nominated by the Democratic convention, against his protest, for the State Senate, from the counties of Henry and Weakley for the years 1885–86, and elected without opposition.

He has served two sessions in the lower and two in the upper house of the General Assembly of the State, and the two first sessions he announced himself as a candidate, but the two last sessions he accepted the office to please his friends—he did not desire or ask for it.

Mr. Martin has never sought popularity, but he values and has received such public approval as follows merit. Popularity that is raised without merit and lost without crime, he has never labored to secure. In his public and private life, his object has always been to do right rather than do what would be popular. He detests show of all kinds, and never makes an effort at display in anything. As a speaker he is dignified and forcible. He deals in facts; and with the aid of his great store of information, is always able to throw much light upon any subject he may discuss.

In the social circle Mr. Martin is particularly fortunate; possessing rare conversational powers, combined with a social, genial nature, which render him a most agreeable companion. He is a man of warm impulses, active sympathy, and while in early years he was somewhat irritable, yet at all times his anger was like the spark, soon gone. He is entirely without malice; is positive by nature, and one will never be misled with regard to his position, as he is never non-committal on important matters. Those who know Mr. Martin best like him most.

He joined the church to which his wife had belonged from infancy—the Methodist Episcopal church, South—in the summer of 1883, and takes a great interest in church and Sunday-school matters.

He has always been ardently in favor of educating the masses, and he is now having a public school taught at his own expense in the town of Martin.

He gives liberally to the church and to all kinds of public enterprises. He is now living at "Malema," one of the most beautiful homes in West Tennessee, just east of the town of Martin, in plain view of the place where he was born.

The last business enterprise he engaged in was the organization of the Bank of Fulton, Kentucky. He was the first president of the bank, but resigned, as he did not desire to engage in active business pursuits.

He is now living upon an ample income, derived from rents, bank stock, interest-bearing securities and the returns from a cattle ranch in western Texas. He has no children.

Mr. Martin is a great reader, and has one of the best private libraries in the country, and many additions of choice books are made every year.

DUNCAN EVE, A.M., M.D.

NASHVILLE.

THIS distinguished surgeon was born in Augusta, Georgia, May 1, 1852, received part of his academic education at White's Creek Springs, Tennessee; next studied four years at the Kentucky Military Institute, near Frankfort, in 1874 took his medical degree in Bellevue Hospital Medical College, New York city, under Profs. Frank H. Hamilton, Louis A. Sayre, Austin Flint, W. H. Van Buren, Isaac E. Taylor, James Woods, and others, and was interne in the hospital for one year thereafter. Returning to Nashville in 1874, he was associated with his father, the celebrated Paul F. Eve, in surgical practice and as associate to his father's chair of surgery in the Nashville Medical College until his father's death, November 3, 1877, since which date he has been senior member of the firm, Duncan & Paul F. Eve, and the successor to his father as professor of surgery in the Nashville Medical College, now the medical department of the University of Tennessee. In 1874–5–6–7 he was also professor of microscopy in the Tennessee College of Pharmacy.

The Nashville Medical College was founded by Drs. Paul F. Eve and William K. Bowling and other prominent medical gentlemen. The Nashville Medical College, after three years of independent existence, was incorporated as a department of the University of Tennessee, and is now one of the leading medical institutes of the South, having in 1882–83 a class of one hundred and seventy-six students.

Dr. Duncan Eve is a member of the American Medical Association, and of the Tennessee State and Nashville city Medical Societies, and for several years was permanent secretary of the State Society. He is now dean of the faculty of the medical department of the University of Tennessee; managing editor of the *Southern Practitioner*, a Nashville journal, devoted to medicine and surgery and collateral sciences; surgeon to Eve's private infirmary, at Nashville; surgeon of the Porter Rifles of that city, and for a time was captain of the Rock City Guards. In politics he is a Democrat; in Masonry a Knight Templar, and for two years was a member of the city board of aldermen. In 1867 and again in 1873 he made the tour of Europe "more to see the world," than for the purpose of visiting the medical institutions, though these did not escape his observation while abroad.

Dr. Eve married in Nashville, November 1, 1876, Miss Alice Horton, daughter of Col. Joseph W. Horton, now a retired merchant, formerly a colonel in the Confederate service. Her mother is the daughter of John M. Thompson, a wealthy planter and trader, originally from Kentucky. Mrs. Eve was educated at Ward's Seminary, Nashville, and is a devoted member

18

of the Presbyterian church. By this marriage Dr. Eve has had three children, Bessie, Paul (died in 1880) and Duncan.

The subject of this sketch is a man of large build and tireless activities, and has the appearance of a man who has no need to be told to "cut boldly." In his entire make-up is plainly written, "*aut Cæsar aut nullus.*" To whatever position in life the destinies might have assigned him he would have stood in the front rank. He has chosen to make his mark as a surgeon, and by unanimous consent he is among the first in that line. Yet he has not reached the meridian of life. Victor Hugo well said to Charles Sumner, "It is not years that make men great, years only make them old." And also, in Dr. Eve's case the writer finds an exception to the general rule that men of success begin life without name or fortune or help from any source. He did not spring from obscurity into prominence. He is a son of one of the most widely known families of the South. His father, Paul F. Eve, made a national and even a European reputation among the most eminent lights in the medical profession.

His mother, Sarah A. Duncan, his father's second wife, was born in Barnwell District, South Carolina, daughter of Rev. Hansford Dade Duncan, a very distinguished Baptist divine," a lineal and most direct heir of "the Jennings estate," his mother being a Miss Jennings, of England. His father was a Scotchman, a lineal descendant of Lord Duncan, or King Duncan, as he was for a short time. Dr. Eve's mother was the Tennessee vice-president of the Confederate Monumental Association, which had its origin in Richmond, Virginia. She has three children: (1). Duncan Eve, subject of this sketch. (2). Paul F. Eve, professor of anatomy in the medical department of the University of Tennessee, and practicing surgery with his brother; married to Miss Jennie Brown, daughter of Maj. W. L. Brown, and grand-daughter of Judge Morgan W. Brown. (3). Sarah A. Eve, wife of Edward Drane, a merchant at Nashville.

Dr. Eve's half-sister, Annie Lou Eve, daughter of his father's first wife (a great-niece of Gen. David E. Twiggs of Mexican war fame), is now the widow of Col. V. K. Stevenson, a New York millionaire, builder of the Nashville and Chattanooga railroad. She has four children, Paul, Elouise, Maxwell and Annie.

Of Dr. Eve's father, Paul Fitzsimmons Eve, who was born on a rice plantation on the Savannah river, near Augusta, Georgia, June 27, 1806, and died at Nashville, November 3, 1877, the medical fraternity will doubtless publish his life in a separate volume, or in connection with those of his two most distinguished associates,

William K. Bowling and Lunsford P. Yandell. He acquired more degrees than are worn by the titled aristocracy of Europe: A.B., A.M., M.D., L.L.D., Bearer of the Golden Cross of Honor of Poland, 1831; president of the American Medical Association, 1857–8, and the Tennessee Medical Society, 1871–2; centennial representative of surgery in the Medical Congress of Nations at Philadelphia, 1876; successively professor of surgery in the Medical College of Georgia, 1832–49; in the University of Louisville, 1850, in the medical department University of Tennessee 1851–68, in the Missouri Medical College 1868–9, in the medical department of the Nashville and Vanderbilt Universities 1870–76, and Nashville Medical College; associate editor of the Nashville *Medical and Surgical Journal*, and of the *Southern Medical and Surgical Journal*; author of "Remarkable Cases in Surgery," and of six hundred original papers, reports and biographical sketches of eminent medical men; volunteer surgeon in the United States army in the Mexican war; surgeon-general of Tennessee in the civil war; member of the American Medical Board; founder of the Nashville Medical College, and seventy times, in seventy-eight operations, successful in the bilateral method in lithotomy, thus winning a name among the most skillful of American surgeons. This eminent man endeared himself to the people of Nashville and the South by his patriotic services in the Confederate army, as a surgeon at Nashville, at Atlanta, at Columbus, at Shiloh and other points. He distinguished himself in the noble offices of human relief, not only on the battle-fields of his country, but in Poland in 1831, in France in 1850, and at the great battles of Solferino and Magenta in the Austro-Italian war of 1859. Though a man of research and thought, and having the appearance of one weighing facts and balancing conclusions, and following out with firmness and decision his own deductions, he was neither a dogmatist in opinions nor imperious in his manner of asserting them. His face was kindly and his presence a social delight. Nor did he seem conscious of his superiority in the profession to which he had consecrated his faculties and his life; though a sage he had that modesty and meekness in his air and bearing that won the hearts of all who knew him. His father, Capt. Oswell Eve (whose mother was a great-aunt of Gen. James Longstreet, of Georgia), was of English descent, while his mother, Alpha Ann —— ——, was of Irish stock. His father was a classmate of Drs. Rush, Shippen and James, of Philadelphia, and is said to have been the first person, or among the first, to take a steamer across the Atlantic.

The predominant of the Eve family on both sides, is best expressed in the word—push. Great families make great States, and Tennessee cherishes the name of Paul F. Eve as that of a man who excelled in his profession, and bequeathed to her a family not unworthy of the name he made illustrious.

HON. EDWIN HICKMAN EWING.

MURFREESBOROUGH.

NO name in Tennessee shines with a more steady radiance than that of the Ewing family. It is one of the immovable jewels of the State, and is connected with its congressional, legislative, judicial, legal, medical, literary and banking history, and dates back to 1780. There is not a stain upon its escutcheon. No member of it has been marked or spotted as addicted to gaming, drunkenness, dissoluteness, nor by the wiles and trickery of the demagogue. The heroic vices never attached to the family. They are society people, distinguished for their culture, refinement and high sense of honor, and are brave without vainglory, proud without being haughty, affluent without arrogance, and prominent without being pretentious.

The oldest living and probably the best representative of the family is the subject of this sketch, Hon. Edwin Hickman Ewing. He was born in Davidson county, Tennessee, December 2, 1809, and there grew up, attending the schools of the city, and graduating in October, 1827, from the University of Nashville, under the celebrated Dr. Philip Lindsley, in a class of twelve, among whom were Gen. Gideon J. Pillow, Hon. David W. Dickinson, for several years M.C., Hon. Ebenezer J. Shields, M.C. from Giles county, G. W. Foster, Thomas Foster, and Dr. Patrick D. Nelson, of Rutherford county.

From the age of fifteen young Ewing determined to be a lawyer, and in school and at college studied with that end in view. After graduation he obtained license to practice, January, 1831, from Supreme Judge John Catron and Circuit Judge James Stewart, and thenceforward practiced regularly in the county, circuit, chancery and Supreme courts. He was in the Supreme court as early as 1833. He practiced at Nashville without any break from 1831 to 1851, except the time he was in Congress and the Legislature, to be mentioned hereafter. In 1837 he took his brother, Hon. Andrew Ewing, into partnership, which continued until 1851.

In 1840 he canvassed the counties around Nashville in favor of the election of Gen. William Henry Harrison to the presidency, during which he got into divers difficulties with Democratic politicians and editors, Judge Ewing's prominence and ability as a speaker making him a standing target for the shots of the Democratic leaders.

In 1842 he was a member of the Tennessee Legislature from Davidson county, elected as a Whig, without opposition. When that General Assembly organized he was made chairman of the committee on federal relations.

In the latter part of 1845 he became the successor of Dr. J. H. Peyton, brother of Hon. Bailey Peyton, who had been elected to represent Davidson, Sumner, Smith and Macon counties in the United States Congress. Judge Ewing was elected in opposition to Gov. Trousdale. He took his seat in January, 1846, after the committees had been formed. In Congress he made a number of speeches on the tariff, the Oregon question, the Mexican war, and the river and harbor bill, which were published and at once gave him a reputation which was an honor to himself and a credit to his State. Hon. Alexander Stephens, then in Congress, said of his speech on the tariff, it was the best he had ever heard on that subject.

Declining a re-election, he returned to his law practice, which he continued with his brother until April, 1851, when, his health failing from his large and laborious law business, he took a trip to Europe, starting April 2, 1851, and being absent eighteen months. He visited England, Scotland, Ireland, France, Germany, Italy and Switzerland, traveling in the latter country six hundred miles on foot, meanwhile recovering his health. He then went to Egypt and up the Nile as far as Assouan, at the cataracts, inspecting the pyramids, the temples and other noted ruins; and, then making a detour to Suez, went down the Gulf of Suez to Mt. Sinai, which he ascended; thence by the Gulf of Akabah visited Petra; thence to Hebron, on the borders of Palestine, and the home of the patriarch Abraham, whose tomb he visited. He then went to Jerusalem; to the river Jordan, and bathed in it; then to Bethlehem, to the Dead Sea, and then north to Damascus—the oldest of cities; saw the rivers Abana and Pharphar, and ascended to the headwaters of the famous stream. On the route from Damascus to Beirout, he took in Baalbec and measured a corner-stone in its walls—66x18x12. From Beirout he went to Smyrna, hence to Constantinople, Trieste, Paris, London and home. These travels in the East made Judge Ewing, who is always an entertaining conversationalist, much sought after by those interested in oriental places of historical interest.

Not long after his arrival at Nashville, he was called upon to pronounce a eulogy on Daniel Webster. This address, delivered in 1852, gave him more fame as a

writer and orator than any other of his numerous addresses and papers, on all manner of subjects, published sometimes over his own name; sometimes under a *nom de plume*.

Judge Ewing continued to practice law, in a perfunctory way, only in important cases, until 1857, at which time he was worth upwards of one hundred thousand dollars. In 1857 he bought a fine plantation in Rutherford county, and moved there, but returned to Nashville in 1859 with his son-in-law and daughter, Mr. and Mrs. Emmet Eakin, and lived with them for a year, when they removed to Saline county, Missouri, near Marshall. In 1860 he again removed to Murfreesborough to live with his son, Josiah W. Ewing, intending to practice law no more.

The war came on and his sons, Josiah and Orville, both went into the Confederate service, and Judge Ewing remained on his son's place, three miles from Murfreesborough. During the war Judge Ewing was under surveillance of the Federal troops on account of his sympathy for the South, though up to the war he had been a Union man, but heartily with the South after Federal invasion begun.

After the war he continued to live with his son until January 1, 1866, when he resumed the practice of law at Murfreesborough, in partnership with Hon. E. D. Hancock. This partnership was dissolved in 1869, after which Judge Ewing appeared in cases mostly at Nashville—bank and railroad cases—meanwhile frequently contributing articles to the press on metaphysics, religion, and politics. He wrote what may be called the basis of the speeches and writings that have since been made on the State debt question, Judge Ewing taking the ground that the State is liable for the whole debt, but that the creditors should allow a large deduction as an equity.

In 1880 he was appointed Judge of the Supreme court of Tennessee, vice Judge Cooper, disqualified on account of his having, as chancellor, decided many of the cases taken by appeal from Davidson county. He afterwards took the place of Judge Peter Turney, absent on account of rheumatism and the old wound he received during the war. In 1881-2, by request of the other members of the court, Gov. Hawkins appointed Judge Ewing special judge in place of Judge Cooper, incapacitated on account of being the owner of State bonds, to sit, in what has since become the "one hundred and three case." Judge Ewing delivered the opinion advancing the case on the docket, and afterwards, in the final disposition of the case, three of the judges, Freeman, McFarland and Turney, enjoined the issuance of new bonds by the funding board. Judge Ewing wrote and delivered the dissenting opinion, which the lawyers speak of as his monument. This opinion was the most labored effort of Judge Ewing's life. [See Lea's Supreme Court Reports, 1881-2.]. For the past three or four years Judge Ewing has been receiving no fees, practicing merely to wind up his old cases, only a few of which now remain.

Judge Ewing married at Nashville, in 1832, Miss Rebecca Williams, a native of Davidson county, daughter of Josiah Williams (at one time Sheriff of Davidson county), a large farmer on the splendid tract since known as "Maplewood." Her grandfather died in North Carolina. His oldest son, William Williams, was at one time a member of the Legislature from Davidson county. The Williams family came from North Carolina, and were quite prominent people in Davidson county. They are of Welsh extraction.

Mrs. Ewing's mother was a daughter of Joseph Phillips, a respectable magistrate of Davidson county. Mrs. Ewing's cousin, Mrs. John Felix Demoville, of Nashville, is a grand-daughter of Joseph Phillips, as is also Mrs. James C. Warner, a sister of Mrs. Ewing.

Judge Ewing and his two brothers, Andrew and Orville, married three sisters, daughters of Josiah Williams. Judge Robert Ewing, of Nashville, member of the board of public works and affairs (facetiously called the "big three"), is a son of Andrew Ewing, and a nephew of Judge Ewing, subject of this sketch. His niece, Rebecca, daughter of Andrew Ewing, is the wife of Henry Watterson, the famous editor of the Louisville *Courier-Journal.*

Of Judge Ewing's five brothers: (1). John O. Ewing became a physician of much merit and prominence, but died at the age of twenty-six in the year 1826. His son, John O., married a daughter of Alexander Campbell, the famous West Virginia preacher, and afterwards married a daughter of John M. Bass, of Nashville. (2). Henry Ewing was clerk of the county court of Davidson, and afterwards in New York. (3). Albert Ewing was a Christian preacher, and died at Eureka, Illinois, sixty-eight years old. He married Jane Caroline, daughter of the celebrated Alexander Campbell. (4). Orville Ewing was president of the Planters Bank of Nashville for many years. Though bred a lawyer he never practiced. (5). Andrew Ewing was a member of Congress as a Democrat from a Whig district. He died at Atlanta, Georgia, in the Confederate service, being judge of the permanent military court of Gen. Bragg's Army of the Tennessee. He left a reputation for being one of the best common law lawyers the State ever had. He was a very eloquent speaker, and being a prominent politician was one of the Democratic leaders of Tennessee.

By his marriage with Miss Williams Judge Ewing has had four children: (1). Josiah W. Ewing, born in 1834; graduated from Bethany College, West Virginia, under President Alexander Campbell; married, in 1855, Miss Ada B. Hord, daughter of Thomas Hord, a wealthy and highly respected farmer and retired lawyer of Rutherford county. He has four children, Thomas H., Orville, Emmet and Josie. (2). Jane Caroline Ewing, born in 1836; graduated from the Nashville Female

Academy; married Emmet Eakin, who died during the war, and by him had four children, Rowena, Florence, Sallie (Lovie) and Arthur D. The latter died at Memphis, at the age of twenty, a professor in the medical college of that city. After the war Mrs. Eakin became the wife of Dr. James E. Wendell, of Murfreesborough, and bore him one child, a daughter, Jane, who died at the age of twelve. The mother died in 1872, aged thirty-five. (3). Florence Ewing, educated at Nashville and married, first, Andrew Fletcher, by whom she had two children, Edwin, and one who died in infancy. After Mr. Fletcher's death she married Dan P. Perkins, of a prominent Williamson county family, and by this marriage has two children, Rebecca and Sarah Lou. (4). Orville Ewing, who went into the Confederate army in Col. Joel A. Battle's Twentieth Tennessee regiment as sergeant-major, and was badly wounded and taken prisoner at the battle of Mill Springs. He was killed in the battle of Murfreesborough, Wednesday, December 31, 1862, the very day he was appointed to a position on the staff of Gen. William Preston.

Judge Ewing has one great-grandchild, Ethel Reed, daughter of Florence Reed, who is the daughter of Jane Caroline Eakin and wife of James H. Reed, a hardware merchant at Murfreesborough.

Judge Ewing's father, Nathan Ewing, was clerk of the county court of Davidson county, a man who sustained a character of exceeding honesty, diligence and attention to business. He was the son of Andrew Ewing, who came from Rockbridge county, Virginia, to Tennessee, in 1780, and was the first clerk of the county court of Davidson county, which, with Sumner county, then embraced nearly all of Middle Tennessee. Judge Ewing's father was born in Virginia in 1776. The Ewings are of Scotch-Irish, deep-dyed, Presbyterian origin.

Judge Ewing's mother, whose maiden name was Sarah Hill, was a daughter of Daniel Hill, a farmer, a native of North Carolina, who came to Tennessee, when she was nine years old. Lieut.-Gen. D. H. Hill, one of Gen. Lee's most distinguished corps commanders, belongs to the same family. Mrs. Ewing's mother was a Hickman, of North Carolina. Hickman county, Tennessee, was named for the brother of Judge Ewing's maternal grandmother, and for him Judge Ewing, himself, was named Edwin Hickman. He was prominent as an Indian fighter, was a surveyor and pioneer settler in Tennessee. He was killed in camp at night by the Indians.

Judge Ewing's mother died in 1855, at the age of seventy-five, a model woman, of fine sense, of extensive reading, a well-balanced mind and fascinating conversational talents, fond of poetry and of quoting the standard poets. She, too, was of Scotch-Irish origin, but in her religious faith a staunch "Campbellite." She had six sons who grew to manhood, and made some figure in life, and there has never been a vice of gaming, drunkenness or dissoluteness attached to their names. Her last child was a daughter, Sarah, who died four years old.

Judge Ewing belongs to no secret society, and to no church, and never had any partnership or formed any association except with lawyers. In religion, he is an agnostic—denying nothing, affirming nothing, as his writings clearly show. Yet he is a man of broad catholicism and liberality of opinion. He is one of the most successful lawyers in Tennessee, and has always been considered a wealthy man. When asked for the methods by which he had succeeded, he replied, "I can't say that I had any method. I lived from day to day and from hand to mouth. In that regard I am like the knife grinder, I have no story to tell."

For an estimate of Judge Ewing's character, the writer sought an interview with Judge W. H. Williamson, of Lebanon, and Hon. James D. Richardson, of Murfreesborough, and from their informal conversation, gathered the following: Judge Ewing is not what is called a social man except with his intimate friends and men of the profession. Yet he is very kind-hearted and sympathetic. He and his brother, Andrew, were always popular but without demagogy. Andrew was a fine popular speaker, persuasive and earnest, and the best jury lawyer Tennessee ever had. It is said their mother never went to rest at night until every one of her sons were up stairs in bed; and she made men of them all, strong men who are as so many monuments to her motherly care, and as so many jewels to the State. There is not a man of the Ewing name, all the way back and all the way down, but is of unblemished character. Judge Ewing has long been considered the Nestor of the Tennessee bar. In ability, wisdom, profound learning in the law, and fine *belles-lettres* scholarship, there is no lawyer in Tennessee that ranks him. He is a hard-working, energetic, brilliant lawyer; an untiring investigator, leaving nothing unturned, working because he loves to work. His style of oratory is earnest, sometimes vehement.

Gen. Joseph B. Palmer, of Murfreesborough, when asked for an estimate of Judge Ewing's character, replied: "Mr. Ewing is a profound and critical scholar, to which he has made the addition of a most extensive and careful course of general reading. Very few business men have read so much. He has frequently filled a place on the Supreme bench for long spaces of time, under special appointments, and his written opinions, published in the reports of the last thirty years, mark him a genius and the possessor of deep learning, of which the most distinguished of lawyers might feel a just and honorable pride. To the younger members of the profession wherever he has lived, he has always been of incalculable advantage, ready to advise and instruct and aid them in the solution of embarrassing difficulties, which often greatly depress young men. This he was enabled to do, owing to his great readiness with the best authorities on almost any legal proposition that might be sprung. In addition to this, his own elevated example and conduct in his profession has been a constant stimulus to every young man who had any ambition to excel in the law. In his profession Judge Ewing has always charged good fees, uniformly, but not extravagantly, nor extortionately by any means, and while he has taken reasonable compensation for his services, his object has been usefulness to others rather than pecuniary profit to himself. He is a very fine business man, giving close attention to all matters entrusted to his care, as well as to his own personal dealings with all men. In his feelings and intercourse with men of whatever creed, he is liberal, catholic and charitable. Taken all in all, he is an honor to his race and a blessing to his country."

REV. THOMAS J. DODD, D.D.

NASHVILLE.

THOMAS J. DODD was born at Harper's Ferry, Virginia, August 4, 1837, the son of Prof. James B. Dodd, a native of Loudon county, Virginia, who, after being professor of mathematics in Centenary College, Mississippi, filled the same chair in the college at Jackson, Louisiana, and was subsequently professor of mathematics, and for a while president, of Transylvania University, Lexington, Kentucky. He was the author of a very popular series of mathematical text-books, Dodd's arithmetic, algebra, geometry and trigonometry, that had a large circulation until the publishers failed at the opening of the late war. He was a man of singleness of aim in his profession, both as an educator and as a Christian gentleman; a man of remarkable courage, physical and moral; a thinking man and honest in his convictions, fearless but not obtrusive in presentation of them. Besides his mathematical attainments, his acquaintance with general literature, and especially with theology and metaphysics, was quite extensive. He died March 27, 1872, aged sixty-four years.

The grandfather of Dr. Thomas J. Dodd was William Dodd, of Loudon county, Virginia, a quiet farmer, of good character, and of Welsh descent. He died in 1837.

Dr. Dodd's mother, Delilah Bartleson Fox, was a daughter of Dr. Fox, of the District of Columbia, and came from a family of refinement and of comfortable circumstances. She was a woman of bright intellect, of fine education, and remarkably conversant with English literature in its highest ranges. She died in Lexington, Kentucky, in 1849, leaving four children of the ten born : (1). Martha Elizabeth Dodd, now wife of William H. Ralston, a capitalist, near Leavenworth, Kansas. (2). James W. Dodd, LL.D., professor of Latin language and literature in Vanderbilt University, Nashville. (3). Thomas John Dodd, subject of this sketch. (4). Virginius W. Dodd, of Texas.

Dr. Dodd passed his boyhood as a student in Transylvania University, at Lexington, Kentucky, from which institution he graduated in 1857. After graduation he taught a few years, and then joined the Kentucky Conference of the Methodist Episcopal church, South, since which time, though he has taught a great deal, he has never severed his connection with that conference. In 1863 he was made principal of the academy at Millersburg, Kentucky, which afterwards became the Kentucky Wesleyan College. After being there a while, he was invited to Paris, Kentucky, by leading citizens, to open a select school, and such advantages were offered that he felt it his duty, as did also his friends, to accept the proposition. After teaching at Paris six years, he was sent by Bishop Paine to take charge of the Methodist Episcopal church, South, at Frankfort, after which he held the pastorate of the Methodist churches in Covington and Maysville, Kentucky. In 1875 he became president of the Kentucky Wesleyan College, at Millersburg, a position which had been pressed upon him several times before. Yet he had only been there one year when he was invited to the professorship of Hebrew in Vanderbilt University, Nashville. For three or four years he was, in connection with his Hebrew professorship, pro tem. professor of English literature, and his classes were among the largest in the university. In March, 1885, dissatisfied with the management of the board of trust, and especially with the peculiar control exercised over the faculty by the president of the board, he resigned his professorship in this institution, and in the following September opened a select high school in Nashville. This institution is in many regards peculiar. In it young men are carried through the most advanced collegiate classes—but all studies are taught with a constant reference to their practical utility, either in business life or in the cultivation of intellectual and moral character. The high estimate in which this institution is held is shown in the fact that though the tuition is two hundred dollars per annum, a larger number of candidates than could be admitted made application for scholarships before the first session was opened.

Though engaged for the greater part of his life chiefly in the educational work, Dr. Dodd has not been idle in the ministry. His pulpit ministrations have been about as constant as those of most pastors, and have been extended cheerfully among all the religious denominations. While a Methodist in heart and in membership, he has never been a sectarian—making a broad distinction between the general Church of Christ and his own division of it, which he holds to be but a subordinate branch of the Church catholic. His readings and studies, like his sympathies in religion, have been varied. In literature his attention has been devoted to the ancient classical and Semitic tongues, especially the Hebrew, with a few of the modern languages, so far as these have been necessary to the prosecution of enlightened scholarship.

Dr. Dodd has had fine literary advantages from the first. His parents were cultivated people, and he has been a hard student from the age of ten, when, as he humorously relates, he received his first whipping from Rev. Wright Merrick, Lexington, Kentucky. In his methods as a teacher, he seeks to impress his students by oral communication rather than by text-book instruction. As a theological professor, he aimed more to teach his students how to think than what to think. He never required them to accept any statement or view on his authority, or that of any man, living or dead, but upon great underlying principles of truth and reason, so far as they may be attained. Both as a theologian and as a scholar, these processes, while they have led him to the earnest advocacy of his own views, have caused him also to see the reasonableness of the views of others; hence, neither in literature nor in theology does he admit the least dogmatism, as the word is generally understood.

In 1873 Dr. Dodd married Miss Eva Baker, of Covington, Kentucky, by whom he has had two children—one of whom, Mary Louise Dodd, born July 17, 1874, is now with him, educated partly by himself and partly at a select school in the neighborhood of the university. The other, Eva Virginia Dodd, sleeps in the most beautiful part of the cemetery at Lexington, Kentucky.

Mrs. Dodd is a woman of remarkably fine practical sense, in addition to a high order of literary culture and social refinement. She finished her education at Notre Dame Convent, Cincinnati, a school of eleven hundred students, from which she graduated as valedictorian. She is a member of the Methodist Episcopal church, South. She is fully in sympathy with her husband in all his literary tastes as well as in his ministerial duties, and is an invaluable assistant to him in all that he undertakes, either in the way of private study or of public office. Few women unite in themselves more harmoniously the literary or artistic talent with the practical or domestic : few are better qualified, in general, for the sphere which woman alone can fill.

THOMAS MARTIN, Deceased.

PULASKI.

FROM 1818 to 1869 no man filled so large a place in Giles county, or so impressed himself upon its history as Thomas Martin, merchant, planter and banker. Upon his death, January 13, 1870, the citizens of Pulaski, where he had lived fifty-two years, held a meeting, at which it was resolved that, " we owe the memory of Thomas Martin a debt of gratitude for a large portion of the public spirit, enterprise and improvement in our county for the last thirty years. Our railroads, turnpikes and public buildings have all grown up intimately connected with his name, and for these things, as well as for his friendship and kind social bearing with us all, we will keep his memory green in our minds as one whose example we would try to imitate."

The ancestry of Thomas Martin were of Welsh origin, and early emigrated to Virginia. His great grandfather's name was John Martin, and his grandfather was Thomas Martin, born in Virginia in 1714, and died in that State, aged seventy-eight years. All of his sons were in the war of 1812. Rev. Abram Martin, father of Thomas Martin, was born in October, 1774, in Albemarle county, Virginia; was a farmer, a minister of the Methodist church, and came to Tennessee and settled in Sumner county in 1809, where he died August 4, 1846. He was a man of uprightness and charity, exceedingly conscientious and religious, and noted for his strong intellect. His wife, *nee* Jane Oglesby Tribble, of a Virginia family, was notably intellectual, very witty, a fine conversationalist, and lived to be ninety-four years old. Her mind was clear as a bell to the last. Within three or four days of her death she solved problems in mental arithmetic.

Of such parentage was Thomas Martin, born near Charlottesville, Virginia, Monday, December 16, 1799, the night George Washington died, or as Mr. Martin used humorously to say to his children, " that night one great man left the world and another entered it." At the age of ten he came with his father to Sumner county, Tennessee, where he lived on the farm, went to school, and clerked two years in Col. Desha's store at Gallatin, till the age of eighteen, when he went to Pulaski, and soon became its most conspicuous citizen. After the age of fifteen he never cost his father a cent. As an example of his devotion as a son, his daughter mentions with pride, that she found among his bank papers, after his death, every letter his father had ever written to him.

A youth in his teens he went to Pulaski, then a new town, a mere village; at twenty-five he had accumulated one hundred and fifty thousand dollars. He died worth more than a million. His marvelous success from the first is instructive, for it came of his fine judgment and foresight, or, as another more happily expresses it, " by his thinking beforehand what he was going to do." That he was a strong man a study of the engraving accompanying this sketch amply shows. The head is at once broad, deep and long ; the firm mouth indicates self-assertiveness, and the will-power to say No. He had a fine physique, robust health, a large brain, a solid character, was a good merchant, a warm-hearted patriot, and above all, a good man—all of which justifies the partiality with which his friends still speak of him. He and his family have done much for the country, yet not one of them has ever asked an office of honor, trust or profit in return, or even in recognition for their valuable services.

Thomas Martin set out in his career on the right foot, and won the admiration of the people of his county by a single decision which only a man of singular devotion to principles of honor could have made under the temptation to save money by taking a legal step which he deemed dishonorable; for what first gave him a business footing and high standing among merchants was this: At the age of eighteen, while absent on a visit to his father, and just after closing a business venture, his partner squandered the money (four thousand dollars) due the creditors of the firm. On his return he found the bills in the hands of lawyers for collection. He had had no hand in misappropriating the funds, but when his own lawyer advised him to plead the infant act, he replied with indignation, "Never! I would sooner die; and if I have two years' time every dollar shall be paid," and he at once pledged all that he had, including his riding horse and its equipments, to satisfy the debt. When the New York creditors heard of his manly reply and upright conduct, they at once granted him extension of time and offered him unlimited credit, and he soon became the foremost merchant of Pulaski.

No investment yields so large a per cent. in the mercantile world as a good name, based on commercial honor. This he always kept so bright that President James K. Polk offered to Mr. Martin the secretaryship of the treasury, but this he declined. Believing that the post of honor is the private station, he replied that no public position could buy his time.

He did not, however, afterwards, refuse to act as mayor of his town as an act of good citizenship. The other positions he held grew out of business, social or religious relations. He was president of the Pulaski Savings Bank; president of the Nashville and Decatur railroad, and loaned that company eighty-seven thousand dollars, besides taking heavily of its stock. He was class-leader, steward, Sunday-school teacher and superintendent in the Methodist church, of which he was a

member fifty-three years, having professed religion in
1817, and it is said the church-bell never rang that he
did not answer it. His daughter, with filial piety, has
had placed in the Pulaski Methodist church, in which
he worshipped so many years, a memorial window, a
perfect gem of stained glass, in honor of him and his
good wife, her mother. The window represents the
four evangelists with their several emblems—the eagle,
the ox, the lion and the angel. These are expressed in
four medallions, twined together with oak leaves and
lilies, the whole representing the strength of the father
and the purity of the mother.

For years Mr. Martin was a pillar in the church at
Pulaski, and attended to its financial interest with the
same system and punctuality with which he managed
his own business. He was a man quick to decide, firm
in his purpose and prompt to execute. It is believed
that to his influence is due in great measure the spread
of Methodism over Giles county.

The financial revulsion of 1837-38, a matter of no
interest now, is recalled here only for the purpose of
showing Mr. Martin's splendid abilities as a manager.
During that crisis he became accommodation endorser
for his neighbors to the amount of one hundred thous-
and dollars, and the banks having given him entire control of the paper, not a dollar was lost.

In 1840-41 he, in connection with Andrew M. Ballentine, built the turnpike road through Giles county, and
at a later day he co-operated with Thomas Buford in
constructing the Southern Central railroad, and after
the death of Mr. Buford, was president of that company until after the war. The older citizens of Pulaski
still have reminiscences to relate of his kindness to the
poor and sick, and his efforts to reclaim the profligate
and dissipated. The first high school for girls in Giles
county, organized in 18—, and to which he gave an endowment fund of thirty-five thousand dollars, still bears
its maiden name of "Martin Female College," and is
one of the cherished institutions of the Tennessee Conference.

The moral of his life—for there is much logic in a
life like this—was the illustrated fact that integrity,
sagacity and persevering industry will, in the end, reap
a commensurate reward. Few young men start in life
with slimmer advantages than he had, yet he became
one of the most influential citizens of the State, and a
standard man of the times. As a financier, he had no
superior in Tennessee. Academies, school-houses and
churches received liberal subscriptions from him. He
loved to aid industrious and moral young men who
were struggling to rise in the world. His benefactions
were, some public, some personal and private. He not
only left his immediate descendants in comfortable surroundings, but, among other bequests, upon his elder
sister and her sons, he settled a fine estate of five
hundred acres of land in Sumner county. The
secret lay in his intense personality, energy, system,

tireless application, foresight, liberality and total abste-
miousness from all sorts of spirituous drinks and
from evil-speaking. He was cheerful and buoyant
almost to gayety, and a hearty laugher. Gambling he
detested, and cards he called "the Devil's darning
needles," for if used in sport they took up time, and if
in play they led to serious consequences.

Mr. Martin married in Davidson county, Tennessee,
October 12, 1824, Miss N. H. Topp, daughter of John
S. Topp, an Indian fighter and pioneer from North
Carolina, and a wealthy planter and mill owner. An
anecdote is told of the old pioneer, occurring early in
life. While descending the Holston river, the Indians
fired on him from the ambush of the dense forest
that, dark and still, grew even to the water's edge. He
fell from the boat desperately wounded—staining the
stream with his blood. His friends picked him up and
supposed him dying, but he opened his eyes and said,
with a brave smile and cheery accents, "Do not grieve;
I shall not die—I am not ready to leave yet." His
father, Col. Roger Topp, was a colonel in the Revolutionary war, and with his five brothers won great distinction at the battle of King's Mountain. Col. Roger
Topp was a fine civil engineer, and he and his five
brothers were rewarded by the United States government with a large grant of land near Nashville. Col.
Topp was subsequently killed by a Tory, whose father
he had taken captive in battle. The Topp family are
of English origin, and came to America from Yorkshire. Dr. W. W. Topp, brother to Mrs. Martin, was
on the staff of Gen. Jackson in his Indian wars. John
S. Topp (the first-named), also served under Gen
Jackson throughout the Seminole war. Another brother,
Col. Robertson Topp, was a very successful lawyer and
railroad president at Memphis. She had two other
brothers who were lawyers—John S. Topp and Dixon
C. Topp. Mrs. Martin's mother, nee Comfort Everett,
was a very remarkable lady, combining the finest attributes of a woman with the strong intellect of a man.
Upon the first arrival of her family at the fort near
"Nash's Lick,"—now Nashville—the little orphaned
brother and sister, under charge of Mrs. Topp (then a
staid matron of sixteen years), strolled from the protection of the fort, being enticed by the birds and the
beauty and bloom of the surrounding woods. They
were missing but a short time when a party, headed by
their fearless sister, went to seek and rescue them.
They were seen approaching, presenting a dread appearance—"like two fountains of blood"—having been
scalped and left for dead by the Indians. Mrs. Topp
gathered them to her loving heart, and with untiring
affection nursed them through long hours of pain and
delirium, back to life. The young girl thus tortured
became famous in after years for her beauty. Her rich
bronze-brown hair fell as a mantle about her, and none
dreamed that beneath the wavy tresses lurked the
mark of the Indian tomahawk.

By this marriage of Miss Topp and Mr. Martin, five children were born: (1). Laura E. Martin; graduated in Nashville; died in 1864, the wife of Gen. Thomas G. Blewett, of Columbus, Mississippi, leaving one child, a son, Claude Blewett, now a planter in Mississippi and Louisiana, and living on the splendid estate given him by his grandfather Martin. (2). William Marcellus Martin; educated at Yale; married Lizzie Otis: died December 13, 1867, leaving one child, a daughter, Laura Marcella Martin, now the wife of Solon E. F. Rose, a planter at Columbus, Mississippi; living on the splendid estate left her by her grandfather Martin. (3). Cornelia Ann Martin, born in December, 1830, died August 10, 1832. (4). Ophelia Jane Martin; educated at Pulaski by Rev. Robert Caldwell, and at Nashville by private teachers; married Hon. Henry M. Spofford, of Louisiana, January 7, 1861, and has three children, Eleanor Spofford, Thomas Martin Spofford and Nina Spofford. (5). Victoria Martin; graduated at Nashville; died single in 1858, aged twenty years.

Judge Abram Martin, brother of the subject of this sketch, was circuit judge at Clarksville, Tennessee.

Hon. Henry M. Spofford, who married Miss Ophelia J. Martin, was born at Gilmanton, New Hampshire, September 8, 1821. He was a graduate, with highest honors, of Amherst College, Massachusetts, and located in Shreveport, Louisiana, in 1845, and at once entered upon the practice of law. He early gave promise of a brilliant future, and rose rapidly at the bar. In 1854 he was elected to the Supreme bench of Louisiana, and filled that exalted station with signal credit until he resigned in 1858, returning to the practice of his profession and to the achievement of those honors which cluster so thickly about his name and make his memory imperishable. Possessing great wealth, and having risen to the highest attainable eminence in his profession, politics had little that could allure him; he nevertheless accepted an election to the United States Senate, in 1877, by the almost unanimous vote of the Nicholls Legislature, but in the complication of the politics of the times, he was cheated out of his seat, through no fault of his, however, for he pursued it with unwavering vigor from a sense of loyalty to the people and State who had conferred the trust upon him. After his death the Senate admitted his title to the senatorship by paying to his widow the eighteen thousand dollars attaching to the office up to the date of his demise. He died at Red Sulphur Springs, Virginia, August 20, 1880.

Judge Spofford was one of the grand men of these later times; profound in the sciences; versed in history and literature; eminent in law and politics; an eloquent speaker; a beautiful writer, and a lecturer characterized not less by the penetration of his research and the close analysis of the subjects he handled—notably his lectures on Goethe, Dante and Milton—than by the elegance of his diction. He was a fine Greek and Latin scholar, and often wrote his briefs entirely in French.

But the grandeur of the man was most conspicuous in his finely balanced character, in the refinement of his manners, his truthfulness, and a modesty that betrayed absolute purity of mind. He had the rare ability to veil the keenest sarcasm with a tenderness so delicate that it reminded one of a Persian scimiter tempered with perfume. With resolute firmness to carry his point, his manners were those of a French statesman—soft, dignified, pleasing, of exquisite tact and consummate address. His was a representative character, both in its symmetry and solidity, whether he be viewed as a professor for two years in Amherst College, as a lawyer in successful practice, a jurist handing down his decisions from the Supreme bench, an author, a statesman, or a family man.

Rev. Dr. W. M. Leftwich, who pronounced Judge Spofford's funeral oration at Pulaski, gives as the factors of his noble character, self-reliance, decision of character, self-control, force of will, exclusive devotion to his profession, a sense of responsibility, and great learning. His was a separate and distinct individuality, yet he was the product of centuries of English history. His genealogy dates back eight hundred years to Gambolier de Spofford, the Saxon thane, who built the Spofford castle, still standing in the West Riding of Yorkshire. John Spofford, a descendant of Gambolier de Spofford, and the ancestor of Judge Spofford, came over in the *Mayflower*, and became a factor in the religious and political history of New England. Judge Spofford's only brother, Ainsworth Spofford, is the well-known and popular librarian of Congress, author of a series of "American Almanacs," valuable as books of political reference, and is also co-editor, with Charles Gibbon, of the "Library of Choice Literature."

The Spofford mausoleum, in Metairie cemetery, New Orleans, is a Greek temple, cut of the purest Carrara marble, and situated on a gently graduated mound. The dome of the temple is supported by elaborately chiseled pillars and capitals, and beneath is a lovely angel of large proportions, with graceful wings and a wonderfully beautiful expression of up-turned face, while it records a favorite passage from the Holy Book with its marble pen. A large gilt cross crowns the monument. This monument was designed and erected by Mrs. Spofford and executed by celebrated Italian artists in Massa-Carrara.

Injustice would be done the memory of Mr. Martin, if more particular mention were omitted here of his only surviving child, Mrs. Judge Spofford, and her family. Mrs. Spofford, more than the wealth he accumulated and the public enterprises he set on foot, is the monument to his worth as a man and wisdom as a father. Mrs. Spofford is among the most brilliant women of the South, remarkable for the reach of her learning, and her fine judgment as a business woman. She is an accomplished artist in oils and pastels; a fine musician and musical composer, and wields the pen of a ready

19

writer. Her parlors at Pulaski and New Orleans are a history of half the world, which only a traveled scholar can read. Half the year the family reside in New Orleans, where they have a beautiful home, 195 St. Charles street; and half the year they live at Pulaski, in the ancestral mansion, now seventy years old, and designed with exquisite architectural taste. Mrs. Spofford visited Europe both for her own gratification and the education of her children. To them it was a great geographical lesson. They studied art in ancient galleries, in the home of the arts; and in the manners, customs, spirit and homes of foreign peoples discovered for themselves the effect of various institutions on nationalities, she herself acting as interpreter, guide and classmate. Such an education is far superior to any course in college, and the results of the methods adopted by the mother for qualifying her children for the duties of life are seen in the son's freedom from vices, his steadiness and

fine business habits, while the daughters are not unworthy of their ancestry.

Mrs. Spofford seems to have inherited with the blood and business tact of her father, his enterprising public-spiritedness, and is now turning her attention to the betterment of her native county by the introduction of fine breeds of stock. She was the only exhibitor from Giles county at the World's Centennial Exposition at New Orleans, 1884–85. Having in vain urged action on the part of others, she chartered a car and sent it to the Crescent City, filled with the products of her county, which fully represented its wonderful resources—from the nuts of oaks, beeches, walnuts, chestnuts, etc., to great disks of these and other giant trees from the primeval forests that still adorn her domain of "Martinhurst. It is needless to say that all agricultural and dairy products were also shown, together with the handiwork of ladies of the county.

JOHN LIGHT ATLEE.

CHATTANOOGA.

DR. JOHN LIGHT ATLEE, for many years a prominent and honored citizen of Athens, Tennessee, but now of Chattanooga, having removed to the latter place in July, 1884, is descended from an old English family, and has a most interesting and distinguished history. He was born at Gettysburg, Pennsylvania, January 9, 1832, the son of Rev. Edward A. Atlee, a minister of the Methodist Episcopal church, a native of Lancaster, Pennsylvania, who married in Gettysburg in 1826, moved to Athens, Tennessee, in 1840, and there died in 1861, at the age of sixty-five years, leaving as an heirloom to his descendants a reputation for being an honest man.

The grandfather, Wm. Pitt Atlee, was born in Lancaster, Pennsylvania; was a colonel in the war of 1812; married, in 1798, Miss Sarah Light, and died in February, 1815.

The great-grandfather, William Augustus Atlee, was born in Philadelphia, July 1, 1735; married Miss Esther Bomes Sayre, of New Jersey; was admitted to the Lancaster bar in 1758; appointed judge of the Supreme Court of Pennsylvania, 1777; was chairman of the committee of safety, and commissary and superintendent of the arsenal at Lancaster during the Revolutionary war. On August 17, 1791, he was appointed president judge of the First district court of Pennsylvania, embracing four counties. He died September 9, 1793.

The great-great-grandfather, the son of William Atlee, of Ford Hook House, England, was the first of the name to come to America. He was the private

secretary of Lord Howe. He married Miss Jane Alcock, daughter of an English clergyman, who was a cousin of William Pitt, the old earl of Chatham. She was a maid of honor to the Queen, who wanted her to marry into the royal family, but she ran away and followed Atlee to America.

The grandfather of the fifth remove was Samuel Atlee, of Brentford, the son of Samuel Atlee, the son of William Atlee, of Ford Hook House, in the parish of Acton, Middlesex, England, who died in 1652.

One "Sir Richard at-the-Lee" figures in the ballads of Robin Hood. His parents lived at the Lee, and the name of the locality was adopted as the surname of the family. At-the-Lee was changed to Atte-Lee, and finally, as now used, Atlee.

Dr. Atlee's mother, nee Delilah Gilbert, was born in Gettysburg, Pennsylvania, September 27, 1809, daughter of Bernhardt Gilbert, a native of Germany, sheriff of Adams county, Pennsylvania. Her mother was also a Gilbert, first cousin of her husband. Dr. Atlee's mother was educated at Bethlehem, Pennsylvania, is a member of the Methodist Episcopal church, South, to which she is remarkably devoted, and exerts her influence in a Christian direction. She is now living with her son at Chattanooga, the mother of ten children: (1). Amelia Atlee, wife of Rev. A. T. Cox, of Texas. (2). John Light Atlee, subject of this sketch. (3). Anna Elizabeth Atlee, wife of Judge John S. McCampbell, Corpus Christi, Texas. (4). Sarah Catharine Atlee, widow of Exum Luther, formerly of Goliad, Texas,

now living with her brother, Dr. Atlee. (5). Marga-
retta S. Atlee, died the wife of Thomas M. Coleman,
Rockport, Texas. (6). Harriet Krauth Atlee, one of
twins, died in infancy. (7). Letitia Smith Atlee, died
the wife of P. C. Wilson, Chattanooga. (8). Mary P.
Atlee, wife of N. T. Ayres, Houston, Texas. (9).
Edwin Augustus Atlee, married Miss Bettie Foster,
daughter of S. C. Foster, and is now a lawyer at Laredo,
Texas. (10). Bernhardt Gilbert Atlee, D.D.S., married
Miss Amanda J. De Ryee, and is now at Laredo,
Texas.

Dr. Atlee went to Athens, Tennessee, in 1840, when
eight years of age. He attended school there and at
Hiawassee College until 1848, when he left Athens,
horseback, and went to Philadelphia, and remained
there reading medicine with his uncle, Dr. Washington
L. Atlee, and attending the Pennsylvania Medical College until 1853, when he took his medical degree under
Profs. Darrach, Grant, Patterson, Gilbert, Reid, Allen
and Smith. After graduation he returned to Athens
and began the practice of medicine there in April, 1853.
He began with a small library and without money, but
succeeded in building up a large and lucrative practice,
and is now in easy circumstances. His rule has been to
do unto others as he would have others do unto him, a
a rule that makes men just and charitable, and oft-
times leads to fame and fortune.

He is now a member of the Tennessee State Medical
Society, and of the American Medical Association. He
is a Democrat, a Master Mason, and a member of the
Methodist Episcopal church, South, and was for a long
time a steward of the Athens station.

Dr. Atlee married, at Athens, Tennessee, May 22,
1856, Miss Sarah Humphreys, daughter of Hilton
Humphreys, a merchant of that town. Her mother,
nee Miss Lucinda E. Toncray, daughter of David Toncray, from near Abingdon, Wythe county, Virginia,
came to Athens in her girlhood, about 1834, and taught
school there until her marriage. She was a finely educated lady and of very superior attainments. She died
in September, 1878, at the age of sixty-eight years,
leaving two children : (1). Sarah Humphreys, now wife
of Dr. Atlee. (2). Mrs. Frank Coleman.

Mrs. Atlee was educated at Athens, and is a member
of the Methodist Episcopal church, South. She is a
lady of much intelligence, and remarkable for the
facility with which she makes friends in all circles in
which she moves.

By his marriage with Miss Humphreys, Dr. Atlee
has four children : (1). James B. Atlee, born December 21, 1861; graduated at Vanderbilt University in
1883, and is now studying medicine. (2). John Light
Atlee, jr., born April 1, 1866. (3). Frank Hilton
Atlee, born May 30, 1868. (4). Sarah Atlee, born
March 29, 1873.

Dr. Atlee's paternal uncle, Dr. John Light Atlee,
now eighty-six years of age, and engaged in the active
practice of his profession, was born at Lancaster, Pennsylvania, November 2, 1799; graduated M.D. from the
University of Pennsylvania, April, 1820; took the degree of L.L.D. from Franklin and Marshall College;
was president of the Lancaster county Medical Society;
president, in 1857, of the Pennsylvania State Medical
Society, and president of the American Medical Association in 1882–83. He is famous as a surgeon, especially for the number of his operations of ovariotomy.
In June, 1843, he, with his brother, revised the operation of ovariotomy that was first performed by Dr.
Ephraim McDowell in Kentucky, in 1809.

His brother, Dr. Washington Atlee (Dr. John L.
Atlee's uncle), studied medicine under Dr. James
L. Atlee, of Lancaster, Pennsylvania ; moved to Philadelphia in 1845 ; filled the chair of medical chemistry
in the medical department of the Pennsylvania College
at Philadelphia, and, during the course of his practice,
performed the operation of ovariotomy three hundred
and eighty-seven times. On the occasion of his death,
Dr. Samuel Gross offered resolutions which were
adopted by the Philadelphia County Medical Society,
complimenting him as an ornament to the profession, as
one of the pioneers of ovariotomy in America, and of
having placed it upon a firm and permanent basis as
one of the established processes of the healing art, thus
conferring immense benefit upon suffering women by
increasing their comfort and prolonging their lives ; also
complimenting his memory as an author and able
thinker, and for his contributions to gynecology and
other branches of medical science. His published
works embrace a volume on ovariotomy, and forty-seven
papers and twenty-one lectures on various subjects.

Dr. Atlee's grand uncle, Col. Samuel John Atlee, of
Revolutionary fame, was born at Trenton, New Jersey,
in 1739, was a commissioned officer in the French and
Indian wars, and was present at Braddock's defeat in
1758. He served under Gen. Forbes, was lieutenant
and afterwards captain in that campaign. He was appointed March 21, 1776, colonel of the Pennsylvania State
battalion of musketry; on the 27th of August, 1776,
he achieved imperishable fame at the battle of Long
Island under Washington. He was a delegate to the
Continental Congress in 1778 and served till 1782. In
October, 1783, he was elected supreme executive counselor of Lancaster county, and served in the General
Assembly of 1782–85–86. In 1784 he was appointed
one of the three commissioners to treat with the
Indians, and his name appears in the treaty of January
21, 1785. He died while a member of the General
Assembly of Pennsylvania, November 25, 1786. A
tablet to his memory has recently been placed in Christ
church, Philadelphia.

PROF. ANDREW H. BUCHANAN.

LEBANON.

THE Buchanans are of Scotch-Irish stock. Thomas Buchanan, grandfather of Prof. Andrew H. Buchanan, subject of this sketch, died a farmer in Arkansas, leaving a reputation for being a correct business man and a good and faithful Christian. Prof. Buchanan's uncle, Rev. John Buchanan, of the Cumberland Presbyterian church, did more to christianize Arkansas than any man who ever lived in that State. He traveled over the State and preached nearly all his life, distributed Bibles, and was a leader in other good works.

Prof. Buchanan's father was Isaac Buchanan, a native of Kentucky, who grew up in Tennessee, was a farmer all his days, a man of small fortune and but little education. He lost his life during the war, at the age of sixty-one. Although a gentleman, honored above most men as a father, he had been required to take the oath of allegiance to the Federal government, which he refused to do, being southern in sentiment, in principle and interest. He was killed at Cane Hill, Arkansas, by a command of Indians, while standing at his own cellar door. He had given them as many apples as they wished, and turned to lock the door, when he was shot down in cold blood by the savages in the service of the Federal authorities. Some months after his death, three of his sons were killed on the same day while in the Confederate service at Cane Hill. Isaac Buchanan was notably firm in his positions for the right, always expressing himself freely and fearlessly, which was one cause of his being killed. He determined in early life to give his children suitable education, if nothing else, and exerted himself in that direction as the leading object of his life. Every one of them received a collegiate education before his death.

Prof. Buchanan's mother was Naomi Crawford, daughter of John Crawford, a successful farmer of Lincoln county, Tennessee. She is now living, seventy-nine years old, with her son at Lebanon, Tennessee. Her mother was Margaret Buchanan. She is the mother of seven sons and one daughter: (1). Andrew H., subject of this biography. (2). Alfred E., a civil engineer; now superintendent of the Cotton Belt Narrow Gauge railroad. He graduated in engineering under Gen. Alexander P. Stewart at Lebanon, and has been in employment as an engineer, except one year during the war, from 1854 until the present time. He married Miss Henrietta F. C. Smettem, and now resides at Little Rock, Arkansas. (3). William M., graduated at Lebanon, and lost his life in the Confederate service at Cane Hill, Arkansas. (4). Pleasant W., graduated at Lebanon, was professor of mathematics in Cane Hill College; was a captain in the Confederate army, and

killed at Cane Hill. (5). John T., graduated at Cane Hill College, and at Lebanon in the theological department; married Miss Alta Russell, and is now a minister in the Cumberland Presbyterian church, at Pierce City, Missouri. (6). James G., graduated at Cane Hill College, and lost his life in the Confederate service at Cane Hill, Arkansas. (7). Cyrus W., died at the age of seventeen. (8). Elizabeth Cyrene, educated at Independence, Missouri; married Prof. W. D. McLaughlin, of Cumberland University, now residing at Lebanon.

Andrew H. Buchanan was born in Washington county, Arkansas, June 28, 1828. He was raised very strictly, trained to work very hard during the summers, but was sent to school during the winters until twenty-one years old. In the fall of 1850, he entered Cumberland University at Lebanon, Tennessee, and graduated in 1853, in the academic and civil engineering departments, under Profs. Anderson, Stewart, Marriner and James M. Safford. He then spent one year in civil engineering on the Missouri Pacific railroad, after which he returned to Lebanon and filled the chair of civil engineering in the university, and of languages in the preparatory department, and remained in that position till 1861, when he joined the Confederate army as an engineer and was attached to the headquarter topographical engineering corps of Gen. Bragg's army, from the fall of 1862 to the battle of Chickamauga, and afterwards under Gen. Joseph E. Johnston till the close of the war, being engaged without intermission in the work of a topographical engineer. Gen. Johnston has stated since the war that he planned many a battle during the Dalton-Atlanta campaign from the maps of Lieut. Buchanan without having seen the ground himself, and from a reference to him in "Johnston's Narrative" (p. 320), it is evident that he placed the utmost confidence in his intelligence and faithfulness.

After the close of the war Prof. Buchanan taught a high school three years at Cane Hill, Washington county, Arkansas, averaging about two thousand dollars a year in tuition fees. In the fall of 1869 he was recalled to Cumberland University, in which he has filled the chair of mathematics and civil engineering ever since, at a nominal salary of two thousand dollars. From August, 1876, he has been engaged in the geodetic survey of the State of Tennessee, under the direction of the superintendent of the United States Coast and Geodetic Survey, working at this some five months each year. In 1882, under appointment of Prof. Hilgard, superintendent of the United States Coast and Geodetic Survey, he assisted in observing the transit of Venus, December 6, at the Naval Observatory, Washington, the party being under the charge of Prof. William Harkness, of the observatory.

Prof. Buchanan married at Spring Hill, Maury county, Tennessee, July 10, 1855, Miss Malinda A. Alexander, a native of Henry county, Tennessee, niece of Dr. J. W. Sharber, of Spring Hill, by whose liberality she was educated. She graduated at Soule Female College, Murfreesborough, is a member of the Cumberland Presbyterian church, taught school a few months during the war, and has made a model wife and mother, characterized chiefly by her ambition to train up her children to be useful Christians. Nine children have been born unto them, four of whom died in infancy. The five living children are : (1). James C., graduated at Cumberland University, and is now an engineer on the Georgia Pacific railroad. (2). Andrew B., graduated in the academic and theological departments of Cumberland University, and is now stationed as a Cumberland Presbyterian preacher at Camden, Tennessee. (3). Isaac W. P., now a student at Cumberland University. (4). Kate Stewart. (5). Blanche Alexander.

All of Prof. Buchanan's family are members of the Cumberland Presbyterian church. He is a member of the temperance order of Good Templars. He was a Whig while there were Whigs, but has been trying to be a Democrat since the war, and though not taking much active interest in politics, may be classed a Democrat.

Prof. Buchanan began life without means, except the education given by his father, and, like bookish men generally, has not had much time to make money. He has had to work hard all his life, and it is probably among the greater of human blessings that a man is compelled to develop his talents and do something to avoid living on the fruits of other men's labor. His preference when he started out in the world was to follow the business of civil engineering above all else, but thinking that his life as a Christian would not be worth as much to the word in that business, he relinquished, with some reluctance, that line of life. While in college Prof. (afterwards lieutenant-general) Stewart suggested to him the advisability of following practical engineering a year or two and then to return and assist him in conducting the university engineering school. This led him to the business of teaching, at which he has been engaged ever since. In teaching, he explains the difficulties of problems first, then requires pupils to explain them at the board to him. The class comes in and presents its difficulties, each pupil being allowed to ask his questions freely, which are then solved, and the pupils required to go to the board and explain whatever may be called for in the whole lesson.

Prof. Buchanan has distinguished himself whenever he has come in contact with intelligence that appreciates a man of real merit. Without the address to attract popular notice in his position as teacher, and in his connection with government service, he has, however, commanded the attention of some of the ablest scientific thinkers in this country. He did the same while he was a soldier, and when he was in contact with the most observant and most capable men in the Confederate army. He is a close thinker on many subjects outside of his profession as a mathematician, and especially in his investigations of Christian theology. He is a thorough worker in the church to which he belongs; a devoted advocate of good morals in the society in which he moves; impartial in his judgment, strict in his morality; an exemplar in all his conduct, both as a citizen and a Christian. His character is felt and appreciated in his own circle, and has a wide influence upon the lives of the young men committed to his care. An earnest and faithful worker in the field of science, he constitutes one of those, to some extent, unseen forces, that control the thought and morals of the people whom he so well serves. As a mathematician, in his connection with the United States Coast Survey, he has been efficient in formulating new methods in that department, and has become distinguished among the oldest scientific men connected with the government in that important department. His connection therewith was not obtained through political influence, but was secured by the intelligence that department, a fact which has reflected credit not alone upon them, but has demonstrated that modest and true merit will sometimes be found out by earnest men in the most exalted positions.

Prof. Buchanan set out in life to be a Christian, to be useful to his generation, and he is training his children in the same direction. Not indifferent to the applause of his contemporaries, he seems mostly controlled by a desire to stand well in the court of his own conscience and in the sight of his Creator.

JAMES ELDER.

THIS gentleman, known far and wide as a successful business man, and one of the leading bankers of Memphis, was born in Dinwiddie county, Virginia, October 8, 1809, the son of William Elder, a farmer, and Miss Mary Towler, daughter of Benjamin Towler, an ex-Revolutionary soldier, of Dinwiddie county, mentioned in further detail in the sketch of Mr. Elder's brother, John W. Elder, elsewhere in this volume.

When James Elder was only six years old, his father removed the family to Rutherford county, Tennessee. James Elder was educated at Murfreesborough, under Samuel P. Black, a teacher, who educated many of the most prominent men of Tennessee. He left school at the age of eighteen, and began business as a clerk in a dry goods store of his brother, Benjamin Elder, at Murfreesborough, and there remained until 1835. He then removed to Holly Springs, Mississippi, and engaged first in the sale of dry goods and next in that of boots and shoes, remaining there until 1850, at which time, his brothers having gone into the cotton and commission business at New Orleans, he moved to Memphis to act as their agent, which he did until 1854.

At this latter date he was elected president of the Memphis branch of the Planters Bank of Tennessee, a position which he filled for two years. He then returned to the cotton and commission business, in which he continued until 1862, when he closed his warehouse on account of troublous war times. He followed no regular occupation from that time until 1864, when he again engaged in banking as president of the DeSoto Bank of Memphis, a position which he filled until 1874, when the bank's charter expired, and the business of the DeSoto Bank having been transferred to the Bank of Commerce, he retired from office, but remained a stockholder and subsequently became a director in the latter institution. Although brought up to mercantile pursuits, Mr. Elder had but little taste for them, always preferring those of finance.

Previous to the war Mr. Elder belonged to the Whig party, but now votes with the Democrats; yet he is by no means an unreasoning partisan, and was never a candidate for political office. He served several terms as councilman of the city of Memphis under the old government, both before and since the war.

He has been a member of the Presbyterian church for about forty-six years, and has been an elder for forty years.

Mr. Elder was married August 23, 1832, to Miss Elizabeth H. Niles, daughter of Charles Niles, of Murfreesborough, Tennessee. Her mother was Miss Wade, of the well-known Rutherford county family of that name, and a cousin of Levi Wade, esq., and Capt. Ethel B. Wade, of Murfreesborough. She died in December, 1882, having borne six children, five of whom are now living; all daughters and all married: (1). Marietta Elder, now wife of S. H. Dunscombe, president of the Bank of Commerce of Memphis; has five children. (2). Sallie E. Elder, now widow of the late Gen. W. Y. C. Humes, and has four children. (3). Susan W. Elder, now wife of Judge W. L. Scott, of St. Louis; has four daughters. (4). Isabella Elder, now wife of John B. Leech, of New York; has nine children. (5). Lizzie Elder, now wife of John L. Norton, of Memphis, Tennessee; has four children.

Mr. Elder is another type of the self-made man. Like most men who are successes, he has worked hard for what he owns. He began life without anything and worked at first for a salary of one hundred and fifty dollars a year, but with a determination to conquer his fortune, a determination which went a long ways in bringing about a happy result. By perseverance and by vigilance, by sober and steady habits, and by an unfaltering determination to discharge his duty faithfully and to act with integrity in all things, he has enjoyed a life full of good deeds and happy reflections. Nay, more. A sterling, quiet, unostentatious man, he has spent his days in assiduous attention to his own business, and careful avoidance of intermeddling with the business of others. A life-long Christian, after the strictest Presbyterian pattern, he has always found time and means for religious duties. Eminently domestic in his nature, no attraction or pleasure has been for him so great as those afforded by the home circle of his love.

His years have passed in the serenity of good health, good conscience, prospering business and happy family relations; and his sunset promises to be as calm and peaceful as that of a long day in June whose sky has known only passing clouds.

HON. W. L. LEDGERWOOD.

KNOXVILLE.

THIS gentleman, whose name is widely known in Tennessee as a lawyer, a politician and a farmer, was born in Knox county, Tennessee, June 4, 1843, and grew up at work on his father's farm, going to the neighboring country schools at intervals, which were the only scholastic advantages he ever had. His parents being strict Baptist people, he was raised under religious influences and early acquired good moral habits.

In August, 1861, at the age of seventeen years, he entered the Union army as a private in company B, First Tennessee infantry, commanded by Col. R. K. Byrd, and served as a private soldier in that regiment until April 8, 1862, when he was transferred to the Third Tennessee infantry as first lieutenant of company I, and served in that capacity until May 25, 1863, when he became captain of the company and commanded it to the close of the war. He was mustered out February 23, 1865, at Nashville, having served in Tennessee, Kentucky, Ohio, Alabama, besides taking part in all the leading battles of the Georgia campaign. The last battle in which he was engaged was that at Nashville, between the forces of Gens. Hood and Thomas.

The war over, he returned home and went to farming again. In 1866, he was forced into politics and was nominated by the Knox county Democracy for the Legislature, but was defeated by Dr. M. L. Mynatt. In 1867 he was appointed by President Johnson second lieutenant in the Eighteenth regular infantry, United States army; was examined on Governor's Island; passed his examination and received his commission; served in that regiment until the army was consolidated in 1869, when he was transferred to the Eighth cavalry, United States army; resigned in 1872, and again returned to Knox county and the farm.

He then read law alone at home for a year; was admitted to the bar by Judge E. T. Hall and Chancellor O. P. Temple in 1873, and began practice at Knoxville, where he lived, until 1884, when he moved to " Cedar Grove farm," two miles from Knoxville, a property which he purchased in 1883. His law practice has been large from the beginning, for he has many warm personal and party friends.

In 1874 Capt. Ledgerwood was again nominated by the Democratic party as a candidate to represent Knox county in the Legislature, and this time was successful, being elected over Hon. S. T. Logan, recently senator from the Knoxville district. In the Thirty-eighth General Assembly (1875), Capt. Ledgerwood was chairman of the committee on military affairs.

In 1880 he was elector for the Second congressional district on the Hancock and English ticket. In 1882 he was again nominated for the Legislature, was again elected, and was chosen speaker of the House of the Forty-third General Assembly.

In 1884 he was nominated for congress in the Second Tennessee district, and though defeated by Judge L. C. Houk, reduced his opponent's majority one thousand and eight hundred votes below the vote of James G. Blaine, Capt. Ledgerwood leading the Cleveland and Bate vote by about that majority.

Capt. Ledgerwood has always been a Democrat—never voted any other way. His father and grandfather and collateral branches of the family were Democrats before him, and the fidelity with which he has served his party no doubt will gain for him even more distinction in the future.

In 1866 Capt. Ledgerwood was made a Master Mason in Master's Lodge No. 244, Knoxville. Since then he has been made Knight Templar in Cœur de Lion Commandery No. 9, Knoxville, and a Knight of Malta; he is also a member of Pearl Chapter No. 24, Knoxville.

His father's family were Baptists. His wife and children are members of the Methodist Episcopal church, South, and while he is only a paying member of the latter communion, he, however, firmly holds that Jesus Christ came into the world to save sinners.

Capt. Ledgerwood married at Louisville, Kentucky, September 20, 1866, Miss Jo Strother, a native of Sumner county, Tennessee, born March 16, 1844, and named " Jo " in honor of the celebrated and greatly beloved Judge Jo. C. Guild. Mrs. Ledgerwood's mother was Mrs. Penina Strother, her maiden name being Penina Pitt, daughter of Gerald Pitt, an Englishman. Mrs. Ledgerwood's father, Henry Strother, was a native of Virginia, and a merchant at Gallatin. He died when the daughter was very young, and left three children, Allen, Jo and Thomas. Thomas Strother lost his life by an accident on the Louisville and Nashville railroad. Allen Strother is now an engineer on the Alabama Great Southern road, and is a somewhat remarkable character; a communist; a prominent member of the Brotherhood of Locomotive Engineers; of high scientific attainments in his profession, and an eloquent speaker on subjects maintaining the rights of labor as against the money power. He married Miss Mary Haslam, of Nashville.

Mrs. Ledgerwood was educated at Louisville, and is a woman of quiet, domestic habits, and though not unsocial, is essentially a home-maker and a home-lover. She is noted for her frankness, and for her generosity, especially to those in distress.

By his marriage with Miss Strother, Capt. Ledgerwood has four children: (1). Claude, born August 16, 1867, in Knox county, Tennessee. (2). Sidney Aline, born March 15, 1869, at Sidney, on the Union Pacific railroad, then in Wyoming Territory, but now in Nebraska. (3). Samuel T., born September 30, 1870, in Knox county, Tennessee. (4). Willie, born June 4, 1872, in Knox county, Tennessee.

Ledgerwood is a compound of two names. Upon the Irish side the family comes from St. Leger; upon the English side from a family named Wood. All the Ledgerwoods in the United States are of the same family, of Irish and English mixture. Capt. Ledgerwood's great-grandfather, James Ledgerwood, came from England and settled in Botetourt county, Virginia; was in the Revolutionary war and also the war of 1812. He was a farmer and married a Miss Pierce, of Virginia.

Capt. Ledgerwood's grandfather was also named James. He was born in Botetourt county, Virginia, and was also a soldier in the war of 1812, from Knox county, Tennessee, under Capt. Gibbs. He married in Greene county, Tennessee, and moved back and located in Knox as a farmer. His wife was also named Pierce, but no relation to his mother's family. He moved to Southern Illinois and died there, in 1846, aged sixty-eight years, leaving four daughters: (1). Mary, wife of Caleb Treece. (2). Sallie, wife of Henry Johnson. (3). Darthula, wife of Abraham Haukley. (4). Luartha, wife of Jefferson Bayless.

The first three daughters named married in southern Illinois, and the fourth married in Knox county, Tennessee, and afterwards moved to Illinois.

James Ledgerwood, the grandfather of the subject of this sketch, also left six sons: (1). James. (2). Samuel, father of the subject of this sketch. (3). John. (4). William. (5). David. (6). Joseph.

It was a family of farmers. Joseph, the youngest son, lost his life in the Mexican war. The father of Capt. Ledgerwood (Samuel Ledgerwood), was born in Knox county in 1808, and died October 18, 1884. He was a magistrate for a number of years, and was a man of incorruptible honesty, leaving behind him an excellent reputation as an honest, upright and useful citizen.

Capt. Ledgerwood's mother, *nee* Miss Scena N. Ruth-

erford, was born in Knox county, daughter of Absalom Rutherford, a large farmer. He had been a soldier in the Revolution from Virginia, was at the battle of Monmouth, and afterwards under Gens. Gates and Greene, in their southern campaigns, including the battle of Camden, where he was wounded, having his right leg broken below the knee. He was a brother of Gen. Rutherford, of Virginia, who distinguished himself in the Revolutionary war.

Capt. Ledgerwood's mother died in 1867, aged sixty years. She was a woman of great industry and deep and undoubted piety. She was the mother of seven children: (1). Elliott. (2). James L. (3). Annie. (4). Absalom P. (5). Mary. (6). Darther. (7). Washington Lafayette, subject of this sketch.

Of these, Elliott Ledgerwood married Peggy Delap, and is now a farmer in Union county, Tennessee. James Ledgerwood was captain of company F, Third Tennessee United States infantry in the late war; married Margarena Hansford, and is now a farmer in Union county, Tennessee, on a part of the old homestead. Annie Ledgerwood died the wife of John Bayless. Absalom P. Ledgerwood was a member of his brother's (James L. Ledgerwood) company, and died in the war. He married Elizabeth Skaggs, and left three children, Orlando, Granville and Lafayette. Mary and Darther Ledgerwood died in infancy.

The only money Capt. Ledgerwood ever had given to him was five hundred dollars, presented by his father after his marriage. All else that he has handled he has made himself by close application to business, by hard work, and by practicing strict economy. Although very cautious about endorsing, he has lost some by security debts. He never sued a client or anybody else in his life on his own account, and has never been sued by any man. A close collector of fees, by making his clients believe he thinks them honest they make unusual exertions to pay him. His standing as a lawyer and a politician comes of his having been always a true man, never lying to or deceiving any one, and fulfilling all promises he makes. He is a man of strong likes and dislikes. His tone of voice indicates a man of decision of character and great self-reliance.

COL. HUMPHREY R. BATE.

MEMPHIS.

HUMPHREY R. BATE was born in Bertie county, North Carolina, December 23, 1813. He studied law in the office of Thomas P. Devereux, esq., Raleigh, North Carolina, and in 1836 moved to the western portion of Tennessee. In 1838 he commenced the practice of the law at Covington, in Tipton county,

where he continued to reside till the year 1884, when, from ill health, he ceased to practice, and moved to Memphis.

As a lawyer he stood at the head of the Covington bar, and is second to no lawyer in West Tennessee, or perhaps in the State, as an advocate, in the thorough knowledge of his profession, or in the successful management of difficult cases.

In politics he has always been a Democrat, and a great admirer of Jefferson and Calhoun, and their theories of government. He cast his first presidential vote for Hugh L White, and has stood by the Democracy, through thick and thin, ever since. Although never an office seeker, he was prevailed upon by his friends to become a candidate for the Legislature in 1847, and was elected to represent Tipton and Lauderdale counties; was re-elected in 1849; again in 1851, and again in 1857, the latter time representing Shelby, Fayette and Tipton counties.

In 1870 he represented Tipton, Fayette and Shelby counties in the State convention that revised the constitution, his great abilities as a lawyer making him one of the most useful and prominent members of that distinguished body.

The qualities of his heart equal those of his head.

Although raised a Protestant he became a member of the Roman Catholic church in 1862, and is very devout in his religion.

As a neighbor, a citizen and a friend, he is said to be almost without a fault. He has always taken great interest in all enterprises for the public good, but is too modest to make himself conspicuous in carrying them forward. His constitution is naturally delicate and his health has never been robust, but with will power and fortitude he has accomplished a fine professional success; yet having never married and being without the chief motive for the accumulation of property, he has spent his means freely for his own comfort; has been liberal, however, to others, and is now in independent circumstances. His townsmen speak of him with enthusiasm as a pure-minded, lovely man, of noble, generous impulses, whose bearing and virtues illustrate "the grand old name of gentleman, debased by many a charlatan."

ALEXANDER ERSKINE, M.D.

MEMPHIS.

THIS gentleman, who, for twenty-seven years, has been a general practitioner of medicine in the city of Memphis, but devoting himself more particularly to the diseases of women and children, and whose success, financial and professional, has given him rank among the foremost men of the city, was born at Huntsville, Alabama, September 26, 1832.

His father, Dr. Alexander Erskine, who died in 1857, at the age of sixty-six, in Huntsville, where he had practiced from 1819 till his death, was a native of Monroe county, now in West Virginia. He graduated in 1817, at the University of Pennsylvania, and spent the two subsequent years in practice in the almshouse of the city of Philadelphia, and then settled at Huntsville, where he made his mark on the profession in Alabama, notably by his being one of the first to discover and introduce into practice the virtues of *Secale Cornutum*, upon which he left a thesis, as yet unpublished, but showing depth and carefulness of research. He was also a pioneer in the use of quinine. The character of this remarkable physician deserves a careful study by the younger men of the profession even at this late day. He was a taciturn man, especially reticent in regard to the secrets of the sick-room. With phenomenal powers of endurance, exceedingly temperate, studying his cases with careful discrimination, he was one of the best diagnosticians of his time. He was the father of eleven children, the two eldest of whom died in infancy. Of the others, Mary Jane Erskine is now the wife of James H. Mastin, a prominent citizen of Huntsville; Dr.

Albert R. Erskine, now a prominent physician at Huntsville; Alexander Erskine, the subject of this sketch; Laura E. Erskine, who died the wife of Dr. Wilkinson, at Huntsville; Thomas Fearn Erskine, James A. Erskine and Miss Kate A. Erskine, now living at Huntsville; William M. Erskine, now in Texas, and Dr. John H. Erskine, who died of yellow fever in Memphis, September 17, 1878.

Further mention should be made of Dr. John H. Erskine. He and his brothers, Albert and Alexander, went through the war as surgeons in the Confederate army. He was acting medical director in Gen. Joseph E. Johnston's army in North Carolina at the time of the surrender, having risen from the position of assistant-surgeon, and was to have received his commission as medical director. At the time of his death he was health officer of the city of Memphis, a position which he had filled for some time previous. He fell a sacrifice to the duties of his office, working night and day to stay the spread of the epidemic of that year. He was a man of high character, bold, determined, decided in his judgments, and fearless in the discharge of his duties. It took a man of his stamp to compel compliance on the part of unwilling citizens with sanitary ordinances. He was a gentleman much esteemed in Memphis, and attached to himself close and warm friendships. His life and character are an interwoven part of the history of that city, and his name and memory among its rarest jewels. Col. J. M. Keating, the cautious, discriminating, yet brilliant author of the history of yellow fever in Mem-

20

phis, pays the following just tribute to the memory of Dr. John Erskine: "Another case, a type of the home physician, is recalled. He was a man of large mold. Physically he was perfect; very tall, very stout, he was the picture of health. His handsome face was lighted by a perpetual smile. Good nature, good heart, and a cheerful soul were the convictions his manner carried to every beholder. He was a manly man. He had been a soldier, and he bore about him the evidences of gallant service. Nervous and eager, devoted and anxious, he went down to his grave the victim of overwork. He was an inspiration to his friends, an example of constancy, steadiness, unflinching courage, and unflagging zeal. To the sick-room he brought all these qualities, supplemented by an unusual experience, an inexhaustible stock of knowledge, and a sympathy as deep as the sad occasion. Tender as a woman, his heart ached at the recital of miseries he could not cure. Besides his duties as health officer, John Erskine was earnest in his attentions to patients, whose demands were incessant. For days before his succumbed, observant friends felt that he must fall. He had tasked his powers far beyond endurance. His heart was, to the last, keenly sensitive to the sorrows about him; the mitigation of them was his anxiety. He chided himself because he could not do more for the people who loved him, and by whom he will ever be remembered; and, to the last, was questioning himself for a remedy for a disease that has so often conquered the ablest of a noble profession. No better man ever laid down his life in the cause of humanity."

Dr. Alexander Erskine's grandfather, Michael Erskine, a native of Pennsylvania, emigrated from Lancaster county, that State, to Monroe county, Virginia, where he married Mrs. Margaret Paulee, *nee* Hanly, by whom he had five children, Dr. Erskine's father being the third son.

The early history of Dr. Erskine's grandmother (Handly) is among the most romantic of family traditions. Her first husband, Paulee, was killed by the Indians, and herself taken captive and kept a prisoner for four years by the Shawnee tribe, in Ohio, the chief adopting her as his daughter. At his death she was ransomed, returned to her family and afterwards married Michael Erskine. [For an interesting account of the incidents of her captivity, see Hardesty's Historical and Geographical Encyclopedia, page 371]. She died at the age of ninety years.

Dr. Erskine's mother, Susan Catharine Russel, now living, eighty years old, in Huntsville, Alabama, was born in 1805, in Loudon county, Virginia, near the city of Leesburg, the daughter of Col. Albert Russel, who was a lieutenant-colonel in the Revolutionary army, and was with Washington in his marches. He moved from Virginia to Alabama in the early days of the latter State, where he resided till his death. He left five children, of whom Dr. Erskine's mother is the third.

She is a woman of remarkable common sense, of fine judgment, of high Christian character and principle, and has been an ornament to the town of Huntsville from her earliest years. She married in 1820 at the early age of fifteen. She is a noble type of the southern women of the past time. She has been a member of the Presbyterian church since 1822. Her mother's maiden name was Nancy Hooe, of an old Virginia family. Her brother, Dr. Albert Russel, who died at Huntsville in 1844, was a partner of her husband, Dr. Alexander Erskine, father of the subject of this biographical sketch.

Dr. Erskine grew up at Huntsville, taking his academic course for eight years under James M. Davidson, the "Irish orator," after which he studied four years in the University of Virginia, where he graduated in chemistry and German. He then studied medicine in 1855–56 in his father's office at Huntsville, and returning to the University of Virginia, took a medical course there in the same class with Dr. R. B. Maury, whose sketch see elsewhere in this volume. He then went to the University of the city of New York, and graduated there in 1858, and in October of that year settled in Memphis. In 1859–60 he, in connection with Dr. D. D. Saunders, (whose biography see elsewhere), and the Drs. Lunsford P. Yandell, sr. and jr., late of Louisville, reorganized the Memphis Medical College, Dr. Erskine taking the chair of obstetrics. After the breaking out of the war this faculty disbanded, but in 1867 the college was again reorganized with Dr. Erskine, Dr. D. D. Saunders, Dr. R. B. Maury, Dr. G. B. Thornton and Dr. R. W. Mitchell as the faculty, Dr. Erskine being dean. These gentlemen carried on the institution till 1872.

Dr. Erskine, though raised by a Whig father, has always affiliated with the Democratic party. His family, on both sides, have been Presbyterians from time immemorial, and he has for many years been an elder in that church. He has been connected with the Second Presbyterian church of Memphis for twenty-six years. He is a member of the Knights of Honor, of the Shelby county and Tennessee State medical societies, and is an occasional writer for the medical journals. He is now professor of obstetrics in the Memphis Hospital Medical College.

The following is a brief resume of his army experience: He served with Gens. Cleburne, Cheatham, Bragg and Polk in the campaigns in Tennessee, Mississippi, Kentucky and Georgia. He was with Gen. Bragg at the battle of Perryville, Kentucky; was taken prisoner and placed in charge of the sick and wounded at Harrodsburg for six weeks, but was afterwards sent via Louisville and Cairo to Vicksburg, where he was exchanged, and from which place he soon rejoined the army at College Grove, Tennessee. He was at the battle of Murfreesborough, and upon the retreat of the army, spent the winter at Tullahoma, being at that time brigade surgeon in Gen. Polk's command. He was next in charge of the Law hospital at LaGrange, Georgia, and continued with it till the surrender.

Dr. Erskine first married, at Memphis, December 10, 1861, Mrs. A. L. White, *nee* Miss Law. She died in 1868. By this lady Dr. Erskine has two children, Alexander and John H. Erskine.

His second marriage, which occurred at Columbia, Tennessee. December 19, 1872, was with a cousin of his first wife, Miss Margaret L. Gordon, daughter of Washington Gordon, of Columbia. By this marriage he has had seven children, Mary (who died in infancy), Louisa, Washington Gordon, William, Albert Russel, Elizabeth and Laura. Mrs. Erskine's father, Washington Gordon, was a farmer in Maury county, and died in the Confederate service at Vicksburg. Lieut.-Gen. John B. Gordon, of Georgia, is her cousin. Her mother was a Miss Bradshaw, of Columbia.

Throughout his life Dr. Erskine has been guided by the highest sense of conscientious rectitude, fidelity to his trusts, energy, zeal and promptitude in execution, and above all by high religious principles. He has always been a very close student; has always tried to be kind to the poor, and has instilled into his children the same principles by which he was reared. His personal boast is that his parents were of the strictest integrity and loftiest moral and religious character. His mother is a deeply pious woman, and while his father was less demonstrative, he was nevertheless upright in all his life, and died a Christian, in communion with the Presbyterian church. He has left the impress of his high character on that of his entire family. His son, Alexander, has ever endeavored to emulate his father's virtues, and has always stood among the foremost in the ranks of his profession in Memphis. His name, with that of his lamented brother, Dr. John H. Erskine, has been long identified with the city, and will be handed down to his children with pride, as pure, unsullied and elevated.

W. G. BIBB, M.D.

NASHVILLE.

THIS gentleman comes of one of the most distinguished families in the South. Its members have filled the responsible and honorable positions of governor, circuit and supreme judges, State senators and legislators, congressmen, United States senator, colonel and secretary of the treasury. Of the subject of this sketch, it may be said in the language of the challenge given by the hero in the "Patrician's Daughter":

"It may be by the calendar of years you are the elder man,
But 'tis the sun of knowledge on the mind's dial shining bright,
That makes true time."

W. G. Bibb was born in Montgomery, Alabama, June 25, 1854. He received his literary education at the University of Georgia and the University of Alabama, from which latter institution he graduated in 1872. He began the study of medicine in 1874, and attended one course, in 1876, at the University of Virginia. He then came to Nashville, and, in 1877, was valedictorian of his class and graduated as an M.D., from the medical department of the University of Nashville and Vanderbilt University. He spent the summer of 1877 in Paris, France, visiting the hospitals there, and upon his return went to New York city, and in 1878, graduated from the Bellevue Hospital Medical College under Profs. Austin Flint, sr. and jr., Sayre, Barker, Mott, Van-Buren, Janeway and others.

In March, 1878, he settled at Montgomery, Alabama, in practice and remained there until the spring of 1881, when he moved to Nashville, having been in that year elected professor of materia medica and therapeutics in the medical department of the University of Tennessee and Nashville Medical College. In 1882 he was appointed surgeon of the Nashville, Chattanooga and St. Louis railway, a lucrative position, which he held during Gov. Porter's presidency of the road. Dr. Bibb is a thoroughly enthusiastic lover of his profession, and his address on "Progressive Medicine," lately delivered, is a credit not only to himself but to the institution in which he is a professor. As a lecturer his style is rather conversational than rhetorical, his object being to instruct in matters of fact rather than make display. His manners are frank and cordial, and such as characterize the typical physician.

In personal appearance Dr. Bibb is a man of medium height and weight. He is a zealous Mason and a member of Nashville Commandery Knights Templar. He is also a Knight of Pythias. In politics, he always votes the Democratic ticket, as he believes that ticket represents the southern white man's idea. Nor could he well vote otherwise and conform to the examples and teachings of his brilliant and distinguished ancestry.

Dr. Bibb's father, Col. Joseph B. Bibb, was a lawyer at Montgomery when the war between the States began, when he raised a company of volunteers, went to Mobile and seized Fort Morgan and garrisoned it until the State of Alabama seceded, when he returned to Montgomery and, with Col. Beck, raised the Twenty-third Alabama regiment, of which he became lieutenant-colonel. On the death of Col. Beck he succeeded to the command of the regiment and served as its colonel in all the campaigns of the western army in Mississippi; with Gen. Bragg in the Kentucky campaign; with Gen. Joseph E. Johnston in the Dalton campaign; with Hood in his Nashville raid, and at the reorganization of the army served with Gen. Johnston in North Carolina, surrendering with that commander at Greensborough. Returning home he engaged in planting in Montgomery county, Alabama, until September 14, 1869, when he died of consumption, brought on by a wound from the fragment of a shell he received at the battle of Nashville. He was a man brave, generous and philanthropic, with a hand open as day for melting charity, and the words applied to the Prince of Orange are quite as applicable to him: "No man ever knew what what that thing was that the Prince of Orange feared."

Dr. Bibb's mother was Miss Martha Dandridge Bibb, daughter of the venerable Judge B. S. Bibb, now living at Montgomery, at the advanced age of eighty-seven years. Dr. Bibb is her oldest son, and her only other child is Peyton B. Bibb, ensign United States navy, at present stationed on the Pacific coast in the United States hydrographic and geodetic survey. The mother has been inspired with an ambition to make her sons worthy of the illustrious name they have inherited. She is a most agreeable conversationalist, possesses a face beaming with intelligence, eyes radiant with good nature, and altogether is one of the most interesting of the high-born southern women.

The maternal grandfather and grandmother of Dr. Bibb are both living, and are in possession of all their faculties. They have been married sixty-five years. Judge Bibb was born in Elbert county, Georgia, September 30, 1796, and is now in his eighty-ninth year. Of this distinguished gentleman the Savannah, Georgia, *Times* recently contained the following interesting sketch: "Judge Bibb comes of a noted family. His elder brother, Dr. William Wyatt Bibb, of Elbert county, Georgia, the home of the family, entered the congress of the United States in 1807, and in 1813 was elected to the senate. In 1817, when the territory of Alabama was opened for settlement, he was appointed territorial governor by President Monroe. In 1819, when Alabama was admitted as a State into the Union, he was elected governor, and died during his term of office in 1820, having scarcely reached the age of forty years. Such a career for a young man was wonderful, and an evidence of his high character. His brother, Thomas Bibb, was then president of the Alabama senate, and succeeded him as governor of the State for the unexpired term. Hon. B. S. Bibb, the surviving representative of this distinguished family, was born in Elbert county, and married Miss Sophia F. Gilmer, a sister of Gov. Gilmer, of Georgia, and a relative of Gen. J. F. Gilmer, of Savannah, and moved to Alabama sixty years ago. His nobility of character was soon appreciated, and he was called frequently to serve the public. He has filled many positions of honor and trust, been elected a number of terms to the lower house of the Legislature and to the Senate; was probate judge of the county for fourteen years, and was the first judge of the city and criminal court of Montgomery, and was the first judicial officer removed by the Federal authorities after the close of the war. He is now in the eighty-ninth year of his age, and has just passed the sixty-sixth anniversary of his marriage. And now, with his noble wife, who, during the perilous days of the late war, labored so earnestly and zealously for the comfort of the soldiers in the hospitals, and was known to thousands as "dear aunt Sophy," he is passing quietly and peacefully the evening of a life full of honor, cheered by the consciousness that his days have been well spent, and that his generation are a credit to him."

The great-grandfather of Dr. Bibb was high sheriff of Prince Edward county, Virginia, during the Revolutionary war. After peace was made he moved to Elbert county, Georgia, where his family was reared. His wife, Sallie Wyatt, was a descendant of Sir Isaac Wyatt, one of the first colonial governors of Virginia, and by blood she was related to the Peytons, Dandridges, Bookers and other first-class families of Virginia. The Bibbs were originally from Wales, and have been in America over two hundred years.

Another distinguished relative of Dr. Bibb was the Hon. George M. Bibb, of Kentucky, a leading jurist, at one time judge of the court of appeals of Kentucky, secretary of the treasury of the United States, and also served a term in the United States Senate.

Dr. Bibb's paternal grandfather, Peyton Bibb, married Miss Martha Cobb, of Georgia, daughter of Thomas Cobb and relative of Gens. Howell and Thomas Cobb, distinguished in the late war. On her mother's side, she was kin to the well-known Martin family of South Carolina.

Dr. Bibb's maternal grandmother, Sophia L. A. Gilmer, was a daughter of Thomas Meriwether Gilmer, of Oglethorpe county, Georgia, a sister of Gov. Rockingham Gilmer, of Georgia, and a first cousin of Secretary of the navy Gilmer, who was killed by the explosion of a gun on board a vessel on the Potomac river during an inspection by the president's cabinet many years ago. She was also a great niece, on her mother's side, of Gen. Andrew Lewis of the Revolutionary army.

Dr. Bibb was married at Nashville, June 25, 1878, to Miss Susie Dunlap Porter, who was born at Paris, Tennessee, September 17, 1858. She is the grand-daughter of Dr. Thomas Kennedy Porter, of Paris, Tennessee, and the only daughter of Hon. James D. Porter, ex-governor of Tennessee, ex-president of the Nashville, Chattanooga and St. Louis railway, and at present first assistant secretary of State in President Cleveland's cabinet. Her mother, originally Miss Sue Dunlap, is a daughter of Gen. John Dunlap, of Paris, Tennessee, and niece of Gen. Richard Dunlap, a distinguished Tennessean—the confidential friend of Gen. Andrew Jackson. Mrs. Bibb was educated at Nashville, and is a lady of very fine presence, remarkable for her womanly virtues, her love of home and devotion to her family, and in all that constitutes true womanhood, she is as true as the needle to the pole. By this marriage there are two children: (1). James Porter, born December 4, 1879. (2). Mattie Gilmer, born June 26, 1882.

Dr. Bibb is at present junior member of the medical firm of Cain & Bibb. Dr. Cain is from Okolona, Mississippi, where he had a very lucrative practice. He is a graduate from the medical department of the University of Nashville, and served with credit and ability as surgeon of Tucker's Mississippi brigade during the war.

P. S.—Since this sketch was written, Dr. Bibb has returned to his old home in Montgomery, Alabama, important private business requiring his personal attention there.

F. S. NICHOLS.

MEMPHIS.

THE subject of this sketch is, in many respects, a remarkable person—a true type of the self-made man. The family from which he came was of English origin. His great-grandfather, William Nichols, came from England and settled in Connecticut. His father, William Nichols, removed from Litchfield, Connecticut, to Michigan and thence to Iowa, where he engaged in farming and died in 1840. His mother, originally Miss Sammons, was a native of Duchess county, New York. Her father, Frederic Sammons, was a man of prominence in Revolutionary times, and was an officer in the American army. He was made a prisoner when New York was invaded by Sir William Johnson, who had been a neighbor of the family on the Mohawk river, and he was confined three years at Quebec, after which he made his escape. His brother, Thomas Sammons, was a member of Congress from New York for several terms during the administrations of Jefferson and Madison.

F. S. Nichols was born in McCombe county, Michigan, February 27, 1828, and lived there until 1838, when he went, with his father's family, to Davenport, Iowa, and grew up there, working on a farm till he was twenty years of age. Reared in a new country, he was deprived of early school privileges, but from his boyhood he had a great fondness for reading, and read everything that fell into his hands. Through this desire, which increased as he grew, he was led to choose the printer's trade, and his education was received in a printing office. In 1848 he entered the office of the Rock Island (Ill.) Advertiser, a Whig journal, and there remained till 1851, when he established a Democratic paper in the same town, and continued as its editor and publisher till 1853. He then took the gold fever and went to Australia, where he experienced the ups and downs of a miner's life for six years. Returning to the United States, he settled in Iowa and engaged in farming for three years, at the end of which time he went into the office of the Chicago Times, where he remained till 1864.

Hearing that there was a great demand for printers in Memphis, he decided to go to that city. Upon arrival there he purchased an interest in the Memphis Bulletin, owned by J. B. Bingham, editor, assuming the position of foreman, and continued with that paper till it suspended publication in 1870. He then became foreman of the Memphis Avalanche. In 1877 he became one of its proprietors, and in 1879, became chief proprietor and editor—his present position. Since he has had control of the Avalanche, it has improved in every way; in character as a journal, in circulation and in value as a newspaper property.

He has always been a Democrat, but has taken no part in politics except through his journal. He is inclined towards independence, and the expressions of opinion through his paper are not controlled by party machinery. He supports a measure not because it is Democratic, but because it is in itself good. To express it briefly, the Avalanche is not a "party organ," but wields a free lance on all subjects, bristling at all times with original, unique and pungent paragraphs.

Mr. Nichols became a Master Mason at Rock Island, Illinois, in 1851, and a Knight of Honor at Memphis, in 1881.

He was married, August 20, 1860, to Miss Josephine Hughes, daughter of Harvey Hughes, a descendant of a Virginia family, one branch of which settled in Ohio and another in Tennessee, where the family is still represented. He is an architect by trade, and still living in Missouri.

One of Mrs. Nichols' uncles is the oldest banker in Cincinnati, Ohio, and the president of Hughes' Bank. Another uncle is judge of the circuit court in Ohio.

To Mr. Nichols and wife there was born one child, a daughter, now wife of William H. Forrest, of Memphis.

Mr. Nichols belongs to a class of men who are rarely appreciated at their full worth by their fellow-citizens, who pass through life quietly, often in a subordinate capacity, and never displaying their real power unless some unlooked for occasion develops it. It was the terrible visitation of yellow fever to Memphis, in 1879, that developed the hidden forces in the character of F. S. Nichols. No reader of the Memphis papers during the prevalence of the fearful scourge, can have forgotten the "old man" of the *Avalanche* and his biting paragraphs. Though the city was nearly depopulated, by flight and death, he remained bravely at his post and daily bulletined to the outside world the ravages of the epidemic. While manfully doing his own duty to his stricken fellow-men and women, he seemed to be inspired with a profound disgust at the conduct of those who had left the city as a matter of safety, but whom he daily lampooned through the columns of the *Avalanche* as "cowards," "skulkers," etc. This persistent line of invective made him many personal enemies, of course, but it served to bring him into general notice as a brave man, a strong writer and a journalist, who dared to think and speak for himself. From an obscure foreman, he became, at once, an editor of recognized ability and influence. In the recent controversies in Tennessee over the State debt, Mr. Nichols was a pronounced "skyblue" Democrat, and the honor of the State had no firmer or more aggressive champion than the *Avalanche*, under Mr. Nichols' editorial guidance.

P. S.—Since the foregoing sketch was prepared, Mr. F. S. Nichols was stricken with paralysis, has died, and the *Avalanche* has passed into other hands, though it still maintains much of that independent Democratic character it acquired under his management.

REV. STANFORD G. BURNEY, D.D., L.L.D.

LEBANON.

THIS eminent clergyman and scholar, celebrated for his splendid abilities, his high character, and his modesty, presents a fine study as a student, teacher and pastor, yet, while his history is connected with some of the most important educational and religious enterprises of the day, he is also to be looked upon as an intellect shining with light for others to work by as well as being a worker himself. He is regarded by learned men, who have known him for thirty years, as one of the best thinkers in the State, advanced beyond his time, and a metaphysician of the highest class.

When Dr. Burney, as a young man, entered upon his active ministry, he made a profound impression on the public mind, as an eloquent speaker, of gentle and pleasant address, and remarkable earnestness. He was even then recognized by thoughtful men as an abstract and philosophical thinker, and a general conviction was then formed that he would reach, as he has done, the front rank among his brother ministers. Although he was fitted for the pulpit in a pre-eminent degree, and capable of gaining great popularity by his cultivated oratory, yet his intense application to the study of the Bible as the great book of Human Philosophy, necessarily carried him at an early day to the school-room and to literary pursuits. From these two callings he had access to the intelligence of the church, and has controlled that intelligence, next to the learned Dr. Richard Beard, more than any other man of his day. These pursuits made somewhat a change in his outward character. His manners became unobtrusive and quiet, and he now impresses one as a reserved student, but gentle and kind in all his relations with men. If he had been as aggressive in his efforts to gain distinction and the plaudits of the world as he has been in his profound study of man and his relations to his Creator, he could have gone to the highest place in that direction. But his ability was well recognized by active leaders in his church, and he was in due time called to the most important position in the leading theological school of his denomination, where to-day he stands among the first and ablest of her teachers. He has been not only a student of the Bible, but also a student of the great secular thinkers. This has freed him from these idiosyncracies usual with men who study only one side of a question, and has given to him a balanced character both in thought and expression. He combines the practical, philosophical character of a Solomon, with the poetic zeal and fire of an Isaiah. To splendid powers of statement as a writer. and of expression as a speaker, he has added wide powers of investigation of philosophy, human and divine, and is regarded as a capable critic of every phase of thought in the field of theology or of agnosticism. With a voice musical and soft, and a nature tender and gentle, he yet has underneath evidences of the fire and zeal of his early manhood. Every one can see and appreciate the actors on the field of great public matters, both in church and state, but only a few know that quiet and thoughtful men like Dr. Burney are at last in real control, and it is the unseen hand that keeps any system together.

Stanford G. Burney was born in Robertson county, Tennessee, April 16, 1814. He is the son of William Burney, a native of North Carolina, born in 1788, moved to Robertson county when twelve years old, became a successful farmer, and died in 1856. Twice married, he raised eleven sons, six by his first wife and five by his last. He first married Miss Annie Guthrie, daughter of Rev. Robert Guthrie, a native of North Carolina, who settled in Tennessee about 1800, and finally moved to Missouri, and died there. His wife was a Miss Smith. Rev. Robert Guthrie was one of the earliest preachers of the Cumberland Presbyterian church—one of the men excommunicated from the old church. He was of a distinguished Scotch-Irish family.

Of the six sons by the first wife, Dr. Burney, subject of this sketch, is the eldest. H. L. Burney is a preacher in the Cumberland Presbyterian church, and resides near Clarksville, Tennessee. J. H. Burney died a farmer. John F. Burney was a professional teacher, educated at Princeton College, Kentucky, and died twenty-six years old. Wesley Monroe Burney was a Confederate soldier, captured at Fort Donelson, and died at St. Louis. Eli Gunn Burney graduated from the Mississippi University; is now teaching at Oakland, Mississippi, and was for a time professor of languages in Cumberland University, Lebanon, Tennessee.

Dr. Burney's father's second wife was Miss Frances Donelson. Of the five sons by her, William Burney was a soldier among the first Confederate troops raised in Robertson county, and is now living on the old homestead. Hatcher Burney joined the army and was killed at Dalton during Gen. Johnston's retreat. Hatton Burney is now living on the old homestead in Robertson county. Marshall Burney died in 1872. Ewin Burney is now a lawyer at Nashville.

Dr. Burney's grandfather was John Burney, of a large family in the North and South Carolinas, of Scotch-Irish descent. He married Miss Mary Parks, daughter of George Parks, who was a colonel in the Revolutionary war from North Carolina.

Dr. Burney was raised a country boy, born feeble, always dyspeptic. He early evinced a marked taste for study and learning, and stood in advance in that time of the boys of his neighborhood, being particularly fond of the natural sciences. After receiving an exceptionally good common school and academic education, he attended, two and a half years, Princeton College, Kentucky, and graduated in 1841. On the 12th of August following, he married Miss Susan Gray, of Princeton, Kentucky, daughter of William and Lydia Gray, formerly from South Carolina. Mr. Gray was a wealthy farmer, trader and shipper. Mrs. Burney was educated at Elkton, Kentucky, and is a highly cultured lady, noted for her practical sense, prudence and discreetness in her intercourse with society.

By this marriage Dr. Burney has had nine children :

(1). Addison G. Burney, joined the Eleventh Mississippi Confederate regiment, and was killed at Spottsylvania Court-house, May 12, 1864, at the age of twenty-two. It was said of him "no better soldier ever shouldered a musket for the Confederate cause." He belonged to Col. Joe Davis's regiment, Early's division.

(2). Theodore C. Burney, born January 1, 1845, left college with his brother, Addison, to join the army. Both were wounded in the battle of Seven Pines; both were furloughed home, both returned and rejoined the army. He was in the battle of Gettysburg, and on the retreat was killed in the battle of Falling Water. (3).

Mary B. V. Burney, born June 6, 1847; was an exceptionally fine scholar, even when young; is highly educated ; now the wife of James H. Howry, oldest son of Hon. J. M. Howry, of Mississippi, a distinguished member of the Masonic order in that State. They have five children, Mary Alice, Burney, Erle C., Eugene H., and Addison Theodore. (4). Herschel P. Burney, born December 25, 1850; educated at the University of Mississippi; spent several years managing his father's farm in Lafayette county, Mississippi; now engaged in teaching at Atkins, Pope county, Arkansas. He married Miss Nannie McKee, daughter of William S. McKee, for many years sheriff of Lafayette county, Mississippi. She is a graduate of the Oxford (Miss.) Female College, and is finely educated. They have three children, Nannie Clyde, Maggie Sue, and William Stanford. (5). Louella Clarissa Burney, graduated from Union Female College, Oxford, Mississippi ; married S. S. Scales, graduate of the University of Mississippi, son of Dr. Nathan F. Scales, of Noxubee county, Mississippi ; is now a successful merchant. They have two children, Lucie Anna and Nathaniel Fields. (6). Auna Z. Burney, graduated at Union Female College, Oxford ; married Rev. W. R. Binkley, pastor of the Cumberland Presbyterian church at Oxford, Mississippi. (7). Susie F. Burney, graduated at Union Female College, Oxford, and is now living at Lebanon, Tennessee, with her father. (8). Geary D. Burney, now a student in Cumberland University, Lebanon. (9). Stanford Corinne Burney, now in school at Lebanon.

Dr. Burney was ordained in March, 1836, in Wilson county, Tennessee, a minister of the Cumberland Presbyterian church, in which he has preached, hardly missing a Sunday, every since. He first located in Nashville, August, 1841, and preached there eighteen months. In January, 1843, he took charge of the Female Academy at Franklin, Tennessee, and taught one year. He then became the first agent for the Cumberland University, and spent one year collecting money for the endowment of that institution. In December, 1844, he settled on a farm near Memphis, and preached several months for the First Cumberland Presbyterian church in Memphis, while the first church-house was building. He remained there three years preaching to a country church, and associated with Robert Fraiser as editor and publisher of the *Religious Ark*, a Cumberland Presbyterian paper. In 1848 he accepted the presidency of Mount Sylvan Academy, in Lafayette county, Mississippi, and conducted that institution two years. In January, 1850, he accepted the pastorate of the Cumberland Presbyterian church in Oxford, Mississippi, and filled the position twenty-five years, with the exception of the year 1860, when Dr. C. H. Bell was pastor. After the war Dr. Bell and Dr. Burney filled the pulpit, alternately, until 1873.

Dr. Burney has always held high position in his church, and has been connected with almost every important committee. He was once appointed on a committee to revise the discipline of the church; twice appointed to revise the theology of the church; was chairman of a committee on organic union with the Southern Presbyterian church; was twice a delegate to represent the Cumberland Presbyterians in the Evangelical Union conference in Scotland, and also a delegate to represent the Cumberland Presbyterian church in the Pan-Presbyterian council at Belfast, Ireland.

In 1852 Dr. Burney established the Union Female College at Oxford, Mississippi, and continued its president until 1860, when he resigned, and became president of the board of trustees of the college, which position he held until 1878. In October, 1866, he was elected professor of English literature in the University of Mississippi, a chair which he filled seven years, meantime performing the duties of the chair of metaphysics in that institution a part of the time, making in these positions a high reputation in the world of letters. In 1873 he resigned this position, and from January, 1874, to September, 1877, he preached at Jackson, Newbern, Dyersburg and other points, besides running his farm in Mississippi.

In September, 1876, he was elected to the chair of biblical literature in the theological department of Cumberland University, Lebanon, Tennessee; in September, 1877, he accepted that position, moved to Lebanon, and entered upon the duties of that chair. In December, 1880, he was elected to the chair of systematic theology in the same institution, Dr. Richard Beard, who had filled the chair twenty-seven years, having died. This position he now holds.

Dr. Burney was made a Mason at Nashville, in January, 1844, and has taken all the York masonry degrees except Knight Templar, and has taken twenty-nine degrees in the Scotch rite. He has filled all the offices in the lodge, chapter and council.

Being a relative of the distinguished statesman, Hon. Hugh L. White, Dr. Burney gave his first vote to that eminent Whig for president, and may be regarded as a life-long Whig, though since the war has been voting with the Democrats. He has never held political office, though for two years accepted the postmastership at Mount Sylvan, Mississippi.

When a boy, Dr. Burney, although of delicate health, was full of vivacity, loving fun and pleasure, but avoided the extremes of dissipation. He loved wine, loved parties, attended balls, and on one occasion was present at a bran dance, where liquor was drank pretty freely, and men got to fighting. That night he reflected that, if this is the best a life of pleasure can do for a man, it is a poor thing; and he then and there resolved on a line of virtue and right living, and now, on the principle that a man's highest interest lies in the line of duty, his proud satisfaction is that his life has smoothly run ever since. He has not selected his fields of labor, but has been urged into them by friends and force of circumstances. His father, who was a man of some fortune, gave him two thousand dollars for a start; by his wife he got as much more, and during life he has made a good deal of money, but like most of students, has made money a secondary consideration. He professed religion at eighteen years of age, commenced preaching at twenty, was ordained at twenty-two, and has preached fifty years, mostly in Mississippi, from 1847 to 1874, preaching at Oxford, alone, some twenty-seven years. The Union Female College founded by him, is the oldest institution of its class in Mississippi.

Dr. Burney's writings have been mostly review articles, which have made him quite famous. The late Dr. Thomas O. Summers, of the Methodist church, regarded him, as a polemic, among the first men of the age. His published disquisitions on subjects connected with psychology, metaphysics and theology, and his reviews of books have given him a place distinctively his own in the world of letters.

MAJ. E. P. McNEAL.

BOLIVAR.

E. P. McNEAL, the subject of this sketch, was one among the earliest of West Tennessee pioneers, and is, perhaps, as thoroughly a representative man of the farmers of West Tennessee, from its first settlement to the present time, as any one now living within its boundaries. He is the son of Thomas McNeal, and of Clarissa, daughter of Ezekiel Polk, of Mecklenburg county, North Carolina, and was born in York District, South Carolina, on September 6, 1804.

In 1806, his parents removed to Maury county, Tennessee, in which county he grew into manhood, alternating work on the farm with going to school, until his father and family moved to Hardeman county, West Tennessee, in 1822. His family were among the first to take possession of the country west of the Tennessee river.

Ezekiel Polk, his grandfather, and also William Polk, Thomas J. Hardeman, and Thomas McNeal (his father), made crops in Hardeman county in the year 1822, by sending out hands to work, in advance of their arrival, on lands near the present site of the town of Bolivar. This was the first year of the settlement of Hardeman county. The county was organized in 1823, and on the place of Capt. Thomas McNeal, one mile north of the present site of Bolivar, a log court-house was built, and the county seat established and kept there until removed to Bolivar, in 1825.

In 1823 E. P. McNeal, then nineteen years of age, made a crop of his own near where Bolivar is now situated. In 1824-25-26, he was occupied as a surveyor in West Tennessee district. In 1827 and 1828, he was in the service of the United States government as deputy-marshal under Gen. Purdy, marshal for the district. In 1829 he was employed in a dry goods store in Bolivar, which had then grown into a town. In the same year (1829) he was placed in charge, as receiver, of the interests of a mercantile concern in connection with Col. John Preston, of Virginia, and in the winter of 1830–31, in connection with J. H. Bills, he built and carried from Bolivar to New Orleans two flat-boats loaded with cotton, to sell for themselves and neighbors.

Upon his return home in 1831, E. P. McNeal formed a mercantile partnership with his brother-in-law, Maj. John H. Bills, and in April of that year Maj. McNeal went to New York and Philadelphia by river and stage to buy goods, which in those days was a tedious undertaking. The firm of Bills & McNeal, merchants, continued in prosperous business from 1831 to 1846, when it dissolved, each partner going into separate mercantile business on his own account, E. P. McNeal continuing therein in Bolivar up to 1856. In the meanwhile Maj.

McNeal dealt extensively in lands in Tennessee, Mississippi and Arkansas, and as early as 1840 began farming on a large scale in Hardeman county, giving to his farming interests the greater part of his time and attention. He closed out all of his mercantile business in 1856, and since that date has devoted his attention exclusively to his plantations, having acquired a large landed estate in Tennessee, Mississippi and Arkansas. In this pursuit he has been very successful. And even after the immense losses resultant from the war in slaves, one hundred and fifty in number, and other property, he has kept his farms and stock to a high standard, which but few farmers in the South have been able to do.

E. P. McNeal, in January, 1835, was married to Miss Ann Williams, daughter of J. J. Williams, esq., of Hardeman county. They had one child, Priscilla, who died just on arrival at womanhood—at the age of eighteen. His beloved wife, who had made home happy for forty years, died in 1875.

Throughout all of his life Maj. E. P. McNeal has been a quiet and modest man. He has been charitable and liberal with his means, without ostentation. He has never sought public place. He has made and preserved from youth to manhood and old age, even to four score years, an enviable record of energy and promptness in business; sincerity and truth in speech; uprightness and honesty in conduct, and in all dealings with his fellow-men, and at this time he stands in the front rank of the men of West Tennessee, having preserved and strengthened, as the years went by, the golden reputation he has earned and kept untarnished as one among his pioneers.

REV. J. W. PHILLIPS, M.D.

TULLAHOMA.

THIS prominent physician and surgeon was born in Mecklenburg county, Virginia, January 11, 1820, worked in the corn-field till he was eighteen years old, taught school in his nineteenth year at Durhamville, Tennessee, read medicine under Dr. W. D. Scott at Trenton, Tennessee, and graduated M.D. in May, 1842, at the University of Pennsylvania, under Profs. Nathan Chapman, William B. Gibson, Robert Hare, Hugh L. Hodge, William E. Horner, Samuel Jackson and George B. Wood, in a class with Dr. A. L. C. Magruder and Dr. R. P. Walton, of Norfolk, Virginia. Between the sessions he attended Wills' Hospital for the Lame and Blind, and Warrington's Obstetrical Department, from each of which institutions he took a diploma in addition to his regular degree. He practiced medicine at Salem, Mississippi, from June, 1842, to December, 1845; next practiced twenty years in Hinds and Madison counties, Mississippi, doing an exceptionally

large practice among the wealthiest people in that State; his fees for eight years averaging five thousand dollars per annum. He was in the yellow fever epidemic at Brownsville, Mississippi, and in the cholera epidemic of 1866 at Memphis.

When Mississippi enlisted her minute men for the Confederate service, he was commissioned by Rev. T. W. Casky (the agent appointed by the Legislature of the State), post surgeon at Bolton's Depot, Hinds county, Mississippi. Ex-officio he became surgeon of Gen. Charles E. Smeed's brigade and served one year, then refugeed to Smith county, Texas, to save his negroes, and there practiced medicine till the war was over; then came to Memphis, practiced one year; next at Mason's depot three years; at Brownsville three years, and at Dyersburg ten years. He located at Tullahoma, April 15, 1884. He was at an early day a member of the Mississippi State Medical Society, and in

21

1866 became a member of the Memphis Medical Society, and in that year was called upon to furnish an essay on *Tetanus*, which was made the leading article in Willett & Ramsey's Memphis *Medical Journal* of that date.

Dr. Phillips is a Royal Arch Mason, a Democrat and a Methodist, and is a licensed elder in the Methodist Episcopal church, South. He began preaching in 1844, and has exercised ministerial functions as a local preacher wherever he has lived, and has never been challenged to answer for any misconduct by the church.

Dr. Phillips has children by two marriages. In 1847 he married at Sharon, Madison county, Mississippi, Miss Harriet Wade Austin, daughter of William J. Austin, a wealthy planter and distinguished financier, a native of Tennessee. The children born of this union are: (1). Flavia, educated at Southern Female College, Port Gibson, Mississippi ; now wife of David H. Poston, a distinguished lawyer at Memphis. (2). Florence, educated at same school ; died in 1873, aged nineteen.

In 1853 Dr. Phillips was again married, in Madison county, Mississippi, to Mrs. Martha Almeda Walker, widow of John F. Walker, of New Orleans. She was born near Columbia, Tennessee, daughter of Gen. Russell McCord Williamson, a graduate of Chapel Hill, North Carolina, and surveyor-general of Mississippi, under Gen. Jackson's administration, which position he held at the time of his death. His wife was a Miss Lindsley, of Williamson county, Tennessee. Mrs. Phillips was educated at Nazareth, Kentucky, is an Episcopalian, an expert in music, a fine writer, and was never known to have a cross word with any one or to be mixed up in gossip or a wrangle. Her leading trait is her domestic habits. By this marriage ten children were born, four of whom, sons, died in early childhood. Of the survivors: (1). Sallie Fredonia, educated at St. Agnes school, Memphis; now wife of Hon. Frank M. Estes, a lawyer at St. Louis ; has two children, Frank and Grace. (2). Mary, educated at Brownsville; married C. C. Walton, a druggist at Norfolk, Virginia ; has three children, Charles Courtland, Kearney Phillips and Almedia Linton. (3). James

William, now in business at Memphis. (4). Charles Thomas, now in his eighteenth year, a cadet at the United States Naval Academy at Annapolis. (5). Jessie, educated at Dyersburg and St. Louis. (6). ——— By her first marriage Mrs. Phillips has one child, a son, John F. Walker, now in mercantile life at Memphis. He married Miss Swan, daughter of Confederate Congressman Swan, of Tennessee, and by her had one child, John F., now being raised in the family of Dr. Phillips.

Dr. Phillips' father, who died in 1867, in Fayette county, Tennessee, at the age of eighty, was a soldier in the war of 1812, was a successful tobacco planter, a good man, and a deacon in the Baptist church.

Dr. Phillips' mother, *nee* Miss Dorcas Pettus, was born in Mecklenburg county, Virginia, daughter of Samuel Pettus, a famous large planter in that county. Her mother was a Miss Shelburn, of an extensive Virginia family. Dr. Phillips' mother died in 1862, at the age of sixty-six. Dr. Phillips' two brothers, Dr. Thomas A. Phillips, of Canton, Mississippi, and Dr. Joseph W. Phillips, of Williston, Tennessee, are physicians of fine standing.

Dr. Phillips began his business life a thousand dollars in debt. He has made a great deal of money, but has been too loose a trader, too liberal and generous-hearted to accumulate a large permanent property. His friends state that his energy is unexampled in his profession, and the amounts he has earned during his professional life are probably without a parallel among doctors, outside of large cities. In forty one years he earned, as his books show, in professional fees, one hundred and twenty-three thousand dollars. But his negroes were set free and his lands rendered valueless, and he sold them for Confederate bonds, which he failed properly to invest in time. He is still a hard student of medicine, aiming to keep himself qualified for his profession, while doing an active practice.

Dr. Phillips is six feet high, weighs one hundred and eighty pounds, has a florid complexion, and the appearance of a thoughtful, careful, busy business man, without any trace of arrogance or self-seeking.

JUDGE JAMES M. QUARLES.

NASHVILLE.

THE distinguished lawyer and gentleman, whose name stands at the head of this sketch, ranks second, perhaps, to no one in Tennessee as a criminal lawyer, while as a jurist he is regarded among the first. He was born in Louisa county, Virginia, February 8, 1823, and lived there until 1833, when his father moved to Christian county, Kentucky, and there young Quarles

was brought up on a farm, near the village of Garrettsburg, receiving his preparatory education under private tutors. In 1844 he went to Clarksville, Tennessee, to study law in the office of George C. Boyd, and was there a companion and fellow-student of Hon. James E. Bailey, late United States senator from Tennessee. He was admitted to the bar in 1845, by Judge Mortimer

M. Martin and Judge Maney. He at once stepped into a good practice, which continued to flourish, as his reputation for criminal practice soon became wide-spread.

Raised a Democrat, he was, in 1854, elected by that party attorney-general for the Tenth judicial circuit which office he filled until 1859, when he resigned. Soon after he was elected to represent his district in the United States Congress, succeeding Gen. Felix K. Zollicoffer, of Nashville, and serving during the stormy period of approaching civil war. After his congressional term expired he returned to Clarksville and resumed practice of the law. Here, he continued during the war and after, up to 1872, when he moved to Nashville to enjoy the advantages of the wider field offered his eminent ability. In 1878 he was elected judge of the criminal court of Davidson and Rutherford counties, from which position he resigned in 1882, and again resumed his regular practice, taking as a partner Mr. W. A. Thoma, lately deceased, and Mr. W. T. Turley, formerly of Franklin. In addition to his services on the bench and at the bar, Judge Quarles is also the author of "Quarles' Criminal Digest," published at Nashville in 1873, by Albert B. Tavel.

Judge Quarles became a Mason and Odd Fellow at Clarksville. After his removal to Nashville, he became a member of the Independent Order of Red Men, and a Knight of Honor.

The Quarles family is of English descent, and is able to trace its ancestry back to a remote period. Among the earliest known ancestors who can be placed accurately, was the well-known English poet, Quarles. However, another member of the family is mentioned as keeper of the rolls in England at a still earlier date. The family in America is descended from three brothers who settled in Virginia. One of them, James Quarles, was the great-grandfather of the subject of this sketch. He married a Miss Pryor, of the Pryor family of Virginia, from whom Gen. Roger A. Pryor, the brilliant criminal lawyer, now of New York, is descended. James Quarles' son, John, or "Jack," as he was nicknamed, was the grandfather of Judge James M. Quarles. He was an associate and warm friend of the celebrated William Wirt. He married into the Minor family, so well and so favorably known in Virginia. This son, Garrett Minor Quarles, was Judge Quarles' father.

Judge Quarles' mother, whose maiden name was Mary Johnson Poindexter, belonged to another old Virginia family, of French Huguenot origin. Her father, Rev. John Poindexter, whose history will be found in "The Virginia Baptists," was a prominent minister in his day. Gov. Poindexter, of Mississippi, was her uncle.

Judge Quarles was married at Hopkinsville, Kentucky, April 3, 1849, to Miss Mary W. Thomas, daughter of Robert W. Thomas, then editor of the Clarksville *Chronicle*. Her grandfather married Miss Lewis, cousin of Meriwether Lewis, and a direct descendant of Fielding Lewis, who married Gen. George Washington's sister, Bettie Washington. Mrs. Quarles' great-grandfather, Robert Walker, was a surveyor and ran "Walker's line" between the States of Kentucky and Tennessee (then Virginia and North Carolina), and named Cumberland Gap, Cumberland river and Cumberland mountains in honor of the Duke of Cumberland, a short time after his victory at Culloden.

By his marriage with Miss Thomas, Judge Quarles has nine children now living: (1). Robert T. Quarles. (2). Ellen D. Quarles. (3). Lucy M. Quarles. (4). Eva Belle Quarles. (5). Fannie Thomas Quarles. (6). David Walker Quarles. (7). Ninte Lee Quarles. (8). Lizzie L. Quarles. (9). W. A. Quarles, jr.

Mrs. Quarles is a devoted member of the Protestant Episcopal church, and is a lady distinguished for her domestic tastes, her intelligence, her amiable character, and devotion to her family.

Beginning life with but little of this world's goods, not even having the advantage of a collegiate education, Judge Quarles has achieved success and prominence in his profession by keeping before him the truth that there is no royal road to success, but that it must be achieved by assiduous study and close attention to business. As an orator he is very captivating—can be vehement at will, and is frequently very eloquent. In the management of cases he is one of the most successful advocates at the Nashville bar, and appears as counsel, either for prosecution or defense, in nearly every important case brought for trial there. His learning is extensive, his literary tastes covering the widest field of standard and sterling knowledge. Socially, he is one of the most companionable of men, an excellent *raconteur*, a gentleman of affable manners, consequently very popular.

HON. JOHN WESLEY BROWN.

ROGERSVILLE.

JOHN WESLEY BROWN, one of the eleven senators who, in April, 1885, broke a quorum of the Senate by absenting themselves from their seats in that body to prevent the passage of the "registration bill," was born at Lee Valley, Hawkins county, Tennessee, November 15, 1852, and made that his home till the age of twelve or fourteen, going to school and farming. In 1868, he went to McMinn Academy, Rogersville, in which he studied some two years, after which he was a student about fourteen months in the Hiawassee College, Monroe county, Tennessee. In 1874 he began the study of law under Judge E. E. Gillenwaters, at Rogersville, and was admitted to the bar in 1875, licensed by Judge Gillenwaters and Chancellor H. C. Smith, and practiced at Rogersville from 1875 to 1881, when he became founder and editor of the Rogersville *Press and Times*. After editing that paper something over a year, he spent six months traveling in the northwestern States. He then returned home and resumed editorial control of his paper. November 15, 1881, he was appointed to a clerkship in the Nashville post-office, a position which he resigned April 30, 1882, to accept a position in the Pension Bureau at Washington, District of Columbia. This latter place he resigned in October, 1882, to accept the position of file clerk of the Forty-seventh Congress. The political complexion of the House changing with the incoming of the Forty-eighth Congress, he went out of that office, and returned to the management of his paper and to the practice of law, in March, 1884. In the Republican convention held at Jonesborough in July, 1884, he was nominated for the State Senate, and at the general election, November 4, 1884, was elected to represent the Second Senatorial district, comprising the counties of Hawkins, Hancock and Greene, in the Forty-fourth General Assembly of Tennessee, being the junior member of the Senate, and the only unmarried man in it.

He has been a delegate to every Republican State convention since 1879; was an alternate delegate to the Republican National convention at Chicago, in July, 1880, from the First congressional district of Tennessee, and cast the vote of that district; was also a delegate from the same district to the Republican national convention of 1884, and was one of Mr. Blaine's warmest supporters. From 1879 to 1881, inclusive, he was chairman of the Republican executive committee of Hawkins county, and in 1880 was elector for Hawkins county on the Garfield and Arthur ticket.

He has been unswervingly Republican in politics from his boyhood, and is ultra, aggressive, and uncompromising in all his political views. He has never sought an elective office except that of senator, and to that he was elected by a vote of some four hundred above the party strength. He has, however, a decided taste for political life, and has taken a very active part in the various campaigns. His speech in the Senate on the bill pensioning Confederate soldiers was noted for its vehemence and aggressiveness, particularly in that portion where he denied the constitutionality of the measure proposed. There chanced to be present on that occasion a large number of visitors from northern States, on their way to the New Orleans exposition, who, after listening to the speech, expressed their astonishment that he should dare to utter views so antagonistic to the doctrines entertained and taught by the opposition. To use his own language, "my politics have been everlastingly Republican, and I have lived and worked that way."

Mr. Brown belongs to no secret organization, nor to any church, though he is a firm believer in the Christian religion, and occasionally has acted as Sabbath-school teacher.

He began life without means, and is now in independent circumstances, the result of a rule to which he has adhered, never to owe anything, and to limit his expenditures to his actual necessities. If he makes but little he also makes it a point to know he is clearing money. With these views, by clear-headed judgment, rigid economy and judicious trading, he has accumulated a respectable property. He has never been given to dissipation, and has never bet on anything. Though ruthlessly assailed by politicians, his character is unblemished. It is a singular fact that few persons are indifferent to him—being either his warm friends or bitter enemies, a fact for which it is difficult to account.

Senator Brown's father, Rev. Iredell Campbell Brown, of the Methodist church, was born in Hawkins county, Tennessee, and had only the advantages of a common school education. He has been a local Methodist preacher from his young manhood, and has the reputation of being one of the finest vocal musicians on the continent. His business is that of farming and stockraising, and he is now living at "High Oaks," three miles east of Morristown, on the East Tennessee, Virginia and Georgia railroad. His charity, sympathy for the poor, and his perfect good will for mankind in general, have attached all who know him as his friends. His father, Thomas Brown, a native of North Carolina, came to Hawkins county, Tennessee, early in the present century; married there; lived a farmer, and died at about the age of seventy-five, leaving ten children: (1). Mary Brown, married Rev. William Wyatt, and has seven children, Iredell Campbell, Thomas Pendigrass, Samuel Patton, Sarah, Matilda, Nannie and John. (2). Rev. Iredell Campbell Brown. (3). Jesse Brown, who married Miss Nancy Charles, daughter of Col. Rogers Charles, of New Canton, Tennessee; died in 1874, leaving five children, Charles, Solomon, Sarah, Susan and Nancy. (4). Thomas E. Brown; married first Miss Eliza Dodson, who died, leaving no issue. He then married Mrs. Mary Kyle, widow of Dr. Robert Kyle, by whom he has two children, Alice and Thomas, jr. (5). Dr. Owen M. Brown, married Miss Nannie Fortner, daughter of Rev. Isaac Fortner, of Hawkins county, and has four children, Luther Fairchild, Paralee, Emma and Owen M., jr. Dr. Brown was the surgeon of the First Tennessee light artillery (Federal) in the late civil war. (6). Clinton A. Brown, married Miss Laura A. Crawford, daughter of Rev. Robert Crawford, of Hawkins county, and has eight children,

Robert A., Clinton, Thomas, Frank, Sallie, Aga and a pair of twin boys. (7). Nancy Brown; died in 1885, wife of Samuel Edison, leaving four children, Joseph, Sallie, Matilda and Samuel, jr. (8). Sarah Brown; died childless, wife of Joseph Anderson, of War Gap, Hawkins county. (9). James Brown, married Miss Rebecca Vermillion, daughter of William Vermillion, and has ten children, Theophilus, George and Frank (twins), Thomas, Clinton, Walter, Nannie, James. Fannie and John. (10). Matilda Brown, wife of Hiram Herd, of Manchester, Kentucky; has one child, John.

Senator Brown's great grandfather, Samuel Brown, came from North Carolina to Tennessee after his son came. He was a farmer, and had been a Revolutionary soldier.

Senator Brown's mother was Mary Ann Willis, daughter of James and Sally Willis, of Lee Valley, Hawkins county. She is the grand-daughter of Larkin Willis, a native of Scotland, a noted philanthropist, especially kind and liberal in his donations to strangers. It is said that he, on three different occasions, gave horses to men who were complete strangers to him. His wife was Elizabeth Sizemore, of North Carolina. Of the Willis family, Maj. W. W. Willis, was major of the Eighth Tennessee Federal cavalry, and represented Hawkins county in the Tennessee Legislature after the war, about 1866. Summerville R. Willis, sister to his mother, married Dr. H. K. Legg, and lives at Seligman, Missouri. Another member of the family, Silas Willis, is now a telegraph operator at Stevenson, Alabama. Mr. Brown's maternal grandmother was Sallie Wilson.

Senator Brown has two brothers and five sisters, all living: (1). Francis Asbury Brown, born May 15, 1851; now practicing medicine and farming at Lee Valley, Hawkins county; married Miss Nellie Schneider, and has two children. (2). Larkin Willis Brown, born December 4, 1854; studied law; was joint editor and proprietor with his brother in the Rogersville *Press and Times* one year; is now farming; is unmarried. He was twice elected county superintendent of public instruction for Hawkins county; was assistant teacher three years in the Sweetwater Male Academy, Monroe county, Tennessee. under Prof. J. L. Bachman. (3). Sarah Elizabeth Brown; married James M. Johnstone, of the firm of Fulkerson & Johnstone, manufacturers of boots, shoes, saddles and harness, at Rogersville; has four children, Charles C., Fannie Matilda, Mary Annie Jackson and Mattie. Mrs. Johnstone is noted for her practical good sense, and dispenses her hospitalities with the grace and dignity of the Lady Bountiful. (4). Annie Rathbone Brown, now wife of J. J. Starnes, a farmer and stock trader of Hawkins county. (5). Argyra Catharine Brown, now wife of J. H. Beal, a farmer near Whitesburg, Hamblen county, Tennessee. (6). Mary Artemesia Brown, now wife of Wm. A. Orr, a lawyer at Jonesville, Virginia. (7). Mattie E. Brown, now living with her parents at "High Oaks."

JAMES M. LARKIN, M.D.

CLARKSVILLE.

THIS gentleman, an impressive conversationalist, entertaining by the variety of subjects he discusses, the scope and accuracy of his knowledge of men and things, the remarkable tenacity of his memory of names, dates, incidents and personal histories, and distinguished also for the magnetism with which he fixes the attention of his hearers, the many agreeable acquaintances he has formed, the earnestness with which he enters into the discussion of any subject which the occasion or the company may suggest, appears in these pages as a representative of the medical profession in Clarksville, and as one of the standard men of Tennessee. To the writer he appears as one of those men about whom there is an air and manner of reserve force and energy, ready to be brought into action at will, thereby making him equal to almost any emergency. Quick, clear, logical and forcible in his arguments, he warms up with enthusiasm until he becomes oblivious to all subjects except the one under discussion, his interest in which is manifested by a flashing eye, animated gestures and a flow of words at once eloquent and interesting. One of his brother physicians in Clarksville says of him: "Dr. Larkin is a close student, and possesses a prodigious memory. Thoroughly honest in word and deed, with no flattery for any man, he is held in high esteem by a wide circle of acquaintances. Possessing a vast stock of general information on historical subjects, as well as upon the general topics of the day, he is ever ready in conversation, and has at the same time an amount of practical common sense which makes him ready in carrying out the views which he expresses. In spite of his feeble constitution, he is a master of his profession, both in medicine and surgery, and had not ill health put bounds to his progress, he must have stood at the top round of the ladder. As a surgeon in the Confederate army he was faithful to every trust."

The subject of this sketch was born on the waters of

Jones' creek, in what is now known as the Larkin and McAdow settlement, in Dickson county, Tennessee, June 29, 1818. The place of his birth is interesting as being only one mile from Laurel Furnace, which was among the earliest iron-works established in Tennessee, and about the same distance from where the organization of the Cumberland Presbyterian church was effected. When nine years of age, his father moved to a farm near Charlotte, and there young Larkin lived until his twenty-fifth year. His education, which had been begun in the common schools of the county, was completed at Tracy Academy, in Charlotte, when he took a course under Prof. Paschall. His early intentions were to study medicine, but on account of ill health he was prevented from doing so until 1843, when he went to Nashville and began study under Drs. Thomas R. Jennings and A. H. Buchanan. Never able to be on his feet long, he prosecuted his studies the greater part of his time in bed, yet, in spite of this, became so proficient that he was made prosector and demonstrator by these eminent physicians in charge of private clinics. He remained in Nashville three years, except when absent attending the medical college at Louisville, where he took his degree in the spring of 1846. After spending the summer with his old preceptors, he returned to his former home, and in the following spring started on a trip in search of health, and spent two years in the vicinity of Covington, Tennessee. He finally, in the fall of 1848, settled at Charlotte, and remained there in practice until the beginning of the war. His practice was largely among the employes of the iron-works owned by the Baxters, VanLeers and Napiers, and his career was both financially and professionally a success. In 1857, the University of Nashville conferred upon him an honorary diploma on account of his skill in surgery.

In May, 1861, he became surgeon of the Eleventh Tennessee Confederate regiment, commanded by Col. James E. Rains, and served in that capacity until his regiment was transferred to the regular Confederate service, when his commission from the governor of Tennessee expired. About this time, his wife having died, he obtained leave of absence from Gen. Zollicoffer, returned home, and did not report for service to be transferred with the regiment. However, rejoining the army, he refused a commission as assistant surgeon, and served under a contract, doing hospital service under Dr. D. D. Saunders, of Memphis, as post surgeon, and Dr. S. H. Stout, as medical director. In November, 1864, broken down by work, he obtained leave of absence, spent the winter in South Carolina, and was at Marietta, Georgia, on his way to join the army again, when news of the surrender came.

While serving as surgeon of the Eleventh Tennessee, and stationed at Camp Cheatham, he conceived the idea of establishing hospital tents in place of the board huts then used, and proposing his plan to Gen. Foster, it was carried out, and became the means of great good to sick and wounded soldiers.

After the war, finding the iron-works where he had practiced wholly destroyed and his old practice gone, he located at Clarksville, where he has since resided in successful practice, and as constant as his health would allow.

Dr. Larkin became a Master Mason at Charlotte in 1847; was made Senior Warden under a special dispensation four months after initiation; was afterwards elected Master of his Lodge, and subsequently became a Royal Arch Mason in Clarksville Chapter.

In early life he voted for Martin VanBuren, a civilian, against Gen. Harrison, a military chieftain, casting no other presidential vote until he voted for Fillmore, and then for John Bell, always refusing to vote for a military candidate for a civil office. All his sentiments were Whig, and he so voted in State elections. Opposed to secession from principle, he however considered Mr. Lincoln's call for troops, without the consent of Congress, an act of tyranny, and entered most heartily into the rebellion. When the war closed, and he came to choose between parties, he was forced to vote with the Democrats, but since that party assumed its present policy on the public debt he has refused to co-operate with any party, but voted for Cleveland and Hendricks.

Dr. Larkin's father, Joseph Larkin, was the sixth child and fourth son of John Larkin, who was born in Dublin, Ireland, the son of a linen draper, and who, when a boy, while spreading linen was, together with two Scotch lads, kidnapped and brought to Philadelphia, where he was apprenticed to a manufacturer, and learned the art of weaving. After attaining his majority he moved to Guilford county, North Carolina, and became a member of the Alamance congregation of Presbyterians. He married Sarah McAdow, daughter of James McAdow, who, together with his brother John, born in Ireland, came to North Carolina at an early day. The family name was afterwards changed to "McAdoo." In 1796, as remembered by this writer, John Larkin and his brothers-in-law, John McAdow, Rev. Samuel McAdow, and the family of James McAdow moved from Guilford county, North Carolina, to Tennessee, and settled in Dickson county, and founded the Larkin and McAdow settlement on Jones' creek.

The Rev. Samuel McAdoo (autography changed to "McAdoo") previously mentioned, *grand uncle* of Dr. Larkin, was a Presbyterian minister, and he, together with Rev. Finis Ewing and Ephraim McClain, of Kentucky, and Samuel King, of Alabama, met at McAdow's residence and constituted a presbytery, thereby organizing and founding the Cumberland Presbyterian church in Dickson county, Tennessee, February 4, 1810. (See *Life of Ewing*, by F. R. Cossitt, chapter 14, page 195.)

Joseph Larkin, father of Dr. Larkin, who died September 23, 1837, in his fifty-second year, was married,

May 25, 1815, to Catharine Clark, who was born in Guilford county, North Carolina, May 25, 1790, the daughter of Hance Clark and Mary Bailey. Hance Clark was an Irishman, and, so the writer is informed, was a cousin of Dr. Adam Clark, the celebrated Biblical commentator. Mary Bailey was descended from the the Baileys and Alexanders of Scotland.

Dr. Larkin was married in Dickson county, Tennessee, December 23, 1847, to Miss D. Jane Coldwell, (cousin of Hon. Thomas H. Coldwell, now of Shelbyville,) daughter of Abiram Coldwell, of Hawkins county, Tennessee, and his wife, Nancy Montgomery, formerly of Richmond, Virginia. Miss Montgomery was a daughter of Maj. James Montgomery, an English officer, and the niece of Gen. Richard Montgomery, who fell at Quebec.

Mrs. Larkin died August 25, 1861. She was a lady of firm and decided character, but exceedingly gentle in her manners, and by her sweetness of temper made many friends. Four children were born to this union: (1). Josephine, born August 22, 1852; died July 10, 1853. (2). Neill Brown, born August 28, 1856; now a citizen of Savannah, Georgia. (3). Charles Hugh, born December 15, 1858; now chief stenographer for the branch of the Standard Oil company, New York city. (4). James Jerome, born August 25, 1861; died in July, 1863.

Dr. Larkin was married a second time, February 10, 1866, to Miss Emma V. Bagwell, daughter of Pleasant Bagwell, of Lynchburg, Virginia. To this union has been born one child, Jennie Finley, born December 15, 1873.

Throughout life Dr. Larkin's motto has been to attend to all duties promptly, and make no engagements which he does not expect to keep. His habits have always been studious and temperate. He never took a glass of grog in a saloon in his life, has been moderate in all things, and has always lived within his income, hence, at this writing, November 30, 1885, is in comfortable circumstances, and owes no man, county or State, a dollar. His never-varying rule is, " do as you would be done by."

JOHN R. FRAYSER, M.D.

MEMPHIS.

DR. JOHN R. FRAYSER was born February 15, 1815, in Cumberland county, Virginia, and there grew to manhood, or till he was twenty years of age. He is descended from a Scotch-Irish family. His grandfather Frayser, a Scotchman, came to America in 1801, and settled in Hanover county, Virginia, near Richmond, and engaged in farming. His son, Robert, father of the subject of this sketch, was a man of very strong character, and rose from the anvil to the bench, having been at first a blacksmith and afterwards judge of the court of Cumberland county. He died at Staunton, Virginia, in 1831, at the age of sixty-one years, leaving six children, one of whom, Robert, went to St. Charles county, Missouri, where he became an extensive planter, and married Miss Spears, niece of Judge Edward Bates, who was a member of President Lincoln's cabinet. Another son, William, went from Virginia to Memphis, where he remained a few years, and then removed to Lexington, Holmes county, Mississippi, where he became prominent as a lawyer. He died there in 1842. A third son, Albert, was a merchant in Powhatan county, Virginia. Benjamin F., another son, graduated with honor at the University of Virginia, and was a successful practitioner of medicine till his death in 1853.

John R., our subject, was brought up on a farm in his native county, obtaining his earliest education in the "old field schools" of the neighborhood, and, for one year, in the academy at Cartersville, Virginia. His tutors were Philip Leak, a very eminent teacher of that day, and Jesse S. Armstead, a Presbyterian minister. At quite an early age he formed the intention of studying medicine, and in the fall of 1832, entered the Medical University of Pennsylvania, where, on account of his extreme youthfulness, he was called "the boy" by his classmates, one of whom was William Gibson, son of Professor Gibson of the university. He graduated in medicine in the spring of 1834, and in the following year, being just twenty years of age, he went to Memphis, where he has been ever since, every year and every month in the year. He was induced to settle in Memphis by the persuasions of two of his brothers then living there; one a merchant and the other a lawyer and editor of a paper in the city. He landed in Memphis with just three dollars in his pocket, and stopped at the old City Hotel, of which Thomas D. Johnson was proprietor. He took the landlord into his confidence, told him that he was without money, and at once received his sympathy and a promise of help. He boarded for three years with Mr. Johnson, who became his warmest friend, and charged him only sixty dollars in money for three years' board, taking the balance out in practice in his family. He did not enter actively into practice at once, but, up to 1840, was connected with a book store in partnership with Jeptha Fowlkes.

During the year 1840 he formed a partnership with Dr. Hugh Wheatley, who had solicited him to join him in the practice of medicine when he first came to Memphis. At the expiration of one year, Dr. Frayser entered into partnership with Dr. Solon Borland, who, after remaining with him one year, turned his attention to politics, moved to Louisville, and, after practicing medicine there for a time, went to Arkansas, took a prominent part in Democratic politics in that State, was elected United States senator, and afterwards appointed minister to Central America. At the beginning of the late civil war he (Borland) entered the Confederate army with the rank of colonel, and died while in the service.

In 1849 Dr. Frayser formed a partnership with Dr. James Chase, who continued with him till his death in 1859. He then entered into partnership with Dr. E. Miles Willett, which lasted till 1878, when he took as a partner Dr. B. G. Henning, his son-in-law, who is now professor in the Memphis Hospital Medical College.

Dr. Frayser was married November 4, 1837, to Miss Pauline A. Brown, daughter of William Brown, a native of Virginia. Her mother was Miss Saunders, sister of Romulus M. Saunders, of North Carolina, who was a member of Congress from that State for several terms, and afterwards minister to Spain. One of Mrs. Frayser's half-brothers, Capt. Henderson, was an officer in the United States army and adjutant on the staff of Gen. Gaines. Mrs. Frayser was left an orphan at an early age, but was tenderly cared for by Mrs. Dunn, wife of Dr. Dudley Dunn, near Memphis. She received her education at Huntsville, Alabama, and was a lady of unusual intellectual powers and unblemished Christian character. She was a consistent member of the Methodist church from her sixteenth year to the time of her death, which occurred February 28, 1884.

The union of Dr. Frayser and wife was a most happy one, and from it were born six children: (1). R. Dudley, a sketch of whom appears elsewhere in this volume. (2). Emma L., born in 1846, now the wife of Col. R. M. Smith, formerly of Nashville, now of New Orleans; they have three children. (3). Julia. (4). Cornelia, born in 1852, now the wife of Dr. B. G. Henning, and mother of three children. (5). John C.,

born in 1857, now shipping clerk to Lynn & Lewis, New Orleans. (6). David, law partner of his brother, R. Dudley Frayser.

In politics, Dr. Frayser was raised an old line Whig. He was a great admirer of Henry Clay, for whom he always voted. Since the war he has voted the Democratic ticket, though he has never taken an active part in politics. He has invariably refused to become a candidate for public office, although often solicited to do so. He has several times been offered a professorship in the Memphis Medical College, but declined, believing that his duty to his clientele required his whole attention.

He became a member of the Independent Order of Odd-Fellows in 1837, but has never held any office in the order. As in politics he has been a quiet voter, so in the lodge he has been a silent member.

Dr. Frayser has been successful in acquiring and holding a very large practice, due alike to his acknowledged skill and attainments, and the fidelity and promptness with which he has always responded to the calls of the sick. For the accumulation of money he never displayed any special talent or desire. He has been fortunate, however, in being associated with business-like partners, and thus abundant financial rewards have accompanied his professional success. In the year 1866, his professional income alone was sixteen thousand dollars—perhaps the largest income of the kind ever enjoyed in Memphis. He has always dearly loved his profession, and devoted all his energies to its practice with becoming enthusiasm in the cause of humanity. One of his professional brethren in Memphis says of him: "Dr. Frayser is a man of high moral character, has stood at the head of his profession in Memphis for many years, and enjoys an enviable reputation." This tribute is simply a just one. There is not in Memphis a more honorable, upright citizen, nor one who enjoys, in a greater degree, the confidence of the people.

Dr. Frayser has passed through all the epidemics with which Memphis has been afflicted for the last fifty years, beginning with Asiatic cholera the first year of his residence there, and ending with the yellow fever in 1879. Dr. Frayser had the yellow fever himself in 1878, but was spared for further usefulness to his fellow-man.

HON. BENJAMIN J. LEA.

BROWNSVILLE.

THE ancestry of Judge Lea were English and Scotch-Irish, but not tracable in this sketch beyond the grandfather, Bennett Lea, who was a well-to-do farmer in North Carolina. The father, Alvis Lea, a native of that State, was a farmer and merchant in Caswell county. He was a member of the Baptist church, a quiet, unassuming man, who looked well after his own household, and also found time and means to make his benevolent nature felt among his neighbors. He had no ambition for any sort of public life, but was content,

> "Along the cool, sequestered vale of life
> To keep the noiseless tenor of his way."

He died at his home in Caswell county, North Carolina, in 1876, at the age of seventy-one years.

Judge Lea's mother, whose maiden name was Nancy Kerr, was a niece of the celebrated Baptist minister, John Kerr, who, for several terms, was a member of Congress from Virginia; and she was also a cousin of John Kerr, jr., who represented a North Carolina district in Congress several years, and died in 1878, while on the superior bench of that State. Her father was a North Carolina farmer. Her mother, originally Miss Cantrell, was of a North Carolina family. The Kerrs are of Scotch-Irish origin.

Judge B. J. Lea was born in Caswell county, North Carolina, January 1, 1833. He was raised in that county, working on the farm and going to school alternately, until he entered Wake Forest College, from which institution he was graduated in June, 1852. Having, at quite an early age, formed the determination to become a lawyer, on quitting college he removed to Haywood county, Tennessee, where he engaged in teaching school, carrying on his legal studies in the meantime. In 1856 he was licensed to practice by Judge John Reed and Chancellor Isaac B. Williams, and at once opened a law office in Brownsville, where he has resided ever since. From 1858 to 1872, he was law partner with Hon. H. J. Livingston, now chancellor of that division. In 1859 he was elected representative from Haywood county, and served in the Legislature of 1859–60, being a member of the committees on the judiciary and federal relations. While still a member of the Legislature, he was appointed by Gov. Isham G. Harris, commissary in the provisional (Confederate) army of Tennessee, and, a few months later, was elected colonel of the Fifty-second Tennessee regiment, and remained its colonel till the close of the war, having been re-elected upon its reorganization in 1863 by an almost unanimous vote. Judge Lea was taken prisoner in West Tennessee, in March, 1865, and kept on parole until after the final surrender.

The war over, he resumed the practice of law at Brownsville, with great success. Like most of his southern brethren of the bar, he had then but little left, beyond his profession, upon which to build for the future, but, with courage and hopefulness, he set himself to work in the new life. In 1876 he was appointed by Gov. Porter special judge of the Supreme court on account of the illness of one of the judges, and served in that office about eight months. In September, 1878, he was appointed by the Supreme court to the position of attorney-general and reporter for the State. This position he still holds, and, during the seven years he has held it, he has served the State with signal ability and fidelity. The work of the Supreme court since he has been in office has been unusually heavy, and his reports are quite voluminous, though exceedingly well prepared.

Judge Lea was married in Haywood county, June 15 1853—the first year of his residence there—to Miss Mary C. Currie, a native of that county, and daughter of George and Judith Currie, both of North Carolina families. Her mother was a Chandler. Mrs. Lea was educated at Brownsville. She is a member of the Methodist church, and is a woman of much force of character, possessed of sound practical judgment, gentle manners, kind disposition, and skilled in all the better ways of the good housewife.

There have been born to Judge Lea and wife four children: (1). Swannanoa, born October 20, 1854; graduated from Ward's Seminary, Nashville. She married Thomas F. Baynes, now deceased, a lawyer of Brownsville. He was a lawyer of great promise and very industrious, having probably hastened his death by excessive work. She has since married Mr. J. P. Eastman, of Lebanon, a lawyer. She has two children, Thomas F. and Effie Baynes. (2). Mary F., born in 1859, and died in infancy. (3). Katie B., born in 1860, graduated at Brownsville and Nashville, and married John C. Sanders, a lawyer at Lebanon. She has two children, Mary Lea and Richard. (4). Alvis G., born April 8, 1868.

Judge Lea is a man of marked personal characteristics. Physically, he is a splendid specimen of his race. In height he measures over six feet, while in weight he "tips the beam" usually at two hundred and forty-five pounds. His robust, hale and hearty look is always suggestive of good living. His eyes are dark and keen, and fairly blaze on occasions of excitement, while his heavy projecting brows impart to his countenance an air of gravity that commands respect, as by authority. Yet austerity is not a characteristic of Judge Lea. In temper, usually, he is as gentle as a woman, and, in the social circle, there is no one more genial. He loves the society of his friends, and, in friendly devotion, there is no man more prompt or true.

In politics, Judge Lea has been a life-long Democrat, though, with the exception of the legislative service already mentioned, has never held political office. In 1872 he was made chairman of the Democratic State convention. In 1855 he became a Master Mason, and afterwards took the Chapter degrees. He has served as Master, King and High Priest. He is also a member of the Order of the Knights of Honor, of the United Workmen, and of the Golden Rule. He is a member of the Methodist church, in which he has been steward and lay delegate to the annual conference. His personal life is, in all respects, exemplary, regulated at all times by the highest standards of propriety and morality.

As a lawyer, Judge Lea has been very successful. His qualities are of the solid, rather than of the brilliant order. His reputation is that of the safe counselor. Strong common sense, subjected to a rigid conscientiousness, is the sub-stratum of his character. His conceptions of professional duty are lofty and liberal.

There is nothing of the pettifogger in his nature. When a man becomes his client, he becomes his *protege* and is held in the light of a friend, whose cause becomes his own. Where a remedy is possible without litigation he invariably urges it, though adversely to his own interest. Ever since he came to the bar he has acted upon the belief that very many of the suits brought before the courts might be compromised by the parties, or their lawyers, more profitably to all concerned, than by a warfare in the court-room; and so it has long been Judge Lea's custom, when consulted or retained, to endeavor first to effect a settlement of the matters in controversy, before resorting to legal process. This failing, however, his zeal in the fight is quite as marked as his previous desire for peace. And in the court-room Judge Lea is very effective. As an advocate he has few equals. Besides, his conduct before court and jury is marked by a degree of candor and fairness that wins confidence and secures conviction. "Smart tricks" and "sharp practice" are foreign to his methods.

Judge Lea is yet in his prime, physically and mentally. The future should have much laid up in store for him.

HON. JOHN FRIZZELL.

NASHVILLE.

JUDGE JOHN FRIZZELL is of Scotch origin. The original family emigrated to Ireland and thence to America, settling in Virginia. His grandfather, Abram Frizzell, and his brothers were tobacco planters in Maryland and Virginia, and from these descended all the Frizzells in the United States, who spell their names in that way. Abram Frizzell's wife was a Miss Williams. She died at the age of forty-five, he at the age of about ninety. Judge Frizzell's father, Nathan Frizzell, was born in Pittsylvania county, Virginia, September 3, 1808, and moved with his father's family to Bedford county, Tennessee, in 1825, where his father lived a few years, returned to Virginia, married again, and died in 1858 or 1859. Judge Frizzell's father married, November 27, 1827, Miss Mary Jones, daughter of Hugh Jones, living near Beech Grove, then in Bedford, now Coffee county, Tennessee. The Joneses were from Buncombe county, North Carolina. Hugh Jones, though at the time over age, was a volunteer under Gen. Jackson, at New Orleans. He was a great lover of his rifle and passionately fond of hunting. He died between eighty-five and ninety years of age. Judge Frizzell's maternal grandmother, Jones, was of a North Carolina family, and, with her husband, settled in Coffee county. Hugh Frizzell, Judge Frizzell's brother, was

elected, in 1870, clerk of the criminal court of Davidson county, and died in office, after two years' service.

Judge Frizzell's father started out in life a poor man. He worked on a farm, as a day laborer, until, becoming corpulent, he taught school for several years in Bedford and Rutherford counties. His teaching did not extend beyond reading, writing and arithmetic. He had the reputation, among other attainments, of being an exceptionally correct speller, a very rare accomplishment even among scholars. He received his education in Virginia. In 1841 he removed to Winchester and sold goods for a time. Shortly after going to Winchester, he was elected magistrate, and served as chairman of the county court. In March, 1844, he was elected clerk of the circuit court, and was re-elected four times successively, holding the office for twenty years without interruption. When the courts were reopened after the war he declined a reappointment to the clerkship tendered him by Judge Hickerson, then presiding. He was an honest man, faithful to every trust, benevolent and just. He was a moral, temperate man, and, in politics, was a Jeffersonian Democrat. He died September 21, 1871.

Judge Frizzell's mother was a devoted member of the Methodist church, and died in May, 1882, at the age of seventy-four, leaving four children surviving her, eight having died before her.

Judge Frizzell's experience in boyhood was somewhat unusual, and it is hardly too much to say that the effects of that experience are still seen in the striking domestic virtues which characterize the man. He was raised in the homestead and trained to do all manner of household work, in assistance of his mother. He had thus but little advantage of farm labor or of school privileges, except as an irregular attendant at his father's school, when he could be spared from home. At the age of about eighteen, however, his father sent him to the county academy one term, which was all the regular schooling he obtained. At the age of fourteen he had begun writing in the office of the circuit court clerk, and, in his fifteenth year, became deputy clerk. For the next ten years, with the exception of the brief period at the academy, he was mainly engaged as deputy in his father's office and in the other clerks' offices of the county. It was this early clerical training, no doubt, that laid the basis of that high business character which he now enjoys. In 1849 he was elected register of the land office at Nashville, by the Legislature, the member from Franklin county, Col. Hayden March, presenting his name in his absence and without his knowledge. He took charge of the office in December of that year, and, for three years, gave his personal attention to its duties. Leaving the office, then, in charge of a deputy, he returned to Winchester, and, for about one year was in charge of a mercantile establishment, meanwhile assisting his father in his office.

Judge Frizzell was born, as should have been earlier stated, in Bedford (now Coffee) county, September 8, 1829, on the Garrison fork of Duck river. Excepting while in Nashville, filling the office of land register, as before related, he lived in Winchester from 1841 till 1868, when he removed to Nashville, and has lived there ever since.

In February, 1854, Judge Frizzell was licensed to practice law by Chancellor B. L. Ridley and Judge Nathaniel Baxter, and practiced at Winchester, except during the war, till his final removal to Nashville. From 1856 to the breaking out of the war, he was in partnership with Hon. A. S. Colyar (whose sketch see elsewhere in this volume). Hon. A. S. Marks was a member of the firm from 1858 to 1861. The partnership was dissolved by the war. (See sketch of Hon. A. S. Marks in this volume). For about two years, after 1865, Judge Frizzell was associated in practice with Hon. Peter Turney, now on the Supreme bench of the State. (See sketch of Hon. P. Turney in this volume).

For several years Judge Frizzell was trustee of the Robert Donnell Female Institute at Winchester. In 1870, after removing to Nashville, he was elected school commissioner in what was then the seventeenth school district of Davidson county. He took an active part in forming the voluntary association which conducted

the public schools of Davidson county until the present system was organized by legislative enactment. He has ever been an ardent friend of popular education, and was one of the most active citizens in urging the passage of the law under which the present system of public schools in Tennessee was organized. For about ten years he was a member of the board of education in the town of Edgefield, while it was yet a separate corporation, and, a greater portion of the time, was president of the board.

Upon the first serious threatenings of civil war, Judge Frizzell was in favor of resorting to all honorable means for the avoidance of bloodshed. But when it became apparent that war was inevitable, he promptly took a decided southern position. He volunteered as a private in Col. Turney's regiment, but before he reached the command, he was intercepted by a telegram calling him to Atlanta, where he was placed on post duty. Shortly afterwards, he was commissioned as captain and placed in charge of transportation and the auditing of railroad accounts. He remained in that department of the Confederate service, mainly engaged in auditing accounts, till the close of the war. The rank of major was given him just before the war ended. During his term of service, he disbursed over seven millions of dollars, and had his accounts audited and passed "O K" up to January 1, 1865, a record that few disbursing officers of the Confederacy can present.

In the ranks of Masonry Judge John Frizzell is a conspicuous figure, not only in Tennessee, but throughout the Union. From the period of his initiation, his "heart received the beauties of Masonry," and he was charmed with its work and its principles. There are but two other men in Tennessee, than Judge Frizzell, who have presided over all the grand bodies of Masonry in Tennessee: Maj. Wilbur F. Foster, Nashville, and H. M. Aiken, Knoxville. Judge Frizzell's petition to Cumberland Lodge No. 8, Nashville, is dated September 8, 1850, his twenty-first birth-day. He was initiated in October, passed in November, and raised December 21, 1850. He has served as Junior Warden and Master of Lodge, as Junior Grand Warden (in 1853), Deputy Grand Master (in 1854), Grand Master twice (1858-59), Grand Secretary since 1868, and as one of the committee to compile the Masonic Textbook of Tennessee. He was made a Royal Arch Mason, April 27, 1852, served as High Priest of the Chapter for several years; was Grand High Priest one year. He received the Council degrees in 1852, and has been Most Illustrious Grand Master of the Grand Council of Tennessee; was made a Knight Templar, Nashville Commandery No. 1, December 17, 1852, and was elected Grand Commander of the State in 1867; received the order of High Priesthood in 1860, and has been Grand President of the Order of High Priesthood of Tennessee. Since 1868, he has been continuously

Grand Secretary of the Grand Chapter, and Grand Recorder of the Grand Council. He received the Thirty-third degree of the Ancient and Accepted Scottish Rite in 1866, having taken the preceding degrees of that Rite in 1859. In 1874 he was elected Deputy General Grand High Priest of the General Grand Chapter of the United States, and, in 1877, was elected General Grand High Priest. Few Masons in the world can present such a record. Judge Frizzell has also been Supreme Master Workman of the Ancient Order of United Workmen. He is also a Knight of Honor and a non-affiliated Odd Fellow.

In politics, Judge Frizzell followed his father, and has always been a Democrat. He has several times been a delegate to political conventions, but has never held any political office. In 1853 he made an experiment for the Legislature as a candidate in Franklin county, and was defeated by one hundred and seventy votes. This was the first canvass made by any candidate in the county on the principles of local option. Since then the county has sent two or three temperance men to the Legislature.

Under the act of 1883, authorizing the judges of the Supreme court to appoint referees for the three divisions of the State, Judge Frizzell was appointed, in connection with Judges John L. T. Sneed and S. J. Kirkpatrick, as one of the referees for East Tennessee. He has earned the reputation of being a clear-headed, painstaking, upright judge.

Judge Frizzell married, in Rutherford county, July 23, 1854, Miss Matilda Winford, a native of Winchester, daughter of William and Sophia Winford, both natives of Tennessee. Her father died in the Texas revolution, in 1837. Mrs. Winford (her mother) died in 1852. She supported herself and family by teaching school, and was a lady of fine mind and high culture. Mrs. Frizzell is a graduate of Mary Sharpe College, Winchester, and has been of great benefit to her husband in his literary labors. She possesses all the traits of a perfect wife and mother, gentleness of disposition and firmness of purpose being her chief characteristics. She is, as also her husband, a consistent and earnest member of the Cumberland Presbyterian church. In regard to the husband, it should have been stated that he joined the church in 1843, and has been an elder for the last thirty years. He was stated clerk of the General Assembly for eleven years, and in 1884, was elected Moderator—the first layman to fill that position in any Presbyterian General Assembly in the United States. He was on the committee that revised the Confession of Faith and Government of the Church, and prepared for that committee the present constitution and regulations of the church. In June, 1884, the degree of LL.D. was conferred upon him by Cumberland University, at Lebanon, Tennessee.

Judge Frizzell and wife have had five children: four living, Sophie, John R., Maude and Charles F.; and one dead, Sallie.

In the narrative of the life of Judge Frizzell, we have sufficiently indicated his character as a man and lawyer. If anything more is lacking to convey to the reader a just idea of the man, his own frank utterances will supply the complement. In response to an inquiry concerning his life, he said: "I started on nothing. I assisted my father in raising his family. Whatever success I have attained in life, I owe to the faith I have had in the providence of God. That God will take care of and prosper those who trust in Him, I honestly believe. In business, my father taught me that whatever is worth doing at all, is worth being well done. Under my father's training, I have given great attention to details, and this is the secret of success." This being the cardinal idea of Judge Frizzell's life, it is easy to see how he came to the front as a business lawyer. He is yet in the vigor of manly strength, and the State has still much to hope from him.

REV. N. M. LONG.

MEMPHIS.

THE distinguished young minister, whose name heads this sketch, was born in Somerville, Fayette county, Tennessee, July 27, 1849. When he was about nine years of age his mother, who had married a second husband, moved to Sullivan county, East Tennessee, and here young Long grew up on a farm. He received his education at King College, Bristol, Tennessee, graduating in May, 1871, as valedictorian of his class, and the winner of the prize medal for oratory.

In his youth Mr. Long had intended to become a lawyer, but having joined the Presbyterian church in 1867, he determined to study for the ministry. Therefore, after leaving King College, he entered the theological seminary at Columbia, South Carolina, and remained there two and a half years, being called in the middle of his third year to take charge of the Presbyterian church at Tallahassee, Florida. Here he remained four years, at the expiration of which he was called to Pulaski, Tennessee, staying there one year. He then took charge of Lauderdale street Presbyterian church, Memphis, one year, and was next called to the Park Avenue church in the same city. In a short time he began to preach at the old First Congregational church, which had been closed for several years on account of the epidemics. After six months' ministration at this church, now called the "Strangers' Church," the congregation had grown so fast as to demand his whole attention, and he resigned the pastorate of Park Avenue church.*

Though brought up in the strictest school of old-style, orthodox Presbyterianism, Mr. Long has always been inclined towards liberalism and independence in religion, and never submitted to some of the iron-clad doctrines of his church. While at the theological seminary he differed with his professors on a number of points. When he went to Memphis he was required by the presbytery to undergo a rigid examination before being admitted. However, he was admitted by a two-thirds vote, in the spring of 1881. After he had preached there one year some of the Presbyterian pastors and elders presented a petition to the presbytery to compel him to cease preaching at an independent church without orders from the presbytery. After three days consideration of the matter the presbytery ordered him to give up the "Strangers' Church." From this decision Mr. Long appealed to the synod of Memphis, which met at Florence, Alabama, in October, 1882, but they refused to consider the appeal, on the ground that it was not a judicial case, and an appeal did not lie. He then withdrew from the presbytery on condition that he was to receive a certificate of good membership, and that he withdrew at his own request, without censure. Since that time he has remained in charge of the "Strangers' Church," which has greatly flourished under his care. When reorganized its membership was only nine, but it has increased tenfold, while the congregations are larger in proportion to membership, perhaps, than any church in Memphis, and composed largely of the professional and leading business men of the city.

Mr. Long has been a strong advocate of temperance, and has delivered numerous sermons and lectures on prohibition. One of his lectures was printed in Chicago and widely circulated. In 1884 he delivered a series of sermons on the vexed question of the Sunday Law. In these sermons, though opposed by all the other ministers of the city, he took the ground that the law is unconstitutional and destructive of the rights of citizens. His utterances on this subject created a profound impression, not only in Memphis, but all over Tennessee and adjoining States. One of his sermons has been printed and ten thousand copies distributed.

The following comment on his second sermon on this subject, delivered March 30, 1884, is from the editorial columns of the Memphis *Appeal:* "The Strangers' Church was filled last night when the Rev. Mr. Long delivered his second sermon on the Sunday Law. His first effort created a decided sensation, and his second was looked forward to with unusual interest. In the audience last night could be seen hundreds of men with whom it is the exception rather than the rule to attend church, and their presence was decided proof of the power of this minister who has risen step by step and day by day in the confidence and esteem of the general public, gathering about him a congregation of men who are not mere figureheads, but sound and logical thinkers, and who attend his meetings regularly, sustaining him because of the broad and liberal views he unhesitatingly expresses whenever occasion requires. His sermon last night was the result of profound study, and bore marks of careful preparation; yet he used no notes, speaking rapidly and without a pause, except to give force to some well-grounded sentence. He was listened to throughout with profound attention."

As a speaker Rev. Mr. Long is clear, forcible and logical. He makes it a point in his public speaking to seek the good of the people; to follow with all his energies whatever he undertakes; maintaining his position with all his earnestness, but at the same time is ever ready to yield when convinced that he is wrong, and to adopt views which he may have opposed when satisfied that they are correct. As a result of this he has been led to renounce many things which were ground into him when a boy, and to adopt others which he was taught to look upon with horror. Consequently, he now does his own thinking and says what he thinks. In whatever he undertakes he endeavors to stand at the head, no matter what it may cost in the way of personal labor or personal study. His course at college fully illustrated this. For languages and the natural sciences he had great fondness and easily mastered them, but for mathematics he had no taste whatever; yet he determined to master their mysteries, and by dint of perseverance eventually stood at the head of his class. His strong points of character are energy, persistentcy and a positive and determined nature.

In 1864 Mr. Long, though only fourteen years old, and very small for his age, enlisted for the Confederate service in Witcher's company of Owen White's battalion. He served several months and was one of the smallest boys in the army. When his command moved out of East Tennessee he was allowed to return to his home to take care of his mother, as his step-father had also gone into the army. When the Federals advanced into that region he was not molested, no one having an idea that a boy so small had been a soldier.

In politics Mr. Long has always voted with the Democrats. He could not well do otherwise, considering his teachings, his temperament and surroundings.

While in charge of the Tallahassee church he was elected to a professorship at King College, but could not accept because his church refused to accept his resignation. On a subsequent occasion the president of the college again tendered him a professorship, which he declined.

Mr. Long was married at Tallahassee, Florida, May 6, 1879, to Miss E. Shirley Wilson, daughter of W. R.

Wilson, a prominent merchant, and an elder in the Presbyterian church of that city. Her grandfather, David Wilson, originally from Virginia, was also a leading merchant at Tallahassee, and married Miss Shirley, of an old Virginia family. Mrs. Long's mother was Miss Frances Maxwell, daughter of Col. John S. Maxwell, of Liberty county, Georgia. The Maxwell family is descended from the well-known family of that name in Scotland. Mrs. Long received her education at Tallahassee. She is a lady of bright social disposition, very genial, and a great favorite. She is a Presbyterian. Two children have been born to this couple : (1). Richard Wilson Long, born December 17, 1881; died June 8, 1882. (2). Margaret Rhea Long, born March 30, 1883.

Rev. Mr. Long is descended from families of soldiers on both sides. His father, Col. N. Long, was born in Maury county, Tennessee, in 1816; graduated with distinction at the University of Nashville; served through the Florida war and was breveted colonel for gallantry on the field. He was a well educated, scholarly gentleman, and had studied law and civil engineering, but after joining the church gave up the law and devoted his whole attention to civil engineering. He met his death from exposure while engaged in the survey and laying off of Obion county, Tennessee, dying in 1849, at the age of thirty-three. His father, Dr. John Joseph Long, was one of eight brothers, natives of Halifax county, North Carolina, and settled in Maury county in the early part of this century. His father, the great-grandfather of Rev. Mr. Long, was Nicholas Long, of Halifax county. The Long family is of Scotch-Irish descent, and has produced many distinguished orators and lawyers.

Mr. Long's paternal grandmother was Miss Quinland, of South Carolina. Two of Mr. Long's uncles, Edward and John Long, died in Texas a few years since. John Long served through the first Texas war, the Mexican war, and, although over fifty years old, commanded a company in the Confederate army.

On his mother's side Mr. Long is descended from the well-known Rhea family of Tennessee. His mother was Miss Margaret Rhea, born in Maury county in 1820; graduated at Nashville under Dr. Lapsley in 1836, and married, in 1848, Col. Nicholas Long, who, as before stated, died in 1849. In 1858, she married her cousin, Col. James D. Rhea (now living in Sullivan county, Tennessee). She died May 17, 1880. She was a lady of rare culture and literary talent, and wrote numerous poems and other articles, many of which were published in the *Western Casket* over the *nom de plume* of "Tennessee." She was a zealous Presbyterian and an earnest Sunday-school worker all her life. Her father was Matthew Rhea, who graduated under Dr. Doak, of Washington county, Tennessee, and was considered one of the finest scholars in the State. He was the author of Rhea's map of Tennessee, the first and one of the best ever made. Matthew Rhea's mother was Miss Preston, daughter of Col. Robert Preston, of the celebrated old Virginia family of that name. Matthew Rhea's father was also named Matthew (great-grandfather of Mr. Long), and served in the Revolution, and was presented a sword by Gen. Nathaniel Greene for gallantry on the field at the battle of Guilford Courthouse, North Carolina. His father, Rev. Joseph Rhea, was a Presbyterian minister, who came to Sullivan county, Tennessee, from Ireland before the Revolution, and was a son of Matthew "Reah" Campbell, who was exiled from Scotland, during the reign of James II., of England. He was a cousin of the Duke of Argyl, and took part with him in the rebellion of 1685. Escaping from prison, on the Isle of Man, he fled to Ireland and changed his name by dropping "Campbell" and transposing the "h," making the family name thereafter "Rhea."

At the beginning of the late war, Mr. Long's uncle, Matthew Rhea, became first-lieutenant in Capt. Burton's company, which was raised at Somerville, and formed a part of the Thirteenth Tennessee Confederate regiment. He took with him the sword which had been presented to his gallant ancestor, by Gen. Greene, and at the battle of Belmont, November 7, 1861, while in command of his company, was killed, and his company cut to pieces, after refusing to surrender. The sword was lost and has never been found. The event was commemorated by a beautiful poem, written and published a short time after the battle, by Mrs. L. Virginia French, one of the sweetest songstresses the South has ever produced.

Hon. John Rhea, for whom Rhea county, Tennessee, was named, was a brother of the great-grandfather of the subject of this sketch. He was the first member of Congress from Tennessee, and represented the eastern district twenty-two years. He was one of seven lawyers first licensed in Knox county, mention of which fact is made in Killebrew's work on Tennessee.

Dr. Abram Rhea, another of Mr. Long's uncles, raised a company which formed a part of the Thirteenth Tennessee, and refusing a commission, went in as a private. After the Belmont battle he was called from the ranks for duty as a surgeon, and afterwards became surgeon-general under Gen. Bragg, with the rank of brigadier, and was regarded as one of the best surgeons in the service. He is now living in Fayette county. Another uncle, Walter Rhea, commanded a company of partisan rangers in the late war. He was a prominent citizen of Fayette county, where he died in 1881.

Robert Rhea, uncle of Mr. Long's mother, served through the war of 1812. He was captured at the battle of Quebec, escaped from prison, was recaptured in the woods of Maine, together with his brother, Joseph Rhea, and was chained upon his back in a prison ship for three months. After the war he went on board a Spanish privateer and served several years. Towards the close of the war between Spain and England, his ship was burnt off the coast of Virginia, and the crew swam ashore. He then went to the valley of Virginia, where he remained several years, engaged in teaching school. He taught the famous Confederate General Thomas J. (Stonewall) Jackson how to read, and was a great favorite with him. Though over seventy years of age, he served in a home guard company during the late war.

He died in Sullivan county in 1872, aged eighty-five years.

Mr. Long's maternal grandmother was Miss Mary Looney, eldest daughter of Col. Abram Looney, of Sullivan county, and a sister of Col. R. F. Looney, of Memphis, and Col. Abram Looney, of Maury county. Her mother was a Miss Gammon, of a prominent East Tennessee family.

MAJ. A. J. McWHIRTER.

NASHVILLE.

WE doubt if there is a more genial, pleasant or popular gentleman in Tennessee than Maj. A. J. McWhirter. Fully six feet in height, weighing one hundred and ninety pounds, of spendid physique, blue eyes, a large head with very high forehead, and face expressing a kind and benignant nature, with courtly, winning manners that invariably convert strangers into friends, this gentleman's history will prove interesting to many people.

He was born in Wilson county, Tennessee, June 15, 1828, of Scotch-Irish parentage, and spent the early years of his life on his father's farm, where he attended the school of his grandfather, George McWhirter, who died in 1836, after which he attended Campbell's Academy at Lebanon, until old enough to enter Cumberland University, where he remained for two and a half years, and only withdrew to accept the deputy county court clerkship under Josiah McClain, who was clerk of Wilson county for forty years. In 1847 the Hon. John Bell tendered him a cadetship at West Point, which he declined, preferring to enter commercial life, which he shortly afterwards did with the wholesale dry goods house of H. & B. Douglas at Nashville, Tennessee. So valuable did he become to this then famous firm, that on the first January, 1850, he was admitted into the concern as a junior partner, and continued with them in business, amassing considerable wealth, until 1856. Retiring from this firm, he formed a copartnership with Col. Thomas L. Bransford and Russell M. Kinnaird, and opened a wholesale dry goods establishment. At the expiration of three years Maj. McWhirter bought out the firm and ran the business on his own account until the civil war commenced. He was an ardent Whig and bitterly opposed secession, but when he saw the war was inevitable, raised a company of one hundred and six men, known as the Edgefield Rifles, which became company A, of the Eighteenth Tennessee infantry, then commanded by Col. (now Gen.) J. B. Palmer. As captain of this company he was captured at Fort Donelson, and after being exchanged at Vicksburg, received orders to report at Richmond,

Virginia, whence he was assigned duty under Maj. J. F. Cummings, of the commissary department, and was stationed in northern and western Georgia, and continued in that department with the rank of major, purchasing supplies for Bragg, Johnston and Hood until April 20th, 1865.

The war being over, Maj. McWhirter went to New York and engaged in the brokerage and commission business, but returned to Nashville in 1867, and has made it his home ever since.

In 1867 he became connected with the wholesale clothing house of Bolivar H. Cooke & Co., and was recognized far and wide as the leading and most influential salesman in the southern States, in appreciation of which fact this firm paid him for years a salary of seven thousand five hundred dollars per annum. In January, 1882, his friend, Gov. William B. Bate, appointed him commissioner of agriculture, statistics and mines, which position he is now filling with distinguished ability—indeed, at this writing (1885) it is almost impossible to pick up a Tennessee paper that does not contain complimentary notice of him. His speeches at various agricultural conventions in and out of his State, stamp him a man of broad and comprehensive intellect, breathing a spirit that is in unison with the rapid progress of the times. While his memory is wonderful, his information is even more so. As a writer, he is fluent, forcible and pungent. As a worker, he is tireless. His policy as commissioner can be commended to the officials of other States, and if followed by them, will revolutionize many things South during the next few years. The organization of the Southern Immigration Association is alone due to his efforts, and as its first president he has given it an impetus that causes the entire South to manifest the livliest interest in its success.

Maj. McWhirter as before stated, is descended from the Scotch-Irish stock so numerous in the Carolinas, Virginia, Kentucky and Tennessee. His father, George F. McWhirter, was born in Davidson county, Tennessee, in 1787, and was a farmer in Wilson and Davidson counties for more than eighty years. He was a soldier under Gen. Jackson during his Indian campaigns, participating in the battles of Talladega, Emuckfaw and the Horseshoe, and was a man of strong sense and thorough education. His grandfather, George McWhirter, was born in Mecklenburg county, North Carolina, in 1759, and was educated by the distinguished Hezekiah Balch, the author of the " Mecklenburg Declaration of Independence." After the death of Balch, George McWhirter married his widow, Mrs. Balch, who became the grandmother of the subject of this sketch. He was the first man who taught the classics in Tennessee; was a great student and one of the few thoroughly educated men in this section at that time. His pupils came from far and near, among whom were the Hons. John Bell, Bailie Peyton, James C. Jones, Jo. C. Guild, the Yergers and others of eminence. This grandfather changed the name of MacWhorter to McWhirter. Mrs. Balch's maiden name was Mac-Candlis, of Philadelphia, Pennsylvania, and one of her ancestors was martyred on the coast of Scotland for espousing the Presbyterian faith.

Maj. McWhirter's great-grandfather, William Mac-Whorter, a farmer and physician, was born in South Carolina. His father and mother came over from the north of Ireland in the latter part of the seventeenth century. Two of William Mac-Whorter's brothers continued to live in Georgia and South Carolina, where their descendants are now living, and have changed the spelling of the family name to McWherter and Mc-Whorter.

On the maternal side, our subject's mother was a Miss Blair. She was born in 1796, at Mul Herron Fort, about five miles from Nashville, and is now living. Her father, Samuel Blair, one of the first settlers in Tennessee, was born in Mecklenburg county, North Carolina, in 1769, participated in the defense of Buchanan's fort and the battle of Nickajack, and lived to the ripe age of ninety-six. His wife, Maj. McWhirter's maternal grandmother, was the daughter of Gen. Simpson, a celebrated Indian fighter. He was killed and scalped by the Indians in 1794, near a fort on what is now a part of the Vaulx estate, on the Franklin pike.

Maj. McWhirter married, in 1853, Elizabeth Marshall Bransford, at Glasgow, Kentucky, daughter of Col. Thomas L. Bransford, who was then a wholesale merchant, at once in Louisville, Kentucky, Nashville and Memphis, Tennessee. Col. Bransford was a prominent and influential politician ; was the first president of the Nashville and Danville railroad ; often in the State Legislature, and at times a State elector. He was born and raised in Virginia. Col. Bransford's wife was Miss Settle. Her mother was Miss Pickett, of Virginia, who was closely related to the Picketts and Marshalls of that State.

Maj. McWhirter has two sons, Louis and George.

HON. JOHN OVERTON, JR.

MEMPHIS.

THE history of the Overton family is intimately connected with that of Tennessee. Hon. John Overton, the grandfather of the subject of this sketch, was one of the early Supreme judges of Tennessee, and a contemporary and warm personal friend of Andrew Jackson. He was the founder of the city of Memphis, and at one time owned the land upon which the city now stands, having purchased a tract of five hundred acres from Elijah Rice for the sum of five thousand dollars. At a subsequent period Andrew Jackson and Gen. James Winchester were associated with Judge Overton in the ownership of this tract. It was conveyed by them to a company, and the town of Memphis was planted.

Judge Overton was of Scotch-Irish descent, and came to Tennessee from Virginia about the time, or soon after, the foundation of Nashville. His son, Col. John Overton, of Nashville, is the father of Hon. John Overton, jr. Col. John Overton is one of the leading and one of the wealthiest citizens of the State. He is an extensive real estate owner, was the founder and is still one of the owners of the Maxwell House, Nashville, and is also heavily interested in the city of Memphis.

Hon. John Overton, jr.'s, mother was Miss Rachel Harding, daughter of Thomas and Elizabeth Harding, and a cousin of Gen. W. G. Harding, of Nashville, whose biography appears elsewhere in this volume.

Hon. John Overton, jr., was born in Davidson county, Tennessee, April 27, 1842, and grew up there on a farm, attending the common schools until his fifteenth year. He then went to school for two years to Profs. Frank and Charles Minor in Albemarle county, Virginia, in 1857-58. Returning to Tennessee in 1860, he entered the University of Nashville and there remained until April, 1861, when he left to enter the service of the Confederacy. He enlisted in the Tennessee State troops and became a member of the Forty-fourth Tennessee regiment of infantry, in the company of Capt. Reid. In 1862 he was transferred to the staff of Gen. Bushrod R.

Johnson with the rank of captain, and served with him till Gen. Forrest was transferred to the Western District, when he became a member of his staff, still with the rank of captain. He served with Gen. Forrest till the close of the war. He participated in all the battles of the army of Tennessee up to the time he became a member of Forrest's staff, including the battles of the Kentucky campaign, Murfreesborough and Chickamauga. During the latter part of the war he took part in all the fights and raids of Forrest, including Fort Pillow, Tupelo, Nashville, and the battles of Hood's campaign in Tennessee, in 1864. He surrendered with Forrest at Gainesville, Alabama, May 13, 1865.

In 1865 John Overton, jr., located at Memphis and engaged in the real estate and brokerage business, which he has followed up to this time. In 1882 he took as a partner Mr. Charles N. Grosvenor and formed the firm of Overton & Grosvenor, which now represents the largest real estate interests of any firm in Tennessee. They handle, rent and sell on an average two millions of dollars' worth of property annually.

John Overton, jr., has been prominently connected with all of the most important commercial and financial enterprises of the city of Memphis for a number of years. He has been a director of the Bank of Commerce since its organization, and also of the Peoples Insurance Company from its foundation to the present time. He is vice-president and director of the Planters Insurance Company; president and director of the Vanderbilt Insurance Company, besides which he has been a director in numerous railroad companies, including the Mississippi River railroad, now the Chesapeake and Ohio; the Kansas City, Springfield and Memphis railroad, and others. His career as a business man has been one of uninterrupted success, and through the vicissitudes of flood and pestilence he has maintained his position as one of the substantial men of Memphis.

Hon. John Overton, jr., has always been a Democrat. In 1873 he was elected to the lower house of the Legislature, receiving the unanimous vote of his county, a larger vote than has ever been cast for any other candidate in the county. In 1875 he was elected to the Senate over an opponent who received about one hundred and sixty votes out of sixteen thousand. After one term in the Senate he declined a re-election. While in the House he was chairman of the committee on commerce, and during his term in the Senate was chairman of the committee on finance.

When the old city government of Memphis was abolished by an act of the Legislature, under an act providing for the appointment of two commissioners, one to be elected by the people, owing to his popularity with all classes he was compelled to become a candidate for membership on the board of fire and police commissioners, was elected, and was a member of the same while the great sanitary and street improvements were carried out. After he had been a member of this board for two and a half years, upon the resignation of Dr. Porter he was elected president of the taxing district and served until the expiration of the term of office, when he declined to be a candidate for re-election, although it was known he could have had the position without opposition. He has taken no part in politics except at the solicitation of his friends, and has never been a candidate for an office to which he was not elected.

Hon. John Overton, jr., was married on October 23d, 1866, to Miss Matilda Watkins, of Davidson county, Tennessee, daughter of William and Jane Watkins, and grand-daughter of Col. Mark R. Cockrill, the well-known stock raiser of Middle Tennessee. Mrs. Overton was educated in Davidson county, Tennessee, and in Philadelphia. She is a woman of strong and sterling traits of character, and one who never neglects her duty. She delights in the cultivation of flowers and the performance of household and family duties. She is a member of the Presbyterian church.

Hon. John Overton, jr., began business after the war, barehanded. His father's property had been confiscated but he took charge of his business in the city of Memphis, and has been actively engaged for himself and for others ever since that time. He now possesses a comfortable fortune. He has ever given close and energetic attention to his business. Whatever he had to do he has done thoroughly. He has always dealt on a cash basis, engaging in no reckless speculations, but going gradually up the hill. First-class credit, a protection of business character, and a thorough knowledge of his business in all its details, is the basis of his success.

Moreover, he has been an eminently public-spirited citizen, and has always taken a lively interest in the prosperity of the city of Memphis, ever ready to do his duty in whatever promoted her welfare and advanced her lines along the way to prosperity and metropolitanism. A gentleman of Memphis who has had ample opportunity to observe Hon. John Overton, jr., during the whole of his business career, says of him: The real secret of John Overton's success is his strict integrity, sober habits, close attention to his profession, rare good judgment, perseverance, and a strong and determined nature.

23

HON. COLUMBUS MARCHBANKS.

SPARTA.

THIS gentleman, so well known in Tennessee for his popular style of oratory and eloquence on the stump, was born in Overton county, Tennessee, September 28, 1843. He comes from excellent families on both sides. His father, Burton Marchbanks, was a farmer and tanner, a native of Overton county, born September 28, 1801, and died in 1861 on his homestead in Putnam county. He was a Baptist, and a Whig until the days of Knownothingism, but then became a Democrat, and remained one ever afterwards. He was a successful man, accumulated a fortune of about seventy-five thousand dollars, by his own exertions, and left a reputation for scrupulous honesty and faithfulness in his statements and actions.

Mr. Marchbanks' grandfather, William Marchbanks, was from South Carolina, and his people were Scotch. He was himself born in Scotland. William Marchbanks became a wealthy farmer in Overton county, was an old line Whig, and died at the age of seventy-five years. He married Jane Young, a sister of James Young, a man of considerable prominence in Jackson county, Tennessee. William Marchbanks and his wife were both members of the old Baptist church. They left a large family of sons and daughters, among whom was Judge Andrew J. Marchbanks, who, for a number of years, was judge of the circuit which included the county of Warren. It is said among lawyers that his decisions were reversed fewer times than those of any other circuit judge in the State.

Mr. Marchbanks' mother, *nee* Miss Julia F. Goodbar, of the only Goodbar family in the United States, is the daughter of Joseph Goodbar, a Virginian by birth. Joseph Goodbar settled in Overton county, Tennessee, about the year 1800, and spent his life as a farmer and trader. He was a Democrat of the Virginia type. He died a few years prior to the late war, leaving seven sons, Hilary, William P., James M., Joseph Lafayette, Andrew J., Jesse F., and Thomas Porter, and several daughters. Of these sons, Hilary Goodbar died soon after his marriage. W. P. Goodbar was the president of the Sparta branch of the Bank of Tennessee for many years. His son, James M. Goodbar, is now a prominent merchant at Memphis. The sons are all successful business men, well known in Arkansas, St. Louis and Memphis commercial circles. For a fuller account of the Goodbar family see sketch of James M. Goodbar, in this volume. Mr. Marchbanks' mother is a member of the Methodist Episcopal church, South, and is a sprightly, vivacious, intelligent lady of the old school. Her mother's maiden name was Masters. Mrs. Marchbanks is the mother of six children: (1). Columbus, subject of this sketch. (2). Brice, who died in 1861, aged sixteen. (3). William, now a trader at Sparta; married Miss Amanda Hunter. (4). Frank, now a farmer and machinist; married Miss Amanda Johnson. (5). Burton now a druggist at Sparta; married Miss Margie Sanders. (6). Isabel, now wife of Dr. S. E. Snodgrass, brother of Judge D. L. Snodgrass of the Court of Referees. Dr. Snodgrass lives at West, McLenan county, Texas.

Mr. Marchbanks was raised on his father's farm, and when a young man, worked five years in his father's tanyard. After the war he ran a tanyard in Putnam county on his own account, and says of this period of his life, "I was a tanner, and a good one too, and could go back to the business if I had occasion or a mind to do so." His early education was obtained in the common schools of his native county, after which he went to Burritt College in the years 1858–59, where he mastered the curriculum as far as the junior year.

When the war came up he went into the Confederate service as first lieutenant of company D, Eighth Tennessee infantry, Col. Alf. Fulton commanding. At the reorganization in 1862, he went into McMillan's cavalry, originally raised by James W. McHenry, and which became a part of King's First Confederate cavalry regiment. His service was chiefly on detached duty. He served in Tennessee, Kentucky, Virginia, Georgia, South Carolina and Mississippi. He was captured February 5, 1864, in Putnam county, was paroled and sent across the Cumberland river and there kept till the war ended, and was never exchanged.

The war over, he attended the law school at Lebanon two sessions, and was admitted to the bar in 1866, by Judges W. W. Goodpasture and Andrew McClain, began practice at Cookeville, Putnam county, and practiced there till 1870, when he quit law practice and went into mercantile life two years. He returned to the law in 1872, and removed to Sparta, where he has resided and practiced ever since, being most successful as a criminal lawyer, but preferring chancery practice, because it is smooth and quiet, as are his tastes. Mr. Marchbanks being a very stalwart man in his appearance and manner, and emphatic in his oratory, is at once over-awing and overpowering. This, in a measure, accounts for his fine success in criminal practice, and has brought to him a number of noted criminal cases.

Mr. Marchbanks has always been a Democrat, and is now a Prohibitionist also. In 1875–76 he was State senator for the counties of White, Putnam, Fentress, Morgan, Scott, Cumberland, Roane, Campbell and Overton. He is the author of the present law under which the State has a Bureau of Agriculture, Statistics and Mines. In 1884 he was Democratic elector for the Third congressional district, and made a vigorous canvass for Cleveland and Hendricks. Indeed, he made more reputation as an elector in that campaign than any speaker who has canvassed the district for years—many men following him from county to county to hear him speak. In 1868 Mr. Marchbanks was made a Master Mason. He is also a Knight Templar of Baldwin Commandery No. 7, Lebanon, Tennessee. He has been Worshipful Master, Most Excellent Master and High Priest, and has filled nearly all the offices in the Blue Lodge, Council and Chapter. In 1874 he became an Odd-Fellow, and has been Noble Grand, and also belongs to the Encampment. He is a Knight Templar, and also Worthy Chief Templar of Sparta Good Templar Lodge. He is an earnest advocate of temperance, and throws all his influence and talent into the cause of prohibition.

He was raised a Methodist, and is now a steward and trustee in the Methodist Episcopal church, South, at Sparta. For eight years he has been a Sunday-school superintendent, and it is said that his school is the best organized and best conducted about Sparta. He has been known to ride eighteen miles on Sunday morning to get to his Sunday-school. He is chairman of the Sunday-school Board of the Tennessee Conference of the Methodist Episcopal church, South, to which he was appointed in 1882. He has been twice a lay delegate to the Tennessee Conference—Lebanon in 1882, and Shelbyville in 1883.

Mr. Marchbanks married in Livingston, Overton county, Tennessee, February 5, 1863, Miss Linnie Hart, who was born August 28, 1844, daughter of John Hart, a merchant, now county court clerk of Overton county. Her mother, nee Miss Lucinda Cullom, is a sister of Judge Alvin Cullom and Gen. William Cullom, both of whom were members of Congress. (For a fuller account of the Cullom family see the sketch of Gen. William Cullom elsewhere in this volume.) Mrs. Marchbanks had two brothers, James and William C. Hart, both now deceased. Her sister, Elizabeth, is now the widow of James Cash, of Livingston, and her sister Sue is now the wife of W. W. Harris, of Livingston. Mrs. Marchbanks was educated at Livingston, is a most elegant and beautiful lady, refined, intelligent and remarkably modest; never has a harmful word to say of anybody; attends to her own family; looks neat, and keeps her children neat and her house tidy; is an incessant reader, and is beloved far and near for her hospitality. Five children have been born of this marriage: (1). Florence, educated principally at the Cumberland Female College, McMinnville; married Mr. William Rhea, now in business at Sparta; has one child, Mamie. (2). Minnie. (3). Alice. (4). Nellie. (5). John Burton, named for his two grandfathers.

Mr. Marchbanks began life without money, but owned some wild lands, and is now comfortably well off. He has been engaged in several lines of business—always making a trade if he saw anything in it. His success comes of sobriety and honest dealing with everybody, especially since he became a member of the church in 1876. Prior to that time he made much but saved little. His success has been attained since he joined the church and became a Sunday-school worker. He wants no publicity, but desires to live a quiet life. He has been in military and civil public life, and as it has been no pleasure to him, he lately remarked, " I intend to buy me a farm and live retired with my family."

Gen. George Dibrell says of his neighbor and friend: " Marchbanks is a man of fine ability, a first-rate lawyer, one of the best political stump speakers in Tennessee, a zealous member of the church, and a most efficient Sunday-school worker. He is also an enterprising man; will risk anything he thinks will develop his section of country. He spends his money freely, has an interesting family, of whom he is very proud, does a great deal to help his younger brothers along, has been the main man in getting up the White County Agricultural Association, has been engaged largely in the lumber business and in developing the mineral resources of his county, and has made considerable money. He is devoted to his friends, and sometimes makes enemies by speaking his sentiments too freely about everybody and everything."

JOHN PITMAN, M.D.

MEMPHIS.

DR. JOHN PITMAN was born in Shenandoah county, Virginia, October 14, 1807. He was brought up on a farm, and was sent to an academy at Mossy Creek, in Augusta county, Virginia, to be prepared for the University of Virginia, which institution he entered in 1831, and there remained one year. He early made up his mind to study medicine, and in 1833 entered the medical department of the University of Pennsylvania, from which institution he graduated in 1834, after which he began practice in his native county, where he remained until 1836. He then moved to Alabama, and settled at Talladega. After remaining there about five years, he married, and moved to Holly Springs, Mississippi. He continued in the practice of his profession at that place until 1851, when he moved to Memphis, where he still resides. With unvarying fidelity and zeal he has made the practice of medicine his life work. Since going to Memphis he has never been out of harness, remaining at his post of duty all the time, and passing through all the epidemics—five of yellow fever and several of cholera, notwithstanding he had the fever himself in 1873.

At one time, previous to the late war, he filled the chair of the practice of medicine in the medical college at Memphis for two years, occupying the position up to the time the college was dissolved.

Dr. Pitman became a Mason at Holly Springs, Mississippi, and took all the degrees of Ancient York Masonry there, and filled nearly all the offices in the lodge, but after going to Memphis did not connect himself with any lodge.

He was raised a Whig, and like most other Whigs, was opposed to secession, but when the war actually came on he sympathized with the South. Since the war he has voted the Democratic ticket, though not considering himself as belonging to that party. He has never held any political office, always refusing to become a candidate, though often solicited to run. At one time, while residing in Alabama, he was solicited to become a candidate for Congress, but declined to do so, as he has all other political preferment.

Dr. Pitman's father was Lawrence Pitman, a farmer, of Shenandoah county, Virginia. He was a man of plain education, but was distinguished for his fine common sense, and noted as one of the best farmers in his community. He died about 1860, at an advanced age.

Dr. Pitman's grandfather, a native of Saxony, came to America at an early day and settled in Virginia.

The late Philip Pitman, of Virginia, who was a member of the convention which framed the former constitution of his State, and also of that which framed the present constitution, was a brother of the subject of this sketch.

Dr. Pitman's mother was Miss Catherine Wills, of a family of German descent, who settled first in Pennsylvania, and moved thence to the valley of Virginia at an early day.

Dr. Pitman has been twice married. His first marriage took place in Alabama, in 1836, to Miss Mary Ragland, daughter of John Ragland, a native of Halifax county, Virginia, who moved from there to Georgia, and thence to Alabama, and finally, after the marriage

of Dr. Pitman, settled at Holly Springs, Mississippi. Mrs. Pitman's grandfather was Lipscomb Ragland, of Halifax county, Virginia, a merchant and a farmer, who was noted for his love of fine stock. By this marriage there were four children, three of whom died in infancy. The other, a son, Warren T. Pitman, entered the service of the Confederate States, and was killed at the sanguinary battle of Franklin, Tennessee, in 1864. Mrs. Pitman died in 1846.

In April, 1851, Dr. Pitman was married to his second wife, Mrs. Watkins, who was a Miss Martha Armistead Booth, a daughter of William Booth, of Virginia, a wealthy farmer. This was the same Watkins family to which Benjamin Lee Watkins belonged. Mr. William Booth's wife was a daughter of Col. Green, of Virginia, and the mother of Mrs. Dr. John Pitman, of Memphis, Tennessee. Mrs. Booth was the only daughter of Col. Green by his second wife, whose maiden name was Armistead. Mrs. Booth was the niece of the Amblers, Pendletons, Allens, Pegrams, Seldons, Carys; and related to a number of distinguished "Old Dominion" families.

Dr. Pitman was raised a Presbyterian, but has been a Methodist for many years. His wife is also a member of that church.

In early life Dr. Pitman was a close and hard student, and it was his love and desire for study that led him to choose the noble profession of medicine. He has followed its requirements with commendable fidelity, and kept fully abreast of the progress made in this branch of science. His life has been one of constant labor and conscientious discharge of duty towards his patients. Inspired by a love of humanity and a desire to ameliorate the condition of the suffering and the afflicted, he has attended to the calls of the rich and poor alike—thus illustrating the nobility of " Tillan the merciful "—for when the angel of affliction knocked at some sufferer's door, the first to hear and the second to call was "Tillan the merciful." In his profession he has always been successful, and has all the time had a large practice. In the city of Memphis alone, he has received more than one hundred thousand dollars in fees, though much of the fortune he has made has been lost by sympathising too closely with friends, and by endorsing for those who failed to meet their obligations with him.

JUDGE CARRICK W. HEISKELL.

MEMPHIS.

ONE of the youngest colonels in the Confederate service, who won his title by his blood, was Col. (now Judge) Carrick White Heiskell, of Memphis. He was born in Knox county, Tennessee, July 25, 1836. He

lived there upon a farm and attended the common schools until he was thirteen years of age. He then entered East Tennessee University, now the University of Tennessee, at Knoxville, and remained one year.

Leaving there he entered Maryville College, at Maryville, Blount county, Tennessee, and graduated under Dr. Isaac Anderson in 1855. He was fond of books and had little taste for farm life. His favorite studies were mathematics and the languages, and when he left college he was a good Greek and Latin scholar, besides being well grounded in English, the natural sciences, mathematics and kindred branches. Shortly after graduating he went to Rogersville, Hawkins county, Tennessee; and taught for two years in McMinn Academy, in the meantime studying law with his brother, J. B. Heiskell. At the expiration of the two years, he was admitted to the bar at Rogersville, by Judge Patterson and Chancellor Luckey, and practiced there until the breaking out of hostilities between the States.

Young Carrick Heiskell was one of the earliest to enlist in his county, and became first-lieutenant of company K, Nineteenth Tennessee infantry regiment, the first company that went from his county into the Confederate service. When the regiment was organized he was elected captain of his company, and served with this rank through the Kentucky campaign with Gen. Zollicoffer, and was with him when he fell at Fishing Creek. After the battle of Murfreesborough he was made major of his regiment, and served as such till the battle of Chickamauga, where he was severely wounded in the foot, which compelled him to leave the service for twelve months. Rejoining the army before he was able to throw aside his crutches, he took command of his regiment on the retreat from Tennessee, after the Hood campaign in 1864. The colonel and lieutenant-colonel of his regiment both having been killed, he became colonel of the Nineteenth Tennessee infantry regiment. He was with Gen. Forrest and commanded the remnant of the brigade of Gen. Strahl, who fell at the battle of Franklin ; participated in all the skirmishes on that retreat ; remained with the army till the close of the war ; took part in the battle of Bentonville, North Carolina, and surrendered at High Point, North Carolina, April 26, 1865.

After the war Col. Heiskell located at Memphis and engaged in the practice of law in partnership with his brother, Hon. J. B. Heiskell, and Col. Moses White, of Knoxville, Tennessee. After this firm had existed for several years he and his brother went into partnership with Judge W. L. Scott, now of St. Louis, the style of the firm being Heiskell, Scott & Heiskell, and which lasted till May 28, 1870. He was then elected judge of the first circuit court of Shelby county, and held the position for eight years. That part of his history which illustrates his career as a judge has been written in the judicial records of the State, and will be found in *Heiskell's Reports* (volumes 1 to 12), edited by Hon. J. B. Heiskell.

Before leaving the bench Judge Heiskell was elected city attorney of Memphis, and as soon as his term as judge had expired he entered upon the duties of the office and served till the old city government

was abolished in 1879. He was an earnest colaborer with those who had the old government abolished, and worked faithfully and ardently to have the present admirable system of city government adopted. He continued as city attorney under the new regime, brought the legal battles of the taxing district through its infancy, and served till March, 1884, when he returned to the practice of his profession.

Judge Heiskell was an old line Whig and a thorough Union man up to the firing on Fort Sumpter. He took up arms in defense of his State, and though he voted to call a convention to decide on the question of secession, he also voted after he was in the army for Union delegates to the convention, being unwilling to go out of the Union till a majority of the people of Tennessee had decided that it was best. When the war went on he had no hesitancy in standing with his people. Since the war he has co-operated with the Democratic party, but has never been an ultra-partisan.

The Heiskell family is of German descent. Judge Heiskell's father, Frederick Heiskell, was born at Frederickstown, Maryland, in 1786, and moved to Knox county, Tennessee, in 1815. He was one of the pioneer printers of Tennessee, and established the Knoxville *Register* in 1816, and published it till 1836. All of the statutes of Tennessee from 1820 to 1836, were printed by him at Knoxville. In 1836 he gave up printing and retired to his farm. He served several terms in the Legislature of Tennessee, and died in 1882, at the advanced age of ninety-six. He was a man of strong, practical, common sense, and met with fine success in business. His brother, William Heiskell, was also a member of the Tennessee Legislature for several terms.

Hon. J. B. Heiskell, brother of the subject of this sketch, was a member of the Confederate States' Congress during the whole period of the existence of the Confederacy. He was also attorney-general for the State of Tennessee since the close of the war, and is regarded as one of the ablest lawyers in the State.

Judge Heiskell's mother, *nee* Miss Eliza Brown, was of Scotch-Irish descent, and a daughter of Joseph Brown, one of the earliest sheriffs of Washington county, Tennessee, and resided at Jonesborough. She married Frederick Heiskell at that town in 1816, and died in 1854. Her brother, Hugh Brown, was a professor in East Tennessee University during its early years, and was also the partner of Frederick Heiskell in the printing business. Her father emigrated from Ireland to this country in his youth.

Judge Heiskell was married at Rogersville, Tennessee, October 21, 1861, to Miss Eliza Netherland, daughter of Col. John Netherland, an eminent lawyer of Rogersville. He was a member of the Legislature for several terms prior to the war ; was several times elector on the Whig ticket, and ran against Hon. Isham G. Harris for governor in 1859. He is now living at Rogersville. His father was a native of Virginia.

Mrs. Heiskell's mother was Miss Susan McKinney,

daughter of John A. McKinney, a prominent lawyer in East Tennessee, during the early days of the State. Her cousin, Judge Robert McKinney, was on the Supreme bench of Tennessee for several years prior to the war, and was the colleague of Judge Archibald Wright, of Memphis, and Judge Robert L. Caruthers, of Lebanon.

By his marriage with Miss Netherland, Judge Heiskell has seven children now living, four sons and four daughters. Mrs. Heiskell has been a member of the Presbyterian church for many years. She is a lady of a remarkably genial disposition and possesses all the elements of a good wife and a good mother. Judge Heiskell has also been a member of the Presbyterian church for many years.

The secret of Judge Heiskell's success is energy. He believes that persistent hard work is the only talisman in life, and that we should unite with this morality, honesty and integrity of purpose, together with a Christian walk and conversation.

One of Judge Heiskell's brother-lawyers says of him: "The key-note of his character and his success is his earnest, enthusiastic pursuit of what he believes to be right and a fearless discharge of what he feels to be his duty. If he has a fault it is over earnestness, but that earnestness is always directed towards the right side. Going upon the bench at a very early age, he made a careful, faithful and capable judge, and his decisions in many difficult and important cases were sustained by the Supreme court. Filling the office of city attorney in Memphis at a time when the difficulties of the position were greatest, he helped to engineer the affairs of the taxing district during the stormy period of its infancy, and fought and won for it many battles in the courts at a time when many were doubting the success of this new form of government, and were asking the question, 'Will the taxing district stand the ordeal of the courts?' His life has been but a fulfillment of the promises of his youth. Entering the Confederate army at a very early age, he was one of the youngest colonels in the service, and it was this same earnestness and enthusiasm that made him a good soldier. United with these traits he has a positive, decided nature, habits of strict morality, and talents of a high order."

JAMES H. DICKENS, M.D.

READYVILLE.

DR. JAMES H. DICKENS was born in Rutherford county, Tennessee, June 11, 1823. His father was B. B. Dickens, a farmer, in moderate circumstances, a justice of the peace and an elder in the Christian church. He was a native of North Carolina, and came with his widowed mother from that State when in his fifteenth year; lived in Warren and Bedford counties until grown, when he settled in Rutherford county. He was a man of firm character, of conscientious conduct and sterling integrity. He married in Rutherford county, raised a family of eight children, and died in 1860, at the age of sixty-five. Of these children, only three sons are now living, James H. Dickens, subject of this sketch, and J. F. and W. B. Dickens; both of the latter farmers. Two of Dr. Dickens' paternal uncles, William and John Dickens, settled in Jackson county, Tennessee, as farmers. William Dickens, the grandfather of Dr. Dickens, was a farmer in North Carolina.

Dr. Dickens' mother, whose maiden name was Miss Nancy Holt, was the daughter of Fielding Holt, a farmer in Rutherford (now Cannon) county, by birth a Virginian, and one of three brothers born and raised in Henry county, in the "Old Dominion." Dr. Dickens' mother was one of those kind, honest, unassuming, true-hearted ladies of the old school, so famous and so honored in Tennessee pioneer history. She died in 1855, at the age of fifty-three.

James H. Dickens was raised on a farm and had a rough and tumble farmer boy's life. His early opportunities were quite limited. Outside of the schooling he got in the county schools of his neighborhood, his education was obtained at Woodbury and at the Milton Academy, under Moses W. McKnight, where he learned Latin and mathematics. He was a quiet and studious boy, and obediently did all he could at whatever he undertook, bringing all of his ability to bear upon his task—a trait that has characterized him through life. He was free from the vices common to boys, having been trained by his parents to control and keep himself within bounds.

He began the study of medicine in 1844, in the office of Dr. M. W. Armstrong, at Milton, Rutherford county, and read with him a little over two years, meanwhile practicing a little. He attended two courses of lectures at the Memphis Medical College, in the years 1846-7-8, graduating as an M.D., in 1848, under Profs. Cross, Grant, Miller, Doyle, Donn, and Ramsey. He began practice without a dollar of capital, at Readyville, in March, 1848, remained there till January, 1849, when he went to Carollton, Mississippi, in March, 1849, and practiced there till November, 1850. He then returned to Readyville, settled permanently, and has been actively engaged in practice in Rutherford county ever since—now about thirty-five years. His practice up to 1878 was very heavy, his attention being devoted exclusively to his profession, with the exception of running a farm, which at present consists of some eight hundred acres, of which about five hundred acres are in cultivation.

Dr. Dickens' success in life has come to him as a natural sequence of his merit, and because he has first gained the approval of his own conscience and judgment, and has followed out his business on that line, with whatever energy and ability he possessed. He has never used money to bring money in, but invested it in property, mostly real estate, and before the war owned a few negroes.

During the year 1869 he was president of the Rutherford County Medical Society, and was one year vice-president of the Tennessee State Medical Society. In politics, he was an old line Whig, and gave his first vote for Henry Clay, but since reconstruction has been a Democrat, at least has acted with that party. In 1844 he joined the Christian church, of which he is still a member.

Dr. Dickens married in Rutherford county, Tennessee, January 25, 1849, Miss Melissa McKnight, daughter of Capt. James McKnight, a farmer, originally from Virginia. Her mother was Nancy Doran, also of Virginia. Mrs. Dickens was educated at the McKnight Academy, in Rutherford county, is a member of the Christian church, and is noted for her domestic virtues and especially for her industrious habits. It is said of her, she is a self-supporting woman, and has made more money than she has spent, which entitles her to the distinction of filling woman's divine mission, as expressed in the words of the Creator, "I will make an help-meet for man." Her kindness and devotion to home duties and relations are her chief characteristics.

Dr. Dickens' has been a close student and a hard-worker all his life, doing an active and laborious practice. Since early manhood he has lived at one place and filled all the conditions of success, and is an example of what a man can do for himself by the right kind of a life. It is all a mistake that success comes by chance. It follows a law. A man must be a good financier and a money saver, without being miserly; must be energetic and industrious, and taking Dr. Dickens as an illustration, must marry a woman of similar qualities. He has been wise enough to avoid going security. He has not been a close collector, his disposition being to indulge debtors—resorting to persuasion and not to coercion for collecting debts, and the result is that he has not lost more than one-third of his professional fees; before the war not more than one-fourth.

In personal appearance Dr. Dickens is a man to be noted. He is about six feet high, looks tall and slender, has blue eyes and plentiful gray hair, worn in a high roach. He has always been a temperate man, and though not totally abstemious has never been in the habit of even taking toddies, and has not used tobacco for thirty years. He has never gambled, knows nothing practically about dissipation, and has never had a fight since boyhood. He is literally surrounded by troops of friends. He is the most successful physician in Rutherford county in point of property. His standing in every way is very high as a citizen, a gentleman and a physician.

THOMAS BLACK, M.D.

McMINNVILLE.

THE original family of Blacks came from Scotland. The great-great-grandfather of Dr. Thomas Black was a Scotch clergyman. The great-grandfather emigrated to America and settled in Kentucky. The grandfather, Samuel Black, a Kentuckian, moved to Warren county, Tennessee, and there died. The father, Alexander Black, was born in Kentucky, in 1804, came with his father to Warren county, and after his father's death was bound to Alexander Shields, a merchant, and was raised in mercantile life, clerking for Shields, at McMinnville. He also clerked, a year or two for Kirkman & Irwin, merchants in Nashville, then returned to McMinnville, went into business with P. H. Marbury, as a merchant, until the year 1856, after which he retired to his farm in the country, and died in 1859, at the age of fifty-five. He was an elder in the Cumberland Presbyterian church, lived a very exemplary life, and left a name of which both his family and town are justly proud. Henry Watterson, the distinguished editor of the Louisville *Courier-Journal*, is a descendant of the same stock, his mother, *nee* Talitha Black, and Dr. Black's father being cousins.

Dr. Black's mother, *nee* Miss Mary A. Smith, was the daughter of Meriwether Smith, of Kingston, Tennessee, and, like her husband, left a reputation that is at once an honor and an incentive to her descendants. She died in Nashville, in 1873, at the age of sixty-five, leaving seven children—six sons and one daughter: (1). Samuel Black, now a farmer. (2). John Black, now a lawyer at Bentonville, Arkansas. (3). Thomas Black, subject of this sketch. (4). Mary L. Black, now wife of R. H. Mason, a merchant and farmer at McMinnville. (5). Robert Black, a merchant and manufacturer of stoneware at Smithville, Tennessee. (6). Alexander Black, a merchant at Leiper's Fork, Williamson county. (7). Meriwether Smith Black, now in the hotel business at Cincinnati.

Dr. Thomas Black was born at McMinnville, Tennessee, June 13, 1837, and was educated there in the old Carroll Academy, occasionally clerking in his father's store, and had a fondness for general literature, and especially for botany and chemistry, in which branches of science he has since made fine reputation.

He began the study of medicine in 1857, in the office of Drs. Hill & Smartt at McMinnville. After reading with them one year he began practice and continued it until the war, when he went into the medical department of the Confederate army, and was detailed as a hospital steward, but sometimes acted as assistant-surgeon. Having no diploma at that time, he could not be commissioned as surgeon or assistant-surgeon, though he practiced through the entire war and until the surrender at Greensborough, North Carolina, May 10, 1865. He served the entire time in Col. John H. Savage's Sixteenth Tennessee regiment, and his history in connection with that gallant command runs through Virginia, North Carolina, South Carolina, Georgia, Florida, Alabama, Mississippi, Kentucky and Tennessee, and includes the battles of Murfreesborough, Chickamauga, Missionary Ridge, and the Georgia campaign from Dalton to Atlanta.

After the war he practiced two years in Warren county and then removed to Nashville. In 1868 he graduated as M.D. from the medical department of the University of Nashville, under Profs. Paul F. Eve, Thomas R. Jennings, W. T. Briggs, C. K. Winston, J. B. Lindsley and Joseph Jones. He lived in Nashville eight years, practicing medicine and teaching chemistry to private classes in the medical department of the University of Nashville. Part of this time he was professor of analytical chemistry and materia medica in the Tennessee College of Pharmacy at Nashville.

Dr. Black passed through the cholera epidemic at Nashville in 1873, and in November, 1874, moved to McMinnville, where he has been doing a general practice as physician and surgeon ever since, and occasionally has contributed articles on chemistry and kindred topics to the medical journals. He is now a member of the fac-

ulty of Cumberland Female College, at McMinnville, and is highly esteemed as a clear and forcible lecturer on scientific subjects.

Dr. Black married at McMinnville, February 13, 1867, Miss Emma J. Young, daughter of the late Dr. John S. Young, of Nashville, formerly—for eight years, from 1840 to 1848—secretary of State, during which time he superintended the building of the Tennessee Hospital for the Insane and other noted public edifices. Mrs Black was born May 6, 1845, on the site where the State capitol now stands. Her mother, nee Miss Jean L. Colville, was the daughter of Maj. Joseph Colville, one of the founders of the town of McMinnville. Samuel Colville, Esq., the banker at McMinnville, is the son of Lusk Colville, brother of Mrs. Black's mother. Mrs. Black was educated at Cumberland Female College, McMinnville, and at the famous and dearly beloved old Nashville Female Academy, under Rev. Dr. C. D. Elliott. She is a Cumberland Presbyterian, and to the excellencies of an intelligent Christian lady she has added those domestic virtues that make home happy.

By his marriage with Miss Young Dr. Black has eight children: (1). Jean Young Black, born March 12, 1868. (2). Mary Alice Black. (3). John Young Black, born December 20, 1871. (4). Sallie Colville Black. (5). Susan Black. (6). Emma Black. (7). Clara Josephine Black and (8). Leah Black.

Dr. Black is an elder in the Cumberland Presbyterian church, which denomination he joined when a youth. In politics he is a Democrat. He is the mayor of the town of McMinnville; a Knight of Honor; a Master Mason, and medical examiner for several insurance companies. He is a man of handsome *personnel*, a gentleman of most affable manners and social attainments—a good companion, a good citizen and a most excellent physician. He has succeeded in life by always trying to do the right thing and to help along his fellow-man. It is a pleasure to write of one who possesses such sterling traits of a noble manhood.

CAPT. JAMES HARVEY MATHES.

MEMPHIS.

THE Mathes family is of Scotch-Irish extraction. The remote ancestor of Capt. James Harvey Mathes, subject of this sketch, was Alexander Mathes (or Matthews, as he spelt the name), who came to America about 1720, first settling in Pennsylvania, and afterwards removing to Virginia. Some forty years after, four Matthews brothers, and their families, including Capt. Mathes' great-grandfather, George Mathes, removed to Washington county, East Tennessee, a period long anterior to the admission of the State of

Tennessee into the Union, and it is a tradition that even up to this time the family name was spelled Matthews. They settled near what is now known as Washington College, then known as Martin's Academy, an institution in the establishment and support of which they and the Doak family, and other pioneers, took an active part.

The Mathes family has been very prolific in preachers and doctors, and as their history shows they have, from early times, been the friends of education and the upbuilders of society. During the late war, most of the descendants were on the Union side. There was an Ebenezer Mathes, a very wealthy man for that country, years ago, who "set his negroes free" before the war, by sending some of them to Liberia and some to the "free-soil States of the north." He also gave liberally for the endowment of institutions of learning and charity, and to colonization societies. At his death, since the war, he left all his property to charitable causes, excepting some small legacies to relatives.

George Mathes, great-grandfather of Capt. Mathes, was a Virginian by birth, and, as stated, removed to Washington county when a young man, subsequently removed to Blount county, and was killed by a famous Indian chief, John Watts, a few miles west of where Maryville now stands. His son, William Mathes (Capt. Mathes' grandfather), was born in Washington county, and is said to have been the first white child born in Jonesborough. He grew up to be a prosperous farmer and a man of fine character, noted for his high sense of honor and fair dealing. He was an elder in the Presbyterian church at Dandridge; was a magistrate and held the office of county trustee. He married in Jefferson county, Miss Rachel Patton Balch, of an old Revolutionary family, niece of one of the signers of the Mecklenburg Declaration of Independence. He reared a large family, but only one of his children now survives, Rev. William Alfred Mathes, father of Capt. J. Harvey Mathes.

Capt. Mathes' father inherited the old homestead, and the deed to it, by some means, was signed by James K. Polk. He still lives, aged seventy-one years, in the home which his father built when he was an infant. He is a Presbyterian minister and a farmer; has always been a strictly religious man, devoted to Sunday-school work and to the cause of temperance.

The mother of Capt. Mathes was Miss Margaret Maria Hart, daughter of Edward and Elizabeth Hood Hart, the latter a relative of Lieut.-Gen. John B. Hood. She was born three miles east of Maryville, Blount county, Tennessee; married in 1837, and died in December, 1881. She was a true, good wife and mother, and of a peculiarly sweet temperament. She was the mother of eight children: (1). James Harvey Mathes, subject of this sketch. (2). A daughter, who died in infancy. (3). Dr. George A. Mathes, who was a member of the Thirty-seventh Tennessee Confederate regiment; died in Memphis, July 31, 1881. (4). Rachel Emma Mathes, now wife of J. S. Barton, a lawyer at McMinnville, Tennessee. (5). Edward H. Mathes, now a lawyer at Ozark, Arkansas. (6). John T. Mathes, now a lawyer in Uvalde county, Texas. (7). Nathaniel Beecher Mathes, now a theological student at the Southwestern University at Clarksville, Tennessee. (8). Cordele Mathes, now instructor in painting in a college at Pine Bluff, Arkansas.

The history of the Hart family is exceedingly interesting. The remotest direct ancestor of Capt. Mathes' mother that can now be traced, was a merchant in London, extensively interested in shipping and a trader in the Levant. About the year 1606 he was captured by pirates, had his eyes put out, and was made a galley slave for fourteen years. He, however, escaped with others in a boat, was picked up in mid-ocean by a trading ship, and brought to Norfolk, in the colony of Virginia. He afterwards married there and had one son, Thomas Hart, from whom sprang a very numerous family that subsequently settled in Kentucky and other States west, and intermarried with the Clays, Bentons, Breckinridges, and other prominent families. One branch of the family came to Tennessee at a very early day, one of whom was Joseph Hart (Capt. Mathes' great-grandfather), who became the head of a very large family, consisting of ten sons and two daughters. He removed to Bartholomew county, Indiana, about 1834, and died there. One of his sons, Samuel Hart, now lives at Carrollton, Mississippi; another, James H. Hart, lives at Shawneetown, Illinois; another, Rev. Charles H. Hart, is a Presbyterian minister in Logan county, Ohio. Another son, Edward Hart (Capt. Mathes' maternal grandfather), was born, lived and died in Blount county, Tennessee.

Of the sons of Edward Hart (Capt. Mathes' maternal uncles), one of them, Thomas Hart, still lives at the old homestead in Blount county; another, Joseph Hart, lives in Knox county; another, Dr. Nathaniel Hart, formerly surgeon in Orr's First South Carolina regiment, now lives near Brooksville, Florida. Two daughters of Edward Hart, Mrs. Abigail Boyd and Mrs. Hettie Aiken, now live in Blount county.

Capt. James Harvey Mathes was born June 29, 1841, in Jefferson county, Tennessee, and grew up on his father's farm, leading the life and doing the work of a farmer's boy. His parents being upright, strictly honest and prudent people, his early moral training was in the right direction. He attended the neighboring country schools until his sixteenth year, when he entered as a student Westminster Academy, East Tennessee, then under control of Prof. A. W. Wilson, a Presbyterian minister and a noted educator, now president of a college at Dodd City, Texas. He remained there three years, during which time he assumed especial prominence in rhetoric and composition, wherein he evidenced the instincts and preferences which, in after life, led him to embrace the profession of journalism, in which he has achieved enviable distinction. During his scholastic days he enjoyed the reputation of being one of the best read young men in Jefferson county, and he was always known to seize with avidity only the healthiest literary productions, both modern and ancient. When nineteen years of age he accepted a position as teacher in an Alabama school, where he pursued his duties as tutor in the daytime, read law at night, and at the same time prepared himself for col-

24

lege. But his coveted diploma was never received, for on the very day that Fort Sumpter fell he closed his school and started home to Jefferson county. Here he heard Andrew Johnson, Horace Maynard, Gov. Brownlow, T. A. R. Nelson, and other noted men of East Tennessee, make Union speeches, some of which were so bitter against the South that his sympathies were at once aroused for the southern cause, notwithstanding his father and the majority of his relatives had adopted Union views.

He at once raised a company for the Confederate service, was made captain, and drilled his men for two months, but his company was finally distributed into different branches of the army, and young Mathes enlisted as a private in the company commanded by Capt. S. M. Cocke, which afterwards became a part of the Thirty-seventh Tennessee regiment. He was first elected orderly sergeant of his company, and at Germantown, near Memphis, was appointed sergeant-major by Col. (afterwards brigadier-general) William H. Carroll. The regiment encamped at Knoxville for some time and did guard duty around the jail while Parson W. G. Brownlow was a prisoner there, but there was no bitterness or unkindness shown the prisoner, a fact which Mr. Brownlow kindly recognized in a book which he afterwards published, although he was severe in his opinions of Gen. Carroll, and subsequently refused to allow him to return home from Canada, where he died an exile. While at Knoxville Mathes was detailed and assigned to duty in the adjutant-general's department, under Gen. George B. Crittenden, but returned to his regiment when it was ordered to Mill Springs, Kentucky, where he participated in the battle at that place.

When the army was reorganized at Corinth, Mississippi, in April, 1862, he was elected first-lieutenant of his company, and soon after was commissioned as adjutant of the Thirty-seventh Tennessee regiment, a position he held until the close of the war. At the battle of Perryville, where the regiment lost nearly one-half its strength in killed and wounded, he took an active and conspicuous part. At the battle of Murfreesborough, Col. Moses White and Lieut.-Col. Frayser were wounded and Maj. J. S. McReynolds was killed, and the young adjutant was practically in command of the regiment after the field officers fell. Subsequently the regiment was stationed at Chattanooga and other points down the railroad to Dalton, Georgia. After being recruited they were sent to the front near Wartrace, and at a later period, consolidated with the Fifteenth Tennessee, a regiment that had been formed under Col. Charles Carroll, a brother of Col. William H. Carroll, of the Thirty-seventh. The colonel commanding at that time, however, was Col. R. C. Tyler, who succeeded to the command of the consolidated regiment. The colonel of the Thirty-seventh and Adjutant Mathes, together with a number of other officers, were assigned

to duty elsewhere, Capt. Mathes being sent on detached service for several months in north Georgia, at Knoxville and Jonesborough, East Tennessee, and finally into Virginia, the Carolinas and Georgia. Returning to the army he was assigned to duty in southern Alabama. After two or three months' perilous service in chasing down deserters and breaking up bands of bushwhackers, who had fled from both the Federal and Confederate armies to the swamps and wilds of southern Alabama, along the Florida line, he made application to Gen. Bragg for permission to return to the army front. The request was granted, and during the latter part of '63 he rejoined his old regiment and declined a captaincy in favor of his old position, where he would not have to give up his tried and faithful war horse. Shortly after he was appointed inspector of Tyler's brigade, Col. Tyler having in the meantime become brigadier-general, succeeding Gen. Bate, who had been promoted to a major-generalship, succeeding Gen. John C. Breckinridge in command of the division.

Capt. Mathes participated actively in the Georgia campaign all the way from Dalton, being under fire fully seventy days out of seventy-five, and although in all the prominent engagements as a staff officer, he yet found time to write frequently to the *Memphis Appeal* (then published at Atlanta), over the *nom de plume* of "Harvey." His letters were highly interesting, plainly bearing the stamp of ability, and were valuable contributions to the war literature of the day.

On July 22, 1864, while acting as assistant adjutant-general, on the staff of Gen. Thomas Benton Smith, he received a frightfully severe wound in the left knee, from a shell which exploded so close to him that he could feel the concussion. His horse was killed instantly. Capt. Mathes was carried off the field on a blanket by some of the Ninth Kentucky mounted infantry (Gen. Cerro Gordo Williams' brigade), to a small cabin being used as a hospital by the Kentucky brigade. Some time later an ambulance drove up with Col. R. Dudley Frayser, who was also very badly wounded. That afternoon the two wounded friends and officers were removed to the division hospital, some miles in the rear, where between eight and nine o'clock, Capt. Mathes' injured leg was amputated just above the knee, by Dr. Joel C. Hall, of Mississippi, acting surgeon of the brigade. The next day Capt. Mathes was removed to Atlanta, placed on a train and moved out to Lovejoy's, and the day following was carried on, with numerous other badly wounded soldiers. At Griffin he was compelled to disembark, on account of the intense pain of his wound, but four weeks later was able to go on crutches, and six weeks from the date of the operation was removed to Columbus, Georgia, in a box-car, and was three days in making the journey, accompanied only by a colored servant. From Columbus he went to Silver Run, Alabama, but his injured limb being attacked with gangrene, caused his return to Columbus, where he became so prostrated with the disease and numerous surgical operations, that he was reduced to the lowest possible point of life, and became a mere skeleton. In the midst of his multiplied sufferings, however, he was the object of the kindest attention from the ladies and citizens of Columbus, and was visited by his aunt, Mrs. Dr. N. Hart, of Ninety-six, South Carolina, who, with a mother's care and solicitude, nursed him through the crisis. Yet he improved very slowly, and on March 22, 1865, left for Grenada, Mississippi, hoping to communicate with his parents, from whom he had not heard in six months. While at Grenada news of the surrender came. Gen. Marcus J. Wright was in command of that district, and Gov. Isham G. Harris and his sons were there awaiting results, keeping their horses saddled and hitched day and night, ready to leave at a moment's notice, which they did when the news was confirmed, Gov. Harris going to join Forrest's command which had not surrendered. Capt. Mathes went on through to Memphis by private conveyance, arrived there May 13, 1865, and was paroled by the Federal provost-marshal on Court street. This parole, and his Confederate commission as first-lieutenant, a surgeon's certificate signed by Dr. Hall, July 23, 1864, a pocket testament from his father, carried through the war, and a diary kept during the greater part of the strife, being about his only souvenirs of the great struggle, except a Federal sword he captured at the battle of Murfrees borough, which is now at his old home in East Tennessee.

That Capt. Mathes has been through the fiery furnace of war needs no further attestation from this chronicler. The lost limb is an eloquent reminder of the fearless devotion with which he served his country. But the disturbed condition of things in East Tennessee just after the war made it unsafe for him to return to his old home, and at this period his experience as an army correspondent stood him in good stead, and he soon succeeded in securing the city editorship of the Memphis *Daily Argus*, a position he held with credit to himself and employers from December 25, 1865, until the paper ceased to exist, early in 1867. During his service on the *Argus* (which toward the last became the *Commercial and Argus*), he received severe injuries in a terrible railroad accident near Iuka, Mississippi, which hastened what he had felt would come sooner or later— another amputation of his wounded leg, which had never entirely healed after the gangrene was eradicated. This was performed in Memphis by Dr. Voorhees, in the presence of a number of prominent physicians and surgeons, in the latter part of October, 1866. After a month's confinement to his bed, and a trip to New Orleans by boat, he went on duty again December 1, 1866, and a year later was able to dispense with his crutches and use an artificial limb.

He next cast his fortunes with the Louisville *Courier*, remained nearly a year on its editorial staff, was again forced to resign regular work on account of ill health, and acted as special correspondent at Indianapolis and Chicago for various journals. In the spring of 1868 he became connected with the editorial staff of the Memphis *Avalanche*. On March 1, 1869, he became city editor of the Memphis *Public Ledger*, and in 1872, was appointed chief editor, succeeding Col. F. Y. Rockett, who died in the summer of that year. During the sixteen years and more that Capt. Mathes has been the editor of the *Public Ledger*, the most amicable relations have existed between Mr. E. Whitmore, the proprietor, and himself. The paper has grown almost without a precedent in the South, is now the oldest afternoon journal in the South, has outlived more than a dozen rival cotemporaries, and is to-day in a solid, financial condition. Under the editorship of Capt. Mathes it has taken high conservative ground on leading questions of the day, and while Democratic in politics, is very independent as well as liberal, fearless as well as bold, a leader in progress, development, and the social and educational advancement of Tennessee. The noble people of Memphis have been ever quick to recognize his efforts and to hold up his hands in the cause of truth and justice, and he has never betrayed their trust, but grown with that public-spirited city and become one of the standard men in their midst.

Capt. Mathes was married December 2, 1868, at Forest Hill, near Memphis, to Miss Mildred Spotswood Cash, daughter of Col. Benjamin Cash, a native of North Carolina, and a planter, who died December 14, 1874. The mother of Miss Cash was Mildred S. Dandridge, from near Richmond, Virginia. By blood connection Mrs. Mathes is related to a number of leading and time-honored families in Virginia, Mississippi, Tennessee, Alabama and the Carolinas. She is highly educated and a graduate of the best schools of Memphis. The marriage of Capt Mathes and Miss Cash was the romantic result of an acquaintance formed during the first year of the war, when she was a mere child of twelve or thirteen. The bright eyes, sweet face and winning manners of the little southern girl won the heart of the young soldier, and his manly and chivalric bearing fired her tenderest sentiments even then. The distress of war did not disturb the glowing picture of future happiness drawn by the young people, and one day when she was told that her hero was frightfully wounded and had lost a limb, she was asked if she would still marry him should he live to return. "Yes," she replied, " bring him on, if he has only body enough left to hold his heart." A noble sentiment direct from the true heart of a noble woman. They became formally engaged shortly after Lee's surrender, and were married nearly four years later. By this marriage five children have been born: (1). Mildred Overton Mathes, born July 28, 1870. (2). Lee Dandridge Mathes, born January 12, 1872. (3). Benjamin Cash Mathes, born January 1, 1875. (4). James Harvey Mathes, born December 12, 1877. (5). Talbot Spotswood Mathes, born May 6, 1881.

Capt. Mathes was reared in the Presbyterian church, but is now a member of the Strangers' church (Congregational, Rev. N. M. Long, pastor), Memphis, and is chairman of the board of trustees. He became a Mason in 1864, while in army winter quarters at Dalton, Georgia, under a dispensation from the Grand Lodge of Alabama ; since the war, has become a Royal Arch Mason, and at one time served as secretary of South Memphis Lodge, No. 118, of which he became an affiliated member in 1868. He is also a Knight of Honor ; was the first Dictator of the first lodge (No. 196) in Memphis and in West Tennessee. This is now the largest lodge in the State. He was also a charter member of Johnson Lodge, No. 21, A. O. U. W., the first lodge organized in Memphis, and has attended Grand Lodges of both these orders in Nashville.

Capt. Mathes was raised a Whig, but since the war has been a Democrat. Soon after the war he became prominently identified with local and State politics and took an active part as long as the people labored under the disabilities of disfranchisement. In April, 1870, he was elected tax collector on privileges—an office that existed only in Shelby county—held the position two years, and in 1872 was re-elected by the almost unanimous vote of the county, receiving over fourteen thousand votes.

In 1874 he was elected to the lower house of the Legislature, and served as chairman of the committee on printing, and as a member of other committees. In 1878 he visited Europe, carrying a commission from Gov. A. S. Marks as representative of Tennessee to the Paris Exposition. This tour was taken on his own account, mainly for recreation and health. While abroad he wrote a series of letters from Scotland, England, Ireland and France, which were published in the Memphis Ledger and extensively copied. He returned to Memphis in August, 1878, after the yellow fever broke out, resumed his editorial chair on the Ledger, but was taken with the fever September 7, and had a very violent case, but with the advantages of a good constitution, the best of medical attention, the kind offices of his lodge brethren, and the devoted nursing of his faithful wife, he partially recovered, only in time, too, to assist in nursing and caring for the wife who was stricken at his bedside just as he had passed the crisis. Mrs. Mathes also had a very violent case of the fever, and for three days was entirely speechless. Two of their nurses died, one in the house and the other elsewhere, and it was some months before either husband or wife were wholly themselves again.

While still weak from the fever and scarcely able to walk, Capt. Mathes was again nominated for the Legislature, and was elected by a handsome majority, in No-

vember, 1878. He became a candidate for speaker of the House, but being physically too weak for the fight, and in order to break a dead lock, withdrew in favor of Hon. H. P. Fowlkes, of Williamson county, who was immediately elected, and subsequently appointed Capt. Mathes chairman of the committee on finance, ways and means. With other members from Shelby he took an active part in procuring the repeal of the charter of Memphis, and in passing the act under which the pres ent taxing district of Memphis was established. In connection with his political history as a legislator, it may be stated that in the Legislature of 1875, he was one of the "immortal nine," comprising the Shelby delegation, which voted for Andrew Johnson for United States senator in opposition to his personal friend and old commander, Gen. Bate, feeling bound to obey his constituency, who virtually instructed him to cast his vote that way or resign.

Since serving his last term in the Legislature, he has been a candidate for no office on his own account, but has devoted his attention entirely to his editorial duties. However, in 1879, he was appointed by Gov. Marks as a member of the board of visitors to the University of East Tennessee (now University of Tennessee); was reappointed in 1883 by Gov. Bate for another term, it being an honorary office without compensation. Without being an aspirant for office he has attended as a delegate from his county, most of the State Democratic conventions since the war. In the State convention, June, 1884, he was unanimously, and without solicitation on his part, chosen as elector on the National Democratic ticket for the Tenth (Memphis) Congressional district, and afterwards made a brilliant canvass as such in behalf of Cleveland and Hendricks. At the same convention he was appointed an alternate delegate to the Chicago National Democratic convention and attended in that capacity. As a popular speaker, Capt. Mathes is held in very high esteem for his eloquence, solid information, logical and well-balanced views. He is an excellent raconteur, a fine " after dinner man," and a pleasing conversationalist. Besides his visit to Europe, he has traveled extensively in the United States, Canada, New and old Mexico, acquiring a large acquaintance with men and matters, which he never fails to put to good use.

He has succeeded well in a financial sense ; is now a director in the Vanderbilt Insurance company, Memphis, and has a fair property. He has always taken good care of his family, is charitable to the unfortunate, has lived within his income, and avoided debt with a holy horror. His greatest fortune has been his wife, who, although reared in luxury, has done her full share in helping him to succeed in life. And he has returned this devotion with a loving and a loyal gallantry that well merits for him the noble title of a born gentleman.

COL. MOSES H. CLIFT.

CHATTANOOGA.

THE word Clift, meaning stability, as a family cognomen, is a perpetual incentive to high endeavor and fixedness of purpose. The great ancestor, James Clift, an Englishman, came over to North Carolina in 1712. His son, James Clift, was in the war of the Revolution and in that of 1812, and was at the battle of Cowpens and at New Orleans. He married a Hitchcock, of North Carolina, related to the celebrated geologist. She was a niece of Dr. Benjamin Franklin.

Col. Clift's father, William Clift, was born in North Carolina, in 1795, moved with his father to Knox county, Tennessee, about the year 1800, and resided there until 1825, when he settled in Hamilton county, Tennessee, where he still resides. He has been engaged in farming and the lumber business most of his life. He was colonel of the Seventh Tennessee Federal regiment, and served till captured in the fall of 1863, in Rhea county, Tennessee. Singular to say, while the father was a colonel in the Federal army his son, subject of this sketch, was also a colonel on staff duty on the other side. The elder Clift was colonel of militia many years before the war, and before he entered regular service. He was for many years a magistrate of Hamilton county and has always been a citizen of weighty influence. For forty-five years he has been an elder in the Presbyterian church. He married Nancy Arwin Brooks, daughter of Gen. Moses Brooks, of Knox county, Tennessee, a gentleman of Scotch blood and birth, and a soldier in the war of the Revolution. Her brother, Joseph Brooks, of Knox county, now deceased, was also general of militia. Her brother, John, died in the Mexican war. Her mother was an Arwin. Col. Clift's mother died in 1846, leaving seven children: (1). America W., died the wife of R. W. Coulter. (2). Agnes E., now the widow of Johnson Coulter. (3). James W., a farmer, and now secretary of the Soddy Coal company, and of the Walden's Ridge Coal company. He was a lieutenant in the regular army of the Confederate service. (4). Mary A., wife of J. W. C. Henderson. (5). Robert B. (6). Moses H., subject of this sketch. (7). Joseph J., a justice of the peace and a farmer in Hamilton county.

Col. Clift was born at Soddy, Hamilton county, August 25, 1836. He was raised to do farming, flatboating and steamboating on the Tennessee river, and from his earliest boyhood throughout his career, has been distinguished for his untiring energy. In the war he was brave, pushing and fearless. To-day, at his home in Chattanooga, he is universally popular, and, indeed, all over East Tennessee. His education was neglected when he was a boy. He had the advantage of only fourteen months' schooling, and hence deserves praise for attaining eminence in a learned profession by hard work and diligent self-application. He began studying law at the age of twenty-two at Chattanooga, in the office of Judge John L. Hopkins, was admitted to the bar in 1861, by Judges T. Nixon Van Dyke and John C. Gaut. But before beginning practice he entered the Confederate army and raised company H, of the Thirty-sixth Tennessee regiment, his brother, J. W. Clift, being made its captain. After serving seven months he left the Thirty-sixth Tennessee and went to the Fourth Tennessee cavalry, Starnes' regiment, Forrest's old brigade. He remained in that regiment until the battle of Fort Donelson, when he was promoted to a captaincy on the field and assigned to duty on the staff of Col. Starnes, who was then commanding the brigade. He remained with Col. Starnes until that gallant officer was killed at the battle of Tullahoma, in August, 1863, when Clift was assigned to duty on the staff of Gen. George G. Dibrell with rank of captain, but was afterwards promoted to major at the battle of Kennesaw Mountain, and to colonel at Waynesborough, Georgia, in 1865. Col. Clift served with honor and great gallantry in Tennessee, Kentucky, Virginia, Alabama, Mississippi, Georgia, South and North Carolina, surrendering at Washington, Georgia, being at the time with the troops accompanying President Davis and his cabinet.

Col. Clift took part in the battles of Fort Donelson, Parker's Cross-roads, Jackson, Lavergne, Murfreesborough, Chickamauga, Knoxville, Dandridge, Spring Hill, Franklin, Pulaski, Philadelphia, Loudon, Tennessee; Saltville, Tunnel Hill, Resaca, Kennesaw Mountain, Cassville, Buckhead church, Waynesborough, Georgia; Aikin's Bridge and Columbia, South Carolina, Greensborough and Charlotte, North Carolina. He was wounded at the battles of Fort Donelson, and at Cassville and Waynesborough, Georgia. At Fort Donelson, Tennessee, he had twenty-three bullet holes shot through his clothes, but without abrasion of the skin. At Fort Donelson, it is said, the Federal officer in command offered a reward of five thousand dollars for the capture of Col. Clift. After the battle of Chickamauga he was ordered into the Federal lines across the Tennessee river, and remained there several hours gathering information, which he communicated to Gen. Bragg at Missionary ridge. Just before the battle at Tunnel Hill he was ordered into the enemy's lines on the scout again, watched the movements of the Federal troops while concentrating before moving on their march into Georgia, all of which he promptly and accurately reported to Gen. Joseph E. Johnston, then commanding the Confederate army. Gen. Bragg offered Col. Clift a generalship at Chattanooga, in 1863, but he declined the distinction.

The war over, he returned to his home at Soddy,

when, after remaining a few weeks, he went to Fort Valley, Georgia, and there opened a law office and made his first fee. He remained there only two months and then went to Atlanta, where he remained until February, 1866, when he went to Murfreesborough and practiced until the December following. He then located permanently at Chattanooga. Since then he has diligently, and with great success, practiced law. He is now president of the Soddy Coal company, and of the Walden's Ridge Coal company; is a director in the Chattanooga cotton factory; the Citico furnace; the Chattanooga Electric Light company; owns two farms in Hamilton county, and, besides his palatial residence, several business houses and unimproved real estate in Chattanooga, and is classed among the solid men of that city.

It is true of this gentleman that he is a self-made man, for he began life when the war ended on a dollar and fifty cents, and his fortune is due to himself. His system is that of persistent, energetic industry, and to this day he has never invested a dollar from which he did not realize fifty per cent. He is said to be brave, tender-hearted, charitable and generous to a proverb. He risks his own judgment, and close investigation and judicious investment will account for his financial success. As a lawyer he consults nobody; acts on his own opinion, and keeps his own counsel. Self-reliant always, he first learns the facts of a case—from which he forms his conclusions as to the rights of his client and the law applicable; it is then the object to sustain these conclusions by authorities. He refuses to take a case unless he thinks his client has a chance to win.

In religion Col. Clift is a Presbyterian, and has been an elder in that church some fourteen years. In politics he is a Democrat. He has held the positions of alderman, notary public, special judge, and was a delegate to the National Democratic convention at St. Louis, in 1876, and at Cincinnati, in 1880.

Capt. Clift first married in Monroe county, Tennessee, in September, 1866, Miss Attie Cooke, daughter of Dr. R. F. Cooke, a distinguished physician, whose father was for two terms a member of Congress from East Tennessee, and originally from South Carolina. Mrs. Clift's uncle, Hon. J. B. Cooke, is now on the Supreme bench of the State. Her mother was Charlotte Kimbro, of Monroe county. Mrs. Clift died at Chattanooga, in

February, 1876, at the age of twenty-nine, leaving three children: (1). Attie Arwin. (2). Mary Roberta. (3). Moses H., the latter dying in infancy.

Col. Clift's second marriage occurred at Cartersville, Bartow county, Georgia, June 28, 1883, with Miss Florence V. Parrott, who was born in that town, April 24, 1858. She was the daughter of Judge J. R. Parrott, a native of Cocke county, Tennessee, born February 25, 1827, and died at Montvale Springs, Blount county, Tennessee, June 10, 1872. He was educated at Emory and Henry College, Virginia; moved to Georgia in 1848; went to the bar in 1851; was a delegate from Gordon county, Georgia, to the Union convention of 1850, and was the youngest member of that body. In 1856 he was an elector on the Fillmore ticket, and in 1860 on the Bell and Everett ticket; was a member of the constitutional conventions of 1865 and 1868, and was president of the latter. In 1863 he was appointed quartermaster, with the rank of major, of Gen. Wofford's brigade, and was afterwards solicitor-general of the Cherokee (Georgia) circuit in the latter part of that year. In 1868 he was appointed judge of the Cherokee circuit, and filled that position until his death. In politics he was a Republican; in religion a Protestant Methodist. In everything in his life's conduct he endeavored to rely on reason, common sense and fact; his speeches were pointed, forcible, eloquent, and in his bearing he was a fine type of the cultivated gentleman.

Mrs. Clift's grandfather, Jacob Parrott, was a native of Tennessee, and died at Parrottsville, a town named for the Parrot family, a member of which invented the famous Parrott gun.

Mrs. Clift's mother's maiden name was Mary Trammell, and she is now living in Cartersville, Georgia. She was born in Nacoochee Valley, Georgia, a daughter of John Trammell. Her mother was Elizabeth Fain. Mrs. Clift's maternal uncle, Leander N. Trammell, is a prominent politician, and now a railroad commissioner of the State of Georgia. Mrs. Clift was educated at the Augusta Female Seminary, Staunton, Virginia, and received the highest medal given for English composition. She is distinguished for her superior mental endowments, high literary attainments and her gracious disposition and graceful manners. By his second marriage, Col. Clift has one child, Rhoton Parrott, born August 9, 1884.

JOHN P. BLANKENSHIP, M.D.

MARYVILLE.

DR. JOHN PATTON BLANKENSHIP was born at Friendsville, Blount county, Tennessee, December 6, 1839, and grew up there, working on his father's farm, going to school during winter months, and studying from early boyhood, with a view of becoming a physician. His habits in boyhood were good, due in part to his good mother's admonitions. For four and a half years he was a student in the Friendsville Institute, taking most pleasure in the study of languages. The last term he attended that college he studied physiology, anatomy and chemistry under Dr. David Morgan, the president and founder of the school. He began the study of medicine at the age of twenty, in the office of Dr. Isaac Taylor, in Maryville, and read with him two years, practicing some in the second year. In February, 1862, he was appointed by Col. L. C. Houk to the position of assistant surgeon of the Third, Tennessee Federal infantry regiment, and was with that regiment from its organization throughout its campaigns in Tennessee, Georgia and Kentucky, when he was discharged at Murfreesborough, Tennessee, on account of ill health.

In the fall of 1862, he occasionally attended medical lectures at Louisville. In June, 1866, he returned to Maryville, and again entered into practice there. In 1874-75 he studied medicine in the Vanderbilt University at Nashville, and graduated March, 1875, under Profs. Paul F. Eve, W. T. Briggs, Thomas L. Maddin, W. L. Nichol, Van S. Lindsley, Thomas Menees, J. M. Safford, Thomas A. Atchison and John H. Callender. In March, 1883, the Nashville Medical College conferred upon him the *ad eundem* degree. From 1866 to the present time he has been engaged in the general practice of medicine and surgery at Maryville and in Blount county, confining himself exclusively to his profession. During the summer of 1884, he was resident physician at Montvale Springs, whither he went for the benefit of his own health, a spell of typhoid-pneumonia during the war having seriously injured his constitution, from the effects of which he has never entirely recovered. Dr. Blankenship deserves credit for the tenacity of purpose with which he has, over all obstacles, pursued the study of his profession, and risen to a high standing in it.

The Blankenship family, mostly farmers, are noted for being a working, determined, energetic people. Dr. Blankenship's great-grandfather, Isham Blankenship, was raised near Richmond, Virginia, and first went to North Carolina, and from the latter State came to Tennessee, the family locating in Blount and Monroe counties. Isham Blankenship had seven sons, each one of whom had seven sons, four of whom came to Tennessee, and so the race has spread all over East Tennessee, and the State, and even over other States. It is a tradition in the family that no less than fourteen of the Blankenships were the fathers of seven sons each, though this is not stated as a positive fact.

Dr. Blankenship's grandfather, Gilbert Blankenship, was a successful farmer on the Tennessee river, in what is now Loudon county, and there died in 1875, at the age of eighty-four. He married three times, his last wife being Elizabeth Hughes. He left eleven children by the three wives, Dr. Blankenship's father, Isham Blankenship, being a son of the first wife, Bertha Davis, a native of Virginia, brought to Blount county at the age of fourteen years, where her father and mother died. Her father was a farmer.

Dr. Blankenship's father, Isham Blankenship, died, thirty-eight years old, near Friendsville, Blount county, when the son was only eleven years old. He was born in Blount (now Loudon) county and was a farmer. When a young man he was a lieutenant in the army which removed the Indians from the Hiawasse country, mention of which is made in *Ramsey's Annals of Tennessee*. The Blankenship family are related to the Moore family—prominent people and among the early settlers of North Carolina.

Dr. Blankenship's mother, *nee* Mary McClain, of Scotch-Irish descent, was born near Morganton, now in Loudon county, daughter of John McClain, a farmer from Virginia. Her mother was a Miss Stephens and came either from Maryland or Virginia. Mrs. Blankenship's brother, Andrew McClain, was county register of Blount county, sixteen years. In 1865, he removed to Lincoln county, Tennessee, where he died in 1881. Her brother, Alexander McClain, is now a prosperous farmer near Fayetteville, Tennessee. Dr. Blankenship's mother died in 1877, aged fifty-eight, leaving three children: (1). John Patton Blankenship, subject of this sketch. (2). Gilbert Blankenship, married Jane Bryant, daughter of Esq. John Bryant, of Loudon county, and has five children. (3). Jannette Blankenship, who died in 1881, wife of D. J. Baldwin, a merchant and miller at Clover Hill, Blount county, leaving six children.

Dr. Blankenship married at Clover Hill, Blount county, May 10, 1860, Miss Sallie A. Edmondson, daughter of John H. Edmondson, who grew up in the same neighborhood with the celebrated Gen. Sam Houston. Mr. Edmondson was an original abolitionist and Republican, and is now living, at seventy-one years of age, on his farm in Blount county. His son, Matthew Houston Edmondson, is now sheriff of Blount county, as his brother Capt. James P. Edmondson, was for four years previously. It is said he is the most popular man in Blount county. The Edmondson family in Virginia are a somewhat noted family, one of whom was a colonel in the Confederate army. Mrs. Blankenship's mother was Margaret Dunlap, daughter of John Dunlap. Mrs. Blankenship was educated at Clover Hill and Baker's Creek, was a Presbyterian, and noted for her strict piety, kindliness of disposition, her talent for economical management and her quiet, retiring nature. She died January 24, 1884.

By his marriage with Miss Edmondson, four children were born to Dr. Blankenship: (1). Leonidas Cæsar Blankenship, born June 10, 1861; educated at Maryville College; now reading law in Knoxville; married in June, 1884, Miss Bertha Adams, of Indiana. (2). John Horace Blankenship, born March 24, 1865; now studying in Maryville College. (3). Margaret Lillie Blankenship, born September 7, 1867; now in same college. (4). Minnie Blankenship, born February 20, 1870; now in same college.

Dr. Blankenship was married the second time at Macon, Georgia, November 4, 1885, to Miss Alice S. Taylor, daughter of Charles Taylor, Esq., at his residence. The Taylor family are related to the Brantly family of Georgia and North Carolina; and also to Rev. George Taylor, a noted Baptist divine, of Richmond, Virginia, now missionary at Rome, Italy. Mrs. Alice S. Blankenship is a member of the Episcopal church.

Dr. Blankenship is a member of the Presbyterian church, an Odd Fellow, and in politics a Prohibitionist and Republican, though a Democrat before the war. In 1883, he was president of the Blount County Medical Society, and is now a member of the State Medical Society. In 1882–3, he was the temperance and educational editor of the *East Tennessee News*, published at Maryville. For four years he served at Maryville as examining surgeon for pensioners, under appointment from the general government.

So far Dr. Blankenship has made a success of his life. He owes no man a dollar, has raised a family, has a comfortable property, and is contented and happy in the practice of his profession. His success is due to perseverance and application to his calling ; to staying at one place; being honest in his dealings with mankind, and liberal to the poor. He began without inheritance and owes his position to his own efforts.

On April 7, 1884, he delivered an address before the Blount county Medical Society which attracted attention from the leading medical journals of the country. The following extracts show Dr. Blankenship's estimate of medicine as a science, the duties of a physician, and the honors to which he is entitled: " A profession that has such noble objects in view must be noble. The good that has been conferred on mankind by it is beyond all human calculation. Even among the ancients it was believed to be a gift from God. There are those to-day who hold the same opinion, and are sustained in their belief by the following: ' Honor the physician, because he is indispensable, for the Most High hath created him ; for all medicine is a gift from God, and the physician shall receive homage from the king.' Christ said on a certain occasion, 'They that are whole need not the physician, but they that are sick.' The disciples of medicine, regardless of self, have ever been the friends of humanity. The physician must seem calm and serene though his heart be troubled. He must not lose his reason, but on the contrary think well and apply his remedies promptly and under all circumstances. The physician is not only entrusted with the life of his patient, but also, to some extent, the social, moral and intellectual welfare of the people he practices his profession among are in his hands; for sometimes the domestic curtain is drawn aside, and the troubles are confided to him by the family, as a peacemaker and moral guardian of those interested, whose words of advice and consolation restore hope and bring a calm to the troubled heart, and life is made bright again. How great, then, should be his acquirements, how extensive his knowledge of medicine. Should it be the love of money alone that urges the physician on in the discharge of his duty, his expectations in life, in a certain sense, will be realized; but his life will go out in the end, and the profession will be made no better for his living, for other fields offer more gold. But money cannot pay for the labor that the conscientious physician performs, nor the blessings he bestows; gold cannot buy what charity gives. There is a higher and nobler impulse that prompts the physician to do his duty to his fellow-man and his high and responsible calling in life—that he has the conviction in his own heart that he is doing his duty in relieving suffering humanity, and has the consolation to know that his labors are appreciated by some of the human race, if not by many; by the tears shed by some poor woman, and that emanate from an angelic heart and flow out to soothe the sorrow within, and are like the pearls of the ocean, and more precious than all the gold of earth. Humanity calls the physician from the mansion of the rich to the hut of the poor; and the honest physician will receive his reward here and after he crosses the river of time. Then he will be paid for all his labors."

HON. WILLIAM H. DeWITT.

CHATTANOOGA.

THIS sturdy, self-made lawyer was born October 24, 1827, in Smith county, Tennessee, and is well-known in the legal and political history of the State. Born of parents who were far from wealthy, his father being a preacher and small farmer, young DeWitt, enured in boyhood to the toils of farm life, was in the habit of studying to improve his mind at night as well as in the day, when not otherwise engaged, and in this way became, in a great measure, his own school-master, and learned almost as much without an instructor as with one, mastering some of the branches of mathematics and the first books in Latin without scholastic assistance. In search of knowledge he worked his passage on a flat-boat to Nashville, on his way to Berea Academy, near Chapel Hill, Tennessee, where he studied ten months under Rev. John M. Barnes, one of the best old-time educators in Tennessee. On his return he carried his books and clothing in a pair of saddlebags, thrown across his shoulder, and footed his way home, a distance of one hundred miles, and with only three dollars and a half in his wallet, borrowed from George W. McQuiddy.

After he grew to manhood he lived two years, 1847-8, at Gainesborough, Tennessee, teaching in Montpelier Academy. The next two years he taught in Jackson county. From 1850 to 1856, he lived at Lafayette, Tennessee, teaching in the academy one year, and practicing law five years. In law, also, as in literature, he became his own school-master, thus illustrating the time-worn saying, "The boy is father to the man." But he determined in early boyhood to gain as good an education as perseverance, energy and industry would bring, aided by very limited pecuniary means. This view met the approval of his father, by whom, long before he reached manhood, he was permitted to teach in common schools, and with the money thus accumulated go to various seminaries of learning.

He was licensed to practice law in November, 1850, at Lafayette, by Judges B. L. Ridley and William B. Campbell, and became a member of the American Legal Association in 1851. In 1856-58, a little over one year, he practiced law at Lebanon. From 1858 to 1875, he resided at Carthage, county-seat of his native county. On January 8, 1875, he settled in Chattanooga where he still resides. Both before and since the war, some of the best educated and most intellectual men of the State became lawyers under his instructions, for which he refused compensation. It is a part of his reputation, and one reason for his personal popularity, that he has ever been ready to aid and encourage all worthy and aspiring young men.

Meanwhile, Judge DeWitt represented the counties of Smith, Macon and Sumner in the Tennessee House of Representatives in 1855-6; was renominated in 1857, but declined. He was elected a member of the constitutional convention of 1861, he opposing the convention, which was voted down. In August, 1861, he was elected to the Confederate Congress. The Tennessee delegation to the Confederate Congress stood among the most distinguished men in the whole country, and consisted of W. H. DeWitt, Robert L. Caruthers, James H. Thomas, George W. Jones, John F. House, John D. C. Atkins and David M. Currin. (See Alexander H. Stephens' *War Between the States*, Vol. 2, p. 464.) The proceedings in that body are comparatively unknown, as all the sessions were secret while Judge DeWitt was a member.

In 1872, Gov. John C. Brown appointed him special chancellor in the Fifth chancery division of Tennessee, pending the contest of the election of W. W. Ward by Combs and Cox.

In politics Judge DeWitt was a Whig, and was one of those who lingered long and worshiped devoutly at

25

the abandoned altars of his party, opposing secession with all his might till the war came on, and even then his sympathies and not his judgment led him to espouse the Confederate cause. Since the war he has acted with the Democratic party, but has always been conservative in his views. Though he was always successful in his contests for office, yet, since the war between the States, he has never sought office of any kind though often urged to stand for political and judicial positions. He has never been ambitious for office, and never became a candidate except at the earnest solicitation of his friends, and though conscious of his powers, has been unpretending, and prefers a retired life.

In 1878, he was a member of the judicial convention, held at Nashville, to nominate candidates for judges of the Supreme court. He was chairman of the committee on resolutions in the State Democratic convention in 1876, which nominated delegates to the St. Louis convention which nominated Tilden for the presidency.

Judge DeWitt is a member of the Methodist church. He became a Mason at Lafayette, Tennessee, in Lodge No. 149, has taken all the Chapter degrees, and was one year Worshipful Master of the lodge at Carthage. He was made an Odd Fellow in Martin Lodge, No. 32, at Lafayette, and has passed all the chairs of that order.

Judge DeWitt first married in Jackson county, Tennessee, May 30, 1847, Miss Emilia Price, daughter of Thomas Price, Esq., a large land owner and farmer. Her mother was a Miss Van Hooser. To this marriage were born five children, two of whom died suddenly on the same day with the mother, in 1863; two died in infancy, and only one child survives: Lade DeWitt, born in 1852; educated at the Catholic school, Bardstown, Kentucky; married December 5, 1871, in Smith county, Kentucky, Mr. James Monroe Fisher, a lawyer at Carthage, and has three children, DeWitt, Julian and Bessie.

Judge DeWitt's next marriage, which occurred in Smith county, Tennessee, May 30, 1867, was with Miss Bettie Wilson (a direct descendant on the paternal line of Daniel Boone), daughter of Hughlette Wilson, of Barren county, Kentucky. Her mother was Kitty Bird Wooten, of a leading old Kentucky family. Mrs. DeWitt's grandfather, Gen. Sam Wilson, was one of the pioneers in surveying and laying off entries for land grants in Kentucky and Tennessee. Her sister, Kate, now living at Nashville, is the widow of the late Judge Samuel M. Fite. Her sister, Nelia, married H. M. Hale, a lawyer at Carthage, and her sister, Josie, is the wife of Carroll Denny, a farmer in Smith county. Mrs. DeWitt was educated in Kentucky, by Rev. Dr. Isaac T. Reneau, but finished her education under Rev. Dr. Lapsley, of Nashville. She is a member of the Methodist church. By his marriage with Miss Wilson Judge DeWitt has two children: (1). William Eugene and (2) Hughlette.

Judge DeWitt's parents were both born in 1792, in

South Carolina. His father, Rev. Samuel DeWitt, was an officer in the company of Capt. Wilkinson (grandfather of Peyton Wilkinson), in the war of 1812, under Gen. Jackson. The ancestors of Judge DeWitt's father and mother were in the Revolution of 1776. Judge DeWitt's mother was a McWhirter, and her grandfather, McWhirter, was killed in the battle of King's mountain. Her uncle, Henry Wakefield, was shot through the breast in that war, but lived to the age of one hundred and six years.

In addition to his attainments as a lawyer, Judge DeWitt's literary culture has been so highly appreciated that he has often been selected to deliver addresses on Masonic occasions, fourth of July celebrations, college commencements, and other occasions, calling for varied historical, philosophical, literary and political learning, and oratorical abilities of a high order. His memorial addresses on the deaths of members of the bench and bar have also helped to spread his reputation among the first orators of Tennessee, for he has few equals for pathos and logic. Moreover, he is not infrequently spoken of as a ripe scholar and a gentleman of elegant tastes and manners, but had he cultivated the talent which expressed itself in his young manhood in essays in verse, he might have been classed among the poets. A few only of his poetical attempts remain.

Judge DeWitt is truly a self-made man. By perseverance and industry he overcame all obstacles and obtained a classical education and finally became learned in the law. In his career of life he was given to no evil habits whatever. Truthfulness and integrity were the stars that guided him. He resolved in early manhood to become at least the equal of any one in his profession, if hard study, good morals, energy and diligence would accomplish it. He chose his profession early and bent every effort to succeed. In this time of thought and action he drew much inspiration and lasting benefit from the teachings of his venerated father, and from the "Lectures of Rev. Dr. Hawes to Young Men."

One great fault of his life, however, growing out of kindly nature or his want of power to say " no," is that he has, from time to time, lost heavily by endorsing for others, though he is now, notwithstanding this, in very independent circumstances. As a lawyer, he stands in the front rank of his profession in the highest courts of the State and of the nation, before which he has been almost uniformly successful, though he has never brought all his intellectual resources into full play, except upon occasions that demanded it. As a man he is upright and just in all his transactions, allowing nothing to come between him and the discharge of what he believes correct and honorable. The elements of his character are so fashioned as to imbue him with the strongest sympathies for the poor and the unfortunate through all the grades of society; while his integrity and chivalry command the admiration of all who know him.

HON. THOMAS J. FREEMAN.

TRENTON.

JUDGE THOMAS J. FREEMAN is a native of West Tennessee, having been born in Gibson county, on the 19th day of July, 1827. His parents were of the best class of Tennessee citizens.

Freeman is an English name, and the American families of the name are descendants from an English ancestry. The genealogy of this family, however, is not clearly traceable for more than three or four generations back. The grandfather of our subject, John H. Freeman, was a Virginia planter and slaveholder. The father, Dr. John H. Freeman, was a native of Brunswick, Virginia, and, about 1819, removed to Nashville, where he was engaged for a time in a mercantile establishment. From Nashville, he went to Columbia and merchandised, marrying there in 1825. He died in Gibson county, in 1879, at the age of seventy-four. He was a man of strong and active intellect and nervous temperament, devoting himself the greater part of his life to his practice of medicine, without much thought of accumulating property.

Judge Freeman's mother, *nee* Priscilla Jones, was o rn in Smith county, Tennessee, but raised in Maury, where she married in May, 1825. She was the daughter of Capt. Thomas Jones. originally from Wake county, North Carolina, a cousin of Hon. Nat. Macon, United States senator from North Carolina, at an early day. Her grandfather, Thomas Jones, was a captain in the Revolutionary war. She died in Gibson county, in 1857, leaving ten children, of whom the subject of this sketch is the oldest.

Judge Freeman received a common school education up to the age of fifteen. His early opportunities were limited to the country schools and the county academy. By the time he was seventeen, he had taken a course of medical reading, but he soon determined not to adopt that profession. In March, 1845, he began the private study of law in borrowed books, teaching neighborhood schools in the meantime, until he reached the age of twenty-one. At that period he obtained from Judges Turley, of the Supreme court, and Calvin Jones, chancellor of the district, a license to practice law. He at once opened an office in Trenton, where he practiced till 1861, when he moved to Haywood county. At the close of the war he moved back to Trenton and awaited future developments. In November, 1865, when the courts were reopened, he removed to Brownsville and there resumed the practice of law. He continued to practice there and in the neighboring counties till the spring of 1870, when, by the Democratic State convention, he was nominated, and by the people elected, to the Supreme bench of Tennessee, a position which he has now held fifteen years, having been renominated and re-elected in 1878. His life thus divides itself into two sections—that of lawyer and that of judge.

Judge Freeman grew up in a Whig family, and his first vote was cast for Gen. Taylor for president in 1848, but, at the age of twenty-three, he allied himself with the Democratic party and has ever since been a strict construction Democrat of the Jeffersonian school. In 1855 he made the canvass for Congress against Emerson Etheridge, then regarded as invincible, and reduced his large majority to a very small one. He was a delegate to the Cincinnati national Democratic convention in 1856, that nominated James Buchanan for the presidency. He was ever a man of strong political feeling, but, since going on the bench, he has refrained from any participation in the political contests of the State or nation, beyond the exercise of the elective franchise and the frank expression of his opinion on all questions of public policy, at proper times and places.

Judge Freeman married at Trenton, July 28, 1852, Miss Martha Lois Rains, daughter of the leading lawyer at the Trenton bar, and his own legal preceptor, Rolla P. Rains, a native of Georgia, but who grew up at Winchester, Tennessee. Her mother, originally Elizabeth Evans, was a native of Huntsville, Alabama. Mrs. Freeman was educated at Trenton. She is yet a remarkably handsome, well preserved woman, and is famed for her excellent domestic qualities.

Judge Freeman and wife have had born to them five children, all at Trenton: (1). Willis J., born July, 1854; now deputy clerk of the Supreme court; married Willie Mays, daughter of J. M. Mays, a banker at Columbia, Tennessee, and has one child, Irene. (2). Helen, graduated at the Methodist Female College, at Jackson ; married W. L. Hall, of the Dallas (Texas) Herald, and has one child, Dudley Freeman. (3). Cora, graduated at Jackson ; wife of Mr. J. Dawson, and now residing at Kansas City, Missouri. (4). Thomas J., born November 29, 1859; is a lawyer of the firm of Harris, Turley & Freeman, at Memphis. He married Miss Sallie Matthews, of Trenton, and has one child, Cora. (5). O. B. C., born August 6, 1861 ; now a lawyer at Trenton.

Judge Freeman is a Royal Arch and Select Master Mason and a Knight of Honor. In religion he is a Baptist, and a distinct and affirmative believer in the Christian religion. He joined the Baptist church when but fifteen years of age.

In regard to the civil war, Judge Freeman was a pronounced southern man, and had the courage of his convictions. He promptly enlisted in the Confederate service and, in August, 1861, was chosen colonel of the Twenty-second regiment, Tennessee infantry. He commanded the regiment in the battles of Belmont and Shiloh. At a later battle he was severely wounded and disabled for a month, which was followed by an attack of camp fever, which kept him out of the service till the fall of 1862, when he was transferred to Gen. Forrest and remained with him till the winter of 1864, on staff duty. At this junction, Judge Samuel Williams, of the Ninth judicial circuit, having died, Gov. Isham G. Harris commissioned Judge Freeman as judge of the circuit, but he never qualified. Under the commission he returned home, however, having been released and discharged on account of ill health.

Judge Freeman has been too close a student—too faithful a devotee to his profession—to have given much of his time or thought to the matter of accumulating money. Nevertheless, notwithstanding he found himself at the close of the war ten thousand dollars in debt, he is now in fairly independent circumstances.

In personal physique, Judge Freeman is tall, slender, lithe and sinewy; his face, regularly featured, is intelligent and pleasing and surmounted by a high, intellectual forehead. His eyes are dark, of mild expression ordinarily, but beaming with intellectual light on occasions of exciting interest. To persons not familiar with his capacity for long-sustained work, Judge Freeman's physical appearance is suggestive of a delicate constitution, and even his best friends have sometimes feared that the sword of the spirit would cut through its fleshy scabbard. But an examination of the Supreme Court reports for the last fifteen years will demonstrate that Tennessee has had but few Supreme judges capable of as much judicial labor as Judge Freeman has perfomed within that time.

While Judge Freeman has always kept himself abreast with the learning of his profession, he has found time to sweep the fields of literature, ethics and philosophy, gleaning the richest treasures of thought and storing them in his well-ordered mind until it has been justly said of him that he is one of the most broadly-cultured men in the State of Tennessee. As in legal science, so in current literature, he never allows himself to drop behind the advanced thought of the times. He is an omnivorous reader, devouring book after book, as they are cast from the press, with the avidity of a hungry man. And what is most notable in his case, the argument, the thoughts and, oftentimes, the very language, are transferred from the pages of the book to his receptive mind and held distinctly there, in the keeping of a memory remarkable for the power and accuracy of its retentativeness. His brothers of the bar frequently speak of him as "the walking encyclopedia," or "the peripatetic library." His social qualities are of the most pleasing order and are remarkably well developed. His conversational gifts are brilliant and charming. Especially is he fond of the society of the younger members of the bar, being ever ready to aid them with friendly suggestions and wholesome counsels.

As a lawyer, Judge Freeman was eminently successful in practice. He was critically careful in the preparation of his cases, and was a skillful and eloquent advocate. But it was his mastery of technical pleading that gave him his first and best assurance of success. At the time he came to the bar, the loose methods of pleading, now in vogue under our simplified court procedure, were unknown, and would have seemed to court and bar ridiculously absurd. No man could then hope to successfully conduct a suit at law unless he were able to thread the labarynthine mazes of Stephens and Chitty. A recent writer in the Nashville *American*, speaking of Judge Freeman, relates an incident illustrative of the Judge's readiness and skill as a pleader: "Well do I remember," he says, "a sharp contest between this gentleman and the lamented Scurlock, in the court-room at Brownsville, Judge W. H. Stephens presiding. It was a case of unusual importance. A demurrer was heard and disallowed; then came a plea and a replication; now a rejoinder and surrejoinder; then a rebutter and surrebutter. No Damascus blades ever flashed more rapidly in the hands of skillful duellists than did these steel-bright weapons before an admiring court in the hands of those accomplished pleaders. I recall to-day the delight with which I witnessed the contest. According to the rules of practice, either might have claimed indulgence and delay at any step of the proceedings; but, no, at each succeeding step, the plea was drawn without a moment's delay or reference to the books."

The well-earned reputation which Judge Freeman acquired at the bar, has been well-sustained on the Supreme bench. His love of professional work seems to have grown upon him in his higher sphere of action, and the fruits of his judicial labors have proven that his associates at the bar had not overestimated his learning or his discriminating powers of analysis; neither has there been any disappointment or betrayal of the

universal confidence, based upon an honorable professional career, that he would acquit himself on the bench as an able and upright judge. His decisions command the respect of bar and people. The criticism has been sometimes made by such as prefer the blunt, ponderous, pregnant phrases of a Wright or a Turney, or the sharp, clear and conclusive sentences of a McFarland, that Judge Freeman's opinions are usually too elaborate. But logical elaboration is preferable to insufficiency of argument and authority. One of the Judge's professional brethren, referring to this line of criticism on his opinions, very truly says: "But, for logical precision, chaste diction and strict adherence to the traditions of American law, as they have come down to us, filtered through the minds of Marshall, Story, Webster and Kent, his friends believe, with all due appreciation of the merits of his associates and contemporaries at the bar, that he will bear comparison with the best and noblest of Tennessee's judges." The works of no man are perfect. The highest excellencies in the best must make compensation for some minor defects, and it is a marked compliment to the superior ability and accomplishments of Judge Freeman that the merciless eye of criticism has detected no graver fault in his splendid work than the studious elaboration of argument by which he has taken care to sustain his decisions. His opinions, recorded in the annals of the Supreme court of Tennessee, will be his imperishable monument, than which his ambition could demand nothing worthier or more honorable.

The influences of Judge Freeman's personal life have ever been on the side of morality and religion. As before stated, he is a devoted member of the Baptist church, strongly attached to its doctrines, and a thorough believer in the divinity of Christ and his religion. He is fond of the Sunday-school and neglects no opportunity for mingling with children and addressing them. He is also an ardent friend of the temperance cause. Though he has accumulated no great fortune in worldly goods, he is rich in the consciousness of a life well-spent, and, as has been well said, has achieved for his children the heritage of a "good name," which Solomon says, "is rather to be chosen than great riches."

HON. EDWARD H. EAST.

NASHVILLE.

THE name of Edward Hazzard East, has, for years, been conspicuous on the roll of eminent lawyers in Tennessee. He was born in Davidson county, October 1, 1830. His father, Edward Hyde East, emigrated from Virginia as early as 1806, and settling upon a farm in Davidson county, devoted himself to agricultural

pursuits. He was a man of strong mental characteristics and of much local influence. He was chosen justice of the peace at an early day, and as far back as 1833, became chairman of the county court of Davidson county, a position which he held for many years. With the first appearance of the Whig party in the political arena, he became a Whig and continued in that faith through life. He was one of sixty citizens of Davidson county who cast their vote for Hugh Lawson White in 1836, against Andrew Jackson, for the presidency of the United States. He died at the advanced age of fourscore years and upwards, leaving a handsome estate to his children.

The grandfather, Benjamin East, was a native of England. He came to America and settled in Virginia while it was yet a colony. He served through the Revolutionary war and lived to the ripe age of eighty-odd years.

Judge East's mother, Cecelia Buchanan, came of a family well known as among the earliest of pioneer settlers in Tennessee. Her brothers were Capt. John K., Robert and Thomas Buchanan. She was a woman of quiet, unobtrusive disposition and liberally endowed with those domestic virtues which constitute the crown of the model wife and mother. She instilled into the minds of her children, from infancy, those principles of virtue that have so notably marked their lives. She died in 1870, at the age of eighty years, leaving four of her ten children surviving her, viz.: (1). Malvina, widow of John J. Gowen, who died in Mississippi, in 1842. (2). Louisa, wife of Alexander Buchanan, a farmer of Davidson county. (3). Edward Hazzard, the subject of this sketch. (4). Dr. A. A. East, a physician of Nashville.

The youth of Judge East was that of a farmer boy, though his advantages for early education were quite good and were by no means neglected. When about sixteen years of age, he entered the old Washington Institute in Davidson county, and was graduated in literature from that school in 1850. Having early resolved to become a lawyer, he next entered the law department of Lebanon University, from which institution he was graduated in 1854, with the degree of Bachelor of Laws in a class of eight, among whom were Dr. W. E. Ward (a sketch of whom appears elsewhere in this volume); Levi W. Reeves, of Louisiana; Alfred Elliott, of Nevada; Charles Ready, jr., and Richard A. Keeble, jr., of Murfreesborough. The two last named died during the late civil war. From the date of his graduation to the present time, he has practiced law in Nashville, with the exception of the interruptions caused by the war, and the period during which he occupied the bench as chancellor. During this period, he has held many positions of honor and trust. Indeed, there are few men of his age to be found anywhere upon whom have been bestowed so many marks of confidence and esteem by their fellow-citizens. He was for several years, president of the board of directors of the Tennessee Hospital for the Insane. He is one of the original members of the board of trust of Vanderbilt University, and, for a time, served as the first president of that board. He has been for many years a member of the board of trustees of the University of Nashville, which institution, in 1880, conferred on him the honorary degree of LL. D. He is now president of the board of trust of the Tennessee School for the Blind at Nashville, and has, from its establishment, been a member of the board of managers of the State Normal School, also located at Nashville. Besides these, from time to time, there have been many other like philanthropic positions in the higher line of social duty, though less permanent in character, that his fellow-citizens have called on him to fill, and he has always served with cheerfulness, ability and fidelity.

Judge East has never been a politician in the common partisan sense of the term, though there has never been a time since he attained his manhood, when he has not felt an intelligent and earnest interest in the policies of his State and nation. It may be said of him that he was born and bred a Whig, and when, amid the dark foreshadowings of gathering war, it became only too manifest that the "old Whig party was dead," there was no sadder mourner at its bier than Judge East. At the time his young mind was unfolding to a perception and conception of the politics of his country, the genius of Webster and the spirit of Clay, and, nearer home, the calmer statesmanship of Bell, were improving the mind of the nation. Such men charmed his youthful fancy and became his political exemplars. It was no wonder, then, that he looked with abhorrence upon every movement looking to a dissolution of the Union. Southern by birth and southern in sympathy, he not only felt that the rights and safety of the southern people could only be preserved and protected "in the Union and under the constitution," but that, by the very nature of American citizenship, and in view of the untold disasters that must necessarily follow all attempts to dissolve the government, it was a patriotic duty to maintain the federal Union as the only hope of assured peace and of republican freedom on this continent. Thus impressed, he could not be false to his solemn convictions, despite the obloquy to which he was, for the time, subjected. He did not, nor could not, lift his hand against his southern brethren, neither could he be induced to deal a blow which his conscience forbade. In 1859, he was elected to represent Davidson county in the State Legislature. Our State and presidential elections were not then, as now, held simultaneously. The State election in 1859 took place in August, the legislators being chosen for two years, or until August, 1861, so that the members chosen in 1859 were in office at the time of Mr. Lincoln's election. This Legislature—1859-60—was twice called together in extra session. Judge East had opposed every proposition looking to secession, but when, after President Lincoln's call for troops, he found he was no longer supported by a majority of his constituents, he conscientiously handed back to them his trust and tendered to the governor his resignation as representative. He withdrew from public position and, as before intimated, took no active part in the war.

Upon the occupation of Nashville and Middle Tennessee by the Federal army, in the spring of 1862, Judge East was induced to accept the position of secretary of State. By his conservative counsels and humane suggestions in this position, he was enabled to contribute much—more, indeed, than the public ever knew, toward a mitigation of the necessary severities of the situation. When Mr. Johnson became president, he invited Judge East to a position in the White House, but he declined to accept; and, notwithstanding the president placed the Blue Book at his service to make choice of such office as he desired, he respectfully declined to accept any position that the president could give him. On reaching home from Washington, he found that the president had sent his name to the senate and that he had been confirmed as United States district-attorney for the Middle district of Tennessee. Notwithstanding this was then a far more important office than now—involving as it did, many new and interesting questions growing out of the war—and was quite lucrative withal, he nevertheless declined it with thanks. Subsequently Judge East was twice elected chancellor for Davidson county, but in 1874, he resigned that position and accepted the one he now holds—that of counsel for the Nashville, Chattanooga & St. Louis railway company. His character as chancellor will be treated further along.

In 1874, Judge East was induced to stand as a candidate to represent Davidson county in the Legislature of 1875, and was elected. He was made chairman of the committee of ways and means, the duties of which laborious position he performed with distinction. He was conspicuous during the session for his able and earnest championship of the honor and credit of the State, as against the arguments of those who denied the legal validity of the bonded debt of the State. It was during this session of the Legislature that ex-President Johnson was elected to the United States senate after one of the most exciting contests ever witnessed in our State capitol. To this result the personal influence of Judge East largely contributed.

In 1878, Judge East was nominated for governor by a State convention of the Greenback party of Tennessee, but, although he was strenuously urged to make the race by influences more potential than the organization that nominated him, he could not be induced to take the field.

This completes the list of notable political points in the life of Judge East. Before touching upon his professional career, some points in his personal life may as well be recorded here. Judge East was married in 1868, to Mrs. Ida T. Ward, of Mississippi, daughter of Rev. Henry C. Horton, of the Methodist Episcopal church, South. They have two interesting daughters, Edine H., and Bessie Cecelia—and their family circle, though not a very extended one, is a very happy one. Judge East has demonstrated in his own career, that a professional business life and a religious life are not incompatible, but, on the contrary, may be rendered beautifully harmonious. From an early period, he has been a member of the Methodist Episcopal church, South—not simply a passive layman, making easy his church relations by periodical contributions to its treasury, but an active, zealous member, taking a lively interest in all the enterprises and institutions of the church. He has, for a number of years, been one of the stewards of McKendree church, Nashville, and has served as lay delegate to annual conferences. He was a delegate from the general conference of the Methodist Episcopal church, South, to the Methodist Ecumenical Council, at London, in 1881. As already stated, he was one of the original members of the board of trust of Vanderbilt University. Whatever service the church may require at his hands, or a sense of duty may suggest, is rendered with genuine Christian zeal. He is esteemed by the authorities of the church, as one of the sincerest and wisest of their counsellors.

In personal *physique*, Judge East is of tall, slender figure, and has something of the "lean and hungry" Cassius-like appearance that would indicate a man who does not "sleep o' nights." His face is of the classical type, with an aspect of strong intellectuality and deep thoughtfulness, not "sicklied o'er," indeed, but strikingly suggestive of the constant working of the brain within. His conversational gifts are charming, which his explorations into every field of literature, and his critical observations of every type of humanity and civilization, keep continually supplied with richest material upon which to exercise themselves. Outside of the home circle, he enjoys no greater delight than when finding himself in the midst of a genial and responsive company of friends. He is excessively fond of literary and scientific studies. While he has neglected no branch of the law in the range of his conscientious study, neither has he slighted any opportunity for testing the merits of a new author, or of investigating any novel philosophical problem.

But after all, it is as a lawyer and jurist that he is best known. In the chosen profession of his life, he has best laid the foundations of a great character, to which other personal accomplishments are but ornaments. The way to eminence at the Nashville bar has never been an easy one. Only that merit which has been tried and proven through a long, hard series of laborious years, in daily competition with the best products of the profession, who, themselves, have only developed through the like long, hard series of laborious years, has ever been permitted to stand pre-eminent at the bar of the capital city of Tennessee. There is no royal road to success for a Nashville lawyer, and that any one has attained it, strictly within the line of his profession, is pretty good evidence that he has deserved it. That Judge East has already justly achieved the reputation of a great lawyer is the unanimous verdict of his professional brethren of Nashville and throughout the State. To offer proofs on that point, by way of reciting the various notable triumphs he has enjoyed, would not only be superfluous, but would extend this sketch far beyond allowable limits.

A lawyer is best known to his professional associates, and it must be said to the honor of the legal profession that, while it is subject to the jealousies and envies that afflict humanity in all its branches, there is among the better class of the profession an *esprit du corps*, under the influence of which the true lawyer takes pleasure in bearing testimony to the worth of an honorable associate. Judge East could well afford to commit his reputation, both as a man and lawyer, to the members of the bar among whom, for the last thirty years, he has spent his professional life. Nor can the writer of this sketch do Judge East, or the truth, a better service than to let a few of the lawyers speak for him. One who often crosses swords with Judge East at the bar, and who, himself, has always wielded a Damascus blade—who, besides, is a critic among critics—thus speaks of Judge East: "As an advocate, he has few peers if any in the State of Tennessee. He is a lawyer of extensive and varied attainments, and is equally successful in all the departments of his profession; whether it be in the Supreme, the circuit, the chancery or the criminal court.

"I know no lawyer of as great versatility, nor of as great success; he seems to combine all the elements that are necessary for a successful lawyer and advocate. Besides this, he is a man of extensive literary and scientific culture, and one of the finest conversationalists I ever knew. In this respect, he is absolutely fascinating, and he can be interesting and entertaining alike to infancy and to old age, to the most ignorant and the most intelligent, to white and black ; for he can take the most ignorant negro that ever lived in the South and can charm and fascinate him, and will take pleasure in doing so ; and, in a minute, will be eminently interesting and entertaining in the most refined, elegant literary and scientific circle. The very expression of his face is a pendulum between a smile and a frown ; the frown impressing solemnity, and the smile illuminating pleasantry. He is gentle, amiable and tender ; and yet possesses, and can exercise, the most caustic satire and the most withering sarcasm.

"He has the singular faculty of drawing to himself personal friends, despite political and party ties. He was elected chancellor by the votes of both parties. In a heated contest, in which all parties were anxious for the control of the Legislature, he distanced all his competitors, without a pledge to any line of policy or an enunciation of an opinion on any question involved in the canvass ; and in the House of Representatives was the efficient controlling cause of the re-election of Andrew Johnson to the senate of the United States. No man could have been a more successful politician, but

politics, as far as office is concerned, seemed to have no attraction for him. Even as chancellor, a non-political office, he grew weary of it and resigned.

"He is a firm believer in the Christian religion, a devout Methodist, and has delivered lectures on historic characters of the Bible which have excited warm admiration, and clearly disclosed an ability which would have elevated him to the utmost prominence as a pulpit orator." "I regard his success as being the result of his native ability, his industry, and his warm, genial, kind and noble heart, and an eloquence that is peculiar to himself, and that shines alike in the social circle, on the rostrum, and in the forum. In a word, I think he has more genius than any man I am acquainted with in Tennessee."

The chancellor who succeeded him on the bench, says of Judge East: "He is a first-class lawyer, both in point of learning and ability. As a practitioner, he comes as near being the best lawyer in the State as any man in it. His success is the result of his ability, learning and attention to his business. He is a clever, amiable, agreeable man, and universally popular among all classes, as much so as any man I know. His popularity results from his kind and affable manner, being accommodating and generous to a degree that amounts to self-sacrifice."

An ex-senator of the United States, himself a profound jurist, who had often met Judge East at the bar, offers this pronounced and characteristic opinion :

"Lawyers who have tested the strength of Judge East at the bar, apologize for their defects by speaking of him as the ' great white-washer ;' by which they mean that he is a man who can paint every picture in the brightest colors, bring out the strongest points of a case in the best light, and make the worst cause appear to best advantage. He is wonderfully powerful in advocacy. His ingenuity is most remarkable in reducing his opponent's position to an absurdity. Though he has an office, he can be found anywhere else with as much certainty as there ; for, like Socrates, the philosopher, he spends his time in the streets, mingling with men engaged in the rough roll and tumble of business, in which common sense and the dominant traits of human character have fullest play, and it is doubtless to this fact that he owes much of his power as a lawyer. In this respect, he resembles the late Judge Archibald Wright, of Memphis, who seemed never to study, but was in fact a most diligent student, not of books merely, but of men and business."

A distinguished member of the Supreme court of Tennessee bears this honorable testimony : "Some lawyers excel in chancery suits, some in land litigation, some as advocates, but the best general lawyer in the State—excelling in all departments—is Judge East."

A mere biographer can add nothing to such testimony as all this. There is nothing that needs to be added except a brief reference to his character as chancellor. It could hardly have been otherwise than that a lawyer possessed of the gifts and legal accomplishments above set forth, based upon a moral character that was unassailable, and in which a sense of justice was a cardinal element, should have been an able and upright dispenser of equity from the bench. Gifted with the most subtle powers of analysis, his mind, rapidly and with intuitive accuracy, separated the chaff from the substance and discriminated between the false and the true. The ingenious sophistries of counsellors could not mislead him, nor could extraneous considerations sway him a hair's breadth from the line of duty. The rich litigant and the poor one met "on the level" in his court, and his decrees were accepted as the conclusions of a head and heart, well educated and thoroughly honest. The reversals of his decrees were very rare, and, indeed, except for the purpose of gaining time, not many appeals were taken. There was in Judge East a pleasant freedom from the strained dignity too common to the judicial position, that rendered him, at all times and at all places, easy of access by the legal fraternity. It has been said of him that in light or perfunctory matters, he would "sit at chambers" in a barber shop, a counting-room, or even on a street corner, whenever the inconvenience of repairing to the court-room or his office seemed rather greater than the importance of the matter involved. In short, he had not a particle of the vanity or affected dignity of office. His bearing on the bench or off the bench, towards the profession, was always marked by courtesy, affability and patience. His retirement from the chancellorship was a source of unusual regret.

Judge East is yet comparatively young—just of the age at which English lawyers reach their prime, and English statesmen come to be regarded as fit to deal with the graver matters of state. Though by no means physically robust in appearance, his composition is of that tough and sinewy sort whose capacity for endurance is unmeasured. According to the probabilities of vital statistics, he has yet many years of good life ahead of him. He has prospered financially, and taken bond against the too frequent calamities of old age. His possibilities are yet great, and his capabilities are sufficient to convert them into probabilities and these last into realizations. He is yet one of the live, progressive men of Tennessee.

HON. ROBERT J. MORGAN.

MEMPHIS.

THE paternal ancestry of Judge Robert J. Morgan is of English origin. Three Morgan brothers emigrated from England to America in colonial days, and settled, one in Connecticut, one in Pennsylvania, and the third, from whom Judge Morgan descended, in Virginia. Gov. Morgan of New York, descended from the Connecticut branch of the family, and Gen. Daniel Morgan, of Revolutionary fame, from the Virginia branch. The Morgans of Virginia became connected with the Barbours, a family well and widely known in that State.

Judge Morgan's grandfather, John E. Morgan, was a Virginian by birth, and lived and died in that State. Other members of the family removed to Kentucky and Tennessee, in both of which States there are now a large number of living representatives of the name. Judge Morgan's father was also named John E. Morgan. He was a wealthy merchant and banker at LaGrange, Georgia, and also a successful planter. He was a prominent member of the Methodist church for fifty years, and was noted for his fine business capacity and the highest integrity of character. During the late war, he was appointed by President Davis commissioner of the Confederate government for the State of Georgia. He died in 1868, aged seventy years.

Judge Morgan's mother was Miss Mary T. Brown, daughter of Jere Brown, a native of North Carolina, who moved to Georgia. Her mother was a Miss Beasley, of a well known Georgia family. Mrs. Morgan was reared by her uncle, Hon. Jarrel Beasley, a man of some distinction as a member of the Georgia Legislature.

Judge Robert J. Morgan was born in LaGrange, Georgia, March 25, 1826. He was educated at the University of Georgia, and graduated there in 1847. Having previously determined to study law, he entered the office of Bull & Ferrell, at LaGrange; was admitted to the bar in 1849 by Judge Edward Young Hill, and taken as a partner by his preceptors. Shortly afterwards, Judge Bull went upon the bench, and the firm became Ferrell & Morgan, continuing as such until 1859, when Morgan removed to Memphis with a view of practicing law and engaging in planting in the rich Mississippi bottoms. He was at that time in affluent circumstances, having been very successful in his profession as well as inheriting a comfortable estate. Opening an office in Memphis, he remained there until the beginning of the war.

In 1861, he raised and organized at Chattanooga, the Thirty-sixth Tennessee Confederate regiment of infantry, and being made colonel, held the command for two years, when the regiment was consolidated and he was assigned to duty on the staff of Lieut.-Gen. Leonidas Polk, as adjutant-general, and had to deal with the organization and supervision of Gen. Polk's courts martial while he commanded a corps, and afterwards when he commanded a department. He remained with Gen. Polk until the death of the latter, after which he was assigned by the Confederate war department to the adjustment of claims against the government in Georgia, and served in that capacity till the surrender, when he received his parole at Atlanta. Col. Morgan saw service in the Tennessee, Kentucky and Georgia campaigns, being stationed at Cumberland Gap during the early part of the war, and afterwards participating in the battles of Murfreesborough and Chickamauga, after which he was transferred to the western department with Gen. Polk.

After the surrender, he returned to Memphis and resumed the practice of law. In 1867, he was elected city attorney, and filled the office three years. During all this time he was not allowed to vote, but held the position without taking any other oath than the ordinary oath of office.

In November, 1869, without his previous knowledge, Gov. Senter sent him a commission as chancellor, to fill the vacancy occasioned by the resignation of Hon. Wm. M. Smith, and at the earnest solicitation of the bar of Memphis, he accepted it. An election was ordered in January, 1870, to fill the vacancy, and Judge Morgan was elected over his opponent, Judge John P. Caruthers. This office he filled until the constitutional convention of 1870 declared all the offices of the State vacant. He was a candidate for re-election under the new constitution, and was elected over Col. T. S. Ayres, and held the office until September, 1878. He received three commissions as chancellor within six months—once appointed by the governor, twice elected by the people. Judge Morgan occupied the bench as chancellor of the chancery court of Shelby county for about ten years, first under executive appointment, and then by popular election. In 1878, he voluntarily retired from the bench and resumed the practice of his profession at Memphis. His administration of the judicial office was eminently satisfactory to the bar and to the people, and reflects honor upon his name. He exhibited rare qualifications for an equity judge; for, added to his culture as a lawyer, and his experience at the bar, his natural gifts of fine common sense, discriminating judgment, and a quick appreciation of the right, fitted him peculiarly to administer the system of equity jurisprudence. These qualities served to enable him to reject sophisms and the mere technicalities of the law, and to reach almost unerringly the merit and justice of the cases brought before him; and it may be safely affirmed that no inferior judge in Tennessee ever had fewer of his decisions reversed by the appellate courts. During the period of his incumbency of this office, the business of his court was im-

26

mense, yet by unceasing labor he dispatched it without showing signs of physical or mental exhaustion, which too often begets in judges irritability of temper and a tyrannical bearing towards the members of the bar. While he was impartial and unflinching as a judge, he was uniformly kind and courteous, alike to the older and more eminent and to the younger and more obscure members of the bar, so that he won the respect and confidence of all. During a decade of laborious service, and while constantly passing upon the novel and difficult legal questions that were then before the courts, frequently involving very large interests, he so conducted himself, and so administered the delicate trusts committed to him, that he voluntarily laid aside the ermine unstained by the slightest breath of suspicion that in any instance he was controlled by unworthy influences or motives. After quitting the bench he resumed his practice, which he still continues.

Judge Morgan belonged to the old line Whig party, and was opposed to secession, believing that the southern States had not sufficient grounds for such action. In February, 1861, he voted against calling a convention looking to the withdrawal of Tennessee from the Union, but after the Atlantic and Gulf States seceded, he voted, in June, 1861, for Tennessee to unite with her sister States. When he returned to Tennessee after the war, he joined the Democratic party, and has been one of its ardent supporters ever since. In 1880, he was elector for the Tenth Congressional district on the Hancock ticket, canvassed his district, and also made speeches in other parts of the State.

Judge Morgan has been twice married, first in January, 1851, at LaGrange, Georgia, to Miss Mary H. Battle, daughter of Dr. Andrews Battle. She died in less than one year after her marriage.

In September, 1854, he was married, at Milledgeville, Georgia, to Miss Martha F. Fort, daughter of Dr. Tomlinson Fort, an eminent physician, who wrote a work on the practice of medicine, which has become very popular in Georgia and the southwest. Dr. Fort served several terms in both branches of the Georgia Legislature; was a member of Congress from that State, and was also president of the Georgia State Bank for several years. During all this time he did a large and lucrative practice. He was one of the projectors of the railroad from Atlanta to Chattanooga, and when Chattanooga was a mere landing on the Tennessee river, he made extensive purchases there, having faith in Chattanooga's future, and that it would some day become an important point. He died at Milledgeville, in 1859, at the age of seventy-two. The family was from North Carolina, but removed to Georgia before the Revolution.

Mrs. Morgan's mother, was Miss Martha Fannin, of a prominent Georgia family and a cousin of the celebrated Col. Fannin, who was massacred at the Alamo with Davy Crockett. She was gifted with strong powers of mind, judgment and will, and her impress upon her family has been beneficial and lasting. She died at Macon, Georgia, in 1883, in the eightieth year of her age. Mrs. Morgan was educated at Milledgeville, Georgia, and is distinguished for her gifts in conversation and writing, for her clear conception of every question that is presented, and the vigor of her elucidation. Few ladies in Tennessee have better claims to be called intellectual, while her cultured mind is scarcely surpassed anywhere. By this marriage, Judge Morgan has two children: (1). Mary L. Morgan, born in 1856, now the wife of Mr. John A. Keightly, formerly of Louisville, Kentucky, now of Leesburg, Florida. (2). John E. Morgan, born February 5, 1861 ; now in business with Orgill Brothers, Memphis.

Judge Morgan's family on both sides have been Meth-odists for several generations, and he and his wife are both members of that church. He was made a Master Mason at LaGrange, Georgia, where he also took all the Chapter degrees.

By his personal appearance, Judge Morgan would attract attention in any assemblage. He is a man of fine, portly physique; broad shouldered, and with a well balanced head that at once declares him a man of big brain. As a speaker, he has few equals in the South. His voice is deep, rich, sonorous—of great compass and power. Both at the bar and on the stump, he is a quick, ready, weighty debater. He has always done a large and lucrative practice, and when he brings his strong will power and determination in full play, his client can almost certainly count on a verdict in his favor.

HON. WILLIAM GIBBS McADOO.

KNOXVILLE.

HON. WILLIAM GIBBS McADOO, was born at Island Ford, nine miles northeast from Clinton, Tennessee, April 4, 1820. His ancestor, John McAdoo, came from the old world about the beginning of the eighteenth century, landing at Norfork, Virginia. The grandfather of the subject of this sketch, John McAdoo, was born in the valley of Virginia, February 6, 1757; came to East Tennessee in its early settlement, and was with Sevier at the battle of King's mountain. He was also a follower of Sevier through many a bloody fight with the Indians, and was a participant in the rencontre between the forces of Tipton and Sevier in March, 1788, resulting in the downfall of the "State of Franklin." His home in the latter part of his life was at the mouth of Hynds' creek, two miles east from Clinton, Tennessee, where he was the owner and cultivator of valuable lands, and where he died, December 26, 1830. He was married to Martha Grills, September 4, 1787, by whom he had two sons, William, born May 28, 1788, and John, born June 21, 1790. Here his wife died January 8, 1838, and they are buried together in the family burial ground near by.

John McAdoo, the father of William Gibbs McAdoo, together with his brother, responded to the first call for volunteers occasioned by the outbreak of the hostile Creek Indians in 1813, and participated in the bloody conflicts through which Gen. Andrew Jackson broke the power of the Creek nation forever. Soon after his return, he again enlisted, was made lieutenant, and again, under the leadership of his gallant commander, remained in service until the close of the war by the glorious victory of New Orleans, on January 8, 1815. In August, 1815, he married Miss Mary Ann Gibbs,

daughter of John and Anne Gibbs, *nee* Anne Howard, of Anderson county. Hon. William Morrow, of Nashville, formerly treasurer of Tennessee, is a grandson of John and Mary McAdoo, being the only son of Mrs. Emma Morrow (the oldest sister of W. G. McAdoo), and her husband, Robert Morrow.

The Gibbs family deserves mention. Nicholas Gibbs was a native of Baden-Baden, Germany, but was descended, on his father's side, from an English family of Norman-French extraction, which had its representative with the Conqueror at Hastings; and a devoted follower of Charles the First, a member of this family, on the triumph of Cromwell, sought refuge in Germany. There Nicholas Gibbs was born about the year 1735. Joining a recruiting regiment, he came to America in the French service; in 1758, shared in the glory won by the gallant Montcalm in the repulse of the British at Ticonderoga, and coming to the United States, took part once more against the British. He moved to Knox county in the earliest settlement of that region, and left a large family of sons and several daughters. One of these sons, Capt. Nicholas Gibbs, fell at the head of his company in the battle at Tohopeka; and others were in the same war. One of his sons, George W. Gibbs, was, for a long time, a prominent citizen, lawyer and banker at Nashville; and one of the sons of the latter, Hon. C. N. Gibbs, was recently secretary of the State of Tennessee. Nicholas Gibbs died in 1819, and lies buried at his old homestead, in Grassy valley, Knox county. His son, John Gibbs, born 1769, died, 1840, took part in many of the early struggles with the Indians; was a leading land owner and slaveholder in Anderson county, and was an honored county officer.

He left one son, William Howard Gibbs, and several daughters besides Mary Ann Gibbs, already mentioned, the wife of John McAdoo, and mother of W. G. McAdoo.

Hon. William Gibbs McAdoo, spent his youth on his father's plantation at Island Ford, and at the neighboring county schools, learned to read, and evinced that fondness for books which has been a leading characteristic of his life. His father removed to Knoxville in 1828, and resided there two years to afford his children better facilities to acquire education. Here he made rapid progress in English, and began the study of Latin under Rev. Isaac Lewis. The Union Academy being established at Clinton, his father purchased a farm near that village, and for several years young McAdoo pursued his studies under the teaching of the distinguished Dr. G. W. Stewart, of Midway, Mississippi. In 1835, he entered Rittenhouse Academy, in Kingston, where he made progress in his English, Latin and Greek studies. In 1838, then but eighteen years of age, he was appointed principal of Union Academy, at Clinton, a high compliment to one so young. There he taught two years. In 1840, he was made principal of Franklin Academy, at Jacksborough. After teaching there a year, he was induced to return to Union Academy, where he taught in 1841 and in the earlier half of 1842. In the autumn of this year, he entered the University of Tennessee, at Knoxville (then East Tennessee University), where he took a regular classical and scientific course, graduating in August, 1845. Among his fellow students were Hon. J. B. Cooke, now one of the judges of the Supreme court of Tennessee; Hon. W. C. Whitthorne, ex-member of Congress; Hon. J. D. C. Atkins, United States commissioner of Indian affairs; the late Prof. R. L. Kirkpatrick, of the University of Tennessee, and the late J. C. Ramsey, United States district attorney. On the day following his graduation, Mr. McAdoo was elected to the Legislature to represent the counties of Campbell and Anderson. He was a member of the old Whig party—a party then having a decided Democratic majority against it in the Legislature. In this period, he was one of a committee sent to Memphis at the time of the meeting of the great internal improvement convention of 1845, over which Hon. John C. Calhoun presided, and where he uttered his famous doctrine in relation to the duty and the power of the general government to make internal improvements, wherein he spoke of the Mississippi river as "a great inland sea."

On the opening of the Mexican war, in the spring of 1846, Mr. McAdoo hastened home from an absence, joined a company of volunteers as a private, and sought the Rio Grande. Before marching into the interior, he was elected to the first lieutenancy of the company. His friend, John L. Kirkpatrick, was captain. A long march of the regiment—the second regiment of Tennessee volunteers, the brave and eloquent William T.

Haskell being the colonel—lay through the beautiful valley at the eastern base of the Sierra Madre mountains, through Victoria, the capital of Tamaulipas, to the city of Tampico, a distance of five hundred miles. Thence the regiment embarked for Vera Cruz, and took part in the siege ending in the capture of that city, March, 1847. After a long illness, Capt. John L. Kirkpatrick died at Vera Cruz, after which Mr. McAdoo commanded the company, and led it in the charge at the battle of Cerro Gordo in April, 1847. This charge became the subject, soon afterward, of acrimonious controversy between Brigadier-Gen. G. J. Pillow and Col. W. T. Haskell. The war assuming greater proportions than was anticipated, a sufficient quota of volunteers for three years was called to the field, and the twelve months' men were discharged by reason of expiration of service, and were sent home.

Soon afterward, Mr. McAdoo entered the law office of Judge Edmund Dillahunty, of Columbia, and in 1849, received license to practice law. Early in 1850, he opened a law office in Knoxville; was elected by the Legislature attorney-general for the second judicial circuit of Tennessee; was afterward re-elected by the people and held the office until the spring of 1860. In this position, he won a distinction for vigor and impartiality in the discharge of his duties well remembered by those connected with the administration of justice at that period. In the State convention to nominate a candidate of the Whig party for governor in 1847, he was offered the candidacy by the committee on nomination, but being averse to political struggles, declined the honor.

The war between the States found Mr. McAdoo's health shattered by dangerous disease. The better to protect a slave-property, he removed to Georgia, where he entered the southern service in 1863, and continued therein until the war closed. He participated in the struggles at Kennesaw mountian, about Atlanta, at Macon, and throughout the rest of of the war in Georgia. On its close, he opened a law office in Milledgeville.

On the re-organization of the State government, he received the appointment of district attorney, and afterward was made judge of the Twentieth judicial district. He resigned these to accept the presidency of the St. Mary's and Western railroad company. In 1877, he was offered a position in the *corps* of instructors in his old *alma mater*, the University of Tennessee, at Knoxville, which he yet holds, thus returning to the work which most delighted his early life—*teaching*. Judge McAdoo is the author of an *Elementary Geology* of Tennessee, numerous alumni addresses, literary lectures, centennial poems. etc., etc. He has written much for the press, contributing to the journals of the day editorials, criticisms and news letters. He has unpublished manuscripts, intended for publication, sufficient to make a large volume.

Judge McAdoo has been twice married. In 1849, he married Miss Anna Cleopatra Horsley, eldest daughter of William and Catherine Horsley. Mr. Horsley was a native of Yorkshire, England; married Miss Catharine Arnold in North Carolina, by whom he had two sons, John and Alfred, and three daughters, Anna (Mrs. McAdoo), Eliza (Mrs. Helm), and Catherine (Mrs. McNutt). By the marriage with Miss Horsley, he has two daughters: Catherine, the wife of Mr. Edwin F. Wiley, residing in Knoxville, and Miss Emma McAdoo. Mrs. Anna McAdoo died in 1853, in Knoxville, and lies buried in Knoxville, in Gray cemetery.

In 1857, Judge McAdoo was married to Mrs. Mary McDonald, of St. Marys, Georgia, widow of Randolph McDonald, who died at Savannah from the yellow fever scourge in 1854. Mrs. McAdoo is a great-grand-daughter of Charles Floyd, of North Hampton county, Virginia, a member of the St. Helena Guards in the Revolutionary war, and whose son, John Floyd, located in Camden county, Georgia, having married Miss Isabella Maria Hazzard, of Beaufort, South Carolina. From John and Isabella Floyd, were born four sons and four daughters, whose descendants reside in Georgia and Florida. Of these sons, the oldest, born in 1797, was Charles Rinaldo Floyd, the father of Mrs. McAdoo. He was married to Miss Julia Ross Boog, at St. Marys; and from this marriage were born: (1). Mary Faith Floyd, the wife of W. G. McAdoo. (2). Rosalie Sarah Humes, widow of James W. Humes, of Abingdon, Virginia. (3). Charles R. Floyd, deceased. (4). Richard S. Floyd, of San Francisco, California. The maternal grandfather of Mrs. McAdoo, Mr. John Boog, was a native of Dornoch, Scotland, and married Miss Isabella King, of Falmouth, Jamaica.

Mrs. McAdoo has in her possession, a silver crescent worn on his cap by her great-grandfather, Charles Floyd, as a member of the St. Helena Guards, and bearing the inscription, " Liberty or Death." Her grandfather, Gen. John Floyd, was commander in chief of the Georgia troops called into service at the outbreak of the Creek war in 1813. He led his troops into the hostile country, and fought the Indians in the battles of Chalibbee, Tallassee and Autossee; was afterward in command of the American forces in Savannah until the war was ended. He was a member of Congress afterwards; was a large planter; and his hospitable mansion, on the border of the sea, was the resort of hosts of friends. He died June 20, 1839. His son, Charles R. Floyd, while a youth of sixteen years, took part in the battles fought with the Indians in the Creek war. For his gallantry, he was appointed to a cadetship at West Point, where he received a military education. In 1821, he traveled in Europe and visited Waterloo and other great battle fields. He was appointed by Gen. Winfield Scott to the chief command of the Georgia troops engaged in the removal of the Cherokee Indians in 1838, and performed the duty with such celerity and dispatch, that bloodshed was averted. He received the warm commendation of Gen. Scott. He was an exquisite scholar, poet, painter, and noted for his chivalry, which never knew a stain. He died at his home in Camden county, in March, 1845.

Judge W. G. McAdoo, by his second marriage, is the father of three sons: John Floyd, William Gibbs, and Malcolm Ross; and of four daughters: Caroline Blackshear, Rosalie Floyd, Nona Howard and Laura Sterrett.

As adjunct professor of English and modern languages, Judge McAdoo has under his instruction the classes in higher English grammar, rhetoric, and English literature and history, in our State University; and he still retains the full measure of his vigor and promptitude in the discharge of duty.

HON. SOLON E. ROSE.

PULASKI.

THE lineal ancestry of Judge Solon E. Rose, subject of this sketch, dates authentically, back to Scotland, and the year 1740. Prior to that, however, it is known that the " Clan of the Roses " were located about thirty miles from Inverness, Scotland, and that they were a little noted for their intermarriages with the Campbells and Grahams. The mother of William Wallace, was a Rose, as is stated in the history of the Clans of Scotland. The Rose family coat-of-arms, was a shield with a diagonal bar, having three roses upon it, the whole surmounted by a stag, and bearing the motto, " *Virtus incendit vires*"—" Virtue kindles the strength."

The genealogical tree of the Rose family, reaching back three hundred years, was destroyed during the late civil war. It was transmitted to the youngest son of the oldest son, in continued succession, and in its absence the data herein recorded is given from family tradition. Rev. Dr. Robert Rose, the executor of the vast estate of Gov. Spottswood, of Virginia, a man of eminent ability and social worth, came over to America with Gov. Spottswood, who died about 1740. He had four sons, Henry, Hugh, William and Charles, one of whom, probably Henry Rose, was the direct ancestor of the subject of this sketch. He was related to many prominent families of Virginia.

Henry Rose's grandson, John Rose, was the father of William Rose, the father of Solon E. Rose. John Rose married Elizabeth Davis, and settled on Rose creek, Brunswick county, Virginia, when twenty years old, and there died when near the age of eighty. His relative, Dr. Robert H. Rose, married the sister of James Madison.

Col. William Rose, father of Solon E. Rose, was born on Rose creek, Virginia, December 19, 1779, and moved to Giles county, Tennessee in 1813. He married in Virginia, Miss Elizabeth Winfield Meredith, whose mother was a Winfield, and a relative of Gen. Winfield Scott. Col. William Rose was a farmer; was elected colonel of the county militia; was a Democrat; a Methodist from early youth; a man who never drank a drop of liquor in his life; a remarkably well rounded character, distinguished for his devotion to his church, for his numerous charities, his hospitalities and agreeable, social manners. He was one of the first aldermen of the town of Pulaski, and was associated with Aaron V. Brown and others, who afterwards became prominent. One of his favorite sayings was, "If you meet a Scotchman who seems to be a gentleman, trust him; he'll do to trust." He died May 25, 1851, at the age of seventy-two. His wife, a most heavenly minded and lovely woman, long preceded him to the grave, dying in Giles county, Tennessee, December 31, 1820, at about the age thirty-five. She was born in Brunswick county, Virginia, daughter of David Meredith, whose father came over from Wales. She bore Col. William Rose seven children, all sons, to-wit: (1). Edward Winfield Rose, who was chairman and county judge of Giles county twenty-three years; was also once a member of the Legislature, and next to Thomas Martin, filled a larger space than any man ever in the county. (2). William Meredith Rose, now living in Nashville, was long a merchant and farmer in Giles county. One of his daughters, Henrietta, is the wife of Col. Hume Field, of Confederate army fame. (3). Alfred Hicks Rose, now a farmer in Hardeman county, Tennessee, and was for some years judge of the probate court there. (4). Robert Henry Rose, now a lawyer of fine standing at Lawrenceburg, Tennessee; was chancellor for eight years and circuit judge two years, at Lawrenceburg, before the war. He has never married. (5). Fielding Rose, died, aged thirty, a successful merchant. (6). David Erwin Rose, was a physician and a fine belles-lettres scholar; died at the age of thirty-one. (7). Solon Eldridge Rose, subject of this sketch.

Col. Solon Eldridge Rose was born in Giles county, Tennessee, August 18, 1818. He was educated in the Pulaski Wurtemburg Academy, having previously studied under James McCallum, one of the sterling characters of Tennessee. When eighteen years old, he went to the Florida war and was in the battles of the Withlacoochla, Panasophca and the Wahoo swamp. At the two battles of the Wahoo, he attracted the at-

tention of Gov. Call and Col. Bradford, by his dash in leading the charge. After the battle, Gov. Call called on him and said, "You have won the golden spurs;" and Col. Bradford said, "I have a beautiful daughter that is your prize."

For awhile after, as before the Florida war, he was clerk in a store at Pulaski at liberal salaries. In 1839, he commenced studying law in the office of Shields & Rose, procured license in his twenty-second year, practiced awhile at Pulaski, but shortly afterward located at Lawrenceburg, where, in February, 1843, he was elected attorney-general of that circuit, and held the position six years. At the expiration of his term, every lawyer in the circuit assured him, either in person or by letter, he would have no opposition if he wanted the office again. He, however, declined re-election. He did a very lucrative practice at Lawrenceburg for the ten years succeeding his attorney-generalship. From 1848 to 1859, he was president of the Lawrenceburg bank, one of the banks that paid every dollar of its currency after the war. During that time he was also engaged in manufacturing business, and in connection with Gen. Allen and others, built the Crescent mills in Lawrence county, at an expenditure of $46,000. He moved from Lawrenceburg to Pulaski early in 1859, and formed a partnership with Judge John A. Tinnon, which continued till Tinnon's elevation to the bench, June, 1883. He has, himself, been repeatedly commissioned special judge of the chancery and circuit courts. He has, for many years, been a director in the Nashville & Decatur railroad, and in 1869, succeeded Mr. Thomas Martin, deceased, as president of the Giles National Bank, of Pulaski. In his professional career, Judge Rose has practiced at the courts with President Polk, Govs. Neill S. and John C. Brown, Hon. A. O. P. Nicholson, Judges Archibald Wright and Milton Brown, Gen. Gideon J. Pillow, and others who became distinguished in political life and in their profession.

Judge Rose however is not more noted for his legal learning and facility of speech, than for his literary acquirements. He has long been regarded as one of the most eloquent orators in the State, while he has ever proven himself exceedingly felicitous with the pen. As early as 1844–45, he edited, for twelve months, the Academist, a literary paper published at Lawrenceburg, and demonstrated his ready acquaintance with the classics, and was perfectly at home among the standard literati. He has been always an active supporter of schools and other public enterprises. He is a member of the American Legion of Honor, and in religion, his proclivities are Methodistic, though he is not a communicant; and while the rubric of his faith is not so diversified as that of some, yet he is orthodox.

Judge Rose was raised by a Democratic father, but up to the war he himself was a Whig—every drop of blood in him. In 1848, he canvassed his congressional district as the Whig presidential elector on the Taylor and Fillmore ticket, associated in the campaign with Gov. James C. Jones, Hon. Thomas A. R. Nelson, Hon. John Netherland, Col. Searcy and other Nestors of the days of old line Whigism. He made a brilliant reputation as a political orator in that campaign. During the war, he was in active sympathy with the Confederate cause, though up to the time Lincoln's proclamation for troops was issued, he was a strong Union man, and made the last speech in Giles county for the Union cause. Since the war, he has been among the great leaders of the Democracy of Tennessee, one of the ablest and most ardent.

In 1881, he was elected, and stood elected three-quarters of an hour, United States senator from Tennessee, but was defeated at the last, by what means the following impromptu speech by Col. Rose will show. This speech was delivered before the joint convention of the Legislature—an exceptional honor, as no man not a member of either house had ever before been called to address a joint convention of the Legislature. He was escorted to the stand and and being introduced by his successful competitor, Judge Howell E. Jackson, spoke as follows: "Gentlemen of the convention: This call is unexpected, but I thank you for the privilege of tendering my profound thanks to the convention for the expression of their confidence and their zeal in my behalf during the recent contest for United States senator. To those who supported me, I feel that I could coin my heart into words of gratitude for their earnest support. Although I did not announce myself a candidate, asked no man to vote for me, nor wrote a single letter to forward my election, yet I am no less grateful for the distinguished honor paid me. Not that I was indifferent to so proud a position, for it is an honor the most exalted ambition might covet. If I had been elected, others could have carried more ability to the discharge of its duties, but none more zeal and devotion to the interest of our common country. I should have given my support to questions that were national, if I believed them just and would subserve the general interest of the country. Not that I would forget my own loved South. Thou land of my nativity!

> "Where e'er I roam, what other lands to see,
> My heart untraveled fondly turns to thee."

Tennessee has given her share of genius and valor to the world, has kept step in accord with the graced rythm of human progress, and her destiny and her prosperity are linked with the entire country. The election of Judge Jackson will add luster to the name of Tennessee, and the manner of his election I hope will redound to the common good. I hope ere long all political asperities shall vanish—the winter pass, the spring-time come and the voice of peace be heard in the land, from the Aroostook to the Rio Grande, from Puget sound to Tampa bay, from lake to gulf, and from sea to sea—united in one bond of brotherhood, moving on

to the developing of our mighty material wealth, and accomplishing our sublime future. Notwithstanding these reflections, I can but regret that having been twice elected to the proud position of United States senator I yet failed to retain it. As the contest waged, like a sea when conflicting winds sweep its troubled surface, there arose one amid the storm—one who I had seen but once before in life, when all my preconceived opinions of him vanished. Frank, open, manly in his bearing—he seemed the very embodiment of pluck and generous rivalry; while the waves were rolling, alternating me victory and defeat, he waved over the distracted elements the wand of the magician, and the line gave way; my friends faltered.

> 'Clan Alpine's hosts were backward borne[*]
> Yea, where was Roderick then?[*]
> One blast upon his bugle horn
> Were worth a thousand men.'

And the sequel of the story was my defeat. Then vanished the dream of my youth, the earnest wish of my manhood, and the solace of my declining years. But with the memory of such an honor, I can well afford to fold around me my political robe and "lie down to peaceful slumbers." Why regret? Fame is but the castle ambition builds, and like the cloud pavilion in the sky is ever at the mercy of the inconstant winds. Now, in the presence of Judge Jackson, with my hand on my heart, I thank him for his magnanimous conduct during the fervor of the contest. Gentlemen of the convention—without regard to party—I hope your lives may be long, prosperous, useful and happy. May the Christian's hope guide you through life's devious journey; may "all your ways be ways of pleasantness and all your paths be peace." May your roof-trees distil blessings as did the sky of Hermon, and around your firesides cluster life's fondest endearments."

Since the foregoing memorable episode in the life of Judge Rose, he has not sought or held political office, except in 1884, when he was unanimously elected by the State Democratic convention of Tennessee, as a delegate for the State at large to the national Democratic convention at Chicago, which nominated Cleveland and Hendricks.

Col. Rose's reputation as an orator, which has caused his selection as orator of the day on numerous notable occasions, was enhanced by the eloquent and brilliant speech he delivered on "Giles county Day," May 17, 1880, at the Nashville Centennial Exposition—the occasion being the dedication of Giles county's tribute, the burthen of the speech being the history of the county, and especially of the three governors that county has furnished the State. The *Pulaski Citizen*, May 20, 1880, says of that speech:

"Giles county has reason to be proud of the manner in which Col. Solon E. Rose represented her people at

---

[*]This in reference to Hon. Roderick Random Butler (Republican), who influenced the votes that defeated Judge Rose.

the Centennial Exposition Monday last. His oration was a chaste and finished effort, perfectly adapted to every requirement of refined and cultivated taste, and so exquisitely in harmony with the inspiration and patriotic purposes of the day as to attract general attention to its marked superiority over any similar effort, either written or uttered, that the Centennial season has yet given birth to. For delicacy of conception, elevation of thought, brilliancy of style, and poetic fervor, it is worthy of being classed with the finest literary productions of the day. It is the superb contribution of a scholar, a poet and a patriot to the annals of the time, and one that Giles county will feel an especial pride in preserving."

Col. Rose married in Lawrence county, Tennessee, November 14, 1843, Miss Marcella Buchanan, who was born in that county, June 25, 1823, daughter of M. H. Buchanan, Esq., once sheriff of Giles county; a farmer and large slaveholder. Her paternal grandfather, William Buchanan, was from South Carolina, and settled on Buchanan's creek (named for him), in Giles county, about 1810. His mother was the daughter of Maximilian Haynie, the South Carolina astronomer—an historical character.

Mrs. Rose's mother, nee Miss Ethalinda Bumpass, was daughter of Dr. James Bumpass, and niece of Dr. Gabriel Bumpass—the latter a remarkable but eccentric physician, who afterwards settled in Lawrence county, where he died, ninety-nine years old. Mrs. Rose's oldest brother, Franklin Buchanan, was speaker of the Tennessee House of Representatives in 1847–48. Another brother, Dr. Robert M. Buchanan, is now a prominent physician at Okalona, Mississippi, and her brother, Gabriel J. Buchanan, is a brilliant lawyer at Aberdeen, in the same State. Her nephew, Col. John M. Simonton (son of her oldest sister, Mrs. Gilbreath Simonton), was a colonel in the Confederate service, and president of the Mississippi senate.

Mrs. Rose was finely educated at Pulaski, and has all her life borne the reputation of being a woman surpassingly handsome, and is an exceptionally lovely character, from what is the brightest page in human life—her devotion to duty. Through all his trials in life, Col. Rose confesses to have found in her an admirable aid. Though a comfortable and hospitable housekeeper, she is noted for her good, sound common sense economy, always avoiding extravagance. The children born of this union are four in number: (1). Solonia Marcella Rose, born November 16, 1844; studied first under Mrs. Adams; then at Dr. Prettyman's Female College, Louisville; graduated at the Columbia Athenæum; married Capt. John D. Flautt, cashier of the Giles National Bank; has four children, Marcella Rose, Solon J., Mary Lizzie, and John Haynie. (2). William Haynie Rose, born April 23, 1847; educated at Pulaski; now a farmer in Giles county; married Miss Maria Louisa Stacy, daughter of Major J. B. Stacy, clerk and

master at Pulaski; has one child, William Haynie. (3). Elizabeth Ethalinda Rose, born in 1849, died in May, 1858, aged about nine years. (4). Solon Edward Franklin Rose, born December 19, 1850; educated first at Pulaski; graduated at Washington Lee University; for a time was cashier of the Giles National Bank, but is now a large planter in Lowndes county, Mississippi. He married Miss Laura Marcella Martin, granddaughter of Thomas Martin, of Pulaski, and niece of Mrs. O. M. Spofford. She is the daughter of William M. Martin, now deceased (see sketch of Thomas Martin elsewhere in this volume). Her mother, nee Miss Lizzie Otis, is a niece of the late Mrs. Dr. Thomas A. Atchison, of Nashville, and of Mrs. Tyree Rodes, of Giles county. They have one child, Lizzie Otis.

Col. Rose prides himself on the fact that his children are of exemplary habits, of high social standing, prosperous in life, and have been signally fortunate in their marriages.

Col. Rose began life without means, though at one time his father was a man of fortune, but was so reduced by his exceeding kindness of heart in assuming suretyship for others, his estate was much diminished. On this account, the son was compelled, the last few years, to educate himself, yet he bravely devoted himself to his profession; was prompt in meeting his obligations and faithful in the discharge of his duties. In this way he got a start, acquired a reputation, and when he had surplus money, invested it in bank stock or manufacturing enterprises. He has never failed to be at his banking office on time in fifteen years, unless seriously absent. His chief characteristics as a business man and a lawyer, are his punctuality—attending to business at once—seeing to his cases in all their detail, and pursuing them with indomitable perseverance. He now owns and is interested in three fine farms, and is reckoned among the solid men of the State. He owes his success in life to his father's temperate example, never having taken a drink in a saloon in his life; to abstaining from vices; to being just to all men, and to assuming the demands of duty with courage and determination.

When Col. Rose was asked what counsel, drawn from his experience and a review of his own history, he wished to transmit to his posterity, he said: "Have some definite aim in view; select some pursuit and follow it with perseverance and fixedness of purpose; labor assiduously. Few things of value are acquired without labor. Labor is our heritage, but the parent of success. Accumulate, but accumulate honestly. Carry conscience into business and politics as well as into ethics. Always be prompt in the discharge of duty. Promptness is a high virtue. 'Punctuality is the politeness of kings.' Cultivate the social virtues, for they are the graces of life, but not to the neglect of the sterner virtues, for devotion to duty is the brightest page in the book of life. Be always polite; politeness is the cheapest of all investments for the profit it brings. Be proud but not vain; pride is the strength of character; but vanity is its weakness. Never forget you are a gentleman! Never forget you are a lady! Restrain your temper, but preserve your manhood. The beauty of female character is in the cultivation of the gentler and nobler graces of the head and the heart, and a patient discharge of the duties in her sphere. Restrain the extravagances of

prosperity, but meet misfortune with fortitude; for human virtue should be equal to human calamity. Avoid indebtedness. Be temperate. Aid religious progress by an exemplary life, rather than by doctrinal theories. Christianity, by the spread of the blessings of civilization beyond all other creeds, is alone sufficient to inspire faith in its truth, and command our zealous support."

COL. JOSEPH RHEA ANDERSON.

BRISTOL.

THE Andersons are of Scotch-Irish origin. The lineal ancestors of Col. Joseph Rhea Anderson, subject of this sketch, were rebels in Scotland, settled in the north of Ireland, and subsequently emigrated to Augusta county, Virginia. The grandfather, John Anderson, in 1773, moved to what is known as the "Block House," an old fort, at the head of Carter's valley, Scott county, Virginia, when the country was a wilderness. He raised a family of four sons, William, John, Audley and Isaac, and four daughters, Mary (who married John Skillern), Elizabeth (who married William Christian), Sarah (who married Rev. Andrew Galbraith), and Jane (who married Rev. John Heniger). The family was twice run out from their dwelling there by the Indians, and took refuge in Fort Clapp, near Abingdon, Virginia. John Anderson died October 13, 1817. His wife, *nee* Rebecca Maxwell, was a descendant of the Campbell family, of whom Alexander Campbell was the most notable. She died February 21, 1824.

The youngest son of John Anderson was Isaac Anderson, father of the subject of this sketch, who raised a family of twelve children on the old homestead. He never accumulated much property except in lands. His character was that of a careful, God-fearing man. He was a Sunday-school teacher, and every Sunday evening he asked and rehearsed the questions in the catechism to his family, and it was the regular Sunday work of his children to get those lessons. He was known as Col. Isaac C. Anderson, of Scott county, Virginia, having charge and control of the militia of his day. He filled the office of magistrate in Scott county over twenty-five years. His leading trait of character was unswerving integrity. He could not bear to hear a man tell a falsehood, and was apt to tell him of it if he did. His death occurred February 7, 1872.

Col. Isaac Anderson's wife was Miss Margaret Rhea, who was born on the homestead of her father, Back creek, Sullivan county, Tennessee, August 7, 1791. She was the daughter of Joseph Rhea, a descendant of Rev. Joseph Rhea, who lived at Pontotoc, Pennsylvania, son of Rev. Joseph Rhea, of the Presbyterian church. Her mother, *nee* Frances Bredin, came from Ireland to this

country, a widow with five daughters, and settled at what is now known as the Byar's farm, Washington county, Virginia. Mrs. Anderson was well educated in the common English branches. Her characteristics were firmness, decision, industry and perseverance. In the rearing of her children she made persistent effort in teaching them to be self-sustaining and self-reliant, and always to keep out of debt. She was exceedingly economical and taught her children economy and saving habits. She died April 24, 1873, having been the mother of twelve children : (1). Rebecca, who married Joseph Newland. (2). Joseph Rhea, subject of this sketch. (3). John, died March 12, 1849. (4). Audley, married Miss Cornelia Alexander. (5). Samuel Rhea, married Miss Mary Rader. (6). Frances, married J. J. Hughes. (7.) Eliza, married D. J. Carr. (8). Sarah Ann, married H. S. Kane. (9). Caroline, died unmarried, June 27, 1830. (10). Mary, married J. H. Earnest. (11). Isaac C., married Nannie Stuart. (12). Jane, married William Stuart. The most of those surviving are now living in Sullivan and Washington counties, Tennessee.

Joseph Rhea Anderson was born October 25, 1819. His first fourteen and a half years were spent on the farm with his parents. His principal book talent was in mathematics, and he studied the rudimentary branches by himself, as also grammar, dictionary, geography and astronomy later on, when he went to live with his uncle. The first money he ever made was fifty cents, received for a bushel of Irish potatoes, which he raised on his own patch on the farm. He kept that half-dollar two or three years, thus laying the foundation of his future banking house. In March, 1834, being not yet fifteen years old, he began as a clerk in the store of his uncle, Samuel Rhea, at Blountville, Tennessee, on a salary of fifty dollars a year and board, and remained there until October, 1842—eight years—in which he acted as salesman and deputy postmaster. During this time he saved seven hundred and fifty dollars, his salary having been gradually increased. When twenty-one years of age he borrowed five hundred dollars from his father and five hundred dollars from an uncle, and went into business for himself on one thousand, seven hundred and fifty dollars capital, at Eden's Ridge, Tennessee. He remained there till March, 1844, paid back the five hundred dollars borrowed from his uncle, but his father would never receive the money borrowed from him, as he intended, as he said, to give it to his son, but the son redeemed the note, with interest, in February, 1872, after his father's death, and the money went to the heirs of the estate.

In March, 1844, he went into partnership at Blountville, with his uncle, Samuel Rhea, and remained equal partner, taking charge and conducting the business, until September, 1853, when they dissolved partnership, he having previously purchased of his father-in-law, Rev. James King, one hundred acres of land at what is now known as the town of Bristol. Col. Anderson is the founder of the town of Bristol. He laid out the lots and made a plat of the town in 1852, and is now the only man living there that was there at the time. This one hundred acres, lying partly in Virginia and partly in Tennessee, he named Bristol, after the great manufacturing city of Bristol, England, in the hope that it might some day become a great iron manufacturing center. In September, 1853, he moved his family to Bristol, when it was a large meadow, and commenced business as a merchant, in the house now standing at the corner of Fourth and Main streets.

He conducted that business in his own name until 1860, when he took two of his clerks—young men—John P. Wood and J. M. Hicks, into partnership, the firm name being changed to Anderson, Wood & Hicks. Col. Anderson went into the banking business, leaving his partners in charge of the mercantile house. Both businesses were abandoned in 1862, in consequence of the war, and he kept out of the strife as long as he could, but finally acted as assessor and collector of war taxes, collecting only Confederate money, from 1862 to 1865.

He resumed business as a merchant in the spring of 1866, and continued alone until 1870, when he formed a partnership with his brother, Audley Anderson, and nephews, John C. Anderson and A. B. Carr, under the firm title of J. R. Anderson & Co. He left control of this house in charge of the other members of the firm, and in 1870 re-engaged in banking. The firm continued until March, 1882, when Mr. Anderson sold out to J. C. Anderson and A. B. Carr, who are still in the trade at Bristol.

In 1876, he established the First National Bank of Bristol on a paid up capital of fifty thousand dollars. After running that bank awhile he took up the State charter bank, October, 1879, until October, 1883, when he formed the National Bank of Bristol, of which he is now president. The capital has not been changed, though it has been increased, which is a matter private. The bank is reported on a good footing, and does a general banking business. In 1842, Col. Anderson was worth seven hundred and fifty dollars; in 1852, seven thousand dollars; in 1862, twenty thousand dollars; in

1872, twenty thousand dollars; and in 1882 he paid taxes on sixty thousand dollars, his property consisting chiefly of real estate and bank stock, while as a banker he does a business of over two million dollars per annum.

Col. Anderson, from his early life and throughout, as clerk, merchant, trader and banker, has conducted his business upon the enduring basis of honesty and truthfulness. These principles he inculcates in his family, and also impresses the great principle that man makes nothing unless he saves it, and nothing only by practicing self-denial through life. Young men experiment at something and fail, then strike out at something else; this, he believes, is getting out of a safe boat into one that is leaky. He has had but two occupations in life, merchandising and banking, both in the same line, and his advice to boys is, "stick to one business and make a success of it, as you can, no odds what the business is." He has cultivated staying power, saving power, and worked on an average eleven hours a day.

Col. Anderson married at Sapling Grove (now Bristol), June 5, 1845, Miss Melinda W. King, born June 27, 1821, daughter of Rev. James King, a Presbyterian minister, of a Virginia family. Her mother, nee Miss Mourning Micajah Watkins, was born in North Carolina, daughter of Col. Watkins, a planter, near Halifax. Mrs. Anderson on her mother's side, is related to the Williams family, of Tennessee. Mrs. Anderson graduated at the Young Ladies' Seminary, Knoxville, under Dr. Esterbrook. She is noted for her traits of kindness and her work with the infant classes in Sabbath-school, and having joined the Presbyterian church in 1836, has been a faithful and constant Christian worker from that beginning.

By this marriage six children have been born: (1). James, born April 4, 1846; still living with his father, an afflicted child. (2). Sarah Ann, born August, 1847; died May 6, 1853. (3). John Campbell, born March 27, 1850; graduated at Princeton, New Jersey, 1872; now a merchant at Bristol; married his cousin, Sarah Ann Anderson, daughter of Audley Anderson. She died in September, 1884, leaving five children, Audley King, Joseph Rhea, Margaret Melinda, Alice Florence, and an infant, who died the week after the mother. (4). Isaac Samuel, born December 9, 1854; attended King College, Bristol, and graduated at Hampden-Sidney College, Virginia; unmarried; is now a Presbyterian minister, and has been an evangelist six years in Lee and Scott counties, Virginia; present residence, Jonesville, Virginia. (5). Margaret Micajah, born November 4, 1857; graduated at Rogersville Female College, and afterwards at Oxford, Ohio; married John H. Caldwell, son of Rev. George A. Caldwell; now book-keeper in the First National Bank, Bristol; has three children, Margaret Melinda, John Hardin, and Joseph Rhea. (6). Joseph King, born August 10, 1861; died January 3, 1863.

Col. Anderson's boyhood was exemplary, so much so

27

that he thought himself as good as members of the church, and he did not see the necessity of joining a church until, when eighteen years of age, he attended a revival in 1838, at the Presbyterian church in Blountville, conducted by Rev. Daniel Rogan. He kept up his connection with the Blountville church from 1838 to 1853, when he removed to Bristol, and joined the church there. He has been an elder for the past twenty-seven years, and a Sabbath-school teacher forty-five years; was superintendent of the school at Bristol from 1853 to 1860. He regularly attends the Sabbath-school to this day; however, preferring to teach, loving to study the lessons and to investigate the Bible.

Col. Anderson does not know the taste of brandy or whiskey; never drank a drop of intoxicating liquor in his life, and has never tasted wine, only in the sacrament of the Lord's Supper. He has never chewed tobacco. He smoked cigars occasionally, after his majority, but since his marriage has not used tobacco in any form. When a boy he never dissipated his nights, but stayed in the counting-room at the store, studying. He has never been sick in bed a day in his life, all attributable to his regular habits of eating and drinking wholesome diet. In personal appearance, he looks glad and grateful; stands five feet ten inches high, and weighs one hundred and sixty-eight pounds.

In politics, he began as a Democrat, but as is natural to suppose, he believes in paying every dollar of the State debt, and opposed the 50-3 settlement. The only office of a political nature he has ever held was from 1858 to 1876, when he was either the mayor or

a member of the board of aldermen of Bristol. In 1862 he became a Mason, and has taken twelve degrees, including Knight Templar, and is now Eminent Commander of Johnson Commandery at Bristol, and has served as Worshipful Master and Captain of the Host. Since 1842 he has been a Son of Temperance, and has occasionally lectured on temperance. He is now Grand Worthy Patriarch of the State of Tennessee, elected in October, 1883, and again in 1884. Outside of the church, his principal work has been that of advocating temperance, organizing societies and conducting "Bands of Hope"—taking little boys into the pledge, some of whom are now grown men, and frequently write him letters of thanks for his care in setting them out in life on a temperance basis. Ninety per cent. of the members of his "Bands of Hope" have stood faithful to the pledge.

Col. Anderson was a railroad director from 1863 to 1865, having at that time charge of the funds of the East Tennessee and Virginia road. In 1868 he became a director again and continued such until 1883, under the auspices of the East Tennessee and Georgia railroad.

His life is one of great simplicity and directness of manner and unimpeachable integrity, his object and aim being to elevate the morals of the people and bring them up to a higher standard. As a rule he has few intimate, personal friends outside of his family, and very few persons know much about his business. But his philanthropic life has won for him the reputation of being "a good man," and what title is higher or more honorable than that?

PROF. A. T. BARRETT, LL.D.

WINCHESTER.

A TEACHER whose pupils in their junior year can calculate eclipses, and develop all the formulas of plane and spherical trigonometry, is entitled to the notice of a biographer, and the attention of those who would assist in moulding the institutions of the country and leave their impress on the times.

Prof. A. T. Barrett is such a man. He was born at Kingsville, Ohio, April 12, 1847, and there spent his boyhood, working on a farm in the summer and going to school in the winter till 1858, when he went to Detroit, Michigan, and spent one year with his oldest brother, Myron E. Barrett, then president of the Bryant & Stratton Mercantile College, that city. He then returned to Kingsville, entered the academy there, under the tuition of Profs. C. W. Heywood and A. J. Barrett, LL.D., the latter being his brother, a graduate of the University at Rochester, New York, and now pastor of the Baptist church in that city. Under their tuition he

studied four years, but for lack of means did not go to college. Instead, he went to Niles, Michigan, in 1863, and entered the service of J. S Tuttle, where he spent two years, when he again returned to Kingsville, where his parents lived, and studied in the academy another year. In 1865, he entered the University of Rochester, remained there four years, and graduated in 1869, having taught school, at odd times, to get means to pay his way. On graduating he took the highest prize given in the university—the Davis gold medal—a prize given for excellence in scholarship and oratory. He then went to Loweville, New York, and became connected with the Loweville Academy, occupying the chair of belles-lettres; thence to Erie, Pennsylvania, where he became associated with his brother-in-law, M. R. Warner (who had married his sister, Emily Barrett), as general insurance agent, his field being western Pennsylvania and eastern Ohio. After remaining in this position nearly two years, he was, in the summer of 1871, elected by the trustees of Mary Sharp College, Winchester, Tennessee, professor of mathematics, and has filled that chair ever since, with honor to himself, to the institution and the South.

In politics, Prof. Barrett is a Democrat; in religion, a Baptist. He is also a member of the Knights of Honor and of the Knights and Ladies of Honor. He joined the church at the age of fifteen, and has always lived the life of a consistent and devoted member. Thus he had a good induction and a good "send off," being well equipped for the contest with a rough roll and tumble world.

Prof. Barrett married at Kingsville, Ohio, August 22, 1871, Miss Kate C. Stanton, born February 23, 1848, daughter of Warren Stanton, a merchant of that place, who was arrested by the Federal authorities during the war for hurrahing for Jeff. Davis, and was confined at the Columbus military prison, where he contracted a cold, which resulted in his death. His father was an old resident, and one of the early settlers of Kingsville, Ohio, having moved there from New York in 1817.

Mrs. Barrett's mother, *nee* Miss Mary Wellman, of a New York family, is now living with Prof. Barrett at Winchester. Her other children, Jimmy and Fred, died in early life. Mrs. Barrett was educated at Kingsville, is a lady of rare culture, and is noted for her exceptional good judgment and administrative ability. Before marriage she had a successful experience as a teacher, and is now a member of the faculty of Mary Sharp College.

To his union with Miss Stanton, three children have been born to Prof. Barrett, all born at Winchester: (1). Daisy A., born September 18, 1872. (2). Maud S., born September 6, 1874. (3). Roy M., born August 7, 1877.

The Barretts are English people. One of Prof. Barrett's ancestors fired the first gun in the American Revolution. There were two divisions of the family; one came south; one remained in New England, and from this latter branch Prof. Barrett is descended. His father, Amos Barrett, was a native of Oneida county, New York, moved to Ohio, a single man, and engaged in farming. He has held several offices in the town of Kingsville, is a man of fine brain, scholarly and of undoubted integrity. His life has been consistent, and he has been a leader in the Baptist church at Kingsville for a generation, and is one of the standard men of that place. He married (1827) Miss Maria Brown, of a New York family, by whom he had ten children, eight of whom are living: Myron, Perry, Judson, Stephen, Clinton, Emily (wife of M. R. Warner, before mentioned), Susan Adelaide and Albert Tennyson, subject of this sketch. The two children that died were Clarinda and Adelaide, the latter Prof. Barrett's twin sister.

Prof. Barrett's mother died in August, 1881, at the age of seventy, a lady remarkable for devotion to her children, making every sacrifice for their education, her life being one of toil for this purpose till her death. All the qualities which adorn woman were conspicuous in her. She was never so happy as when making others happy. She, also, was a Baptist. A few years before her death her golden wedding was celebrated, at which were present her children and nineteen grandchildren.

Beginning life without a cent, Prof. Barrett has achieved financial success as well as distinction in his profession. Strict economy and a sacrifice of every interest in the performance of duty, lie at the bottom of his success. Working with patience, satisfied with moderate income, and with an eye single to the accomplishment of one thing; turning a deaf ear to flattering entreaty from other directions, and with a determination to make character in his chosen profession of mathematics, he has won a most enviable fame as a teacher of rare culture and excellence, and possessing executive ability, which opens the future in most promising aspect.

As a teacher, some of his methods are somewhat novel and peculiar. The fundamental principles to which he adheres in all his instructions are: 1. To generate in the student a love for the *subject* under consideration, and not to move a wheel until he succeeds in that. 2. To generate in the student a desire to acquire an education, as an end rather than as a means; thus reversing the theory so long held by educators of the past. 3. To move upon the principle that education is the growth of the individual mind, and not mere mental accretion. 4. That instruction, unless assimulated, is food undigested. 5. That education is a force which acts from within outward, and an essential element of this growth is the consent of the pupil's *will*. He holds that you can no more educate a child than you can grow an oak. The child is the germ of the man, as the acorn is the germ of the oak; as we may supply moisture, heat and light to the one, to *induce* growth, so we may furnish instruction to the other, by means of which the mind is developed. Instruction is food; but it must be *taken*, masticated, digested and assimilated as material food is. 6. In the government of his school he throws the responsibility upon the honor of the pupil, while recognizing the wisdom of Solomon, that a child left to herself will bring her parents to shame.

It was through the personal persuasion of Dr. Z. C. Graves that Prof. Barrett accepted the chair of mathematics in Mary Sharp College. He received the degree A.B. in 1869, that of A.M. from the university at Rochester, New York, in 1871, and that of LL.D. from the Southwestern Baptist University at Jackson, Tennessee.

Two of his brothers, Judson and Stephen, graduated at the same university (Rochester), the former in 1854; the latter in 1859. Stephen Barrett is now principal of the high school at Lincoln, Nebraska. Perry Barrett is a physician of considerable eminence in Oregon. Clinton Barrett is a prominent and efficient railroad man, now located at Chattanooga, Tennessee. Myron Barrett has attained great celebrity as a penman and business man. His sister, Emily, is a lady of high literary culture, and his sister, Susan, stands in the high-

est rank as a musician, both as a pianist and vocalist. Every member of the family are Christians in fact as well as in name, and adorn society wherever they go. It is a talented and brainy family.

CAPT. W. D. HAYNES.

BLOUNTVILLE.

THE Haynes family is of German origin, as the family features so plainly indicate. The original German name was *Heine.* The celebrated Robert Y. Hayne, of South Carolina, was of the same family though the name is spelled somewhat differently.

Capt. W. D. Haynes' grandfather, George Haynes, was a native of east Virginia, Westmoreland county; was a farmer; a soldier in the Revolutionary war, and a member of George Washington's body-guard. His son, John Haynes, father of Capt. Haynes, was born in Carter county, Tennessee, and was a millwright by occupation. He married Miss Elizabeth Hyder and moved to McMinn county, where he died in 1835, at the age of thirty-five, leaving four children: (1). James. P. Haynes, who married Miss Margaret Elliott, and now lives at Dayton, Nevada. (2). Martha J. Haynes, now wife of John W. Hyder, Carter county. (3). William D. Haynes, subject of this sketch. (4). John T. Haynes, who died in 1865, unmarried.

Capt. Haynes' mother, *nee* Elizabeth Hyder, was born in Carter county, Tennessee, daughter of Michael Hyder, a farmer, who lived to his ninety-ninth year on the place where he was born. His father, John Hyder, came from Germany; was a Revolutionary soldier, and settled in Carter county, near Gen. Taylor's, among the first settlers of the county. Capt. Haynes' mother (who afterwards married John Hill) is now living at the age of seventy-eight, in McMinn county, and is as stout and active as most women are at fifty. She is a Southern Methodist, and is a lady of straightforward, unpretending manners, of simple piety, and strong common sense. She had three brothers, Ben, Hampton and John Hyder. The latter was trustee of Carter county, and also represented his county in the Tennessee Legislature, and won for himself the name of "Honest John Hyder." Her sister, Eleanor Hyder, married James P. Haynes, Capt. Haynes' paternal uncle. Her half-brothers, by her father's second marriage (with Sarah Bowman), were Samuel Hyder, Joseph Hyder, and her half-sister was Catharine Hyder. The latter married Hampton Edens, of Carter county.

William D. Haynes, subject of this sketch, was born in McMinn county, Tennessee, November 15, 1833. His father dying when he was two years old, his mother returned with her four children to Carter county, and

there he lived with his grandfather, Michael Hyder, till 1844, going to school, going to mill, tending stock, making sugar, grinding apples to make apple brandy— in short, a farmer's boy of all work. In the meantime, his mother having married John Hill in Carter county, and moved back to the homestead in McMinn county, ten miles west of Athens, on Rogers' creek, in 1844, William went to McMinn county and worked on his mother's farm the following five years. The best part of his early life was spent in this way. His step-father, John Hill, was an industrious, thrifty man, without education, who kept him at hard work, and frequently against his inclination. Young Haynes had an ambition to educate himself. His step-father tried to persuade him to remain on the farm, but William ran away to Georgia and worked with the Irish laborers near Tunnel Hill, in getting out string timber for the Western and Atlantic railroad, then in course of construction. At this employment he received eight dollars a month for four months, but he had resolved to accumulate money with which to educate himself, and already determined to become a lawyer. He then came to Bradley county, Tennessee, and worked several months as a common laborer at ten dollars per month, in helping to grade the East Tennessee and Georgia railroad. In 1850 he entered Hiawassee College in Monroe county, Tennessee, and remained there till June, 1853, when he began teaching his first school, ten months term, being on Chatata creek, five miles from Charleston, in Bradley county. In 1854 he taught on Chickamauga creek, in Hamilton county, at forty dollars a month. In 1855 he joined the "copper craze" at Ducktown, Tennessee, but after operating there six months was unsuccessful in his speculations, the company spending fifteen thousand dollars, "all for nothing." Undaunted, however, he still persisted in his determination to become a lawyer. So, after selling his interest in the farm in McMinn county for the purpose of educating himself, and being still three hundred dollars in debt for his college expenses, he commenced reading law in March, 1856, with his cousin, Hon. Landon C. Haynes, at "the old Tipton place," eight miles east of Jonesborough, and after reading with him two years, and in the meantime acting as private family tutor, preparing his cousin's sons for college, he obtained license to practice in 1858, from Chancellor Seth J. W. Luckey and Judge D. T. Patterson. When he at last obtained possession of his much coveted law license, he wrote on it "*Nil Desperandum*," a fitting motto, and one, too, which has guided him in his manly struggles all through life. He at once located at Blountville, May, 1859, and has successfully practiced there ever since, except during the war.

In May, 1862, he was commissioned a captain in the quartermaster's department of the Confederate army, and assigned to post duty at Knoxville, Morristown, Jonesborough, and other places; in 1863 was assigned to duty as brigade quartermaster on the staff of Gen. William E. Jones, and served in East Tennessee and southwestern Virginia from the summer of 1863 to the spring of 1864, when he was transferred to the army of northern Virginia; assigned to duty as quartermaster of the Sixteenth Virginia cavalry, Col. Ferguson, and part of the time, in 1864, as brigade quartermaster with Gen. McCausland's cavalry brigade, and as such was in the last raid made into Pennsylvania in 1864, when McCausland was ordered to burn the town of Chambersburg. In December, 1864, he came home on furlough, and was captured by Gen. Stoneman on his Salt Works raid near Bristol, December 14, 1864. He was then sent as a prisoner, *via* Nashville, Cleveland, Ohio, Buffalo, New York, and Philadelphia, to Fort Delaware, where he was kept in confinement till June 17, 1865.

In July, 1865, he resumed his law practice at Blountville, and has continued there, practicing in that and the adjoining counties, and in the Supreme court. In 1870 he was nominated on the Democratic judicial ticket for attorney-general, with Hon. Robert McFarland (afterwards Supreme judge) for chancellor, and Hon. Felix A. Reeve for circuit judge, but was defeated by Hon. Newton Hacker, who obtained two hundred and fifty-six majority, the usual Republican majority being about two thousand.

Capt. Haynes was chairman of the Democratic executive committee of the First congressional district from 1876 to 1882; has attended about all the State conventions of his party, and generally taken an active and more or less conspicuous part in the proceedings. He was originally a Whig, voted for Bell and Everett in 1860. He became a Mason in 1868, in Whiteside Lodge, No. 13, Blountville; has taken the Chapter degrees and served as Master of his lodge sixteen years, from 1869 to 1884, inclusive. He is a Southern Methodist, and has been for ten years a Sunday-school superintendent.

Capt. Haynes married first in Carter county, Tennessee, his first cousin, Miss Margaret Haynes, youngest sister of Hon. Landon C. Haynes, daughter of David Haynes, a plain, unlettered farmer, trader and ironmaster, who was at one time a man of considerable wealth. Her grandfather, George Haynes (also the grandfather of Capt. W. D. Haynes), left nine sons and

three daughters. The sons were David, James, John, George, Joseph, Jonathan, William, Christopher and Aaron. Of these David Haynes married Rhoda Taylor, a first cousin of Nat. M. Taylor's father, Andrew Taylor, who was a brother of Gen. Taylor. (For a history of the Taylor family, see sketch of N. M. Taylor, elsewhere in this volume). David Haynes had seven sons and five daughters. The sons were Landon C., George, Matthew T., David, James, Napoleon and Nat. T., and the daughters were Lavinia, wife of George F. Gammon; Mary T., wife of Lawson Gifford; Edna, wife of Alexander Harris; Emma, wife of Nat. G. Taylor, and Margaret, wife of Capt. W. D. Haynes.

Of the sons, Hon. Landon C. Haynes was the most noted of the family. He ran two unsuccessful races for Congress against Andrew Johnson and one against Hon. T. A. R. Nelson. He was a member of the Tennessee Legislature at one time, and speaker of the Senate; was a member of the Jonesborough bar, and prominent among such distinguished lawyers as Judge Deaderick, Gen. Thomas D. Arnold, Hon. T. A. R. Nelson, Judge Milligan, Hon. John Netherland, and Hon. Joseph B. Heiskell. He was an elector for the State at large in 1860, on the Breckinridge ticket. He served with Hon. Gustavus A. Henry as a Confederate senator from Tennessee during the war, and left a reputation as one of the finest orators of Tennessee, ranking in eloquence and ability with Bailie Peyton, Meredith P. Gentry, William H. Polk, Gus. A. Henry, Jo. C. Guild, James C. Jones and Andrew Johnson, with all of whom he made canvasses. His son, Hon. Robert W. Haynes, now living at Jackson, Tennessee, has twice represented Madison county in the Legislature.

Of David Haynes' daughters, Emma is the wife of Rev. N. G. Taylor, and mother of Hon. Robert L. Taylor, both ex-members of Congress. Her son, Hon. A. A. Taylor, made a brilliant canvass as elector for the State at large for Garfield in 1880; has once represented Carter and Johnson counties in the Legislature, and is now engaged in the practice of law and in farming on Nolachucky river.

Mrs. Haynes' sister, Edna, is the wife of Rev. Dr. A. N. Harris, a prominent Southern Methodist minister, and her son, Nat. E. Harris, is now a leading lawyer at Macon, Georgia.

By his first marriage Capt. Haynes has three children : (1). Rhoda E., born June 24, 1860; graduated from Sullen's College, Bristol, 1882. (2). Mary T., born December 25, 1861. (3). William Lee, born March 2, 1865.

Capt. Haynes next married at Blountville, Tennessee, September 30, 1869, his second cousin, Miss Maggie Haynes, daughter of Matt. T. Haynes, a lawyer, and brother of Landon C. Haynes. Her mother, *nee* Miss Margaret Dulaney, was the daughter of Dr. William E. Dulaney, of Blountville. Her grandfather, Dr. Elkana Dulaney, of "Medical Grove," his home near Blountville, was a member of the Tennessee Legislature. The Dulaney family is famous for the number of physicians among them for generations back. They are of French Huguenot extraction. Dr. Joseph E. Dulaney, Mrs. Haynes' uncle, was a surgeon of note in the Confederate army. Her uncle, Dr. N. T. Dulaney, represented Sullivan county two terms in the Tennessee Legislature, and is considered a leading physician in upper East Tennessee. Mrs. Haynes is a grand-daughter of Mrs. Mary Dulaney, who was a daughter of Gen. Taylor, the grandfather of Nat. M. Taylor, of Bristol. Mrs. Haynes has one brother, Hal. H. Haynes, a lawyer, at Blountsville. Her sister, Lannie, married N. C. St. John, a lawyer, in Smith county, Virginia. Her half-sister, Mattie J., is the wife of Dr. J. M. King, of Bristol. Her aunt, Eva, is the wife of Rev. J. W. Bachman, of

Chattanooga. (See Dr. Bachman's sketch elsewhere). Her aunt, Carrie, is the wife of Judge Charles J. St. John, chancellor First division of Tennessee. Her aunt, Mary, is wife of Dr. M. M. Butler, a leading phy sician at Bristol. Her aunt, Lolie, is wife of George B. Smith, an artist and merchant at Bristol. Her aunt, Ellen, is-wife of Fulton St. John, a successful farmer in Smith county, Virginia.

By his second marriage Capt. Haynes has three children : (1). Lannie May, born January 6, 1875. (2). Roberta Young, born September 7, 1878. (3). Matt. Dulaney, born August 29, 1882.

Capt. Haynes has stuck to one business, to one place ; has avoided extravagance and dissipation, and won his standing by hard work, economy and steady purpose to achieve success.

HON. NEWTON WHITFIELD McCONNELL.

HARTSVILLE.

NEWTON WHITFIELD McCONNELL, now of Hartsville, was born in Marshall county, Tennessee, May 22, 1832, and was raised there, near Mooresville, on his father's farm, plowing, hauling, going to mill, splitting rails and doing everything a boy ever did on a farm. As a boy he was full of mirthfulness, fond of sport, fond of athletic play at school, and, after the crops were laid by, was always a regular attendant at the neighborhood schools until his sixteenth year. He then spent five months at Pleasant Grove Academy, near Culleoka ; five months at the Mooresville Academy ; four months at the Lewisburg Academy, and five months at Jackson College, Columbia, Tennessee. He then entered Alleghany College, Meadville, Pennsylvania, and after a course of two years and three months, graduated an A.B., in 1855, taking the Latin salutatory in his class of twenty-one members. Three years after he had the degree of A. M. conferred on him by his *alma mater*. In 1856 he married and taught school at the academy at Girard, Pennsylvania, two years, having under him some one hundred and fifty pupils.

In May, 1857, he came to Wilson county, and taught school at the Taylorsville Academy two years, then removed, September, 1859, to Hartsville, where he has lived ever since, teaching school from September, 1859, to February, 1862. From February, 1862, to the end of the war, he was in the Confederate army, and in prison. He first enlisted in Col. James D. Bennett's Ninth Tennessee cavalry, and was with this command until after the reorganization of the regiment immediately following the battle of Shiloh, when Col. Bennett, having raised a new cavalry command in Tennessee, Judge McConnell joined Company G, Fourth Tennessee

cavalry, known afterwards as Ward's cavalry, in Gen. John H. Morgan's command. He remained with Morgan until after Bragg's retreat from Kentucky and location at Murfreesborough, when he was commissioned as captain to raise a company. After having recruited the company, he was captured near Hartsville, in February, 1863, and lay in jail in Gallatin for two months, and was then taken to Fort Delaware and held with fifty-nine other officers, as hostages, subject to retaliation for any harm that might befall Streight's men, who had been captured by Forrest at Rome, Georgia. From Fort Delaware he was taken to Johnson's Island in the latter part of 1863, and remained there until the night of January 1, 1864, when with four others, he made his escape, crossing Sandusky bay on the ice, but was recaptured at Toledo, taken back to Johnson's Island, and remained there until he was taken to Richmond, March 2, 1865, and never was exchanged. He, however, went to his command, Ward's cavalry, then in Gen. Breckinridge's department, at Abingdon, Virginia. When Gen. Lee surrendered, Gen. Breckinridge disbanded his army, and Capt. McConnell went with Col. Giltner to Mount Sterling, Kentucky, where he surrendered, in May, 1865. He was in the battle at Shiloh, April 6, 1862 ; battle of Hartsville, December 6, 1862 ; in Morgan's " Christmas raid " into Kentucky, and in various skirmishes.

While Judge McConnell was in the army his wife and child (Frank W.), were at Hartsville until September, 1864, when Mrs. McConnell went to her father's in Pennsylvania, and remained there until the war closed. Peace established, he brought his family back to Hartsville, where he taught in the academy two years. In August, 1867, he was licensed to practice law by Judge Andrew McClain and Chancellor Barry, the law having been his objective profession for years. He practiced in the courts of Sumner, Smith and Macon counties, and in the State Supreme court until February, 1875, when he was commissioned circuit judge, by Gov. James D. Porter, and held the position under that appointment until August, 1876, when he was elected by the people to fill out the unexpired term of Judge S. M. Fite, which expired September 1, 1878. In August preceding he was elected for the full term of eight years, which expires September 1, 1886.

In 1872, Judge McConnell was elected State senator for the counties of Sumner, Trousdale, Macon, Smith, Jackson and Clay, and served in the senate of 1873, as chairman of the committees on corporations, and tippling and tippling houses. He introduced and had passed the "Local Option Bill," but Gov. John C. Brown vetoed it, on the ground that it had passed irregularly in the house.

In 1872, he was a candidate for Congress from the Fourth Tennessee district, but in the congressional convention the "two-thirds rule" was adopted, and though at one time he came within one-sixth of a vote of getting the requisite two-thirds, finally failed, Judge Fite getting the nomination, and McConnell the judgeship made vacant by Fite. Judge McConnell laughingly says he "shot at the buck and killed the doe that time," which only shows, however, that the Lord knows better how to take care of a man than he does himself.

Politically speaking, Judge McConnell sucked Democratic milk when a baby, and has been a Democrat ever since. When eighteen years old he joined the Presbyterian church and is now an elder, and has often attended as a lay delegate the presbyteries and synods of the church. Raised and educated in that church, he loves it dearly and is orthodox in his faith, though liberal in his views of other denominations. He is an active churchman, as indeed he is active from his temperament in everything he goes about, and could not well be any other way. He began his business life on limited means, but is now in comfortable circumstances. He has been heard to say: "The only lamp that has guided my feet along the pathway of life is, whatever my convictions taught me was right and my duty I have unfalteringly done it."

But this biographical sketch would not be complete without a more specific notice of his judicial career. In his administration of both the civil and criminal law, he has shown rare ability, and achieved signal success. In civil controversies he has given litigants general satisfaction. And when appeals have been prosecuted to the Supreme court, his judgments have borne the closet scrutiny and seldom been reversed. Possessing a mind thoroughly trained, and capable of correct discernment of the most intricate distinctions, he successfully masters the most difficult legal problems.

In his administration of the criminal law, he has made himself an indispensable factor of our State judiciary. He has held the reins of the law with a firm hand, and always unflinchingly adhered to the discharge of his duty. He has superior administrative ability, as shown by the clearing up of the crowded dockets of his circuit. He is an enemy of all crime, and pursues with an unsparing hand the gambler, illegal liquor seller and pistol carrier. He often reminds the grand juries in his charges that sober people rarely commit crime, hence their duty by every lawful means to suppress the sale of liquor to them, and thus prevent crime.

As a public speaker he is fluent, never wanting for language, earnest and magnetic.

In 1883, he was Grand Master of Masons of the State of Tennessee, having previously filled the office of Master of Union Lodge No. 113; Grand Orator of the Grand Lodge, 1873; Grand Senior Warden, 1874; twice Deputy Grand Master, and is a Knight Templar of Baldwin Commandery, Lebanon. He is also a Knight of Honor.

Judge McConnell is the uncompromising foe of intemperance. When a child his father, who was a very ardent temperance man, made the son pledge eternal animosity against liquor and the liquor traffic; hence, his well-earned reputation as the leader of the temperance movement in Tennessee. He has closed every saloon in his judicial circuit by the enforcement of the four-mile law. So much for what a father can do through a fearless and obedient son. More than this, the family name is unsullied throughout, not a drunkard among them.

Judge McConnell married his wife near Meadville, Pennsylvania, February 26, 1856. She was Miss Nannie Elizabeth McCall, daughter of Capt. Samuel and Martha McCall. Her father was a prosperous farmer, of Scotch-Irish stock. Her mother was pure Welsh, daughter of David Morris, a native of Wales. Mrs. McConnell comes of a plain, unpretentious, common-sense family of the very highest reputation, belonging to the great middle class of society, and is connected with the Campbell family, of Pennsylvania, the same family that Gen. Robert Hatton, of Tennessee, was connected with, Gen. Hatton's father and Mrs. McConnell's father being cousins. Her salient traits are self-sacrificing devotion to her family and the good of others, intelligence, good strong judgment about affairs, benevolence, being specially kind to the sick, and possessing the highest sense of honor; hence, she is beloved by all who know her. She is naturally lively and cheerful, consequently is often taken for Judge McConnell's second wife, and her son has not infrequently been asked if she was not his sister, so well preserved, youthful and happy does she appear.

By this marriage three children have been born: (1). Francis Winston (Frank) McConnell, born January 26, 1861; graduated B.S. at Vanderbilt University, May,

1883, and is now a professional teacher; married, August 20, 1884, Miss Mollie C. Corley, of Davidson county. (2). Odell Whitfield McConnell, born July 4, 1868. (3). Annie Eloise McConnell, born April 26, 1873.

The McConnell family is of Scotch-Irish stock, and came from the north of Ireland. Judge McConnell's grandfather, Emanuel McConnell, was born at Port Tobacco, Maryland, and was left an orphan at eight years old, in the care of his uncle, who joined a colony to move to South Carolina. The colony started, but the uncle remained behind to attend to some business, sending Emanuel on with the colony. Soon after, the uncle was killed by the Indians, hence, when Emanuel reached South Carolina, he was cut off from his immediate relations, and never knew much of the history of his family. He joined the regular army in the Revolutionary war and participated in the battle of the Cowpens, the siege of King's mountain, and was under Sumpter and Morgan, and fought in the partisan wars in South Carolina. He married Miss Armstrong, of South Carolina, and left a large family, three sons, John, Jeremiah and James; and five daughters, Elizabeth, Nancy, Tabitha, Rachel and Patsey. He died in March, 1843, in Marshall county, Tennessee, at the very advanced age of ninety years. He was a pioneer settler in that part of the country—a plain man, noted for his firmness, honesty and patriotism. His son, Jeremiah McConnell, was Judge McConnell's father. He was born in Georgia, came from there to Tennessee when a small boy and died, in 1871, at the age of seventy-four,

leaving seven children: (1). Calvin Luther McConnell. (2). Harriet Atwood McConnell, wife of Nicholas Cheatham. (3). Newton Whitfield McConnell, subject of this sketch. (4). Amanda Edwards McConnell, widow of William Rutledge. (5). Aseneth Morrison McConnell, wife of William Bryant. (6). Jackson Watts McConnell, a farmer on the old homestead in Marshall county. (7). Washington Emmons McConnell, a farmer in Marshall county.

Judge McConnell's father was a man of very strong native intellect, of rugged honesty; unambitious, would never hold an office; profoundly religious, a very great student of the Bible, and in his latter days would read little else; was cautious and prosperous in business, accumulated a good estate and took care of it, and, as said before, was a very ardent temperance man. His wife, *nee* Annabel D. Martin, was born in North Carolina, daughter of William and Mary Martin. She came with her parents to Tennessee when a small girl, and is now living, at the age of eighty-one, with her son, Jackson McConnell, in Marshall county. She is a woman of great purity and goodness of character, devoutly religious and noted for her benevolence. She is a model housekeeper—a lady of the old school—self-reliant, self-helpful, and takes great pride in her children and grandchildren, the latter of whom now number twenty-three. Her mother's maiden name was Barbour. Her brothers fought on the patriot side in the war of the Revolution. One of them rose to the rank of colonel in the Continental army.

CAPT. WALTER S. BEARDEN.

SHELBYVILLE.

THIS ripe scholar, successful lawyer, ex-soldier, and popular gentleman, was born in Petersburg, Lincoln county, Tennessee, January 10, 1844. As a child he was fond of study, was an apt scholar, and by the time he was twelve or thirteen years of age was in the leading classes in mathematics and the classics in the academy he attended. At fifteen he began to assist in teaching, always choosing the advanced classes, and began to support himself " before there was a hair upon his face." Since fifteen years of age he has cost no man a cent. At sixteen, he carried a class through Davies' Bourdon (algebra), having himself solved every problem in it. He had mastered the curriculum in the schools near his home before he was old enough to go to college, and continued to assist in giving instruction till the fall of 1860, when he entered Emory and Henry College, Virginia, and remained till the following spring, when the college closed on account of the war. From his earliest years he has been a great reader and studied with keen interest a great variety of miscellane-

ous works. Often he and his brother would lie in bed at night and read until 2 o'clock. In this way he acquired a valuable stock of information on many subjects besides cultivating facility of expression and becoming familiar with the language of standard writers. Returning to Tennessee in the spring of 1861, he taught a country school near Petersburg a few months.

He next assisted in raising a company for the Confederate service—company E, Forty-first Tennessee regiment—and was made second-lieutenant, although not quite eighteen years old. At the battle of Fort Donelson he was captured with his regiment and imprisoned several months at Camp Chase and Johnson's Island. After the exchange and reorganization of his regiment he was elected first-lieutenant, and during the last two years of the war was captain of his company. He saw war in all its vicissitudes—cavalry fights, infantry fights and fights with gunboats—the field, the march, the camp and the prison. He was in the campaign around Vicksburg, during which his regiment formed a part of Gregg's famous brigade, and went through one of the toughest campaigns endured by any body of troops during the struggle. He was in the Dalton and Atlanta campaign from New Hope church to Jonesborough, during which time his company suffered severely, and Capt. Bearden was three times wounded. He was at Peachtree Creek, Georgia, on July 20, 1864; on the right of Atlanta in the same month, and at Jonesborough, Georgia, August 31, 1864, where he received a severe wound in the thigh, which disabled him and put him on crutches for the rest of the war. After the Jonesborough battle he went to Aberdeen, Mississippi, and there remained till the surrender.

During the latter part of the war Capt. Bearden organized a body of men and protected the cotton in a large section of the country from persons who were trying to get it away before the arrival of the Federal troops, who expecting to find it would probably have laid waste the country if disappointed in what they regarded as war booty. Hearing that the planters would be held accountable for all of the cotton that ought to be in that region, Capt. Bearden and the men whom he drew around him, protected it until the arrival of the Federals and thus saved many plantations from pillage and destruction. At the close of the war he went to Meridian, Mississippi, to get his parole, and was pressed into service by the Federal commander to assist in preparing paroles, and made them out for nearly five thousand Confederate soldiers. His twin brother, Edwin R. Bearden, who was a lieutenant in his company, and had commanded it at Chickamauga, where he was severely wounded, was with him on this occasion, and was also pressed into the same service of paroling Confederates.

Capt. Bearden returned to Petersburg, Tennessee, after the war was over, and being in very poor health took to doing all sorts of hard work, such as cutting and hauling wood, in hope of restoring his health. In the latter part of 1866, he moved to Shelbyville and assisted Maj. Randolph in Dixon Academy several months, teaching a part of each day and spending the rest of his time reading law in the office of Samuel Whitthorne, Esq. Early in 1867 he was admitted to the bar by Judge Henry Cooper and Chancellor Steele, and at once began practice in partnership with Mr. Whitthorne, continuing with him a little more than a year, since which time he has practiced alone, always doing a large business and leading a very active life.

Previous to the war all of Capt. Bearden's political predilections were in favor of the Whig party; in later years he has been a Democrat, but never an "offensive partisan." He has been chairman of the Bedford county Democratic executive committee, has presided at numerous political meetings and attended various conventions, but while taking a lively interest in politics, and freely expressing his opinions on whatever

28

questions came up, he has steadily refused to become a candidate for any office whatever, though often solicited to do so.

Capt. Bearden became a Mason in Mississippi during the war, and was made a Royal Arch Mason, under a special dispensation from the grand Masonic bodies of Mississippi, about one month after he was twenty-one years old. He became High Priest of Tannehill Chapter, No. 40, R. A. M., at Shelbyville, about 1870, and held the position for ten years. He became a Knight Templar in Murfreesborough Commandery, No. 10, in 1877, and attended the Triennial Conclave of the order at Chicago in 1880. He has taken a great interest in Masonry, and has collected many rare and valuable books on that subject.

Capt. Bearden has at different times taken a considerable part in newspaper work, and during 1870 and 1871, wrote for the Nashville Banner over the nom de plume of "To Date," and contributed a column or more each week, which formed a complete history of Bedford county during those years. He also took a warm interest in newspaper work in his own town, and though not officially connected with any of the papers, assisted greatly in establishing the Shelbyville Commercial, and wrote for it about one year during its infancy. He has always been esteemed a ready, pointed and effective writer.

He has been interested actively in fire insurance for a number of years, representing the Liverpool, London and Globe, the Home, of New York, the Phoenix, of Hartford, and for a while the old Franklin, of Philadelphia, as well as numerous other companies, and has done a large business for them in his part of the State. He has been attorney for the Nashville, Chattanooga and St. Louis railroad for several years. He was one of the promoters of the Sylvan mills, near Shelbyville, and has been a director in the company since its organization; is also a director of the Charter mills at Wartrace.

Capt. Bearden's father, Dr. B. F. Bearden, a native of South Carolina, came to Tennessee in his youth. He was a man of great breadth of mind, a leader in his profession, a thinker, and a man of learning, but withal very modest. He died in 1870. All of the Beardens in this country are related, and are supposed to be descended from the early French settlers of South Carolina. As a family they have been remarkable for their sound, practical, common sense. Capt. Bearden's mother was Miss S. M. Blake, of Lincoln county, a lady of Scotch blood, and a sister of Rev. Dr. T. C. Blake, of Nashville.

Capt. Bearden married in February, 1874, Miss Maggie C. Whiteside, daughter of Thomas C. Whiteside, a well-known lawyer of Shelbyville. Her mother was Miss Robinson, of Winchester, Tennessee. To this union have been born two sons and three daughters.

Capt. Bearden has been a member of the Presbyterian church about twelve years.

He began life with nothing in the way of capital, but with a good education, backed by industry and energy, punctual attention to business and an earnest desire to succeed. He always strikes while the iron is at welding heat. His methodical arrangement of his business, as well as his information on a great variety of subjects, has contributed largely to his success. Every paper is kept in its proper place, every stray bit of information is carefully noted down. He has ever striven to check litigation. Conservative in disposition, he aims to get the rights of his clients and then stop the case, and loves justice for its own sake. But whenever there are hard blows to be given, whenever wrong-doing is to be crushed, he goes in to deal sledge hammer blows. Striving to do justice to all men, he never charges his clients according to what they are worth, but for the value of his services and no more.

He is now said to be a candidate for the chancellorship of the Fourth chancery division of Tennessee, at the next judicial election.

GEN. JOHN FAIN.

BLOUNTVILLE.

THE Fains, from whom the subject of this sketch is descended, came originally from France, being driven from that country by religious persecution. They went first to the north of Ireland, and thence to America, settling in Virginia before the Revolution. The great-grandfather of Gen. Fain (John Fain) was killed near Lookout mountain, nearly a century ago, by an Indian's arrow. He was captain of a company organized to protect the early settlements from the inroads of the savages. The grandfather, John R. Fain, was born in Sullivan county, Tennessee. He was for a time a merchant at Dandridge, and afterwards at Blountville. He married Ellen Crawford and died about 1869, leaving three sons, Thomas, Hugh C. and John H., and daughters, Hannah (Anderson), Ruth (Anderson)—three sisters having married brothers—and Amelia (Mitchell). Of the children who died before the father's death, Nancy married Henry Anderson, Elizabeth married W. B. Neil, and Ellen died unmarried. The father, Thomas Fain, was born July 31, 1809, and has been a merchant and farmer all his life. He was, for a time, justice of the peace. He has a reputation unblemished, and is noted for his charity and unostentatious benevolence. Although a slaveholder, he was a Union man during the civil war and is now. In politics he is a zealous Republican. He is a man of great firmness and has long been distinguished as an earnest advocate of temperance. He was the principal founder of Reedy Creek Academy, and is a strong friend of education. The mother, formerly Rachel Anderson, was born in Sullivan county, February 14, 1814, and died July 10, 1884. Her life was devoted to her domestic duties. She was a devoted member of the Presbyterian church, and is remembered by her family and friends for her firmness of principle and purpose, and her uniform and unfailing kindness. She was the mother of ten children: (1). John, the subject of this sketch. (2). Ellen R., who died the wife of John G. Lynn. (3). Nancy Jane, who is the wife of Lott Pence. (4). Will. H., who is a merchant, lawyer and clerk and master at Blountville. He married Alice Spurgeon and has four children, Rachel, Maggie, Samuel Patton and Carrie. (5). Hugh, who is unmarried and at home with his father. (6). Hannah A., who is unmarried. (7). Samuel A., who married Jennie R. Hicks and has five children, Thomas H., Ellen, Hugh Lott, Mary and Mattie Bell. (8). Belle R., who is the wife of John P. Gardner, and has six children, Rachella, Maggie, Mattie, Thomas, Alice and William. (9). Amelia, who died in infancy. (10). George Thomas, also died in infancy.

Gen. John Fain was born in Sullivan county, Tennessee, December 20, 1835, and grew up there till 1858, when he went to Collin county, Texas, and there engaged in farming and teaching school. He remained there until the breaking out of the war, when he entered the Confederate service (though against his will) as a private in Martin's Texas Rangers (cavalry). He saw service in the Indian Territory, in Arkansas and in southern Texas. He was in a number of battles and skirmishes, among them the fights at Elk creek and Saline river, Arkansas.

The war over, he returned to Collin county, Texas, and re-engaged in farming and teaching. In October, 1868, he moved back to Sullivan county, Tennessee. In 1870, he resumed the study of law, which he had partially read in early boyhood. In 1869, he was licensed by Judge Gillenwaters and Chancellor Smith to practice law, was admitted to the bar and immediately commenced the practice at Blountville, where he has resided up to the present time. It should have been stated that he received his early education at Washington College and Rotherwood.

In politics Gen. Fain was originally a Whig, as were his father and grandfather. Since the reconstruction of parties in the southern States, however, the old Whig party having disappeared, he has been a pronounced Republican. In August, 1878, he was elected attorney-general for the First judicial circuit of Tennessee, his term expiring September, 1886. His circuit comprises the counties of Johnson, Carter, Sullivan, Washington, Unicoi, Greene, Hawkins and Hancock. In religion, Gen. Fain is a member of the Presbyterian church.

Gen. Fain married near Gladeville, Virginia, December 17, 1857, Miss Carrie V. Bickley, who was born February 7, 1842, the daughter of William Bickley, a farmer and owner of mills in Scott county, Virginia. Her mother was Jane Kilgore, of a Virginia family. Mrs. Fain's cousin, George W. L. Bickley, a man of brilliant attainments and a pleasing writer, is somewhat famous as the founder of the order of the Knights of the Golden Circle, that had for its object the conquest of Mexico. Her uncle, Hiram Kilgore, frequently represented Scott county in the Virginia Legislature. Another uncle, Dr. William Kilgore, was for many years a prominent physician at Franklin, Louisiana. He died in Milam county, Texas. Her father died while she was quite young. Her mother died in 1875, being over seventy years of age, and leaving six children, viz.: John, Joseph P., Elizabeth (wife of Judge H. C. Bruce, Wise county, Virginia), Sallie (married John M. Ballow), Malinda (now wife of Peter Day), Hiram A., and Carrie V. Mrs. Fain was educated at Estellville, Virginia, and Reedy Creek Academy, Tennessee. She is a member of the Methodist church, is a lady of culture and literary taste, and is noted for her splendid domestic qualities.

Gen. Fain and wife have had born to them twelve children: (1). William Thomas, died in infancy. (2).

May R. J., educated at Blountville and married W. K. Yost, carriage manufacturer, at Blountville. They have three children, John W., Claude Henry, and Carrie Kate. (3). Belle E., educated at Blountville and Bristol; married, April 22, 1884, Walter H. Wiley, a farmer of Fincastle, Virginia. (4). Sallie B. (" Pet"). (5). Hannah A. (6). Ellen Malinda, died fourteen months old. (7). Thomas J. (8). Will. Hugh. (9). Nannie E. V. (10). Carrie Amelia. (11). Alice Eugenie. (12). Florence.

Gen. Fain, since commencing the practice of law, has devoted himself to his profession. As a prosecuting attorney he is diligent, but humane. While he prosecutes the guilty felon with all the energy of his nature, he does not seek to magnify the errors of the unfortunate, or crowd the criminal docket with frivolous cases for his own emolument in the way of multiplied fees. Gen. Fain was trained to habits of industry. His father, being a man of fair fortune, might have raised the son in comparative idleness, but he wisely preferred to teach him the necessity of work. He put him at an early age to clerking in the store and occasionally to work on the farm.

Gen. Fain has been a reading man all his life, keeping himself posted in general literature as well as in his profession. He began life with but a small outfit and now he is comfortably well off, the result of diligence and economy in his practice, and the good management of his wife, who brought to him as her dowry a handsome sum of money. Gen. Fain is yet in his prime, and there is but little danger that he will ever retrograde, either professionally or financially.

C. B. McGUIRE, M.D.
FAYETTEVILLE.

THE McGuire family are of Irish extraction. John McGuire, the grandfather of Dr. Calvin Bridges McGuire, subject of this sketch, was born in Ireland, and came, when a child, with his father to Charleston, South Carolina. He was one of three brothers, one of whom went to Kentucky, one to Virginia, while he, John McGuire, came to Giles county, Tennessee, where he located at an early day in the settlement of that county.

Cornelius Wesley McGuire, father of Dr. McGuire, was born in Lincoln county, January 1, 1801. He was a magistrate in Lincoln county for nearly twenty years, though his education was limited to what he acquired without going to school. He was a devoted Methodist and a moral and strictly upright man. He was also a man of fine common sense and much native talent, and was much sought after as the business man of his neighborhood, in such matters as making surveys, writing deeds and bills of sale. He died September 18, 1859.

Dr. McGuire's mother was Miss Sallie Meloney, of Scotch descent. Her father, John Meloney, was a manufacturer of cedar ware in Limestone county, Alabama, where he died. Dr. McGuire's mother died in April, 1873, at the age of sixty-nine, having borne thirteen children, seven sons and six daughters: (1). Elizabeth J. McGuire, unmarried. (2). William H. McGuire, died in 1875. (3). Sarah L. McGuire, died the wife of J. C. Butler. (4). Nancy H. McGuire, died the wife of James N. George. (5). Calvin Bridges McGuire, subject of this sketch. (6). John P. McGuire, now a wholesale grocer and commission merchant in Nashville. He was colonel of the Thirty-second Tennessee Confederate infantry regiment at the time of the surrender, and has a very gallant military record—a full account of which may be found in Dr. J. B. Lindsley's "Military History of Tennessee." (7). James S. McGuire, died a farmer in North Alabama. (8) Robert R. McGuire, residing in Giles county, Tennessee. (9).

Cornelius N. McGuire, who was killed at the battle of Fredericksburg, Virginia, December 13, 1862. He was first-lieutenant of company K (Turney's First Tennessee Confederate regiment), and was commanding the company when he fell. (10). George W. McGuire, now a practicing physician in Lincoln county, Tennessee. (11). Mary D. McGuire, died the second wife of J. N. George. (12). Narcissa E. McGuire, now wife of William S. Owen. (13). Docia A. McGuire, unmarried.

Of the seven sons, all were in the Confederate service; one was killed, and five wounded.

Dr. Calvin Bridges McGuire was born on his father's farm near Millville, Lincoln county, Tennessee, July 1, 1831, and worked on the farm till he was twenty years old, going to school meantime in a class with Dr. J. F. Grant, the two boys growing up together. Dr. McGuire and Dr. Grant both finished their education at Forest Hill Academy the same day, and both graduated in medicine in the spring of 1856, though in different schools. (See Dr. Grant's sketch elsewhere in this volume). While in school, chemistry, anatomy and philosophy were Dr. McGuire's favorite studies, which he prosecuted mostly with a view to the future practice of medicine.

He began the study of medicine January, 1853, at Millville, in the office of Dr. M. P. Forehand, and, after reading with him two years, attended the medical department of the University of Nashville, 1854-5-6, taking two courses of lectures and graduating M.D. in February, 1856, under Profs. John M. Watson, Paul F. Eve, W. K. Bowling, C. K. Winston, W. T. Briggs, J. Berrien Lindsley and Thomas R. Jennings. After graduation he practiced medicine in Lincoln county till April, 1861, when he enlisted as a private in company K, of Col. Turney's First Tennessee Confederate infantry; was elected lieutenant soon after the regiment reached Virginia; was appointed surgeon of the regiment early in 1862, and soon after was appointed senior surgeon of Archer's Tennessee brigade, Army of Northern Virginia, and in this capacity served until Gen. Lee's surrender.

After the war he returned to his old location at Millville, Tennessee, and there practiced till January, 1871, when he located in Fayetteville, where he has practiced ever since.

Dr. McGuire married in Lincoln county, Tennessee, January 27, 1863, Miss Lizzie P. Green, who was born in that county, October 15, 1843, daughter of A. B. Green, a successful farmer. Her mother, nee Miss Sarah O. Dobbins, now living, at the age of sixty, with her daughter at Fayetteville, is a native of Lincoln county, daughter of Samuel Dobbins, who emigrated from East Tennessee at a very early day and became one of the pioneer settlers of Lincoln county. Mrs. McGuire's brother, Perry H. Green, is a farmer near Tupelo, Mississippi. Her sister, nee Theodocia O. Green, is now wife of George E. Suttle, a large farmer in Giles county, Tennessee. Mrs. McGuire is a member of the Presbyterian church.

By his marriage with Miss Green three children have been born to Dr. McGuire: (1). Jimmie McGuire, born October 18, 1866; graduated at the Columbia Athenæum in 1883; married November 28, 1883, Mr. Horton C. Lamb, a merchant at Fayetteville. (2). Frank McGuire, born May 20, 1871. (3). Myra McGuire, born July 22, 1881.

Dr. McGuire became a Mason in 1859; is an Odd Fellow, a Knight of Honor, a Knight of Pythias, a member of the Ancient Order of United Workmen, and of the Knights and Ladies of Honor, and is the examining surgeon for the four last named organizations. He is the vice-president of the First National Bank of Fayetteville; belongs to no church, though a believer in the Christian religion; and in politics is a Democrat, as was also his father. He served one year (1872) as an alderman of Fayetteville.

He began life without patrimony, came out of the war with nothing, but was free from debt, a leading trait in his character being a holy horror of owing any man anything. By his wife he received a small estate, and is now in easy and even independent circumstances, and does not owe a dollar in the world. He made his money by saving what came to him through his profession. It is not that he has made it so marvelously fast, but that he saved what he collected in fees, has been prompt in meeting obligations, and has avoided speculation.

Dr. McGuire has a strongly marked character. His intellect is vigorous and healthy, with a predominant resolution and will, hence he has the surest elements of success in life. He has encountered and overcome many obstacles that laid in his path, and is now established in a well-earned practice. He has a steady nerve and great skill with the knife, hence has acquired considerable local reputation as a surgeon. Had he a wide field of operation, no doubt his professional character would become very extended, if not national. He is devoted to his profession and makes it alike useful and profitable. He is a gentleman of high moral standing, agreeable manners and fine social qualities. He is a good type of a useful and honorable citizen.

MAJOR WILBUR F. FOSTER.

NASHVILLE.

WILBUR F. FOSTER was born April 13, 1834, in Springfield, Massachusetts. His ancestors on both sides were among the early English settlers of that State. His father, Dexter Foster, originally a machinist, became a civil engineer, and was one of the leading spirits in the construction of the Boston and Albany railroad, upon which he designed and constructed the first railroad tunnel ever built upon a curve. He was a son of Lewis Foster, who was born in Massachusetts in 1764. Maj. Foster's mother was Miss Allin, daughter of D. Allin, who also belonged to the Puritan stock.

While yet in his youth, Maj. Foster removed with his father to Montgomery county, Maryland, seven miles from Washington City. Here his father soon afterward died, leaving him an orphan at the age of nine years. About a year or two later he returned to Massachusetts to be educated, and spent several years at academies in Northampton and Springfield, graduating at the latter place, at the age of seventeen. He soon obtained a position under Capt. John Childe, chief engineer of the Mobile and Ohio railroad, and spent two years assisting in locating and laying out that road. Transferred, in the early part of 1853, to the Tennessee and Alabama (now the Nashville and Decatur) railroad, he was, from that time till the beginning of the war, engaged in the location and construction of the Nashville and Decatur, the Edgefield and Kentucky, and the Henderson and Nashville roads, and had charge, during the time, of the construction of the bridge across the Cumberland river at Nashville, the first railroad bridge constructed across that stream. Beginning as rodman, he had risen to the position of first assistant.

In April, 1861, he joined the First Tennessee Confederate regiment, as a private in the Rock City Guards. About ten days after joining the service, he was detailed for engineering duty and sent to superintend the construction of forts Donelson and Henry. Requesting to be sent back to his regiment, after these forts were built, he was ordered with it to Virginia, but, in three weeks from the time of his arrival there, he received an appointment as first-lieutenant in the engineering corps, and was ordered to report to Gen. Zollicoffer at Cumberland Gap. When Gen. Kirby Smith moved into Kentucky, Lieut. Foster was made captain of engineers and assigned to duty with Gen. McCown. After the return from the Kentucky campaign, he was made chief engineer of the department of East Tennessee, serving on the staff of Gen. Buckner. After the battle of Chickamauga, he was made major of engineers and placed in charge of topographical work with Gen. Johnston, serving in this capacity till that officer was relieved of command. He was then assigned to

duty as chief engineer of Gen. Stewart's corps, and served as such till the surrender of the Confederate armies, at which time he was at Greensborough, North Carolina.

Returning immediately to Nashville and engaging in the practice of engineering, he was, in 1865, elected city engineer, and, with the exception of two years of Republican regime in 1866–67, held the position till March, 1884, engaging at the same time in engineering in various directions, and doing more or less of work for all the railroads running into Nashville, though not officially connected with any of them. He has served as a director of the First National Bank of Nashville and of the Phillips & Buttorff Manufacturing Company. The latter position he now holds.

Too young to take any part in politics previous to the war, his sympathies were all with the Whig party. Since the war he has been a Democrat, but has taken no active part as a politician.

In Free Masonry he has taken all the degrees up to the fourteenth degree, Scottish Rite. He became a Master Mason in 1857, took the Chapter degrees in 1859, the Council degrees in 1861, and became a Knight Templar in 1865. He was elected Grand Master of the Grand Council of Tennessee in 1869; Grand High Priest in 1873; Grand Master of the Grand Lodge in 1879; Grand President of the Order of High Priesthood in 1871–72, and Grand Commander of Knights Templar in 1878. He is one of two men in Tennessee who alone have filled all these offices. (See sketch of Hon. John Frizzell elsewhere in this volume).

Maj. Foster became a member of the First Presbyterian church of Nashville, in 1867, and has been chairman of its board of deacons since 1870. He takes a lively interest always in the welfare of his church.

Maj. Foster was married in Nashville, June 19, 1866, to Miss Lizzie Nichol, daughter of John Nichol, one of the oldest citizens of the place. She, too, is a Presbyterian in her religious faith. She is a lady of domestic tastes, splendid social qualities, and most charitable impulses. They have one living child, a daughter.

Maj. Foster is in a great degree a self-educated man. Even while acquiring his academic training, he aided largely in defraying the expenses by his own labor. From the time he embarked in life for himself, he has been self-reliant. The very nature of his profession required accuracy and promptness, and he made it a vital point never to be delinquent and never to submit his work till he had thoroughly proven its correctness. Having conscientiously schooled himself by this rule, his rise was, very naturally, steady and rapid. Personally, he is universally esteemed by his fellow-citizens, while, in his profession, he is accepted as an authority wherever known.

HON. WM. M. RANDOLPH.

MEMPHIS.

WILLIAM M. RANDOLPH was born near La-Grange, Fayette county, Tennessee, June 16, 1837. When about two years of age his parents moved to Clark county, Arkansas, where they remained about two years and then returned to Tennessee, and lived in the vicinity of Somerville till December, 1844, when they removed to Memphis, and after remaining there a few months, returned to Arkansas in May, 1845. They settled in Clark county, near Arkadelphia, where they remained till 1849, and then moved into the town of Arkadelphia, where they are still living, both at a very advanced age.

Young Randolph received nearly all of his early education from his mother, having no advantage of a school until he was thirteen years of age. He then went to school about four months, but stopped on account of sickness, started again within a year, and continued for about a year and a half, and subsequently attended another school for about the same length of time. He also attended a grammar school for about six weeks, taught by Allen M. Scott, at which he attained marked success. In 1852, he went into the post-office at Arkadelphia as clerk and assistant post-master, and remained about four months. In August, 1854, he became the deputy of Isaac W. Smith, who filled the offices of clerk of the circuit court, probate court, chancery court, county court and recorder. In August, 1856, Newton S. Love was elected to succeed Mr. Smith, and after remaining with him long enough to instruct him in the duties of his office, Mr. Randolph retired, January 1, 1857.

In the meantime, he had been reading law with Hon. Harris Flanagin, afterward governor of Arkansas, and in January, 1857, he went to Little Rock to read law with Ebenezer Cummins and Augustus H. Garland, the latter of whom was subsequently United States senator from Arkansas, and is now attorney-general of the United States. A short time after Mr. Randolph entered this office Mr. Cummins died, and Mr. Garland kept a place for Mr. Randolph as partner till he got license to practice law. He was licensed in February, 1858, by Chief Justice Elbert H. English, of Arkansas, before whom he had practiced in a moot court, and by whom he was told that his license was ready whenever he wanted it. He was then admitted to a partnership by Mr. Garland, and they practiced all over the State, but particularly in the Supreme court, having as large a practice as any firm in Arkansas, till the secession movement began.

Mr. Garland became a delegate to the State convention in Arkansas, which was called to pass upon the question of secession; was also a delegate to the convention when it met a second time, and afterward a delegate to the provisional Congress at Montgomery, after which he had very little to do with the business of the firm. Mr. Randolph remained at Little Rock attending to his practice till December, 1861, when, through the influence of Mr. Garland, he was appointed Confederate States district attorney for the eastern district of Arkansas, which position he held till January, 1864, and then resigned. He continued living at Little Rock till it was occupied by the United States forces in September, 1863, retiring before them into south Arkansas, where he remained till January, 1864, and then having received assurances from the Federal military authorities at Little Rock that he might pursue his ordinary avocation there unmolested, he returned to that city. In April, 1865, he removed to Memphis, where he has since resided, continuing in the practice of his profession. Upon going to Memphis, he formed a partnership with Samuel T. Morgan, who died in 1867, and after that he was in partnership for one year with Abram R. Herron and Leopold Lehman; after that firm was dissolved, went in with Treadwell S. Ayres and James C. Calhoun, and after the death of Mr. Calhoun, continued with Mr. Ayres several years, and then formed a partnership with Hon. E. S. Hammond, now United States district judge. The firm lasted untill Judge Hammond went upon the bench, in 1878. During a part of the time Mr. R. D. Jordan was a member of the firm. One year of the time, Mr. Samuel S. Wassell, of Little Rock, was also a partner in the firm. After this firm was dissolved, Mr. Randolph practiced alone for several years. In 1882, he was in partnership with Mr. E. B. McHenry; and after that firm dissolved, continued business with Robert M. Heath, as Randolph & Heath, for a year or more, and since that time has been practicing alone.

In early life, Mr. Randolph was a Democrat, and following the teachings of that party, he believed the right of secession was reserved to the States under the constitution, and that in the then existing circumstances, the Southern States were justified in resorting to it in 1861. He was kept out of the army by physical disability, and as the war progressed, he saw that the failure of the South was beyond question, and also decided in his own mind that it was not best that it should succeed. He had never believed that slavery was right, nor did he believe that any government founded on slavery could be a good or a just government. After his views changed he kept quiet till the war was over, remaining at his home and doing what practice he could. After the war he was disfranchised, along with the great mass of people in the South, and did not vote till 1869. All his advice and influence were exerted toward having the people of the South acquiesce in the state of affairs and give their active, hearty support to the government and the party which controlled the government, feeling that all opposition was not only futile but injurious. Entertaining such views, he very naturally coalesced with the Republican party, and has continued to vote with them up to this time. He was city attorney of Memphis from December, 1869, to February, 1874, with an intermission of about six months. In 1874 he was a candidate for the State senate, but failed to secure his seat; in 1876, was a delegate to the Republican national convention at Cincinnati, and in the fall of 1876, as also in 1878, was a candidate for Congress against Hon. Casey Young, but again failed to secure his seat. He has never sought office and has never been a candidate, except at the solicitation of his party and his friends.

Mr. Randolph was married at Little Rock, January 17, 1861, to Miss Rebecca E. Wassell, daughter of John Wassell, a gentleman of English birth, who was a prominent lawyer at Little Rock, a leading member of the Episcopal church, in early times was one of the publishers of the *Arkansas Whig*, and at different times served as mayor of the city, judge of the probate court, and filled numerous other positions. Mrs. Randolph's mother was Miss Margaret Spotts, a native of Delaware, but raised in Louisville, Kentucky. Mrs. Randolph has been a member of the Episcopal church from her girlhood. By his marriage with Miss Wassell, Mr. Randolph has five children now living: (1). Laura. (2). George, aged seventeen, now in his father's office. (3). Edward, aged fifteen, at Christian Brothers' College, Memphis. (4). Amy, aged ten. (5). Wassell, aged five.

Mr. Randolph's father, Rodolph Randolph, is a native of Virginia, born in Amelia county, near Farmville, on the Appomattox river. His father, Henry Randolph, was a soldier in the body-guard of Gen.

Washington during the Revolution. He was married to Mary Poytress and moved to West Tennessee in 1827. The mother of the subject of this sketch, was Miss Lucretia A. Greene, daughter of Mial Greene and Nancy Jackson. She was born in Dinwiddie county, Virginia, and came to Tennessee with her parents from that State. Like most men of success, Mr. Randolph is emphatically a self-made man. When he began the study of law, he determined to make that his business and to follow nothing else. This plan he has assiduously and faithfully pursued through life, and devotes now a considerable portion of each day to the study of his profession. His father had not the means to give him an education or a start in life, and many years ago became an invalid, dependent upon his son for a support. Thus he started in life with no money and very little education, but with native talent, studious habits and indomitable will-power, he has persevered and conquered success. He has been continually at work from the time he commenced till now, with never an idle day or an idle minute. He is a constant reader, yet never neglects his duty to his clients or to his family. Raised in a new country, with no books, no teachers, few churches and few educated people, his early ambition was to get all the knowledge he could from every possible source, and to do what he had to do with all his might, energy and intelligence.

His success in Memphis has been quite remarkable, hardly surpassed by any member of the bar of that city. He has been president of the Memphis Bar and Law Library Association since 1878, and looks with considerable pride upon his efforts toward building up the very excellent library that Association now owns. He is temperate in his habits and never gambled in his life. In his youth he was very fond of the sports of hunting and fishing, pastimes in which he still indulges with keen enjoyment.

CAPT. THOMAS H. PAINE.

NASHVILLE.

HARDEN PAINE, the grandfather of Thomas H. Paine, was born in Person county, North Carolina, March 4, 1783. He married Nancy Bumpass, of the same county, February 15, 1807. She was a descendant of one of the early pioneers of that county, who came from Petersburg, Virginia, where he had long been a merchant and a prominent man, but whose fortune had been impaired by adverse circumstances. Here, in the wilds of the Roanoke, he commenced anew the struggle of life with the heart and courage of one unsubdued in the purposes of honorable manhood, and again won the independence of his former standing and

the means of liquidating a debt of three thousand pounds entailed upon him by the dishonesty of a business associate. He became the progenitor of an extensive family distinguished by men of high respectability. Harden Paine came of a sturdy English ancestry. His grandfather, Dr. James Paine (the great-great grandfather of Capt. Thomas H. Paine), emigrated to America about 1740, and settled in Granville county, North Carolina. He married in Virginia an estimable lady by the name of Harden, a name that became prominent in the family nomenclature. Having acquired a large fortune, he erected a goodly mansion and surrounded himself with all the comforts of a "fine old English gentleman of ye olden time." He was educated to the profession of medicine and surgery in London, whence he emigrated and practiced that profession for a number of years in his colonial home. His residence was in the midst of one of the earliest settlements of that section, and his house was long known by way of eminence as the "brick house." He was the founder of a large and extensive family, distinguished in genealogical annals as the Roanoke branch of the Paine family in the South.

He had four sons, Robert, John, James and William, from the first of whom was descended the late Bishop Paine, of the Methodist Episcopal church, South. William, the youngest, was the father of Harden, of whom we write. He was born in Person county, North Carolina, December 19, 1751, and on arriving at maturity became a planter—a pursuit he followed the remainder of his life. Although of limited education, he was a man of good judgment, of great industry and withal, like old Simeon, he was "a just man and devout." Of him it has been said by the most eminent man of the name: "I remember him and his good wife very well. He was greatly respected and loved by his family and neighbors—cheerful, amiable, a strict member and attendant of the church."

During the Revolution he was a firm patriot, sharing throughout in the toils and privations of the North Carolina militia, and when the conflict was over, he returned to the peaceful pursuits of the soil. He married in 1781, and became the father of nine children, five sons and four daughters. He resided all his life in the county of his birth. He died about 1814. A short time before his death, Harden, the oldest son of the family, emigrated to Tennessee. He first settled in Giles county, but removed to Lawrence county. It was here, in imitation of his grandfather, Dr. James Paine, he built a brick house near Lawrenceburg, where he remained many years. It was a goodly home, among a refined and Christian people, where his days might be rounded out in the fruition of peace and happiness; but such was not to be. He again sought a new home in the then unbroken wilds of southwest Missouri. There he reverted to the pursuits of agriculture and laid the foundation of a new home. Peace, happiness and prosperity came to his doors. As the new country grew in population, his name became honored as a good citizen. Though never in political life nor a seeker for its offices, he was often placed in positions of public trust. When the civil war came on he was "old and well stricken in years," and sought to avoid the trials of the impending strife by removing to Texas. But his mission was soon to terminate. He lived to the end of the war, and calmly awaited the final summons. It came December 9, 1865, when he passed away in his eighty-third year.

Harden Paine was endowed by nature with great qualities which but needed the refining touches of educational training to make him a man capable of taking high rank. He had a splendid *physique* and deported himself with dignified demeanor. Politically, he was a Democrat of the Jeffersonian-Jackson school. In religion, a Baptist, and his convictions were emphasized by a deportment that bespoke him a Christian gentleman. Among his acquaintances his word was the synonym of truth. His friendships were enduring—his benefactions liberal. He was exact in all his obligations to others and demanded the same in return. He sought no distinction among men but preferred the humble walks, which he adorned by a consistent and honorable devotion to duty. To his life the lines of the poet might well apply:

> "'Tis only noble to be good ;
> Kind hearts are more than coronets,
> And simple faith than Norman blood."

The father of Capt. Thomas H. Paine was Maj. Sidney S. Paine, a farmer by occupation, a major in the days of the militia, a prominent member of the Primitive Baptist church, in which he preached some in his latter days. He was a warm advocate of education and literary in his tastes—in short, an intelligent, upright, honorable and useful citizen. He died in 1868, at the age of sixty years. He was one of twin brothers, the other of whom, Jesse L. Paine, was a successful business man, and quite a prominent citizen of Dallas county, Missouri. Having settled there at an early day, he "grew up with the country" and became well known, not only in his own, but in other counties of the southwestern part of that State. He was clerk of the circuit court of his county for about twenty years. At the beginning of the war, to save his property, and avoid the sanguinary strife that threatened his immediate vicinity, he moved with his father to Texas, where he died within a day or two of the same time of the death of his twin brother in Tennessee.

Capt. Paine's mother, *nee* Susan J. Allen, now living, at the age of sixty-three, in Wayne county, Tennessee, is a native of Davidson county, Tennessee, daughter of Jeremiah Allen. Her mother was Mary Ann Daniel.

Thomas H. Paine was born in Lawrence county, Tennessee, December 1, 1836. He grew up there, working on his father's farm and going to school when in session, until the age of eighteen years, when he went to his grandfather's in Missouri, and attended school at Lebanon Seminary one year. He then came back to Tennessee. Soon after his return from Missouri he entered Jackson College, Columbia, Tennessee, where he completed his collegiate education under President B. F. Mitchell, and the noted surveyor and mathematician, Prof. O. H. P. Bennett. After leaving college, he read law at Lawrenceburg, in the office of Attorney-General Lee M. Bently, and was admitted to the bar in 1861, by Judge Elijah Walker and Chancellor Stephen C. Pavatt, and had just gotten fairly into practice at Lawrenceburg, in partnership with Caleb B. Davis, when he, although just of age, was elected to the Tennessee Legislature from Lawrence county. He had, however, a few months previous to this, been elected by the county court as county trustee, to fill the vacancy occasioned by the death of Isaac W. Alford, Esq. This unexpired term he filled with credit to one so young.

He entered the General Assembly of 1861-62, the youngest member of the body, and assumed and maintained a high position throughout the session. While this Legislature was in session at Nashville, the fall of Fort Donelson necessitated its adjournment to Memphis, February 16, 1862. It remained in session there for some weeks, and upon its adjournment *sine die*, in March following, Capt. Paine returned to his home in Lawrence county, where he at once raised, organized, and was elected captain of a company of cavalry, which he reported to Lieut.-Col. Cooper, of Biffle's regiment, with whom he served, with his company, for some time on recruiting service in Middle Tennessee, after which he reported to Col. G. H. Nixon, and his became company A of Nixon's regiment Tennessee cavalry, Confederate States army. He served in that command until its surrender, under Gen. Forrest, in the spring of 1865. A considerable portion of this time, Capt. Paine, as senior officer, was in command of the regiment, Col. Nixon being on detached service or in command of the brigade, and the lieutenant-colonel and major being prisoners of war. He was in active service with this command during the remainder of the struggle, taking part in many of the brilliant operations of Gen. Forrest in Tennessee, Alabama, Mississippi and Georgia.

After the war, instead of resuming the practice of law, he was prevailed upon by the trustees of Jackson Academy at Lawrenceburg, to become principal of that institution, and held that position until again elected to the Legislature in November, 1870. Immediately after the adjournment of that Legislature (1871), he was elected president of Savannah College, at Savannah, Tennessee, which position he filled until June, 1874, when he resigned, and was soon thereafter nominated by the Democratic convention as a candidate for the State senate from the Eighteenth senatorial district, to which he was elected by a large majority. Upon the organization of the Legislature he was elected speaker of the Senate—the second office in the State, ranking next to governor—and presided over that body with marked dignity, ability and impartiality.

As an evidence of the high appreciation of his services as speaker, the following complimentary resolution, proposed by senator Ellis, a Republican, was unanimously adopted just previous to the adjournment of the senate, and ordered to be spread upon the journal:

Resolved, That our thanks are due, and are hereby tendered, to the Honorable Thomas H. Paine, speaker of the senate, for the able and efficient manner in which he has presided over the deliberations of this body. Prompt in attendance upon his official duties, presiding with dignity and firmness, quick in perception, his impartial rulings have defied criticism, and his candor challenged admiration, while his courteous demeanor has reflected honor and credit upon an honorable position.

When the senate adjourned, he again taught in the Savannah College, and at Ross Academy, in Hardin county, until January 22, 1883, when he was appointed by Gov. Bate, and unanimously confirmed by the senate, as State superintendent of public instruction, the position which he now holds, and the arduous duties of which he has discharged with signal success.

In February, 1880, while quietly discharging his duties as a teacher in the college at Savannah, and without his knowledge, he was, upon the recommendation of Hon. J. D. C. Atkins and Hon. W. C. Whitthorne, members of Congress, appointed by the president as supervisor of the Tenth Census for the fourth district of Tennessee, comprising seventeen counties. He accepted the appointment, and at once went to work, and divided his district into one hundred and seventy-one enumeration districts, for each of which he appointed one enumerator of census. He was remarkably successful in securing good business men for this important and very particular work, and by the first of June following, he had blank schedules in the hands of every enumerator, and all were ready for the work. During the month of June he received daily reports from these officers as to the progress of the work. After the close of the labor of enumeration, he carefully examined and corrected all the accounts for the services of his enumerators and recommended their payment. In all this, and in the report of his work made to the department of the interior, he gave universal satisfaction.

Capt. Paine, though nominally a lawyer, has practiced but little, his time having been taken up by his service in the army, and as teacher and also as a politician, stumping various portions of the State on important issues of the various canvasses. In politics, he is a Democrat. He is a Royal Arch and Council Mason, a member of the Methodist Episcopal church, South, a Knight of Honor, having organized a number of lodges of that order in Tennessee and Alabama, and is also a member of the Tennessee Historical Society.

Capt. Paine married in Lawrence county, Tennessee, May 24, 1859, Miss Minerva A. Kelly, daughter of John J. Kelly, a planter, formerly of Alabama. Her mother, Susan M. Boswell, was the daughter of William Boswell, of Lawrence county, originally from North Carolina. Mrs. Paine is a member of the Methodist Episcopal church, South, and was educated near Florence, Alabama. Three children have blessed their union, all born in Lawrence county: (1). Susan Ida Paine, a graduate of Hardin Female College, Savannah, Tennessee. (2). Thomas Harden Paine. (3). Memphis Kelly Paine.

Capt. Paine's only living brother, Dr. Jere. A. Paine, is a prominent physician in Wayne county, Tennessee. His brother, Jesse Allen Paine, died in the Confederate

29

army, a private in Capt. B. F. Matthews' company K, Third Tennessee regiment.

Capt. Paine's cousin, John H. Paine, son of Jesse L Paine, to whom reference has been made in this sketch is quite a prominent citizen of Springfield, Missouri. He was, for a long time, clerk of the circuit court, and is now recorder of deeds in that city.

His only surviving uncle on his father's side is James W. Paine, of Macon county, Missouri, now a merchant of Callao, in that county. Judge Paine, as he is familiarly called, is a man of a high order of intelligence and very popular. Without seeking the position, he was elected by the people to the office of judge of the county court, which he filled with credit to himself and satisfaction to the people. Preferring to give his attention to his private business, he declined a re-election. He is now growing old, but is still vigorous and industrious.

Capt. Paine is six feet high, slightly stooping, weighs one hundred and seventy-five pounds, is of large, stron build, and has the appearance of a man of force and ye of kindness. His profile shows him to be what is calle a long-headed man, and his projecting brows and promi nent chin at a glance indicate him a man of energy an character. He has risen to the highest honors of th educational profession, has been able in all stations, an makes a fine representative Tennessean. Kindness i one of his chief characteristics. The clasp of his han tells you at once he is a whole-souled man and a winne of hearts. The lesson that his father taught him, tha kindness and politeness cost nothing and pay well, h has put to a severe test by standing security for other and finally having their debts to pay. But anothe striking characteristic is, that he has always made it point to do well what he does at all, and to make th most of every undertaking, being faithful to ever charge entrusted to his hands.

GEN. GEORGE GIBBS DIBRELL.

SPARTA.

THIS distinguished soldier, statesman and civilian, one of Tennessee's ablest and most honored citizens, one of the most useful men the State ever had in Congress, and one of the bravest generals that ever drew blade in defense of the old "Volunteer State," richly deserves an honored place among her representative sons. His life has been varied, interesting, romantic and thrilling.

Gen. Dibrell's great-grandfather, Dr. Christopher DuBrey, was a Huguenot refugee from France, and with the Huguenot colony settled on the James river in Virginia, in the year 1700. After coming to America he changed the family name to DeBrill. Subsequently, it was changed to its present style of orthography, Dibrell. He had two sons, Charles and Anthony. All the Dibrell family in the United State sprang from these two sons.

Gen. Dibrell's grandfather, Charles Dibrell, was a patriot soldier in the Revolution, and was a pensioner up to his death at Union City, Tennessee, at the residence of Gen. G. W. Gibbs, who had married his daughter, Lee Ann Dibrell. Charles Dibrell's first wife was a Miss Burton, of a branch of the Lee family, of Virginia. He married her in Buckingham county, Virginia. His second wife was a Miss Patterson, of good family, by whom he had four children : Patterson, Panthea, Elvira and Agnes.

By the first wife, Charles Dibrell had eight children: John, Elizabeth, Polly, Lee Ann, Anthony (Gen. Dibrell's father), Judith, Charles and Joseph.

Of these, Judith Dibrell married Temple Poston, of Elizabethtown, Kentucky, by whom she had a son, Charles Dibrell Poston, who represented Arizona Territory in Congress two or three terms since the late civil war.

Gen. Dibrell's father, Anthony Dibrell, married in Wayne county, Kentucky, and was deputy sheriff at the time of his marriage. He moved to White county Tennessee, in 1811 ; was appointed receiver of the land office at Sparta ; was clerk of the circuit court at Sparta for twenty-one years ; was a member of the Tennessee Legislature ; in 1839 was a candidate for Congress, and for ten years was Tennessee's State treasurer, elected by the Legislature. After the late war he was appointed clerk of the circuit court again. He died at Sparta in January, 1875, in his eighty-seventh year. He was a warm, devoted friend; a moral, Christian man, and very liberal to the poor and needy. He always contended that a man was not a friend to any one whom he would not help when in need. He was a Henry Clay Whig, a Methodist, a bank director and successful farmer and trader.

The mother of Gen. Dibrell was Miss Mildred Carter daughter of William Carter, of New River, Wythe county, Virginia. Her father was a blacksmith and farmer, had been a soldier in the Revolution and was a pensioner. The East Tennessee Carters are of the same stock. John Carter, Gen. Dibrell's maternal uncle, died in Monroe county, Tennessee. The well-known families—Scruggs, Yearwood and Carter—in upper East Tennessee are all maternal relatives of Gen. Dibrell. The wife of Judge George Brown, of Knoxville, is also related to him, her maiden name being Scruggs.

William Carter, Gen. Dibrell's maternal grandfather,

moved from Wythe county, Virginia, to Wayne county, Kentucky, when Gen. Dibrell's mother was quite a girl. There she was reared and there she married. She was exceedingly industrious and economical and devoted to bringing up her children in the proper walks of life. She was a devoted Methodist, a warm friend of the church, liberal and charitable, and a great hand to look after the sick. She died in 1883, in her eighty-third year. She was the mother of ten children: (1). Montgomery Dibrell, deceased. (2). Elizabeth Dibrell, now widow of C. J. Sullivan. (3). Crockett Dibrell, now in the stock business at Austin, Texas. (4). Joseph B. Dibrell, deceased. (5). George G. Dibrell, subject of this sketch. (6). Lucinda Dibrell, widow of James R. Herd; now living with her son, James R. Herd, in Lavacca county, Texas. (7). Sarah B. Dibrell, widow of John W. Whitfield; now living in Lavacca county, Texas. (8). William C. Dibrell, now in the cattle business in Coleman county, Texas. (9). John Anthony Dibrell, deceased. (10). Martha F. Dibrell, widow of J. N. Bailey; now living near Sparta, Tennessee.

Hon. Barney Gibbs, lieutenant-governor of Texas, is a second cousin of Gen. Dibrell, being a grandson of Gen. Gibbs, who married Gen. Dibrell's aunt, Lee Ann Dibrell. Col. Charles N. Gibbs, now of Chattanooga, also a son of her's, secretary of State of Tennessee for eight years, is a cousin to Gen. Dibrell. Charles Anthony Sullivan, who was chancellor at Starksville, Mississippi, is Gen. Dibrell's nephew, being a son of his sister, Elizabeth. Isaac Sullivan, another of her sons, is now clerk at an Indian agency, having been appointed by Gen. J. D. C. Atkins. Gen. Dibrell's brother, Montgomery Dibrell, who died June 6, 1881, aged sixty-nine years, was clerk and master at Sparta, Tennessee, before the war, and clerk of the circuit court at the time of his death.

George Gibbs Dibrell was born April 12, 1822; raised on a farm; attended country schools in winter and worked during the summer. In the spring of 1838, he went one session to the university at Knoxville, and studied under president Esterbrook. The fall before his father had sent him to Virginia with a drove of cattle, and in the winter following he went to Mississippi with a drove of hogs. In 1839 he worked on the farm, and the first money he earned was while his father was candidate for Congress in that year, his father having given him a horse as pay for managing and working his farm. Young Dibrell made the crop and in the fall after sold the horse for one hundred and forty dollars. He then began trading and shifting for himself. In March, 1840, he was elected clerk of the branch of the Bank of Tennessee at Sparta, and held the position until March, 1846, at a salary of five hundred dollars per annum. He commenced life without patrimony, his father having been broken up by security debts. He was not a wild or dissipated boy, though fond of fun and enjoyment. He never swore nor used tobacco, and

never drank spirits to excess, but was always sober and steady. His boyhood was joyous. He was fond of nature and fond of stock, staying on the mountain weeks at a time, looking after his father's cattle, sheep and mules, which is so picturesque and suggestive, as to remind one of David, the shepherd boy, who afterwards became the king of Israel and the "Royal Psalmist."

From 1846 to 1860, he was in mercantile life at Sparta, and again, from 1865 to 1875, and was a successful money-maker both times. He began merchandising on one thousand six hundred dollars, furnished him by a man named Officer, the business being carried on under Mr. Officer's name, and two years after Dibrell gave Officer back his one thousand six hundred dollars and two thousand five hundred dollars besides, as his share of the profits. Meanwhile, from January, 1848, to April, 1860, he was county court clerk at Sparta.

He was elected to the State constitutional convention, called in 1861, as a Union candidate, but the convention, having been voted down, never met. Dibrell advocated the meeting of the convention, but opposed secession, promising, however, that if the worst came to the worst he would prove himself a sound southerner. He was elected to the Legislature, regular session, 1861, without opposition, but served only two or three weeks, preferring to be with his regiment, the war meanwhile having broken out.

Gen. Dibrell entered the Confederate service July 20, 1861. He enlisted as a private in Capt. J. H. Snodgrass' company, Twenty-fifth Tennessee infantry regiment, Col. Sidney S. Stanton commanding. He was elected lieutenant-colonel August 10, 1861. He served in Tennessee and Kentucky under Gen. Zollicoffer, and was in the battle of Fishing Creek, January 19, 1862; and afterwards at the battle of Farmington, Mississippi, May 7, 1862. At the reorganization of the army at Corinth, he was defeated for the lieutenant-colonelcy, whereupon he went home and raised the Eighth Tennessee cavalry regiment, behind the enemy's lines, and was made its colonel. It was raised as an independent partisan ranger regiment, but it went into service in Forrest's command, at Murfreesborough, in October, 1862.

Gen. Dibrell's service extended over Kentucky, Tennessee, Mississippi, Alabama, Georgia, South Carolina, North Carolina and Virginia. He took part in the battles of Neely's Bend, October 19, 1862; Triune, Tennessee, 1863; Franklin, Tennessee, 1863; Florence, Alabama, in the spring of 1863, against two Federal gunboats; two fights near Sparta, Tennessee, August 9 and 17, 1863; Chickamauga, September 19 and 20, 1863; Philadelphia, Tennessee, October, 1863, in which he captured seven hundred prisoners and all of Gen. Woolford's artillery, camp equipage, ambulances, wagons and one thousand two hundred horses; at Maryville, Tennessee, November, 1863; siege of Knoxville, November, 1863; Lone Mountain, Tennessee, December 2, 1863;

Mossy Creek, Tennessee, December, 31, 1863; Dandridge, Tennessee, January 17, 1864; Dibrell's Hill, Tennessee, January 28, 1864; from Resaca, Georgia, back to Atlanta, and in the daily fights from Dalton to Atlanta, from the spring of 1864 to August, 1864, three months of rough riding and rough fighting.

Meanwhile, Gen. Dibrell had succeeded to the command of Gen. Forrest's "old brigade," July 1, 1863, after the death of Col. Starnes. This brigade Gen. Dibrell commanded till the close of the war. The last six months he also commanded Williams' Kentucky brigade, formerly under Col. W. C. P. Breckinridge, now member of Congress from the Lexington, Kentucky, district.   Gen. Dibrell was commissioned brigadier-general in July, 1864, though Gen. Forrest had recommended him for the position a year before—in July, 1863.

In August, 1864, Gen. Dibrell commanded a column under Gen. Wheeler in his raid into Middle Tennessee, and was, while *en route*, engaged in the fights at Tilton, Maryville and Strawberry Plains. At Readyville, Tennessee, September 7, 1864, was the only time his command was stampeded or surpised during the whole war. He was next at the battle of Saltville, Virginia, October 7, 1864; next near Forsyth, Georgia, against Gen. Sherman on his march to the sea; then at the battle of Griswoldville; two fights at Waynesborough; one near Ebenezer swamps, and various minor brushes in opposing and harassing Sherman on his march. Then came the battles of Grahamville, South Carolina, Salkahatchee river, Lawtonville, Columbia, South Carolina, Blackville, Orange Court-house, Stony Point, Fayetteville, North Carolina, Averysborough, Bentonville, and Raleigh, April 12, 1865. At the latter place he was ordered to report to President Davis at Greensborough, North Carolina, and in two days and nights he marched eighty-five miles, reported with his command to the Confederate president and escorted him on to Washington, Georgia, where the command was surrendered. Gen. Dibrell was paroled May 11, 1865.

At Lone Mountain, East Tennessee, on the Knoxville and Cumberland Gap road, December 2, 1863, Gen. Dibrell was wounded by a minnie-ball through the right groin, and, by a pistol, shot through the right arm, breaking one bone in the arm. During the war he had several horses shot under him.

In the spring of 1862, he was in the brigade of Gen. (now Governor) Marmaduke, of Hardee's corps. The Federal Gen. Pope's celebrated dispatch that he had captured four thousand men came of Gen. Dibrell's losing forty-one men, all told, killed, wounded and captured, May 7, 1862, in a conflict with Pope at Farmington, Mississippi, while on picket duty. Dibrell went into the fight with two hundred men, and lost forty-one. Pope's dispatch was a gross exaggeration.

Gen. Dibrell's two sons, Waman and Joseph, were with him in the army, both of whom were lieutenants at the close of the war. (For a fuller account of Gen. Dibrell's military history, see Dr. J. B. Lindsley's "Military History of Tennessee," and Gen. Jordan's and Col. John P. Pryor's "History of Forrest's Campaigns.")

When the war closed Gen. Dibrell returned to his home near Sparta, and re-engaged in the more peaceful pursuits of a merchant, farmer and trader. In 1870 he was elected to the State convention which formed the present State constitution. In that distinguished body he was a useful and prominent member. He was the author of the clause to make clerks and masters elective by the people, and offered an ordinance that representatives in the Legislature should not exceed seventy-five in number, and that each county with one thousand five hundred qualified voters should have one representative, but both of these measures failed, the latter by only two votes.

Gen. Dibrell never had political aspirations until his friends importuned him to stand for Congress. His leading ambition when a young man was to make money in order to give his children a better start in life than he had had. He was a Whig up to the war, and voted for Taylor in 1848 and Fillmore in 1852. Since the war he has been a Democrat—one in whom there is no guile nor shadow of turning. In November, 1874, he was triumphantly elected to Congress, and was re-elected in 1876, 1878, 1880 and 1882. In 1880 he was appointed a delegate to the national Democratic convention at Cincinnati, but did not attend.

Ten years in Congress, consecutively, from 1875 to March 4, 1885, the nominee of Democratic conventions, the record he made, and the zeal and faithfulness he displayed in looking after the interests of his constituents, made him so popular the nomination was again tendered him in 1884, but he declined re-election. He was the first man to introduce a bill in Congress making it a misdemeanor in a Federal officer to demand, receive or contribute money to be used for election purposes; was the first to introduce a bill to make all public roads post roads. He got more money appropriated for the improvement of the Tennessee river than any other member of Congress from Tennessee. He had a United States court established at Chattanooga, and Chattanooga made a port of entry, and secured an appropriation of one hundred thousand dollars to have a custom house built there. Whether the business he was asked to do in Congress came from black or white, Republican or Democrat, or whether the matter was great or small, he attended to it promptly and faithfully, deeming himself the servant of the people as their representative. During his ten years of service he was not absent from roll-call a dozen times. He spoke but little, but in the last Congress in which he served had as much influence as any member, however old. He was on the committees on military affairs, agriculture and pensions. He was the author of the bill permitting producers to sell tobacco by the one hundred pounds. It was remarked by the Hon. Leopold Morse, of Massachusetts, that he could get business through easier than any other man in Congress. Gen. Dibrell replied: "That is because I always have my business in right shape and ready to be passed." At the commencement of the Forty-seventh Congress, the file clerk (Francis, of Alabama), paid him the compliment, of saying, " You have your bills and reports in better shape than any other member of the House." At the last Congress he had a bill passed to pay a war claim over the adverse report of the committee on war claims —the first instance of that committee being defeated— members voting for the bill because " old man Dibrell ' said " it was right," the House taking his judgment in preference to that of the committee.

Gen. Dibrell is now engaged in farming and stock raising near Sparta, and looks much like a well-to-do farmer, cheerful, grateful, happy, and contented to live a plain life. His mansion in the edge of town is a long two-story frame building, standing in a yard full of shade trees and flowering shrubs—a happy-looking home, where one may pass his days enjoying what an apostle seemed worthy of a blessing to be prayed for— " a quiet and peaceable life." His farm at Sparta contains some eight hundred acres, and he owns three others in White county. His success in life is due to his own efforts—to his self-dependence and his economy; and though he has always been liberal to church and school enterprises, he has never wasted money foolishly; never was sued in his life, never was protested on his own paper, but has lost much money by going security, therefore, has cautioned his boys against that hazardous practice. He got into the way of endorsing for people when a candidate for public office, and has suffered from it. He has been a successful trader in stock and is " a good judge of horse-flesh."

In 1866 he was elected a director of the Southwestern railroad, and elected president of it in 1869, a position he held till the road was sold to the Nashville and Chattanooga company, by the State, and afterwards till the road was completed to Sparta, October, 1884. He is now a director in the Bon Air Coal company, of which Ex-Gov. John C. Brown is president, Gen. Dibrell owning one-fourth of the stock.

Gen. Dibrell never belonged to any secret organization except the Grangers, which he joined in 1872. He has been a member of the Southern Methodist church since 1842, has been steward and trustee, and twice a delegate to the General Conference—at Memphis in 1870, and at Nashville in 1882.

Gen. Dibrell married at Sparta, Tennessee, January 13, 1842, Miss Mary E. Leftwich, a native of that town. born October 1, 1824, daughter of Waman Leftwich, a merchant, a native of Wytheville, Virginia, for several years a justice of the peace and county trustee of White county, Tennessee. He died in 1877, at the age of

seventy-five years. Her mother, nee Miss Rebecca Rowland, was raised in Sumner county, Tennessee, and died in 1878, the mother of five children: (1). Mary E. Leftwich, now Mrs. Gen. Dibrell. (2). Matilda J. Leftwich, the wife of Hugh L. Carrick. (3). Louisa M. Leftwich, who died the wife of Joseph Snodgrass. (4). Emily C. Leftwich, now the widow of B. F. Smith. (5). Capt. Jefferson Leftwich, now deceased, and who was captain of company D, Eighth Tennessee cavalry, under Gen. Dibrell.

Mrs. Dibrell's uncle, Isaac J. Leftwich, a lawyer and banker at Wytheville, Virginia, was for many years a member of the Virginia Legislature. His granddaughter, Nannie, is now the wife of Mr. Wadley, a large farmer and lumberman, at Nashville, Tennessee. Mrs. Dibrell was educated by Rev. Dr. C. D. Elliott at the old Nashville Female Academy. She has been a pious member of the Southern Methodist church since 1842. She is a Sunday-school worker, and a member of the Good Templars. She has been economical, prudent and careful, and after the war, when her husband was stripped of his fortune, she came down to work and never complained. She is an exceptionally good manager, and it is probable no lady living so near a town makes bills so seldom as she. Her children idolize her. She spent three winters with Gen. Dibrell in Washington City. They have eight children, seven sons and one daughter: (1). Waman L. Dibrell, born December 3, 1842; educated at Sparta; served through the war and became lieutenant of cavalry under his father; now postmaster at Sparta; has been a notary public, and was for six years clerk and master of the chancery court at Sparta. He married Miss Eveline Morgan, daughter of Rev. James H. Morgan, and has three children, Harvy, Mary Lou and Eugene. (2). William C. Dibrell, born May 7, 1844; now member of the wholesale boot and shoe firm of Murray, Dibrell & Co., Nashville; married November 11, 1869, Miss Kitty Stratton, of Nashville, daughter of Col. Madison Stratton, and has two children, George and Mary L. (3). Joseph A. Dibrell, born November 17, 1845; educated at Sparta; served through the war and became lieutenant of cavalry under his father; now farming in White county, Tennessee; married December 11, 1872, Miss Ritha Brewster, daughter of T. J. Brewster, deceased, of White county. His wife and two children are dead also. (4). Mary Louisa Dibrell, born June 30, 1850; educated at Ward's Seminary, Nashville; married December 12, 1872, James T. Officer, son of Gen. Dibrell's old friend, James C. Officer. She died August 19, 1877, leaving two children, George and Mamie, both of whom are now being raised by Gen. Dibrell. (5). James Dibrell, born June 8, 1852; educated at the University of Knoxville; now farming in White county; married Miss Dora Jett, daughter of John W. Jett, deceased, and has one child, Mary. (6). Jefferson Dibrell, born April 14, 1856; educated at Sparta; now farming in White county; married Miss

Cora Taylor, daughter of John D. Taylor, of White county, and has two children, Frederick and Jane. (7). Frank Dibrell, born August 6, 1868; educated at Emory and Henry College, Virginia, and in the law department of Vanderbilt University, Nashville; now a farmer; married in 1880, Miss Louisa Rhea, of Sparta, daughter of John S. Rhea, deceased; has three children, Rhea, Kate and Aquilla. (8). Stanton Dibrell, born July 24, 1860; educated at Sparta and at Burritt College; now depot and express agent and telegraph operator at Sparta; married October 10, 1883, Miss

Elizabeth Carey, daughter of Prof. J. L. Carey, Franklin, Tennessee, and has one child, Willie.

When the note-gatherer for this volume met Capt. Marchbanks, one of Gen. Dibrell's neighbors, the latter said: "When you find Gen. Dibrell you will see a noble-looking man, of simple, unpretentious manners, but of intelligent, glad, kindly face, and as honest as daylight." The gentleman spoke truly, for Gen. Dibrell's record and character is one which his fellow-citizens throughout the State delight to dwell upon in words of highest encomia.

HON. GEO. W. T. HUGHES.

COLUMBIA.

AMONG the early immigrants to the province of Pennsylvania, and first settlers on the upper branches of the Schuylkill river, in and near the town of Reading, were two brothers of the name of Hugh (afterward changed to Hughes), who came to America from Wales, and one, if not both, of whom were eminent preachers of the Society of Friends. In the same party were two other brothers named Yarnell, from each of whom has sprung a numerous progeny, now scattered over various portions of the United States. Other families of Hugheses, but no other Yarnells are known to have immigrated to America.

As the aborigines retired, the immediate descendants of those four individuals located on the frontier—in many cases the Indians their nearest neighbors. Whenever hostilities occurred they suffered severely in the disasters incident to Indian warfare; their houses were burned; their property destroyed, and yet often among the first to extend the brotherly hand in aiding them to retrieve their fortunes were those same Indians, who, so soon as peace was established, invited them back to the settlements from whence they had been driven.

Prior to the American Revolution, the family of Yarnells located beyond the Broad mountains, at the intersection of the creek which flows between the Mahony and the Mahontaga mountains—the road leading through the then wilderness which separates Shawmaking Fort, at the junction of the two branches of the Susquehanna (now Stansbury) from the settlements near Reading. Very few, if any, families were within twenty miles of them. Still further up the "New Purchase," as it was then called, in virtue of recent treaties with the Indians, upon a most beautiful spot which he had himself as pioneer and surveyor selected, where the Otawassa empties into the Susquehanna, and about half way between Shawmaking Fort and Wyoming settlement, Ellis Hughes (grandson of one of the aforementioned brothers), with his wife (a grand-daughter of one

of the Yarnells), with their young family, had settled. They had already collected many comforts around them, built commodious dwellings, planted orchards, constructed a saw-mill, grist-mill, tannery and smithery. It was about this time that the terrible massacre at Wyoming occurred. The whole of that frontier was abandoned by the settlers, and hundreds of families, destitute of every thing, fled to the settlements below. The improvements at Catawassie were reduced to ashes. When peace was restored and the enemy driven beyond the scene of their depredations, the Yarnell family returned to their former settlements and continued to occupy them, where their descendants are to-day quite numerous. Ellis and Hannah Hughes with their family, now increased to ten children, removed to Chester county, Pennsylvania. He associated himself with a capitalist in Philadelphia, in locating and purchasing lands covering about twenty-five thousand acres, and embracing much of the now valuable coal lands in that section. Before completing their enterprise, Ellis Hughes, while from home employed therein, died at Catawassie, October 6, 1785, aged forty-six years. The lands were lost to the family. "His partner held all the writings." . . . It was amidst the most trying difficulties, and the embarrassments which the war had superinduced, bereft of husband and property, that Hannah Hughes became a widow with a family of ten children. . . . To a meek and truly feminine delicacy of mind, she united, with the most endearing disposition, an uncommon share of both fortitude and perseverance, a quick and steady presence of mind, and a sound understanding which, improved by a large share of eventful experiences, eminently qualified her for the duties of a parent, which now devolved upon her in double measure. . . .

Such, in part, is the record left of Hannah and Ellis Hughes by one of their sons.

After the death of her husband, Hannah Hughes

removed to Baltimore with her ten children, these quite young. The record adds that "the enterprise was blessed of God." She died in April, 1816, and the record is thus closed: "The sermon preached by that eminent minister of the gospel, Mary Mifflin, upon the occasion of returning from the grave, just inclosed, to the meeting then convening, was among the most consoling and eloquent discourses ever listened to by him who leaves this testimony upon record, with the hope that the lesson which he has learned of so impressive a character may not be lost to others. 'Trust in the Lord, O my soul.'"

Phoebe Hughes, the eldest child, married John Skelton, and her family were amongst the earliest settlers of Cincinnati, the Stansburys of that place being descendants of hers. Annabella Hughes, another daughter, married Peter Little, a man of considerable prominence in Maryland, who represented his district for many years in the United States Congress, and whose only son and child married the daughter of Dr. Chapman, a man of note in Baltimore. Mary Hughes, another daughter, was married to Benjamin Fowler, of Washington, by whom she had three daughters, one of whom married A. B. Murray, another Thomas Harrison, and the third Dr. Riley, all of Washington, where their families still reside. The late Mrs. Robert Garrett, of Baltimore, was a daughter of Mrs. Harrison. Elinor Hughes married William Buel. Jeremiah Hughes, a son, located in Baltimore and was, at the time of his death, and for years prior thereto, owner and proprietor of *Niles' National Register*, a paper of wide and powerful influence. Gideon and Thomas Hughes both moved to Ohio, where they settled.

Elijah Hughes, another son, grandfather of the subject of this sketch, removed to Tennessee early in the present century, and settled in Robertson county, near Turnersville, where he continued to reside up to his death, honored and respected by all who knew him. He brought with him to Tennessee a young and beautiful wife, *nee* Miss Ellen Hamilton, a native of Baltimore, who survived him but a short time. By her he had four children, two daughters and two sons: Elizabeth Hughes, who married Rev. Simon Peter, of Kentucky, and removed to Illinois, carrying with them several valuable slaves and emancipating them because they were convinced the institution of slavery was wrong. It need not be added that the courage to do right under such temptations sustained them in a life of usefulness and great prosperity. Mary Hughes married a Mr. Whitehead, and settled at Natchez, Mississippi. Jesse Hughes removed to Louisville, Kentucky, where he married a Miss Buckner. His family now reside at South Bend, Indiana.

Richard E. Hughes, the father of George T. Hughes, remained at the old home, and in early life married a distant relative, Miss Amanda Oursler, whose parents had also emigrated from Baltimore and settled first in Sumner county. Richard E. Hughes possessed to an uncommon degree, those traits which characterized his ancestors, pertinacious resistance of wrong, a clear conception of the rights of his fellow-man, and unswerving devotion to principle. It may be imagined that the immoral and vicious dreaded his power and influence. For years before his death, he succeeded in preventing the sale of liquors in the village in which he lived—by persuasion, by buying the property in which it was sold, even at exorbitant prices, and refusing to allow it to be used for that purpose, and finally, to perpetuate his influence as far as possible, provided in his will that no whisky or intoxicating drink should ever be sold upon any of the lands devised by him, and in case it was done the title should revert to others. When but a boy he learned the trade of a blacksmith, and although in after years he accumulated a considerable estate, yet he never abandoned his hammer and his apron, and to impress upon his only son the dignity and importance of labor, he once went into the rooms of an artist in his working garb, with his arms bare, and steady hand grasping his hammer, which on the "sounding anvil" had wrought out his fortune, his face begrimed with dust, and in this plight, with his boy beside him, had his picture taken.

Richard E. Hughes died at the early age of fifty-two, in the year 1855, leaving surviving him his widow and six children, five daughters and one son, all of the latter comparatively young. His industry and prudence had accumulated sufficient property to secure his family in ease and comfort, which was added to by his wife, who took the entire management of the business, and conducted it with the rarest of good judgment and skill, but unfortunately, most of the property consisted of slaves which were emancipated by the results of the war; and thus mother and children, or those who were still under her roof, consisting of three daughters and the son, the latter being quite young, were thrown upon their own resources.

Nothing but an uncommon share of fortitude and perseverance on the part of the mother, and unquestioning obedience and submission to her guidance on the part of the children, enabled her to complete the education of her children, hold together the remnant of their estate, and start them out into the world with a small competency unencumbered with debts, and, best of all, unencumbered by habits of prodigality. She still lives, beloved and honored by her children, at the advanced age of seventy-three years, with her daughter, Mrs. Minnie Fizer, in Robertson county. She is a member of the Methodist Episcopal church, South. Her children now living are six in number: (1). Emma Hughes, now widow of Dr. C. H. Lockhart, formerly of Clarksville. (2). Ellen Hughes, now wife of Maj. A. J. Allensworth, of San Antonio, Texas. (3). Mary Hughes, now wife of William Darden, a farmer in Robertson county. (4). Sarah Hughes, widow of

Maj. A. W. Bently, formerly of Lawrenceburg, Tennessee, brother of George W. T. Hughes' wife. (5). George W. T. Hughes, subject of this sketch. (6). Minnie Hughes, wife of George M. Fizer, of Robertson county, Tennessee.

George Washington Taylor Hughes was born in Robertson county, Tennessee, February 22, 1847, the day on which the battle of Buena Vista was fought; this coincidence coupled with the fact that it was also Washington's birthday, accounts for his name doubtless. He received his education at the schools of his native village, until the age of twelve, when he entered Stewart College, at Clarksville, Tennessee, in the freshman class, and remained there until the commencement of hostilities. In the fall of 1864 he entered school at Eminence, Kentucky, and remained until the summer of 1865, having completed only a portion of his studies, expecting to return and complete his course the ensuing session. As the representative of his literary society, he delivered an address on February 22, 1865, which was complimented in the papers of Louisville, and he was unanimously selected as the representative of his class at the close of the term. On his return home his mother did not think the condition of the estate would justify the expense of returning him to college. He then, after some hesitation, and not until persuaded to that course by friends, commenced the study of law, under the direction of Hon. James E. Bailey, of Clarksville. After spending several months in study he entered the law school at Lebanon, Tennessee, and left that school in the summer of 1868; first located in Sprinfield, Tennessee, where he was licensed to practice law by Judges Alexander Campbell and Frazer, but after a few months removed to Lawrence county, Tennessee. He practiced at Lawrenceburg from June, 1869, to June, 1876, and then moved to Columbia, Tennessee, where he has practiced ever since, first in partnership with Maj. Isaac N. Barnett, until the latter's death, in September, 1884, and since in partnership with Mr. E. H. Hatcher, the style of the firm being Hughes & Hatcher.

Mr. Hughes is a Democrat, though his father was a zealous Clay Whig. He has, however, never been a candidate for office, and never held office except that of alderman of Lawrenceburg two or three years, and at Columbia, where, as the first president of the board of education, he assisted in the organization of the public schools. One thing of which he is proud, that he has never attended a political convention, never had much to do with politics, though by no means neutral in matters pertaining to the welfare of his country. At twenty-one he joined the Masons at Springfield, but has taken only the Blue Lodge degrees. He is a Knight of Honor; a member of the Methodist Episcopal church, South, as were all his people on both sides before him, since the organization of that church; is a Sunday-school teacher, and for fifteen years a Sunday-school superintendent, and is now a trustee of the church at Columbia.

Mr. Hughes married at Lawrenceburg, June 3, 1869, Miss Lilly V. Bently, daughter of Daniel Bently and Matilda Bently, nee Miss Matilda Lindsley, of Maury county. Mrs. Hughes' father was a capitalist and the first president of the Lawrenceburg bank; was a self-made man; started in life without means, and made his fortune merchandising and trading, and later in life went into the banking business and loaning of money.

By his marriage with Miss Bently Mr. Hughes has two children: (1). Leonard Hughes, born at Lawrenceburg, September 18, 1871. (2). Emma Clare, born at Lawrenceburg, May 5, 1874.

Mr. Hughes began life on a small patrimony, and his wife brought him a small estate. He is now reckoned among the few Tennessee lawyers who are good financial successes. He has faithfully met the duties his profession imposed upon him; has never had any bad habits; never drank a quart of intoxicating liquors in his life; never made a bet; has been content to make money in a légitimate way; never deals in futures, and avoids going security. He is now a director in the Columbia Cotton Mill company, and also in the Columbia Water company. He has occasionally acted as special chancellor by election of the members of the bar. He is regarded as a very fine chancery lawyer; a careful, industrious, thorough investigator, of a logical turn, a good reasoner, and progressive in his profession.

RICHARD R. DASHIELL.

JACKSON.

DR. RICHARD R. DASHIELL is descended of a Maryland Huguenot family. His great-grandfather fled from France to England, where he married a sister of Lord Fairfax, came to America, and settled on the eastern shore of Maryland about 1750. His son, Rev. George Dashiell, was rector of St. Peter's church in Baltimore in 1790, when Baltimore was a little village. He married a sister of Gen. W. S. Winder, a Baltimore lawyer of political and social distinction, and who was defeated by the British at Bladensburg in the war of 1812. Rev. George Dashiell was the leader of the movement in the division of the Protestant Episcopal church into high and low parties, he adhering to the low church party.

Dr. Dashiell's father, Alfred H. Dashiell, was born in Baltimore in 1794, was a clergyman in the Episcopal church, going with his father, and finally joined the Presbyterian church. He was pastor of a Presbyterian church in Philadelphia ten years; then pastor of a church three years in Jacksonville, Illinois; next was president of the Nashville Female Academy four years; then was pastor of the Presbyterian church at Franklin, Tennessee, four years; then for fifteen years was pastor of the church at Shelbyville, Tennessee; afterwards for two or three years was president of the Rogersville College, East Tennessee, and finally removed to Brooklyn, New York, where he died in 1882, at the age of eighty-six, leaving a reputation for unyielding courage in standing for whatever he thought right, and for boldness in the declaration of his convictions, however unpopular. He was a man of great force as a speaker. He left living seven children, of whom Dr. Richard R. Dashiell is the oldest. His son, George Dashiell, is a cotton merchant at Memphis. His son, Rev. A. H. Dashiell, is pastor of the Presbyterian church at Lake View, New Jersey. His son, Dr. W. B. Dashiell, is a large farmer at Kaufman, Texas. His daughter, Emily E. Dashiell, is now the widow of Jesse H. McMahon, widely known as the editor of the old Memphis Enquirer. His daughter, Sophie R. Dashiell, is now the wife of Capt. Carter Harrison, of Murfreesborough, grandson of President Harrison. His daughter, Lavinia C. Dashiell, is now the wife of Dr. William Lytle, of Murfreesborough.

Dr. Dashiell's mother, nee Miss Ann Ridgely, was the daughter of Judge Richard Ridgely, of the Supreme court of Maryland. Her mother was a Miss Dorsey. Dr. Dashiell's mother was, on her mother's side, a cousin of Judge Chase, of the Supreme court of the United States, who was appointed by Gen. Washington. She was also cousin of Hon. Reverdy Johnson, and of Gov. Howard, of Maryland, and was a niece of Nicholas Ridgely, the leading merchant of Baltimore in his day. She died at Brooklyn, New York, in 1880, at the age of eighty-one. Her leading characteristics were religious fervor and devotion to her children.

Dr. Dashiell was born in Baltimore, August 18, 1816, and lived in that city until ten years of age. His next ten years he passed in Philadelphia. He graduated at Amherst College, Massachusetts, in 1833; afterward studied medicine four years in the University of Pennsylvania, graduating in 1837, under Profs. Chapman, Gibson, Dewees, Horner, Rogers and Jackson. He settled in St. Louis in 1837, where he practiced nine months, when that city had only twelve thousand inhabitants. He next settled at Nashville and practiced there, 1839-40, when he was invited to take charge of the iron works below Clarksville, and there he practiced and farmed nine years. In 1847 he removed to Jackson,

30

Tennessee, where he has practiced ever since, farming before the war, but not since.

During the war he was appointed by Gov. Isham G. Harris, surgeon of the Sixth Tennessee Confederate regiment (Col. William H. Stephens), and in this capacity served through the war, in Tennessee, Kentucky and Georgia. He had charge of the Beauregard hos-. pital at Jackson, in 1862, and retained that position till ordered to the field.

Dr. Dashiell was one of the earlier members of the Medical Society of the State of Tennessee, at Nashville, of which Dr. Felix Robertson was the first president. He occasionally contributes articles to medical journals, chiefly on diseases peculiar to the Forked Deer valley.

Dr. Dashiell is an Entered Apprentice Mason, an ancient Odd Fellow, a member of the Knights of the Golden Rule; in politics a Democrat, though formerly an old line Whig; for two years was an alderman of Jackson, and in religion has been a Methodist for forty-five years, and has served as steward and trustee. In 1850-51-52, he was a partner of Col. W. W. Gates, of the West Tennessee Whig, and edited that paper two years in the interest of the Whig party, and supported Gen. Scott for president.

Dr. Dashiell first married in Stewart county, Tennessee, in 1841, Miss Louisa Jane Kizer, by whom he has one child, Miss Emily E. Dashiell, a graduate of the Conference Female Institute at Jackson, in which she taught music one year, and is now teaching music in that city. She is also highly educated in other branches.

Dr. Dashiell's first wife dying in 1848, he next married at Jackson, January 15, 1850, Miss Eliza Jane Taylor, daughter of Col. Richard Taylor, a planter, originally from North Carolina. Her mother was a daughter of Philip Alston, a planter of Madison county, Tennessee, originally from Chatham county, North Carolina. Mrs. Dashiell graduated at the school of Rev. William Findley, at Jackson, Tennessee, and is a lady noted for her devotion to her church and for her domestic economy.

By this marriage Dr. Dashiell has four children: (1). George T. Dashiell, born in October, 1850; educated at West Tennessee College; was for four years private secretary of Gov. Richard Coke, of Texas, and is now engaged in stock raising and railroading at Kaufman, Texas. (2). Annie Ridgely Dashiell, graduated at Conference Female Institute, Jackson. (3). Richard H. Dashiell, born in February, 1856; educated at West Tennessee College, and is now in mercantile business at Jackson. (4). Alfred T. Dashiell, graduated from the Southern Baptist University at Jackson, and died in 1881, at the age of twenty-one.

In setting out in professional life, Dr. Dashiell aimed to attain high standing as a surgeon and practitioner, and has succeeded, both professionally and financially, and built up for himself a high character, and a reputation as one of the standard men of his city and State.

MAJ. HENDERSON MITCHELL FOLSOM.

ELIZABETHTON.

THE subject of this sketch, residing within the romantic mountain region of upper East Tennessee, can justly lay claim to a proud English lineage. Many distinguished persons, bearing the name of Folsom, figured in English civil and military history. The American Folsoms are descended directly from the Earl of Percy. Persons who mention with commendable pride their distinguished ancestry are not infrequently ridiculed by people whose plebeian motto is, "Let every tub stand on its own bottom," and who are unwilling to give credit to father, mother or remote ancestor for any of their own better characteristics. After interviewing more than twelve hundred persons and studying their family histories, the editor is of opinion that an honorable family pride is a very potent factor in the formation of individual character, and is oftentimes the main inspiration of lofty endeavor. No one of proper sentiment can fail to feel a pride in ancestry which was the boast of chivalrous days, especially if, like the Folsoms, he can trace his lineage back to the grand old days of the Crusaders, when his progenitors left home and friends and battled against the followers of Mohammed for the sepulchre of Christ.

Three brothers, sons of the Earl of Percy and the Countess of Foulsham, found it necessary, in 1760, to leave England on account of their sympathy with the American colonies in their complaints and struggles against the mother country. They very naturally bent their course toward America, landing at Portsmouth, New Hampshire, where two of the brothers settled. The other settled in South Carolina. Only one of the Portsmouth brothers married, and from him descended the northern branch of the family, including the California Folsoms, for whom Folsom City, California, is named. The brother who settled in South Carolina, the great-grandfather of Maj. Folsom, was a captain in the Revolutionary army. His descendants are settled in South Carolina, Florida, Georgia, Arkansas, Indian Territory and Tennessee.

The grandfather of Maj. Folsom lived in Moore county, North Carolina. He died in the service of the United States, at Norfolk, Virginia, where he is buried.

The father, Malcolm Neilson Folsom, was born in Moore county, North Carolina, December 5, 1792, was married in that county and moved to Tennessee about 1820. He settled first in Greene county, but afterwards removed to Carter, where he farmed and held a number of public offices, among them, register of the county, county court clerk and justice of the peace for eighteen years. During the eighteen years he tried six thousand recorded civil causes, and but three of his decisions were ever reversed on appeal, an extraordinary record. His education was limited to ninety days' schooling, but he had strong native sense, and was a man of strong convictions and undoubted integrity. He was a soldier in the war of 1812. He had three honorable discharges from the army during that war, having enlisted three several times for limited periods. He died February 22, 1878.

The mother of Maj. Folsom, Nancy Hughes, was a native of Moore county, North Carolina. She was, in all respects, a model woman, industrious, frugal, gentle in her disposition, and noted for her hospitality. She was a member of the Methodist church, as was also her husband. She died at Elizabethton, April 16, 1877, about seventy-five years of age.

There were left surviving Malcolm and Nancy Folsom, eight children, viz.: (1). William James. (2). George W. (3). Nancy. (4). Thomas S. (5). Mary. (6). Henderson M., subject of this sketch. (7). Benjamin F. (8). Sarah.

Maj. H. M. Folsom, the subject of this sketch, was born at Elizabethton, Tennessee, October 4, 1831, and has made that his home all his life. He has been, in great degree, the architect of his own fortune. He began life for himself at the age of sixteen, at which time he set out for Missouri to enter Ebenezer High School, ten miles north of Springfield. After two years' study there he went to school no more. Previous to his going to Missouri, he had spent a short while at Emory and Henry College, Virginia, and also about a year at Holston College, New Market, Tennessee, under president Allen H. Mathes, who, leaving that institution for Missouri, persuaded young Folsom to accompany him, promising that his board and tuition should cost him nothing. After quitting school, Maj. Folsom went to merchandising in partnership with Dr. G. T. Magee, at Elizabethton, meanwhile, as opportunity offered, reading law under the instruction of Gen. James T. Carter. In 1856 he was licensed to practice by Judge Seth J. W. Luckey and Chancellor Thomas L. Williams. Soon afterward, he was appointed clerk and master, a position which he held for six years. Since his retirement from that position he has devoted himself closely to his profession, excepting the interruption caused by the war, and has had an exceptionally successful career at the bar.

Maj. Folsom entered the Confederate service October 23, 1862, as major and quartermaster on the staff of Gen. Alfred E. Jackson. In June, 1864, he was transferred, with same rank, to Gen. John C. Vaughn's command, Army of Northern Virginia, and was quartermaster on his staff for three months. He was then transferred to Gen. Wharton's brigade, Northern Virginia, in the same capacity, but, after one month in that position, he was ordered to Gen. Joseph E. Johnston's army, then in Georgia, but never reached it, owing to the Federal occupation of East Tennessee, and western North Carolina. In November, 1864, he rejoined Gen. Jackson's command and remained with him till the close of the war. Maj. Folsom took part in the battles of Piedmont, Lynchburg, and Liberty, Virginia, in June, 1864; in the capture of Martinsburg, Virginia, July 4, 1864; Winchester, September 19, 1864; Cedar Creek, October 19, 1864. The commission which he held—that of major—was the highest in rank from Carter county in the Confederate army.

In regard to politics, under the old division of parties Maj. Folsom was a Whig, and voted for the last ticket that party ever put into the presidential race, Bell and Everett. Since the war, he has been a Democrat. Not approving the course of reconstruction and disliking the feeling evinced by the Republican party towards the people of the South, he felt constrained to co-operate with the Democratic party as the one from which the South had most to hope. He has never taken an active part in politics in any way, and was never a candidate for public office, though his friends, without any offering on his part, have several times had his name before congressional conventions. Though very decided and steadfast in his political views, he has no taste for the business of politics.

In 1854, Maj. Folsom was made a Master Mason, at Elizabethton, Dashiell Lodge, No. 238, and has served in every office in the lodge. For ten years he has been attorney for the Knoxville Car Wheel Company. He is a member and steward of the Methodist Episcopal church, South, and several times has been a lay delegate to the Holston annual conference and to the district conference. Though now in his fifty-fifth year, Maj. Folsom has never in his life sworn a profane oath, having, from boyhood, refrained from the habit, under the solemn conviction that it was wrong to swear. It would seem that a man who had served through the war as quartermaster, and had encountered the vexatious experiences of the court-room for nearly thirty years, without swearing at all, deserves a place in this volume alongside of the venerable Dr. J. B. McFerrin, who is on record as having never told a lie in his life. Maj. Folsom himself said to the writer: "I am not conscious of having ever told a wilful, mischievous lie in my life; nor, in a married life of thirty years, have I ever been unfaithful to my marriage vows." He joined the church in 1854, and was for many years Sunday-school teacher, deeply interested in the welfare of the rising generation.

Maj. Folsom was married at Elizabethton, September 30, 1854, to Miss Sarah Elizabeth Berry, who was born in Carter county. She is the daughter of John Berry, a soldier of the war of 1812, one of the defenders of Fort McHenry, near Baltimore, upon the storming of the fort by the British in 1814. He was a printer by

trade and a native of Virginia, and came to Tennessee with his wife, whom he married in Shenandoah county, Virginia. His wife, neé Catharine (Kitty) Shryock, now living in Bristol at the age of ninety years, is the sister of United States Senator Riddleberger's mother, so that Mrs. Folsom and the senator are first cousins.

Mrs. Folsom was educated at Rogersville Female College, and has the reputation of having done her whole duty as a Christian lady in all the relations of life. She is a woman of fine practical sense, patient, gentle, affectionate, and commands the love of all who know her. In her girlhood, she was somewhat noted for her personal beauty and sweetness of disposition, but her highest encomium is to be found in the fact—which both husband and wife concern—that during the thirty years of their married life, not a cross or harsh word from either side has passed between them.

Maj. Folsom and wife have had four children: (1). John Malcolm, born January 5, 1857; was educated at Bristol and Athens, Tennessee; now a druggist at Elizabethton; married, March, 1884, Miss Amelia Stover, daughter of Dr. S. M. Stover, of Carter county; they have one child, Henderson Matson, born July 19, 1885. (2). William Berry, born November 17, 1859; educated at Morristown and at home under private teachers; died May 5, 1878. The morning before he died he said to his father at his bed-side: "I have been thinking over my whole life, and I cannot remember an unkind word you ever said to me." It is a comforting remembrance of the son, to the parent, that he never tasted strong drink nor swore an oath in his life. (3). Ida, born August 21, 1862; was educated at Sullins College, Bristol, but after going through the entire course, she declined the diploma offered her. (4). Minnie, born January 1, 1867; graduated June, 1885, at Sullins College. In her junior year, she won the reader's medal from the senior class.

Of the southern Folsoms, Col. Folsom, of Gordon, Georgia, commander of the Fourteenth Georgia regiment, Confederate States army, was killed in the battle of the Wilderness. A commission promoting him to the rank of brigadier-general reached army headquarters the day after his death. Col. James M. Folsom, brother of the last-named, was adjutant-general of the State of Georgia during the war, and is now a commission merchant at Gordon, Georgia. He is the author of the "History of the Georgia Regiments in the Confederate Service." Capt. W. W. Folsom was in the Confederate service, and after the war edited a paper in Arkansas, where he still lives.

Nathaniel Folsom, a great-great uncle of Maj. Folsom, when about twenty years of age, left home and took up his residence with the Choctaw Indians. He married a daughter of the Choctaw chief, and by her had a large family of children, the descendants of whom, some two hundred in number, live now in the Choctaw Nation, Indian Territory. Of these there have been quite a number of men distinguished among the Indians, notably Hon. Israel Folsom, who, for many years, was agent of the Choctaw tribe at Washington, and also acted as government agent in its dealings with the tribe.

Enough has been said, probably, to carry a pretty clear idea of Maj. Folsom's character as a man and lawyer. If anything be lacking in this regard, however, the opinion of one of the judges of our Supreme court, before whom Maj. Folsom has practiced for many years, may well round up this sketch. The distinguished jurist says: "Maj. Folsom is a man of more than ordinary modesty, but calm and self-possessed in debate, always having perfect command of his faculties. Within the range of his investigation, he is one of the most accurate and thorough lawyers in our State. His preparation of his cases is thorough—his mastery both of details and the principles governing them, always full. His briefs are among the best in form, neatness of arrangement and precision of statement, that come before our court. He is always clear and understood at once, and at times rises to the height of a chaste and well-tempered eloquence. If he had a larger field, with his habits of thorough mastery of all he undertakes, he would rise to the front rank of useful men in the State. His eminent fairness and truthfulness of statement, as well as argument, always give him command of the earnest attention of the court. He is incapable of any trickery or cunning. All he does is the work of a man who seeks to win his cause by manly grapple. What cannot be done by fair argument and the force of truth, would not be sought by him, for either himself or clients. Take him altogether, he is an ornament to the bar of his section, and he would grace any court in our State, as a judge, by his fine judicial qualities, both of head and heart, especially the latter. His nice sense of right is the equivalent of a large share of simple intellect. He is emphatically a specimen of God's noblest workmanship—an honest man."

The ordinary language of panegyric could add nothing to such a testimonial as that. That it is deserved is abundantly proven by the success that has attended Maj. Folsom's professional labors. And he is yet, in reality, a comparatively young man. Though fifty-four years of age, there is not a silvered hair on his head, and he seems to be yet in his physical prime. He may well still look ahead and aloft, for there are no doubt greater triumphs yet awaiting him.

HON. GEORGE K. FOOTE.

JACKSON.

THE Footes came originally from England before the revolt of the colonies, and settled first in Connecticut. Thence most of them moved south, some taking up their abode in Virginia, and others settling in North Carolina. From the Virginia branch of the family was descended the late Hon. Henry S. Foote, for many years a conspicuous figure in politics. From the North Carolina branch, the subject of this sketch is descended. His grandfather, George Foote, was born in North Carolina and became a farmer in that State. He was a soldier of the Revolution and fought with distinction in the battle of Guilford Court-house. He removed at an early day to Kentucky, being one of the first settlers in that State. About the year 1818, he pushed still further west, locating in Indiana, not far from the residence of Gen. William Henry Harrison. Here he spent the remainder of his life, dying at the advanced age of eighty-seven years. He was a man of solid character—a true type of the old-school gentleman. His wife was Lucretia Nance, daughter of Thomas Nance, of South Carolina, a relative of the Ruffin family of North Carolina. She was a worthy helpmeet to her husband, whom she outlived, having died at the extreme age of ninety years. She left four children surviving her: William, Kinchloe, George and John Foote.

Rev. William Foote, father of the subject of this sketch, and a prominent minister of the Methodist Episcopal church, was born at Guilford Court-house, North Carolina. He was a farmer as well as preacher. He was married in Indiana, where the greater portion of his life was spent, and where he died in 1846, in the forty-sixth year of his age. In politics he was an ardent Whig. His wife, the mother of our subject, was Naomi Bell, daughter of Samuel Bell, of Kentucky. She was born near Harrodsburg, Kentucky. Her mother was a Ross, and became noted as one of fourteen women who volunteered to venture out of the fort near Harrodsburg, to get water for the famishing garrison when it was surrounded by Indians, knowing it would be certain death for the men to expose themselves within range of the savages' rifles. She lived amid the tragic events that gave to the soil of Kentucky the name of "the dark and bloody ground." Her father was Judge Ross, one of the most noted of the blue-grass pioneers.

Judge Foote's mother lived but about a year after the death of her husband. She was a woman of much fortitude and energy, a devoted wife and mother, and exceedingly careful in the training of her children. She died at Corydon, Indiana, November, 1847, at the age of forty-six, leaving three children: (1). George K., subject of this sketch. (2). Robert, now in Memphis.

(3). Jabez, who lost his life by the explosion of the steamer "Andrew Jackson," on the Ohio river, near Shawneetown, Illinois.

Judge Foote grew to manhood in Harrison county, Indiana. He was a farmer boy, and learned to lay brick and plaster when a youth, and was especially fond of field-sports, hunting, fishing and fox-chasing, though he was free from the too common vicious habits of youth. He was educated in the old Corydon University. When twenty-one years of age, he married, settled in Corydon and engaged in general speculation. In 1847 he removed to Leavenworth, Indiana, where he began the practice of law. He remained there but two years, however, when he removed to Cannelton, Indiana. Here he practiced his profession about eighteen months, when he moved to Golconda, Illinois, where, in addition to the practice of law, he engaged in the real estate business and lead-mining for ten years, doing a very prosperous business. In 1866 he removed to Decaturville, Tennessee, where he remained about eighteen months. Next he moved to Lexington, Tennessee, and thence, in 1873, to Jackson, where he has resided ever since, engaged chiefly in the practice of law.

In politics, Judge Foote was a Whig until the disintegration of that party. In 1860 he voted for Abraham Lincoln, and has been a Republican ever since. The first office he ever held was that of constable, in Cannelton, Indiana. In 1879 he was appointed special commissioner of the Southern Claims Commission, and discharged the duties of that position some four years. In June, 1881, he was appointed by President Garfield postmaster at Jackson, and on the 14th of October following, was reappointed by President Arthur to the same position, which, at the time this sketch is prepared, he still holds.

In June, 1863, Judge Foote was mustered into the United States volunteer service, as a member of the One Hundred and Thirty-sixth Illinois infantry, but on account of his business qualities he was assigned to permanent duty in the commissary department and was not engaged in battle afterward. He remained with the army in Kentucky and Missouri until 1864.

Judge Foote was an alternate district delegate to the national Republican convention at Chicago, in 1884, and favored the nomination of President Arthur by that body. He became a Mason in Cannelton, Indiana, in 1851. He is also an Odd Fellow.

In 1846, October 16, Judge Foote was married, in Harrison county, Indiana, to Miss Mary Falkenburgh, who was born and reared at Cape May, New Jersey. She is a member of the Christian church, and is a lady noted for her piety and charity to the poor and distressed. Mrs. Foote's father was a captain in the war of 1812. Her mother was Elizabeth Sullivan, also a native of New Jersey.

There were born to Judge Foote and wife the following children, none of whom are now living: (1). Samuel, who was in the gunboat service during the war. He married a Miss Clore and died in 1868, aged twenty-four. (2). William, died February, 1874. (3). Mozella, died the wife of William Wilson, a merchant, of Lexington, Tennessee, leaving one child, George. (4). George, died March, 1884, at the age of twenty-three. (5). Ada, died in 1884. This daughter contributed to various periodicals and was remarkably gifted. Three children died in infancy.

Judge Foote began life with no resources but his own talents. He had plenty of pluck, however, and struck boldly out into the world with the determination to succeed. The first money he ever earned was as a hired plow-boy, at eight dollars a month. Being paid off at the end of three months, he went proudly home and laid his twenty-four silver dollars in his mother's lap. He was never after that either ashamed or afraid of work. Whenever the practice of the law became a dragging business (as it will periodically in nearly all communities), he did not sit down, fold his arms and wait for business to come to him. He turned his hand at once to whatever honorable enterprise promised reasonable profits. His first substantial profits were realized as contractor in brick-laying and plastering in the town of Cannelton, Indiana. Industry and economy have ever been his leading characteristics, and these constitute the secret of his success. He is now in quite independent and comfortable circumstances, and is reckoned one of the solid men of his county.

CAPT. WILLIAM STOCKELL.

NASHVILLE.

CAPT. WILLIAM STOCKELL, the veteran "fire chief," the successful merchant and business man, and one of the most popular citizens of Nashville, whose face and form have long been familiar to almost every man, woman and child in that city, well deserves a place n these pages. He was born in Malton, Yorkshire, England, October 17, 1815. His grandfather, William Stockell, born at Malton, sprang from an old English family that lived for many years in that vicinity. He raised a large family of sons and daughters, the sons being chiefly distinguished as successful merchants. One of his daughters, Margaret Stockell, married a Mr.

Jewett, and lived to the good old age of eighty-four years.

Capt. Stockell's father, also named William Stockell, was a son of William Stockell, of Malton—thus grandfather, father and son being born in the same town. Capt. Stockell's father was a seafaring man, came to America, bringing his family with him, in 1824, and settled in Baltimore. In 1829 he moved to Cincinnati, where he remained three years, then purchasd a farm in Brown county, Ohio, and lived there until 1839. In the latter year he removed to Nashville, Tennessee, and took charge of the construction of the buildings and grounds of the University of Nashville, then under the presidency of Rev. Dr. Philip Lindsley. In 1845, while walking through the grounds, he accidentally stepped on a rusty nail, which penetrated his foot, produced lockjaw, resulting in his death. He was one of those energetic, pushing, go-ahead men, who build up society, and leave the world better for having lived in it. He was a bountiful provider for his family, and gave his children the best educational advantages for those times.

Capt. Stockell's mother, nee Miss Jane Gray, was born in Pickering, Yorkshire. England, daughter of William Gray, a merchant miller. She was a member of the Methodist church, a lady of great piety, and remarkable for her energy, industry and domestic management. She died in Nashville, at the home of her daughter, Mrs. Carrie Hight, wife of Capt. O. H. Hight, now secretary of the Nashville Merchants' Exchange. She was the mother of five children: (1). William Stockell, subject of this sketch. (2). Elizabeth Stockell, died the wife of George W. Lincoln. (3). Mary Ann Stockell, who also became the wife of George W. Lincoln, and after his death, married Howell Huddleston Averitt. (4). Jane E. Stockell, died the widow of David C. Love, for a long time circuit court clerk at Nashville. (5). Caroline Stockell, now wife of Oliver H. Hight, above mentioned.

Capt. Stockell in his boyhood had but limited educational advantages, but having learned the bricklayer's and plasterer's business in Cincinnati, and carried it on there until 1846, at odd moments and during leisure time, he applied himself closely to such books as would qualify him in making calculations for a business of that description. He also studiously and diligently applied himself in learning drawing, designing and modeling ornaments of every conceivable pattern for the interior decoration of churches, public edifices, and fine private buildings. In the latter particular he was eminently successful, producing numberless exquisitely beautiful and refined specimens, wonderful both as to their great variety and finished workmanship. The finishing and interior decoration of the State Capitol at Nashville, the Masonic Hall, the Maxwell House, the Tennessee Hospital for the Insane, and numerous other public and private edifices in Tennessee are specimens of his superb handiwork. There was a time when he

was the only decorator of the interior of buildings in stucco work at Nashville, and all of the parties now engaged in that business in the city learned their trades with him, and are recognized as master workmen in their lines. The house in which he now lives, No. 63 South Cherry street, was one among the first modern houses in the city of Nashville, the interior finish of which would do credit to any city in America, and is recognized by architects who come to see it as of superior finish and original design. During Capt. Stockell's entire business life in Nashville, his relations with all he ever worked for or with, have been of the most pleasant character. To a man doing so heavy a business for so many people over so long a period of time, it must be a most happy reflection that he has never had to sue for his collections, and that his social relations are not marred or embittered by unpleasant memories. Everybody knows Capt. Stockell; even the children cannot meet or pass him on the street, without giving him that hearty salute that only kindly natures and long established characters can command; an incident recalling Homer's lines:

> " 'Till late in life, descending as to rest,
>   His people blessing, by his people blest."

But it is perhaps chiefly from his honorable record as a fireman, and as chief of the fire department of the city of Nashville for many years, Capt. Stockell is best known by the general public. His gallantry and bravery on trying occasions; his cool-headed wisdom and executive ability in hours of peril; his many sacrifices of personal comfort to save the lives and property of others; his promptness in responding to the first tap of the alarm bell—in rain or shine, night or day, winter or summer—these have been themes of praise for two generations past, and must bring to the fearless "old chief" many pleasant recollections of good service, well and faithfully done. In 1840 he became president of the Independent Western Fire Company of Cincinnati, and filled that position until November 12, 1846, when he left Cincinnati to make his home at Nashville. Just before his departure, the members of his old company each took from their pockets a silver dollar and had them melted into a beautiful and heavy silver speaking trumpet, which they presented to him "in remembrance of his services." It is a souvenir which the Captain shows with much pride, and regards as an heirloom money could not buy.

He connected himself with the volunteer fire department of Nashville in 1847, soon after his arrival in Nashville, joining " Broad-street Fire Company, No. 2," and a few months thereafter was elected its presiden and remained as such until 1859, when the paid steam fire department was organized. Being in a lucrative business which he could not sacrifice, he retired at that time from the department, having been requested, however, at all times to attend fires and give his counsel which he did, always having the confidence and goo will of the chief in charge and of the firemen. He was appointed by the city council December 28, 1866, to go East and purchase steam fire apparatus for the city, a letter of credit being given him by the city authorities for the purpose to the amount of twenty thousand dollars. He made the purchase, which resulted in a large saving to the city, the apparatus then bought being still in use and in good condition.

In July, 1869, Hon. John M. Bass having been appointed by the chancery court receiver of the city of Nashville, called to his aid and counsel the wisest men of undoubted character and standing highest in public esteem, among them Anson Nelson, whom he appointed treasurer, and Capt. William Stockell, whom he placed in charge of the fire department, Capt. Stockell accepting the position at the urgent request of leading citizens, and especially of the insurance companies. His appointment by Mr. Bass, dated July 28, 1869, empowered him "to organize the fire department as his agent and conduct the same on the most economical plan, having a due regard to efficiency." From that date until his final retirement in 1883, he was elected by the city council from time to time, and served altogether in that capacity fourteen consecutive years. During this time he was also secretary of the board of building commissioners, making annual reports of the lumber business, buildings erected, and progress of the city in general, many of his reports having been commended very highly by the press.

He was one of the organizers of the national convention of chief fire engineers of the United States at Baltimore; has been president of that body, and is now chairman of its finance committee. At the meeting of the association at Chicago, September 9, 1884, Capt. Stockell read two remarkable papers, one "an essay on the best methods of supplying cities with water for fire purposes," and one "on the importance of introducing fire drills into all the schools."

In 1884, by request of the Tennessee Historical Society, of which he is a member, he prepared and submitted an elaborate "history of the fire department of Tennessee," which was replete with many pleasant reminiscences and practical suggestions, and was received with great favor.

He is a member of the A. O. M. C., now styled the Robertson Association, and in 1884, in connection with Anson Nelson, Esq., and Dr. John Berrien Lindsley, revised its constitution.

Capt. Stockell was made a Mason in Claiborne Lodge in Nashville; is now a member of Cumberland Lodge, No. 8, and is president of the board of trustees, having charge of the property of that lodge. On October 24, 1882, he was made a 32° Mason by Gen. Albert Pike. He is also a Knight of Pythias of the endowment rank; was one of the organizers of Myrtle Lodge, and is a member of the Grand Lodge of that order. He is a member of the Cumberland Presbyterian church. In

politics he was a Whig till the Know-nothing issue came up, when he voted for Andrew Johnson for governor, and has been a Democrat ever since. In 1850 he was elected from a Democratic ward—the Sixth—a member of the city council, and re-elected in 1852-3. He was a member of the city board of education with such men as Francis B. Fogg, Return J. Meigs, Col. M. H. Howard and W. F. Bang, in the early organization of the public schools of Nashville. He was for a long time a director in the State Bank of Tennessee, appointed by Gov. Johnson and afterwards by Gov. Harris. He was also a director and one of the organizers of the Mechanics National Bank of Nashville; also a member of the State Agricultural Bureau, appointed by Gov. Johnson and also by Gov. Harris. He was one of the organizers of the first mechanics' fairs ever held in the city of Nashville. The first fair was held in a store on the Public Square. He has also been connected with all the industrial expositions that have been held in the city of Nashville, being president of the exposition in 1873, and chairman of the Nashville Centennial Exposition in 1880. In 1885 he was assistant commissioner for Tennessee at the Cotton Centennial Exposition and World's Fair held at New Orleans.

Capt. Stockell married first in Brown county, Ohio, in 1838, Miss Gelina Records, daughter of Josiah Records. She died June 11, 1839. He next married in Cincinnati, Ohio, May 3, 1840, Miss Rachel Wright, daughter of Joseph Wright, formerly from New Jersey. Her mother, Sarah Bowers, was also a native of New Jersey. Mrs. Stockell was born, raised and educated in Philadelphia, and moved to Cincinnati, in 1839. Her father was a farmer, who lived to be eighty-three years old, active to the very last. She is a devoted and active member of the Cumberland Presbyterian church at Nashville.

By his marriage with Miss Wright, Capt. Stockell had nine children, four of whom died in childhood. Those who reached maturity were: (1). Charles Henry Stockell, born in Cincinnati, April 8, 1841; was a member of the Rock City Guards, and afterward an officer in the Tenth Tennessee, and served in the Confederate army four years; married December 19, 1875, Miss Winnie Hollis, of Louisville, Kentucky, and has one child, Dake; now residing in Atlanta, Georgia, and connected with an extensive commercial firm. (2). Louisa J. Stockell, born in Cincinnati, June 14, 1844; graduated at Loretta and at Nashville; married W. R. Rankin, an attorney at law, July 18, 1865; has five children, David, Charles, Mary, Albert and Turley. (3). William Franklin Stockell, born in Cincinnati, March 7, 1846; enlisted in the Confederate army and was drowned while crossing a river, December 25, 1863. (4). Albert W. Stockell, born in Nashville, August 8, 1848; graduated from the literary and law departments of Cumberland University; practiced law successfully at Columbia, Tennessee; married, January 4, 1876, Miss

Eloise Cooper, daughter of Matthew D. Cooper, and sister of Judge William F. and Ex-United States Senator Henry Cooper; has four children, Marian, Patty, Albert and Henry. (5). George W. Stockell, born at Nashville, April 2, 1852; now head of the firm of George W. Stockell & Co., in the wholesale agricultural implement business at Nashville. (6). Orville Ewing Stockell, born September 14, 1855; now a partner in the house with his brother, George W.; married November 8, 1877, Miss Ida F. Gower; has one child, Rachel.

Capt. Stockell began married life with ninety-six dollars, and by hard work and honesty of purpose has made a fortune and a name among the most honored citizens of Nashville. Still happier, no man can say Capt. Stockell ever wronged him out of a cent, or that he came to his office Saturday nights and went away without the money due for his week's work. Happiest of all, he and his companionable wife have lived to raise their sons in a city and see them every one doing well and standing high in good society. This result is largely due to the mother, who, naturally of a sunny and benignant temper, very early adopted the policy of making her home happy and attractive to her children. For this purpose she herself, when thirty years old, took music lessons with her daughter, that she might amuse and entertain her sons and their visiting friends. She encouraged her sons to have a club room at home, and their principal evening amusements there, she making herself one of the company, and by her presence both enlivening and adding dignity and grace to their entertainments. The results justify one in commending her example to young mothers desirous of seeing their boys successful and honored. In declining years it is a gratifying reflection that no one can call up wrong things about him; more pleasant still, to have, as Capt. Stockell has, a scrap-book full of the most friendly and flattering notices—the result of a busy life conducted on manly, benevolent and Christian principles.

His old friend, Anson Nelson, Esq., who has known him intimately for many years, gives this estimate of Capt. Stockell's character: "Capt. William Stockell came to Nashville in 1846, and soon showed himself a good, steady mechanic. His industry and faithfulness were developed to such an extent that he soon obtained as much work as he could do, even with the skilled workmen he employed. He acquired, as a natural result, a fine property of his own, and a competency to live on. He was happily married, and reared a family of children, of which any man might be proud. His children are all married and well settled in life.

"Capt. Stockell was a natural fireman, and his services

as captain of the old volunteer company, Broad street, No. 2, were relied upon in all cases of fire, in any part of the city. After the organization of the paid steam fire department, he was not, for several years, actively engaged in this arm of public service. Upon the going out of the notorious Alden administration, in 1869, the Hon. John M. Bass was appointed receiver for the city, and he at once selected Capt. Stockell to take charge of the fire department of Nashville. He was elected chief by the incoming Morris administration, and re-elected year after year, during different administrations of the city government, for fourteen consecutive years. This was a wonderful compliment, considering the fact that there were always so many applicants for every office in the gift of the municipal government. He was selected solely on account of his superior qualifications for the position; for it was well known that, as a matter of pecuniary consideration, he did not need the office. While fire chief, he made many advantageous improvements, among the most notable being the introduction of the fire alarm telegraph, which has worked successfully since its introduction. The management of the department, under his wise and careful supervision, was a source of gratification to his fellow-citizens. He retired from this service in the autumn of 1883. As a member of the Association of Fire Chiefs of the United States, Capt. Stockell has been for several years one of the most prominent and useful. His papers, read before that body, have attracted more than ordinary attention.

"In all the public offices of the city, in every important movement for the public good, Capt. Stockell has always been a prominent factor. He never failed to do his whole duty, and never shirked any labor or pecuniary demand to aid his people. His services as a director in many mechanical and other associations, were invaluable. He was one of the working directors of the Centennial Exposition of Nashville, in 1880, and no one did more to insure the successful accomplishment of that grand enterprise. As an active member of the Tennessee Historical Society, and in the Robertson Association, his services are well-known and duly appreciated.

"Capt. Stockell's reputation as a man of progressive ideas, as a stirring, active member of society, as a good citizen, ready always to discharge his whole duty, is universally acknowledged. Numerous testimonials of respect, by different organized bodies, and by individuals, have been presented to him; all testifying to his active labors and to his worth as a man. His services will probably be more appreciated after his death, than they will be while he is alive."

G. B. THORNTON, M. D.

MEMPHIS.

DR. G. B. THORNTON, of Memphis, one of the ablest and most widely known physicians and surgeons in Tennessee, is a Virginian by birth, though his whole life, since 1847, has been identified with the city of Memphis, his longest periods of absence therefrom being during his academic and collegiate years, and the four years of military service he gave to the cause of the Confederacy.

He received a liberal literary education, and medicine being chosen as a life profession, he commenced its study in the office of Dr. H. R. Roberts, professor of surgery in the Memphis Medical College, from which institution Dr. Thornton graduated in March, 1858. He next graduated from the medical department of the University of New York, in March, 1860, and commenced the practice of medicine in Memphis in the spring of the same year.

On the breaking out of the war in 1861, he identified himself with the Confederate cause, and in July or August of that year passed a satisfactory examination before the state board of medical examiners at Nashville, and was commissioned assistant surgeon for the Tennessee State troops, by Gov. Isham G. Harris, and assigned to duty with the artillery arm of the service, stationed above Memphis, on the Mississippi river. In November, 1861, he was present at the battle of Belmont, Missouri. In March, 1862, he was with his command at the engagements at Island No. 10, and New Madrid, Missouri. In May, 1862, he was commissioned surgeon by the war department at Richmond, and was made surgeon of division on the staff of Major-Gen. J. P. McCown, who commanded a division of Gen. Earl VanDorn's corps, then at Corinth, Mississippi. This was rapid promotion for so young a man, but subsequent events proved that Surgeon Thornton well merited such distinguished recognition. He was on Gen. McCown's staff at the battles of Perryville, October 8, 1862, and Murfreesborough, December 31, 1862, and January 1, 1863.

In the summer of 1863, he was assigned to duty as chief surgeon of division on the staff of Major-Gen. A. P. Stewart, at Chattanooga; was with this division at the battle of Chickamauga, September 19 and 20, 1863, and at Lookout Mountain and Missionary Ridge in November, 1863; was with this division at Dalton, Georgia, in the winter of 1863-4, and in all the engagements of the Army of Tennessee, throughout the bloody summer of 1864.

He was on the staff of Major-Gen. H. D. Clayton, of Alabama, as chief surgeon of division, at the battle of Franklin, and in front of Nashville, in the fall of 1864. At the re-organization of the army in North Carolina, in the spring of 1865, he was assigned to duty on the staff of Major-Gen. E. C. Walthall, of Mississippi, with whom his military career terminated. He was with the Army of Tennessee from its organization in Tennessee, in 1861, to its capitulation in North Carolina, in 1865; with the exception of Shiloh; was present at every great battle it fought; was with his command on all its marches and campaigns; was present at its organization and at its dissolution—in other words, saw its Alpha and its Omega.

It is but just to note that Dr. Thornton was the youngest division surgeon in the Confederate army. Being fond of operative surgery, and having acquired a good theoretical knowledge of its principles prior to the war, his position afforded him the amplest opportunity for practicing the art in his field hospitals. This large and valuable experience rendered him *au fait* subsequently, when in charge of the City Hospital at Memphis, or as occasion offered, in private practice. The knowledge gathered and the experience acquired in these four years of active military life were likewise beneficial to him in the administration of the civil offices he held.

He returned to Memphis in August, 1865, and resumed practice. In September, 1866, he was elected assistant physician for the City Hospital of Memphis, then under the charge of Dr. J. M. Keller, now of Hot Springs, Arkansas, the office of assistant resident physician, being made necessary to meet the demands caused by an epidemic of cholera which occurred in Memphis that year. He resigned this position in 1867, and was elected physician in charge, October, 1868, by the city council, which position he held until February, 1879, when he resigned. This was a general hospital for the treatment of all kinds of medical and surgical cases. The official reports show an average of about two thousand patients treated annually. During Dr. Thornton's administration, Memphis was visited by four epidemics of infectious diseases: One of smallpox, in the winter of 1872-3; a limited epidemic of cholera in the spring of 1873; an epidemic of yellow fever in the latter part of the summer and early fall of 1873, and the great epidemic of yellow fever in 1878, commencing in August and ending in November, in which Memphis lost not less than three thousand of its population by death.

Dr. Thornton's professional experience during the years of his official connection with this institution was certainly varied and extensive, and his abilities as a professional man and administrative officer are fully attested by his being retained for nearly eleven consecutive years, through all the changes incident to municipal government, and that, too, when its local political affairs were very unstable. In February, 1879, he resigned his office as physician to the City Hospital, his

31

health being much impaired by his duties during the last named epidemic, with the determination to devote himself exclusively to private practice.

Under the newly organized city government he was offered and accepted the position of president of the City Board of Health. The sanitary condition of the city at this time was dreadful. The following extract from the first annual report of the Board of Health, published in 1880, for the year 1879, but partially expresses its condition: "On the subsidence of the epidemic of 1878, the city seemed literally paralyzed, besides being in a worse sanitary condition in every respect than ever before; and the winter passed without an effort being made worthy of mention toward general sanitary work. Consequently, on the organization of this Board of Health, in February, 1879, the task of perfecting a system of sanitation to an extent at all commensurate with the necessities of the occasion, with the facilities at its command, was more than could be reasonably expected of the new board," etc. In July of 1879, yellow fever again appeared and lasted until frost—late in October. This office Dr. Thornton has held to the present time. The same earnestness of purpose and fidelity to duty has characterized him in this, as in the preceding office. Within the period of five years, from being one of the most unsanitary places in the country, Memphis is now one of the most cleanly, and is fully abreast with the most advanced in all things pertaining to public hygiene. As president of the Board of Health, he has enjoyed the full support of the city government and the confidence of the people.

Aside from his official life, Dr. Thornton has devoted his time to private practice, and taken active part in the medical organizations of the day. He was a member of the Memphis Medical Society during its existence before and after the war; is a member of the Shelby County Medical Society from its organization; one year was its vice-president; is a member of the Medical Society of the State of Tennessee, since May, 1878, and was made vice-president from West Tennessee in April, 1879, and was its president in 1881–82; is a member of the American Medical Association since 1877; a member of the American Public Health Association since 1879; was a member of the advisory council of this association in 1883–84; of its executive committee for 1884–5, and one of its vice-presidents for 1885–86. In the fall of 1879 he was appointed a member of the Tennessee State Board

of Health, by Gov. A. S. Marks, to fill a vacancy occasioned by the resignation of Dr. R. B. Maury, and on the expiration of his term, was re-commissioned by Gov. W. B. Bate, April 4, 1883.

Dr. Thornton is the author of several essays which have attracted favorable comment from the medical and sanitary journals, and were received with great favor by those interested in these subjects—one on yellow fever, its pathology and treatment, with clinical notes on one hundred and forty cases treated in City Hospital in 1878, which he read before the State Medical Society at its annual meeting in Nashville, April, 1879, and which was published in the transactions of that year; one on "open treatment for amputations, pyæmia and septicæmia," with notes on a number of cases illustrating this method, treated in the same hospital; read before the society at Knoxville, and published in its transactions for 1880; an address as president of the society, delivered at the annual meeting in Memphis, May, 1882, and published in transactions of that year; an essay on the yellow fever epidemic of 1879, as it occurred in Memphis that year, and read before the Public Health Association at its seventh annual meeting in Nashville, November, 1879, and published in vol. 5 of "Reports and Papers" of that society; one on "Memphis sanitation and quarantine, 1879 and 1880," read before the same body at its meeting in New Orleans, December, 1880, and published in vol. 6; one on "negro mortality of Memphis," read before the same society at Indianapolis, October, 1882, and published in vol. 8; also five annual reports to the Legislative Council of the city of Memphis, as president of the Board of Health; a report to the State Board of Health on the epidemics in Tennessee in 1881 and 1882. He has also contributed several other papers to medical journals on professional subjects.

Dr. Thornton married Miss Louisa Hullum, of Memphis, in December, 1869, a lady of culture and refinement; a true type of a Southern gentlewoman, and a member of the Protestant Episcopal church. She died in June, 1875, leaving him two young children—a daughter, Anna May Thornton, and a son, Gustavus B. Thornton, jr., both at present at school in Virginia.

In politics Dr. Thornton has been a Democrat all his life, as were his ancestors before him, since the organization of the party. He was never a member of any church; has been a Master Mason about twenty years.

JUDGE SAMUEL A. RODGERS.

LOUDON.

THIS prominent jurist, whose time off the bench is pleasantly occupied in farming on a large scale— raising wheat, corn and cattle, and in rearing his family in the happy simplicity of old-fashioned country style--

presents a fine type of a judge who has attained a competency by methods of strict integrity, knows the value of success and how to enjoy it.

He was born in Knox county, Tennessee, March 5,

1830. He was brought up on a farm at hard labor—his father being a solid, well-to-do farmer; a man of unusual energy and firmness of character, who taught his children to work and to avoid idleness as one of the direst evils. In this way young Rodgers' earliest struggles began in driving wagons and following the plow, in hauling logs and assisting about his father's mills. By these means he built up a good constitution, grew to manhood a strong, hearty, robust specimen of the young mountaineer. He was fond of the chase and rifle, but his early prevailing tastes were for literary pursuits and the practice of law. His early school opportunities were limited until he was sixteen years old, when he was sent to the private county schools of the neighborhood some three or four years. Afterward becoming tired of school, in the winter of 1851-2, he went to California, where he stayed until 1853, spending a year in the gold mines. In the fall of 1853 he returned, and remained through the year 1854 on his father's farm as general manager.

In September, 1855, he entered the literary department of Cumberland University, Lebanon, remained there three years, graduated in 1858, completing a course of Latin, Greek, French and Spanish, besides the regular curriculum. While at college he was president of his society—The Amasagassian, and passed through the course with honor. He returned to Knox county, studied law about a year under Hon. John Baxter, present United States circuit judge; in the fall of 1859, obtained license to practice from Chancellor T. Nixon Van-Dyke, and Judge George Brown, and entered into partnership with Hon. O. P. Temple (whose sketch see elsewhere), and with him practiced until the courts were closed, in 1862, by the presence of the armies and the disturbing influences of the war. During the war he remained in East Tennessee, taking no part in the contest, believing that course his duty as a private citizen. His attachment to the government of the United States was firm and unwavering during the entire struggle; he not believing in the doctrine of secession, either upon legal principles or principles of sound policy. Upon the return of order and the re-opening of the courts, he again went into the practice of his profession in partnership with Judge Temple. After a few months' practice, the firm found it necessary to take in another partner, which they did in the person of Judge Andrews, since one of the supreme judges of the State. After a still further continuance of the business until the beginning of the winter of 1867-8, he withdrew from the firm, sold out his interest in the partnership to his partners, and took his wife and her grandmother to California, via New York and Panama—for the wife's health. After spending something over a year in Santa Cruz county, California, his wife's health being restored, he returned to Tennessee and opened a law office at Loudon, where he remained till 1878, when he was elected to the office of judge of the Third judicial circuit, embracing the counties of Knox, Blount, Loudon, Monroe and Roane, term expiring September 1, 1886.

Before the war Judge Rodgers voted the Whig ticket, but since the war he has been a Republican, though never actively engaged in politics. He is a Master Mason, a Cumberland Presbyterian and an elder in his church. He states with commendable pride that he has been for some fifteen years a Sunday-school superintendent.

A distinctive characteristic of Judge Rodgers in the ethics of a practitioner of law, is to compromise suits and thus remove or soften the asperities of life between fellow-citizens. This he has often done from a sense of loyalty to duty, and oftentimes, too, at his own pecuniary sacrifice.

It is said he has kept hundreds of people out of law suits by advice of this kind. He himself refers to his course in this part of his history as the most pleasant of his life. The Master of us all, in his wonderful sermon on the mount, said: "Blessed are the peace makers."

Judge Rodgers' father, William Rodgers, was born and raised, lived and died in Knox county, Tennessee. He accumulated considerable property as a farmer and mill owner. His integrity was beyond question, and he was a leading, strong-minded man, who forced his way and left his impression on the world. He was a soldier in the war of 1812; for twenty-five years was a justice of the peace, and was an elder in the Concord church, the first Cumberland Presbyterian church planted east of Cumberland mountains. Judge Rodgers' grandfather, Joseph Rodgers, was an Irishman, who early immigrated to this country, and lived and died a farmer in Knox county. His wife was formerly Miss Elizabeth Donelson, an immediate relative of the well-known family of that name living in Jefferson county, Tennessee.

Judge Rodgers' mother, nee Miss Mahala Lowe, was born in Knox county, daughter of Abram and Elizabeth Lowe, and lived from an early day at what is now known as Lowe's Ferry, on the Tennessee river—in a block house built at that place, and which was a general rendezvous for the white settlers, who had often to defend themselves from the incursions of the Choctaw Indians. Abram Lowe came over to this country from Germany. His wife was the daughter of an Englishman named Martin.

Gen. S. D. W. Lowe, of Knox county, is Judge Rodgers' maternal uncle. He is a large farmer and stock raiser, and now owns and occupies the old homestead described above. He is distinguished for his elevated bearing as a militia man and for his splendid character.

Judge Rodgers' only sister, Ann Amanda Rodgers, is now the wife of S. L. Russell, a merchant and farmer at Concord, Knox county. Judge Rodgers had five brothers, viz.: James M., Joseph N., Abram W., George D. and William D. Rodgers, all of whom except Joseph N. Rodgers, went to California to reside at various dates since the war. Abram W. Rodgers died at Mazatlan, Mexico, September 5, 1883, of yellow fever. The other three brothers—James, George and William—are farmers, fruit growers and stock raisers in California. Joseph N. Rodgers still lives a farmer in Knox county, Tennessee. One of Judge Rodgers' nephews, Arthur Rodgers, son of James M. Rodgers, has risen to distinction as a lawyer at San Francisco, and is one of the regents of the University of California. He spent some two or three years in traveling around the world. He is a fine speaker and writer, and a man of broad culture. Onear Rodgers, another son of James M. Rodgers, is a prominent physician at San Francisco—a graduate of Bellevue Medical College, New York.

Judge Rodgers married in what is now Loudon, (then Roane) county, Tennnessee, May 10, 1863, Miss Sarah E. Rhea, who was born in that county, November 15, 1843, daughter of John W. Rhea, a native of Sullivan county, Tennessee. He has a first-class character and belonged to one of the most prominent families of East Tennessee. Mrs. Rodgers' great uncle, Hon. John Rhea, was a congressman from Tennessee two or three terms, and a large land owner. Her second cousin, Rev. Samuel Rhea, a minister in the Presbyterian church, went as a missionary to Persia, and died there. There are upward of twenty ministers in the various branches of the family, among them Rev. John Bachman, (whose sketch see elsewhere in this volume), Rev. Nathan Bachman, the well-known evangelist, and Rev. Lynn Bachman. Chancellor Seth J. W. Lucky married a Miss Rhea, a second cousin of Mrs. Rodgers. The county of Rhea was named for the Rhea family. This family settled years ago in Sullivan county, and is one of the strongest and best families in the State. They are connected with the Prestons, of Virginia. Mrs. Rodgers' cousin, Dr. Rhea, of the firm of Cowan, McClung & Co., Knoxville, married Miss Bella Cowan, daughter of the late James Cowan, of that city. Mrs. Rodgers' mother was Miss Adaline Dodson, daughter and only child of Alexander Dodson, a farmer and stock raiser in Tennessee, originally from North Carolina, where he married Elizabeth Roberts, a lady famous in her family for strong natural talent and individuality of character. Alexander Dodson died January 27, 1862. Mrs. Rodgers' uncle, Jesse Roberts, was a prominent Methodist minister in North Carolina. Mrs. Rodgers' only brother, Alexander D. Rhea, now of Tehuacana, Texas, a farmer and stock raiser, married Mary F. Hatchett, of Monroe county, Tennessee. They have eight children: John, Addie, Robert, Joseph, Bettie, Louise, Rodgers, and Cleaves. Mrs. Rodgers was educated at Athens Female College; is a member of the Cumberland Presbyterian church; is a lady of bright, sunny disposition, and is eminently utilitarian in her views.

By his marriage with Miss Rhea, Judge Rodgers has

seven children: (1). California—"Callie,"—born in Santa Cruz county, California, February 17, 1869. (2). Addie M., born in Loudon, July, 27, 1871. (3). Samuel Rhea, born October 8, 1873. (4). Mary Bell, born October 7, 1875. (5). Annie E., born June 20, 1877. (6). William Arthur, born November 17, 1879. (7). Minnie, born April 12, 1882; died March 27, 1883.

Judge Rodgers began the work of his life in a struggle and has long since won a fair success, and besides being a useful citizen, has never failed to give a word of encouragement and a smile to men in trouble to drive away a pang, and given many men a push to help them up. When he left college he was one thousand dollars in debt. He was not born great, but has won recognition by hard toil and struggle, and a disposition to do good and diffuse happiness around him. He has risen to the honors of his profession, and financially is in a fair condition.

Judge O. P. Temple, for many years Judge Rodgers' law partner, and one who knows him well, by request, has furnished the following estimate of his character: "Judge Rodgers possesses a clear, level, well-regulated intellect. He is thoroughly of the strong, practical, common sense order. He is not brilliant nor sparkling, but always cool, deliberate and comprehensive, and eminently judicial in tone. Having an almost instinctive sense of justice, it is easy for him to apply the principles of law in every case coming before him. He has moral courage also, without which there can be no safe judge. But few judges have been so near universally popular and acceptable. It is impossible to do exact justice, and decide property rights against men, however just the decision, without making enemies, few or many. Judge Rodgers has, perhaps, made as few as any judge ever on the bench of the State. On the bench he is mild and gentle, never noisy, abrupt or scolding, but a soft word always commands silence and obedience. There is never any wrangling in his court, and yet no judge so gentle in the preservation of order. The moral tone of Judge Rodgers is, perhaps, his most conspicuous trait of character. This is in the highest state of development and activity. To do right seems to be his first and highest aim, not as a means of popularity, but from principle and for the love of right. His conscientiousness is great, almost intense. Added to this, nature blessed him with a kind heart, a serene temper, happy, joyful spirits, and a large, sympathetic heart, full of charity and good will toward all. Withal he is firm, sincere and truthful. He does not wear all these qualities as a cloak to win popularity, but they are the real manifestations of his nature. If asked the secret of the success of Judge Rodgers as a public man, I should say his conscientiousness, truthfulness, justice, and fidelity to duty and friends, combined with energy and fine sense."

CAPT. JAMES M. GOODBAR.

MEMPHIS.

JAMES M. GOODBAR was born in Overton county, Tennessee, May 29, 1839, and lived there until he was eleven years of age. His father then moved to White county, Tennessee, where he lived on a farm adjoining the town of Sparta until he was eighteen years of age. Like many of the men who have become successes he did not have the benefit of a college course, but received his education in private schools. His last teacher was William H. Marquess, formerly of Nashville. Young Goodbar's father was a merchant in the town of Sparta, and being about the store from his early youth, he, too, naturally acquired a taste for merchandising, and determined to make that his calling. In 1857 he went to Nashville and began his career as a clerk for Bransford, McWhirter & Co., wholesale dry goods merchants, beginning with a salary of four hundred dollars a year. With this firm he remained till 1859, when its name was changed to A. J. McWhirter & Co., and with the new firm he remained till 1860, his salary having been in the meantime increased to one thousand five hundred dollars a year. In 1860 he went to Memphis with Thomas L. Bransford, who had been the head of the firm by which he was first engaged, and his son, Maj. John S. Bransford, now of Nashville, Tennessee. They there engaged in the wholesale boot and shoe business. Mr. Goodbar had been in business long enough by this time to learn the methods of business men, and though he had but little capital he was taken as a partner by Mr. Bransford on account of his business capacity, and the firm of Bransford, Goodbar & Co. was formed. They continued in a very flourishing business for a little more than one year, and then closed up their house on account of the war.

Early in 1862, Mr. Goodbar entered the Confederate service as a lieutenant in the company of Capt. George Carter, of the Fourth Tennessee regiment of cavalry, Col. John P. Murray commanding. He served in Kentucky, Tennessee and Georgia, and surrendered with Gen. Dibrell's command at Washington, Georgia, in May, 1865. He took part in the battles of Murfreesborough, Perryville, and all the other fights of Bragg's Kentucky campaign, in 1862. In the latter part of that year he was made quartermaster of his regiment with the rank of captain, and served in that capacity until the regiment was reorganized during the summer of 1863, when he was assigned to duty in the commissary department, where he served till the close of the war.

After the surrender of the Confederate cause he returned to Memphis and resumed the wholesale boot and shoe business in company with J. R. S. Gilliland in the firm of Goodbar & Gilliland. After a few months they associated with them in the firm Mr. Goodbar's uncle, J. L. Goodbar, and continued under the same firm name till 1876. Messrs. Goodbar & Gilliland then

sold out to J. L. and A. B. Goodbar, and the firm then became Goodbar & Co. In July, 1878, Mr. Goodbar again purchased an interest in the firm and continued with them until July, 1883, when, in company with A B. Goodbar, he bought out the interest of J. L. Goodbar and admitted as partners William L. Clark and J. H. Goodbar. The firm is now composed of these members.

Mr. Goodbar is a stockhholder and director of the Planters' Insurance company, and has also been a stockholder, director and vice president of the Mercantile Bank since its organization.

Mr. Goodbar has always been a Democrat, but preferring to concentrate his energies upon his business has usually taken little part in politics. He took an active part in the movement to abolish the old city government of Memphis and substitute for it the taxing district mode of governing, and by his efforts contributed no little to the planning as well as the execution of this movement, so important to Memphis. When the citizens of Memphis, driven to desperation by the condition of their city government, held a public meeting to discuss the propriety of abolishing it, he was one of a committee of seven appointed to prepare a new form of government to be recommended to the Legislature. This committee drafted the present form of government, which was adopted by the Legislature, and has become a noble municipality. After the new government was adopted Mr. Goodbar was elected a member of the board of public works, and thus had the opportunity of helping to carry out the plan which he had assisted in forming.

Capt. Goodbar was married, September 10, 1867, to Miss Mary E. Morgan, of Hernando, Mississippi. Her father, Judge John H. Morgan, was originally from Lincoln county, Tennessee, and during the early days of Memphis, resided there and was mayor of the town. He was a cousin of Hon. John M. Bright, of Fayetteville, whose sketch appears elsewhere in this volume. Mrs. Goodbar's mother was Miss Edmondson, of Lincoln county, Tennessee. Mrs. Goodbar's three brothers were all officers in the Confederate service. Col. W. E. Morgan and Capt. John H. Morgan both fell at the battle of Murfreesborough. Her third brother, Hon. J. B. Morgan, now of Hernando, Mississippi, served through the war as colonel; was several times wounded but recovered, and after the war engaged in the practice of law, and was elected chancellor of his district. To this union have been born four children: (1). Willie Morgan Goodbar, born August, 1868. (2). Mamie Oliver Goodbar, born July, 1872. (3). Jennie Edmondson Goodbar, born January, 1875, died in July following. (4). James Bright Goodbar, born July, 1881.

Mrs. Goodbar is the happy possessor of a disposition

that makes her popular with all who know her, and wins for her a large circle of friends. She has been a member of the Presbyterian church for many years. Capt. Goodbar has been a member of this church for ten years.

Capt. Goodbar's father, William P. Goodbar, a native of Overton county, Tennessee, died in October, 1878, at the age of sixty-eight. He was a successful merchant for many years. He served as sheriff of Overton county for two terms, and as clerk of the circuit court for two terms. After moving to White county he was president of the branch Bank of Tennessee, at Sparta. He was a man of great energy, sound, practical judgment, fine business capacity, and accumulated a very comfortable estate, which was, however, invested principally in slaves and was swept away by the war.

The Goodbar family is of English descent. Joseph Goodbar, grandfather of the subject of this sketch, came from Virginia to Tennessee, and was one of the early settlers of Overton county. Several of Mr. Goodbar's uncles were prominent and successful merchants in different parts of Middle Tennessee. His only brother, Joseph H. Goodbar, entered the Confederate service as major of the Sixteenth Tennessee regiment, commanded by Col. John H. Savage, and died at Morristown, Tennessee, in 1862, of disease contracted while in the service.

Capt. Goodbar's mother was Miss Jane McKinney, daughter of Henry McKinney, a farmer, of Overton county, and a descendant of a family originally from North Carolina, who settled in Overton county at an early day. She died in 1867, at the age of fifty-five years. She was for many years a member of the Cumberland Presbyterian church, and was an earnest, pious Christian woman.

Capt. Goodbar had five sisters: (1). Mary Goodbar, who married the late Col. Thomas B. Murray, of McMinnville, Tennessse, a prominent lawyer in that part of the State. (2). Fannie B. Goodbar, who married James L. Jones, and died at McMinnville, in 1861, leaving an infant son, Frank Goodbar Jones, now a salesman for Goodbar & Co. (3). Lou B. Goodbar, who married William L. Clark, now a partner in the firm of Goodbar & Co. (4). Clementine Goodbar, who died in 1863. (5). Miss Maggie Goodbar, now residing in Memphis.

Capt. Goodbar is essentially a self-made man, and his career has been one of uninterrupted success. Begin ning after the war with a very small capital, he ha gradually built himself up to a position of high com mercial prominence and influence. The trade of hi firm is now about six hundred thousand dollars pe annum, which is believed to be the largest busines done by any one house in this line south of the Ohi river, except one in Galveston, Texas. Its able an successful management gives it a leading place amon the substantial mercantile firms of Memphis.

Capt. Goodbar's success, like that of all other men has been the result of well defined principles and meth ods, which were laid out in early life, and have bee closely followed. It is no secret to state that his goo fortune is attributable to economy, untiring energy an perseverance, close attention to business, and a stric adherence to a rule to deal fairly and honestly with a men. His life is an illustration of the great advantag to be derived from concentrating one's energies upo one thing, for he has never allowed anything to dive his attention from his business, and by constant har work he has mastered it.

Mr. W. D. Beard, of Memphis, says of him: "M Goodbar has been the founder and the builder c his own fortune. In 1866 he established, in compan with Mr. J. R. S. Gilliland, in Memphis, the wholesal boot and shoe house of Goodbar & Gilliland. Bot were young men of small monied capital. Their bus ness was carried on in the second story of a house o Main street. It was unpretending, but in its manag ment Mr. Goodbar manifested those traits of characte personal habits or methods, that have since made hi eminently successful in life. He was sober, economica prompt, energetic, painstaking and the thorough mast of his business. His mental equipoise then, as no was great. A man of facts rather than of fancies, me theory never ran away with him. To every invitir scheme or business emergency, he brought the measu of a sound, and at all times reliable, common sense, an the result is that mistakes with him have been rare. is this conservative faculty that has made him so val able as an adviser. In every business enterprise wi which he has been connected, where amounts of capit and action were required, whether it be an insuran company or a bank, he has been regarded as a sa counsellor."

HON. F. M. FULKERSON.

ROGERSVILLE.

HON. F. M. FULKERSON was born in Washington county, Virginia, January 18, 1825. The Fulkerson family came originally from Holland, the branch from which the subject of this sketch descended, having finally settled in Virginia. His grandfathe James Fulkerson, married Miss Mary Van Hook ar died in Washington county, Virginia. The fathe Abram Fulkerson, was born in Washington count

Virginia; married in that county, and removed in 1835, to Grainger county, Tennessee, where he continued the pursuit of farming; a captain in the war of 1812; was afterward a justice of the peace for a number of years, and was a man of high esteem among the people of his county. He died in 1860, at the age of seventy.

The mother of Col. Fulkerson, Margaret L. Vance, was a daughter of Samuel Vance, of Washington county, Virginia, a farmer. He was a Revolutionary soldier and participated in the memorable battle of King's Mountain. The Vances, it is claimed, entered England in the fifth century with Hengist and Horsa. The name was originally De Vaux, which, in Scotland, became changed to Vaus (the De being dropped), and in Ireland it came to be pronounced and written as Vance. (See sketch of Charles R. Vance in another part of this volume). The mother of Mrs. Abram Fulkerson was Margaret Laughlin, of a Virginia family.

Mrs. Fulkerson (mother of F. M. Fulkerson) was a devoted member of the Presbyterian church. She was a woman of marked traits of character, of excellent judgment, positive in her convictions, skilled in domestic duties, and exceedingly careful in the training of her children, who have felt her benign influence through life. She died in 1864, at the age of sixty eight, the mother of nine children, viz.: (1). James. (2). Margaret. (3). Mary. (4). Samuel V. (5). Francis M., subject of this sketch. (6). Harriet. (7). Isaac. (8). Catherine. (9). Abram.

Of these, James married Alice Armstrong, and was successively bank clerk, postmaster and hotel-keeper at Rogersville. He died in 1849. Margaret married Dr. A. W. Armstrong, of Knox county, and died in Indiana. Mary is now the widow of Archimedes Davis, of Washington county, Virginia. Samuel V. fell in battle near Richmond, in the Confederate service. He was unmarried, and was judge of the circuit court at Abingdon, Virginia, at the time of his death. He served as adjutant in the Mexican war. Was a member of the constitutional convention that revised the Constitution of Virginia. He was colonel of the Thirty-seventh Virginia Confederate regiment, and served under Stonewall Jackson. His death was deeply lamented, especially in southwestern Virginia, where he was greatly beloved. The two following brief letters concerning him, from the pen of Stonewall Jackson, will no doubt be read with interest:

[Gen. Jackson to Capt. James Vance, Thirty-seventh Virginia Regiment.]

HEADQUARTERS, VALLEY DISTRICT, July 17, 1862.

CAPTAIN—Your letter of the 8th inst. has been received. If your brave kinsman (Samuel V. Fulkerson) was neglected by others, he was highly prized by me, you may rest confident, and should my report of the battle of Kernstown *ever* be published, those who read it will see the high estimate in which he was held. In his death the army and myself, as well as you, his kinsman, have sustained a great loss. I hope soon to see you exchanged.

Respectfully yours,
T. J. JACKSON.

[Gen. Jackson to Hon. F. M. Fulkerson.]

GORDONSVILLE, VIRGINIA, September 2, 1862.

Mr. F. M. Fulkerson:

SIR—In reply to your letter of the 7th ult., permit me to say that Col. S. V. Fulkerson was an officer of distinguished worth. I deeply felt his death. He rendered valuable service to his country, and had he lived, would probably have been recommended by me before this time for a brigadier-general. So far as my knowledge extends, he enjoyed the confidence of his regiment and all who knew him. I am, sir, your ob't servant,

T. J. JACKSON.

Harriet married W. P. Armstrong, of Rogersville, and has eight children, viz.: Charles, Robert, Margaret, Kate, Mary, Arthur, Samuel and William. Hattie, the youngest, remarkable for her Christian graces, died at about fifteen years of age. Isaac married Miss Cel. Roberts, and is now living at Bryan, Texas. He served through the Mexican war in the Fifth Tennessee regiment, under Col. George R. McClelland. He also served through the late civil war as a member of the celebrated Texas cavalry (Rangers), participating in probably an hundred battles and skirmishes. He has been treasurer of his county. Catharine married B. F. Hurt, a merchant of Abingdon, Virginia, and has four children, viz.: Maggie, Nel, Floy and Katie. Abram married Miss Celevia Johnson, of Clarksville, Tennessee, and has been for years a practicing lawyer at Bristol, on the Virginia side. He was major of the Nineteenth Tennessee Confederate regiment, and colonel of the Sixty-third Tennessee regiment. He has been a prominent member of the Virginia Legislature; was a member of Congress from the Ninth Virginia district four years ago, and was re-elected to Congress from the same district, November, 1884. He was several times severely wounded during the war, and was one of the prisoners whom the Federals placed under fire of the guns at Fort Sumpter. He has but one son, Samuel, a graduate of the Virginia Military Institute. Francis M., subject of this sketch, married, first, near Rogersville, Miss Elizabeth M. Hale, who was born May 29, 1827, the daughter of Col. George Hale, merchant, farmer and bank cashier, and once member of the Legislature. Her grandfather, Philip Hale, a Virginian, who removed to Jefferson county, Tennessee, at an early day, was of Scotch descent. Her mother was Margaret Hamilton, daughter of Joseph Hamilton, a lawyer, of Jefferson county, of prominence in his time. Her grandmother was Penelope Outlaw, daughter of Alexander Outlaw, who is frequently mentioned in the histories of Tennessee as commissioner and holder of various civil offices. He was one of the pioneers of Jefferson county, and was, in many respects, a noted character in his day.

The first Mrs. Fulkerson was educated at Salem, North Carolina, and was a devoted member of the Presbyterian church. She is remembered as an excellent wife and mother—affectionate, prudent, industrious and faithful to all her trusts. By his marriage with her, Col. Fulkerson has six children, viz.: (1). Margaret H., born March 11, 1856; educated at Rogersville and

Staunton, Virginia. She is now the widow of Dr. F. C. Painter, formerly of Virginia, and by him has two children, Frank F. and Annie Bell. (2). Mary C., born January 15, 1858; educated at Rogersville Female College; married, May 26, 1881, to John K. Shields, a lawyer, and son of Hon. James T. Shields, of Bean's Station, and died October 1, 1881. (See sketch of Hon. James T. Shields elsewhere in this volume). (3). Amanda Vance, born June 24, 1860; educated at Rogersville Female College, in which she is now teaching drawing and painting. She was educated in these arts in the Conservatory at Boston, Massachusetts. (4). Evan Neill, born April 17, 1863; educated at Rogersville, Baltimore and Boston, and now principal music teacher in Rogersville Female College. (5). Kate P., born January, 1866, and educated at Rogersville Female College. (6). Hattie S., born May 4, 1863.

Col. Fulkerson was next married at Rogersville, November 18, 1874, to Miss Penelope Elizabeth Neill, daughter of James K. Neill, merchant of Rogersville, and niece of Samuel Neill, banker at same place. She was born October 21, 1842, and is a grand-daughter of Samuel Neill, sr., formerly a merchant of Rogersville. Her mother was Catherine D. Hale, daughter of George Hale. Her only full sister, Mary S., is wife of James G. Mitchell, secretary and treasurer of the East Tennessee, Virginia and Georgia railroad company, at Knoxville. Her two half-sisters are Eva, wife of C. A. Dosser, lawyer of Jonesborough, and Sarah, wife of John Grisham. Her two full brothers are George H. Neill, of Columbus, Georgia, and William H. Neill, of Louisville, Kentucky. Her half-brother, Alfred T., resides in Oregon. Mrs. Fulkerson is a graduate of the Rogersville Female College, and is a zealous member of the Presbyterian church. She is a lady of pronounced character, energetic in whatever she undertakes, and is noted for her devotion to church interests. Two children have been the result of the second marriage: (1). Elizabeth Sidney, born August 24, 1875. (2). Frank Neill, born September 17, 1877.

We return now to the principal subject of this sketch. When about ten years old, Francis M. Fulkerson came with his father's family to Grainger county, Tennessee, where he grew to the age of twenty, working on the farm and attending school. He then entered a store in Rogersville as clerk, on the not very princely salary of one hundred dollars a year and board. At the end of the year he found himself with but little money, though with some knowledge of business. The Mexican war breaking out about this time, he caught the volunteer spirit that prevailed throughout Tennessee, and, in 1847, entered as a private in company I (Capt. James H. Evans), Fourth Tennessee infantry (Col. Richard Waterhouse). He served through the war in the capacity of ordnance sergeant, to which position he was appointed soon after the organization of the regiment. The regiment was at Vera Cruz, Jalapa, Puebla, and the City of

Mexico, being stationed at the last named place at the time the treaty of peace was concluded.

Returning to Rogersville in 1848, Col. Fulkerson read law in the office of Col. John Netherland for about two years, when (in 1851) he was licensed to practice by Chancellor Thomas L. Williams and Judge Seth J. W. Luckey, of the circuit court. After two years' practice at Rogersville, he removed to Tazewell, Tennessee, where he practiced law about eight years, being five years of the time clerk and master by appointment of Chancellor Luckey. In 1859 he returned to Rogersville, where he has ever since resided and practiced his profession. For about six years he practiced in partnership with Hon. John Netherland and James T. Shields, and at different times since has had as partners S. L. Chesnutt, L. G. Walker and A. D. Huffmaster, the last named being now associated with him.

In 1863 Mr. Fulkerson was elected to the State senate, but owing to the disturbed state of the country, by reason of the war, the General Assembly failed to meet.

Before the war Mr. Fulkerson was a Democrat, during the war he was a pronounced "southern man," and since the war has been a Democrat. In 1861 he was elector for the Tenth district, on the Davis and Stephens ticket, but made no canvass, there being no opposing ticket. In 1883-4 he represented Hawkins county in the Legislature, having been elected by several hundred majority, notwithstanding there is a steady majority for the opposite party in the county. One term seemed to have satisfied him with legislative service and honors, since no amount of persuasion could induce him to stand for re-election, which he could certainly have secured.

In 1859 Col. Fulkerson became a member of the Order of Odd Fellows, and in 1883 of the Knights of Honor. He is now president of the board of trustees of the Rogersville Female College. He is an active member of the Presbyterian church, having joined the church at Tazewell, in 1852. He was for five years a ruling elder in the church at Tazewell, and has been such for four years at Rogersville.

Col. Fulkerson may justly be called a successful man. He has always stood deservedly high in his profession. His devotion to his clients' interests is proverbial, and yet he would scorn to advance his client's cause by any of the "sharp practices" characteristic of the pettifogger. While conscientiously attending to his professional engagements, his business education has served him a good purpose, enabling him to carry profitable interests in several enterprises. He is a successful farmer, as well as lawyer, and takes great pride in his herd of Jersey cattle. He has also been engaged in the tanning business, and has an interest in a boot and shoe factory in Rogersville. Besides, he is a member of the firm of Fulkerson, Chesnutt & Co., engaged in quarrying the beautiful Hawkins county marble.

Col. Fulkerson is a man of pleasing manners and honest methods. There is probably not a man in the whole State who enjoys to a higher degree than he the esteem and confidence of the community in which he lives. As a citizen and neighbor, he is prompt to do whatever a sense of duty suggests to be right. As a lawyer, while he is zealous, he is also conscientious, neither grinding the unfortunate with exorbitant fees, nor leading the litigiously-inclined into lawsuits which his own judgment condemns. When called by the people of his county to represent them in the Legislature, he showed that he could lay aside the mere partisan and vote and act according to the dictates of his judgment and conscience. His personal influence is ever on the side of virtue and in the interest of law and order. The Christian church has no better friend than Col. F. M. Fulkerson, nor the State a more pure and upright citizen.

COL. WILLIAM F. TAYLOR.

MEMPHIS.

THE gentleman whose name heads this biographical sketch presents a splendid type of a gallant soldier, an excellent civilian, a successful merchant of high-toned integrity, and a modest, sincere Christian, whose good fortune has been carved out mainly through his own indomitable energy and business probity.

William F. Taylor was born in Madison county, Alabama, July 11, 1835, and remained there until February, 1848, when he moved with his grandfather, Charles Taylor, to Shelby county, Tennessee, and with the exception of four years spent in the war, has lived in that county ever since, residing in Memphis since January, 1853.

The Taylor family is distinctly connected with the family of which President Zachary Taylor was a member—a fact, however, which Col. Taylor's grandfather, Charles Taylor, refused in his modesty to admit, and used to say, with pride, that he "was not a member of a branch of the Taylor family; was never indicted or sued in his life, and never ran for office," traits which have been transmitted and are characteristic of the family, who are rather retiring in their disposition, avoiding all publicity not necessarily incident to the post of duty. Charles Taylor was born in Granville county, North Carolina; was a farmer, and, indeed, almost the entire family were agriculturists. He married Miss Mary Turner, and died near Hernando, Mississippi, in his seventy-sixth year. He was the father of six children, three of whom preceded him in death. Of his children who survived him: (1). Lucy Ann Taylor, died the widow of Stephen W. Rutland, DeSoto county, Mississippi. (2). Edmund J. Taylor, is now living, a farmer, at Elgin, Arkansas; was a soldier in the Mexican war from Alabama, and merchandised in Memphis a number of years. (3). Martha J. Taylor, died the widow of George Douglass, a farmer, first in Alabama and then in Mississippi. Of the children who died before their father: (1). Charles Taylor, died in DeSoto county, Mississippi. (2). John T. Taylor, father of the subject of this sketch, died in Alabama when the son was only five years old. (3). Robert H. Taylor, died in DeSoto county, Mississippi.

John T. Taylor, the father of Col. Taylor, was born in Granville county, North Carolina; moved to Alabama when quite young; there married, lived a planter and school teacher, and died at the age of thirty-three, leaving four children: (1). John H. Taylor, now in Memphis in mercantile life. (2). Charles N. Taylor, died forty-five years of age, a successful planter in Shelby county, Tennessee. (3). William F. Taylor, subject of this sketch. (4). Mary T. Taylor, died in childhood.

Col. Taylor's mother, nee Miss Martha A. Ford, was born in Cumberland county, Virginia; was a Methodist; a lady of quiet, unpretending nature; a noble character, endowed with goodness of heart, and was noted for allaying of strife in her circle, and blessed by all who knew her as a Christian peace-maker. She managed the small estate left her by her husband so as to give her children a liberal education. She was herself a good biblical scholar, fond of reading, and set her children the example of self-denial and almost of self-abnegation, and was one of those intelligent, practical women, all devotion, who fill the world with sunshine and with happiness. She died at her home in Memphis, in March, 1872, at the age of sixty-three. She was a paternal niece of Dr. Hezekiah Ford, a celebrated physician of Virginia. She had no sister, and but one brother, Newton Ford, a merchant at Memphis, and a member of several firms in that city; in 1847-8 of the firm of Ford, Taylor & Robinson (dry goods); from 1849 to 1859, a planter in Shelby county, Tennessee; from 1859 to 1862, of the firm of F. Lane & Co., grocers and cotton factors; after the war, 1865 to 1870, of the firm of Newton Ford & Co., in the grocery and commission business; from 1870 to 1873, of the firm of Ford, Porter & Co. He died in 1873, at the age of sixty-two. He was at one time vice-president of the First National Bank of Memphis.

William F. Taylor, under the benign influence of a

true and good mother, was trained in his boyhood in the path of rectitude and duty. He was educated principally at Macon College, Tennessee, and at Chalmers Institute, Holly Springs, Mississippi. He was educated for a physician, but his health failing, in 1852, he labored in the crop that year, and then began his his apprenticeship as a merchant in 1853, beginning as a clerk for Strange, Goodwin & Co. one year. From 1854 to 1859, he clerked for Speed & Strange; from 1859 to January, 1860, for W. B. Miller & Co., and in 1860 became a member of the latter firm.

An ardent, patriotic southerner, and always loyal to the cause of the South, in May, 1861, he went into the Confederate army as lieutenant of cavalry in the Memphis Light Dragoons. A few months afterward he was elected captain of the company. When the dragoons were organized into a regiment at Columbus, Kentucky, William H. Jackson (whose sketch see elsewhere in this volume) was elected colonel. In 1863, Capt. Taylor was promoted to the lieutenant-colonelcy, and commanded as such till the close of the war. He saw service in Tennessee, Missouri, Kentucky, Alabama and Mississippi, under Brigadier-Gens. Wm. H. Jackson and Ed. Rucker; Maj.-Gens. W. H. Jackson, Jos. Wheeler and J. R. Chalmers, and under Lieut.-Gens. Stephen D. D. Lee and N. B. Forrest. He participated in the battle of Belmont, and in innumerable raids and all of the battles of Forrest's command. He was twice slightly wounded; first on the right ear at Pulaski, and in the right hand at Columbia, Tennessee. He remained in the army till the surrender at Sumterville, Alabama, May, 1865. (For a fuller account of Col. Taylor's regiment and services, see Dr. J. B. Lindsley's Military History of Tennessee). Col. Taylor was never absent from his company or regiment during a battle or a raid throughout the war—a record which shows his sense of duty and his loyalty to it.

When the war closed he returned to Memphis, and in 1867 became a member of the firm of Newton Ford & Co.; next of Ford, Porter & Co.; then of Porter, Taylor & Co. till 1882. Since that time he has been in the cotton commission business of the firm of W. F. Taylor & Co., 314 Front street, Memphis. He came out of the war with nothing except a mule and a horse—without real estate or a dollar in money. He is now reckoned among the solid business men of the city.

Col. Taylor married in Memphis, December 13, 1866, Miss Sallie S. Ford, a native of Shelby county, Tennessee, born April 15, 1843, daughter of Newton Ford, before mentioned. Her mother, nee Miss Appless Frazer, was of an Alabama family. She was a cousin of John Frazer, of Holly Springs, Mississippi, whose children, Martha, Phebe Ann, Fanny, and Charles W., are well known prominent people of Memphis. Martha Frazer died the widow of Richard B. Brown, a lawyer of Memphis; Phebe A. Frazer is now the widow of C. W. Edmunds, a Memphis tobacco merchant; Fanny Frazer is

the widow of Rev. Mr. Graham, a Presbyterian minister, late of LaGrange, Tennessee; Charles W. Frazer is a prominent lawyer at Memphis.

Mrs. Taylor's mother, Mrs. Ford, died at Memphis, November, 1882, at the age of sixty-two years, a bright, attractive lady—a splendid type of southern womanhood of two generations ago. She was the mother of six children: (1). Ann E. Ford, unmarried. (2). Mary F. Ford, now widow of Samuel L. Raines, a planter of DeSoto county, Mississippi. (3). Bettie F. Ford, who died the wife of Dr. D. W. Bynum, of Memphis. (4). Sallie S. Ford, wife of Col. Taylor. (5). Augusta F. Ford, married Maj. F. Molloy. (6). James N. Ford, now a lawyer at Memphis.

Mrs. Taylor was educated at the celebrated Nashville Female Academy, under Rev. Dr. C. D. Elliott. She is a member of the Methodist church. Col. Taylor joined that church in 1857, and soon after their marriage, though a great favorite in fashionable society, his wife joined the church with him, and now three of their oldest children are members of the same denomination. Like her husband, Mrs. Taylor is of a modest and retiring nature, avoids extremes, and though one of the most accomplished women in Memphis, gives far less attention to society than to the training of her children. She is wise in counsel, economic in habit, and a good manager; of high cultivation and positive character, but like her father, withdraws herself from conspicuity, even in her church relations. By his marriage with Miss Ford, seven children have been born to Col. Taylor—all sons, and all born in the same house at Memphis: (1). Pope Taylor, born May 26, 1868. (2). Wm. F. Taylor, born June 21, 1870. (3). Walter D. Taylor, born June 10, 1872. (4, 5). Ford and Frank Taylor, twins, born July 9, 1874. (6, 7). Emmet and Edwin Avent Taylor, twins, born November 28, 1877.

Although he has never run for office, except military positions, Col. Taylor is Democratic to the core. He is steward of the First Methodist Episcopal church, South, at Memphis; was made a Mason in a floating lodge during the war, but is not affiliated, being too much devoted to his family to go to any organization at night, except his church or to a meeting of ex-Confederates. For several years he has been a director in the Bank of Commerce and various manufacturing establishments and insurance companies—facts which show his standing in the industrial and commercial circles.

Col. Taylor, from his first start in mercantile life, has practiced frugality and endeavored to keep down his expenditures within his income. He has made nothing by speculation, but by plodding, close application to business—"slow by slow," always making something, saving something; husbanding his resources, and guarding his commercial honor with strict integrity. He never had a note protested—never allowed a paper to go unprotected—has lost heavily by going security, which taught him a lesson, and should be a warning to others.

COL. W. D. ROBISON.

MURFREESBOROUGH.

THIS self-made man, distinguished as a Mason and as a soldier, was born in Rutherford county, Tennessee, about five miles from Murfreesborough, June 30, 1840, the son of Dr. Samuel B. Robison, a native of North Carolina, who came to Tennessee when a young man, and settled in Rutherford county, where he continued the practice of medicine up to the time of his death, which took place in 1871, at the age of sixty-seven. Col. Robison's mother, was Miss Mary North, daughter of William North, a native of Virginia, who came to Tennessee with her father when quite young. She was married to Dr. Robison in 1836, and became the mother of three daughters and one son, the latter the subject of this sketch.

Col. Robison was educated in the common schools of the county and in Union University at Murfreesborough, which latter institution he entered in the fall of 1854, and remained there one year. He was brought up on a farm till he reached the age of fifteen years, when he went to Murfreesborough and began life as assistant to Col. W. R. Butler, postmaster at that place. After remaining at the postoffice three years, he became engaged in the dry goods business as a clerk, and so continued until the beginning of 1861, when he returned to his father's house and began going to school again.

At the outbreak of the war he left school and joined the army of the Confederacy. After the war he studied medicine at the University of Nashville, and graduated from the medical department of that institution, but never practiced his profession. While at the medical college, he was elected county trustee for Rutherford county, and served two years. After this, he clerked in a drug store for one year. While in the drug business he was elected county tax collector and served two years, after which he went into the dry goods business again, as clerk and book-keeper, and so continued for three years, when he became a partner in the firm of Kerr & Robison, grocers, and continued in this business for two years. At the expiration of this time he was elected clerk of the county court of Rutherford county, the position he now holds, having been first elected in 1878 and re-elected in 1882.

Leaving school in the spring of 1861, he entered the company of Capt. Thomas White, of the Second Tennessee regiment of infantry, as a private, and served in this capacity for eight months, being connected with the Army of Virginia. He was then elected to the first vacancy which had occurred in his company—that of third lieutenant—November, 1861, and with his command was transferred to the Army of Tennessee in the spring of 1862. In May of that year he was made captain of his company, and held that rank through the

Kentucky campaign, and finally, on the return to Knoxville, after this campaign, on the promotion of Col. W. B. Bate to the rank of brigadier-general, Robison was made colonel of his regiment, and held this rank till the close of the war.

Col. Robison took part in the following important battles: Bull Run, the first great battle of the war, July, 1861; Acquia Creek, Virginia, autumn of 1861; Shiloh, April, 1862; Corinth, April, 1862; Richmond, Kentucky, August, 1862, where he received a wound; Perryville, Kentucky, October, 1862; the battles of Murfreesborough, December, 1862, and January, 1863; Chickamauga, September, 1863, where he was again wounded; Missionary Ridge, December, 1863; Ringgold Gap, December, 1863, where he received a wound in the wrist, but did not leave the field until the fight was over. He also took part in the battle of Resaca, in the spring of 1864; the battle of Kenesaw Mountain, July, 1864, and all the other battles of the famous Dalton and Atlanta campaign, and finally in the battle of Jonesborough, Georgia, August 31, 1864, where he received a severe wound in the left hip, which confined him to his bed for eight months, until the war had closed, and from which he has never entirely recovered.

As a soldier, Col. Robison was brave and self-sacrificing, and distinguished for his kindness to his men, by whom he was dearly loved, for they would have followed "Tony" Robison into the very jaws of death. What others thought of him is attested by his rapid rise in rank. He was one of the youngest colonels in the army, having reached that rank when just past the age of twenty-two.

Col. Robison joined the Masons at Murfreesborough, in 1868, and has passed through all the degrees of Masonry up to the eighteenth degree, Scottish Rite. He has filled the offices of Worshipful Master, High Priest of the Chapter, and all the offices of Knights Templar, from Warden up to Grand Commander of the State, which office he held from May, 1882, to May, 1883. Upon the organization of Sinai Lodge of Perfection at Murfreesborough, he was made Sovereign Master and has held the position up to this time.

Col. Robison was raised a Whig, but since the war has been a Democrat. He has never been actively engaged in politics, and with the exception of the offices of county trustee, tax collector and clerk of the court, before mentioned, has never held civil office.

Col. Robison was married, September 15, 1869, to Miss Fannie Rice, daughter of John P. Rice, a native of Alabama, who came to Tennessee in 1867, and located at Murfreesborough. Mrs. Robison's mother was Miss Annie Dunn, daughter of Isham Dunn, a native of Alabama. She was educated at St. Agnes Academy, in

Memphis, and at Soule Female College, Murfreesborough, from which latter institution she graduated in 1869. Mrs. Robison died on the 6th day of March, 1885, after a lingering illness of five months. Thus passed away a noble, Christian woman, a true and faithful companion, and a devoted, loving wife. They had no children.

Col. Robison has been a member of the Methodist church since 1866. Mrs. Robinson was a Presbyterian. Col. Robison began life with nothing, and has made for himself a competency, and is now in comfortable circumstances. He has always adhered strictly to a res-olution to live within his income and keep out of debt. As a man of business he is correct, careful and attentive in all his transactions. As a soldier, he was the idol of his comrades, and never ordered his men into any position of danger he was not willing to lead them. He possesses that calm, quiet, cool and collected bravery that distinguishes the hero, challenges the admiration of the historian, and enkindles anew in the breast of every patriot the fires of patriotism. Beloved by all who know him, a man of strong friendships, and with a host of strong friends—such a man cannot fail to be a good citizen.

COL. R. DUDLEY FRAYSER.

MEMPHIS.

THE subject of this sketch belongs to that generation whose youthful hopes and plans were rudely smitten by the blasts of civil war. He was born in the city of Memphis, June 4, 1840, the son of Dr. John R. Frayser, an eminent physician of that city. His early education was acquired in the public schools of Memphis, though he was sent to a special teacher, Prof. Whitehorn, to prepare for college. In the fall of 1858 he entered the Kentucky Military Institute, and graduated in the spring of 1861, as valedictorian in a class of twenty-two, nearly all of whom lost their lives in the civil war, holding some rank, some on the Confederate, some on the Federal side. Young Frayser had determined, at an early day, to be a lawyer, and during the summer vacations, had been reading law at the school of the celebrated Thomas B. Monroe, United States district judge for the Louisville district. He took the degree of Bachelor of Laws at this school, and the degree of Bachelor of Arts at the Institute. He returned to Memphis, where he had hoped to embark at once in the practice of his profession, only to find that the dread confusion of impending war had given pause to all professional business in his chosen department, as well as in most others, and that the only refuge of a young man was to become a soldier. He accordingly enlisted in company F, 37th Tennessee regiment of infantry, first commanded by Colonel, afterwards Brigadier-General, William H. Carroll, of Memphis. Soon after enlisting, he was made adjutant of the regiment, and served as such until the reorganization of the army at Corinth, in the summer of 1862, when he was made lieutenant-colonel. After the battle of Murfreesborough, December 31, 1862, to January 3, 1863, his regiment was consolidated with the Fifteenth Tennessee, and he was continued as lieutenant-colonel till the close of the war. He surrendered at Charlotte, North Carolina, being at the time, as senior officer, in command of T. B. Smith's, formerly Tyler's, brigade, Bate's divis-ion. The first battle in which he was engaged was that at Fishing Creek, Kentucky, in which Gen. Zollicoffer was killed. January, 1862, at Murfreesborough, he was severely wounded in the neck, being shot from his horse as he went into the fight on the first day of the battle.

After this, on account of his wound, he was made post commandant at Ringgold, Catoosa Springs and Dalton, Georgia, until just before the battle of Chickamauga, when he became engaged in active service again, took part in the battle of Chickamauga and all the battles of the Dalton and Atlanta campaign. After the battle of Atlanta, he was taken severely ill which kept him from the field until just after the battle of Bentonville, North Carolina, when he rejoined his command. Receiving his parole at Charlotte, North Carolina, he, with several other officers, rode across the country to Columbus, Mississippi, where they sold their mules and wagons, and took the cars for Memphis, where he landed in May, 1865. Shortly afterward he resumed the study of law with Judge R. J. Morgan, who subsequently became chancellor, was admitted to the bar in the fall of 1866, and formed a partnership with his preceptor in the firm of Morgan & Frayser, which firm continued until 1870, when they took into partnership Mr. Milton P. Jarnagin, and formed the firm of Morgan, Jarnagin & Frayser. The firm always had a large and lucrative practice. After Judge Morgan went upon the bench, the firm of Jarnagin & Frayser was formed, and continued until the fall of 1883, when Mr. Jarnagin gave up law, moved to East Tennessee, and engaged in farming and stock-raising. Col. Frayser then took into partnership his younger brother, David, a recent graduate of the Harvard law school, and Mr. Thomas M. Scruggs, a graduate of the University of Virginia. The firm of Frayser & Scruggs was formed and has continued to the present time, one of the leading firms of the Memphis bar.

Col. Frayser was raised a Democrat, but was opposed to the war and to sececsion, and while at college would often tell his associates what must be the results of such a war, and often referred to the proclamation of Andrew Jackson during the nullification struggle. But when he returned to Tennessee he went with his people, and fought through the war, to find at its close that his prediction to his classmates, four years before, had been fulfilled. He has never held office, and has never been a candidate, except on one occasion, in 1872, when his name was before the Legislature for nomination for the Legislature. He has frequently been a delegate to political conventions, but has never assumed the role of a politician. On the contrary, he has sought to avoid complicating himself with the business of politics, feeling that whatever attention he might give in that direction would be bestowed at the expense of his professional and other business. While this is so, he has never been indifferent to the political condition of the country, nor has he been lacking in positiveness of political opinion. He is a man of conservative views, and during the agitation of the State debt question in Tennessee he co-operated with what was known as the "sky-blue" wing of the Democratic party. He was sternly opposed to any " forcible adjustment" that excluded the creditors of the State from any participation in the settlement. He regrets Tennessee's course in regard to her debt, but is willing now to let by-gones be by-gones, and join hands with the majority.

Col. Frayser became a Mason in 1863, at a lodge in DeSoto county, Mississippi, where he was raised to the degree of Master Mason. He is now a member of DeSoto Lodge, Memphis. He joined the Independent Order of Odd Fellows, at Memphis, in 1873, filled all the subordinate offices of the order, and became Grand Master of the State in October, 1880. During the summer of 1881, he visited the different lodges of the State, lecturing upon the principles and ceremonies of the order, to which he is much devoted. He is now one of the trustees in the Odd Fellows' Hall and Library Association of Memphis, and a member of Chickasaw Lodge, I. O. O. F. He is also a member of the Knights of Honor. He is largely interested in railroad enterprises. He was, for several years, a director in the Memphis and Charleston railroad company. He owns valuable interests in the Mississippi and Tennessee railroad, and is one of the chief owners of the Memphis city railway—one of a syndicate that controlled a majority of its stock, and has since been elected president of the company, which position he now holds. He is also a stockholder in several banks, being a director and attorney for the Union and Planters' Bank of Memphis, one of the largest and most reliable monied corporations in the southwest. He is a director in the Vanderbilt Insurance Company, the Pioneer Cotton Mill, and has filled that position in several other companies. He is also a director of the Memphis Law Library Asso-

ciation, and president of the Odd Fellows' Relief Association, and Memphis Abstract Company. This mere recital shows that Col. Frayser is no common man.

Col. Frayser was married, February 5, 1867, to Miss Mary F. Lane, daughter of Fletcher Lane, of Memphis, who was one of the leading cotton factors and commission merchants of the city, was connected with many of the most important banks and insurance companies prior to the war, and was a leading man in all public enterprises of the city. His father was Sampson Lane, a native of Georgia, and a prominent man in that State.

Col. Frayser has three children: (1). Pauline. (2). Florence. (3). R. Dudley Frayser, jr.

Mrs. Frayser is a lady of domestic tastes, fond of her home, her husband and her children. She is remarkable for attractiveness of manners and amiability of disposition, and is a great favorite in the social circle. She is an earnest and consistent member of the Methodist church, which she joined in her girlhood, and while always taking a great interest in church matters, and always willing to assist and do her utmost in her church, at the same time she does not forget home and household duties. Col. Frayser is strictly orthodox in his belief, and, while not a member of any religious organization, believes in encouraging all evangelical denominations. He is charitable when a proper object presents itself; and has an abhorrence for display of any kind in such matters.

When Col. Frayser returned to Memphis after the war, he started from the "ground floor," having nothing to begin on but his education, which he feels is a sufficient start for any young man, and a sure basis for obtaining a competency, when backed by proper energy. He has made an independent fortune by his own exertions, owning, in addition to his railroad and banking interests, a large plantation in Shelby county, and another in connection with Col. John Overton, jr., in Tipton county; also a large interest in the Bon Aqua Springs Association, in Hickman county, Tennessee, of which he is secretary and treasurer. He is a great believer in life insurance, and carries policies to the amount of over $30,000.

His motto has been, never to buy any thing unless he needed it, and not then unless he had the money to pay for it. He has always had an abhorrence of indebtedness and of promises to pay without paying.

Col. Frayser is not only an able lawyer, but a sound, judicious operator in general business. He is a man of great correctness and positiveness of character, guided rather than by convictions of right than by considerations of policy. Hence his position on questions that concern society is never equivocal or doubtful. He is a man of small stature, weighing now only about one hundred and nine pounds, and never having exceeded one hundred and twenty pounds in weight, but he possesses any amount of energy and capacity for work.

He wears his hair cut short, and it is roached back over his head, has a long flowing black silken beard, and dresses scrupulously neat. He has yet a youthful appearance. A gentleman visiting Memphis in 1885, who had not seen Col. Frayser for over twenty years, saw him on the street and remarked to a friend: "Yonder goes a gentleman whom I have not seen since the war began, and I see only the back of his head now, but fifty cents to a pretzel I can name him." "Who is he? asked his friend. "R. Dudley Frayser." And it was. "Neither of us weighed much over ninety then—and Frayser holds his own, though eighty-five of it is back-bone and brains and beard, his friends say. He was lieutenant-colonel of the Thirty-seventh Tennessee, and a gallant soldier. Col. Frayser is the only valedictorian I have ever known who made money after leaving college. He graduated at the Kentucky Military Institute, June, 1860. He is now president of the only street railway company operating in Memphis, his lines aggregating sixteen miles in length."

He is strictly temperate in habits, eschewing strong drink and tobacco in any form. A prominent Memphis lawyer says of him; "He is remarkable for his close attention to business, his devotion to the interests of his clients, his clear conception of every man's rights, and for the great force and power with. which he executes every thing he undertakes. He is also remark-able for his ability in handling financial matters. He is now, and will always be, a financial success, and pos-sesses wonderful nerve in executing his plans. When he has once made up his mind as to a particular policy, he moves forward in its execution without hesitancy, and with that energy which is so distinguishing a trait in his character. He is a good lawyer, works hard, and studies closely, and is growing daily in his profes-sion."

For the further family history of Col. R. Dudley Frayser, the reader is invited to examine the sketch of his father, Dr. John R. Frayser, which appears else-where in this volume.

JUDGE T. W. TURLEY.

FRANKLIN.

THIS distinguished jurist and erudite lawyer was born at Bean's Station, Grainger county, East Tennessee, January 18, 1820. His paternal grandfather came from Ireland when a child, and with his parents located in the colony of Virginia. When the war for independence began he enlisted on the patriot side and served almost from the beginning of the Revolution to the siege of Yorktown, at which place he was made an invalid for life by the bursting of a British bombshell near his head, shortly before the surrender of Lord Corn-wallis. He lingered and suffered from his wound sev-eral years, but finally died from its effects. His wife also died about the same time.

They left an orphan son, Thomas Turley, who subse-quently became the father of Judge Thomas W. Turley, subject of this biography. At the early age of eighteen Thomas Turley left Virginia, his native State, and set-tled in Grainger county, Tennessee. Here he married, in 1811, Miss Desdemona Taylor, and here he died of pneumonia, December 6, 1833, leaving his widow with nine children. When a young man he served a cam-paign against the Creek Indians, under Gen. Jackson, in 1812. He was a man of good morals and unusual industry, but was only able to provide a support for his large family, without leaving them any estate.

Those who travel on the railroad leading from Nash-ville to Chattanooga, by looking across the bottom at Shellmound station, can see the historic cave called Nickajack. Near there a bloody battle was fought about

the year 1790, and a signal victory achieved by the whites over the Indians. Ten years afterward that same cave was occupied by Thomas Turley (Judge Turley's father), for three weeks under peculiar circumstances. As before mentioned, he left Virginia at the age of eigh-teen. When he reached the Tennessee river, at the mouth of German creek, in what is now Grainger county, he found a keelboat loaded with such merchandise as was suited to Indian traffic, which, with the cargo, be-longed to Col. Ore, who lived in the neighborhood. It was destined for Nickajack cave, and was put in charge of three men, with instructions to float down to the cave, then at least one hundred miles west of any of the white settlements of East Tennessee. Young Turley came up just before they pushed off, and asked permis-sion, as a volunteer, to accompany the expedition. His services were readily accepted, and in due time the voyagers reached the cave and unloaded their boat. This they securely fastened, intending to load with such articles of barter as they might receive in exchange for their trinkets, and carry back to the owner. Although it was a time of peace (the year 1800), the Indians were very shy. Very few came to the cave the first day, but they could be seen standing on logs and projecting rocks in almost all directions, and a very noticeable fact was, they all carried scalping knives in their belts. The first night one of the boatmen deserted without notice to his companions. The next day the Indians seemed still very shy, but more numerous. The two men who remained became very uneasy and made some reconnoisance, and found that the Cherokees who were sitting around at so many points not only had their scalping knives, but all seemed engaged in whetting them and feeling the sharp edges. The men told what they had seen, but never disclosed to Turley their intentions. The next morning both of Turley's companions were gone and he was left alone to barter with the savages, and perhaps to become the victim of their treachery. But he boldly faced the responsibility and remained at his post. Three weeks afterward other men were sent down who reloaded the goods and returned with them. Turley, although very young, had had some experience in Indian life, and said he was not the least afraid of them. He took care of the goods, and not an article was stolen or otherwise lost. He trafficked with the Indians a little and returned with the boat, when he received the warm thanks of Col. Ore. He died thirty-three years afterward, within half a mile of the bank where he boarded the keelboat for the Nickajack expedition.

Judge Turley's mother was a splendid specimen of the pioneer women who acted such conspicuous and heroic parts in the settlement of the western country. She was born in Virginia, but was brought by her father, also a Revolutionary soldier, to the banks of the Holston, in East Tennessee, while the territorial government of Tennessee was in force, and upon, or near the banks of that river she lived for more than eighty years, dying in 1879, in the ninetieth year of her age. For robust health and the amount of household labor she could, and did perform, she had no superior in her day. For a period of fifty-eight consecutive years, she never used a particle of medicine, such as doctors prescribe. In 1876, a family reunion was held at her house. She had raised nine children, all at that time living. It had been thirty-eight years since they were all with her at the same time. She and her descendants on that day numbered precisely one hundred, quite a remarkable coincidence, it being the centennial year of American Independence.

The literary and legal attainments of Judge Thomas W. Turley were acquired by solitary study. It may be truthfully said he was a scholar without a teacher, and a lawyer without a preceptor. Fifteen dollars would cover all tuition fees paid his school masters. He was, from a child, remarkably fond of reading, and eagerly devoured every book he could find or borrow. In East Tennessee, fifty or sixty years ago, pineknots, usually called "lightwood," were the principal illuminator in the absence of the sun. Most families made it a point to keep *pine* on hand as regularly as they did *meat* or *meal*. It was well understood in the family that *Tom's* seat was in the chimney corner on the pine. Seldom of winter nights, from the time he was a small boy to eighteen years old, was he absent from his seat in the corner, on or near the pine, keeping

up his own light, and reading some book, giving no attention to the conversations and pastimes engaged in by the rest of the family. In this way a habit of abstraction, while reading, from what might be passing in his presence, was formed, which was utilized to much advantage in after life when his business had to be transacted in the bustle and confusion of a court-house. He thinks he has not met any one who could more effectually confine his mind to reading or writing without disturbance by things in sight or hearing around him.

Although when he had almost no advantages of schools—public schools were not in vogue in that day—and had lived a very laborious life, working on the farm, and in saw and grist mills, reading only at night, on Sundays and during such rest hours as could be snatched up; yet at the age of twenty he was a pretty accurate English scholar, and had few superiors in English grammar, geography, history and arithmetic. After leaving his mother, the first business he was engaged in was teaching school, which was somewhat in the line of his taste.

On the 20th of June, 1840, he heard the first political speech he ever listened to from any speaker of note. It was delivered by Hon. Ephraim H. Foster, at that time a senator in congress from Tennessee, made in advocacy of Gen. Harrison, the Whig candidate for president. He has heard no address since that interested or impressed him so much. He asked a bystander what that man followed as a business, and was answered that he was a lawyer. Instantly he determined to devote his life to that profession, and from pursuit of that purpose he never afterward faltered for a moment. Up to that time he had formed no plan of life, and was only drifting along, simply gratifying a taste for reading and a desire for all such information as was to be found in books. By a seeming accident, and in an instant, a plan of life was fixed, and the destiny of the man was shaped. So soon as the crowd dispersed he went straight to a lawyer's office and asked to borrow the book first to be read by one intending to become a lawyer. He was handed Blackstone's Commentaries, which he read that night after returning home, a distance of fifteen miles, till a late hour, and has been reading, with more or less assiduity, that and other law books from that day to this. As a means of support while reading law, he taught several little schools of the "old field" character, and was admitted to the bar in his native county, January 1, 1843. His receipts for the first two years from his practice did not amount to fifty dollars a year. The following amusing incident, recently published in the Nashville *Banner*, illustrates some of the trials and tribulations through which Judge Turley passed when a young barrister: "Judge T. W. Turley, an eminent barrister of Franklin, who began the practice of law some forty years ago, in an East Tennessee town, has now in his possession the first fee he received. He had just hung out his shingle when a hog-drover, who, passing through the town, became involved in a lawsuit, and called on the young attorney to defend his cause. He responded, winning his client's case. In consideration of his services he charged one dollar and a half. The drover handed him a two-dollar bill on the Bank of North Carolina, at Raleigh, and receiving back the requisite change, departed. The young attorney pocketed his two dollars with a light heart, but imagine his feelings when he subsequently learned that it was a counterfeit, and he had given in change a genuine half-dollar, and all the money he possessed. The judge has kept the bill ever since, preserving it with as much care as he would a much larger sum."

Judge Turley took an active part in early life in the building of the Cincinnati, Cumberland Gap and Charleston railroad. He made the first public speech ever made in Grainger county in advocacy of that enterprise. It was many years after the charter was obtained before the work could be put under way. The road is now in successful operation, running from Morristown, Tennessee, to Asheville, North Carolina. He was made a director and continued in the active duties of the position till he left East Tennessee.

He settled and opened a law office in Rutledge, county seat of his native county, where his business steadily increased till 1856, when he was elected by the people to the office of judge of the Second judicial circuit of Tennessee, beating, by a handsome majority, Judge Barton, the popular incumbent, then a candidate for re-election.

Judge Turley never in his life took much part in politics and never made a political speech, a thing that can be said of but few Tennessee lawyers. He uniformly voted the Whig ticket while that party existed, and was a pronounced opponent to secession, but when President Lincoln made his first call for seventy-five thousand troops to invade the South, he decided to go with his people and share their fortunes, and during the war was classed as a Southern man, but took no active part in the struggle, continuing to hold his courts regularly to within eighteen months of the surrender, though but little business was done after July, 1861. Toward the close of the war, finding prejudice against those who were termed rebels very strong in East Tennessee, he quietly took his family into Carolina, and finding himself superseded by a judge appointed by the military governor, and afterward the prejudice by no means abated, during the Brownlow reign of terror, he preferred to locate where the general sentiments of the people would be more congenial. In the fall of 1865, he located in Franklin, Williamson county, Tennessee, and resumed the practice of law, in which he has been actively and successfully engaged ever since. He has not engaged in the criminal practice at all, and has confined himself mostly to practice in the chancery and Supreme courts. He was appointed and acted as Supreme judge in the celebrated "new issue" case. His opinion in that case is published in the

fifth volume of Baxter's reports. The practice of law having of late years dwindled down to a small business, his principal source of income is from a cotton plantation he owns in Bolivar county, Mississippi.

While a young man Judge Turley took much interest in Masonry, was considered a bright Mason, and was several times elected Master of the lodge to which he belonged; frequently attended the Grand Lodge, and was at one time Deputy Grand Master of the State, at another Grand King in the Grand Chapter of Royal Arch Masons. Turley Lodge, at Maynardville, East Tennessee, an active working lodge, was named in recognition of his Masonic labors.

On the 8th of October, 1844, Judge Turley was married to Miss Mary R. Cocke, daughter of Dr. W. E. Cocke, and granddaughter of Gen. John Cocke, a major-general in the war of 1812, and for many years a member of congress from the First district of Tennessee.

Mrs. Turley's great-grandfather, Judge William Cocke, was with Gov. William Blount, the two first senators in the United States congress from Tennessee. The way in which his election was secured will illustrate how elections were carried in 1776, in the first Legislature that ever met in the State. William Blount was very popular; had been the Territorial governor, and his election was a foregone conclusion, but who should have the honor of the other senatorship, was a matter of heated contest. Cocke was a noted Indian fighter, and had warm and determined friends, but not quite strength enough to defeat his popular opponent. His son, John Cocke, then just twenty-one years old, was a member of the Legislature, which was a small body of men sitting in a log meeting-house at Knoxville. John Cocke, the day before the election was to come off, canvassed the house and found his father would be beaten by one vote. Though young, he had experience enough of the world to learn that flattery is a powerful agent in controlling the actions of mankind, male as well as female. A few days previous he had an act passed laying off a new county in the one he represented—Hawkins—which was named Grainger, in honor of the maiden name of Mrs. Gov. Blount. There was an old Dutchman in the house, representative from Sullivan county, named Rutledge, who was not a Cocke man for senator. So John Cocke schemed for his capture. On the morning of the day the election was to come off, as soon as the house came to order, John Cocke arose and addressed the speaker, remarking that he held in his hand and offered as a bill, an act to establish a county seat for the new county of Grainger, and said he, "In honor of my distinguished friend from Sullivan, I have named the county seat Rutledge." Nothing more was said. Soon the election for senator was gone into, and when the clerk called for the vote of "the gentleman from Sullivan," Rutledge responded in an emphatic tone, "Cocke!" Judge Cocke went to the United States senate and was also re-elected, and there stands Rutledge, still the county seat of Grainger, but there is not a citizen in it who knows under what circumstances its name was given.

Judge and Mrs. Turley have had but three children. The eldest, a daughter, died at nine years of age. T. J. Turley, the oldest son, is an active business man in Nashville, Tennessee. William Turley is practicing law at Nashville, in partnership with Judge James M. Quarles, with a bright future before him.

Judge Turley and wife have been members of the Presbyterian church from early life. He was ordained an elder in 1851; takes a deep interest in church affairs, particularly ecclesiastical courts, and has been twice a member of the general assembly of the church to which he belongs. As a Sunday-school worker he has as much reputation as any man in his county, and has been president of the Middle Tennessee Sunday-school Association. He has been president of the Williamson County Bible Society during most of the time he has lived in the county.

One of Judge Turley's cardinal resolutions, from a very early age, was to *do whatever he undertook thor-*oughly, hence he adopted that as a motto, as second to none, and which he wrote on the fly-leaf of several of his books, and under its inspiration he undertook to make himself as good an arithmetician, as good a geographer, historian and grammarian as the country afforded, and flattered himself that he succeeded. But as he grew older, he felt very much like his motto was too ambitious, and abandoned it. While on the bench he made it an invariable rule to open his court on time, sharp. When he adjourned to meet at 8 o'clock the court met at 8 o'clock. He says in the seven years during which he held his courts, he never was ten minutes behind the time fixed in opening his court. In that time he only failed to hold one term of his courts, and that was caused by high water. Another rule was, that he would never go to the court-house before the time of opening. When he reached the door, he always went straight to the bench, and would engage in no social conversation in the court-house. If there were more judges who would act on these rules, the effect on the dockets would be striking, and it might enhance the esteem of the courts in the public mind.

HON. J. D. C. ATKINS.

PARIS.

THIS eminent and distinguished statesman, whose fame is co-extensive with the boundaries of the nation, and whose political services are intimately interwoven with the political history of the country for a third of a century past, is one of Tennessee's brightest jewels. His proverbial popularity with the people of his native State, is due doubtless to his confidence in the sober second thought, the good sense and ultimate wisdom of the masses, who are enabled by their own modes of thought, and their social discussions, to arrive at just conclusions as to the effect of laws, modes of government, and the usefulness of public men. The people follow no man blindly. While they are apt to repose great confidence in public men who have shown themselves in sympathy with popular rights, and who have made consistent records, they at last assert their own independence, both in thought and action. Should any leader exhibit selfishness, or unsoundness, or indifference to public interests, he at once falls beneath the ban of their condemnation. Tried by this crucible test of worthiness, Gen. J. D. C. Atkins has proven himself as made of the purest metal, and, therefore, his people honor and love him.

The Atkins family is of Welsh and Irish blood. Gen. Atkins' great-grandfather, John Atkins, was a native born Welshman, as was also his great-grandfather on the maternal side. His paternal grandfather (also

named John Atkins) was born in Anson county, North Carolina; married a Miss Richards of a North Carolina family, daughter of a Revolutionary soldier, and moved to Stewart county, Tennessee, where he died. He was a farmer and a citizen of considerable wealth. He, raised a large family of sons and daughters, every one of whom succeeded well in life and became wealthy for their day.

Gen. Atkins' father who was also named John (a favorite family name), was born in Anson county, North Carolina, January 28, 1787, and died December 30, 1845, in Henry county, Tennessee. He was a wealthy farmer and bequeathed Gen. Atkins the homestead upon which he now lives. He was a Democrat, and held some minor county offices. For forty years he was a member and a liberal supporter of the Methodist church, and his house was the home of Methodist preachers. He never in his life owed a debt overdue for a day, and when he died did not owe a dollar to any man. His prominent trait of character was promptness in the discharge of duty, whatever he believed it to be. He was a man of action and of very few words. He was kind and liberal to the very poor, and as charitable towards the weaknesses of human nature as any man who ever lived could be, who had at the same time his detestation of falsehood, treachery, meanness and insincerity. He was modest to a fault, and never spoke

33

unkindly of others. One of his maxims was, "If you can't speak well of a man, don't speak of him at all." Another was, "Never feel yourself above the influence of any one, however humble."

Gen. Atkins' mother, *nee* Miss Sarah Manly, was born in Anson county, North Carolina, daughter of Richard Manly and Keziah Freeman. She had a brother, Rev. John Manly, who was a leading Methodist preacher in West Tennessee in the early settlement of that portion of the State. Manly's Chapel, in Henry county, named for him, bears evidence as to his prominence and popularity. Gen. Atkins' mother was a devout Methodist. She died at the age of thirty-two, when the son was an infant.

The Atkins family has produced mostly farmers and a few merchants, the subject of this sketch being the most prominent one in politics. Gen. Atkins' brother, Eldridge G. Atkins, who died at Memphis in 1866, was a lawyer, and practiced at Paris and in the adjoining counties. He left one son, J. W. G. Atkins.

John D. Clinton Atkins, was born in Henry county, Tennessee, nine miles east of Paris, near Manly's Chapel, June 4, 1825; grew up in the same county; was educated at the Paris Male Academy, and at Knoxville, graduating with the first honors of his class, from the East Tennessee University, August, 1846. His earliest political proclivities were Democratic, his ancestry on both sides being Democratic as far back as family tradition goes. In the American Revolution, they were Whigs. Young Atkins began taking a lively interest in politics as early as his fifteenth year, in the campaign of 1840 between Messrs. Van Buren and Harrison, and in 1843 in the contest for congress in his congressional district between Hon. Cave Johnson and Hon. Gustavus A. Henry. When only nineteen years old, he took an active part, while at the East Tennessee University, in the campaign of 1844, between Messrs. Polk and Clay. He first began making political speeches in 1848, in the campaign between Messrs. Cass and Taylor. He was elected to the Tennessee House of Representatives in 1849, in opposition to extending State aid to railroads, but in the progress of events changed his opinion on this subject, and in 1851, was re-elected to the Legislature, being then in favor of State aid to the railroads, and in that Legislature he was one of the committee of nine that inaugurated the internal improvement system of the State. In 1855, he was elected to the State senate from the counties of Henry, Weakley and Obion, and in that body opposed the "omnibus railroad bill," in conjunction with Hons. W. C. Whitthorne, Neill S. Brown, Frank C. Dunnington and others. On January 8, 1856, Gen. Atkins was elected chairman of the Democratic State convention at Nashville, which sent delegates to the national Democratic convention, which nominated Buchanan and Breckinridge. The same year he was presidential elector for the Ninth congressional district, on the Buchanan and Breckinridge ticket.

In 1857, Gen. Atkins was nominated by the Democrats as their candidate for Congress from the Ninth congressional district, composed of the counties of Henry, Weakley, Obion (which then embraced Lake), Dyer, Lauderdale, Tipton, Gibson, Carroll and Henderson. He was elected by one hundred and twenty-nine majority in a district which had been Whig by six hundred or seven hundred majority, overcoming the celebrated Emerson Etheridge, who, in 1853, represented the district without opposition, and, in 1855, had defeated Judge T. J. Freeman, by between five hundred and six hundred votes. In 1859, Gen. Atkins was again a candidate, but after a still more heated and animated campaign, was defeated by Mr. Etheridge by only eight votes.

Gen. Atkins was a delegate for the State at large to the Charleston and Baltimore conventions of 1860, and acted with the Tennessee delegation, withdrawing from the Baltimore convention when Virginia withdrew, because the delegates were admitted from the States which had already seceded, and who were, therefore, without a constituency. In the interval between the Charleston and Baltimore conventions, Gen. Atkins was again made presidential elector for the Ninth congressional district on the Breckinridge and Lane ticket, but the Bell and Everett ticket was successful in the State.

Sectional agitation ensuing, and feeling rising so high as to result in the secession of the southern States, it became necessary for Tennessee to take action one way or the other, and Gen. Atkins, without hesitation, acted with the southern wing of the Democracy, and thinking Tennessee had just cause for complaint as to her treatment by northern agitators, he favored a State convention on the basis of the Crittenden compromise. The majority of people in the State thought otherwise, and the convention was voted down in February, 1861. Events transpired so rapidly throughout the nation, especially in the southern States which had seceded, Tennessee could no longer occupy a quiescent or neutral ground, and in June, 1861, voted herself out of the Union.

Meanwhile Gen. Atkins had volunteered for the Confederate service, had been elected lieutenant-colonel of the Fifth Tennessee regiment, and like everybody else in the army, voted for the State's withdrawal from the Union. He remained in the army but a short time, his health being very poor, when, without being a candidate, he was elected to represent his district in the provisional Confederate Congress, and took his seat at Richmond, in August, 1861, Tennessee having seven representatives only, viz.: Judge Robert L. Caruthers, Col. John F. House, Hon. David M. Currin, Hon. Thomas L. Jones, Hon. James H. Thomas, Col. William H. DeWitt and Gen. J. D. C. Atkins. In November, 1861, he was elected a member of the House of Representatives of what was called the permanent Confederate Congress, and was re-elected in 1863, when the army nominated candidates at Winchester, Tennessee. In that body he served on the post-offices and post-roads, army and foreign affairs committees. He introduced, as a member of the foreign affairs committee, of which William C. Rives, of Virginia, was chairman, the resolution which led to the appointment of Messrs. Stephens, Campbell and Hunter to the Hampton Roads conference. (See Hon. A. H. Stephens' correspondence with Hon. Ben Hill).

The close of the war found Gen. Atkins in very straightened financial circumstances; his family were in Texas, and he returned home in the latter part of 1865, and set about recuperating his broken fortunes, accepting the situation and trying to make himself the best citizen he could. In connection with two other gentlemen, he founded the *Paris Intelligencer*, in 1867, and published it for several years as a means of support. In the meantime he returned to his farm and lived upon it, and has been in that business, as an occupation, ever since, making stock-raising and grass culture a specialty.

The partialty of the Democratic party, however, again called him into service. In 1872, he was nominated as a candidate to represent his district in the United States Congress, and was elected by a large majority. He was nominated without opposition, and was re-elected in 1874, 1876, 1878 and 1880, each time receiving large majorities over his Republican competitors.

During eight of the years he has served in the United States Congress, he was a member of the committee on appropriations, four of which years he was chairman of the committee, and during his entire twelve years of service there he was identified with questions of economic reform. He had charge of the army bill when the Democracy purposely defeated it, which caused a change of policy in the iron will and military despotism the administration had so long maintained toward the southern States. He was one of the selected committee of sixteen appointed by the Democratic senators and representatives in the Forty-fourth Congress, which finally consented to and advised the adoption of the electoral commission as a mode of settling the presidential difficulty, and which the country generally regarded as necessary to prevent civil war and much bloodshed. He also served as a member of the special committee appointed by the Democrats of the two houses of the Forty-fifth Congress, to formulate the policy of the Democratic party in that Congress upon the subject of the repeal of the test oaths and supervisor of election laws, of which committee Hon. Allen G. Thurman, of Ohio, was chairman.

On the Tennessee "State debt" question, Gen. Atkins has always acted with the State credit party, and voted for Gen. William B. Bate for governor, in the canvasses of 1882 and 1884, believing that the policy advocated by Gov. Bate was the best solution of the State's financial difficulties.

In 1882, Gen. Atkins voluntarily retired from public life, more warmly regarded by his constituency than ever before, seeing that his retirement was a detriment and a loss to the public service, yet after a long life of activity, he found social and domestic quiet stronger charms. In 1884, he was sent as a delegate from his county to the State Democratic convention, and without solicitation, and even against his protest, he was made president of that body, which nominated delegates to the national Democratic convention, at Chicago, which nominated Cleveland and Hendricks. At the same convention, and against his personal wishes, he was unanimously chosen as one of the presidential electors for the State at large on the Cleveland and Hendricks ticket. His much impaired physical health, however, forced him to relinquish many of his appointments in that campaign, and again he retired to the privacy of his home. But the signal triumph of the national Democracy in that memorable contest, demanded, in order that the victory might be made more complete, that the ablest statesmen of the party should be placed in charge of affairs. President Cleveland having selected Hon. L. Q. C. Lamar, United States senator from Mississippi, as secretary of the interior in his cabinet, the next selection in that department was Gen. J. D. C. Atkins as United States Indian commissioner, which was tendered him and accepted March 26, 1885. To this position Gen. Atkins brings his great abilities, his wise judgment and his life-long experience in public affairs—qualifications that will add additional lustre to his fame, and greatly advance his country's interests.

Gen. Atkins was married in Paris, Tennessee, November 23, 1847, to Miss Elizabeth Bacon Porter (cousin of ex-Gov. James D. Porter), daughter of William Porter, a farmer, a very popular man, who was for many years county court clerk of Henry county. Her grandfather, William Porter, sr., a native of Pennsylvania, moved in early life to Kentucky, thence to Tennessee. He was the son of one of seven brothers, who came to this country from Ireland (see sketch of Gov. Porter elsewhere in this volume). The Porter's are related to Gen. Patterson, of Pennsylvania. Mrs. Atkins' mother's maiden name, was Miss Sarah Ware, of a Kentucky family of considerable wealth. Mrs. Atkins' uncle, Thomas K. Porter, father of Gov. Porter, was a prominent physician at Paris, and her uncle, Dr. James D. Porter, is now a prominent physician in Hill county, Texas. Mrs. Atkins was educated at Paris, under Prof. Ball. She is pre-eminently a charitable woman, noted for her kindness of heart, her strong common sense, and her ability to make everybody around her her friend. By this marriage, Gen. Atkins has five children: (1). Sallie Atkins, educated at the Holly Springs Institute, at Mrs. Pettitt's select school at Mound Prairie, Texas, and at Paris; married in 1867, Hugh Dunlap, son of Gen. John H. Dunlap, and has six children, Clinton, Hugh, John, Porter, Evelyn and William. (2). Bettie Atkins, graduated at the Paris Female College, under Prof. Sterling; married, in 1880, Prof. T. H. M. Hunter, of Paris, formerly of Lewisburg, Tennessee; has one child, Atkins. (3). John D. Atkins, born January 20, 1857; educated at the East Tennessee University and at Cecil College, Kentucky; now farming in Henry county; unmarried. 4). Mattie Green Atkins, graduated at Jackson, Tennessee, under Prof. Jones. (5). Clintie Atkins, married, in 1885, Dudley Porter, son of ex-Gov. James D. Porter, now assistant secretary of State for the United States.

Gen. Atkins was elected, when quite a young man, and commissioned by Gov. Neill S. Brown, as brigadier-general of the State troops in the peace establishment. Hence, he is called General—a title universally given him, though in the late war he only held the rank of lieutenant-colonel. He became a Mason at Knoxville, Tennessee, in 1846, and has taken all the Chapter degrees. He is also a member of the Knights of Honor and of the order of the Golden Cross. Beginning life on a handsome patrimonial estate, he has been prudent and economical, and now finds himself in very easy and comfortable circumstances. Besides his farm property and other investments, he is a member of the Bon Air Coal, Land and Lumber company.

Personally, Gen. Atkins does not appear over fifty years of age. He is somewhat tall, slender, and of very lithe build. His countenance is frank and honest in every lineament. He is quick spoken, and with a soft-ness of voice that indicates a kindly good nature, and has that look of self-confidence and self-satisfaction that Cicero points out as the principal factor of success in a candidate for the public suffrages. The writer found the General at his farm, among his stock, and he at once commenced dilating upon the delights of country life, dwelling with enthusiasm upon the notes of the wood-thrush that made vocal with the most delicious music his fine forest of poplar, oak and chestnut. And here, perhaps, was the best place to study the man.

One of the strongest traits of his character is his fidelity to his word; faithfulness to his obligations. But the foundation corner-stone of his character is to do injustice to no man, and to guard, if necessary with his heart's blood, his own good name. No man who does this can be far out of the way, for he must be fair, honest, liberal and correct, if he preserves a good name. Although he once changed front on an important State question, the people still adhered to him as being a man open to conviction, and honest and brave enough to avow belief in his new position. His name has never been smirched. He has no false pride that makes him feel superior to the people who have conferred honors upon him. The people believe he has an identity of interest with them, and that he is fearless in the advocacy of what he believes to be right, and what he believes are the people's rights. He is a noble specimen of a noble Tennessean.

WILLIAM H. MORGAN, M.D., D.D.S.

NASHVILLE.

THE distinguished gentleman and eminent dental surgeon whose name heads this biographical sketch, is of Welsh extraction. It is a well authenticated fact that nearly all of the American Morgans are the offspring of three brothers Morgan, who came over from Wales, and who were descendants of the celebrated Morgan, the buccaneer, one of the boldest, most noted and most successful that ever sailed the seas. It is this same stern perseverance of the Welsh blood that has given the American descendants success in various callings in life. The members of the family who have most illustrated the name are: Gen. Daniel Morgan, the famous American patriot; the late Gov. E. D. Morgan, of New York; Col. William A. Morgan, of Gen. J. E. B. Stuart's Confederate cavalry, and senior captain in Stuart's old regiment; the late Dr. Jacob Bedinger Morgan, once president of the Union Bank of Mississippi, whose daughter, Miss Sallie Bedinger Morgan, has attained some literary celebrity as the author of "Tahoe, or Life in California," and by her frequent contribu-tions to leading journals of the country, and last, but by no means least, Dr. William H. Morgan, of Nashville, subject of this sketch.

Dr. Morgan's great-grandfather, William Morgan, was born in New Jersey, settled at Shepherdstown, Virginia, and died there. His grandfather, Hon. Abram Morgan, was born in Jefferson county, Virginia; was a soldier in the Revolution; served ten years in the Virginia Legislature, and died in Logan county, Kentucky. He was a cousin of Gen. Daniel Morgan, mentioned above.

Dr. Morgan's father, Joseph Morgan, was born in Jefferson county, Virginia, emigrated with his father in 1809, and settled as a small farmer in Logan county, Kentucky. He was in the war of 1812-14, in the campaign under Gen. Hopkins, in what was then known as the "Territory of Indiana;" was under Jackson in Gen. Coffee's brigade of mounted rifles in Florida, and was at the battle of New Orleans, in a company thirty-two strong which came out of the fight without a commissioned officer. This was on the night of December 23,

1814, preceding the general engagement. Mr. Morgan died, at his home in Logan county, Kentucky, in 1871, in his seventy-ninth year.

Dr. Morgan's paternal grandmother was Miss Mary Bedinger, daughter of Henry Bedinger, a Revolutionary soldier, and a prominent citizen of Jefferson county, Virginia. She was a sister of Hon. Michael Bedinger, who served in Congress from Kentucky, and an aunt of the distinguished Henry Bedinger, who was in Congress from Virginia, and afterwards United States minister to Holland.

Dr. Morgan's mother, *nee* Miss Elizabeth Adams, was born in Montgomery county, Maryland, the daughter of Alexander Adams and Sallie Beall. She died in 1824, at the age of twenty-five years, leaving four children, of whom William H. Morgan was the oldest. Her only other surviving child, Sarah A. Morgan, is now the wife of Erasmus A. Apling, of Illinois.

William H. Morgan was born in Logan county, Kentucky, February 22, 1818. He was raised on a farm, and received his education, which was very meagre, in the country schools, near his father's homestead. At the age of thirty years he graduated from the Baltimore College of Dental Surgery, March 1, 1848, when there had been issued only fifty-one regular dental diplomas in America, not counting honorary degrees. After practicing a short time in Russellville, Kentucky, he located in Nashville, Tennessee, in 1849, and has lived there ever since—now thirty-seven years. When he came to Tennessee there was but one other regular dental graduate in the State. As an evidence of the interest he takes in the profession outside of his office, it is pertinent to mention, as a part of the dental history of the country, that he was present at and assisted in the organization of the American Dental Association in 1860, and has rarely missed a meeting of that body since. At its session in Boston, in 1866, he was made first vice-president, and in 1870, at Nashville, its president. By appointment of the Tennessee Dental Association, he delivered the address of welcome on the assembling of this national body at Nashville. He was chosen the first president of the Central State Dental Association; has also served as president of the Nashville Dental Association; president of the Mississippi Valley Dental Association, and president of the Ohio Dental College Association, having been for many years a member of the board of trustees of the Ohio Dental College, and for a time was its president. He called together, by his individual card, the convention that formed the Southern Dental Association at Atlanta, in 1869, which is now one of the most prominent and prosperous associations in the United States, more than one hundred members being present at its meeting in Atlanta, in 1882.

In 1879, Dr. Morgan was elected to the chair of clinical dentistry and dental pathology in the University of Nashville and Vanderbilt University, and has served as dean of that faculty since the organization of the dental department. No man in America has labored harder, and no man in the South has done so much to elevate dentistry to the dignity of a separate and distinct science as Dr. Morgan, nor more successfully used his time, talent and influence to raise the standard of dental education. It was no idle compliment of the late Dr. C. K. Winston, when he said of him, "Dr. Morgan is not only an eloquent speaker, but an honor to his profession and a benefactor to his race."

His contributions to dental literature, published in the dental journals of the country, bear ample evidence of his ability as a writer, clear, concise and pointed. As a lecturer and debater, he is earnest, enthusiastic, direct, comprehensive and convincing.

Though professionally known as a dentist, and as a most skillful operator, recognized as ranking among the most eminent in the United States, Dr. Morgan's name and fame are not confined to that one field of usefulness. In the Methodist church he has held, almost continuously, for upward of forty years, official relations, from class-leader to delegate in the annual and general conferences. For sixteen years he has been a member of the book committee of the Southern Methodist Publishing House, and secretary of the committee for that time; for the past seventeen years has been president of the Nashville and Davidson County Bible Society; is a director in several insurance companies; holds several trusteeships; has been secretary of Masonic lodges; chaplain in his Commandery, and is a member of the Vanderbilt senate. In all these trusts he has been exceptionally punctual in attendance, and in whatever body found is known and spoken of as "a working member." At the age of sixty-eight years, the Nestor of his profession, full of honors, it must be a proud satisfaction for his posterity to read that he has done more for the advancement of dental science than any other man in the southern States, that he stands among the foremost in every good work, eminent among prominent Tennesseans, and has a national reputation. Yet, if one should enter his office, he doubtless would be found as hard at work as if he had his name and fortune still to make.

The life of such a man is worth the study of young men who would rise in the world, and of parents who would point out to their children the path to success. In boyhood, Dr. Morgan had and cultivated a natural taste and love for mechanics, and the one predominating trait in his character has ever been an ambition to excel, to do better than any other could, whatever he undertook. It is this principle that gives cunning to the hand of the artisan, keenness to the eye of the explorer, eloquence to the orator, energy to pride, and perfection and finish to those who would triumph in architecture, manufactures and the sciences. It is a quality found in the *noble few* who do all the work in building up the world's civilization.

Dr. Morgan married in Logan county, Kentucky, November 30, 1852, Miss Sarah A. Noel, who was born in Shelby county, Kentucky, daughter of Garnett B. Noel, of the Garnett family of Virginia. Her mother, *nee* Miss Caroline H. Rouse, was a daughter of William Rouse, a merchant at Shelbyville. Mrs. Morgan's mother was one of the two first graduates of Mrs. Tevis' noted school, Science Hill Academy, Shelbyville, Kentucky. Mrs. Morgan is a lady of fine education and excellent judgment, and her husband (competent authority) " praiseth her when he sitteth among the elders of the land," as a lady endowed with the three highest womanly graces: modesty, industry, and domestic skill. By this marriage Dr. Morgan has four children, all born in Davidson county, Tennessee: (1). Henry William Morgan, born October 25, 1853; graduated from the Nashville High School; was the first matriculant and first graduate of the medical department of Vanderbilt University; graduated in 1876, from the Philadelphia College of Dental Surgery; now in successful practice in partnership with his father. He married, November 3, 1880, Miss Tillie Evans, daughter of the late William M. B. Evans, a druggist, formerly of Troy, New York. Her mother, *nee* Miss Irene Mc-Nairy, is a grand-daughter of Dr. Boyd McNairy, an eminent physician in the early days of Nashville, noted for his hospitality, having entertained Gen. LaFayette on his visit to Nashville in 1825, and other distinguished men, Clay, Calhoun, Jackson, and others. By this marriage Dr. Henry William Morgan has one son, William Henry, jr., and one daughter, Irene. (2). Effie Morgan, born January 24, 1855; graduated at the Nashville City High School, (3). Joseph Bedinger Morgan, born April 30, 1856; graduated at the Nashville High School; now of the firm of Morgan & Hamilton, manufacturers, Nashville; married, January 17, 1883, Miss Jennie Gibson, daughter of the late Nathan Gibson, of Nashville. (4). Garnett Noel Morgan, born March 12, 1861; finely educated; now in commercial life in Nashville. Thoroughness is his principal characteristic. For this he won the praise of the Vanderbilt faculty, especially of Bishop McTyeire, president of the board of trust.

Dr. Morgan is a man of large, well-proportioned physique, full of energy and push, and this, too, notwithstanding he has been lame from his childhood from rheumatic affection. Yet no one ever saw him blue.

He is always cheerful and full of business. Moreover, he is a most companionable gentleman ; affable without affectation, and polite because suavity is inherent with him. He is in comfortable, independent circumstances, and owns several valuable buildings in Nashville. By the war he lost twenty thousand dollars, yet Bradstreet now rates him as worth forty thousand dollars, with first-class credit. A determination to excel, and the concentration of his powers upon the work of his profession, account for his success. He is universally regarded as an honest and a just man. In the community where he is best known and best beloved, his integrity is beyond question. As a dentist he has never advertised, except in a simple business card. The characteristic of stern Welsh perseverance, not easily turned from a purpose, is brightly illustrated in his life and his work.

In politics Dr. Morgan was an old line Whig, and in feeling still adheres to that celebrated party, though of late years he has acted mainly with the Democrats. He has never claimed to be an orthodox Democrat ; has voted for principles and not for party ; for measures in preference to men. It was, therefore, a matter of great surprise to the hide-bound, dyed-in-the-wool Democracy, when the telegraph announced, on November 11, 1885, that President Cleveland had appointed Dr. Morgan as a member of the board of Indian commissioners, in place of Hon. Orange Judd, resigned. The appointment was unsolicited, unsought by Dr. Morgan, and was as much of a surprise to him as it was to the spoilsmen and office-seekers. The following editorial from the Nashville *Union*, November 14, 1885, will show, however, the wisdom of the selection: "The appointment of Dr. W. H. Morgan, by the president of the United States, as a member of the board of Indian commissioners, is to say the least of it, a safe appointment, so far as the government is concerned. The office is one without a salary, only actual expenses paid while on official business, and is limited to a very few and very simple duties, the principal qualification being incorruptibility, with prudence and discretion. Where the president got his information about Dr. Morgan nobody seems to know ; but if he was simply looking out for a man whose character was a guarantee that there would be no public scandal or jobbery where he presides, then the president stopped at the right man in taking Dr. W. H. Morgan.

REV. ACHILLES D. SEARS, D. D.

CLARKSVILLE.

THE venerable and devoted man of God, who is the subject of this sketch, now in charge of a pastorate in Clarksville, is of English descent, both his grandparents having immigrated from England and settled in Virginia. His paternal grandfather, William B. Sears, who was a cousin of Gen. Charles Lee, of Revolutionary fame, was at one time, sheriff of Fairfax county, Virginia. He married Elizabeth Whaley, and their oldest son, Charles Lee Sears, who died in Virginia during the late civil war, married Elizabeth Worster, daughter of John Worster, an English gentleman who had settled in Virginia. From this marriage was born the subject of this sketch. The Whaley and Worster families are still numerously represented in Fairfax county, while the Searses are plentifully scattered throughout the northwestern States. The ancestors of William B. Sears lived in Normandy, before the Norman invasion. One of the name came to England with William the Conqueror. The name, under various modifications, is found numerously spread throughout England. Two of them are known to have come to America. One, Richard Sears, landed at Plymouth, Massachusetts, in 1640. The other, William B. Sears, came to Fairfax county, Virginia, in 1755.

Dr. Sears was born in Fairfax county, Virginia, January 1, 1804. He was brought up to work on a farm, and derived his early education from the common English schools of the neighborhood, his principal teachers being Profs. Klepstein and Richardson, two well known instructors in their time. The only one of his early school-mates now known to be living, is Henry Millan, of Lucas county, Iowa.

In 1823, being then but nineteen years of age, Dr. Sears removed to Kentucky, and settled in Bourbon county, where he engaged in teaching school for about five years, in the meantime studying law with Lucien J. Feemster. In 1828, he married and removed to Fayette county, near Lexington, and engaged in farming for several years. In 1838, he became a member of the Baptist church, and was ordained for the ministry at Davis Fork church, by Revs. Darnaby Leake and Dr. Dillard, in 1839, and began his labors as a home missionary in northern Kentucky, with headquarters at Flemingsburg.

In 1842, he was called to take charge of the First Baptist church of Louisville, where he remained for seven years. He then became general agent of the Baptists for Kentucky, in which capacity he served for two years, after which he took charge of the church at Hopkinsville, Kentucky, in 1851, where he remained till the beginning of the war of secession. Being an ardent supporter of the South, he was forced to leave

Kentucky when the Federals occupied the State, and, retiring to Mississippi, spent the next four years in the South, most of the time supplying the Baptist church at Columbus, Mississippi. The remainder of the time, under the auspices of the Southern Baptist Board of Missions, he was a missionary to the Confederate soldiers, to many of whom he administered baptism.

While endeavoring to reach his family in Kentucky, he got as far as Clarksville, Tennessee, but was not allowed to enter Kentucky until martial law was abolished by President Johnson. He was called to the Baptist church in Clarksville, and has continued in charge of it up to the present time—a period of twenty years. The church during that time has increased from twenty-five to two hundred and twenty-five members, while a new house of worship has lately been erected at a cost of twenty-five thousand dollars. During the forty-six years of his ministry, he has baptized between two and three thousand persons, and, though now upwards of eighty years of age, he is in good health and performs the regular duties of his church with as much ease to himself as he did twenty years ago. He has been a delegate to the following general conventions of the southern Baptists: At Richmond, Virginia, in 1846; at Nashville, Tennessee, in 1851; at Baltimore, Maryland, in 1853; at Montgomery, Alabama, in 1855, where he preached the conventional sermon; at Louisville, Kentucky, in 1857; at Russellville, Kentucky, in 1866; at Memphis, Tennessee, in 1867.

He has frequently been called to deliver commencement sermons to various female colleges, including those at Lebanon, Bowling Green, Bardstown, Hopkinsville and others. He was for four years moderator of the Cumberland Baptist Association, after which he declined a re-election. Prior to the war, he was, for several years, associate editor of the *Western Recorder*, published at Louisville.

Politically, though never conspicuous as an "offensive partisan," Dr. Sears has ever had very decided convictions. He was reared a Calhoun Democrat, and was, and still is, a thorough believer in the doctrine of State's rights. As a matter of course, he was a warm sympathizer with the South in the late civil struggle.

The warm interest Dr. Sears has taken in Masonry, and the number of high positions he has held in the order, render that portion of his history specially important. He became a Master Mason, a Royal Arch Mason and Knight Templar, at Hopkinsville, Kentucky, in 1850, and affiliated with Clarksville Commandery, No. 8, in 1867. He was Commander of a Commandery in Kentucky for twelve years, and for a like number of years in Tennessee. He has been Worshipful Master, and is now Prelate of his Commandery. In 1870, he became Grand Commander for the State of Tennessee. As Past Grand Commander he has been a prominent member of the Grand Encampment, and attended the triennial conclave until prevented by age. In 1849, he became a member of the order of Odd Fellows. In both orders he has frequently been called on to deliver addresses on important occasions; among which he recently delivered an address at the laying of the corner-stone of the first Baptist church, Nashville.

Dr. Sears was married, March 25, 1828, to Miss Ann B. Bowie, daughter of William Bowie, of Frederick county, Virginia, a descendant of the Bowies of Maryland. She is a cousin of Col. James Bowie, of " bowie knife " fame. Her mother was Miss Card, of Raleigh, North Carolina, a member of the family who are the maternal ancestry of Hon. William Windom, late secretary of the treasury. By his marriage with Miss Bowie Dr. Sears had four children, one of whom is now living, the wife of Jno. N. Major, formerly of Christian county, Kentucky, and the mother of one daughter and four sons, the oldest of whom, A. D. Sears Major, is now a practicing lawyer of Clarksville. Mrs. Sears is a member of the Baptist church, is full of energy and vivacity, though now more than eighty years old, and has always been a woman of strong mental powers and keen perceptive faculties.

Dr. Sears is a close student. Beginning life with no other education than that acquired in common schools, he applied himself to his books at every opportunity, and acquired a fair knowledge of Latin, Greek, Hebrew and French by private study. Essentially the architect of his own fortunes, he has made himself by work and study. Choosing a profession, he devoted himself to it closely, and has made it his aim to get and use whatever would be of advantage in his calling. His grandfathers were both free-thinkers, of the school of Tom Paine, and he himself, raised in an atmosphere of that sort, was brought to reflection by family sorrows. He began to read the Bible, got all his denominational views therefrom, was converted to God, and joined the church without having listened attentively to a single denominational sermon.

A late newspaper correspondent, writing of a recent Baptist assembly, speaks thus of Dr. Sears: "The most remarkable man present was Rev. A. D. Sears, D. D., who is eighty-two years old, and is yet hale and vigorous in body and mind, and is abreast of the age in all mission and educational progress. His stirring words to the people on the duty of giving liberally of their means for the extension of Christ's kingdom, were received with marked attention. If all the pastors in this association were as thoroughly missionary in spirit and practice as he is, where hundreds are reported now, we'd have thousands. The writer spent the night with this venerable man, and was much interested in his talk. One or two of his utterances I venture to give: ' I am eighty-two years old; I can't live much longer; as I look back over a checkered life, I find that I have not one kind word nor kind act to regret, and I wish all my actions and words had been kind.' Another: ' I am glad to say I never had a doubt that Jesus Christ came into the world and died to save sinners, and I never doubt that I have an interest in His blood and shall live with Him forever in Heaven."

J. H. VAN DEMAN, A.M., M.D.

CHATTANOOGA.

DR. J. H. VAN DEMAN, of Chattanooga, justly regarded as one of the leading surgeons and physicians of Tennessee, is a native of Ohio, born in Delaware county, of that State, October 27, 1829. He is a bright example of the self-made man, of an ambitious young American who, without inherited wealth or influential friends, overcomes obstacles, conquers difficulties and at last achieves success. Thus, while a mere youth, he had to work hard for the money necessary to obtain an education. He graduated, June, 1849, in the classical course from the Ohio Wesleyan University, Delaware, Ohio, and in the spring of 1852, graduated in medicine at the Cleveland (Ohio) Medical College, under Profs. De La Meter, H. A. Ackley, J. L. Cassells, Jared B. Kirtland, and others, and in the same year received, unsolicited, the degree of A.M., from his literary alma mater.

He then engaged in practice at Delaware and vicinity, but still labored under financial difficulties, for when he quit the medical college he did so without a dollar in his pocket, and besides was in debt for his horse, his buggy, his books and his last course of lectures. But he possessed what is oftentimes of more real value— he had pluck and energy, and a resolute will. He continued in practice at Delaware until 1857, when, in order to better his pecuniary situation, he became a candidate and was elected clerk of the Ohio senate two terms, 1857–58 and 1858–59, while Hon. Salmon P. Chase was governor of Ohio. With the money thus made he resumed his chosen profession, and practiced at Delaware until 1861.

When the rebellion broke out, he at once espoused the cause of the Union, and was made captain of company K (which he raised), Sixty-sixth Ohio volunteer infantry. He participated with gallantry in the battles of Winchester, Port Republic, Larue and Cedar Mountain, Virginia. In the latter engagement he was slightly wounded in the head and was captured, while leading a reconnoissance, at ten o'clock at night. He was then taken to Libby prison, kept five months, paroled, and exchanged January 10, 1863, after which he rejoined his command, resigned his captain's commission, and went into the medical department, Army of the Cumberland. He was assigned to duty as assistant-surgeon, and joined the Tenth Ohio infantry regiment at Tullahoma, Tennessee, May 5, 1863. He remained with that regiment one year, when, on May 5, 1864, he was promoted to be chief surgeon and medical purveyor of the United States military railroad department, division of the Mississippi, and remained at Chattanooga in that capacity until October, 1865. In December, 1865, he took charge at Chattanooga as surgeon of the refugee and freedmen's department of the United States government, of which he had charge until the following July, when that division of the department was abolished. A short time after this he was made post surgeon of the regular United States army, stationed at Chattanooga, and acted as such most of the time until 1879, when the post was discontinued and the troops moved to the West.

During his residence in Chattanooga, Dr. Van Deman has passed through three epidemics of small-pox, two of cholera, and one of yellow fever, remaining at his post during the existence of each.

Dr. Van Deman was president of the Tennessee State Medical Society in 1873, and presided over that body two years, one time by filling the vacancy caused by the absence of Dr. J. B. Murfree, of Murfreesborough, president of the society at that time, and who was detained at home on account of sickness in his family. Dr. Van Deman is also a member of the American Medical Association, and was for three years, 1876 to 1879, a member of its judicial council. He has been a member of the American Public Health Association since 1874; is an honorary member of the Delaware (Ohio) County Medical Society; has served as examining surgeon for the United States pension bureau at Chattanooga for eleven years, being surgeon now; and has also been surgeon of the marine hospital service since April, 1879, appointed by Hon. John Sherman, secretary of the treasury. Meanwhile, he has frequently contributed to medical literature—notably two articles, one on cholera in 1873, and one on the yellow fever epidemic of 1878—published in the reports and papers of the American Public Health Association. He retired from active practice in 1883, except as to surgery, which he still continues.

Dr. Van Deman joined the Masonic order in 1867; has taken the Chapter and Council degrees, and is now serving his seventh term as Worshipful Master of Chattanooga Lodge, No. 199. He has also served as High

Priest of Hamilton Chapter, No. 49, two years, and as Thrice Illustrious Master of Mount Moriah Council, No. 50, four years, and is thought to have conferred more degrees than any other Masonic officer in the city of Chattanooga. He is also a Knight of Pythias; was the first presiding officer of the lodge at Chattanooga, and has served four terms in that capacity; also is a member of the endowment rank, and has been its president five years, or ever since its organization. He is also a member of the Grand Army of the Republic, and was the first Post Commander of Lookout Post, No. 2; indeed, of whatever local body of similar character of which he is a member, he has been its presiding officer one or more terms.

The first political vote Dr. Van Deman ever cast was for the Whig ticket in 1852. But when the Whig party of the North was merged into the Republican party he went with the Democracy, and, singular to say, his company was the only one in the army that gave a majority for Hon. Clement L. Vallandigham, for governor of Ohio, in 1863.

Dr. Van Deman was a member of the Chattanooga city council in 1871. With the exceptions named in the foregoing record, he has been engaged in nothing but his profession, to which he has devoted his life with zeal and fidelity, his medical library being his only company in a literary point of view, and his chief forte operative surgery. One of his grand passions is to have the finest library and the finest set of surgical instruments of any doctor in the town, and he has them, and their use is free to any physician who may ask them.

Dr. Van Deman married in his native town, May 27, 1854, Miss Rebecca M. Norris, daughter of Hon. William G. Norris, of New England descent, a leading judge, a prominent citizen, and a large farmer, of Delaware county, Ohio. Mrs. Van Deman's mother was Miss Phœbe Main, formerly of Connecticut. She died of cholera in 1869, leaving seven children. One of Mrs. Van Deman's brothers, Dr. James B. Norris, was for six years, from 1872 to 1878, Dr. Van Deman's partner in the practice of medicine at Chattanooga, from which place he went, in 1878, with a corps of sixteen nurses, to Vicksburg, during the yellow fever epidemic, and there the brave and noble fellow died. By special order of President R. B. Hayes and the secretary of war, his remains were removed from Vicksburg and buried in the national cemetery at Chattanooga, in 1879, in compliance with a wish Dr. Norris, expressed prior to his departure for Vicksburg. The record of his noble life closed with his martyrdom in his profession, in the cause of humanity, and his is an honest fame that should long outlive the boasted deeds of reckless valor.

Mrs. Van Deman was educated at Granville Female College, Ohio. She in an ardent member of the Protestant Episcopal church, takes active interest in charitable enterprises, and is a leader in social circles. Dr. and Mrs. Van Deman have no children, but in 1881 adopted Alice Elrod, an orphan girl, born in Hamilton county, Tennessee, August 29, 1868, and now being educated in Notre Dame Academy, conducted by the Sisters of the Roman Catholic church, at Chattanooga. Dr. Van Deman's father, Rev. H. Van Deman, a Presbyterian minister, preached thirty-nine years to one congregation in Delaware, Ohio. He was born in Holland, but was raised in Ohio, and lived and died, at the age of seventy-eight years, in Delaware, Ohio. In early life, he served as private in the war of 1812. Dr. Van Deman's paternal grandfather, John Van Deman, a native of Holland, died a wealthy farmer, near Chillicothe, Ohio, eighty years old. His wife, who died in the same year, immigrated from Holland to America with him.

Dr. Van Deman's mother, *nee* Miss Sarah Darlington, is now living, eighty-three years old, at Delaware, Ohio, where she has lived since 1824. She was born in Virginia, daughter of Joseph Darlington, who was, for fifty-five years, county clerk of Adams county, Ohio, and was also a member of the convention that framed the first constitution of the State of Ohio. His wife, *nee* Miss Sarah Wilson, was also a Virginian. Dr. Van Deman's mother is a Presbyterian, and noted as a pious, consistent Christian woman.

One peculiarity of the entire Van Deman family is, that neither within the memory of man, or in written record or tradition, has there ever been known a single member who drank intoxicating liquors. They have all been temperate men. Dr. Van Deman has never yet, in all his life, drank a glass of liquor; and being now a man of considerable property, in every lease he makes he inserts a clause that no liquors shall be sold on the premises, yet he belongs to no temperance organization. Perhaps, also, his temperate habits greatly account for his robust and vigorous health—for he stands six feet high, weighs one hundred and ninety-nine pounds, and was never sick a week at one time.

In business, Dr. Van Deman attends to his own affairs, lives up to the Golden Rule, pays what he owes, and demands what is due. He attended, while in practice, to calls when they came; if he got his money, well and good; if not, he forgave those who were unable to pay. He has never had a note go to protest, and as a physician lives strictly up to the code of ethics of the American Medical Association—never having a secret remedy he is not willing to impart to any medical man for the benefit of the sick. His chief ambition has been to make property enough to support his wife should he die first, and his greatest desire is to stand well through life, in the community where he has cast his fortunes. Comfortable in his circumstances, he now has a rent-roll income of over five thousand dollars a year, independent of his professional fees, owes no man anything, and enjoys the respect and confidence of his fellow-citizens. Would that our State had many more such native born or adopted sons, quite as worthy to be enrolled among " Prominent Tennesseans."

COL. JOSIAH PATTERSON.

MEMPHIS.

THIS gentleman, who ranks among the foremost lawyers of Tennessee, and whose reputation as an advocate of popular rights is co-extensive with the borders of his adopted State, first saw the light in Morgan county, Alabama, April 14, 1837. There he grew to manhood, doing all manner of work on his father's farm. He received a fair English and classical education in the academy at Somerville, Alabama, and his tastes being in the direction of the law, from a boy of fifteen he stood on tiptoe, looking eagerly forward to the time when, as a man, he should take his place among men. In order to accomplish this cherished desire, he taught school several sessions, studying law in leisure hours. In April, 1859, he began practice in his native county, having been admitted to the bar by Judge John E. Moore. Although quite young when he commenced practice, he soon had a good clientage, but the war coming on, he at once joined his fortunes with those of the Confederacy.

He entered the Confederate service as first-lieutenant in Clanton's celebrated First Alabama cavalry regiment, participated in the battle of Shiloh, and was there promoted to captain of company D, Clanton's regiment. After the evacuation of Corinth he was detached from the regiment, and, in connection with Capts. Roddy and Newsome, ordered to operate on Gen. Buell's connections through North Alabama, over the Memphis and Charleston railroad. During the summer of 1862, and up to the time of the evacuation of North Alabama, these three companies harrassed the Federals at every point, captured two trains, over five hundred prisoners, over three hundred horses and mules, over two hundred wagons, and three hundred thousand rounds of fixed amunition, camp equipage, baggage, etc., effectually destroying the connections of the Federal army between Decatur and Corinth, for which they were complimented in a general order issued to the army. Next he participated in the battles of Iuka and Corinth, and in December, 1862, although only twenty-five years old, was promoted to the full rank of colonel and placed in command of the Fifth Alabama cavalry regiment.

In 1863, Col. Patterson operated in Middle Tennessee until the army fell back from Tullahoma, when he retired into North Alabama with his regiment. In the fall of 1863, just after the battle of Chickamauga, Col. Patterson crossed the Tennessee river, at what is known as the "Tow-head," near Larkinsville, above Guntersville, Alabama, and made a daylight attack on a force of between four hundred and five hundred Federal troops, stationed at Hunt's Mill, engaged in gathering in all the grain in that section and grinding it up for Rosecrans' army, which was then penned in at Chattanooga. Col. Patterson succeeded in surprising the enemy, completely routing them, capturing one hundred and fifty prisoners, all their horses, arms and munitions of war, and burnt the mill, making a clean sweep, and gaining a most brilliant little victory.

Reporting his achievements to Gen. Bragg, he was then ordered to take a force, composed of picked men of his own regiment, and those of the Fourth Alabama cavalry regiment, commanded by Col. W. A. Johnson; to recross the Tennessee river; make a forced march to the tunnel running through the Cumberland mountains, at Cowan, on the Nashville and Chattanooga railroad; drive away the force guarding the tunnel, and so obstruct it as to prevent trains passing through to supply the Federals cooped up at Chattanooga. The tunnel was guarded by a regiment of Federal infantry, so distributed as to protect the three shafts which had been sunk down from the top of the mountain to the track below. Col. Patterson disposed his troops so as to attack the three garrisons simultaneously, which was done with great gallantry by the men under his command, a large number of prisoners being captured and the mountain cleared of Federal soldiers. The road was then obstructed by rolling huge stones, which had been excavated out of the mountain, down the shafts to the track below.

Returning into North Alabama, after a hot pursuit on the part of a large body of Federal cavalry, Col. Patterson next participated in repelling Sherman's attempt to reinforce Grant, by passing through North Alabama, over the Memphis and Charleston railroad. The entire force of the Confederate cavalry operating in that section was commanded by Gen. Stephen D. Lee, and the resistance was so effective, and the railroad so completely destroyed, that Sherman abandoned the attempt, crossed the Tennessee river, and made his way by forced marches, overland to Chattanooga.

In 1864, Col. Patterson was in command of the district of North Alabama, when Gens. Forrest and Roddy were engaged in the Mississippi campaign, in which Gen. Sturgis and Gen. Smith, commanding the Federal forces, were so signally defeated. While in command of this district he was very active in his operations. Crossing the Tennessee river at Gillsport, with less than

three hundred and fifty men, at nine 'o'clock in the morning, he attacked the Thirteenth Illinois infantry regiment, numbering over five hundred men, at Madison Station, Alabama. So sudden was the attack, that the enemy, although they were entrenched in a stockade, threw down their arms and fled. He captured two hundred and fifteen prisoners, a number of wagons and ambulances, a large amount of army supplies, and such as he could not take with him he burned. That evening, while recrossing the river, he was attacked by a large force of Federal cavalry, but succeeded in repelling them and gaining the south bank with all his prisoners and booty, with the loss of only one man killed and one man wounded.

He commanded the post at Corinth, in December, 1864, when Gen. Hood made his campaign in Tennessee, rejoining the defeated army at Bainbridge, on the Tennessee river. After the retreat of the Confederate army from Tennessee, in view of the general demoralization that took place, Col. Patterson was directed by Gen. Hood to go on a mission through the counties of North Alabama, addressing the people at various points, and persuading the discouraged soldiers to return to the service. The speeches made by Col. Patterson in this crisis were thought to be the ablest of his life, his whole soul being thrown into this effort, and resulting in thousands of men rejoining the army. Returning to his regiment at Moulton, Alabama, about the latter part of March, 1865, he operated in front of Gen. Wilson's celebrated cavalry raid from the Tennessee river to Selma, burning bridges, felling trees, and resisting Wilson's progress at every step. He was captured at the battle of Selma, owing to a severe wound in the left knee, which he had received by a fall from his horse, during a night attack at Salem church, the night before, while on the retreat, and which incapacitated him from making his escape otherwise than on horseback. He made his escape, however, the first night the enemy marched with him, and returned, as best he could, into North Alabama, to find the country overwhelmed with the news of Gen. Robert E. Lee's surrender.

The most of his regiment having escaped capture at Selma, he rapidly reorganized them, and learning that President Davis was attempting to make his escape through the mountains of North Alabama, he held his troops in hand, refusing to surrender until May 19, 1865, hoping that he would be able to assist in the flight of the president.

After the war, Col. Patterson practiced law with marked success in his native county one year, next for five years at Florence, Alabama, and in March, 1872, located at Memphis. He has been remarkably successful in his profession in his new home, being now the junior member of the well-known firm of Gantt & Patterson.

Col. Patterson has always been a Democrat on principle, believing, as he does, in the absolute right of the people to control their own affairs. However, he never took any active part in political matters until 1882, when he was called upon to preside over the State Democratic convention which nominated Gen. William B. Bate for governor, for his first term, and during the session Col. Patterson made a speech which attracted attention throughout the State, and at once brought him into prominence in political circles. Being an ardent admirer and personal friend of Senator Isham G. Harris, he consented, in order to secure his return to the United States senate, and to secure the enactment of such local legislation as was needed by the people of Memphis, to become a candidate for the lower branch of the Legislattre. His ticket was elected, overcoming a Republican majority of one thousand five hundred. In the Legislature Col. Patterson was prominent as an earnest advocate of the railroad commission bill, the bill for the settlement of the State debt (known as the 50–3 bill), the return of Gov. Harris to the United States senate, and the passage of measures looking to the settlement of the debt of Memphis.

Col. Patterson, when a very young man, married Miss Josephine Rice, youngest daughter of Judge Green P. Rice, who was at one time prominent in the political history of Alabama. Mrs. Patterson's mother was Miss Ann Eliza Turner, of a well-known Virginia family, and connected with the Blount, Sykes and Bynum families of Tennessee, Alabama and Mississippi. Mrs. Patterson was educated at the Somerville (Alabama) Female Academy, and is remarkable for the elegance of her deportment, her charity, and her modest, retiring ways. She is sincerely beloved by a host of friends. To this marriage were born three children: (1). Mal-

colm R. Patterson, now twenty-two years of age; educated at Vanderbilt University, Nashville; and now a rising young lawyer of great prominence at Memphis. (2). Mary Lou Patterson, educated at Sayre Institute, Lexington, Kentucky. (3). Ann Eliza Patterson, yet at school.

Col. Patterson and family are Presbyterians, as were all their people before them. His father was an elder in the Presbyterian church for forty-five years before his death. Col. Patterson became a Mason in Somerville in early manhood.

Col. Patterson's father, Malcolm Patterson, was born in Abbeville, South Carolina, of Scotch-Irish parentage. He was a farmer, emigrated to North Alabama in 1817, and lived there, an honored citizen, until his death, in February, 1859, at the age of seventy. Col. Patterson's paternal grandfather, Alexander Patterson, was a patriot soldier in the Revolutionary war, and was wounded at the battle of Cowpens. He, also, was a farmer.

Col. Patterson's mother, nee Miss Mary Deloache, was of French extraction. She was born on Stone's river, Rutherford county, Tennessee, and emigrated with her father, John Deloache, to Jefferson county, Alabama, after she grew up to womanhood. She was born in 1802, and belonged to a hardy pioneer family. Her elder brother, William Deloache, was a soldier under Gen. Jackson throughout his Indian wars. Col. Patterson's maternal grandfather, John Deloache, was a farmer in comfortable circumstances, and highly respected. He died in 1820, near the spot on which the city of Birmingham, Alabama, now stands. The whole family, on both sides, have been mostly farmers from time immemorial.

HON. BENJAMIN J. TARVER.

LEBANON.

THIS modest gentleman, never much in public life, nor ambitious for preferment out of the line of his profession, appears in these pages as a representative Middle Tennessee lawyer and jurist, and Christian gentleman.

Benjamin J. Tarver was born in Warren county, North Carolina, July 1, 1829, but came with his father to Wilson county, Tennessee, when three months old, and there has lived ever since. He received a fair literary education at the common schools in his father's neighborhood, near Tucker's Gap, mixing, in his boyhood, study and farm labor. From the age of fourteen he was devoted to books, being especially fond of philosophical, mathematical and scientific studies, and becoming at an early age, a good Latin scholar. He studied law in the Lebanon law school in 1849–50–51,

graduating the latter year. Among his classmates were Robert Weakley Brown, Judge J. D. Goodpasture, Hon. E. H. East, Gen. Robert Hatton, Judge Abe Demoss, Hon. Mr. Halsey (now M. C. from the Bowling Green, Kentucky, district), and Judge Wm. S. McLemore.

After graduation he opened an office at Lebanon, and at once entered upon a good practice. It was a strong bar he had to compete with, composed of such men as Judge John S. Brien, Hon. Jordan Stokes, Hon. Charles Ready, Hon. Jo. C. Guild, Col. William L. Martin, Gen. Robert Hatton and Judge Nathan Green. Beginning his career with only ten dollars, three dollars of which he gave for a "shingle," and three dollars for a subscription to the National Intelligencer, he is now reckoned among the solid men of his county. He is a director in the Tennessee Pacific railroad company, and a director in the Second National Bank, at Lebanon. From the early part of 1852, to January, 1878, he was in partnership with Hon. Ed. I. Golladay. This partnership was dissolved by his going on the bench as chancellor of the Sixth division, under appointment from Gov. James D. Porter, a position which he held nine months, and for which he was an unsuccessful candidate before the people in 1878.

Judge Tarver's practice has been confined mostly to civil cases in the chancery, referee and Supreme courts, but he has occasionally appeared in important criminal cases. His professional and financial success is due, not to outside influences or family connections, but to the fact that he has never dissipated any; was never in politics; has made it a point to be always at his office or at the court-house in business hours, instead of hanging about the streets and loafing. A similar history will be found in the biography of Gov. John Ireland, of Texas. Judge Tarver has made it a rule to be frank with courts and never to mislead; consequently, his practice before courts has invariably won their confidence, and his success before jurors is largely attributable to the same fact. He never submits propositions of law or fact unless he believes them himself to be true. It is lawyers of this class who give high moral tone and credit to a bar and add dignity to a profession—the most important known to society or the history of nations. As a speaker, Judge Tarver is neither noisy or florid, but aims to convince the judgment and to awaken and strengthen the conscience of the court or jury to decide on the conviction his logic has carried to their minds.

Before the war, Judge Tarver was a Whig of the Henry Clay and John Bell school, and made speeches in opposition to secession. But when the war had actually begun at Fort Sumter, he soon after joined the Confederate army, enlisting as a private in Col. Robert Hatton's Seventh Tennessee regiment, and staying in that regiment until the spring of 1862. He was made a lieutenant of his company while in the camp of instruction at Camp Trousdale, Sumner county. He served in Virginia and Tennessee, and took part in the battle of Murfreesborough, four days, and numerous other engagements. In the summer of 1863, his health failed and he left the service.

In 1866, he was a delegate from his congressional district, with Gov. William B. Campbell, to the Philadelphia convention, called to organize a national political party with which the South could affiliate. Since then, Judge Tarver has voted the Democratic ticket.

Judge Tarver is a Methodist, as were his parents. He joined the church when twelve years old and has served as trustee, steward and delegate to the annual conference; has been a Sunday-school teacher twenty-five years, and is now president of the Wilson county Auxiliary American Bible Society. In 1865, he became a

Master Mason, and is also an Odd Fellow. Occasionally, he contributes to the agricultural, political and religious literature of the times, and has now and then taken the place of an absent or sick editor of his town papers, editing them for a month at a time. He has frequently delivered agricultural and literary addresses, mostly the former, as he was raised a farmer and always delighted in agricultural pursuits.

Judge Tarver married in Wilson county, July 28, 1875, Miss Sue White, daughter of Dr. James B. White, a prominent physician and agricultuist of that county, originally from Virginia. Her mother was a Miss Shelton, daughter of James Shelton, of a Virginia family. Mrs. Tarver is a niece of Rev. Dr. William Shelton, of Nashville, and of Daniel Shelton, a prominent lawyer at Jackson, Mississippi. Her aunt, Martha, is the widow of Hon. H. Y. Riddle, formerly member of Congress from the Lebanon district. Mrs. Tarver's paternal lineage is traced back to the Marshall, Jefferson and Commodore Baron families of Virginia. Mrs. Tarver graduated in Rev. Dr. C. D. Elliott's Academy at Nashville, and is a lady of high culture, and in all the relations of life is attractive and amiable, with an exceptionally large amount of practical common sense in the management of her affairs.

Judge Tarver comes direct from old American Revolutionary stock. His grandfather, Benjamin Tarver, had five brothers in the patriot army in the war for independence, and he himself, when only sixteen years old, was at the battle of Guilford Court-house. Benjamin Tarver settled on Hickory Ridge, Wilson county, Tennessee, in 1808, and died there. His son, Silas Tarver, was Judge Tarver's father.

Silas Tarver went to North Carolina on business when a young man, and there met Miss Nancy Harris, whom he married, and there the subject of this sketch, named for both grandfathers, was born, before the family moved to Tennessee. Silas Tarver was a plain farmer and justice of the peace, and a soldier when a boy in the Indian wars under Jackson. He had two brothers, Ben and Edmond, who both lived in Wilson county several years, moved to Texas and there died, leaving families. One of Edmond's children, Benjamin E. Tarver, became a prominent lawyer and politician in Texas. One of Ben's sons, Charles Tarver, became an editor in Texas. Both these cousins of Judge Tarver died in Texas in early life.

A branch of the Tarver family settled at Macon, Georgia, and another in Selma, Alabama, where they became prominent as large property holders. Micajah Tarver, of Tuscumbia, Alabama, went to St. Louis, was a prominent lawyer there, and for several years edited a monthly, devoted to the improvement of the valley of the Mississippi; he died there in 1861.

One of the Misses Tarver, of the Alabama branch of the family, became the wife of Gen. Bee, of Texas.

Of the five brothers of Judge Tarver's grandfather,

one came to Tennessee; one went to Alabama; one to southern Mississippi; one to Georgia, and one remained in Virginia. The family are of Welsh extraction, and noted for their fertility of resources and energy, notably so were Judge Tarver's grandfather and father. His father was thoroughly posted in the history and measures of the political parties of the country, and was a fine judge of law, and a considerable theologian, though neither a lawyer or preacher.

Judge Tarver's mother, *nee* Miss Nancy Harris, who died in Wilson county in 1845, aged fifty-five, was a relative of Gov. Isham G. Harris. She was born in Warren county, North Carolina, daughter of James Harris, a Revolutionery soldier, whose father immigrated from England before the Revolutionary war and settled in Warren county, and that portion of the county called

Harristown took its name from his family. A large number of the Harris family in the South and West sprang from that stock.

The Tarver family in England trace their ancestry back to Cromwell's time. One of them, Canon Tarver, was private tutor to the present Prince of Wales. But the data in possession of the writer is too meager on which to base more than a mere mention of the English family.

Through his paternal grandmother, Judge Tarver is a kinsman of Hon. John V. Wright, whose sketch see elsewhere in this volume.

Judge Tarver's brother, John Bell Tarver, is a farmer on the paternal homestead in Wilson county. Of his two sisters, Mary died unmarried; Hannah died the wife of Judge Claiborne, of Texas, leaving one child, Kate.

JOHN D. SMITH, M. D.

DYERSBURG.

ONE of the best specimens of a self-made, yet successful and representative Tennessean, that has come under the observation of the writer hereof, is Dr. John D. Smith, of Dyersburg. His grandfather, Thomas Smith, was a native of Wake county, North Carolina; removed to Anson county, North Carolina, at an early day, amassed a fine estate, and died at the age of forty, leaving two children, John Alls Smith (father of Dr. John D. Smith) and Ellen Smith, who died the wife of James Capel, of Wadesborough, North Carolina. His father, John Alls Smith, was born in Anson county, North Carolina, was a successful farmer, and a Whig, though not a church member. He immigrated to Henderson county, West Tennessee, in 1838, and there died in 1847, at the age of fifty-five years. His mother was Miss Lucy Williams, daughter of Benjamin Williams, a farmer of good estate, who removed from Wake county, North Carolina, to Anson county, in the same State, and died at the advanced age of eighty years. Dr. Smith's mother was one of God's noble women; a devoted member of the Missionary Baptist church; an active, energetic Christian, the chief object of whose life was the correct and upright training of her children—her example in this respect furnishing a model for even the best of mothers. She was, moreover, a lady of exceptionally fine mind and judgment, and held a high position in society as a woman loyal to all the best and most elevating relations of life. She died in 1853, at the age of fifty, having been the mother of thirteen children, seven of whom survived her: (1). William Thomas Smith, now a farmer in Henderson county, Tennessee. (2). Susan Smith, who died the wife of William Rhodes, of Henderson county. (3).

Dr. John D. Smith, subject of this sketch. (4). Eli Smith, who married Miss Elizabeth York, and is now a farmer in Dyer county, Tennessee. (5). Ellen Smith, who married James Fesmire, now a farmer in Henderson county, Tennessee. (6). Martha Jane Smith, died the wife of Park Rhodes, of Henderson county, Tennessee. (7). Elijah Flake Smith, married Miss Elizabeth Argo, and is now farming in Texas.

Dr. John D. Smith was born in Anson county, North Carolina, March 18, 1829, and went with his parents to Henderson county, Tennessee, in 1838, and there grew up. He received his academic education at the neighboring country schools, and at the age of eighteen commenced reading medicine with Dr. C. W. Hays, at Red Mound, Tennessee. After reading two years, he next practiced medicine four years, in Benton county, Tennessee. He then entered the Memphis Medical College, and graduated in 1854, under Profs. Wooten, Merrill, Quintard (now Protestant Episcopal Bishop of Tennessee), Robards, Taylor, Shanks, Millington, and D. F. Wright—the latter then demonstrator of anatomy. After graduation he settled at Friendship, a village in Dyer county, and was building up a fine practice when the war broke out.

In the spring of 1861, he volunteered in the Forty-seventh Tennessee Confederate infantry regiment, Col. M. R. Hill, of Trenton, commanding; served as assistant surgeon in that regiment until after the battle of Murfreesborough, when he was, without application on his part, promoted to surgeon and assigned to duty with the Twenty-ninth Tennessee regiment, commanded by Lieut.-Col. Rice. He served in the latter regiment till after the battle of Chickamauga, when he was transferred to the hospital department, and placed in charge of the Dawson hospital at Greensborough, Georgia, and remained there till the downfall of Atlanta. He was next ordered to Andersonville, Georgia, remained there but a short while, when he was ordered to Iuka, Mississippi, to assist in fitting up the hospitals at that place for Hood's army. After Gen. Hood's defeat, Dr. Smith returned home on furlough, having contracted a severe attack of opthalmia, from exposure, which, together with a broken down state of health, confined him to his room thirteen months, hence he was never able to return to the army. Dr. Smith made a fine reputation among the soldiery while he was their surgeon. He modestly says he cannot lay claim to the discovery of any new method of treating soldiers in hospital or in trans-itu, but it is one thing to handle tools well and another to introduce new ones. As a surgeon, he ranks high with the profession for various difficult and delicate capital operations which he has successfully performed.

Having once more fairly recovered his health, Dr. Smith resumed the practice of his profession at his old home, Friendship, and continued to practice, excepting two years, 1869–71, he spent railroading, until October, 1882, when he moved to Dyersburg, and has resided and practiced there ever since. He is a member of the West Tennessee Medical Society, and of the Tri-State Medical Society, the latter body being composed of physicians and surgeons residing in Mississippi, Arkansas and Tennessee. He has contributed quite a number of valuable and interesting articles to medical journals, by which he is, perhaps, best known to the profession at large. In the *Southern Practitioner*, Nashville, Tennessee, in 1880, appeared an article from Dr. Smith, on *Rotheln*, or German measles, which was extensively recopied by the medical press of the United States. He contributed the report of a case of pulsating tumor, or "Aneurism of the Tibia," to the *American Journal of Medical Science*, for January, 1882, which has been used by medical journals for statistical purposes. But the two articles which gave him most reputation, almost national fame, in fact, are: one on the treatment of "Pneumonia" (see *Mississippi Valley Medical Monthly*, March, 1883), and one (in the same journal, January, 1885) on "Malarial Fever."

In religion, Dr. Smith is a Methodist, having joined that church in 1851, and is now a steward in the church at Dyersburg. During the war he preached some as a licentiate among the soldiers, having been licensed in 1858, though he was never ordained. He was made a Mason at Camden, Tennessee, in 1851, and has taken the Chapter degrees. He is also a member of the order of the Golden Cross, of which he is examining surgeon, as he is also for two or three other insurance organizations. Dr. Smith was originally a Whig, but since the war has acted with the Democrats, though he has held no office and has not been an active partisan.

In 1870 he was elected president of the Brownsville and Ohio railroad company.

Dr. Smith married, in Benton county, Tennessee, December 8, 1850, Miss Vetury White, a native of that county, born January 5, 1833. Her father was Capt. James White, who came of a pioneer Hickman county family, and was in several skirmishes with Indians in an early day in the settlement of that county. He was a well-read man of fine sense, although a plain, practical, successful farmer. He died in 1882, at the age of eighty-two years. He was twice married. His first wife was a Miss McSwine, by whom he had two children, Andrew White and Patsy White; the latter was the first wife of J. C. McDaniel, a farmer and tobacconist at Camden, Tennessee. Capt. White next married Miss Elizabeth Matlock, by whom he had nine children; Mary White, who married Joseph Peacock; Thomas White, now a farmer, married a Miss Johnson; Vetury White now wife of Dr. J. D. Smith, subject of this sketch; Hugh Lawson White, now a farmer, married a Miss Walker; Eliza and Ellen White, twins, who married respectively Clark Hubbs and James Walker; Lovilla White, married Clinton Walker; Caroline Victoria White, married James Bealough; Henry Clay White, unmarried. Mrs. Smith was educated at country schools, and is a lady of fine domestic and religious habits and culture. Her life has been devoted to the care of her family, and to the discharge of charitable and Christian duties. She professed religion at an early age and joined the Cumberland Presbyterian church, but after marriage withdrew from that communion in order to join the Methodist church with her husband.

By her marriage with Dr. Smith eleven children, ten sons and one daughter, have been born, to-wit: (1). Millard McFarland Smith, born September 15, 1851; married Miss Allie Hinckle; has five children, Lothaire, Vala, Almonte, Vetury Esther, and ———; graduated M.D., at Cincinnati, and is now practicing medicine in Hardeman county, Tennessee. (2). Chelius Cortes Smith, born February 21, 1853; died in infancy. (3). James Robley Smith, born April 8, 1855; died in infancy. (4). Richard Fillmore Smith, born October 4, 1856; now a farmer at Friendship; married Miss Alice Buckley, of Mifflin, Henderson county, Tennessee; has four children, Alice Irene, Gertrude, Orion and Richard. (5). John Devergie Smith, born February 4, 1858; now a farmer; married Miss Lina Warren, near Friendship, Tennessee, who died in February, 1884. (6). Benjamin Franklin Smith, born July 12, 1861; married Miss Izora Bond, Bell's Depot, Tennessee; has one child, a daughter. (7). Julius Alexander Smith, born January 19, 1866, now reading medicine. (8). William Thomas Smith, born December 26, 1868. (9). Lucy Elizabeth (Bettie) Smith, born July 24, 1870. (10). Josiah Weightman Smith, born May 17, 1873. (11). Walter Scott Smith, born February 20, 1875; died in infancy.

Dr. Smith began life on his own account at the age of seventeen, without patrimony, and in spite of the frequent buffets of fortune, is now in comfortable and independent circumstances, owning a fair amount of real estate in Dyersburg and vicinage. Up to ten years ago his financial career was a success in every respect, for he was particular never to allow his expenses to exceed his income, but to live economically and save some of his earnings. But about 1875, in the kindness of his heart, he was induced to endorse for friends, by which he lost heavily—a warning a thousand times repeated in every generation, which should be given heed to by all readers who would be admonished for their own good. He has always been a close student; has zealously devoted his time to the study and practice of his profession; has ever tried to systematize and store away in convenient form his fund of knowledge; has ever avoided dissimulation; lived the life of a plain, matter-of-fact man, and held sacred every trust committed to his care, and compromised no interest over which he has had charge. He has also been a liberal financial supporter of his church and of the charitable institutions of his county.

Personally, he is a very attractive gentleman. He stands five feet, ten inches high, has a large, round head, and a stout round body, no where presenting what is called an angular appearance. And his character and reputation, like his physical make-up, is that of a well-rounded man. In manners he is exceedingly affable,

and wins friends because he is the ideal family physician.

Perhaps, however, the following from his friend and medical partner, Dr. T. R. Moss, will best give an estimate of his character. Speaking of his medical ability, Dr. Moss says: " He is a man of extraordinary mind. He is to-day one of the most diligent of students, and judging from the vast fund of knowledge of which he is the possessor, it is very plain that he has ever been studious. He is a man of never-ceasing and untiring energy, and in a struggle, whether it be to solve a difficult problem, or unravel some mysterious subject, worthy of investigation, or to cure some old chronic case of ankle-joint disease, which demands wisdom, skill, patience and perseverance, long, long after others would have despaired and quitted the field, he is still to be seen, as fresh and vigorous as when the struggle began, contending for victory. He is a firm and faithful friend to the sick, whatsoever be their troubles, and fortunate may one consider himself who, when stricken with some terrible malady or meets with some fearful injury, if he can call to his aid the wise counsel and steady hand of Dr. J. D. Smith. He never deserts or forsakes, but lends the best of his aid and skill during the most dangerous periods, and if it be the will of an all-wise Providence that his patient must go, then he can console those who need consolation, and advise those who need advice, with that Christian spirit which should characterize every practitioner of medicine."

JAMES F. GRANT, M.D.

NASHVILLE.

THIS eminent surgeon, whose medical record is among the most brilliant in Tennessee, was born of Scotch parentage, at Mulberry village, Lincoln county, Tennessee, in 1836, about three months after his parents' arrival there from Scotland. His grandfather, James Grant, was a native Scotchman, and settled in Lincoln county about 1835.

Dr. Grant's mother is a native of Scotland, and is a stout, vigorous lady, of strong sense, of positive character and influence, yet, withal, a plain, practical woman.

Dr. Grant left home when only eleven years old, and did not return until fifteen years after, when he came back a full-fledged doctor. He carved out his own career. He was the architect of his own fortune. When he first left home he hired himself to James McCallum, of Pulaski, to drive a two-horse wagon at seven dollars per month. He stayed with Mr. McCallum one year, and then went on horseback to Oakland, Mississippi, and hired to Mr. J. Kuykendall to work on his farm a year at sixteen dollars a month. At this

time he could neither read nor write. Returning to Tennessee in 1850, for the next three years he attended a private school taught by Prof. Barber (formerly from Pennsylvania), at Bethany, in Giles county. Under this fine scholar and preceptor he obtained a very good literary and classical education, but he had to work hard on Saturdays, and in the garden, evenings and mornings, to pay his board and save up enough to accomplish the ambition of his life—that of becoming a physician and surgeon. Through the kindness of Dr. Jesse Mayes, afterwards his father-in-law, he was finally enabled to go to Philadelphia to obtain his medical education. He spent five years in Philadelphia in perfecting his medical knowledge; two years he was under Dr. James M. Course and Dr. D. Hayes Agnew as his private preceptors in medicine; one year he spent in the Pennsylvania Marine Hospital, and two years he attended lectures at the University of Pennsylvania, graduating M. D. from that institution in 1856, under Professors Carson, Gibson, Rogers, Hodge and Leidy.

After graduation he practiced medicine with considerable success in Giles county, Tennessee, from 1856 up to the breaking out of the war between the States, when he volunteered for the Confederacy as a private soldier, and went with the First Tennessee Confederate regiment to Virginia. Although but a mere youth, he was given one of the first commissions in the army as a regimental surgeon, and assigned to duty with Col. Cook's regiment, then at Camp Cheatham, Tennessee, He was present at the first important battle of the war, Bull Run, and at the last one, at Bentonville, North Carolina, having served through the entire four years of bloody conflict—most of the time with the Army of Tennessee. He was captured at Fort Donelson February 22, 1862, and kept six months on Johnson's Island, a prisoner of war. He served in Kentucky, Tennessee, Alabama, Mississippi, Georgia, North and South Carolina, and was present at the battles of Bull Run, Fort Donelson, Murfreesborough, Chickamauga, Mission Ridge, Cassville, New Hope Church, Rocky Face Gap, Kennesaw Mountain, Resaca, Atlanta, Jonesborough, Franklin and Nashville. His service was exclusively in the field. He served two years as surgeon of Gen. John C. Brown's brigade; was temporarily surgeon of Breckinridge's division. He was next made assistant medical director of the Army of Tennessee, then medical inspector of the Army of Tennessee. On the reorganization of the army in North Carolina, Gen. John C. Brown was placed in command of one of the divisions, and Dr. Grant gave up the position of medical inspector of the Army of Tennessee, at the request of Gen. Brown, and was assigned to duty as chief surgeon of his division. Dr. Grant was among the first surgeons in the army who commenced the operation of resection instead of amputation, thereby preserving the limb, and for which scores, maybe hundreds, of hapless, mangled soldiers have blessed his name.

After the war Dr. Grant practiced medicine sixteen years at Pulaski, and in 1879 settled in a wider field at Nashville, where he has practiced ever since, from 1882 to the present time, associated part of the time with Dr. N. D. Richardson, whose sketch appears in another part of this volume.

In surgery Dr. Grant has performed almost every capital operation—lithotomy, strangulated hernia, cataract, ovariotomy, ligation of the principal arteries, subclavian and femoral, trephining, etc. He has made quite a reputation in orthopedic surgery. In 1876 he was a member of the International Medical Congress at Philadelphia. He is a member of the American Medical Association; of the State Medical Society; of the Nashville Medical Society; of the Historical Society of Tennessee; is corresponding member of the Gynæcological Society of Boston; has been vice-president and president of the Tennessee Medical Society, and has occasionally, by invitation, lectured before the medical colleges of Nashville, to fill the places of absent professors.

Dr. Grant is a born naturalist and mechanic, fond of experiments and original investigations, as the numerous wonderful and valuable specimens in his private cabinet abundantly show. His devotion to his profession is absolute. Indeed, it amounts to enthusiasm. He studies questions closely. His papers on bloodletting, medical ethics, the influence of mercury on the biliary system, attracted marked attention from the most learned men in the medical fraternity. He not only loves his profession, but is a true friend to medical men, and takes great interest in their history. He has written the Medical History of Tennessee in Dr. J. B. Lindsley's "War History of Tennessee."

In 1868, Dr. Grant became an Odd Fellow, and 1872 a Knight of Pythias. He is also a member of the Ancient Order of United Workmen and of the Red Men. He has always been a Democrat from early boyhood.

Dr. Grant married in Giles county, Tennessee, February 18, 1858, Miss Julia Mayes, daughter of his old friend and patron, Dr. Jesse Mayes, a native of Rockbridge county, Virginia, who settled in Pulaski about the year 1833. He was a soldier in the Florida war, and a surgeon in the Indian emigration, about 1837. He is a man of highly cultivated intellect, of true nobility of character, a popular, standard man. He is now living at his country home in Giles county, at the age of seventy-one.

Mrs. Grant's paternal grandfather, Fletcher Mayes, was a Virginian. His wife was a Miss Hill, of the same family to which the celebrated Gen. A. P. Hill, of Virginia, belonged. Mrs. Grant's paternal uncle, Hill Mayes, was an engineer in Texas before Texas was a State. Her uncle, Johnson Mayes, was a prosperous merchant at Gonzales, Texas. Her only surviving paternal uncle, Fletcher H. Mayes, was for a number of years a member of the Virginia Legislature, and a member of Congress from Virginia, and is now living, eighty-nine years old, and in successful practice as a lawyer at Fincastle, in Botetourt county, Virginia. His son, Robert Mayes, is judge of the criminal court of Botetourt county, and is a man of remarkable genius.

Mrs. Grant's mother was Miss Mary E. Cook. Her maternal grandmother was a Miss Clay, a cousin of Henry Clay. Mrs. Grant's maternal great-grandfather, Cook, was a prominent German physician—a "Dutch doctor"—who came to America from Holland. Mrs. Grant's only sister, Sarah, is now the wife of J. E. Morton, a large farmer in Giles county, Tennessee.

Mrs. Grant was educated at the Soule Female College, Murfreesborough, and is a lady remarkable for her glad, sympathetic nature, her bright, winsome, cheerful disposition, and is among the most highly cultivated and intellectual ladies of the State. She is a member of the Methodist church, as is also Dr. Grant, though he is not a sectarian.

Dr. Grant is not a rich man, but is in comfortable

circumstances. The natural impulses of his nature are to confer favors and gratify his friends, and the result is that he has had very many security debts to pay. By his profession he has made over one hundred thousand dollars, but being a poor collector, never asking any man for money, even when due, and having a boundless charity and overwhelming hospitality and generosity, he has not accumulated a large property. He is said to be wholly unfitted for any business in the world except medicine. He is actively absorbed in his profession; charitable to the limit; entirely forgetful of self where others are concerned; a firm, true friend; a vigorous hater of his enemies; warm-hearted and impulsive; generous to prodigality.

As a physician and surgeon, he stands in the front rank of the medical men of the South.

DR. J. H. HOWELL, M. D.

BROWNSVILLE.

DR. J. H. HOWELL was born in Greensborough, Alabama, October 11, 1824. When about five years of age, his father moved to Haywood county, Tennessee, and there he was brought up on a farm and taught to do all manner of farm work. He went to school in the old field schools, and his teachers were Maj. Thomas Owen and Dr. Elijah Slack. His father was a physician, and through his example and influence, the son was led to choose medicine as his own life-work and profession. In 1841, he entered the Medical University of Pennsylvania, and graduated in 1844. He then located at Brownsville, met with fine success, built up a large practice, and remained there until the war came on. In 1863, he went to Memphis and engaged in merchandising with Nixon, Wood & Co. Here he remained for six years, and not having been prosperous in his mercantile life, returned to his profession, going back to Brownsville in 1869. From that time on he has been very successful in his calling, and has built up and enjoyed a very extensive and lucrative practice. When Brownsville was desolated by an epidemic of yellow fever in 1878, he was one of the few physicians who remained there and bravely fought it, and was himself taken down with the fever, though he had previously suffered from an attack of that dreadful disease while living in Memphis, in 1873.

Dr. Howell has been a faithful, conscientious worker, and a close student in the field of medicine, since he first adopted it as a profession. He has passionately loved it, not only for the sake of science, but on account of the great good he was thus enabled to do for his suffering fellow mortals. He began life with nothing but his education, yet, by his own individual efforts, had amassed a handsome property when the late civil war began. Much of his means was invested in slave property, hence was swept away by the results of that war.

and when he resumed practice in 1869, he did so with an unconquerable determination to build himself up, and has been steadily succeeding.

Dr. Howell was raised an old line Whig. When the war came on he was a Union man, and since then has voted with the Republican party. He has, however, taken no active part in politics, and though often solicited, has always refused to become a candidate for any political office.

He was made a Mason at Brownsville, in 1846; has taken all the degrees of the order up to and including Royal Arch Masonry, and has held most of the offices of the subordinate lodge. He is a charter member of Ivanhoe Lodge, No. 14, Knights of Pythias, and is now holding the office of Chancellor Commander.

Dr. Howell's father, Dr. William Howell, who was born in 1801, and died in 1844, was a native of East Tennessee. He practiced medicine very successfully at Greensborough, Alabama, for several years, and then moved to Brownsville and engaged in farming, continuing also the practice of his profession, in which he achieved considerable prominence. The Howell family is of English descent.

Dr. Howell's mother was Miss Sarah Jane Bell, daughter of John Bell, a prominent citizen of North Carolina in Revolutionary times. She is a sister of Commodore Henry Bell and of Gen. William Bell. Her mother was Miss Haywood, daughter of Judge John Haywood, one of the Supreme judges of Tennessee.

Dr. Howell was married, in December, 1845, to Miss Virginia L. Scott, daughter of Robert Scott, a native of Virginia, who moved to Haywood county, Tennessee, in 1833, and became a large and successful farmer.

Dr. and Mrs. Howell are both members of the Baptist church. Their only child, a daughter, died of yellow fever in 1878.

JAMES D. RICHARDSON.

MURFREESBOROUGH.

ONE of the ablest, as well as one of the most promising, men of his age in Tennessee, either as lawyer, politician, parliamentarian and statesman, is the brilliant and distinguished gentleman whose name heads this sketch—Mr. James D. Richardson, of Murfreesborough. He was born in Rutherford county, Tennessee, March 10, 1843. After attending Central Academy from the age of six to seventeen, he entered Franklin College, near Nashville, under President Tolbert Fanning, and studied there one year.

The civil war broke out and young Richardson, at the age of eighteen, at once volunteered as a private in the Confederate service, joining Mitchell's (afterwards Searcy's) company, Forty-fifth Tennessee regiment of infantry. In this regiment he served as a private till the battle of Shiloh, when he was made adjutant-major of the regiment, and filled that position till the surrender at Bentonville, North Carolina. He served in the campaigns in Tennessee, Kentucky, Mississippi, Alabama, Georgia and Louisiana, taking part in the battles of Shiloh, Vicksburg, Baton Rouge, Murfreesborough, Chickamauga, Missionary Ridge, and the battles of the Johnson and Sherman campaign, in which he was wounded at Resaca, by a minnie ball, through the left arm, which, for some time, disabled him for service. He wore his arm in a sling up to the surrender. Two of the fingers of his left hand appear noticeably drawn and cannot be straightened, as the result of this wound, but making only a slight disfigurement.

In 1865, he married, before the surrender, and in the same year just after the surrender, read law with Judge Thomas Frazier, was admitted to the bar by judges Frazier and Henry Cooper, in 1866, and commenced practice at Murfreesborough, for twelve years as a partner with Gen. Joseph B. Palmer, and since that time as a partner with his younger brother, John E. Richardson, the firm style being James D. & John E. Richardson.

In politics, Mr. Richardson is a reformed Whig, being a descendant of an old line Whig who never went into any of the " isms." Not being old enough to vote in the days of the Whig party, he has never cast any but a Democratic vote.

In 1870, he was elected to the Legislature from Rutherford county, and on the assembling of that body, was elected speaker of the House, being then about twenty-eight years old, probably the youngest speaker in the history of the State. In 1873, he was elected State senator from the counties of Rutherford and Bedford, and in the senate was a member of the judiciary committee. Like Henry Clay, of Kentucky, he was elected by his people before constitutionally of age. In 1876, he was a delegate to the national Democratic convention at St. Louis, which nominated Samuel J. Tilden for president. As a political speaker, he has canvassed almost every portion of the State, electrifying the Democracy with his superb oratory, his brilliant eloquence, his graceful mastery of forensic arts, while at every State convention of the party held within the past fifteen years, the towering figure of the " tall cedar of Rutherford " has risen above the storms of party and commanded attention as few other men in the State are able to do.

In 1884, in the nominating convention held at Tullahoma to select a Democratic candidate for Congress from the Fifth congressional district of Tennessee, after a stormy session of several days, the convention enthusiastically united on Maj. Richardson as their standard-bearer, and at the ensuing election he defeated his opponent by a handsome majority, and at the writing of this volume is serving his admiring constituency at Washington.

Mr. Richardson became a Mason in October, 1867, in Mount Moriah Lodge, No. 18, at Murfreesborough, and has been in one or another Masonic office ever since. He has taken all the degrees of ancient craft Masonry, Knight Templar, and Scottish Rite, to the thirty-third inclusive, is now the active member for this Rite in Tennessee, and has been Master, High Priest, Illustrious Master and Eminent Commander of the Commandery, and for ten years filled the latter station. In 1873, he was Grand Master of Masons of the State, and in 1883, Grand High Priest of the Grand Chapter of the State, and has delivered various Masonic addresses over the State on invitation. He delivered the address before the Grand Lodge in 1872. His most famous Masonic speech was his eulogy on the life and character of Hon. Robert L. Caruthers, delivered before the Grand Lodge in 1883. He has been, for many years, chairman of the Masonic committee on jurisprudence. He is the author of a handsome volume, entitled " Tennessee Templars," two hundred and fifty pages, illustrated with steel engravings of some nineteen of the most eminent Masons in the State.

Mr. Richardson married in Greene county, Alabama, January 18, 1865, Miss Alabama Pippen, a native of that county, born the daughter of Eldred Pippen, a large cotton planter, originally from North Carolina. He died when the daughter was twelve years old. Her people are mostly planters. Her brother, Eldred D. Pippen, was a member of Fowler's battery from Tuscaloosa, and fell in the battle of Chickamauga. Her brother, Samuel C. Pippen, is a planter and stock dealer in Phillips county, Arkansas. Mrs. Richardson was educated at the Howard Institute, at Tuscaloosa, and Judson Institute, Marion, Alabama. By his marriage with Miss Pippen, Maj. Richardson has five children: (1). Annie, born November 21, 1865, graduated at Murfreesborough Female Institute. (2). Ida, born May 3, 1867, graduated 1884, at the same college. (3). Allie, born November 6, 1869. (4). John W., born April 27, 1872, died November 19, 1873. (5). James D. jr., born January 4, 1875.

Mr. Richardson joined the Christian church while at Franklin College, and is now a deacon in that church. His wife is a member of the same communion, as is also his daughter, Miss Annie. Mr. Richardson is a progressive man in all his habits of thought, and would favor a re-statement of theologies and creeds.

Mr. Richardson began business life on a good inheritance and acquired a fair estate by his marriage, which he has added to by his professional fees, having been exceptionally successful, as his practice has always been very heavy. He has the reputation of being a hard worker, without having any special object in view beyond the discharge of the day's duties. With the very many irons he has had in the fire, he could hardly form a systematic method, but by dint of constant application of time, energy and ability, he has taken care of them all and neglected nothing. Politics, Masonry, the law, divide his attention. The enterprises of his town have commanded much of his time. He has been president, director and treasurer of the fair association of his county; was director of the Stones River National Bank, and is now a director of the Safe Deposit, Trust and Banking company of Nashville.

Mr. Richardson is descended of Scotch stock. His grandfather, James Richardson, was a native Virginian, who moved, in 1815, to Rutherford county, and settled lived and died there a farmer. His son, Dr. John W Richardson, father of the subject of this sketch, was born in Charlotte, Virginia, November 23, 1809, graduated in medicine at Transylvania University, Lexington, Kentucky, in 1830. He married, in 1833, and lived at Old Jefferson, in Rutherford county, till 1841, when he settled where he died, on a farm eight miles from Murfreesborough. He practiced medicine from the time of his graduation till his death, November 19, 1872. In religion, he was a member of the Christian church from about 1835, and his whole life was characterized by religious devotion. He was a trustee of Franklin College, and helped to sustain the educational and benevolent enterprises of his denomination. In politics, he was an old line Whig, and was a member of the lower House of the Tennessee Legislature in 1843, 1845, 1847, 1849, 1851 and 1857, and of the State senate in 1853 and 1859. He was a political speaker of great force, though not considered an eloquent orator. His manner was impressive, persuasive and convincing, and he was, during all his active life, the leader of his party in his county, so great was the public confidence

in his wisdom and integrity. He had the reputation of being the best manager in the Whig ranks in the State. He published many pamphlets on political, medical and religious subjects. His last production was an essay on puerperal convulsions, read before the State Medical Society, of which he had been president two or more times. He was a very modest man; was several times voted for for speaker when his party was in the minority in the Legislature, and so he was not elected. He was a thoroughly practical man, quiet in his manner, firm in his principles and character, not given to saying things hard of any one, temperate and methodical in his habits, and had among his personal friends who visited him, such men as John Bell, Meredith P. Gentry, James C. Jones, John Marshall, F. K. Zollicoffer, Tolbert Fanning and many others of the most eminent men of the State in ante-bellum times. He was kind hearted, affectionate, and his children regarded him with a reverence akin to awe. He led a busy life, and notwithstanding losses by the war, left some forty thousand dollars to his children. He was an ardent Union man and never consented to the Confederate movement till the war began, when he told his friends, "We must defend ourselves." He was a man of clearness, dignity and simplicity of character. No man was freer from making a display. There was no affectation about him.

Mr. Richardson's mother, Augusta Mary Starnes, a sister of Hon. E. Starnes, judge of the Supreme court of Georgia, and a cousin of the late Gen. J. W. Starnes of Williamson county, of Confederate cavalry fame, is the daughter of Daniel Starnes, of Georgia, who died in 1817, when she was only two years old. Her paternal ancestry was of Scotch-Irish descent. Mr. Richardson's mother is now living with her son at Murfreesborough. Mr. Richardson's only brother, John E. Richardson, born January, 1857, is his law partner. His oldest sister, Susan W., is the widow of Col. John J. Jolly, colonel of the Forty-third Alabama regiment, who died in 1882. His sister, Mary, married John B. Batey, a farmer in Rutherford county. His oldest brother, William T. Richardson, was a physician of much prominence, who entered the Confederate army and died in 1862. He was a graduate of Franklin College and of the medical department of the University of Nashville.

During Mr. Richardson's congressional candidacy, in 1884, the Shelbyville Gazette contained the following well merited estimate of his character: "Mr. Richardson is no stranger to the people of this congressional district, nor, in fact to the people of this State, as he has been prominently connected with the politics of Tennessee from his early manhood, and has already won for himself a State reputation. When quite a young man, he was triumphantly elected a member of the House of Representatives of our Legislature, by the people of his native county, and although it was his first experience in public life, he was honored with the position of speaker, being elected over the Hon. Andrew B. Martin, of Wilson, after a spirited contest, which position he filled with signal ability, presiding with such grace, dignity and impartiality as to secure to him high rank among the best parliamentarians of the land. His constituents, being so well satisfied with his course during his first term, promoted him to a seat in the senate of the next General Assembly, electing him by a handsome majority over two of the most popular citizens of his county. During this session, by his close application to business, untiring energy and commanding influence, he soon became one of the leaders of the senate, and did much towards shaping the legislation of that General Assembly. The brief political career of this distinguished gentleman has clearly illustrated two things: That he has natural gifts, as a pre-

siding officer, possessed by but few men, and that as a legislator, he is faithful, honest and capable. So that if the people of this district should confide their interests to his hands in the next Congress of the United States, they can draw assurances from his past faithful services as a public servant, that he will be eminently conscientious in the discharge of his trust."

Judge E. H. East, of Nashville, in speaking of Mr. Richardson, said: "He is a reliable, safe, conscientious lawyer; stands high in his profession; is endowed with unusually attractive powers of personal address and polish of style; is gentle and undemonstrative in his manners, and entirely sincere—his forte before a jury is his sincerity. He is of a kindly, generous nature, dignified and elegant, without the least trace of arrogance or affectation, and without haughtiness of character or manner."

WILLIAM L. NICHOL, M. D.

NASHVILLE.

COMPARATIVELY few men rise to eminence on their native heath. The transplanting process is not less successful with the human species than in the lower natural kingdoms, and the young man of lofty ambition, upon attaining his majority, usually concludes that it is better to escape the besetting conditions and occurrences of his youthful period and take his chances in a new field of enterprise. The old saying that "a prophet is not without honor save in his own country" applies with peculiar force to the young man who undertakes to rise to professional distinction in the community where the days of his boyhood have been spent. In such case success can spring only from genuine merit. No false veneering, however plausible, can avail to win it.

The subject of this sketch, Dr. William L. Nichol, has achieved his success in the town of his nativity, literally growing up with the city and holding his place in the front rank of its citizens and in the highest grade of his profession. If, like most others, he had committed his share of youthful follies, he boldly faced them and lived them down.

The oldest inhabitant of Nashville at this time, can scarcely remember when the name of Nichol was not closely associated with the success and material prosperity of the city. The grandfather of Dr. Nichol came from Ireland. He settled at King's Salt Works (now Saltville), in southern Virginia, where he married. Subsequently, he became a wholesale merchant in Knoxville, where, for several years, he carried on a successful business. Thence he removed to Nashville, where he soon became a leading commercial man. His business qualifications were of a very high order. They soon attracted the attention of President Andrew Jackson—

than whom there was no better judge of men—who appointed him to the presidency of a branch of the United States Bank at Nashville. He continued successful in business until his retirement, and died, leaving a handsome patrimony to his children.

William Nichol, the father of Dr. Nichol, was born at King's Salt Works, Virginia, in the year 1800. He removed, when quite young, with his parents to Knoxville, and thence to Nashville, where he grew to manhood under the excellent business training of his father. He married, in Rutherford county, Miss Julia Lytle (now living in Nashville at the age of seventy-four), daughter of William Lytle, a farmer, originally from North Carolina, where he served in the Revolutionary war as captain. He amassed a large fortune by land speculations in Rutherford and adjoining counties.

William Nichol, at the time of his father's death, was already a well-equipped business man, the peer of any in Nashville. Among the incidents of his training, illustrating the strict methods of his father, it is related that, on one occasion, according to the modes of travel in those days, he made a sixteen days' horseback journey to Baltimore to make purchases for the house; but it was discovered, on his return, that he had neglected to purchase a certain article that had been set down in his list. His father started him back to Baltimore the next morning to get it, which he did, thereby acquiring a lesson which made a life-impression. He was long a most successful merchant, and was for a time a partner of Harry Hill, the famous New Orleans merchant, with whom it is said he never had any written articles of partnership. He was at one time mayor of Nashville. He served for many years with conspicuous ability as president of the State Bank of Tennessee, and wound up his active business career as a planter in Davidson county, besides carrying on a plantation in Arkansas. He died at his residence near Nashville, in 1878.

Dr. William L. Nichol was born in Nashville, Tennessee, October 8, 1828. He was educated in the University of Nashville, graduating in 1845, and receiving his literary degree at the hands of President Philip Lindsley. After a three years' course of study he was graduated in medicine in 1849, from the University of Pennsylvania, then under charge of Profs. Jackson, Horner, Wood, Hodge and Chapman. He was a private pupil of Dr. W. W. Gerhard. After graduation, he was, in 1849, elected resident physician of the Philadelphia Hospital and Almshouse, where he remained about eighteen months, and then entered the United States Navy as assistant surgeon. Under orders from the navy department, he joined the Pacific exploring expedition under Commodore Ringgold, and served in that expedition over the Pacific, Atlantic and Indian oceans, visiting China, Japan, Capetown and Australia. In 1856, on account of ill health, he resigned in San Francisco, returned to Nashville and entered upon a course of private practice, which he continued till the breaking out of the war, when he entered the Confederate service as surgeon and served through the entire war, first as regimental surgeon, then as brigade surgeon, and, lastly, as surgeon in charge at various hospital posts.

The war over, he returned to private practice. In 1868, he was elected to fill the chair of diseases of the chest and clinical medicine in the University of Nashville. In 1870, he was transferred to the chair of materia medica and therapeutics, and, again, in 1874, to the chair of obstetrics. Upon the establishment of the chair of diseases of women and children, he was elected to fill that place, which he now holds. From 1869 to 1874 he was in partnership with the celebrated surgeon, Dr. W. T. Briggs (whose sketch appears elsewhere in this volume). For several years, between 1866 and 1873, he was editor-in-chief of the Nashville *Medical and Surgical Journal*, discharging the duties of the position with marked ability and to the great satisfaction of the profession. He is a member of the city and State medical societies.

As to his personal life, Dr. Nichol has been thrice married. He first married in Nashville, 1858, Henrietta, daughter of Sterling R. Cockrill, a planter, now at Pine Bluff, Arkansas. Her mother was Ann H. McDonald, daughter of Col. McDonald, of the United States army, a resident of New Orleans. By this marriage, Dr. Nichol has one child, Henry, born April 26, 1859. Mrs. Nichol died in 1859, at the birth of her son. In 1864 Dr. Nichol married Ella, daughter of John Fackler, of Huntsville, Alabama, and by this marriage has a daughter, Bessie, born in Cuthbert, Georgia, 1865, who graduated from Ward's Seminary in 1882. The second Mrs. Nichol died in 1868. His third marriage was with

Mrs. Martha DeBow, widow of the late J. D. B. DeBow, the distinguished editor of the once well-known periodical, *DeBow's Review*. She is the daughter of the late John Johns, a successful farmer of Davidson county. She is a lady of queenly presence and manners, representing the classic style of female beauty in its loveliest type, yet she is no less conspicuous in society for the uniform display of those refined virtues which are, at once, the guarantees and the ornaments of noble womanhood. She is not only the light of the social circle, but home is always the brighter for her presence. Mrs. Nichol is a member of the Missionary Baptist church. The result of the third marriage is one son, William L., born at Nashville, July 5, 1872.

Dr. Nichol's devotion to his profession has been almost absolute. He chose to dedicate himself to its labors and its duties at a time when it was fashionable for the "sons of rich men," as he then was, to pass through the forms of a collegiate education, to gain a smattering of the classics, and cram their heads with as many excerpts from the poets as their memories would bear, perhaps obtain a professional degree by way of personal ornament, and rely upon the father's exchequer for support. Dr. Nichol might have made himself that style of man and been an elegant gentleman in his day, "for a' that." But there is an activity —a restless energy—in his very nature, that, from boyhood, has rendered a state of " elegant ease " an impossibility in his life. At quite an early day the desire to become a physician became the ruling ambition of his life. He began his professional studies at the age of seventeen, and before he was twenty-one he had graduated and entered upon his life duties and business. To the practice of medicine he dedicated his life, and, if the expression be allowable, he has been true to his professional vows. He has always been fully alive to the duties of citizenship, and taken a lively interest in whatever concerned the welfare of the community. He has ever been a man of positive political convictions— first a Whig, then and now a Democrat—but he has never allowed himself to be tempted from the true course of his professional career. Few men have been more successful than he in the practice of medicine— none more prompt and accurate as a diagnostician. In the lecture-room he is perfectly at home. His method in the treatment of his subjects is thoroughly and severely analytical, and his own enthusiasm inspires zeal on the part of his classes in their investigations. He is scholarly in his profession, yet he scorns all pedantic show in the lecture-room. He is fluent without verbosity, and copious without redundancy. He is apt in illustration, and frequently indulges in appropriate anecdote ; yet all mere superfluity is rigidly discarded. To impress his own idea upon his students seems to be his chief ambition, and this he usually succeeds in accomplishing. Dr. Nichol is yet comparatively young, and it is safe to say that further professional honors await him.

HON. ANDREW B. MARTIN, LL.D.

LEBANON.

THE life-history of this eminent and very excellent gentleman presents one of the most interesting sketches in this volume, and should be an incentive to the perseverance and ambition of young Tennesseans who may encounter obstacles in the pathway of their fortunes.

Andrew B. Martin was born at Trousdale's Ferry, Smith county, Tennessee, the son of Dr. Matthew Martin, a native of Barren county, Kentucky, who was the son of Edward Martin, of Virginia, of English parentage. Dr. Martin died at the age of forty-nine, leaving three sons, Robert P., Andrew B. and Monroe; and five daughters, Fannie, Susan, Margaret, Lavinia and Rebecca, Andrew B. being the sixth child.

Andrew B. Martin's mother, *nee* Miss Matilda Crow, who died in 1876, was born in 1804, in Ireland, daughter of Jane Crow, *nee* Porter. She was a lady of culture for her times, and was noted for her vigorous mind, practical turn and energy. Her first husband was William Walton, of Smith county, Tennessee, by whom she had four daughters, Sarah, Penelope, Matilda and Mary.

His education was obtained under very embarrassing circumstances. He attended common schools until the death of his father, which occurred in 1849, but shortly after that event, it became necessary for him to take care of himself, and, acting upon this necessity, he left home with thirteen dollars in money, which he had earned by working in a brickyard. Having never been from home before, circumstances directed him to Lebanon, Tennessee, where he was wholly unknown, but where, although only fifteen years of age, his manly manners and his straightforward way of acting, soon secured for him a clerkship in a drug store. This business was distasteful to him, but it was the only thing that was open. He took hold of it, however, with the well defined purpose in his mind to some day become a lawyer. Perhaps the legal atmosphere that surrounds the place stimulated his ambition; perhaps it was destiny that directed him thither. However that may be, it was up-hill work with him for a while, but still the ambitious boy persevered, and he held his position for five years, pursuing at odd intervals a course of study, and thus completing a fair academic education—his studies being directed by the curriculum of Cumberland University, with the students of which institution he was thrown in daily contact. In 1856, without having added anything to his finances, but largely to his experience and knowledge of the ways of the world, he entered the law school of Cumberland University, paying his way as best he could by labor performed at night and on Saturdays, as book-keeper for two or more

business houses in Lebanon. At length, after studying in the university two years, he graduated in June, 1858, receiving his diploma from those eminent jurists and legal educators, Judges Abram Caruthers and Nathan Green, sr. and jr. When he had completed his course in the law he had neither money nor books, but had made many friends, and had met with nothing to seriously discourage a brave young fellow in his purpose to conquer success. Shortly after graduation, he became a candidate for attorney-general of the Seventh judicial circuit, but was defeated, being second, however, in the race against some twelve or more candidates. The time taken up by his canvass and the excitement at that period, just preceding the war, prevented him from meeting with any marked success in the practice of the law.

On May 20, 1861, he enlisted in Capt. John K. Howard's company (H), which afterwards became a part of Col. Robert Hatton's Seventh Tennessee Confederate infantry regiment. He was elected lieutenant in the company. He remained in the regiment until Col. Hatton became brigadier-general, when he was made adjutant-general on Gen. Hatton's staff—a position very pleasing to both gentlemen, as they had been intimate personal friends for many years, Mr. Martin being a special favorite of Gen. Hatton's from boyhood. Mr. Martin served in Virginia, Tennessee, Georgia, North Carolina and South Carolina; participated in the battles of Cheat Mountain and the Romney expeditions in the early part of the war; afterwards at Seven Pines, Murfreesborough, Tullahoma, Chickamauga, Resaca, Dalton and Kennesaw Mountain. When the lines of battle were drawn around Atlanta, Mr. Martin was sent on detached service with Wheeler's cavalry, which made a raid in rear of the enemy, passing through the State of Tennessee, Mr. Martin serving on this raid as adjutant-general on the staff of Gen. George G. Dibrell. After this he was transferred to the staff of Gen. Joseph Wheeler, and continued with that commander until the close of the war, participating in the last battle at Bentonville, North Carolina, and surrendering at Charlotte, North Carolina, in April, 1865.

After the surrender Mr. Martin returned to his home at Lebanon, and resumed the practice of law, but he was still without funds and had to borrow money to buy clothing to take the place of his Confederate jeans. His determination to succeed as a lawyer was still unshaken. The condition of the country was favorable to litigation, and his gallant record during the war recommended him to the favorable consideration of the people of his county, and, as a consequence, practice began to set in in his direction. He formed a partnership with

Maj. (now Judge) William H. Williamson, which continued six years, or until Maj. Williamson was elected to a judgeship.

Mr. Martin married at Murfreesborough, Tennessee, May 6, 1868, Miss Alice Ready, daughter of Col. Charles Ready, an eminent lawyer, and for many years a member of Congress from that district. Her mother, *nee* Miss Martha Strong, was a daughter of Dr. Strong, of East Tennessee. Mrs. Martin's sister, *nee* Miss Mattie Ready, first married Gen. John H. Morgan, the celebrated Confederate cavalry chieftain, and is now the wife of Judge William H. Williamson, of Lebanon, whose sketch appears elsewhere in this volume. Mrs. Martin's brother, Col. Horace Ready, who commanded the Twenty-third Tennessee Confederate infantry regiment, is now a lumber merchant in Florida.

Mrs. Martin graduated from Patapsco Institute, Maryland, in 1860, and is distinguished for conservatism of sentiment upon all subjects, strong and vigorous intellectuality, and for her extensive reading. She is a lady of unusual intellectual culture. Indeed, few women have read more or read more profitably than she. Her father being a man of wealth and high social position, she had the advantages of Washington society, and of mingling with the most intellectual people of the country, attracted to her side, not alone by her pronounced beauty, but by all the graces that make a beautiful woman attractive. Higher and better than all, she is a Christian woman in all the walks of life, and her husband credits her with having made him a better man and helped him in every way. She has the reputation of being exceptionally well-balanced—never saying indiscreet things or doing foolish ones. She is a cousin of Gen. William T. Haskell, his mother being her father's sister. Gen. Haskell was one of the most brilliantly eloquent orators Tennessee ever produced.

By his marriage with Miss Ready, Mr. Martin has had six children, the first two of whom, Alice and Ella Love, died in infancy. The surviving children are Mary, Martha, Andrea and Helen.

In politics Mr. Martin was originally a Whig, but since the war has been in full accord with the Democratic party. In 1871, he was elected to the Legislature from Wilson county, and served as chairman of the judiciary committee of the House, in which capacity he made a reputation over the State. He was a delegate to the national Democratic convention at Baltimore, in 1872, and at St. Louis, in 1876, casting his vote in the former for Horace Greeley (under instructions), and in the latter for Gen. Hancock. In 1880, he was Democratic elector for the State at large on the Hancock ticket, and canvassed the State, adding greatly to his reputation as an effective speaker.

In July, 1878, he was elected professor of law in Cumberland University, a position he has filled ever since. In 1883, he was elected by the literary societies of Lincoln University, Illinois, to deliver the commencement address. It was on this occasion that the trustees and faculty of that university conferred upon him the degree of LL.D.

Mr. Martin became a Master Mason in 1861, has taken all the Chapter, Council and Commandery degrees, has served as Master, King, High Priest, Eminent Commander, Generalissimo and Prelate, and in 1870 delivered the address at the meeting of the Grand Lodge in Nashville.

Mr. Martin and his wife are members of the Cumberland Presbyterian church, of which he is a ruling elder. In 1883, he was a delegate to the general assembly of the church at Nashville.

Thus honors have clustered thick about the brow of this man, who started out in life a poor and friendless boy. But his record only shows that determination and purpose, backed by a good character and standing in society, and the use of honorable means, are almost sure to achieve vicotry. He has never drifted nor lived aimlessly, but has had a purpose which he has sedously followed, and after all, it is strong will power, guided by [conscience, that works out an honorable destiny.

BENJAMIN W. USSERY, M.D.

CLARKSVILLE.

THIS gentleman is a native of Montgomery county, Tennessee, and was born July 21, 1829. He grew up in the same county, and received his literary education, first at the school of Prof. John T. Richardson, and afterwards at the Masonic College (now the Southwestern Presbyterian University), at Clarksville. Before graduating he began the study of medicine in the office of Dr. A. D. Cage, Clarksville, and from there went to Philadelphia and studied in the office of the celebrated Dr. William E. Horner, professor of anatomy in the University of Pennsylvania. After spending two years at that institution, he graduated in April, 1853, receiving his diploma and the degree of M.D. from Profs. William D. Horner, William Gibson, George B. Woods, Joseph Carson, Hugh L. Hodge, Robert E. Rogers and Samuel Jackson. The intervals between sessions were spent at the Pennsylvania and Wills Hospitals. He returned to Montgomery county July, 1853, and for the five following years practiced medicine with pronounced success, his practice being both large and lucrative.

In 1859–60 he spent the greater part of his time in traveling over the country—from Canada to Mexico, including twenty-six States and Territories of the Union, his object being to gratify his love of observation.

In October, 1861, he went into the Confederate army as surgeon of the Forty-second Tennessee regiment, under Col. William A. Quarles, and in this regiment served till it was captured at Fort Donelson, in February, 1862. When the troops were about to be surrendered Col. Quarles informed him that the officers would not be allowed to go with the men. Dr. Ussery instantly replied: "With your permission, then, I will not go to prison." Making his escape, he proceeded to Murfreesborough, joined the army under Gen. Albert Sidney Johnston, and was by him assigned to duty as surgeon of Col. Stanton's Fourteenth Mississippi regiment of Zollicoffer's brigade, and was, by seniority of his commission, brigade surgeon until after the battle of Shiloh, when, at his own request, he was detached to rejoin the Forty-second Tennessee, which had just been exchanged and was then at Jackson, Mississippi. Arriving there, he was ordered to report to Gen. Bragg at Chattanooga, where he was appointed by Gen. Polk as assistant medical inspector of his corps. He served in this capacity seven months, after which, his health being broken down by dysentery, he was transferred to hospital service at Lagrange, Georgia, by order of Adjutant-Gen. Cooper, Confederate States Army, and remained there eleven months as a member of the reserve surgical corps and in charge of a hospital of three hundred beds. He was then ordered to Atlanta and participated in the surgical duties of the battles of July 23 and 28, 1864. Returning to his post at Lagrange, he remained three months in charge of the sick and wounded who could not be moved after the battle of Atlanta. At the end of this time he was ordered to West Point, Mississippi, with his hospital, and there remained three months in comparative idleness. After Gen. Hood retreated from Tennessee, he removed his hospital to Enterprise, Mississippi, where he remained in charge till the surrender, having done service at the battles of Fort Donelson, Shiloh, Corinth, Stones River, Chickamauga, Missionary Ridge, and Atlanta. At Fort Donelson he was shot through the clothing and also stunned by the bursting of a shell in such close proximity to him that it produced severe bleeding at the nose.

The war over, Dr. Ussery returned to Montgomery county, completely broken down in fortune, but resumed practice and has been practicing till this time, a good deal of the time, however, trading successfully in tobacco and land. He is now in partnership with J. Edwards, dealing in leaf tobacco, at Clarksville.

Dr. Ussery spent four years of the best part of his life preparing for his profession, studying nothing else. He next went to what he considered the best school as a private student under one of the oldest and most widely known professors in the United States, his ambition being to give himself, by this means, a professional standing, subscribing wholly, cordially and practically to the code of ethics of the American Medical Association, which has been his uniform guide in his relations with the profession. Adding to this first-class training his methodical habits of study, and by means of his honesty and fair dealing, he has made a name among the standard physicians of his country. He is a member of the Montgomery County Medical Society, and was formerly a member of the Tennessee Medical Association.

Politically, Dr. Ussery was an old line Whig until the revolution and breaking up of parties by the war, which threw him into the Democratic party, with which he has acted and voted since that time. While taking no active part in politics, he has felt a sufficiently warm interest to vote intelligently.

He is a director in the Grange Warehouse Association, at Clarksville, a position he has held since 1877, when the association was organized, and when he was the purchaser of the building which they now occupy. This association has been eminently successful, and its sales of tobacco, which were eleven thousand hogsheads in 1878, now average some seven thousand hogsheads per annum.

He was made a Mason in Clarksville Lodge, No. 89, in 1854, and has taken all of the Chapter degrees. He has been a member of the Methodist church since his sixteenth year; was at one time class-leader, is now steward, and has been twice elected a lay delegate to annual conferences of his church, serving once in 1873. His parents were zealous Methodists, and all of their children and grandchildren, who have lived to adult years, have joined that church. No member of the family has ever been known to be drunk or to have sworn an oath. Family pride, based on such a record as this, is at once pleasing and honorable.

Dr. Ussery's father, John W. Ussery, a native of Lunenburg county, Virginia, born in 1798, immigrated to Tennessee in 1816, purchased a farm in Montgomery county, where he lived until his death, in April, 1879, at the age of eighty-one. He married, in 1822, a lady who had been raised in Virginia with him, boy and girl together, and who had come to Tennessee in the same wagon train. He was a very successful trader in land, and was punctiliously honest in all his dealings. His characteristics were promptness and decision. His father, William Ussery, of English blood, died in Lunenburg county, Virginia, in middle age.

Dr. Ussery's mother, nee Miss Rebecca Neblett, was a daughter of William Neblett, who died in Franklin county, Virginia. He was a soldier in the war of 1812, as was also his son, John L. Neblett. Her mother was a Miss Love, of Irish stock. The Neblett family is one of the most numerous in Montgomery county, and were among its early settlers. They are still numerous in Virginia, and are largely and creditably represented in

36

Louisiana and Texas. Dr. Ussery's mother, eighty-two years of age, is now living with her son. A Methodist, the strictest of the strict, tolerating nothing mean, dishonorable or prevaricating in her children, she is still as zealous as ever for her church and all its institutions, giving freely to all its charitable enterprises. Dr. Ussery was the fourth of seven children, and is now the youngest living. His brothers, William and John R. Ussery, are successful farmers in Montgomery county.

William Ussery married his cousin, Miss Ann Elizabeth Neblett, daughter of Dr. Josiah Neblett, a prominent physician of Montgomery county, and has ten children, Josiah Neblett, Ethelbert, Lucy (now wife of Alexander Lyle), Sterling, Wilmur, Lewis, Katharine V., Mary, Benjamin and William.

John R. Ussery married Miss America Smith, of Montgomery county, also has ten children, Ida (now wife of John R. Steele, Esq.), George, William, Elizabeth, Maud, Robert, Edwin, Eloise, Frank and Norman.

Dr. Ussery's sister, Sarah Ussery, married Rev. James M. Smith, a Methodist minister and a magistrate of Montgomery county. They have eight children, Eugenia, John, William, Dean, Benjamin, Fannie, Rebecca, Jane and Mary. Another sister, Mary Ussery, died the wife of P. H. Keesee, leaving three children, two of whom survive, Charles C. and Virginia Lee.

Dr. Ussery himself has never married.

JABEZ P. DAKE, A. M., M. D.

NASHVILLE.

DR. DAKE was born at Johnstown, New York, April 22, 1827. His father, Dr. Jabez Dake, was born at Saratoga, New York, and his paternal grandfather at Bennington, Vermont, where he took part in the famous battle with the British. His mother was born at Smithfield, Rhode Island, as also were her ancestry for several generations.

The paternal stock was English, first located at Hopkinton, Rhode Island, about 1680; and the maternal was Welsh, first entering Rhode Island with the colony of Roger Williams. His father emigrated to what was called "the West," locating in the fertile valley of the Genesee, about the year 1830.

Of relatives there was quite a large settlement in the town of Portage, and village of Nunda, Livingston county, as there had been for two generations before at Greenfield, Saratoga county. His mother's maiden name was Sophia Bowen; and the Bowens, like the Dakes, were numerous and well known in Saratoga county. The Dakes and Bowens of Chicago, Pittsburg and Michigan sprang from the Saratoga stock.

The subject of this sketch inherited from his father the sturdy enterprise of the English, and from his mother the untiring industry and perseverance of the Welsh. He also, if such a thing be possible, inherited the gift of healing from his father, who was regarded as almost a natural healer, so great was his success, with limited educational advantages. His eldest brother, David M., and the next, Chauncy M., were physicians, the former graduating at Castleton, Vermont, and the latter at Philadelphia, Pennsylvania. His fourth brother, William H., was also a graduate in medicine, but followed dentistry, when that art was new, as a specialty. David M. Dake, M.D., was well known as a most successful physician and surgeon at Pittsburg,

Pennsylvania, near which city he now resides in retirement, with an accumulated competency. Chauncy M. Dake, M.D., was one of the earliest practitioners of homœopathy in this country, having settled at Geneseo, New York, when there were hardly a dozen physicians of that faith west of New York city. He died at Rochester, New York, a few years ago.

Beside these brothers Dr. Dake had one other, Abram B., who died at Nunda, while yet a young man. He had three sisters, the eldest married to James McClellan, the second to Lyman Hoppins, both having several children, mostly residing in Michigan. The parents have passed away, Mrs. Hoppins leaving a son, Chauncy I. Hoppins, M.D., at present a successful physician at Geneseo, Illinois.

Dr. Dake's youngest sister was married to James D. Crank, a prominent merchant for many years, at Geneseo, New York. She died several years ago, at Cincinnati, Ohio, leaving six children. Mr. Crank is now residing at Pasadena, California, where he is interested in orange groves and vineyards. His eldest son, Hon. J. F. Crank, member of the California Legislature, is one of the leading capitalists of the Los Angeles region. His second son, Charles D. Crank, M.D., is practicing medicine at Cincinnati, and holds a professorship in the Pulte Medical College, of that city. His youngest son is, also, a physician, located at Los Angeles, California.

It may be mentioned that Dr. D. M. Dake's only son is an eminent physician at Belleville, Illinois, and his son-in-law, F. W. Skiles, M.D., till the time of his recent retirement, was in a large and lucrative practice in the city of Brooklyn, New York. The only son and child of Dr. C. M. Dake, is at present a well-known practitioner of the healing art in New York city.

It is a noteworthy fact that every member of this

numerous family of medical men has adopted the views of Hahnemann, including the father of the subject of this sketch, as well as his sons, hereinafter to be mentioned. And it must be said that Dr. Dake's mother was one of the earliest and most active advocates of temperance, urging its claims persistently when social custom and fashion were all in favor of the free use of intoxicants. She favored moral reforms and denounced shams, and urged independence and vigor of action in all good measures, evincing the spirit of her Roger Williams, Quaker–Baptist ancestry. While her husband was a mild-mannered and good man, distinguished among his friends as a great peace-maker and benefactor, she was independent of thought, resolute of purpose and uncompromising in her efforts for what she deemed best. If her sons and her grandsons have shown little regard for the orthodox and the authoritative, the germ of it all must be traced to her as the parent and exemplar.

As a boy, Dr. Dake applied himself diligently to study for several years in the Nunda Academy, and then at Madison University, Hamilton, New York, spending his last, or senior, year of literary study at Union College, Schenectady, then under the presidency of the great Dr. Eliphalet Nott. From this college he graduated as a Bachelor of Arts, in July, 1849. Up to the time of his graduation, at the age of twenty-two, he had been constantly in school, except for one year, 1845–6, which he spent in Tennessee, as principal at the Bethany Institute, about twenty miles east of Memphis. While in Tennessee his father died, occasioning his speedy return for the settlement of the estate and care of his mother. Finding his patrimony only sufficient to start him in some modest business, or to put him through the balance of his college course, he determined to use it for the latter, much against the urgings of his family. Being the youngest and only child left unmarried, his mother would have kept him with her at home, but yielded to his earnest purpose to finish his education.

On his way to Hamilton, having allowed the stage-coach to go on while he stopped to call on an old friend, five miles short of that place, he was walking the distance alone, when, on gaining an eminence, he caught a first view of the old university buildings, three miles away, across the valley, and halted suddenly to take in the scene. After an earnest survey and the recollection of the doubts expressed at home as to his physical ability to continue so long at study, he said aloud, "There I will go through or lose my life in the attempt." With that resolution he went down the road and across the beautiful valley to the battle ground of college hopes and fears. One year his mother took a house and remained with him at Hamilton.

Though obedient to college rules, a time came when he refused to yield to a requirement of the faculty which he and nine-tenths of the students considered an imposition. Seeing a determination to enforce the obnoxious measure, and not desiring to put himself in open rebellion, he asked for and received an honorable dismission to Union College. When the storm broke, and a hundred and fifty young men were suspended for insubordination, he was peacefully pursuing his studies at Schenectady. The independent way of thinking and high resolves, gained by inheritance, were greatly fostered by the teaching and example of Dr. Nott. At that time no American college was turning out larger classes of better and more courageous thinkers, destined to make an impression on the world, than was old Union. Dr. Dake stoutly maintains that no college president and no college system, in America or elsewhere, have been, or ever will be, superior to those of Union in her halcyon days, from 1820 to 1860. The list of her graduates during that period has names that adorn almost every useful walk in American life.

In regard to occupation, the subject of our sketch had not fully determined. At the age of sixteen his mind led toward the law, and he began to read Blackstone in the office of an eminent lawyer; but, coming often upon lengthy Latin quotations, that he could not readily read, he concluded, after a few months, to return to school. Before he had reached the end of his college course, his mind had received strong religious bias, and he felt that he ought to preach. But dyspepsia and throat affection, and a tendency, not unnatural, to the profession of his father and elder brothers, finally decided him to study medicine; and, after leaving Schenectady, he went to Pittsburg and entered the office of Dr. Gustavus Reichhelm, an educated Prussian, the first to bear homœopathy west of the Alleghanies (1837). He took a course at Geneva and another at Philadelphia, graduating from the Homœopathic Medical College of Pennsylvania, in the spring of 1851. His thesis, or graduating essay, on "Medicinal Forces," was afterwards published in the *American Journal of Homœopathy,* and also in some foreign journals.

Returning to Pittsburg, he succeeded his brother in practice, and the following year became associated with his medical preceptor, Dr. Reichhelm. The latter removed to Philadelphia in 1853, leaving him a large clientele.

The ungenerous attacks upon the new school of medical practice in the city papers, found in the successsor of Dr. Reichhelm a ready disputant. Files of the leading daily papers of Pittsburg, from 1849, show controversial articles from his pen that led his opponents to recognize in him a literary as well as medical scholar of no ordinary rank. He was solicited to become an associate editor of the Philadelphia *Journal of Homœopathy,* and, afterward of the *North American Quarterly Journal,* of New York. Both of these have articles showing his ability as a writer.

In 1855, he was called to occupy the chair of materia medica and therapeutics in his *alma mater*, the first fully organized homœopathic college in the world. For two winters he left his practice with his junior associate, Dr. J. C. Burgher, and delivered a course of lectures in Philadelphia. Finding his health impaired by the double work in 1857, he resigned the chair and its agreeable duties at the college, and devoted himself entirely to the work at Pittsburg.

At the meeting of the American Institute of Homœopathy, the national society of the new school, in Chicago, in 1857, he was elected to the presidency of that body. The following year he delivered the annual address before the same, in the city of Brooklyn. In the year 1855, while general secretary of the institute, by an earnest appeal, he succeeded in rallying the profession so as to increase the attendance largely at the following meetings in Washington, Chicago and other cities. In that same year he was one of the orators in Philadelphia, at the great celebration of the centennial birthday of Hahnemann. But, notwithstanding all these public duties, he was constantly building up a large business at home. In 1859, he wrote a small work on " Acute Diseases," for domestic use chiefly, which has appeared in several enlarged editions since.

Much work finally took effect upon his health, and in 1863 he was forced to retire to his farm, at Salem, Ohio. Leaving the choicest medical clientele, up to that time, ever gathered at Pittsburg, he turned his mind and worn down physical energies to the cultivation of fine fruits, especially the grape. Succeeding in that, as in medicine, he was soon at the head of the Grape Growers' Association in Ohio. During his administration Mr. Charles Downing, Mr. Barry and other distinguished pomologists, were brought to the south shores of Lake Erie to see the wonderful display of grapes. But the declining health of his wife and the need of a milder climate, led him to think again of Tennessee. In the spring of 1869, he removed to Nashville and opened a medical office among strangers. It was not long, however, till the reputation made at Pittsburg followed him here. One of his earliest clients said to him one day, " Doctor, you haven't sent me any bill for your services —don't you need some money?"—to which he replied, " No, sir, I brought some money along." He came to Nashville, not as a mendicant, nor as a novice in what he proposed to do. Business came more rapidly than he expected, not through any tricks or adroit advertising, but because he had earned it by study and close attention to business for many years. It was soon discovered that he was not a horse-trader nor a saloon loafer, nor a society seeker, and that he was a physician. Nor was his pen idle. He soon issued a revised and enlarged edition of his work on "Acute Diseases," a pamphlet on the "Remedies We Use," a larger one on "Therapeutics in Outline," this latter being a display of the leading principles and methods of therapeutics, especially showing the true position and relationships of the law, *similia similibus curantur.* He has written

many other pamphlets on medical and sanitary topics, besides numerous papers for the national society and for medical journals. As chairman of the bureau of materia medica in that society, he conducted important investigations and materia medica improvement. On the latter subject he submitted an important paper at the World's Convention, in Philadelphia, in 1876, and on the latter, one at the World's Convention, in London, in 1881. By his efforts in this country, and those of Dr. Richard Hughes, in England, a large Cyclopædia of Drug Pathogenesy is being published, of which Dr. Hughes is editor for Great Britain, and Dr. Dake for America, each being designated for that position by his respective national society.

But, not alone in medicine has the Doctor been interested and at work. At an annual meeting of the managers and friends of the Nashville Woman's Mission Home, the late Rev. Dr. Baird moved the appointment of Dr. Dake as chairman of the advisory board, in order, as he said, to secure the building of a hospital, an addition greatly needed by that institution. Very soon thereafter the new chairman had each manager supplied with a small subscription book, bearing his own name and that of his wife for a liberal sum each, and by the time the architect had his plans and specifications made, money enough was subscribed on the little books to warrant the giving out of the contracts for the building; and in less than a year the hospital addition was ready for use.

And, in 1883, the Doctor, always fond of paintings and other products of the fine arts, believing that the time had come in Nashville for fostering the interests of art, called a meeting of all the artists in the vicinity, and of the friends of art, for the organization of a society. The result was the Nashville Art Association, an institution made up of the best people in the community, already grown beyond the question of success, with him at its head as president.

Dr. Dake has for years contended against legislative enactments for the regulation of the practice of medicine by boards of censors, and has written much on the subject. He objects to the drawing of a line, or basing a license to practice, on the possession of a diploma, since, as he contends, the most dangerous medical impostors and quacks have diplomas. He advocates a law requiring each practitioner to write his personal history on a register, kept for the purpose and open to public inspection, in the office of the county clerk, under oath, telling what he has done to qualify himself for practice and to merit the confidence of the sick. His motto is, " Light for the people and freedom for the physician." Though possessed of as many and as good diplomas as any medical man in the State, he says : " Let every man stand on his practical merits, not on the small gatherings of his school-boy days."

In the spring of 1875, Dr. Dake broke down, from

over-work, and went to Europe, traveling through the British islands, Holland, Belgium, Germany, Switzerland, Italy and France. His active brain found work of a most agreeable and refreshing character in those old countries, with cathedrals, palaces and collections of art. He returned, fully restored, late in the following autumn, and resumed his accustomed work. The following winter he was called to the chair of principles and practice in the old college at Philadelphia, and went there, lecturing through the winter to a large class. At the close of the course, he resigned the chair, being convinced that his wife's health would not allow her to reside so far north in winter, and he not willing to go there alone.

In the summer of 1881, he again went abroad, more for medical purposes, to attend the World's Convention in London, and to visit the hospitals of the old world. He traveled much in England, visiting the great seats of learning and the best hospitals there and in Holland, North Germany, Denmark and Sweden. He traveled, also, in Norway, Finland and Russia, as far as St. Petersburg. He was especially inquiring into the "Swedish movement cure," and the "massage" treatment. In London he visited Dr. Roth, the great translator and writer on those subjects, and Dr. Metzger in Amsterdam, who was treating more patients by those methods than any other physician in Europe.

Dr. Dake has no military record nor political history, having devoted his whole mind and energies to the healing of the sick. He has never sought office and is thoroughly independent in the use of his vote.

He has been a Royal Arch Mason for twenty-five years, though now for several years not an active or affiliated one. On arrival in Nashville he refrained from visiting the order, determined that no one should accuse him of making use of such introductions to gain business.

Going back, we find he was married, April 3, 1851, to Miss Elizabeth Church, daughter of Dr. William Church, a prominent physician at Pittsburg, who died in the year 1829. Her paternal grandfather was also a physician. Her father's brother, Samuel Church, was a leading iron manufacturer and merchant at Pittsburg, a bosom friend of Alexander Campbell, and a great promoter of his Baptist reform. Her brother, William Irwin Church, was also a physician, having studied, and afterwards become a partner, with her husband, Dr. Dake. He died at Pittsburg, in 1862. Though early left an orphan, and inheriting a delicate constitution, Mrs. Dake received a good education in her girlhood. Possessed of a natural fondness for literary work, she has written many lines of great merit, chiefly known, however, to friends in affliction, words of comfort and consolation. With a strong religious bias and inspiration, she has always been devoted to her church, and the interests of the poor and the distressed. Since her children have grown up, so as to engross less

of her attention, she has been a manager in the board of the Woman's Mission Home and of the Protestant Orphan Asylum at Nashville. A more devoted wife and mother and faithful dispenser of charity, all without ostentation, cannot be found.

By his marriage with Miss Church, Dr. Dake has five children, all sons, born at Pittsburg, except the youngest: (1). William Church, the eldest, was born at Pittsburg, January 28, 1852. His literary education was received at Ypsilanti, Michigan, and at Nashville, where he graduated from the high school. He studied medicine in his father's office, and graduated from the medical department of the University of Nashville. He also attended lectures at the New York Homœopathic Medical College and the clinics at Bellevue Hospital. Since 1872, he has been associated with his father in practice. Besides an excellent reputation as a successful practitioner, he has won some fame as a medical writer. His work on diphtheria, founded on a large experience in treating that disease, stands high as an authority in Eurpoe as well as in this country. In 1873 he married Miss Myra Wiggin, daughter of Richard Wiggin, a well known railroad superintendent at Pittsburg. She lived only three months after her marriage. He married a sister of his first wife, Miss Addie Wiggin, in 1878, and by her has had two children, Richard W. and Bessie C. (2). Walter M. was born January 16, 1855, and received his literary education at Nashville; studied medicine in his father's office; attended lectures at the University of Tennessee, at the Pulte Medical College, Cincinnati, and at the Hahnemann Medical College, Philadelphia, taking the diploma of the last named in the spring of 1877. Having a strong love for literary pursuits, he hesitated some time before falling into line with his ancestry in the profession of medicine. After graduation, he located for a short while at Jackson, Tennessee, where he was doing well when called to Nashville to aid his father and elder brother, with whom he has since been associated. He married Miss Fanny G. Ward, eldest daughter of S. M. Ward, a planter, at Jefferson, Texas. In regard to these brothers, it may be remarked, that it seldom happens that such harmony and success are seen to attend two brothers associated in professional life. Each has a strong and enthusiastic following, and is widely known in Tennessee. (3). Jabez P., jr., was born September 15, 1857, and educated chiefly at Nashville, graduating from the Fogg high school, attending lectures at the medical department of the University of Tennessee and the University of Michigan, and taking his medical degree from the latter, in 1879. He located at New Albany, Indiana, but was prevented remaining there long by failure of his health. Giving up practice, he visited the Hot Springs, Arkansas, and other health resorts. So far as able, he now assists his father and brothers in their practice at Nashville. (4). Charles, was born July 13, 1860, and received his literary education at Nashville, and in the Southwestern Baptist

University, at Jackson, Tennessee. He attended lectures at the medical department of the University of Tennessee, and graduated there in the spring of 1881. The summer after graduation he spent at Hot Springs, in charge of the business of a practitioner who had gone to Europe. He afterward located at Louisville, Kentucky, where he remained till the removal of his friend from Hot Springs and the urgent calls of acquaintances there occasioned his return to that place, in the autumn of 1883. Though young, he holds his professional knowledge and measures with such a grip as to command confidence and win success. (5). Frank B., was born at Salem, Ohio, September 10, 1864. He was educated at Nashville, and afterward attended Weaver's Business College, at Louisville, Kentucky. After hesitating as to the profession of his father and brothers, he finally concluded to follow their example, and is now attending lectures at the medical department of the University of Tennessee.

Dr. Dake imbibed the religious beliefs of his fathers, uniting with the Baptist church when he was eleven years old; and, looking back, he now considers his early profession of religion as a great safe-guard during the trying years of youth. Though connected with the Baptist church for so many years, he is not in full accord with its teachings upon all subjects. He claims the right to theorize and generalize for himself upon accepted facts. In religion, as in medicine, he submits to no authority without thinking, and considers free thought and investigation essential to the truth and to the happiness of man, no less in spiritual than in temporal affairs. His wife, at the time of marriage, was a member of the Disciple or Christian church, but removed her membership to the Baptist church soon after.

Dr. Dake, though strictly professional, has given some attention to outside financial ventures, some of which have been unsuccessful, yet he has acquired a competency. Professional men, he thinks, should invest only in the best securities, such as require but little personal attention, even though they afford less income than some others may promise. If there is any special secret in his success it is in *untiring application wisely exercised*, at first in student life and then in professional life. His efforts have done much to forward the interests of the new school of medicine, especially in the South. As a member of the yellow fever commission, in 1878, he endeavored to show, by statistical gatherings, the superior efficacy of the homœopathic treatment in that dreaded disease. His medical writings are recognized in Europe, as well as America, as among the most finished. No American physician of the new school is more favorably known in England.

Besides holding membership in the national society of his school and his State and local medical societies, he has been made an honorary member of numerous other associations of physicians, among which may be mentioned the Homœopathic Medical Society of Mexico; the State Societies of New York, Pennsylvania, Ohio and other States; the Western Academy of Homœopathy, and an active member of the American Public Health Association. Dr. Dake has recently returned from his third visit to Europe, having been obliged to go there with his son, Dr. J. P. Dake, jr., in the interest of health for both. In this last travel abroad his attention was given to matters of art, as well as to the cyclopædia being published in London, under the editorship of Dr. Hughes and himself. He is yet at work, with the prospect of years of usefulness.

WILLIAM T. ARRINGTON, D.D.S.

MEMPHIS.

WILLIAM T. ARRINGTON, of Memphis, now one of the most eminent dental surgeons in the South, was born at Dresden, Weakley county, Tennessee, November 11, 1836, and passed his youth in that place. He was brought up on a farm and received an academic education at Dresden. After this he was engaged in the drug business, as a clerk, for two years, and during that time read a course in medicine, which he at the time contemplated adopting as his profession. In 1853 he went to Hickman, Kentucky, but shortly afterward, his health failing, went to the parish of Plaquemines, Louisiana, where he remained one year. He then went to Goldsborough, North Carolina, and resumed the study of medicine under the tutorship of his brother, Dr. B. F. Arrington, and also took up the study of dentistry. Subsequently, he gave up medicine altogether and devoted himself to dentistry, following the example and advice of his brother. In the fall of 1854, he entered the Philadelphia College of Dental Surgery, and graduated there in 1856, in a class with Dr. J. Foster Flagg, of Philadelphia.

After leaving college he located at Trenton, Tennessee, built up a large practice, and remained there until the breaking out of the war. When hostilities began he went to Union City, Tennessee, where the Confederate troops were assembled, and became connected with the quartermaster's department, serving in that capacity until the evacuation of that place, in 1862. His health again failing, he resigned and returned to his old home at Dresden, where he engaged in farming until the spring of 1864. He then went to Hickman, Kentucky, and engaged in commercial enterprises until the close of the war. After the war he went to Memphis and again resumed the practice of his profession, since which time he has remained there, enjoying a very large and lucrative practice. During all his changes of residence and business he has been uniformly successful and prosperous.

In 1867, he was called to Cincinnati to fill a chair in the Cincinnati College of Dental Surgery, but remained there only during one course, when he resigned.

In 1869, together with Dr. William H. Morgan, of Nashville, and other prominent dentists, he organized the Southern Dental Association, and was elected its first president, at Atlanta, in August of that year. In connection with Dr. Morgan, he was also one of the organizers of the Tennessee Dental Association, in 1867, and was its first secretary and afterwards its president. He is also a member of the National Dental Association.

In recent years, Dr. Arrington has become largely connected with mining interests, and is secretary and treasurer of the Indus Mining company, of New Mexico, and also secretary and treasurer of several large enterprises in old and New Mexico.

Dr. Arrington was raised an old line Whig, but, like most men at the South, abided the wishes of his State and went with her when she left the Union. Since the war he has been a Democrat. He has, however, always avoided politics, shrinking from public life and refusing to hold any political office, preferring to devote himself to his profession. He became an Odd Fellow in 1879, and is also a member of the Royal Arcanum, the Royal Asylum, and the Knights of Honor. He passed through all the chairs of three of these in the year in which he was initiated. He and his wife are both members of the Protestant Episcopal church.

In 1876, he was elected a member of the public school board of Memphis, and, being re-elected from time to time, served until January, 1882, when he resigned. He was an earnest advocate of equal rights and equal compensation for male and female teachers.

Dr. Arrington's father was James H. Arrington, a gentleman of Scotch-English descent, born in North Carolina, January 4, 1801. He was a planter, and in 1826, moved to Tennessee, settled at Paris, and engaged largely in that occupation. He died in 1862, leaving one daughter and five sons, three of whom are now living: (1). Dr. B. F. Arrington, a dentist, and now resident of Goldsborough, North Carolina. (2). Dr. John Arrington, also a dentist, at Jackson, Tennessee. (3). Dr. William T. Arrington, subject of this sketch.

Another son, J. J. Arrington, went to California during the "gold fever," and subsequently took an active part in politics, serving in the State senate of California for several terms. He was the first brigadier-general commissioned in California, and at the beginning of the

war started south to join Breckinridge's army, was detained in St. Louis by the Federal authorities, and while there met with an accident which resulted in his death.

Dr. Arrington's mother's maiden name was Mary Sprouille. She was the daughter of Dr. Sprouille, of Dublin, Ireland, who was educated in that city, came to America, settled in North Carolina, on Albemarle Sound, and there achieved success and distinction as a medical practitioner. Mrs. Arrington was the sister of Gen. Samuel Sprouille and Col. Ben. Sprouille, of North Carolina. Her mother was Miss Mary W. Blount, a member of the Blount family, of North Carolina, from which Gov. Blount, of Tennessee, was descended.

On January 18, 1859, Dr. Arrington was married to Miss Emma C. Levy, daughter of Archibald Levy, then a merchant at Trenton, Tennessee, formerly of Georgia. Mrs. Arrington's mother was Miss Overall, a member of the well-known Rutherford county family of that name. Her grandfather was Louis Levy, a merchant at St. Mary's, Georgia; and her grandmother was Miss Ann Patterson, daughter of Col. John Patterson, of Philadelphia, one of the old Revolutionary patriots. Mrs. Arrington's grandmother was remarkable for her Christian and womanly virtues. She died in Philadelphia at a very advanced age. At the time of her death there were living of her descendants thirteen children, fifty-three grandchildren, and thirty-six great-grandchildren--in all one hundred and two direct descendants.

By his marriage with Miss Levy, Dr. Arrington has two children: (1). William T. Arrington, born in 1868. (2). Guy Arrington, born in 1874.

Dr. Arrington has always loved his profession and faithfully devoted the best years of his life to it, strictly adhering to the policy of having no partner, and saying but little of his successes or failures. While socially inclined, he has never formed many confidential friendships, but has confided in his wife for counsel and assistance. He has always conducted his business on the principle of never putting off till to-morrow what can be done to-day; has studiously avoided all lawsuits or controversies of any sort, believing in the settlement of disagreements by milder means. He has always been temperate in his habits, and has but few troubles, studying always to avoid them. He is fond of scientific investigation, which he follows as a labor of love. Courteous to all men, respecting rich and poor alike, he never makes discriminations under any circumstances. A member of the medical profession in Memphis says of him: "He stands at the head of his profession, and is a gentleman of the highest tone—of veracity, integrity and morality."

He has a fine store of general information, and is perfectly at home upon a great variety of subjects. In disposition genial, and inclined toward social conversation, he is also scrupulously particular about treating all men, high and low, with the utmost courtesy, which at once makes them at ease in his presence. He never says anything which would wound the feelings of any one, and demands the same treatment from others, despising, as he does, discourtesy and impoliteness. As a friend, he is faithful, and will not allow an absent friend to be censured without coming to his defense. Affectionate and kind as a husband and father, positive in his nature, quick in his susceptibilities and decided in his views, he is, nevertheless, always willing to yield and make reparation when he is in error. The following is the estimate placed upon him by a leading member of the Memphis bar: "Dr. Arrington has been a resident of Memphis for twenty years. I have known him intimately in all the relations of his life, as a husband, a father and a friend, and he has been all that a

true, faithful, brave man could be. He has no superior in his profession, and there is no man who enjoys more of the confidence of the people of Memphis. He has been eminently successful in his life's work, and belongs to the highest order of manhood."

Dr. Arrington not only ranks all the members of his profession in Memphis, but it may be safely said in Tennessee. It is said his work is even more celebrated in Europe than here, and is readily recognized as his without any other evidence. He is a man of fine accomplishments in every way, and his name is one of the immovable jewels of the proud young city of Memphis —an honor to dentistry, and, in a measure, the redemption of it—a name, indeed, prominent among the eminent gentlemen of the South.

DEERING J. ROBERTS, M.D.

NASHVILLE.

DEERING J. ROBERTS, M.D., was born in Nashville, Tennessee, May 20, 1840. His father was John Roberts, who came to Nashville from London, England, in 1835, a practical printer, and for a number of years was one of the proprietors of the Nashville daily and weekly *Republican Banner*. His mother, Eliza Sheegog, was born in Cheshire, England, her father being John Sheegog, a barrister at law, who removed from Ireland to London a few years before her birth. The subject of this sketch was the third of a family of seven children, six boys and one girl. He was educated in the best private schools of Nashville, until he attained his seventeenth year, when he commenced the study of medicine under Dr. Alfred R. Griffith as a preceptor. He entered the medical department of the University of Nashville in the winter of 1858-9, attending the succeeding summer session, and graduating at the annual commencement of the session of 1859-60. Of the two valedictorians elected that year, he was chosen to represent, and delivered the valedictory address to, the medical society of the class, acquitting himself creditably in his first appearance before a public audience.

He located in Pittsborough, Calhoun county, Mississippi, in the spring of 1860, but his health giving way to the effects of malarial influences, he returned to his native State, notwithstanding he was rapidly acquiring a good and remunerative practice.

On his return to Tennessee, he settled at Nolensville, in Williamson county, where he remained in active practice until the culmination of the civil war between the States, in the spring of 1861.

He first entered company C, Rock City Guards, of the First Tennessee regiment of infantry (Col. George Maney), as a private, and although he received a certificate

of passed examination and was tendered a commission as assistant surgeon, he served in the ranks, making friends of both commanding officers and comrades, until April, 1862. During his career as a private soldier, his regiment served through an arduous and active campaign in western Virginia, under the renowned Gens. Robert E. Lee and Stonewall Jackson. At no time was he ever known to shirk a duty, and was always with the first to volunteer his services when any manner of extra duty was on hand, no matter how difficult or hazardous. In April, 1862, at the reorganization of his regiment, he was transferred and assigned to duty as the medical officer of Col. Joel A. Battle's famous Twentieth Tennessee regiment, serving with it until the Army of Tennessee was surrendered at Greensborough, North Carolina, under Gen. Joseph E. Johnston, in May, 1865. He passed his examination as assistant surgeon at Murfreesborough, in November, 1862, and his examination for promotion to surgeon at Shelbyville, six months later, although, with the exception of but a few months, he was the acting senior medical officer of his regiment. The history of the Twentieth regiment is his history from 1862 until 1865, for he shared its fortunes, its toils and privations, its marches and its battles, its defeats and its glories, until its flag was furled, with the exception of the brief interval from December 1, 1864, when, at the battle of Franklin, Tennessee, he was left on the field in charge of the wounded of Bate's division until January 28, 1865, when he was exchanged as a prisoner of war, and again rejoined his regiment, to remain until his parole was given him with the rest of Johnston's army, in North Carolina, when he returned to his father's residence, at that time in Sumner county, Tennessee.

In the summer of 1865, he commenced once more the

practice of his profession at Palestine, Lewis county, Tennessee, remaining only until the spring following, when, at the solicitation of his sister, then residing in Kentucky, he removed to that State, locating at Breedings, Adair county, Kentucky.

During the winter of 1867, January 20th, he married Rachel Lavina, eldest daughter of Robert M. Breeding. In January of the year following, he removed to Hendersonville, Sumner county, Tennessee, where he soon acquired a large and lucrative practice, enjoying the confidence of all the leading citizens of that community.

In the spring of 1877, he was tendered, unsolicited, and accepted the chair of physiology and clinical medicine in the Nashville Medical College, now the medical department of the University of Tennessee. The following winter session he was transferred to the chair of theory and practice of medicine in this institution, which he has since held, with credit to himself, his associates, and the college.

In 1879, together with his associates and colleagues, Prof. Duncan Eve, and the late Profs. George S. Blackie and T. Chalmers Dow, he set on foot a literary venture, devoted to medicine and surgery, bearing the title of *The Southern Practitioner.* The death of two of his honored and honorable co-laborers left him and Dr. Eve to carry out the undertaking. Under his direction, as managing editor, since 1882, it has far exceeded its former wonderful success, and is now recognized as one of the standard medical journals of the land, with a circulation larger than any publication of like character south of the Ohio river.

In 1876, he was elected to membership in the Tennessee State Medical Society. In 1877, he read a paper on diphtheria, at the annual meeting of this organization, which attracted more than ordinary comment as a paper of original thought. He also read at the same meeting an eloquent biographical memorial of his former beloved teacher in surgery, the late Prof. Paul F. Eve. He has taken an active part in every meeting since, was a member of the committee of publication one year, and chairman of the same committee in a subsequent year. He was elected treasurer of the society in 1883. He

became a member of the American Medical Association in 1876, was elected secretary of the section on practice of medicine in 1881, and chairman of the section on State medicine, chemistry, physiology, etc., in 1883. He was elected vice-president of the American Medical College Association in 1882. He is also a member of the Sumner County Medical Society and the Nashville Medical Society. He was elected a member of the Nashville board of health in 1879, and by the board its secretary. At the expiration of his term, in June, 1883, he was unanimously re-elected by the board of councilmen and aldermen of his city, his past services as a sanitarian being appreciated by the municipal authorities.

He was a delegate to the Democratic State convention in 1878, and was appointed surgeon to the Tennessee State penitentiary by his old military chief, Gen. William B. Bate, when he was elected governor of the State, his appointment having been recommended by leading physicians in nearly every county in the State, by every living president of the State Medical Society, by ex-governors, United States senators and many leading politicians throughout the State.

Dr. Roberts was made a member of Saundersville Lodge, No. 359, Free and Accepted Masons, in 1876, was elected Senior Deacon in 1877, and Worshipful Master in 1878, and represented his lodge at the Grand Lodge in 1879, and subsequently. He has never dimitted from his lodge. He is a member of Gallatin Chapter, Royal Arch Masons, receiving the degrees in 1877, and of Nashville Council, No. 1, Royal and Select Masters. He is also the representative of the Grand Lodge of Missouri, near the Grand Lodge of Tennessee.

Dr. Roberts was received into membership in the Presbyterian church at Hendersonville, in 1876, and was made a deacon of the church the year following.

Dr. Roberts has a family of five sons and three daughters (two sons having died in infancy), to-wit: Annie, John, Harry, Rachel Eugenia, Deering, Albert, Joseph E. (died at the age of nine months), Bessie, George B. (died twelve days after birth) and Robert.

Dr. Roberts is a hard-working, faithful, zealous practitioner, of quiet, modest, gentlemanly manners, and highly esteemed by all who know him.

HON. JOHN C. FERRISS.

NASHVILLE.

JOHN C. FERRISS was born, May 21, 1837, in the county of Rutherford, Tennessee. He was the third of twelve children. His parents were of the highest respectability, esteemed by all who knew them for their fine neighborly qualities. Their circumstances were not such, however, as to enable them to afford to any of their children more than a limited English education.

In 1853, John C. Ferriss removed with his parents to Gibson county, West Tennessee, where he remained with them about two years, assisting in working the farm. At this time (1855), having reached his eighteenth year, he became inspired with natural youthful desire to "see the world for himself." So, without risking the parental refusal by applying for "leave of absence," in company with James McGaw, of Columbia, Tennessee, he came to Nashville. Here he succeeded in obtaining a situation in the office of the *Tennessee Baptist*, published by Graves, Marks & Co., where he remained long enough to acquire a pretty fair knowledge of the printing business. He then became publisher of the old Rutherford *Telegraph*, for Northcott & Ott, proprietors. In 1859, he went to Pine Bluff, Arkansas, and became publisher of the *Jefferson Independent*, a Democratic organ. For some years his heart had been set on the profession of law, and at odd times he had been availing himself of the opportunities afforded to read such elementary works as he could get hold of. In the fall of 1859, having made sufficient accumulation to justify him in the enterprise, he entered the law department of Cumberland University as a student. He had made sufficient advancement in his private study to render his collegiate course a brief one, so that, on the 27th of June, 1860, he was graduated from the university with the degree of Bachelor of Laws. On the 7th of September following he began the practice of law at Nashville.

The civil war between the States soon afterward began, and among the earliest volunteers, Ferriss enlisted as a private in company C, Second Tennessee infantry, William B. Bate, colonel. Ferriss was promoted to a captaincy for gallant conduct on the battlefield of Murfreesborough, or Stones River, as it is called by the Union army. For his gallantry on this occasion, his name was placed on the "Roll of Honor" by the Confederate war department. After the war, penniless, he resumed the practice of his profession, and with great zeal and industry followed it a period of six years, when he was elected the first public administrator of Davidson county. This office he filled for half the term, to the satisfaction of the public, when in a hotly contested campaign, with highly popular and worthy competitors, he was elected to the office of county judge, in 1872. In 1878, he was re-elected judge, and holds the office until September, 1886.

By a life of rectitude and strict morality, Judge Ferriss has established a high character for integrity and as a just and righteous judge. In the discharge of the duties of his station, following the dictates of duty and of a benevolent heart, he has gone out into the city and the country, and gathered in the neglected orphans, and provided for them homes, and in instances numberless, had them adopted into reputable families. In this, he has established for himself a monument more enduring than marble. Had he discharged no other of the various functions of his office (all of which he has discharged with efficiency, ability and great fidelity), this one duty, performed so well, would crown him with laurels. Scattered through Tennessee, here and there, are bright eyed orphan girls and youths, who owe to this great-hearted man the first ray of sunshine that ever brightened the threshold of their existence.

Judge Ferriss is a consistent member of the Methodist Episcopal church, South. In politics, he is conservative and liberal, a true Democrat.

He married, while a soldier in the Confederate army, Miss M. L. Nolen, of Triune, an excellent lady, of remarkable culture and intelligence. By this marriage they have nine children, all of them liberally endowed with pluck, energy and good promise.

If it be true that those are great whose lives benefit their fellow-men (and who shall gainsay it?), then is John C. Ferriss' title to greatness already well established. Better than warrior's wreath or monarch's crown will be such a title, when the grand final adjustment of human accounts shall come to be made.

HON. WILLIAM R. MOORE.

MEMPHIS.

THE subject of this sketch was born in Huntsville, Alabama, March 28, 1830, the son of Robert C. Moore, who died the same year, at the age of twenty-four, leaving two children, William R. Moore and Martha J. Moore, the latter of whom married Alney H. McLean, of Middleton, Rutherford county, Tennessee, and died there in 1883. Her husband still resides at Middleton, on a farm which has been in his family for more than a hundred years.

Mr. Moore's grandfather was Charles Moore, a native of Virginia, born near Charlottesville. Mr. Moore is a man of pure southern blood, never having had a relative born north of the Ohio river. His family on both sides came from the four Virginia towns—Charlottes- ville, Petersburg, Fredericksburg, Lynchburg, and the country around them. Very few surviving relatives of his family name are now living. The family has been made up chiefly of farmers for the last one hundred and fifty years, who have never had much to do with public life, being content to live as quiet, unostentatious agricultural people; well to do, but not wealthy; land and slave-owners, belonging to the self-sustaining class; never pretentious, but modest and retiring men of business, who paid their debts, kept their pledges, and retained plenty of this world's goods about them. A principle which has pervaded the whole family, has been a great pride of integrity, and a firm adherence to their word.

Mr. Moore's mother, yet living, was Miss Mary F. Lingow, daughter of Archibald Lingow, descendant of another old Virginia family. Her mother was Miss Martha Cleveland, daughter of Jeremiah Cleveland, descendant of Col. Ben Cleveland, a Revolutionary soldier, who bore a conspicuous part in the battle of King's Mountain. The characteristics of Mr. Moore's family on his mother's side, have been much the same as those of his paternal ancestry. They have always been a peaceful, strifeless people, never mixing with troubles, personal or political, and peculiarly free from military or official ambition. The family on both sides have been religionists—members of the Presbyterian and other Protestant churches, and always consistent in their faith.

After the death of his father, which occurred when William was six months old, Mr. Moore's mother moved to Tennessee and settled at Beech Grove, then in Bedford (now Coffee) county, and lived there, a widow, seven years, at the expiration of which time she married John M. Watkins, near Fosterville, Tennessee, where she has since lived in the same house for the past fifty years.

Mr. Moore was brought up on a farm, receiving only partially the advantages of the common schools, and in the log school houses of his day laid the foundation upon which he built his self-taught education. In early boyhood he had a strong desire to go out in the world and make his own way, and at fifteen his mother finally consented for him to go. Fortunately, he found employment in the store of Mr. William R. McFadden, merchant and postmaster at Beech Grove, Coffee county; fortunately, because Mr. McFadden was one of the kindest and most fatherly of men, of fine business capacity and integrity, whose personal character was a fine model for the ambitious young business man. His salary, for the first year was only twenty-five dollars, but being quick, active and willing to work, he soon learned to manage the store and to keep the post-office. When he had been there about a year, he was sent by Mr. McFadden with a four-horse team to haul goods from Nashville to Beech Grove, and for the first time in his life saw a city. After this he was dissatisfied with his life in a country store, and desired to go to Nashville for business. His employer consented to his leaving, proffering him letters of introduction to merchants in Nashville, which he declined, holding that a boy who could not get a situation himself, did not deserve one, and never once doubting his ability to succeed, a feeling which he has carried through life. Having saved enough money to pay his way, in 1847, he traveled by stage to Nashville, and arrived there knowing no one, and with no clearly defined purpose beyond seeking employment and connecting himself with some big house. With this view he visited the principal business firms. The first man who noticed him was Maj. R. C. McNairy, then a leading retail dry goods merchant, who consented to employ him if he would bring a letter of recommen-

dation from his last employer. He wrote for the letter and secured the position at a salary of one hundred and fifty dollars for the first year. His strong point was his willingness to work, which soon gained for him the favor of his employer. He would rise before the other clerks were up, sweep the store, and go out among the marketers drumming for custom. At the end of the year, Maj. McNairy, unsolicited, raised his salary to three hundred dollars, which stimulated him to greater exertion, and the next year he received five hundred dollars. He remained with this firm three years. He was fond of reading, and invested his spare money in books, and in this profitable manner, spent most of his evenings' leisure time. Having no one to direct him, he read promiscuously, thereby acquiring a fund of miscellaneous information, which proved of great benefit to him in later years.

In the meantime, gaining experience in business, he became reflective, and began to cast about for a permanent pursuit for himself. Noting that many of the rich men of Nashville were wholesale dry goods merchants, he resolved on that branch, and accordingly applied to Eakin & Co., then the largest house of the kind in Nashville, for a situation, which he obtained, as a salesman, and remained with them six years, with a salary beginning with six hundred dollars per year, which was gradually increased to two thousand dollars. It was here that his views of business began to widen. Twice a year, during this period, he was sent out by his employers as a drummer through Middle Tennessee. Often regretting his own meager opportunity for an education, when only twenty-one years of age he gave to Rev. W. D. Chadick, of the Cumberland University, at Lebanon, Tennessee, five hundred dollars from his earnings, to aid in the endowment of a professorship in that school, hoping that thereby some young man like himself might be benefitted.

Conceiving a desire to go into business for himself, in yet a wider field, he made up his mind in a single night to go to New York. Having learned the value of letters of introduction, he procured these from the Nashville merchants to several New York firms, and on presenting them was offered a situation by each house. Informing himself of their respective characteristics, he found one firm, S. B. Chittenden & Co., a reputed anti-slavery house, which had no southern trade. To this house he offered his services, hoping to build up a custom from the South which would show for itself, the firm agreeing to give him five thousand dollars for the first two years, and a partnership thereafter, on condition that he realized his expectations. He remained in New York but one day, when he returned to canvass the southern States in the interest of this house. Succeeding beyond his expectations, at the end of two years he received his five thousand dollars and the partnership in the firm for three years, but after he had been there about two years he met Mr. Joseph H. Shepherd, of the firm of Shepherd, McCreery & Co., of Charleston, South Carolina, but originally of Nashville, who told him he had sold out at Charleston and was going to Memphis, and wanted him to go with him, which, after much persuasion, Mr. Moore reluctantly consented to do. Mr. Chittenden consented to his withdrawal from the firm, paying him sixteen thousand dollars for his interest.

The firm of Shepherd & Moore was established at Memphis, in December, 1859, and had a very prosperous year in 1860, but the war coming on in 1861, unexpectedly to him, they lost every thing by their credits among country merchants. The partners also disagreed in their political views. Mr. Shepherd was almost religiously wedded to secession, while Mr. Moore, who was a natural born Union man, was as religiously inclined the other way. After the sequestration act was passed by the Southern Confederacy, Mr. Shepherd gave to the Confederate authorities, undr Mr. Moore's protest, an inventory of the firm's northern debts, but after the Federal occupation of Memphis, June 6, 1862, Mr. Moore went to New York to see his creditors, announcing his intention to pay dollar for dollar, if they would give him additional time. His proposition was accepted, all the debts afterward paid, one hundred cents to the dollar, and his credit in New York established on a firm basis, and has so continued. Soon after this Mr. Shepherd died, and the firm of William R. Moore & Co. was established, and has continued successful to this date, paying its liabilities dollar for dollar, with interest, through all the vicissitudes of war, panics and epidemics, during the last twenty-six years.

Mr. Moore was raised a Henry Clay Whig and an American policy man, as opposed to the doctrines of Calhoun, always strongly opposing the Democrats. He believes that while States have rights and counties have rights, the Nation is the only sovereignty, and that the Union is greater than any of its thirty-eight parts, and must be placed first in any controversy. His politics are broad, taking in the whole country represented by the "old flag." In 1860, he voted the Whig ticket for president, headed by "Bell and Everett," upon the platform: "The Union, the Constitution, and the enforcement of the laws," and when that party went out of existence he joined the Republicans, voting for Lincoln. He was an uncompromising Union man, but did not go into the army because his tastes were not military. He has never owned a weapon, and never has been in a difficulty, doing his own thinking and allowing others to do the same. Since the beginning of the war, he has written a great deal, doing his fighting with the pen, leaving the sword to those whose tastes ran in that line. He has never desired or sought office, the public and official positions he has held having been urged upon him without his solicitation.

The following extract from a letter written by Mr. Moore to the Memphis *Argus*, in 1864, will show his position at that time: "By love of country, I do not mean an attachment to some particular spot, because we may happen to have lived upon it, as for instance, Maine or Mississippi, but an abiding love of the *whole* country."

In May, 1865, he introduced, in a mass meeting in Memphis, a set of resolutions, accepting the results of the war. During the war, he was made military alderman in Memphis.

In 1868, he was a candidate for the Legislature on the platform of "reduced taxes, Senter and suffrage," and was the fourth man on the list, but as there were three to be elected, and the third man had not taken the "iron-clad oath," Mr. Moore was, by law, entitled to the seat, but desiring to take no advantage of an informality, he went to Nashville, was sworn in and then resigned, and compelled Gov. Brownlow to order another election, which, contrary to his wishes, he did.

In 1880, he was nominated for the Forty-seventh Congress, he knowing nothing of the nomination till it was published in the newspapers. He accepted with reluctance, and was elected over Hon. Casey Young, the most popular Democrat in West Tennessee. He was renominated in 1882, but declined to run. While in Congress, he was prominently mentioned in connection with a place in President Arthur's cabinet, and a letter signed by a large number of the business men of Memphis and elsewhere, irrespective of party, was sent to the president, requesting his appointment. He took part in the discussions in Congress, and made speeches on all the great questions and issues which were before that body. His speeches, especially upon "Chinese Immigration," "Civil Service Reform," "Contested Election case of Lynch vs. Chalmers," "American Shipping," "Common Schools," "Improvement of the Mississippi River," etc., are marked by that broad and forceful vigor which is the chief characteristic of his nature.

Mr. Moore, though fond of the society of ladies showed for a long time little inclination to marry, but finally did marry, February 14, 1878, Miss Lottie Haywood Blood, who was born in Hamilton, Canada, daughter of George H. Blood, a native of Massachusetts, late engaged in the manufacture of cotton-seed oil at Memphis. Her mother was Miss Margaret Thompson, formerly of Edinburgh, Scotland. Mrs. Moore was educated at the State Female College, at Memphis, and afterward under private tutors. She is distinguished for her personal beauty, her wit and grace, and art in dress, and during her husband's stay at the national capital, took rank in Washington society as one of its fairest ornaments, restoring, in a measure, the pristine glory of ante-bellum days. They have no children.

Mr. Moore was raised in the Presbyterian faith, but adheres to no sect, because he finds none broad enough. His decalogue is the Golden Rule: "Do unto others as you would have others do to you." His creed is best expressed in the couplet:

" For modes of faith, let graceless zealots fight,
His can't be wrong, whose life is in the right."

Believing that every man should worship according to the dictates of his conscience, he entertains no prejudice, on account of religion, for Protestant, Jew or Catholic, and desires, after his death, no better epitaph than the six monosyllables, " He did the best he could."

He belongs to no society or secret organization, holding the same views in regard to them as he does toward churches—not through prejudice, but because he does not desire to bind himself by any oath or obligation. His preference has always been for a business under his personal control, so he has kept out of public corporations and companies. He was at one time a member of the Chamber of Commerce, and took a prominent part in organizing and carrying it through, during its days just after the war. He is a quiet, earnest, capable business man, of unimpeachable integrity, of great force of character and striking individuality. He has, under all circumstances, maintained his financial and commercial standing. He is also a man of decided opinions and of outspoken convictions, frequently arraying himself in opposition to current public sentiment, but never flinching from what he believes to be right. His patriotism takes in his whole country, and his religion all mankind.

COL. EDWARD W. MUNFORD.

McMINNVILLE.

THE Munford family sprang from English Welsh blood. Thomas Bowling Munford, grandfather of Col. Edward W. Munford, was a member of the Virginia House of Burgesses from Amelia county. He left four sons, William, Richard, Thomas and James, who settled in Hart and Green counties, Kentucky. Richard Munford built the town of Munfordville; was a farmer, a merchant, and several times a member of the Kentucky Legislature. James Munford settled in Green county, Kentucky.

William Munford, father of Col. Edward W. Munford, was born in Amelia county, Virginia, went to Kentucky when a young man, was one of the early settlers, and died at Lebanon, Tennessee, in 1844, at the age of sixty-six. He was a very successful farmer ; a man who lived in his affections, greatly beloved by his family and friends, and was the peace maker of his neighborhood. Col. Munford says of his father, that he, Albert Sidney Johnston, and William B. Munford, of Clarksville, Tennessee, were morally the three purest men he ever met, combining all the sterner virtues with amiability and sweetness of character ; true manhood, without double dealing or chicanery, and without a particle of deceit in their natures or transactions.

William Munford, a cousin of Col. Munford's father, was a finished scholar, author of a very celebrated literal translation of *Homer's Iliad*, which gave him a European reputation ; author of other able literary productions, and was associated with Henning as reporter of the decisions of the Supreme court of Virginia (see Munford's Reports, and Munford & Henning's Reports), a library of themselves. George Wythe Munford, son of William Munford, just mentioned, was, for many years, librarian and secretary of the State of Virginia, and was distinguished as a polished scholar and fine orator; a man of intellect and culture, universally respected as one of the first gentlemen of Virginia, pure in principle and refined in manners and tastes.

Col. Munford's mother, *nee* Miss Lettice Ball, was born in Lincoln county, Kentucky, daughter of Thomas Ball, originally from Virginia, but who early started out for himself, went to Kentucky, took up the carpenter's trade, at which he worked at Lexington, became a prominent farmer and owner of a large tannery. He married a Miss Reid, of a family distinguished in the legal profession in the early history of Kentucky, and through his maternal grandmother, Col. Munford is connected with the Marshalls, Reids and Greens of that State. Col. Munford's maternal grandfather, Thomas Ball, was a man of decided force and integrity of character, very eccentric, a great humorist; universally respected, and possessed of a contempt for worldly honors. Col. Munford's mother died at her home on the farm, in Lincoln county, Kentucky, when he was only five years old. She was a most loveable woman, very devout, and her daily habit was to take her children with her into a room and pray for them. When on her death-bed, she pointed to heaven, and said to her husband, "meet me with the children there." She left eight children, one having died previously: (1). Matilda Munford, who died the widow of Maj. Mooney, a United States officer in the Mexican war. Her first husband was Joseph N. Hudson. She was phenomenally gifted, brilliant with pen and tongue, of resplendent beauty, and had a magnetism that drew people around her and made her the center of attraction. Her son, Samuel, was a soldier in the Mexican war, was prostrated with sickness in the city of Mexico, and the mother made her way to that city, nursed him to health and brought him home, which for those times was the act of a heroine. (2).

Mary Jane Munford, married Albert G. Ward, in Davidson county, Tennessee, near the Hermitage. (3). Thomas J. Munford, married three times. Though weighing but one hundred and forty-five pounds, he was a remarkably athletic man, of almost superhuman activity and strength. He was a fine classical scholar; was a member of the Tennessee senate from Wilson county; was for a long time clerk and master of the chancery court at Clarksville, Tennessee, and died on his plantation in Kentucky. (4). William B. Munford, represented Montgomery county in the Tennessee Legislature. He was a very conscientious man, a good man through and through, like a pure diamond, without fleck or flaw. He was an elder in the Presbyterian church, a praying, devout member, without affectation, with a fine, manly, open face, with implicit faith in the Bible and tranquil confidence in the Christian religion. He literally walked with his God, and when he died those who knew him said, "We shall never again see a man so pure, so grand, so splendid, so symmetrical." (5). Sarah Watkins Munford, who became the wife of Tennessee's famous Whig orator, governor and United States senator, James C. Jones. This lady was famous for her fine humor, her fund of anecdotes, her charming manner of relating family histories, and her power of entertaining company by her brilliant conversational powers, and yet was withal a superb business woman. (6). Robert Munford, died early in life. (7). Kitty Ann Munford, wife of Dr. Miles McCorkle, who formerly represented Wilson county in the Legislature, a very prominent physician, distinguished in his profession. (8). Richard Munford, died early in life. (9). Edward W. Munford, subject of this sketch.

Edward W. Munford was born in Lincoln (now Boyle) county, Kentucky, near Danville, October 16, 1820. Edward was placed in the primary department of Center College, Danville, at eight years old, and among his fellow students were John C. Breckinridge and Beriah Magoffin, the latter, afterward governor of Kentucky. Edward soon became irregular, got ahead of his classes in some studies, was advanced to higher classes, believed everything he heard or read with blind credulity, believed even Ovid's stories, made himself a master of the Latin, and left college without graduating, but with letters from his professors to his father very highly creditable to the young student. With all his college learning he had never been taught the multiplication table, English grammar or geography, the college curriculum of that day being exceedingly defective as to the rudiments. About 1835, his father came on a visit to Lebanon to his children, Mrs. James C. Jones, Thomas J. Munford and Mrs. Kitty McCorkle, and Edward accompanied him, and the latter was entered at Campbell Academy under Rev. Thomas Anderson, afterward president of Cumberland University, to perfect his English studies, Euclid and the natural sciences. On suggestion of his brother, William B. Mun-

ford, he clerked in his store some three months, but his inclination being toward the law, he read under Judge Robert L. Caruthers one year, made a journey to Kentucky to visit the grave of his mother and see the old home, when he next joined his brother, William B. Munford, at Clarksville, where he studied law under George C. Boyd, at the same time that James E. Bailey was a law student under Boyd. He obtained license to practice in 1840 (before his majority), from Judge Mortimer A. Martin, and in 1841, from Judge William B. Turley. He practiced at Clarksville till 1850, "receiving employment," he says, "far beyond his merits," he and James E. Bailey being on one side or the other of most of the important cases in the courts there, and usually on opposite sides.

In 1846, he unwisely endorsed notes and bills to the amount of some sixty thousand dollars. Out of this impulsive venture he came out with the clothes on his back, his law library, and a large amount of very valuable experience. While thus involved, he told his bride elect that if money was essential to her happiness she must discard him. She nobly replied, she would marry a *man* and not his estate. In 1849 they married. She was Miss Amelia A., daughter of Paul J. Watkins, of Alabama.

In December, 1850, Col. Munford moved to Memphis and practiced law there till 1858, with the exception of 1853–54, which he spent on his plantation in Lawrence county, Alabama, for the sake of his health. In 1855, his wife died, leaving him two children, one having died before and one soon after the mother's death. The sole surviving child, Paul Edward Munford, lived to be nearly twenty-one years old, and died in 1873, having made a most enviable business reputation. In 1858, Col. Munford closed business in Memphis, having made a satisfactory fortune, with the intention of taking his son, Paul Edward, to Europe to be educated orally, particularly in the French and German, but the war coming on soon after, he gave up the trip.

Very soon after the breaking out of the war, he was offered the command of a regiment, but declined it, saying to the men: " I do not feel competent to lead you— I might get you killed, and will not accept the trust." Afterward he accepted the position of major on the staff of Gen. Albert Sidney Johnston, joined that command in October, 1861, at Bowling Green, and served with him till he was killed at Shiloh, April 6, 1862. "The greatest man the South had fell that day," said Col. Munford, "and Shiloh was the only battle I was ever in where true military genius was displayed by the commander." He served in the campaigns in Tennessee, Mississippi, Alabama and Georgia, and with the Army of Tennessee generally; was in the battles of July 22 and 28, 1864, at Atlanta, and in many minor engagements, not necessary to mention in this sketch. In 1864, he was appointed by President Davis judge of the military court of the department of which Gen.

Dick Taylor was chief, and in that capacity served till the close of the war.

After the war, he became a director in the Carolina Life Insurance company, at Memphis, of which Jefferson Davis was president. His physical health being too feeble to justify regular practice of the law, he moved to McMinnville, in 1872, as president of the Tennessee Company. In 1877, he moved back to Memphis, and in 1880, back again to McMinnville, on account of failing health, and there settled for life, and is now so stout and robust as to not appear a day over fifty years old. In 1867, Col. Munford married at Memphis, Mrs. Mary E. Gardner, widow of William Ross Gardner, a liuetenant in the United States Navy, a meritorious officer, who had served through the war with Mexico with considerable distinction. Mrs. Munford is the daughter of John Kerr, an old merchant of Augusta, Georgia, who removed to Memphis and died there. Her mother was Miss Catharine Burke, of Augusta. Mrs. Munford is descended from Gov. Elbert, of Georgia, an old Revolutionary soldier. Mrs. Munford was educated at Augusta; is a member of the Cumberland Presbyterian church, and is beloved for her unswerving loyalty to truth. She is a woman of much intellectual culture and fine social character, with a face fascinating by its sweetness and innocence of expression. He never lost a sweetheart in the wife, nor she a lover in the husband, and their lives are beautifully domestic and happy. Col. Munford was a Whig up to Know Nothing times, when he began voting " striped tickets." Since the war he has been a Democrat, there being no other alternative for a true southerner. He has been occasionally appointed special judge to hold court when the presiding judge was sick, but with these exceptions and his military commissions, he has never held office. He is a Master Mason. In religion, he believes in God as a Heavenly Father, but is non-sectarian. Nature gave him energy; a fine constitution; a cheerful, social disposition; a manly, generous, keen ambition to attain excellence, in harmony with an unsullied honor, which he would not exchange for profit, position or power. He would never besmirch a spotless citizenship by demagogism. He won his success by honest, hard work, and by a life of truth and candor, and a scorn of hypocrisy and pretense. He is a man elastic in his organization, a brilliant conversationalist, an eloquent orator, with a boundless command of language, which, together with his sympathetic, friendly manners, make him a boon companion and a man much sought after as a friend.

HON. AUGUSTUS H. PETTIBONE.

GREENEVILLE.

THE ancestry of Augustus H. Pettibone is English Puritan, Scotch (clan Grant), and French Huguenot. He is the sixth in descent from John Pettibone. a Huguenot Frenchman, who was admitted a freeman in the colony of Connecticut, in 1658, and from whom all the American family of the name have sprung.

On his mother's side, he is the seventh in descent from John Alden, the clerk of the Mayflower, immortalized in Longfellow's "Courtship of Miles Standish." He is also a descendant of Capt. Matthew Grant, who was the first American ancestor of Gen. U. S. Grant. through his (Capt. Matthew Grant's) daughter, Priscilla Grant.

Augustus H. Pettibone's grandfather, Elijah Pettibone, a native of Norfolk, Connecticut, born in 1748, was a soldier in the Revolutionary war, from Bunker Hill to the surrender of Burgoyne, and drew a pension till he died, in 1818. His thirteenth child and youngest son was Augustus N. Pettibone, father of the subject of this sketch; born January 29, 1802, at Norfolk, Connecticut; was a clothier and cloth dresser; moved in 1822, to Ohio; built the first cloth dressing and carding mill in northern Ohio, at Newburg, now a part of Cleveland; was sheriff of Cuyahoga county, Ohio, and held several other county offices, though his business was a manufacturer of cloth. He died in 1849, in Greene county, Wisconsin, where he had removed in 1846. He was an old line Whig, and was noted as a self-taught elocutionist and a fine reader.

Maj. Pettibone's mother, nee Nancy L. Hathoway, was born near Burlington, Vermont, in 1803, daughter of Zephaniah Hathoway, a native of Taunton, Massachusetts, who afterwards became a pioneer in the woods of Ohio, and died an extensive farmer in that State. He married Miss Silence Alden, descendant of John Alden before mentioned. Maj. Pettibone's mother was a woman of decided force of character, as were all her sisters—Sally, wife of George Comstock; Demaris, wife of Samuel Barney, and Hartie, wife of William Barney—two sisters who married two brothers. Mrs. Pettibone was a member of the Christian Baptist church, and died in 1842, leaving three children: (1). Julia, now wife of Reuben Parkinson, Bedford, Ohio. (2). Augustus Herman, subject of this sketch. (3). Lorette H., now wife of William Green, Waukesha, Wisconsin.

Maj. Augustus H. Pettibone, was born at Bedford, Cuyahoga county, Ohio, January 21, 1835. He attended Hiram College, and Ex-President James A. Garfield was his leading teacher, and under him Maj. Pettibone read Virgil and studied geometry, and with him began the study of Greek. While Maj. Pettibone was at Hiram College, Gen. Garfield wrote a drama entitled "Burr and Blennerhassett," which was enacted with Pettibone as "Burr," and Mrs. Garfield as "Mrs. Blennerhassett."

He next entered the University of Michigan, spent four years there, during which time he took a long course in history under Andrew D. White, and graduated in 1859; studied law eighteen months with Hon. Jonathan E. Arnold, at Milwaukee, Wisconsin, then the great lawyer of the Northwest; was admitted to the bar at Jefferson, Wisconsin, January, 1861, by Judge Harlow Orton, recently chief justice of Wisconsin, and entered on the practice at LaCrosse.

In 1861, he entered the Federal army as a private in company B, Nineteenth Wisconsin infantry; was promoted to sergeant, but soon after was appointed by Gov. Ed. Salomon to recruit for the Twentieth Wisconsin regiment; was mustered in as second lieutenant; promoted to captain of company A, and at Vicksburg, just before the surrender, was promoted to major and served the rest of the war in that capacity; saw service in Missouri, Arkansas, Mississippi, Louisiana, Texas and Alabama; participated in the battles of Prairie Grove; siege of Vicksburg; operations on the Atchafalya, in Louisiana; capture of Brownsville, Texas; siege of Fort Morgan; battle of Pascagoula, and siege of Spanish Fort, before Mobile. He was mustered out at New Orleans, June, 1865. He was twice wounded; served on courts-martial several times, and for several months commanded his regiment.

The war over, he settled at Greeneville, Tennessee, as a lawyer, where he has continued to reside ever since.

In politics, Maj. Pettibone was a Whig and is now a Republican. In 1867-68, he was an alderman of Greeneville; was presidential elector for the First congressional district of Tennessee on the Grant and Colfax electoral ticket, in 1868; was elected attorney-general for the First judicial circuit of Tennessee, in 1869-70; was assistant United States district attorney for the eastern district of Tennessee from 1871 to 1880; was elector for the State-at-large on the Hayes and Wheeler ticket in 1876; was a candidate for Congress in 1878, but was defeated by Hon. Robert L. Taylor; was elected to Congress in 1880, re-elected in 1882, and again in 1884, his majorities increasing at every election.

In Congress, he was always on the committee on elections—one of the most laborious committees of the house. Of his twenty-five speeches, made while a member, two were eulogies, one on Gen. Burnside, which has been embodied in Ben. Perley Poore's "Life of Burnside," and one on Dudley Haskell—model eulogia, remarkable for their difficult combinations of historic reference, differentiation of personality, and choice language, which only a trained thinker can com-

mand. In the Forty-seventh Congress, Maj. Pettibone led the fight in having Chalmers, of Mississippi, put out, and in the Forty-eighth Congress led the fight in having him put in. He gave his best efforts for educational interests, working for the Blair bill, for internal improvements (river and harbor), and for a protective tariff, and though not often on his feet, won the name of a good worker for his constituents.

In 1860, Maj. Pettibone became a Mason at Palmyra, and is now a member of Greeneville Royal Arch Chapter; is an Odd Fellow; member of the Delta Kappa Epsilon Fraternity, and a member of the Christian church, which he joined in 1853. He frequently delivers lectures and addresses to colleges, on commencement occasions, on various literary topics. As a lawyer, either as prosecutor or defender, he has had twenty-seven murder cases.

Maj. Pettibone is five feet eleven inches high; weighs one hundred and fifty-five pounds, is very active, lithe, quick spoken, and his leading characteristic is patent—pluck and energy, or rather personal courage, intellectual, moral and physical. Naturally he is brave, and by culture, a courageous man. He has been a hard student all his life. He knows what a dollar is worth; never incurs a debt he does not intend to pay; in business matters is prompt and faithful to the last letter; is against repudiation in every possible form—individual, municipal or State; began life without a dollar, and is now, financially, among the solid men of East Tennessee, the result of industry, economy and business integrity.

Maj. Pettibone married first at Twinsburg, Ohio, September 10, 1863, Miss Sarah Young, daughter of Hezekiah Young, a farmer. She died in 1867.

He next married at Rogersville, Tennessee, July 16, 1868, Miss Mary Speck, daughter of Thos. J. Speck, a merchant tailor, once associated with ex-President Andrew Johnson. Her mother, Mary Russell, was a daughter of ——— Russell, a soldier with Gen. Jackson in the war of 1812. Mrs. Pettibone graduated from Rogersville Female College, in 1859; is a highly educated and elegant lady, and it is believed no human being has ever spoken an evil word of her, because she speaks evil of no one. Her expression is that of goodness, grace and graciousness, and sprightliness. By this marriage, Maj. Pettibone has one child, Herman, born at Greeneville, October 2, 1875, and under his father's direction is an exceptionally gifted reader for a youth, is an indomitable student of Shakespeare, Tennyson, Macauley, Bancroft and kindred authors—a talent which he seems to have inherited from his grandfather Pettibone.

Maj. Pettibone has been a delegate to all the Republican State conventions in Tennessee, from 1870 to 1885. In 1884, he was a delegate to the Republican national convention at Chicago, and espoused the cause of Mr. Blaine, who has long been his warm personal friend.

JOHN R. BUIST, M. D.

NASHVILLE.

THE Buist family name is French, and was originally De Buest; but the ancestors of the subject of this biographical sketch moved to Scotland, in the time of Mary, Queen of Scots, where the "De" was dropped and the name became Buist.

Dr. John R. Buist was born in Charleston, South Carolina, February 13, 1834, and graduated in literature from the South Carolina College, at Columbia, in the year 1854. After studying medicine two years at the Charleston Medical College, under Profs. Geddings, Dickson, Frost and Moultrie, he entered the medical department of the University of New York, whence he graduated M.D., in March, 1857, under Profs. Paine, Metcalf, Draper and Mott. He served as interne fifteen months, 1857–8, in Bellevue Hospital, New York. He next attended medical lectures in the University of Edinburg, Scotland, during the winter of 1858–9. In the latter year he went to Paris, France, and was a student under the celebrated Trousseau, Nelaton, and other distinguished professors. In January, 1860, he settled at Nashville, Tennessee, and began practice. In May, 1861, the war having broken out, he was appointed assistant surgeon of the First Tennessee regiment, Confederate States army, but was promoted surgeon, May, 1862, and assigned to the Fourteenth Tennessee regiment, Col. Forbes, of Clarksville, commanding, and in a few months was again promoted, this time to brigade surgeon, and transferred to Gen. George Maney's Tennessee brigade, under Gen. Bragg, with which he continued until the close of the war.

During the time of his connection with Maney's brigade, Dr. Buist was chief surgical operator in Gen. Frank Cheatham's division. He was present at the battles of Shiloh, the seven days battles around Richmond, Chickamauga, Missionary Ridge, Perryville, Johnson's retreat from Dalton, and at the battle of Franklin, in all of which he had the very arduous duties of a surgeon to perform. Several of Dr. Buist's more difficult surgical operations in the army, together with his views as to the proper treatment of wounded soldiers, both in transitu and in hospitals, are recorded in the "Surgical History of the War," by Surgeon-Gen. Woodward, of the United States army.

Dr. Buist was left in charge of the Confederate wounded at Perryville, Kentucky, after Gen. Bragg's retreat, in October, 1862, and remained with them until February, 1863. After the battle of Nashville, in December, 1864, he was taken prisoner at Franklin, while in charge of the wounded of Gen. Hood's army, and was detained a prisoner at Nashville, Louisville and Fort Delaware, in all three months. He rejoined the army in North Carolina, and surrendered at Greensborough, under Gen. Joseph E. Johnston.

After the surrender he went to Richmond, in June, 1865, and in the senate chamber took the oath of allegiance to the United States. Returning to Nashville, he formed a partnership and practiced medicine one year with Dr. R. C. Foster, son of Hon. Ephraim H. Foster, formerly United States senator from Tennessee. Dr. Foster retiring, he next formed a partnership with Dr. John H. Callender, which continued until Dr. Callender was elected superintendent of the Tennessee Hospital for the Insane, in 1869. Since that date, Dr. Buist has practiced alone, giving his undivided attention to private practice, except when engaged in the sanitary affairs of the city of Nashville, he being a member of the city board of health from its foundation in 1874, to June, 1880. He was at times both secretary and president of the board. He was active in the discharge of his duties through the cholera epidemics of 1866 and 1873, and a member of the board of health during the exciting times of the threatened yellow fever epidemics of 1878–79.

He was also professor of oral surgery for three successive sessions, from 1879 to 1883, in the dental department of Vanderbilt University, but retired in the spring of 1883, on account of the arduous duties of his increasing private practice.

Dr. Buist is a member of the Edinborough, Scotland, Medical College Society; the State Medical Society of Tennessee, and the City Medical Society of Nashville. In personal appearance Dr. Buist is of medium height and weight, is compactly built, has light gray eyes, and the mild, benevolent face of the typical physician. He is modest and quiet in demeanor, but a gentleman of culture, rare social attainments and of great popularity.

Dr. Buist married in Nashville, July 3, 1876, Miss Laura Woodfolk, a great beauty and a reigning belle. She is the daughter of Gen. W. W. Woodfolk, of a leading North Carolina family. Her grandfather, Maj. William Woodfolk, of Jackson county, Tennessee, was a pioneer of that section, and a large planter and influential man. Gen. Woodfolk, her father, was a member of the Legislature from Jackson county; served on Gov. Carroll's staff; was a man of fine ability and large fortune, being one of the richest men in Tennessee when the war broke out. Mrs. Buist's mother, nee Ellen Horton, was a daughter of Joseph W. Horton, a sheriff, county court clerk and otherwise prominent in the early history of Davidson county. Mrs. Buist was educated at the famous old Nashville Female Academy, under Rev. Dr. C. D. Elliott. By this marriage Dr. Buist has one child, a son, William Edward Buist, born December 27, 1871. Dr. Buist and wife are both members of the Presbyterian church.

Born and raised in South Carolina, Dr. Buist has

always affiliated with the Democratic party, and in Tennessee politics is a very ardent State credit man, abhorring repudiation; but is catholic in feelings and views, and too independent to be called a strict party man. Financially, Dr. Buist, after losing his all in the war, has accumulated a comfortable property. His success in life, in point of character and usefulness, he has been heard to say, is due to his father, a Presbyterian divine and a great thinker, having profound views upon the subject of education, considering the style of education then existing in books, schools and colleges as in the main failures. His views on education were, that in the first place the physical, intellectual, and moral man should be all cultivated and trained in harmony; that health of body, mind and heart constitute the perfection of character. With such views, the plan he put in practice in his own family was, living on a farm, making his children work in all departments of the farm, teaching them that manual labor is honorable; instructing them himself at home, with the aid of books, he imparted to them what he thought much more important than what is contained in books—the impress of his own mind and character. He taught them that the object of their intellectual culture was to think for themselves; to recognize truth and to hold to it; that virtue and religion are one, and that without these no education is complete. On these principles Dr. Buist's eduction was conducted from infancy to the time of his leaving the paternal mansion, in 1855, at the age of twenty-one. These are the grounds of his success, both as a physician and a man. He belongs neither to the Bourbon nor to the progressive school of medicine, so-called, but is essentially conservative, believing in progress, but progressing slowly, and changing only after due experimentation and observation.

Dr. Buist's father, Rev. Edward T. Buist, D.D., graduated, in 1827, from the Charleston, South Carolina, College, and from Princeton Seminary in 1832, under Profs. Alexander and Miller. He supplied churches in and around Charleston for several years, and then located at Greeneville, South Carolina, where he was successively pastor of the congregations of Nazareth, Fairview, Mt. Tabor and Greeneville churches. He was for several years president of the Laurensville Female College; a very popular preacher wherever he went, a man of general information, well read on almost every subject, with wonderfully attractive powers of conversation. His predominant traits of character were his love of truth, his catholicity of spirit, and loyalty to his own convictions. He made it a point to love truth for its own sake, and not merely for personal relations to it. He died in 1878, at the aged of sixty-eight.

Dr. Buist's grandfather, Rev. George Buist, D.D., a native Scotchman, graduated from the University of Edinborough, and was sent to Charleston, South Carolina, in 1792, to fill the Scotch Presbyterian church at that place, and was its pastor up to the time of his death, in 1808. He was president of the Charleston College for many years, and reputed to be one of the most thorough scholars and able preachers of his day. He left four sons, all of whom became eminent in professional life.

Dr. Buist's mother, nee Margaret Robinson, born in Charleston, South Carolina, was, on her father's side, Scotch-Irish, and on her mother's side of French Huguenot extraction. Her father, John Robinson, was a cotton commission merchant and banker at Charleston all his life. Her mother was Susan Thomas, daughter of a Huguenot exile from France. Dr. Buist's mother died in 1849, leaving two children : (1). John R. Buist, subject of this sketch. (2). Edward Somers Buist; graduated at the University of Virginia in 1856; studied medicine in 1859–60, first at Charleston and then at New York, and graduated as an M.D., just before the breaking out of hostilities; entered the Confederate service and was killed at the bombardment of Fort Walker on Hilton Head, in October, 1861, while operating upon a wounded soldier.

GEORGE W. JONES.

FAYETTEVILLE.

GEORGE W. JONES was born in King and Queen county, Virginia, on the banks of the Mattipony river, March 15, 1807. In March, 1816, his father moved to Giles county, Tennessee, where he died, May 20, 1820. His father was a captain of militia in the war of 1812, and held the office of sheriff in Virginia. A year after the death of his father, Mr. Jones was apprenticed by his guardian to learn the trade of saddlery. He served his term at Fayetteville and worked at that business for several years afterward. His young manhood was sober, discreet and well ordered, and his after life justifies the proverb that the boy is father to the man. Though of a highly social nature, he was never married, but in the absence of family ties the circle of his friends was the circle of his acquaintance, and those who knew him best were warm and devoted.

In 1832, under the administration of Gov. Carroll, he was appointed by the Legislature, as the constitution of 1796 prescribed, a justice of the peace for Lincoln county. This position he filled until January 1, 1835, and was one of the three justices composing the court of common pleas and quarter sessions, having jurisdiction of all causes except felonies and ejectments. He was then elected clerk of that court, and filled that office until the abolishment of the court, under the operation of the constitution of 1834.

The public career of George W. Jones may be said to have commenced with the adoption of the constitution of 1834, in the State of Tennessee, its ratification by the people taking place in March, 1835, and his election to the house of representatives of the General Assembly in August of that year. The cardinal features of that instrument, as contrasted with that of 1796, were distinctively democratic, in that it framed a government more immediately responsible to the people through popular elections. This was in entire accord with the ruling principle of Mr. Jones' political faith, viz., that the people are fully capable of self-government, and are the rightful source of all political power, and that the honest mistakes of which they may occasionally be guilty are more tolerable and of less harm to the cause of good government than the view which assumes the people to be ignorant, and would permit them but a remote and indirect control over their laws and the functionaries appointed to administer them. He was a firm believer in the doctrine that everybody is wiser than anybody. The chief duty of the Legislature of 1835 was to organize the State government under the new constitution, and harmonize its laws with the principles therein set forth. Mr. Jones participated actively in that work.

His service was acceptable to his constituency, and in 1837, he was returned to the popular branch of the General Assembly. One of the important measures of that year was the project for the establishment of the Bank of Tennessee, and it was zealously opposed by Mr. Jones, though ineffectually. He had been an opponent of the Bank of the United States, and was antagonistic to governmental banking institutions on principle, and as promotive of favoritism and corruption, and, despite of the fiscal advantages claimed for them, prone to become political agencies and of detriment to the public good. In August, 1839, Mr. Jones was sent to the State senate from the district of Lincoln and Giles. In the meantime, the Bank of Tennessee had been organized, its capital being the State school fund, the Federal surplus revenue deposited under the act of Congress of 1836 with the State, and the proceeds of two and a half million of State bonds issued for the purpose. The report of its president to the Legislature showed that one million of these bonds were still held by the bank, and Mr. Jones promptly introduced a bill directing their return to the secretary of State, and that they should be cancelled by the governor of the State. At this session, he opposed a recommendation of the message of Gov. Polk, that bonds of the State should be payable in sterling money, and in the city of London, and contributed to the defeat of the proposition in the General Assembly.

Among the most signal of his acts while serving in the State Legislature, was his earnest support of a bill abolishing imprisonment for debt, and there is none which he recalled with a fonder satisfaction than the part he bore in obliterating from the statute book that odious heritage from the days when the personal liberty of free citizens was sordidly set in the scales of dollars and cents, and mistake and misfortune were made as infamous as crime.

In 1840, while a candidate for presidential elector on the Democratic ticket, a vacancy occurred in the office of county court clerk of Lincoln county, and the county court, in August of that year, elected Mr. Jones to fill the unexpired term, to March, 1842, when he was elected by the people for a full term of four years. This office he resigned, however, at the July term of the court, in 1843, and at the State election in the month following, was elected the representative of his Congressional district in the house of representatives of the United States, and took his seat in the December following, as a member of the Twenty-eighth Congress.

This Congress witnessed the advent on the theater of national affairs of quite a number of men who were destined to attain distinction and exert a wide influence in subsequent years—among them Andrew Johnson, Stephen A. Douglas, Robert Toombs and Alexander H. Stephens. Of the subject of this sketch it may be said, that while not rivaling these and others of his Congressional contemporaries in brilliancy of attainments and oratorical gifts, no man preceding him in the popular branch of Congress, or then or since entering it, surpassed him in efficient usefulness as a legislator, and none of those named, and but one or two in the history of the government, ever, for so long a term of service in that body, and so implicitly, held the confidence of an immediate constituency and that of the country at large. He was continued in membership by successive elections for sixteen years, or until 1859, in the most of the elections the opposition being nominal and his majorities always overwhelming. It is doubtful if there is another instance in the history of Congress—unless it be that of John Quincy Adams and his constituency—in which the relationship between the representative and the represented was more thorough and cordial. The most important national question, during the first Congress of his service, was the annexation of Texas, of which he was a staunch advocate, and gave support, both to the resolution of the house of representatives on the subject, and the alternative bill from the senate, for a commission to negotiate the matter, when the two propositions were conjoined. In the Twenty-ninth Congress —the first of the Polk administration—he advocated, by speech and vote, the act declaring a state of war with Mexico, and in that and the succeeding Congress, ardently supported all measures for its vigorous prosecution. He voted for the act organizing the territory of Oregon, in which the Missouri compromise line was incorporated, on the ground that it lay north of the line. He supported the *ad valorem* tariff act of 1846, which contained no feature of protective duties for protection's sake, but which was a tariff for revenue, yielding, as such a tariff must inevitably do, some degree of incidental protection to domestic industries. That act was an efficient one for revenue, in spite of the prediction of advocates of high tariff duties that it would fail in producing an amount sufficient for government necessities. The revenue, indeed, increased and sufficed, not only for the ordinary needs of the nation, but for the extraordinary expenditures of the Mexican war, and under it, domestic manufacturing industries did not languish for lack of due protection. His view of the whole question of the tariff then was neither those of the free trade or protection duty *doctrinaire*, holding the former to be impracticable, as the revenues must be collected by impost taxes, and the latter wrong in principle, tending, under certain conditions and circumstances, to defeat its own object, as well as to decrease revenue, and, under others, to create and foster monopolies. He held the primary object of a tariff to be revenue, and the protection given by its rates, within that limit, to be secondary and incidental, and that, with the increasing need of revenue, the manufacturing and productive interests of the country would always receive legitimate protection. During this period he opposed the recharter of local banks in the District of Columbia, and, as he had done in his own State, favored the act abolishing imprisonment for debt in the district.

In the fierce agitation of the slavery issue which ensued upon the acquisition of territory from Mexico, and during the stormy period of 1849 and 1850, Mr. Jones was eminently conservative. The representative of a southern State, and firmly loyal to all the interests of her people, he was never betrayed into extremism. He was impressed with the delicate and embarrassing nature of the question and recognized the necessity of compromise, and judging that his section lost none of its substantial rights in the compromise measures of 1850, he yielded the several features of that series of bills his earnest support. He voted for the admission of California as a State with a constitution interdicting slavery, because it was the will of the people who framed it, taking the broad ground that he would force no domestic institution or system of laws on any people who did not desire them, and he as strenuously opposed the right of any community to interfere with the domestic institutions as they existed by the will of the people of other States or communities.

Mr. Jones at that time, and up to the culmination of the slavery contest in the civil war, never gave his adhesion to the extreme constitutional doctrines maintained in regard to slavery and State's rights, of which Mr. Calhoun was the arch apostle. He believed neither in the right of nullification or secession. He was a Democrat of the strictest sect, but it was of the school of Jefferson, Jackson and Benton. He recognized two sets of agitators among the ambitious politicians of the country—those in the North, using anti-slavery sentiment for the foundation of a sectional political organization, in order to aggrandize themselves in official station, and those in the South, championing the technical and abstract rights of slave-holders, for the purpose of "firing the southern heart" and precipitating disunion, and erecting a separate government in which they would rule as chiefs. He deprecated the disruption of the Democratic convention at Charleston, in 1860, and in the contest of that year, gave his support to Stephen A. Douglas, as the representative candidate of the conservative and national Democratic party.

During Mr. Jones's long service in the national house of representatives, he was a member at various times of the most important committees of the body, and punctual and laborious in the discharge of duty. He served on the committee on the District of Columbia; on that of territories with Stephen A. Douglas; on that of post-offices and post-roads with Abraham Lincoln; on that of rules of the house, of which he was chairman in the Thirty-second and Thirty-third Congresses, and on that of ways and means. In 1851, the speaker of the house, Lynn Boyd, of Kentucky, named Mr. Jones for the chairmanship of the ways and means committee, with Mr. George S. Houston, of Alabama, as second on the committee. With characteristic modesty, Mr. Jones declined this eminent position, and requested of the speaker a transposition of names in the formation of the committee with Mr. Houston. This was done, and he remained in that position for four years. He also did service on various select committees, and on conference committees on disagreeing votes with the senate, and as one of the tellers in the count of electoral presidential votes in February, 1857. In 1853, William R. King, of Alabama, who had been elected vice-president of the United States, was in ill health, and absent from the country, on the island of Cuba. Under an act of Congress, the United States consul at Havana was appointed to administer the oath of office to Mr. King, and Mr. Jones was designated to bear a copy of the law and instructions thereunder to the consul, and was the official witness to Mr. King's subscription to the oath of office.

The leading feature in Mr. Jones's congressional service, and in his character as a public man, was his devotion to the idea that it is not in a splendid and extravagant government, giving support, and in turn supported by, powerful monopolies and aristocratic establishments, that the people find the best security for their liberties, or means for the promotion of individual prosperity and happiness. He held that this government was formed by the people distinctly to attain these ends, and in its administration he followed simplicity, economy and honesty as cardinal precepts, and was the consistent and outspoken opponent of every species of legislation that fostered the wealth of the few and facilitated the growth of private fortunes out of the common wealth of the republic. He opposed the creation of useless and unnecessary offices, and the payment of salaries beyond the limit of just and adequate compensation. In regard to all forms of government expenditure he was economic, but never narrow-minded or niggard. He held that the burden of taxation should fall as lightly as possible on every man's purse, that he might be enabled, under just and equal laws, to develop the enterprise and industry of which he might be capable, and elevate himself as best he might in fortune and social rank. He was a strict constructionist of constitutional grants and limitations of power, and did not believe that the "general welfare" clause of the constitution conferred sovereign power on Congress to do anything and everything, whether prohibited or permitted, expressedly or impliedly, with the public purse or the public lands. He opposed a bank of the United States, and held that gold and silver only were money, and that paper of any kind claiming to be such should be representative of, and convertible into it, on demand. He did not favor institutions like the United States Naval and Military Academies.

He opposed service pensions for soldiery, and civil pensions of all sorts. He opposed a large standing army, and a large naval establishment, and especially the creating of public debts, State or national, and believed firmly in John Randolph's philosopher's stone —"pay as you go," as the better rule for States as well as individuals. While he advocated the policy of taking as little from the public wealth as was possible for governmental use, he scrutinized with scrupulous care every channel through which it was sought to disburse it, and his name as a public servant was synonymous with faithful and vigilant guardianship of the public treasury. And this he did without fear, favor, affection or offensiveness.

After the election of Mr. Lincoln, in November, 1860, Mr. Jones, having supported Mr. Douglas for the presidency, continued to counsel a prudent and conservative course to the people of the southern States. When the conflict of arms was precipitated in 1861, he deemed it the wise alternative to espouse the southern side, on the ground that unanimity of the southern people would tend to temper the character of the strife and probably shorten it. In November, 1861, he was elected to the house of representatives of the Confederate States, and assumed his seat in February, 1862. At the end of this service, in 1864, he declined a re-election, and, his home being within the lines of the Union military forces, he accepted the hospitality of a friend in North Carolina, where he remained until the cessation of hostilities. Repairing shortly thereafter to the seat of government, he was cordially received by his friend and former colleague, Andrew Johnson, the president,

and promptly pardoned and relieved of political disability.

Until 1869, Mr. Jones was in private life, when he was elected a delegate to the convention to revise and amend the constitution of Tennessee. The body assembled in January, 1870, and he participated in its deliberations until a few days before its final adjournment. A clause had been inserted in the instrument empowering the Legislature to impose a poll-tax as a preliminary requisite to the exercise of the franchise privilege. This feature was repugnant to the principles uniformly advocated by him, and regarding it as a most objectionable form of property qualification, and restrictive of political rights, he refused his assent, and declining to affix his signature to the proposed constitution, withdrew from the convention, and afterward voted against the ratification of the instrument.

In 1871, he was appointed by Gov. John C. Brown a trustee of the Tennessee Hospital for the Insane, was reappointed by Gov. James D. Porter in 1877, and by Gov. A. S. Marks in 1879, and occupied that position at the time of his death, the duties of which he discharged with the zeal and fidelity that marked his course in other places of trust and responsibility.

In 1878, at the request of the family and immediate friends of the late ex-President Andrew Johnson, he delivered the oration at the unveiling of the monument erected to his memory at Greeneville, Tennessee. His intimate personal relations and political affiliations with that distinguished man eminently qualified him to review his remarkable career and analyze his public character and vindicate his place in history, and the task was performed in a manner befitting the theme and the occasion.

Though it had been several years since Mr. Jones passed the Psalmist's allotted period of three score and ten years, his physical vigor was remarkably preserved, and his mental faculties were unimpaired to the hour of his death. He maintained a proper interest in public affairs in his latter years, but resolutely refused to listen to all solicitations to be recalled into active political life. Several occasions since his retirement caused his name to be considered with reference to high positions in the State and Federal governments, but with positiveness and the utmost sincerity, he declined to listen to the appeals of his friends. The retrospect which he was able to cast over his public service, extending to nearly fifty years, was in the highest degree satisfactory to him. An acute and sagacious observer —the late John C. Rives, of the Washington *Globe*— once remarked of him to the writer, that the public character of Mr. Jones might well be envied by any man who had ever served the government. His uniform reply to suggestions of his re-entry upon public life was, that no man should presume to think himself capable of being useful to two generations in a political trust, and that one he had some reason to believe regarded his service as worthy, had passed away. And therein was expressed the wisdom of a sage.

George W. Jones most resembled, in the qualities which for so long a time attracted the public confidence and esteem, an eminent character in the early days of the republic—Nathaniel Macon, of North Carolina. Simple in tastes, courteous to all, modest in appreciation of self, exact in methods, well informed on subjects requiring an opinion, of sterling good sense, of comprehensive knowledge of men, of unbending integrity, and of elevated devotion to the cause of popular government, the useful and blameless records of both of them signally illustrate the truth, that the best type of public officials is not always found in association with brilliant intellectual gifts and acquirements, but rather in lucid judgment, honest conviction and unostentatious courage.

JAMES RODGERS, M. D.

KNOXVILLE.

DR. RODGERS is descended from Scotch-Irish parentage. His great-grandfather was a Pennsylvanian. His grandfather, James Rodgers, was a native of Pennsylvania, went to Rockbridge county, Virginia, and from there to Washington county, East Tennessee, when a young man, in the first settlement of the country, and married Rhoda Alexander, daughter of Francis Alexander, one of the pioneer settlers of Washington county, a native of Virginia. He moved to Knox county about the year 1800, and engaged in farming, being at the same time a blacksmith. He (the grandfather) was in the war of 1812, and died about 1836, at the age of some seventy-five years, a stanch old Presbyterian, and an old Clay Whig. The grandmother died at an advanced age, leaving six children, one of whom, Samuel R. Rodgers, was chancellor at Knoxville since the war, under appointment from Gov. Brownlow. Two of her sons, William and Alexander Rodgers, were physicians; the former died in Knox county, the latter in Mississippi. Her two daughters, Lavinia and Lucinda, died unmarried, in Knox county.

Dr. Rodgers' father, Thomas Rodgers, was born in 1794, in Virginia, came to Washington county in early life, and from there to Knoxville, when eighteen years old (1812), married in Knox county, and carried on the blacksmithing business at Knoxville until about 1840. He then purchased a farm within two miles of Knoxville and removed to it, lived a farmer, and died December 22, 1870. He held the office of magistrate fifteen or twenty years. In politics, Hugh L. White and Henry Clay were his idols, and he remained a Whig all his life. He joined the Presbyterian church in early life, was ordained an elder October 24, 1829, and was an acting elder in the Second Presbyterian church at Knoxville till his death. He was a very quiet man, attending to his own business and nobody else's.

Dr. Rodgers' mother, Annie Patton, was born in Knox county, daughter of Robert Patton. She died in 1820, a Presbyterian, leaving three children : (1). Mary, married a Mr. Bryant, moved to Middle Tennessee, and died there. (2). James, subject of this sketch. (3). Elizabeth, married James Randles, from Sevier county, moved to Texas and died, leaving several children.

Dr. James Rodgers was born in Knoxville, July 2, 1818, and has lived in that town ever since. He was raised to work until he entered Knoxville College, in which he studied some three or four years under President Joseph Estabrook. Leaving college, he clerked in a drug store six years, during which time he studied medicine under Dr. James Morrow. He took lectures in Lexington, Kentucky, in 1842–43, under Dr. Ben Dudley, and has been practicing medicine ever since. In 1870, the faculty of the University of Nashville conferred the degree of M. D. upon him, on account of his age and experience. The names attached to his diploma are a sufficient guarantee of the merit of its recipient, to-wit: Professors W. T. Briggs, T. L. Madden, Paul F. Eve, W. L. Nichol, Van S. Lindsley, John H. Callender, W. K. Bowling, C. K. Winston and J. Berrien Lindsley.

Both professionally and financially, Dr. Rodgers has been a success. He began life on nothing, and after paying fifteen thousand dollars security money, is now in independent circumstances. He is a member of the County and State Medical Societies, of the American Medical Association, and of the National Board of Health, and has been president of the East Tennessee Medical Society, and of the Knox county Medical Society. It is nobler mention to say that he stood by his people through every epidemic that has visited the town; of cholera in 1854, and of small-pox during the war.

In politics, Dr. Rodgers was first a Whig, but has been a Republican ever since the disintegration of the Whig party. He was postmaster at Knoxville four years under appointment from President Grant, in 1869. He was appointed by Gov. Brownlow State director of the Knoxville and Kentucky railroad, and served three years. He was examining surgeon of the United States pension department from 1870 to 1883. He is a Royal Arch Mason, and has held all the offices in the Independent Order of Odd Fellows, including that of Grand Master of the State. In religion, he is a Presbyterian, was ordained elder June 16, 1872, is clerk of the session; has frequently been delegate to the synods, and was delegate to the General Assembly at its session in Madison, Wisconsin, in 1880. Dr. Rodgers married at Knoxville, in November, 1843, Miss Rosanna McMullin, who was born in that town, July 20, 1820, daughter of Daniel McMullin, a native Irishman. Her mother was a McCaughan, also a native of Ireland, where she married her husband. She died young, leaving three children: (1). Rosanna, wife of Dr. Rodgers. (2). Thomas, a merchant at Waco, Texas. (3). Isabella, who died at Knoxville, wife of David Solomon, leaving three children, William, a printer; James, now in Kansas City, Missouri, and Fannie, unmarried.

Mrs. Rodgers was educated at Knoxville, is a Presbyterian, and is notably domestic in her ways and habits. By his marriage with Miss McMullin, Dr. Rodgers has ten children: (1). Isabella, wife of M. C. Wilcox, who came to Knoxville from Ohio in the Federal army. They are now living at Mt. Airy, Georgia. (2). Thomas, a druggist at Knoxville; married Miss Lucie White, and has six children, James, Margaret, Charles, Cowan, Flora and Don. (3). James, in mercantile life in St. Louis; married Miss Lillian Branner, in Knoxville, and has two children, George and Ruth. (4). Samuel, graduated in medicine in Vanderbilt University, Nashville; now practicing at Mt. Airy, Georgia (5). Charles, in the drug business, at Knoxville. (6). Wallace, farming in Knox county; married Miss Jewie Jackson, has three children, Lizzie, Rose and Jewie. (7). Anna, wife of E. G. Oats. (8). Hugh, died in infancy. (9). Hugh (second), in mercantile business at Knoxville. (10). Lillie, a young lady now at home.

Since 1832, Dr. Rodgers has lived a Christian life, with Presbyterian strictness, trained his children in the ways of godliness, and has lived to see them all, from the oldest to the youngest, baptized into the Presbyterian church, thus achieving the greatest success a father can accomplish. He never took a chew of tobacco, was never intoxicated, does not know one playing card from another, never had a fight, and having the universal esteem and confidence of his city, where he has lived sixty-six years, and of which he is a representative physician, he is presented to the distinguished company whose biographies fill this volume as a standard Tennessee man.

J. J. HARRISON, M.D.

LOUDON.

THE Harrison family is of Scotch-Irish stock, the ancestors of this branch coming to America from "Auld Scotia's flinty glebe." Dr. Harrison's grandfather, John Harrison, moved from Virginia to East Tennessee, at an early day in the settlement of that section. He married Miss Susan Jackson, in Roane county, and by her had only one child, James F. Harrison (father of the subject of this sketch), who was born near Loudon, in 1809; raised on a farm; read medicine under Dr. Tom Anderson; attended one course of lectures in Washington City; graduated at Lexington, Kentucky, and located at Loudon, where he had an extensive practice until his death, in 1861. He was a very positive, determined man, and upright in all his dealings and transactions in life; was an elder in the Presbyterian church; born and raised a Whig; sympathized with the southern cause, and was a member of the Masonic fraternity.

Dr. Harrison's mother, *nee* Miss Sarah D. Merrick, was born in New Orleans; was educated in Roane county; was a member of the Presbyterian church, and noted for her overflowing hospitality, and a charity limited only by her means and opportunities for doing good. She died from the effect of injuries received in being thrown from a buggy at Red Clay, Georgia, in 1859, at the age of forty-six, and left three sons and two daughters: (1). John Henry Harrison, who became a captain in the Confederate army, and was killed at the battle of Piedmont. (2). Josiah J. Harrison, subject of this sketch. (3). James M. Harrison, died at Huntsville, Alabama, of heart disease. (4). Rachel Susannah Harrison, widow successively of Dr. R. W. Adams and George W. Mayo. (5). Sarah Adaline Harrison, now wife of John B. McGhee, of Monroe county, Tennessee, nephew of C. M. McGhee, of Knoxville.

Dr. Harrison was born in Roane (now Loudon) county, Tennessee, February 13, 1834, and there grew up, working on his father's farm, and going to school in the winter months. He commenced the study of medicine when eighteen years of age, under his father at Loudon; attended the medical department of the University of Nashville two sessions, and graduated in the winter of 1853–4 under Profs. W. K. Bowling, A. H. Buchanan, Paul F. Eve, C. K. Winston, J. Berrien Lindsley, John M. Watson, and Robert M. Porter. In 1854 he located at Loudon, associated in practice with his father, and in 1858 returned and took another course in the University of Nashville. He has had a successful practice ever since including an extensive surgical practice. He was a contract surgeon in the

Confederate service for a while during the war, but being in bad health during that time, was exempted from military duty.

Dr. Harrison became a Mason at Loudon, in 1855; has taken all the Chapter, Council and Commandery degrees, and has been Master of his lodge eighteen years. He has passed all the chairs of Odd Fellowship; has served as Dictator of the Knights of Honor; is an elder in the Presbyterian church, and served as delegate in presbytery and synod. Although raised a Whig by a Whig father, he is now a Democrat; has been an alderman, and served as delegate to the county and State conventions of the Democracy.

Dr. Harrison first married, in Loudon county, in 1863, Miss Lizzie M. Abbott, daughter of R. H. Abbott, of a Virginia family. Her mother was a Miss Pepper, also of Virginia. Mrs. Harrison died in 1866, at Huntsville, Alabama, to which place Dr. Harrison had removed. She left one child, Miss Lula May Harrison, born in Loudon county, June 22, 1864, and graduated at Shorter College, Rome, Georgia, in 1883.

Dr. Harrison's second marriage, which occurred at Loudon, in 1870, was with Miss Mary B. McCray, daughter of Gen. Thomas H. McCray, a native of Monroe county, Tennessee. When the war broke out Mrs. Harrison's father, who was then living in Texas, raised a regiment for the Confederate army, and afterwards became a brigadier-general. Her mother, nee Miss Angeline Galbreth, was a daughter of Rev. John T. Galbreth, a Methodist preacher. Mrs. Harrison is the elder of two children. Her sister, Alice McCray, is now the wife of John Cole, a farmer in Monroe county, Tennessee. Mrs. Harrison was educated in Bishop Pierce's school in Georgia, and is a Presbyterian. Her crowning characteristic is to make home home-like and comfortable, and to raise her children correctly. She has won the reputation of being a kind and devoted step-mother, showing no partiality as between her step-daughter and her own children. She has borne Dr. Harrison seven children, all born in Loudon: Frank Rhea, Henry M., Fannie A., Joe J., Thomas H., Emmett M., and John McGhee.

Dr. Harrison has made a success in life by self-reliance and self-exertion. His father had accumulated some property, consisting of lands and negroes, most of which was swept away by the war, or went to pay security debts. This left his children to begin life where he began it—on about nothing. Dr. Harrison, therefore, has made what he now possesses by faithful and constant attention to his profession, to which he has exclusively devoted his time, his talents and his influence.

ANSON NELSON.

NASHVILLE.

THIS gentleman appears in this volume of "Prominent Tennesseans" without a title, but as he has a reputation for honesty as wide as that of any man in the State, the author is half-tempted to style him, Anson Nelson, the Honest. Not that he is more honest than any other honest man, but because his uniform and undeviating integrity and faithfulness in the many important private and public trusts he has held has caused him to be universally recognized as a conscientious, faithful and punctual man from inborn principle, and which has given him the unlimited confidence of the people of Tennessee, and especially of the city of Nashville, who would readily avouch that Aristides of Athens was not more worthy the title of "Aristides the Just," than is this beloved citizen of the "Athens of the South" worthy to be called Anson Nelson, the Honest.

He was tax-collector of the city of Nashville from 1853 to 1862, eight years, and city treasurer of Nashville from October, 1869, to November, 1883, fourteen years, making twenty-two years of public service, and in these capacities handled and disbursed more than fifteen millions of dollars, requiring his signature to coupons or checks more than two hundred thousand times, and no paper bearing his personal or official signature has ever been protested or thrown out of bank or unpaid when due on demand. In all this immense business with officials and private individuals, it is said no complaint has been heard, either on account of delay or incorrectness of settlement. For this great—indeed, fearful—responsibility, he had to give bond in the sum of from fifty thousand to seventy-five thousand dollars, while receiving a salary of only from one thousand five hundred dollars to two thousand dollars per annum.

In his manners Mr. Nelson is modest and deferential, even to apparent diffidence; but when duty or honor demands he is self-assertive and unflinchingly faithful over the many things entrusted to him. The net results of his life clearly show that he is not honest from policy, but because he loves to do right for right's sake.

After so long a time in the service of the public, in 1883, Mr. Nelson determined to retire from office, a step he had long contemplated, and in the following address "To the People of Nashville," returned to them, with clean hands and unsullied name, the trust they had imposed upon him: "It has become generally known that I am not a candidate for re-election to the office of city treasurer, or an applicant for any official position. The new reform movement, just starting, gives me an excellent opportunity to step aside and pursue another calling, after two or three months of necessary rest. This fact was known to the present members of the city council several days ago, and is not a new or sudden decision. More than a year ago I made up my mind to retire from office, and two or three times I was on the point of resigning, but was prevailed upon to postpone the matter, when, finally, I concluded to fill out my term. My decision not again to run for the office was known to a few friends many months ago, and has nothing whatever to do with the recent election or its results.

"And now it is proper for me to say to the good people of this city that I feel, as I have felt for years past, the profoundest gratitude to them for long continued favors, and for their unwavering and unabated friendship. For fourteen years past I have held the office of city treasurer, without a break or interruption. Before the war I was tax-collector for over eight years, which makes more than twenty-two years of municipal service. This is unusual, almost without precedent, and I am doubly thankful for these home honors, and for such continued manifestations of public confidence. I was voted for by members of the city council, year after year, with a unanimity that was almost surprising. Democrats and Whigs, Republicans and anti-Republicans, temperance men and anti-temperance men, white men and colored, and men of all shades of opinion in politics and religion, have cheerfully and uniformly supported me, believing it to be their duty to their constituents. I never had an opponent for either office, except upon a single occasion, and then the opposition was very slight.

"My accounts have been examined annually by competent committees, and passed upon as correct. For the last year this has not been done, but soon will be. No blunder or mistake has ever been made, so far as I know or believe, save two or three clerical errors, of minor importance, which were easily corrected. My books have been accurately kept, and they are simple and easily understood. The business of the city treasurer is to receive money and pay out the same according to law, and, until about two years ago, to report monthly to the city council, in detail, all receipts and expenditures. This was done every month until the office of city auditor was created, when it was made his duty to so report. He has done so ever since. Numbers of men, as part of the finance committee, have gone over my books, and, I am proud to say, have always found them to be correct. The city, however, had a regular book-keeper in its employ until the creation of the office of city auditor, who now performs the duty.

" I have handled, on an average, about half a million
39

of dollars annually. I have been under bond for about fifty thousand dollars all the time, and was fortunate enough always to obtain good names, without applying to those that I thought would ask in return pecuniary favors of me or the city. The labors of my office, as every one knows, are responsible and arduous, and I trust my successor will be better remunerated for his work than I have been. My salary has been comparatively small.

" It is unnecessary for me to say that I wish the new form of government complete success. The system I believe to be a good one, and it ought to succeed. I greatly desire the prosperity of all the people of this good and growing city, and with grateful thanks to all, I am, respectfully, ANSON NELSON."

This determination on Mr. Nelson's part met with universal regret—the people felt they had sustained an almost irreparable loss, while the press, of all shades of political complexion, bore willing testimony to his unblemished record. The *American*, in it editorial columns, said: " There are few, if any, who will read the card of Anson Nelson, Esq., published in to-day's *American*, without regretting his announced intention to retire from the management of the city's financial affairs. If there is one man in Nashville, who, above all others, is respected by every class of the community for his sterling honesty, faithful service in the public interest, and high Christian character, that man is Mr. Nelson. As stated in his card, his intention has not been hastily formed. It was certainly not based upon the idea that he would not be retained by the new city council. On the contrary, there is ample authority for stating that, had he been disposed to hold the office longer, he would have been unanimously re-elected. Capable, honest and experienced public servants like him are but too rarely found in these days, and it is a matter of regret that the reform government is not to have the benefit of his skill and sagacity as a financial officer."

The Nashville morning *World*, of the same date, contained the following : " Mr. Anson Nelson, after serving the city in the capacity of treasurer for fourteen years, makes the announcement that he will no longer be a candidate for any office. He says it is no sudden notion, but that he intended, and would have retired long ago, had not his friends urged him to continue. Six months ago he again fully concluded to retire, the duties of the office confining him so closely, and had gone so far as to draw up his resignation, but again his friends urged him to continue, on the ground that it would be very difficult to get a man who would be willing to give a fifty thousand dollar bond for that length of time. He says he has now fully determined to no longer seek official position. For fourteen years he has been the choice of the people, through the board of aldermen, and is the only city official, with the exception of Capt. Stockell, who has been honored successively for so long a period, now in office. Before the war, Mr. Nelson served as revenue collector over eight years, and never had any opposition for either treasurer or collector, except on one occasion. As treasurer, Mr. Nelson has handled over half a million dollars a year, making about fifteen millions during the fourteen years in office. His bond has been variously fixed at from thirty thousand dollars to seventy-five thousand dollars, which he has never had any trouble in making. The bond at the present time is fifty thousand dollars. His accounts have been passed on annually by an auditing committee, with the exception of the past year, which will be done in a few days. In retiring from the office he desires to tender his profound gratitude to all the members of all councils during the time he has served, and to the citizens of Nashville, for the continued confidence and honor shown him."

The evening *Banner* said: "The announcement that Mr. Anson Nelson has determined to retire from the service of the city, is received with regret as deep as it is universal. For fourteen years he has faithfully discharged the duties of treasurer, receiving and disbursing millions of dollars, and during that long period not one word of criticism of his official action has been uttered. His close attention to business and his affability toward all with whom he has come in contact, won for him the hearty commendation and the good will of his fellow-officials, the conductors of the government and the general public. Wearied with years of constant toil, Mr. Nelson will shortly give up his position and take a rest, to which he is justly entitled, and which his friends hope will be full of enjoyment. It is his intention to resume work in another sphere several months hence, and we cordially join the citizens of this city in wishing him the greatest success."

The *Artisan* contained the following tribute, which but reflects the love and sentiments of thousands of his fellow-citizens: " As a rule the resignation of a public official (a very rare occurrence) is no loss to the public service, but occasionally there is a very marked exception. One of these is the resignation of Anson Nelson, as city treasurer. His experience and knowledge of that office would have been of very great value to the new government, and his example as an honest and upright financier, of inestimable worth. For twenty-two consecutive years he has served this city, eight as collector, and fourteen as treasurer, and but for his refusal, would have continued to do so as long as his life was spared to us. Except once, his election from time to time has been unanimous, and that time the opposition was but trifling; his unblemished integrity, genuine truth and uprightness, and eminent fitness, were such that no one ever ventured to suggest a change, and after all these years of service and handling of public funds, he retires from office without the slightest taint on his character, or a breath of suspicion attached to him, and without a dollar that the strictest or most sus-

picious could intimate was not justly or righteously his own. Of what immense value in these times of speculation and shortage is such a record; such a financial career and such a record is worth as an example, and a beacon to the young business men, more than a thousand sermons or essays on honesty and integrity. We trust we may long continue to meet him and his good wife—one of the very few mated, and not merely matched, couples in this world—in our daily walk, and that for many, very many years, they may together reap the happiness of a well-spent life, and well-earned comforts, and that far distant may be the time when either will be called to mourn for the other, or to vainly long for

' The touch of a vanished hand
And the sound of a voice that is still.' "

Mr. Nelson was born in Washington county, Tennessee, November 19, 1821, and spent the first seven years of his life in the " Hiawassee Purchase," now McMinn county, and at Maryville, and his next twelve years at Knoxville. When only ten years old he entered the office of Maj. F. S. Heiskell's Knoxville *Register* to learn the printer's business. Among the boys employed at that time in the same establishment were others who afterwards became prominent men: Gen. F. K. Zollicoffer, Midshipman Harrell, William Fields (editor of *Fields' Scrap Book*) and William Clayton, of Alabama.

Having completed his apprenticeship and become a full-fledged journeyman printer at Knoxville, Mr. Nelson went to Nashville, in 1840, and soon after took charge of the Nashville *Whig* as foreman. In 1849, he bought the *Daily Gazette* and established a job office in connection with it, publishing by contract the *Presbyterian Record* and the *Western Boatman*. He purchased the *Tennessee Organ* and edited that paper in the interest of temperance, as advocated by the Sons of Temperance, of which order he was elected Grand Treasurer, and subsequently filled all the higher offices of that organization. But the general public had need of his energetic and reliable services, and, as before stated, from 1853 to 1862, he was, by successive elections, revenue collector of the city of Nashville. From 1864 to 1869, he engaged in the real estate business. When Hon. John M. Bass became receiver of the corporation of Nashville, which had just been rescued from a plundering band of irresponsibles who drifted to Nashville during the war, Mr. Nelson was appointed to take charge of the city tax-books. In October, 1869, he was elected treasurer of the city by the new council, and held the office continuously until November 16, 1883.

In 1855, he was elected recording secretary of the Tennessee Historical Society, and has held that office ever since. In 1880, the society had his portrait painted and hung in the library room of the State capitol, in appreciation of his services as their secretary for twenty-five years.

At the organization of the Mt. Olivet Cemetery company, in 1855—the principal burying ground of the city —he was elected a director of the company and is still a director. He was instrumental in building the South Nashville street railroad, in 1865—the first street railway in Nashville—and was president of the company the first year of its existence. He was a director in the Nashville and Chattanooga railroad company for three years, under the administration of Hon. M. Burns, its president, and was one of the executive committee for the term of his directorship. He was a director of the Second National Bank of Nashville, in 1865-6. He was one of the board of managers of the city's Centennial Exposition, in 1880, and prepared and had read by W. K. McAllister, jr., esq., a sketch of the history of Nashville for its first one hundred years. That sketch, with the author's *addenda*, was deposited in the cornerstone of Wesley Hall, at Vanderbilt University, in 1881. A Statistical View of Nashville, a magazine article by Mr. Nelson, was deposited in the corner-stone of the State Capitol, in 1845. He is vice-president of Goodman's business college, Nashville, and for thirty years, has been one of the business advisers of Mrs. ex-President James K. Polk.

For forty-two years Mr. Nelson has been a member of the Baptist church, for twenty-seven years one of its deacons, and was for four years its Sunday-school superintendent—during the war.

In 1847, he became a Master Mason, and has taken all the degrees up to and including Knighthood. For many years he has been treasurer of Phœnix Lodge, No. 131, Nashville, and has served as Warden in the lodge, and as King in the chapter. He is also a member of the Royal Arcanum.

He was an old line Whig until that party ceased to exist, but since the war, has co-operated with the Democrats. He was a delegate, in 1857, from Davidson county, to the State convention that nominated Gen. Robert Hatton for governor.

Mr. Nelson first married, in Knoxville, February 18, 1840, Miss Eliza Ann Grady, a native of Hawkins county, Tennessee, daughter of John Grady, a farmer, of a Virginia family. She was a handsome woman, of intelligence and strong convictions, and a member of the Baptist church. She died at Nashville, February 1, 1866, leaving one son, Henry, born in Nashville, November 20, 1844; educated at the Nashville high school; was at one time auditor of the Nashville and Chattanooga railroad, and previously a clerk for the Adams Express company; married Miss Henrietta Cheney, daughter of H. J. Cheney, and maternal granddaughter of Col. Samuel D. Morgan, the noted wholesale merchant of Nashville. He died December 12, 1879.

Mr. Nelson's next marriage, which occurred August 6, 1868, was with the lovely Miss Fannie Dickinson Howell, eldest daughter of Rev. Robert Boyte C. Howell, D. D., the famous pastor of the First Baptist church, of Nashville. She was born December 29,

1838; educated at Nashville and Richmond, Virginia, and is a spirited lady, graceful in person and manner, and noted for being a fluent and elegant writer, having contributed articles, occasionally, both prose and poetry, to the newspapers and magazines. She reads French and German, understands music thoroughly, and is a very devoted member of the Baptist church. In the ladies' weekly devotional meetings of that church, she is a leader, and has been for several years past. In the Sunday-school she is also a teacher, having a class of some fifteen young men—clerks and students in the normal and dental and other schools of the city, they attending that class on account of her intellectual vigor and high culture. Withal, she is a thoroughly domestic woman.

Dr. Howell, her father, was born in Wayne county, North Carolina, March 10, 1801; died at Nashville, April 5, 1867, and was followed to the grave by an immense concourse of his fellow-citizens, who respected, loved and venerated him. He was one of the most remarkable ministers of his times. In his pulpit, whether praying or preaching, he was a magnificent man, of varied and profound learning, and of deep and undoubted piety. In his style of oratory, he was a man to whom one had to listen with his eyes. No man of his day in Tennessee did so much to increase the numbers of the Baptist denomination, to make it respectable, or to elevate the standard of ministerial education. An evidence of Dr. Howell's personal popularity is found in the fact that he performed the marriage ceremony for five hundred and forty-six couples. He was, for forty years, a distinguished divine in Virginia and Tennessee, and was the most celebrated Baptist preacher in the South. He was also the author of a number of valuable works. One of his published volumes, "Terms of Communion," went through several editions in the United States and four in Great Britain. Besides a number of pamphlet addresses on various occasions, he was the author of "The Deaconship," "The Cross," "The Covenants," "The Way of Salvation," "Evils of Infant Baptism," and "The Early Baptists of Virginia," standard denominational works. One of his unpublished works, "The Christology of the Pentateuch," may yet be given to the public.

Mrs. Nelson's oldest brother, Alfred T. Howell, is now a lawyer near Granberry, Hood county, Texas. Her brother, Hon. Morton B. Howell, a lawyer at Nashville, was formerly clerk and master in chancery, and mayor of Nashville in 1874, and is a gentleman of much culture and fine literary attainments. Her brother, Robert H. Howell, for a long time a leading publisher, is now secretary of the Oman & Stewart Stone company. Her brother, Joseph T. Howell, is cashier of the Fourth National Bank, Nashville. Her sister, Jennie Howell, is now wife of Rev. Dr. D. W. Gwin, pastor of the First Baptist church, Atlanta, Georgia. Her sister, Anna Howell, is now wife of Dr.

Frank Hollowell, physician in charge of the Nashville Medical Hospital. Her sister, Serena Howell, is now wife of Andrew J. Grigsby, business manager of the Nashville *Spirit of the Farm*, an agricultural journal. Prof. C. H. Toy, of Harvard College, is a cousin to Mrs. Nelson.

Mr. Nelson's paternal ancestry is of English extraction. His grandfather, Berryman Nelson, was, however, born in Virginia, was a farmer and a patriot soldier in the Revolutionary war. Mr. Nelson's father, Daniel Nelson, was a native of Virginia, married in North Carolina, moved to Jefferson county, East Tennessee, and there followed his occupation as a millwright and farmer. He died, in 1856, at the age of fifty five. He was a Baptist and a Whig. He had an extreme fondness for the science of mineralogy, and went one trip with the celebrated Dr. Gerard Troost, State geologist, on his exploring trip through East Tennessee, in order to gratify his taste in that direction, and was of much service to Dr. Troost on account of his knowledge of the country and its minerals. He left but little property, and the son has humorously remarked, "he had the honor of being born poor and has kept his inheritance."

Mr. Nelson's mother, *nee* Miss Dorcas Howard Ellis, was born in Iredell county, North Carolina, daughter of Jonathan Ellis, of an educated, prosperous family. Among her relatives, was Hon. Vespasian Ellis, formerly United States consul to Venezuela, and Gov. Ellis, of North Carolina. She died in Iowa, at the age of sixty-two. She was a well educated lady, and the son owes his first love of learning to her, though she found within him an ambition for knowledge and for being good from earliest childhood.

Rev. William A. Nelson, D. D., of Raleigh, North Carolina, is a brother of Mr. Anson Nelson. His brother, Rev. Daniel B. Nelson, is a retired minister in Henderson county, North Carolina. His brother, Maj. John Howard Nelson, is a farmer at Farmerville, Union parish, Louisiana. Another brother, H. H. Nelson, of Richland, Iowa, is one of the three supervisors of Keokuk county, Iowa, and still another brother, Samuel E. Nelson, is a farmer at Delta, Keokuk county, Iowa. Of his sisters, Eliza Nelson died the wife of Mr. Stone, at Bloomington, Illinois, leaving two children; and Mary Nelson died in Iowa, wife of Mr. Stone, leaving four children.

In personal appearance, Mr. Nelson may be described as of medium height, erect figure, compactly built, and weighing about one hundred and forty-five pounds. A study of his portrait shows a projecting brow, keenness of perception, and a forehead corrugated with the lines of earnest thought. His expression is that of intentness, as if following Solomon's advice, "Let thine eyes look right on, and thine eyelids straight before thee." One would at once proclaim him a man of fixed purpose and dignity of character. Financially, he has been a fair success for a man who seems never to have "made haste to be rich," or even to covet a large estate. When he first entered public office he adopted for his motto, "A good name is rather to be chosen than great riches," and this has greatly influenced his life, and, in turn, the influence of such a man must and will survive him for generations.

HON. D. W. C. SENTER.

EX-GOV. DeWITT CLINTON SENTER, was born in Rhea county, Tennessee, March 26, 1832, the son of Hon. William T. Senter, who, although a slave-holder, taught his son to look upon slavery as a misfortune and wrong in principle. Young Senter grew up, from the age of ten to twenty-one, on a farm in Grainger county, going to the neighboring country schools when they were in session. He attended Strawberry Plains College ten months, in 1851-2. He commenced reading law at home, in 1852, under the instruction of Hon. T. W. Turley, but had only read in a desultory sort of way about a year, when he was elected, in his twenty-third year, to represent Grainger county in the Legislature. He served not only that term, but by successive re-elections, in every Legislature up to 1861.

He was a stanch Union man, as were many of our best citizens among the liberty-loving mountaineers, and in the spring of 1862, was arrested by the Confederate authorities and made the grand southern tour, as a political prisoner, for about six months. Returning home and remaining about twelve months, he went into Kentucky, and remained there until quiet was partially restored in East Tennessee, by Federal occupation.

After the reorganization of the State government in 1865, he was elected to the State senate from the counties of Grainger, Anderson, Union, Claiborne and Campbell. In 1866-67, he was re-elected from the same counties; and when that body was organized, he was elected speaker of the senate. During this session, Gov. Brownlow being elected to the United States senate, Speaker Senter filled out his unexpired gubernatorial term of eighteen months as governor of Tennessee.

In 1869, he was elected governor by the people by the overwhelming majority of seventy thousand votes, defeating Gen. William B. Stokes. This campaign was one of the most notable in the annals of Tennessee politics. The difference between Gov. Senter and his competitor was on the franchise law, Gov. Senter taking position for the repeal of the law, upon the ground that every man who pays taxes ought to be entitled to vote. On this issue, he made a bold, brilliant campaign, completely routing his opponent, gaining one of the most signal victories in State politics, and wresting the State government from the hands of men who had hitherto administered its affairs with oppression and bitterness. After his election he induced the Legislature to call the State constitutional convention of 1870, which repealed the franchise law, which he had previously favored, prior to the reorganization of the State government, in the hands of loyal men. His party fealty was challenged by many Republicans in the State, but experience has vindicated the wisdom of changing policies with a change of the spirit and circumstances of the people and times.

Since the completion of his gubernatorial term, Gov. Senter has been engaged in farming, having served in the house of representatives six years, in the senate four years, and three and a half years as governor.

Prior to the war, Gov. Senter was a Whig, born, bred and early instructed in the principles advocated by Henry Clay. He afterward became a Republican, and has never cast a Democratic vote on principle, and was never defeated before the public for any office to which he aspired. In 1864, he was district presidential elector on the Lincoln and Johnson ticket, and in 1868, was an elector for the State at large on the Grant and Colfax ticket. His political record has been so satisfactory to his own feelings that he has retired from politics without a remorseful reflection upon himself, or a reproach from his fellow-citizens, whom he served so ably and faithfully.

Though raised by strict and pious Methodist parents, Gov. Senter has never attached himself to any church, a motto of his life being that if he once undertook anything he would go through with it. Never having felt the change called conversion, he deemed it would be unwise, if not hypocritical, to join a church and assume the responsibilities of a Christian character without first having had an experience of that change that would enable him well and truly to meet its obligations. A striking trait in Gov. Senter's character is his confidence in the ability and inclination of the American people to rectify wrongs or oppressions whenever they feel them, and to know when they are well off. In other words, he believes in the stability of the American republic.

Gov. Senter is a Master Mason, but belongs to no other secret society. He is in comfortable financial circumstances, and seems to enjoy very much the healthy and independent life of a prosperous and prudent East Tennessee farmer. In 1865-66, he was president of the Cincinnati, Cumberland Gap and Charlston railroad.

Gov. Senter married, in Grainger county, Tennessee, September 1, 1859, Miss Harriet T. Senter, a distant relative, daughter of Gen. P. M. Senter, county and circuit court clerk of Grainger county for about twenty years; a soldier in the army that moved the Cherokees from Florida, in 1837; a lieutenant in the Mexican war, and now practicing law at Rutledge, Grainger county. Mrs. Senter's mother, nee Miss Adeline E. McCraw, is the daughter of Gabriel McCraw, whose name is signed to more surveys and locations of lands than that of any man ever in East Tennessee. He was for many years sheriff of Hawkins county. Mrs. Senter was educated at the Female College, at Rogersville, and is an industrious home-woman, remarkable for her household economies, not addicted to extravagant living, fine dressing, nor fashionable life. While, strictly speaking, not a literary woman, she is well posted on the topics of the day. She prides herself more on making a greater quantity and nicer butter than any woman in the country.

The grandfather of Gov. Senter, was Tandy Senter, a native of Virginia, who lived to be one hundred and nine years old, and died near Kingston, Roane county, Tennessee, in 1866. He was in the war of 1812, was a life long farmer, and noted for raising fine horses. He married Miss Susan Lyon, of a Virginia family. He left twelve children by two marriages, six by each marriage.

Gov. Senter's father, Hon. William T. Senter, was born in Grainger county, married in Hawkins county, was first a merchant, then a minister of the Methodist Episcopal church, and later in life, in 1833, was a member of the State convention that revised the constitution of Tennessee. He was next district elector on the Harrison and Tyler ticket, in 1840; was the nominee of the Whig party for Congress against Abraham McClellan, but was defeated. In 1842, he was elected to Congress from the Second congressional district (then including Grainger county), served in 1843-44, and died in 1847, aged about forty-seven years. He was noted as being the most popular local preacher in East Tennessee, and had the power of carrying an audience, not alone by his brilliant eloquence, but by his known integrity, high moral character, and his even temperament, which kept him from quarreling with his neighbors about religion or politics.

Gov. Senter's mother, whose maiden name was Nancy White, was born in Hawkins county, Tennessee, daughter of Rev. George White, a Virginian, and a Methodist minister in the itinerant service. He was a strict family disciplinarian, and would stop any time in the middle of his sermon to rebuke any disorder he saw in church. He was a godly man of the old school, revered by young people as well as feared, and beloved by all. He married Miss Sarah Snodgrass, a daughter of Col. David Snodgrass, of Sullivan county, Tennessee, who was a colonel in the Revolutionary war, and for forty years before his death treasurer of Sullivan county. Gov. Senter's maternal grandmother, was a woman of remarkable piety, and religious without ostentation. Gov. Senter's mother, now in her seventy-fifth year, is still living on the old homestead. She has been the mother of seven children: (1). DeWitt Clinton Senter, subject of this sketch. (2). Susan Sarah Senter, now wife of Dr. Jos. P. Conway, in Hamblen county; has seven children, Sarah Porter (widow of Jacob Baker), Nancy, William, Charles, Joseph, DeWitt and Edward or "Pudgy." (3). Mary Lucinda Senter, unmarried. (4). Ann Eliza Senter, who died the wife of George M. Murrell, leaving three children, Martha, Ada and——— (5). Rebecca Senter, now wife of George A. Hodges, of Texas. (6). Nancy Senter, widow of Dr. John H. Everett; has three children, Wilmer, Robert and Sallie. (7). William T. Senter, now a Methodist minister in itinerant service; married Miss May Mayes, and has five children, DeWitt, Nancy, Rebecca, Harriet and William.

One of the cardinal points in Gov. Senter's character, even when a young man, was this: "Do nothing that will offend mother, or cause her to blush for anything I may do." And though wild and fond of gay life, he never did, even in his younger days, anything that was dishonorable. His mother, an old-fashioned, strong-minded woman, of the keenest, shrewdest observation, and of the strictest religious code, morning and night, invariably called her children together, read the Bible and prayed with her family and whoever might be present. And to the restraining influence of her counsel and example, to her ambition for her children to excel, Gov. Senter, with true filial gratitude, attributes his success in life. If he thought a thing was right, his principle has been to carry it out, regardless of cost or trouble or time.

COL. EDWARD I. GOLLADAY.

NASHVILLE.

EDWARD ISAAC GOLLADAY, subject of this sketch, widely and favorably known for his great abilities as a lawyer, a politician and a statesman, was born in Lebanon, Tennessee, September 9, 1831, the son of Isaac and Elizabeth Golladay. He began his school life, after some instruction at home, at the age of nine years, under Miss Harriet Abbe, formerly of Connecticut, who founded Abbe Institute, and afterward attended a classical school, Campbell Academy, under Prof. W. R. McDougall, an excellent New York educator, at that time located in Wilson county, Tennessee. At the age of twelve years he entered the literary department of Cumberland University, Lebanon, graduating at eighteen, with the degree of B.A. Among his schoolfellows were Wiley M. Reed, who became pastor of the First Cumberland Presbyterian church, Nashville, and afterward was a colonel in the Confederate army, and was killed at Fort Pillow; also Rev. W. E. Beeson, now president of a college in Texas, and Judge Samuel B. Vance, an eminent lawyer, formerly of Henderson, Kentucky, now of Evansville, Indiana.

He entered the law department of Cumberland University, under Judges Abram Caruthers and Nathan Green, sr., and was contemporary in the school with Hon. John F. House, Gen. Robert Hatton, Hon. H. Y. Riddle (who represented the Fourth congressional district in the Forty-fifth Congress), and several others who have attained eminence on the bench in other States. After graduation, he began practice at Lebanon, and, with the exception of intervals, which will be hereafter mentioned, remained there until March, 1881, when he moved to Nashville.

He married, in 1851, at the age of twenty, Miss Lou L. Cossitt, daughter of Rev. F. R. Cossitt, president of and professor of theology in Cumberland University, and one of the most profound classical scholars in the Cumberland Presbyterian church of that time. By his marriage with Miss Cossitt, he has one child, Fanny C. Golladay, born July 28, 1864, in Lebanon; educated at Lebanon and at Ward's seminary, Nashville.

In 1857, he was elected to the Legislature from Wilson county, on the conservative opposition, or Whig ticket, leading the ticket by about five hundred majority. At this session of the Legislature the adoption of the Code of Tennessee was passed upon, and he was a member of the judiciary committee; was also a member of the committee on corporations. In 1859, he was tendered the nomination of candidate for the State senate, but declined, being then under thirty years of age. In 1860, he was nominated at Murfreesborough, congressional elector on the Bell and Everett ticket; accepted; had as a competitor Gen. William B. Bate (now governor), who represented Breckinridge and Lane; was elected, being the youngest member of the electoral college.

In September, 1861, he enlisted as a private in the Confederate service, in a company called the "Caruthers Grays," and was elected captain of the company. In October, 1861, he was elected lieutenant-colonel of the Thirty-eighth Tennessee infantry regiment, Col. R. F. Looney, of Memphis, in command. The regiment was composed of Tennesseans, Alabamians and Georgians. He participated in the engagements at Hartsville, Shiloh, Pittsburg Landing, Chickasaw, Monterey, and Corinth. In November, 1863, he was captured in Wilson county and sent to Gen. Lovell H. Rousseau, commanding at Nashville; gave his parole, and a bond not to engage further in hostilities; was released and remained within the Federal lines. He resumed his law practice, both at Lebanon and Nashville.

In 1870, he became a Democratic candidate for Congress from the Hermitage district, embracing Davidson, Wilson, Williamson, Robertson, Cheatham and Trousdale counties; canvassed the district against Hon. William O'Neill Perkins, Gen. Tom Benton Smith, Col. James J. Turner, Col. Joseph Mottley and the Hon. Bailie Beyton. He received the nomination in convention at Nashville, and was opposed in the election before the people by the Hon. Bailie Peyton, an eminent politician, and the Hon. William F. Prosser (Republican), then sitting member for the district. He was elected, beating Prosser by nearly six thousand, and Peyton by over three thousand votes. He took his seat as a member of the Forty-second Congress, March 4, 1871. The right of the whole Tennessee delegation to be seated was disputed, and an especial contest of Golladay's seat was made by Prosser. Col. Golladay delivered an effective written argument in behalf of the Tennessee delegation before the committee on elections, which was ordered to be printed. The report of the committee was unanimous in favor of seating the whole Tennessee delegation; Congress adopted it without a dissenting vote, and the contest by Prosser was dropped. He was a member of the committee on patents, and of the committee on mileage. He delivered speeches against the famous "kuklux" and "civil rights" bills, both of which measures have since been pronounced unconstitutional by the Supreme court of the United States. In common with Hons. Daniel W. Vorhees, James A. Garfield, S. S. Cox, Samuel J. Randall, and the great majority of the eminent Republican and Democratic members of the Forty-second Congress, he voted for what was known as the "salary grab bill," and has always possessed the sturdy manhood to defend his action and maintain his integrity in this matter. He introduced and secured the passage of the bill for the purchase of the property for the construction of the custom-house at Nashville. He secured appropriation for the first time in congressional history for the improvement of Cumberland river, securing as much as two hundred and forty-five thousand dollars in his one term, making the river a familiar in the river and harbor bills since passed, for further appropriations. He also introduced a bill for the dedication of all the public lands belonging to the United States for educational purposes, and for an equal distribution of the lands or their proceeds for this use among the respective States, according to population, and asking for an account from all the States that had received such grants from Congress.

In 1872, a year made famous by what is known as the Johnson-Cheatham canvass, he was the nominee of the Democratic party in the Nashville district for Congress, but was defeated by Horace H. Harrison (Republican); a defeat brought about by dissensions produced in the Democratic ranks by reason of Mr. Johnson's candidacy.

He was, in 1874, a candidate for nomination before the Democratic convention, which met at Hartsville, and came within a few votes of being nominated. The convention could not agree on any of the aspirants before it, and took up Hon. S. M. Fite, of Carthage, who had not been a candidate, and who, having been elected, died before taking his seat. Strangely enough, Col. John W. Head, of Gallatin, who was elected to fill the vacancy, also died before taking his seat, when Hon. H. Y. Riddle, of Lebanon, was elected, took his seat, and sometime after committed suicide, during a temporary mental aberration.

In 1878, at the instance of many friends, Col. Golladay made an independent canvass for Congress, in the Fourth district, against Hon. Benton McMillin, who had been nominated, without having been a candidate, over the heads of all aspirants, including Col. James J. Turner, Col. John P. Murray and R. C. Sanders. Col. Golladay refused to go into convention, claiming that the Democratic majority was so large that no convention was needed. In this race he was defeated, receiving, however, a very handsome vote, and carrying Wilson county triumphantly.

Col. Golladay was, for many years, a trustee of Cumberland University, his old *alma mater*, which position he resigned in 1881, on removing to Nashville. Since 1878, he has not been an aspirant for any public honors.

Whatever success Col. Golladay has attained, is due to his education and the practice of integrity and industry in his profession, coupled with his powers of public speaking, at the bar and on the hustings. There are few better debaters in Tennessee, and still fewer who can win the hearts of an audience and carry them along *en rapport* with his fervid, burning, fiery eloquence.

He was brought up in the Cumberland Presbyterian church, of which his parents were members, but is strongly attached to the doctrines and ritual of the Episcopal church. He is a Mason of the Royal Arch degree; has passed all the chairs in Odd Fellowship; is a member of the Improved Order of Red Men, having attained the degree of Chief; also of the Knights of Pythias; but is not a frequent attendant at the meetings of any of the societies mentioned, his occupation in life being such that he has but little time to keep up his associations with these excellent orders.

Col. Golladay's father was born near Staunton, Virginia, and, when about four years of age, was bound out, being an orphan, to a kinsman, a farmer. At the age of seventeen he ran away and went to Maryland, and became clerk in a dry goods store in Hagerstown.

At that place he met Miss Elizabeth Shall, whom he married. In 1816, he moved to Lebanon, Tennessee, and engaged in merchandising with his brother-in-law, Michael Yerger, the father of the distinguished family of Yergers of Tennessee and Mississippi, famous as lawyers, judges and law reporters. By his marriage with Miss Shall he had ten children, eight sons and two daughters, Col. Golladay being the youngest. Of these children: (1). Samuel Golladay, was for many years a merchant in Nashville and Lebanon; died at Col. Golladay's residence, in 1873, unmarried; one of the purest and best of men. (2). George Shall Golladay, was a lawyer in Mississippi, and several times elected to the Legislature of that State; died in Memphis, in 1872. (3). Hon. Jacob S. Golladay, now a farmer and lawyer in Logan county, Kentucky; was several times a member of the Legislature of Kentucky, and twice a member from his district to the Fortieth and Forty-first Congresses. (4). Frederick Golladay, now a farmer in Wilson county, and resident in Washington, D. C. (5). Robert H. Golladay, is a lawyer of superior ability in Grenada, Mississippi, and a man of great modesty and worth. (6). David Golladay, died in infancy. (7). John Golladay, died also in infancy. (8). Carrie M. Golladay, died in 1865, the wife of Thomas J. Stratton, cashier of the Second National Bank, Lebanon, leaving four sons, all in business in Lebanon. (9). Sarah Ann Golladay, married Rev. W. W. Bell; now a widow, living in Kansas. (10). Edward Isaac Golladay, subject of this sketch.

Col. Golladay's father was a man of very strong common sense, of high morals and integrity; economical and strict in the government and management of his family; of great sobriety; of limited education, but a good letter writer and a correct speller, writing a very fine hand. He was a man of magnificent personnel; a devoted friend and admirer of Andrew Jackson, and a man very warm in his friendships and attachments. He was appointed postmaster directly after he began merchandising in Lebanon, and remained in office through all the successive changes of administration—Whig and Democratic—till his death, which occurred at Lebanon, October 6, 1848, at the age of sixty-seven years.

Col. Golladay's paternal grandfather was a soldier under Washington, being at Valley Forge and at Trenton, where he was wounded.

The Golladays are of French extraction, the family name, as originally spelt, being Gallaudet.

Col. Golladay's mother was born in Hagerstown, Maryland, in 1787, and was the youngest of six children. Her sister, Margaret, died the wife of Michael Yerger, by whom she had eleven children, ten sons and one daughter. Col. Golladay's mother was an eminently domestic woman, occupied entirely in the care and training of her children and the comfort of her husband and family. She was very strict, yet very tender and kind and motherly. The children were all taught to work and to be useful. She, as well as her husband, made every effort to afford them the best education the means and the times and country afforded. She was of German or Dutch origin, and possessed all of the sturdy, sterling qualities of that people. In June, 1872, Col. Golladay, accompanied by his wife and daughter, visited Hagerstown, Maryland, and was shown by an old aunt, Mrs. Kittie Kausler, the parlor in which his mother and herself were courted by the young gallants, who afterwards became their respective husbands; also, the old spring from which the family obtained water, and the ancient Lutheran church in which his father and mother were married, now somewhat changed in its architecture.

In physique and facial expression, Col. Golladay is a most attractive man. He stands five feet ten inches in height; weighs about two hundred and six pounds; has dark, piercing black eyes; intensely black hair, slightly streaked with gray; looks the very picture of robust good health, and impresses one with the idea that he sprang from good, strong stock, physically, mentally and morally.

THOMAS E. MOORE, M. D.

BOLIVAR.

THIS gentleman, who is justly regarded as one of the representative physicians and surgeons of Tennessee, was born in Huntsville, Alabama, August 18, 1819. His ancestors on both sides were originally from Virginia. His grandfather, Rev. John Moore, was a Methodist minister and farmer, a pioneer settler in Alabama. His father, John F. Moore, was a prosperous farmer, born in Brunswick county, Virginia; emigrated to Alabama when it was a territory; located in Madison county, Alabama, where he died, in 1835, at the age of fifty-five years. Of Dr. Moore's paternal relatives who distinguished themselves, there were his uncle, Dr. David Moore, of Huntsville, who served several terms in the senate and lower house of the Alabama Legislature; his cousin, Hon. Suydenham Moore, son of Dr. Alfred Moore, who was a congressman from Alabama when secession took place, and his brother, John E. Moore, who was circuit judge in the Florence, Alabama, district.

Dr. Moore's mother was Miss Nancy Fletcher, daughter of Richard Fletcher, a native of Brunswick county, Virginia, and one of the early settlers in Alabama. She died in 1832, at the age of forty, having borne twelve children, nine of whom survived her: (1). James Moore. (2). Maria Moore, who died the wife of John Malone. (3). Dr. John R. Moore, now a large farmer near Greensborough, Alabama. (4). Leonidas Moore. (5). Dr. Thomas E. Moore, subject of this sketch. (6). Martha Moore, who died the wife of John M. Moore. (7). Matthew Moore. (8). Robert Moore. (9). Albert Moore.

Thomas E. Moore was raised at Huntsville, and educated in the schools and academies there. At eighteen, he began the study of medicine with his brother, Dr. John R. Moore, of Greensborough, Alabama, and after reading with him two years went to the Transylvania University at Lexington, Kentucky, in 1838, graduating there in the spring of 1842, under Profs. Dudley, Bush, Mitchell, N. R. Smith, Cross and Peter. Returning to Alabama, in June, 1842, he soon afterward removed to Bolivar, Tennessee, and permanently located, where he has practiced ever since, now forty-four years. His practice has been extensive and lucrative from the first. Before the war he invested his surplus income in land and negroes. Since the war, also, he has been a financial success, and this too, notwithstanding the fact that the legitimate medical fraternity is not protected in Tennessee, the country abounding in so-called physicians, almost totally incompetent, but patronized out of the comity of the neighborhoods where they live. Whether the Legislature or the medical colleges are responsible for this grievous state of affairs, and are to be held accountable because the medical profession is so poorly represented, or rather so badly misrepresented, it matters not, yet it is as certain as that health and life are preferable to sickness and death, that no man without an honestly-earned diploma should be allowed to practice medicine, and that the standard of qualification for a diploma should be measured by the most advanced medical science. The skill, experience and learning of Dr. Moore have been widely appreciated, both profess-

ionally and financially; is recognized over the State, and he presents in himself a notable example of that elevated dignity which the profession in general should attain.

Dr. Moore is the president of the medical board at Bolivar, and stands high in the profession. He is especially successful in the management of diseases of women and children. His success came of strict attention to business, economical habits, and a sober life, never dissipating in any way. In politics he has always been Democratic, as were his father and relatives before him, but he has never taken much part in party contests, confining himself strictly to his profession. He is an Odd Fellow, and a strong Methodist in principle, though not a communicant.

Dr. Moore has been twice married. He first married, in Bolivar, in 1848, Miss Elizabeth Joy, daughter of Levi and Martha Joy, nee Johnson. His wife died in 1849, leaving one child, a daughter, Alice, now wife of Mr. M. B. Hardaway, a planter, in Benton county, Mississippi, who has six children, Lizzie, Alice, Virginia, Lucie, Mingibus and Morgan.

Dr. Moore next married, in Marshall county, Mississippi, March 20, 1855, Miss Susan Morgan, daughter of Maj. J. H. Morgan, a planter. Her mother was Miss Lucie Jeffreys, originally from North Carolina. The second wife died December 25, 1879, at the age of forty years, leaving one child, a son, Thomas Morgan Moore, born March 5, 1856; educated at the University of the South, Sewanee, Tennessee; now a druggist and farmer at Bolivar.

Dr. Moore is a man of noble physical proportions stands six feet two and a half inches in height, and weighs two hundred and twenty-five pounds. His features are strongly marked, and the impression he makes is that of a man of force, while his promptness in speaking, and the clear, confident tones of his voice, indicate a man who has strong faith in his own rectitude and convictions. He is a man of sterling integrity, conservative in all things, radical in nothing, and with much of the milk of human kindness in his nature.

DAVID JOBE GIBSON, M. D.

JONESBOROUGH.

THE subject of this sketch was born on his grandfather's farm, near what is now Johnson City, Washington county, Tennessee, April 17, 1822, and grew to ten years of age in that immediate vicinity. His father then located near Jonesborough, and in that town Dr. Gibson has had his home ever since, with the exception of some three years, which he spent at Asheville, North Carolina.

In his boyhood he worked some on the farm, but went to school most of the time, intending, from the age of sixteen, to become a physician. In his case is but another illustration of early inclinations being turned in the right channel, and should prove to parents that children ought to be permitted at an early date to begin preparation for the special pursuit or profession for which nature seems to have destined them. He spent

40

three years, 1840–43, as a student in Washington College, then under President Alexander Doak, whose grandfather, Samuel Doak, founded that school, the first institution of learning in Tennessee. After leaving college, he studied medicine under Dr. Samuel Cunningham three years, at Jonesborough, occasionally visiting his patients with him, and assisting in numerous surgical operations. He then attended one course of lectures in the medical department of the Transylvania University, Lexington, Kentucky, and afterward went to Asheville, North Carolina, where, for three years, he practiced medicine. He then attended a course of lectures at the Philadelphia College of Medicine, and graduated in 1851, under Profs. Mitchell, Van Dyke, McClintock, Fickardt, and others. After graduation he came to Jonesborough, where he has practiced his profession ever since, doing an extensive and laborious practice, during which he has performed such surgical operations as strangulated hernia, amputations, etc. He is president of the Medical Association of Washington county, and president of the examining board of United States surgeons for applicants for pensions, and was secretary of the board for ten years.

Before the dissolution of the Whig party, Dr. Gibson was a Whig; since then he has been a Republican, but has never held office, except that of alderman of Jonesborough. He joined the Presbyterian church at the age of thirty, and has been an elder in that church the past twelve years.

Dr. Gibson married, first, in Asheville, North Carolina, in 1850, Miss Harriet E. Johnston, daughter of William Johnston, a wealthy merchant, general trader and cotton manufacturer, a native of Ireland. Her mother was Lucinda Gudger, daughter of James Gudger, a prominent citizen of Buncombe county, North Carolina, and member of the Legislature of that State. Mrs. Gibson died in 1852.

Dr. Gibson next married, at Jonesborough, Tennessee, in June, 1859, Miss Sarah A. Kelly, a native of Atkinson, New Hampshire, daughter of John Kelly, a lawyer. Her mother, Mary Chase, was a relative of Judge Salmon P. Chase, the famous secretary of the treasury under Mr. Lincoln. Mrs. Gibson's only paternal uncle, Dr. Nathaniel Kelly, is a prominent physician at Plaiston, New Hampshire, now eighty-four years of age. Her only brother, Henry A. Kelly, is a lawyer, recently in government employ at Washington. Her only sister, Miss Mary E. Kelly, resides at Atkinson, New Hampshire. Mrs. Gibson was educated at Mount Holyoke, Massachusetts; is an active working member of the Presbyterian church; a woman of very positive character, untiring in her efforts at any thing she undertakes, especially church work, in which she has been prominent ever since she came to Jonesborough. She has a very vigorous and well trained mind, and is in full sympathy with the independent spirit and progressive aspirations of East Tennesseans. She has strong convictions of right and wrong, and adheres to them so rigidly that it has been said of her that she would make fine material for a martyr. She was first president of the Woman's Synodical Missionary Society, and is president of the Jonesborough Women's Missionary Society. She came to Jonesborough with a class-mate and fellow-teacher, Miss Sarah Jane Foster, now the widow of Rev. Samuel Rhea, who died a missionary in Persia. His widow now resides at Lake Forest, Illinois.

By his marriage with Miss Kelly, Dr. Gibson has three children : (1). Harriet Elizabeth Gibson, born June —, 1860; graduated at Andover, Massachusetts, in 1881; is a member of the Presbyterian church, and a very active and devoted worker in her church, indefatigable in every work she undertakes, in this respect a reproduction of her mother. She has taught private literary schools at Jonesborough, is a Sunday-school teacher, treasurer of the Woman's Presbyterial Missionary Society, and leader of the Juvenile Missionary Board, Jonesborough. She married, April 23, 1885, John W. Heron, M.D., of Jonesborough, an Englishman by birth, and in May following sailed with him for Corea, where he is medical missionary under the auspices of the Presbyterian Board of Foreign Missions. (2). John Henry Gibson, born May, 1862; educated at Jonesborough; now engaged in business at Asheville, North Carolina. (3). David J. Gibson, jr., born ——, 1873.

The Gibsons are of Scotch-Irish stock. Thomas Gibson, the grandfather of Dr. Gibson, came from Dublin, Ireland, and settled in Washington county, at the " stone house," near Carter's depot, and engaged in school teaching. He died at an early age. He married a Miss Dungan, daughter of Jeremiah Dungan, a prominent citizen of his time, and the owner of a mill and other property, including the "stone house." He left three children : (1). Jeremiah Gibson, father of Dr. Gibson. (2). Thomas Gibson, who died in Washington county, a farmer. (3). Orphia Gibson, who died the wife of Seth Thompson.

Dr. Gibson's father, Jeremiah Gibson, was born at the " stone house," lived a successful farmer, was in the war of 1812, and died at the age of eighty-four, distinguished for those sterling East Tennessee virtues, integrity and truthfulness, and for being kind-hearted and generous to the poor. It is said he never turned want away from his door, and was esteemed highly by his neighbors and friends. He was not a man to color the truth, but uniformly made his statement cover the exact facts of the situation. A singular and a commendable peculiarity of this gentleman was, that whenever he told his servants to do anything, he told them the reason why he wanted it done.

Dr. Gibson's mother, nee Phebe Jobe, was born in Shenandoah county, Virginia, daughter of David Jobe, a farmer, who moved to Washington county, Tennessee, when the daughter was a child, located at the place now known as Johnson City, which is situated on what was his farm. He was a very quiet man, and possessed of considerable property. Dr. Gibson's mother held to the Baptist faith. She was self-sacrificing and kind-hearted, especially to the distressed, of most excellent practical sense, and ruled her household by kindness. Dr. Gibson, with some pride, states that his mother never struck him a lick, and that he always obeyed her. One of the few instances parallel to this is in the history of Bishop Kavanaugh, of whom his biographer relates that he never disobeyed his mother. All honor and blessing is the promise to sons who thus honor father and mother. She died at the age of eighty-four, the mother of but one child, the subject of this sketch.

Beginning life without inheritance, he is now in comfortable circumstances, owns a drug store and considerable real estate in Jonesborough. It is not so much owing to want of personal pride or energy that some young men become failures, but from ignorance of the science of success, the law of thrift. Dr. Gibson,

though reared tenderly, had pride of character and ambition to get a start, accumulate property and make his mark in the world. He has never been extravagant or wasteful, but has been a bad collector, too lenient and indulgent with his numerous dilatory patients. A man may be so good to others as to be unjust to his own family, but Dr. Gibson's desire has been to do right and so conduct himself as to win the confidence, respect and approbation of his fellow men. One of his aims is to bring as much sunshine as he can into the world, and, so far as his professional abilities enable him, to relieve human suffering. It seems an absolute pleasure to him to speak a kind word to a ragged, or make a sorrowing child happy by a kind word or act. Affectionate in disposition, exceedingly sympathetic, modest and candid to a fault, he is one's beau ideal of a family physician. He has strongly marked features, a Roman nose, very gray and plentiful hair, and a voice so very tender that it must be itself a tonic and a hope to one on a sick-bed. Indeed, he is one of those men, of whom people are apt to say, "It is a great pity the State has not a hundred thousand such men as he."

HON. CHARLES BRYSON SIMONTON.

COVINGTON.

THE following biographical sketch of Hon. Charles Bryson Simonton, one of the most distinguished and promising of the younger generation of Tennessee lawyers and statesmen, furnishes another striking example of what a Tennessee boy can do to rise superior to his circumstances, and, by force of that genius and merit which ever assert themselves, compel public recognition of an inherited manhood. It is always a pleasant task to extol merit, but it is eminently so when the subject is as modest as praiseworthy, and when the record will prove as interesting and instructive as it is true to life.

Charles Bryson Simonton is of Scotch-Irish parentage, and was born near Porterville, Tipton county, Tennessee, September 8, 1838. His paternal grandfather, John Simonton, came over from Ireland about 1757, when but fourteen years of age, an orphan, and, with his three sisters, settled in York district, South Carolina, afterward removing to Fairfield district, on Little river, in the same State, where, after a successful career as a planter, he died, leaving four sons and four daughters. He married Martha Strong, sister of Christopher Strong, of Dickson county, Tennessee, who was a very successful farmer and business man, accumulated a large property, and made many benevolent bequests at his death. He is the ancestor of many highly respected families in Middle and West Tennes-

see, Arkansas and Mississippi, bearing the names of Strong, Dickson and Bowen.

A large family of sons and daughters was reared at the Fairfield home, and many of their descendants today are citizens of South Carolina, among whom may be mentioned the Brices, Wilsons and Douglases—names that have figured in useful and honorable pursuits, many of them as ornaments in the learned professions. Of the latter, no citizen of the Palmetto State enjoys a larger share of the confidence and esteem of his people, than Col. Charles H. Simonton, the well-known lawyer and distinguished politician. He is the son of Charles Simonton, uncle of Charles B. Simonton, subject of this sketch. Two of his sisters married Brices, gentlemen of wealth in South Carolina, and their children occupy positions of influence as ministers, lawyers and physicians in that State.

Charles B. Simonton's father, William Simonton, the fourth son of John Simonton, was a native of South Carolina, born in 1790. His wife, nee Miss Katie Ferguson, was born in the same State. They removed to what was then the wilderness of West Tennessee, locating in Tipton county, in the winter of 1829–30. With his brother, Robert Simonton, he cleared a farm, and soon after erected the first cotton gin-house in the county. The venture was not financially successful, and four years after the birth of the subject of this sketch, the father died (in 1843), at the age of fifty-three, leaving his widow with eight children, and provided with but a meager support. The youngest of the eight children, Charles B. Simonton, was brought up to labor on the farm—a task which in the South means the most arduous toil for the greater portion of the year. With his brothers he wielded the hoe and followed the plow from day to day, and in the fullness of time helped to gather in the crop that was the support of the family. If he ever repined, it was at the thought that fate had denied him the advantages of education; the only facilities in that regard being the wretched winter schools of the period. When he was fifteen years old, his uncle, John Simonton, of Fairfield, South Carolina, a man of means, while on a visit to Tennessee, observing the intelligence, sobriety and studious habits of his nephews, determined to afford them the opportunity for a classical education. His proposition was to first educate an older brother, William W. Simonton, but to this generous proposition, Charley, emboldened to improve this chance in life, suggested as an amendment that it would be still better if the uncle would send two of the boys to school instead of one, himself to be the second. Thus taking the tide at its flood shaped his future. The amendment was accepted, and the two brothers were sent, first to a school at Porterville, then taught by Rev. J. A. Dixon, now a Presbyterian divine at Pine Bluff, Arkansas (who had married their niece, Miss Kate McCain), and Rev. James H. Strong, now pastor of Salem church, Tipton county. Here they completed a preparatory course prior to entering Erskine College, South Carolina. This latter institution the boys attended three years, graduating in August, 1859, Charley being elected by the Euphemian literary society to represent it on commencement day, a distinction which, added to the honor of receiving the long coveted diploma on the same occasion, made that the proudest day of his life. The members of the society were gratified at his effort as their representative, the audience was delighted, and his friends interpreted his oration as indicating future eminence and usefulness.

The young Tennessean left college utterly without means in a pecuniary sense, but rich in grand possibilities. He had acquired the right to advancement, and he intended to advance. The school-room was his arena for a time, where he intended to achieve that success, and therefore, after graduation, he returned home and taught school in the academy where he had formerly been a student, and continued to teach with acceptance until the day he heard of the firing on Fort Sumter.

The boom of those guns echoing through the land, transformed the quiet and studious young teacher into the ardent and impetuous soldier. He did not wait for the secession of his State, but joined the first company raised in Tipton county for the Confederate service, company C, under Capt. D. J. Wood, of the famous

Ninth Tennessee infantry, Col. H. L. Douglass commanding. Company C was composed of the flower of Tipton's young men, and no one was permitted in its ranks without the unanimous consent of its members. Charles B. Simonton was elected second-lieutenant without opposition. He was present at the battle of Belmont. At the battle of Shiloh he commanded his company in the second day's action, and at the reorganization of the army at Corinth, May, 1862, he was chosen captain, receiving ninety-six votes of ninety-seven cast in the election. In the engagement at Perryville, Col. Buford having been disabled, Capt. Simonton took command and pressed the enemy until he too fell, very seriously wounded. Here company C lost more than half its members in killed and wounded. Left upon the field, the young officer was taken prisoner, and for six months lay at the point of death. Lingering in hospitals, unable to sit at the table for his meals, from the date of his wound, October 8, 1862, till the following Christmas, he at length partially recovered. The cartel for exchange of prisoners being abrogated and paroles revoked, on March 10, 1863, he and two comrades quietly procured horses, and, unobserved, started for Dixie, thus undertaking a task for which his frail body was in nowise fitted, and would not have sustained had he not been upheld by an iron resolution that surmounted all obstacles.

He rejoined the army at Shelbyville, Tennessee, after an absence of seven months, though unable for duty. He, however, remained with his command until the following August, when, being advised by his surgeon that he could not again be fit for service, he resigned. He was then the senior captain of his regiment, had been in the campaigns in Missouri, Mississippi, Tennessee and Kentucky, and participated in at least three of the hottest fights in the west—Belmont, Shiloh and Perryville. His reluctant resignation, however, was compelled by despair of ever recovering from the wound he received at Perryville—a minnie-ball having shattered his left shoulder—and which totally disabled him for over two years, and from the effects of which now, twenty-two years later, he has not the full swing of his left arm. The close of the war found him at the bedside of a brother, who shortly afterward expired from wounds received in battle. So cruel were the desolations of war that they robbed his family of four members, himself of four brothers.

Of these brothers, Christopher Simonton was successfully engaged in agriculture before the war; went into the Confederate army; had his house and barn, crib and stables burned by the Federals; died in hospital in Dallas county, Alabama, and now lies buried at New Hope church, near Forts, in that county. Presley Simonton, also a farmer, served in the Fifty-first Tennessee, Col. Browder's (afterward Chester's) regiment; returned home, and sickened and died in August, 1862. His sister, Miss Mary Simonton, who waited on him, also sickened, and survived him only six weeks. Robert C. Simonton was a merchant at Salem, Arkansas; enlisted in the Twelfth Tennessee regiment (Richardson's brigade); served under Forrest during the whole war; fell a victim to camp fever in 1865, and died just as the news of Lee's surrender reached his brother, Capt. Charles Simonton, who was standing at his bedside. William W. Simonton, after leaving Erskine College, taught school in Dallas county, Alabama; married Miss Maggie Moore, daughter of Col. Robert Moore; went to farming after his marriage; enlisted as a private in the Twenty-seventh Alabama regiment; was twice wounded in battle; surrendered at Goldsborough, North Carolina; returned home and died two years afterward of wounds received in service.

Capt. Simonton's oldest sister, Martha Simonton, first married Albert McCain, and afterward her present husband, J. C. Davis, and now resides in Dorsey county, Arkansas. His sister, Sarah A. Simonton, married Charles F. Strong, a farmer, residing near Atoka, Tipton county. Capt. Simonton's half-sister, Margaret, married Ross McCain, a prominent citizen of Tipton county. Their son, William S. McCain, is an attorney of reputation at Pine Bluff, Arkansas.

After his resignation from the army, Capt. Simonton returned home and resumed teaching at Porterville While engaged in teaching there he married, October 16, 1866, Miss Mary McDill, daughter of Capt. Robert McDill, a merchant of that village, a Presbyterian elder, and of Scotch descent. United States Senator McDill, of Iowa, is a member of the same family. Mrs. Simonton's mother was a Miss McCreight, of a South Carolina family, also of Scotch blood. Mrs. Simonton was educated at the schools at Porterville and Covington, and is characterized by gentleness, devotion to duty, wonderful fortitude and unusual resolution. Her charms of mind and manner make her a prime favorite in the social circles in which she moves.

By his marriage with Miss McDill, Capt. Simonton has five children: Anna, Ella, William M., Charles P. and Nannie May.

Mrs. Simonton had three brothers in the Confederate service. Scott McDill fell at Chickamauga, William S. McDill was killed at Franklin, and George W. McDill was shot through the right breast at Perryville, and was thought to be mortally wounded, but recovered; rejoined his command, Ninth Tennessee regiment, Maney's brigade, Cheatham's division, and surrendered at the close of the war, at Greensborough, North Carolina.

Capt. Simonton is an hereditary Democrat. Trying to rebuild his shattered health and shattered fortunes, he was occupied in the school-room until 1870, when he announced himself a candidate for circuit court clerk, and made the race against Nat Tipton, a very influential and popular citizen, defeating him by the handsome majority of six hundred and fifty votes. Having studied

law at intervals, and whenever he could spare the time from the serious business of making a living, he was admitted to the bar, in 1873, by Judges Flippin and Walker, and has since continued the practice very successfully, financially, and gaining reputation, especially as an advocate. In 1874, after a bitter contest, he was re-elected clerk by a greatly increased majority. In 1876, he resigned this place, having been nominated as the Democratic candidate for the Legislature from his county, and was elected, though the Dorsey B. Thomas opposition carried the county by more than two hundred votes. This canvass was exceedingly bitter and personal, and the tact and ability displayed in it, especially his self-possession, under trying circumstances, laid the foundation for Capt. Simonton's future promotion. In the Legislature he served on the judiciary and federal relations committees.

Two years later, that is, in 1878, he was a candidate for Congress in the Ninth congressional district, comprising the counties of Tipton, Lauderdale, Dyer, Obion, Lake, Weakley, Gibson, Crockett and Haywood. He came to the convention with four opponents, one of whom was the son of the late Hon. John Bell, of Tennessee, and the equal of his distinguished father in ability and attainments. Capt. Simonton received the nomination, and was elected to the Forty-sixth Congress. He defeated Mr. Bell again in convention in 1880, and was returned to his seat in the Forty-seventh Congress. During the canvass for this term, he was opposed by a coalition candidate, nominated by the low-tax greenback convention, in the person of Mr. George Mathis, of Trenton, a gentleman who had gained considerable reputation as an expert stumper and debater. Mr. Mathis abandoned the race after the first meeting.

Of Capt. Simonton's ability as a congressman, the Baltimore (Maryland) *Baltimorean* said: "Mr. Simonton, as a legislator, is for the useful and practical, a thorough economist, and the enemy of class legislation and jobs. He is a good parliamentarian, and was often called during the Forty-sixth Congress to preside in committee of the whole, during the consideration of most important and difficult matters, which he did with much credit to himself and satisfaction to the house. His knowledge of parliamentary details enable him always, in connection with intelligent attention to the proceedings, to understand the status of pending measures. He is up with the business, attentive and watchful. He is not often address the House, but when he does, has the satisfaction of receiving its respectful and considerate attention. In committee work, the most important legislative duties, he is painstaking and laborious, and has made a number of reports, involving much labor and research—prominent among which was his report on the claim of certain descendants of officers of the Revolutionary war, involving more than sixteen million dollars, and the investigation of which requires a knowledge of the proceedings of the continental Congress, as well as the fiscal history of the government after the adoption of the constitution of 1789."

During his service in Congress Capt. Simonton also made considerable reputation by the able speech he delivered on the bill for appointing a tariff commission.

By the redistricting of his congressional district by the Legislature of 1882, his county was attached to the Tenth or Memphis district, and the people whom he had so acceptably served that he had broken down all opposition to his re-election, were thus deprived of the opportunity of returning him to Congress; hence his retirement from that branch of the public service.

To the honor of his Christian mother is due the fact that Capt. Simonton was a regular attendant at Sunday-school from a boy, and probably also that he is now a Sunday-school teacher and an elder in the Presbyterian church. He is a Knight of Honor, a member of the order of Knights and Ladies of Honor, and Master Workman of the Ancient Order of United Workmen. For ten years he has been a member of the board of trustees of Tipton Female Seminary.

It is said he has made more speeches than any other man in Tipton county and on many subjects—temperance, education, Sunday-school celebrations, Young Men's Christian Association, literary addresses, and on commencement occasions, anniversaries, and the like.

Since he has been keeping house, there has been no time when he and his wife have not had in their home at least one, and often two or even three orphans, schooling and caring for them—most of them related either to himself or her, thus paying to others the debt of gratitude he owes to the uncle who sent him to college and helped him to a start in life.

During the year 1875 he edited the Tipton *Record*. While running this paper he made it a lively sheet, calling public attention to many official irregularities, as well as making it educational in its progressive tone.

Briefly stated, the elements that have combined in Capt. Simonton, and enabled him to succeed, are: first, determined effort; second, to never miss an opportunity he thought he could honorably improve to his advantage. He found out very early in life that if he waited for somebody to find places for him and put him along, he would never reach the desired end; that he had these things to work out for himself. His observation had taught him that success rarely comes with a single effort, but by repeated effort and the use of many expedients, and victory has often to be snatched from the jaws of seeming defeat. The man who succeeds is he who can fight hardest when fortune seems against him. The most useful lever of success is a well-schooled mind, coupled with a resolution to conquer obstacles and attain excellence.

In person, Capt. Simonton is of medium height, well and compactly built, has a fine eye, whose glance is shot square and straight at his auditor, most pleasant and engaging manners, and is in the very prime of life; a life wholly pure and unsullied—one that is a pride to possess, and should be an honor to uphold.

NICK D. RICHARDSON, M. D.

NASHVILLE.

THIS popular and successful physician and surgeon was born at Athens, Alabama, November 30, 1832. His father was William Richardson, a prominent lawyer at that place, for several years attorney-general of Alabama, and representative of Limestone county in the Alabama Legislature, from 1830 to 1833. He died in 1866, in his sixty-ninth year. He stood in the front rank of Alabama lawyers; was a man of the highest integrity; never sought office, and at one time declined appointment to a judgeship. He stood particularly high as a chancery lawyer, and had a legal reputation as the peer of the best and ablest men in Alabama. He was a Virginian by birth and education; for a time, about 1819, filled the chair of ancient languages in Washington-Lee University; came to Alabama in 1821, and settled as a pioneer.

Dr. Richardson's grandfather, William Richardson, was a Virginia planter, slave-holder and fine stock-breeder. He was a patriot soldier in the Revolutionary war. On his father's side he was of English, and on his mother's side of Irish blood.

Dr. Richardson's mother, *nee* Miss Ann Davis, was a native of Hanover county, Virginia, daughter of Capt. Nick Davis, an officer in the war of 1812. He emigrated to Alabama at an early date; was president of the Alabama senate thirteen years; a member of the Alabama State constitutional convention, in 1819, and the recognized leader of the Whig party in that State during its existence. He was a close and intimate personal friend of Henry Clay—the two being raised as boys, within a stone's throw of each other, in "the slashes of Hanover." Capt. Davis died at his homestead in Alabama, in 1856, at the age of seventy-five years, a man universally beloved, wealthy, charitable, hospitable, and a great lover of fine stock, especially thoroughbred racers. It is related of him that he was particularly partial to hard working men, who always found welcome at his house and table. He married Miss Patsey Hargrove, of a

Virginia Quaker family. His son, Col. Nick Davis, jr., maternal uncle of Dr. Richardson, was a brilliant lawyer at Huntsville; was attorney-general of the State; a Whig leader; a fine stump orator, and a representative of Madison and Limestone counties in the Alabama Legislature, also a member of the State secession convention of 1861.

Dr. Richardson's maternal aunt, *nee* Miss Martha Davis, is now the widow of Judge George W. Lane, for many years a circuit judge in Alabama, and from 1861 up to his death, in 1864, United States district judge.

Dr. Richardson's mother died May 3, 1861, at Athens, Alabama, at the age of fifty-one years, leaving seven children: (1). Mary P. Richardson, now wife of Thompson Anderson, a leading wholesale dry goods merchant at Nashville, Tennessee. (2). Nick D. Richardson, subject of this sketch. (3). William Richardson, a prominent lawyer and politician, now judge of the probate court at Huntsville, Alabama. He married Miss Lizzie Rucker, of Lynchburg, Virginia. (4). Edwin R. Richardson, a wholesale shoe merchant of the firm of Richardson, Mason & Co., Nashville. He married Miss Sue Hamilton, daughter of Mortimer Hamilton, a merchant, and niece of James M. Hamilton, now a large hardware merchant at Nashville. (5). James B. Richardson, of the firm of Richardson, Mason & Co., Nashville. He married Miss Sallie Evans, daughter of William H. Evans, for many years one of the largest wholesale merchants, and also a banker, at Nashville. (6). Ann E. Richardson, now wife of H. E. Jones, a prominent lawyer at Nashville. (7). David Michelle Richardson, graduated M.D. from Bellevue Medical College, New York, and died unmarried, in 1879.

Dr. Richardson was raised in Athens, attended the schools there till his sixteenth year, then went to the University of Virginia and studied two years. In 1852-3, he attended the Jefferson Medical College, Philadelphia, and graduated M.D., in 1853, under Profs. Pancoast, Dunglison, Bache, Mutter, Huston, Meigs and J. K. Mitchell. He remained six months after graduation in practice at the Pennsylvania hospital. In 1854, he returned to Athens and commenced practice in partnership with Dr. T. S. Malone, then the most prominent physician in North Alabama.

He practiced at Athens till 1861, when he went into company F, of the Twenty-sixth Alabama regiment, as a lieutenant, and shortly afterward was commissioned by President Jefferson Davis as a surgeon in the Confederate States army, and served as such till his surrender at Macon, Georgia. He served almost exclusively in the field, and was in the campaigns in Alabama, Tennessee, Kentucky, Georgia, Texas, Mississippi and South Carolina, including the battles of Shiloh, Murfreesborough, Chickamauga, and those from Dalton to Atlanta, Jonesborough, Franklin and Nashville.

The war over, he returned to Alabama and resumed practice "with nothing but a home, a wife, three children and a horse." He, however, followed his practice closely till 1873, when he was taken down with inflammatory rheumatism, and was sick for five years. In 1881, he moved to Nashville, where he is now in practice. Financially, he has been, by means of his profession, and by farming in Alabama, a fine success, and is now estimated to be worth fifty thousand dollars. His business principles are of the highest order—to live within his means, buy nothing unless he is able to pay for it, and never buy anything on credit. These principles are inherited from his progenitors on both sides—families proud of their standing in the community in which they lived, and ever given to recognizing and encouraging merit wherever found, whether in the hovel or in the mansion.

He was raised a Whig, but since the war has voted the Democratic ticket, though he has never held or wanted civil office. He is a Royal Arch Mason, and a member of the Ancient Order of United Workmen. He belongs to no church, but is a warm friend of the Christian religion, and especially of the Methodist denomination.

Dr. Richardson first married, at Athens, Alabama, October 27, 1858, Miss Bettie Hine, only daughter of Roswell Hine, a leading merchant of that place, of a New York family. Her mother was originally Miss Mary P. Malone, daughter of Capt. John P. Malone, a large Alabama planter, and a soldier in the war of 1812. Mrs. Richardson died at Athens, in 1874, at the age of thirty-eight, leaving six children: (1). Roswell H. Richardson, born at Athens, November 7, 1859; now a merchant at that place; married Miss Ellie Walker, daughter of Judge William H. Walker, a prominent lawyer at Athens, and has one child, Walker. (2). Ann Davis Richardson, born November 15, 1861; graduated at Athens Female College; married, in 1881, T. N. Hobbs, a planter, in Limestone county, Alabama, and has one child, Richardson. (3). Charles B. Richardson, born at Cartersville, Georgia, November 22, 1863; now in commercial life at Nashville. (4). William E. Richardson, born at Athens, February 27, 1866; now at school. (5). Mary Pleas. Richardson, born August 12, 1868. (6). Nick D. Richardson, jr., born August 9, 1871.

Dr. Richardson's second marriage, which occurred at Huntsville, Alabama, May 1, 1879, was with Mrs. A. E. Sledge, widow of O. D. Sledge, a merchant at that place. Her father was William H. Echols, a merchant and planter in North Alabama, and her mother was Miss Mary Hobbs, of a Virginia family.

Personally, Dr. Richardson is a most attractive and companionable gentleman. He is six feet high; weighs one hundred and eighty pounds; has the face and manners of the typical, warm-hearted, impulsive southern planter, and looks fearless, unsuspecting, independent and very self-conscious.

HON. THOMAS C. MUSE.

JACKSON.

HON. THOMAS C. MUSE was born in Pittsylvania county, Virginia, January 23, 1834. When he was only five or six years old, his father moved to Henderson county, Tennessee, where he grew up. When sixteen, he clerked on the Tennessee river in the commission business one year. His father, Daniel C. Muse, a farmer, was a native of Pittsylvania county, Virginia, exceedingly fond of politics, a Henry Clay Whig, and when dying, January, 1865, left an injunction that his children should all be educated—a wish which was carried out. He came to Tennessee with one child and one negro, and notwithstanding losses by the war, left an estate of thirteen thousand dollars, besides his lands. After his death his widow "broke up," moved to Jackson, and there died in 1878, at the age of fifty-eight. She was originally Eliza, daughter of Isaac Stone, of Virginia. She was a lady remarkable for her fine management, economy and domestic qualities, and her devotion to husband, children and servants. The clothing for her entire family she had made at home.

His father trusted almost entirely to his memory in his transactions with his neighbors, though he could keep books. After his death many of his neighbors came to his administrator and paid several hundred dollars of which there was no account in writing. He was a remarkably healthy man, his last sickness being his first. His grandfather, William Muse, was a Virginian, of Scotch-Irish blood. One of his sons, James Muse, was a man of fine literary attainments; located near Lexington, Kentucky; taught a private school; made a fine fortune by speculating in lands, moved near Lexington, Missouri; remained there several years as a teacher, and also as a minister of the Christian church; from there he moved to Collin county, Texas, and died. He was an eloquent man, and distinguished as a leader in his church wherever he resided.

Of his brothers: (1). Dr. John A. Muse resides at Pinson, Madison county, Tennessee, engaged in the practice of his profession. (2). Henry Muse, who was educated at Ann Arbor, Michigan, and West Point, New York, resigned his position after remaining two years at West Point, is now farming in Johnson county, Texas. (3). William A. Muse is principal of the public school at Rutherford station, Gibson county, Tennessee. (4). Etheridge Muse was educated at the Southwestern Baptist University, and is now merchandising at Jack's creek, Henderson county, Tennessee. (5). James D. Muse, graduated June, 1884, from the Southwestern Baptist University. Of his sisters, Jennie E., widow of Milton S. Edwards, is postmistress at Lexington, Tennessee. Callie A. is the wife of Ed. McCollum, a merchant at Henderson station, Chester county, Tennessee. She was educated at the Conference Female Institute, Jackson. Ida, the youngest sister, educated at the same school, is living, unmarried, with her sister at Lexington.

The subject of this sketch was educated at Clinton Academy, Hickman county, Kentucky, and graduated in law at the Cumberland University, Lebanon, Tennessee, in 1855; practiced law at Lexington, Tennessee, till the war; after which he moved to Jackson, Tennessee, continuing his law practice.

In 1874, he made a canvass for Congress against Hon. J. D. C. Atkins, but was defeated, one of the issues in the canvass being the civil rights bill, on which he took the same view precisely that the Supreme court of the United States has lately laid down, viz.: That all men are equal before the law, and that negroes must obtain their rights through the same channels with the white race. In that canvass also he took ground for a tariff for revenue, with incidental protection.

He became a Mason at Jackson, Tennessee, in 1870, and has taken all the degrees, including Knight Templar.

In religion, he inclines to the Methodist church, but is not a communicant. His first wife was a Methodist. The present Mrs. Muse is a Presbyterian.

He married first in Madison county, in 1855, Elizabeth, daughter of William R. Collier, of that county, a native of North Carolina, a prominent citizen of the county, and a large farmer. Her mother was a Robinson, of a North Carolina family, grand-daughter of Battle Robinson, a large slave-holder, who moved from North Carolina to Madison county, where he died. From this marriage were two children: (1). William C., born March, 1860, graduated at the Southwestern Baptist University, Jackson, now on the editorial staff of the Louisville *Courier-Journal*. (2). Albert D., born February, 1867, now studying in the Southwestern Baptist University, taking a full course, as did his brother.

Mrs. Elizabeth Muse dying, he married at Paducah, June 6, 1872, Mrs. Theresa, widow of Capt. Charles C. Smedley, daughter of Mr. Edrington, who, for a great number of years, was clerk of the county court of Ballard county, Kentucky. She is a step-daughter of Hon. John W. Crockett, at one time member of the Confederate Congress from Kentucky. Her mother was a Robertson, of Kentucky. Her daughter, Fannie Smedley, married Charles C. Harris, a druggist at Jackson, and has two children, William and Charles. Mrs. Muse is a lady of fine literary attainments, well read in poetry, a good French scholar, and is noted for her tireless industry, family pride and ambition, especially for the success of her step-sons.

In February, 1861, Mr. Muse was elected from Henderson county to the convention to consider whether the

State should remain in the Union. The convention was voted down, Mr. Muse advocating "No convention." His father being a Whig and an uncompromising Union man, he inherited those principles, and was a Union man during the war, and on that account was arrested, in 1862, by the Confederate authorities and held a prisoner at New Orleans until Gen. Butler took the city, and released him. He then took a sailing vessel, and after twenty-eight days, landed at Boston, went to New York, and thence, via Louisville, home, which he reached July, 1862, finding the country in possession of the Federals. When the Confederates regained possession, he was again arrested, in 1863, but the citizens of Lexington, Henderson county, interfered and procured his release, at the instance of his wife, who claimed that in reciprocity she was entitled to her husband's release, she having favored several distinguished Confederates. She went further, and assured the Confederates that, if her husband was taken off, she would have Lexington burned, including her own house, which argument prevailed. On his release, he took his wife and child to Paducah, where he remained two years, until about the close of the war.

In 1865, he was elected from the Twenty-first senatorial district—Henderson, Decatur, Humphreys, Perry and Benton counties—to the State senate, in which he voted for universal suffrage, and against the issuance of State bonds, under Brownlow's administration, for the purpose of rebuilding and re-equipping the railroads of the State, that had been neglected and worn out during the war. In 1867, he was appointed by Gov. Brownlow, chancellor of the division composed of Haywood, Dyer, Gibson and Madison counties. In 1868, he was elected to the same position and held it till the change of the constitution, in 1870, when he was defeated by Hon. James Fentress, of Bolivar. In 1868, he was elector for the Eighth congressional district, and voted for Grant and Colfax. The same year he was chairman of the Republican executive committee of that district. In 1876, he was a delegate to the national Republican convention at Cincinnati, and in 1880, to the national Republican convention at Chicago. In 1880 he was a candidate for the United State senate, but was defeated by Hon. H. E. Jackson, and returned to his home and was sent to the State senate, taking the position that all men should be held equal before the law, and that no man, white or black, should be disfranchised. He was elected, in 1882, judge of the common law and chancery court of the Democratic county of Madison, which position he now occupies. His term expires September, 1886.

Judge Muse, "the oldest of the nine Muses," is, in every sense, a self-made man, socially, professionally, politically and officially, having received little or no assistance from relatives or partial friends. He is one of the exceptions to the rule that Republicans are ostracised socially, as his last election as judge sufficiently evinces. All the family, from the father to the youngest son, were uncompromising Union men during the war, and are all Republicans since, a remarkable record for so large a family, and illustrative of that loyalty to conviction that all men respect as one of the chief elements of genuine manhood. His decisions as chancellor and common law judge have been, almost without exception, sustained by the Supreme court. His reputation for impartiality on the bench has never been questioned. His first ambition in life was to acquire a good education, even while assisting as foreman on his father's farm. His motto has been to do correctly whatever he had to do. He chose the profession of the law, and devoted himself assiduously to learn all the elementary principles of it, and was not ambitious to be other than a lawyer till after the war, when he went into politics in the interests of the country, as he understood and had them at heart. His father gave him one thousand one hundred dollars after he quit school, and though too kind to his friends by going their security, he is now in very comfortable circumstances. He was never drunk in his life; his chief ambition was to be an examplar for others. From the day he was twenty-one, till now, he has uniformly had some business in hand and plenty to do. He never broke a promise, never did injustice to a fellow man, and never knowingly told an untruth. The world is always full of work for men of this stamp, for such qualities win confidence, and surround a man with troops of friends from the best and most influential classes of society.

CAPT. BENJAMIN F. HALLER.

MEMPHIS.

BENJAMIN F. HALLER was born in Marion, Smyth county, Virginia, March 4, 1836. He remained at home until he reached his seventeenth year, attending school the greater portion of the time, acquiring the elements of a good education. He then, of his own accord and at his own expense—the only way he has ever traveled—went to Wilmington, North Carolina, where he engaged a short time as reporter on the Wilmington *Herald*, and afterward, for two years, as salesman in a dry goods establishment. From Wilming-

41

ton he went to Memphis, Tennessee, arriving there March 4, 1858, with only a few hundred dollars in hand. Having letters of introduction to Bishop Otey and other prominent citizens, he soon obtained the responsible position of cashier in one of the largest mercantile houses in the city, which place he retained until May 15, 1861, when he went into the Confederate army, joining the "Shelby Grays," which afterward became company A of the Fourth Tennessee infantry regiment (Col. R. P. Neely), and remained with that command till August, when he was commissioned captain and authorized to raise a company for himself, which, after being partly formed, he merged into the "Sumpter Grays." This company became company A of the Thirty-eighth regiment Tennessee infantry, Col. R. F. Looney commanding. With this command he served till after the battle of Shiloh, when the company was detached and assigned to artillery service, in which capacity it commanded the position on the lower Farmington road at Corinth until the evacuation of that place, when it was ordered to Columbus, and there Capt. Haller was appointed by Gen. Dick Taylor, provost marshal of the first military district, extending from Corinth to Meridian, Mississippi, and remained there till early in 1864, when the company was assigned to duty with Gen. Forrest, and with him remained till May 15, 1865, when the forces were surrendered, at Gainesville, Alabama.

Capt. Haller returned to Memphis, June 23, 1865, and engaged in business in the ensuing fall, but after several business changes, in February, 1876, he engaged in cotton seed oil manufacturing, in which he has continued ever since, and is at present secretary and treasurer of a leading company in that line. After twenty-six years in Memphis, including four years in the army, he has risen from a stranger, with less than a thousand dollars, to a comfortable social and financial position; and this, not by speculation, but by hard work, by taking care of what he makes, by staying at one place and pursuing one line of business. In 1867, he lost some twelve thousand dollars by the operation of the bankrupt law; but to-day he has the happiness of saying, "I don't owe a living soul a nickel," and besides that he is never five minutes behind with an engagement, unless something very serious detains him. His family before him were old line Whigs, and so was he until the war, but since then the only course left him was to vote with the Democrats. He is a stockholder in various companies, but director in none. In religion, he is Presbyterian, as is also his wife.

Capt. Haller was made a Mason at Columbus, Mississippi, while on duty there during the war, in 1863, and has held the position of Worshipful Master four terms, at Memphis; High Priest of the Chapter two terms; thrice Illustrious Master of the Council; Eminent Commander of Knights Templar three terms; Venerable Master of the Lodge of Perfection, Scottish

Rite; Grand High Priest of the State of Tennessee; Most Illustrious Grand Master of the Grand Council of Royal and Select Masters of Tennessee; Grand President of the Order of High Priesthood of Tennessee; Grand Commander of Knights Templar of Tennessee; is a 32d° Mason of the Scottish Rite; has had the honorary title conferred on him, of Knight Commander; is elected to receive the 33d° with the rank of Inspector General, and is General Grand Principal Sojourner of the General Grand Chapter of the United States; General Grand Recorder of the General Grand Council of the United States; represents the Grand Commandery of Maine near the jurisdiction of Tennessee, and also represents the Grand Council of Maryland in the Grand Chapter, and the Grand Lodge of Texas, and is a member of the standing committee on Appeals and Grievances in the Grand Lodge of Free and Accepted Masons of Tennessee.

Capt. Haller married, in Memphis, October 10, 1868, Miss Clemmie Fisher, daughter of Maj. G. W. Fisher, who represented Shelby and Fayette counties in the State senate two or three terms before the war. He was originally from Pennsylvania, and was a wealthy planter. Her mother is now living in Memphis at the age of sixty-eight. Mrs. Haller's brother, John H. Fisher, a cotton buyer at Memphis, married Miss Bettie Matthews, and has four children, Cora, Henry, Thomas and George. Mrs. Haller's sister, Elizabeth Fisher, died in 1883, wife of J. C. Johnson, leaving seven children, Ida, Carrie, Edwin, Lily, Anna, William and Cynus. This sister left a reputation, almost national, for her liberality to the poor, and for being an effective worker in benevolent enterprises. She was vice-president of the Woman's National Christian Association at the time of her death. Mrs. Haller's sister, Barbara Fisher, is now the widow of John R. Garrison, and has one child living, John R. Her sister, Georgia Fisher, is the wife of B. W. Capps, of Memphis.

By his marriage with Miss Fisher, Capt. Haller has one child, a son, Frank Elma Haller, born July 11, 1869; now being educated at Memphis.

Capt. Haller's father, Dr. George W. Haller, was born in Wytheville, Virginia, in 1800. After taking his literary degree, he graduated in medicine at Jefferson Medical College, Philadelphia, became distinguished as a physician and surgeon in Virginia; married at Liberty, Bedford county, Virginia; settled at Marion, Virginia, in 1836, and died in 1860, while on a visit to his son, Booker Calland Haller, in Texas. He left nine children, Richard J., Mary, Booker Calland, James F., George W., Jane E. (wife of Robert H. Woodson), Benjamin F., subject of this sketch, Sallie A. (wife of L. G. Trent), and Sue J. (now Mrs. Williams, of North Carolina). Of these, Booker Calland Haller, was wounded and died in the war, in Gen. E. Kirby Smith's command; George W. Haller, was killed in battle, in Gen. William Walker's expedition to Central America, in 1857; Mary Haller, died in 1856, at Tazewell, Court house, Virginia, wife of Dr. J. R. Doak, leaving four children, Nannie, William, Reese and Rachel. Four of the brothers served in the Confederate army; two with Stonewall Jackson, Richard J. and James F. Haller, the former a major.

Capt. Haller's mother, *nee* Miss Ann Fullerton Webb Johnson, was the daughter of Richard Johnson, of Liberty, Virginia, and grand-daughter of Maj. James, of the Revolutionary army, who died in February, 1827, and maternal grand-daughter of Maj. White, also of the Revolutionary army, from Virginia. Her brother, James F. Johnson, was a prominent lawyer and politician at Liberty, Virginia, and represented his

district in the Virginia Legislature a number of terms. She was related to the Edmondson's of Halifax county, to the Stones of Danville, and the Moormans of Pittsylvania, all of English descent, and among the early settlers of the Old Dominion. Of Capt. Haller's paternal uncles, five were physicians in Virginia. The character of Capt. Haller may be readily inferred from the fact, that he has never yet tasted one drop of beer or ardent spirits of any kind, and this statement should be accepted as a factor in his success. It is not the province of a biographer to make predictions, but the editor feels safe in saying that a man who went through four years' service in the army without drinking, can not be induced to become intemperate hereafter.

REV. JOHN BUNYAN SHEARER, M. A., D. D.

CLARKSVILLE.

THIS eminent theologian, educator and scholar, now professor of biblical instruction in the Southwestern Presbyterian University at Clarksville, Tennessee, author of "Bible Course Syllabus, a Formulated Course of Study in the English Bible," etc., properly takes rank among the foremost Christian educators of the South.

John Bunyan Shearer was born in Appomattox county, Virginia, July 19, 1832, and received his primary education in Union Academy, in that county. He was taught by Henry F. Bocock (brother of Hon. Thomas F. Bocock, the distinguished congressman), on the principle of learning one thing at a time. For example, he was taught Latin, exclusively, from ten to thirteen, until pages of Latin classics were read with almost the ease of English; then Greek, direct, from thirteen to fifteen; then mathematics from fifteen to seventeen, when he entered the junior class of Hampden-Sidney College, graduating, with distinction, June, 1851, under the presidency of the distinguished Rev. Lewis W. Green, D.D., and Profs. Charles S. Venable and Charles Martin.

He next entered the University of Virginia, prosecuting the academic course and taking the master's degree, in 1854, under Profs. McGuffey, Gessner Harrison, Courtenay, and other distinguished educators associated with them. After this he spent one year, 1854–5, as principal of Kemper's boarding school for boys, at Gordonsville, Virginia, which position he left to study theology at Union Theological Seminary, Virginia. He remained there three years—from 1855 to 1858—graduating the latter year, and was ordained to the gospel ministry in December, 1858. From 1858 to 1862, he was pastor of the Presbyterian church at Chapel Hill, North Carolina. While a student at the Theological

Seminary, he preached two years at Bethlehem and Concord churches, in Prince Edward county, Virginia, during which time the membership of those churches was more than doubled. From 1862 to 1870, he was pastor of Spring Hill church, Halifax county, Virginia, and at the same time principal and proprietor of the Cluster Springs boarding school for boys.

Dr. Shearer came to Tennessee in 1870, and located at Clarksville, as president of Stewart College, which position he held nine years—from 1870 to 1879—and until that institution was reorganized as the Southwestern Presbyterian University—being connected with the institution altogether some fifteen years. He was for three years, 1879–80–81, professor of history and English literature in that institution, but has taught biblical science during the whole period of his connection with the school, 1870 to 1885, at present filling the chair of biblical instruction.

Stewart College owes its origin to the Masons of Tennessee, who founded it about 1850. They erected buildings and conducted a school for five years. Failing to meet with satisfactory success, they transferred the institution to certain gentlemen of Clarksville, who paid the debts of the college, and in turn transferred it to the Presbyterian synod of Nashville. The college was named in honor of Prof. William M. Stewart, who was its leading patron and benefactor, and who served the institution, gratuitously, as president, and then as professor of natural sciences. The college was achieving a reasonable success when it was broken up by the war. Its libraries and cabinets and other appliances were destroyed and the buildings dismantled during the varying struggles of internecine strife. No effort was made to resuscitate the institution until the arrival of Dr. Shearer, in 1870.

At that time there was neither school, faculty, apparatus, libraries nor cabinets; part of the buildings had not been repaired since the ruthless hands of the soldiery had been laid upon them, and the small nucleus of endowments had been saved from the wreck by the skill and fidelity of Hon. D. N. Kennedy, acting for the board of trustees. The institution, being then under the care of the synod of Nashville, and its patrons necessarily few, Dr. Shearer immediately opened negotiations with the southwestern synods of the Presbyterian church, with a view to founding a university common to them all and worthy of them all. These negotiations resulted in the agreement of the synods of Nashville, Memphis, Alabama, Mississippi (including Louisiana), Arkansas and Texas, to join in founding a school on the basis of a more distinctively Christian education. A plan of union was adopted, almost unanimously, and a directory, consisting of two members from each of the six synods, was given charge of the enterprise. In the meantime, Stewart College was achieving a remarkable initial success, so that at the proper time it was adopted as the nucleus of the desired university, though many other places competed with Clarksville by generous offers for the location. The new institution—the Southwestern Presbyterian University—was chartered by the State of Tennessee, in 1875, a new directory taking charge of Stewart College and continuing the old faculty and curriculum until the reorganization, in 1879.

On tendering Stewart College as the foundation for the university, Dr. Shearer insisted on vacating all the chairs in the institution, in order that the board of directors might be wholly unembarrassed in reorganizing, himself being a member of the board of directors. A dangerous spell of sickness laid him on the shelf almost the whole of the year 1878-79. At the reorganization, in 1879, he nominated the distinguished educator, Rev. J. N. Waddel, D.D., LL.D., as the chancellor of the university, and was himself elected to the chair of history and English literature, including, for the time, biblical instruction, as before mentioned, though his health was still so poorly re-established that he seriously doubted his ability to ever again do regular work. Happily, however, his health was regained, though slowly, and since that time, in the judgment of his friends, he has been able to do the best teaching work of his life. With the reorganization he very properly retired from the directory, but the board saw fit to place in his hands the entire business interests of the institution, and also to make him *ex officio* a member of the executive committee of the board, who have the management of all matters *ad interim*.

For nine years the entire financial interests of the institution were laid upon Dr. Shearer, and its affairs were conducted on the principle of a clean balance sheet, and freedom from debt. Unusual difficulties beset the path of the institution, both by reason of the narrowness of its means and the peculiar state of public credit in Tennessee. It became necesssary for him to labor for years in the interest of the literary and charitable institutions of the State, which, like Stewart College, were largely interested in the condition of State finances. The endowments were steadily increased from about thirty thousand dollars, in 1870, to one hundred thousand dollars, in 1879, at which latter date the Southwestern Presbyterian University owned about seventy thousand dollars of State bonds. The necessity of constant watchfulness during the sessions of the Legislature, from year to year, in order to secure the regular payments of interest and the final safety of the principal, amid political wrangling, won for Dr. Shearer the reputation of being a most successful "lobbyist"—in the better sense of the term—and without drawing upon himself or his cause any of the odium usually thereunto attached. The schools of the State readily concede to him a large share of the credit of the refunding and safety of educational endowments, and their final removal from politics, even to the extent of making the State the custodian of such funds, so that they can neither be stolen, lost, or squandered by a reckless board of trustees.

During the period of his connection with the university, Dr. Shearer has been doing what may be called a pioneer work, in placing the Scriptures as the central figure in a liberal education, and requiring all forms of human learning to make their obeisance to them. In all his teaching he has sought to make his school more distinctly a Christian school than the schools of the past. The Church, he maintains, has no mission to educate unless she can make her schools more specifically Christian than can the State schools. Dr. Shearer places the English Scriptures on the same basis as the severe studies—Latin, Greek and mathematics—and holds that education is insufficient without a thorough mastery of revealed truth. He makes the Bible course the unifying course of all sound learning. He teaches that there is nothing good in human thought for which we cannot find the authority in the Scriptures, or at least the concrete illustration, and that there is no heresy for which we do not find the answer, either directly or by necessary implication, in God's word—notably in history; the historian who fails to recognize God in history gives but partial and inadequate views of the whole, because the "seed of the woman"—the seed of Abraham—is "head over all things to the Church." This proposition, he maintains, runs like a red thread through all history.

In a notable sermon which Dr. Shearer delivered at Monteagle, in the summer of 1884, he illustrated these views, as a theologian, on the proposition that the evangelical Christianity of do-day is in approximate conformity with Scripture warrant—in its organization, government, franchises, forms and modes of worship. In that discourse, he treated the historic development of the Abrahamic covenant, through the Mosaic economy, and through the later superadded synagogue system, into Christianity, this last being a continuation of the organic life of the church, set up in the family of Abraham, and now become universal.

Teaching seems to have been a sort of second nature with Dr. Shearer from very early life. He was employed, when sixteen years old, as assistant in the academy where he was educated; and at the University of Virginia he was employed two years of his course by the professors to teach their sons and daughters, besides having private classes among his fellow-students during the whole of the three years he remained there. This work was wholly unsolicited on his part, but most welcome, on account of the necessity of relieving his father from the burden of a protracted attendance at school. This private teaching was kept up to the end of his theological course so successfully that by this means, and by preaching and colporteur work, he earned and spent two thousand five hundred dollars on his education, losing only one year from actual attendance at school.

In boyhood he had no bad habits—never using profane language nor contracting any of the usual youthful vices. He was consecrated from birth to the gospel ministry by a devotedly pious mother, but never made up his mind to preach until his twentieth year. He joined the church at the age of ten. From fifteen to nineteen he had a varied religious experience, in which he encountered all the difficulties, doubts and battles of his life.

Since coming to Tennessee, Dr. Shearer has not had a regular pastorate, though, in 1871–72, he had charge of the Presbyterian church at Clarksville. While he never misses an opportunity to preach a sermon, and in fact preaches nearly every Sunday, most of his work is missionary work.

Dr. Shearer is descended from Whig ancestry, but since the disastrous results of secession, has advocated Democratic doctrines and politics. He, however, draws his views of republican government largely from the model divinely given in the Hebrew commonwealth, and in which, he holds, is to be found all the safe-guards of civil and social liberty, in perfect adjustment; that apart from the theocratic features of the Hebrew commonwealth, there is found the earliest and highest form of a confederated republic of sovereign States (the twelve tribes), with perfected constitution; and, that the exact adjustments of their executive, judicial and legislative bodies have been unequalled by any republic of mere human origin. A proper understanding of these things, he insists, furnishes a safe-guard against the Jacobite on the one hand and a licentious democracy on the other; and, besides, in that commonwealth was found the only perfect adjustment of civil and ecclesiastical law, which secured liberty of worship on the one hand and freedom from priestcraft on the other.

Dr. Shearer married, in Prince Edward county, Virginia, September 5, 1854, Miss Lizzie Gessner, who was born at Munster, Westphalia, Germany, November 19, 1832, the daughter of Johan Gessner, who emigrated to Texas, where he died in 1839. Her mother was Katrina Blumenthal, with no blood-kindred living. The same is true of Mrs. Shearer. A lady of indomitable energy and perseverance, her husband ascribes to Mrs. Shearer no small part of his success in life, and he is frequently guided by her judicious counsel, and aided by her strong womanly help. She shares absolutely in every project he undertakes, and prosecutes it as her own. They have no children, but their house has been filled with the children of others during almost the entire period of their married life. The sick, the suffering and the poor bless her in every community in which she has ever lived.

The family name, Shearer, is Irish, but it came through William the Conquer to England, and the Irish ancestors of the family in America are descended from members of Cromwell's famous Ironsides, whom he settled in Ireland. Wherever those descendants are found, either in this country or abroad, are found many of the best characteristics of that devoted band. No one who bears the name has ever been known to disgrace it by drunkenness or any other form of vicious indulgence. The grandfather of Dr. Shearer, James Shearer, a soldier of the war of 1812, died in Appomattox county, Virginia, in 1872, aged ninety-six years. He was born in Pennsylvania, and married Miss Elizabeth Akers, daughter of Peter Akers, whose grandson, Rev. Dr. Peter Akers, now ninety-four years old, but with eye undimmed and force unabated, is the great apostle of Methodism and president of a college in the northwest. Both of Dr. Shearer's grandmothers were sisters of the same family, and out of a family of eleven, who all lived to be over eighty years old.

Dr. Shearer's father, now living in Appomattox county, Virginia, at the age of seventy-seven, and in full vigorous health, is one among few men who has devoted his life wholly to the raising of his family and the service of his church and community, without ever seeking or accepting civil office, or ever engaging in any enterprise for the increase of his fortune. He has always been considered free for any service that was needed by his fellow men.

Dr. Shearer's mother, nee Miss Ruth Akers Webber, who died in Appomattox county, Virginia, at the age of thirty-seven, was the daughter of John Webber. She was the mother of seven children, six of whom, John B. (subject of this sketch), Elizabeth M., Richard B., James W., Mary R. and Henry C., survived her. Of these, Elizabeth M. Shearer died the wife of W. A. LeGrand, leaving three children, John A., Richard B. and Lillie R., who married Eldridge P. Carson, and has one child, Lizzie Gessner. Richard B. Shearer was a Confederate soldier, and was killed at Monocacy,

Maryland, at the head of his company, in 1863. James W. Shearer is now a Presbyterian minister. Mary R. Shearer has been twice married, and has five children. Henry C. Shearer is a farmer in the home county, Virginia, and an elder in the Presbyterian church, and has three children.

Dr. Shearer has been, financially, far more successful than most men of his profession. The first money he ever earned he adopted the theory of the tithe as the minimum that a man should give of his gross earnings to religious and charitable uses, but he has given beyond this rule, time and again, even to half his income. It is a common saying in Clarksville that everything he touches prospers. Has not God said, "Them that honor Me, I will honor?" and again, "There is that which scattereth and yet increaseth." He lost everything he had by the war, and the property he now has is the aggregate of little accumulations, year by year, mainly from professional sources, aided by the economy and prudence of his enterprising and faithful wife.

ALONZO W. BROCKWAY.

BROWNSVILLE.

ALONZO W. BROCKWAY was born near Malone, Franklin county, New York, September 22, 1824. His father, William C. Brockway, was the youngest of a large family of brothers and sisters, and was born at or near Walpole, New Hampshire, in 1786, his father, originally a native of Ellington or Lyme, Connecticut, having moved to Walpole a short time previous to the breaking out of the Revolution, and there lived and died. He had been a captain in one of the New Hampshire regiments, and a gallant soldier in many battles of the Revolution ; was several times severely wounded and carried a British bullet in his leg to his grave.

The Brockways are of English descent, and about all the persons of that name in the United States are supposed to have descended from Walston Brockway, who is shown by the records to have owned real estate in Lyme, Connecticut, as early as 1679. He is believed to have emigrated from England about 1660, only forty years after the landing of the pilgrims at Plymouth Rock, and no other emigrant of the name is known to have come over, hence the conclusion that he was the progenitor of all the American Brockways. This is the view of William L. Brockway, of New York city, and Beman Brockway, of Watertown, New York, who are compiling the genealogy of the family.

Mr. A. W. Brockway's father was a soldier in the war of 1812. . He was a farmer and mechanic ; a man of vigorous mind and body, and died about twenty-five years ago, at a very advanced age.

Mr. Brockway's mother was Miss Betsey Hadley, a direct descendant of the Putnam family, and was a cousin of Gen. Israel Putnam. Her mother's maiden name was Elizabeth Putnam, and her father was a soldier in the Revolution ; was at the battle of Bunker Hill, at the very beginning of the war, and served faithfully till the close. The family seem to have been very numerous and very long lived on both sides. Both the parents of Mr. Brockway lived to be over eighty years of age, and his grandparents were both over ninety years of age at death, and he, though now over sixty years of age, has all the activity and energy of thirty years ago.

Mr. Brockway's youth was passed at Malone. The usual routine of life incident to a new country and a very cold climate was his lot. Hard work, even in young boyhood, alternating between the field, the forest, and the workshop, and attending the district school for a few months each year, made up the record of his early life, with very few embellishments, either in the way of recreation, fine clothes or luxurious habits of living in any sense. He now recalls, as the most pleasant of those early days, the few on which he was permitted to go to the village, about two or three times a year, with the other boys, and enjoy the festivities which in those days attended the fourth of July, and the annual gathering of the militia, usually termed the "general muster." If he was the master of fifty cents on an occasion of this kind, to spend in ginger cakes, soda water, firecrackers, and the like, he was rich, and so felt, because it had been accumulated gradually, by dint of some skill and extra work during the preceding days and weeks.

All these things, however, had a tendency to develop the perseverance, energy, resolution and self-reliance which have characterized him in later years. His training was of the kind best calculated to develop the sterling elements of a boy's character, if he possesses any. At sixteen or seventeen years of age he was permitted, though under many difficulties, and with few of the real necessities of such schooling, to attend, for a few terms, the old Franklin Academy, and was for a time the school-fellow of ex-Vice-President William A. Wheeler, who was a native of Malone. Many pleasant recollections occur to him now, more than forty years after, of his daily life with young Wheeler and his cousins, who were near neighbors, and some of the other young men who have, like him, attained distinction in life.

When about nineteen years of age, Mr. Brockway went west " to grow up with the country." This was about

1843. With a few dollars which he had scraped together, and a few more which had been generously sent him by an older brother, Rev. William H. Brockway, then chaplain in the United States army, and stationed at Fort Brady, at the outlet of Lake Superior, he started for that place, more than a thousand miles distant, nearly all by water, except seventy miles, from Malone to Ogdensburg. This distance he made, mostly on foot, in the space of two days, his little blue 7x9 trunk having preceded him by stage, at a cost of fifty cents. Toward the close of this trip, a pleasant incident occurred. When about eight or ten miles from Ogdensburg, he was overtaken by the mail stage, a four-horse Concord coach, the grandest and most rapid style of inland travel in all that region in those days. The driver, who knew him well, halted the stage and invited him to mount the box with him, and he so rode into town, much refreshed by the ride and thankful for the kindness. For this act of kindness to him, tired, foot sore, and almost discouraged, as he was, the name of Irwin Heath, the stage driver, has ever been held in grateful remembrance, but from the time that he boarded the old steamer Ontario, the same night, and took an affectionate farewell of his friend, they have never met.

He took a deck passage for Detroit. The voyage, which lasted a week, was attended with hard fare, sea sickness, and almost starvation toward the latter part. There were then only a few old-fashioned steamers on the lake, and the "deck passengers" had to sleep on deck and take their meals at the second table, for twenty-five cents each. When he reached Detroit he was out of money and had been without food for thirty-six hours. A rascally restaurant-keeper had passed a counterfeit dollar upon him, which left him without means to procure anything to eat during the latter part of the trip. Though he had a draft for twenty dollars, which his brother had sent him, on a house in Detroit, yet, with the timidity of a country boy, he was afraid to show it to the captain, thinking he would be put down as a humbug. In Detroit he put up at the old City Hotel, on Woodbridge street, and went to bed supperless. Rising early next morning, he found the firm on which he had the draft—John Owen & Co., druggists—on Jefferson avenue, had his draft cashed, and felt that he was in possession of untold wealth. He remained in the city a few days, and was very kindly treated by his brother's friends, Mr. Owen, his partner, Mr. Henchman, and the Rev. Mr. Fitch. He then embarked on a sailing vessel for Mackinaw, and arriving there safe, coasted with French Canadian voyagers to Fort Brady, being several days on the way, camping out at night, and coming near being wrecked in a storm.

At Fort Brady he remained for two or three years, doing all sorts of work, not hesitating to seize any opportunity that presented itself. He was employed in clerking at the military post, exploring, and working in the copper mines, and generally "roughing it." All of that country was then strictly Indian lands, but the year after he went there the Indian title was extinguished, and then people began to flock thither, from every nation and every clime, to the copper mines, which had just been discovered, and have since proven by far the richest in the world. Mr. Brockway was in the midst of all this movement from its very inception, and experienced all the incidents of camp life—"all of which he saw and a part of which he was." He was a friend of Dr. Houghton, State geologist of Michigan, by whom the copper mines were brought into notice, and was one of the first to go into the enterprise. He attended to transportation, exploration, keeping the accounts of the company, and a great variety of other work connected with the business in its every department. While there he fell in with John Hays, of Pittsburg, who was representing the Pittsburg and Boston Mining company. Mr. Hays took a great fancy to him, and one day made the, to him, very startling proposition that he should come to Pittsburg the next year to be his partner in the drug business. This offer, which was made on account of his known honesty and integrity, was accepted.

He went down to Detroit and went into the house of John Owen & Co. (who had cashed his draft when he first came to Detroit), as a clerk, and remained from fall till spring. With only such experience as he had gained here, he went to Pittsburg and became the partner of Mr. Hays, in the firm of Hays & Brockway. His capital was only two hundred dollars and his experience. Mr. Hays' capital was five thousand dollars, but they were equal partners. This was the move which first brought him out of the position of a working man and introduced him to mercantile life. At Pittsburg he remained for several years in a flourishing business.

After awhile, at the request of Mr. Hays, Dr. C. J. Hussey, and other wealthy gentlemen, who controlled the Pittsburg and Boston Mining company, Mr. Brockway was sent back to the Lake Superior copper regions to attend to the transportation of a mass of copper which had just been taken out of the company's mine. This piece of copper, weighing about four tons, was the largest mass of native copper that had been mined in the world up to that time. In the face of many obstacles he got it shipped to Fort Brady and thence to Detroit, and finally got it safely to New York. Here his partner, Mr. Hays, took charge of it, shipped it on the old steamer Sarah Sands, one of the first stern-wheelers which crossed the ocean, carried it to London, where it was put in the British museum, and there remains to the present day. An article written by Mr. Brockway on this mass of copper, and giving some outlines of the mines, was published in the London *Times*, and this, with the arrival of the copper, produced more excitement in England than anything of a similar nature that has ever happened. A year or two after this, Mr.

Brockway sold out his interest in the drug business to Mr. Hays.

Having become a favorite with Dr. Hussey, he was made a confidential friend by that gentlemen. In the winter of 1848-9, he went to Louisville with Dr. Hussey to buy a stock of pork, and before they had been there long the Doctor was called back by sickness in his family, and Mr. Brockway was left in charge with forty thousand dollars to invest. The money was invested and the pork shipped to Pittsburg. The steamer on which Mr. Brockway started back home was never able to get beyond Wheeling, Virginia, and he was compelled to stage it from that point across the country eastward, and suffered greatly on account of cold weather and exposure.

Mr. Brockway is an original, genuine "Forty-niner." Just at this time the gold fever was breaking out, and one day—shortly after his arrival home—Mr. Hussey asked him how he would like to go to California. His reply was, that it would please him if he only had money to go on. He was then informed by Dr. Hussey that he and other gentlemen had made up a purse of ten thousand dollars to be invested in California, provided he, Brockway, would go out to take charge of the enterprise. Preparations for the trip were at once begun. Supplies were shipped in March, 1849. Mr. Brockway and a few companions proceeded to St. Louis and thence to West Port landing, where Kansas City now stands. Here they started for the journey of over two thousand miles across the plains, through a country uninhabited, save by hostile Indians. A large company of emigrants had been formed at West Port landing, and was commanded by Col. William H. Russell, who had previously crossed the plains. About half way across part of the company became dissatisfied, seceded and elected Mr. Brockway captain. This trip, the incidents of which are like a romance, lasted more than three months, and was attended by many hardships—hard work, hard fare, in the face of scalping Indians, fording rivers, scaling mountains and cliffs, and drawing their wagons after them over weary miles of arid, almost burning, plains; snow banks hard as ice, in the mountains, in the month of July, were some of the many interesting incidents. From West Port landing to San Francisco, there was only one United States post, a small fort in the valley of the Platte, and white men were seen by them only three times on the journey. They arrived in the valley of the Sacramento, in a very dilapidated condition, the latter part of July, 1849. After a few days' rest he bought a lot and began to build, erecting thereon the first brick house in Sacramento City, and helping to make the brick with his own hands. Labor had to be paid five to ten dollars a day, and the little lumber they could get cost one hundred dollars per thousand feet, as there was only one saw-mill in the State. This was Suter's mill, where gold was first discovered. Mr. Brockway at once em-

barked in trade and did a flourishing business until a year later, when his building and stock were swept away by the great floods in the Sacramento valley. After the waters had subsided, he rebuilt and began again, under very depressing circumstances, but built up a good business and made money rapidly. About a year after he took to mining, and located the first gold bearing quartz vein at Mariposa. The land afterwards turned out to be the property of Gen. Fremont, and the result of the venture was somewhat disastrous.

The machinery which the company had sent, by way of Cape Horn, to operate the mines, and which proved unfit for the purpose, was put into a small boat and made a rude but real steamer, the first that ever navigated the inland waters of California, and ran on the Sacramento and Feather rivers. In the summer of 1851, he sold out and started on his return to Pittsburg.

Proceeding by steamer to Panama, he crossed the Isthmus, partly on foot, partly by canoe, and partly on the back of a jackass. On one occasion, his party, who had with them about thirty thousand dollars in gold, were in danger of being robbed by a band of desperadoes who watched them closely all night, but being confronted with arms loaded and cocked, they withdrew. Two of Mr. Brockway's companions on this trip were Dr. Brandies, of Erie, Pennsylvania, and Mr. Rhodes, of Mansfield, Ohio. Sailing from the east side of the Isthmus, by way of Kingston and Havana, they arrived safely at New York. Mr. Brockway's idea at this time was to form a large mining company and return to California, but not succeeding in this, he went into banking, investing his capital in that business.

His same old friends established the Forest City Bank, at Cleveland, Ohio, and put him at its head as cashier, which position he filled from 1851 to 1857, his bank all the time in a flourishing condition. In 1858, he went to Flint, Michigan, established the Peoples Bank, and conducted it for several years. While there he built Brockway block, on Main street, still one of the finest blocks in that city.

When the oil fever broke out, during the late war, he immediately went into the business and was very unfortunate, being brought to bankruptcy. Giving up his all, he went to work, nothing daunted, to pay off the remainder of his indebtedness, and has done so, by hard and successful work, during the eighteen years he has been in Tennessee.

Feeling that he would have a better chance in a new country, in 1867 he came to Tennessee, and organized the Shelbyville Savings Bank, which he conducted with marked success for two years. In 1869, he sold out there and removed to Brownsville, Tennessee, which was then a very flourishing town, and there established the Brownsville Savings Bank, of which he has been cashier up to the present time. The banking business was at first carried on in a small room at the back of a jewelry store, but when he was about to resign on account of ill health, brought on by hard work in such quarters, the stockholders and directors built the present handsome bank building, at a cost of about twenty thousand dollars, it being one among the finest in the State, and was designed by Mr. Brockway and erected under his personal direction. Mr. Brockway is now the owner of a controlling interest in this bank, besides having other property, altogether making up a comfortable estate.

A natural born Union man, Mr. Brockway has usually voted the Republican ticket, but has taken no active part in politics. He was a delegate from Michigan to the great conservative Republican convention which met at Philadelphia, in 1866, with a view to organizing a new party out of the better elements of the two old ones, and healing the breach between North and South. He was one of a committee sent by this convention to Washington to wait upon President Andrew Johnson, who tendered them a reception at the White House.

Mr. Brockway was first married at Malone, New York, in December, 1851, to Miss Juliet Meigs, daughter of Guy Meigs, of the firm of Meigs & Wead, old and prominent lumber and dry-goods merchants. The only child living, by this marriage, William Guy Brockway, is now a banker in Gadsden, Alabama; was born at Cleveland, in 1858.

Mr. Brockway was married a second time, at Detroit, in October, 1868, to Miss Nellie Scott, daughter of Capt. James P. Scott, of the United States army, who died in the service, after the war. To this union have been born three children: (1). Frank Thatcher Brockway, born in 1873; died in infancy. (2). Alonzo W. Brockway, jr., born in 1875. (3). Violette Mary Brockway, born in 1877. Both Mr. and Mrs. Brockway are members of the Methodist church, and he has been an official member for many years.

In his business principles, the views of Mr. Brockway have corresponded with his actions. Beginning life with no money, and without the advantages of a liberal education, his success has been the result of honest, hard work. He is a man for honest labor, in any field in which a man can be useful; has a morbid horror of idleness; would take to sawing wood to prevent being out of employment. Added to this, he has a firm self-reliance. He has never *waited* for a position, or sat under a shade tree and cut off coupons whenever there was a cord of wood to be sawed. He believes that life is too short to be wasted in trifling. He can find no excuse for a lack of faithfulness to any trust reposed, and feels that integrity and a faithful discharge of duty, are the greatest essentials of success.

During his forty years of an active business life, in which industry and faithful devotion to his business have been Mr. Brockway's chief characteristics, it is not saying too much to add, that during all this time only a small portion of it has been spent elsewhere than in the midst of a loving family, surrounded by the comforts of a model *home*, with a well selected library of standard works, where the most of his leisure hours are spent in perusing their contents, and where his hand and his purse are, and ever have been, open to every legitimate business enterprise, to every call of religion, or any benevolent object, local or otherwise. In connection with this last, and showing the estimation in which he is held, we add, that Mr. Brockway was recently appointed and commissioned by Governor Bate, as one of the three commissioners for the building of the West Tennessee State Hospital for the Insane, a position of much responsibility, for which he is peculiarly fitted, by reason of considerable experience in the construction of buildings, both public and private. Here, as in every other trust, he will be found in the conscientious discharge of his duty to the public; and in the satisfaction of having contributed his best talents for the comfort and amelioration of that most unfortunate class of his fellow men for whom the institution is designed, will consist his highest and most satisfactory reward.

NAPOLEON HILL.

MEMPHIS.

THIS gentleman, whose history illustrates so well the fact that well directed energy leads to success in life, appears in these pages as a representative Tennessee merchant. The following sketch of Mr. Hill, as a business man, from a work entitled "Memphis—Past, Present and Future," is strong testimony as to his worth and the regard the people of Memphis have for him: "No pleasanter task falls to the duty of the editor and statistician than that of presenting to the world the character and *personnel* of the leaders of thought and action, and reviewing the results of their energy and enterprise in the busy drama of every-day life. Men who give both impress and impulse to commercial history are not only 'the abstract chroniclers of their day,' but they are the guides of the people in mercantile education and heralds of the broad progress which marks American trade and commerce. For broad and comprehensive executive abilities for leadership, men moving

42

upon the active stage of business life, have proven their superiority in the estimation of the American people, not only in the ordinary pursuits of business, but to grapple with and manage the most abstruse points and parts of social and political economy. The true American statesmen of broad views and successful action are the leading merchants—the founders and heads of great commercial establishments. The firm of which Mr. Hill is a member has made a rare record of business success, and gained a position among commercial leaders throughout the country. The history of the commercial advancement and progress of the city of Memphis has produced few examples of success so marked and substantial as that which has attended the efforts of Messrs. Hill, Fontaine & Co. Within the period of its existence, this house has taken a position and achieved a success which would be surprising but for the known ability of its management."

Mr. Napoleon Hill, the head of this firm, has resided in Memphis for twenty-five years. He is one of the most widely known and highly esteemed citizens of the community in which he lives, and closely identified with Memphis in the development her various financial, commercial and productive enterprises, he exerts an active influence in the development of her resources and the fostering of her best interests.

As viewed by Col. J. M. Keating, the brilliant editor of the Memphis *Appeal*, Mr. Hill appears as follows: "Mr. Napoleon Hill is, perhaps, one of the very best examples of success furnished by the South since the war. He is a type of the class that leads in all our industrial and commercial pursuits. Self-reliant, energetic, prudent, pushing, thoughtful, conservative, full of expedient, always ready, broad and liberal, cheerful in disposition, thoroughly democratic in manner and habit, carrying the details and cares of his business with a light heart, because he never steps beyond the limits of his capital, and keeps before him constantly a high and manly sense of the obligations that rest upon him as the head of a great commercial house, the second in point of cotton sales in the world. He learned many valuable lessons in the mining camps of California in the early days of that State. These were invaluable to him, the best of them being the self-control and self-discipline which none of his contemporaries have ever seen him break through. His evenness of temper and *bonhomie* of manner are proverbial, as is his constancy and devotion to his relatives and his friends. He ties to these as with hooks of steel. His success since 1865, that year so memorable for an overwhelming disaster, which brought poverty and despair into all parts of the South, is one of the marvels of our time, especially when the ups and downs of Memphis are considered. He began with bare hands; to-day, twenty years after, he is a millionaire. This result, so creditable to him, is the outcome of well directed and constant labor, the careful avoidance of reckless speculation; the

concentration of all his forces in one channel; the mastery of all technical difficulties, and a stern determination always to be at the head of the cotton business. Placable, pleasant and good-natured, he is beloved in social life. There his utter simplicity of character and his ingenuousness are felt to be the products of a good heart. He is the idol of his home circle, in which he finds a recompense for all the cares of a life whose burdens have been in proportion to the rapid growth of his business. Napoleon Hill is winning the title of merchant prince. Far seeing, he is far reaching; hence his name is listed among the railroad, bank and insurance officers and directors, and those who have invested in and control great mechanical enterprises in Tennessee and Alabama. His life is a lesson for the generations to come, as it is an example for that which is contemporary with him. Honored by all men, he is looked to by all classes of his fellow-citizens as one worthy the highest public trusts."

Napoleon Hill was born in Maury county, Tennessee, near Columbia, October 25, 1830. When he was about five years of age his father moved to Marshall county, Mississippi, where he grew up, living on a plantation until his seventeenth year. He received his education in the old field schools of Mississippi, never attending any college. When he was about fourteen years of age, the death of his father put an end to his school days, as he was the oldest son, and had to take charge of the plantation. Determining to adopt a mercantile life, he went, in 1847, to Bolivar, Tennessee, and began his business career as a clerk in the store of his uncle, John H. Bills, and there remained till April, 1850. The California fever having broken out, he left Tennessee and went across the plains to that State in search of gold. For two years he lived the life of a miner, working in the placer diggings. Getting tired of this business, in which he had met with partial success, at the end of two years he left it. After this he opened a trading post at the junction of the Trinity rivers, mining streams in the northern part of California. There he built boats and established ferries across the two streams, opened and conducted a ranche. Gold had just been discovered upon that stream, and miners were flocking thither from every nation and every clime. Among these he built up a flourishing trade, and remained there about four and a half years. In 1857, he returned to Tennessee, having accumulated about ten thousand dollars during the California trip. He settled at Memphis and engaged in the cotton and commission business, as a member of the firm of Hill & Dorion, till the beginning of the war. At the close of the war, he resumed business at Memphis, as a cotton factor and wholesale grocer, in the firm of Williamson, Hill & Co., which lasted till the spring of 1868, when the partnership was dissolved by the death of Mr. Williamson. The name of the firm was then changed to Hill, Fontaine & Co., the name under which it now exists.

Mr. Hill has been identified with all the commercial and financial enterprises of Memphis for many years, and has been an officer in numerous banks, railroad and insurance companies. A few years subsequent to the war, he filled the position of president of the Memphis Chamber of Commerce for two terms, and was president of the Cotton Exchange for two terms, during the years 1880–81. He is now president of the Memphis City Fire and General Insurance company, the largest in the State, and is also a director of the Memphis and Charleston railroad. He was one of the organizers of the Union and Planters Bank of Memphis, the largest bank in the State, and has been one of its directors since its foundation. He is largely interested in the Pratt Coal and Iron company of North Alabama, he and his partner holding about one-fourth of the stock of the company, which owns and operates the largest bituminous coal mines in the United States, producing over two thousand five hundred tons of coal daily, besides operating iron furnaces of which the daily product is from one hundred and fifty to two hundred tons, in addition to which he is the owner of a large area of iron lands in Franklin county, Alabama, and coal lands in the adjoining counties. He is the head of a house which does the third cotton business in the world, handling as much as one hundred thousand bales per annum. The firm has also a large branch establishment at St. Louis, and their trade in the departments of their business— groceries and cotton—is more than five and a half millions of dollars per annum.

Up to the war, Mr. Hill was a Whig, and since the war has voted with the Democrats, but has never been a candidate for office, and seldom takes any part in politics, devoting his whole time to his business. He is essentially a business man.

Mr. Hill was married, in Hardeman county, Tennessee, July 8, 1858, to Miss Mary W. Wood, whose father, William H. Wood, a gentleman of large success as a banker and planter, now lives in Memphis, and is engaged in planting in Arkansas. He was born in Albemarle county, Virginia, in 1814, and came to Tennessee in 1833. The family is of Scotch descent. Mrs. Hill's mother, nee Miss Benigna Polk, daughter of Col. Ezekiel Polk, one of the earliest settlers of Hardeman county, belongs to a family of Scotch-Irish descent, which traces its ancestry through many generations back to Ireland and Scotland. She was a half-sister of the father of James K. Polk. Mrs. Hill's sister, Miss Nina Wood, is now the wife of James H. Martin, of Memphis. By this marriage with Miss Wood, Mr. Hill has four children : (1). Olivia P. Hill, married Charles Grosvenor, of the prominent real estate firm, Overton & Grosvenor, Memphis. (2). Napoleon Hill, jr. (3). Mary M. Hill. (4). Frank Fontaine Hill.

Mrs. Hill has been a member of the Presbyterian church since her youth. She is a lady of genial, sunny disposition, fond of her household, and is a good neighbor, a good wife and a good mother.

Mr. Hill's father, Dr. Duncan Hill, a gentleman of English descent, was born in North Carolina, and came to Tennessee in his youth. He was a planter as well as a physician, and met with marked success in both lines. He died in 1844, at the age of forty years. Mr. Hill's mother was Miss Olivia L. Bills, daughter of Isaac Bills, and sister of the late Maj. John H. Bills, a prominent citizen of Bolivar, Tennessee. Her grand parents, Daniel and Deborah Bills, were natives of North Carolina, and were Quakers. She was born in Maury county, Tennessee, in June, 1807, and died at St. Louis, Missouri, in September, 1883. Her mother, Miss Lilias Houston, was a daughter of John Houston, a first cousin of Gen. Samuel Houston. After the death of Dr. Hill, she married Col. Josiah DeLoach, of St. Louis, Missouri. She was a member of the Christian church, and an earnest, faithful Christian. She was characterized by the sweetness, and, at the same time, the strength of her character, and exercised a great influence upon her family. Her ancestry on her father's side were Welsh, while the Houstons were of Scotch descent, and settled on the Susquehanna river, in Pennsylvania, about 1730.

Mr. Hill's brother, Jerome Hill, is the head of the branch house of Hill, Fontaine & Co., in St. Louis, and another brother, Harry M. Hill, is a lawyer in Memphis. Mr. Hill has also two sisters now living, Mrs. Joy, of St. Louis, and Miss Emily E. Hill, of St. Louis, Missouri.

When Mr. Hill began life, he was ambitious to make money, and when the gold fever of California broke out, he thought there was the place to make it, but after working in the mines for a while, he came to the conclusion that a man could succeed in anything if he would bring all his energies to bear upon it and persevere in it. He has kept ever before him a determination to succeed, and feels that, without a motive in life and an object to work for, no man can be either happy or successful, but having these, and backing them with perseverance and energy, he is certain to achieve his object. He believes that for a man to be a financial success, he must be liberal ; that a penurious man is seldom a success, and that liberality is always well rewarded. He thinks that any business well conducted leads to fortune, while the best business poorly followed will eventually lead to ruin. The reports which have come to the writer's ears, in Memphis, of the liberality of Mr. Hill, bear ample testimony to the truth of his theory, that liberality is an essential of success. Memphians say that he is as liberal as he is successful.

PROF. HUNTER NICHOLSON.

KNOXVILLE.

THIS distinguished son of a distinguished father, was born in Columbia, Maury county, Tennessee, June 9, 1834. His father, the Hon. A. O. P. Nicholson, was United States senator from Tennessee, in 1841–2, first appointed by Gov. James K. Polk, to fill the vacancy occasioned by the death of Hon. Felix Grundy. At the expiration of this term, he was nominated by the Democrats for election to the senate, but owing to a defection, and the forming of a combination with the Whigs, Hon. Hopkins L. Turney, a Democrat, was elected. In 1857, however, Judge Nicholson was elected to the United States senate by the Tennessee Legislature, and served until the breaking out of the war, when he left the senate, Tennessee having seceded from the Union. He was two or three times a member of the Legislature, elected first before he was twenty-one years old. He was chancellor in the Columbia district four years, as successor of Chancellor Terry H. Cahal. He was chief justice of the State at the time of his death. He was a member of the State convention of 1870, and chairman of the committee on suffrage in that body. He was twice elector for the State at large, in 1840 and 1852. He began life as the editor of the *Mercury* at Columbia, and edited the Nashville *Union* during Polk's campaign in 1844, afterwards was editor of the Washington *Union* during Pierce's administration, 1852 and 1857, and was during this time printer to Congress. At Chapel Hill, where he graduated in 1827, he was long afterward spoken of as a rounded man, who was a born student, and who in every department took first rank. But he was more at home on the bench than anywhere else, and was pre-eminent as a judge. Judge Nicholson was born in Williamson county, about two miles from Spring Hill, Tennessee. His father died when he was four years old. He went to school to Esq. Black, grandfather of Henry Watterson, editor of the Louisville *Courier-Journal*, and afterward to Dr. Jordan, near Mount Pleasant, and finally to Chapel Hill, North Carolina. After graduating, he studied medicine at the Jefferson Medical College, Philadelphia, but never intended to practice medicine. He studied law after he was married, and practiced at Columbia, which was his home. His first partner was Hon. Sam. D. Frierson, whose sketch appears elsewhere in this volume. While he lived at Nashville, Russell Houston was his law partner, as was also Hon. William F. Cooper, and subsequently William J. Sykes. He belonged to no church, though he read the Bible with assiduous zeal, and to no secret order. Judge Nicholson, whether considered as member of the Legislature, United States senator or judge, always appears a strong man, who has left his mark upon the history of his State, but he shone most conspicuous as a member of the Columbia bar, universally celebrated as the most brilliant in the State, composed of Russell Houston, James K. Polk, Gideon J. Pillow, James H. Thomas, Edmund Dillahunty, M. S. Frierson, Judge W. P. Martin, L. D. Myers, George Gantt and others. Judge Nicholson was appointed with Judge Caruthers, by the Legislature, to revise the statutes of the State. That work is yet the standard authority, and is a model of its kind. About ten years after the completion of this work, he issued an additional volume, known as Nicholson's Supplemental Statutes.

The trait that most characterized Judge Nicholson, was his extreme modesty and purity of thought and speech, never using an oath, or language in any company unfit for the most refined ears. During his whole life he kept up his classical reading in his vacations, Horace being his special favorite. Such was his uniform courtesy that, although engaged actively from early manhood in the most heated political campaigns of the State, he retained throughout life the warmest friendship of his most prominent political opponents, among whom were such men as John Bell, James C. Jones, Gustavus A. Henry and Edwin H. Ewing.

The Nicholson family is originally of English blood. It is a very numerous family, represented, historically, in England, by Gov. Nicholson, of colonial fame, Peter Nicholson, the distinguished mechanic and author of a series of books ("Nicholson's Encyclopedia"), and Gen. John Nicholson, the gallant English commander, who fell at the siege of Delhi.

Judge Nicholson's father, O. A. Nicholson, was born in Guilford county, North Carolina, and located in Maury county, Tennessee, among its earliest settlers. He was a mill-wright, carpenter and surveyor, and had rather a better education than a majority of the people of his day in that county, but died not over thirty-five years old, leaving three children: (1). Maria Nicholson, who married, first, Simpson Walker, a merchant at Columbia, and after his death, Elias J. Armstrong, a farmer in Maury county. (2). Calvin H. Nicholson, a farmer in Tennessee and a planter in Mississippi. (3). Alfred Osburn Pope Nicholson, the father of Prof. Hunter Nicholson.

Prof. Nicholson's mother, *nee* Miss Caroline O'Reilly, was born in Maury county, Tennessee, daughter of Dr. James Charles O'Reilly, a native of the city of Dublin. He was a graduate of Edinburgh medical school, came to the United States, practiced his profession for a while in North Carolina, and finally settled in Maury county, in 1808. Mrs. Nicholson's mother was Miss Mary Gordon, a cousin of Gen. John B. Gordon, United States senator from Georgia, and of Gen. James B. Gordon, who fell in the Confederate service in Virginia. Prof. Nicholson's mother was educated at the old Nashville Female Academy, is a Methodist, and though fond of society and a great reader, is thoroughly domestic in her tastes and habits. She is the mother of seven children, namely: (1). Osburn P. Nicholson. (2). Hunter Nicholson. (3). A. O. P. Nicholson, jr. (4). Andrew J. Nicholson. (5). Charlie O'Reilly Nicholson. (6). Mary Nicholson (now Mrs. A. B. Estes). (7). Anna Nicholson (now wife of Hugh Gordon).

Prof. Nicholson graduated, first, at Franklin College, Tennessee, in 1852, under President Fanning, and next, in 1855, at the University of North Carolina. After graduation he became associate editor with his father of the Washington *Union*, and while at the capital studied law with Hon. Caleb Cushing, then attorney-general of the United States. From 1857 to 1861, he practiced law at Columbia as a member of the firm of Nicholson, Sykes & Nicholson, meantime editing the Columbia *Herald*, from 1858 to the breaking out of the war.

In 1857, when Hon. Isham G. Harris became governor of Tennessee, young Nicholson was appointed on his staff as adjutant-general of the State. From the battle of Fort Donelson to the surrender of Forrest's command at Gainesville, Alabama, he was actively engaged as major and assistant adjutant-general, and saw service in Tennessee, Virginia, Alabama and Mississippi. (See History of Forrest's Campaigns by Jordan and Pryor).

The war over, Prof. Nicholson returned to the editorship of the Columbia *Herald*. In 1868, he established and edited the *Dixie Farmer* at Columbia, but subsequently moved the paper to Nashville, Paul & Tavel becoming the publishers. In 1869, he was called to the chair of agriculture in the East Tennessee University, at Knoxville, and has been connected with the college ever since, at present being professor of natural history and geology.

In 1871, he was actively instrumental in organizing the bureau of agriculture of Tennessee, and was appointed by Gov. John C. Brown one of its commissioners, and continued as such during four years, the existence of the bureau. (See Resources of Tennessee by J. B. Killebrew). He has been continuously connected with the press from his boyhood to the present, either as editor, contributor or author.

He married, first, at Harmar, Ohio, in 1855, Miss Lottie Stone, a graduate of the high school at that place, and daughter of Col. Augustus Stone. Her mother, Charlotte Putnam, was a lineal descendant of the celebrated Israel Putnam, of Revolutionary fame. Her uncle, Col. A. W. Putnam, was for many years president of the Tennessee Historical Society, and is the author of a most excellent and valuable work, "The History of Middle Tennessee." Mrs. Nicholson died, January 7, 1873, leaving five children: (1). Caro Nicholson. (2). Maury Nicholson. (3). Augustus Nicholson. (4). Loring ("Lora") Nicholson. (5). Rebecca Nicholson.

Prof. Nicholson's next marriage, which occurred October, 1875, was with Miss Kate D. Martin, daughter of Dr. Robert Martin, of Nashville. Her mother, Miss Eliza Dickinson, is the daughter of Dr. J. Dickinson, of Williamson county, Tennessee. Mrs. Nicholson was educated at Dr. Elliott's Female Academy, at Nashville, is an Episcopalian, and combines, in a remarkable degree, domestic and literary tastes. By this marriage Prof. Nicholson has two children: (1). Hunter Nicholson, jr. (2). Bessie Nicholson. Prof. Nicholson is also an Episcopalian, and in politics a Democrat.

Prof. Nicholson has been governed in his whole life by a conscientious desire to occupy no position which he did not feel himself competent to fill, seeking by preference those in which he could do most good to others. He has never used wine, brandy or tobacco—and yet never belonged to a temperance society. He has been an inveterate reader from nine years of age. His omnivorous reading, his inordinate fondness for books, and his wide and intimate knowledge of them, acquired for him the appointment of librarian of the university, in addition to his regular duties as professor. He pays a severe penalty for his revels in the luxuries of so many branches of learning, for by reference to the catalogue of the university, it will be seen that he has at present assigned to him no less than twelve topics, an amount of brain work that would break down many men.

PROF. ZUINGLIUS CALVIN GRAVES, A. M., LL. D.

WINCHESTER.

MARY SHARP COLLEGE, founded in 1849, which has brought one million dollars to Winchester, and now stands in the front rank of the female colleges of the Union, owes the system of discipline which has given it success mainly to Prof. Z. C. Graves, who has been at its head for thirty-five years. His theory of female education is: that culture gives both tone and direction to the charms of womanhood ; that

;t is instruction as a means of development of personality; that systematic study is thinking; that habits of industry are chief objects of scholastic training, and that culture should at once be broad, liberal, thorough and progressive, and include the truths connected with temporal and eternal destiny. Its teachers engaged, its equipment and methods founded upon this philosophy, it has stood the test of time and acquired a reputation that has drawn to it large patronage and created a wide demand for its alumnæ, and even its undergraduates, for teachers, four hundred of whom are now in the field.

The man who has, through this institution, impressed himself upon his times, is the subject of this biography, Z. C. Graves. Their histories are inseparable. To speak of one is to think of the other. For forty years he has been a teacher, working seven hours a day—not superintending merely, but actually teaching, and of those scholastic years has not lost forty days' time—an extraordinary record. The first woman's college requiring a liberal education, including higher mathematics and Latin and Greek, was the Mary Sharp, and in 1853, it conferred the degrees named on the first two women in the world's history who had received such diplomas. The graduates were Miss Nannie Meredith (now Mrs. Embrey) and Miss Mary A. Falmer (now Mrs. Forbes). Since that time three hundred and ten young ladies have received the degree at the Mary Sharp College.

Mary Sharp College began as an experiment. The problem was whether women can be educated in the higher branches equally with men. A visit to this institution ought to convince the most hardened skeptic that they can, for the junior classes in mathematics are uniformly required to calculate an eclipse and develop all the formulas for plane and spherical trigonometry; and the same enthusiasm is manifested in astronomy, and even the little children exhibit it in the primary branches. It depends upon how a dish is cooked whether one takes to it with relish. The thoroughness and extent of the studies and methods of this institution ought to be known over the South, and its patronage trebled. It is a true statement that the curriculum here is the same as that of boys' colleges, plus music. There are five professors and five under teachers, and twelve pianos in use, all new, and an *esprit du corps* that is best translated by calling it *the enthusiasm of confidence.* A primary school and a normal department are features of the institution. It is not architectural piles only, but men, that make colleges. There are names connected with the universities of Oxford, Edinborough, Dublin, Berlin and Yale as lasting and as monumental as the buildings in which they are taught. And the name of the master spirit of Mary Sharp College is passing into a fame that will survive the edifice in which he has instructed five thousand girls.

Prof. Graves is a great enthusiast in the teacher's profession; he is wholly absorbed in the teacher's work. In the school-room he has wonderful power over his pupils in directing those energies—to make students of them—to make thinkers of them; to inspire his students with a love of their work. As an instructor before his class, possessing ability to impart and impress—in all this lies the secret of his success. The members of the faculty, while not imitators of him, are equally enthusiastic in their several departments. The fact that their freshman classes start with sixty or seventy pupils, and the senior classes run out with sixteen or twenty members, demonstrates that other fact, that their pupils are not advanced without being thorough and "sure enough" scholars. In Latin and Greek, the class in Horace, examined in 1883, was pronounced by competent linguists superior to any in any college, male or female, in the United States, known to the gentlemen witnessing the renderings and listening to the history of the odes. In fact, it has long been a saying about Winchester, that if Graves cannot get an idea into a student's head, no one else need to try it, for he will get on top and stamp it in.

Prof. Graves is a native of Chester, Vermont, born April 15, 1816, and there grew up at his books, doing the common work of that country, as required on a farm, but his mind ever upon his studies. He graduated from the Black River Institute, of Vermont, in 1837. and at the age of twenty-one, left home for the Western Reserve of Ohio, where he founded and became principal of Kingsville Academy. He had taught common schools, winter sessions, in Vermont. His success at Kingsville was brilliant—his pupils coming from many States, and some of them becoming distinguished in after life, among them: Prof. Lucien Osborn, forty years a professor in Madison University; Prof. J. W. Fowler, president of Michigan University; Rev. J. W. Knopp and Rev. William Ward, missionaries to Burmah; Rev. Daniel Bliss, president of Bryant College, in Syria, and others.

After teaching at Kingsville twelve years, he was called to the founding of Mary Sharp College, where he has spent the remainder of his life, so that since he formally entered upon his profession, he has been in only two places. As previously stated, Mary Sharp College was in its inception a new departure, its purpose being to demonstrate the problem whether the female mind is capable of that development in science equal to that of the male mind. It was once thought exceptional that Caroline Herschel should be the equal of her brothers, as a mathematician, but Prof. Graves has demonstrated the fact that the feminine mind generally is susceptible of the same degree of development as the masculine in the abstruse sciences—mathematics, metaphysics, æsthetics and ethics. That his efforts in this direction have met with success, and received due recognition by other eminent educators, the honors that have been conferred upon him bear testimony. The degree of A.M. was conferred upon him in 1846, by Madison University, New York, and later, that of

LL. D., by the Union University of Murfreesborough, Tennessee.

Prof. Graves is one of three children, he being the eldest. His sister, *nee* Louisa M. Graves, is now the widow of Prof. W. P. Marks, late superintendent of the Edgefield schools in Nashville. His brother, Rev. J. R. Graves, is the celebrated Baptist preacher, editor, author and polemic, now of Memphis. The family is of Huguenot descent, and it was always a custom in each branch of the family to name its first born male Zuinglius Calvin, the name Prof. Graves bears, though he himself has departed from that rule. The most remote known ancestor of the family fled to America at the revocation of the Edict of Nantes and settled in New England. The grandfather, Graves, was a merchant, a member of no church, and of no special note above that of an ordinary business man.

The father of Prof. Graves, also named Zuinglius Calvin, was also a merchant, and died at the age of thirty, leaving a widow and the children above mentioned, the mother at that time being about twenty-eight years old, and, although remarkably beautiful, never married again, but devoted herself wholly to the education of her children, with results that must have been highly gratifying to her, as witnessed in their brilliant careers. The mother, Lois M. Snell, was born in Hopkinsville, Massachusetts, daughter of Samuel Snell, a Revolutionary soldier, a manufacturer, and of New England Puritan stock. She was remarkable for her decision of character. When she had once formed a plan, she executed it. Her mind was given to all the theological questions that agitated her times, being a great reader of theological works. That her mind was of a metaphysical cast, is evident from the fact that one of her favorite books was "Edwards on the Will." Her method of training her children was to cultivate their will power by seeing that they executed any plans they had formed. She was a member of the Baptist church, and very zealous. She died at the age of seventy-eight years, and if it be true, that the good works of this life follow the saints departed, how true in her case must be the poet's words:

" Who to dumb forgetfulness a prey,
This pleasing, anxious being e'er resigned ;
Left the warm precincts of ethereal day,
Nor cast a longing, lingering look behind ? "

Prof. Graves married, in Kingsville, Ohio, July 3, 1841, Miss Adelia C. Spencer, a native of that place, born in 1821, daughter of Dr. Daniel M. Spencer, and a niece of Platt R. Spencer, author of the Spencerian system of penmanship. Her mother, *nee* Miss Marian T. Cook, was the daughter of Erastus Cook, a graduate of Williamstown College, a very eccentric man, spending most all his time in reading Latin, Greek and the old masters. Mrs. Graves' education was completed in the Kingsville Academy, under Prof. Graves. She is familiar with French and Latin, excels as a writer, and

is classed among southern poets. She is the author of "Jeptha's Daughter," and "Seclusaval, or the Arts of Romanism," of which ten thousand copies have been printed and sold. For her literary labors she has received more than three thousand dollars. She is the author of twelve volumes of Sabbath-school literature, and is known as the editor of the "Child's Book," under the *nom de plume* of "Aunt Alice." She has, for more than thirty years, been matron of Mary Sharp College, and is professor of literature in that institution. She is one of the few women of high literary culture who is a good business manager, lays hold with her hand, and knows how to manipulate and materialize the advantages and forces within her reach. She owes nothing, and will not permit her husband to owe a cent if she can help it ; he being so absorbed in his profession, it became a necessity that she should become the financier of the firm. Mary Sharp College is as much indebted to her for its life as to Prof. Graves himself.

By his marriage with Miss Spencer, Prof. Graves has four children : (1). James R. Graves, a freshman in Dartmouth College at the breaking out of the war, when he entered the Confederate army and lost his life at Ringgold, Georgia, in 1863, at the age of twenty-one years. (2). Florence M. Graves, a graduate of Mary Sharp College; married Henry Green, of Columbus, Georgia. (3). Zuinglius Dickinson Graves, an invalid, now thirty-six years old. (4). Hubert A. Graves, a graduate of Mary Sharp College, in 1877; now a farmer in Franklin county. He was, for two years, principal of the Masonic Academy, at Wooley's Ford, Georgia.

Prof. Graves, when a student, became an investigator and made up his mind that the presentation of science, *i. e.*, school culture, was on a wrong method, and he conceived a method by which the minds of students might become interested in the sciences, if they were presented correctly—that is, if the then mental food was cooked rightly. Having formed his plan, with him original, he entered the profession, and in his own peculiar manner presented the sciences in such a way that he has in his whole professional life had all the patronage he desired or could possibly attend to, both in Ohio and Tennessee. He introduced the first blackboard ever seen in the Western Reserve. He introduced the object method system of teaching in that section. His method may be styled tact. He insists that teachers, like poets, are born, not made. Mechanical teachers are not successes.

On the death of Rev. Dr. Joseph Eaton, he was elected chancellor of the Union University at Murfreesborough, and has been called to at least fifteen other places, but he kept his eye single to this one institution, thus developing a staying power which is a principal factor of his success. He has given ten thousand dollars of his earnings to the institution to preserve it. He has given his life and his earnings to his college.

In religion he is a Baptist. At the age of nineteen, he was licensed to preach, but having a talent to be a teacher, he felt more called to be a teacher than to be a preacher. Consequently, he has always refused to be ordained, as he felt he could do only one thing, though during his licentiate he has delivered perhaps hundreds of sermons. In politics he is Democratic, but has never held political office, his eye being kept single to his profession.

Prof. Graves is a man of medium height, weighs one hundred and fourteen pounds, has a benevolent and authoritative expression, without the appearance of either timidity or arrogance. He is a man of intensity of will, clearness of purpose, and a tireless worker. The wonder has been expressed that a man of his age can do so much work and enter with spirit into the studies of young people. Perhaps his enthusiasm and longevity may be set down as cause and effect. As a class, the greatest students, e. g., jurists, are the longest lived men in the world. Is it not the *mens sana* that preserves the *corpore sano?* When the mind gives way to despair the body sinks. When business men retire on their wealth they die of *ennui.* Mental activity in the direction of public benefaction leads to long life—a deduction which this single instance, in the absence of facts to the contrary, clearly supports.

CHARLES R. VANCE, ESQ.

BRISTOL.

CHARLES R. VANCE, the prominent and well-known attorney of Bristol, who is descended from leading East Tennessee families on both sides, was born at a place called Cherokee, in Washington county, Tennessee, August 22, 1835. From infancy until fourteen years of age, he grew up in Jonesborough, and then his father, a physician, moved to Kingsport, and there the son was reared, alternately working on the farm and going to school. In 1856, he entered upon the study of law under Hon. Thomas A. R. Nelson, read under him until 1858, when he was licensed to practice by Judge D. T. Patterson and Chancellor Seth J. W. Luckey, and began to practice in the courts of the First judicial circuit, embracing the counties of Hawkins, Greene, Sullivan and Washington, his office being at Kingsport. Shortly after admittance to the bar he ran for the office of attorney-general of his district against Sam Powell, but was defeated by a small majority.

He continued to practice law until the war broke out, when he entered the Confederate army as a private in company K, Nineteenth Tennessee regiment, but not being able to do field duty, was appointed agent for the First congressional district, to make out the claims of citizens for forage taken by the Confederate soldiers. About twelve months before the close of the war, he was appointed by the Confederate secretary of war, under an act of the Richmond Congress, agent for making out and reporting the claims of citizens for property taken or destroyed by the Confederate armies. In this position he continued until the close of the war, when he was indicted for treason at Knoxville, on account of his connection with the Confederate army, but the case was dismissed upon payment of costs.

When Mr. Vance began life as a young lawyer, he did so on one hundred dollars, which he borrowed to purchase a library. By 1861, he had made enough to buy a residence in Bristol for one thousand five hundred dollars, got it paid for, but during the war, in 1863, was compelled to sell the property to keep it from being damaged by the Federal soldiers. He sold it for ten thousand dollars in Confederate money, which he invested in tobacco at Lynchburg, had the tobacco shipped to Bristol, just before the Stoneman raid, and the soldiers of Stoneman's command helped themselves to it, and so it was all lost. When he resumed business as a lawyer, after the war, he was five hundred dollars in debt. Having located at Bristol, he again began practice in the same counties as previously, and with the addition of Washington and Scott counties, Virginia, and in the Supreme court at Knoxville. He has continued there ever since, engaged in no other business. From 1871 to 1877, he was attorney for the East Tennessee, Virginia and Georgia railroad, for the counties of Sullivan, Washington and Carter. He now owns a residence in Bristol, one hundred and forty acres of good farming land within a mile of that town, and is in independent circumstances.

Prior to the war, and until the reorganization of political parties, Mr. Vance was a Whig, but after the close of the war, he espoused the cause of Democracy. The only active political work he did, however, was in the campaign of 1880, when he canvassed the First congressional district for Hancock and English. He was a member of the board of aldermen for Bristol from 1870 to 1877. He became a Mason in 1862, in Shelby Lodge, Bristol, and has taken the Chapter degrees. He joined the Presbyterian church at eighteen years of age; has been an elder in the First Presbyterian church, Bristol, since 1874; was a delegate from Holston presbytery to the general assembly in New Orleans, in 1876, and was superintendent of the Sunday-school for six years, ending January, 1885.

Mr. Vance married, in Sullivan county, Tennessee, October 16, 1860, Miss Margaret J. Newland, who was born on Reedy creek, Sullivan county, at the old Newland homestead, March 28, 1838. Her father, Joseph Newland (now dead), was born on the same place, of a Virginia family of Irish and Scotch blood. He was a farmer and large land owner, a magistrate, an active worker as a member of the Presbyterian church, and was noted for his Christian piety. Mrs. Vance's mother, *nee* Rebecca H. Anderson, is the daughter of Isaac Anderson, of Scott county, Virginia, and sister of Joseph R. Anderson, the Bristol banker, in whose sketch, elsewhere in this volume, will be found a full account of the Anderson family. Mrs. Vance was educated partly at an academy on Reedy creek, but finished her education at Abingdon, Virginia. At an early age, she joined the Presbyterian church, at Blountville, under the ministry of Rev. Daniel Rogan, from which time she has lived a devoted and consistent Christian life. In her girlhood, she was educated in all the domestic duties, is an economical manager, conscientious and strict in the performance of duty, and enforces that principle in her family, and relies devoutly upon earnest prayer to Almighty God. She has taught her children the catechism with diligence and regularity, and is an active worker in the church and a teacher in the Sundayschool. By his marriage with Miss Newland, Mr. Vance has five children: (1). James Isaac Vance, born September 25, 1862; graduated at King College, Bristol, in 1883, and has just completed his course of theology in the Union Theological Seminary, Hampden-Sidney College, Virginia. (2). Joseph Anderson Vance, born November 17, 1864; graduated at King College, in 1885, and is also preparing for the ministry, in the Theological Seminary, Hampden-Sidney College, Virginia, having just passed his first year in the same. (3). Charles R. Vance, jr., born October 1, 1867. (4). Margaret J. Vance, born December 9, 1869. (5). Rebecca M. Vance, born January 20, 1874.

Mrs. Vance's brothers and sisters are: (1). Martha Newland, who married William A. Dooley and is now living on their farm on Reedy creek, Sullivan county. They have four children, Joseph, Earnest, Rebecca, and Nellie. (2). Isaac Anderson Newland, married Miss Mattie Lewis, of Georgia, and is now farming in Scott county, Virginia. (3). Ellen A. Newland, now wife of Prof. James P. Doggett, of King College, Bristol. They have five children, Eliza, Hallie, Fannie, Joseph and Maggie Nell. (4). Joseph M. Newland, married Miss Jude Leslie, and is now living on his farm in Sullivan county, Tennessee. (5). Samuel A. Newland, who has recently married Miss Helen Brown, of Sullivan county, Tennessee, and is living with his mother on the old homestead, Sullivan county. (6). Fannie A. Newland, married Cain Pence, a farmer and cabinet maker, Sullivan county. (7). Robert Newland, who has recently married Miss Bettie Welford, of Sullivan county, Tennessee, and is living with his mother. (8). Eliza B. Newland, married William P. Duff, a farmer in Lea county, Virginia.

The history of the Vance family dates back beyond the times of James the First of England, and is of Scotch-Irish descent. The Tennessee Vances are related to the Vances of North Carolina. Three brothers came to this country from England, Patrick, David and William. From Patrick Vance the Tennessee family is descended. Patrick Vance was a physician, and graduated at Edinburgh, Scotland. He was a native of Ireland, but came to America from England, and settled in Campbell county, Virginia. His son, William K. Vance, grandfather of Charles R. Vance, subject of this sketch, was born in Virginia, and married Miss Keziah Robertson, daughter of Charles Robertson, prominent in the early history of Tennessee as a pioneer, who made large surveys on the Holston, Nolachucky and Tennessee rivers, and was a brother of the Secretary of State of Franklin. (See Ramsey's History of Tennessee). William K. and Keziah Vance left eight children, viz.: Dr. James H. Vance, father of the subject of this sketch; Charles R. Vance and Mona Vance, both of whom died in early life; David G. Vance, who died in Georgia; Dr. William N. Vance, now a prominent physician at Bristol, where he settled in 1866; Patrick H. Vance, who died in Cincinnati during the war; Caroline Vance, married P. M. Craigmiles, a banker at Cleveland, Tennessee, and died there in 1883, leaving two children, Walter and Gussie; Keziah Vance, married Dr. O. P. Herndon, of Barboursville, Kentucky; Harriet Vance, married — Thornton, and is now living in Arkansas; Susan Vance, married James S. Patton, and died in Kingsport, leaving two children, William and Florence, the last named being dead.

Dr. James H. Vance (father of Charles R. Vance), was born at Greeneville, Tennessee, educated at Tusculum College, under President Doak, and took his medical degree at Transylvania University, Lexington, Kentucky. He first practiced at Greeneville; then at Cherokee, Washington county, two years; next at Jonesborough, fourteen years, and then moved to Kingsport, where he is now living on his farm, at the age of seventy-six. He is a leading East Tennessee physician, a man of excellent memory, of fine intellect, and extensive information on scientific, literary and political subjects. He is a Presbyterian and an Odd Fellow; during the war was a conservative Union man, and since the war a Democrat. His wife was Miss Jane Sevier, who has borne him eleven children: (1). Charles R. Vance. (2). Maria C. Vance, now wife of Rev. John R. King, Leesburg, Virginia. (3). Anna Elizabeth Vance, who died at the age of six years. (4). Keziah Vance, unmarried, at home. (5). James N. Vance, who graduated at King College; completed his theological course at the Union Theological Seminary,

Hampden-Sidney; was married to Miss M. Foster Tad-lock, daughter of Rev. J. D. Tadlock, D.D., and president of King College; was installed pastor of a church in Mississippi; and died December 29, 1881. (6). William V. Vance, a lawyer at Union City, Tennessee; married Miss Fannie Miller, of Hawkins county. (7). Nannie V. Vance, unmarried, at home. (8). Joseph Vance, who married Miss Mattie M. Fain, of Hawkins county, Tennessee, and now resides with his father; there have been two children born of this marriage, viz., James Foster Vance, who died in early infancy, and Charles Rutledge Vance, who is living. (9). Jennie Vance, unmarried and living with her parents. The other two children of Dr. James H. Vance were sons, who both died when only a few days old.

On his mother's side, Mr. Vance is descended from the famous Sevier family. His maternal great-grand-father, Capt. Robert Sevier, was a Revolutionary soldier, and was killed at the battle of King's Mountain. He was a brother of John Sevier, the first governor of Tennessee. He left two sons, Valentine and Charles Sevier. Valentine Sevier was bound out when a boy, but afterward was taken as a clerk into the store of a Mr. Jones, at Jonesborough, where he lived for a number of years; and afterward went into a store as clerk for Mr. Deaderick, remaining with him until Deaderick made him his partner and opened a store at Greeneville. Here he remained until he was elected clerk of the circuit court at Greeneville, a position which he continued to hold by re-elections for forty years. He was twice married. His first wife was a Miss Dinwiddie, of Greene county, by whom he had twelve children: (1). Jane Sevier, who became the mother of Charles R. Vance, and died at her home near Kingsport, March 1, 1886. (2). Robert Sevier, educated at West Point, served a while in the United States army, and afterward moved to Missouri, where he died. (3). Charles Sevier, died in Mississippi, leaving two children, Thomas and Nannie. (4). David Sevier, was clerk and master at Greeneville many years; married a daughter of George W.

Netherland, Sullivan county, and settled on a farm at Kingsport, where he now lives. (5). Dr. William R. Sevier, graduated in New York and practiced medicine at Jonesborough until his death, in 1883; married Miss Martha Ellen Cunningham, daughter of Dr. Samuel B. Cunningham, an eminent physician at Jonesborough, and the first president of the East Tennessee, Virginia and Georgia railroad. (6). James Sevier, was a merchant at Rogersville for a number of years; moved to Jonesborough, where he has been for many years proprietor of the Washington hotel. (7). Edward Sevier, who married a Miss ——, and who resides at Asheville, North Carolina. (8). Joseph Sevier, married Miss Nannie Broyles, of West Tennessee, where he resided until the war broke out, when he entered the Confederate army as a member of Wheeler's cavalry, and while leading his regiment, in the absence of its commander, fell in an engagement in Georgia. (9). Keziah Sevier, now the widow of George Jones, a merchant at Greeneville. (10). Isabella Sevier, died the wife of Dr. F. A. McCorkle, at Greeneville. (11). Elizabeth Sevier, died the widow of Rev. Whitfield Cunningham. (12). Susan Sevier, unmarried, now living at the age of seventy, with Dr. James H. Vance's family, at Kingsport.

Valentine Sevier's second wife was a Miss Cannon, by whom he had two children: (1). Charles Sevier, who married Miss Julia Brown, and is now a hardware merchant at Bristol. (2). Henry Sevier, a lawyer, now at Greeneville.

As to Mr. Charles R. Vance's legal methods, and the manner in which he attends to business, he is everywhere recognized as an honest, prompt and faithful man. He always advises a client for his best interest; is rather brief in his speeches; speaks to the point, in simple, earnest, clear and forcible manner; avoids irrelevant and immaterial issues—and in his practice complies rigidly with his promises made to fellow-attorneys. Socially, and in all other relations of life, he is a gentleman of sterling and sturdy integrity.

JUDGE JESSE H. GAUT.

CLEVELAND.

THE Gaut family of Tennessee, chiefly distinguished through its members of the bar, are the descendants of Irish ancestry. The grandfather, John Gaut, was born in 1760, in Ireland, and there married. He and Lutitia, his wife, and his two brothers, James and Matthew, and a sister, came over to America after the Revolutionary war, and settled near Philadelphia, Pennsylvania. The two brothers came South, but of their descendants the editor finds no trace. It is probable, however, that the Gauts, of Chaleston, South Carolina, are among them. John Gaut, after remaining in Pennsylvania a few years, moved to Washington county, Tennessee, and six years later, permanently settled on French Broad river, in Jefferson county, where he carried on a tannery and farm till his death, March 5, 1833. He left nine sons, James, Matthew, Benjamin, John, William, Samuel, Joseph, Robert and George W., and four daughters, Mary, Nancy, Betsy and Patsey.

The sons were all farmers, and every one but Samuel lived to be seventy-five years old. Their descendants are mainly in Arkansas, Missouri and Texas. Of these uncles of Judge Jesse H. Gaut, Joseph Gaut is yet living at the age of eighty-five. He has three sons, John, Rufus and S. P. Gaut, the latter an able and successful lawyer at Cleveland, Tennessee.

James Gaut, father of Judge Gaut, was born in Washington county, Tennessee, September 19, 1786, and died February 13, 1875. He followed for many years the tanning business. He married, in 1810, in Jefferson county; in 1820, moved to McMinn county, where for many years he operated a tannery, but finally went to farming, which he continued until his death. He was a man of exceeding fine morals, a strict member of the Cumberland Presbyterian church, very temperate in all his habits, did but little outside or speculative trading, and was for those times successful in business. In politics, he was a remarkably strong Henry Clay Whig. He was in all things, a straightforward, honest, plain man, forming his own opinions, to which he adhered with great tenacity. His wife, nee Miss Rosamond Erwin, was born in Jefferson county, Tennessee, August 25, 1792, an only daughter, having an only brother, Jesse Erwin, who went to Indiana and served several terms in the Legislature of that State. The subject of this sketch was named Jesse for him. Judge Gaut's mother's half-brother, Dr. Joseph Erwin, was a physician of prominence, and practiced in Texas, where he died. Judge Gaut's mother was a woman of strong intellect, a Cumberland Presbyterian, and a leader in her neighborhood in church and social matters. She died in Bradley county, July 12, 1869, having borne nine children, only three of whom survived her, namely: (1). Judge John C. Gaut, of Nashville, born February 27, 1813; graduated from the University of Knoxville, in 1837; read law one year in Athens, Tennessee, under Hon. Spencer Jarnagin, afterward United States senator from Tennessee; was admitted to the bar in 1838; settled in Cleveland, in 1839, when there were only a few houses in that place, and practiced law there until 1853, when he was elected by the Legislatue judge of the Fourth judicial circuit, to fill the vacancy left by Judge Keith Under the amended constitution of the State he was elected by the people to the same position in 1854, and re-elected in 1862, and held the office till he moved to Nashville, where he has practiced law ever since. He stands prominent among the eminent lawyers of the State, and has several times sat on the Supreme bench to try special cases. He has been twice married. First, to Miss Sarah Ann McReynolds, near Athens, Tennessee, in 1837, and had by her two children, John M. Gaut, now an able lawyer at Nashville, and Anna E. Gaut, who married Patrick H. Manlove, a leading Nashville merchant. Judge Gaut's second marriage, was on February 16, 1875, to Mrs. Sallie A. Carter, of Franklin

Williamson county, Tennessee, a lady of much beauty, and intellectual and social attractions. (2). George W. Gaut, born December 9, 1816; married in McMinn county, Tennessee, in 1841, Miss Adeline Dorsey, daughter of Rev. Micajah Dorsey, a Methodist minister; followed farming in McMinn county until 1855, when he moved to Missouri, where he died, July 14, 1874, leaving nine or ten children. (3). Judge Jesse H. Gaut, subject of this biography.

Of the children who died before the mother, two died in infancy. A daughter, Mahala Gaut, died the wife of John Dorsey, son of Dimmon Dorsey, a farmer, leaving two children, James A., and Celina Jane, the latter now wife of John Selvidge, of Bradley county. Nancy and Mary Gaut both died unmarried. Minerva Gaut, died in 1852, in Arkansas, wife of A. Taft.

Jesse H. Gaut was born near Athens, McMinn county, Tennessee, November 25, 1824, and grew up in that county; was required to work on his father's farm till seventeen years of age, going to the common schools of the neighborhood, which lasted only a few months each year. By this means, and by studying at home, he acquired a good rudimentary education. When seventeen, he taught school a year at twenty dollars a month. He then attended school at Cleveland one year, under a teacher named H. W. Von Aldehoff, a Prussian, of fine education. He next attended the university at Knoxville two years, studying Latin, geometry, chemistry, surveying, philosophy, etc. March 1, 1848, he began to read law with his brother, John C. Gaut, in Cleveland and after reading with him closely for two years, obtained law license from Charles F. Keith, judge of the circuit court, and Thomas L. Williams, then chancellor of all East Tennessee. He then went into the practice of law at Cleveland, and formed a partnership with his brother, John C. Gaut, which lasted till his brother became judge in November, 1853. Has lived there ever since, in the practice of his profession, and has practiced before the Supreme court of the State every year from 1853 till the present. He has also practiced before the circuit, district and Supreme courts of the United States. He was, for thirty-two years, attorney for what is now the East Tennessee, Virginia and Georgia railroad, and was attorney for the branch Bank of Tennessee, at Athens, from 1855 till 1861. Among the most noted cases in which he was leading attorney, may be mentioned the case of Thomas Hopkins' heirs against Thomas H. Calloway, known as the "Jolly Island case," he being of counsel for Calloway. Another noted case was the Union Consolidated Mining company of Polk county against Black, McCauley and others, involving over half a million of dollars. The Jolly Island case was in the Supreme court several times, where he argued it twice alone. The last time it was argued, his brother, John C. Gaut, and John M. Gaut, nephew of Jesse H. Gaut, aided him and rendered valuable service. The case was finally compromised and settled according to the decision they obtained. In the cases of the Union Consolidated Mining company of Polk county against Black, McCauley and others, he argued it before the circuit court of the United States and got it remanded back to the chancery court, his associates having no confidence in the motion and declining to aid him in it. These facts are mentioned merely to show the accuracy with which Judge Gaut examines the cases entrusted to his care.

On October 1, 1881, Gov. Hawkins commissioned him special judge of the Supreme court at Knoxville, in the place of Chief Justice J. W. Deaderick, who was unable to attend the court on account of sickness, and he has several times served as special chancellor and circuit judge, either under appointment from the governor, or by election of the lawyers.

He was elected to the Legislature in 1865, and served in the session of 1865–66, as chairman of the judiciary committee and of the committees on incorporations and on Federal relations. In 1868, he was defeated for the chancellorship of the Third chancery division, by Hon. D. M. Key. In politics, he was a Whig until that party went down; since then he has been a Republican. In 1882 and 1883, he was each year unanimously elected mayor of the city of Cleveland, and served those two years in that capacity, and did much to preserve peace and good order, and to establish a good system of schools in the city. In 1884, Judge Jesse H. Gaut was elected to the State senate, and served his district in that capacity.

Judge Gaut married first, in McMinn county, near Athens, December 6, 1849, Miss Sarah E. Isbell, who was born in that county, September 29, 1829, daughter of Benjamin Isbell. Her mother was Martha Parks. Her paternal uncle, James Isbell, was a noted banker at Talladega, Alabama. Her four brothers were Thomas, John W., Howard and Dennis R. Isbell. The first was a Baptist minister; John W. and Howard, young men of fine talent and good education, both died in the Federal army, and Dennis R., a man of excellent education, is now a farmer, surveyor and stock dealer in McMinn county. Her sister, Francis D., is the widow of William L. Rice, her first husband being John Hughes. Her sister, Martha, died, the wife of Robert A. McMillan, a merchant at Talladega, Alabama. Her sister, Missouri, is now the wife of Robert A. McMillan above named.

Judge Gaut's first wife died at Cleveland, May 28, 1864, leaving three children: (1). Thomas Isbell Gaut, born July 18, 1856; educated at Richmond College, Virginia; read law with his father, obtained law license and had practiced his profession only a few months when he was employed as clerk in the Fifth auditors' office in the treasury department at Washington, where he has served the government honorably and efficiently nearly four years. He married Mary M. Lee, daughter of William M. and Matilda Lee, both now deceased,

and has two children, Ione and James W. (2 and 3). Oscar Hamilton and Orlando Parks Gaut, twins, born July 15, 1863, educated together at Cleveland. Oscar is clerk, salesman and book-keeper for Manlove & Co., Nashville. Orlando is book-keeper for R. A. McMillan & Co., at Talladega, Alabama.

Judge Gaut's next marriage, which took place at Jonesborough, Tennessee, March 8, 1866, was with Miss Ella A. Luckey, a native of that place, born February 18, 1836, second daughter of Hon. Seth J. W. Luckey, circuit judge and chancellor for thirty-six years, a native of North Carolina. Her mother was Sarah Rhea, of a noted and numerous family in East Tennessee, for one of whom, Hon. John Rhea, who was an uncle of Mrs. Gaut's mother, Rhea county was named. Mrs. Gaut's elder sister, Jane, died in 1884, the wife of Col. William K. Moore, of Dalton, Georgia, leaving five children, Alice, Elizabeth (married, May, 1884, Rev. W. K. Walker, a Presbyterian minister of marked ability, a graduate of Albany Seminary, New York), John R. Rhea and Ella. Mrs. Gaut's sister, "Pet," is now the wife of John E. Williams, of Knoxville, and has five children, Luckey, Neil, Annie, Agnes and Bessie. Her sister, Elizabeth, is the wife of George W. Hamilton, a merchant at Dalton, Georgia, and has five children, Jennie, Bessie, George, Seth and Cornelius. Her sister, Agnes, is the wife of Dr. Joseph K. Walker, of Rogersville, Tennessee, and has five children, Cornelius, Seth, Margie, Jesse Gaut and Mary. Her brother, Cornelius E. Luckey, a prominent Knoxville lawyer, married Miss Julia Simms, of Georgia, and has one child, Mary.

Mrs. Gaut went to school at Jonesborough and Rogersville, and like her sisters, is a strict Presbyterian and well educated. These sisters all lead in the society in which they move, and exercise their influence against all immorality. They are all women well informed; well posted in religion and politics; fond of reading, and are devoted to their church and their prayers, never retiring to bed at home or abroad without their secret prayers, and they raise their children to this devout and wholesome custom. They are also all noted for being diligent women and fine house-keepers. By his marriage with Miss Luckey, Judge Gaut has six children: (1). Sarah Luckey Gaut, born February 1, 1868. (2). John Watson Gaut, born January 28, 1870. (3). Jessie Rhea Gaut, born August 16, 1872. (4 and 5). Agnes Moore and Luella Erwin Gaut, twins, born January 17, 1875. (6). Cornelius Luckey Gaut, born August 4, 1877.

Judge Gaut is a member of the Cumberland Presbyterian church, as is also his wife, who joined that denomination since her marriage.

The only method Judge Gaut has in his business affairs is to be prompt. In the court-room, as out of it, he treats everybody with becoming respect. In the management of a law suit, if there is no proof against his client to hurt him, he stops the case without introducing any. His mind is essentially of the judicial cast. He eliminates all surplusage from the proof, and addressing himself directly to the judgment of the court or jury, selects the strong point in the case to argue and argues that well. An old lawyer once said of him in open court, " He has such an affidavit face it is impos-

sible to answer him successfully." His personal habits from boyhood have been good. He has never played cards or been intemperate. His greatest ambition is to provide for his family and educate his children well. He is a most sociable man in his manners, and very fond of anecdotes and reminiscence.

HON. PRESLEY T. GLASS.

RIPLEY.

PRESLEY T. GLASS was born in Halifax county, Virginia, October 16, 1824. His parents, Dudley Glass and Nancy Carr, were of Scotch-Irish descent, his remote ancestors having settled in Virginia during the colonial period. His grandfather, Dudley Glass, was a farmer by occupation, a frugal man, of practical good sense, and a Baptist in religion. He was a captain in the Revolutionary war, as was also Maj. Glass' maternal grandfather. He died in 1827. His father, who also bore the name of Dudley, was raised on the farm and inured to habits of industry, thrift and economy. In October of the year following his father's death, he removed with his wife and younger children, three in number, Elizabeth, Presley (the subject of this sketch), and John, the youngest, then an infant, to Tennessee, and settled three miles west of Dresden, the county seat of Weakley county. That section of the State was at that time an almost unbroken wilderness, and the new settlers went to work vigorously to make homes for themselves. Mr. Glass was the owner of a few slaves, whom he put to work clearing land and building houses. A few cabins were erected, and about ten acres of land cleared in time for the next year's planting. He was successful in his farming operations, his economical habits and sound judgment standing him in good stead in his new home. At that early period, neither cotton or tobacco were grown in that section as market crops, the cereals and forage, together with hogs and such vegetables as the immigrants required, being raised. Mr. Glass generally sold his corn and oats to his merchants in sacks, and the first money his son Presley ever earned was for sewing up these sacks at a cent apiece. The father never held office of any kind, but devoted himself wholly to his farm, and soon accumulated a competency, and was regarded as a prosperous man. He was not permitted to enjoy the fruits of his well directed labors in his new home but a short time, having died in the winter of 1834, about six years after his removal to Tennessee. He was prompt and faithful in the discharge of every public and social duty, and his death was a severe loss, not only to his family, but to the new community, in the development of which he had taken an active and useful part.

Maj. Glass' mother was a daughter of Thomas Carr, a

well to do farmer, who lived and died in Halifax county, Virginia. Like her husband, she was industrious and frugal, engaging with great energy in all the household duties and industries of the early days, superintending and aiding with her own hands in the spinning and weaving of the cloth which clothed her entire family, both white and black, at least during the milder seasons of the year. In those early times in West Tennessee, a patch of flax was cultivated by almost every family, and the fibre manufactured for home use. Many hours of her children's early life were spent in listening to the whirr of Mrs. Glass' little old fashioned flax wheel, watching the unwinding of the fibres from the reel and the thread taking shape under the dexterous manipulations of her fingers. This flax was often woven into cloth by the colored women, and made into garments for her two small boys. This truly good woman died in 1859, at a ripe old age, respected and beloved by her children and neighbors. She was never a devotee of fashion, her sphere being the domestic circle, and she justly prided herself upon her skill and taste in the management of her household affairs. She was a member of the Baptist church. Industry and piety were her leading characteristics. Of nine children born to her, she left six surviving her, viz.: Thomas, Dabney, Dudley, Elizabeth, Presley T. (subject of this sketch), and John. Elizabeth is the widow of Jeptha Rogers, and has nine children. John, the youngest child, served in the Confederate army, and after the war, was a prominent newspaper editor at Trenton for sixteen years. He died in April, 1882. Dabney was a merchant, and Thomas and Dudley were farmers. The oldest daughter married W. Martin, who came from Virginia to Weakley county, Tennessee, about 1835, and accumulated there a large estate. Their descendants now reside in the town of Martin and vicinity, and are among the most intelligent and influential citizens of that section. One of the sons, Hon. George W. Martin, has been a member of both houses of the General Assembly of Tennessee, and traveled extensively abroad. (For a full account of the Martin family, see sketch of Hon. George W. Martin elsewhere in this volume).

Maj. Glass was raised on the farm of his parents, and

in his youth enjoyed such educational advantages as the then sparsely settled condition of the country afforded. The log school house, with its stick and dirt chimney, puncheon floor and benches, and its broad plank writing desk, extending across the entire width of the building, and lighted by means of an opening made in the wall by cutting out one or two logs, was his *alma mater*, and his instructors the illiterate pedagogues of the backwoods. At the age of fourteen, his widowed mother put him to work on the farm, upon which he labored continuously for four years, performing the hard tasks incident to the primitive modes of farm work of that day. Tobacco being the principal money crop of the region at that period, young Glass learned all about its culture and curing, from burning the plant-bed to preparing and packing the product for market, doing much of the labor with his own hands. At eighteen, he again entered school for a short time, going to the county academy, of which Jesse Leigh, a man of some culture and learning, but not an accurate scholar, was principal. He afterward attended one session of the Lexington, Kentucky, law school, and obtained his license in 1847, from Judge William C. Dunlap and Chancellor McCampbell. He began the practice of law in Dresden shortly afterward in connection with Hon. Emerson Etheridge, but the partnership lasted only one year, being terminated on account of the widely divergent political views entertained by the two members of the firm.

Maj. Glass first married, on December 20, 1848, in Lauderdale county, Tennessee, Miss Sarah C. Partee, who was born in the adjoining county of Haywood, April 3, 1831, and by her had two children: (1). Hiram D., born September 12, 1849, who is now a successful merchant at Ripley; married Miss Virginia Palmer, daughter of William E. Palmer, of Lauderdale county, and has six children, Mary, Laura, Presley, Hiram, Ada Sue and Frank. (2). James Nelson, who died in infancy. Mrs. Glass died July 2, 1852, at Gibson Wells, Gibson county, Tennessee. Maj. Glass' next wife, was Miss Maria S. Partee, a cousin of his first wife, to whom he was married August 15, 1855, in Panola county, Mississippi. She was born in Henry county, Tennessee, October 18, 1831, and was a daughter of S. B. Partee, her mother being a Miss Edwards, of that county. By this marriage there were two children: (1). Ada Pauline, born in Lauderdale county, June 18, 1857; educated at Brownsville and Trenton, Tennessee, and Bellwood, Kentucky, at which latter place she graduated. She was married July 4, 1877, to W. P. H. Butler, a farmer, son of a Baptist minister of Georgia. They now live at Flippin, Tennessee. (2). Mattie Irene, who died when one year old.

After the death of the second wife occurred—November —, 1860, Maj. Glass married, in Haywood, county, Tennessee, December 15, 1868, his present wife, Miss Susan Taylor Barbee, daughter of Dr. Allen J.

Barbee, of that county, a relative of Rev. Dr. Barbee, of Nashville. Her mother, Susan Taylor, was a daughter of John Y. Taylor, of Haywood county. Mrs. Glass was educated at Brownsville, and is a zealous and earnest member of the Methodist church, to which both her parents belonged. She is a lady of strong intellect and great force of character, plain and simple in her tastes, and frugal and domestic in her habits. She has made household economy, horticulture and floriculture matters of careful study all her life, and is exceedingly well informed upon all these subjects. Being gifted with superior taste in all matters in the sphere of woman's duties, she has at all times ordered her household economy with a view to her husband's happiness— in other words, possessing, in an eminent degree, those qualities that make her a help-meet indeed, and truly lovely in her husband's eyes.

The many public positions occupied by Maj. Glass during his life, show in what high esteem he has always been held by his fellow-citizens. At the age of eighteen, he was elected colonel of a regiment of State militia in Weakley county, and held the office two years, 1843 and 1844. In 1847–8, he represented Weakley county in the General Assembly of the State, having been elected as a Democrat. At this time he was only twenty-two years old, and was, by a few days, the youngest member of that Legislature. In 1848, he was presidential elector for his county, Gen. Lewis Cass being at the head of the ticket. During his first legislative experience, he was a member of the committee on the State lunatic asylum, of which Hon. John M. Bright was chairman. At this session, the plan for the establishment of the asylum, presented and urged by the great philanthropist, Miss Dix, of New York, was adopted by the General Assembly, Maj. Glass earnestly advocating the measure, both in committee and in the house of which he was a member. He regards with a just pride the part he took in founding that grand charity of our State, the Tennessee Hospital for the Insane. After removing to Lauderdale county, which was in March, 1849, he served as one of the magistrates of that county several years, from 1851 to 1857; from 1850 to 1857, he was one of the trustees of the Ripley Male Academy, and was an alderman of the town of Ripley from 1851 to 1855. Upon the breaking out of the civil war, he joined the forces of the Confederacy, and in May, 1861, was appointed commissary with the rank of major, which position he held until May 10, 1865. His first service was with Gen. Cheatham, at Union City, from May, 1861, until the removal of the forces to Columbus, Kentucky, in the autumn following. After the evacuation of Columbus, he went with the army to Island Ten as commissary on the staff of Gen. McCown, where he remained until shortly before it fell into the hands of the Federal forces. He was with McCown at Corinth, until that place was evacuated, in July, 1862, when he was ordered to Chattanooga, where he collected one million of rations for the subsistence of Gen. Bragg's army on its campaign into Kentucky. He accompanied Gen. McCown on his march from Knoxville, and was with him at the battle of Perryville, returning to Knoxville, in October, 1862, going thence to Readyville, and soon afterward engaging with McCown's command in the memorable battle of Murfreesborough. On the evacuation of Murfreesborough, he was ordered to Shelbyville, traveling all night in the rain. Soon afterward he was relieved from duty with Gen. McCown and ordered by Gen. Polk to report to Gen. Pillow, at Huntsville, Alabama, where he remained on duty until the place was evacuated, July 4, 1863. From Huntsville he went to Marietta, Georgia, where he was stationed until November, when he accompanied Gen. Pillow to Montgomery, Alabama, where he remained until the following June, going thence to Talladega in the same State. He accompanied Gen. Pillow in his expedition to Tunnel Hill, near Dalton, Georgia, where the latter had been ordered to proceed and do what he could toward damaging the tunnel on the Western and Atlantic railroad, in order to cut off supplies from Sherman's army, then commencing its march to the sea. While on the march, Gen. Pillow, learning there was a brigade of Federal troops at LaFayette, determined to make a night attack upon them. The enemy was fortified in the court-house at LaFayette, and after eight or ten hours of fruitless fighting, and the loss of several valuable men, Gen. Pillow concluded to retire. Owing to considerable random firing by the enemy, the horses belonging to the Confederates, which were being held by a small number of men detailed for the purpose, became restive and finally stampeded. The enemy keeping up a damaging fire all the time, the retreat became almost a rout. Maj. Glass, having engaged actively in the conflict, rode among the disordered and scattered troops, composed of Tennesseans and Alabamians, endeavoring to restore order. The first field officer he met was Col. Ball, of Alabama, and having asked him if he could do anything to stop the wild stampede, Ball replied: "Help me to rally them behind this fence." Failing in this effort, Maj. Glass rode a little further and met Col. Neely, who had his brigade drawn up in good order. On putting the same question to him, he replied: "Yes; let the Alabamians get to the rear and I will put a stop to the stampede." Maj. Glass rode down Neely's lines and appealed to the men as Tennesseans to stand firm and do their duty, which they did. Order was soon restored and the Confederate troops marched quietly off, the enemy giving no further pursuit. Gen. Pillow being released soon after this, Maj. Glass was ordered to report to Gen. Dan Adams, then on duty at Talladega, and was then charged with procuring supplies for the commands at Cahaba and Opelika. He was with Gen. Adams when Gen. Wilson assaulted and captured Selma, but succeeded in crossing the river and making his way to Montgomery. Being separated from his official papers, which had been sent with his servant to Demopolis, Alabama, Maj. Glass was permitted by Gen. Adams to go in that direction, with Lieut. Donelson, of Forrest's staff, and made his way to Uniontown, where he found his papers and servant, and remained a few weeks. While there he heard rumors of the surrender of Gen. Johnston, and later on, of Gen. Lee. In the meantime, Gen. Adams had gone to Meridian, Mississippi, from which point Maj. Glass received a dispatch to report there immediately. To that place he repaired promptly, and was paroled, May 10, 1865.

The war over, Maj. Glass returned to his home at Ripley, and spent the remainder of the year in trying to collect up the remains of a once prosperous mercantile and farming business. After settling up his old matters he removed to Memphis and engaged in the commission business for two years. He then moved to Trenton, and conducted editorially the Trenton *Gazette* for one year. Marrying his present wife about this time, he spent one year (1869) on a farm, returning in September of that year to Ripley, and resuming his mercantile business. The business proved a prosperous one, and he continued in it until 1877, when he turned it over to his son and devoted himself exclusively to farming, in which he is at present engaged.

In 1882, he was elected representative from Lauderdale county in the State Legislature. He was made chairman of the committee on agriculture, and was recognized as the leader in the house of the agricultural interests of the State. He was the author of the bill making important and valuable changes in the fish laws of the State, and also of the act creating the agricultural experiment station at Knoxville, under the direction of the University of Tennessee, at that place. He supported by his vote and advocacy the act creating a railroad commission, and took an active and leading part in all the important legislation of the session. He was the friend and advocate of all measures looking to the suppression of the use of ardent spirits, and introduced and warmly supported the bill to pay in full all bonds of the State held by educational institutions, in or out of the State, including especially the three hundred thousand dollars of Tennessee State bonds held by the Peabody Institute, of Baltimore. The advocacy of these measures attracted public attention to Maj. Glass, and gave him a position among the foremost of Tennessee legislators. He voted for the 50-3 settlement of the State debt, but would have preferred a settlement at 60-6, if such a settlement had been practicable; but the temper of the public mind was such that fear was felt upon the part of conservative State credit men that, should the proposition to settle at 50-3 fail, from any cause, repudiation of the entire debt would probably be the final result.

Maj. Glass was a candidate for the Democratic nomination to Congress before the convention of that party at Dyersburg, September 9, 1884. After more than two thousand ballots had been taken, he withdrew from the contest, although he had frequently come within three or four votes of the necessary two-thirds of all the votes cast. After a session of five days, the convention adjourned, late on Saturday night, September 13, having failed to make a nomination. The adjournment was to the following Thursday, and the convention met pursuant thereto at Trenton, Tennessee. Maj. Glass was not present at Trenton, nor was his name placed before the convention until after several hundred ballotings had taken place. He was then brought forward by the delegations from Gibson and Crockett counties, and nominated under the majority rule, it having been found impossible to effect a nomination under the two-thirds rule. He immediately entered the field and made a thorough canvass of the entire district. Hon. Emerson Etheridge became his competitor, but no proposition being made by him for a joint canvass—Maj. Glass being already in the field—they each canvassed separately. Mr. Etheridge being decidedly the strongest Republican in the district, brought out the entire strength of his party, increasing his vote more than three thousand over that of Capt. Lyle, who had made the race against Hon. Rice A. Pierce, two years previously. Maj. Glass was also strongly opposed by two of the Democratic newspapers of the district, on account of the manner in which he was nominated, and many of the personal friends of Hon. Rice A. Pierce opposed him with intense bitterness. Notwithstanding all this opposition, he was elected by a majority of nearly twenty-five hundred over his competitor, and the two papers of his own party that opposed him ceased to exist immediately after the election.

Maj. Glass' politics began to take shape when he was very young. His father was a Jackson man. When Crockett and Fitzgerald made the race for Congress, Maj. Glass took sides with Fitzgerald's followers, and as he investigated the political history of the country he began to allign himself with the Democratic party. He has always taken a leading interest in politics, but has been uniformly conservative; for example, he did not believe in the expediency of secession, and doubted the constitutionality of it. In his contests for the Legislature and for Congress his speeches have been mainly on the agricultural and business interests of the country—first, to show that agriculture is the great industry of the country; that more than one-half the population are engaged in it; and, consequently, are entitled to a large recognition at the hands of the Federal government. He is in favor of a tariff for revenue, so adjusted within revenue limits as to afford protection to all American industries, and believes that the protective policy, together with our navigation laws, has been the chief cause of the loss to America of the carrying trade which we enjoyed in 1855. In other words, we have fostered our manufacturing industries to the great detriment of our carrying trade, building up the one as hot-house plants, and almost destroying the other.

His election to Congress by a brilliant majority, is to be accounted for on two grounds: First, his moral character; and, secondly, the interest he has always manifested on the stump, in the Legislature, and as editor, in the agricultural interests of the State, and especially of his own district, comprising the counties of Haywood, Lauderdale, Dyer, Obion, Lake, Weakley, Gibson, and Crockett—one of the most productive agricultural districts in the State. Secondly: In 1860, he supported Stephen A. Douglas, believing he was one of the few men living who was able to prevent war between the States; and being devoted to the union of the States, Maj. Glass did not favor secession till the integrity of the Union was broken by the secession of South Carolina, when he thought it was better for the South to stand together, and favored the secession of Tennessee.

As a speaker, he has good command of language, and states his propositions with a clearness that shows he has mastered the subjects he handles, and is familiar with the history of political questions. His ambition seems all unselfish, and he aims only at the good of the country with which his own interests are identified.

His character was formed on the farm. His parents were never rich, and their children were required to do some farm work. He had but little money during his minority, and was never disposed to be extravagant. His tastes were simple and his habits economical. His patrimony was quite small, and he early recognized the fact that he must use both economy and industry in order to rise in the world; and in not having the advantage of a collegiate education, he was put at a disadvantage with many of his contemporaries; but having ambition to do good and make himself useful, he engaged in mercantile business, and pursued it with diligence and energy, and whilst he gave up the practice of law very early, he kept up his habits of reading, and studied closely the history of his own country, and especially the lives of the founders of American institutions. He mingled freely with the masses, learned their struggles and difficulties, and was always in sympathy with them. He studied closely the industrial interests of the people, and was always opposed to monopolies, and regarded with keen apprehension the growing corporations of the land, believing that there is intelligence and virtue enough in the masses to govern the country successfully, and that capital in the hands of a very small minority ought not to be allowed to direct the legislation of the country in its interest, to the detriment and partial enslavement of the majority. Being a practical man, on the stump he does not say sharp things, nor tell anecdotes, but any assemblage of people that listens to him must see clearly his positions, and the reasons that sustain them. Hence, his powerful influence as a speaker. He is always calm, collected, dealing in facts and figures, and draws his illustrations of an idea or a policy from the results of its own history, and back through American history, and into the depths of antiquity, where it first began. He never possessed great money-making capacity, and worked harder than most men to accomplish what he has in the way of property.

He has drawn around himself a following, because the people came to have confidence in his honesty and integrity; and when in office he always guarded the public treasury with great vigilance. Hence, he was not looked on with great favor by those having jobs; and never considered popularity worth the cost, unless it followed as the reward of correct conduct.

In religion he is a Baptist, and has been liberal to the Baptists and Methodists especially, as his wife is a member of the Methodist church. He is a Sunday-school teacher, but not an officer in his church.

As a speaker and conversationalist, he is always instructive, and always a surprise, for the reason that he is so original in his expressions and modes of thought. Very clearly he is a man that wears his own head, does his own thinking, and is utterly free from pretense and mere sham and show. He appears in this volume, not only as a representative Tennessee congressman, but a representative Tennessee man, of the best type.

During his brief service in Congress, Maj. Glass has shown himself an attentive and useful member, ever alive to the material interests of the country, and laboring earnestly to promote the welfare of the farming and industrial classes, whose claims on the fostering legislation of the government have been, to a great extent, subordinated to far less important matters. On March 6, 1886, he delivered a well prepared speech upon a bill, introduced by himself, to promote agriculture. The intention of the bill was to enlarge the scope of commercial agents, by requiring them to embrace in their reports to the State and treasury departments the subject of agriculture as well as of commerce and manufactures, and in its advocacy Maj. Glass delivered a most practical argument. The limits of the present sketch allow only the publication here of the following extracts, which will give a fair sample of the speaker's style, and his strong, effective manner of presenting facts and arguments: "Under the present law, our consuls are required to procure and transmit to the department of State accurate commercial information of their districts, and to report the prices-current of merchandise as often as may be required to the treasury department. Now this bill would have them to procure and transmit through the same channels, information of the condition and prospects, monthly, of the crops within the limits of their consulates, so that the facts may be compiled and embraced in the monthly bulletins of the crop reports of the commissioner of agriculture; and also to

give at least once a year, or oftener if so required by the State department, the prices-current of all such merchandise and farm products, orchard and garden, as are imported into the ports of their consulates, thereby giving to the farmers of our country a full knowledge of the character and quantity of the products of the soil of the countries where this government has a consul, in order that our people may be informed as to when there may be a demand and a market for their surplus products of the soil and the prices-current of the same. We can not give to the farmer too much information on this subject. And it is certainly the duty of the government to do this much to advance so great and overshadowing an industry, particularly when it can be done at so small a cost. The agriculturists of the country must become more self-asserting and enforce their just demands for larger and broader recognition in the legislation of Congress. It is the duty of the government to provide for this large and useful class of our population all such information as will entitle them to know where to find the best and dearest markets for their products and to remove as far as practicable all obstacles to their access to them. This becomes imperative, in view of the fact that most of the farm products have tended downward for years in price, and many have reached a price below which there is no margin above the cost of production.

"Legislation should be directed to the end that the farmer be given the freedom of the open markets of the world and all proper facilities afforded him for the transportation and exportation of his products to any market, domestic and foreign. This very numerous class seeks no exclusive privileges, but only such as are enjoyed by every other class in the land. This they have a right to demand, and Congress should not deny it to them. The law should compel our consuls to gather and furnish this agricultural information, that the commissioner may scatter it broadcast over the land.

"There is no good reason why our consuls should confine their reports to the commodities exported from the countries to which they are accredited. Let them embrace all articles imported of considerable value, especially of the products of the soil, the mine, and the workshop, the character of farm tools used in cultivating crops, and whether of domestic or foreign manufacture. This will give our industrial population a better idea of the best markets for their surplus products, and when and where to export them. The masses need information on these subjects, and it is the duty of the government to procure and furnish it. It can be done through government agency at much less cost to the citizens than through private channels. A broad and liberal policy in this direction should be inaugurated and carried out.

"The farms of the United States are worth more than ten billions, a larger sum than is invested in any

44

other single industry, and the annual returns from these farms exceed three billion dollars. The manufacturing industries of our country produce annually, in round numbers, five billions three hundred and sixty-nine millions, but more than half of this is the cost of raw material, leaving as the gross value of the products of manufacture one billion nine hundred and seventy-five million—little more than one-half the value of the farm products. Agriculture furnishes employment to a greater number of laborers than any other occupation. About fifty-two per cent. of our entire population are engaged in this industry or are dependent upon it for a living. Of the seven million six hundred and seventy thousand farmers, about four millions own the farms they cultivate, and nearly four millions are farm laborers. Let us dignify this great industry by giving to it a larger and broader recognition in the legislation of this body. Let tardy justice be done that class who toil in the field and the shop, and are the most law-abiding, patriotic and useful class in the land. This country is pre-eminently agricultural, and in the very nature of things must continue to remain such."

COL. MATTHEW C. GALLAWAY.

MEMPHIS.

THE eminent editor whose name stands at the head of this biography, and who is recognized as one of the ablest, most erudite, and most successful journalists of the South, was born in Huntsville, Alabama, March 5, 1820, but was raised in Morgan and Lawrence counties of that State. His father, Wiley Gallaway, was a native of Oglethorpe county, Georgia, came to Alabama, in 1818, located at Huntsville, moved from that place to Morgan county, in 1822, and settled near where Danville in that county now is, and was one of the first school teachers in the State of Alabama. He married, at Bowling Green, Kentucky, in 1817. In 1824, he moved from Morgan to Lawrence county, and taught school there until about 1830, when he was elected probate judge of Lawrence county, which office he held about twenty-seven years. In 1859, he moved to Texas with his two daughters, Mrs. James Townsend and Mrs. James Wise, and there died and was buried at a place called Lone Pine, in his seventy-fifth year. Judge Gallaway was known as the finest scholar of his day and State. He was also a most popular man, as is evidenced by his having held an elective office for so long a time, his integrity, honesty and inflexibility of character winning for him the implicit confidence of the entire community. The family strength in the county is also seen in the remarkable fact, that at one time, while he was the probate judge, his son, William M. Gallaway, was the circuit judge, elected by the Legislature, and his nephew, Amos P. Gallaway, was, at the same time, sheriff of the same county. This concentration of office in his family, however, defeated him at the succeeding election, but at the election next ensuing, he was re-elected probate judge by an almost unanimous vote, the people not appreciating his services until they had had a trial of getting along without them four years. He was succeeded by his brother-in-law, Judge Charles Gibson, and Judge James H. McDonald, his son-in-law, now fills the position, showing that the office has been in the family ever since 1830, except the brief interval before mentioned.

The Gallaway family is of Scotch-Irish origin, and came over to Oglethorpe county, Georgia, just prior to the Revolution, in which three brothers took part on the patriot side. Many descendants of the stock now live in North Carolina and Georgia.

Col. Gallaway's paternal grandfather, Matthew Gallaway, a native of Oglethorpe county, Georgia, died in Morgan county, Alabama, in 1822. He married Mary East, who lived to the advanced age of ninety-six, and died in Oglethorpe county, Georgia, having gone back to that State after the death of her husband. Hon. E. H. East, of Nashville, whose sketch appears elsewhere in this volume, is a descendant of the same East family.

The "C" in Col. Gallaway's name stands for Campbell, he having been named for Colin Campbell, a conspicuous character in Scottish history, and the Gallaways and Campbells being of kith and kin.

Col. Gallaway's mother, née Miss Mary McDowell was the daughter of John McDowell, a native Irishman, who came to this country, the only one of his family when a boy. He settled first in Oglethorpe county, Georgia, moved to Bowling Green, Kentucky, thence to Lawrence county, Alabama, and thence to Moulton, where he engaged in the hat trade and made a handsome property. In early manhood, he served as an American soldier in the Revolutionary war, for which he drew a pension till his death at Moulton, Alabama, in 1841, eighty odd years of age. Col. Gallaway's mother was a member of the Baptist church, and was celebrated for her piety, charity and fine practical sense, just the wife, indeed, for an educated man like her husband. The fine vein of broad, every-day business sense that characterizes the son, was derived from the mother, whom, in this respect, and in his keen sense of the ludicrous, as well as in physique, he more resembles than he does his father. As will be seen, however, from his portrait accompanying this sketch, Col. Gallaway takes also after his father's side, whose mother was an East, and there is a striking resemblance between Judge East and Col. Gallaway, as will appear on comparing their portraits in this volume. Col. Gallaway's mother died at Moulton, Alabama, in 1855, at the age of fifty-seven, leaving six children, all of whom are dead, except the oldest, the subject of this sketch. He has adopted two of his nieces, Lucille and Mary Mc. Wise, daughters of his sister, Elizabeth Gallaway Wise, who died in 1867, leaving these two daughters to his care. Lucille Wise is now the wife of James V. Fussell, a leading merchant at Forrest City, Arkansas, and has one child living, Annie, and one dead, Fanny Gallaway, named in honor of Col. Gallaway's wife. Mary Mc. Wise married James A. White, a stock dealer at Pulaski, Tennessee, and has three children, one, Fanny Wilkes, also named for Mrs. Gallaway.

One of Col. Gallaway's cousins, Mrs. John Malone, *nee* Miss Sallie A. Reedy, is distinguished for having written more poetry of a high order than any poetess in the South.

Having received the advantages of a common school education up to the age of sixteen, Col. Gallaway's father then placed him in his office as deputy clerk, and there his history begins, which, *en passant*, it may be well to say, was rather boisterous and tempestuous. Indeed, he was celebrated as being the wildest boy in the county. When his father found he could not manage him, he entered into a conspiracy with Hon. Thomas M. Peters, since chief justice of Alabama, for the purpose of bringing about a reformation in the wayward youngster. The terms of the conspiracy were, that his father should disinherit him and Judge Peters, then editor of the Moulton *News*, should take him into his printing office to see what could be made of him. They did not have to wait long for the opportunity, for one day young Gallaway whipped a youngster about his own age most terribly. According to the programme, then, when Gallaway went to his father's office as usual, his father took him to the door and told him to go; never to put his foot in his father's house or office again; that he had tried to control him and had failed, and now he must face the world and take care of himself. Gallaway flew to his mother for comfort and intercession, but she being in the secret also, ordered him out of the house. Here was a perplexity. Although the mother permitted him to get his clothes, she would not relent in her banishment. Taking a seat on the court-house fence steps, the young man seriously contemplated the situation, and was lost in wondering what he would do, when Judge Peters, answering to his cue, saw him, and, as if by accident, passed by, and inquired, "Why so sad? What's the matter?" The matter was explained. Peters seemed greatly distressed, offered his sympathy and promised to intercede, provided Gallaway would go to work in his office and change his wild course of liv-

ing. He promised to give him one hundred dollars for his services the first year, without board, and try and induce his parents to let him board at home, provided he promised to do better. That night the arrangements were perfected, and next morning young Gallaway was duly installed in the printing office. It was in November, 1836, the day of the presidential election between White and Van Buren. The foreman tied a newspaper around him and put him to rolling off election tickets. Three hours' work blistered his hands till they bled. Next day he was put to learning the cases, and in three months from that day he could beat any man in the office setting type, and did set up most of the type for the weekly paper that year. He not only did that, but rolled the forms, did most of the press work on an old-fashioned hand press, mailed the papers to subscribers, and was so energetic and so changed in his conduct for a year, that, at the end of his engagement with Peters, his father purchased the office and made him a present of it. Accordingly, he became a newspaper proprietor and publisher, in November, 1837, when only seventeen years old, and continued to publish his paper in Moulton from that date until August, 1840. About that time he was visited by John H. Tice, since celebrated as a meteorologist, and who recently died at St. Louis, who came at the instance of the Democrats of Tuscumbia, Alabama, and induced him to remove his office to Tuscumbia, at which place he and Tice started the first Democratic paper, the *Franklin Democrat*, in opposition to the *North Alabamian*, then edited by Asa Messenger. The contest of 1840 was celebrated for its excitement and bitterness, and Gallaway, young as he was, took an active part in that canvass, and made quite a reputation in it as an editor. In 1841, he sold out the *Democrat* to A. C. Matthews, removed to Decatur, Alabama, and bought an interest in the *Southern Murcury*, in connection with William G. Stephenson. There he married, July 21, 1842, Miss Fanny B. Barker, at the residence of her uncle, Col. L. S. Banks.

In December, 1842, he sold out and did not again engage in the newspaper business till January, 1844, when he purchased the Florence *Gazette*, the oldest paper in the State, having been established in 1819. At that place, he was eminently successful in the newspaper business. There were many bitter contests for Congress in the Florence district, in which he always took a prominent part. In 1850, there was much excitement in regard to the passage of the compromise measures. Gen. George S. Houston, afterward governor and United States senator, had long represented that district in Congress, but had retired and was succeeded by David Hubbard, who announced himself an avowed disunionist, on account of the compromise measures. Gallaway, although a secessionist, did not believe those measures cause sufficient for a dissolution of the Union, and determined Hubbard should be beaten. On account of his ability as a canvasser and stump speaker, aspirants were reluctant to oppose him. Three weeks before the election, Gallaway hoisted at the head of the *Gazette*, the name of George S. Houston as candidate for Congress. Houston, after making an experiment of a week, became alarmed, withdrew from the canvass, and failed to fill his next appointment. Gallaway hearing of this, said he must be elected, whether a candidate or not, and should be; kept his name at the head of the paper, urged his support, printed ten thousand circulars, distributed them over the district, went over the district, encouraged Houston, who continued in the canvass from that day and was triumphantly elected, the Whigs rallying to his support. In every canvass thereafter, Gallaway took a prominent position, especially in the contest between Joshua L. Martin, an independent candidate, and Nathaniel Terry, Democratic nominee for governor. He made more character in that exceedingly bitter canvass than in any other up to that time. He made a State reputation. He went to Florence with only two hundred dollars in money; when he left there in September, 1855, he was independent, with upwards of twenty thousand dollars, so successful had he been in the newspaper business. He located, in 1855, at Aberdeen, Mississippi, and started a newspaper called the "*Sunny South*," which was also a success, as evidenced by the fact that the original cost was one thousand eight hundred dollars, and in August, 1857, less than two years, he sold the paper for three thousand seven hundred dollars.

He attended the great celebration at Memphis, in May, 1857, of the completion of the Memphis and Charleston railroad, and was so pleased with the prospects of Memphis and its great future, and desiring a larger field to operate in, having exhausted the field already occupied, he determined to move there. Returning home and selling out in August, he commenced preparing for a newspaper which he was anxious to commence on the first of January, and had already ordered materials, but had not issued a prospectus, because he was perplexed as to the name of the new paper, having a contempt for old worn-out and insignificant names and wanting something new and attractive. Out of a list of about a dozen new names thought of, he had nearly made up his mind to select "Sesame," but a friend pronouncing it "Se-same," he rejected it. At a church meeting he heard a preacher use the words, "The great avalanche of public opinion," and thereupon he determined, after some thought, and discussing it with his wife, to adopt for the title of his new paper, the word *Avalanche*, and that night issued his prospectus. The novelty of the name attracted universal attention. When he started the paper, he deposited ten thousand dollars in Wicks' bank, which he proposed to risk in the enterprise. Although there were three morning papers then in Memphis—the *Appeal*, *Eagle and Enquirer*, and *Bulletin*—at the end of three months, the *Avalanche* was paying expenses, and a half

interest was sold to Colin Campbell, of Columbia, Tennessee, for a large advance on the cost. Campbell soon afterward dying, his interest was purchased by Col. M. W. Cluskey, author of "Cluskey's Political Text Book," and a brilliant and able journalist. The paper grew in popularity and value, having taken a prominent part in the contest which brought about the war, and being regarded as the exponent of extreme southern sentiment. On the night South Carolina seceded from the Union, thirty thousand dollars was offered for the paper.

In the meantime, in 1860, Col. Gallaway was appointed postmaster at Memphis, by President James Buchanan. He was not an applicant for the office, and was astonished when he received official notice of his appointment. He served as postmaster, still editing the *Avalanche*, until the surrender of Memphis, June 6, 1862.

When that event came, Col. Gallaway joined Forrest's cavalry as aide-de-camp on Gen. Forrest's staff, and served with him till the end of the war. He served in East Tennessee, Georgia and Mississippi, taking part in the battles of Chickamauga, Bryson's Cross-roads, the raid into Memphis in August, 1864, and was in the battles of Nashville and Murfreesborough; at the storming of Fort Pillow, and on many raids, capturing troops, etc. At Chickamauga, he was slightly wounded, and his horse was shot in the head, while in the charge upon the enemy at Pulaski. He was also in the fight at Selma, and in numerous other engagements. For a fuller account of Col. Gallaway's military career, see "Forrest's Life and History of the War," by Gen. Jordan.

The war over, he returned to Memphis, in May, 1865. When Memphis fell he had disposed of the *Avalanche*, and the parties who purchased becoming bankrupt, he was forced to commence life over again without a dollar. He determined to revive the *Avalanche*, and for this purpose, went on to Washington and procured a pardon from Andrew Johnson, returned to Memphis and applied to his friends, Capt. Dan Able and Col. Samuel Tate, who were then doing a prosperous business, making known to them his desires and wants. They asked him how much money he would require? He told them he could start the paper with three thousand dollars. They told him to call next morning, when they gave him a letter of credit for ten thousand dollars, only three thousand of which, however, he used. Through this aid, the *Avalanche* was revived in January, 1866, with W. H. Rhea as his partner. The paper was more successful than ever before. The money borrowed was paid back at maturity, and the *Avalanche* was more prosperous than any paper had ever been in Memphis. The *Avalanche* fought a bitter fight against the objectionable men put in office, and controlling the negroes there, who were enfranchised, while the white citizens were disfranchised. Gallaway's articles were terrific in their personality, and for some of them he was arrested—probably a dozen times—and confined in jail one night, only for utterances in a free and unshackled press, which, however, the judge, a carpet-bagger, regarded as contempt of court. The citizens of Memphis came to tear the jail down, but Gallaway forbade them. These events, and the fierce and bitter tone of his articles, made the *Avalanche* the most noted paper of the South for the time. This war of the *Avalanche* continued till August, 1869, when Hon. D. W. C. Senter, having been elected governor with the avowed purpose of enfranchising the rebels, the tone of the *Avalanche* was modified, having gained the important point for which it had so persistently contended, the enfranchisement of the rebel soldiers and their sympathisers.

In the meantime, Col. A. J. Kellar, who had become a part owner in the *Avalanche*, seemed disposed to go too far in the opposite extreme. This produced a disagreement between Gallaway and Kellar, resulting in the latter purchasing the former's interest in the *Avalanche*, in April, 1870.

Col. Gallaway then bought stock in the Memphis *Appeal*, and became connected with that paper in May, 1870, at which time there were thirty stockholders. He and Col. J. M. Keating, his present partner, began purchasing the interests of the other stockholders, and these two now own the entire paper and edit it. To show the success of this paper, reference need only be made to the fact that, in 1868, the *Appeal* sold at public auction for twenty-one thousand dollars, and that in August, 1883, one hundred thousand dollars was offered for it and refused.

Col. Gallaway has become celebrated in the South as authority on the *code duello*, and has acted as second in two *affaires du honeur*. He has favored and still advocates duelling as a peace measure, believing that when the code is established and punctiliously observed, it prevents instead of causing the shedding of blood. He was second in the celebrated duel in which H. C. Chambers killed Col. W. H. Lake, both of Mississippi; was also second in the duel between George R. Phelan and James Brazzallaire, in which the latter was badly wounded. On account of his recognized familiarity with the code, he has been selected as referee during the last twenty years in scores of personal difficulties, which were all satisfactorily settled, except in the two cases named, and which were considered impossible to adjust amicably. Col. Gallaway is an extremist in everything—friendships, enmities and charities, but is very magnanimous and forgiving, and without malice. As long as the cause exists he is pugnacious, but as soon as that is removed, he relents and shows an unbounded generosity.

In politics, he has always been a Democrat without variation, and though he has made more office-holders than any man in the South, has never sought or held office himself, except that of postmaster, before mentioned. He has been a delegate to nearly all the party State conventions, and twice a delegate to national Democratic conventions. He has never been a public speaker, for the reason that he can never think consecutively on his feet, becoming bewildered as soon as he rises to speak. On this account, as well as for other reasons, he has never been a candidate for office, and declined nomination for the Legislature.

As an evidence of his generosity and kindness, he and his wife, though they have no children of their own, have raised, during the forty years of their married life, some thirty children, who needed protectors, orphan kin, either on his or her side. Col. Gallaway joined the Odd Fellows when a young man, but has not taken any interest in secret societies. Though a firm believer in the Christian religion, he belongs to no church, entertaining liberal views, and opposing sectarianism. In his younger days, he lived a stormy life that led to excesses, but for several years past has been living in quietness and tranquillity. The conflicts which he used formerly to engage in, and which were suited to his nature, are now abhorrent to him in his anxiety for peace and a serene old age.

When the war began, he had, as postmaster, ten thousand dollars belonging to the United States government. This amount was seized by military force of the Confederate government, but so soon as peace was declared, he was sued for the recovery of this money by the United States government and judgment obtained, which was subsequently paid by him. Per contra, the Federal forces used his house in Memphis as headquarters for nearly two years after the war, took about two thousand dollars' worth of furniture and silverware when they left, and did him other damage, but for all this he has never received anything.

The episode in his life, when his father disinherited him, marks the beginning of the manhood of Col. Gallaway. From that day, he resolved to be a man, and by energy and close attention to business, has succeeded in every newspaper with which he has been connected, until now he is half owner of one of the finest newspaper properties in the South, and is classed among the solid men of his city. His caustic style of writing has given him his success, for it gave notice to all the world that the editor is a man true to himself, swearing in no man's word, *librata suis ponderibus.*

The following extract from a biographical work, recently published in Memphis, shows how he is estimated as an editor in that city: "Col. M. C. Gallaway commenced his editorial career in 1837, when only seventeen years of age, and has been connected with the press ever since, and during that time has written more than any southern journalist now living. In May, 1870, he purchased an interest in the *Appeal*, which, outside of Louisville, is regarded as the ablest and most popular of all the southern Democratic newspapers, as is attested by its large circulation. Col. Gallaway is ardent and enthusiastic in his temperament, and is therefore extreme in his friendships and his enmities. He defends his friends with the same energy that he attacks his opponents. Without the wit of Prentice, he more nearly approaches the great Kentucky editor in withering sarcasm, biting irony, and crushing ridicule, than any writer of the South."

Mrs. Gallaway was educated at Huntsville, Alabama, and was teaching school when Col. Gallaway married her. She is a lady of extraordinary character, of strong, vigorous intellect, judgment almost infallible, and is consulted, not only by her husband, but by friends, for her advice in important matters. She is a strong advocate of woman's rights, but has never gone to the extreme of woman suffrage, which she thinks would sink rather than elevate her sex. In her own vigorous mind, she believes woman intellectually the equal of man, and consequently ought to have the same rights. Her charity has been unbounded. She was elected president of the Home for the Homeless prior to the war, and bought a lot on which to build a charitable institution, which was not constructed, on account of the war coming on. After the war, she converted this institution into a refuge for maimed Confederate soldiers, which, for several years, she kept up by soliciting contributions from the public, and often from her own means. The first few years after the conflict between the States, her door was the hammering place for maimed Confederate soldiers, their orphans and widows. In order to benefit this class, she got up what was called the "Fanny

Thruston Society," and invited distinguished lecturers throughout the South to address the public, and from the proceeds of these lectures, she raised thousands of dollars, which were appropriated for the benefit of this class. In 1866, she conceived the idea of erecting a monument to the Confederate soldiers, and by persistent importunities, succeeded in raising about five thousand dollars, which built the splendid monument now in Elmwood cemetery, Memphis, erected to the memory of those noble men.

Mrs. Gallaway is first and foremost in all works of charity in Memphis; is the oldest communicant of the Cumberland Presbyterian church in that city; when able, has been a regular teacher in the Sunday-school; and has always been president or controller of societies for the benefit of the church. Justice is the star that directs her footsteps, and her regard for truth and her aversion for falsehood, are leading traits in her character. Her sense of duty controls her in everything. Every one who knows her—so implicit is their faith in her sense of justice and her fine judgement—refers to her for opinions. But the highest praise of all is, that though married forty-two years, she has never given her husband a cross word. Her motto seems to have been, "Beware of the first quarrel." No woman in the South is better known or more respected than she for a character which all who know her regard as faultless, and in Memphis she is treasured as one of the jewels of the city.

MAJ. GILBERT V. RAMBAUT.

MEMPHIS

MAJ. GILBERT V. RAMBAUT was born in Petersburg, Virginia, February 13, 1837, and lived there until his twenty-first year. He never attended college, but took a thorough course in the academies of Petersburg, beginning his education under Prof. McGhee, continuing it under Prof. Thomas D. Davidson, now of Abingdon, Virginia, and finishing at a military school under Lieut. Bass, at the age of seventeen. His tastes all ran in the direction of a mercantile life, and as soon as he left school, he went into the tobacco business with his father at Petersburg. Wishing to get into a newer and wider field of enterprise, he concluded to take the advice of Horace Greeley to "go west and grow up with the country." In February, 1858, he moved to Memphis, Tennessee, and engaged in the tobacco business, which he followed for one year. He then sold out and went into the hotel business as clerk at the Worsham House, and shortly afterward bought out the proprietor and formed the firm of Rambaut & Cox, who carried on the hotel until the begin-

ning of the war. In the meantime, he had become engaged in railroading, in company with the firm of Hopper & Co., and had taken a contract to build a railroad through Attala county, Mississippi, the road being an extension of the New Orleans, Jackson and Great Northern railroad, which was projected from Canton, Mississippi, to Tuscumbia, Alabama.

When the war broke out, he left Mr. Cox in charge of the hotel and enlisted for the Confederate service, entering Forrest's old regiment as a private in company H, commanded by Capt. McDonald. He served through the war with Forrest, and took part in all his battles and campaigns, with two brief exceptions; once during the Fort Pillow raid, when he had been left in command at Columbus, Mississippi, and the other time at the Memphis fight, when, having been ordered back to Macon, Mississippi, from Oxford, Mississippi, on business, and though telegraphed by his general, failed to join his command before they left.

After the battle of Fort Donelson, when Forrest, who

had cut through the enemy's lines and escaped with his regiment, was called upon by the war department to make a report, it was written by Maj. Rambaut, at the dictation of Forrest. After the battle of Shiloh, where he was slightly wounded in the hand, he was one of ten men who went with Forrest, who had been brevetted brigadier-general and sent into Middle Tennessee, and when Forrest was put in command of a brigade of cavalry and sent with Bragg on his Kentucky campaign, he acted as commissary of the brigade. He and his friend, Maj. John P. Strange, and Gen. Forrest were all promoted for gallantry in the battle of Murfreesborough, which was fought on Gen. Forrest's birth-day—July 21, 1862—but their commissions were not received before going into the Kentucky campaign, and after the the return to Murfreesborough, Strange and Rambaut were offered commissions as colonel and lieutenant-colonel, respectively, in the field, in the new command which Forrest was forming. On the morning that they were to be assigned to duty, they were about to part from Gen. Forrest, in the office of Gen. Joseph B. Palmer, at Murfreesborough, when Forrest, who had become deeply attached to them while they had served on his staff, expressed with great feeling his regret that their relations were to be severed. Moved by this, they threw up their appointments as field officers, and continued on the staff, Maj. Rambaut starting for Richmond that night to bring out the commissions for the whole staff, his, Strange's and Forrest's bearing date July 21, 1862.

In February, 1863, while returning from the second fight at Fort Donelson, he was captured near Kinderhook, Tennessee, by the command of Gen. Jeff. C. Davis, whom he had known at Fortress Monroe, Virginia, when Davis was a lieutenant in the regular United States army. He was treated with great kindness, and after being kept at Nashville on parole for about three weeks, was sent to Camp Chase and thence to Fort Delaware. After two weeks at Fort Delaware, he was exchanged at City Point, Virginia, reported to the war department at Richmond, and rejoined his command during the Streight raid, having been in the hands of the enemy about three months. Maj. Strange, who was his most intimate friend before, during and since the war, was with him in prison.

In a skirmish at Dillard's plantation, between Pontotoc and Harrisburg, July 12, 1864, Maj. Rambaut was wounded in the knee, but did not leave the field. During the campaign in the "western district," he was in seventeen fights in thirteen days. On one occasion, he was in command, with Gen. Forrest serving on his staff. Forrest had left him at Trenton, Tennessee, in command of one company, a lot of dismounted men, and Morton's battery of four guns and seven ammunition wagons, the whole force amounting to about one hundred and twenty-five men, with orders to proceed to Kenton station, while he, with the rest of the command, was engaged in tearing up the railroad. When

within about two miles of Kenton, he was informed by a citizen that it was occupied by the enemy, two hundred and fifty strong, entrenched in a stockade. Having his orders to camp at the place, and being convinced that Gen. Forrest was aware of the fact that it was in possession of the enemy, he concluded to make an attack and dislodge them, if possible. Having made his plans, he was advancing to the attack, having driven in the Federal skirmishers, when Gen. Forrest galloped up and called to him to know what he had done, and being informed, told him to carry out his designs, but instead of taking command himself, acted as a member of Maj. Rambaut's staff during the fight. This was a very neat compliment from a gallant commander to an equally gallant subordinate. Maj. C. S. Seay, of Gen. Forrest's staff, acted as Maj. Rambaut's adjutant. The enemy were driven in, and fire from the artillery being opened upon them, they surrendered at the second discharge.

He served through the Hood campaign in Tennessee, in 1864, and when Gen. Forrest, commanding the rear guard on the retreat from Nashville, after holding the town of Columbia for five days, had fallen back and routed the enemy between the Tennessee river and Pulaski, thus putting an end to the pursuit, he sent Maj. Rambaut to bear the dispatch to Gen. Hood.

Surrendering at Gainesville, Alabama, on the 13th of May, 1865, he returned to Memphis with the intention of going at once to Mobile, Alabama, to enter into business with Mr. Weaver, of Columbus, Mississippi. Changing his plans, he went into the grocery and cotton business with his father-in-law, Mr. E. M. Apperson, at Memphis, and remained with him up to June 1, 1885, and is now devoting his time to the management of the Union Stock Yard and Fertilizer Company, of which company he is the largest stockholder.

Previous to the war, Maj. Rambaut was a Whig, and twice voted against secession, but went into the war in defense of his adopted State. Since the war, he has voted with the Democrats, but has never sought or held political office.

He has been actively connected with the public interests and public education in Memphis, and has served as a member of the city school board for the past twelve years. He served as president of the board for two years, under the old system, and when the charter was amended, in 1883, vacating all the offices, he was one of five commissioners appointed by the governor, was elected by them president, and served until January, 1884, when he was elected by the people, and again made president. He was re-elected a commissioner by the people in January, 1886, with the present taxing district officers, for a term of four years. He was a director in the Planters Insurance Company of Memphis, from its organization till 1882. He has been president of the Mechanics' Building and Loan Association from its organization, in 1877, to the present time. He is one of the originators of the Memphis Union Stock Yard and Fertilizer company, which has a capital stock of two hundred and fifty thousand dollars, and is composed of the solid men of Memphis, having in its board of directors seven of the presidents of the leading corporations of the city. He is also president of the North American Holstein Cattle Registry and Breeders' Association, and he is a stockholder of various other corporations. He has been for several years president of the Mozart Musical Society of Memphis, having been elected to the position without solicitation on his part, and not knowing of the action of the society until told of it by a friend the next day. This society is now one of the institutions of Memphis. It is conducted in connection with the conservatory of music, and has an associate membership of two hundred and fifty, composed of the leading business men of the city, who keep it up, while an active membership of one hundred and seventy-five gentlemen and ladies compose the chorus. Here the people of Memphis receive at their doors the best musical instruction which the country affords, and in the festivals which are given by the society, the best musical talent of Europe and America is employed. When Maj. Rambaut was elected its president, there were only eighteen members and a class of eleven. In sixty days, there were two hundred members and a class of one hundred. He became a Mason in Leila Scott Lodge, Memphis, in 1860, and has filled nearly all the subordinate offices, served one term as Master of the lodge, and is now Eminent Commander of St. Elmo Commandery, Knights Templar. He is also a member of the Knights of Honor and the Royal Arcanum.

Maj. Rambaut was married at Memphis, March 5, 1860, to Miss Sue Apperson, daughter of E. M. Apperson. Her father was born in Charles City county, Virginia, and moved to Memphis nearly fifty years ago, and is now about the oldest merchant in the city. He is well and widely known in business circles, and has been connected with most of the principal banks and insurance companies of the city, and is also largely engaged in planting in Mississippi, Tennessee and Arkansas. The family of Apperson is of Welsh descent. Mrs. Rambaut's mother, Miss Moorcock, a lady of Scotch-English descent, was born at Berkley, Virginia, the daughter of a Methodist minister. Mrs. Rambaut was born in Halifax county, North Carolina, in February, 1839, and was educated at Memphis and at Somerville, Tennessee. She is domestic in her tastes, and devoted to her home and her children. She is a member of the Protestant Episcopal church, of which Maj. Rambaut is also a communicant. To this union have been born six children: (1). Susie, born February 10, 1861, now wife of J. Monroe Williamson, a planter near Helena, Arkansas. They have two children; a son, Vincent R., born November 11, 1879, and a daughter, Irene, born January 1, 1884. (2). Maggie Elise, born August 6, 1865; a young lady of rare accomplishments,

who graduated in two institutions of learning before attaining her seventeenth year. (3). Edna, born November 3, 1867. (4). Vinnie, born August, 5, 1870. (5). Maybelle, born May 9, 1872. (6). G. V. Rambaut, jr., born September 6, 1873.

The Rambaut family is of French descent. Maj. Rambaut's father was Capt. G. V. Rambaut, a tobacco merchant at Petersburg, Virginia. He was born at Bates' Spring, near Petersburg, in 1799, and died November 21, 1874, being at the time of his death the oldest native-born citizen of Petersburg. He was the first and only commander of the Petersburg Guards, a prominent military organization forty years ago, and at the beginning of the war of secession, though more than sixty years of age, entered the Confederate service as a captain of artillery. In 1867, he moved to Memphis and remained five years, and then returned to Petersburg, Virginia, where he died. He left five children: (1). Mrs. William E. Morrison of Petersburg, Virginia, a lady of remarkable culture and literary attainments, particularly in history. (2). Gilbert V. Rambaut, subject of this sketch. (3). Robert D. Rambaut, of Memphis. (4.) Mrs. Louis Warrington, of Baltimore. (5). Mrs. Nannie Hill, of Richmond, Virginia.

Maj. Rambaut's grandfather, Richard Rambaut, a merchant of Bordeaux, France, came to America shortly after the Revolution. His paternal grandmother had one of the most eventful lives ever known by any woman. She was the daughter—in fact the only child—of the Count De LaRoche, of Saint Domingo (a younger son of the famous LaRochefoucald family), being, by virtue of this, sole inheritor of the Saint Domingo estates, and a countess in her own right. She was betrothed in early childhood to her cousin, the only son of the Duc De Tour LaRoche, and sent to France to be educated there, in the old family chateau, as its future mistress. The Revolution, with all its horrors, broke out. All aristocrats were either killed or thrown into the Bastile and afterward guillotined. Her uncle, the Duke, and his son, were both victims, the father being guillotined, the son dying in prison from want and confinement. The little countess was stolen off by an old family retainer, and after many hardships and hair-breadth escapes, returned to her father in Saint Domingo. Then, after a few years of comparative peace, she was again betrothed to another more distant cousin, Eugene LaRochefoucald, heir to the duke of that title, and also, should they ever regain their rights, to the dukedom of De Tour LaRoche. The insurrection took place directly after the marriage. She and her mother, after seeing the father and young husband massacred before their eyes, escaped, through the fidelity of two old negroes, to Baltimore, where these two faithful creatures supported their mistresses by their work—the man, Jacques, by his trade of ship caulking, the woman, Lucinde, by mending fine lace in pattern, which she had learned while with her young mistress in the convent in

Paris. Richard Rambaut, a merchant at Petersburg, went on to Baltimore to buy his flour, met the young and beautiful widow at the house of a friend, also a French *emigre*, and courted and married her. The mother married again, a Captain La Touche, of the French navy, whom she also met in Baltimore, at the house of Madame LaMoricire, one of those unfortunate refugees also. The famous French philosopher, the Duke De La-Rochefoucald, was a direct ancestor. The early history of the family is that of the "*LaRoche,*" who founded the town of LaRochelle, in France. It is related of the Duc De Tour LaRoche that he was considered the most polite gentleman at the court of Louis XVI., and that he walked on the scaffold with a rose-bud in his button hole, for which he spent his last franc, and taking his laced chapeau from his head, placed it under his left arm and bowed with inimitable grace to his executioner. This incident is related in an account in *Harper's Magazine* of famous French aristocrats. Maj. Rambaut's grandmother was the Countess Elize Warrenne De LaRoche, and the Duchess LaRochefoucald, at the time of her second marriage, but as *all* titles had been done away with by the Revolution, she was only called Mademoiselle and Madame.

Maj. Rambaut's mother, Miss Jane Hammond, was the daughter of Joel Leroy Hammond, who was born in South Carolina, at Hammond's Mountain, and was of the same family with Senator Hammond. He moved to Petersburg, Virginia, in early manhood, and was for many years a merchant in that city, and held, for a long time, an office in the civil service of the United States. His wife (Maj. Rambaut's maternal grandmother) was a Miss Durell, the daughter of Rebecca Douglas, the only daughter of Sir Robert Douglas, of Tiddesdale, Scotland. She was accustomed to wear the old Douglas crest, and at the burial place of the family, in old Blandford church, Petersburg, one of the tombs also bears the crest of the Douglases. A picture of the old family home is painted on a panel over the mantel in the dining-room of the old Rambaut homestead in Petersburg.

Maj. Rambaut began life with nothing but his talents and his energy. He received no inheritance, but has made what he has by working for it. He is upright in his transactions, looking well to his reputation. He has few enemies. He is characterized by strength of determination and tenacity of purpose. When he undertakes an enterprise he brings all his energies to bear upon it. His strong points are perseverance and the power of concentration.

GEN. JOSEPH B. PALMER.
MURFREESBOROUGH.

THIS gentleman, distinguished as a lawyer, a political orator, a Confederate general, a Mason of prominence, and a man of high-toned honor and fidelity to principle in all the walks of life, appears in this volume as one of the best specimens of the native-born, representative Tennessean. He first saw the light in Rutherford county, Tennessee, November 1, 1825. His father, Dr. W. H. Palmer, a native of Halifax county, Virginia, came to Tennessee and married about the year 1822, and settled in Rutherford county. His uncle, Dr. Jeffrey Palmer, of Halifax county, Virginia, was a man of considerable distinction as a physician and scholar in his day, and died leaving an only daughter, now residing in Richmond, Virginia. Gen. Palmer's grandfather, Moses Palmer, was a man of prominence and ability in the "Old Dominion," and by his exertions, and through his means, the thriving town of Halifax Court-house was chiefly built.

The mother of Gen. Palmer was Miss Mildred Johns. Her father was Joseph B. Johns, a native of Halifax county, Virginia, who married in Virginia, and came to Tennessee about the beginning of the present century. He first settled near Nashville, but subsequently moved to Rutherford county and became a large planter. He died, leaving four sons and five daughters.

Gen. Palmer's parents both died when he was very young, leaving him their only surviving child, consequently he was raised by his grandfather. The mother died first, and shortly after the father went to the Northwest country and took a prominent part in the Black Hawk war, settling, at its close, in Illinois, where he practiced medicine until the time of his death.

Thus left an orphan, he was brought up by his grandparents, on their farm, and was taught to do all the work incidental to the life of a farmer's boy up to the age of seventeen, which was the means of inculcating habits of industry, and laid the foundation of his splendid physical constitution. His educational advantages were at first confined to the old field schools, which were then so common in the country. On January 1, 1844, he entered Union University at Murfreesborough, where he pursued his studies more than two years. After leaving the university, he was under the private tutorage of Rev. Dr. Joseph Eaton for several years. He then began life for himself as a school-teacher, his institution being located about four miles west of Murfreesborough, where, for one year, he conducted one of the largest and most successful schools ever taught by any one man in Rutherford county, the school often reaching over one hundred pupils. The

45

students of this school are now scattered all over Rutherford county, heads of families, and still greatly attached to their teacher, personally and otherwise. After this he began to read law at Murfreesborough, in the office of Hardy M. Burton, who died in 1852, United States consul at the island of St. John. He was admitted to the bar at the March term of the circuit court of Murfreesborough, in 1848, by Judge Samuel Anderson, one of the ablest circuit judges who ever presided in Tennessee, and has, with the exception of the period of the war, continued to practice successfully, with a full practice in all the courts up to this time. He has always been fond of his profession, very studious, and very attentive to the causes of his clients.

In the sectional strife which preceded the outbreak of the war, Gen. Palmer, who had always been a straight Whig, was a stanch Union man, and made many speeches to the people of Rutherford and adjoining counties in favor of the Union, and against a resort to arms to settle the difficulties of the country, maintaining throughout that the genius of our government implied a settlement by reason and diplomacy, and not by force, but when force came, and President Lincoln called troops into the field to settle the difficulty, as a melancholy fact he recognized that the Union was broken, and that there was no other chance to adjust the strife except on the field. When this assurance came, he unhesitatingly took sides with the South, and raised for the southern service, first a company, and then a regiment, of which he was made colonel by unanimous vote. This was the Eighteenth Tennessee regiment of infantry, a gallant body of soldiers, which afterward became so distinguished for its services under him. He continued to command the Eighteenth Tennessee till the summer of 1864, when he was made a brigadier-general and placed in command of the brigade originally organized by him, and, previous to that time, commanded by Gen. John C. Brown. After this promotion, there were added to his command the Fifty-fourth and Sixty-third Virginia regiments, and the Fifty-eighth and Sixtieth North Carolina regiments, which gave him the largest brigade in the Confederate army of Tennessee. He continued in command of this brigade through a part of what is known as the Dalton and Atlanta campaign, and in Gen. Hood's campaign in Tennessee, in the fall of 1864, and on down to the reorganization of the Army of Tennessee, under Gen. Joseph E. Johnston, at which time he was placed in command of all the Tennessee troops in Johnston's army then in the field, and so continued till the date of the surrender at Greensborough, North Corolina, April 26, 1865, his brigade not being paroled till the 2d of May following. After the surrender he marched all the Tennessee troops into their State, and delivered them to their homes, during the month of May, 1865.

Gen. Palmer was at the battle of Fort Donelson, and was surrendered there, with the whole of Buckner's army, February 16, 1862, and was imprisoned in Fort Warren, Boston harbor, Massachusetts, until a general exchange of prisoners, which took place in September, 1862, when he was re-elected colonel of his old regiment. He was actively engaged in the battles of Murfreesborough from December 28, 1862, to January 2, 1863. This was his home, and as the whole country was familiar to him from early boyhood, Gen. Bragg relied upon him very largely for information. On the last day of the battle, he was in the celebrated fight known as the Breckinridge charge, during which his horse was shot under him, and he was himself three times wounded, though he refused to leave the field till the fight was over. Though a colonel in rank at the time, he was in command of a brigade in this fight. This was a most desperate battle; more than two thousand men, including several field officers, being killed and wounded in one brief hour. By the wounds received at this battle he was disabled till the 12th of April following, when he again took the field.

In the battle of Chickamauga, September 19, 1863, he was desperately wounded while leading a successful charge against the enemy, on the first day of the fight, a little before sunset. This wound was for a long time considered mortal, but from it he finally recovered, leaving his right shoulder badly injured and his right arm partly paralyzed, which has so continued through life. He rejoined his command on the 12th of July following, and took part in all the battles in front of Atlanta, and the battle of Jonesborough, where he was again slightly wounded. After this he, with his command, came into Middle Tennessee with Gen. Hood, and in connection with Gen. Forrest's cavalry. His brigade bore a conspicuous and gallant part in the bloody battle at Franklin, in November, after which he was sent on an expedition against the strongly fortified town of Murfreesborough. Here he was engaged in a heavy fight near Murfreesborough, December 7, 1864, in which fight the division of Gen. William B. Bate also partictpated.

After the battles around Nashville, he retreated with Hood's army southward, by way of Tupelo, Mississippi, Mobile, Alabama, and thence by way of Augusta, Georgia, Columbia, South Carolina, into North Carolina, where he took part in the battle of Bentonville, under Gen. Joseph E. Johnston, March 20, 1865. In this battle his brigade was made the directing column, and drove the enemy before them, successfully leading a charge of more than one mile, and carrying two strongly fortified lines. His brigade lost heavily, and he himself was again slightly wounded, but did not leave the field. His inspector-general, Capt. Gideon H. Lowe, was killed at his side, and his horse was shot from under him. Among others killed on this day were Col. Saffles and Lieut.-Col. Borgas, both of the Twenty-sixth Tennessee regiment. Thus ends the military career of Gen. Palmer, in which, as one who knows him well says, he made a record of which any man would have a right to be proud. In military affairs he was essentially a man of duty. He never got a furlough, never missed a fight or a drill, or any other camp duty, except when actually shot away from his colors. He always gave the strictest obedience to orders, and when he received instructions from his commander, carried them out, if he could, not stopping to count up the difficulties.

About the beginning of the war, one of Gen. Palmer's Whig friends met him on the public square, in Nashville, and observing his Confederate uniform, asked him, "What does this mean?" "It means," said he, "that I am doing my duty by going as my people are going." His men would follow him anywhere, for the love which they bore their trusted and idolized commander. In Hood's Tennessee campaign, in November and December, 1864, Gen. Palmer's men, many of them barefooted and half naked—some of them with old blankets tied around their feet by way of shoes—followed him as enthusiastically as ever, and when he drew them up and made a speech to them, cold and shivering and hungry as they were, they cheered him to the echo, and bade him lead them forward once more to face the guns of the enemy.

Gen. Palmer has been twice married. His first wife, to whom he was married February 15, 1854, was Miss Ophelia M. Burrus, daughter of Fayette Burrus, a farmer, of Rutherford county, who was socially highly connected throughout Middle Tennessee, being related to the Browns, Haskells and Readys, names so familiar throughout the State. Mrs. Palmer's mother was Miss Eliza Ready, daughter of the late Charles Ready, sr., of Readyville. Mrs. Palmer died in July, 1856, leaving an only son, Horace E. Palmer, now the law partner of his father, at Murfreesborough, an attorney of unusual ability, and a gentleman worthy of his distinguished sire. Mrs. Palmer was a graduate of Soule College, at Murfreesborough, and was noted for her many accomplishments and for her great personal beauty, being one of the most beautiful women that Tennessee has ever produced.

The second marriage of Gen. Palmer, which took place in June, 1869, was to Mrs. Margaret J. Mason, of Pulaski, Tennessee, a daughter of Andrew M. and Mary T. Ballentine, of that place. The Ballentine family is well known in Tennessee, and has produced some distinguished men. One of Mrs. Palmer's brothers, John G. Ballentine is now a member of Congress from the Seventh district of Tennessee. A second brother, W. F. Ballentine, represented Giles county in the Tennessee Legislature in 1882 and 1883. A third brother, ——— Ballentine, is a wealthy merchant and farmer, at Sardis, Mississippi; and a fourth, Andrew, is a farmer, at Pulaski, Tennessee. Mrs. Palmer is a graduate of Nashville Female Academy, under Dr. C. D. Elliott, and is well known in the social circles of

Nashville and throughout Middle Tennessee, as a well-read, highly accomplished and intellectual woman.

Gen. Palmer was made a Master Mason in Mount Moriah Lodge, No. 18, at Murfreesborough, July, 1847; became a Royal Arch Mason in Pythagoras Chapter, No. 23, in 1848; a Knight Templar in Nashville Commandery, No. 1, in 1850; is a charter member of Murfreesborough Commandery, No. 10; has been Master of Lodge, High Priest, Eminent Commander of Commandery, Grand Commander of Knights Templar, in 1872, and is a charter member of Sinai Lodge of Perfection, No. 4, Ancient and Accepted Scottish Rite.

Before the war, Gen. Palmer was a straight Whig, and was opposed to the Know Nothing movement of his party, but remained in the party, and took an active part in every presidential campaign from 1851 up to and including 1860, and made many speeches for the Whig presidential candidates. In 1849, he was elected to the Legislature, from Rutherford county, on the Whig ticket, with Dr. George D. Crosthwait as colleague, and was re-elected in 1851, with Dr. John W. Richardson as colleague, and remained in the Legislature till 1853, four years in all. While in that body he was a member of the committee on federal relations and the committee on ways and means. During the sessions that Gen. Palmer was in the Legislature, many important measures were before that body, and much of the legislation out of which has grown the subsequent debt troubles of Tennessee, was done. Gen. Palmer always voted against issuing a large amount of bonds, and imposing a large debt upon the people of his State.

Gen. Palmer was mayor of Murfreesborough from 1855 to 1859, inclusive, serving four successive terms in that office. Since the war, he has been a Democrat, zealous, faithful and unswerving, but never a seeker of office.

In 1845, he joined the Methodist church, and has been, to quote the words of a gentleman who has known him well, "a most consistent Christian all his life." His first wife was a Methodist, while the present Mrs. Palmer is a Presbyterian in faith.

In his business, as in military affairs, Gen. Palmer has always been a man of duty, of constant labor, and of marked devotion to business in preference to pleasure. Moreover, he is temperate in his habits, and it is to these things that he owes his success, socially, financially, as a lawyer, and as a general. His object in life has been usefulness to his country and love to his race, and in these conscientious reflections of a well-spent life, he finds ample compensation. His friendships are firm and lasting. A man of soul, men love him for his ready outflow of sympathy. His face gladdens when he meets you, and his whole manner, while you are with him, seems to say, "I am glad you are here, and would like to contribute to your happiness." A wonderfully retentive memory, he often recalls incidents of meetings with friends many years before, which at once reminds them he has not forgotten them, and binds them to him with hooks of steel. Brave as a soldier, he is yet as gentle as a woman in disposition. Modest in manner, he avoids publicity, and shrinks from seeking those positions to which he is richly entitled by reason of his splendid abilities. He is a self-made, self-educated man of the highest type. For a man so gentle, so amiable, and so peaceful in private life, it amazed all his soldiers to see how utterly careless of himself he was in battle, exposing himself on every field, and receiving numerous wou nds, which are his badges of an honorable and patriotic gallantry. He was a magnificent soldier—Tennessee had none his superior. He is a superb gentleman—Tennessee has few his equal.

HON. WILLIAM M. SMITH.

MEMPHIS.

THIS well-known lawyer, jurist and politician was born in Mecklenburg county, Virginia, May 8, 1830. In 1831 his father moved to Haywood county, Tennessee, where the son grew up, there receiving his education in the common schools of the county and at LaGrange College, Alabama, graduating from that institution in 1848. After leaving college he returned to Tennessee and began the study of law, at Brownsville, with his brother, Thomas G. Smith, afterward judge of the law court in Memphis. During the year 1849, he was engaged in teaching school in Haywood county, Tennessee. In September, 1850, he entered the law school at Lebanon, and graduated in the summer of 1851, in a class with Gen. A. W. Campbell, of Jackson, Judge John A. McKinney, of Knoxville, James R. Cocke, of Knoxville, Col. Edward I. Golladay, of Nashville, Judge W. S. McLemore, of Franklin, Hon. Atha Thomas, ex-State treasurer of Tennessee, and other prominent men. He received his license from Judge Nathan Green, of the Supreme court, and professor in Cumberland University, and Chancellor Ridley, of Murfreesborough, and began the practice of law in partnership with his brother, Thomas G. Smith.

In 1853, he was elected to the Legislature from Haywood county, and served one term, the colleague of Hon. James E. Bailey, Hon. Henry Cooper, Judge James B. Cooke, now on the Supreme bench of Tennessee, William J. Sykes, Maj. George W. Winchester, Col. John F. House and others, since prominent in the State.

Resuming the practice of law at Brownsville, he continued there until 1860, when he was elected chancellor for the division composed of the counties of Henry, Weakley, Obion, Gibson, Dyer, Haywood, Lauderdale, Tipton and Fayette, and held the chancery courts of those counties until they were suspended by the war. From 1857 to 1860, he was attorney in Haywood county for the Memphis and Ohio, now the Memphis branch of the Louisville and Nashville railroad. After the war he was State director in the same road, beginning in 1866. He took no part in the war, though a Union man throughout.

Judge Smith was raised a Whig, and continued one up to the time the party broke up, but did not approve of the Know Nothing movement in his party, and never belonged to that organization. When the Republican party was organized in the State he joined it, and has been a consistent Republican ever since.

In 1864, he was appointed by Gov. Andrew Johnson as judge of the common law and chancery court of Memphis, moved to that city in December of that year, and continued as chancellor until December, 1869, when he resigned. In 1868, upon the resignation of Judge Hawkins, he was offered the position of Supreme judge, but declined. After his resignation he resumed the practice of law in Memphis. In 1874, he formed a partnership with Mr. W. A. Collier, which has continued till the present time.

In 1870, he was nominated for Supreme judge by the Republican convention, but declined the nomination, and in 1878, declined a nomination for chancellor. In 1880, he was elected to the State senate from Shelby county, and when the Legislature assembled, received the Republican nomination for speaker of the senate, and also received the Republican vote for United States senator on several ballots. In 1882, he was the Republican nominee for Congress in the Tenth district.

Judge Smith was married, September 28, 1853, to Miss Julia Taylor, daughter of Edmund Taylor, of Fayette county, Tennessee, who was descended from a Virginia family, which removed to West Tennessee and settled in Haywood and Fayette counties. The family were noted for their honesty, modesty and piety. To this union have been born six children, four sons and two daughters: (1). Paul, born in 1854; died at Memphis, February 3, 1881. He was a promising young lawyer. (2). Edmund J., born in 1856. (3). Hunt Macon, born in February, 1860, died July 4, 1885; intelligent, pure, and deeply lamented by a large circle of friends. (4). Willie V., born in 1862. (5). Julian, born in October, 1864, and died at West Point, New York, February 24, 1884, while a cadet at the United States Military Academy. He was a young man of great promise. (6). Martha Augusta, born in July, 1867; died in January, 1868.

Judge Smith's father was Rev. James Smith, a Methodist preacher, who was one of the earliest settlers of Haywood county. His mother was Martha Macon, niece of the Hon. Nathaniel Macon, of North Carolina, at one time speaker of the lower house of Congress, and afterward president *pro tempore* of the senate—a very able and distinguished man.

The following from the leading members of the Memphis bar is the best and truest estimate of Judge Smith's character, formed, as it was, by men who knew him well. The extract is taken from a series of resolutions passed by the lawyers of Memphis when he resigned the office of chancellor in 1869: "The retirement of Judge William M. Smith from the bench of the chancery court of Memphis, and the termination of the relations that have so long and pleasantly connected him with this bar, present an opportunity to us, which we cheerfully embrace, to declare thus publicly our sense of his merits. We have known Judge Smith during his protracted and arduous service as chancellor, discharging the laborious and delicate duties of office, under a condition of things that tried his capacity, temper and integrity; and thus knowing him, we bear cheerful testimony that he has not failed in either of these high qualities. Presiding in the most important chancery court in the State, with a crowded docket, full of cases presenting new and vexed questions growing out of circumstances incident to the late war, for the decision which he was often without precedent in history or adjudged cases to guide him, his position was both trying and responsible, and if sometimes the soundness of his legal conclusions was questioned by the bar, yet it was not to the disparagement of his legal attainments, nor did the taint of suspicion attach to the judicial integrity which guided him to, or the conscientious conviction which accompanied, these conclusions. In the vindication of his integrity and conscientiousness, as well as of his ability and legal attainments, we cheerfully pronounce Judge Smith, as chancellor, to have been eminently satisfactory, and we submit, as the sense of this meeting, as follows: Be it resolved, that we take pleasure in expressing to Judge Smith the assurance of our high regard, and in bearing testimony to the uniform patience, courtesy, integrity and ability that have characterized him as a legal officer, and extend to him a cordial welcome to the bar as a brother lawyer."

In 1883, the leading Republicans of Memphis prepared a letter to President Arthur, asking him to appoint Judge Smith to a place in his cabinet, and thus make him the leader of the southern Republicans. This letter shows the integrity of his motives and the honesty with which he adheres to his principles, as well as the high estimate in which he is held by his fellow-citizens. It says: "Give to southern Republicans a leader that they can follow with honor and credit. Such a representative, such a leader, we beg leave to recommend in the person of Hon. William M. Smith, one of the most distinguished native-born citizens of the State, and one of the most loyal and devoted Republicans in the South. Never a spoilsman or a place hunter, but always true to his convictions, he allied himself to the Republican party at the very hour of its birth; and through all its vicissitudes and struggles, has stood steadily by it, braving every criticism that is brought upon him, and by his integrity and purity of character, disarming hostility and winning public confidence. Though unswerving in his political convictions and conduct, even in the most heated party excitement his honesty, purity and patriotism have never been assailed, and he commands the respect of every one who knows him."

Judge Smith has always been modest and retiring, as is evidenced by the number of times he has declined to be brought forward when party and friends wished it. He is a member of the Methodist Episcopal church, South.

PROF. JAMES E. SCOBEY.

MURFREESBOROUGH.

THIS gentleman, who has long been prominently identified with the educational interests of Tennessee, was born near Lebanon, in Wilson county, Tennessee, January 3, 1834. He was the son of John B. Scobey, a native of the same county, whose father, James Scobey, came to Tennessee from North Carolina, before Tennessee was admitted to the Union as a State, settling at Station Camp Fort, in what is now Sumner county.

Prof. Scobey's mother was Miss Sallie Sweatt, daughter of Edward Sweatt, who moved to Tennessee from North Carolina, in 1822. Her father was a prominent man in North Carolina, and represented his county in the Legislature for several years. After coming to Tennessee, he became distinguished as a teacher and a preacher. He was a good linguist and a good man, of broad scholarship.

Prof. Scobey's great-grandfather, on his maternal side, came from England, and his great-grandmother from Ireland. They settled in Maryland at an early day, and moved from there to North Carolina, whence the family migrated to Tennessee. Paternal ancestors were all from Ireland.

Prof. Scobey was brought up on a farm and sent to

the common schools until his nineteenth year. Although his parents were in easy circumstances, he was taught to work hard. His father, believing in physical labor to develop a boy, placed him in a blacksmith shop at the age of seventeen, and he remained there for two years. He then entered as a student at Franklin College, near Nashville, and graduated in July, 1854, in a class of six, all of whom are now dead, with the exception of himself and Dr. T. K. Powell, a prominent physician, of Haywood county, Tennessee.

After completing his education, he chose teaching as his profession, and immediately entered upon the work at Green Hill, in Wilson county. In April, 1855, he became principal of Union Academy, at Tucker's Crossroads, six miles east of Lebanon, and conducted there a large and flourishing school till the outbreak of the war. At the close of the war he again entered the educational field, and in 1867, established, near Green Hill, in Wilson county, an academy called Oakland School, which continued in a flourishing condition, and became quite famous under his presidency, until 1872, when he moved to Murfreesborough, and became president of Murfreesborough Female Institute, now Haynes Institute, which position he still fills. He has been one of the foremost educators of the State, a live, wide-awake, progressive advocate of the school interests of Tennessee ever since the war, and has attended a great number of educational conventions and teachers' institutes, always taking a lively interest in schools, both public and private. In 1867, he was a delegate to the educational convention at Nashville, and introduced in that body a resolution to establish a State normal school, since which the State Normal College of Tennessee, an institution justly regarded as one of Tennessee's brightest jewels, has been established. In 1883, he was made principal of the summer normal school, at Monteagle, on the Cumberland mountain, a compliment which was at once a tribute to his ripe scholarship, and a recognition of his eminent and constant services in the cause of education.

In 1860, Prof. Scobey was made a colonel in the Tennessee militia. In December, 1861, he volunteered for the Confederate service, and, becoming captain of company C, Fifty-fifth Tennessee regiment, Col. G. L. McKoin commanding, was mustered into service at Camp Trousdale, Sumner county. He took part in the two days' battle at Shiloh, in April, 1862, commanding his company on both days, and after the fight, being the only officer of his regiment left in line, he conducted its retreat to Corinth. Immediately after this he was taken sick with putrid sore throat and fever, and was sent to West Point, Mississippi, on the sick list. During this illness, from the effects of which he has never fully recovered, his regiment was consolidated with the Forty-fourth Tennessee regiment, and he received an honorable discharge from the service, signed by Lieut. Gen. Hardee. However, in December, 1862, he again entered the service as a commissary, with the rank of captain, and was stationed at Cartersville, Georgia, for nearly a year, collecting supplies for the army. He remained in the service this time till near the close of the war.

Prof. Scobey was a Whig before the war, and in 1861, was the Whig candidate for the Legislature from Wilson county. Being opposed to the war, and in favor of a compromise, he made the canvass on that issue, and though a young man, and opposed by two very able men, William L. Martin and Judge Abram Caruthers, he had every prospect of a triumphant election until the whole aspect of affairs was changed by the battle of Bull Run, and he was defeated by a majority of eighty-seven votes. After it was found that the war was a fixed fact, he took sides with the South. Since the war, he has taken no active part in politics, but when voting has voted with the Democrats.

Prof. Scobey was married, near Lebanon, August 31, 1859, to Miss Alice Harris, daughter of Maj. James S. Harris, a prominent citizen of Wilson county, and a successful business man. Her mother was Miss Waters, of a well-known Wilson county family. Mrs. Scobey was educated under Mrs. Charlotte Fanning, at Franklin College, near Nashville, and graduated there in June, 1859, just two months before her marriage. She was a lady of fine accomplishments, and assisted her husband, teaching in his schools from the time of their marriage up to 1872. She was a devout member of the Christian church, and noted for her sweet and amiable disposition, and her charities. She died August 29, 1881, having been the mother of six children: (1). Jennie, now a teacher in Haynes Institute, Murfreesborough. (2). Gussie, now a teacher in Haynes Institute, Murfreesborough. (3). James B. (4). John E. (5). Alice. (6). Robert.

Prof. Scobey is a member of the Masonic fraternity, having been made a Master Mason at Lebanon, in 1858. He has been a member of the Christian church since 1849. Mrs. Scobey was a member of the same church.

As a man, Prof. Scobey has an air of friendliness about him which makes him popular with all who know him. As a teacher, he is a success, being a fine scholar and having always conducted flourishing schools with increasing reputation. This is the verdict of those who have had opportunity to judge. He has devoted himself exclusively to the profession of teaching, and has followed it with close attention, being always ready to seize any opportunity for improvement. He has been a constant reader of all sorts of educational works, and a participant in educational meetings. Such a man, so ardent and devoted to a calling so important, is worth much to a State, and deserves to be honored.

REV. JOHN BERRY McFERRIN, D. D.

NASHVILLE.

THIS remarkable man, whose name is reverenced and beloved in thousands of households, not only in Tennessee, but throughout the length and breadth of the country, is one of the best and purest types of the native Tennessean. He was born in Rutherford county, June 15, 1807. He was a most extraordinary child, grew very rapidly, and walked when only seven months of age; was never sick a day, never took a dose of medicine, and never had a headache until after he was eighteen.

He was placed in school at the very early age of four years, and he has no recollection of the time when he could not read the alphabet. He learned moderately fast, and received a plain education in the English branches only, at such country schools as were then accessible, supplemented by studious habits and self-culture at home.

He joined the church at thirteen, and from his early days led a life of strict morality and obedience. His habits have always been as regular as the measure of well-written music—a time to rise, a time to eat, and a time to sleep. He never committed a wrong intentionally, never swore an oath, was never in a circus, never witnessed a theatrical performance, and such was his early moral training, and so thoroughly did his parents impress upon him the value and importance of truth that, if he ever told a lie, he has no recollection of it. He never received but one correction at school, and but one punishment from his parents, and that was administered with a small twig, not more than eight inches in length. In after years, Dr. McFerrin ruled his own children by the laws of love and kindness, and never chastised them, except with a straw.

His early life was made up of the ordinary routine of farm work, following the plow, going to mill, driving wagons, etc. He first felt that he was called to preach at the age of eighteen, and became a licensed minister of the Methodist Episcopal church, October 8, 1825. He became a member of the Tennessee conference, as a traveling preacher, in November, 1825, and preached his first sermon at Tuscumbia, Alabama. He then traveled three circuits—Franklin, Lawrence and Limestone, Alabama; was two years among the Indians, as a missionary; was stationed at Huntsville, Alabama, at Pulaski, Tennessee, and three times at Nashville; was presiding elder of the Florence, Alabama district, and of the Cumberland district, in Tennessee; was editor of the Nashville *Christian Advocate* from 1840 to 1858; was missionary in the Confederate army, and faithfully accompanied the Tennessee troops throughout the arduous campaigns and perilous struggles of the late war, administering to the sick and wounded, helping to bury the dead, and preaching sal-vation to the living. He has been twice book agent for the Methodist Episcopal church, South, serving in that capacity eighteen years; was secretary of the board of missions, for the same church, twelve years, and has been a member of the general conference, continuously, from 1836 to 1886. He is the author of "The History of Methodism in Tennessee," which has been printed in three volumes, octavo, of five hundred pages each, and has met with extensive sale; is also author of several published sermons, numerous addresses, and many contributions to the press of Tennessee and other States.

Accompanied by his daughter, Miss Kittie Lou McFerrin (now Mrs. Robert W. Bryan), Dr. McFerrin went as a delegate to the Ecumenical Conference, which met in London, England, in September, 1881. During this tour, he visited and held services in various churches in London, Dublin, Edinburgh, Paris, and New-castle-on-Tyne, and was one of the editors of the history of the meeting of this conference.

He was early connected with the missionary society, and interested in all the general movements of the Tennessee conference and of his church, and was one of the prime movers in originating and building La Grange College, in Alabama. The title of Doctor of Divinity was conferred upon him by this college, in 1847, and by Randolph Macon College, Virginia, the same year. He has been a general conference officer longer than any man in the church, North or South, a period of forty-four years. He was never nominated for any office to which he was not elected, and was never censured for his official conduct in any position he has held. While editor of the *Christian Advocate*, he, through the press, entered into all the theological controversies, discussing the dogmas that divide the denominations, and especially those conflicting with his own creed. He has made no departures; the Methodist creed, as taught by the standard writers, and set forth in the Discipline, he holds now, without any abatements or innovations. But, as he grows older, he becomes more catholic in his feelings; not less a Methodist, but more philanthropic, and more charitable toward other denominations.

Personally, and in physique, Dr. McFerrin bears out the sturdy quality of his moral character, the sturdy purity of his piety. He has a large frame, strongly built, stands six feet in his boots, and has an average weight of two hundred and ten pounds. His features are all prominent and pronounced; craggy, projecting brows; eyes blue and penetrating, capable of varied expressions and emotions, and seem to speak and give emphasis to the language he utters. Capable of great endurance, hard work and close application, his bearing is stalwart and self-reliant, and he has the appearance of one who has been exposed to all weathers, but which only seems to have doubled his capacity for more labors to come. Perfectly composed, of wonderfully even temperament, he has the look of a man who is never surprised, but always calm, cool, and collected. A person would have to travel far and search diligently for a man whose eyes are capable of such varied expression, and whose manner is so perfectly free from self-consciousness. But one other such man comes to the memory of the writer, and that is Joseph Jefferson. Both of these men "hold the mirror up to nature," and each hides himself from his audience by losing himself in the subject he handles.

The question naturally presents itself to one studying the life and public services, and considering the intellectual potency and the reputation of Dr. McFerrin, why his church has not made him one of its general superintendents—elevated him to the episcopacy. In Nashville, the theory is that he and Rev. Dr. A. L. P. Green were both equally worthy, but as both lived in Tennessee, the general conference could not elect both, and so elected neither. He has been voted for several times for bishop of the church, and undoubtedly would have been elected in 1854, had it not been for the death of his first wife, and the consequent state of his home affairs, which forbade his acceptance. Again, in 1866, his friends would have called him to fill this position, but just prior to the meeting of the conference he was crippled by a fall from a railroad train, and his recovery was then very doubtful.

Not only is Dr. McFerrin a Methodist in faith, but he is methodical in the preparation of his sermons. Yet his plans are very simple. He first studies his subject carefully, then blocks it out in his mind, and makes it a uniform rule to speak extemporaneously. This, perhaps, is one of the secrets of his great success as a pulpit orator. His manner is that of deep and serious earnestness; his discourses bear the stamp of his own intellectuality and originality, and his powerful exhortations make their way and find lodgment in the hearts of his hearers. His motto in life has been: one business, punctuality, energy, strict fidelity, and love to God and man.

Dr. McFerrin has been twice married. His first marriage occurred September 18, 1833, to Miss A. A. Probart, of Nashville, only child of William Y. and Sarah Probart, who became the mother of five children, Sarah Jane, James William, John A., Elizabeth Johnston and Almira Probart, and died near Nashville, in May, 1854.

He married the second time, November 12, 1855, Miss Cynthia T. McGavock, daughter of John and Elizabeth McGavock, of Nashville. The present Mrs. McFerrin is the great-granddaughter of Gov. McDowell, of Virginia. Her sister, Mary McGavock, was the wife of E. P. McGinty, formerly editor of the Nashville *Whig*,

and at one time a member of the Legislature from Montgomery county, Tennessee. Mrs. McFerrin was educated at the old Nashville Female Academy, is a cheerful, active, industrious home-loving woman, and has discharged the offices of wife, step-mother and mother to her husband's perfect satisfaction. She is the mother of three children—Kittie Lou, Mary McGinty and Elizabeth McGavock.

Dr. McFerrin's oldest child, Sarah Jane McFerrin, was born March 6, 1842; graduated at Columbia, Tennessee, and married, November 15, 1860, to James Anderson, from Virginia, formerly a school teacher, now a farmer, in Sumner county, Tennessee. Their children are, John McFerrin Anderson, a rising young lawyer of Nashville, William Wade, James Douglass, Walter Leake, Ewell Avery, Mary Mira, Virgie Lou, Dora and Frank. The second child, James William McFerrin, was born July 2, 1846; entered the Confederate army a lad of seventeen; was wounded and captured by the Federal forces at the battle of Nashville, in December, 1864, and remained in prison at Camp Douglas, near Chicago, till the close of the war. He was for several years connected with the wholesale shoe house of Settle & Kinnaird, at Nashville. He married in December, 1868, Miss Dora Cook, of Nashville, and while on their wedding tour were on board the steamer United States when it collided with the America, burnt and sunk in the Ohio river, above Louisville, barely escaping with their lives. His wife died, April 25, 1875, leaving one child, Annie. The father met his death by a railroad accident, near Birmingham, Alabama, November 16, 1881. The third child, John A. McFerrin, was born March 26, 1848; was educated at Nashville, and at Emory College, Virginia; united with the Methodist church in 1865, and was granted license to preach in 1869; now stationed at Ashland City, Tennessee. He married Miss Martha Abston, June 28, 1871, and has five children, John B., Mary D., Almira, James Abston and Virginia. Elizabeth Johnson McFerrin was born December 15, 1850, and died at the age of three. Almira Probart McFerrin, was born May 8, 1852; married Rev. P. A. Sowell, in September, 1877, and has one child—Tennie McFerrin.

The Doctor's oldest child, by the second wife, is Kittie Lou McFerrin, who was born December 24, 1856; graduated at Ward's Seminary, Nashville; married, February 15, 1882, Robert W. Bryan, of the Nashville Transfer Company; has one child—Claiborne Nelson. Mary McGinty McFerrin, was born March 1, 1859, and died in infancy. Elizabeth McGavock McFerrin, was born July 23, 1861, and married, June 15, 1881, J. H. Yarbrough, real estate broker, of Nashville.

Dr. McFerrin's great-grandfather, William McFerrin, sr., was one of three brothers who came from Ireland about 1730, and resided, for some time, in York county, Pennsylvania. The Doctor's grandfather, also named William McFerrin, was a patriot soldier in the Revolutionary war, and was at the battle of King's Mountain. He died in Mississippi, more than ninety years of age. The Doctor's paternal grandmother was the daughter of James Laughlin, whose family came from Belfast, Ireland. His maternal grandmother was a Miss Campbell, of an extensive Virginia family. The parents of Dr. McFerrin, James McFerrin and Jane Campbell Berry, were born in Washington county, Virginia. Both families came from Ireland more than one hundred and fifty years ago, and stopped in York county, Pennsylvania, where they separated, part going to Western Pennsylvania and Ohio, and the immediate family coming to Kentucky and Tennessee. Dr. Mc-Ferrin's parents settled in Rutherford county, Tennessee, in 1804, just one year after the county was organized.

The McFerrin family were originally Presbyterians, but became Methodists in 1820. James McFerrin, Dr. McFerrin's father, was with Gen. Jackson, in the Creek war; was, for a number of years, colonel of the Fifty-third Tennessee regiment; became a Methodist preacher, in 1821, and preached twenty years. He died in September, 1840, at the age of fifty-six, and was buried with Masonic honors. He left two daughters and four sons, three of whom were Methodist preachers, and four of his grandsons are now licensed ministers of the Methodist Episcopal church, South. The family is noted for its preachers, there having been thirteen in the immediate family, all Methodists.

Dr. John B. McFerrin is a double cousin to James McFerrin Berry, whose son, ex-Gov. Berry, of Arkanas, is now one of the United States senators from that State. He is also a double cousin to B. H. Berry, whose son, Hon. C. P. Berry, is a member of Congress from California.

If the young men of to-day, who read this biography, ask how Dr. McFerrin became a leader, and one among the great men of his church, they may be answered: 1. He has lived a long time and usefully. 2. He is endowed by nature with a strong mind. 3. He is devoted to doing God's work, and from this consecration comes his courage. Truth and right, in all their power, have taken hold upon him, and he is, like John the Baptist, a "voice;" not proclaiming himself, but giving utterance to the truth that has inspired him. 4. He has followed one calling, and given all his powers to the work of the ministry. As a pulpit orator, his success is largely attributable to the fact that he knows humanity, its sorrows and sufferings, its passions and prejudices, as the musician knows the stops of the church organ. 5. And lastly, but not to be lightly esteemed, since it is also a gift of God, comes his physical power and capability of endurance, which have enabled him to work on untiringly, where other men must have faltered and suffered defeat. No man in Tennessee has impressed himself more deeply and permanently upon the public mind than John B. McFerrin; because he is justly regarded as a good man. He is a profound thinker, a ready writer, a forcible preacher, a man of faith, a muscular Christian, a first-class financier and business man, as the general conference has most reason to know, from his superb management of the publishing house. He will go down as an historic character, eminent among the most prominent Tennesseans of his time, and his memory will be embalmed in the hearts of his people, and future generations will rise up and call him blessed.

GEN. MATT. MARTIN.

TULLAHOMA.

THIS distinguished orator, soldier and patriot, whose mother was a cousin of Henry Clay, of Kentucky, and whose paternal grandmother, Betty Marshall, was a cousin of Chief Justice Marshall, of the supreme court of the United States, was born the youngest of a family of thirteen, in Bedford county, Tennessee, June 18, 1812—on the same day that the formal declaration of war was made against Great Britain by Congress, which was proclaimed by President Madison on the following day.

He was educated—partly at the Manual Labor School at Princeton, Kentucky, and partly at the University of Nashville, under President Philip Lindsley. At the age of twenty-three, he married, went to farming in Bedford county, made money very fast, and became, for those times, very wealthy. But having no power to refuse a friend a favor, he went security too liberally, and, per sequence, much of his wealth took wings and flew away. He became not only eminent as a farmer, but was one of the most prominent citizens in his section, occupying a position so reputable that his political party urged him repeatedly to accept a nomination for Congress when it was useless to run—he being a Whig, and the congressional district (James K. Polk's) overwhelmingly Democratic. Again, his personal party friends urged him to announce himself a candidate for governor against Hon. Isham G. Harris, but this he also declined.

In the meantime, he had devoted his leisure to the study of law, and having been licensed to practice, he opened an office at Shelbyville, in 1851, and practiced with much success until 1861; his great popularity as

46

an orator, his knowledge of human nature, his adroit manner of handling facts in a case, added to his extensive acquaintance, gaining for him a very large clientele. After the war he practiced at Manchester until 1877, when he settled at Tullahoma, where he has since continued to reside, devoting his time mainly to recovering his valuable property in Independence and Izard counties, Arkansas. This property consists of a large tract of land purchased by him some forty years ago, and on which are rich mines of manganese ores. The discovery of the manganese deposits was made by Smith, the Arkansas assistant State surveyor, over forty years ago. Samples of the ore were sent to Prof. Gerard Troost, of Nashville, who was Gen. Martin's old teacher, for analysis. Prof. Troost pronounced the ore very rich, and advised his pupil to purchase. But from the neglect of Gen. Martin's agent, who failed to keep him posted, the lands were sold under a tax sale. It was further given out that Gen. Martin, who was a resident in the mountainous districts of Tennessee, had been killed during the war. "These reports coming to my ears," said the General, "I went down to attend my own funeral and administer on the estate." He succeeded in recovering the property through the courts, and this, added to his previous possessions, gives him a fair share of this world's goods.

Gen. Martin has always been an enterprising and public-spirited man. While a farmer he established a pork-packing house in Nashville, one among the first in the State. In 1848-9, he was a member of the company, consisting of himself, James H. Wilson and Gen. F. K. Zollicoffer, that built the wire suspension bridge at Nashville, at that time reckoned as one of the finest and most substantial bridge structures in America, and the longest in the South. This bridge was destroyed by having its wires cut upon the evacuation of the city by the Confederate army under Gen. Albert Sydney Johnston, in February, 1862.

Prior to the war, as before stated, Gen. Martin was a Whig. When the war broke out he espoused the Confederate cause, but with great agony of spirit, saying to a friend in 1861: "We must go with our people." Since the war he has been a Democrat, but has never voluntarily sought office, and never wanted it. He has repeatedly declined nominations when there was every prospect of a successful canvass. In 1869, he was elected, without canvassing or making a speech, a delegate from the counties of Coffee, Grundy and Van Buren to the State constitutional convention of 1870, and in that body was chairman of the military committee.

To most Tennesseans, however, Gen. Martin is best known by his career as a soldier, for a martial spirit and love of country were born in him. He volunteered for the Mexican war, but his company disbanded before reaching the seat of hostilities. In the great war between the States, however, he bore a conspicuous part. In June, 1861, he was called upon to command the "Erwin Guards," as their captain, but in a few days thereafter, without opposition, he was elected colonel of the Twenty-third Tennessee volunteer infantry, which was soon after brigaded under Gen. Pat. Cleburne.

About this time, the call of the militia being determined upon, he was solicited to allow his name to be voted for as major-general of the third division of Tennessee State troops. His answer was: "In time of war no man should seek or decline an office." On receiving this reply, the citizen soldiery took up his name and triumphantly elected him their major-general. He was still at Bowling Green, Kentucky, in camp, commanding the Twenty-third regiment, one of the best drilled and best disciplined regiments then in the Confederate service, when Gov. Harris made a call on him for one-half of his militia division, comprising eighteen regiments, to be chosen by the draft. On receiving this order he was in doubt as to his exact duty, for, being then performing service as an officer in the regular Confederate army, he could not determine the proper line of duty—whether it would be right to resign his rank in the regular service and accept a position in the militia of still higher rank. He consulted with Gen. Cleburne, assuring him that he was undecided as to what he should do; that duty, instead of promotion, was his ruling motive; that the cause was everything, the man nothing, and he would abide the advice of his superior officer. Gen. Cleburne answered that, while unwilling to forego his services, he was undecided what advice to give, and referred him to Gen. Hardee. He went to Gen. Hardee, who was unwilling to decide the matter, and referred him to Gen. Albert Sidney Johnston. The latter said this was not a time for delay or hesitation. He would decide at once, and that was that he (Gen. Martin) should resign his rank in the Confederate army and accept the office of major-general of militia, tendered him by the citizen soldiers, and that no time was to be lost. He accordingly tendered his resignation, but it happened about that time that the demand for troops elicited great enthusiasm in his part of the State, and he found that the militia who were to fill out his division had entered the army as volunteers, instead of waiting to be drafted. The upshot was that, instead of organizing his division, Gen. Martin hastened to his regiment and "joined the boys" again. He was in time to take part in the battles of Shiloh and Pittsburg Landing.

The brigade of Gen. Cleburne, in which Gen. Martin fought, attacked the Federals, commanded by Gen. B. M. Prentiss, who was at the extreme front. The Confederates advanced to the brink of a ravine, Prentiss' brigade occupying the opposite side of the ravine, when the most furious artillery duel took place which occurred during the war. The limbs on the trees were cut down by the cannonade, and were very destructive to the men. Gen. Martin was wounded in this part of the battle in seven places. A limb fell on him, doubling him up on his horse. His wounds were severe and his sufferings extreme. The slope of the ravine was very steep, but the Confederates made the descent into the chasm, the banks being over one hundred feet high, when Prentiss, holding his position on the crest of the ridge, delivered a plunging fire from his batteries on their heads, which was very destructive and murderous. Gen. Prentiss held his position with dogged bravery, standing as firm as a rock, until subsequently, being surrounded by a superior force, he had to surrender.

The following anecdote, published in the Detroit *Free Press*, illustrates so well, and so truthfully, Gen. Martin's conspicuous bravery on the field of Shiloh, it seems very appropriate in this connection: " During the battle of Shiloh, as the First Tennessee regiment of Confederate infantry was advancing to attack, lying on the edge of the battlefield, some of the boys saw a big, fat colonel, badly wounded. He proved to be the gallant Mexican and Confederate veteran, Col. Matt. Martin, of the Twenty-third Tennessee. As the column came up on the double-quick, and, with a yell, Col. Martin lifted his head and roared out in stentorian tones, give 'em goss, boys—that's right, my brave First Tennessee--give 'em Hail Columbia!' The regiment halted but a moment, and one of the boys inquired, 'Colonel, where are you wounded?' He answered in a deep bass voice, 'My son, I am wounded in the arm, in the leg, in the head, ¡in the body, and in another place I have a delicacy in mentioning; but don't mind me; go ahead, give 'em fits!' And the truth of it is, he *was* wounded in seven places, and, besides, a limb had fallen upon him, doubling him up on his horse."

In the subsequent struggle of the Confederacy, Gen. Martin filled various positions of honor and responsibility. He remained with the Twenty-third until after the battle of Chickamauga, being called upon by the men to command them, and thus he served with " the boys " through the campaigns in Tennessee, Mississippi, Alabama and Georgia. The remainder of the time, after Chickamauga, he was mostly with Gen. Clanton, upon Clanton's request. His bravery during the war was recognized by Generals Cleburne and Hardee in the most complimentary terms. His conduct throughout the struggle was reckless of danger—exposing himself at the most dangerous points of the conflict whenever necessity required. More particularly, however, is Gen. Martin gratefully remembered by the people, both for his bravery and for the promptness with which he gave his name, his eloquence and his commanding influence to the cause of the South.

Gen. Martin was first married in Maury county, Tennessee, September 24, 1835, to Miss Sarah Quincy Williams, daughter of Gen. Samuel H. Williams, a

large farmer, and a gentleman prominent in that county as a sheriff, brigadier-general of militia, and member of the Legislature. Mrs. Martin's mother, *nee* Miss Ruth Davidson, was a relative of Gen. William Davidson, of Mecklenburg county, North Carolina, an intrepid officer of the American army, who lost his life at the battle of Cowpens, South Carolina, and in whose honor Davidson county, Tennessee, was named. Mrs. Martin was one of eight sisters, all noted as ladies of great refinement and model housekeepers. She was a Presbyterian, and a graduate of the Nashville Female Academy, a remarkably fine mathematician and accomplished in music. She died in 1851, having borne nine children, four of whom are now living: (1). Barclay Martin, married Miss Kate Fogleman, of Shelbyville, and has three children, Barclay, Louie Queen, and Johnnie. He is now living at Wichita Falls, Texas, a lawyer. (2). Sarah Clay Martin, now wife of William J. Armstrong, of Maury county, has seven children, Quincy, Matt., Mary Barclay, George, William and Maury D. (3). Margaret F. Martin, now wife of Augustus F. Sowell, of Maury county, has three children, Jennie Pearl, Augustus, and Lizzie Martin. (4). Marshall Abram Martin, now practicing law at Burnett, Texas; married Miss Emma Walker, daughter of Thomas Walker; has six children, Barclay, Thomas Walker, Matt., Anna, Emma J. and Armstead Fisher. Gen. Martin has four great-grandchildren: Quincy Armstrong, oldest daughter of William J. Armstrong, married J. T. Cochran, and has three children, William, Thomas, and Matt .Martin. Mary Gordon Armstrong married Milton Bunch, and has one child, Hugh. Gen. Martin's present wife was Miss Elizabeth D. Martin, his second cousin, whom he married March 5, 1865, in Montgomery, Alabama. She was born in Shelbyville, Tennessee, February 2, 1824, daughter of Hon. Abram Martin, war tax-collector of the Confederate States for the State of Alabama, and for many years a circuit judge in that State. Her mother, Jane Patton, was the daughter of Thomas and Jane Patton, both native Irish.

The Martin family is of Scotch-Irish descent. Gen. Martin's portrait, accompanying this sketch, plainly shows in its strong Scotch-Irish lineaments. His grandfather, Abram Martin, commanded a company under Washington at Gen. Braddock's defeat. A short time before the Revolution he moved from Virginia to Edgefield district, South Carolina, and was killed by the Indians, in the State of Georgia, while with a surveying party locating lands. He left his widow with eight sons and one daughter. All of these sons were officers in the American army during the Revolutionary war, except Matt. Martin, the youngest, Gen. Martin's father, who was a private. Gen. Martin's oldest uncle, William Martin, was a captain of artillery, and was killed at Augusta, Georgia. Barclay Martin was a captain in a cavalry regiment, and afterwards became a colonel. John Martin was a major, George a captain of infantry, and Edmund, James and Marshall Martin were lieutenants. All who know Gen. Martin will remember with what pride and animation he recalls and dwells upon the Revolutionary history of his ancestry, and there may be found in these reminiscences an explanation of his own lion-like courage and dauntless patriotism. Having inherited with his blood a name honored in history, it seems to be his ambition to transmit it untarnished, and illustrated with his own prowess, to his posterity.

The Martin blood was up during the struggle for American independence. The day after the battle at Augusta, in which Capt. William Martin was killed, the British evacuated that city and were en route to Ninety-six, in South Carolina, Col. Brown being their commander. An officer was sent forward to order breakfast at the house of Mrs. Betty Martin, grandmother of Gen. Martin, and this, too, the very day after her son had been killed. The British officer asked her if her name was Martin, and upon being answered in the affirmative, informed her that he had seen her son killed the day before—had seen his brains shot out. She replied that she wished she had five thousand sons to fight in the same cause. When Col. Brown came up he went into the house, and seeing that the lady was in great distress, and presuming that she was apprehensive of improper treatment or of losing her property—she being of a noted rebel family—assured her she might rest easy on that score, that both she and her property should be protected. She replied: "It is not that; but the anomalous position I am in of being compelled to feed those who killed my own son but yesterday." "Who informed you that your son was killed yesterday?" inquired the British commander. She pointed out the man, one of his own officers, whereupon Col. Brown reprimanded the officer severely, struck him with his sword, and threatened to have him cashiered for bearing such tidings to a mother.

The personal courage, the daring spirit and patriotism of the Martin family, were finely illustrated soon after this event by a thrilling adventure of Gen. Martin's aunts, Grace and Rachel. The former, an English lady, originally Miss Grace Warren, was the widow of Gen. Martin's uncle, Capt. William Martin, who had been killed at Augusta. The latter, whose maiden name was Miss Rachel Clay, a cousin of Henry Clay, was the wife of Col. Barclay Martin, Gen. Martin's uncle. These two ladies captured a British officer, with his escort, and took from them an express which they were carrying to the British commandant at Ninety-six. They dressed themselves in their husbands' clothing and armed themselves, one with an old pistol, the other with a bayonet fixed to a staff like a pike. While dressing for the enterprise, Rachel Martin suggested that they would better represent men if they could swear at them while attempting the capture.

Grace promptly replied: "If you can't swear, I can. They have killed my husband, and d—n them, I can curse them with all my heart." Concealing themselves in an ambush near the way along which they knew the bearer of the coveted dispatches must pass, they sprang into the road as the two men rode up, pointed their weapons, and ordered them to surrender. They took the officer and his escort prisoners, disarmed them, secured the dispatches, and conducted their captives back to Martintown, to the house of their mother-in-law, Mrs. Betty Martin, Gen. Martin's grandmother. The old lady twitted the officer that he and his orderly had surrendered to such youthful soldiers. "Why, madam," said he, "they attacked us so suddenly we had no time to defend ourselves. The wicked eyes of the youthful soldiers were so determined and piercing, I am confident they would have run us through or shot us dead, had we offered the least resistance." Thereupon the old lady turned to her daughters-in-law and said: "Soldiers, what are you going to do with your prisoners?" They replied: "We ought to have killed them at first, but now we know not what to do with them, unless we confine them as prisoners in the swamps until the war is over." The old lady suggested that they be paroled, which gave great relief to the prisoners. Rachel Martin, being the wife of an officer, and knowing something about the paroling of prisoners, put them under oral obligation not to fight any more during the war, and especially to protect the women and children wherever they went, and not rob them of the necessaries of life. The officer begged for the dispatches, but the ladies kept them, and had them delivered, post haste, to Gen. Nathaniel Greene, and the patriot cause. For other and fuller information of these ladies, see Mrs. Ellett's "Women of the Revolution."

Gen. Martin's father, Matt. Martin, the youngest of the eight brothers, was born in Charlotte county, Virginia, grew up in South Carolina, but went back to Virginia, and married after the Revolution. After this, upon the reorganization of the South Carolina militia, he was elected captain of an artillery company. He remained in South Carolina several years, then moved to Bourbon county, Kentucky, remained two years, and then, with his brother, Col. Barclay Martin, settled in what is now Bedford county, Tennessee, shortly after the Duck and Elk river purchase was made from the Indians. He died in that county, October 16, 1846, in his eighty-fourth year. He was a man noted for firmness, strong will and superior judgment; and his deportment in life was such that he had the unbounded confidence and esteem of the whole community, and great influence in political, social and church affairs, though not belonging to any communion. He always refused to become a candidate for any trust, though he was a justice of the peace from 1807 to 1834.

Col. Barclay Martin, Gen. Martin's uncle, after his

settlement in Bedford county, was a member of the Tennessee Legislature for that county. He was a very popular man, and of high character. He died childless, and now lies buried alongside of his wife, Rachel, and Gen. Martin's father and mother, Matt. and Sally Martin, in the family graveyard on the old homestead of Gen. Martin's father, in Bedford county.

Gen. Martin's mother, originally Miss Sally Clay, sister of Rachel Clay before mentioned, was born in Charlotte county, Virginia, daughter of Henry Clay, "the tobacco maker." He became very wealthy, and emigrated to Bourbon county, Kentucky, where he died. As before stated, she was a cousin of Henry Clay, the great Whig orator and statesman, and it is through his mother and paternal grandmother, Marshall, that Gen. Martin has inherited the oratorial power for which he has been so long distinguished in Tennessee. Gen. Martin's maternal grandmother was Miss Rachel Puvall, a Virginia lady. Gen. Martin's mother was a member of the Baptist church, and a lady noted for great energy and industry and fine common sense. She died at the age of seventy-nine, having borne thirteen children—four sons and nine daughters.

Of Gen. Martin's brothers and sisters, it may be said: Barclay Martin was a member of the Tennessee house of representatives and of the senate, and also a member of congress from that State.

Miss Lucy G. Martin married Theodrick Bradford, who represented the Bedford county district in the Tennessee senate for many years, in the early history of the State.

His sister, Miss Rachel P. Martin, married Hon. John Tillman, a member of the Legislature from Bedford county for many years. She was the mother of Hon. Lewis Tillman, M. C., and Judge B. M. Tillman, chancellor. Her grandson (son of Lewis Tillman), Col. Samuel Tillman, is now a distinguished professor in West Point Military Academy. Another grandson, Col. James D. Tillman, was a colonel in the Confederate army; afterwards represented Lincoln county in the lower house, and Lincoln and Franklin counties in the State senate. Another grandson, George Newton Tillman, is now United States marshal for Middle Tennessee, and a lawyer who, perhaps, has no superior of his age in the State.

Gen. Martin's oldest sister, Miss Polly Marshall Martin, married her cousin, John Marshall, a gentleman of high standing and culture. Their son, Rev. Matt. Martin Marshall, is a noted Presbyterian clergyman and revivalist. His son, also named Matt. Martin Marshall, is a prominent lawyer at Dyersburg, Tennessee. A grandson of Rev. M. M. Marshall, Matt. Marshall Neill, is a rising lawyer of much promise at Trenton, Tennessee.

Gen. Martin's sisters, Rebecca Martin and Betty Marshall Martin, married brothers, both farmers. Rebecca married Thomas B. Mosely, and Betty M., married

Edward A. Mosely—both gentlemen of respectability and wealth. Gen. Martin's sister, Mattie Bedford Martin, married Samuel R. Rucker, a lawyer of distinction, who was formerly in the State senate from Rutherford county. Gen. Martin's seventh sister, Sally Clay Martin, married Col. John L. Neill, a lieutenant under Jackson. He was captured by the British on the evening of their landing below New Orleans, in the night attack made by Jackson upon them. He was a popular man, and at one time sheriff of Bedford county.

Many members of the Martin family have been prominent. William D. Martin (Gen. Martin's cousin), was a member of Congress, and afterwards judge of the South Carolina supreme court. Abram Martin was a circuit judge in Alabama. Edward Martin was a member of the South Carolina Legislature, and a very successful planter in Beaufort district of that State. These were the sons of Gen. John Martin, of South Carolina, one of the eight patriot brothers. Two of Gen. John Martin's daughters married gentlemen of prominence. The youngest, Sarah, was the wife of governor and United States senator, Fitzpatrick, of Alabama. The eldest, Susan, married Dixon H. Lewis, United States senator from Alabama. John A. Elmore (Gen. Martin's cousin), was an eminent lawyer at Montgomery, Alabama. His reputation was such that the supreme judgeship of the State was repeatedly tendered him, but he uniformly declined it. The county of Elmore, in Alabama, was named for him.

By way of anecdote, it might be related here that prior to the war Gen. Martin's brother, Barclay, had a wide reputation as a Democratic speaker, and the General himself as a Whig orator. Frequently Barclay would have appointments in various parts of the State, and the Whigs would send for Matt. to answer him, and in like manner Barclay was often sent for to answer Matt., but neither would accept the invitation, so high was their mutual brotherly regard. They differed politically till the war came up; since that they are one in politics, as always in brotherly love. Family pride is a characteristic of the entire family, and their adherence to each other has never been equalled outside of the clans of Scotland.

After the war, Gen. Martin returned home and advised everybody to abide by the result or leave the country, as he was anxious to see the Union brought back to the standard of the fathers. He refused to take a fee, either from a rebel or a Federal soldier, when arrayed against each other for injuries done during the war, on the ground that such suits would reopen wounds that should be given time to heal. In this way he did a great public service.

Gen. Martin is a man distinguished, not alone for personal courage and public spiritedness, but for firmness of character and fine social qualities. He is a true man, true to his friends, true to principle, and true to his State—an honorable, hightoned, high-minded, refined gentleman; a great favorite in social circles, which he always enlivens with anecdote, wit and humor. Though not a vindictive man, his repartee, when attacked, is sudden and withering. His sympathies are easily excited, and, when defending a criminal, his lips are tremulous with emotion, and often his tears

flow. He is a man of large build, frank and outspoken, and carries in his conversation the unmistakable lines of an honest man, a man of push and nerve and sincerity. In appearance he resembles Gen. Robert E. Lee. So striking is the likeness that it is frequently alluded to.

J. BUNYAN STEPHENS, M. D.

NASHVILLE.

THIS distinguished gentleman is presented in these pages as a type of strong mental, moral and physical manhood; of medium height, compact build, large frame, weighing one hundred and seventy-five pounds; of dark complexion, clear brown eyes; a face radiant with intelligence, and with a serene, collected appearance, as of a man who sees his way before him, and has his mind made up to do or suffer whatever duty may demand. The impression he makes on one seeing him for the first time is that he is a man of positive character. And such is the reputation he has made for himself throughout the South, as professor of obstetrics in the Nashville Medical College, a chair which he has filled for the last nine years; as editor of the *Baptist Watchman;* as an eminent physician, and as pastor of the Primitive Baptist church. His location in Nashville was brought about by the celebrated Dr. John M. Watson, who, seeing his own end approaching, selected Dr. Stephens for his successor in charge of the Baptist church in that city. Yielding to his solicitations, he settled there in March, 1867, and by a very active life has made a name among the standard men of the State, and acquired a comfortable fortune.

Of the mental make-up of Prof. Stephens, a fair estimate may be formed from the following sentences gleaned from a speech he made to his graduating class of 1881: "Another element of success is self-reliance. The mainspring of all individual growth and vigor, the master key which unlocks all difficulties in the medical profession, as in other callings, is a determination to be your own helper. The men who have won distinction in the marts of commerce, or have become lights in the intellectual firmament—the stars that shine with steady radiance through the ages of medical literature, emerged to eminence from the chilling depths of obscurity and destitution. They are men of humble parentage, whose cradles were rocked in lowly cottages, buffeted the billows of fate and worked out their own distinction with an ardor that could not be quenched, and without dependence, save upon the mercies of God and their own energies. Above all, a deep and burning enthusiasm is needed in every one who would accomplish great ends in any calling."

These, and similar memorable utterances in the

speech, made a deep impression, and were much talked of in Nashville. They fell from the lips of a man who had himself experienced what it is, and how it pays, to courageously grapple with the rough roll and tumble of practical life.

Dr. Stephens, undoubtedly, owes much of his solidity of character to his parentage, and much of his success to a judicious marriage. He was born in Marshall county, Tennessee, February 5, 1836, and as his name, John Bunyan, indicates, of Baptist parents. His father, Rev. Jeremiah Stevens, a native also of the same county, and now over seventy years old, is a Baptist minister, a farmer in moderate circumstances, a son of James and Frances Stephens, originally from North Carolina. His mother was Emeline Ezell, daughter of Rev. Balaam Ezell, an old Baptist minister of eminence, also of North Carolina stock. Thus the Doctor is at once the son and grandson of Baptist preachers.

The Primitive Baptist people are proverbial for their stability of character. There is less of volatility among them than among the Scotch themselves. In Tennessee, as elsewhere, they are noted for their loyalty to their creed and church; for honesty in their commercial transactions, and for being the only people whose letter will admit its bearer into any communion whatever. Their ministry and baptism are almost universally recognized as orthodox. The writer heard a story about town that on at least two occasions Dr. Stephens, not long after settling in Nashville, applied to a broker in the city to cash drafts from Gen. Anderson Gordon, of Arkansas, upon a Memphis house. The broker declined, as he knew neither Stephens, Gordon, nor the Memphis firm. The Doctor brought in a jeweler, who vouched for him. "Well, but," said the broker, "I don't know Gordon, nor those Memphis people either." "Neither do I," replied Dr. Stephens, "but I know that Gen. Gordon is an old Baptist of high standing in Arkansas." "That being the case," interposed the jeweler, "I'll vouch for Gordon and I'll vouch for that Memphis house too. Cash the draft, and if it comes back to you dishonored, bring it to me, and I'll pay it." The Doctor got the money. After this he again applied to the same man for accommodation. The broker humorously replied, "Well, I suppose it was predestinated from the foundation of the world that I should let you have it," and he did.

The writer is not trying to picture a rough man. Dr. Stephens has the happy faculty of refusing without a repulsive air, but even a book agent knows from the tone of voice with which he declines, the discussion is closed.

At a meeting of preachers of several denominations in a merchant's store in Nashville, Dr. McFerrin, Methodist, pointing to Dr. Stephens, said : " And here is Dr. Stephens, who belongs to a church that always pay their debts; I never knew one of them to fail." " Yes," said the merchant, "I never lost a cent by one of them in my life." Dr. McFerrin then inquired, " How about your own people?" " Why," the merchant responded, "they have broken me up three times."

Dr. Stephens' mother died when he was only four years old, leaving three children, himself, James B., and Joseph K., the latter now also an old Baptist preacher, and all three practicing physicians.

In boyhood Dr. Stephens received only a limited education, and the learning he has was acquired since he became his own man. He was a moral boy, having a father and step-mother who knew how to "train a child in the way he should go." From early childhood he inclined to be a physician, another proof of a valuable truth, that whoever would succeed in life must fit himself for some particular line of business that is suited to his natural bent. Like many successful men, Dr. Stephens had no collegiate education, yet his reputation for both literary and scientific attainments is very high. At the age of eighteen, he began reading medicine under Dr. Edward Swenson, at Chapel Hill, Tennessee. He attended two courses of lectures in 1856–7, and received his diploma in 1867, and has been practicing medicine in Nashville ever since. He began to read medicine with only one-half dollar in his pocket, and in debt sixteen dollars. With some assistance from his uncle, George W. Ezell, he made his way through.

In 1875, he was elected first to fill the chair of theory and practice of medicine in the medical department of the Nashville Medical College (now University of Tennessee), but soon after became professor of obstetrics, a position which he still ably fills. In addition to his professorship, and large private practice, he has been for fourteen years physician to the small-pox hospital, at Nashville, by election of the county court.

In 1862, Dr. Stepens became a Master Mason, but dimitted in 1868. He has also been connected with the Odd Fellows, Knights of Honor, and the Ancient Order of United Workmen. He is a Democrat.

Dr. Stephens married, in Marshall county, Tennessee, August 28, 1856, Miss Amelia L. Ferguson, who was born November 1, 1835, daughter of John Fleming Ferguson, a farmer and a magistrate in his district for many years. Her grandfather, John Fleming Ferguson, was of Scotch descent, a native of North Carolina. Her

grandmother was of Irish stock. Her mother was Amelia Britton, daughter of Joseph Britton, originally from North Carolina, of English descent. Mrs. Stephens has a good English education, and the reputation of being possessed of every grace that adorns a lady. She is a woman of great firmness and decision of character and good sense, and is noted for her unerring judgment of human nature.

By his marriage with Miss Ferguson, Dr. Stephens has two children: (1). Jeremiah Fane Stephens, born June 15, 1857; graduated in medicine in 1876, and in dentistry in 1877, and is now practicing dentistry in Nashville, and has already made a sterling reputation. He married, in Nashville, September 5, 1878, Miss Willie Mallory, daughter of William Mallory, of Nashville. (2). Ophelia Elizabeth Stephens, born June 30, 1860; graduated at the high school at Nashville; married, March, 1881, Robert M. Dudley, a merchant of the firm of Dudley Bros. & Lipscomb, of Nashville, and has one child, Bunyan Stephens, born February 2, 1882.

Dr. Stephens was baptized into the Old Baptist church in October, 1854; began preaching in 1859, and was pastor of Mount Olivet church, in Lincoln county, from 1860 to 1866, when he took charge of the church at Nashville, of which he is still pastor. In some respects he is in advance of his church in matters of faith. He believes in the renovation of the earth and the personal reign of Christ on earth, which will be the Kingdom spoken of in the Bible. He believes in the resurrection of the body and the actual existence of soul and body on the earth after resurrection. The first resurrection he holds is from among the dead—that is, the resurrection of the saints and no others. "The rest of the dead," he understands, will live not again until the one thousand years are ended. More succinctly stated, he believes in the personal return of Christ to this earth, at which time will occur the resurrection of the saints, and that thereafter the earth will be the home of the Redeemer and His redeemed ones.

Mrs. Stephens is also a Primitive Baptist, and in full harmony with her husband, though her parents were attached to no denomination. To fill at once the difficult and delicate position of wife to a man who is both physician and preacher, is an honor equalled only by that other honor she has achieved—of raising up children who have always been obedient and courteous to their parents; uniformly respectful to their authority and deferential to their superior experience and wisdom.

Dr. Stephens' motto has been to live a Christian life, to live at the head of his profession (medicine), and to die the death of the righteous. Honest dealings, an energetic, earnest life, account for his success. He never had a note to go to protest, and has made it a rule to be punctual to meet his promises, and he says, with laudable pride, no man has ever suffered to the amount of a dollar on his account.

WILLIAM C. SHEPPARD, D. D. S.

COLUMBIA.

THE ancestry of Dr. Sheppard is traced back only to his grandfather, James Sheppard, who died in Williamson county, Tennessee, about the year 1830, at the age of about sixty, the richest man of his day in that county. He married Phebe Mastin, in Halifax county, Virginia, and settled on the Yadkin river, in North Carolina. Somewhere about 1815, he purchased five thousand acres of land on Hickory creek, Warren county, Tennessee, where he farmed till about 1820, when he moved to Williamson county, engaged in stock raising, farming, merchandising, and trading till his death. Those were pushing, pioneer times, and he was a pushing man, personally superintending all departments of his business. He was himself fond of his dram, but when not entirely sober he would sign no papers, nor receive or pay out money or transact any business whatever. He had four sons: Austin, Andy, James, and Clinton; and five daughters: Betsy, Polly, Sally, Patsey and Phebe. It was a common remark that the girls were like their mother—devout, godly women; bright and shining members of the church. The boys were not reckless, nor as money-makers failures, but neither they nor their children or grandchildren have been so successful as their ancestors. The sons were industrious, stirring men, and raised respectable families. No stain is upon their records, but it is doubtful if all of his descendants together have as much property as he had. He made his money by trading with the Indians, by speculating in lands, and by tireless industry. The first bed he slept on, after going to housekeeping in North Carolina, was made of leaves gathered by his young wife out of the forest. The same year he gave his only hat to a man who helped him fence in his clearing. He was a soldier and teamster in the Revolutionary war, and was at the battle of King's Mountain. His stout, compact build, and especially his facial features, are unmistakably traced in nearly every one of his descendants. His children are all dead but one, James Sheppard, of Dallas, Texas, now eighty-three years old—a fine specimen of noble manhood.

The religion of the family was the old Baptist, but the grandchildren now belong to various denominations. Reviewing the history of the Sheppard family, how they are scattered—not one of them living on the ancestral lands—the first reflection that rises is, how soon fortunes are wasted, and how soon we all turn to ashes! James Sheppard's children, one only excepted, are all dead. His history itself is forgotten, except the legendary fragments of it herein related. His grandson remembers that his grandfather, in his last sickness, had his favorite horse led into his room and turned round, that he might see whether it was being taken

good care of. His character was that of a genial, jovial, pushing, gathering man of the world, and his memory is lovingly cherished.

Dr. Sheppard's grandmother, Phebe Mastin, was one of the excellent of the earth. Her patience, piety, fortitude and sweetness of disposition, are the most precious heirlooms in the families of her descendants. Her saying, which seemed a plaster for every sore, her panacea for all incurable wounds, " It is as it is, and it can't be any tisser," an admiring and grateful grandchild thinks the wisest philosophy he ever learned. She was buried at Columbia at the great age of ninety, after living to see about one hundred and forty-one of her descendants; now probably four times that number are scattered in Kansas, Arkansas, Texas, Missouri, Tennessee, and elsewhere. Of her ancestry no trace remains.

Dr. Sheppard's father, William Clinton Sheppard, the youngest of nine children, died in Columbia, at the age of sixty-two. He was born in North Carolina, and grew up in Warren and Williamson counties, Tennessee. He was twice married. By his first wife, Polly Riggs, he had five children, James M., Elizabeth, who married Mr. Watson, Joseph, Marietta, who married Mr. Joyce, and Josephine, who married Mr. Lancaster. By his second wife, née Mrs. Parthenia Moore, whom he married at Mount Pleasant, Tennessee, January 18, 1845, he had three children: (1). William Clinton, subject of this sketch, born in Columbia, Tennessee, November 4, 1845. (2). Eurilda, died the wife of Thomas Whittaker, leaving four children, Moore, Homer, Stella and Emma. (3). Andrew, died eighteen months old. Dr. Sheppard's father was a man of generous impulses, and in the earlier part of his life was too liberal with his money and too convivial, qualities which soon dissipated a very large estate. But misfortune only brought out the energy that was in him, and he soon became independent again. He used to say: " I would make a living if I were set down on a flat rock;" and the son, a chip of the old block, says: " You can never keep a Sheppard down in the world." His career in Columbia, where he spent the last twenty years of his life, was in all respects satisfactorily successful. He lived and died universally respected for his business qualities, and for his high-toned bearing as a Christian gentleman. He was eminently a family man, courteous and indulgent to his children, a good provider, very fond of his kin, and lavish in his outlay upon the education of his children.

Dr. Sheppard's mother, now living with him at his home in Columbia, at the age of seventy-seven, is one of the most remarkable women in Tennessee. With the vivacity of a girl, the gayety of a belle, the fortitude of a heroine, the tact of a diplomat, and the energy of a will bent on victory, she is celebrated in Columbia society as a leader in church enterprises and other public charities, and for her skill and kindness as an amateur "doctor," especially in calls to relieve the perils of maternity, and for her high character as a lady. She is a strong woman, standing back from no obstacle, never knowing how to accept defeat, rising superior to every difficulty, spreading sunshine over every circle she enters, the friend and counselor of young people, and mentioned by old and young, high and low, only to be praised as an unapproachable model. She was thrice married. The first husband, whom she married at Athens, Alabama, February 14, 1826, was Dr. J. B. A. Thevenot, by whom she had five children, Amanda, Evelina, Napoleon, Sally E., and Ann Maria. Of these, only one survives, namely, Sally E., widow of John Neely, by whom she has two children, Eddy Orion and Joseph Thevenot. Her second husband, whom she married at Mount Pleasant, Tennessee, December 4, 1835, was J. M. Moore, by whom she had two children, Mary Eliza Moore, now dead, and Dr. J. J. Moore, now lying in San Francisco, California. Her third husband was William Clinton Sheppard, father of Dr. Sheppard, whom, as before stated, she married January 18, 1845.

Dr. Sheppard married in Rutherford county, Tennessee, December 2, 1869, Miss Idell Johns, who was born September 24, 1851, daughter of J. B. Johns, an uncle of Gen. Joseph B. Palmer. Her mother, *nee* Maggie Wade, was cousin to Levi and Samuel Wade, of that county, and related to the Randolphs of Virginia. Mrs. Sheppard was educated at Soule Female College, Murfreesborough, is a member of the Presbyterian church, and is noted for the mildness of her disposition; her great presence of mind in cases of danger; is even-tempered in the government of her family; high-minded in her aspirations for her children; relies upon reason for their control, and with the happiest results.

By his marriage with Miss Johns, Dr. Sheppard has nine children: (1). Maggie C., born in Rutherford county, September 8, 1870, and has already become a local celebrity as a musical performer on the cornet. (2). Lucy Idell, born in the same county, October 28,

1871; deceased. (3). Eula Kate, born in the same county, September 8, 1872. (4). Joseph P., born in Columbia, April 6, 1874. (4). Robert Russell, born in Columbia, July 9, 1876; died September 8, ——. (6). James Ernest, born in Columbia, June 21, 1877. (7). Pattie, born in Columbia, March 4, 1879. (8). Minnie, born in Columbia, December 9, 1880. (9). Died an infant, unnamed.

Dr. Sheppard, from his earliest boyhood, was always full of energy. He worked on a farm, assisted his father in the livery business, and, at twelve years of age, hired himself to work on the streets of Columbia at fifty cents a day. He was educated at Jackson College, Columbia. In his eighteenth year he went into the Confederate army; joined no command, but was with his brother, J. D. Sheppard, in Bate's Second Tennessee regiment, one year. At nineteen he began the study of dentistry, and studied two years at home. He next was a pupil for some seven years under Dr. Robert Russell, at Nashville. In 1869, the year of his marriage, he began the practice, and also farmed, in Rutherford county, where he remained three years, when he moved back to Columbia, where he has resided ever since, doing a practice so large and lucrative that Chancellor Fleming said of him: "He makes more money than any merchant in the town, and ought to be the richest man in it. In 1878, he was appointed clinical operator in the dental department of the University of Tennessee, at Nashville. In 1881 he had the degree of doctor of dental surgery conferred upon him by the same institution, of which honor he is justly proud.

He is a Master Mason and a Knight of Pythias. In religious faith, he is a Presbyterian.

Inheriting from his mother, who has been often spoken of as "a chain-lightning woman," an active, nervous, energetic, and proud nature, he made a resolution in early childhood to conduct himself so that everybody would respect him, and, as far as possible, be independent of the world, instead of dependent. On first acquaintance, he appears only as a bright, sprightly man; but he is a deep thinker, a close reasoner, a shrewd observer of events, and reader of character, and, like his father and grandfather, has made a great deal of money, but has been too generous with it.

J. C. ROSS, D. D. S.
NASHVILLE.

JAMES C. ROSS, D.D.S., of Nashville, was born in Hamilton county, Ohio, July 16, 1815, the son of Thomas Ross. His father was a native of Pennsylvania, born in Lark county, of that State, May 19, 1769, the son of John and Eleanor Ross. The family is of

Scotch descent, Ross being the name of a Scottish clan. When a young man, Thomas Ross emigrated to Warren, Ohio, where he was a farmer for a number of years, and from there went to Cincinnati, in 1810, arriving at the foot of Main street in a flat-boat, when that city had a

47

population of only twenty-six hundred. In 1821, he removed from Carthage, Hamilton county, to Butler county, Ohio, where he died, in 1825. He was a very industrious and hard-working man, and became quite prosperous. His eleven children all lived to maturity. The mother of Dr. Ross was Miss Rosalinda Cobb, daughter of Samuel and Sarah Cobb. She was born in New Jersey, May 8, 1779; married July 9, 1799, and died in New Albany, Indiana, in 1836. She was a lady remarkable for her motherly kindness and devotion to her church, her even temper and placidity of disposition. She was, at her death, a member of the Methodist Episcopal church, but during the lifetime of her husband was, with him, a Presbyterian. Her brother, James Cobb, was for many years a prominent saddler of Cincinnati.

John D. Ross, the second child, and Dr. Ross' oldest brother, now living at Buchanan, Michigan, has reached the age of eighty-three years. He was the founder and president of the Farmers' and Manufacturers' Bank of Buchanan, of which his son, Alfred F., is now cashier. He himself has retired from business. He married early, his family increased rapidly, and the first twenty years of his married life was a struggle, but after that time fortune smiled upon him, and he went on from one degree of prosperity to another. He was for some time a merchant, and was once elected to the Legislature of Michigan, and for many years was president of the town council of Buchanan.

Dr. Ross' brother, William B. Ross, was for several years a Methodist minister, preaching in Ohio and Indiana, but living, a part of the time, at Newport, Kentucky. He lost his life in attempting to stop a runaway horse. His three sons, James H., Lewis L. and George S., now live in Newport, and are engaged in business in Cincinnati.

His next brother, Dr. Henry L. Ross, now deceased, was a physician, practicing at Newport, Kentucky, and at one time held the position of physician at the Newport arsenal, under the United States government.

His sister, Sarah Ross, the oldest child of the family, was born in 1800; married, in 1821, Edward Noble, a farmer, and died in 1825. After her death Mr. Noble went to Lebanon, Ohio, engaged in mercantile business, and was afterward elected to the Ohio Legislature from Warren county.

Dr. Ross' sister, Annie Ross, is now wife of Rev. John G. Bruce, D.D., of the Kentucky conference of the Methodist Episcopal church, and is living near Danville, Kentucky.

His sister, Elizabeth Ross, was born October 7, 1810, and died at Cincinnati, the wife of Joseph Lindley Conkling.

Dr. Ross' next oldest brother, Samuel C. Ross, the seventh child and fourth son, was born in Ohio, in the year 1813; was raised and educated in Cincinnati; taught school for a time, but soon turned his attention to dentistry. He married Mrs. Agnes Rouse, daughter of Mr. John Bradshaw, of Shelbyville, Kentucky. After marriage, he practiced his profession for several years in St. Louis, but finally returned to Shelbyville, where he continued to practice until failing health compelled him to retire. He died in 1855.

His brother, Joseph R. Ross, born April 20, 1818, was a school teacher in Cincinnati. He died in Newport, Kentucky, in 1840. He was the only member of the family·who never married.

His brother, Alfred N. Ross, born May 23, 1820, was a druggist. He died in 1847, on the anniversary of his birthday.

Dr. Ross' youngest sister, Ellen Luella Ross, born August 10, 1822, died near Danville, Kentucky, wife of Walter Scott Powell.

Dr. Ross obtained his academic education at the common schools at intervals till the age of sixteen, when he was apprenticed to a manufacturer of furniture, in which business he distinguished himself by such superiority and excellence of workmanship, that before the expiration of his apprenticeship he was made foreman. He remained in the furniture business until the age of twenty-two, when he began the practice of dentistry, the study of which he had commenced one year previous. He began practice in Lawrenceburg, Indiana, in 1837, and then traveled till the time of his marriage, in 1841. He practiced three years in Frankfort and three years in Lexington, Kentucky.

In 1847, he removed to Nashville, where he settled, and has resided and practiced ever since, with the exception of the time between February, 1858, and June, 1859, which he spent in Huntsville, Alabama. From the age of twenty-two, when he commenced the practice of dentistry, he has devoted all his energies to that pursuit. He has now been practicing for forty-eight years, and is the oldest practitioner of dentistry in Nashville, probably in the State. He is a professor in the dental department of the Vanderbilt University, and one of the original faculty, having participated with Dr. W. H. Morgan (whose sketch appears elsewhere in this volume) and others, in the organization of the dental department. He was elected at that time professor of operative dentistry and dental hygiene, and president of the faculty, a position which he has filled ever since. He has, also, occasionally contributed to the literature of the profession. In 1873, he was elected president of the State Dental Association, which was organized at Nashville, in July, 1867. He was a delegate from the State Association to the National Association twice; first at Cincinnati and afterward at Detroit.

On January 12, 1841, Dr. Ross was united in marriage, at Harrodsburg, Kentucky, to Miss Lucy J. Fairman, the daughter of Richard Fairman, an ingenious and enterprising machinist and mill-wright, originally from Connecticut. Her mother was Sarah Parks. Mrs. Ross was educated at Harrodsburg, Kentucky. She is a very devoted and active working member of the Protestant Episcopal church, and a lady whose kindness of heart and many deeds of charity have endeared her to a large circle of friends. By this marriage Dr. Ross has five children living: (1). William B. Ross, born April 17, 1844; educated at Nashville, and is now a civil engineer. He was a gallant soldier in the Confederate army four years, going out as a private in the famous Rock City Guards, afterward the First Tennessee regiment of infantry, under Col. George Maney. He served in Virginia, Mississippi, Tennessee, Kentucky, Georgia and Alabama; participated in the battles of Perryville, Atlanta and Jonesborough; was wounded at Perryville, taken prisoner several times, and came out with the ranking title of plain "Mr." He married, January 12, 1881, Miss Harriet A., daughter of Maj. Alexander Warfield, superintendent of several mining companies in Colorado. They have one child, Mary Christine, born Christmas, 1883. (2). Annie Ross, educated at Nashville, under Rev. Dr. C. D. Elliott, and at the Columbia (Tennessee) Female Institute; now the wife of James A. Thomas, a leading insurance agent, of the firm of Gale, Thomas & Sharpe, Nashville; has three children, James Ross, Mary Weakley and Rachel. (3). Mary Ellen Ross, educated at Louisville (Kentucky) Female College; married James Thomas, jr., January 12, 1876, of the firm of Pendleton, Thomas & Co., wholesale druggists, Nashville; has one child, Annie Lou. These two sisters married gentlemen of the same name, but not related. (4). James S. Ross, educated at Montgomery Bell Academy, Nashville; is an electrical engineer. This gentleman organized the "Telephone Exchange" in Nashville, one among the first organizations of the kind in the world, and is now manager of the Nashville Electric Time Telegraph company. (5). Frank Fairman Ross, born in 1862; educated in the Nashville public schools, and has been engaged with his brother in civil and electrical engineering.

Of the eleven children born to Dr. Ross, six have died. Of these, the first, Horace C. Ross, was born November 3, 1841, in Frankfort, Kentucky, served in the Confederate army four years, and died in Nashville, July, 1882. He married Miss Laura Anderson, daughter of Thompson Anderson, of the wholesale dry goods firm of Anderson, Green & Co., Nashville. He was educated in Nashville and was a member of the leading insurance firm, Ross, Gale & Thomas. As a Mason, he was an untiring worker, being a Knight Templar. He was a devout Methodist, and the Sunday-school found him a ready, punctual and zealous worker in any post to which he was called, from that of secretary and librarian to that of superintendent—a faithful and fruitful teacher. For twelve years he was the leader of the choir at the McKendree Methodist church, Nashville. Coming from a family of highly artistic organization, in him the artistic trait took the direction

of music, and through it he became an inestimable blessing to his church. His love of music was intense, his taste highly cultivated and refined; his musical conscience ever impelled him to give to the service of the sanctuary the best music which industrious and painstaking practice could attain.

In a memorial discourse delivered at his funeral service at McKendree church, July 2, 1882, Rev. D. C. Kelley, D.D., paid the following beautiful tribute to his memory: "As son, few men have such a record of obedience and tenderness; as brother, none knew more gentle and unselfish devotion; as husband, he had all of the manly devotion and unreserved self-renunciation that this sacred relation brings as its crown of earthly bliss. A thoughtful woman, warped by no peculiar relationship, said to me to-day, 'I have never known two lives to run so harmoniously together for so many years.' As a man of business, he was transparently honest. He would never have objected, in any matter of business, for the person with whom he dealt to see every entry on his books which could in any way throw light on the remotest history of the transaction. More than this, he might have looked back of the ledger into the heart of him who kept it, and found every motive clear in the light of the crucial Christian rule, Do unto others as you would have them do unto you. Thank God for the privilege, ever and anon, of pointing the fault-finding world to a man in whom religion and honesty were alike conspicuous. But, as son, brother, husband, man of business, he was subordinate to Horace Ross the Christian. More than all and every thing else, he was a Christian; it was his interest in Christianity that entered into and glorified all these other relations, and gave them their mellow tenderness and their rich beauty."

Of Dr. Ross' other deceased children, Lucy Ross, born in 1852, died in 1875; John Ross, died in his twelfth year; the other three died in infancy.

Dr. Ross affiliated with the Odd Fellows for twenty-five years, and passed all the chairs, but of late has not attended the lodge. He was also a member of the Sons of Temperance. He joined the Methodist Episcopal church in Cincinnati, at a watch-night meeting, in 1832, and has since served as class-leader and steward, and is now trustee of Elm Street Methodist Episcopal church, South, Nashville. All of his children are members of the Methodist church except William B.

The first presidential vote he cast was for William Henry Harrison, being at that time an old line Whig, but since the war he has been identified with the Democratic party.

In his earlier married life, he felt that, as the head of a family, there was a responsibility resting upon him not to be shirked. Whatever he might be able to give his children, he wished to advance them in mental and moral culture. It was his idea to bring his children as near to him as possible, and with this in view he made associates of them, and sought to make home the most attractive place that could be found. The wisdom of this course is seen in the fact that his children have been only a comfort to him.

As a dentist, Dr. Ross has made it a matter of conscience always to give the best service without regard to the prospect of compensation. As showing the methodical character of the man, it may be mentioned that he has, from the beginning of his letter writing, kept notes of letters written and received, and for many years was in the habit of preserving all letters. From 1848 he has kept a diary, both for convenience of reference to his past life, and also as an heirloom for his children, that they may trace his history.

Dr. Ross stands about five feet ten inches in height, and weighs one hundred and twenty pounds, has blue eyes and an expression of benignity and clearness of character. He is slightly stooped from the long habit of bending over the dental chair. When he was a boy he was of a somewhat timid nature, needing encouragement and stimulation rather than repression. He is a modest man, finding his greatest pleasure in pleasing the company in which he may be placed, and doing service rather than seeking to be a leader. The impression he makes on one is, that he is a man who wants to know his duty and is always ready to do it. He has the appearance of a careful man; always busy, but never in a hurry.

Dr. William H. Morgan, who has known him intimately for many years, furnishes the following estimate of his character : " Dr. Ross is a Christian gentleman ; a man who has no bad traits—in short, essentially a good man. The measure of professional and social success to which he has attained is largely due to his known honesty and integrity of purpose. The excellence of his social and professional character is the legitimate outgrowth of his deep religious convictions."

WILLIAM J. McMURRAY, M. D.

NASHVILLE.

THIS gentleman, whose record as a soldier, a citizen and a physician, is at once an honor to the State and the pride of an extensive circle of friends, is justly entitled to rank among representative Tennesseans. He was born in the Sixteenth civil district of Williamson county, Tennessee, September 22, 1842, and grew up on his father's farm. When only seventeen years old, he entered the Confederate army as a private in the company raised by Col. Joel A. Battle, the "Zollicoffer Guards," which was mustered into service, May 17, 1861, and organized with the Twentieth Tennessee regiment, at first a part of Gen. Zollicoffer's brigade. He remained in this one company and regiment till its surrender, and except when off active duty on account of his wounds, of which he received more than his share, he was with his regiment from Wild Cat, in Eastern Kentucky, to the plains of Louisiana. On the Georgia campaign of seventy-five days, he was under fire sixty-five times. He was elected first corporal in 1861, next became second sergeant, then second lieutenant, at the reorganization of the Army of Tennessee, at Corinth, in May, 1862, was promoted to first lieutenant, in 1864, at Dalton, Georgia, and commanded company B of the Twentieth Tennessee regiment, as its gallant captain, C. S. Johnson, could never learn to drill.

He was in the famous charge made by Gen. Breckinridge's division at Murfreesborough—the command going into the engagement with four thousand six hundred men, of whom two thousand two hundred were lost. In that desperate battle, young McMurray was wounded in the left breast by a minnie ball, and left to lie all night on the battlefield, in the dead of winter. The ball passed between his heart and a Bible which he carried in his left coat pocket. From this wound he was disabled two months.

At the battle of Chickamauga, he was wounded by a piece of shell in the right groin, and was again left for dead all night on the field. From this wound he was disabled four months.

He received a third wound at Resaca, Georgia, in May, 1864, a minnie ball striking him in the left leg below the knee, which disabled him two or three weeks.

He lost his left arm in a skirmish in front of Atlanta, August 5, 1864. His armless left sleeve, armless from the shoulder down, is a silent but eloquent reminder that he has deserved well of his country, and is entitled to the praise of a brave man, cool and intrepid, doing his duty with unflinching courage.

Dr. McMurray is a tall, trim-made, handsome man, perfectly erect, and with an expression that precisely indicates his military history. He entered the army from principle, based on that pride that characterized the flower of the southern troops, and is a fine specimen of the noble and manly young men who constituted the southern chivalry, and many of whom now sleep on the plains where the flag of the South needed friends.

He served in Tennessee, Kentucky, Mississippi, Louisiana, Georgia, Alabama and North Carolina, and took part in the battles of Laurel Bridge, October, 1861 ;

Wild Cat; Fishing Creek, January 19, 1862; Shiloh, April 6 and 7, 1862; around Corinth, in 1862; Vicksburg, 1862; Baton Rouge, 1862; Murfreesborough, December 31, 1862, and January 1 and 2, 1863; Hoover's Gap, in the spring of 1863; Bethpage Bridge, June, 1863; Chickamauga, September 19 and 20, 1863; Rockyface Gap, Resaca, Dallas, Pine mountain, Kennesaw mountain, Peach Tree creek, and in the various skirmishes before Atlanta. He surrendered at Marion, Alabama, May 17, 1865. His regiment went out nine hundred and ninety-eight men strong, was recruited to one thousand three hundred, but surrendered with only thirty-four. His company, which numbered, first and last, one hundred and fifty-three, surrendered with seven men. For a fuller account of Dr. McMurray's military career, see "History of Davidson County," pages 457-8-9.

Up to the time of the war, Dr. McMurray had only received the limited educational advantages of a country school, his father having died when the son was only twelve years old. After the war, he studied one year and a half in the academy at Nolensville, under Prof. Joseph D. Didiot, of Paris, France, and graduated in 1867, having the honor of delivering the valedictory address. He next read medicine two years under Drs. William Clark and Thomas G. Shannon, and then attended two courses of lectures in the medical department of the University of Nashville, graduating February 26, 1869, under Profs. William K. Bowling, Paul F. Eve, Thomas L. Maddin, T. B. Buchanan, J. Berrien Lindsley, Van S. Lindsley and W. T. Briggs. He also had the honor of the unanimous vote of his class for valedictorian.

After graduation, Dr. McMurray began practice three miles south of Nashville, but on January 1, 1872, moved into the city, as from the effects of his wounds he was unable to endure the fatigue of saddle practice. In 1872, he was elected jail physician for the county of Davidson, and appointed physician to all the Supreme court prisoners held for trial in the Middle district of Tennessee, and kept that position eight years through successive appointments and elections. During the first thirteen years of his practice, he only lost twelve days from his professional business. He was at one time a member of the city board of health; at one time (1876) a member of the board of aldermen, and is now vice-president of the Nashville Medical Society, and is a member of the Tennessee State Medical Society. He is the author of the historical sketch of the Twentieth Tennessee Confederate regiment, in Dr. J. B. Lindsley's Military Annals of Tennessee, and is at this writing the efficient chairman of the Democratic executive committee of Davidson county.

Financially, Dr. McMurray has made a fine success. He started in life in 1869, with two hundred and fifty dollars less than nothing, and is now thought to be worth forty thousand dollars. Raised by a mother who always

taught him to guard well his credit, he has acted upon her good advice, and has made it a rule when he earned a dollar to have something to lay by of that dollar, i. e., never allow his expenditures to overrun his income. Five cardinal points in life he has always tried to work to: first, competency; second, strict attention to business; third, frugality; fourth, integrity and preservation of character; fifth, hope in the midst of direst defeat. On this line he has fought the battle of life. He has been heard to say, with filial gratitude, that he owes these principles to his mother, and, with a gallant pride, to his wife for her fine judgement, whom he has uniformly consulted on the propriety of business investment—like Lord Brougham, who uttered the memorable words, "Were I about to embark in some important enterprise, my first step would be to consult a sensible woman." Dr. McMurray is fortunate in having one of those sensible women for a wife.

Dr. McMurray's great-grandfather, of Scotch-Irish stock, was one of the early settlers of Kentucky. His great-grandmother was a Miss Kinkade, whose father was Irish and her mother Welsh. In 1790, they settled near Nashville, where the great-grandfather was killed by the Indians, in 1792. His second son, Samuel McMurray, married Levicy Morton, and had eight children, the eldest of whom, John McMurray, by his marriage with Miss Mary J. Still, became the father of seven children : (1). Sarah A. McMurray, died in 1863. (2). Samuel J. McMurray, was sergeant-major of the Twenty-fourth Tennessee Confederate regiment, and was killed at the battle of Franklin, November 30, 1864, at the age of twenty-four. (3). William J. McMurray, subject of this sketch. (4). Lucy Ellen McMurray, wife of William Smith, a farmer near Trenton, Tennessee. (5). John H. McMurray, graduated in pharmacy at Nashville; now a druggist in that city; married Miss Mary Morton, a daughter of George Morton, a Williamson county farmer of high standing and wealth. (6). Joel A. McMurray, died in 1856. (7). Thomas M. McMurray, now a practicing physician at Nolensville, Tennessee; married Miss Sallie King, daughter of David King, who fell at Dr. McMurray's side, at the battle of Chickamauga.

The McMurray family has had many participants in every war in which the United States have been engaged, from the Revolutionary struggle down to the recent strife between the States. In the latter they fought exclusively on the Southern side. Of five of Dr. McMurray's brothers and cousins, two were slain outright on the field, and the other three disabled for life. A cousin, Col. Sam. McMurray, is now in command of all the Texas State troops.

Dr. McMurray's mother, also of Irish descent, was born near Danville, Virginia, but from the age of nine months, grew up in Williamson county, Tennessee, where she married and reared her family. She is now living at Nashville, experiencing a mother's highest ambition—the gratitude of a son whose early training she so wisely planned, and which has made of him a success. Her relatives, the Stills, are mostly in Virginia.

Dr. McMurray's uncle, Dr. Thomas M. McMurray, died a bachelor, in 1864, at Spring Hill, Maury county, Tennessee, where he had practiced twenty years, and had the reputation of being a most excellent physician, and the neatest man in his dress in his county.

Dr. McMurray married in Davidson county, October 22, 1872, Miss Fannie May McCampbell, who was born in Nashville, November —, 1854, but was raised on her father's farm near the Hermitage. She is the daughter of Hon. Thomas McCampbell, who, when quite young, was a State senator from the Knoxville district. She is paternally descended from the McCampbells and Andersons of Knoxville—families noted for the legal talent they have given to the bar. Mrs. McMurray's mother, was a Miss Gowdey, daughter of Thomas Gowdey, a wealthy jeweler of Nashville, who, in early life, was an Irish soldier, under Wellington, at Waterloo. Mrs. McMurray is a lady of fine culture, and graduated from Ward's seminary, Nashville, in 1871. By his marriage with this lady, Dr. McMurray has one child: (1). Addie Morton McMurray, born June 30, 1876.

Mrs. McMurray is a second cousin on her father's side to the late Judge John Trimble; a paternal cousin to the wife of Gov. Neill S. Brown, and a second cousin of Judge Frank T. Reid, of the Davidson county circuit court. Her brother, John McCampbell, is a clerk in the employ of the Louisville and Nashville railroad company. Her sister, nee Miss Mary Lou McCampbell, is now the wife of Edward Gaines, a hardware merchant, at Nashville. Her brothers, Thomas and Arthur McCampbell, are farmers in Davidson county. She also has a single sister, Miss Nannie McCampbell, living with her. Her aunt, Mary McCampbell, died the wife of Enoch Ensley, a wealthy merchant and planter in Mississippi and West Tennessee, but who resided at Nashville.

In politics, Dr. McMurray is a strict Democrat, though his father and uncles were Whigs. In 1869, he became an Odd Fellow. Dr. McMurray and his wife are Methodists, but in religion as in other matters (excepting only politics), he is a liberal, independent thinker, tolerant of the opinions of others. He is a close thinker, a philosophic reasoner, a determined man, with strong faith in the ultimate issue, and of solid character. Whoever and whatever the McMurrays have been, the name of the brave young Confederate lieutenant, the subject of this biography, will doubtless long continue to be mentioned with pride by the family as one of its most conspicuous members.

JAMES D. PLUNKET, M. D.

NASHVILLE.

THIS gentleman, now in the meridian of life, appears in these pages, not only as a prominent Tennessean, but as one of the most widely known representatives of the medical profession in the State. In personal appearance he is tall and somewhat slender, but of strong build, and well fitted for the activities of a busy life. He has dark hair, calm, inquiring eyes, and the look of a man of system, promptness and prudence. His manners are frank and easy, without ostentation, yet his character is bold and essentially aggressive.

He was born in Williamson county, Tennessee, of wealthy parentage, and received his primary education under private tutors and at academic schools. For three years, from 1854, he was a clerk in the wholesale dry goods house of Morgan & Co., at Nashville, and next spent one year with D'Arman & Co., commission merchants, New Orleans.

In the fall of 1859, he began the study of medicine in the office of Dr. George A. J. Mayfield, at Nashville. In 1860, he went to Philadelphia, where he became the private student of Dr. Joseph Leidy, professor of anatomy, and entered the medical department of the University of Pennsylvania, from which he graduated, in 1863, taking his degree under Profs. Wood, Jackson, Pepper, Agnew, Hodge and Henry H. Smith. During his stay in Philadelphia he spent the summers as an interne in the city hospitals.

On his return home he accepted the invitation of Surgeon-Gen. Moore, to enter into the medical service of the Confederate States, as assistant surgeon; was on duty successively in the (Frank A. Ramsey) hospital, first, at Knoxville, and afterward at Cassville, Georgia, and then " in the field " with the Fortieth Georgia regiment of infantry, Gen. Stovall's brigade, and lastly with the Fifty-second Georgia regiment, in the same brigade. He served until the close of the war, when he began practice, in May, 1865, at Nashville.

He is entitled to the honor of having first agitated and taking a leading part in the establishment of the Nashville Board of Health, of which, from its organization, June 4, 1866, to the time it ceased to exist, in the spring of 1869, he was secretary and president.

In 1873, in view of a threatened epidemic of Asiatic cholera, which soon afterward burst in all its fury upon this community, the mayor of Nashville appointed a sanitary commission, composed of seven leading medical practitioners of the city, and of this commission Dr. Plunket was made president. In May, 1874, the Board of Health was reorganized and Dr. Plunket again made president. In June, 1876, he was elected city health officer, but declined the position. In 1879, he retired from the Board of Health, his private practice taking up all his time. At his instance the State Medical Association petitioned the Legislature to establish the State Board of Health. In March, 1877, the bill for that purpose passed, and Gov. James D. Porter, after appointing Dr. Plunket as a member of that board, asked him to name the other " four physicians of skill and experience, regular graduates of medicine, and who had been engaged in practice not less than ten years," as the law required, and he would commission them, which was accordingly done. The board, as first organized, was composed of Drs. T. A. Atchison and J. M. Safford, of Middle Tennessee, E. M. Wight, of East Tennessee, and R. B. Maury, of West Tennessee; and Dr. Plunket was elected president, and served as such four consecutive years, till May, 1880, when he resigned, as before, on account of the steadily increasing duties of his private practice. As president of the State Board of Health, he, in 1879, had the city of Memphis quarantined, on account of an epidemic of yellow fever developing there, a measure that met with vehement opposition from traders, and the local press in their interests but public opinion finally endorsed his action, as it resulted in confining the pestilence to the city limits, and applauded the courage of an official, who, for the safety of the public health, did his duty at the cost of being hung and burnt in effigy by the rabble in the streets of Memphis.

Upon the motion of Dr. Plunket, then president of the State Board of Health, there was assembled for conference, at Memphis, June 30, 1879, representatives from the several boards of health in the Mississippi valley, in which eighteen States were represented. The convention resolved itself into a permanent organization as the Sanitary Council of the Mississippi Valley, and Dr. Plunket was chosen president. He is a member of the American Public Health Association, and has been twice elected a member of its executive committee. He is a member of the American Association for the Advancement of Science, and in 1878, was chairman of the committee on meteorology. He is a member of the American Medical Association, and of the Medical Society of the State of Tennessee, of which latter body he was, from 1865 to 1875, the permanent secretary, and for sixteen years its treasurer. He is a member of the Davidson County Medical Society, and of the Nashville Medical Society. In 1868, he was elected to the chair of surgical anatomy in the medical department of Cumberland University. In 1870, he was elected president of the city council of Nashville.

To the medical journals of the country he has con-

tributed a large number of interesting and valuable papers, notably among them, one on " Disinfection of Sewers by Ozone," " Cotton as a Fomite," " Vital Statistics in Tennessee," " Bovine Tuberculosis; a Fruitful Source of Human Disease and Death," and " Ozone and its Relation to the Public Health." He is regarded as one of the foremost authorities in the South on sanitary matters.

Of Irish parentage, his character is naturally persistent and self-assertive. In the " History of Davidson County," from which the editor has culled most of the foregoing facts, it appears that on the paternal side, he is descended from Lord Plunket of Queen's counsel in the trial of Robert Emmet, in 1805, and that in the collateral branches of his ancestral family have been priests and bishops of the Catholic church in Ireland. His mother, nee Miss Anna Smyth, was a well rounded character; possessed of many noble womanly attributes, and a mental strength and range of culture seldom found. She died in her sixty-second year, upon December 7, 1877. She, as also all his maternal ancestors, were Scotch-Irish Presbyterians. The Magee College at Derry, Ireland, was endowed by his great-aunt, Magee. One of his near relatives—a Plunket—is a member of the present British Parliament.

Dr. Plunket's father, James Plunket, was a native of Edgeworthstown, county Longford, Ireland, and a graduate of Trinity College, Dublin. He was a man of superb education and skilled in scientific mechanics. Coming to this country, he was, for many years, a manufacturer of cotton mill machinery at Paterson, New Jersey, whence he moved to Dayton, Ohio, lived there four years, and finally settled at Franklin, Tennessee, where he took charge of and finally became a leading member of the firm that owned the large cotton mill and mercantile establishment connected with it at that place. He was a well-read man, had a fine memory of names, dates and authorities, and did business on the old time principle that honesty is the best policy. In religion he was a Roman Catholic. He died January 31, 1874, at the age of sixty-eight. His brother, Judge Joseph Plunket, resides at St. Maries, Ohio.

Dr. Plunket married, in Danville, Kentucky, November 19, 1872, Miss Jennie E. Swope, a native of that place, daughter of Col. John B. Swope, who died June 28, 1881, one of the standard men of Kentucky, a scholar and a retired merchant. Her mother, nee Miss Fannie Hunton, of a Virginia family originally, was a sister of Mrs. Judge Fox, of Danville, of Judge Logan Hunton, of St. Louis, and Col. Thomas H. Hunton, of New Orleans. Mrs. Plunket's brother, Col. Thomas H. Swope, is a capitalist at Kansas City, Missouri. Her brother, Logan O. Swope, is a large stock farmer near Independence, Missouri, and her brother, John Swope, is a stock raiser at Midway, Woodford county, Kentucky. Her sister, nee Miss Margaret Swope, is now the wife of William M. Fleming, a farmer of Maury county, Tennessee. Mrs. Plunket was educated in Danville and at Stewart College, in Shelbyville, Kentucky, and from the readiness with which she reads human nature, seems to have inherited this, the striking, characterstic of her father. Like him, also, she is devoted to literature, and is a lady of rare mental culture.

By his marriage with Miss Swope, Dr. Plunket has only one child living, Gertrude M. Plunket, who was born January 20, 1883.

Dr. Plunket and wife are members of the First Presbyterian church, of Nashville. He is a Master Mason, and in politics a Democrat, although reared by a Whig father.

Financially, Dr. Plunket has been quite successful, and is in very easy and comfortable circumstances. He began professional life without inheritance, and has accumulated his fortune mainly in the line of his practice and by judicious investment. He is the only physician who has immediate family has produced, except his younger brother, Dr. Joseph M. Plunket, who died in Nashville, January 31, 1873, at the age of thirty-two. He took up medicine from pure love of it, and has stuck to that profession, as it correlates the natural sciences, of which he is a devotee.

His brother, Thomas Smyth Plunket, was a lieutenant in the United States navy; appointed to the Naval Academy at Annapolis by President Johnson, in 1867, and from which he graduated in the class of 1872. He distinguished himself by his fine scholarship in that institution. He lost his life accidentally while skating, at Erie, Pennsylvania, January 31, 1882. He was in his thirty-second year at the time of his death.

Dr. Plunket's brother, John Thompson Plunket, graduated from the Southwestern Presbyterian University, at Clarksville, and afterward from the Union Theological Seminary, Columbia, South Carolina, and after preaching several years at Raleigh, North Carolina, is now pastor of the Madison Avenue Presbyterian church at Covington, Kentucky. He married Miss Sallie Kennedy, a daughter of Hon. D. N. Kennedy, of Clarksville, Tennessee, and by whom he has had three boys, Thomas, Henry and Paul.

Dr. Plunket's sister, nee Miss Ann Plunket, is the wife of Thomas M. Brennan, who was, before the war, a large manufacturer of machinery, in Nashville, who built the first locomotive engine constructed in Tennessee. She has five children, Thomas, Isabella, Anna, Joseph and Harry.

Dr. Plunket's sister, nee Miss Isabella Plunket, is now the wife of Henry Clark, of Nashville, for many years connected with the Nashville, Chattanooga and St, Louis railway. Her first husband, Willis Long, of Versailles, Kentucky, was a merchant at New Orleans. by whom she had one child, nee Miss Anna Long, now wife of P. J. Sexton, a wealthy retired contractor, of Chicago. Her second husband, Dr. Alfred Rolls, a native of Toronto, Canada, was a physician at Nashville.

HON. THOMAS WASHINGTON NEAL.

DYERSBURG.

COL. THOMAS W. NEAL, or, as his friends delight to call him, "Tom Neal," one of the most popular and successful newspaper men in Tennessee, a man who numbers his friends by legions, a typical southern gentleman, frank, sincere, generous and brave, well deserves a place in the Valhalla of " Prominent Tennesseans."

He was born in Nashville, Tennessee, April 11, 1836, and grew up there till eighteen years of age. He comes from old Virginia stock; his grandfather, Bartholomew Neal, was a planter in that State. His father, Richard P. Neal, was born in Virginia, emigrated to Davidson county, Tennessee, where he married, and died. He was an industrious, sober man, a good citizen, an earnest Methodist, and at one time held an important county office. The son was an infant at the time of the father's death.

Col. Neal's mother, nee Miss Caroline Buck, is a native of Nashville, and is now living in that city, at the advanced age of seventy-eight. She is an affectionate mother, of the kindliest disposition, an exemplary Christian, being a devoted member of the Methodist church. She has only had two children, Thomas Washington Neal, the subject of this sketch, and Richard Henry Neal, a faithful soldier in the Confederate army, under Gen. Bragg, and now a clerk in the Davidson county trustee's office.

Thomas W. Neal was educated at Irving College, in the literary department, but regards the printing-office as his *alma mater*. Indeed, he may be taken as a typical typographer, for he learned the art preservative of all arts in the office of the time-honored Nashville *Republican Banner*, then edited by Gen. Washington Barrow. Graduating from that institution of glorious memory, he next went to Shelbyville, Tennessee, where, for a few months, he edited the Bedford *Yeoman*, an independent sheet in his hands. He was next employed in different capacities in printing offices at Nashville, Memphis, Helena, Arkansas, Louisville and Henderson, Kentucky. Next he edited, for two years, the Trenton, Tennessee, *Southern Standard.* From there he went to Hickman, Kentucky, and edited the *Times.* In 1858, he edited the Dyersburg, Tennessee, *Recorder* in conjunction with F. G. Samson, a lawyer and clerk and master of the chancery court. He then crossed over the river and founded the Warren *Sunbeam,* at Warren, Arkansas, and was engaged in that occupation until the breaking out of the war. He then laid aside the "shooting-stick" and took up the "shooting iron," enlisting as a private in the Ninth Arkansas Confederate infantry regiment, under Col. John M. Bradley. Upon the expiration of his term of enlistment, he returned to Nashville and became city editor of the *Daily Press* for six months. He left Tennessee on account of the war troubles, and went to New York where, for several months, he was employed as proof-reader. After this he returned to Memphis, was city editor of the *Daily Bulletin,* and at the same time edited the *Play Bill,* a theatrical sheet, devoted to fashion, gossip, society *on dits,* etc. We next find him at Pine Bluff, Arkansas, as editor of the *Dispatch,* and then he returned to Dyersburg, in October, 1865, and established *Neal's State Gazette,* with which he has had unbroken connection, as editor and proprietor, ever since.

So far this sketch reads like the record of a newspaper man, given to roaming and without fixed aim in life. This usually falls to the lot of the Bohemian, who, like the migratory bee, sips honey on the wing, and goes on and on in his happy pursuit of sweeter flowers; but the truth is, Col. Neal has been remarkably devoted to one line of thought and action, and for a newspaper man has developed fine staying power, having remained a fixture at Dyersburg more than twenty years, and made a name as the most successful country newspaper man in Tennessee. He has filled every position in a printing office, from roller-boy to the editor's chair, and, as a consequence, the *State Gazette* is not only one of the best weeklies in the State, but from its foundation has been a financial success.

In *ante-bellum* times, Col. Neal was a Henry Clay Whig, but *post-bellum* has been a Democrat, yet with a considerable dash of independence. He founded the *State Gazette* during Brownlow's administration in Tennessee, when it took some nerve to edit a Democratic newspaper in this State. In the meantime, the people of his town, county and district have called him to occupy various positions of honor and trust. He has been mayor of Dyersburg two years, president of the Dyersburg Town Board of Education, president of the Dyer County Fair Association, secretary of the Sunday-school (though not a member of any church), and, as an evidence of his popularity among the younger "boys," president of the Dyersburg Base Ball Club. He is an Entered Apprentice Mason, an Odd Fellow, and a Knight of Honor. In 1883, he was elected Dictator of the Knights of Honor, at Dyersburg,

and is now Grand Assistant Dictator of the Grand Lodge of that order for the State. In 1882, he was elected president of the Dyersburg Building and Loan Association. He has also been president of the Tennessee Press Association, and no annual meeting or "annual jaunt across the country" is complete without the presence of "handsome Tom Neal." In 1877, he was elected to the Tennessee Legislature from Dyer county by the largest majority ever received by anybody in that county. In 1884, he was nominated by acclamation, in the convention at Union City, as the Democratic candidate for joint representative of Dyer, Lake and Obion counties, in the forty-fourth General Assembly of Tennessee, and was triumphantly elected, having received the largest majority of any Democratic member of that body. In that Legislature he was appropriately made chairman of the committee on public printing, being the only editor in that body. He has been a delegate from Dyer county to every Democratic State convention held at Nashville since the war, and was alternate delegate for the State at large to the national Democratic convention at Chicago that nominated Cleveland and Hendricks. As a speaker, he is earnest and forcible, with considerable of the brilliancy of the finished orator. Thoroughly posted in State and national politics and appreciative of the wants and feeling of the people; painstaking, yet quick and persevering in all his undertakings, he may be regarded as conservative and liberal, yet firm and unyielding in his positions on questions of right. Honest and sincere, especially in taking the weak side early, which afterward became the strong side, gave the people confidence in him, and hence his large majorities. He has frequently been on the right side in his judgment, even against popular judgment, and has at times succeeded in producing a revulsion of sentiment in his constituency, thus showing that his first opinions were correct.

He began life without patrimony, and without capital, save his brain and brawn. He now owns valuable real estate in Dyersburg, a farm in Dyer county, and is in very comfortable circumstances. Liberal in spirit and energetic by nature, he has never regarded stinginess as an element of success. He is not a close collector, has lost some money by going security, but he never appears over-anxious about debts due him. He thinks kindness will collect a debt from a certain class of people more promptly than "dunning," or otherwise pressing his claims. Hence, he frequently gets his money, and at the same time extends his friendship and his popularity. His object and desire is to live pleasantly and to make those around him pleasant, without vaulting ambition for either riches or honor. His home at Dyersburg is an ideal one, as all who have enjoyed its generous hospitality will testify.

Col. Neal has been twice married; first, at Dyersburg, December, 1859, to Miss Fannie Benton, daughter of Dr. Abner Benton, of Dyersburg, a promi-

48

nent physician, at one time State senator from that end of the State, and a near kinsman of the celebrated United States senator, Hon. Thomas H. Benton, of Missouri. Her mother, now living at Dyersburg, at the age of fifty-seven, was originally Miss Mary Ann Wardlow, daughter of Joseph Wardlow, a very wealthy farmer, in Lauderdale county, Tennessee. Mrs. Neal was educated at Brownsville, Tennessee, Female College, and was a pure, good woman, noted for her sense of right and justice and conscientious discharge of duty. She was a Methodist from early girlhood. She died in 1880, at the age of thirty-nine, having borne two children: (1). Ella Neal, born in Nashville; finished her education at Greenwood Seminary, near Lebanon, Tennessee, under Mrs. N. Lawrence Lindsley; is an exceptionally fine vocalist, and a zealous Methodist. (2). Lillian Neal, born in Dyersburg; now in school.

Col. Neal next married in Sandgate, Vermont, June 15, 1881, Miss Alice Hoyt, daughter of William and Esther Hoyt. Her father is a farmer. Her mother comes of a literary family. Mrs. Neal is a member of the Presbyterian church, and an accomplished performer on both the piano and organ. She graduated with honor from the Fort Edward Institute, New York, and is of fine literary attainments.

Col. Neal is a very attractive gentleman, personally, and was voted "the handsomest and most polished member" of the Legislature of 1884–5. Courtly in his manners, refined in his tastes, with the air of a king, yet the dash of a cavalier, you know when he looks you in the face and gives you his hand you are taking the hand of a loyal-hearted gentleman. He is of medium height, "five feet, eight and three-quarter inches, by Confederate measure," and weighs one hundred and sixty pounds. His hair, moustache and imperial, liberally sprinkled with iron-gray, give to him a nameless air of grace and gallantry. Benignity of disposition, sincerity of conviction, impulsive generosity, yet modesty of mein—these are written in indelible lines upon his features, for a kindlier nature it were difficult to find. His career as editor, legislator and business man has been built up by industry, fidelity and ability, and this is why he has attached to himself whole troops of friends.

MR. JOHN McLEOD KEATING.

MEMPHIS.

THE scholarly gentleman whose name heads this sketch, and whose position is in the front rank of the ablest and most refined and polished American journalists, is a native of Ireland, and comes of Scotch-Irish stock. He was born in Ireland, Kings county, June 12, 1830, grew up and was educated in Scotland until his ninth year, and afterward in Dublin. At the age of thirteen he was apprenticed to the printer's trade, entered the office of the Dublin World, and at the end of five years reached the highest position— foreman of the office—when only eighteen years of age. He was also an amanuensis to the editor-in-chief. He was very studious and very rapid in acquiring the dextrous facilities of a printer, a knowledge of newspaper work —composition, press work, etc.

In 1846, he became a member of the Young Ireland Club, of which John B. Dillon was president. After the fiasco that followed in 1848, he emigrated to America, and settled at New York, where he resided until December, 1854. In New York he was foreman of an illustrated weekly paper, known as the New York Journal; was also foreman, six months, of the Leader, a noted political newspaper.

During his residence in New York city, of nearly eight years, he served six years and three months in the New York State militia, more than two years of that time in the famous Seventh regiment. He was induced to this service in the hope that by completing seven years' service, he would be exempt from certain duties as a citizen, and would thus be free to prosecute his labors and purposes in his profession.

But on account of ill health, he went to New Orleans in December, 1854. There he worked for a short time in the printing business, then went to Baton Rouge, and thence to Nashville, where, as foreman of the composing room, he helped to open the Methodist Book Concern, now known as the Methodist Publishing House. Shortly after, he returned to Baton Rouge and became superintendent of State printing, a position he held two years. In 1856, he returned to Nashville and married, and went back to Baton Rouge. In 1857, he returned to Nashville for the third time, and became managing editor of the Daily News, of which Allen A. Hall was the editor-in-chief. The next year, 1858, he went to Memphis, was employed as commercial and city editor of the Bulletin, and that city has been his home ever since.

He remained with the Bulletin until the commencement of hostilities, when he was employed as a clerk and acted for a short while as private secretary on the staff of Gen. Leonidas Polk, and was with that commander from the beginning of the war until October 1861, when he was taken ill with a serious attack of typhoid fever, which confined him to his bed four months and incapacitated him for military duty of any kind, as per report of Dr. Joseph Newnan. Partially recovering his health, he engaged with the Southern Express company, as money clerk, and so continued until the capture of Memphis by the Federal army. After that event he was employed as city editor of the *Argus*, the only Democratic paper then published there, and known as the " secesh organ," with which he remained until the close of the war. He then established the *Daily Commercial*, which existed for over one year, when it was merged in the *Argus* and was published some months as the *Commercial and Argus*.

Mr. Keating spent the winter of 1867-8 in Washington in confidential relations with President Andrew Johnson, and returning to Memphis in August, 1868, purchased Gen. Albert Pike's interest in the Memphis *Appeal*, with which journal he has been identified ever since. Three times he gave up journalism, as he supposed, never to return to it, because its money remuneration did not enable him to do what he desired for a young and growing family. He went into the cotton and grocery business, at which he did well, but was compelled to give it up by the Federal authorities in 1863. He was, as has already been stated, in the express business, and also gave up a lucrative insurance business—life, fire and marine—to return to his first love, and take charge of the *Appeal*, in 1868, as managing editor.

When Mr. Keating landed in this country, in 1848, he became a student of the politics of the country of which he determined to become a citizen, and thus was persuaded into becoming a Democrat, as he says, an humble disciple of Jefferson and of Calhoun. He did not believe in slavery, but in settling in the South, as a law-abiding man, had nothing to say; though he would have had, as all who know him admit, if ever the emancipation of the negro had become an open question. He was opposed to war, but believing in the right of secession, early espoused the cause of the South as one that he believed to be the logical result of a long train of events, beginning before the Revolution and gathering strength with every cycle after. Earnestly and heartily and manfully he wrote for the people with whose fortunes he has been so intimately identified for more than a quarter of a century. He held his allegiance to the Confederacy sacred until it went down forever, and then turned to the work of guiding the hapless, helpless and hopeless people out of their individual and their national distresses. Believing in individual liberty, he readily adapted himself to the changed situation and urged the acceptance of the inevitable, the rehabilitation of the country, and the restoration of the old soldiers to their places as citizens, and of the States to the Union. Negro emancipation being the great and lasting and most tangible result of the war, he believed in the education of the freedmen as necessary to their comprehension of the duties devolving upon them as citizens. He did not oppose nor did he regret their being made citizens. They could not be otherwise, being free. The decision

of Judge Gaston, of North Carolina, on the rights of bond and free, which he early met with in his studies, made a lasting impression upon him, and has been his guide ever since, where citizenship was concerned. He has always, therefore, been an ardent and uncompromising friend of the negro, as he has been the champion of the rights of women to the same freedom as is enjoyed by men—to labor and participate in the affairs of government; to vote and hold office, and help in all the affairs of State. He was one of the editors who met in Nashville, in 1869, in the *Banner* office, to concert measures for the restoration of the State to the people and for the enfranchisement of the ex-Confederate soldiers and citizens. He helped to secure the adoption of the present constitution—adopted in 1870—and sustained Gov. John C. Brown's administration with something like enthusiasm. He was an advocate of the financial policy of that statesman, and was an uncompromising advocate for the payment of the State debt, proving by the incontestible figures furnished by the census of 1860 and of 1870, and subsequently by that of 1880, the ability of the State to meet all its obligations. The failure to do this he regards as a grave mistake, and one that will recoil upon the people and give them trouble. During the reconstruction period he waged in the *Appeal* a relentless war upon the carpet-baggers in Mississippi, Alabama and Arkansas, where his paper circulated, and has ever regarded those repressive and oppressive measures as the greatest of all the many curses entailed by the civil war. His advocacy of manufactures; of diversity of pursuits; of good turnpikes as a necessity to facilitate inter-county traffic; of common schools, and the utmost stretch of freedom in opposition to all class restrictions and legislation, and the dogmatic bigotry of sects, is known far and wide. He believes, as he says, that the less government has to do with the people, the greater their advance; that, thrown upon themselves, there is a direct appeal made to the individual conscience, and each man is more or less upon his good behavior. The progress of the United States, as compared with any of the nations of Europe in the last one hundred years, proves the correctness of his position. He says that no man can rise above himself, and thus he cannot be freer than nature made him. Hence, the diversity and divisions among men. He loves America, and believes in American methods, in social as in political life, as incomparably superior to those of European countries. Of the history of Tennessee he has been a close student, and he loves to strengthen his defense of the common people, among whom he counts himself, by pointing to the heroic self-sacrifices of the fathers and founders of the State, and the superb legacy they have left their sons in their subordination to a self-elected government, when the first colony was but a puling infant, surrounded by Indians thirsting for its annihilation. He is proud of his citizenship and position in a State, the founders of which were law-abiding and God-fearing men, lovers of liberty, and moved by well defined comprehension of the powers of government, and that it was theirs to make, to amend or abolish at will.

In 1874, Mr. Keating went, by special invitation from ex-President Jefferson Davis, as his friend and companion, on a trip to the Rocky mountains through Missouri, Kansas and Colorado, a trip during which Mr. Davis broke through the reserve he had imposed upon himself after the war, and delivered several addresses on agriculture. Mr. Davis counts Mr. Keating among his stanch friends, though not a partisan one; that he could not be with any man. He sees and admits the good points of all public men, makes allowance for their surroundings, their political and social connections, and the possibility of their judgments being warped and sometimes obscured. He was thus enabled to be, and consistently so, the friend of President Andrew Johnson, who was the antipodes in many respects of Mr. Davis, and of Senator Isham G. Harris, whom he admired and long sustained as one of the most manly and truth-loving of the public men of the country; a fearless man, because he tries to be right and believing himself to be, pushes on to the conclusion, regardless of consequences. Mr. Keating, a positive character himself, admires positive men with definite aims, and has always been attracted to them, holding the other sort in contempt.

Mr. Keating was married, in Nashville, Tennessee, October 30, 1856, by the Rev. Dr. Edgar, of the First Presbyterian church, to Miss Josephine Esselman Smith, daughter of Mr. John Smith, a native of Pennsylvania, related, on his mother's side, to the Norris family, of Norristown, Pennsylvania. Mrs. Keating graduated from the Columbia (Tennessee) Female Institute, under Rector Smith, whence she emerged with a diploma that attests a scholarship which she has always kept alive by constant, earnest and faithful study, notwithstanding her absorbing duties as wife and mother and housekeeper. She has been the faithful friend, companion and counselor of her husband; has seconded all his ambitions for success and distinction in his profession, and has kept pace with him in all the channels of culture and cultivation. She is one of the most accomplished women in the State. In music, is thorough as a vocalist, pianiste and harpist, and excels in a knowledge of French history and literature. Handsome of face and form, and dignified in carriage, she is beloved by all who know her for her wit and repartee and brilliancy as a conversationalist, and for her excelling abilities as a letter writer. She is also noted for her great good sense—common sense—and her love of truth, even in little things. She was a devoted daughter, and has given herself with singleness of purpose to the promotion of her husband and children. They have two children, a son, Neil McLeod Keating, and a daughter, Caroline Morton Keating. Agreeing

with her husband that their children should be taught to work at what they were best fitted for, Mrs. Keating, for several years, resided in New York, and there superintended the studies of the daughter as a pianiste in preparation for an artiste's career, and of the son, who is now in Paris, whence he went from the Art Student's League School, of New York, where, last year, he was pronounced by Prof. Dewing, the president of the school, to be the leading and best pupil, his work being regarded as equal to the best imported French work. Both the children of Mr. Keating have a promising career before them.

Mr. Keating traces his lineage back to the first of his name, Halis Keating, who landed with FitzStephens in Ireland, in 1169, one among the first of the Norman invaders, who, as he says, had once been murdering and plundering the people of that unfortunate country. Dr. Geoffrey Keating, who was the first historian of Ireland after the "Four Masters," and who wrote much poetry and many religious works, was of the same family, the origin of which is thus traced by the late Michael Dohemy in John O'Mahoney's translation of Keating's "History of Ireland": "According to the traditions of the family, adopted and, so to speak, legalized, by the Books of Heraldry in Ireland, the founder of the house, whose original name is now unknown, was one of the pioneers of the Norman invaders, who kindled the beacon fire that lit the way of Fitz-Stephens into the Cuan-au-Bhainbh. The story goes, that as he lay by his watch-fire, a wild boar, chancing to prowl that way, was proceeding to attack him, until frightened by the sparkling of the fire, when he fled in dismay. The watcher, thus providentially saved, adopted for his crest a wild boar rampant rushing through a brake, with the motto, *fortis et fidelis*, and his name became, we are not told how, Keating or Keting, from the Irish words, *cead tinne*—first fire." In all his life in Tennessee, Mr. Keating has been true to this motto, and was conspicuously noted, in 1878, for fortitude and fidelity. The Keatings passed through many vicissitudes in Ireland during the civil wars and rebellions, but furnished many distinguished priests to the Catholic church in Ireland; general officers in the British army; a great many judges to the English and Irish bench, and several diplomatic agents, notable among them Col. Keating, who, after twenty-four years at the court of Persia, wrote a history of that country that is yet highly valued as a standard. Another colonel of the same name, wrote a compendious history of India. Gen. Keating, who commanded the expedition that captured the Mauritus, and was afterward governor of that island, was a distinguished military and civil servant of Great Britain. In this country the Keatings of Philadelphia, New Orleans and western Virginia have distinguished themselves in the profession of engineering and medicine, being conspicuous in the latter. One of the name, Dr. J. M. Keating, of Philadelphia, traveled with Gen. Grant through India, and on his return home published his impressions of the tour. The branch of the Keating family to which the subject of this sketch immediately belongs, was of the yeoman or farmer class, and was settled in the north of Ireland, where its members were identified with the Tory or dominant faction, and were ardent churchmen. Mr. Keating early imbibed from his Scotch-Presbyterian mother the love of liberty and breadth of view that has always distinguished him in public life. Her teachings and explanations, her promptings and the auguries of her ambition for her boy, sent him into the world thirsting for knowledge in the solemn conviction that it *is* power. She, like his father, was of humble origin, but of the sturdy stock that stood behind John Knox in his contest as the great Reformer. The spirit of freedom burned brightly in her breast, and she hated the oppressions which her husband's Tory kindred aided in inflicting upon their own people, blinded, as they were, by bigotry and the intolerance born of it. Mr. Keating, profiting by these lessons learned at his mother's knees, availed himself of the first opportunity to manifest his love of country and, as before stated, joined the "Young Irelanders," in 1846, when yet scarce sixteen, uniting with the Curran club of Dublin, and pledging himself to help in the regeneration and for the liberty of his native land.

Mr. Keating was a director, in 1867, in a company which formed to bridge or tunnel the Mississippi river at Memphis, and which made extensive surveys for that purpose. He was also secretary and treasurer of the first elevator company in Memphis, in that year, and in 1872, was a director in the Mississippi railroad company, which anticipated the line recently constructed to New Orleans, via Vicksburg, from Memphis. He was also about that time a director in a company to build a railroad from Memphis to Jeffersonville, Texas, and another to build a railroad to Kansas City. He was also a director of the company that turned over the charter and right of way to the present Kansay City, Springfield and Memphis railroad. This latter road has been completed, and at a banquet given in Kansas City, in June, 1884, to the guests from Memphis, Mr. Keating was selected to respond to the toast, "Cotton, corn and cattle, the links of destiny that bind us in commercial unity." His response was not only able and brilliant, but elegantly eloquent, worthy of reproduction here, if space would admit, and in its peroration was as follows: "Cotton, corn and cattle bind the cities we represent in commercial unity through the medium of the Memphis, Springfield and Kansas City railroad, and we can never be separated again. We are the latest expression of American grit, pluck and enterprise, and our future is assured. With the Union restored, and sectional bitterness entirely wiped out, greater possibilities are to come as a result of the enterprise of the people of the whole country. With the curse of

slavery removed, the incubus that weighed upon the energies of the white man and limited his horizon, there has come to the South a wonderful quickening. We are now free indeed. Diversity of pursuit, a more certain knowledge of our duties and best possibilities, have come to us, and we are ready for them."

In 1876, Mr. Keating was a member of the committee, appointed by Mayor Loague, to compromise the debt of Memphis with the creditors. He has never held office, and was but once before a convention as a candidate. In 1868, his name was sent to the United States senate, by President Johnson, for the postmastership of Memphis, but the mere mention of his name created a storm, and it was promptly, and by a full vote of the Republicans present, refused the courtesy of being sent to the committee. It went in at one door and was sent out at the other, and in not more than five minutes.

Mr. Keating passed, unscathed, through the yellow fever epidemics at Memphis, in 1868, 1873, 1878 and 1879. During 1878, he edited the *Appeal*, and when the compositors and pressmen, the business manager and others, went down or perished, he nobly stood at his post, and, with the assistance of but one man, Mr. Henry Mood, set up the type and made up the forms every day, for several weeks, besides doing the reportorial and editorial work, and responding to all his duties as a member of the executive committee, which really governed the city during those trying and distressful days. Thus was he true to the motto of his family, "*Fortis et fidelis.*"

In the spring of 1879, after he had written and put to press his "History of the Yellow Fever," he delivered an address at the theater, before an audience composed of the merchants, bankers and manufacturers of the city, and at which all the physicians of the city were present, in which he explained, with technical accuracy, the necessity for sanitary reform, painting in truthful colors, at the same time, the then very unsanitary condition of Memphis, which he was enabled to do from a personal inspection. This was the beginning of the sanitary work that has made Memphis one of the model cities of the world in a sanitary point of view.

Mr. Keating is president of the Memphis branch of the International Association of the Red Cross of Geneva. He is also a member of the American Health Association, and has contributed to the papers published by that organization, in 1880, "The Value of Sanitation from an Economical Standpoint," in 1882, "The Cremation of Excreta and Household Wastes," and, in 1884, "The Ultimate of Sanitation by Fire," a paper that has attracted attention in Europe as well as throughout America, and has generally been endorsed by the press. In September, 1881, he published a report on the sewer system of Memphis, and the epidemics of preventable diseases that have visited that city and its site since 1740.

He is an honorary member of the Memphis Society

for the Prevention of Cruelty to Animals and Children; and also of the Memphis Typographical Union; is a member of the Memphis Mozart Society, also of the Mendelssohn Society, the two leading musical organizations of that city, and is regarded as the best musical critic south of the Ohio river. He is also a member of the Tennessee Historical Society, and has written a memoir for Dr. J. B. Lindsley's History of Tennessee, covering all the operations of the Confederate armies in the State, from the inception to the close of the late civil war. He has also written a great deal on negro education, and in the *Popular Science Monthly*, for November, 1885, published "Twenty Years of Negro Education," a careful, exhaustive and convincing review.

He was made a Mason in 1853, and in 1879 an Odd Fellow. He began to study for the ministry in the Protestant Episcopal church, in 1857, under Bishop Quintard, then rector of Holy Trinity church, in Nashville, and during 1860, and until 1862, continued under the immediate supervision of Bishop Otey, of the diocese of Tennessee, then residing at Memphis. Bishop Otey was his warm personal friend, and during the last six weeks of his life Mr. Keating nursed him day and night. He reveres the memory of Bishop Otey as that of a second father, and owes much to his advice. He was fully prepared to take orders in the church, but gave up what had long been a cherished design, because he could not give his adhesion to the cardinals of the creed of a Christian body for which he says he has always cherished a tender love, and will ever hold in reverence, and whose prayer-book he has always held to be the best book in his library. He is, in the better sense of the term, a free-thinker. He believes in God as the beginning and end of all things, and holds, with Jesus Christ, that the Golden Rule is the sum and substance of all religion. He is grateful for the example of Christ; for His espousal of the cause of the poor; for the truth He preached to the people; His commisseration and compassion for the erring and suffering; His manly vindication of Himself and His mission; the God-like simplicity of His life, and above all, for the courage with which He died.

Mr. Keating is a great reader, and has one of the best working libraries in the State. He has followed, with absorbing interest, the progress of modern science, and the great religions of the world have, ever since he took up theology, been a particular study, and one that is still an absorbing one. He begins with Nature-worship, and ends with Christ, to whom he clings as the greatest of all teachers, the Master, the sublime exemplar, the elder brother of all mankind who seek Him diligently. Medicine and surgery have always had attractions for him, and he sometimes regrets that he did not devote himself to a profession for which he entertains a very high respect. History and geography have been his delights from childhood, and to travel is his favorite

recreation. Politics, in the best sense of the term, have claimed much of his best thought, and he has been a close student of the constitution of the United States, and of the several States, and of colonial and early State history, that of Tennessee especially, of which he has made extensive notes, with a view to publication, in connection with a history of Memphis, which he has been writing on, as he could take time from his too engrossing editorial duties, for the past two years. He has also made extensive notes on the subject of slavery in the Southern States, with a view to the preparation of a work that will show the attitude the South has always maintained toward the negro as slave, freeman, citizen and voter.

Mr. Keating has, for nearly thirty years, suffered from a troublesome disease which necessitated, in 1864, and in 1866, two severe surgical operations, and he has found only in silence and seclusion the relief he craved from its attacks. This, perhaps, accounts for much of his studiousness and love of retirement. For the last twenty-five years he has been a close and methodical reader. He had acquired from his parents the reading habit, and though, for a few years, he threw away much valuable time in "seeing the world," he yet made it a point first, to do some reading during a week, and finally mastered himself sufficiently to do some every day. After a few years he found that this desultory sort of reading would not do, and he began carefully to formulate his studies, to make mental notes of his progress on the particular subjects to which he devoted himself. Upon these methods he founded the success which he marked out for himself, when yet a boy, setting type, when he said one day to some companions, who laughed at him, that he would not be content until he owned, edited and controlled a newspaper, little dreaming then that this prediction was to be realized, on the far away banks of the Mississippi. He was always anxious to be right, and always anxious to escape from prejudice of any form. He has often said he arose every morning as near like a white sheet of paper as possible, ready for all good impressions. His desire was always for freedom, and to see others free. He has not now, and never has enjoyed, any privilege or right that he was not willing that all other men, and every woman, should enjoy. On this basis of freedom he has built for success, asking nothing of the world but a fair field and no favors. He is not, in the sense in which it is generally understood, self-assertive. With all the sturdy qualities of his race, he contends manfully for his principles, leaving himself out, satisfied that the people are quick to recognize and acknowledge ability and merit, and that in time, if he deserved it, he would find a high place in their confidence, esteem and respect, as a leader among men. As to political office, he holds that, as a rule, an aspirant for office is not fit for office. Of a retiring disposition and modest, he yet clings, with death-like tenacity, to what he believes is right. He loves his books, next after his wife and children, and these after his God.

Mr. Keating's success as a journalist is due to his conviction that a newspaper must, first of all, be devoted to news, news that will satisfy all classes, and to a rigid impersonal management. He believes that the newspaper should subserve the general and not particular interests; that it should represent all classes fairly, frankly, and as fully as space and opportunity will admit, and that when editorial comment is made, it should be short, pointed and comprehensive. Parties and partisans should be sustained when they are right, and unsparingly condemned when wrong. An editor should not have any friends to reward, nor enemies to punish. He must always be impartial, to enjoy the confidence of the public. The newspaper belongs as much to the public as to him. The people of the city, town or county he publishes in should be first with him, then those of the State, and next, those of the nation, and, after that, the world at large. Wrong should be unhesitatingly denounced, and the right always fearlessly sustained, no matter who it may hurt. He is the implacable foe of the personal puffery by which villainy has sometimes been shielded by the press, and men, without fitness, ability or character, foisted into high places. An unswerving Democrat, he has always held his opponents in respect, believing that they have the same rights as he, and convinced that, so long as the world lasts, there will always be two sides to a question. Opinion, political, social and religious, he holds to be a matter largely of education, influenced by surroundings, and no man can, from any fair, reasonable, just or feasible standpoint, denounce another because he cannot or does not agree with him.

The following remarkable article from Mr. Keating's pen, published in the *Appeal*, March 24, 1886, may be taken as a specimen of the philosophical mode of thought, comprehensive cast of mind, and philanthropic yearnings of an editor, who ought to be classed rather as a statesman: "No man can read the news of strikes, and impending strikes, of combinations of labor and combinations of capital, with which the papers are daily filled, without a feeling of apprehension of an impending crisis. No man can read the news of to-day without a feeling of coming calamity worse than civil war. One million of workingmen, according to the report of the United States Labor Bureau, are out of employment and without the means of buying bread. They have no funds to draw from for support, and are without hope—destitute. Enforced beggary and destitution make desperate men. Beggary, enforced by cupidity, make despairing men. It is hard to die of starvation in the midst of plenty. It is hard to go hungry in a country where wealth is flaunted as as aggressive force by men whose elevation on pedestals of gold is due to questionable, many of them, unlawful measures. Such a man can have no bowels of compassion, for no robber can sympathize with industrious labor. What he has, has come to him without manual labor, and by the subversion of conscience, and he laughs at the hard-working and honest toiler as a simpleton. If he is appealed to for aid, his answer is: "Let them go and make money as I did." But a poor man can not buy railroads at twelve thousand dollars a mile and water them up to one hundred and twenty-eight thousand dollars a mile, and compel the farmers, the merchants and manufacturers to pay six per cent. per annum on the water. Such wholesale robbery, perpetrated in defiance of the plainest and simplest dictates of fair dealing, are not within the workingman's reach, even if he desired to be dishonest, but he is within the reach of these, the most powerful combinations of modern times, to be ground into subjection to a tyranny worse than that of the robbing barons of William the Conquerer's day. Reduced to a mere machine, imbruted by continuous labor, extending, as in the case of street-car drivers, to fourteen and sixteen hours in the twenty-four, the workingman has not time, even for a moment's serious thought, for his future or that of his children. Whatever of civilization he may have had when he began the race of life is thus being steadily stamped out of him, and he is gradually becoming a sullen savage. Out of this slough of despondency a cry has gone up for counter-combination, and the Knights of Labor have been organized to stem the broad, deep and sweeping current of degradation and slavery, and prepare for a contest that may end in anarchy, if a way is not found to meet the honest, earnest appeal of the workingmen for a chance to improve their condition by lessening the hours of labor to eight per day, and making such a standard of wages as shall reduce the averages of beggary to the lame, the halt and the blind. War, in any guise, is to be avoided, but a war that would find the poor arrayed against the rich, is one that must be prevented, and it can be. All sense of justice has not perished out of the country. The standards of fair dealing have not been lost. Apply these, square the differences between employer and employed by the rule which Christ said embraced "all the law and the prophets," and there can not be a moment's doubt as to the result. Let the rich man, the railroad combinationist, the monopolist and the manufacturer put himself in the place of the workingman, if only for a moment, and strikes will become impossible. Let them remember that men, women and children must live, and that if they do not live by work they will by beggary or by robbery. Let them remember that it is easier, as well as better, to support a poor man in work than in pauperism, and that by lifting him above the accidents, the contingencies and the exigencies of life, they are increasing the ranks of good citizenship, lessening the ranks of crime, and making for civilization in its highest and best sense by raising the average of self-reliant, self-respecting and self-dependent men. There are large bodies of intelligent workingmen who have willing allies among the professions. These have been discussing the disparities between extreme indigence, squalor and wretchedness and the expense of indulgence, of palatial splendor and plenty. They have been asking the question, how and by what means can a man in less than thirty-five years amass or acquire control of six hundred and fifty million dollars worth of property, a sum greater by nearly one hundred thousand dollars than the estimated true valuation of all the taxable property in each of the States of Georgia, Kansas and Maine, and nearly as much as that of Tennessee, of Virginia and Minnesota? How few men have made one million dollars, even in a long life-time, by their own unaided efforts? In a country whose constitution declares for the equality of all men, the means and measures that enable one man to absorb and monopolize the wealth that belongs to honest industry to an extent like this, are the agencies of wrong and of crime. This it is that lies at the basis of all strikes; this it is that has put labor and capital at bay, confronting each other as they do to-day, with an avowed purpose, the one of defense and the other of aggression, regardless of consequences. It is, as Henry George says, the "House of Have" and the "House of Want" that are occupying this attitude, and are preparing for a collision, and that everywhere jostle and scowl at each other. What is to prevent encounter? What is to prevent this threatening war of classes? Compromise— which is better than bloodshed, turmoil, confusion and destruction of property. The South would to-day be better off by nine million dollars and six hundred thousand valuable lives had the negro been voluntarily set free and the civil war been averted."

As an earnest of the fairness of Mr. Keating in politics, and as further illustrating his style as a writer, the following article, written some years ago, and published in his paper on the morning that Gen. Grant was the guest of the city of Memphis, is here given: "The people of Memphis will greet Gen. Grant to day with a generous and manly welcome. They will recognize in him the great leader of the northern people during the civil war, the man whom that people delight to honor as their hero. They will greet him as the soldier whose magnanimity twice prevented the humiliation of our greatest soldier—our hero, the immortal Lee. They will greet him as the soldier who refused to make a scene of the surrender at Appomattox, and whose thoughtfulness and generosity preserved to our officers their swords and to our men the mules and horses with which to begin the labors of civil life after four years of bloody, fruitless strife. They will greet him as the soldier who interposed to save our brave Confederate soldiers from the harrassments and annoyances, and the degradations that radical malignancy had prepared for them as the finale of a petty vengeance. They will greet him as the idolized leader of the millions who, from every part of the northern and western States of the Union, sent us

in the years of plague an unstinted help in money, and men and women, accompanied by a tender and Christian solicitude for our sick and dying. He is their representative, the man whom above all others they delight to honor. For this, putting away the record of the party whose instrument, possibly against his better nature, he became, the people of Memphis will take him cordially by the hand. They will recall the traits of a character whose most prominent faults, even from our extreme point of view, lie at the door of his good nature, his love of friends, his devotion to those who, at any time, especially in his hours of need, have kindly served him. They will put aside political differences, and self-respecting, will entertain the soldier who, fifteen years ago, rounded a great career by acts that sounded the very depths of a noble nature, and that were a contrast with the then prevalent sentiment that he stemmed in their accomplishment. He is our fellow-citizen—he is an American. Now, while the record of the sections is still open, while history is still recording the evidences of the great struggle, while so many of the participants on both sides still survive as active agents of the people in the administration, or in legislating for the administration, of the restored government, it is too much to expect oblivion as to acts that have left their sting and smart to fret and worry us, even to this very hour. But if we recall the events that have chased each other so rapidly since the eyes of the beloved commander at Appomattox were blinded by the tears of the sorest trial of his life, we shall find that we have reason, abundant reason, to be thankful that in so short a time we are again as free men, with none to make us afraid, that we are again in possession of the States the fathers and pioneers fashioned out of the wilderness, that all the comities between the States of the American Union are restored, that the Union itself, to which the South contributed so much of brains and blood, is stronger than ever, stronger in its attitude toward the world beyond, and stronger in the affections of the people. Looking back along the pages of the history of our race, we find no parallel to this. Even to our own day, the hate of England's greatest ruler, Cromwell, is perpetuated by intelligent men. The discords, contentions and feuds born of political differences have for seven hundred years marked the course of parties in Ireland. In Spain three factions, fired to an intensity of zeal by the remembrances of the past, wait the opportunity to seize the throne of Alfonso; and in France, the legitimist, the Orleanist and the imperialist perpetuate contentions which daily threaten the safety of the republic. Unlike Germany, we have neither an Alsace nor Lorraine. We cannot afford to transmit animosities as heirlooms. Only here, in this land, where strong common sense tempers all we do, was it possible for the surging sea of war to subside and for the genius of the people to evoke by their fiat and their will an effective 'Peace, be still.' In the life of a nation, fifteen years is but as a day. Yesterday we were at each other's throats, to-day peace reigns in all our borders, and we are enjoying the overflowing fruits of many industries, making the whole world our market. The wounds of war are almost healed. We already read of it in histories. We do not forget it; we do not forget the noble men who gave their lives for us—but the fierceness, the passion and the prejudice of the strife have died out, and tender, grateful recollections of them survive. The history of both sections, like the stars upon our flag, are merged. We are, let us hope, upon the threshold of the new era, when all trace of the bloody contest will be blotted out, and we shall be able to say that in a generation we had fought through years of bloody war and wiped out all its stains. A man can win no nobler victory than to triumph over himself, to subject himself to law, to restrain his impulses, to put passion and belittling prejudices under foot, and people can offer no higher evidence of their civilization than their subjugation of passion, prejudice and hate and the uncharitableness of sectional strife and party animosities. Looking abroad through all the States, while we find those who would yet warp the judgment of the nation and strain the endurances of the republic, we find the great mass yielding to those kindly influences which strengthen the bonds of the Union, sustain mutual confidence and cement brotherly love. What part this man or that man took in bringing this about, we will not to-day stop to inquire. We will enjoy the retrospect. We will halt on the first step toward an engrossing political contest, and will indulge ourselves in one of those pleasant episodes that prove the picture we have drawn. We will entertain Gen. Grant as our guest, and by another generous, hospitable act, hasten forward the day when only the greatest of the achievements of both North and South, a common heritage, will be remembered or recalled."

Notwithstanding Mr. Keating's great abilities as an editor, and as a speaker, one is delightfully surprised to find that one of his chief accomplishments is that of a conversationalist. Not before ordinary company, but with his friends, selected or invited, because they are congenial, and in his own home surrounded by books and pictures and works of art; business all forgotten, extraneous care banished from his presence. It is then that the heart of this man talks through his intellect to his delighted auditors. It is a good education to be able to listen to him, for his conversation is a flowing rivulet of information, and as the current of his speech sweeps on, one is fascinatingly amazed that an editor, tied down to the treadmill work of commenting upon current events gathered by the telegraph wires, has had time or nerve left to revel in the luxuries of science, philosophy, belles-lettres and art, and to become a critical master of subjects embracing so wide a range of information. A cultivated Irishman, only a trace of the wit and humor for which the Irish race is celebrated appears in his conversation. His phrases are diamonds

of thought, simply philosophy, yet mixed with heart and soul. One knows not whether he takes more interest in his subject or his company; the current of his words, the eloquence of his diction, the depth of thought, and the happy combinations of his ideas, so charm the listener, one has no disposition to enter into the conversation further than to show attention and appreciation, throw in a word here and there to give direction to it, and encourage the speaker to go on. From his readiness on all subjects, it would seem he has no favorite branch of knowledge, or if he has, it is sociology. It is painful to think of such a mind as an editor, for a newspaper is the property of the public, and the editor has contracted to please them. Worse still, the newspaper belongs to the party, and the editor must give up to the party what belongs to mankind. He must suppress the rising thought, conceal the honest admission, and if he escapes the advocacy of party wrong against opposition right, finds it indeed difficult not to at least color his own party statements and discolor the position of his opponents.

Gen. Colton Green, of Memphis, who has known Mr. Keating long and intimately, says of him: "He is a man of a great deal of earnestness, full of enthusiasm, full of gentleness and sympathy, and strong desire to better the condition of his fellow-man. He is a humanitarian of very broad views, i. e., whose views go beyond *ex cathedra* ideas, and in all public affairs he is free from provincial prejudices. These traits were illustrated, first, by the conduct of his paper, the *Appeal*, for as an editor he has been a teacher, and a moralist as well; then his course during the yellow fever epidemic of 1878, brought him more prominently before the people than ever. He was an active working member on all the various committees, laboring, counseling and giving them his advice, when it took a brave man to preserve a clear head. He was one of the most prominent actors during those terrible days. After the epidemic had passed, he made persistent effort to educate the people in the ways of sanitary reform, pointing out defects in the systems of engineering that then prevailed in the city, the want of proper drainage, sewerage and a garbage service. The articles he wrote led to a meeting of the citizens, in which the first steps were taken out of which grew the Sanitary Association, which inaugurated the reforms which have since taken place. He took a special leadership in promoting and accomplishing the fine system of sewerage which the city of Memphis now possesses. Through his activity and his intelligent advocacy of it, the system was perfected. He does not mix much with people, being a student and an editor, but socially he is a charming man, and has a charming family."

In the *Appeal* of November 27, 1878, we find this testimonial to his deservings and high estimate of his abilities: "Now that Mr. J. M. Keating is absent for recreation and to recuperate the waste produced upon his

49

system, his partner and editorial associate takes the liberty of stating that it was through his extraordinary exertions that the *Appeal* was published during the epidemic. He was a pillar of strength to the paper. He was never bewildered in the mazes of difficulties that surrounded him; but was always equal to the emergency. When the number of compositors was reduced to only two, he was enveloped in the midnight gloom of hopeless despair. But he fell back upon himself, marched into the composing-room, put in type his own editorials and prepared the forms of the paper for the press. But for his unconquerable will and energy the *Appeal* would have been suspended. The prudence and ability with which Mr. Keating conducted the paper, under such appalling circumstances, has received the universal commendation of the public. He added much to his reputation as an enterprising newspaper man, which was already extended; for it is now generally conceded that Mr. Keating has no superior in the South. He has been trained to journalism from earliest boyhood, and is familiar with every department of a newspaper. His natural powers, great industry and patience would have made him successful in any career he might have chosen. But it was fortunate that he so early comprehended, as it seems he did, his own aptitudes and tastes; that he found scope for his talents, or rather conquered a place for their exercise, in a profession for which he is pre-eminently fitted, and in which he has won a name and achieved a success with which the most ambitious might be justly proud. He understands journalism in its every part, from the tripod to the newsboy. He can serve as leading, financial, local or river editor. There is no department in journalism he can not fill, and 'make noble and dignified by his way of filling it.' "

BRYCE STEWART, ESQ.

CLARKSVILLE.

THIS gentleman, one of the pioneer citizens, and for many years a leader in the leading industry of his town—the tobacco trade—appears in this volume as one of the substantial business men of Clarksville, and as a man who has made his way to the top of the ladder by his integrity, enterprise, energy, assiduity and faithful attention to business. He was born in the town of Rothesay, Isle of Bute, Scotland, and was sent to school there, becoming, at the age of fifteen, a fair English scholar, and having a good knowledge of Greek and Latin. At the age of fifteen, he emigrated to America to join his brother, John Stewart, who had preceded him several years, and was then a tobacco merchant in Richmond, Virginia. Here he remained with his brother about two years, during which time he received good training and had become well acquainted with the tobacco business.

About the year 1833, he went to New Orleans, and together with his brother, erected a tobacco factory, of which he became manager, but during the year he was stricken down with the yellow fever, and on recovering left the city for a more healthy locality.

Coming to Clarksville, he found it a good point for the tobacco trade, and during the latter part of 1834, located there, and though then not more than eighteen or nineteen years of age, he at once took charge of a tobacco factory which his brother assisted him in starting. Clarksville was then a very small town, and had only three tobacco houses. Here he has remained, witnessing its growth and development during fifty years of progress and pause, building himself up in the tobacco trade and amassing a handsome property. A few years previous to the war, he severed his active connection with the business, and after the war began, closed out entirely. In the meantime he had been operating establishments in Glasgow and Brunswick, Missouri, and Mayfield, Kentucky, and was doing business in Nashville, Tennessee, and St. Louis, Missouri, and also dealing in cotton in Memphis. Financially considered, his history was one of steady progress up to the time he retired from business.

Mr. Stewart was in early life a Whig, of the Henry Clay school, in favor of peace and the preservation of the Union, if possible. Since the war he has voted with the Democrats. He took the degree of Master Mason at Clarksville many years ago. He became a member of the Presbyterian church at Clarksville, in early life, and helped to build the first Presbyterian church ever erected in the town, where there were on his arrival only five or six persons of that faith.

Mr. Stewart's father, Bryce Stewart, was a merchant and ship-owner in Scotland, and the descendant of an old Presbyterian family. He was a man of success in his business, a prominent member and an elder in the Established church. His father was a Scotch farmer. Mr. Stewart's mother was a Miss Kerr. Two of his brothers, John and Daniel Stewart, now retired merchants of Richmond, Virginia, were for many years leading tobacco men in that city.

Mr. Stewart was first married, at Clarksville, Tennessee, in 1839, to Miss Eliza J. McClure, daughter of Alexander McClure, a merchant, and the descendant of a family who were among the earliest settlers of Clarksville. The family was of Scotch-Irish descent. By this marriage he had three sons and one daughter, all of whom are now dead except the youngest, Bryce Stewart, jr., who is now a lieutenant in the British army, and stationed in India. The daughter, Marion, married Mr. Hume, a banker of Louisville, Kentucky, and left one son, Bryce Stewart Hume. Mrs. Stewart died in 1866.

Mr. Stewart was married a second time, in 1873, at Clarksville, to Miss Sallie West Cobb, daughter of Dr. Joshua Cobb, a prominent citizen of Clarksville. By this second marriage he has one son, Norman Stewart, born in 1874, now living with his father. Mrs. Stewart is a member of the Presbyterian church.

Mr. Stewart revisited Europe in 1866; again in 1873, and a third time in 1881, spending on each occasion nearly two years traveling over the continent, enriching his already well-stored mind with practical knowledge of interesting historic places. This knowledge he has a most pleasant manner of imparting, and therefore, is a most companionable gentleman, a man of culture and refined education. It is not difficult to account for Mr. Stewart's success in life, for he has been a hard worker, a punctual, attentive, industrious, energetic business man, and good fortune has followed his footsteps and crowned his efforts with plenty. He is a man of kindly nature, charitable in disposition, gentle-natured and firm in his friendships. In short, he is a model citizen and a good man.

HON. E. L. GARDENHIRE.

CARTHAGE.

JUDGE E. L. GARDENHIRE, of Carthage, one of Tennessee's ablest lawyers and most distinguished judges, was born in Overton county, Tennessee, November 12, 1815, and there grew to manhood, assisting his father in farm work, who, although a man of considerable property, thought it his duty to train the son to work. In the winter months he attended the neighborhood schools until just turned into his nineteenth year, when his father sent him to Clinton College, in Smith county, where he studied two years—1834-5-6—Latin, Greek, mathematics and the natural sciences. After leaving college, he continued his studies privately at home one year, when he took charge of the Livingston Academy and taught school one year. In 1838-9, he studied law under Judge Cullom, and obtained license to practice, in August, 1839, before Judges Caruthers and Andrew J. Marchbanks. From this time, he read diligently until 1844, in the early part of which he began practice at Livingston, and did an exceptionally large and remunerative practice, making six thousand dollars a year. From the very beginning, he refused bad debts. If a man would not pay him, unless it was a charity case, he refused his services. November 27, 1851, he moved to Sparta, Tennessee, where he resided until 1876, when he settled permanently at Carthage. At the breaking out of the war he was worth in negroes, lands, good debts and money in bank, some forty thousand dollars. By the war he lost not less than thirty thousand dollars. Since that time, however, he has recovered his fortune, by dint of hard work and close application to his business, and is now in very independent and comfortable circumstances.

In August, 1849, Judge Gardenhire was elected State senator from the counties of Fentress, Overton, Jackson, White and Van Buren, and served in the Tennessee Legislature of 1849-50, and was chairman of the committee on public grounds and public buildings.

In May, 1858, he was elected judge of the Fifth judicial circuit, comprising the counties of Scott, Morgan, Fentress, Overton, White, Bledsoe, Sequatchie and Marion, and held that position until December 1, 1861, when he resigned on account of the impossibility of holding courts during the war.

In November, 1861, he was elected to the Confederate Congress, and served in the sessions of 1862 and 1863. In this Congress he urged and voted for every measure which he thought would promote the interests of the South, and was regarded as an able legislator. After the war, in 1875, he represented White and Putnam counties in the Tennessee Legislature, and in that body served as chairman of the committee on judiciary. In the spring of 1877, Gov. James D. Porter appointed him one of the Supreme court of arbitration, which position he filled one year. October 11, 1883, he was appointed by the unanimous vote of the Supreme court one of the judges of the court of referees for West Tennessee, the position in which the editor hereof found him.

In politics, Judge Gardenhire has always been a Democrat, of the strictest and straighest sect, being very decided in his political views but always respecting the views and feelings of gentlemen differing with him on party issues. In 1856, he was a delegate from the State at large to the Cincinnati convention that nominated Buchanan for president, and on his return home was nominated presidential elector for the Fourth congressional district, canvassed the district, and was elected over his Whig competitor, Judge William Hickerson.

Judge Gardenhire was made a Master Mason in Sparta Lodge, No. 99, in 1866. In religion, he is a believer in the doctrines of the Christian or Campbellite church, of which his wife and children are members. He has had some editorial experience, having edited the *Mountain Democrat*, at Sparta, in 1856–7, for the benefit of his friend, William Holton, owner of the paper.

Judge Gardenhire married, in Overton county, Tennessee, December 5, 1839, Miss Mary McMillin, a native of Kentucky, daughter of James McMillin, esq., a gentleman of Scotch blood, and for several terms a member of the Kentucky Legislature, noted for his good humor, anecdote and hospitality. His father, a Presbyterian preacher, left Scotland and went first to France, thence to Kentucky, with his father, in 1805, where he married and afterward settled in Overton county, Tennessee. He died in 1876, at the age of ninety years.

Mrs. Gardenhire's mother, *nee* Miss Katharine Halsell, was of Irish descent. Mrs. Gardenhire's nephew, Hon. Benton McMillin, of Carthage, son of her oldest brother, John H. McMillin, is now a member of Congress, from Tennessee, from the Fourth congressional district, this being his third term, to which he was elected without opposition. He is chairman of the committee on claims, and stands very high in Congress. He married, in 1886, Miss Marie Brown, of Pulaski, Tennessee, daughter of Hon. John C. Brown, ex-governor of Tennessee. John H. McMillin represented Monroe county, Kentucky, in the Legislature of that State, and died in 1883. Mrs. Gardenhire was educated at Centre Point, Kentucky, and, like her family generally, is very popular; an intellectual woman, with a fine sense of the ludicrous, and possessed of that agreeable vivacity and witty turn that intelligent Irish people generally have.

To this marriage were born eight children, one of whom died in infancy. The living are: (1). James Alexis Gardenhire, born December 23, 1840; educated at Lebanon University; was licensed to practice law, but is a farmer in Smith county. He served in the Confederate army as captain of a company in the Twenty-eighth Tennessee, and as aid to Gen. Marcus J. Wright. He married Miss Florence Carrick, of Sparta, daughter of H. L. Carrick, a merchant. (2). Alice Catharine Gardenhire is now wife of J. F. Goodbar, a merchant at Lonoke, Arkansas, and has five children: Joseph L., Frank, Leslie, Lafayette and Alice. (3). John Halsell Gardenhire, born in Overton county, December 24, 1845; married Miss Elizabeth Snodgrass, daughter of Joseph Snodgrass, a merchant of Sparta, and has six children: Erasmus Lee, Joseph, Mamie, Fannie, Alice and ———. (4). Mary Gardenhire, married Mark L. Clark, a farmer and mill owner in White county, and has five children: Erasmus, Lee, Elizabeth, Annie, Ella and Rosalee. (5). Ellen Gardenhire, married James T. Quarles, a prominent merchant at Sparta, and has two children, Joseph and Freddy. (6). Ada Gardenhire, married John H. McMillin, a lawyer at Celina, Tennessee, brother of Congressman

Benton McMillin. She has three children: Ella, Elizabeth and John H. (7). Rosalee Gardenhire, married Cornelius Cullom, a farmer near Carthage, and has one child, Mary.

Judge Gardenhire's great-grandfather, Jacob Gardenhire, emigrated from Germany to Pennsylvania. His grandfather, also named Jacob Gardenhire, setted in Virginia; was a soldier seven years in Washington's army; was a regular old Virginia gentleman, fond of his horse, his hounds and his children. He moved to Tennessee in 1790, and settled at Campbell's Station, Knox county, fought the Indians there, and died in September, 1824, in Overton county, where he had moved in 1811. Rev. James Godwin, the celebrated soldier in Marion's army, was a personal friend of this old gentleman, and preached his funeral. (See Weems' Life of Gen. Marion).

Judge Gardenhire's father, Adam Gardenhire, born August, 1792, in Knox county, was a successful farmer, a man of strong good sense and business judgment, amassed an estate of seventy-five thousand dollars, and was a careful, vigilant, economical, money-making man, leaving nothing undone, who never had a lawsuit on his own account, was liberal and hospitable, and a Methodist for forty years before he died, August 4, 1851.

Judge Gardenhire's paternal uncles, William, Thompson, George and John, were all distinguished for fine courage, and were prosperous business men. His paternal aunt, Margaret, married John Carmichael, and lived and died in Roane county, Tennessee.

Judge Gardenhire's mother, *nee* Miss Ailsey Tippet, born June, 1792, in Rowan county, North Carolina, was the daughter of Erasmus Tippet, a farmer, who served for two and a half years, in the latter part of the Revolutionary war. He was a man of good estate, owned some forty negroes, but never owned land. Her mother, Lucy Bierling, was a daughter of John Bierling, of Rowan county, North Carolina, where Judge Gardenhire's mother was born. Judge Gardenhire's mother died in Overton county, April 17, 1873. She was a woman uniformly kind to her children, and to her negroes, whom she treated with genuine humanity; was a member of the Methodist church for sixty years before her death, and died as she had lived, thoroughly honest in her convictions. She had more courage than ordinary women, but was gentle, rather than demonstrative.

Faithful and candid are the two words that distinguish the character of Judge Gardenhire. In his law practice he has always hesitated in broaching bad news or discouraging views to his clients, but never takes advantage of his client's ignorance to make money unprofessionally or to his client's detriment, and never takes an exhorbitant fee. His reputation is that he deals justly with all men, and this reputation is sustained by an upright record in the community in which he has lived and practiced law for forty years.

HON. THOMAS MENEES, M. D.

NASHVILLE.

DISTINGUISHED for his eminent rank in the medical profession, for the high political honors he has won, and for being the oldest living representative of a family that assisted in laying the foundations of the civil and social fabric of Middle Tennessee, Thomas Menees first saw the light in a cabin on Mansker's creek, in Davidson county, Tennessee, June 26, 1823, under circumstances little prognostic of the distinguished career he was to run.

The family is of sterling Scotch origin, and the original way of spelling the name was McNees, but of the history of the clan there now remains no accurate tradition. Benjamin Menees, great-grandfather of Dr. Menees, was a native of Amherst county, Virginia, served with credit as a patriot soldier in the American Revolution; emigrated as a pioneer and settled on Sulphur fork of Red river, in what is now Robertson county, Tennessee, of which county he was county court judge in 1791. "He died in his block house in 1811." A fuller account of his life and services, as well as of the Menees family, may be found in Putnam's "History of Middle Tennessee," and Clayton's "History of Davidson County."

Dr. Menees' grandfather, James Menees, was a noted Indian fighter and Tennessee pioneer. He was a member of Capt. John Donelson's party of hardy emigrants, who started from the settlements of East Tennessee, in the spring of 1780, and steered the first keel-boat from Knoxville to Nashville. The adventure was by a long, hazardous and unexplored route by water—with hostile Indians continually harrassing them, but they made the voyage successfully, down the Holston, down the Tennessee to its junction with the Ohio, then up the Ohio, and up the Cumberland to the French salt spring, where the city of Nashville now stands. The buoyant, cheerful spirit of the women on that memorable voyage seemed never to fail, and they permitted not the men to do all the hard labor in the navigation, often would not be denied the privilege of lending a helping hand, for, as it is told:

"They worked with paddle, pole, and oar;
They worked when every hand was sore;
They worked with cheerful heart and more—
They worked with paddle, pole and oar,
Until they need to work no more,
Now landed at the wished for shore."

Such were the pioneer mothers and fathers who laid the foundations of a city so beautiful and so beloved. May their noble examples stimulate the present generation, and be not lost to posterity! James Menees, one of the boldest and bravest of this daring party, became a successful farmer, and for many years was sheriff of Robertson county. His wife, *nee* Miss Rebecca Williams, was a most excellent woman, well educated, and a grad-

uate of the Moravian Female College, at Salem, North Carolina. She died when her only child, Benjamin W. Menees (Dr. Menees' father), was an infant.

Dr. Menees' father, Benjamin W. Menees, was born and raised in Tennessee, and died in Robertson county, in 1863, at the age of seventy-four years. He served with his father and several uncles under Jackson, in the war of 1812-15. He was a thrifty, hard-working, pushing farmer and stock-raiser, and left, besides a comfortable estate, the more valuable heirloom of a character for integrity and broad common sense. Family pride, founded on an inheritance of this kind, is a potent factor in the formation of the manhood of children and of their success and high standing in life.

Dr. Menees' mother, *nee* Miss Elizabeth Harrison, was the daughter of Thomas Harrison, a successful Sumner county farmer, and sister of the late Judge Orville Harrison, of Panola county, Mississippi. She was a broad brained, intellectual woman, highly educated, of deep and earnest piety, devoted to her husband and children, and earnest in teaching and training them in religion, in morality, integrity and energy. It is to her good influence the son mainly owes what he is and has been, and to his father those habits of industry and probity by which he became systematic and business-like, even when a boy.

Dr. George W. Menees, brother of the subject of this sketch, is now one of the leading practitioners of medicine at Springfield, Tennessee. Their only living sister, Emily Elizabeth Menees, is now the wife of Dr. J. W. Dunn, of Turnersville, Tennessee, and has but one child, Dr. J. W. Dunn, engaged in practice with his father. Dr. Menees lost two sisters and one brother, all dying in childhood, within ten days of each other. His sister, Rebecca W. Menees, lived to be a young lady, was remarkably brilliant and gifted, the most intellectual member of the family. She died, in 1852, just as she was blooming into a lovely womanhood.

Although born in Davidson county, Dr. Menees was raised in Robertson county, and lived there until February, 1862. He was brought up on his father's farm to habits of systematic industry, received a country school education, and taught school himself one term, when a young man. In 1841, he commenced the study of medicine in the office of Dr. Robert K. Hicks, at Springfield, Tennessee; next took a course of lectures in the medical department of Transylvania University, Lexington, Kentucky, and from 1842 to 1845, practiced in his father's neighborhood with exceptionally good success. In 1845, he returned to Transylvania University and there received the degree of M.D., March 6, 1846. From that date his professional career was satisfactorily successful; from 1845 to 1855, in partnership with Dr. Hicks, and from 1855 to 1871, with his younger and only living brother, Dr. George W. Menees. In October, 1865, having meanwhile been a member of the Confederate Congress, and a refugee from his native State four years, he commenced practice in Nashville, where he still resides. In 1873, he was elected professor of materia medica and therapeutics in the medical department of the University of Nashville. In 1874, he was elected professor of obstetrics and dean of the faculty in the combined medical departments of the University of Nashville and Vanderbilt University, positions he has held uninterruptedly from that time until now. He is a member of the American Medical Association, of the Tennessee Medical Society, and of the Nashville Medical Society, and for many years represented the institutions in which he is a professor in the association of the American Medical Colleges; besides, has given much of his time, talent and influence to the elevation of the standard of medical education. Among the papers contributed by him to the Tennessee Medical Society may be mentioned, "A Paper upon Placenta Prævia," "Use of Obstetric Forceps in Delivery." "Hour-glass Construction," and other subjects.

Not less brilliant is his political record, for from the date of his medical graduation in 1846, his name is prominently connected with the political history of the State. He has always been a stanch, unswerving Democrat; was born and raised that way. He took an active part in all the presidential contests from that of Polk and Clay to that of Lincoln and Breckinridge. In 1849, he was the party nominee for the General Assembly, but was defeated by his Whig competitor, Col. Wiley Woodard, the latter having a political majority of five hundred in the county to begin with, but which Dr. Menees reduced to thirty-eight. In 1857, he was elected State senator for the counties of Robertson, Montgomery, Stewart and Cheatham, and served one term, being chairman of several committees, among them a special bank committee. In 1859, he was the candidate of his party to represent the Hermitage district in the United States Congress, but was defeated by Judge James M. Quarles, who had the advantage of an overwhelming political majority in the district. In 1860, he was a delegate to the national Democratic convention at Charleston, and advocated the nomination of Breckinridge, as also at the subsequent Baltimore convention. In 1861, and again in 1863, he represented his congressional district in the Confederate Congress, to which he was elected over strong opposition, by a majority of five to one. He served in that body, with zeal and activity and marked ability, a cause which he had espoused as the only logical and honorable solution of the political problems of those dark and stormy days.

Dr. Menees married, first in Davidson county, Tennessee, April 21, 1853, Miss Elizabeth Hooper, who was born in that county, daughter of Claiborne Y. Hooper, a native of the same county, and a large and prosperous farmer. Her mother was originally a Miss Keeling, a native also of Davidson county. Mrs. Menees graduated at the Columbia Institute, under Rector Smith; was a member of the Methodist church; much esteemed for her culture and intelligence, and especially for her amiability and benevolence. In social circles she was unusually gifted. She died, April 24, 1861, at the age of about twenty-five years.

By his marriage with Miss Hooper, Dr. Menees had four children. The eldest, a daughter, Mary Rebecca Menees, died in infancy. The eldest son, Thomas Williams Menees, M.D., was born at Springfield, Tennessee, January 15, 1855; graduated from the medical department of Vanderbilt University in 1876; practiced with his father from the time of taking his degree; was made associate demonstrator of anatomy in Vanderbilt University; died, September 15, 1878, while in the service of the Howard Association, during the yellow fever epidemic at Memphis. He had married Miss Mollie Loftin, of Nashville, and by her had one child, a son, Thomas Williams Menees. The second son, Young Hooper Menees, M.D., was born at Springfield, August 15, 1857; graduated in medicine from Vanderbilt University; married Miss Alma W. Bunch, of Springfield, by whom he had one child, a daughter, Elizabeth Menees. He practiced at Springfield with his uncle, Dr. George W. Menees, with remarkable professional success for one of his age, when suddenly he was cut down by death, December 12, 1883. The following obituary notice of this brilliant and promising young physician appeared in the Nashville American: "Young Hooper Menees, M.D., died at his residence, in Springfield, Tennessee, December 12, 1883, in the twenty-seventh year of his age. In his premature removal from the scenes of life, a career whose opening was auspicious and presaged great success, has been closed, and the insidious disease which cut him down has scored another illustration of the saying of the ancients : ' Whom the gods love die young.' The subject of this notice was the second son of Prof. Thomas Menees, M.D., of the medical department of the University of Nashville and Vanderbilt University, and an elder brother of Prof. O. H. Menees, of the same institution, and a junior brother of the late Thomas W. Menees, M.D., one of the noble sacrifices to professional duty, who fell in the epidemic at Memphis in 1878, and in all respects was worthy of such a record of professional lineage and connection. Though reared in great part in this city, since 1880 he had been engaged in the practice of medicine with his uncle, George W. Menees, M.D., of Robertson county. After a studious course, evincing great aptitude for the profession, he acquired his degree in the medical departmnt of Vanderbilt University, and at once entered upon its exacting duties. The comparatively brief period of his service sufficed to display a proficiency of knowledge and skill unusual in one of his age, and was laying the foundation for an honorable and prosperous sphere of usefulness. His deportment was amiable and attractive, and the list of his devoted friends widened with the circuit of his professional labors. His assiduous attention to those who came beneath his care, and his warm, genial nature inspired confidence, and won their esteem and affection in a remarkable manner. The quality of his intellectual gifts was superior, he was an independent and original thinker, tenacious of his convictions, and firm and manly in their assertion. While duly deferential to the judgment and views of elders and those in whom he confided, he possessed the elements of a strong individuality which impressed his associates. Such endowments and traits were earning for him an enviable position in the ranks of his calling, and in the community, when the symptoms of a fatal disease appeared, which was gradually sapping his physical constitution. With still buoyant and unflagging spirit, he was reluctant so soon to yield up a life so bright and promising, and to which he had added the endearing responsibilities of a fond wife and child; yet, when the summons was felt to be inevitable, he calmly confronted the issue, and surrendered in entire resignation to the inexorable fiat. The last days of his young life, so inscrutably clouded, were sustained and soothed in the consolations of a firm religious faith, and so he passed away amid the tears of his family, and the sincere regret of the community in whose midst his labors gave promise of a benefaction. The death of such a son is a peculiarly poignant sorrow to his distinguished father, who has twice been smitten with such a blow, and is a loss to the ranks of the younger members of the profession. His brief life was an honor to both, and the remembrance of his worth is a proud consolation that may temper the keenness of the grief at his untimely taking-off." The youngest son of Dr. Menees, Orville Harrison Menees, M.D., was born at Springfield, April 15, 1859; graduated M.D. from Vanderbilt University in 1879, and succeeded his deceased brother, Dr. Thomas W. Menees, as associate demonstrator of anatomy; in 1880 was elected demonstrator of anatomy; soon after made a medical tour of Europe, visiting the hospitals and colleges of Edinburgh, London, Paris, Berlin and other noted places; continued to hold the position of demonstrator until the spring of 1883, when he was elected to the chair of anatomy and histology in the medical department of the University of Nashville and Vanderbilt University, a professorship which he is filling with complete satisfaction to his colleagues and classes. A separate sketch of this gentleman will be found elsewhere in this volume.

Dr. Menees' second marriage, which occurred at Nashville, August 14, 1868, was with Mrs. Mary Jane Walker, widow of Hiram K. Walker, editor of the Nashville True Whig and Republican Banner. This lady was born in Nashville, daughter of John Austin, a leading and prosperous builder, a native of Maryland. She was educated at Dr. Elliott's Nashville Female Academy. She is a Methodist; a vivacious, sprightly lady, distinguished for her charities and especially for her domestic qualities—being a devoted home-maker. By this marriage, Dr. Menees has one child, a daughter, Mary Elizabeth Menees, born December 14, 1873; a bright, joyous universal favorite in church, school and wherever she goes. She has carried from her infancy a life membership in the Methodist Missionary Society.

For forty-three years Dr. Menees has been a member of the Methodist church, and for a long time was a steward. In 1858, he was made a Royal Arch Mason at Springfield, and has repeatedly represented Western Star Lodge, No. 9, Springfield, in the Grand Lodge of Tennessee. As a doctor, he makes it a point to stand strictly upon the ethics of the profession. In forty years practice he has not deviated from them, though, at times, he has lost friends by this course. Financially he is in very comfortable circumstances. Before the war he had accumulated a fortune of sixty thousand dollars, and at one time was a director in the Edgefield and Kentucky railroad, though he began his professional life without capital and in debt.

Dr. Menees has a commanding presence and manner, whether before an audience discussing the politics of his country, or in the class-room demonstrating the great truths of medical science to students. As a political stump speaker, he is reckoned as one of the most eloquent and effective in Tennessee, while, as a lecturer, he is at once the delight and the instructor of his pupils. With a voice ranging through all the tones of the diatonic scale, his mouth is as full of eloquence as is the throat of a mocking-bird with song. But his power over men in the class-room is based on the principle that treating medical students as gentlemen, they being gentlemen, will reciprocate the courtesy. This suaviter in modo makes him a charming companion socially. As a lecturer, he makes the impression that his objective point is the elevation of medical practice to the highest plane of science. Faultlessly clean in his dress, he speaks in the proud tone of authority, but with the air of a whole-souled, warm-hearted and impulsive gentleman to gentlemen. His style is by turns didactic, familiar, humorous, and with frequent outbursts of impassioned declamation that awaken the enthusiasm of his spell-bound class, who respond with hearty applause. Running through the entire lecture, which he delivers with the fluency of a master of his subject, is a feeling of responsibility which he attempts to impress upon his class. Here is a man born in a log cabin lecturing the scions of aristocracy and inculcating, along with his instruction, the great principles of personal dignity and professional honor and pride, of which he is himself a fine type. He is what he teaches his students to be, prompt and decisive in action, practicing with the precision of science, and moved by honor, integrity and purity. His painting of a scene to impress the paramount importance of a physician being equal to the emergencies, when the life of a mother depends upon the decision and action of a moment, was a master-piece of eloquence, and would have done honor to the Roman forum, or the senate hall of the United States. Dr. Menees, both in and out of the lecture-room, is in manner and bearing a typical southern gentleman of the old regime, whose ideal is that personal honor that comes of seeking to ennoble and exalt a profession which is at once "a service and a sacrifice to save a human life."

As a specimen of the fervid eloquence and rich imagery of the oratorical style that characterizes Dr. Menees, the following address, delivered by him on behalf of the faculty, to the graduating classes of the medical departments of the University of Nashville and Vanderbilt University, in the Masonic theater, Nashville, February 22, 1877, is reproduced here entire:

"*Gentlemen of the Universities, of the Classes, Ladies and Gentlemen:* I appear before you this evening, by appointment of my colleagues, to represent the faculties of the medical departments of the University of Nashville and of Vanderbilt University, upon this commencement occasion; a time-honored custom, requiring that there shall be a valedictory address upon the part of the faculty, now commonly called a 'charge to the class.'

"The themes common to such occasions have been so hackneyed and worn as to raise the question, perhaps, in the minds of some, whether the custom would not be more honored in the breach than in the observance. If, however, you scrutinize the objectors, it may be that you would find that their locks have already been whitened by the frosts of age, and thinned by the winds of time.

"Then, to the audience generally, and to these young gentlemen particularly, such occasions have not yet become so common as to divest them of interest. I say to these young gentlemen especially, who are just entering upon the threshhold of professional life, with all the ardor of youthful ambition, inspired by a noble emulation and animated by sanguine hopes and fond anticipations, are eager for the responsibilities which are pressing so closely upon them—to them the occasion is one of no ordinary interest.

"All this, however, is no answer to the objection, that the subjects common to such occasions have been so rehashed as to render it difficult to present anything having the freshness of originality. Indeed, it was said by Hippocrates, twenty-three centuries ago: 'He that, rejecting all that is already known, should pursue another plan for his researches, and boasts of having found out something that is new, deceives alike himself and others.'

"The difficulties involved in selecting a subject are thus apparent. A didactic lecture would be out of order; what we may have failed to teach you of the science and art of medicine, during the five months of arduous labor just closing, would scarcely be supplied in this parting hour; and clinics, we presume, you have had *ad nauseam.*

"Then we will away with all these, and talk to-night of the medical departments of the University of Nashville and of Vanderbilt University.

"More than a quarter of a century ago, the idea of establishing a medical department in connection with the University of Nashville was conceived by some great minds, in order to furnish the medical students of the South and West an opportunity to prosecute their professional studies without necessarily being driven, at great expense and inconveniences, North and East to do so.

"The university was a part of the heritage which that noble old historic State, one of the original thirteen, North Carolina, bequeathed to us. Munificent as was the benefaction, and glorious as its results, I say it was but a part of our heritage from her. She gave us the iron-willed, lion-hearted, incorruptible, immortal Jackson; the pure patriot and eloquent, gifted statesman Polk; in unbending will, matured and enlarged statesmanship, and incorruptible integrity, a second Jackson in the person of the lamented Johnson—characters alike above the blandishments of wealth or the menaces of power—three names which are household words in a nation's vocabulary, gems in fame's immortal chaplet.

"Then should we honor North Carolina as our territorial, political and literary mother. She gave us this university, upon the achievements of the literary department of which, if we had time to do so, it would be pleasing to dwell, and to recount some of the great names which it gave to history (while under the chancellorship of that profound scholar and distinguished educator, Philip Lindsley), as well as many of its living alumni, who are benefactors of their race and ornaments to mankind.

"We can not dismiss this part of the subject without paying tribute to one name associated with this department, which deserves to be handed down to coming ages, with the blessings of each succeeding generation. Need I say that I allude to Montgomery Bell? and cherished and embalmed with it should be the name of George Peabody.

"Successful and brilliant, as has been the past history of the literary department of this institution, we cherish the fond hope that in the new field to which its energies have been directed, that of a Tennessee State Normal College, under its present wise and able management, its future may be, if possible, even more so.

"What a grand purpose, to prepare teachers properly trained and qualified to teach the young idea how to shoot. A great scientific nursery from which the destitution of teachers of the proper culture, training and competency is to be supplied throughout the South and West, by transplanting from this central point material of the first-class. Think of the immensity of its possibilities, each teacher constituting another focal point, a new source of scientific, intellectual and moral light, diffusing an enlarged intelligence, a higher civilization and a purer Christianity among the common millions, thus blessing mankind and honoring God.

"Then, I would say to the distinguished chancellor, go on in your good work; you handle a lever more powerful than that of Archimedes; its fulcrum is all time, and its sweep is eternity.

"We, however, propose to speak more particularly of the medical department. From its first annual announcement, published in 1851, we learn that its faculty was composed of John M. Watson, professor of obstetrics and diseases of women and children; A. H. Buchanan, professor of surgery; W. K. Bowling, professor of institutes and practice of medicine; C. K. Winston, professor of materia medica and clinical medicine; Robert M. Porter, professor of anatomy and physiology; J. Berrien Lindsley, professor of chemistry and pharmacy and dean of faculty; William T. Briggs, demonstrator of anatomy. In a second edition of that announcement appears the name of Paul F. Eve, professor of surgical anatomy and clinical surgery. From the same announcement, I also make the following extract:

"'The medical department of the University of Nashville was organized on the 11th day of October, 1850, at a full meeting of the board of trustees, by the unanimous appointment of the present faculty. By arrangement made with the trustees, the faculty are secured in the exclusive management of the department, a feature in its organization calculated to have the most beneficial effect upon the prosperity of the school.'"

"Thus, gentlemen, we have the organization of this department which has run such an unparalleled career of prosperity.

"And, in my humble judgment, the wisdom in its plan of organization which led to such brilliant achievements, was developed in an address by my distinguished colleague, Prof. Bowling, to the trustees, urging upon them the founding of this department, and suggesting the basis upon which it should be established. From that address, I make the following extract:

"'We have no hesitation in believing that the popular voice here is in favor of a medical school. Many attempts have heretofore been made in vain to meet the expectations of the public upon this subject. The great difficulty in the way of this enterprise, as is shown by its history, running through a period of fifteen years, has been, means to put it into successful operation. We propose to supply this desideratum from our private resources, and to chance the result for reimbursement.

"'We ask of you, gentlemen, only a recognition, and the loan of your college buildings for the period of twenty years. We wish to have the sole management of the department ourselves.

"'First—Because experience and the history of sim-
50

ilar institutions show that this power is safest with those most deeply interested; and,

"'Second—Because this will be an enterprise in which we have invested no inconsiderable amount of money, and would, on that account, desire to be untrammelled in the management of it.'

"The wisdom of the suggestion 'to leave the sole management of the department to those most deeply interested,' and certainly under the circumstances, most competent to do so, was appreciated and adopted by the board of trustees, in most broad and liberal terms, granting the faculty all they asked in that direction. This feature in the management of the department reflects great credit upon the foresight and sagacity of the trustees, as time has most fully demonstrated, and is still retained.

"Thus we have the beginning of this brilliant and glorious success. The faculty immediately provided all the paraphernalia of an elaborate and elegant museum, cabinets and ample chemical laboratory, etc. The college buildings were enlarged, and so arranged as to adapt them to the purpose of medical teaching, there being, in addition to two large and well arranged lecture halls, each capable of accommodating five hundred students, an elegant and commodious amphitheater of equal capacity.

"All things being now ready, the next step in the development of a medical school was to command a class. The department, guided by the wisdom and impelled by the ardor and enthusiasm of its gifted founders, 'burst like Minerva from the head of Jupiter, at once into maturity, in full panoply, and rich in all the appointments of utility,' and commanded the largest first class that any institution of the kind had ever done in this country, and I doubt not, I may add, in the world.

"At the opening of her second course, in 1852, in discussing the advantages of Nashville as an educational point, Prof. Bowling said in the course of his remarks upon that subject:

"'Medical instruction is consequently in the most perfect harmony with her taste and usage, as will hereafter be that of law and divinity. Destiny has associated her with all that is great in learning, and to insure that end has placed her beneath an Italian sky, where the northern breeze meets and tempers the hot breath of the sunny south, while each is chastened and purified by the commingling. She has given her for a throne the everlasting hills, whose marble bases are but symbolical of perpetuity, while the evergreen, which decorates their summits, is but another emblem of immortality. She has surrounded her with teeming hills and fertile valleys that luxuries unbidden might flow in spontaneously upon her, and crown her happy. Is it to be wondered at, that stern philosophy, exact and exacting science, the fitful but inspiring muses, and the kaleidoscope of letters should seek such a paradise for a perpetual jubilee? We need scarcely allude in this connection to the courtly elegance of her social circles, and her warm and generous hospitality, for these are indigenous to the soil.'

"Such, gentlemen, were the auspices under which she began her second course, which was equally successful and brilliant as its predecessor, and on she went in her triumphal march, until soon she was in the very front ranks of medical schools in America, as was predicted in the address already referred to, 'she would be in less than ten years.'

"So pleased were the trustees with the management and success of the department, that early in the period of the first lease to the faculty they added twenty years additional time to their right to occupy and control it, provided, they would still add to and amplify their museum and apparatus, which was agreed to, and done. She continued to add to her success and achievements, to the luster and brilliancy of her fame, until, in the language of the distinguished gentleman already quoted: 'When the war came, the eagle plumage of our medical school was already bathing in the sun, the cynosure of the republics of science throughout the world.'

"By the convulsions and vicissitudes of war, she was crippled but not crushed. Cato, when informed that his son had been slain in battle, answered something like this: 'I should have blushed had my house stood and prospered amid scenes like these.'

"Though wounded, and temporarily arrested in her progress, she still lives, and in the spirit of honorable and glorious rivalry, offers again the gauntlet to those of her competitors who were more fortunately situated in relation to the calamities of that struggle, with the assurance that she will not only deserve victory, but again wrest it from temporary defeat.

"In carrying out this determination, we are being nobly sustained by the trustees, who, less than two years ago, came forward and added thirteen years to our existing lease, giving us an aggregate of thirty years of unexpired possession, conditioned that the lessees would build a hospital attached to the college buildings.

"Already, with all modern improvements, the beautiful, magnificent and imposing structure is there, and has been utilized during two sessions. Thus fully equipped with all the appointments of a first-class medical college, I say we again kindly and fraternally, yet boldly, offer the gauge in honorable rivalry to the most flattered, proud and petted of fortune's favorites, and are willing to abide the arbitrament of time for the result.

"The faculty of this institution has furnished to the American Medical Association two presidents and five vice-presidents, an honor which, I believe, has been conferred upon no other college in America.

"I will not stop to panegyrize the great names of its founders. Their works are their proudest eulogists. They have erected for themselves a monument imper-ishable as the noble profession to the culture and elevation of which they have contributed so much, and high upon whose roll of fame have inscribed their names in letters of living light, to cheer and animate its votaries who are to follow them to high resolves, lofty aspirations and noble achievements.

"So much for the medical department of the University of Nashville, which has been adopted by Vanderbilt University. This medical department now represents each one of these universities, distinct in their faculty organizations, yet joint in their teaching. We have their endorsement, with the power of conferring the degree of doctor of medicine in the name of each institution. We teach the classes jointly, each having all the facilities of the other.

"How honored we are, my colleagues, to enjoy the confidence and official recognition of two such universities, and with what ceaseless diligence, assiduity and fidelity, should we labor to prove ourselves worthy of such confidence, and safe repositories of such trusts. Two great benefactors, alike herculean giants, combining the strength, manhood and wisdom of age with the bloom, beauty, energy and activity of youth.

"To you, young gentlemen, students of two such institutions, twin brothers, as you are, in science, let the only rivalry known among you be that spirit of noble emulation of who can best work and who best agree.

"We come now to consider Vanderbilt University:

"While yet in its infancy it rears its massive proportions in architectural beauty within our suburbs. Chartered in 1872, as the central university of the Methodist Episcopal church, South, the impoverished condition of the country embarrassed its friends in the raising of funds for its organization, and threatened to disappoint the hopes of its wise and sagacious projectors, when, in 1873, Cornelius Vanderbilt gave the institution five hundred thousand dollars, thus insuring its establishment.

"He subsequently increased this amount to one million dollars, making it at once a rich institution, with ample means to guarantee success. The board of trust, upon his first donation (which large sum at once constituted him its founder), without any intimation or expressed desire upon his part, gave the institution his honored name, 'Vanderbilt University.'

"Already, for over a year, has it been in full operation in all its departments, of theology, law, philosophy, science, literature and medicine. We, of the medical department, had the honor of starting first, and are now celebrating our third commencement.

"It numbered, in its various departments, over three hundred students in 1875 and 1876. It now has a library of over six thousand volumes, scientific apparatus which cost more than fifty thousand dollars, and extensive geological and mineralogical cabinets. Tuition is free to all in the theological department, and in the scientific and literary departments to all who are preparing for the ministry.

"Thus it will be seen that, by the munificence of its great founder, the university is placed upon a solid and substantial basis, which, under the wise and discreet management of those to whom his sagacity entrusted its care, insures not only its permanent, but, we trust, its brilliant success.

"He made but one condition to his bequest, and that was that its present honored head, Bishop McTyeire, should remain, during his life, president of the board of trust, thus giving, as we hope, permanency and wisdom to the policy of its government. This furnishes another illustration of the intense foresight and immense powers of combination so characteristic of the man. To that board, with such a head, he might well confide the trust.

"While we may congratulate ourselves upon the establishment in our favored city of such an institution, while as citizens of Nashville and Tennessee and of the entire country, we have reason to be, and are, justly proud of it, and look forward with sanguine hopes and anticipations to the possibilities of its future. Yet this is an occasion not of unalloyed joy. The institution is now in mourning for its founder. Cornelius Vanderbilt is no more. On the 4th of January last, that insatiate archer, which spares neither age, sex nor condition, that leveler of all human distinctions, death, claimed him for its victim.

"It is a time-honored custom to commemorate the death of the great and good, and justly so. Nations mourn the death of the patriot statesman, whose wise counsels have blessed their nationality. The warrior, too, the track of whose triumphal car is all stained with human blood and strewed with weeping widows and helpless orphans, desolation, poverty and ruin, commands the homage of mankind in honors lavished in all the 'pomp and circumstance of glorious war.'

"We come not to-night to do honor to the statesman or orator who, by the terseness of his logic, the brilliancy of his conceptions, with imagery instinct with life and sparkling with jewels, has enchained a senate, or taken captive an admiring world; nor of the warrior, whose glory is red with human gore, and whose hands are wreaking in the blood of those whose fall was his success; not one whose unbridled ambition drove him through slaughter to a throne. No, but one whose laurels are gathered from the nobler spheres of life; one who, with a smile for every difficulty, superior genius, indefatigable energy, wonderful powers of combination and incorruptible integrity, carved his way upward from poverty and obscurity to the pinnacle of commercial and financial fame and success. While other men studied the laws of commerce and finance, he was their monarch, and, as their master, prescribed their laws, and they being proud of their sovereign, delighted in doing him honor by pouring their treasure in rich profusion at his feet. Thus he achieved a success greater in its glory and nobler in its influence than all the blood-bought victories of the world's proud conquerors.

"This is he whose name we propose to honor in memory this evening. What has he done for us? When the clouds of adversity were lowering heavily over our southern land, everything dark as Erebus, our land all drenched in the blood of its best and most chivalrous; crushed as we were, overthrown and oppressed, the world against us, nothing to hope for but destitution and distress; when our noble chieftain lay with his wasted limbs manacled behind the gloomy dungeon walls of Fortress Monroe, dragging out an existence already made miserable by misfortune and disaster, Cornelius Vanderbilt came to his rescue, and with his golden pen wrote freedom to the prisoner and happiness to the hearts of the people he loved so well.

"Nor did he stop here. With a deep, earnest interest in the great social sphere of that metropolis in which he moved, and a heart beating with sympathy for the lonely stranger, flung out upon the temptations of a great city, he took liberally of his means, and dedicated a temple to the living God, and appropriated it to the 'strangers' of New York, and placed there to minister at its altars one whose great accomplishments, intellectual, social and religious, rendered him peculiarly fit to assume the charge of so grand and noble an enterprise.

"Nor did he stop here. He looked with a sad and sympathizing heart once more to our stricken and devastated southern land, and saw our youths with no inheritance but poverty, and nothing but their strong arms and stout hearts to carve their way to fortune and success. He saw genius crushed and talent hampered, and in the munificence of his mighty soul, again he stretched out his hand and spoke into being the grand institution which bears his name, to which our youths may come, as pilgrims to a 'Mecca,' from every portion of this impoverished land, and enjoy advantages and opportunities equal to any the world can offer.

"Let us contemplate for a moment what may be accomplished by the immense field of this benefaction. It proposes to educate the youth of the country and prepare them for all the walks of life; to educate them in the honorable professions, to teach the jurist to rightfully adjust the balance in which controverted interests tremble, to enforce justice and protect the innocent and helpless; to instruct aright the doctor in his high calling, and enable him not only to carry hope and confidence into the stricken palace, whose loved ones in affluence are racked with pain and writhing in anguish, with power, under the blessings of Providence, to soothe, tranquilize and cure; but also to carry consolation and relief to the poverty-stricken in destitution and distress in the lowly hovel, where affection may be equally as tender, heart sentiments as pure and exalted, sympathy as sincere, and grief as poignant as among the more favored of fortune.

"Here, let me charge you, young gentlemen, never allow an unfortunate man, an afflicted woman, or a sick child to be too poor to command your services. Let this be without ostentation, however; let not your right hand know what your left hand doeth.

"But this benefaction does not propose to stop here; it has still higher, more exalted and glorious purposes. It has a theological department, cramped by no narrow sectarian boundaries, in which is taught to theological students of all denominations the unsearchable riches of the Gospel, that they may go the ends of the earth proclaiming the glad tidings of great joy, and offering in the name of our blessed Saviour eternal salvation to all who will believe upon Him, without money and without price.

"Think of it! How vast is destined to be the influence of these cultivated and pious young men, and many of them gifted, too, servants of the Master, commissioned as so many ministers of mercy to carry consolation, joy and hope, not only to the 'fertile regions of the earth, the hospitable homes of virtue, cultivation and morality,' but to the fastnesses of the mountains, the abodes of wretchedness and want, to the far-off isles of the sea, and to the heathen, even, wherever accessible.

"Nor does the munificence of this wonderful man stop here. His sympathies have gone out to the poor, helpless and disabled railroad man, and he orders half a million to a home for the relief of that unfortunate class.

"While upon the subject of his liberality, it is proper to mention that, much as he has done for us, it was from the noble generosity of his soul. In the civil war his sympathies were with the Federal government. When the Merrimac had disabled some of her naval vessels he gave her his proud steamer, bearing his own name, in recognition of which Congress voted him a gold medal.

"We will tax your patience with the recital of but one more act characteristic of this noble, generous man. Cornelius Vanderbilt did not forget his doctor. He left him thirty thousand dollars; a noble example, worthy of commemoration at least, if not of imitation. He seems to have been particularly partial to our profession. 'When, in about 1853, in one of his best steamships, he took his family and a select company of friends abroad, visiting England and France, and the principal ports of the Baltic and Mediterranean,' of whom do you suppose that select company consisted? Of a minister and his family, and his physician and his family. See his wisdom in taking a doctor along, to say nothing of his good taste. Some one might have been taken sick, and he was too smart to be caught without a doctor in that event.

"In every sphere of life, from the young boatman, protecting his passengers from the impertinent insolence of an intermeddling military officer, to the 'king of commerce,' with his ships fretting every harbor and every sea, and to, perhaps, the heaviest and most successful operator in stocks the world has ever known, we find the same bold, comprehensive, successful elements guiding this man of destiny.

"He not only knew how to accumulate, but he had the higher faculty of knowing how to dispense. He was no accident. God had a purpose in his creation. There was a divinity shaping his ends. The conception was divine, the honored instrument was Vanderbilt. The fidelity with which he carried out his trust will make his name immortal. When monuments of brass and marble shall have crumbled into dust, his name, embalmed in the gratitude and love of succeeding ages, will be praised and honored by generations yet unborn.

"This man was the founder of Vanderbilt University. This much, gentlemen, for the two universities, the medical department of each of which we have the honor to represent. Such are the institutions the honors of which you are to take to-night, and as the representative of the faculties, it is my pleasing duty to pronounce you, alumni, worthy of such almæ matres, and welcome you into the profession of your choice, a profession which has commanded the time and attention, and indeed absorbed the lives, of many of the brightest, best and most gifted names which adorn the pages of history.

"Let us, who would presume to be the successors of such men, prepare ourselves for all the acquisitions within our reach, and by constant study and watchfulness, be ever ready to maintain the dignity, integrity and efficiency of the healing art.

"What the future may be, depends upon us. It has been well said, 'the present is ours, the past is ours also, for medicine is not a science of yesterday, nor the dream of a wild schemer, but originating in antiquity, practiced by the Redeemer, handed down, enriched and improved, through centuries, to be perfected only in eternity. The greatest minds of the earth have given it the admiration of their youth; their manhood has improved, ornamented and simplified, and their old age has relied upon it. The vegetable and mineral kingdoms are closely allied to, and kindred sciences give it their strongest support. This is the lofty fabric, planned by the great Architect, founded upon a rock of adamant, which has resisted the storms of time, the floods of persecution and ridicule, the stormy gust of passion and envy, and remains not only unscathed, but whose fair proportions are daily more colossal and finished.' Its reputation is now to be entrusted to your keeping. I charge you, preserve untarnished its honor. Regard those of your profession, by whom you are surrounded, not as rivals, but as colleagues. Observe scrupulously, in your intercourse with your professional brethren, the code of ethics of the American Medical Association.

"I need not urge upon a class of such honorable and intelligent young gentlemen that you should resort to no unprofessional means to gain success. Shun the charlatan or mountebank with his disgraceful and murderous practices as you would a pestilence or plague, whose atmosphere is death. While the latter can only destroy your life, the former breathes a withering sirocco which will blast your reputation as well.

Do not underbid for patronage, thereby degrading your profession, stultifying yourselves and advertising your own consciousness of inferiority. It is weakness and imbecility that vacillates, always; conscious power never. Then, 'with hearts filled with enthusiasm for your profession, cultivate virtuous ambition with all its golden principles.' Let truth, honor, energy and fidelity be your motto, and success awaits you.

"But, gentlemen, time moves on, and the hour has arrived when we must utter that sad, sad word, farewell! No more is the light of your bright, happy faces to greet us with cordial welcome to the halls of science.

"Upon the occasion of the death of Daniel Webster, a plain, honest old neighbor of his, in one sentence, uttered the sublimest eulogy ever pronounced upon his great character, and it was this: 'Daniel Webster, the world will be lonesome without you.' Gentlemen, we shall be lonesome without you.

"Already does the restless locomotive, which is to bear you to your homes, steam upon its rumbling track, impatient for its start, and we must not be selfish, but bid you go. Go to the welcome of those bright eyes, which are to grow the brighter at your coming, make glad the fond hearts of your aged parents, your pure, beautiful, lovely and loving sisters, to say nothing

of the shy sweetheart, to whose modest cheek may steal the timid blush. And to those of you who are blessed with them, go, and again let your presence make happy your dear wives and little ones.

Yes, God bless the babies! Mark the man who does not love babies; there is something wrong in his make-up. I know no place congenial to such a character. The earth is not, for it is dotted all over with the little buds; Heaven is not, for Christ himself has informed us that of such is the Kindom of Heaven, and that we cannot enter there until we become as one of them. As there is but one other locality left, we will press the search for his congeniality no further.

"Then, gentlemen, go to the blessings of your homes and loved ones, and bless them in return; and permit me to assure you, upon the part of the faculty, that you carry with you our best wishes and sincere prayers for your future success, prosperity and happiness. God bless you! Farewell!"

An accurate estimate of the character of Dr. Menees can, perhaps, be better formed from a study of his splendid steel-engraved portrait that illustrates this sketch, than from any words at the command of his biographer. It is the picture of a southerner, of English and Scotch-Irish descent. The chin, lips and nose indicate coinage of the Roman order; the eyes, fixedness of purpose; the projecting eyebrows, quickness of perception; the lofty forehead, a comprehensive mind and moral dignity. The entire facial expression is that of will-power and self-assertion. Withal, it is the face of a much-enduring man with faith in the final result.

JUDGE M. L. HALL.

KNOXVILLE.

HERE is a gentleman who is truly a Tennessean. Born in Knox county, of this State, August 16, 1814, he has never lived outside of that county. Raised a farmer's boy, trained to such work early by an industrious father, he sometimes says he "knows all about it." When a boy he went to the common schools of the county, and there obtained all the education he has ever received. Always fond of reading, he was in the habit of borrowing books wherever he could find them, and of reading everything that came within his reach. The books he most liked were those which told of the discovery of America, the Indian wars, the Revolutionary war, and whatever pertained to the history of the United States. This class of studies he is still partial to, and there are few men so familiar with ancient and modern history of all countries. He has also

always been exceedingly fond of standard poetry, particularly blank verse, e. g., Milton, Pollock, Thompson and Prentice. In boyhood, he was uniformly obedient to his parents, lively, loved to fish and hunt, and became a crack marksman at rifle shooting. He was never guilty of excesses of any kind, unless it was fox hunting, coon hunting, and the like, at night, The result was his physical constitution has always been hardy and his health good.

At the age of twenty-two, he married, settled on his father's farm, studied law at home under the intruction, first of his brother-in-law, Judge Robert M. Anderson, and next under Judge Samuel R. Rodgers, afterward chancellor; was licensed by Judge Scott and Chancellor Thomas L. Williams, in January, 1841; was admitted to the bar at Maryville the same month, and at Knoxville, in February of the same year. He, however, still depended on his farm labor for support, as his practice was limited. In 1852, he was elected clerk of the circuit court, at Knoxville, and held that office till the war came on. In the spring of 1864, he was reelected without opposition, but never qualified, and in April, 1864, he was appointed, by Judge Connally F. Trigg, clerk of the circuit and district court of the United States, for the eastern district of Tennessee, and held that office until August, 1870, when he resigned and stood for the office he now holds, judge of the criminal court of Knox county, a position which he has filled by successive re-elections now fifteen years, the present term expiring in September, 1886.

It will thus be seen that his mind has been occupied thirty-four years with the public business, and that he has won and retained the confidence of the people of his native county. There are only a few men whose biographies appear in this volume that are representatives of the counties where they were born. It is a pet theory of the editor that men should grow up identified with the interests and people of their native localities, as the surest means of forming a high moral character, leading successful business lives, and of being at once happy and useful, and it is with unwonted pleasure that he cites the life and character of Judge Hall as illustrating this theory.

In May, 1864, Judge Trigg appointed him commissioner of the circuit court of the United States, for the Eastern district of Tennessee, and he resigned that office, with his clerkship, in August, 1870.

Judge Hall was raised a Democrat, and was "a Jackson boy." In 1836, however, he voted for Hugh L. White for president, and after that was a Whig till the war came up, since when he has been, as he is now, an unflinching and uncompromising Republican, but has uniformly declined the solicitations of his friends to go into politics beyond doing his duty as a citizen. He belongs to no secret society, and in religion is a Swedenborgian, or New Churchman.

In 1867, he was appointed by Gov. Brownlow State director of the Knoxville and Kentucky railroad, and filled that position one year, but resigned, not approving of the methods of the directory with whom he was associated.

Judge Hall married, in the Second district of Knox county, Tennessee, February 4, 1836, a neighbor girl, Miss Sarah Adaline McCampbell, who was born February 23, 1809, daughter of John McCampbell, who came from Kentucky to Knox county in 1820, a farmer, blacksmith and surveyor, an elder in the Presbyterian church, and of Scotch-Irish stock. Thomas and Andrew McCampbell, of Nashville, were of the same family. Mrs. Hall's mother, Martha Bennett, came from Virginia with her husband to Kentucky, and from there, in 1820, moved to Knox county, Tennessee. The mother, nee Miss McCamp-

bell, died in 1837, and the father, John McCampbell, died in 1853, leaving nine children, namely: Flora, wife of Judge William E. Anderson, formerly of the Supreme court of Tennessee; Catharine, wife of Robert M. Anderson, brother of Judge William E. Anderson—brothers marrying sisters; Elizabeth, died in Livingston, Sumter county, Alabama, wife of James Hare, a lawyer and a Pennsylvanian; Jane, married a cousin, John McCampbell, and both died in Knox county; Mary, died wife of Henry T. Mitchell; Ellen, died at Nashville, unmarried; Sarah Adaline (Mrs. Hall); Benjamin B., a farmer; John M., a farmer. These are all dead, except Mrs. Hall.

Mrs. Hall was educated in the common schools of Kentucky and Tennessee. Like her husband, she has been a reader of everything she can get her hands upon; is a member of the Presbyterian church, but a full believer of the doctrine of the New church, Swedenborgian. She is a lady of determined character, kind and charitable to worthy distressed persons. During the war she was outspoken for the Union cause, but was alike swift to relieve sick, wounded or distressed Confederate or Federal soldiers. Her husband has often consulted her on legal questions, as to how he should decide a case, first submitting to her the facts and asking her opinion as to the right or wrong of the case, on the principle that what a woman knows she knows quick, as by intuition. During the war, Judge Hall remained at Knoxville, with his family, speaking freely his opinions, but was never very seriously molested, though sometimes annoyed with threats held in terror over him. He and his brave wife were determined to live and die at their own home.

By his marriage with Miss McCampbell, Judge Hall has had eleven children, only three of whom are living. Three died in infancy, Ellen, Samuel and Nancy. Three sons, William, John and Robert, when grown, went to Kentucky and joined the Federal army. At the close of the war, William was killed at Knoxville. John first joined the army in Kentucky, was taken sick and captured at Cumberland Gap, but was afterwards with the army in Kentucky and Ohio. He finally enlisted in the United States navy, as mate on the "Narcissus," and perished, January 4, 1866, with all on board, the ship being lost in a storm. John and William were both in the battle of Stones River. In that battle William was wounded, and was lame till his death, in September, 1865. John took part in all the fights with Admiral Farragut, at Mobile, New Orleans, and other points. Robert joined the army at eighteen, took cold from exposure, and finally died of consumption, in November, 1869. William married, in 1864, a Kentucky lady, named Susan Jones, of Louisville. Judge Hall's daughter Martha, twin child with William, married Rev. C. L. Bowling, a Baptist preacher, of Campbell county. She died in 1871, at the age of thirty-two years, leaving an infant that died two weeks after her death. Another of Judge Hall's daughters, Frances, died in 1875, wife of A. Tindell, of Knox county. The children living are: Helen, Evelyn and Mary F., young ladies, still under the paternal roof, educated at Knoxville, and are of the New church faith.

The Halls are of English descent. The grandfather of Judge Hall, Thomas Hall, was a native of Orange county, North Carolina, married Nancy Hay, of that State; was a soldier in the Revolutionary war, was taken prisoner and confined for six months in Charleston, South Carolina, a circumstance he could never mention without his anger rising up at the recollection of the cruel and beastly treatment the king's soldiers heaped upon him. He settled in Knox county just before Tennessee was admitted into the Union. He left ten children, nine sons and one daughter, all of whom lived to be old, the youngest dying at seventy years of age. Their descendants are nearly all farmers. This family came to Knox county when it was a wilderness, which they helped to subdue. They have never been a litigious people, have been good neighbors, and made their living by hard licks. Some of them have been justices of the peace, and a very few merchants.

Judge Hall's father, William Hall, was born in Orange county, North Carolina, in 1788; came with his father's family to Knox county about 1796, had a moderate education, lived a farmer's life, was prosperous, lived well, and never held an office, except that of school commissioner. He belonged to no church, was a Jackson man, but after the Hugh L. White split-off, was a Whig and Union man. He died in March, 1868.

Judge Hall's mother, nee Nancy Nelson, was born in Rockbridge county, Virginia, in 1797, daughter of Elijah Nelson. She came with her father to Knox county about the year 1800. She married in Knox county, in 1813, was a constant reader, and a kind, obliging, industrious woman. She died in 1837, leaving eight children: Major Leroy Hall, subject of this sketch; Joyce Lawson Hall, who married a distant relative, Pulaski Hall, of Knox county; Fanny, now wife of John C. Mynatt, of Knox county, and has four children living, Oliver, John, Flavius and Clack; Elijah Thomas Hall, a lawyer of Knoxville, formerly judge of the Knox county circuit court; Parmelia, who died the wife of Alfred Mitchell; Martha Jane is the wife of J. L. Brown, of Knox county, and has one child, Pink Lawson; Louisa, who died the wife of Joseph R. Dew, leaving two children, Willie and Martha; William Hall, a merchant at Jacksborough, Campbell county, Tennessee.

The first principle taught Judge Hall by his parents, was to be honest, and to correct any mistake made in his favor. He has been true to friends, studious, industrious, always busy, always engaged at something useful, at the same time adhering to principle, but not opposing the holders of errors on personal grounds. He is a strong advocate of religious principles, without which he believes a people must soon go to destruction; takes a deep interest in the welfare of his country, but avoids the scrambles of politics. When he has anything to do, he does it without putting it off; avoids debt, does not owe a cent, and never sued but one man for a fee. As a judge, he looks at things in a common sense way, his main reliance being on the natural right and wrong between parties, but yields to statutes and authorities, when they are clearly applicable. Plain, common, good sense, he maintains, with reason, when applied to the facts, will reach the law of a case, ninety-nine times in a hundred.

HON. JO. C. STARK.

SPRINGFIELD.

JUDGE JO. C. STARK, of Springfield, Robertson county, one of the best and most favorably known jurists in the State, was born in Sumner county, Tennessee, December 29, 1817, and there reared and educated, being raised as a farmer. He taught school some eighteen months, in Sumner county, to improve himself, and at the same time to make money enough to educate himself for the legal profession, which calling he determined upon when a mere youth of seventeen. He read law under Maj. John J. White, at Gallatin, in 1840–41, and went to Springfield, in July, 1841, where he began practice, having been licensed at Gallatin in that year by Chancellor Bramlett and Judge Thomas Maney. Being of a studious nature, and taking to his books with alacrity and assiduity, he did not mix much with the public, hence his growth in practice was rather slow at first, but steadily increased until within a period of three years it had grown quite lucrative. From 1844 to 1851, under the appointment of Chancellor Terry H. Cahal, he was clerk and master of the chancery court at Springfield. In 1851, he purchased a farm of some eight hundred acres, near Springfield, stocked it, and ran it for a while, and then sold it for twelve thousand dollars. In 1851-52, he was elected

State senator from Robertson and Montgomery counties, and on his return from service in the Legislature, the chancellor, John S. Brien, again tendered him the clerk and mastership, which he declined, as it interfered too much with his practice. In 1858–59, in connection with E. A. Williams, he built eleven miles of the Edgefield and Kentucky railroad. He was, for a short time, a director of the company, and for many years, before and after the war, an attorney for the road. In 1859, he and Mr. Williams built the large flouring mills at Springfield. In 1860–61, having bought Williams out, he ran the flouring mills, to which he attached a saw mill, and then sold them, in 1864. Since the war, he practiced law until elected judge, also farming to some extent, which latter occupation he still keeps up. In 1878, he was elected, for a term of eight years, circuit judge of the Tenth judicial circuit, comprising the counties of Sumner. Robertson, Montgomery, Stewart, Houston, Humphreys, Dickson and Cheatham. This position he now holds, his term expiring September 1, 1886.

Judge Stark was originally a Henry Clay Whig, and so remains, in principles, to this day, though in the present formation and attitude of political parties, has been impelled to go with the Democracy, and has so voted since the close of the late war. In 1860, he was a delegate from his congressional district to the national Whig convention, at Baltimore, which nominated Bell and Everett. While in the State senate, he was chairman of the committee on common schools and education. He has three times canvassed his district for congress, subject to the nominating convention, but was defeated.

In 1842, Judge Stark became a Mason, at Springfield, in Western Star Lodge, No. 9. He has taken the Chapter, Council and Commandery degrees, and has served as Master, King, Priest and Scribe. He has occasionally delivered Masonic public addresses, but on one occasion an old negress, listening to him, and mistaking him for a preacher, commenced shouting, an incident which made Judge Stark rather sensitive on that subject, and he has not delivered many Masonic addresses since. Judge Stark belongs to no church, though a believer in the Christian religion, and is a contributor to the support of charitable enterprises. Owning three thousand acres of land at the Greenbrier station, on the St. Louis and Southeastern railroad, he laid off on it town lots, and donated lots for church purposes, to both white and colored, from a desire to improve the human race, and from his respect for the Christian religion.

Judge Stark married, in Fayette county, Tennessee, in April, 1847, Miss Lamiza A. Baird, daughter of Capt. Charles Baird, a native of North Carolina, son of a farmer, Thomas Baird, of Robertson county, originally from North Carolina. Her mother, Nancy Robards, daughter of Rev. William Robards, of Williamson county, died in Fayette county, leaving five children, two of

whom, Benjamin F. and W. L. Baird, are now physicians, in Hardeman county. Mrs. Stark's sister, Emma H., is the wife of L. T. Cobbs, a lawyer, at Springfield. Mrs. Stark graduated from the female college at Somerville, is the "literary department" of the Judge's family, and is remarkable for her piety, her love of the Methodist church, of which she is a devout member, and for her kindness to the poor. By his marriage with Miss Baird, Judge Stark has six children living: (1). Charles B. Stark, now a lawyer, practicing at St. Louis, and ranks exceptionally high in his profession. (2). Jo. C. Stark, jr., is a merchant, at Laredo, Texas. (3). John Lee Stark, is practicing law at Springfield. (4). Robert Lee Stark. (5). Felix J. Stark. (6). Annie Stark, now in school, and admirably proficient in music and literature. Three of Judge Stark's children died in early childhood.

The Stark family is of Scotch origin, the most noted of whom, in early times, was Gen. John Stark, made famous by the battle of Bennington, and his saying to his soldiers, "Do you see those red-coats yonder? They have to be taken or Molly Stark is a widow!" (See Bancroft's History of the United States). Judge Stark's grandfather, John Stark, was a native of Virginia, where he married, and afterward emigrated to Sumner county, Tennessee, and engaged in farming and school-teaching. He helped to build the first Baptist church on Drake's creek, in Sumner county. Judge Stark's father, also John Stark, was born in Virginia, came with his father to Tennessee, lived in Sumner county all his life, a farmer, and died in 1862, at the age of seventy-five, leaving a reputation for being conscientious in all his dealings with men, a principle which he took pains to inculcate in the mind of his son, the subject of this sketch. Judge Stark's mother, Margaret Stark, who died at his house, at the age of eighty-four, was a daughter of John Primm, a Virginian by birth, who moved to Illinois, not far from St. Louis. She left five children living, of ten: Jo. C., Ann (wife of Enoch Cunningham, of Davidson county), Mary (wife of Alexander Cartwright, of Nashville), John P., living near Salem, Illinois, and Catharine, who died the wife of Benjamin Reives.

From early life, Judge Stark has never dissipated, and has been remarkably free from the vices on which, as upon sunken reefs, many lives and characters and fortunes are wrecked. He has always impressed upon his boys the importance of good character and habits of industry, and to his great gratification, they are following both his precept and example. As a lawyer, he has never advised a man to take an appeal, a thing very unusual in the history of a lawyer. He has never abused witnesses, to gain a law suit by that process, and he has long borne the name of an honest lawyer. These particulars serve to throw light upon his character, and evince that his is the highest type of the judicial mind, logical and impartial. On the bench, he is an early, late and laborious worker, and has great partiality for the young men of the profession, encouraging and aiding them in their pleadings and practice. At his election to the judgeship, his county of Robertson cast three thousand five hundred votes, and there were only two hundred and fifty cast against him, and they on account of relationship to a competitor, a fact that indicates his high character where he is best known. He stands tall, erect, and dignified as a Presbyterian divine or a West Point cadet, has an intellectual face, and eyes that seem to be looking inward, as if weighing, considering and balancing the facts, the law and the arguments, *pro* and *con*, to ascertain just what the right and justice of the case is. His appearance is that of a modest and gentle-natured man, loyal to logic and utterly incapable of being flattered or terrified from laying down or following out his own convictions of honor, truth and duty.

PROF. VAN S. LINDSLEY, M. D.

NASHVILLE.

PROF. VAN SINDEREN LINDSLEY fills the chair of opthalmology and otology in the combined medical departments of Nashville and Vanderbilt Universities. As a skillful surgeon and operator upon the eye, ear and throat, he is widely known. A large number of essays, addresses and lectures have been prepared by him and delivered before various scientific societies. He was again and again elected president of the Nashville Medical Society, and is an active member of the leading associations of his profession in the country.

From "Physicians and Surgeons of the United States," we find he is a member of the American Association for the Advancement of Science, is a member of the American Medical Association, and was a delegate to New York in 1880, and to New Orleans in 1885; was a delegate from the State Medical Society to the International Congress at Philadelphia, in 1876, is a member of the Public Health Association, and a member of the State Historical Society. Dr. Lindsley spent some time in Europe, visiting the hospitals and medical centers of the old world. He contributes largely to medical literature, his papers always attracting marked attention, and are widely noticed and copied. Papers on the "Reproduction of Bone" and " Orthopædic Surgery," and " Disease of Mastoid Region," have been read by him before the State Medical Society, besides, lectures on " Sound and Hearing practically Illustrated," The Eye as an Optical Instrument," etc.

Dr. Lindsley's practice comes from fourteen States, besides a large local practice. He has operated more than one hundred times for cataract alone. One of the most remarkable of these cases was that of a man born blind. He had consulted many surgeons and oculists who declined to operate. Dr. Lindsley thought differently, and his judgment was vindicated in the finding of perfect sight through his skillful operation. He was associated, as office partner, for years in general

practice with the late eminent physician, Dr. W. K. Bowling, whose confidence and friendship he prized. He was drawn very near to the hearts of the people of Nashville, as a skilled and faithful practitioner and a fearless worker throughout the terrible epidemics which have devastated Nashville since the war, giving his service as freely to the poor for their blessing as to the rich for their reward.

Dr. Lindsley was born at Greensborough, North Carolina, October 13, 1840. His father was Silas Condict Lindsley, native of New Jersey, and a distinguished graduate of Princeton College. His mother's maiden name was Amelia Spottiswood, of an honorable Pennsylvania family, a woman of great piety and noble Christian character. He was a nephew of Dr. Philip Lindsley, founder and president of Nashville University, and of the eminent physician, Dr. Harvey Lindsley, of Washington, D. C. The family is old in the history of England. The American branch descends from John Lindsley, one of the earliest English settlers of the New Haven colony, Connecticut, who came from London before 1640. Dr. Lindsley's ancestry shows an American record of eight generations, embracing a period of two hundred and forty years.

Primarily educated at Greensborough Institute, of which his father was principal, he was graduated A.M. at the University of Nashville, in 1861, and immediately commenced the study of medicine, and in 1863 received his diploma from its medical department, by whose faculty he was subsequently elected demonstrator of anatomy. After his return from Europe he was elected professor of surgical anatomy, which position he occupied until 1871, after which he filled successively the chairs of physiology and anatomy. In 1876, he was elected to the chair of opthalmology and otology. His profound knowledge of the human system, its mechanism and all its functions, combined with a fearless boldness in operating when required, and a rare delicacy of manipulation, led the faculty to unanimously entrust this highly scientific chair to him, though its youngest member. A few years have sufficed to make him known most favorably among scientist, and to render his reputation national.

Having for over twenty years met the combined medical classes of the Nashville and Vanderbilt Universities, Dr. Lindsley is personally known to several thousand students, and by this large clientage he is esteemed as a friend, and respected, admired and beloved as an instructor. He is justly appreciated as a learned medical educator, and, as a lecturer, he is especially gifted. While lecturing without notes, he is thorough and conscientious in preparation, logical and perspicuous in matter, emphatic and eloquent in delivery, bringing himself *en rapport* with the student, with the earnest desire to impart instruction. The writer was present at a brilliant lecture, practically illustrated, when the enthusiasm of the class of nearly three hundred students was unbounded. They cheered the Doctor to the echo. Magnanimity is a distinguishing trait of his character. In the controversies, in which official position or a sense of duty have compelled him to engage, he has ever been the champion of principles, harboring no ill will to his opponents, always feeling that they were actuated by expediency rather than personal motives.

Dr. Lindsley married Lucy, daughter of Col. J. George Harris, United States Navy, at Harvard-street church, Charlestown, Massachusetts, April 16, 1868. This has proven a most happy union. He has four children, one daughter, Joy Lindsley, aged sixteen, and three sons, Harris, aged fourteen, Van Sinderen, aged ten, and Joseph, eight years old. Mrs. Lindsley is called the most beautiful woman in Tennessee. While an art student at Boston, in her *premiere jeunesse*, her Grecian features were the admiration of artists in the studio building, and she was often importuned to lend her features for ideal portraiture, on canvass and in marble. This compliment was also paid her by a distinguished sculptor at Rome. She has a genuine taste for literature, and was the founder and first president of the Nashville Reading Club, the first literary club in this city, in 1872. The writer recalls many enjoyable literary reunions and charming amateur theatricals under the auspices of this club. It existed for several years, until it numbered more than a hundred members, and was finally dissolved into several smaller clubs. Her daughter, Joy, inherits her mother's beauty, and is already an artist of taste. Her crayon work from nature, received complimentary notice at the World's Exposition, at New Orleans, and her flower painting at the first Nashville art exhibition. Harris, the oldest son, is a bright lad, giving promise of noble manhood, and the little boys are charming children. Dr. Lindsley, assisted by his beloved wife, delights in gathering his friends, both in and out of the profession, about him in his elegant mansion, where they enjoy a refined, graceful hospitality.

Nearly six feet in height, with broad shoulders, his is a handsome *personnel*. He has a noble head, with oval contour of feature, a nose indicative of great force of character, blue-gray eyes, light brown hair and moustache, fair complexion, and the high-bred manner which stamps the gentleman, added to bright humor and the ever ready passing jest.

He united with the Presbyterian church at an early age, and is a true adherent to the doctrines of the communion to which he—as were his fathers before him—is ardently attached. He is a public-spirited citizen, aiding in all worthy public enterprises, and is the dispenser of liberal charity, contributing to public and private need with a large-hearted generosity.

———

While this work has been going through the press, Dr. Lindsley has passed away, dying at his residence, No. 50 South Spruce street, Nashville, on Sunday, November 15th, 1885. This announcement grieved the entire community of Nashville, and a large circle of friends, extending over many States. For twenty-five years he had lived in their midst, and his name and fame were known to all. His life has been one of activity and constant usefulness, and peculiarly identified with public interests. To show the great estimation in which he was held by his church, his associates in the medical faculty, his professional brethren, and, indeed, the whole community of citizens, the editor deems it unnecessary to do more than compile from the columns of the public newspapers the many warm tributes of respect which the sad occasion of his death called forth. Coming as they do from those who knew him best and appreciated him so highly, they constitute a memorial of his worth and virtue which his bereaved family and stricken friends can contemplate with feelings of a just and pardonable pride.

The funeral of Dr. Van S. Lindsley was preached in the First Presbyterian church at Nashville, by Rev. Jere Witherspoon. Every seat in the church was occupied by friends of the deceased, there being a full attendance of the medical and dental students of Vanderbilt University, who had come to pay their last respects to their dead teacher and friend. The coffin was covered with beautiful and appropriate floral offerings. The text was from Psalms cxvi., 15 : " Precious in the sight of the Lord is the death of His saints." Several beautiful hymns were rendered during the services. The remains were escorted to the grave by a large number of friends. The pall-bearers were Drs. T. L. Maddin, John H. Callender, William L. Nichol, James M. Safford, Thomas Menees, T. A. Atchison, Charles S. Briggs and O. H. Menees. The burial was at Mount Olivet cemetery.

There was a good attendance of the physicians of the city at the First Presbyterian church, to take action regarding the death of Dr. Van S. Lindsley. The following were present: Drs. Thomas Menees, W. P. Jones, J. R. Harwell, W. W. Corbitt, C. L. Eves, R. Douglas, W. J. McMurray, J. B. W. Nowlin, J. F. Grant, N. D. Richardson, J. L. Watkins, J. W. Maddin, sr., W. A. Atchison, G. S. Allen, J. G. Sinclair, R. O. Tucker, C. W. Patterson, D. J. Roberts, M. H. Bonner, James B. Stephens, C. C. Fite, R. G. Rothrock, John B. Stephens, Ambrose Morrison, R. Cheatham, W. D. Haggard, J. D. Wallis, W. S. Vertrees, E. Stephens and O. H. Menees. Dr. Thomas Menees was chosen chairman and Dr. J. L. Watkins secretary. In accepting the position of chairman, Dr. Menees made an eloquent speech, which reflected, not only the high esteem which the speaker entertained for the deceased, but the high regard of the profession for him. A committee, to which Dr. Menees was added on motion, composed of Dr. J. F. Grant, chairman, Drs. W. P. Jones, W. C. Cook, J. W. Maddin, sr., W. A. Atchison and C. C. Fite, was appointed to draft suitable resolutions. While the committee were preparing their report, remarks concerning the life and character of Dr. Lindsley were made by Drs. James B. Stephens, W. J. McMurray and Charles L. Eves, who were followed by Drs. W. P. Jones, W. C. Cook, J. W. Maddin, sr., J. R. Harwell, D. J. Roberts and J. D. Wallis. It was then moved and carried that the physicians of the city assemble at the gentlemen's parlor of the Maxwell House at 10 o'clock, whence they would proceed in a body to the late residence, where the funeral services were to be held.

The committttee presented the following resolutions, which were adopted:

" Resolved, that in the death of Dr. Lindsley, the medical profession loses a devoted, intelligent, painstaking and accomplished physician, an ornament alike to society and to the profession. To the luster of an honorable and proficient physician, he added the still more enduring virtues of an exemplary moral and Christian character. A man well endowed by nature, blessed by education, possessed of large attainments, ambitious in his vocation, fortunate in social relations, discharging with full and liberal hands the good deeds of a noble profession, which he pursued with a singleness of heart and scrupulous professional honor, and which had brought him many trophies of victory from the contests of life—we lament that all these he and his family can no longer enjoy, and that we too must surrender our friend and brother to the cold embrace of death. For consolation we commend the bereaved family to God and the divine promise, ' He that believeth on Me, though he were dead, yet shall he live; and whosover liveth and believeth on Me shall never die.'

" Resolved, that in token of our high appreciation of his excellencies as husband, father, citizen, Christian gentleman and doctor of medicine, we will meet together to attend his funeral.

" Resolved, that a copy of these resolutions be furnished the family; also to the city papers for publication.

J. F. GRANT, M.D., Chairman.
W. P. JONES, M.D.
THOMAS MENEES, M.D.
W. C. COOK, M.D.
W. A. ATCHISON, M.D.
C. C. FITE, M.D.
J. W. MADDIN, SR., M.D.
J. L. WATKINS, M.D., Secretary."

At a meeting of the faculties of literature and science, theology, law and pharmacy, held in the office of the chancellor at Vanderbilt University, the following resolutions were adopted:

" Whereas, it hath pleased God in his inscrutable wisdom to take from the university circle our honored colleague, Dr. Van S. Lindsley, a true-hearted, noble Christian gentleman, a ripe scholar, earnest in his profession, who had prepared himself by study and travel for great usefulness in his day and generation, and who seemed to have a long career of prosperity and brilliancy before him:

" Resolved, that we, the academical, biblical, law and pharmaceutical faculties of Vanderbilt University, in joint session assembled, do hereby make expression of our deep regret for this great loss to the university, and of profound sorrow and sympathy with his stricken family, his colleagues and many friends, in this sad bereavement.

" Resolved, that we adjourn all exercises in the university to-morrow in honor of his memory, in order that the faculties and students may attend his funeral; that copies of these resolutions be tendered his bereaved family and to the city papers for publication.

L. C. GARLAND, Chancellor.
WILS. WILLIAMS, Secretary."

The faculty of the medical department of the University of Nashville and Vanderbilt University, and the medical class in attendance, adopted the following memorial in respect to the distinguished and lamented deceased:

"Prof. Lindsley was a native of Greensborough, North Carolina, and was in the forty-sixth year of his age. He came to this city before he arrived at manhood, and has continuously resided here since. Sprung from a family many of whose members were devoted to the pursuits of science and literature—the most eminent of whom was Philip Lindsley, for long years the president the University of Nashville—his labors were given to the science of medicine. He received his degree from the medical department of that institution in 1862. When its exercises were resumed at the close of the civil war, he was made demonstrator of anatomy in his alma mater, and in 1868 was advanced to a professorship. He has filled several important chairs acceptably to his colleagues and the classes which have assembled in its halls, and at the time of his death was professor of diseases of the eye, ear and throat. For a number of years he had practiced that specialty, and had achieved a high reputation for diagnostic and operative skill.

"In September last, while on a visit of recreation to the eastern cities, he was stricken with a painful illness, and was unable to meet the class now in session at the institution, and at length, in the morning of life, comparatively, he succumbed to its ravages. The numerous alumni of the medical department of the University of Nashville and Vanderbilt University, who have gone forth during the long period of his professional connection therewith, will hear the announcement with deep regret, and hold him in appreciative remembrance as a faithful and capable instructor, and an urbane and accomplished gentleman.

"His associates in the faculty, while bearing testimony to the estimable qualities of his character, his abilities as a teacher, his correct and dignified deportment in that relation, and to the just distinction his pen and tongue had acquired for him as a devotee of medical science, and in recording their sense of the loss the institution has incurred in his death, would tender to his bereaved family their condolence in the great grief which overwhelms them in the removal of a beloved husband and father, and in respect to his memory adopt the following resolutions:

"Resolved, that the exercises of the medical department of the University of Nashville and Vanderbilt University be suspended until the day after the funeral services of Prof. Van S. Lindsley, and that the faculty and members of the class attend in a body at their performance; that the lecture desk be draped and the faculty and class wear mourning on the occasion, and that a copy of this minute be transmitted to the family of the deceased and entered on the records of the faculty.

JOHN H. CALLENDER, M.D.
THOMAS MENEES, M.D.
T. A. ATCHISON, M.D.
AMBROSE MORRISON, M.D.
W. G. EWING, M.D.
J. W. GRACE, of Arkansas.
R. L. VAUGHT, of West Virginia.
J. G. FRIERSON, of Alabama.
J. S. PALRIE, of Kentucky.
NOLAN STEWART, of Mississippi.
J. H. WAY, of North Carolina.
IRA BOWMAN, of Georgia.
W. G. NOBLE, of Texas.
W. W. THOMPSON, of Tennessee.
G. J. GILL, of Virginia.
S. P. BARKER, of Missouri.
D. G. LASS, of Iowa.

The faculty of the Vanderbilt dental department met to take suitable action with regard to the death of Prof. Lindsley. It was decided to suspend the exercises for

the day. Drs. D. R. Stubblefield and R. R. Freeman, the committee appointed to draft resolutions, reported the following, which was received and adopted: "Whereas, inscrutable Providence has taken away Prof. Van S. Lindsley, of the medical department, this department tenders its sympathy for the loss of such high moral and intellectual worth, also heartfelt condolence is offered the bereaved family upon whom the irreparable blow has fallen."

At a called meeting of the faculty of the medical and dental departments of the University of Tennessee, to take action in regard to the death of Van S. Lindsley, M. D., professor of diseases of the eye and ear in the medical department of the University of Nashville and Vanderbilt University, the president, W. P. Jones, M. D., appointed a committee to draw up suitable resolutions, consisting of Drs. Deering J. Roberts, J. Bunyan Stephens and Paul F. Eve, who submitted the following, which were unanimously adopted: "Whereas, it has pleased the infinite wisdom of an all-wise Providence to call from the scenes of his earthly labors our friend and professional brother, Prof. Van Sinderen Lindsley, M. D.; to remove from our midst, we may hope, to the full enjoyment of a blissful eternity, one who, by strict probity, integrity of character, and all that makes up a true Christian gentleman, and has well earned and justly merited the glorious award of 'Well done, thou good and faithful servant;' therefore, be it

"Resolved, that in the death of Prof. Lindsley we sincerely mourn the loss of one whose medical skill, whose professional attainments, gentle, kind and courteous manners, and high sense of professional honor, have justly won our sincere admiration and esteem.

"Resolved, that, regarding him in his life as an accomplished Christian gentleman, refined, modest and courageous, a skillful physician, endowed with a logical, earnest and penetrating mind, we heartily commend his example as one well calculated to advance the progress and uphold the honor of a most noble science.

"Resolved, that we tender to his bereaved family and relatives, to his colleagues, and to the students of his college, our most sincere sympathies in their great loss.

"Resolved, that our faculty attend his funeral in a body, suspending the regular exercises in our institution for that purpose, and that a copy of these resolutions be published in the daily newspapers and medical journals of this city.

W. D. HAGGARD, M. D.,
Secretary of the Faculty.

At a called meeting of the Tennessee Historical Society, there were present the Hon. John M. Lea, Judge James Whitworth, Col. E. W. Cole, Rev. M. M. Moore, Col. A. S. Colyar, Dr. W. J. McMurray, J. A. Cartwright, Rev. Dr. W. C. Gray, Capt. Thomas H. Paine, Dr. N. D. Richardson, Col. W. D. Gale, Gen. G. P. Thruston, Judge Pitkin C. Wright, Rabbi J. S. Goldammer, W. A. Goodwyn, Capt. William Stockell, Rev.

Dr. C. D. Elliott, Dr. C. C. Fite, A. G. Adams, Rev. Dr. Dodd, Anson Nelson and several others. The following paper was read and adopted, to-wit: "The Tennessee Historical Society has been exceptionally favored in escaping the loss of members by the hand of death. Very seldom has the twin brother of sleep gathered to himself any one from those we are accustomed to welcome at our social meetings. But suddenly he has extended his icy grasp and taken from our midst one who was near and dear to us all. Dr. Van S. Lindsley was one of those who, very often, was present, and always was interested in our meetings, and aided in the discussions which usually arose. And, although a quiet member among us, he was one whom we will sadly miss. He was always conservative, always thoughtful, always firm in his opinions, yet not insisting on their acceptance by others. We have taken counsel together more than once in his hospitable mansion, at regular meetings, and we have frequently enjoyed the luxury of his hearth and home. He exhibited at all times an earnest interest in the great work in which we are engaged. He was a true-hearted, noble Christian gentleman, a ripe scholar, devoted to the profession which he adorned, and in which he had promise of great usefulness; a friend, whose kindly, courteous greeting and genial, hearty hand-clasp will never fade from our minds. He was born in North Carolina, in 1840, the descendant of a long line of distinguished educators, physicians and divines, showing an untainted and ever useful and honored American ancestry for eight generations, and two hundred and fifty years, and of that line of ancestry he was a worthy and true representative. He was married, in 1868, to the only daughter of our esteemed personal associate, Col. Jeremiah George Harris, a retired officer of the United States navy. This union was a happy one, in every respect, and its severance brings great grief to the companion of his bosom and to their four bereaved children. He was truly a devoted husband and a tender, loving father. At the early age of ten years, our departed colleague gave his heart to Christ and united with the Presbyterian church. He was a genuine disciple, and always walked worthy of the profession he had made when a boy. He was, too, a true adherent of the doctrines of the church to which he, and his fathers before him, were so ardently attached. He died the death of the righteous. We, as a society, tender to his bereaved family and relatives our most earnest and heartfelt sympathy, and we set apart a page in our records to the memory of our loved and departed associate. His life's duty is done. His work is accomplished, and he waits to welcome us on the other side of the dark valley. May we all be as faithful in the discharge of every trust and duty as was the dear departed one."

The above, on motion of Rev. Mr. Moore, was ordered to be transmitted to the family of the deceased, and the city papers were requested to publish the same.

The learned and venerable Chancellor Garland, in illustrating the idea that no man should live unto himself, said to the graduating class of Vanderbilt University, on the occasion of Dr. Lindsley's death: "As an illustration of this truth, to what an illustrious example can I point you in our lately deceased colleague, Dr. Van S. Lindsley. He was every inch the physician, learned, skillful, successful, meeting all the requirements of his ever enlarging profession. These, however, were but a small part of the qualities that adorned his character and made him the idol of his home and the admiration of the circle in which he moved. As husband, father, neighbor, friend and citizen, as well as physician, he has left us a model for our imitation. And, most of all, does he deserve to be imitated in that early consecration of himself to Christ, which brought to his spirit tranquility in life and peace in death. His name does not appear upon those parchments which you are presently to receive, but it is engraved upon the tablets of our hearts, not thence to be effaced by the lapse of time."

In his charge to the graduating class of the medical department of the Vanderbilt University, Dr. Menees said: "That insatiate archer, who spares neither age, sex nor condition, has invaded our faculty, and stricken down, in the midst of his usefulness, one of its youngest members, Prof. Van S. Lindsley. He was young, cultured, and justly ambitious, an ornament alike to his profession, which he loved and cultivated, and to society, which he honored and adorned. His death was a public calamity, and the providence which ordered it to us inscrutable. His ways are past our finding out. Let us, in this sad bereavement, as in all things else, bow submissively to the divine will. I knew Prof. Lindsley long and well, and had much professional, as well as professional and social contact with him, and it affords me a mournful pleasure to bear testimony, to-night, to the fact that in his professional relations, he was one of the most scrupulously ethical and honorable gentlemen I ever knew. It is sad to see one already so distinguished and useful, so full of future promise, and with rapidly growing fame, cut down in the bloom of his manhood; but our loss is his eternal gain. Then we sorrow not as those who have no hope. Sleep on, Lindsley. 'Though thou art gone to the grave, but we will not deplore thee. He gave thee, He took thee, and soon will restore thee, where death hath no sting, since the Saviour hath died.'"

HON. NOBLE SMITHSON.

PULASKI.

NOBLE SMITHSON was born near Noblesville, Williamson county, Tennessee, December 7, 1841; resided in that county until January, 1853, when he moved with his parents to Lexington, Lauderdale county, Alabama. He resided there until 1865, when he moved to Pulaski, Giles county, Tennessee, where he has ever since resided.

His father was the Rev. John G. Smithson, of the Methodist Episcopal church, South, who was born near Danville, Pittsylvania county, Virginia, June 10, 1820, and immigrated with his parents to New Market, Jefferson county, Tennessee, about 1830, remaining there a few years, when the family came to Williamson county, Tennessee. He now resides on his farm, near Pulaski, Tennessee. He is distinguished for energy and industry, and is a first-class farmer, having been quite successful in that pursuit.

Noble Smithson's grandfather, on the paternal side, was Hezekiah Powell Smithson, who was born in Pittsylvania county, Virginia. He was a soldier in the war of 1812, and at one time sheriff of Pittsylvania county. He was the grandson of Capt. Powell, of the Revolutionary army. H. P. Smithson died at Lexington, Alabama, in 1870. Mr. Smithson's great-grandfather was Francis Smithson, born in Pittsylvania county, Virginia, and died in Maury county, Tennessee. Francis Smithson was descended from the Smithson family of Northumberland county, England. Mr. Smithson's paternal grandmother was Henrietta Carter, a member of the Carter family of East Tennessee.

Mr. Smithson's mother was Ann Vaughn Ladd; born in Williamson county, Tennessee, November 10, 1818. She was the daughter of Noble Ladd and Mary Burton; and her mother was the daughter of Peter Burton, an Irishman. Her parents were born in Rockingham and Stokes counties, North Carolina, and were married in that State. She is still living, in good health and spirits. Mr. Smithson is the oldest of fifteen children, all of whom are living except one.

The early life of Mr. Smithson was spent on the farm. His father being in humble circumstances, he labored to aid him in supporting and rearing the family. But from early childhood he evinced a strong desire for education and knowledge, and diligently applied himself to his books, reading more or less every day, and going to school whenever he could be spared out of the crop. In this way he acquired a good English education, including mathematics, but did not study the classics. When only nineteen years of age, he taught school in Alabama and Tennessee, in 1860–61. In 1865, he taught school again near Pulaski, and then read law in books borrowed from Pulaski lawyers. In December,

1866, he obtained license from Judges David Campbell and Hillary Ward, and at once began practice at Pulaski. In 1868–9, he was a State director in the Nashville and Decatur railroad. From 1870 to 1872, his brother, Fontaine Smithson, was associated with him in the practice of the law at Pulaski.

He was district attorney-general for the Eleventh circuit, composed of the counties of Williamson, Maury, Marshall, Giles, Lawrence, Lewis and Hickman, from November, 1867, to September, 1870. At this time the bar of that circuit was exceptionally strong, having among its members some of the ablest lawyers in the State. This office was, therefore, a splendid school for the young attorney-general. Since then he has, on several occasions, acted as special judge and chancellor, appointed by the governor and elected by the bar.

He was elected State senator, in the thirty-eighth General Assembly for the Fifteenth senatorial district, composed of the counties of Giles, Lawrence, Wayne and Lewis, November 6, 1872, for the years 1873 and 1874, and was chairman of the senate committee on judiciary. He was also chairman of a special joint committee to investigate the affairs of the Bank of Tennessee, which sat at Nashville, after the adjournment of the Legislature. He was an industrious and efficient member of the senate, his committee doing a large portion of the work of the session. He was one of the thirteen senators who voted for the public school law of 1873, under which the present system of popular education has grown so efficient and beneficial to the State. Of the measures introduced by him that became statute law, may be mentioned the act for the better enforcement of mechanics' liens, and another, allowing attorneys to appeal from judgments striking them from the roll for contempt of court.

He has been a member of Pulaski Lodge, No. 12, Independent Order of Odd Fellows, and of the Encampment, in which he held the chief offices. He is now a member of the Knights of Honor, American Legion of Honor, Ancient Order of United Workmen, Pulaski Lodge of Free Masons, and of Pulaski Commandery, No. 12, Knights Templar, having held the offices of Captain-General and Generalissimo in said Commandery. He is a member of the Tennessee Historical Society, and of the Bar Association of Tennessee.

In politics, he is independent. He was always opposed to slavery. Having read Wayland's Moral Philosophy, when a boy, he was thereby convinced that slavery was unjust and morally wrong; that it was impolitic and ruinous to the country. He has ever since held these views. He has always held that all citizens, rich and poor, great and small, should have equal rights before the law; that the legal rights of each and all should be precisely the same. He also advocates woman's right to vote, to hold property independently of their husbands, and to participate in the affairs of State, believing that the restrictions upon them and their subjection to the men are relics of barbarism. He believes in the utmost freedom of thought and action, in society, politics and religion, consistent with the rights of others. He was a delegate to the national Greenback convention which convened at Indianapolis, Indiana, in June, 1876, by which Peter Cooper was nominated for the Presidency, he putting Mr. Cooper in nomination before the convention. He was also a member of the national executive committee of that party during the canvass of 1876.

He was married in Giles county, Tennessee, April 2, 1865, to Miss Alice Patterson. Mrs. Smithson was educated in Giles county, is a member of the Methodist church, and is noted mainly for the domestic virtues. There have been born unto them six children, Anna Laura, a graduate of Martin Female College, Pulaski, Noble Smithson, jr., John, Tully, Guy and Alma.

He was a director in and the attorney for the National Bank of Pulaski, from 1878 to 1882. Financially, he is to-day in excellent circumstances, owns a beautiful farm of three hundred acres on Richland creek, three miles west of Pulaski, on the Pulaski and Vale mills turnpike, which is well stocked and in a high state of cultivation. He and his father, J. G. Smithson, own the Vale mills property, consisting of a merchant and custom grist mill, cotton factory, warehouse, store-house and other buildings, the mills and factory being operated by the water power of Richland creek. Said mills and factory are in active operation and doing a thriving business.

His motto has always been to merit success by energy, industry and close applicaion. He believes that fortune helps those who help themselves; that every one is, to a certain extent, the architect of his own fortune; that he who would succeed, must rely upon himself; he believes that few, if any, will aid another unless such aid will profit him who gives it, or gratify some of his passions or prejudices. He attempts to view human affairs as they are, not as they should be. He has a large practice in the local courts and in in the Supreme court of Tennessee, and is an attorney of the Supreme court of the United States. As a lawyer, he is chiefly distinguished for the labor and care bestowed upon his cases, and the thoroughness with which he prepares them.

BISHOP H. N. McTYEIRE.

NASHVILLE.

HOLLAND NIMMONS McTYEIRE was converted at the age of twelve, at Cokesbury school, South Carolina, in 1837, and since he put his hands to the plow has not looked back. He had a good induction, his parents, moreover, being love-feast and class-meeting Christians, whose overflowing hospitality made their home a stopping place for the preachers. All these influences had their effect on his character, and gave direction to his after life.

At the age of twenty he began to preach, the very year he felt called to the ministry. He has preached constantly ever since. He joined the Virginia conference November, 1845, was sent to Williamsburg, Virginia, and preached there until May, 1846. At that time the first general conference of the Methodist Episcopal church, South, was held in Petersburg, and that general conference elected Rev. Dr. T. O. Summers to be editor at Charleston, Dr. Summers at that time being pastor of the principal church at Mobile. Young McTyeire being at the conference to see the great men of the church, Bishop Andrews picked him up there and sent him to take Dr. Summers' place at Mobile. He reached Mobile July 1, everybody assuring him he would have the yellow fever. He was at once introduced to the quarterly conference, which he found in session, occupied in discussing the startling question of buying a lot in the new city cemetery for the purpose of burying preachers who might die of the fever. The lot was not bought in vain, for, in 1854, three preachers were buried in it who had died of the yellow fever. He preached there until the end of the year, and although he did not take the fever himself, the first man he was called on to bury had died of it. While in Mobile he made the acquaintance of the lady who became his wife, a cousin of the lady whom Commodore Cornelius Vanderbilt afterward married. This is one of the secret links of a chain of causes that ultimately gave origin to the great Vanderbilt University, located at Nashville.

His next station after Mobile was Demopolis, Alabama, in 1847; next at Columbus, Mississippi, in 1848. He was then transferred to New Orleans, where he spent ten consecutive years, first as pastor of Felicity Street church, which he built, and then, from 1851 to 1858, as editor of the New Orleans *Christian Advocate*, which he founded in 1851. In 1858, he was elected by the general conference to edit the Nashville *Christian Advocate*, a position which he filled until February

1862, when he left the city, on the fall of Fort Donelson, and did not return until February, 1867.

While within the lines of the Confederacy, in 1863, he took charge of the church at Montgomery, Alabama. In 1866, he went to the general conference at New Orleans, as a delegate from the Montgomery conference, and was there, in April, 1866, elected bishop, together with three others—Wightman, Marvin and Doggett. Since his election as bishop, he has presided in each of the thirty-seven conferences of the church.

Bishop McTyeire has been rather a builder up of the church, looking after its doctrine, discipline, pastoral visiting and general edification, than a revivalist. His most important contribution to the church was to codify its laws in a volume called "The Manual of the Discipline for the Direction of Church Courts and Conferences." He was the author of the resolution, which he introduced in 1866, for the admission of lay delegations, and lay delegates took their seats in the general conference in 1870, for the first time. That legislative act was a great crisis in the affairs of the church, and is now generally conceded to have resuscitated the church from its depression and almost collapsed condition after the war. The Northern Methodist church followed the example in 1868, and lay delegates took their seats in 1872, in the general conference of the northern church. The lay addition brings in and concentrates all the forces of the church. The result is that the southern church doubled its membership in fifteen years, and is the stronger on account of the measure.

In addition to his seven years' editorial experience in New Orleans, and three years in Nashville, Bishop McTyeire has led a busy literary life otherwise. In 1851, the Baptist convention of Alabama offered a prize of two hundred dollars for the best essay on the duties of Christian masters. He competed for the prize, his essay was accepted, and published under the title of "Duties of Christian Masters"—(300 pp., 16 mo.) In 1869, he wrote, at the request of the bishops of his church, his "Manual of the Discipline," (320 pp., 16 mo.) Since its publication appeals from quarterly and annual conferences have greatly diminished, the volume having given uniformity to the administration of church affairs. His next work, written in 1871, was "A Catechism of Bible History," (240 pp., 16 mo.); in 1874, "A Catechism on Church Government," (200 pp., 16 mo.) In 1884, he wrote his "History of Methodism," (octavo, 688 pp.) This is a history of Methodism from a southern point of view, not a history of southern Methodism. A recent writer in the Nashville *American* says of this remarkable work: "It enjoys the rare distinction of being the only history of the church by a southerner. Every page reveals the hand of a master word-builder and faithful historian. He discusses the great subject of the church's disruption, and its concomitant issues, in a spirit of utter impartiality, and with an argumentative power that carries conviction to

every unbiased mind. The work as a whole is justly esteemed a classic by the educated of all Christian sects into whose hands it has gone. The author and the communion he represents are signally honored in the fact that this history has won such high favor within a twelve-month."

In March, 1873, Commodore Cornelius Vanderbilt, of New York, made a donation of five hundred thousand dollars for founding Vanderbilt University at Nashville, making it a condition of the donation that Bishop McTyeire should be president of the board of trustees for life, with a veto power, assigning as a reason that he knew Bishop McTyeire and wanted him to be to the university what he himself was to the magnificent railway system known as the New York Central. He afterward added five hundred thousand dollars, and his son, William H. Vanderbilt, subsequently donated two hundred and fifty thousand dollars, making the entire donation one million two hundred and fifty thousand dollars. Bishop McTyeire expended five hundred thousand dollars of these funds for the grounds, buildings and apparatus of the institution. The grounds comprise seventy-five acres, beautifully situated, and have all the requirements for health, eligibility, etc. The various buildings are thirty in number. The institution has six departments and employs forty professors. Thus, with its munificent endowment, learned faculties and magnificent scheme of buildings, Vanderbilt University has become the greatest institution of learning in the South or Southwest, and equal to the famous old institions of the North and East.

Bishop McTyeire married, in Mobile, Alabama, November 9, 1847, Miss Amelia Townsend, a native of that city, born in 1827, daughter of Maj. John W. Townsend, founder and for many years editor of the Mobile *Register*, and postmaster at Mobile, under Presidents VanBuren and Polk. The Townsend family were formerly New Yorkers, and bought Oyster Bay, Long Island, from the Indians. Originally, they were Quakers of English descent. Mrs. McTyeire's maternal grandfather was Judge John F. Everett, a native of Georgia, and one of the first mayors of Mobile. He died at a good old age, but his mother survived him many years and died in southern Georgia, over one hundred years old. Mrs. McTyeire's mother was Jane Independence Everett. She died in Bishop McTyeire's house at Nashville, in 1876, at the age of sixty-six. Mrs. McTyeire's grandfather, Judge Everett, married three times. His second wife, a Miss Hand, was a first cousin of Commodore Vanderbilt. Mrs. McTyeire was educated in Mobile and in New York, and was in her youth reputed the most beautiful woman in Mobile; and though now fifty-seven, has not a grey hair, does not use spectacles, and is very active and vigorous. Her leading characteristic is fondness for domestic life, a keeper-at-home. She is not fond of general society, but cultivates a few friends, who are closely knit to her.

By his marriage with this lady, Bishop McTyeire has had eight children, two of whom died in infancy. The surviving are: (1). Mary Gayle McTyeire, born in 1848; educated at New Orleans and Nashville. (2). John Townsend McTyeire, born in 1850; graduated at Emory and Henry College; now in railroad business. (3). Walter Montgomery McTyeire, born in 1852; now in railroad business. (4). Amelia McTyeire, born in 1856; educated at Nashville; married Prof. J. J. Tigert, of the Vanderbilt University, and has three children, Mary, Holland and John. (5). Holland N. McTyeire, born in 1859; educated at Nashville; now in business in the Southern Methodist Publishing House, Nashville. (6). Janie McTyeire, born in 1862; graduated at Ward's seminary, Nashville; married, in 1882, Prof. W. M. Baskervill, of Vanderbilt University, and has one child, Amelia.

Bishop McTyeire was a Whig until the Whigs got lost, since which time he has been an eclectic Democrat. He belongs to no secret society, once assigning as a reason, " it took all his time to be a Methodist."

Bishop McTyeire was born in Barnwell district, South Carolina, July 28, 1824, and there grew up to the age of thirteen, when his father moved to the old Creek Nation, Russell county, Alabama, in 1838. There he went to school, worked on a farm, and trapped wild turkeys until 1840, when his father sent him to a manual labor school at Talbotton, Georgia, where he studied and worked two years. He then went to Randolph-Macon College, Virginia, and entered the sophomore class under President Landon C. Garland, now chancellor of the Vanderbilt University. In 1844, he graduated fourth in a class of twelve. After graduation he was elected to act as tutor of mathematics and ancient languages, and, after filling that position one year, joined the conference, as before stated.

McTyeire is a Scotch name. Nimmons is Irish. The Bishop's grandfather, John McTyeire, was born in the northern neck of Virginia, was a farmer, and married Lucy Shelton, of Virginia. The Bishop's father, John McTyeire, was called Capt. McTyeire, because he raised and drilled a company in 1832-3 in South Carolina, in the nullification cause, he being a Calhoun man. His politics and his religion are indicated in the fact that he had one son named John Calhoun and another named William Capers. He was a successful planter, and remarkable for decision and force of character. An instance is related of that decision which made him a leader of men : Once, while traveling through south Alabama, he stopped at a village where he was an entire stranger. During the night a fire broke out, the people were in confusion, and he stood there giving directions, nobody knowing who he was, then or afterward ; but he had an air of command about him, the people obeyed, and the fire was extinguished. He died at his home, in Russell county, Alabama, in 1860, aged sixty-seven years.

Bishop McTyeire's mother was Elizabeth Nimmons,

daughter of Andrew Nimmons, an Irishman, who came over in time to fight the battles of the Revolution. He was for many years the high sheriff of Barnwell district, South Carolina—loved his toddy, loved his country, and loved his children. He was a cotton raiser and a thrifty man. He had the best Irish qualities—was popular, energetic and hospitable. He died at the age seventy. His wife was Miss Jemima Montgomery, born on the Savannah river, of Irish descent. Her five sisters married influential citizens of that country—Cato, Furz, Provost, Noble and Hutto—all planters in the Savannah river bottoms. Bishop McTyeire's mother had a very full development of poetic feeling, was of tender sentiments, a great lover of her home and children and neighbors, and beloved by them all. She was exceptionally attentive to her sick servants and the aged and infirm among them. Her husband was an iron-willed man ; she was gentle. He was stern ; she was tender. Such were the pair that gave to the church one of its ablest and most useful bishops. She died in 1861, leaving four sons, Henry, Holland N. (subject of this sketch), John C. and William C.; and three daughters, Jane (Hurt), Elizabeth (Harris) and Emma (Harris)—two sisters marrying two cousins.

Two qualities, essential to a pastor, are, in equal proportions, blended in the character of Bishop McTyeire—one, the iron will inherited from his father ; the other, the tenderness derived from his mother. He is a gentle, manly man ; a thinker, prompt to decide and execute with force. It will interest young parents to know something of his boyhood. At a very tender age he got an impression at home that made him revolt against drunkenness, laziness, sabbath-breaking and vices generally. His father had a fine knack of holding up a bad case to make his children abhor a vagabond or a drunkard, and to admire an industrious, sober, truthful man. His father would cite these personal instances, not for subjects of gossip or scandal, but as warnings or examples. He would tell the sons how, by study, by labor, and by honor, certain poor boys had risen to be great men : would point out successful poor young men, who had struggled up from poverty to distinction. The father never allowed liquor in his house, and created in the son an abhorrence of that class of vices, and took pains to keep him under good moral and religious influences, especially in the matter of selecting schools for him—passing by four State universities to take him to Randolph-Macon, because he had learned that there his son's morals would be safer. At the age of twelve the boy joined the church. Parents who would learn how this man came to succeed in life must take into account that he had a good send-off at the hands of a systematic, laborious, and, as the result proves, far-seeing father, who had faith in Solomon's axiom, "Train up a child in the way he should go, and when he is old he will not depart from it."

There remains one other factor of his success, and

that is the rule the Bishop laid down for himself: To undertake, not what he thought he could do, or would like to do, but what he thought ought to be done. This often involved him in perplexities and troubles, and subjected him to the criticism of being wanting in prescience; but once committed to a work, he must pull through it, always finding it was nearer the shore he started for than the one he left.

JUDGE JOHN C. GAUT.

NASHVILLE.

THE subject of this biography was born in Jefferson county, Tennessee, on French Broad river, about seven miles below Dandridge, February 27, 1813. When the son was eight years old, his father moved to the Hiawassee district, and settled four miles southeast of Athens, Tennessee. There our subject was reared, working upon his father's farm until he was twenty-one, going to school very little. Upon reaching his majority, he hired out to get money to go to school. In 1833–34, he attended Forest Hill Academy, then under Charles P. Samuels; taught a school himself, in Monroe county, five months, and, at the request of his employers, continued the session three months longer. In April, 1835, he went to the Theological Seminary, at Maryville, presided over by the distinguished Dr. Isaac Anderson, and remained there one year. In April, 1836, he entered the East Tennessee College, at Knoxville (now the University of the State of Tennessee), but his funds having been exhausted by the fall of the same year, he left school, and again taught near his home, in McMinn county, until the spring of 1837, when he returned to college at Knoxville, and remained until the following October, leaving without graduating.

He commenced studying law, January 1, 1838, with Hon. Spencer Jarnigan, at Athens, Tennessee, and November 13, 1838, was admitted to the bar by Judges Charles F. Keith and Edward Scott. He practiced around the circuit till February 19, 1839, when he located at Cleveland, and practiced there until October, 1853, at which time he was elected, as a Whig, over his competitor, George W. Rowles, by the Tennessee Legislature, to the circuit judgeship of the Third (now Fourth) judicial circuit, comprising the counties of Bradley, Polk, McMinn, Meigs, Rhea, Bledsoe, Marion and Hamilton. In May, 1854, under the changed constitution, he was elected to the same position by over one thousand one hundred majority, having the same opponent. Again, in May, 1862, he was re-elected by the popular vote.

In April, 1865, he resigned his judgeship, moved to Nashville, and resumed his private practice, after having been on the bench nearly twelve years. During that long period he missed only one court, and that from the extreme illness of his daughter, Mary L., who afterwards sickened and died at Nashville, in June, 1865, aged twenty-four. From 1846, to 1854 (seven years and eight months), he was a director, in behalf of the State of Tennessee, in the East Tennessee and Georgia railroad company. Under this directory the road was built from Dalton, Georgia, to Knoxville. At a time when railroads were not very popular, he was their friend, joining with James Whitesides and others in advocating the granting of charters to them over the State. Though an old line Whig, when he came to Nashville, he opposed many of the measures of the Brownlow administration as being "too extreme," among which were the disfranchisement of ex-rebels and rebel sympathizers, and the enfranchisement of the negroes. This rendered him obnoxious to the then State government, causing him to be threatened with arrest by Gov. Brownlow for his published articles in opposition to these measures.

At Nashville, in 1867–68, Hon. Robert L Caruthers, ex-judge of the Supreme court of Tennessee, was associated with Judge Gaut in the practice of law. This partnership was dissolved by Judge Caruthers accepting a position in the Lebanon law school, in the latter part of 1868.

Judge Gaut became a Mason at Cleveland, in 1853, and has taken the Royal Arch degrees. In religion, he is a Cumberland Presbyterian. The Gauts are of Scotch and Irish descent, and blue-stocking Presbyterians.

Judge Gaut's great-grandfather died a soldier in the Revolutionary war. The grandfather, John Gaut, was bound out to learn the tanner's trade, in the State of Pennsylvania. Being pretty self-willed, and not liking his employer, he left him and went to Virginia, where he married a Miss Irwin. He moved to Tennessee and settled, first, in Washington county, and next, on the French Broad river.

Judge Gaut's father, James Gaut, was born in Washington county, Tennessee. He died, February 13, 1875, nearly ninety years old. He was a farmer, a strictly honest man, and did not like anybody that was not honest or refused to pay his debts. He was one of the commissioners to locate the county site and lay off the town of Athens.

Judge Gaut's mother, nee Miss Rosamond Irwin, was born in Washington county, near Jonesborough, and reared on Little river, in Blount county, Tennessee. She died in June, 1869, aged seventy-seven years, ten months and five days.

For morality, mildness, discreetness and propriety, and for the assiduity with which she inculcated principles of integrity and honor in her children, she was a model mother, and a woman of very excellent judgment.

Judge Gaut was the oldest of nine children, namely, John C., Mahala S., George W., Nancy, Mary, Jesse H., Minerva, James C. and Robert D. For a fuller history of the family, see sketch of Hon. Jesse H. Gaut elsewhere in this volume.

Judge Gaut was first married in McMinn county, September 26, 1839, to Miss Sarah Ann McReynolds, a grand-daughter of Isaac Lane, of that county, who was in the battle of King's Mountain. Her grandmother was a daughter of Major Russell, of Virginia. Mrs. Gaut was a member of the Cumberland Presbyterian church, a gentlewoman in all her ways, very affable and popular, and the possessor of the very first order of discretion and good sense. She died, June 9, 1873, of cholera, in Nashville, aged fifty-four. By this marriage were born seven children: (1). Mary L. Gaut, born July 11, 1840; graduated at Mary Sharp College, in 1860; died June 12, 1865. (2). John M. Gaut, born October 1, 1841; graduated from Rutgers' College, New Jersey, 1866, and is now a law partner with his father, He married, May 5, 1870, Miss Michel M. Harris, a very accomplished lady. She died in the fall of 1871. He married the second time, October 25, 1876, Miss Sallie Crutchfield, the only daughter of Thomas and Amanda Crutchfield, of Hamilton county, Tennessee. Thomas Crutchfield was a distinguished farmer and stock-raiser, near Chattanooga, and a prominent and leading man of his county. He died at the residence of his son-in-law, John M. Gaut, near Nashville, March 29, 1886. Mrs. Sallie C. Gaut is a graduate of Mary Sharp College. John M. Gaut has had four children, Thomas C., Sarah M., Amanda K., and Mary Ann. The oldest son, Thomas C., died of diphtheria, July 24, 1885. Mr. Gaut is an elder in the Cumberland Presbyterian church, and president of the publication board of that church. (3). Ann E. Gaut, born October 15, 1843, and graduated at Mary Sharp College, in June, 1861. She was married May 5, 1870, to Patrick H. Manlove, a Nashville merchant, and has had two children, Joseph E. and Horace C., the last named dying of diphtheria, March 30, 1886. Her husband is an elder in the Cumberland Presbyterian church, and is also a member of the publication board. (4). Hugh Lawson Gaut, born November 22, 1845, and died, May 28, 1854, of scarlet fever. (5). Albert Coleman Gaut, born August 23, 1851, and died, May 24, 1854, of scarlet fever. (6). An infant, unnamed. (7). Horace C. Gaut, born December 19, 1856, died of scarlet fever, July 17, 1863.

Judge Gaut married the second time, in Franklin, Tennessee, Mrs. Sallie A. Carter, who, at the age of

sixteen, in May, 1843, married Boyd M. Sims, a lawyer, and by him had two children: Annie A. Sims, who married, in 1875, John W. McFadden, who is now with the firm of Thompson & Kelly, merchants, in Nashville, and has one child, Sarah H., born January 5, 1879; Marienne H. Sims, who married, in 1871, R. N. Richardson, a lawyer, at Franklin, Tennessee, who lives on a farm, a portion of his wife's grandfather's old estate. Boyd M. Sims died, in 1848, and in May, 1853, his widow married Joseph W. Carter, a prominent lawyer and politician of Winchester, Tennessee, a Knight Templar Mason, a Democrat, who represented Franklin and Lincoln counties in the Tennessee State senate three consecutive terms. To Col. Carter were born two sons, William E., now in mercantile life at Nashville, and Joseph W., now a railroad officer; married Miss Katie R. French, and has one child, Joseph W., jr. Col. Carter died, July 16, 1856, from which time Mrs. Carter lived a widow till her marriage with Judge Gaut, in 1875. The present Mrs. Gaut is a cultivated lady, of · fine taste, great vivacity and beauty, a high sense of honor, liberal and charitable to a fault. She is a descendant of Revolutionary stock, was born in Franklin, Tennessee, daughter of Alexander Ewing, a large stock-farmer of wealth and prominence in Williamson county, Tennessee. Her grandfather, Alexander Ewing, a raiser of fine stock, was one of the pioneers of Davidson county, where he settled after his service in the Revolutionary war. He built and owned the first brick house in Davidson county. He married Miss Sarah Smith, also of a Virginia Revolutionary family, a sister of Mrs. R. R. Hightower, one of the first settlers of Williamson county. Mrs. Gaut's mother, Chloe Saunders, daughter of Herbert S. Saunders, was also of a Virginia family of Revolutionary fame. Mrs. Gaut's father died in 1835, and her mother, in 1839, leaving five children: Sallie Ann (Mrs. Gaut); Alexander C., who died at twenty years old; Herbert S., now a farmer, in Williamson county, on a part of the old homestead; Melvina, who died the wife of H. B. Titcomb, a druggist and capitalist at Columbia, Tennessee, leaving one child, Alexander Titcomb, now a farmer, near Columbia; William R., who married Miss Johnnie Brown, of Franklin, Tennessee, died of heart disease, 1880, at Franklin, leaving one child, William Wheless, born November 22, 1869, and who, with his mother, still resides in Franklin.

Mrs. Gaut's most marked trait of character is her living up to the Golden Rule, her abounding charity, and devotion to principle. She has been president of several benevolent societies in Williamson county, and is a pronounced prohibitionist. During the war she was truly Southern, and kind to soldiers on both sides, and after the war was one of the most prominent members and ruling spirits of the Ladies' Tennessee Memorial Association, which had for its object the care of maimed soldiers, and supplied artificial limbs to many of the disabled and impoverished heroes of the "lost cause."

Judge Gaut's success in life, and his eminence in the legal world, are due to industry, economy and integrity. He has made it a rule to live up to his contracts, to be punctual in his engagements, making his word his bond. He early learned that it was easier to say "no" than to say "yes," and pay security debts. He has always dealt with high and low, rich and poor, with strict honor. He never had a dollar given to him, and what he has and what he has earned, are the legitimate fruits of his own toil. As a judge, he was conscientious and impartial, and noted for hard work. These characteristics he preserves in private life, and no man in Tennessee stands higher for honesty of purpose and strict integrity.

WILLIAM PALMER JONES, M. D.

NASHVILLE.

THIS gentleman, distinguished for his versatility of talent and executive ability, was born in Adair county, Kentucky, on the 17th day of October, 1819. His father, William Jones, a native of Lincoln county, that State, was a plain farmer, in moderate circumstances, and of Welsh descent. When a young man he took part in the battle of New Orleans, under Jackson. He died in Adair county, in his forty-second year. He was a man of much will force, a good manager of affairs, and was in politics a Democrat. Dr. Jones' great-grandfather, David Jones, was from Wales, and his wife, Polly McCann, from Ireland. Dr. Jones' grandfather, John Jones, a native of Maryland, came West and lived as a farmer in Lincoln county, Kentucky, where he died about the year 1827. Two of his sons were farmers, and one, Rev. John Jones, was a Christian preacher. The father of Dr. Jones' grandmother Jones was Robert Elrod, from Germany, and his wife was Sarah Wilson, from England. The Doctor's mother, whose maiden name was Mary B. Powell, was born in Virginia, daughter of Robert Powell, a farmer, who was a major in the Revolutionary war. Her mother was a Miss West, a relative of the family of the renowned English painter, Benjamin West. This family has also other representatives in America. Capt. John West Jacobs, of the United States quartermaster's department, now superintending the building of a hospital at Little Rock, Arkansas, for disabled soldiers, is the Doctor's maternal cousin.

Dr. Jones' mother, left a widow early in life, with nine children, devoted herself with singular assiduity to their interests till her death, at Bowling Green, Kentucky, in 1851, at the age of forty-five. She was a zealous member of the Methodist church, and noted for the two chiefest of all womanly virtues, modesty and piety. Doubtless the son is as much indebted to her for his religious impressions and inclinations, as to his father for administrative and managing talent, for the Doctor has been a member of the Baptist church ever since 1836; is now, and has repeatedly been elected, president of the Tennessee Baptist convention, and is the only layman who has ever enjoyed such distinction at the hands of the State convention.

Of the early life of this prominent Tennessean, the editor has but scanty trace. His literary education was limited to some eighteen months' attendance at school in Kentucky. But when a mere boy, having elected to be a physician, he read medicine two years under the special instruction of Dr. T. Q. Walker, and in 1839–40 attended lectures in the Louisville Medical College, and subsequently took the degree of M.D. from the Medical College of Ohio, at Cincinnati, and also from the Memphis Medical College.

He engaged in practice before he was twenty-one years old, first at Edmunton, Kentucky, then at Bowling Green, Kentucky, from the fall of 1840 to 1849, when he settled at Nashville, where he has resided ever since. His life in Tennessee has been crowded with events. Indeed, the Doctor is of that type of men that make history in their several specialties. His name figures conspicuously in the reports of the transactions of the American Medical Association, the American Association for the Advancement of Science, the Tennessee Medical Society, and the Medical Society of Davidson county. For several years, from 1853, he was an associate editor of the *Southern Journal of Medical and Physical Sciences*, published at Nashville. Among the most noted of his contributions to medical literature, are his hospital reports and articles entitled " Necessities of the Insane in Tennessee," and " Adequate and Impartial Provision for the Insane of the State."

In 1852, he established the *Parlor Visitor*, and, in 1874, became associate editor of the *Tennessee School Journal*. In 1858, he, with a number of other physicians, founded the Shelby Medical College, of which he filled the chair of professor of materia medica. On the arrival of the Federal troops in Tennessee, and the establishment of the Academy hospital at Nashville, he was placed in charge of it—the first Federal hospital established in Nashville after the beginning of the war. In 1862, he was made superintendent of the Tennessee Hospital for the Insane, at Nashville, Tennessee, by Gov. Andrew Johnson, for a period of eight years, and while there built a separate and suitable hospital for the colored insane; perhaps, the first in the United States, and was unanimously re-elected to the same position, but in 1870 resigned, on account of an injury which he had received from an insane patient, resulting in temporary paralysis.

The responsible position of superintendent he filled with commendable fidelity to the interest of the patients and the State, until January 1, 1870, the date of the acceptance of his resignation. While in charge of this institution, Dr. Jones (as State papers show) received from time to time the highest commendation of the trustees and legislative committees. Indeed, during all this critical period, he succeeded in giving entire satisfaction to financial officers and political parties.

In 1873, he was elected president of Nashville Medical College, now the medical department of the University of Tennessee, and made professor of psychological medicine and mental hygiene in that institution, a position which he still holds, though he does not lecture regularly.

Though never a professional politician, yet from personal acquaintance with Mr. Clay and admiration of his statesmanship, together with earnest convictions of the nobility of purpose which characterized the Whig party, it was his pleasure to co operate with that party until its disorganization, when he joined the ranks of the Republican party, with which he has sympathized and co-operated ever since. Though interested in slave property, by inheritance and marriage, he never in any manner encouraged the rebellion, but throughout the war was a stanch Union man—yet liberal and tolerant to those who differed from him politically. In 1862, he was chosen president of the Nashville city council.

In 1873, he was nominated by the Republicans and elected State senator in the Tennessee Legislature from the Nashville district, by a large majority. The Nashville *Union and American*, a Democratic journal, said of Dr. Jones at that time: "Although he declined making a race, on account of bad health, after a like nomination two years ago, on this occasion, however, accepting the nomination, he was elected by a large majority. Though under existing circumstances, with present political divisions, decidedly a Republican, as indicated by his voting that ticket, he is, nevertheless, believed to have the conscientious independence to

' Dare do all that may become a man.'

and therefore to vote for just such men and measures, and only such, as, in his judgment, will most likely bring the greatest good to the greatest number of people. He is already thoroughly committed to the use of his influence in favor of free public schools, such as shall pervade every county, town and civil district, and permeate every department of society in Tennessee; to the re-establishing of the State credit by funding the

State debt, and thereafter providing for the payment of the interest; to the protection of wool growers, the elevation of the laboring classes, and the consideration of the merchant's tax. The senator from Davidson has been favorably mentioned in each of the divisions of the State as one suitable to be made speaker of the senate."

While senator he proved a most useful member. He was designated by the speaker of the senate as chairman of the committee on public charities, but declined to serve because for many years he had charge of the largest public charity in the State, and did not choose to supervise his successor. He was then made chairman of the public school committee, and introduced, and with others, procured the passage of the present public school law—then so far in advance of legislation in other southern States—which provides for " equal educational advantages for all the children of the State without regard to race, color or condition," though in separate buildings. He also introduced and obtained the passage of the law establishing two additional hospitals for the insane—one for the eastern, the other for the western division of the State. Under this law, Lyons' View was purchased, and the hospital near Knoxville located.

In May, 1877, he was appointed by President Hayes, and confirmed by the United State senate, postmaster at Nashville, and was reappointed by President Arthur, October 28, 1881. This position he held eight years five months and thirteen days, until the incoming of the Democratic administration, and the appointment by President Cleveland, of Gen. B. Frank Cheatham. Under Dr. Jones' management the net earnings of the postoffice at Nashville increased from twenty-nine thousand eight hundred and twenty-eight dollars, in 1877, to seventy-three thousand seven hundred and four dollars, in 1882, a fact in itself of no importance in this volume, except as showing the splendid talent of the Doctor for marshalling affairs, controlling large forces of men, and reducing the complicated machinery of the office to the regularity of clock work. It is only a well balanced mind, and the steady eye and hand of a master, that can achieve results so universally satisfactory to the business men of so large a city. Questioned as to the methods by which he has made his career successful, he replied : " My motto has been, ' In all things to acknowledge God and beg His direction.' "

The Doctor has been frequently and favorably mentioned in connection with gubernatorial honors. He could once or twice undoubtedly have had the nomination of the Republican party, had he consented to make the race. He has been a director in the First National Bank, director of the State prison, and trustee of three universities, and is a member of the State Board of Education, and since this article was written, has been offered the superintendency of the West Tennessee hospital for the insane, but declined to accept.

One of the wisest and best acts of his life, he thinks, was to marry Miss Jane Elizabeth Currey, which he did, in Nashville, October 28, 1851. She is a native of Nashville, and was born in April, 1834. Her father was Robert B. Currey, esq., a native of North Carolina, who, in 1801, was appointed postmaster at Nashville, by President Thomas Jefferson, and served through Mr. Jefferson's administration of eight years. He was retained by President Madison as postmaster through his two terms of the presidency, and also by President Monroe for eight years more—making in all twenty-four consecutive years—a compliment rarely bestowed in an office of such labor and responsibility; and it is gratifying to know it was worthily bestowed. During the time he was postmaster he entertained Gen. Lafayette at his house, in Nashville, in May, 1825. Mr. Currey died in 1848. Mrs. Jones' mother was Miss Jane G. Owen. Mrs. Jones graduated from the time-honored, thrice-illustrious old Nashville Female Academy, under Dr. C. D. Elliott, and was ever remarkable for personal beauty, equanimity of temper, kindliness of heart and womanly graces. She joined the Baptist church in early life, and all her children, except one, are Baptists.

By his marriage with Miss Currey, Dr. Jones has had nine children, six of whom are living: (1). Jennie Ermine Jones, graduated from Ward's seminary; married, in 1870, Prof. S. Y. Caldwell, who has been for fifteen years superintendent of the Nashville public schools. They have four children, Robert, Samuel, Lucien and Albert. (2). Quintard L. Jones, educated in the East Tennessee University; married, in 1882, Miss Elizabeth Porter, daughter of William Porter, a merchant, of Nashville. This son was for a time book-keeper in the American National Bank, Nashville, but is now in the gents' furnishing business, senior member of the firm of Quintard & Arthur Jones. He is also a member of the Nashville city council, and has one son, William Porter. (3). Mary Bell Jones, educated at Ward's seminary; now wife of A. J. Wheeler, senior member of the book and publishing firm, the Wheeler, Osborne & Duckworth company, Nashville. They have four children, William, Edward, Jennie and Melville. (4). Arthur Jones, educated at Nashville; was for a while stamp clerk in the Nashville post-office; now of the firm of Quintard & Arthur Jones. (5). Medora Jones, now a student at Ward's seminary. (6). Roberta Jones, also at Ward's seminary.

Three of the nine children "are not"—William Palmer, Lucien Gaither and Algernon Earle Jones.

Dr. Jones became a Mason in 1840, at Bowling Green Kentucky, and the same year delivered the address on the anniversary of St. John, and represented his lodge in the Grand Lodge at Lexington, Kentucky.

The life of this useful citizen has not been without pecuniary reward. Beginning on a capital stock consisting of a borrowed horse, one-half dollar, the blessing of his mother, and a confident determination to be a success, he is known to own lands in the country, and city real estate, and is understood to be in easy circumstances. In business transactions he is a good listener, systematic, careful, prompt; in all things collected and dignified, with no appearance of ostentation. In early life he was raised a plain farmer's boy—his father owning a few negroes and about one thousand acres of land. After his father's death he continued at farm work, and walked two miles to town twice a week at night for examination in the studies he was privately pursuing. This indomitable energy, this born resolution to succeed honorably in life, has characterized this man's career and brought him the respect and reverence of his fellow-citizens of all classes and of all parties. No man in Tennessee more deservedly enjoys the confidence and esteem of the public.

ROBERT A. YOUNG, A. M., M. D., D. D.

NASHVILLE.

NO name is better known in the church circles of Tennessee, and of a greater portion of the South, than that of the distinguished Methodist divine which heads this biographical sketch. He is distinctively and peculiarly a Tennessean and a southerner, having been born, January 23, 1824, in Knox county, Tennessee, of a southern family, without a relative north of Mason and Dixon's line.

His grandfather, Henry Young, was an Englishman, a ship-carpenter by occupation, who came to America and landed at Baltimore. He was in affluent circumstances, sufficient to educate all of his children up to the high-water mark of that day. He left a very handsome fortune to each of his three children, all sons.

The father of our subject was Capt. John C. Young, born in 1796, in Orange county, North Carolina, and educated at the famous University of North Carolina, at Chapel Hill, in that county. He became a captain in the United States army, and served with credit and distinction under Gen. Jackson. Emigrating to Knox county, Tennessee, he was a large farmer and slaveholder there up to his death, in 1831, which occurred when Robert A. Young was only six years old.

Dr. Young's mother, nee Miss Lucinda Hyder, was

a native of Carter county, Tennessee, daughter of John Hyder, a large farmer, formerly of Pennsylvania, and of German extraction. The Hyders are an "endless generation" in East Tennessee. Hon. Michael Hyder, at one time a member of the Legislature from Carter county, was a maternal uncle of Dr. Young. Dr. Young's mother was born in 1800, and died in 1875, leaving four children, namely: Eveline Decatur Young, who died the wife of W. F. Medearis, of Washington county, Arkansas; Thirza Ann Young, who died the wife of Capt. J. R. Smith, of Sharpe county, Arkansas; Rev. John Henry Young, who was finely educated by a private tutor, Jeremiah R. Moore, a famous East Tennessee teacher, and died in Marion, Kentucky, in 1858, a preacher in the Methodist Episcopal church, South. The fourth, and last child, was Robert A. Young, the subject of this sketch. Of his childhood the biographer has little information beyond the fact that he spent his time at home, on the farm, and in a first-class district school, near Campbell's Station, Tennessee. His schoolmates there were the Bells, the Mabrys, the Martins, the Leas, all members of prominent families of that section. When not at school, or engaged in farm work, he had his room at home, and lived among his books, reveling in them, and taking most delight in history and biography. On his sixteenth birthday, his mother "set him free," saying, at the time, she never expected to have one unpleasant care or concern for him, so great was her confidence in him, and so pleased was she with the habits he had formed. Fifty years later, and shortly before the good mother died, she said: "I have never had an anxious care about you, Robert, since the day I set you free."

On that memorable day in the young man's life, he determined to finish his education at some good college and be a physician. In August, 1842, he made a profession of religion and joined the Methodist church, an event which was the turning point and epoch of his life, for he had been seeking religion regularly from his fifth year up to that date. The following December, he entered Washington College, near Jonesborough, for, having been reared under the influence of the old school Presbyterian church, it was natural that he should thus select an old school Presbyterian college, an institution in which every professor was a graduate, either of Princeton or Edinborough. Here he graduated in 1844, having among his classmates Judge O. P. Temple, of Knoxville, and Hon. Zeb. Vance, the celebrated United States senator from North Carolina.

After graduation, he went into the office of Dr. Brabson, of Rheatown, and with him read medicine, for a few months. But, in the meanwhile, his heart was turned toward the ministry. Therefore, in September, 1845, he was admitted on trial in the Holston conference of the Methodist Episcopal church, South, and traveled Dandridge circuit one year. He had the im-

pression all his rational life, when seeking religion, when at college, when reading medicine, that he must abandon his own plans and preach. When fully convinced that he was called of God to preach, he gave up everything else and turned all his thoughts and studies to the work. It was a complete surrender, and from that day to this he has been in the regular work, without a day's intermission. He has had no other vocation.

In the fall of 1846, he went to Nashville and united with the Tennessee conference, and was stationed chiefly by the advice of Dr. A. L. P. Green, the leading man of the Tennessee conference, and was stationed at Cumberland Iron Works, where he remained two years. About this time he began to write for newspapers and magazines. In October, 1848, he was stationed at Columbia, Tennessee, where he remained two full years, during which time he received his degree of A. M., from Jackson College, of that town. In the fall of 1850, he was stationed for two years in Huntsville, Alabama, a place then considered second only to McKendree church, Nashville, in the bounds of the Tennessee conference. At the close of his term in Huntsville, he was elected president of the Huntsville Female College, but declined. In the fall of 1852, he was stationed in Lebanon, Tennessee, but at the end of his first year, he was transferred to the pastorate of the First Methodist church at St. Louis, Missouri, the transfer being made without his previous knowledge or consent. He remained pastor of that church two years, at the end of which time he was made presiding elder of the St. Louis district, a position which he filled two years. During his pastoral life in St. Louis, he wrote a series of articles for the *Home Circle*, a magazine published at Nashville, Tennessee, under the head of "Characters that I Have Taken a Pen To." These articles were afterward published in a handsome volume called "Personages." About this time he began to be in demand for annual commencement sermons, annual literary addresses and popular lectures. In October, 1857, he was presiding elder of the Lexington district, St. Louis conference, and filled the position three years.

In the fall of 1860, when war was ominous and imminent, Dr. Young, being of strong southern sympathies, was transferred back to the Tennessee conference, and stationed at Lebanon, Tennessee. At the end of that year, he was elected president of Wesleyan University, at Florence, Alabama, and accepted the position at a salary of three thousand five hundred dollars, and a house to live in. This institution enrolled more students than any other in the southern States, excepting only the University of Virginia. Here he remained till near the close of the war. While at Florence, he received the degree of D. D. from the institution over which he presided, but of which he knew nothing till he received his diploma from the secretary of the board.

In the fall of 1864, he was again stationed at Columbia, Tennessee. In the fall of 1865, he was stationed at Tulip Street church, Edgefield, Tennessee, and elected to the general conference, which met in New Orleans, Louisiana, and has been a member, elected on the first ballot, of every general conference from that day to this. In the fall of 1866, he was stationed at McKendree church, Nashville, where he remained four consecutive years. During this time he wrote " A Reply to Ariel," on the ethnological status of the negro, of which five thousand copies were sold in one week. In the fall of 1870, he was stationed at Elm Street church, in Nashville, where he remained four years, which was the close of his active pastoral life, though he has been actively engaged since then in other departments of church work.

In 1874, he was elected financial secretary of the board of trust of Vanderbilt University, at a salary of two thousand five hundred dollars, and continued to devote his time to the duties of that office until May, 1882, when he was elected by the general conference, at Nashville, secretary of the board of missions of the Methodist Episcopal church, South, in which he has been diligently engaged to the present time. For this he receives a salary of two thousand five hundred dollars and his traveling expenses.

He is the editor of the *Advocate of Missions*, the organ of the board of which he is secretary. Many of his sermons and addresses have been published in pamphlet form. He was secretary of the Tennessee conference for twenty-one consecutive years. He is a member of the book committee of the Southern Methodist Publishing House; member of the board of trust of Vanderbilt University; of the board of trust of the Nashville College for Young Ladies; of the board of missions of the Methodist Episcopal church, South; director in the American National bank, Nashville; served three years as a member of the Nashville board of education; became a Mason in Edgefield Lodge, and has taken all the fourteen degrees up to Knight Templar; has belonged to every temperance society as they arose in his neighborhood, and has experimented with the American people by frequent lectures on that subject. He was born and raised a Whig, but since the war, having no choice except to be a Republican or a Democrat, he has acted with the Democrats.

Dr. Young has been twice married; first, in June, 1847, while yet a pastor, at the Cumberland Iron Works, Tennessee, to Miss Mary A. Kemmer, of Bledsoe county. She died in 1879.

His second marriage, which occurred at Nashville, Tennessee, August 18, 1880, was with Mrs. Anna Green Hunter, youngest daughter of Rev. A. L. P. Green,

D. D., LL.D., the most influential man in the southern Methodist church of his day, the bishop excepted. It used to be said, " When Dr. Green speaks, the meetin' is out." Dr. Green was probably the wealthiest Methodist preacher in the South. He died, July 15, 1874, at the age of sixty-eight. Mrs. Young's mother, *nee* Miss Mary Ann Elliston, was the only child of John T. Elliston, of one of the pioneer families of Nashville. The history of the family dates back to 1780, and to Fort Buchanan, in which they lived. Mrs. Young's mother died, March 28, 1881, aged sixty-three years, a lady remarkable for a very high degree of intelligence, and of almost unbounded influence in society and in the church. Mrs. Young graduated from the Nashville Female Academy in 1858, in her seventeenth year. Dr. Young has no children. Mrs. Young, by her first husband, Capt. R. P. Hunter, has three children, Mary Green Hunter, Alexander Green Hunter and Susie Hunter.

Mrs. Young is a member of the Methodist Episcopal church, as are her two brothers, Frank W. Green, of the firm of Anderson, Green & Co., wholesale dry goods merchants, in Nashville, Rev. William M. Green, pastor at Franklin, Tennessee, and her sister, Laura Elliston Green, now wife of Thomas D. Fite, of Fite, Porter & Co., the largest wholesale dry goods firm in Nashville. It may be said, in this connection, that all the descendants of Dr. Green, without exception, are Methodists.

Throughout life, Dr. Young has been recognized as a man of one purpose and one work, "drawing all his thoughts and studies one way." Not only is he a man of stability in this respect, but, to so phrase it, is one of "breath and bottom." His financial success is attributable to industry, economy and the scrupulous avoidance of debt. He has never said to any one who presented a bill, "Call again," but paid it then and there. His leading distinguishing trait of character is punctuality. In the pulpit, he is an orator of great power, extraordinary learning, and wonderful convincing ability. He never had a charge in which he did not hold a successful revival, but he was not known so much as a revivalist as he was for his successful pastoral influence, the upbuilding and strengthening of his congregations. He has been an extemporaneous preacher from the beginning, and this proves him a great student, and a close reader and observer. In personal appearance, Dr. Young would attract attention among any select body of ten thousand men. He weighs two hundred and thirty pounds, stands six feet eight inches high, and like Saul, the son of Kish, towers a head and shoulders above his brethren.

JOHN H. WHITE, M. D.

MILLERSBURG.

IT does not often occur that a teacher lives to become the biographer of his pupils. This volume, however, contains sketches of three gentlemen of distinction who were once students under the editor, to-wit: Hon. James D. Richardson, now member of Congress from Tennessee, Hon. Ethelbert B. Wade, and Dr. John H. White, subject of this article.

John H. White was born, October 6, 1849, at Millersburg, Rutherford county, Tennessee, grew up and has lived there all his life, on the same place where his father was born, lived and died. He took his first lessons in literature at Zimmerman Institue, a school founded and taught by William S. Speer. At the age of twenty he attended college five months at the Ashland University, Lexington, Kentucky. He next attended Union University, at Murfreesborough, Tennessee, ten months, and then began the study of medicine in the office of his brother, Dr. B. N. White, at Christiana, Tennessee. He graduated M.D., from the medical department of the University of Nashville, February 22, 1872, under Profs. Bowling, Eve, Briggs, Maddin, Callender, Buchanan, J. B. Lindsley, Nichol, V. S. Lindsley, and Sneed, and returned to Rutherford county, where he has been engaged in the practice of medicine and in farming ever since, excepting such times as he represented his county in the Legislature. He is a member of the Rutherford County Medical Society, and of the State Medical Society, and is justly regarded as one of the rising members of the profession in Tennessee.

Dr. White is an hereditary Democrat—comes by his Democracy honestly—his father and all the male members of his family on both sides being of that sturdy and unswerving political faith and complexion. He never drew any but Democratic breath in his life. In 1883, and again in 1885, he served in the Tennessee House of Representatives as a representative from Rutherford county, and was considered one of its ablest and most useful members. He was made chairman of the committee on public grounds and buildings, and was temporary speaker of the House in 1885.

In religion he is a member of the Christian church, which he joined at the age of twenty-one, and at present is an elder in his home congregation. In 1872, he became a Mason in Charles Fuller Lodge, No. 426, Carlocksville, Rutherford county, Tennessee.

Dr. White married, in Rutherford county, Tennessee, February 16, 1876, Miss Mattie Pruett, who was born in that county September 15, 1859, the daughter of F. M. Pruett, a farmer, native of the same county. Her mother was Miss Catharine Davis, daughter of Rev. Nathan L. Davis, a noted Baptist preacher, of Rutherford, a farmer and stock trader, who acquired a handsome fortune. Mrs. White was educated at Bellbuckle, Tennessee; is a member of the Christian church, and is one of the most kind-hearted and affable of women, bowing to God's will, asking God's guidance, and ever striving to make her husband and family comfortable and happy—a disposition which extends its influence to others in the form of good neighborly feeling and in acts of.charity. Her husband takes commendable pride in praising her, which is probably the highest compliment in men's estimation a woman can receive.

By his marriage with Miss Pruett, Dr. White has had four children, three of whom survive : (1). Buford M. White, born April 12, 1877. (2). Ella Mary White, born May 1, 1879. (3). Francis Pruett White, born February 16, 1881; died January 31, 1885. (4). Burrell G. White (named for his grandfather), born April 6, 1883.

The Whites are an English family. Stephen White, grandfather of Dr. White, was born in North Carolina, was an officer in the American army in the Revolutionary war, and acquired a good deal of fame in that war. He married a Miss Searcy in North Carolina, and had six sons, Franklin, William, Harvey, Nat, Stokely and Burrell G., and one daughter, Susan, wife of Hugh B. Jameson—all of whom are dead. Two of the sons of Dr. Harvey White, Stephen N. and Thomas D., were captains in the Confederate army. Both of these are dead. Stokely White left one son, William B., now merchant in Kosciusko, Mississippi; has been tax collector of Attala county, and is a citizen of considerable influence. Stokely White, also, left two daughters, Anna and Susan, the latter now wife of Dr. Jo. Collins, at Kosciusko, a leading physician there.

Dr. White's father, Burrell G. White, was born May 20, 1808. He was a man of wide influence in his county, a warm politician, a merchant, a fine financier, of fine property, and a warm friend of education. He was a man who threw his whole soul into his business, his politics, his religion, and into the educational and railroad enterprises of the country. He was a zealous party man; in politics a Democrat; in religion a member of the Christian church. A desire for the promotion of the happiness and advancement of his fellow-beings was his strongest trait of character. He was of strong likes and dislikes, of strong sympathies and antipathies—indeed, a man of very strong individuality. He died, October 31, 1884, leaving six children : Robert M. White, now a farmer and justice of the peace in Rutherford county; William N. White, a farmer in the same county; Dr. B. N. White, a prominent physician and farmer in the same county; Frank White, now deputy county court clerk of Rutherford county, is also a merchant; Catharine G. White, now wife of Benjamin Fugitt; Dr. John Howland White, subject of this sketch.

Dr. White's mother, originally Miss Mary Donelly, now living at the age of sixty-three, was born December 11, 1821, in Dublin, Ireland. She is the daughter of Peter Donelly, a wealthy Irishman, who came from Ireland and settled at Shelbyville, Bedford county, Tennessee. He died of cholera, in 1833, leaving six children: Lucy Donelly, who died the wife of Dr. John W. Wilburn, a member of Congress from Missouri; Mary Donelly, mother of Dr. White; Bartley Donelly, a captain in the Mexican war; Catharine Donelly, now widow of Thomas Jameson; Elizabeth Donelly, who died the wife of Dr. Thornton Matson, of Louisiana, Missouri; Honora Donelly, now the wife of Dr. P. H. Manier, of Wartrace, Bedford county, Tennessee.

Dr. White's mother is a lady of very positive character and pronounced opinions; is very frank; of unusual mental ability; and is both progressive and aggressive.

Honesty, sobriety, veracity, and attention to business and with a determination, even in boyhood, to make life a success if possible—these are the distinguishing characteristics of Dr. White. His father and mother stimulated his ambition to be something and to do something for himself. From them he had a most excellent education; from them he had wise advice and good example. Thus he had a good send-off, and he has made a man of himself. The editor knew his family well, and furthermore knows whereof he speaks.

Dr. White's father married twice. His first wife was Elizabeth Miller, daughter of Esq. Robert Miller, by whom he had three children: Robert White; William White; Elizabeth White, who died the wife of Thomas D. White, her cousin. She left one son, Otie R. White. Dr. White's own brothers are Bartley and Frank, and his own sister, Catharine, wife of Benjamin Fugitt, all of whom have been previously mentioned.

W. M. VERTREES, M. D.

NASHVILLE.

DR. WOODFORD MITCHELL VERTREES, professor of materia medica and therapeutics in the medical department of the University of Tennessee, was born in Brownsville, Kentucky, March 23, 1827, the son of Jacob and Catharine Vertrees.

His grandfather, John Vertrees, was a farmer, of Pennsylvania-German stock, and emigrated to Kentucky in the same party with the father of Gov. Helm, Haycraft and other well-known pioneers, shortly after the arrival of Daniel Boone on that extreme frontier. The Vertrees-Helm party built a fort a very short distance from what is now known as the public square of Elizabethtown. The family name at the time of their emigration to Kentucky was Von Treese, which was afterward anglicised to Vertrees. John Vertrees, therefore, was the first to spell the name in its modern form. He was, also, the first judge of the Hardin county court (Hardin being one of the three counties into which the territory of Kentucky was then divided), and he tried the first murder case in Kentucky, which resulted in the hanging of the murderer.

John Vertrees and his sons, in the early days of their settlement, were engaged in many fierce battles with the Indians. One of their battles, which was fought near Rolling Fork, eight miles from Elizabethtown, is said to have been the hardest fight which ever occurred on the "dark and bloody ground." John and Daniel Vertrees, with a party of eleven other white men, were pursuing a band of Indians, numbering thirteen, who had committed some depredations near Elizabethtown. Daniel Vertrees, being an expert in wood-craft and the modes of Indian warfare, was "trailing" the savages when he suddenly came upon them in a sink-hole, where they were cooking their breakfast. He at once fired upon them, but on turning to gain the protection of a tree, he himself fell dead, pierced by the bullets of the Indians, who, running out to scalp him, were themselves fired upon by the remainder of the whites who came up at that moment. A hand to hand fight ensued, and in the desperate struggle all of the Indians and five of the white men were killed, John Vertrees being one of the survivors.

Some time after, Joseph Vertrees—son of John Vertrees—when nine years of age, was captured by the Indians near where the public square at Elizabethtown now is. His captors started with him to cross the Ohio river on a raft. John Vertrees followed with a band to rescue the little fellow, but when the Indians, hotly pursued, threatened to kill the boy if they were fired upon, the white men desisted from the pursuit and the Indians pushed off and crossed the river with their prisoner. The boy was kept in captivity nine years, but finally made his escape at the age of eighteen, returned to Kentucky, married and brought up a large family, all of whom have Indian peculiarities—love of hunting and fishing, love of solitude and life in the woods. Joseph Vertrees was an uneducated man, but lived to accumulate considerable property, after his return.

Jacob Vertrees, son of John Vertrees, and father of Dr. W. M. Vertrees, subject of this sketch, was a man of strong native sense, and of great honesty and integrity. Indeed, it is the pride and boast of the family that, since the name has been borne, no Vertrees has ever appeared in a criminal court on any criminal charge whatsoever. Jacob Vertrees was also a great lover of fishing and hunting, and retained a fondness for hazardous field sports to the day of his death. He married, in 1812, at Leitchfield, Kentucky, Miss Catharine Davis, then recently from Virginia. She was a most excellent and a most devout Christian woman, and, it is said, not an idle word ever escaped her lips, for she sought to live by the teachings of the Bible, as she understood them.

By his marriage with Miss Davis, Jacob Vertrees had ten children, four sons and six daughters: (1). William Duval Vertrees, the oldest son, was born March 21, 1816, at Brownsville, Kentucky; was educated there; was a sergeant in Col. Churchill's command in the Mexican war, and was wounded at Palo Alto. Returning to Kentucky, he was elected and served several terms in the Legislature, after which he was county judge of Hardin county for fifteen years. He married, in 1855, Miss Haynes, of Elizabethtown; she died in 1876, leaving four children : Mattie Vertrees, now wife of Mr. Bernard, dealer in agricultural implements, New Orleans; John Vertrees, a telegraph operator in the employ of the Louisville and Nashville railroad; Catharine Vertrees, now living in Elizabethtown; Charles Vertrees, who died at the age of eighteen. (2). James Cunningham Vertrees, born in Brownsville, Kentucky, in 1825, and educated there; married Miss Susan Lee, of North Carolina, now a merchant in Palatka, Florida; has three sons : John J. Vertrees, who graduated at the Lebanon law school, and is now a distinguished attorney at Nashville, and regarded as one of the ablest lawyers in the State; James Cunningham Vertrees, jr., born in Missouri; now with his father in business at Palatka; William Otter Vertrees, now law partner with John J. Vertrees; received his literary education at the University of Nashville, and graduated from the law department of Vanderbilt University in 1883. (3). Woodford Mitchell Vertrees, subject of this sketch. (4). John L. Vertrees, born at Brownsville, Kentucky, March 21, 1829; graduated from the medical department of the University of Louisville, in 1857; practiced in Glasgow, Kentucky, until the outbreak of the war, when he joined the Confederate army and was made surgeon of the Sixth Kentucky regiment, Col. Joseph H. Lewis commanding. When Col. Lewis was made brigadier-general and given command of the famous Kentucky "Orphan Brigade," Dr. Vertrees was made brigade-surgeon. He has, ever since the war, been disabled by paralysis, the result of his labors and exposure while in service. The daughters of Jacob Vertrees were: (1). Nancy R. Vertrees, who became the wife of John D. Otter, a leading wholesale grocer and commission merchant, of Louisville, Kentucky. Mr. Otter died in June, 1883, leaving four sons, who succeeded him in the management of the business carried on at the corner of Sixth and Main streets, Louisville, one

of the largest wholesale and commission houses in that city. (2). Rebecca B. Vertrees, married Dr. D. J. L. Ford, of Rocky Hill, Kentucky. (3). Sarah Wright Vertrees, married James H. Wortham, of Leitchfield, Kentucky, who died in 1857, leaving two sons: James Wortham, an attorney, and Woodford Wortham, druggist; both now living at Leitchfield. (4). Zerelda Hopkins Vertrees, married Thomas Hardey, son of Lieut.-Gov. Hardey, of Kentucky; now resides at Horse Cave, Kentucky, and has four children. (5). Mary H. Vertrees, died in 1857, the wife of Charles Wortham. (6). Elizabeth Vertrees, died at the age of sixteen.

Dr. Vertrees attended literary school at Brownsville, Kentucky, until he was twenty years old, when he entered Wirt College, Sumner county, Tennessee, remaining there two years, under President Thomas Patterson. During his collegiate course among his class-mates were Hon. Atha Thomas, ex-treasurer of Tennessee, and Hon. Thomas B. Ivie, of Shelbyville. He then read medicine under Dr. John Sweeney, at Smith's Grove, Kentucky, and afterward attended the medical department of the University of Louisville, where he graduated, in 1851, under President James Guthrie. He practiced at Smith's Grove one year, then moved to Elizabethtown and remained there until 1857, when he went to Mattoon, Illinois, and practiced until the beginning of the war. He was elected mayor of Mattoon in 1860, on the Democratic ticket, but resigned and removed to Franklin, Kentucky, remaining there until he removed to Nashville, in 1871.

Dr. Vertrees was one of the founders of the Nashville Medical College (now medical department of the University of Tennessee), the charter being granted to Drs. Duncan Eve, J. B. Stephens, W. F. Glenn, W. C. Cook and W. M. Vertrees. At the organization of the faculty, he was elected professor of materia medica and therapeutics, but resigned in 1881. In 1883, he was elected to the chair of medical chemistry and toxicology, and in 1885, was transferred to the chair of materia medica and therapeutics, which he now fills.

Dr. Vertrees was a charter member of Tennessee Lodge, No. 20, Knights of Honor, the lodge being organized about six months after the founding of the order, and at a time when it had not more than five hundred members. He afterward withdrew and was a charter member of Cumberland Lodge, Edgefield. He has been a member of the Christian church twenty-five years, and was on the building committee of the first Christian church built at Mattoon, Illinois. In a State where he is so well-known, it is almost superfluous to say he is a Democrat of the loyalest and most unswerving type. He cast his first vote for Franklin Pierce, and has voted the Democratic ticket ever since.

Dr. Vertrees married, in 1857, Miss Martha Ford, daughter of Dr. William Ford, of Dripping Spring, Warren county, Kentucky. By this marriage he has six children : (1). Catharine Elizabeth Vertrees, born January 13, 1860. (2). William Simon Vertrees, born April 1, 1862; a graduate of the medical department of the University of Tennessee. (3). John Columbus Vertrees, born January 5, 1864. (4). Hallie Ellen Vertrees, born January 29, 1867. (5). Mattie Vertrees, born April 13, 1870. (6). Charles Cantrell Vertrees, born August 20, 1879.

The five eldest of Dr. Vertrees' children were educated in the Nashville public schools.

Mrs. Vertrees' eldest brother, Dr. D. J. L. Ford, is now practicing medicine at Rocky Hill, Kentucky. Her youngest brother, William C. Ford, is a successful attorney at Russellville, Arkansas. She had six sisters, all of whom married into excellent families. Elizabeth became the wife of Dr. John Sweeney, of Warren county, Kentucky, with whom Dr. Vertrees read medicine; has five children. Ellen is the wife of Louis D. Shobe, a stock raiser, of Miami, Missouri; has four children. Ermine is the wife of Wilbur F. Moore, a merchant at Franklin, Kentucky; has four children. Mary is the wife of Woodford Dunn, a successful

farmer at Castalian Springs, Tennessee. Nancy is the wife of H. T. Arnold, a retired farmer of Edgefield, Kentucky; has four children.

As to an estimate of Dr. Vertrees' character as a man, as a physician and as a medical educator, the following from Dr. W. P. Jones, of Nashville, his colaborer in the great field of medical science, is well worth quoting: " I regard Dr. Vertrees as a gentleman of the highest honor and strictest integrity. He is an excellent physician, and while not remarkable for fluency of speech, is a careful teacher of medicine. The students of the medical college of the University of Tennessee hear him gladly, because of the exactness of his information and teachings. ' The foundation of his success ' was laid by his noble mother, from whom he inherited vigorous powers of thought as well as will force. The Doctor is eminently social by nature, but does most in the counsel of his own will; hence, in the language of the poet,

' Keeps something to himself
He'd scarcely tell to any.' ''

WILLIAM E. WARD, A. M., D. D.

NASHVILLE.

THIS eminenent educator, whose name appears in numerous sketches throughout this volume, is familiar, by reputation, to thousands of persons in all portions of the country. Tall and spare-made in physique, he has less of the sedentary scholar than of the pushing business man in his dress, his manners and general appearance. His hair and long flowing beard are gray—almost patriarchal, and decidedly venerable. His eyes are penetrating and his facial features sharply outlined; complexion clear, without being pale or ruddy —he looks more like a lawyer or congressman than an orthodox clergyman. Least of all does he resemble in any way the typical teacher. Yet, it is as a teacher, the founder and proprietor, and, for more than twenty years, the conductor of the celebrated Ward's Seminary for Young Ladies, at Nashville, that he is known, and for generations will be honored in Tennessee and the surrounding States. One remarkable trait in this teacher's character is, that he is mild and gentle-mannered, kind and considerate, without being patronizing or lax in his duty toward pupils. The young ladies in his care read in his methods that he expects from them the conduct and duty of brave, industrious and intelligent women, rather than of girls who need the mock sympathy called indulgence.

William Eldred Ward was born near Huntsville, Madison county, Alabama, December 21, 1829, and was

raised on Brier Fork, near Hazel Green, in the same county. His father, John C. Ward, was a large cotton planter and slave-holder, a native of Georgia. He was a leading person in his section, a prominent Democrat and an influential man, the associate of Hon. Clement C. Clay, and his father, Gov. Clay, Hugh L. McClung, and other noted politicians. Honesty of purpose, faithfulness to obligations, and fine judgment and reasoning powers were among his salient characteristics. It used to be said of him that he was a born lawyer, though he never studied or practiced law. In 1847, he removed to Texas and was an extensive cotton planter on Red river, in that State. He died there in 1856, at the age of fifty-six years, having been born at Augusta, Georgia, October 23, 1796.

Dr. Ward's grandfather, Matt. Ward, was a native of Dublin, Ireland, the son of Thomas Ward, a large land owner in the city of Dublin. On the second marriage of his father, Matt. Ward went to sea when a mere boy, and remained a sailor before the mast till he became a captain. On the close of the Revolutionary war, he settled at Savannah, Georgia.

The name, Ward, means a guard, one who takes care of or protects—very beautifully significant of the chosen profession of the subject of this sketch. The Hon. Matt. Ward, Dr. Ward's uncle, was a congressman of the old Republic of Texas for many years, and was fourth United States senator from Texas. His brother, Dr. William Ward, went to Texas with Col. Matt. Ward, and was prominent in his profession in that State.

Dr. Ward's mother, whose maiden name was Sarah Clark, was born in Hancock county, Georgia, in 1807, the daughter of Robert Clark, an Indian fighter under Jackson, a planter and slave-holder. Her mother was originally Miss Rebecca Sledge, of a large, wealthy and influential Georgia family. Her brothers, Robert and Silas Clark, were large planters and men of note in Alabama. Silas Clark raised and equipped a company and fought with it till he lost his life in the Confederate army. Dr. Ward's mother had only a fair English education, but her integrity, purity of character and unselfishness made her the life of her family and neighborhood. Her charity was boundless. Her executive ability was shown in her managing a large plantation and forty slaves after her husband's death. She sympathized with her husband in his eagerness to educate their offspring. She died at Nashville, in the home of her son, in 1869, at the age of sixty, leaving four children surviving of six she had borne: (1). William Eldred Ward, subject of this sketch. (2). John Shirley Ward, now a planter and orange grower at Colton, California. For a short time he edited the Nashville *Union and American*, and the *Ladies' Pearl*, the latter a literary magazine of fine merit. He is a Democratic politician and orator, and of high grade as a literary man. He was a captain in the Forty-ninth Tennessee Confederate infantry regiment, and distinguished himself throughout the war. (3). Rebecca E. Ward, graduated from the Athens (Alabama) Female College and married Col. Frank E. Williams, a distinguished lawyer at Nashville, for nineteen years the partner of Gov. William B. Bate, and now the law partner of Judge John V. Wright. (4). Laura V. Ward, graduated from Ward's seminary, and is now the wife of Col. William Williams, nephew of Col. Frank E. Williams, just named. (5). Robert H. Ward, graduated in law at Cumberland University, Lebanon, Tennessee; married Annie Allen, of Texas, and died just after the war, through which he fought as a Confederate soldier. (6). Silas M. Ward, the youngest child, enlisted in Gregg's Texas regiment, was captured at Fort Donelson, and died a prisoner of war at Camp Douglas, near Chicago, Illinois.

As early as the age of six Dr. Ward was placed in a country school and pursued the ordinary branches with considerable success, and was considered a quiet, studious boy, somewhat abstracted, and not much given to play. He soon got ahead of his classes and began the study of Latin at the age of ten, which excited the derision of his school companions. Nothing daunted, however, he mastered history, arithmetic, grammar and the other rudimentary branches, and having a great taste for oratory found time to cultivate that talent. At

the age of sixteen his father sent him to Green Academy, in Huntsville, taught by James M. Davidson, the great Irish scholar, from Dublin. It was through his instructions that young Ward was inspired with a love for the classics, ancient history and geography, and in that academy he was prepared for college, and was noted as an excellent student. His health was never very good from the age of thirteen to sixteen, and he attended school under this disadvantage. But having a strong ambition to be a scholar and a writer, at the age of seventeen he left Green Academy and went to Cumberland University, Lebanon, Tennessee, where he studied four years in the literary department, graduating A.B. in 1851, and two years in the law department from which he graduated, in 1853, under Judges Nathan Green, sr., Abram Caruthers and Chancellor B. L. Ridley. After leaving the law school, he settled in Henderson, Texas, and was partner in law for one year with Hon. William Stedman, a distinguished jurist, formerly of North Carolina. At the end of one year he went to Jefferson, Texas, and practiced two years with fine success as a partner with his brother, Robert H. Ward.

In 1855, he joined the Marshall, Texas, Presbytery of the Cumberland Presbyterian church, having long labored under the impression, even while studying law, that he ought to be a minister. Thereupon he immediately turned his whole studies and course of life into a preparation for the ministry. To carry out this purpose he entered the divinity school at Lebanon, Tennessee, and studied ecclesiastical history, the Greek and Hebrew languages, and divinity one year. He then spent a year—the first of his ministerial life—in traveling through Texas, Arkansas, Missouri and the Indian nations, preaching everywhere, at camp meetings and other meetings, and raising money for the endowment of the theological school at Lebanon, the year's work yielding about ten thousand dollars. It was a year of very great labor, hardships and dangers, traveling alone and especially in the Indian nations, swimming rivers and under other circumstances requiring a good deal of nerve. He had a library of books in his buggy for study at odd hours, which he thoroughly saturated in swimming rivers in the Indian nation. Some of these volumes, "Horne's Introduction," "Barnes' Notes," etc., bear the marks of their itineracy to this day.

At the end of that year, 1856, he reported his year's work back to the university that sent him out, and he was discharged from further work. He then bought the *Banner of Peace*, the leading organ of the Cumberland Presbyterian church, and settled in Nashville, in March, 1857, and remained as editor and proprietor of that paper till February, 1862. His editorial career is known to all the church, and recognized as really the starting out of a new life in Presbyterian church work, the Doctor's extensive travel and learning giving to it a high tone and value. The fall of Fort Donelson stopped the paper, and it was discontinued during the war. Being now much exhausted by constant work, he moved with his family five miles out of Nashville, and lived a quiet life, to rest and take care of his family. During the last year of the war Dr. Ward lived in the city of New York, observing schools and educational matters in New York and the New England States, studying the life of those institutions that had attained to success, with a view of establishing an institution of his own as soon as the war should close. When that event arrived, in April, 1865, Dr. Ward had his plans fully matured, and left New York in July, 1865, and opened Ward's Seminary for Young Ladies, in September, 1865, in the Kirkman building, near the State capitol, which he rented for the purpose. It was a boarding and day school, and began with six boarders and about forty day scholars. It continued in that building till March, 1866, when he bought the building on Spruce street, where the school has ever since remained. From that date till the present his life has been that of an educator, and his success is known throughout the country. Over three thousand young ladies have been taught in this famous school from Tennessee, Kentucky, Alabama, North Carolina, South Carolina, Florida, Georgia, Mississippi, Louisiana, Arkansas, Texas, California, Missouri, Illinois, Indiana, Ohio, Wisconsin, Iowa, Pennsylvania, and the Indian nations. Few if any schools in the United States can show such a uniformly large list of alumnæ as Dr. Ward's catalogue exhibits.

This school has been built on personal exertion, without a dollar of contribution or donation from any source. It has been directed by the mind of the principal, without a board of trustees, which, in the editor's opinion, hampers more institutions than they have ever benefited. Trustees are not necessary to the success of institutions of learning, as Dr. Ward's experience shows. Where a building or a teacher or apparatus is wanted, or an art gallery, or any thing pertaining to educational advancement is needed, the principal has chosen and procured it of his own accord, and with his own means. This school has always been undenominational, and has educated the daughters of the most distinguished clergymen, lawyers, planters, judges, physicians, merchants and politicians in the country. Dr. Ward has traveled in most countries in Europe, especially England, Germany and Switzerland, noticing the forms of education in vogue in those countries, and adapting them to American ideas so far as he deemed them useful. A feature of the school is to embrace lectures on the various countries of Europe every Saturday evening, when a levee of music and elocution is held in connection with these lectures of the principal. These lectures have opened the minds of thousands of young ladies to the importance of history, the manners and customs of foreign countries, contributing largely to that broad culture, which it is a leading object of this school to impart. These lectures incite to the reading of history by the pupils, and have proven eminently beneficial.

About one hundred young ladies, graduates of this institution, are teachers of music and literary branches, one or two of these being Indians and teaching Indians, and two others are teaching in China as missionaries of the Methodist church. Gen. John Eaton, United States commissioner of education, says: "As an individual educator, Dr. Ward has had greater educational success —i. e., built up a larger school with his unaided exertions, without endowment, than any other man." He furthermore states that Ward's seminary stands first in the South in respect to numbers and general facilities for education. The buildings and furniture and apparatus cost one hundred thousand dollars. There is a large art building erected, arranged and furnished on the most improved ideas as an art hall. The curriculum in the collegiate department embraces five years. The school has paid teachers one hundred and twenty thousand dollars, employing twenty teachers, all of the highest grade. The French language is spoken daily at three tables, and the German language at one. The school has brought about one million dollars to Nashville. It was chartered by the State in 1869.

The high character which this seminary maintains, and the commendatory manner in which it is spoken of, may be seen from the following notices of the press throughout the country—North and South:

The New York *Mercantile Review*, speaking of the schools of Nashville, says: "The chief and oldest established of these is W. E. Ward's seminary. As a private educational enterprise, it is unquestionably unequalled in the country."

The Boston *Journal of Education* says: "Nashville still remains the headquarters of academic education for girls in the Southwest. Dr. W. E. Ward's seminary contains the daughters of the most distinguished families of a dozen States as boarding pupils, with a large number of Nashville girls. In all respects it seems to be abreast of similar institutions elsewhere."

It has a wonderful history.—*Christian Observer*, Louisville, Kentucky.

The leading female seminary at Nashville.—Atlanta (Georgia) *Constitution*.

The standard of this school is of the highest order.—Gallatin (Tennessee) *Examiner*.

With confidence we commend this seminary to parents.—Waco (Texas) *Examiner*.

The institution has no superior, and but few equals, in the South.—Nashville *Banner*.

This school stands deservedly high throughout the southern States.—Austin (Texas) *Statesman*.

The principal is well known to us as a Christian gentleman, an eminent scholar, and most excellent teacher. The seminary buildings are the finest in the State, if not in the entire South.—Memphis *Avalanche*.

This institution is becoming, under the management of Mr. Ward and his accomplished wife, one of the most prominent institutions of learning in the South.— Memphis *Ledger*.

Parents wishing to send their daughters out of the State would find Nashville a fine, healthy city, and Mr. Ward's seminary to offer every educational advantage.— Montgomery (Alabama) *Advertiser*.

This institution has rapidly risen to high position. It has just closed a very prosperous season.—Nashville *Christian Advocate*.

Ward's seminary, at Nashville, Tennessee, has a distinguished reputation for the education of young ladies. —Houston (Texas) *Telegraph*.

It has gradually worked its way till it justly occupies a position in the front rank of American institutions.— Galveston (Texas) *News*.

One of the most flourishing institutions of learning in the country. Those who wish to give their daughters a thorough education, not only in the elegant acquirements of life, but in all the studies going to make the accomplished scholar, cannot do better than place them in W. E. Ward's seminary, Nashville, Tennessee.—New Orleans *Picayune*.

The late commencement exercises of Ward's seminary were highly interesting, attracting large and delighted audiences of the *elite* of Nashville society. Dr. Ward exhibits the qualities of a live educator, and his seminary is one of the fixed institutions, not only of Tennessee, but the whole South. Its continued and increasing success is the just reward of energy, talent, and public spirit.—Nashville *Christian Advocate*.

Ward's Seminary for Young Ladies is an instance of individuality applied to schools. Discarding boards of trustees, visiting committees, baccalaureate orators, and the common machinery of all other schools, it has been managed by one mind, and its grand object has been to find the want in all matters of training, and to strike for it on the most direct line.—Nashville *American*.

The school is in the prime of its vigor and reaching out for more patronage than ever, and receiving more. It is a solid, permanent institution, destined, let us trust, to be perpetuated. So much of Dr. Ward's time is taken up with care for this, his sacred charge, he finds but little leisure to devote to aught else. In 1860, he became a Master Mason. In politics he is an hereditary Democrat, but has never taken more active part in politics than exercising the right of suffrage.

Dr. Ward married, at Nashville, February 24, 1859, Miss Eliza H. Hudson, eldest daughter of Dr. John R. Hudson, a Virginian, distinguished in his profession, and a large practitioner in his earlier manhood, now in his eighty-fourth year, living in Nashville. Her grandfather, Charles Hudson, of Mecklenburg county, Virginia, was a distinguished citizen of that county, a large tobacco grower. Her mother, *nee* Miss Minnie Napier,

was the daughter of John Napier, an iron-master of Dickson county, Tennessee, and niece of Dr. Elias W. Napier, the originator of iron manufacture in Tennessee. Mrs. Ward was born in Dickson county, Tennessee, February 10, 1839, and graduated from C. D. Elliott's Nashville Female Academy. She is tall, commanding and graceful in appearance, and has a remarkable degree of energy and candor and unselfishness of character; a refined Christian spirit with a great and inherited knowledge of medicine, sickness and disease, and the proper remedies, rendering her in this respect a matron unsurpassed for the training of young girls. For more than twenty years her unremitting hand and heart have nobly and faithfully seconded her husband in the great work of education. She has stimulated the ambition of hundreds of timid girls, repressed and reformed many spirits violent by nature, and built up the true idea of refined womanhood in nearly every case brought within her influence. Meanwhile, she has cultivated art to such a degree as to have become distinguished in the city as an amatuer in painting and all artistic work. Like her husband, she is a Cumberland Presbyterian. To her good sense and refined taste, the success of Ward's seminary is perhaps as much due as to the superior management of her husband.

By his marriage with Miss Hudson, Dr. Ward has five children living, four having died in infancy. The living are: (1). Sallie Ward, now the widow of John W. Conley, iron merchant, deceased. She graduated from Ward's seminary in the class of 1877. (2). Florence Ward, graduated from Ward's seminary in the class of 1879; now the wife of Robert H. Chaffe, a commission merchant at New Orleans. (3). Eunice Ward, graduated from Ward's seminary in the class of 1883. (4, 5). William E. Ward, jr., and Rebecca Ward.

A principle with Dr. Ward has been to seek the best associations in college when a boy, and in society, and even to stand aloof from all, until he could find congenial associates, as he did when he came a stranger to Nashville. Another rule of his is to prepare well for work and responsibility by a broad substratum of study and knowledge, and trust that the time would come when he could abundantly use them. Still another trait is not to say what he was going to do, but keep his own counsel, and let his actions speak to the world for themselves. Young men should derive great encouragement from this example—not to feel discouraged when men tell you you cannot succeed, but redouble your energies, keep your own counsel and go ahead. If Dr. Ward had listened to the wisest men in Nashville, he would have abandoned his educational work long ago, for they said it was impossible to succeed in so great an undertaking without pecuniary help. He has lived to demonstrate that they were mistaken. He planned, he resolved, he worked, and extraordinary success has crowned his efforts.

HON. HOWELL EDMUNDS JACKSON.

NASHVILLE.

THIS gentleman, now United States senator from Tennessee, and noted as one of the most profound and erudite lawyers in the State, was born at Paris, Tennessee, April 8, 1832. Just now in the prime of life, with his great intellectual abilities and capacities daily unfolding, he is destined, without doubt, to retain distinction and to have his name enrolled among the *nomina clara* of the nation. He is the son of the late Dr. A. Jackson and wife, *nee* Miss Mary Hurt, of Jackson, Tennessee. A full account of his ancestry will be found in the sketch of his brother, Gen. William H. Jackson, published in another part of this volume.

Howell E. Jackson obtained his academic education in the "old field schools," in the vicinage of Jackson, and his first diploma from the West Tennessee College at Jackson, from which latter institution he graduated, in 1849, with the highest honors of his class. In 1850, he entered the University of Virginia, and completing the customary course there, again graduated with distinguished honors. Returning home he read law for one year under his distinguished kinsman, Judge A. W. O. Totten, then a member of the Supreme court of Tennessee, and Judge Milton Brown. Next he attended the law school at Lebanon, Tennessee, in the fall of 1855, and graduated thence in the summer of 1856.

While *en route* home from the law school, he and his brother, Gen. William H. Jackson, who had just graduated from the West Point Military Academy, met in Nashville, spent a day or two in visiting points of interest about the city, and for the first time visited, together, the friend of their father, Gen. William G. Harding—quite a coincidence when it is stated that the two brothers, years later, married the only two daughters of Gen. Harding. From Nashville, the brothers repaired in a stage coach to their home in Jackson, Tennessee, where their fond father met them at daylight, as the stage stopped at his front gate, filled with joy that his two only sons should have filled the full measure of his hope by graduating at the institutions of his choice—a proud reflection for any young man to have.

Beginning the practice of the law at Jackson, our subject met with fine success. Subsequently, in 1858, he removed to Memphis, where he formed a most desirable law-partnership with Hon. David M. Currin, ex-member of Congress.

At the beginning of hostilities, he was appointed receiver under the Confederate sequestration act for West Tennessee. He shifted about at different points in the South, his duty being to take care of sequestered effects during the war.

After the war, he returned to Memphis, resumed the practice of law, having associated with him B. M. Estes, under the firm name of Estes & Jackson, one of the leading law firms of Memphis; subsequently associating with them Judge Ellet, ex-member of the Supreme bench of Mississippi, under the firm name of Estes, Ellet & Jackson.

Judge Jackson has been twice married; first, in 1859, to Miss Sophia Malloy, daughter of David B. Malloy, a banker of Memphis. Her mother was a Miss Shapard. To this marriage were born four children, Henry, Mary, William H. and Howell. The first Mrs. Jackson died in April, 1873.

In April, 1874, Judge Jackson married Miss Mary E Harding, daughter of Gen. W. G. Harding, of Nashville, whose sketch appears elsewhere in this volume. Like many other men in public life who have been extraordinarily successful, he has had the assistance of a faithful and sympathetic wife. Mrs. Jackson possesses, as her more prominent characteristics, energy and industry. She is domestic in her tastes, loving home and home life better than society, fashion and gayety. She is economical in general matters, but very liberal in her gifts to the church and all religious objects. She is cheerful and even-tempered, not subject to extreme fluctuations of spirits, is cordial and pleasant in manner; is a devoted mother, a genuine help-meet to her husband, and in short, is all that the mistress of a Christian household should be. By this marriage, Judge Jackson has three children, Bessie, Louise and Harding Alexander.

Shortly after his second marriage, Judge Jackson removed to his old home at Jackson, Tennessee, and there formed a partnership in law with Gen. Alexander W. Campbell, under the firm name of Campbell & Jackson. He continued the practice of law there successfully until the fall of 1880, when he was elected to the Tennessee Legislature, upon what is known as the State credit platform, this being his first experience in politics, never having been a member of any political convention. However, he at once became the leading member of that Legislature, and was elected to the United States senate by that body in 1881, his term expiring in 1887.

Upon his entrance to the United States senate, Judge Jackson began at once making his mark in committee work—especially as a member of the committees on claims, pensions and agriculture. In the second session the senate and the country discovered that they had in the quiet and modest senator from Tennessee, one of the profoundest legal minds in the Union. His opinions on constitutional law are regarded as *ex cathedra*. A recent Washington correspondent of the Nashville *Union* says of him: "A good deal of interest is felt in the senate in Senator Jackson's speech on the pending question regarding presidential suspensions and appointments, and the right of the senate to demand papers touching the suspension. Senator Jackson has attained a high rank in the senate in regard to his views on legal and constitutional questions such as these. This is especially shown by the fact that a very large proportion of the bills pertaining to judicial questions and those looking to the reform of the judicial system are referred in the judiciary committee to the sub-committee of which he is a member. Some of the most important judicial questions that have been before the senate this session have been intrusted to this sub-committee."

Cool, direct, and patient, he is a man of deliberation and weight, given to profound thought, but with courage and candor to speak his views when the occasion demands. Judge Jackson's salient characteristics may be summed up as follows: From early boyhood he has been a remarkably close student; of the most exemplary habits; a constant reader, especially of history; a man of scholarly attainments; possessed of an analytical mind; a clear, forcible speaker and writer; of fine constitution; a laborious worker; a most highly successful lawyer; a prudent, sagacious, economical business man, constantly accumulating. He has filled all positions on the bench; has been the attorney of several leading lines of railroad in the State; in politics is a State credit Democrat, and as a politician is conservative, believing in an economical administration of the government. Upon the subject of the tariff he holds that, while revenue should be the primary object in laying duties upon imports, these duties should be laid or adjusted with discrimination, so as, incidentally, to afford that much protection to home labor and capital against foreign competition; and that these duties should be heaviest on luxuries and lightest on the necessaries of life, and that the protection aimed at should, as far as possible, be made to apply to the three great interests of agriculture, manufactures and commerce, so as to give harmonious development to the country.

He has a strongly marked face, a compact, well-knit frame, and a stout, if not robust, constitution. He is an earnest man. Constitutional law is his strong point; difficult legal problems his forte. His tastes have always led him to the vocation of farming, and it was with difficulty that his father could turn him to the law after his graduation at Lebanon. He loves rural life. He is no fancy farmer, but finds a natural, inborn delight in agricultural pursuits, and believes the farmer's life the true source of peace and contentment.

On the 12th of April, 1886—since the opposite page of this sketch was printed—Judge Jackson was nominated by President Cleveland, and unanimously confirmed by the Senate, as circuit judge of the United States for the Sixth judicial circuit, to fill the vacancy occasioned by the death of the Hon. John Baxter. This appointment reflects the more credit upon the gentleman from the fact that he was not an applicant for the position, but was earnestly pressing the name of another Tennessean for the place. The following letter from the president to Judge Jackson shows the ground of his action: " *My Dear Senator*—The applications on behalf of all classes to fill the place made vacant by Judge Baxter's death are so numerous that the matter promises to degenerate into an unseemly scramble. To avoid this I have determined to send the name of Judge Baxter' successor to the Senate at once. In the interest of this important branch of public service, and very clear conception of my duty in the matter, I have determined to say to you, you must abandon all scruples you have entertained and permit me to nominate you to the vacancy. Your reluctance to consent to this action, growing out of the consideration for constituents in your State desiring the place, does you great credit, and increases my estimate of your value. You have no right to attempt to control my action or limit my selection in this way. I am quite willing that all other aspirants and their friends should know that your nomination is my own act and result of conviction of what ought to be done, from which I cannot be moved by your arguments, or by presenting the claims of other aspirants. Fully expecting you will not be insubordinate in the face of plain duty,

" Yours sincerely,

" GROVER CLEVELAND."

HON. WILLIAM HENRY WILLIAMSON.

LEBANON.

JUDGE WILLIAMSON was born in Wilson county, Tennessee, October 28, 1828, and for a man of his age, looks remarkably robust and well preserved, his hair being only slightly tinged with gray. He grew up in that county, on his father's farm, leading the life of a farmer's boy, until twenty years old, when he entered Cumberland University, in October, 1848, from which he graduated in 1852, in a class of six, among whom were Rev. D. C. Kelly, for four years pastor of McKendree church, Rev. E. D. Pearson, D. D., of Missouri, and

54

Rev. E. B. Chrisman, of Tennessee, now of Trinity University, Texas.

In early life, Judge Williamson had an inclination toward the medical profession, and read some in that direction, but abandoned the idea on account of his delicate health. He took to the law, under the advice of Hon. Abram Caruthers, and gave up his earlier taste for farming and medicine. He graduated in law in 1854, under Judge Caruthers and Judge Nathan Green, sr., was admitted to the bar the same year, at Lebanon, where he has resided ever since, commanding a good practice ever since the war. Previous to the war, his health was very feeble, but since the war he has grown strong and robust. In this respect, the war was the making of him, in a degree compensating him for the loss of his right arm.

On the 20th of May, 1861, he went into the Confederate service as orderly sergeant of Company H, commanded by Capt. John K. Howard, of the Seventh Tennessee infantry regiment, under Col. Robert Hatton, and followed the fortunes of that noble command to the close of the war. He was made captain, at the organization of the regiment, May 25, 1861, and was promoted to major of the regiment in March, 1863, at Fredricksburg, Virginia. He served in Virginia, Maryland and Pennsylvania, all the time in Lee's army, under Stonewall Jackson and A. P. Hill. He took part in the battles in western Virginia; in the battle of Seven Pines, where Gen. Hatton fell, May 7, 1862; in the seven days' fight around Richmond; at Fredricksburg, December 13, 1862; at Chancellorsville, May 2, 1863; at Gettysburg, July 3, 4 and 5, 1863, at which battle his brigade (Gen. Archer's Tennesseans), was in the advance of the army and fired the first guns in the battle, and on the last day of that famous engagement, Archer's Tennesseans and the Thirteenth Alabama, with Pettigrew's South Carolinians, were attached to Pickett's division, and these two brigades participated in Pickett's celebrated charge at Cemetery Heights. The map of that battle-field, published by order of the United States Congress, will show that these two brigades, represented by a red line, intermingled with the blue. The men mixed and fought across the breastworks, clubbing their guns. Major Williamson next participated in the opening combats between Grant's and Lee's armies, at Petersburg, March 28, 1865, after which he was furloughed, about fifteen days before Lee's surrender, and the Petersburg fight was his last active military engagement.

Maj. Williamson was three times wounded during the war, and bears upon his body the honorable scars of a brave and gallant soldier. His first wound was received at the battle of Gaines' Mill, while fighting under Gen. A. P. Hill, an inch ball, from a piece of ordnance, going through his right thigh, cutting the leaders, slightly shattering the bone, and from which he at times still suffers pain and from weakness in the limb. He was next wounded at the battle of Chancellorsville, being knocked senseless while standing on the enemy's works, taking observations, just after they had been driven out, but the bullet glanced and killed another man who was standing by his side. He was next wounded at Gettysburg, in the charge on Cemetery Heights, by a minnie ball striking him just below the right shoulder, shattering the arm so that amputation was necessary. His armless sleeve silently proclaims to all who see him that he has been through the fiery furnace of war, and it is an eloquent reminder, too, that he never shrank from his duty, and deserves well of his country.

After the war, he resumed the practice of law, at Lebanon, in July, 1865, in partnership with Hon. Andrew B. Martin, now professor of law in Cumberland University, Lebanon, which partnership lasted until he went on the bench, in 1870. In that year he was elected judge of the Seventh judicial circuit, comprising the counties of Cannon, Rutherford, Bedford and Wilson, a position which he filled for the term, eight years, distinguishing himself, specially as a merciful judge in the administration of criminal law. Like Samuel, the prophet, Judge Williamson can lift his hand and ask, "Whom have I oppressed?" Moreover, it may be said that nothing excites Judge Williamson so quickly and so much as the infliction, too common of late, of unreasonable fines and punishments, worthy only the times of Draco or the Middle Ages. At the expiration of his judicial term, in 1878, Judge Williamson returned to the practice of law in partnership with Andrew B. Martin and E. E. Beard, under the firm style of Williamson, Martin & Beard.

A Democrat, born and bred, Judge Williamson is firm and unflinching in advocating that loftiest of Democratic principles—the greatest liberty to each, consistent with the greatest liberty to all. He has attended political conventions, but has not been active in politics, except in trying to shape a correct political policy for his State. On that great politico-economical question, the tariff, he is for a tariff for revenue only. In December, 1869, he was elected a delegate, from Wilson county, to the State constitutional convention, in which distinguished body, though a young man, he took an active part.

When asked if he was a Mason, he replied, "No; I never joined but two societies, one, the Democratic party, and the other, the Cumberland Presbyterian church, and," he added, jocularly, "I have had hard work to maintain my position in them." He has, for twenty-five years, been a member of the board of trustees of Cumberland University.

Judge Williamson married at Murfreesborough, Tennessee, January 31, 1873, Mrs. Mattie Ready Morgan, widow of Gen. John H. Morgan, the celebrated cavalry chieftain of the Confederate army, and daughter of Hon. Charles Ready, the distinguished lawyer and congressman, of that city. Her mother, nee Miss Martha

Strong, was the daughter of Dr. Strong, of East Tennessee. Mrs. Williamson's sister, nee Miss Alice Ready, is now the wife of Hon. Andrew B. Martin, at one time a member of the Tennessee Legislature, presidential elector for the State at large, on the Hancock ticket, in 1880, and now professor of law in Cumberland University. His biography appears elsewhere in this volume. By her former husband, Gen. Morgan, Mrs. Williamson has one child, Miss Johnnie H. Morgan, who recently graduated with distinction at Patapsco, Maryland. In appearance, she is very much like her father, has a gifted mind, particularly in elocution, and in her manner has that peculiar magnetism that so characterized her father and gave him influence over men.

Mrs. Williamson was educated by Dr. C. D. Elliott, at the old Nashville Female Academy, and is noted for her fine address, intellectual vigor and cultivation, her strength of character and devotion to her children. Handsome in person, and clothed with the graces of the highest order of womanhood, she is naturally of great influence in the community in which she lives. By her marriage with Judge Williamson, she has had five children: Henry, born November 8, 1873; Martha; Charles; Alice; Nannie, died, May, 1883, aged two years.

The Williamson family originally came from Northumberland, England, and settled in North Carolina. Judge Williamson's grandfather, John Williamson, entered the Revolutionary army when he was fifteen years old, and had served one year or more when the war closed. He was married on his way home, on New river, Virginia, to Miss Margaret Cloyd, she being only fifteen years old and he seventeen. They emigrated to Tennessee in 1785, with Gen. James Robertson, the celebrated pioneer soldier and founder of Nashville, and under Gen. Robertson he served as a captain in all his combats with the Indians along the Cumberland river. They first settled in Sumner county, but after the Indians were driven from the country, he settled at the place, now in Wilson county, and built the house where Judge Williamson was born, the original house being built with port-holes in it. He died about 1829, his widow dying in 1842. His brother, Thomas Williamson, was one of Gen. Jackson's officers in all his wars, Indian and British, and all of his sons were in the army in the Indian wars, except William (Judge Williamson's father), who was then only eleven years old. Judge Williamson's uncle, Col. George Williamson, and Gen. Zachariah Taylor, were appointed lieutenants at the same time and in the same regiment, in the United States regular army.

Judge Williamson's father, William Williamson, was born September 14, 1806, in the same house in which his son was born, twenty-two years later. He was a farmer, a Cumberland Presbyterian, a Democrat, and a justice of the peace. He was a man of fine education, a good classical scholar, and, for a time, was a teacher. In early life, he was a dashing man, later, more quiet; remarkable for never speaking evil of any one, man or woman. He died August 22, 1883.

Judge Williamson's mother was formerly Miss Nancy Crutchfield, daughter of Rev. William Henry Crutchfield, of the Methodist church. Her mother was Hannah Mayberry, daughter of William Mayberry, an old pioneer family from North Carolina. Mrs. Williamson died, July 27, 1852, at the age of forty-one, leaving nine children, eight of whom survive, seven of them now living in Wilson county, and one, Elizabeth H., wife of Dr. John B. Talbot, now living in East Nashville, Tennessee. Judge Williamson's maternal uncle, Dr. Oran Crutchfield, was a prominent physician, in Wilson county, but died young.

Judge Williamson has paid little attention to making money, except by his profession. He has been a student all his life from a boy. He was well taught by his scholarly father, and has indulged in a wide range of reading. He was well educated as a lawyer, not only in the curriculum, but outside of that. After he commenced the law, he devoted himself to that science assiduously, and to tracing it to its original sources, Jewish, Roman and English. Young men, aspiring to be lawyers, and to obtain the honors of that profession, will not be throwing away their time if they study carefully the history of this man and his methods. He studied the Pentateuch as diligently as he studied Blackstone, as a preparation for the law.

Of Judge Williamson, his friend, Gen. J. B. Palmer, who has known him long and well, says: "As a judge, he ranks high with the profession as a jurist of ability, impartiality and independence. His administration was distinguished by firmness and fairness and the utmost courtesy, his endeavor being to administer the law on the basis of justice to litigants, and he always extended to all parties every opportunity to present all the merits of their case. Both the bar and the people entertain for him the highest respect. The bar were more than ordinarily attached to him. The whole being said, he was a most excellent circuit judge."

HON. DAVID P. HADDEN.

MEMPHIS.

ALTHOUGH justly entitled to rank among "Prominent Tennesseans," the Hon. David P. Hadden, of Memphis, is by birth a Kentuckian, having been born in Elkton, Todd county, of that State, March 27, 1835. Up to his twentieth year, he followed agricultural pursuits, worked on a farm and tended stock in summer and went to school in winter. To finish his education he, himself, taught school one year and made enough money to complete his studies, which included mathematics, Latin and Greek. In 1857, he graduated from the Jefferson Male Academy, at Elkton, where he had been the classmate of Hon. B. H. Bristow, late secretary of the United States treasury, Hon. Roger Q. Mills, the able and eloquent member of Congress from Texas, and of Frank Jay McClean, of Kentucky. Very many of the students of this academy have turned out to be men of prominence in the various professions and avocations they have chosen subsequently. After graduation, Mr. Hadden went to Memphis, and was engaged there one year in the cotton business, with his uncle, David Park, after which he returned to Kentucky and began the study of law. Meanwhile, he was employed at writing in the offices of the circuit and county court clerks of his native county. He was admitted to the bar, but never practiced. Subsequently, he moved to Clarksville, Tennessee, where he was employed several years as a book-keeper and notary public to the various banks. When the war broke out, although he was southern in all his prejudices and associations, he did not go into the army, but remained at Clarksville, in business, until the town was occupied by the Federals, when he went to New York and engaged in the cotton business with Watts, Crane & Co., one of the largest firms that ever went from the western country to the metropolis. After remaining in that city about two years, he came back to Tennessee, and to Memphis, which he had in his "mind's eye" as a most excellent place in which to locate permanently. He embarked in the grocery and cotton business, in the firm of Simpson, Hadden & Co., of which firm his cousin, William Park, was also a member. That firm was afterward dissolved and succeeded by David P. Hadden & Co., afterwards Hadden & Avery, and then Hadden & Farrington, which has continued to the present time.

Mr. Hadden was brought up a Whig, yet, since the war, he has been a Democrat, and, though classed with that party, has never been a partisan, but has always supported the men he considered safest and best. The business men of Memphis have always shown confidence in him, and have placed him forward in various enterprises of the city. He has been president of the cotton exchange for two terms, and has been sent to various commercial bodies to represent his city and his friends. In 1882, he was taken up by the business men of Memphis, regardless of party, as a candidate for president of the taxing district of Shelby county, and though there were two tickets in the field, his name was upon both, and he received nearly all the votes cast, being elected for a term of four years.

Since the day of his election, he has given up his private business and devoted his time, attention and energy exclusively to the interests of the taxing district, which engages his attention from 7 A. M. to 5 P. M., daily. During his administration, by the aid and counsel of the able men associated with him, the taxing district has seemed to improve and go forward more than at any other time, and it has been his pride to see a debt of more than six millions of dollars nearly all settled, on terms satisfactory alike to the bondholders and the citizens. The system of improvements inaugurated by his predecessors has been carried vigorously forward until the city is now in the healthiest condition since its foundation. Miles upon miles of solid pavements have been laid, as well as a still more extensive sewer system. The government of the city of Memphis, which is looked upon as a model of municipal government, is conducted by a board of three commissioners, of which he is president, and is run upon strictly business principles. The office came to him unsought, and was accepted, not as a political, but as a business position, and has been conducted by him upon that principle. He has no further political aspirations in connection with that or any other office, his sole desire being to see the city prosper under his administration, at the end of which he is ready to turn it over to the people. The vast sanitary improvements which have rendered Memphis one of the healthiest cities in the West, have been carried out mainly under his direction, and that of Dr. G. B. Thornton, the president of the Memphis board of health. Both gentlemen are now valuable members of the Tennessee State Board of Health, having been placed there in consideration of their capacity in sanitary matters manifested in their own city.

Mr. Hadden was made a Master Mason at Clarksville, Tennessee, took all the Council and Chapter degrees there, and was made a Knight Templar at Nashville, in 1860. In 1877, he was elected president of the Masonic Temple Association at Memphis, by the stockholders of that institution. The building had been commenced, but the association was so involved in debt, and the members of the fraternity so much disheartened, that no one seemed willing to take hold of it, but having been elected, he put his wits to work, and, with the aid of an able directory, the temple was completed and is now one of the most ornamental buildings in the city, and is occupied by the postoffice and the various Masonic bodies. He looks upon his connection with the temple with more pride than anything he has ever undertaken. He has been a director in the German National Bank, since 1875, and vice-president of the Bluff City Insurance company for the past eighteen years.

He started in life without a dollar, and has always been reasonably successful, but has never had a desire to amass a large fortune, preferring to enjoy what he makes. His life has been a happy one, and the world has dealt gently with him from infancy up, for he has always numbered his friends by legions.

Mr. Hadden's father, Thomas N. Hadden, a native of Spartanburg district, South Carolina, went to Kentucky when a boy, and died there at the age of seventy-four, at the family residence, which has been in the family since 1790. The family is of old Presbyterian stock, zealously devoted to their church, and none of them have ever sought political preferment or filled political office. Rev. Joseph B. Hadden, uncle of the subject of this sketch, was for many years a prominent Presbyterian minister in Kentucky.

Mr. Hadden's mother was Jane Park, a lady of Irish descent, the sister of ex-Mayor John Park, of Memphis, and of David and Samuel Park. She was a woman of strong traits of character, extraordinary religious temperament, and a member of the Presbyterian church. Her father was John Park, who came to America from Ireland in 1825, and settled in Elkton, Kentucky, where he died, in 1837.

Mr. Hadden is the only surviving representative of the family, and has no children. He was married on the 25th of September, 1873, to Miss Mary Boyd, daughter of A. M. Boyd, a native of Georgia, now living in Memphis. Mrs. Hadden was educated at Vassar College, graduated there in 1872, and is distinguished for the wide range of her accomplishments, which embrace music and drawing, as well as the domestic arts.

HON. DAVID N. KENNEDY.

CLARKSVILLE.

THIS gentleman, now president of the Northern Bank of Tennessee; president of the Clarksville American Bible Society; president of the Clarksville Board of Underwriters; member of the board of directors and secretary of the Southwestern Presbyterian University; member of the board of directors and treasurer of the Clarksville Gas Company; member of the board of directors of the Clarksville Water Company; member of the board of directors and secretary and treasurer of the Greenwood Cemetery Company (which was established mainly through his influence, and, it is due to him and to Clarksville to say, is the most beautiful in the State, excepting only Mount Olivet at Nashville, and Elmwood at Memphis); an elder in the Presbyterian church for the past twenty-five years, and Sunday-school superintendent for fifteen years; now the senior bank officer in Tennessee; president of the oldest bank in the State, and the senior business man of Clarksville, having been a citizen of that town for forty-two years, and of Tennessee for forty-eight years—his life presents many points worth the study of young men who would rise in the world. It may be observed that his rise has been gradual, his capital being at first very small.

His grandfather, James Kennedy, removed from Mecklenburg county, North Carolina, to Garrard county, Kentucky, when that now highly cultivated county was but a wilderness, and improved one of the first places outside of the forts. The father of Mr. D.

N. Kennedy, William Kennedy, in the same spirit of adventure, displayed equal energy in removing to what is now known as the "Green river country," in Kentucky, and settled in Logan county (now Todd), near the present town of Elkton, where the subject of this sketch was born, February 28, 1820. Although his father was a farmer with a limited estate, and with a large family to provide for, he was unsparing of his means and time in promoting all public and benevolent enterprises. He was a devoted Presbyterian, and did not fail to impress, by strict discipline and instruction, the spirit and genius of the religion of his church on his children. In advance rather of the times, with the view of giving an impetus to the cause of education and religion, he gave the ground and other means and much of his time and attention to the erection of what was well known as the "Presbyterian Seminary," an institution most eligibly situated near Elkton, but which, from a variety of causes, has since been permitted to go down, and in its abandonment the aims of a most noble heart were entirely defeated. The cause of education being so dear to him, it was doubtless his intention to give his son a most liberal one, but while taking the initiative, he died, September 22, 1832.

Then began the self-relying exertions of David N. Kennedy. Leaving school, of his own choice, shortly after the death of his father, he took a situation with his brother as common laborer in a wool manufactory in Elkton. After some months faithful toil, with the consent of his relations, he accepted a situation in a retail dry goods store four years in the same town, and removed to Nashville, in 1838. His unremitting attention and fidelity to business was soon rewarded by his employers in that city, who made him their confidential clerk until the cessation of their business in 1840. On being notified of his release from his former engagement, R. H. Gardner & Co., wholesale merchants of great sagacity, who had observed his habits and knew his qualifications, offered him a similar situation, which he accepted, in 1840, and retained until his removal to Clarksville, in 1842, to go into business, on his own account, in connection with Mr. John S. Hart (who had been for some time his co-laborer as a clerk). The firm of Hart & Kennedy continued in business till 1850, when Mr. Kennedy, in consequence of ill health, retired, leaving his partner in possession of a highly lucrative trade, built up by the most assiduous attention and adherence to such principles as rarely fail to secure the confidence of communities and the approbation of an enlightened conscience. Although their capital was limited in the beginning, they competed successfully with their neighbors enjoying the benefits of longer acquaintance and more extensive means.

Antecedent to his marriage, in 1843, his residence in Clarksville was not regarded as so permanent as subsequent changes in his relations caused it to be. Hence, in 1844, he was made a director in the branch bank of Tennessee. In 1845, his appointment was renewed and the directory elected him president, although the junior member of the board. In 1846, the Legislature, with a view of winding up the bank, put the Clarksville branch, with others, in a state of gradual liquidation, appointing an agent through the parent board with an advisory committee, of which Mr. Kennedy was a member. It eventually appearing impolitic to wind up the bank, and highly desirable that the State should participate in the profits which might be obtained from the extensive trade of Clarksville, the Legislature, in 1850, re-established the branch, devolving upon the parent board the duty of reorganizing it. In pursuance of this injunction, a new directory was formed, among whom was Mr. Kennedy, and by whom he was elected president, which office he filled till November, 1850. The resignation of the cashier, Thomas W. Barksdale, at this time devolved upon the directory the necessity of electing another. In casting about Mr. Kennedy was thought the most suitable person to fill the vacancy, but it was not known whether he would accept it, as he would have to give up the presidency as well as his commercial operations. On being approached it was found agreeable to him to do so in view of his feeble health. Thereupon he resigned as president and was unanimously elected cashier.

Having organized the Northern Bank at Clarksville, on January 1st, 1854, he became its president, which position he has filled continuously till the present time.

This bank, organized by the same stockholders that now own it, and with the same leading officers, viz., Mr. Kennedy as president, and Mr. James L. Glenn as cashier, maintained its existence during the war, the assets being removed to a safe place, the cashier remaining on hand, ready to meet all claims, though business had to be done on street corners and in private chambers. Of the thirty-six firms or persons on whom the bank purchased bills during the first year of its existence, only one, Messrs. Sawyer, Wallace & Co., of New York, are now doing business; of their twenty-two bank correspondents, all but five afterward failed, and only three, the American Exchange Bank and the Metropolitan Bank of New York, and A. D. Hunt & Co., o Louisville, are now engaged in business; of the three hundred depositors there were living in the vicinity of Clarksville, in 1879, only twenty two, eighteen of whom continued as depositors. During the seven years prior to the war, the entire losses of the bank did not exceed five hundred dollars, and it has never suspended payment, though it has passed through four years of war and the commercial panics of 1857, 1861 and 1873.

In 1860, Mr. Kennedy was unanimously elected president of the Memphis, Clarksville and Louisville railroad, but declined the position.

A pronounced Henry Clay Whig up to the war, in favor of a protective tariff and internal improvements, and a stanch Union man, Mr. Kennedy voted, in 1860, for Bell and Everett, but when it became evident, in 1861, that the Union could not be saved, he went with the secessionists, and was, in August, 1861, unanimously elected to the lower house of the Tennessee Legislature from Montgomery county, was made chairman of the committee on finance, and upon the resignation of the chairman of the committee on military affairs, was elected to that position.

Tennessee being overrun by the Federal troops, the Legislature having first moved to Memphis and adjourned, and he being physically unable to bear arms, cast his lot with the southern army, and rendered service in the treasury department, under appointment from President Davis, remaining in that position until Gen. Johnston's surrender, when he returned to his home, where, as soon as a pardon was obtained from President Johnson, he reopened the Northern Bank.

In November, 1869, he was unanimously elected from Montgomery county a delegate to the Tennessee State constitutional convention of 1870, in which he was an active, energetic and influential member. This closes his political career, his resolution being then taken never again to accept any public office. Since that time he has been an active church worker.

Mr. Kennedy married, at Clarksville, November 22, 1843, Miss Sarah A. Bailey, a native of Wilkinson county, Mississippi, daughter of James Bailey, originally from North Carolina, and of Scotch blood. He was a cotton planter in Mississippi, and was a brother of Maj. Charles Bailey, of Montgomery county, Tennessee, a prominent and honored citizen, the father of the late United States senator, James E. Bailey.

Mrs. Kennedy's mother, nee Miss Lucinda Brown, of Wilkinson county, Mississippi, died when the daughter was an infant; and her father dying when she was ten years old, she was raised by her uncle, Maj. Charles Bailey, before mentioned. She graduated from the old Nashville Female Academy, under Dr. C. D. Elliott, and is noted for her finely balanced character, the leading traits of which are benevolence and firmness, blended with gentleness. She has been admirably successful in training her daughters to become women, filling their positions with credit and distinction. She is a very efficient and earnest church worker, and her charities are limited only by her means and opportunities.

By his marriage with Miss Bailey, Mr. Kennedy has six children : (1). Mary B. Kennedy, graduated at the Clarksville Female Academy; married, in 1870, B. H. Owen, a druggist at Clarksville, and has three children, Sallie K., John D. and Mary K. (2). James T. Kennedy, born June 21, 1853; educated at Stewart College, Clarksville, and is now a tobacco warehouseman and commission merchant at that place; married, December 1, 1885, Miss Lois Viser, daughter of James H. Viser, of Manatee, Florida. (3). Sallie G. Kennedy, graduated from the Clarksville Female Academy; married, in 1879, Rev. T. J. Plunket, a graduate of the Southwestern Presbyterian University, at Clarksville, and of the Union Theological Seminary, Columbia, South Carolina (a brother of Dr. J. D. Plunket, of Nashville, whose sketch appears elsewhere in this volume), and now pastor of the Second Presbyterian church at Covington, Kentucky. They have three children, Thomas Smythe, Henry Clark and Paul Wood. (4). Clara Stuart Kennedy, educated at Miss Baldwin's Female Seminary at Staunton, Virginia, graduating in several schools without taking a full course; married, in 1881, to Robert H. Burney, a prominent lawyer, and at present attorney-general of the Clarksville criminal

court. They have two children, Robert H. and Sarah K. (5). David Newton Kennedy, an afflicted son. (6). Ellen B. Kennedy, graduated in several schools at Miss Baldwin's Seminary, Staunton, Virginia; married, in October, 1882, J. W. Clapp, jr., son of Hon. J. W. Clapp, of Memphis (whose sketch see elsewhere in this volume). They have one child, James Alston.

Mr. Kennedy and all the members of his family are members of the Presbyterian church.

Beginning life on a very small patrimony, Mr. Kennedy has acquired fortune by industry, sagacity and economy, close attention to business in all its details, and by a determination from the very outset of his business career never to spend as much during a year as he made in that year, and never to engage in outside speculations. From the time he received only seventy-five dollars a year as salary, he has carried out this plan, except during the war. He never engaged in anything he did not understand and that he could not give his personal attention and management except once, in 1853, when he engaged in the iron business, and lost fifty thousand dollars. He has been always temperate, though not totally abstemious; always moral, never having any of the vices supposed to be common to boys, and from the age of twenty-four has been a consistent member of the church. His purpose in life from the beginning was to be a success, and to win it in an honorable way, and to be useful as a member of society.

The late Hon. James E. Bailey, speaking to the editor, said of Mr. Kennedy: "His success is due to himself and to no one else; to his energy, capacity and devotion to business, whatever it was, whether as cashier of the branch bank of Tennessee, or as president of his own bank. All his undertakings are carried on with all his might and main, neglecting nothing which is necessary to success. He is a man who thinks, and is ever ready to carry out his thoughts by action, both in church and State. I regard him as one of the ablest and wisest men in Tennessee in my day. His policy has always been the safe one. You have, in Mr. Kennedy, the most distinguished character who has lived in Clarksville for many years."

HON. ABSALOM ARTHUR KYLE.

ROGERSVILLE.

ABSALOM ARTHUR KYLE was born February 20, 1818, upon a farm on the Tennessee river, six miles west of Rogersville, Hawkins county, Tennessee. He was a son of Absalom Kyle, who was born in the same county, November 4, 1789, and whose father, Robert Kyle, was an Irishman, having emigrated to this country from the north of Ireland, and was one of

the early pioneers to Tennessee, while that territory formed a part of North Carolina. The mother of Absalom Kyle was a Brooks, of English extraction, and was blessed with a numerous progeny, of whom Absalom was the youngest. The latter, in 1812, married Beersheba, daughter of Pharaoh and Beersheba Cobb, who were from North Carolina, and of English descent.

Thirteen children—eight sons and five daughters—were the fruits of this marriage, the subject of this notice being the third son in the order of birth. He was raised upon the farm, receiving, in early youth, such instruction as in that primitive day was given to children of his age, in the "old field," or common schools of his section. His father, however, being determined to give him a classical training, sent him, when in his fifteenth year, to McMinn Academy, at Rogersville, Tennessee, and placed him under the tutelage of Stokely D. Mitchell, who graduated in the class with President James K. Polk, at Chapel Hill, North Carolina. There young Kyle remained for three years, and completed his academic course in 1835. In 1836, he was sent to the university at Knoxville, where he finished his education and graduated in 1838.

Returning home after his graduation, he remained upon the farm until 1840, when, choosing the law as his profession, he went to Rogersville, and read law with Col. John Netherland, until September, 1842, when he was called to the bar, Judges Edward Scott and Robert Anderson signing his license. He at once entered upon the duties of the profession, which he actively prosecuted for several years.

On the 11th of June, 1846, at Tazewell, Tennessee, he married Mary A., daughter of Hugh and Catharine Graham, then in her twenty-sixth year. This pious lady was, for forty-five years, an exemplary member of the Presbyterian church, coy and reserved in her nature, beloved by all who knew her, and distinguished by her noble and unostentatious charities. She died, in the year 1884, deeply lamented by all who ever came within the circle of her acquaintance.

In October, 1847, he was elected by the General Assembly of Tennessee attorney-general for the First judicial circuit for six years. He accepted the office and discharged its functions with much ability.

In April, 1854, he was chosen a delegate to represent his people in the commercial convention, then held at Charleston, South Carolina; after which he continued the practice of law until the late civil war.

In 1861, he was a Union candidate for the convention at Nashville, to which he was elected, beating his competitor, Reuben Arnold, son of the late Gen. T. D. Arnold, by over six thousand votes, in the counties of Jefferson, Greene, Hancock and Hawkins. With all the power and ability he possessed, he combated the doctrine of secession, both upon the rostrum and in the walks of private life, until the question ceased to be debatable, and passed beyond the influence of argument or reason.

After the commencement of hostilities, he remained quietly at his home, in Rogersville, until the Federal forces occupied East Tennessee, when he passed through the Confederate lines and resumed the practice of his profession at Knoxville, where he stayed till May, 1865. In 1864, he supported Lincoln for the presidency.

In the winter of 1863–64, he visited Washington City, in company with Gov. Johnson, by whom he was introduced to President Lincoln. Remaining there six weeks, he and the President became quite intimate, and so prepossessed was the latter with Mr. Kyle that he tendered him the office of United States district attorney for East Tennessee, which, however, was declined, but he requested that the office be given to a friend, Col. C. W. Hall, which was done. In 1865, he became supervisor of banks in Tennessee.

In 1866, he was appointed, without solicitation, by President Johnson, and confirmed by the senate, United States direct tax commissioner of Tennessee. While in this office, three hundred thousand dollars were collected, every dollar of which was paid over and faithfully accounted for.

In the representative district, composed of the counties of Hancock, Hawkins, Greene and Jefferson—all Republican counties—he was elected as a Democrat to the constitutional convention of 1870, over W. P. Gillenwaters, Republican. In 1865, he became a prominent candidate for the United States senate, but was defeated by David T. Patterson, son-in-law of President Johnson.

In 1866, he allied himself with the Democratic party, in consequence of his repugnance and opposition to the radical reconstruction measures and the disfranchising policy of the State, under Gov. Brownlow's administration. In 1868, he was the elector in the First district of Tennessee on the Seymour ticket, since which time he has been frequently mentioned, by the press and by the people throughout the State, as a fit person to occupy the gubernatorial chair.

At the close of the war he owned considerable property, but being kind-hearted, generous, and liberal to a fault, had endorsed for many friends, which utterly ruined him, financially. Yet, in the general wreck, he sought not to conceal or cover up his property from his creditors, but surrendered all he had, thus exemplifying, in an eminent degree, one of the principal traits of his character, that of honesty and scrupulous integrity. After his financial failure he continued to practice law up to the fall of 1875, when he retired to a farm, on the East Tennessee railroad, at Russellville, where he quietly lived until the 22d of April, 1884, when death deprived him of his beloved wife, at the age of sixty-four. The happening of this sad event caused him to make a change of domicile, and his children, being all married and forisfamiliated, he returned to Rogersville, where he made his home with his son, Hugh G. Kyle, esq.

Mr. Kyle died at the residence of his brother, Gen. W. C. Kyle, near Whitesburg, Tennessee, while there on a temporary visit, on the 15th of November, 1885. His death was sudden and unexpected, without the least premonition or warning, and was, doubtless, caused by a stroke of heart disease, of which he previously had an attack. He retired to rest, in his usual health, on the night of the 14th, and next morning was found in his bed a corpse, having manifestly passed away without a pain or a struggle.

The untimely death of this good man, for he was only in his sixty-eighth year, with an apparent promise of great longevity, cast a gloom over the entire community, a people who had known him and loved him for years. It has been said that it is difficult for public men to live and flourish without making enemies. Mr. Kyle, however, it may be truthfully remarked, was an exception. He had no enemies, but lived respected, and died much regretted by all who knew him.

Mr. Kyle practiced law for thirty-five years, and his intercourse with the bench and bar was distinguished for courtesy of deportment and probity of character. He preferred rather to lose a case than gain it by unfair means, or a disreputable act. Although fond of politics, he was not a politician, in the modern sense; his reputation being chiefly attained as an honest man, a fair-minded, just and skillful lawyer. So notorious was his integrity that he acquired the sobriquet of "Honest App."

But the strong natural powers of Mr. Kyle's mind lay dormant until 1861, when the stability of the Union was threatened and assailed. Then it was that his latent energies were aroused, and he became conspicuous as one of the Union leaders of the State. In connection with such men as President Johnson, Col. John Netherland, Judge Nelson, Judge Luckey, and others, he breasted the coming storm and sought to avert the impending calamity. His exertions and example in this direction fostered loyalty to the Union among the people of East Tennessee, for which they have ever since been distinguished. He, like his father before him, was a man of great individuality, and a natural leader of men. Mr. Kyle's devotion to the principles of the constitution which ordained these States into one strong general government, was sincere and unaffected. While conceding the right of the several States to regulate their own municipal affairs, he had no patience with the theory of secession, or the right of each State to withdraw from the Union at her own will, and establish independent governments. Hence, when the late conflict of arms ended, and it became a question whether the southern States were in or out of the Union, Mr. Kyle opposed the measures of reconstruction, logically maintaining that the States had never gone out, within the purview of the constitution, and were, therefore, entitled to representation in the American Congress. This drove him into the Democratic party, although a great Unionist, and a Whig, in ante-bellum days. The policy of disfranchisement, too, adopted by the Republican—then called the Radical—party in Tennessee and other southern States, was distasteful to him, and not congenial to his nature. While the conflict was raging, none desired the success of Federal arms and overthrow of the Confederates more than he, yet when the latter were finally defeated and subjugated by the armies of the Union, instead of pursuing a policy of vindictiveness and disfranchisement toward a fallen foe, he would treat them as wayward brothers who had, like the prodigal of old, left their father's house, but now returned, restore them to all the rights of citizenship and invite them to again participate in the liberties of a great republic. This sentiment exemplified the forgiving nature of the man, and did credit to his goodness of heart.

Other celebrities in Tennessee may have possessed more versatility of genius, their erudition may have been deeper and more profound, but in strong native intellect and common sense, embellished with much culture, unselfish patriotism and devotion to the principles of government which he deemed best for the common weal, leaving out of view his personal preferment, he was almost without a compeer.

Had he sought his own aggrandizement, to the sacrifice of his convictions and principles, he was in a position, as a distinguished Unionist, at the close of the war, to have sought and obtained any judicial or political office in the gift of the people of East Tennessee, by allying himself with the Republican or Radical party, then, as now, largely in the majority in that section of the State; but, like the illustrious Clay, of whom he was a worthy disciple, he would rather be right than be president.

Mr. Kyle was a fine specimen of the mountain man of culture. Possessing a splendid physique, six feet high, well proportioned, with an olive complexion, and dark or hazel eyes, his appearance was marked and prepossessing. He was frank and open in his manners, with a smile and kind word for all, which endeared him to the hearts of his associates. His temperament was mild and placid, and in his generous nature he was wont to cover the foibles of others with the mantle of a broad charity.

In early youth he was fond of music and the sports, and at one period of his life was a fine performer on the violin. He had a passion for the saddle-horse, and spent much of his time in equestrian exercise. Although not an orator, he had a strong, musical voice, combined with a rare faculty of presenting his thoughts in terse, epigrammatic phrase, which made him an interesting speaker in the forum or upon the rostrum.

Four children—three daughters and one son—survive to mourn the loss of a beloved father and sainted mother. The eldest, Lucy A., was born on the 3d of May, 1848, educated at Salem, North Carolina, and is an accomplished lady. In 1877 she married Dr. F. A. Shotwell, of Rogersville, where they still reside. The second, Hugh G. Kyle, was born December 29, 1849, finished his education at Princeton, New Jersey, where he graduated with high honors in 1870. Returning home, he read law with his father, and was licensed in 1871. In 1879, he married Bertha, daughter of Tyre

55

Glen, on the Yadkin river, North Carolina. One child blessed this union, a daughter, Margaret, now four years old. He also resides at Rogersville. The third child, Annis, was born in 1853. She was also educated at Salem, North Carolina, receiving a classical training. In September, 1875, she married Judge H. S. K. Morrison, of Estillville, Virginia, where they have since resided. Maria Louise, the youngest, was born in September, 1862, and received her education at the Rogersville Female College. In 1882, she was wedded to W. B.

Robinson, a merchant, of Newport, Cocke county, Tennessee.

Though their father left them no patrimony of a pecuniary value, it must be the chief solace of these children to reflect now, and in after years, that he left them a patrimony of infinitely more value, the character of a just and honest man, whose very name was a synonym for integrity, which is the greatest panegyric that could be written of his fame. May they follow the example of their illustrious sire.

ORVILLE H. MENEES, M. D.

NASHVILLE.

LOOKING at the two principal factors of the greatness of a State—mind and pride—and taking the medical profession as the measure of both, it is safe to say there is no reason to be found, either in climatic influences, or the products of its soil, to prevent the development of character and talent here in Tennessee equal to any on the globe. The State has already developed surgical talent equal to Gross, "the best in the world," practitioners equal to Flint, and diagnosticians that have no superiors on the continent. The more prominent physicians of the State are not only masters of their profession, but men of broad culture, and of the highest sense of honor, making themselves—to use the language of the most eloquent of them all—"both a service and a sacrifice," and to honor their work the only legitimate way to get honor from it. The medical schools of Tennessee are already commanding the respect of the nation, and have given three presidents and five vice-presidents to the American Medical Association, one president to the association of superintendents of insane asylums of the United States, sent their accredited representatives to the World's Medical Congress at London, and the Centennial Medical Congress at Philadelphia, and, the most significant fact of all, are attracting students from the immediate neighborhoods of older institutions, and even from localities beyond them.

Nor are the older medical men the only representatives of the profession that are entitled to a place in this book. There are young men developing among the faculties that have already achieved something of distinction, and are a promise that the standard of the profession shall not be lowered when committed to their hands. Of these, Dr. Orville Harrison Menees, of Nashville, son of the eminent professor, Dr. Thomas Menees, deserves a separate mention.

He was born at Springfield, Tennessee, April 15, 1859; received his literary education in Vanderbilt University, Nashville; graduated M.D., first from the medical department of the Vanderbilt, in 1879, and took the degree of M.D. in the medical department of the University of Nashville, in 1880, and succeeded his deceased brother, Dr. Thomas W. Menees, as associate demonstrator of anatomy. In April, 1880, he was elected demonstrator of anatomy in the same institution. Born on the high plane of an inherited profession, there he played and grew up and studied under the judicious training of a father ambitious to be excelled by his son. After taking his degrees, and having seen some of the practical work of the profession here, his father advised him, before entering upon his professional career, to visit the famous medical colleges and hospitals of Europe, study the methods of the professors there, attend their lectures, read their books, and thus thoroughly qualify himself for his life's work. Accordingly, in 1881, he made a medical tour of Europe, and visited the medical institutions of Edinburgh, London, Paris, Berlin and Vienna.

He continued to hold the position of demonstrator until the spring of 1883, when he was elected to the chair of anatomy and histology in the medical department of the University of Nashville and Vanderbilt University, a professorship which he now holds with great credit to himself and brilliant promise for the future.

Dr. Menees became a Mason in 1882, in Phœnix Lodge, No. 131, Nashville, and has taken all the degrees in the York Rite, including Knight Templar, and the 32° of the Scottish Rite. Like all his family and relations, in politics he is an hereditary Democrat, and in religion a Methodist. He is unmarried.

HON. NATHAN GREEN, LL. D.

LEBANON.

THE reputation of this distinguished educator in the law is one that is not confined to Tennessee alone, but is co-extensive with the geographical boundaries of the Union, and particularly with those of the South. Thousands of men, now eminent in judicature and statesmanship—many of them enrolled among the *nomina clara* of the Republic, and thousands of others struggling up the rugged paths to eminence, with hearts of steel and intellects of fire—bear the impress of this master mind, and testify to his great abilities.

Judge Green was born in Winchester, Tennessee, February 19, 1827, and in that vicinity grew up to the age of sixteen, alternately going to school and working on his father's farm—his father's policy being to train his children to respect the dignity and acquire a knowledge of manual labor. It was a wise policy, too, for it strengthened the boy's physical constitution and taught him, besides, to appreciate school learning the more when he could get to it. In 1843, his father sent him to Cumberland University, at Lebanon, where he entered the junior class and graduated A.B., in two years, under Rev. T. C. Anderson, president, and Profs. N. Lawrence Lindsley and A. P. Stewart. After graduation he served five months as tutor in the preparatory school of the university. After this he returned home to Winchester and began reading law, and in September, 1847, entered the first class of the law school, founded at Lebanon, by Judge Abram Caruthers. In two years he graduated, receiving the degree of LL.B. under Profs. Caruthers and Judge Nathan Green, sr., father of this subject. He then formed a partnership with Judge Robert L. Caruthers and began the practice of law at Lebanon in the fall of 1849, and remained in this partnership twelve months, until Judge Caruthers went upon the Supreme bench. In 1853, he associated with himself in the practice of law the late Gen. Robert Hatton, and with him remained in practice three years, doing a good business, when they dissolved partnership, Gen. Hatton going to congress, in 1856, and Judge Green taking the professorship of law in Cumberland University, in which he was associated with his father, Judge Nathan Green, sr., and Judge Abram Caruthers, until the breaking out of the war between the States, in 1861. During this period, before the war, the law school was remarkably successful, numbering as high as one hundred and eighty pupils. At the breaking out of the war, Lincoln's proclamation of April 13, 1861, caused the suspension of its operations, its five hundred students in all departments scattering everywhere, most of them going into the southern army, and Judge Green's occupation as a law teacher was gone.

Shortly after the beginning of the war his old friend, Prof. A. P. Stewart, having been made general in the Confederate States army, invited him to accept a place on his staff as first aid-de-camp, which he accepted and afterward became adjutant-general. He remained in the army while it was at Columbus, Kentucky, and was afterward at Fort Pillow, Island Ten, New Madrid, and Shiloh. He was exposed to fire at New Madrid and Shiloh only. Shortly after the battle of Shiloh, his health failing, he resigned his position, but rejoined the army in the fall of 1863, having been appointed, May, 1864, superintendent of engineering works, located first at Atlanta and then at Macon, Georgia. This position he filled till the surrender. In April, 1865, he was captured by the Federal General Wilson at Macon, Georgia, and paroled. In company with hundreds of other Tennesseans he started home, but at Chattanooga he and they were perfidiously arrested and imprisoned by the Federal authorities, and detained prisoners till they took the oath of allegiance, ten days afterward. While in prison they were treated contemptuously in all ways, with one exception. A sergeant of the Federal army, finding that Judge Geeen was destitute of money and of all things, gave him a horse on which he made his way home to Lebanon, after two years' absence. On arriving home, his beard having become gray, and his clothing being the regulation rebel gray, rather coarse gray at that, his children did not know him.

Although the country was in a desolate and disrupted condition, the mails had been stopped and the means of communication were limited, Judge Green and his father, who was then in feeble health, reopened the law school in September, 1865, Judge Abram Caruthers having died during the war. They succeeded in collecting some twenty-five young men, every one of whom had been an officer or soldier in one or the other of the contending armies. All of them being beginners, the work of the law school necessarily devolved on Judge Nathan Green, jr. His father having attempted to teach law a few months, sickened and died, March 30, 1866. On his death-bed the eminent gentleman called the son to him and said, "If you fail to get Judge Ridley or Judge McKinney to take my place your law school is gone." He got neither, both having declined. He, however, in September, 1866, secured the services and co-operation of Hon. Henry Cooper, late United States senator, and the law school, instead of dying, as the father had predicted, doubled in numbers within six months after his death—so true it is that the success of no enterprise is dependent upon any one man, however great he may be. There is always somebody raised up in the providence of God to take one's place. Judge Green has been connected with the law school ever since as one of its professors, and it has been the most successful law school in the State. His professorship in the law school extends over a period of twenty-eight years, and during this time he has had the honor of teaching more than two thousand young men, many of them now creditably representing the institution and him in congress, in legislatures, and at the bar in all the States south of the Ohio river. Among the distinguished *alumni* are ex-Gov. James D. Porter, now assistant secretary of the United States, Gov. William B. Bate, of Tennessee, United States Senator Howell E. Jackson, Hon. John F. House, Hon. E. H. East, and many others.

Upon the resignation of Dr. McDonnold, in 1873, Judge Green was elected chancellor of the university, and has held that position ever since. In 187-,the trustees and faculty of Center College, Danville, Kentucky, on motion of Col. W. C. P. Breckinridge, member of Congress from Kentucky, conferred upon Judge Green the degree of LL.D.

Judge Green's ability, however, is not confined to his eminent qualifications as a teacher and expounder of the law—his work of unifying the different departments —law, theological and literary—of the university, is recognized by those most interested and best acquainted with the history and needs of the institution, and marks him a man of fine administrative abilities, entitling him to the gratitude of the faculty, students and patrons of the university.

Judge Green became a Mason at Lebanon, in 1850; in religion, he is a Cumberland Presbyterian, and an elder in that church, and in politics acts with the Democrats, though a Whig before the war. He is the author of a volume entitled " The Tall Man of Winton," a book designed for the young, the copyright of which he gave to his church, and they have sold several editions of many thousand copies of it. He delivered, in August, 1883, an address before the Monteagle Association on the subject of "Government of Families and Schools," which has attracted wide attention.

In 1876, he became president of the National Bank of Lebanon, and still fills that position. When he was married, twenty dollars in his pocket and good claims for about three hundred dollars were the sum total of his earthly possessions. Before the war he was worth twenty thousand dollars, mostly slave property. His life work has been teaching law, but, unlike most bookish men, he has managed to accumulate a very pretty property, keeping him in very independent circumstances.

Judge Green married, at Lebanon, October 15, 1850, Miss Betty McClain, daughter of Josiah S. McClain, for forty years clerk of the county court of Wilson county, remarkable for his great integrity, particularly as a custodian of the public funds. He died, April, 1876, seventy-seven years old. Her mother, *nee* Miss Martha Johnson, who died in 1880, at the age of sev-

enty, was a native of Wilson county. Mrs. Green graduated from Abbe Institute, Lebanon, in 1848, and, like her father, is without hypocrisy, and remarkable for her straightforwardness and honesty, without any trace of guile, yet agreeable, warm-hearted, full of sympathy and an earnest, working Christian.

By his marriage with Miss McClain, Judge Green has had eight children, five of whom died in infancy. Those now living are : (1). Ella Green, graduated from Corona Institute, Lebanon, and afterward from Ward's seminary, Nashville; married, in 1873, Hon. W. C. Caldwell, a lawyer, of Trenton, Tennessee; now one of the judges of the court of referees. They have four children, Gertrude, Albert, Mattie Ross and Willis. (2). Mattie Green, graduated at Ward's seminary; married, June 28, 1883, Reagan Houston, a successful lawyer of San Antonio, Texas. (3). Grafton Green, born August 25, 1872.

Judge Green's most remote known English ancestor was a tallow chandler in London. His grandfather, Thomas Green, was a soldier in the Revolution from Virginia, and fought under Washington. He began life as an overseer in Virginia, and by taking care of what he made, he was soon better off than his employer, and became a rich man and raised a large family, of whom Judge Green's father, Judge Nathan Green, was the seventh son, born in Amelia county, Virginia, December, 1792, moved to Winchester, Tennessee, when a young man, practiced law there successfully, was a member of the State Legislature from Franklin county, was elected by the Legislature chancellor of the division, including his county—Franklin—was then placed upon the Supreme bench of Tennessee, where he remained by successive elections twenty-five years. He had much to do with formulating and settling the peculiar jurisprudence of the State. He was elected a law professor in Cumberland University, in 1849, resigned his position as judge of the Supreme court in 1852, and died March, 1866. He was universally considered by the profession as one of the greatest and purest judges that ever adorned the bench of this or any other country. He was remarkable for the purity of his private character, and his great activity and zeal as a worker in the church of Christ.

Judge Green's mother, *nee* Miss Mary Field, a native of North Carolina, was born in 1792. Her influence and character had much to do with the formation of her husband's character. She also distinguished herself for her piety and her work in the church; was a sweet-natured, gentle-spirited woman, whom everybody respected and honored. Her father, James Field, was a farmer in North Carolina. His family claimed to be descendants of Mary Queen of Scots. Judge Green's mother died, in 1849, leaving seven children, one of whom, Gen. Tom Green, the oldest son, fought in the battle of San Jacinto, in the Mexican war, and was a major-general in the Confederate service at the time of his death, April, 1864, in a skirmish on the Red river. Tom Green county, Texas, perpetuates his memory, and marks the honor in which Texas held his name. Judge Green's second brother, William S. Green, was a prominent physician in south Georgia, now deceased. His third brother, Dr. Hal. Green, is a successful and prominent physician at Okolona, Mississippi. His fourth brother, John A. Green, is one of the oldest lawyers in Texas—at San Antonio—and was secretary of State under Gov. Throckmorton. His fifth brother, Robert Green, died, at the age of thirty, in Texas, having acquired very great reputation as a lawyer, and of whom the Texans used to say, "the best lawyer among us." Judge Green's only sister, nee Miss Ann Green, is the widow of the late Dr. James C. Bowdon, an eminent minister of the Cumberland Presbyterian church, and for years president of Lincoln University in Illinois. It is a strong, able family, and has given to the State and country worthy sons and daughters.

Judge Green's father, by a second marriage, had one daughter, Miss Mary Field Green, who died the wife of M. Merritt, esq., a successful lawyer of Henderson, Kentucky.

Judge Green's success in life has grown out of his faithfulness to engagements, punctuality to his appointments, to his pursuing with unswerving fidelity one line in life, to his exalted character for probity and justice, thus winning for him the public confidence, and giving him a place among the standard men of Tennessee.

ALEXANDER B. WILSON, A. M.

GREENEVILLE.

ALEXANDER B. WILSON, the well-known attorney, is a native of Greene county, Tennessee, born February 26, 1838. He grew up in that county and has lived there all of his life, excepting the winter of 1865–6, which he spent in Illinois. After going to various country schools, he attended the old Greeneville College three years, graduating thence in 1858, under President John L. Lamson and Prof. A. J. Brown. After graduation he followed no special business until the war came up, when, being a Union man, he joined the Federal army as a non-commissioned officer in company F, Fourth Tennessee infantry regiment, commanded by Col. Stover, son-in-law of ex-President Andrew Johnson. Shortly afterward he was promoted to a second lieutenancy and again to a first lieutenancy, and served in Kentucky and Tennessee. His regiment was captured at McMinnville, Tennessee, by Gen. Wheeler's Confederate cavalry forces; was paroled and disbanded, but reorganized a few months thereafter, at Lexington, Kentucky; crossed the mountains into East Tennessee and served in that section until the close of the war. He was mustered out of service in August, 1865, at Nashville, Tennessee.

After the close of the war he went to the home of his brother, John P. Wilson, now a merchant at Olney, Illinois, and spent the winter there prospecting, but the vigorous climate not agreeing with him, he returned to Greeneville and resumed the study of law with James Britton, and was admitted to the bar, in 1867, by Judge R. R. Butler and Supreme Judge Sam Milligan. Shortly after he became the law partner of Mr. Britton, under the firm style of Britton & Wilson, a partnership which lasted until Mr. Britton's death, since which time he has practiced alone—having business in all the courts of the State.

Politically, Mr. Wilson has been a Republican since the war, but previously was a Democrat, as was his family. In 1861, at the State election to decide whether Tennessee should secede from the Union, he voted against secession. In 1877, he was appointed a commissioner of the United States circuit court, and has held that position ever since. In 1880, he was elected to represent Greene county in the Tennessee Legislature; served in the session of 1881; was a member of the judiciary committee, and during the session voted to settle the State debt at 60–6.

He became a Mason at Greeneville, and is now a member of the Royal Arch Chapter. He is a member of the Presbyterian church; is a member of the board of trustees of Greeneville and Tusculum College, from which institution he received the degree of Master of Arts, conferred in 1869. In addition to his heavy law practice, he has done a good deal of newspaper writing, without being formally an editor.

Mr. Wilson first married, in Chester county, South Carolina, September 7, 1875, Miss Sue Cartledge, daughter of Rev. A. M. Cartledge, of the Baptist church. Her mother was originally Miss Louisa Haygood. The first Mrs. Wilson was educated at Winnsborough, South Carolina. By this marriage two children were born, James C. and Lula Belle.

The first wife dying, Mr. Wilson next married Miss Sallie J. Cartledge, a sister of his first wife, by whom he has two children, a daughter, Madge, and an infant son.

The grandfather of our subject, John Wilson, came from Pennsylvania and settled in Greene county, Tennessee, among its early pioneers. He was of Scotch-Welsh stock. He married a Miss Weir. The father, James C. Wilson, was born in Greene county, Tennes-

see ; was a justice of the peace, a farmer, and a Democrat in politics. He died at the age of sixty-four years,
in 1872.

Mr. Wilson's mother, *nee* Catharine Rice, was a native
of Greene county, the daughter of David Rice, who
came from Rockbridge county, Virginia, and settled in
Greene county as a farmer. She died in 1873, at the
age of sixty-four years, leaving eight children : (1).
John Wilson, now a merchant at Olney, Illinois. (2).
Mary Wilson, wife of Dr. G. H. Evans, now living near
Sacramento, California. (3). David Wilson, a merchant
at Eufalua, Alabama. (4). Alexander Benjamin Wilson,
subject of this sketch. (5). Margaret Wilson, married
Dr. D. W. Rankin, now in Washington county, Arkansas. (6). Samuel D. Wilson, now in business at Knoxville. (7). Belle Wilson, now wife of J. L. Marsh,
depot agent at Home station, on the East Tennessee and
Virginia railroad. (8). James Theodore Wilson, who
died in 1881.

Not only is Mr. Wilson a successful lawyer, but he
ranks among the leading members of the East Tennessee bar. He specially excels in chancery practice, and
his name is associated with many of the most important

cases that have come before the courts in his section
of the State. His life has been upright and honorable.
He has been strictly temperate—was never even a dram
drinker ; never bet on games of chance ; has always
tried to keep his business up, and be prompt and ready
for the trial of his cases.

Without solicitation on his part, he was nominated to
the Legislature and served one term, but has refused to
be a candidate again under any circumstances. In his
case it will be observed that he has staid at one place ;
concentrated his energies upon one business ; has friends
because he is a friendly man—and has fixed habits and
fixed principles—and thus has secured the full confidence of the public. A gentleman of culture, he is not
the mere lawyer, but stands high in social circles also.
As a speaker, he is forcible ; is a thoughtful, studious worker ; a safe counselor, and as a lawyer, is
prompt, faithful and energetic in the management of
his client's cases. Living among people who have
known him all his life, he is esteemed by them for
his professional ability and personal integrity, which is
a better eulogium, perhaps, than anything an editor can
write.

MAJ. JOHN T. WILLIAMSON.

COLUMBIA.

MAJ. JOHN T. WILLIAMSON, lawyer, editor
and State senator, was born the second of three
children, all sons, in Maury county, Tennessee, August
11, 1839, and, with the exception of two years of his
early boyhood, that county has been his life-long home.
He received his education at Pleasant Grove Academy,
in Maury county, and at Lebanon, Tennessee, closing in
the sophomore class in 1860.

In May, 1861, he enlisted in Capt. George W. Jones'
company, raised in Maury county for the Confederate
service, and was made brevet second lieutenant in that
company, when it was organized as a part of Col. John
C. Brown's Third Tennessee infantry regiment. He
saw the war to its close, surrendering at Greensborough,
North Carolina, in April, 1865, having served in Tennessee, Kentucky, Alabama, Mississippi, Georgia and
North Carolina, under Gens. Albert Sidney Johnston,
Bragg, Joseph E. Johnston and Hood. He took part
in the battles of Fort Donelson, Perryville, Murfreesborough ; in Hardee's fight in Georgia, July 22, 1864,
and in the numerous and continued battles of the Georgia campaign of 1864. At Fort Donelson he was wounded
by a minnie ball through his left arm, and disabled for
a month. The same ball after passing through his arm
mashed flat around the barrel of his pistol in his side
pocket as if it had been hammered there of purpose.

On the reorganization of the Fifty-first Tennessee regiment, at Shelbyville, Tennessee, he was elected major
of the regiment, and served in that capacity the balance
of the war.

After the great civil struggle had closed, finding
himself without property, and without trade or profession, he first taught school five months, in 1865, at Brick
Church, in Giles county, Tennessee, after which he
clerked twelve months at the same place. In 1867, he
commenced studying law with Frierson & Fleming at
Columbia ; was licensed to practice in March, 1868, by
Judges H. H. Harrison and A. M. Hughes ; began
practice at Columbia, where he has since continued
with fair financial success.

In politics, Maj. Williamson is a Democrat, and has
taken an active part in the political contests—national,
State and county—that have come before the public in
his time. The first civil office he held was that of alderman of his town, of which, in 1877-8, he was also
mayor. In November, 1882, he was elected State senator, as a " Bate Democrat," from Maury and Lewis
counties, and during the session of the senate of 1883,
was chairman of the committee on new issue Tennessee
money. He has been frequently sent as a delegate to
the congressional and State conventions of his party,
and was chairman of his county executive committee.

He was president of the Tilden and Hendricks club of Columbia, in 1876. While always a warm friend of the Democratic party, and active in it, he has worked in a quiet way rather than as seeking its honors. He took the position of State senator somewhat against his wishes, and only made the canvass, upon the representation of his party friends that the success of the contest depended upon his making the fight.

He became a Mason, in 1867, in Pleasant Grove Lodge, No. 138, and has taken all the degrees up to and including Knight Templar, and has served as Master, High Priest and Eminent Commander. He is also a member of the Royal Arcanum.

He married, in Charlotte county, Virginia, June 22, 1869, Miss Albina Goode Bugg, a native of that county, born the daughter of Zachariah Bugg, a tobacco planter and trader, also a native of Virginia. Her mother was Mary J. Goode, daughter of a Mr. Goode, of the family of Goodes who for many years have furnished members of Congress from that State. Mrs. Williamson was educated at Danville, Virginia. By this marriage, Maj. Williamson has five children: Mary G. Williamson, born August 12, 1870; Ella Vernor Williamson, born in April, 1873, and died in August of the same year; George Bugg Williamson, born September 6, 1874; Lucy Mildred Williamson, born October 8, 1877; Lotta Gray Williamson, born August 21, 1880.

Maj. Williamson and lady and their daughter, Mary, are members of the Cumberland Presbyterian church, of which he is a deacon.

His parents having started in life poor, their children were brought up to work and labor on the farm; some were sent to school, while the others were kept at home to "keep the plows a-going," yet, by alternating work and schooling, the boys managed to get as good an education as any of the boys in the neighborhood. From an early age, our subject had an inclination to the law, was a studious boy and raised under strict moral training of Presbyterian parents. His father, G. C. Williamson, now living on his farm in Maury county, is in his seventieth year, but quite stout and active, and in comfortable circumstances. He was raised in Giles county. He is a fine specimen of the Tennessee farmer, and throughout life has maintained a reputation for honor, integrity and industry, and for devoted attachment to his family—watching and following even his grown children with paternal help, assistance and counsel. Maj. Williamson's grandfather, Samuel Williamson, was a Virginia farmer; married, in that State, Miss Judith Woodfin, and settled in Giles county at an early date.

Maj. Williamson's mother, formerly Mildred Angeline Brown, now living at the age of sixty-six years, was born in Maury county, the daughter of Charles Brown, a farmer, and a native of Virginia. Her mother, Elizabeth Akers, a native Virginian, was the daughter of Peter Akers, who settled twelve miles south of Columbia, where he lived and died a farmer. The whole family, after settling in Tennessee, seem possessed of exceptional staying power. Maj. Williamson's father is now living on the place settled by his great-grandfather, Peter Akers, and many of the old generation now lie buried in the same graveyard. Maj. Williamson's brother, Charles S. Williamson, is a farmer in Maury county, and his brother, Dr. James G. Williamson, is a practicing physician near Culleoka. Both these brothers were in the Confederate service, Charles S. in the cavalry, and Dr. James G. in the same regiment with our subject.

In 1882, Maj. Williamson, immediately after the nomination of Gen. Bate for governor, in connection with others, purchased the Columbia *Independent* and changed its name to the *Maury Democrat*, of which he and Col. J. L. Bullock were the editors, Maj. Williamson being also the business manager. Subsequently they sold the paper and both resumed their law practice.

In personal appearance, Maj. Williamson is a very attractive man. He stands five feet nine inches high, has a Grecian cast of face, with large perceptive and concentrative power, and makes the impression of a kindly-natured man, making his way in the world in moderation, without the restlessness, worry and hurry that characterize too many of our business men, and which shorten the lives of half that die.

The purposes of his life, he said to the editor, have been "to put myself and family in comfortable circumstances, but I have never sought or craved riches; to be liberal and fair with everybody with whom I have dealings. I have never had but little security money to pay, and never had a note to go to protest. I have endeavored so to act as to merit and retain the confidence and esteem of my associates. The history of my family has been that of a fight to come up in the world. One of the ruling motives of my father's life has been that his children might not have to start where he did; one of his desires that they might have advantages he never had, and my feelings are the same toward my family." On such foundations noble families are built. "To found a noble family is a noble ambition—for great families make great States."

DAVID A. NEILSON, M. D.

MORRISTOWN.

THIS gentleman was born in Greene county, Tennessee, March 25, 1825, the son of Col. William D. Neilson, a soldier in the Indian wars, under Jackson, a native of Virginia, who came with his father to Greene county when he was quite young. He married, in Claiborne county, Tennessee, lived a farmer, was a Whig in politics, a colonel of militia, and a man of great energy. He went into business, as a merchant, when very young, had a partner, broke for thirty-six thousand dollars, and, in seven years, paid up his indebtedness, thus showing both energy and honesty. He lived to the good old age of eighty, and died, in 1864, respected and beloved by all who knew him. Dr. Neilson's grandfather was Hugh Douglas Neilson, a native Scotchman, and a man of fine education. He married Miss Sarah Hale, of Virginia, came as a pioneer settler to Greene county, Tennessee, and died there a large farmer.

Dr. Neilson's mother, *nee* Miss Eliza Evans, was born in Claiborne county, Tennessee, daughter of George Evans, of Irish descent. She was a woman of sterling character, noted for her industry, economical habits, and model housekeeping. Neither she nor her husband were members of any church, nor is the son, though all are believers in the Christian religion. She died at the old homestead, in Greene county, in September, 1843, leaving five children: David Alexander Neilson, subject of this sketch; William D. Neilson, died, unmarried, while mining in California; Sarah Jane Neilson, married John D. McCurly, a merchant, at Greeneville, Tennessee, and has nine children; James S. Neilson, who married Miss Martha Baker, is now a very successful farmer, in Greene county, has two children, J. T. and Jesse Neilson, the former of whom is a physician, practicing at Emory, Virginia; Eliza Neilson, married James L. Cain, a farmer, in Greene county, now merchandising in Mississippi.

The Neilson family are a thrifty people, mostly farmers and merchants. Hugh D. Neilson, an uncle of Dr. Neilson, was a well-known and prominent merchant, at Somerville, Tennessee.

Dr. Neilson, from infancy till thirteen years old, being afflicted with a skin disease (*eczema*), was confined to the house in winters, and only went to school in summer. From that time on, continuously, he went to school, attending Tusculum College four years, and two years at the college in Greenville. He began reading medicine when twenty years old, under Dr. F. M. Compton. In 1846, he entered the University of the City of New York, took his medical degree in 1848, under Professors Valentine Mott, Samuel Henry Dickson, Granville S. Pattison, Martin Payne and Gunning S. Bedford. After serving as assistant sur-

geon in the hospital attached to that institution some four months, he returned home, married, and went to practice at his father's, in Greene county. Practicing there till 1853, he moved to Wheelock, Robertson county, Texas, where he practiced two years; moved to Williamsburg, Kentucky, and practiced till 1857, when he moved back to Greene county, Tennessee, to a farm given him by his father, and practiced medicine and farmed till 1868, when he settled in Morristown, where he has practiced ever since, with the exception of the year 1870, when he was in the commission business at Chattanooga, a venture that proved financially disastrous.

During the war, he was a Union man, but practiced medicine all the time, not going into either army as a soldier. Since the war he has voted with the Democrats. For a number of years he was examining surgeon for the pension office at Morristown. He also served as an alderman, at Morristown, several years.

Dr. Neilson first married in Knox county, Kentucky, October 28, 1848, Miss Jane R. Herndon, who was born December 24, 1824, the only daughter of Benjamin F. Herndon, a farmer and stock-trader, originally from Virginia. Her mother, Theodosia Renfro, was the daughter of William Renfro, also a Virginian. Mrs. Neilson's only brother, Dr. O. P. Herndon, is now a prominent physician at Barboursville, Kentucky. Mrs. Neilson was educated at Greeneville, Tennessee, was a woman of great energy, of decided domestic tastes, a member of the Christian (Campbellite) church, and died, February 24, 1876, leaving her husband three children living: (1). Nellie Neilson, educated at Morristown, married George S. Crouch, cashier of the Fourth National Bank of Morristown, has three children, Katie, Jennie and Lillie. (2). Sallie Neilson, educated at Morristown, married A. G. Stewart, now at Buffalo, New York, a fine business man. They have two children, Alexander and Gaines. (3). William B. Neilson, now a practicing physician at Whitesburg, Tennessee. Dr. Neilson's second marriage, which transpired at Russellville, Tennessee, September 11, 1877, was with Miss Mollie M. Burts, daughter of John Burts. Her mother was a Miss Finch. By this marriage, Dr. Neilson has two children: (1). Ludie Neilson. (2). Cora Neilson.

Dr. Neilson became a Mason, in Greeneville, Tennessee, in 1846, has taken the Chapter degrees, and has served as Captain of the Host. He is a quiet, pleasant-mannered man, sociable, friendly, but not obtrusive, is not a man to take trouble to heart, is devoted to his practice, with a ruling ambition to educate his children for advancement in life. A peculiarity of this gentleman is that, when a patient badly needs his attention, he stays with him, treating him conscientiously, and will not leave him to go to a new patient. This has always been his course, and by this means he has saved the life of many a man who, had he left him to attend to another call, must have died. It occurs to the editor that if a physician should leave a patient needing his attention, and he should die, that the doctor must ever thereafter be a miserable man.

Dr. Neilson is about medium height, weighs one hundred and seventy pounds, is of broad, compact build, is very dressy, and impresses one as a man content to do his duty and given to the enjoyment of life.

HON. JAMES M. GREER.

MEMPHIS.

JUDGE GREER, though comparatively young, has made for himself a fine reputation as a criminal judge, and has, besides, the distinction of being the youngest judge in the State. The secret of his eminence is attributable not only to what he believes, but to that which he enforces by practice. Criminal law, he holds, is the enforcement of the demands of a community, that every man shall observe a decent respect for the opinions and rights of mankind. It is not less the prerogative than the duty of man to obey law. Obedience is the expression of his manhood and of his love of liberty. It measures the value he sets on freedom. A criminal judge, sitting to determine whether men properly obey the law, should himself be a man of high moral tone, fine character, a man of mark, quick to perceive, and prompt to act upon his conceptions. The administration of his court should not be harsh, nor yet merciful, but rigid and directed to the suppression of crime and immorality in whatever form they manifest a contempt for organic society, and should guard the statutes designed to protect the public. Though a kind-hearted man, he should be a firm judge, punctual in attendance to business, granting and insisting on the speedy trial of prisoners, and keeping his docket cleared. These are the leading traits in the intricate character of Judge Greer, and which, the lawyers of Memphis say, peculiarly fit him for a criminal judge, especially because he is fearless and cannot be swayed in thought or speech or action by what has become known as the "popular breeze." He is of that class of men who are not for the moment merely, but have lasting qualities, and are destined to live. Remarkable for his skill in the analysis of character, he is likewise distinguished for his discriminating estimates of men. In the administration of his office, he has never been swerved by public clamor. When old evils that had fastened as a sore on the body politic had been given over as incurable, mild salves being applied by others, he, with the boldness of a skillful surgeon, cut them out—gambling, for instance—and received as his immediate reward much hostile criticism and bitter condemnation. The one he accepted good humoredly, and followed the path of duty, unmoved by the other. Per sequence, he instituted many reforms which were at first condemned, but in six months the papers that had censured, applauded him for his achievements.

James M. Greer was born in Holly Springs, Mississippi, October 27, 1847, and there grew to the age of sixteen. After receiving an academic education at Holly Springs, he became a cadet in the Virginia Military Institute, "the West Point of the South." Early in 1864, the battalion of cadets, of which he was a member, went into the Confederate army, Col. Shipp commanding the battalion of four companies, serving in Virginia until April 3, 1865, when, upon the evacuation of Richmond, the battalion was disbanded. Young Greer served throughout as a private, and the gallant body of young soldiers, of which he was a member, served under Gen. Breckinridge in the charge at New Market, in the Shenandoah Valley, in the engagement at Lexington, in defense of Lynchburg when it was attacked by Hunter, and in a number of skirmishes around Richmond.

The war over, he returned, at the age of eighteen, to his father's home in Holly Springs, finding the family so impoverished as to render it necessary to leave their town home and go to their plantation, in De Soto county, Mississippi. There he spent five years, working on the farm, studying law at such intervals as he could find between plowing, scraping cotton, and other work incidental to a Mississippi plantation. Fortunately, he had the assistance of his father, an able, retired lawyer, and, therefore, his nights and odd times were spent profitably. He went to Memphis, completed his law studies, and was licensed to practice by Judges C. W. Heiskell and W. L. Scott, and began practice with three acquaintances and one hundred and fifty dollars in his pocket, showing the confidence he had in himself and the stuff that was in him. While waiting for the coming client, he helped to eke out his existence by writing anonymous articles for the New York *Ledger.* After a while, however, clients did come, and his practice gradually increased until March 24, 1883, when he was appointed judge of the criminal court of Shelby county, his present position. Like his family for three generations before him, Judge Greer is a Democrat, but not a strict partisan, nor has he taken an active part in politics. He is a Knight of Honor,

56

and of the Royal Asylum. In religion, he is a Protestant Episcopalian, as is also his wife.

Judge Greer married in St. Charles, Missouri, September 27, 1877, Miss Betty Buckner Allen, a native of Lexington, Kentucky, a daughter of Dr. John R. Allen, who, from 1860 to his death, in 1877, was a prominent practitioner at Memphis, formerly physician in charge of the Insane Asylum at Lexington, Kentucky. He was a member of the Iowa State senate, from Keokuk, in 1856, and distinguished himself in that body by introducing measures for the care of the insane, a subject which was a specialty with him, and for which he became widely known.

By his marriage with Miss Allen, Judge Greer has three children, all born at Memphis: Allen James Greer, Autry Greer, and Rowan Adams Greer.

Judge Greer's great-great-grandfather, James Greer, came from the north of Ireland, where some members of the family were members of Parliament. He settled in Virginia, on the Potomac river. His son, James Greer (Judge Greer's great-grandfather), was born there soon after the arrival of the family in Virginia. He became a lieutenant in the American army in the Revolutionary war, married a Miss Hayne, of the celebrated South Carolina family of that name, and after the war was a farmer in Virginia. His son, also named James Greer (Judge Greer's grandfather), was born and grew to manhood in Virginia, married a Miss Searcy, emigrated first to Georgia, thence to Sumner county, Tennessee, where James M. Greer, Judge Greer's father, was born, January 22, 1816. Shortly after the birth of Judge Greer's father, the grandfather moved to Paris, Tennessee, and there the son was reared. The family subsequently moved to Holly Springs, Mississippi, where James M. Greer, having studied law, entered upon practice, and won much distinction in his profession. He married Miss Mary Elizabeth Autry, December 22, 1841, and soon after retired from practice, engaged in planting, and subsequently represented De Soto county in the Mississippi Legislature. He removed to Corsicana, Texas, in March, 1876, and there died, March 21, 1879. He was noted for his keen appreciation of humor, for the great strength with which he could use good-humored ridicule as a weapon, and for his large fund of accurate information, historical and political. His detestation of sham and his great sincerity of speech, made him the champion of the weak, but gave him a large number of enemies among the strong. He had no patience with anything that approached pretense, fraud and hypocrisy. He was a man of strong character, but without the training of a mother, as she died when he was only three years old. One of his brothers, Hon. Robert S. Greer, of Marshall county, Mississippi, was for twenty-five years in the State senate, and during that long period of service was identified with the early law-making of that State, and, without being a great man, was conspicuous for his clear, common sense and devotion to honest and economical government. Another brother, Gen. Elkanah Greer, was a lieutenant in Jefferson Davis' regiment in the Mexican war, and afterwards a major-general in the Confederate army, under Gen. Price.

Judge Greer's mother, nee Miss Mary E. Autry, was born in Jackson, Tennessee, February 7, 1827, daughter of Maj. Micajah Autry, whose name is the first on the monument that marks the Alamo, where he died in the struggle for Texan independence. He was of French stock. Born to fortune and reared in easy circumstances, having no business aptitude, he spent his inheritance early in his married life. With Crockett he went to Texas, at the time of the revolution there, in the desperate hope of winning fame and fortune for his family. A descendant of a line of soldiers, he naturally took to this calling. When the bloody massacre at the Alamo came, he fell with Crockett, Travis, Bowie, and the remainder of the one hundred, and as Leonidas and his gallant band at Thermopylæ immortalized Spartan history, so they gave an illustrious page to that of America. His wife (Judge Greer's grandmother), was Miss Martha Wyche Putney, a native of Virginia, and descendant of an English family. When a widow, she removed to Holly Springs, and with an indomitable will that nothing could conquer, succeeded in raising and educating her son and daughter. The daughter became the mother of Judge Greer. The son, Col. James L. Autry, graduated at St. Thomas' Hall, Holly Springs, was elected to the Legislature, and made speaker of the Mississippi house of representatives at the age of twenty-two, the youngest speaker in the United States. He was the military governor of Vicksburg at the beginning of the siege, and at the demand of Admiral Farragut for surrender, made the celebrated response, "Mississippians don't know how to surrender." He was afterward colonel of the Twenty-seventh Mississippi regiment, and was killed at the head of his command, in the battle of Murfreesborough, December 31, 1863. Judge Greer's mother is now living at Corsicana, Texas. She has four children, all lawyers: Hal. Wyche Greer, at Beaumont, Texas, Robert Autry Greer, and De Edward Greer, at Corsicana, Texas, and the eldest, James M. Greer, the subject of this sketch. She inherited from her French ancestry the enthusiasm and courage which marks that people, and has sobered it by taking from her English stock common sense and unflinching perseverance. She is possessed of rare musical and poetic talent, which she has cultivated to an extreme, but used neither, except for the training of her children and the entertainment of her friends. A religionist, whose faith in Jesus as the Son of God has never wavered, she has anxiously read and studied all that Darwin, Huxley and Tyndall have said about the material world, believes in evolution, and reconciles it with Christianity.

Judge Greer has not accumulated a large property.

Like many other lawyers, he seems to have accepted Sydney Smith's idea, to live happily, bring up his family, and seek to do no man harm. Necessarily, therefore, he has spent for them his professional income as he made it, yet he is in quite independent circumstances. His first ambition has been to hand down to his children the same thing he received from his father—a clean and honest name; his second has been to win for himself the reputation of being a just and a truthful man. Incident to these ambitions he has desired, by study and reading, to know what the wise have thought and to apply that thought to his everyday life, so that he might remember that whilst the world was made for him, it was also made for his neighbor. His desire for political distinction, which inspired him in his younger days, he has had to lay aside for the duties devolved upon him as the head of a family. His leading characteristic is dogged, unflinching persistence, which amounts at times to the appearance of obstinacy. His course points out clearly that he does what he deliberately thinks is right. He is inflexibly honest, and has a reputation as a dispassionate, logical and upright jurist.

During the short time that Judge Greer has presided in the criminal court, he has made a distinct and individual impression as a judicial officer. Coming after Judge Horrigan, his career was watched with more than usual interest, and he has not disappointed his many warm personal friends and that element of the people who desire to see the fearless administration of justice. Sentiment has played too large a part in the administration of the law in the South, and the tendency has been toward the exaltation of the criminal. Sympathy for a man in distress, no matter how heinous or disgraceful his offense, not unfrequently plucks the prisoner from a merited punishment, but surrounds him with a halo of glory and innocence. It is hardly

necessary to say that Judge Greer has at no time shown any inclination to yield to sentimentalism, instead of enforcing the law. The tendency of his mind and tastes is pre-eminently judicial. He is a cool, fearless and clear-headed thinker, with one guiding star before him, and that is the conscientious and intelligent enforcement of the laws. When he assumed the bench, there was no laxity in the prosecutions against parties carrying concealed weapons. If anything, he was even stricter than his predecessor, and nothing but good character could mitigate the imprisonment of the criminal. Men high in social position, have been sentenced to the jail, and have had to go there. It is in his stand against gambling that Judge Greer has, probably, in the most conspicuous way, earned the gratitude of the people of Shelby county. When he announced that he intended enforcing the laws against gaming, there were those who sought to ridicule him by calling him a crusader, a moral judge, a visionary. But he had the consolation of knowing that the gamblers have all scattered and fled, and that the last resorts of the guild, maintained in secret and dark places, were raided and almost broken up. This movement has been of lasting benefit to the working-men of Memphis, many of whom spent all their wages in the professional gambling hells. It is unnecessary to call attention to Judge Greer's administration of justice in detail. In brief, he does not know what it is to temporize or compromise with crime, and his one conviction is that there is no need of law unless it is to be enforced, and he has shown the requisite courage, the requisite indifference to unpleasant personal consequences, and the requisite intelligence to enforce it. Though some of his positions on law questions have seemed extreme, yet the results have shown that he is no legal heretic, and it can be fairly said of him that his law is as sound as his administration of justice is fearless.

HON. DAVID M. KEY.

CHATTANOOGA.

HON. DAVID M. KEY, ex-United States senator from Tennessee, ex-postmaster-general of the United States, and now United States district judge, was born in Greene county, Tennessee, January 27, 1824, the son of Rev. John Key, a Methodist preacher and farmer, a native of Greene county, who died in Monroe county, at the age of fifty-six. Rev. John Key was a man of very ardent and enthusiastic temperament, rather distinguished as a revivalist, in the neighborhood of his operations, and of great power over the audiences he addressed, though having but a limited education. He was remarkable for his adherence to principle, and his reputation for honesty was never as-

sailed. His grandfather was a pioneer settler in East Tennessee, came from Scotland, and settled in Greene county in Revolutionary times, and before. David Key, Judge Key's grandfather, was born, lived and died in Greene county, a farmer. In politics, the family were always Democratic—Jeffersonian and Jacksonian. They were plain country folk, farmers of the middle class, none rich, none without property, and all had comfortable homesteads and lived in quiet, easy rural simplicity.

Judge Key's mother, whose maiden name was Margaret Armitage, was a native also of Greene county, born February 18, 1804, the daughter of Isaac Armitage, of an English family. Her mother was Elizabeth

Weston, all pioneers of East Tennessee. The Armitage family came from Pennsylvania, were of good reputation in the localities of their residence, but not known far from home. Judge Key's mother died April 12, 1882, leaving four children: the subject of this sketch; Elizabeth, now wife of Dr. J. H. Brunner, president of Hiwassee College, in Monroe county, Tennessee; John F. Key, who married Miss Margaret Peace, of Monroe county, and is now farming in Texas; Summerfield A. Key, a leading lawyer of Chattanooga. The latter married Miss Mary E. Devine, daughter of John L. Devine, a merchant and planter of that city. This younger brother, though not an aspiring man, served in the Tennessee Legislature, the session of 1877–8.

Judge Key was brought up on a farm and worked industriously, a business that seemed to have begot in him those simple manners and plain tastes that have distinguished him through life. Morally, he was always exemplary and of good home habits, owing to the influence of his parents. The Judge told the editor that he never swore an oath in his life. His education began in the backwoods common schools of Monroe county. His father removed to Monroe county, Tennessee, when the son was only two years old, but he was afterward sent off to better schools, and finally became the first graduate of Hiwassee College, taking his degree in 1850. He had read law in the private office of H. H. Stephens, while attending school, and was licensed to practice in 1850, by Chancellor Thomas L. Williams and Circuit Judge Ebenezer Alexander, both quite distinguished in their day. In 1853, he removed to Chattanooga, where he has resided ever since, in the practice of law, in which he has been quite successful, doing a leading business.

Judge Key married in Roane county, Tennessee, July 1, 1857, Miss Lizzie Lenoir, who was born in Chattanooga, January 28, 1838, the daughter of Gen. Albert S. Lenoir, of a French Huguenot family, who came from North Carolina to Tennessee. On her father's maternal side, she was the great-granddaughter of Waightstill Avery, who was a member of the Mecklenburg convention that made the first American declaration of independence; was the first attorney-general of North Carolina after her separation from the mother country, and noted as Gen. Jackson's antagonist in the first duel he fought, though neither of the combatants were hurt, and Avery was ever after a warm political friend of Jackson. Gen. Lenoir, Mrs. Key's great-grandfather, was president of the North Carolina senate, and was a captain of a company at the battle of King's Mountain. Mrs. Key's mother was a Welcker, of German descent, through Henry Welcker, who came from Germany and settled in Roane county, Tennessee. Mrs. Key's uncle, James M. Welcker, was judge of the Knoxville circuit court, and died, about 1860, during his term of judicial office. Her uncle, Albert G. Welcker, was chancellor of the Chattanooga chancery

division, at the commencement of the war, but was ousted from his office when the Federals took possession of East Tennessee, in 1863.

Mrs. Key received a good education, and is noted for being considerate and cautious. It has been said of her that she does not rush to her conclusions as women are supposed to do, generally, but reasons her way to them. She is doubtless entitled to no small share of the credit for her husband's success. She is quite a handsome woman, tall and graceful, and of commanding presence; a firm, resolute woman, but of a disposition so amiable that it is said all who know her are her friends. Her principal characteristics are stability of character and loyalty to her convictions.

By this marriage Judge Key has nine children, all born during the family residence in Chattanooga: (1). Emma Key, educated at Salem, North Carolina, and afterward graduated at Baltimore. She married, June 20, 1883, to W. B. Thompson, general superintendent of the railway mail service of the United States, a native of New York. She died March 8, 1885. A correspondent of the New York *World*, writing from Washington City, upon the occasion of the death of this most estimable lady says: "The death of Mrs. Emma Key Thompson, which was announced here this morning, created great surprise. It was a shock to a large number of people. Mrs. Thompson was the daughter of Judge Key, postmaster-general of the Hayes administration. Miss Emma Key was the belle of that period in Washington. She was a tall, well-developed, regular-featured blonde. She had very blue eyes, the clearest of clear complexions, while her yellow hair was slightly inclined to red. She was a very matter-of-fact young lady, without the slightest affectation or nonsense. She was thoroughly well educated, and would have been at ease in any society. After her father retired from the cabinet, she went back with him to Chattanooga, Tennessee. She returned here two or three years after marrying Mr. Thompson, who was the superintendent of the railway mail service, under Judge Key. Mr. Thompson is a capitalist. He afterwards established himself in Washington, doing a general speculative business. Mrs. Thompson was one of the most conspicuous of the young matrons of Washington society. She went home for a visit early in the winter. When she went away she was apparently in perfect health. Several years ago she received quite severe injuries by being thrown from a carriage. It is probable that some latent development of the injuries at that time has resulted in her death. She has been ill nearly all of the time since she went home. None of the time has her illness been regarded as serious until very recently." (2). Albert Lenoir Key, was born July —, 1861, graduated from the Annapolis United States Naval Academy, and is in the naval service now, in the Asiatic waters. (3). Kate Key, graduated at Baltimore, with her sister Emma, after attending with her the Salem school. (4). Sallie C. Key, educated at Salem, North Carolina. (5). Maggie Key, now attending school at Chattanooga. (6). John S. Key. (7). David M. Key, jr. (8). Lenoir Key. (9). Lizzie Key.

In the war of the rebellion, the first position Judge Key held was that of adjutant-general, on Gen. Caswell's staff, in the Confederate army. He afterward became lieutenant-colonel of the Forty-third regiment of Tennessee volunteer infantry, which office he held till the end of the war, refusing all promotion, he having loyally assisted in raising the regiment, and many fathers having sanctioned their sons going into the service because he was its lieutenant-colonel, James W. Gillespie, an old Mexican soldier, being its colonel. He was with Gen. E. Kirby Smith and Gen Bragg, in their Kentucky campaigns, and was captured in the siege of Vicksburg. He was at the siege of Vicksburg, and was wounded by a minnie rifle ball.

Judge Key, like his ancestors were, is Democratic, but he takes no part in politics. In 1856, he was on the Tennessee State electoral ticket when Buchanan was elected, and in 1860, was on the Breckinridge ticket, but has never aspired to become a candidate for any political office. In 1870, he was sent, without opposition, to the constitutional convention of Tennesssee, from the counties of Hamilton, Meigs, Rhea, Bledsoe and Sequatchie. In August, 1870, after the adoption of the new constitution, he was elected chancellor of the Chattanooga chancery division, and served until August, 1875, when Gov. James D. Porter appointed him United States senator for Tennessee, to succeed Andrew Johnson, who died in that position. He remained in the senate until January, 1877. In March following, he was appointed postmaster-general of the United States by President Rutherford B. Hayes, and served until August 25, 1880, when he resigned to accept the office of United States district judge for the districts of Eastern and Middle Tennessee, which office he still holds.

Neither Judge Key or his wife belong to any church, though both were brought up by Methodist parents, are orthodox in their views, and understood to be Methodistic in their leanings. As to property, Judge Key is in comfortable circumstances. From boyhood he has been a close economist, from necessity and inclination; was never sued on a note, except as security for others, and has never been a borrower of money. Like all Confederates, he came out of the war with nothing, and, indeed, is not believed to be very ambitious to be rich, but only for excelling in his profession· and to discharge his duties to his clients and the public, when in public position. His methods have been to keep out of debt. Offices he has held, but he never sought one of them; he had not enough audacity. Always honest and truthful, never deceiving the public or individuals, he has so demeaned himself as to win the confidence of the people, of the governor, and the president. He was never a politician, though a party man, and often endorsed by political opponents. He has always sought to be right—never sacrificing a principle for party consistency or party advantage. In fact, as Col. Jeremiah George Harris, of Nashville, has said of Judge Key, "Put him in a company of great men, and he will be the only man present that will not know that he is himself a great man."

Judge Key stands six feet high, is erect, and somewhat corpulent, weighing two hundred and forty pounds. His silver-gray hair, which he wears roached, is luxuriant. His look is like his reputation, quiet, serene, and very benevolent. He appears, also, a largehearted, public-spirited man. His eyes are dark, with a clear, mild expression. He is a man collected, affable, approachable, and of uniform dignity. The qualities of his make-up are so blended in harmony, it is difficult to name the one that is his differentiation.

GEN. WILLIAM H. JACKSON.

BELLE MEADE, NEAR NASHVILLE.

TO a phrenologist, a study of this gentleman's picture reveals a neck and chin indicative of push and force; compressed lips, that speak of determination; arched nostrils, which belong to those who were born to command; eyes of a discoverer, "looking right on and thine eyelids straight before thee;" a brow of depth and breadth, showing quickness of perception; a forehead of concentration of purpose, not given to change, and a coronal denoting dignity and clearness of character. Moreover, one would find in him an illustration of the theory that justifies biographical work, to-wit: that native talent, stimulated by family pride, is the chief factor of individual excellence. Closely akin to this incentive to distinction and success in other directions, is State pride, which blossoms into the activities called public spiritedness, and prompts to lending a helping hand to whatever will elevate and advance one's own native State. In other words, that love of country, which men call patriotism, of the loftiest character and most superb organization.

William H. Jackson was born, October 1, 1835, at Paris, Tennessee, but when four years old, his father moved to the vicinity of McLemoresville, in Carroll county, Tennessee, the motive leading him there being to get near his father-in-law, Rev. Robert Hurt. Remaining there one year, he removed to Jackson, Tennessee, in 1840, and in that town the subject of this sketch was raised. Of the incidents of his boyhood life, one might cull from his father's sketch of him a number of interesting facts. His life has been somewhat eventful. He is a man of strong individuality, both of thought and action. By no manner of means is he a man of dash and show and light weight. His father used to compare that style of man to a "syllabub," from one of Davy Crockett's unique expressions, who, when he had taken his first spoonfull of "syllabub," remarked, "I snapped at it, but by hokey, I believe I missed it." Gen. Jackson's looks and manner make the impression that he might have adopted for his life's motto, " *Festina lente.*" He is deliberate and slow and farmer-like, and for that reason a man of force and a good manager and marshaler of affairs.

He was reared amid good and wholesome precepts in the home circle and sound instruction in the school, and in the Methodist church, of which his parents were members. He gained fast friends for his high spirit and the zeal with which he espoused the cause of the weak or younger children, in his school-boy days, between the age of ten and sixteen. His numerous school broils originated in his fervor in defending the weak against the strong. Naturally of a sanguine temperament, in later years he strove to correct his combative tendencies, never carrying weapons, lest that dangerous temperament might impel him to the use of them, which he might, in cooler moments, regret. It required the severe military training of West Point, where he graduated in his twenty-first year, to subdue this fiery spirit. The future of his manhood was early foreshadowed in the impetuous youth, noted more for energy of action than intensity of application. His fondness for field sports often conflicted with the strict discharge of the duty required in his early school days.

In the spring of 1852, being at that time a member of the senior class in West Tennessee College, at Jackson, he received the appointment of cadet to West Point from his member of Congress, Hon. Kit. Williams. This change brought about higher aspirations, stronger efforts and new associations. He had not applied himself to books, being surrounded by clever chums who were not studious. On entering the Military Academy, he determined to stay where so many from his district had failed, the impelling motive being a desire to please his father, whom he loved devotedly while living, and whose memory is kept ever green and fresh in his mind. There was never greater congeniality in thought, language and sentiment between father and son than between Gen. Jackson and his father. At nine years of age he heard his father remark, in conversation with Judge Turley, of the Supreme bench, Judge

A. W. O. Totten, Gen. William T. Haskell and Judge Milton Brown (the educational institutions of the country being under discussion), that he would be perfectly satisfied to have one of his sons graduate at the University of Virginia, and the other at the Military Academy at West Point. At the time of his entrance to that institution, his brother, Howell E. Jackson, late United States senator, now United States circuit judge (who was always a hard student), was progressing finely, and therefore he determined to carry up his end of the row towards gratifying his father by graduating at West Point, which he did creditably, in 1856, in a large class, many of whom have been very distinguished, among them Gen. Fitz Hugh Lee and Gen. Lomax, of Virginia, on the Confederate side, and Gen. George Bayard, on the Federal side. During his term at West Point, Gen. Robert E. Lee was superintendent of the academy, whom Gen. Jackson speaks of as being the grandest man, in his whole make-up, of any man he ever knew.

After the usual furlough, he went to the camp of instruction, at Carlisle barracks, Carlisle, Pennsylvania, and reported to Col. Charles May, of Mexican war fame, then commanding at that cavalry school of instruction. While there, Gen. Jackson was detailed to conduct a batch of recruits to Fort Leavenworth, Kansas, and turned them over to Gen. Harney. Returning via Washington City, he spent three days in company with Gen. Fitz Hugh Lee, at Arlington, where he met and was greatly interested in old Mr. Custis, the proprietor.

In 1857, he crossed the plains, from Leavenworth to Fort Union, New Mexico, to join his regiment of mounted rifles, two months *en route*, the trip full of novelty and adventure, encountering, as he did, for the first time, the buffalo, the grizzly bear and the antelope, just suited to his ardent temperament and love of field sports.

From 1857 to 1861, he was engaged in the principal Indian fights of that territory, with such men as Kit Carson, Larue and others, as his guides; was complimented several times in orders from department headquarters, also from headquarters of the army, for gallantry, tact and good judgment in Indian fighting.

When war was threatened between the States, he awaited the action of his native State, subscribing to the idea that in a sectional conflict his allegiance was one primarily to his State and his people, the only consideration that caused him to tear himself away from the Federal flag which he had ever cherished and honored, and from those social ties that bound him as with links of steel to his old army associates. He had no voice in precipitating the war, and regretted very much the outbreak of hostilities. Yet, for this act of loyalty to the State which gave him birth, and to the people of his State, whom he has always loved, he remains yet an unpardoned rebel of the government for which he once fought gallantly, often risked his life, and for which, if circumstances rendered it necessary, he would risk his life again. Raised under the Methodist dispensation, he would never apply to the government for pardon, because, under that dispensation, a condition precedent was a confession of enormity of guilt and deep repentance for the humble part that he had performed, neither of which has he ever admitted. And it is a source of proud satisfaction to him that he is in a position where he can stand this implied stigma as long as a great government may see fit to continue it. Of all the participants on the losing side in that great struggle, Gen. Jackson and some thirty others, alone, are thus under the ban.

In 1861, when the war broke out, he was in the United States regular army, stationed at Fort Staunton, New Mexico, with the rank of second lieutenant, in a regiment of mounted riflemen, Col. William Loring commanding the department of New Mexico, and Lieut.-Col. George B. Crittenden, of Kentucky, commanding the regiment. When the first shot was fired on Sumter, he tendered his resignation, turned over to the government every cent of money in his hands, as assistant quartermaster, something over twenty-eight thousand dollars, and proceeded, in company with Col. Crittenden, to Galveston, Texas, where he found the port blockaded. Together with Col. Crittenden, Maj. Longstreet, and Messrs. Terry and Lubbock, of Texas, he ran the blockade and proceeded to New Orleans, from which place he sent a tender of service to the Confederate government, through Maj. Longstreet. Previous to that time, however, he had been appointed by Gov. Harris, of Tennessee, to a captaincy of artillery. On arriving at his home in Jackson, Tennessee, he reported by letter to the governor, who ordered him before the military board of the State, composed of Gov. Harris, ex-Gov. Neill S. Brown, James E. Bailey and Gen. William G. Harding. This board retained him a week, interviewing him in regard to cavalry and artillery equipments, arms, etc. Thence he was ordered to report to Gen. Gideon J. Pillow, then commanding the Confederate forces at Memphis, and served in the capacity of a staff officer to Gen. Pillow, in the army of occupation in Missouri and Kentucky, with headquarters at Columbus. He organized a light battery at Columbus. In the battle of Belmont, which soon after followed, he was ordered with his battery to report to Gen. Pillow, but could not land his guns, by reason of the flying Confederate troops, who would have swamped the boat. But he went ashore himself, secured a horse, reported to Gen. Pillow, and was ordered to the duty of conducting three regiments of infantry in rear of Grant's army. While in the discharge of that duty, his horse was shot from under him, receiving eight bullets, while he received a minnie ball in the right side, supposed, at the time, to be a mortal wound. The ball was never extracted, and Gen. Jack-

son still carries it as a memento. That move, however, was a successful one, routing Grant's army and saving the day to the Confederates.

When the troops were concentrated at Corinth, Mississippi, under Gen. Albert Sidney Johnston, Jackson's battery was ordered there. A week before the battle of Shiloh, Jackson was promoted to a colonelcy in the Confederate service for gallantry at the Belmont battle, and ordered into West Tennessee to take command of all cavalry in that section. He commanded all the cavalry in the minor conflicts in West Tennessee and north Mississippi, frequently capturing trains on the Memphis and Charleston railroad, and on one occasion came nearer capturing Gen. Grant than, according to Gen. Grant himself, he ever was at any time during the war. In the fights about Holly Springs, Mississippi, and Bolivar, Tennessee, and in the vicinity of Corinth, Jackson's command frequently captured whole regiments. He was in that severest of all battles during the war, the attack of the combined forces of Van Dorn and Price on the fortified position of Corinth, commanded by Rosencrans. Subsequently Van Dorn was assigned to the command of all the cavalry in that department, and Jackson was placed in command of a brigade of cavalry under him, his command consisting of one thousand five hundred cavalry, when he moved in the rear of Grant's army and attacked Holly Springs, Grant's depot of supplies. Jackson led the charge upon that place, and with his command captured and paroled one thousand eight hundred infantry with arms in their hands. The command also captured a great many cavalry, and destroyed all the commissary, quartermaster and ordnance stores, estimated at six million or eight million dollars. They also secured all of Gen. Grant's private papers, maps, carriage and baggage, by sending a staff officer into the room of Mrs. Grant, who was present. This brilliant and dashing raid had the effect of changing the plan of the movements of that army, by orders from Washington, caused Grant to retrace his steps and make the river campaign against Vicksburg, his plan before being to destroy Jackson and proceed by land against Vicksburg, in the rear. For this service, Jackson was promoted to the rank of brigadier-general by President Davis, then at Jackson, Mississippi, and assigned to a division of cavalry under Gen. Van Dorn.

Gen. Jackson's next service was at Spring Hill, Tennessee, on the left of Bragg's army, in 1862, Gen. Forrest commanding the First division of Gen. Van Dorn's corps, and Gen. Jackson commanding the Second division. Jackson planned and made the fight at Thompson's Station, his command consisting of Gen. Frank Armstrong's brigade of Mississippians and Tennesseans, and Gen. Sul. Ross' Texas brigade. He lost in that fight, in twenty minutes, two hundred and sixty-five men, killed and wounded, but succeeded in capturing Col. Coburn's Federal brigade of one thousand six hundred infantry.

After various skirmishes with the enemy in front of Gen. Bragg, Gen. Jackson was ordered to join Gen. Joseph E. Johnston, in the fall of 1863, at Canton, Mississippi. He commanded the cavalry of that army in all the movements on the Big Black river, for the relief of Vicksburg, and opposing Sherman's attempted marches to Meridian, capturing a goodly number of prisoners, army trains, and destroying much of Sherman's supplies.

When Gen. Joseph E. Johnston was assigned to the Army of Tennessee, then at Dalton, Georgia, at his request, Jackson's command was transferred there, as previously, at Johnston's request, he was transferred from Tennessee to Mississippi. He was assigned by Gen. Johnston to duty as commander of the cavalry on the left wing of his army, which position he held during the entire memorable Georgia campaign, reporting directly to Gen. Johnston, a member of every council of war that was held, and participating in all the engagements. His command performed very faithful service; among other notable events, the defeat of Kilpatrick, at Lovejoy Station, and again, in conjunction with Gen. Wheeler, at Newnan, Georgia, which resulted in the capture of one thousand five hundred Federal cavalry. Gen. Jackson's command participated actively and most gallantly in the desperate fights around Atlanta, while Gen. Hood was commanding the army; also in the memorable battle Gen. Hardee fought against Sherman's army, at Jonesborough, Georgia.

Gen. Jackson was then selected by Gen. Hood to accompany him in his move around Nashville into Tennessee. On reaching Florence, Alabama, he was put under command of Gen. Forrest. Jackson's column led the advance into Tennessee, pursuing most vigorously the retreating Federal army. Unaided, and alone, it held Schofield's army at bay at Spring Hill, Tennessee, all night, after Hood's disastrous failure to attack that army with his whole force, that afternoon. It participated in the bloody battle of Franklin, one of the most desperate engagements of the whole war, and pursued the flying Federals, leading the Confederate advance up to within three miles of the strongly fortified city of Nashville. Thence it moved with Forrest and operated around Murfreesborough, where Jackson defeated and drove back the enemy to their entrenchments, after the infantry, commanded by Gen. Bate, had fled the field, capturing, while there, a train seeking to succor Murfreesborough, together with a large number of prisoners.

Upon the defeat of Hood's army besieging Nashville, Gen. Jackson was ordered over to the Columbia and Franklin turnpike, to sit in front of the victorious Federals, under Gen. George H. Thomas, who were then advancing. This he did successfully, and his command bore the brunt of the retreat from there to within twenty miles of the Tennessee river, and to their credit be it said, did more than any other command in preventing the capture of Hood's entire army—recrossing the Tennessee river in as good order and as well organized as when they made their march into Tennessee.

Jackson's command was noted for its discipline and famous for its true fighting qualities. For this service Gen. Jackson was assigned to the command of all of Forrest's cavalry troops and the Texas brigade, making three brigades, and was recommended for promotion by Gen. Dick Taylor and Gen. N. B. Forrest, as he had previously often been recommended by Gen. Joseph E. Johnston, Gen. Hardee and Gen. Leonidas Polk. Promotion, however, was never given him, because, while in Mississippi, Gen. Jackson arrested a young friend of Mr. Joseph Davis, a brother of President Davis, for taking government cotton, carrying it into Vicksburg and selling it, and declining to accede to the request of Joseph Davis for the release of his friend. This was regarded as a high-handed offense against the said Joseph Davis, who was all-powerful with his brother Jeff., and which offense was shared in by President Davis.

Gen. Jackson next served with his command in the Alabama campaign, defeating Gen. Croxton and Gen. McCook, of the Federal army, and arrived at Marion Junction, Alabama, where he learned of Forrest's defeat at Selma. Forrest then moved his forces to Gainesville, Alabama, at which time Gen. Taylor surrendered to Gen. Canby the troops of that department. Here Gen. Jackson was appointed by Gen. Dick Taylor, commissioner on the part of the Confederate States, associated with Gen. Dennis, of the Federal army, for the parole of the Confederate troops at Gainesville, Alabama, and Columbus, Georgia. This was Gen. Jackson's last military service. The war had ended. The sword of the dauntless cavalry leader was sheathed. Henceforth the services he saw in the field were to serve him well in the peaceful pursuits of the farm. He returned to his home at Jackson, Tennessee, after the surrender, and his father turned over two cotton plantations to him, which he managed successfully until the fall of 1868.

On December 15, 1868, he married Miss Selene Harding, of Belle Meade, near Nashville, Tennessee, daughter of Gen. William G. Harding, a very full and most interesting sketch of whose life and family connections appears elsewhere in this volume. Mrs. Jackson's sister, nee Miss Mary Harding, is the wife of Judge Howell E. Jackson, late United States senator from Tennessee, and judge of the United States circuit court for the Sixth circuit—two brothers marrying two sisters.

Mrs. Jackson was educated at the old Nashville Female Academy, under Dr. C. D. Elliott, and completed her education in Mme. Masse's private French school, in Philadelphia. She is a highly cultivated lady, speaking French fluently, and, while domestic in her tastes and habits, and supervising her household department, her active housekeeper is her cousin, Miss Lizzie Hoover. A lady of true refinement in every pulsation and thought, cultivated and well read, Mrs. Jackson is also the most devoted daughter, wife and mother. Her sphere and her glory is the home circle. Sociable in her nature, and fond of the company of her friends, her health yet forbids her being a lady of society. She loyally and lovingly subscribes to the idea that her duty is first to the dear ones at home, and the nearer she can attain perfect happiness in this true sphere the more bright are the glimpses of heaven. Thoroughly imbued with the true spirit of Christianity, she is sympathetic in her nature, and given to large yet unostentatious charity. No one possesses a more tender heart for the poor, the needy and distressed than she. Possessed of principle of the highest order, and the personification of truth—pure and unembellished ; a Tennessean, highly charged with pride of ancestry and of State; intensely southern in her feelings, and without concealment in the expression of them; devoted to the Confederate soldier, and sympathizing with and urging on every movement looking to the perpetuation of the memory of the fallen heroes of the Confederate cause—she is endeared, not alone to her family and friends, but is claimed as one of the jewels of the commonwealth, a true-blooded southern lady of the fairest and most delicate organization. How vividly apt, in contemplating this happy union, are the poet's words, " None but the brave deserve the fair." Born, as her father was, on God's beauty spot of earth, the lovely Belle Meade estate, which is her home, as it was and is her father's, and was her grandfather's, she is very pronounced in her preference of a farmer's life for her son, in spite of all the allurements of political or fashionable existence.

By his marriage with Miss Harding, Gen. Jackson has three most interesting, bright and happy children, all born at Belle Meade : (1). Eunice Jackson, was born February 8, 1871. This daughter, now entering her " teens," is distinguishing herself by conducting a Sunday-school for the colored children on the Belle Meade estate, and a charitable society in Nashville bears her name, " The Eunice Jackson Society," in the interest of which a monthly periodical, entitled *Woman at Home*, is published. Her father said of her, " Parents are apt to be partial to their children, but if this daughter has a fault we have not discovered it, which is saying a great deal." With a Grecian face, a graceful figure, and modest manners, she promises to be an honor to the name she inherits. (2). William Harding Jackson, born July 17, 1874. (3). Selene Harding Jackson, born August 20, 1876.

Gen. Jackson and wife, and the daughter Eunice, are members of McKendree church (Methodist Episcopal, south), of which he is also trustee. Originally, Gen. Jackson, as was his father and brother, was a Whig, but since the war he has acted with the Democratic party. He has never held any office, subscribing to the

57

idea that the holding of political office is oftentimes incompatible with a high order of self-respect and personal independence.

Gen. Jackson's father, Dr. Alexander Jackson, was a native of Virginia, and a graduate of the Jefferson Medical College, at Philadelphia. He married in Virginia, and settled first at Paris, Tennessee, where he practiced a few years, and finally located at Jackson, where he died, in 1880, at the age of seventy-six. He was a man of considerable property, which he had accumulated by the practice of medicine and investments in negroes and land. He was one of the remarkable men of the State, of extensive reading, a fine writer, his style being clear, perspicuous and terse. He served in the Legislature two terms, 1849–50 and 1851–52, during the inauguration of the internal improvement system. He was a member of the agricultural board of Tennessee, and took great interest in all matters pertaining to agriculture. He was a member of the Methodist church. Of a philosophical turn of mind, he took life easily and smoothly, never permitting anything to disturb him. Fond of good living, he was exceptionally hospitable to the day of his death. He passed the last half of his life in reading, writing and visiting all portions of America. Though possessed of as much brain as any man in the State, he was not ambitious, and upon his writings and labors many men in Tennessee have risen to prominence. He was one of the remarkable conversationalists of Tennessee ; of a rare jovial and social temperament, not given to excess, however ; fond of the society of young people ; given to music, the arts and sciences, yet possessed of an exceedingly practical turn of mind, and was a man of rare judgment as to men and measures. In the rearing of his boys, his cardinal principles were to impress upon them that truth is the bed-rock of all character, and to establish an intimate companionship with them. Of the paternal ancestry of Gen. Jackson further back, the editor finds no trace, except that the family is of Irish stock.

Gen. Jackson's mother, *nee* Miss Mary Hurt, was born in Halifax county, Virginia, daughter of parson Robert Hurt, a Baptist minister, a man of rare oratorical and conversational powers.

Gen. Jackson's maternal uncle, Maj. Robert Hurt, of Jackson, was a member of the Legislature, and of the bureau of agriculture of the State, a man of most pleasing address and great popularity. He has sons and daughters in Jackson, Tennessee. Gen. Jackson's maternal uncle, William Hurt, was noted as a turf man, in Virginia, a contemporary of William R. Johnson, " the Napoleon of the turf." His children are in Virginia. John and Henry Hurt are influential men in their respective neighborhoods, and both have respresented their counties in the Virginia Legislature. Gen. Jackson's great-uncle, James Hurt, a Baptist minister, a man of strong brain, and of great honor and integrity, was one of the pioneers of West Tennessee. He has left sons and daughters of fine worth, most of whom live near Milan, Tennessee. His eldest son, James Hurt, is the most distinguished member of the Supreme bench of Texas.

Gen. Jackson's father married three times, and had two sons by each marriage. The two middle sons, James and Milton Jackson, are respectable farmers in West Tennessee. By the last marriage, he had two sons, Samuel Miller and Robert Turner Jackson. Samuel Miller Jackson is a hardware merchant in Dyersburg, Tennessee, and the younger, Robert Turner Jackson, of Nashville, has all the elements of a most prominent lawyer, as he is possessed of the most sterling character. He is a member of the law firm of Whitworth & Jackson, of Nashville.

Soon after the marriage of Gen. Jackson to Miss Harding, he sold out his planting interests in West Tennessee and came to Belle Meade, and became the assistant of Gen. Harding in the management of his farm. This was done after the earnest and polite invitation of Gen. Harding, that he would make his home with him, stating that there was plenty of room and plenty of work for them both, and as he was growing old he did not wish to be separated from his daughter, who had charge of his household affairs. The relations between the two in that position have been most pleasant, agreeable and confidential. He has devoted himself to the business with intelligence, energy and assiduity. During this period, from 1868 to 1886, he has occupied a front rank in all that pertains to agricultural matters, either State or national, being the prime mover in organizing and conducting, as chairman of the executive committee, the valuable agricultural journal known as the *Rural Sun*. his idea being that agricultural journals, like almanacs, should be calculated for the latitudes they are designed to serve. His observation had taught him that many young men at the South were swamped in agricultural pursuits, in the effort to apply the teachings of northern agricultural journals to the latitude and conditions of the South, the conditions between the two sections, in point of agriculture, being entirely different. In the East, where land is the principal cost of production, the primary object is to bring about the greatest yield to the acre, which must be done by heavy manuring or most scientific modes of culture. In the South, where land is plentiful and cheap, and labor the principal cost of production, the object is to make the most per hand, going over the greatest number of acres with a given force, relying upon proper rotation of crops and the great fertilizer, red clover, to keep the soil always in good heart.

He has filled the positions of president of the State association of farmers; president of the Bureau of Agriculture of the State, and the financial agent of that bureau, under the administration of Gov. John C. Brown, which bureau got out the work entitled "The Resources of Tennessee," in two volumes, the principal work of reference at this day, as it is descriptive of the State by grand divisions, from east to west, also an an accurate description of each county of the State. In that work is an accurate geological and agricultural map of the State, which originated with Gen. Jackson, his idea being a suggestion, which led to the preparation of this map, that as the agricultural products of a State hinge so intimately upon the geological formation, it was well to have a combined map showing forth both the geological formation and agricultural production of each county. It is a source of pride to him that this work was published at a cost less, by two thirds, than any similar work of equal merit in any State of the Union, and it was gratifying to him that he should have presented the anomaly, hitherto unheard-of, of covering back into the treasury over six thousand dollars of what was considered a small legislative appropriation for the purpose, for which he received the thanks of the Legislature for fidelity and good judgment in the execution of this trust. This work, published in different languages, and scattered abroad, was the initiatory movement which has led to the attraction of immigration and capital to our borders. Regarding it as in the nature of a census, which should only be gotten out at stated intervals, he recommended to Gov. John C. Brown that he, the president, and his associates of the bureau, should resign, and thus save the State that expense, and create the office of commissioner of agriculture, who should be provided with a large room at the capitol, and whose duty should be to collect specimens of minerals, ores and woods, together with agricultural products of the State, and there be prepared to give intelligent and impartial information to the visitor and intending settler in our State, which suggestion was adopted, and is carried out to the present day.

He was the originator of the National Agricultural Congress and held the first meeting in the city of Nashville, was subsequently elected president of that body, and has been among the foremost in advancing the interests of his State. He has written and spoken a great deal in advocacy of reforms tending to curtail extravagant expenditure in State, county and municipal government; also in those measures that tend to lighten the burdens of the tillers of the soil in the State and nation, upon whose shoulders the permanency and splendor of the government rest.

In the fall of 1883, he was selected as the president of the Safe Deposit, Trust and Banking Company of Nashville.

When Gen. Jackson was asked what methods in life—military and civic—he had brought to bear on his efforts for success, he replied: "If I could say that there was one cause above all others that has tended to my success in every position in which I have been placed, it is a commendable pride of character—not content to do as well as others have done, but to study the salient points of successful characters of men in the different fields in which I have been placed, and bring to bear the most careful judgment, coupled with energy, intense application, system and will power to accomplish the greatest results. These qualities, coupled with business courage and dash, account for my success."

He is a man given to boldness of speech without mincing words. His reputation in Tennessee is such that those who know him know they can, by asking, find out where he stands as to persons and measures. Of singular simplicity and transparency of character, he is a strong man, calm, slow, determined, driving right on to his purpose. Of very social disposition, enjoying above all things the society of friends, in his command of language and power of expressing in few words comprehensive views, no man is more entertaining. He is the autocrat of the dinner table. It is one great advantage of a farmer's life that he has no temptation to conceal his opinions lest he lose custom or patronage, for he depends on neither for his support. Still, even if this were not so, Gen. Jackson would be a man of his own mind, with courage to think right, to speak right and to do right. Even his personal appearance declares this. He stands five feet nine and a half inches high, weighs two hundred and twenty pounds, is compactly, even powerfully, built; has blue eyes, auburn hair, a neck of force, a chin of determination, and that look of command that made his soldiers love and obey " Old Red," as they familiarly called him, and to go forward when he ordered—even into the very jaws of death.

BELLE MEADE.

The Creator of the universe honored the vocation of farming by creating a garden eastward in Eden and requiring man to dress it and keep it, and by reason of being surrounded in this calling of agriculturist by nature in its purity and diversity, the desire to be an agriculturist has become ingrained in the composition of man, and all desire to be farmers. This vocation, to insure success, requires greater intellect, better judgment, and more energy than any other, and to the intelligent agriculturist opens up a wider field of thought, in both the science and art of agriculture, than in any other calling. It gives to him a greater breadth of intellect, carrying him out on a broader and higher plane of conservative thought and a purer plane of life, comparatively free from the great conflicts and wranglings of men in the more active trading and commercial pursuits.

To gratify the farmers of the State, the editor presents, from a personal visit, a description of Belle Meade —the largest stock farm in Tennessee, and not exceeded in size by any in Kentucky. The estate contains about five thousand acres in one body, all under fence, the outer fence, which is of stone, being eighteen

miles in length, and of a probable value of fifty or sixty dollars an acre. There are in cultivation two hundred and fifty acres in corn ; cotton, none ; wheat, two hundred acres (but henceforward no more wheat will be grown on the place, as there is no money in the crop); barley, one hundred acres, for grinding and feeding to stock in winter ; clover and orchard grass, three hundred acres ; timothy, four hundred acres ; oats, two hundred and fifty acres—the remainder of this magnificent domain, say three thousand acres, being well set in blue grass and orchard grass pastures.

This Cumberland basin of Tennessee was designed by the Creator to be a grass producing and stock raising section. That farmer who undertakes to deflect it from this idea is going cultivated crops is flying in the face of nature, and undoubtedly pursuing a losing business. Or to frame it differently, the farmer in this section who carries anything in the shape of grain or hay to the man in the city, dealing in those articles, inquiring the price of the man who wishes to buy, and sells to him, is doing a foolish business. Make it a grass producing section, as it was designed, put your surplus produce into stock and let the buyer come to you to inquire the price. This comprises a great deal of the prosperity of the Cumberland basin. On no other basis can the farmers of this section make tongue and buckle meet. The farmers of this section are not in a healthy condition only as they are dealing in stock.

The stock on the Belle Meade farm consists, first in importance, of five thoroughbred stallions of national and international reputation, viz. : Bramble, valued at ten thousand dollars; Enquirer, valued at twenty-five thousand dollars; imported Great Tom (from Lord Falmouth, of England), valued at twenty thousand dollars ; Luke Blackburn, valued at twenty-five thousand dollars, and Plenipo, at five thousand dollars.

Belle Meade was the home of the world-renowned stallion, imported Bonnie Scotland, and Luke Blackburn is his most distinguished son—a worthy son of the old sire who stood at the head of American stallions for three consecutive years. Luke Blackburn was the king of the turf in America, and pronounced the fleetest horse in the world by Col. M. H. Sanford, who owned the " North Elkton Breeding Farm " in Kentucky.

On the farm are ninety thoroughbred brood mares, all of distinguished families, and worth on an average five hundred dollars each. These thoroughbred animals trace their pedigrees in an unbroken line back to the sixteenth century, to the Barb horse of the Arabian desert.

A great feature of Belle Meade, as it is indeed always an epoch in American turf circles, is the annual sale of thoroughbred yearlings. It usually occurs about the latter part of April or first of May, and attracts purchasers from all parts of the United States and the Canadas. Usually about forty-five or fifty head of the beautiful "young things" are auctioned off at each sale. There have been eighteen annual sales of yearlings from Gen. Harding's stud, and in all that time the produce of Belle Meade stallions have never failed to get a large proportion of the plums of the turf. The best year the farm ever had was in 1881, the year after Bonnie Scotland stood at the head of the list of winning stallions, his get that year crediting him with one hundred and thirty-seven races and one hundred and five thousand dollars. So commanding a lead did Bonnie Scotland have that year that Leamington, who came next, was not within sixty thousand dollars of him. The immediate consequence was that the sons and daughters of the old Tennessee stallion brought in 1881 an aggregate of forty-one thousand dollars, eleven head averaging over one thousand nine hundred dollars, and one bringing the phenomenal sum of seven thousand five hundred dollars.

In 1881, the French government sent their representatives, Baron Favorot and Capt. De La Chere, to inspect the horses of America, also the leading breeding establishments of thoroughbreds. Upon their return to France they made a report to the government, comprising five hundred to six hundred pages, descriptive of every species of horse, including " le plug "—the plug horse—so accurate were they. In this work they say : " The best specimen of the trotting horse we found in the State of Kentucky, in America, but the best specimen of the thoroughbred horse we found at Gen. Harding's (Belle Meade), in the State of Tennessee. Indeed, we saw a crop of thoroughbred yearlings there that surpassed anything we had ever seen in England or France "—a high compliment, which Tennessee will not be slow to appreciate.

To the casual observer or thinker this may be surprising, but it should not be when we reflect that Tennessee was far in advance of Kentucky prior to the war in thoroughbred horses, the development of this animal dating back to 1808, in the vicinity of Nashville, and the breed improved by the judicious expenditure of money by such men as the immortal Andrew Jackson, Col. George Elliott, Hon. Bailie Peyton, Col. Berry Williams, Judge Jo. C. Guild, and A. C. Franklin, of Sumner county (now succeeded by his sons, Capt. James C. and A. C. Franklin), and by Gen. W. G. Harding, Mark R. Cockrill, John Harding, sr. (who began on a small scale but never increased it), and Gen. William W. Woodfolk, of Davidson county. This important industry brings a great deal of money and a great many people to Tennessee. It is, therefore, not surprising that the breeding of this stock, started by such men of thought and ability, should have been carried on up to this period by their successors with enlightened judgment, judicious expenditure, care in the selection of the best strains of blood to propagate, coupled with the most careful attention in the breeding and rearing of such valuable animals, aided as this section is by the very best climate known to the new world for this

breed of horses, being nearly identical with the same parallel of latitude as Arabia and the Barbary States, where this stock first originated.

Other branches of animal industry at Belle Meade include the rearing of a herd of from two hundred and fifty to four hundred head of the best grade of Durham cattle that can be obtained in the markets of Tennessee, and about one hundred head of sheep, of the mixed breed of Southdown and Leicester. For a place of this size this would seem a small number of sheep to carry. In explanation, the proprietors deem their land too valuable for sheep except for table use, and unless the range is very extensive of cheap land, the breeding of sheep, including the losses from death and dogs, would be one hundred per cent., which deceives a great many, for the reason that on a place of this size (five thousand acres), you can stock it with one thousand five hundred dollars. Hence, it is readily seen, very little can be made out of it, as compared to carrying ten thousand dollars or fifteen thousand dollars' worth of beef cattle, making fifty to sixty per cent. In other words, the dealing in sheep on a place like this is identical with the foolish experiment of a person trying to eat soup with a fork. It will be readily perceived he will not get much soup. A herd of about two hundred and fifty grade Cashmere goats is kept, designed principally for browsers to assist in cleansing the pastures of the buckle bush, briers, iron weeds and switch cane. Hogs, of the Berkshire breed, are raised sufficient in number, say one hundred and fifty, to provide meat to the quantity of twenty thousand pounds annually, which is required by the laborers on the place. Also, there is a herd of about forty purely bred Shetland ponies, which is being increased annually.

A portion of the place, designed as a hog and mule department, consists of an orchard of one hundred and twenty-five acres, and connected with it three hundred and fifty acres filled with beech trees, which furnish a great quantity of mast, enabling the proprietors to raise hogs as cheaply as any other point in Tennessee.

The entire farm is run by the partnership firm of Jackson Bros., Gen. W. H. Jackson and United States Judge H. E. Jackson. Everything pertains to the firm except separate residences, private stables and private dairies, each one milking from twenty to forty cows, and making butter for market, each cow yielding from four to six pounds of butter per week, buttermilk being given to the laborers to aid them in rearing their children. The labor of the farm consists of about twenty farm hands, about one-half of whom are plow boy size, from ten to fifteen years old ; one man has charge of all the thoroughbred stock, with four assistants ; one man in charge of all out stock, beef, sheep and hogs ; one white man, a mechanic, in charge of the saw mill, grist mill and all machinery. He is the carpenter also, with an assistant negro carpenter, who is also the blacksmith. The wages system has been adopted, on the

idea that the share system is fatal, both to the owner
and the cropper ; for a partnership with a negro is
construed on his part to be absolute freedom to idle
away all the time he, in his judgment or caprice, may
see proper. The system of wages on this place is a
graded one, and consists for the best hands of ten dollars per month for January and February, besides
rations in sufficient quantity of good and healthy food,
house for the laborer and his family, including fuel, a
garden spot of sufficient size to furnish all vegetables
for his family, fruit from the orchard, buttermilk for
the family (medicine, in case of sickness, is furnished
gratuitously—not being a part of the contract), team
and tools to cultivate their garden spots, and every other
Saturday as a holiday. Twelve dollars a month wages
are paid the balance of the year, except during the
harvest months of June, July and August, when fifteen
dollars per month is paid. For plow boy size, eight
dollars, nine dollars and twelve dollars per month wages
are paid, with the house, fuel, and other things as for
the others. The remaining hands are classified between
these two rates, according to their ages, efficiency and
ability to perform work.

The negro quarters (cabins) are arranged on three
sides of an open court or square of five acres, a play-
ground for the children, and where the hands hold their
open air church meetings, when the weather is pleasant.
During inclement weather an ample room is provided
for church services. All of the children of the place
are taught in Sunday-school every Sabbath evening, by
Miss Eunice Jackson, eldest daughter of Gen. Jackson,
the exercises consisting of reading, the catechism and
singing. They all attend the district day school under
a colored teacher. These hands, the oldest ones, slaves
before the war, were born and raised on the place, and
the motto of the management is, they would rather pay
above than below the customary wages of the country,
give them better treatment and in return have better
command of the labor and receive more faithful labor.
The farm is conducted under system—military in its
precision, formulated in rules—not too stringent, distributing the labor and regulating the working on the
principle of deduction from wages for neglect, disobe-
dience of orders, careless breaking or losing of tools, etc.
Yet, all this is based on strict justice and kind treatment, for the negro, like the white child, it seems, can
never be made to understand the sacredness of a contract, as well as how the employer's interest is to neither
forget or neglect the fulfillment of a promise. Gen.
Jackson stated that he had not, in seventeen years of
his management, forgotten or neglected but one promise
made to a hand. He promised a negro, George Thornton, to bring him a pair of pantaloons from the city. As
he stepped out of his buggy at the horse-block, George
was there with an air of perfect confidence that he
would receive his pantaloons. When informed that
Gen. Jackson had forgotten them, his face presented a

dejected appearance. Gen. Jackson said to him, " I am
sorry, George ; and the only way I can rectify it is to
give you the money, which I now do, and loan you my
saddle horse to ride to the city and get them," which
George accepted, perfectly satisfied. This is the treatment, reciprocal in its terms, between employer and
employe at Belle Meade, and this sort of treatment will
always insure interest in the affairs of the employer, and
secure the best description of service.

The glorious forests, the beautiful woodlands around
Belle Meade have excited the unqualified admiration
of thousands. The superb scenery has been likened
to the country around Warwick, in England, but it
is even grander and more beautiful. Here are five
thousand acres in this princely estate—great fields interspersed with parks, groves, forests, the splendor of
feudal years. The match of this place is not to be found
this side of some of the fairest ancient estates of old
England. For this reason one of the most interesting
features of Belle Meade to visitors, and the one in part
conducive to the good living of the family, is a beautiful park containing four hundred and twenty-five acres,
well set in blue grass and supplied with fresh running
water. The forest primeval here displays huge oaks fes-
tooned with vines. The enormous branches hang over
the green turf and unite the beauties of field and forest, of lawn and running brook—and there's your picture ! But it is not yet complete. Within that park is
a herd of about three hundred and fifty deer, the common fallow deer of Tennessee, collected by Gen. Harding, who began with five and added fawns from time
to time, as he might catch them in his hunts. This
animal increases rapidly, each doe adding one or two
a year. The deer furnish royal sport to the members of
the family and their friends, by getting them out of the
park and chasing them with a pack of fox hounds
(thirty being on the place), and ending the chase at
any point with the Scotch stag hounds which Gen.
Jackson imported from Scotland, and of which he now
has three. Many thousands of distinguished persons
have visited Belle Meade and enjoyed this rare treat,
among them, Lord Tarbot, the third son of the Duke
of Sutherland, who not long since was the guest of
Gen. Harding, and while there joined in a deer chase
after the English fashion. It is an agreeable study
of the deer in the park as showing the wonderful instincts with which nature has provided them. The
doe when she drops her fawn will move immediately
away from it. When she returns there to nurse him
she will put him in motion. After nursing, the little
fellow will continue to run as long as he has breath,
the doe following several hundred yards behind him.
When he drops from exhaustion, she immediately turns
at right angles from the track they have been going,
clearly saying thereby that if an animal of prey is coming on their trail, she will divert the pursuer's attention, carry him off after her and not permit him to go

to the fawn, she giving out the stronger scent, while that of the fawn lingers upon the ground but a short time. Now the instinct of the fawn is such that if aroused from the spot where the doe has seen him drop, and he should run for a mile out of the park, it matters not through how many fences, if the observer will station himself a short distance from the spot and remain an hour, he will observe the little fellow creeping steadily back and planting himself in the identical spot he first left. By reason of this animal's instincts it is enabled to live longer, and be preserved in the vicinity of its birth-place, than any other wild animal. The elk, buffalo, bear, wolf, and every other species of wild animal, have been driven out beyond the borders of civilization, while the deer remain.

The deer at Belle Meade are fed with the out stock on sheaf oats and corn, when the weather is so bad they cannot get to grass. Adjoining the park, and separated from it by a low fence is a copse of about thirty acres, in its native growth, thick with vines and dense cane, which is kept as a browsing and hiding retreat for the deer.

The expense of running Belle Meade farm in all its departments, including taxes (two thousand dollars), is about twelve thousand dollars per annum ; gross receipts are about forty thousand dollars, making an income of six or seven per cent. on capital invested in stock. The average farmer in Tennessee makes less than three per cent. on investment.

The family mansion at Belle Meade is a grand old country house, modest in appearance, yet built in the old-time, commodious, and generous southern manner. It stands in the background, far from the highway, and is reached from Harding pike by a luxurious drive, which, in summer, is amid blooming roses and blossoming foliage and the scent of new-mown hay. The house is a two-story brick, and was erected by Gen. Harding in 1853. It has a massive stone front with a pediment supported by a file of six stone columns, twenty-two feet high in two sections, and forming a lovely portico after the southern style. There are four large rooms above and four below, separated by wide halls ; also garret rooms above, and four large cellars underneath. There are library and bath rooms both on the first and second floors, and a broad back porch on each floor. An entry or hallway divides the main house from the kitchen and the summer dining room, while above these two latter are two large chambers, used for linen closets, etc. Water is supplied to the house and kitchen by an Ericsson hot air engine, stationed in one of the cellars, drawing the water from a well and forcing it into a tank located on the back porch above, which has a capacity of eight hundred gallons ; and by means of an overflow pipe from this tank the water is carried to the stable tank, seven hundred and fifty gallons capacity, which furnishes water for the horses at the stables, and is also used for wash-

ing vehicles, etc. In addition, there is a well near the dwelling, with a force pump and hose to throw water on any part of the house, in case of fire. A castellated stone ice-house, a dainty bit of Tudor-gothic, is devoted to the dairy department. Here spring water flows out of the rock.

The furniture of the house is of rosewood and mahogany. The walls are adorned with the old family portraits, evincing that high degree of commendable pride in ancestry as essential to true success in life as the natural oil of the duck is essential to it to prevent its sinking when in water. The portraits and the oil paintings are of Randal McGavock (the great friend of Andrew Jackson) and wife—(father and mother of Gen. Harding's wife); John Harding and wife (Gen. Harding's parents) ; the portraits of Gen. Harding and wife ; of Dr. Alexander Jackson and wife—father and mother of Gen. William H. and Senator H. E. Jackson ; the portrait of the wife of John Harding, son of Gen. Harding ; and the most life-like picture in existence of Gen. Andrew Jackson, "Old Hickory," for whose memory the patriarchal Gen. Harding cherishes the most fond recollection ; pictures of Senator Bayard, of Delaware, Gen. Joseph E. Johnston, Gen. Robert E. Lee, President Jefferson Davis, Gen. Stephen D. Lee, Gen. Fitz Hugh Lee (a particular friend and the classmate of Gen. Jackson at West Point), and a portrait of Dr. George Loring, ex-United States commissioner of agriculture. Gen. Harding, however, takes special pride in his show-case containing the silver premiums taken at fairs by his stock, and the silk purses won by his horses in memorable contests of speed on the turf; the latter he prizes most highly, because the plate was awarded according to the judgment of men, which is often in error as to the most deserving animal in the ring; whereas, on the turf, when the animal went from the tap of the drum, after making the course, contesting against worthy competitors and landing a winner, he was sure his horse was the best in that contest. Hence his reason for valuing the purses more highly than the plate. And so in the race of life, when a man outstrips his fellow man, opposed by foeman worthy of his steel, he too should receive his premium in the plaudits of the multitude and in the refrain, "Well done, thou good and faithful servant." A generous rival in such a race, divested of the slightest tinge of acrimony, is the active and powerful motor to success. This idea was first formulated in the Grecian games, and has found worthy repetition in form of fairs and turf contests in Tennessee.

Such is Belle Meade, the beautiful meadow of Tennessee, and such its surroundings and ennobling influences. What more fitting to close this sketch than the following article, concerning its venerable proprietor, which recently appeared in the *Spirit of the Farm:*

"Wherever the race horse is known, the name of this

distinguished Tennessean (Gen. William G. Harding) is an household word. His life has been a complete success, and furnishes an incentive for high endeavor on the part of the youth of the South. In his quiet retreat, surrounded by those who love him, this venerable man can have a pleasing retrospect. The book of his life is without a blot or a stain. His word is as good as his bond, and that is beyond valuation. No whisper has ever been heard against his name or his character. From a small beginning he has made Belle Meade, as the commissioners of the French government lately said, the most splendid race horse nursery in the world. His career exhibits the rich results of a life anchored to a never-dying purpose. There are ambitious young men in Tennessee, here and there, who have commenced their career in the same line, who can gain immense advantages by a close study of Gen. Harding's life and methods. In the hey-day of youth he caught the spirit of "Old Hickory," and from him he learned to fear "the stain of dishonor as a wound." From him

he imbibed the loyalest of loves for the pure bred horse. With an unflagging energy, and with an elastic hope, he set about the development of the glories of Belle Meade, his ancestral home. Its broad acres and its famous denizens show what a brave and honest man can do. How rich is his experience! How beneficial would be his autobiography! What a tale he could tell of Priam, of Lexington, of Jack Malone, of Bonnie Scotland! In his younger days, Gen. Harding wielded a facile and fascinating pen. In the evening of his life, if so minded, he could enrich the literature of his State by deathless reminiscences of his contemporaries and his horses. He could not withstand the appeal of his friends on this score, and we trust requests may pour in upon him to begin the work. He is the pioneer in one of the most remunerative industries of the South, and his book would be read by all with increasing interest. Besides, his words of experience would greatly aid the rising establishments all over Tennessee, which are destined to bring great revenue to our people."

HON. JOHN A. TINNON.

PULASKI.

THE TINNON family is of Scotch-Irish origin. James Tinnon, the grandfather of the subject of this sketch, came from Ireland with his father when only three years old, settled first in Pennsylvania, afterward in North Carolina, and, in 1806, emigrated with his family to Williamson county, Tennessee, when the country was nothing but a dense wilderness. He remained in Williamson county two years. Cutting his way through the almost impenetrable canebrakes, he finally settled on the fertile lands of Richland creek, five miles north of Pulaski. Here he died, in 1844, at the age of eighty-six, leaving six children, of whom Robert Tinnon, Judge Tinnon's father, was the youngest. His wife, nee Hannah McCracken, was a native of North Carolina, and of Scotch parentage. She died eighty years of age.

Robert Tinnon was about nine years of age when his father took him to Giles county. He grew up to be a good, plain farmer, a good conveyancer, thoroughly posted in the lands of that section. He was a justice of the peace and a member of the county court for twenty years, up to the time of his death, in April, 1862, at the age of sixty-five. He was a class-leader in the Methodist church, a perfectly upright man, genuinely good, quiet in every way, not wealthy, but widely respected.

Judge Tinnon's mother, Elizabeth Abernathy, was the daughter of Joseph Abernathy, from North Carolina, a surveyor and conveyancer in that State, and in Giles county, Tennessee. He was connected with Judge

Haywood and the Shephards in surveying large bodies of land on Richland creek, in Giles county, at an early day—from 1800 to 1810.

Judge John A. Tinnon was born in Giles county, Tennessee, November 28, 1822, and was brought up in that county, on his father's farm, going to the old field schools until sixteen or seventeen years old, when he entered Wirtemburg Academy, in Pulaski, under Profs. Mendum and Hartwell Brown, in 1841-2, and studied there nearly two years. Then he read law about two years with Judges T. M. Jones and Goode, at Pulaski. In 1848, he taught school one year at Lawrenceburg, as an assistant to Prof. J. W. Dana, in the meantime studying mathematics and the languages, and reading some in the law. He obtained license to practice, in the spring of 1848, from Chancellor T. H. Cahal and Judge Scott, and practiced from Lawrenceburg from 1848 to the fall of 1854, when he moved back to Pulaski, and has practiced and resided there from 1855 to the present time. He was in partnership with Col. Solon E. Rose from 1858 to 1882.

In May, 1883, he was appointed by the judges of the Supreme court one of the judges of the court of referees, a position he now holds, at a salary of three thousand dollars per annum. He has three or four times been commissioned by the governor as special chancellor to hold court at Columbia to try causes in which the chancellor, Fleming, was incompetent, and also as special judge, to hold court when the sitting judge, W. P. Martin, was sick.

As a speaker before a jury or court, his style of oratory is earnest and direct, stating the facts and logic of his cases, and not scheming to appeal to the passions, the prejudices or preferences of the tribunal. In politics he was a Whig, "fought, bled and died with Henry Clay." In 1850, he was district presidential elector on the Douglas ticket. Occasionally he has attended State conventions, but since 1860 has taken little part in politics, except to vote with the Democrats as "representing the present state of things."

He became a Mason at Lawrenceburg, in 1843, has filled all the stations in the Blue Lodge, and is a Past Master. He belongs to no church, though a strong believer in Christianity, and a contributor to its benevolent enterprises. His wife is a Presbyterian. He has for ten years been vice-president of the board of trustees of Martin Female College, at Pulaski, one of the finest female schools in the South, founded on a bequest of thirty-five thousand dollars by Col. Thomas Martin, of Pulaski.

Judge Tinnon married, at Athens, Alabama, June 4, 1850, Miss E. Virginia Joyner, daughter of R. Joyner, esq., a justice of the peace, farmer and merchant at that place, of old Virginia stock. Her brother, Dr. Rod. Joyner, of Harrisburg, Arkansas, has been a member of the Arkansas Legislature, and was a member of the constitutional convention of that State. Her sister, Mary P. Joyner, is now the wife of Col. S. O. Nelson, a large commission merchant at New Orleans before the war, now a planter near Athens, Alabama. Her sister, Elizabeth Joyner, married G. B. Parker, a farmer, now near Leesburg, Florida, engaged in fruit culture. Mrs. Tinnon graduated at the Athens Female Institute, and is noted for her high culture, refined manners, overflowing hospitality and her impulsive generosity and charities.

Judge Tinnon's youngest brother, Rev. R. M. Tinnon, D.D., pastor of the Cumberland Presbyterian church in East Nashville, Tennessee, studied for the law, but when the war came on joined the Third Tennessee regiment, under Gen. John C. Brown, and with that regiment fought all through the war; was taken prisoner at Fort Donelson; exchanged; was in the battles around Vicksburg and Port Hudson; had his thigh broken at Chickamauga by a minnie ball; was again captured and exchanged just before the close of the war.

After the war he taught school in North Alabama; professed religion under the ministry of Rev. George Mitchell, studied for the Cumberland Presbyterian ministry, was duly ordained, and took charge of the church at Huntsville; remained there three years, then went, in 1877, to East Nashville and took charge of the church there. He married Miss Sallie Preston, of Decatur, Alabama, about the close of the war, and has five chidren, Meta, Mae, Tullie, Roberta and John Baird. He is a progressive man, one of the best pastors in the church, a natural born speaker, and one of the leading clergymen of Nashville. He has two other brothers, both farmers, William A., near Florence, Alabama, and Capt. J. M. Tinnon, near Alva, Mississippi. They were both soldeìrs in the Confederate army. Also, a deceased brother, Rev. Joseph F. Tinnon, who died in 1852, leaving two sons, one of whom, Rev. James F. Tinnon, of the Methodist Episcopal Church, south, is now stationed at Mount Pleasant, Tennessee.

Judge Tinnon's personality is very attractive. He is about five feet ten inches high, and weighs one hundred and eighty-six pounds. He is of rather stout build, well rounded, almost corpulent; has very dark, luxuriant hair, which he wears roached back as if ready for combat; gray eyes, and the look and manner of a man of the world, surprised at nothing, and easy, whether at home, in his office, at the bar, on the bench, or in any company whatever. He has a very large brain, a big, round, sensible head, and is evidently a man of great force. Like most lawyers, he has a competency, lives well and has a good home. To account for his success, one can readily determine that the only road Judge Tinnon has advanced along is that of work—careful, honest, sincere, intelligent work. He had the right stuff in him to begin with, and he has, put it to good service. A man only fails because he has to succeed upon something that is not in him. He must cultivate himself and get the seed of what is true and right, and then grow. Thoroughly honest with himself and everybody else, whatever he does is without deception. He is not regarded as an ambitious man. He has given more of his time and study to science and literature than a lawyer is generally expected to do. Shakspeare and the Bible are his favorite books, yet in other fields he is a close student.

Judge Thomas M. Jones says of him: "He knows fewer trifles, knows more law and has fewer wants than any man I ever saw. He is a most admirable man in every way."

REV. GEORGE WHITE, D. D.

MEMPHIS.

WHEN the compiler of this sketch was seeking information concerning Dr. White, he was told, "You have one of the richest subjects for a biography, but it will take but few words to tell of him." And, indeed, it does not require volumes to portray the life of a man, who is so uniformly kind and courteous to all; so universally popular with all sects, creeds and all conditions of society; so unflinchingly devoted to duty; so earnest, faithful and tireless in the Master's cause—a man, whose whole existence may be summed up in the sweetest phrase that ever fell on mortal ears, "Glory to God in the highest; peace on earth, good will to man."

All the virtues of a man and a Christian are so harmoniously blended in him and form such a symmetry of character that in looking about to get an estimate of him, it is difficult to find which of the noble traits of manly, mental and spiritual make-up predominates the other.

He was born in Charleston, South Carolina, March 12, 1802, and lived there until he was eighteen years of age. He began his education in Charleston under John Wrench, a very eminent teacher of that day, and subsequently went to school for some time near Statesburg, in Sumter county, South Carolina. When the venerable gentleman—now more than fourscore years of age, and fast traveling toward the nonagenarian period—was asked where he was educated, he replied, with vivid recollection, and with a merry twinkle in his eye: "I went to school for seven years to a teacher who whipped the boys every day, no matter whether they were good or bad ; and to this day the sound of fire bells is sweetest music to my ears, because our teacher was a member of the fire board, and whenever there was an alarm of fire, it meant a brief cessation of hostilities, for the teacher's words were—" Go home boys ; you have a holiday."

After leaving the school near Statesburg, young White entered a law office in Charleston, and devoted two years to the study of the legal profession, which he had determined to pursue. While in this office he, with a number of other young men, went to a camp-meeting, and becoming deeply and seriously interested in the subject of religion, joined the Methodist church, gave up the bar for the pulpit, immediately went to exhorting, and shortly thereafter to preaching.

He remained in the Methodist ministry about ten years, during which time he was the contemporary of Dr. Capers, afterward the celebrated Methodist bishop, and other eminent Methodist divines. Though but a boy in years when he began his ministerial labors, his fame as a preacher spread abroad, and he was known as the "beardless preacher."

In 1822, he went to Savannah and there opened a

school, called at first Savannah Academy, and afterward Chatham Academy, a school which he conducted for more than a quarter of a century, meeting all the time with remarkable success. Few men have been accorded the privilege of laboring so long and so successfully in the cause of education in one place as he did at Savannah. During this period he educated the children of many of the first families in the State of Georgia—the Bartows, Berriens, Laws, Andersons, Bullocks, Screvens, Habershams, Sheftels, Lamars—their name is legion. Many of the men who have been most prominent in the State of Georgia since that time—the great and virtuous in divinity, in judicature, in statesmanship, in commerce and war, have been trained under him, and to-day their children and grand-children refer with pride to the fact that their fathers or grandfathers went to school to Dr. White.

After remaining in the ministry of the Methodist church for about ten years, as a matter of conscience and conviction of duty, he joined the Protestant Episcopal church, prepared for that ministry, and was ordained by Bishop Bowen in St. Michael's church at Charleston, South Carolina, December 31, 1833. During all the years of his teaching at Savannah, he was also engaged in preaching. Indeed, it might be said of him here that he has preached every Sunday of his life for the last sixty-four years, except when prevented by sickness. Likewise, it may be said that one of his strong characteristics, which developed itself then, has stuck to him throughout life, and that is, his extreme kindness to the colored race. Much of his time was spent in ministering to them. His plain, simple, effective and forcible style of preaching suited these people, and they always called upon him, when any prominent member of their congregation died, to preach the funeral. His labors among these humble people were very effective, for moved by the gentleness of his manner, the simplicity and kindliness of his words, they would come about the altar and ask for the prayers of the minister. His years of disinterested labor among them brings out in bold relief one strong element of his character—a genuine and unaffected desire to do good to all men, to lift up the lowly and comfort the humble. For several years of this same period he also preached to the seamen at their chapel, erected by Mr. Penfield, and made many friends among the sailors and sea captains. The founder of this chapel, by his will, left money in bank to employ a pastor, but during the time of Dr. White's pastorate, the bank failed, yet he continued to labor among his charge without money and without price, other than the reward which an approving conscience brings to duty done.

In the meantime he had established, in Effingham

county, Georgia, a parish called St. Michael's, which completed the number necessary for a diocese, and was the means of electing the first bishop of Georgia—Bishop Elliott.

During his residence in Savannah he was prominently connected with the literary and scientific pursuits of the day, and was specially interested in the sciences of geology, conchology and mineralogy, spending much time and study upon them.

In 1852, he published "White's Statistics of Georgia," a volume of wide circulation, which was read and endorsed by the first men of Georgia.

In the same year, desiring to take his family to a more healthy locality, he left the field in which he had so long and so successfully labored and went to Marietta, Georgia, and while there published his "Historical Collections of Georgia," which book was also a great success, and was widely circulated in the State, and it, as well as "White's Statistics," is to this day a standard work of reference in the State.

About 1856, he went to Florence, Alabama, took charge of a church there, and by his efforts during the next two years contributed largely to building it up.

In 1858, he went to Memphis, as rector of Calvary church, which he has made his field of labor up to the present time.

Dr. White is descended from an old Huguenot family, who were among the earliest settlers of South Carolina, where descendants of the family are still living, in the vicinity of Charleston. His father was George White, a cotton factor at Charleston.

Dr. White was married, January 23, 1823, before reaching his twenty-first year, to Mrs. Elizabeth Groves, and for more than sixty years they have toiled along the path of life together. They have had ten children, only four of whom are now living.

Mrs. White's father was John Millen, an Englishman, who came to Charleston and became an indigo and cotton planter. Her mother was Martha Simmons, of an old and aristocratic South Carolina family. Mrs. White was born November 23, 1802, and was first married, at the age of seventeen, to John Groves, who died of yellow fever at Savannah, in 1822. She is remarkable for firmness and decision of character, and is a woman of strong affections, strong impulses, and genial, sunny disposition. During all the years of her husband's ministry, she has been with him, his counsel and his helpmeet, through all the vicissitudes of life—through sickness and sorrow and death, and now, like two ships returning full freighted into port, they are journeying toward their God, borne down by years of usefulness, while three generations of their descendants rise up to call them blessed. Mrs. White is remarkable for the clearness and vigor of her mind for one of her advanced age. She has a memory of dates and incidents which is quite as vivid as in her early youth. In the case of this sweet and lovable old couple, the ancient prayer seems to have been answered—"Mercifully grant that we may grow old together."

Dr. White has been a zealous Mason and an Odd Fellow for many years. He took the degree of Master Mason in Solomon's Lodge, at Savannah, in early life. He has always been active in the fraternity, and has many times been called upon to deliver addresses and memorial speeches. He took the degree of Knight Templar at Memphis, and has been Prelate of the Commandery for more than twenty-two years. Mr. T. J. Barchus, Recorder of Memphis Commandery, No. 4, Knights Templar, says: "Rev. George White, the venerable Prelate of this Commandery, received the orders of Knighthood in this Commandery on the 28th day of January, 1862, and was elected Prelate on the 22nd of September following, an office which he has held uninterruptedly to the present time. The members of the Commandery are closely attached to him by the strongest ties of knighthood, and honor him, not only as the venerable Prelate of our Commandery, but also for the purity of his life and character." Dr. White always loved the order and adhered strictly to its Christian and knightly tenets, and his brother Knights have always shown a more than ordinary appreciation of his virtues. He has also been warmly attached to the Odd Fellows, of which order he became a member soon after its organization at Savannah, and in which he afterward filled the office of Noble Grand.

Twenty-eight years ago Dr. White went to Memphis, where he has spent the ripest years of his life in a labor that has won for him the love of all, for he has proved himself a blessing to all. He is loved, not only by his own denomination, but has the confidence and affection of all classes of people, on account of his piety and liberality. Combining the qualities of the gentleman with those of the Christian philanthropist, he has the love of all creeds and conditions. The benignity of his nature, the affability of his manners, and a bearing venerable and dignified, make an impression upon all blest with the hallowing influence of his society and his ministry. His life has been clear, serene, and full of usefulness. As a theologian, a historian, a profound and ripe scholar, his name ranks among the foremost in his church and State. In modesty, charity and brotherly love, he has no superior. His gray locks, unsullied during the long years of his ministry, add triple force to his sermons. His very appearance bespeaks goodness. The circumstances inducing him to locate at Memphis are quite interesting. The church was without a pastor; one of the members who had lost a son got him to come to Memphis to conduct the funeral services. He was so well liked that he was at once called there by the church, and at once began a career that has embalmed his memory in the hearts of his people for ever. The church immediately began to flourish and has always flourished while under his charge. He has been a faithful rector, has labored ardently for his church, and has always been at his post of duty. Through the trying scenes of the war, and the dreadful epidemics which have ravaged the city, he has kept his church open. Through the dreadful epidemic of 1878, he was indefatigable in his labors in ministering to the wants of his people—his charity was almost a fault, and in visiting the sick he was tireless.

Indeed, this has been true of him at all times and under all circumstances. During all this troublous time his beloved and faithful wife was at his side. In September of that year they lost their son, Eugene D. White, at a time when the city was panic-stricken with the plague, and this aged couple went out to bury their son—the sole mourners at his grave—and while there an incident occurred which beautifully illustrates his character. The remains of a brother Mason were brought to the cemetery for interment; the venerable minister asked the privilege of reading the burial service, and when it was granted, in words most feelingly uttered, and amid tears and sobs that almost choked their utterance, eulogized the character of the deceased. As the sod was falling upon the grave he was approached by a gentleman who asked him to read the service over his wife. The kind old man consented, but first asked that he might bury his own son. In a few moments he was requested to conduct the services at another grave. Even in that hour of trial and suffering, when he had just consigned to the grave his own dearly beloved boy, he did not fail to discharge the duties of his Christian calling.

As a preacher, Dr. White is characterized by simplicity, force and earnestness. He always seems to feel what he is saying, and his sincerity and conscientiousness carry conviction. He is plain and outspoken. If he ever had anything to say, he said it; if he saw anything wrong among his people, he told them of it, but always in the greatest kindness, acting only from a sense of duty—he always did his duty. He has always been prominent in the diocesan conventions in his State, delivering many able and eloquent addresses and sermons. He has three times been a delegate to general conventions of the church—first at Boston, in 1877; then at New York, in 1880, and at Philadelphia, in 1883. Every denomination recognizes the fact that he has stood at the head of the clergy of Memphis, and even after he had reached the age of fourscore he was still eloquent. It was said of him then by one of the papers of his city: "In his sermons his soul seems to triumph over the frailties of his body and pours forth its rich and glowing conceptions with all the fire and energy of youth. There is nothing senile about Dr. White. He is one of that class of men whose intellect will never be impaired by age, for his subjects are thoroughly analyzed; his logic is cogent and conclusive; his sentences are compact; his enunciation slow and distinct; his elocution graceful and emphatic, while he is evidently a man of deep evangelical piety, whose heart is devoted to the Master's work, and the fruits of whose many years of labor will be rewarded in eternity. The prosperity of Calvary church, and its large congregation in regular attendance, show that Dr. White is not wanting in pulpit popularity. He is certainly a faithful and most indefatigable pastor, who seems to be impelled less by ambition than by love; and such is the sweetness and the courtesy of his manner as to endear him to his people and render him useful in their families."

During the plague of 1878, the heroic conduct of Dr. White was noted and commented upon by the press all over the United States. He is popular with all creeds—even Jews come to hear him preach—no man was ever known to speak disparagingly of him. His kindness to the colored race was carried to Memphis with him, and he helped to build them a church there, and by his exertions kept it up.

As a man, Dr. White belongs to the type of old school gentlemen, too courteous to allow etiquette to interfere with naturalness. He meets all men, high and low, with a smile and a kind word. He is remarkable for the child-like simplicity of his character. In disposition he is characterized by the modesty which belongs to all true worth. Never in all his life has he been known to put " Rev." to his name, always signing the plain " George White"; never has he been known to seek advantage from any of those privileges which are sometimes supposed to belong to men in his calling, but in the social and financial world he has been as other men, seeking no honor from his station. His love for children and for animals is almost proverbial, especially is his love for dogs remarkable—for living dogs, images of dogs and pictures of dogs. He has always been fond of work and has led a most active life—a life of energy and ceaseless labor. At seventy-five years of age he moved with almost the vigor and activity of youth. His face betokens a love of freedom and not restraint, and even in his extreme old age bears upon it the glad look of boyhood.

In December, 1881, while conducting divine service at Calvary church, he was stricken at duty's post with a severe fit of appoplexy, and it seemed that his useful career must come to an end, but after a time he rallied and the blessing of his presence has been vouchsafed to his church a little longer, and now, as he nears the end of his " twelve long sunny hours, bright to the close," his people pray that he may be spared to them for many days. The following estimate placed upon him by one of his parishioners testifies the love and reverence his people have for his character and disposition : " Dr. White is beloved by all. He is genial in his disposition, fond of social conversation, gentle in his judgments, avoiding extremes in doctrine, strong in his faith, positive in his influence, decided in his reproofs, harsh in nothing, and withal a kind, good old man."

By request of the biographer, Rev. Davis Sessums

furnishes the following beautiful estimate of Dr. White's character: " The life of this now venerable priest has, throughout its extraordinary long course, been the constant growth and manifestation of those virtues which make the distinctive spirit of Christianity; of humility, of purity and gentleness absolutely without wordliness; of quiet yet persistent and aggressive force in the cause of the gospel. Dr. White, at the age of eighteen or nineteen years, partly by the example of kindred and partly by his own most fervent religious feeling and conviction, entered the Methodist ministry. Subsequently, upon full knowledge of the genius and doctrine of the Episcopal church, the former office was resigned, and he successively took the orders of the diaconate and the priesthood in this latter communion. His ministerial life reaches, in his priestly office in the church alone, over a period of more than fifty years; and his labors during that time have been maintained with an earnestness and a vigor as remarkable in themselves as in the results which they have achieved. For a portion of his early career in the ministry of the church, Dr. White was engaged with educational concerns in Savannah, Georgia, having founded and conducted with rare success a school then instrumental in training many who afterward became prominent in that and other southern States. Literary matters, also, then occupied his attention, finding their outcome in a ' History of Georgia,' which was published at the expense and with the commendation of the State Legislature; a work especially valuable for the detailed materials there gathered as foundations for histories in special lines. The greater portion of his active ministry has passed in Memphis, Tennessee, where for nearly thirty years he has held the rectorship of Calvary Episcopal church. Dr. White has, during this whole period, filled a leading position in the history of the church in the diocese of Tennessee, conspicuous as a pastor, representative as a preacher, a patriarch and father in the annual councils of the church. For many successive triennial conventions of the Protestant Episcopal church in the United States, Dr. White has represented the diocese of Tennessee as one of its clerical deputies. In the conduct of his parish, and in his other official operations, it is the combination of his own high and gentle Christian life with his abilities that has made his work lasting, and his name revered and cherished. A marked power of uttering the hidden things of truth and grace in varied simplicity of language, conjoined with the most earnest, natural and effective art of elocution, has enabled him to wield great influence from the pulpit. The enthusiasm which has ever inspired him in his work, the faithfulness and Christian heroism which have held him at his post, even in the midst of war and the fearful pestilence—these have been outward works to show the world the value and reality of his inward creed. The parish which he has builded up, the lives that trace to him their growth in religious hope, the record altogether that he has made as a true priest of God—these are the assurance of his honor here, the use of the talents which his Master will accept."

———

Since the foregoing was prepared, the venerable and beloved wife of Dr. White has ceased to live on earth. The following beautiful tribute to her many virtues, copied from the editorial columns of the Memphis Appeal, is here inserted as a fitting conclusion to this sketch:

" Verily hath a mother in Israel fallen. Mrs. Elizabeth White, wife of Rev. Dr. George White, long rector of Calvary church, of this city, gently passed away at four o'clock on Friday morning, July 18, 1885. Weak and low the pulse of life had fluttered in her fevered veins for weeks and months, and her friends 'thought her dying when she slept, and sleeping when she died.' It may be truly said of her that

'Of no distemper, of no blast she died,
But fell like autumn fruit that mellowed long;
Even wondered at, because she dropped no sooner.
—Fate seemed to wind her up for fourscore years,
Yet freshly ran she on some winters more,
Till like a clock worn out with eating time,
The wheels of weary life at last stood still.'

Mrs. White was born in Charleston, South Carolina, in 1802. Descending from one of the first families of the State, and possessing beauty, intelligence and many accomplishments, she was a conspicuous belle, a favorite in fashionable society, and married early in life. Her first husband and one child died with the yellow fever. Two years afterward, she married Rev. Dr. George White, and as two placid streams unite and roll their waters in one bright and tranquil current to the sea, so have their happy spirits been borne onward, tender and loving, through light and shade, sunshine and gloom. The friends that cheered their barque as forth it steered on life's long voyage are all gone. But for sixty-two years this happy couple have been lovers, together gazing at the evening twilight and moonlit clouds, listening to the chirp of the cricket, as the stars flashed out in the sky, watching their children as around the crackling fire they joyously danced to the shadows which the prism flung upon the wall, and with clasped hands talked of God, heaven and their love, so pure and holy on earth that it would brighten into a fadeless star in eternity. The tissue of their lives was so wrought as to make them twin spirits. But the harmony of life's chord is broken, and the old, sweet tune is hushed in death. A happier pair never trod life's weary path together. The twain were one in taste and sentiment—in mutual love and trust. United in heart and hand for more than sixty years, they lived in harmony, endeared by joy and sorrow, made closer by death and the bereavement of children, uninterrupted by jar or discord—the parting kiss as fragrant as the nuptial salutation. Both husband and wife were prostrated for weeks, and they could not minister to each other's wants, but they transmitted love and sympathy, and each sigh seemed to ask:

> One of us, love, must stand
> Where the waves are breaking on death's dark strand,
> And watch the boat from the silent land
> Bear the other away,
> Which will it be?'

Natural endowments and high accomplishments made Mrs. Elizabeth White a most lovely character. Mentally, she was strong, had the best culture of her day, and was eminently practical in all the relations of life. Sound in judgment, she was a wise counselor. The Orient is rich in striking symbols, and one of them is to take the veil of a bride when she lays it aside upon her marriage day; to fold it carefully, to lay it tenderly away in a box of sandal or camphor wood; to keep it until the bride who wore it ceases to live, when it is brought forth and wrapped around the face of the dead. And the belief which is taught is that if the bride, as she matured in womanhood and motherhood, was true to her wifely trust, beneath the veil the pinched and withered and wrung face will be restored to bridal freshness and loveliness, and when her eyes shall open in the Beautiful Beyond, they will be filled with their old luster, the lips will call back their carnation, and as youth and purity were on the earth, so the eternal youth will begin. The symbol means that what is beautiful and good cannot be lost; that if the woman causes smiles to be born where sorrow brooded, like the children of the gods, those smiles will be immortal; that if from weeping eyes she has wiped away tears, those tears will turn to diamonds, which all the abrasions of time cannot make dim or wear away; that if the voice has been lifted up in sweet accents for love, duty and charity, it will change to a note of celestial music, the echoes of which will forever swell the grand melodies of eternity, and that the beauties of heaven will be but a magnified splendor of the bride's deeds on earth. If this beautiful custom of the Orient were observed by our people, under the bridal veil that wraps the pallid brow of the deceased the face would grow roseate, and take on a celestial light which all the darkness of death and all the damps of the grave can not extinguish, for her religion was a living sentiment and a conscious reality, and her whole life was set to the music of sympathy, affection, charity, and duty to husband, children and the world. To all who knew her she realized the conception of a faultless, lovely woman. While highly gifted, her spirit was of the most feminine gentleness. She was a devoted and loving mother, maternal affection ever bubbling from her lips. She has been gradually sinking for the past six months. Death seemed to be more the result of a general breaking down and wearing out of the vital machinery than any well defined malady. She bore her long sufferings with a patience and meekness that were sublime. Her mind was occasionally clouded, but it would soon burst forth in all its splendor and beauty. Her sufferings were a whole drama of pathos, but she preserved the harmony of her life to the end, and entered the dark, starless night of death bravely, knowing that the journey to eternal day would be swift, and that the sad wails of loving husband and children would soon be lost in the melody of heaven. The sympathy of the entire community centers around the family of the deceased, and it is especially lavished upon the husband, Rev. Dr. George White. As the clods this morning rattle upon the grave of his lost idol, he will no doubt feel that he has been at the funeral of all his hopes— seen them entombed one by one. In youth he gave his heart to the church, and ever since it has been sweetly attuned to those lofty themes and sublime aspirations which lift man into the splendors that dwell above the earth and beyond the grave. Known and loved alike for unostentatious simplicity, spotless life and the great powers he has consecrated to the highest and best interests of humanity, he will have the sympathies of the whole South in his great bereavement. Rev. Dr. George White has lived through three generations, ministering holy things, and his memory will survive the tomb and ever remain a living presence, fragrant with holy incense. He lingers on the stage, the theater of his usefulness and his triumphs, and with the Bible in his hand, its sacred teachings in his heart, and its sublime promises animating and inspiring his soul, he nobly, bravely labors on. But, tottering with the weight of years upon the brink of the grave, he cannot long survive his irreparable loss. His refrain for the future will be—

> ' Sleep on, my love, in thy cold bed,
> Never to be disquieted!
> My last good night! Thou wilt not wake
> Till I thy fate shall overtake;
> Till age or grief or sickness must
> Marry my body to that dust
> It so much loves, and fill the room
> My heart keeps empty in thy tomb.
> Stay for me there, I will not fail
> To meet thee in that hollow vale;
> And think not much of my delay,
> I am already on the way,
> And follow thee with all the speed
> Desire can make or sorrow breed;
> Each minute is a short degree,
> And every hour a step toward thee.
> At night when I betake to rest,
> Next morn I rise nearer my west
> Of life, almost by eight hours' sail,
> Than when Sleep breathed his drowsy gale.
> Thus from the sun my slow barque steers,
> And my day's compass downward bears;
> Nor labor I to stem the tide
> Through which to thee I swiftly glide.
> But hark! my pulse like a soft drum,
> Beats my approach, tells thee I come;
> And slow how'er my marches be
> I shall at last sit down by thee.
> I am kneeling at the threshold, weary, faint and sore,
> Waiting for the dawning, for the opening of the door;

Waiting till the Master shall bid me rise and come
To the glory of His presence, to the gladness of His home,
But now the morn is breaking, and my toil will soon be o'er.
I am kneeling at the threshold, my hand is on the door,
Methinks I hear the voices of the blessed as they stand
Singing in the sunshine in that far off, sinless land.
O would that I were with them, amid their shining throng,
Mingling in their worship, joining in their song.

The friends that started with me have entered long ago;
One by one they left me, struggling with the foe;
Their pilgrimage was shorter, their triumph sooner won,
How lovingly they'll hail me when all my toil is done.
With them the blessed angels that know no grief or sin,
I see them by the portals prepared to let me in.
Oh, Lord, I wait Thy pleasure, Thy time and ways are best,
But I'm wasted, worn and weary. Oh, Father, bid me rest."

CAPT. HENRY HARRISON TAYLOR.

KNOXVILLE.

BORN on the banks of the Watauga river, which, in the Indian vernacular, means "beautiful river," in the picturesque county of Carter, in Tennessee, June 5, 1841, Capt. Henry Harrison Taylor, now of Knoxville, is a fine specimen of the sturdy young mountaineer manhood of which this State can boast.

He grew up on his father's farm and was taught to work, a rule his father enforced with all his sons, and after attending a neighborhood boarding school, he was next sent to Washington College, then conducted by those famous East Tennessee educators, Archibald Doak, Blair and Tadlock. From there he went to Emory and Henry College, Virginia. In the spring of 1860, he went to Chapel Hill, North Carolina, and there completed the junior course.

But in the spring of 1861 the war broke out, and books and all thoughts of study were laid aside for the rougher and sterner duties of the soldier. He enlisted in the Confederate army as a private for the first year, then became first-lieutenant, and finally captain of company H, Fifth Tennessee Confederate cavalry, commanded by Col. George W. McKenzie. He was captured October 11, 1863, on the retreat from the fight at Blue Springs, Tennessee, between the Confederate forces, commanded by Gen. John S. ("Cerro Gordo") Williams, of Kentucky, and the Federal army under Gen. Burnside. At the time of his capture he was on detached duty as inspector-general of Gen. A. E. Jackson's brigade, the staff consisting of Maj. H. M. Folsom, quartermaster; Maj. W. B. Reese, adjutant-general; Maj. Findley Henderson, commissary, and Maj. Roswell Booth, brigade ordnance officer. Capt. Taylor was sent to Johnson's Island, Ohio, November 15, 1863, where he was detained a prisoner till June 12, 1865, when he was released, the war having terminated.

He was in the several fights around Cumberland Gap, when it was occupied by Gen. Morgan (Federal), and at the battle fought at Tazewell Court-house. He was in the Kentucky campaign with Bragg, and in the engagements at Perryville, Lancaster, Nelson's Crossroads, and Wild Cat; was also in several skirmishes between Burnside's forces and Gen. John S. Williams, in upper East Tennessee and southwest Virginia, in the summer and fall of 1863.

There were in the Confederate army from the county of Carter, about one hundred and thirty-five men, while there were from one thousand two hundred to one thousand four hundred men from the same county in the Federal army. It took a man of determination and strong convictions of right and duty in the face of such odds to go into the Confederate army, and it took a strong—even fool-hardy—man to return there after the war, so bitter and relentless was the hatred entertained for all ex-Confederates.

Therefore, when the war was over, Capt. Taylor went to Marion, Virginia, where he read law with George W. Jones. He was admitted to the bar and licensed to practice by Judges John Fulton and John A. Campbell, and then went to Columbia, Tennessee, where he began practice in partnership with Judge Thomas W. Turley (whose sketch see elsewhere in this volume). He remained at Columbia until February, 1870, when he located at Knoxville, where he has resided and practiced law ever since, in the circuit, chancery, Supreme and Federal courts, but doing no criminal practice. The law firm at Knoxville is Taylor & Hood, who are the attorneys for the Knoxville and Augusta railroad, and also represent the East Tennessee National Bank. Capt. Taylor has been special judge in a number of cases —selected by the lawyers where judges were incompetent by reason of their relations to the causes.

Capt. Taylor has never been in politics as a candidate, but has been a Democrat since he has been of age. In the gubernatorial convention of 1880, at Nashville, he was a delegate from Knox county, and served as a member of the committee on platform, and in that convention favored an honest settlement of the debt of the State, he belonging to what is called the "sky-blue " wing of the Democratic party. His family has figured conspicuously in the politics of East Tennessee, among them Hon. Nat. G. Taylor, who served in Congress before the war; and Hon. Robert L. Taylor, who was a member of Congress, and also Democratic elector for the State at large in the presidential canvass of 1884, and now pension agent at Knoxville.

Capt. Taylor was an applicant for the position of pension agent at Knoxville, in 1885, but the president declined to appoint any man to that position who had

PROMINENT TENNESSEANS. 463

been identified with the Confederate army. On learning this fact Capt. Taylor wrote to Senator Jackson, who was pressing his claims, that he had been identified with the Confederate army, and had no apologies to make for it, and to withdraw his name.

Capt. Taylor married, in Madisonville, Monroe county, Tennessee, November 15, 1877, Miss Inez Johnston, a native of that place, born in the house she was married in, daughter of Joseph Johnston, a merchant, a native of South Carolina, and a relative of Gen. Joseph E. Johnston. Her mother, *nee* Miss Caroline M. Hair, an East Tennessean by birth, is the daughter of James Hair, a farmer and trader. He died in Texas, while on a visit to his daughter, Mrs. Martha Smith. Mrs. Taylor was educated at the Female Institute, Madisonville, and is a member of the Presbyterian church, as is Capt. Taylor, he having joined that church in 1882. Mrs. Taylor is a woman of eminent piety and thoroughness, devoted to home, is thoroughly scrupulous, having a delicate sense of right, and an exquisite regard for the feelings of others.

By his marriage with Miss Johnston, Capt. Taylor has three children: Carrie May Taylor, born September 15, 1878; Elizabeth (" Bessie ") Taylor, born December 30, 1880; Alfred Wilson Taylor, born May 21, 1884.

The original family name Tailor, a maker of clothes, was changed to Taylor in Scotland, the family being of Scotch-Irish extraction. Capt. Taylor's great-grandfather, Isaac Taylor, came to Tennessee from Virginia, and settled in Carter county, among the pioneers of that country. His grandfather, Gen. Nathaniel Taylor, came to Tennessee from Rockbridge county, Virginia, just after his marriage with Miss Mary Patton. He was a general in the United States army, and served under Jackson at New Orleans, and at Emuckfaw and Talladega, in Alabama, in the war of 1812. He died in 1816, about forty-four years of age. He was a man of fine business capacity and great energy, acquired a handsome estate, and gave all of his children a comfortable start in life. His homestead was near Elizabethton, Carter county.

Alfred W. Taylor, father of Capt. Taylor, was born on the Watauga river, Carter county, Tennessee, on a property that has been owned by the family for ninety years. He was a man of more than ordinary intelligence and great modesty, a lawyer by profession, and because of his great aversion to broils and unpleasantness between neighbors and friends, and his efforts to keep his clients out of litigation, was called "the peacemaker" and "the honest lawyer." He died in 1856, at the age of fifty-seven, an elder in the Presbyterian church. He was one of the original projectors of the East Tennessee and Virginia railroad, and was a director in that railroad company at the time of his decease.

Capt. Taylor's mother, *nee* Miss Elizabeth Carter Duffield, was born in Carter county, Tennessee. She was the daughter of Maj. George Duffield, a Philadelphian by birth, of the Pennsylvania Duffield family—a man of fine education and polished manners, a major in the United States army, a circumstance that led to bringing the two families together. Maj. Duffield married Miss Sallie S. Carter, daughter of Landon and Elizabeth Carter, a prominent pioneer couple of East Tennessee. The county of Carter was named for Landon Carter, and the county seat, Elizabethton, was named for his wife, Elizabeth. Mrs. Elizabeth Carter, Capt. Taylor's maternal grandmother, was the sister of Gen. William B. Carter, who represented the First Tennessee district in Congress two or three terms. He is said to have been a man of magnificent size and handsomely proportioned, of popular turn, and to use a homely phrase, was "a good mixer," mingling with the people and swaying them as an electioneerer. The Carter family are said to have been part Indian, having some of the blood of Pocahontas in their veins. They are also related to the Lee family, of Virginia.

Capt. Taylor's mother died in April, 1873, at the age of seventy-three, a woman of decided character, domestic in her habits, an excellent manager of the plantation and negroes in the absence of her husband, while he was attending the courts in Carter, Johnson, Sullivan and Washington counties. She was the mother of six sons and two daughters. All of her sons she raised to be sober and industrious men. Two of them, James P. and Alfred W. Taylor, jr., died just as they passed twenty-one years of age. James P. Taylor died soon after graduating in medicine, and Alfred W. Taylor, jr., was a merchant at Jonesborough. Nat. M. Taylor is a lawyer at Bristol (see his sketch elsewhere in this volume). William C. and George D. Taylor live on the farm, the old homestead in Carter county, unmarried. Henry H. Taylor is the subject of this sketch. Of the daughters, Sarah Taylor died two years of age, and Mary Elizabeth Taylor is now the wife of Dr. Jesse H. Pepper, of Bristol, Tennessee, and has two children, George Henry and Rowena Elizabeth.

When Capt. Taylor began his professional life after the war, he had for a start a capital of some two or three thousand dollars in lands and collectable debts. By dint of economy, and as the result of hard work, applying himself with all his energy and mental capacity, and by earnest devotion to his profession, he has prospered well, and is now in comfortable circumstances. He is a close collector of fees, but has lost some money by indulging in the luxury of security for others. He has always led a sober life, has been attentive to business, has the reputation of fair dealing, and the unlimited confidence of the bar and people.

CAPT. JAMES A. WARDER.

SHELBYVILLE.

ALTHOUGH a Kentuckian by birth, having been born in Mason county, of that State, September 24, 1843, Capt. James A. Warder has been long enough identified with Tennessee to be ranked among her permanent and prominent citizens.

His education was obtained at the private schools in his native county, and one year's attendance at Centre College, Kentucky, which latter institution he left, in 1861, to enlist as a soldier in the Federal army. He went out as a private in company C, Second Kentucky Federal calvary, and fought his way up to a captaincy— attaining the rank of captain of cavalry before his twenty-first year. He served in Kentucky, Tennessee and Georgia, being connected during a portion of the time with the command of Gen. Phil. H. Sheridan, and took part in the battles of Perryville, Chickamauga and Missionary Ridge.

The close of the war found him at Shelbyville, Tennessee, where he had married, and adopting the State, of which his wife was a native, as his future home, he has made Shelbyville his place of residence ever since.

During a visit to his old Kentucky home, in 1865, he began to read law with Hon. John G. Hickman, and returning to Tennessee in 1866, he was admitted to the bar and immediately began practice, in partnership with Hon. Thomas H. Coldwell, under the firm name of Coldwell & Warder, which partnership lasted until 1873, after which he continued his practice alone until 1876.

Capt. Warder is a Republican of the stanchest and truest type. In 1867, he was commissioned as attorney-general of his district by Gov. Brownlow, but declined to serve. In 1876, he was a delegate to the Cincinnati convention which nominated Hayes and Wheeler, and was appointed elector for his congressional district on the Republican ticket, and during the campaign that followed, made an able canvass of his district. When Hayes was made president he was appointed United States district attorney for Middle Tennessee. This office he continued to fill uninterruptedly during the administrations of Hayes and Garfield, and after the expiration of his term served for six or seven months under a special commission from Supreme Justice Stanley Matthews. While holding this position he had to deal with illicit distilling in the mountains of Tennessee, and he virtually succeeded in suppressing the business of the " moonshiners " in that section. He represented the government in the Davis removal cases from the State to the Federal courts, which created intense excitement in Tennessee at the time, and passed into history as a memorable contest between State and Federal authorities. Capt. Warder maintained that in such cases the Federal courts had a right to control the State courts by writs of prohibition. The Supreme court of the United States sustained the jurisdiction of the Federal court, so far as the question of removal was concerned, leaving the right to use writs of prohibition an open question.

After the expiration of his term of office, Capt. Warder resumed his regular practice, in which he has been actively and successfully engaged ever since, with a large business, extending all over Middle Tennessee. He began his professional career without capital, came into Tennessee a Republican and a Federal soldier, but by hard work, earnest effort, strength of will and decided native ability, has overcome adverse circumstances, achieved reputation, firmly implanted himself in the respect and confidence of the people, and accumulated a handsome estate. He is regarded as a sound man, financially, and has been vice-president of the Shelbyville Savings Bank for several years.

The Warder family is of English origin, and the name means " guard over." Capt. Warder's father, Dr. Walter Warder, was a prominent and successful practitioner of medicine in Mason county, Kentucky. Several of Dr. Warder's uncles, as was also the Doctor himself, were prominent in the Baptist annals of Kentucky, in the early days of that State, when log cabins were dedicated as churches. Capt. Warder's mother, *nee* Miss Nancy Artus, was a daughter of James Artus, one of the early settlers in the " dark and bloody ground."

Capt. Warder was married, January 2, 1865, to Miss Laura Gosling, daughter of William Gosling, a cotton manufacturer at Shelbyville, and of an old and highly respectable Middle Tennessee family. To this union has been born one child, a daughter.

Capt. Warder is regarded as one of the rising men of the State. His name has frequently been mentioned as a Republican candidate for governor of Tennessee, and the Supreme bench. In 1884, the Republicans made an earnest effort to carry the State, and as part of the programme, Capt. Warder was requested and unanimously nominated for congress in his district. J. D. Richardson was the Democratic nominee. The canvass attracted general attention throughout the State. The candidates were both young, widely known, warm personal friends, thoroughly posted in political history, and distinguished for the "courtesies" of debate. Capt. Warder was credited with making the ablest presentation of Republicanism ever made in Tennessee, and has since been spoken of, even in the Democratic newspapers, as the "eloquent defender of his faith." It is quite certain the future bears for him additional distinction.

HON. WILLIAM A. HENDERSON.

KNOXVILLE.

ALTHOUGH a citizen of Knoxville for thirty-nine years, the Hon. William A. Henderson is a native of Grainger county, Tennessee, having been born in that county, July 11, 1836. He is descended from an old and highly respectable North Carolina family, who were among the pioneer settlers of East Tennessee, and of English ancestry. That the family is English, is sufficiently evident from the patronymic Henderson, which was changed by aspirating the first letter of the original name, Andrewson, and making the orthography conform to the common pronunciation of it. Thus "Andrew's-son" became Henderson.

Mr. Henderson's grandfather, Thomas Henderson, was a native of the "Old North State," and came to Tennessee among its pioneer settlers. He was a member of the convention that formed the first constitution of Tennessee, and being a prominent politician, after the organization of the State served as a member of the Tennessee Legislature, from what was then called Caswell, now Hawkins, county. Thomas Henderson married Miss Nancy Windom, of a Virginia family, who settled in the town of Somerville. The history of this marriage is more interesting than a romance. Thomas was with his father, moving from North Carolina to Kentucky; Nancy was with her father, moving from Virginia to West Tennessee. The two families met and camped near each other, at the place now known as Cheek's Cross-roads, Hamblen county, Tennessee. Young Thomas became enamored of Miss Nancy, and in three weeks they were married, left their respective parents and "caravans," settled at that place, and there lived and died.

Eldridge Henderson, father of the subject of this sketch, was a native of Grainger county, Tennessee, and a farmer of moderate means. He died when the son was only three months old.

Mr. Henderson's mother, nee Emeline Felts, was a native of Washington county, Tennessee. She was the daughter of William Felts, a carpenter, a soldier in the war of 1812, under Jackson, a quiet, plain, honest, religious man, who lived to be seventy-five years old. His wife was Margaret Lackey, a native of Rockbridge county, Virginia. She died at Knoxville. Six children were born to William and Margaret Felts; three sons, Jackson, David and James, (the two former now at Nashville, the latter at Knoxville), and three daughters, Sallie, Emeline (Mr. Henderson's mother) and Minerva. Sallie died the wife of Wilson Taylor; Minerva died the wife of James O. Allen. Mrs. Henderson, now sixty-nine years old, lives at Knoxville, with her son. She never had but two children, Mary and William A. Mary was born at Knoxville, graduated at the Jonesborough Female College, and died

the wife of Rev. J. L. Lloyd, a Baptist minister, leaving five children, William, Lee, John, Eldridge and Mary. Mr. Henderson's mother is a member of the Methodist Episcopal church, south. Her life has been that of an exemplary Christian, and devoted to her children, their rearing, training, education and culture. Left a widow in their infancy, and being without means, she was ever laudably ambitious to rebuild the fortunes of her family, and struggled for the advancement of her children, and with highly satisfactory results too, both as to the daughter and son, the latter of whom, in addition to his intellectual eminence, it is something exceptional to mention, has never yet had a spell of sickness.

The boyhood of Mr. Henderson was one marked by industrious struggle and genuine hard work. He first worked in a brick-yard, next at a carding machine, and then in a glass factory, going to school at an academy at odd intervals. In 1840, he moved with his mother and sisters, in a flat boat, to Decatur, Alabama, and while there, and in the country near town, he attended school and worked to assist the family. They moved back to Knoxville, in 1845, and he continued his heroic struggle for success. Soon his native talent began to assert itself. There was something in the boy—that rare stuff of which genuine manly men are made. In the summer he taught school to make money enough to attend college during winter. In this way he was enabled to take a four years' course at the University of Tennessee, at Knoxville, entering, in 1852, under the presidency of Hon. William B. Reese, and graduating in 1856, under the presidency of Rev. George Cook, standing second in his class, and receiving the highest encomia from the faculty.

After graduation, he taught school two years, meanwhile reading law under Sneed & Cocke, was admitted to the bar in 1859, by Judges T. W. Turley and George Brown, and immediately became a member of the firm of Sneed, Cocke & Henderson, a partnership which lasted until the breaking out of the late civil war.

A southerner by birth, in feelings and in principles, he joined the Confederate army as a private in Company D, of the Sixty-third Tennessee regiment, Col. Richard Fain, and served in Tennessee, Kentucky, Alabama and Virginia, surrendering at Appomattox Court-house, April 9, 1865, having participated in the battles of Shell Mound, below Chattanooga, Richmond, Kentucky, Perryville, twenty-seven skirmishes in East Tennessee, in the battles from Drury's Bluff around Petersburg, and on the retreat from Petersburg to Appomattox Court-house, seven days. He was captured in front of Petersburg, June 14, 1864, was in prison at the old capitol at Washington City, at Point Lookout,

59

Maryland, and at Elmira, New York, in all, four months. He was exchanged in October, 1864, at Savannah, Georgia. He was twice wounded in action.

His first wound was in the side; the second was received in the knee, causing a dislocation, while engaged in front of the Howlitt House, Petersburg, May 16, 1864, only a few days before his captivity.

He was detailed, in May, 1862, on special court martial service, at Chattanooga. In June, 1862, he was appointed an aid-de-camp to Brig.-Gen. D. Leadbetter, with the rank of lieutenant of cavalry, and served as such till August, 1862, when he was detailed, with similar rank, on the staff of Maj.-Gen. Harry Heath. After the Kentucky campaign, and Bragg's retreat from Kentucky, he was ordered to Mobile, as inspector of Fort Morgan and Fort Gaines. He was then called for by the provost marshal-general (Toole) of East Tennessee, and was detailed for duty as provost marshal of several counties in East Tennessee, with headquarters at Rogersville, where he remained till Burnside captured that post, in September, 1863, when he retired, raised a company of stragglers (men cut off from their commands), and joined the command of Gen. Cerro Gordo Williams, in which he remained till Longstreet's army passed up through East Tennessee, en route to rejoin Lee's army. With them he rejoined his old regiment, and fought with it in the ranks till the surrender at Appomattox Court-house. After the war he returned to Knoxville, was indicted and arrested twice for treason, by the State and the United States authorities. Soon after the war, he resumed law practice, in partnership with his old partner, Cocke, and has been in practice of law at Knoxville ever since.

Before the war he, like his father, was an old line Whig, and his maiden presidential vote was cast for Bell and Everett. Since the war he has been a Democrat, true and tried. He has never held office, except that of alderman of his ward, and as a trustee and one of the executive committee of his old alma mater, the University of Tennessee, yet his lofty integrity of character and his sound and statesman like views of State and national polity have constantly kept him conspicuously before the eyes of the East Tennessee Democracy as a man well suited to fill the highest positions where " public office is a public trust." In particular has his name been mentioned in connection with gubernatorial honors. Mr. Henderson became a Mason at Bristol, Tennessee, in 1863, and has taken the Mark Master and Past Master degrees. He is also a member of the Methodist Episcopal church, south, and a steward of that denomination.

Mr. Henderson married in Knoxville, November 22, 1866, Miss Harriet E. Smiley, who was born in Springfield, Vermont, the daughter of Thomas E. Smiley, a merchant, who moved to Knoxville when the daughter was two years old. He died in that city, in 1866, at the age of sixty-eight. He was a relative of Thomas T. Smiley, author of an arithmetic, once extensively used in southern schools. Mrs. Henderson's mother, nee Miss Nancy Barrett (now living with her daughter, at Knoxville), is the daughter of Col. John Barrett, of Revolutionary war fame. She is also cousin of Dr. James Thompson, author of a mathematical series, and a cousin of the late Prof. Henry Wadsworth Longfellow, one of America's most distinguished poets.

Mrs. Henderson graduated at the Knoxville Female College, under President J. R. Dean. She is a lady of fine intellectual qualities and culture, but is eminently a home woman, though by no means unneighborly or unsocial. By his marriage with Miss Smiley, Mr. Henderson has two children: Mary Henderson, born September 4, 1867, and Anna Henderson, born July 15, 1869.

The elements which have conspired to the success of this self-made man are but the strongly marked characteristics of an intense individuality. His personality is sui generis. He is said to be the best nisi prius lawyer in the State. As an advocate before a jury, he is the strongest man in East Tennessee, and has been often called the George Gantt of East Tennessee, a mutual compliment, however, to the best jury lawyer of West Tennessee. Mr. Henderson is peculiar in a certain tact he has in managing a case before a jury, a wonderful faculty of examining and cross-examining a witness; then he is very witty, and has an unequaled felicity of captivating a jury. He seems to know the prejudices of a juryman by instinct; knows how to get him on his side; seizes upon some little point that escapes from the mouth of a witness, and makes capital of it, either by ridiculing the witness or otherwise turning it to advantage. He sees the points in a case quickly. It is said he will try a case he never heard of, and, without preparation, win it. Natural smartness is his distinguishing trait, and he applies it happily to everything he undertakes. Besides, he is gentleman of fine character, fine education, with a mind stored with many literary excellencies. There are no angularities in his make-up, mental or physical. A well balanced man, with a large frame, a large head, and a large intellect, well trained—it is difficult to point out the peculiarities that distinguish him from other men, though one sees and recognizes them instantly. In one word—his career has been a success. There is no shady side to his life; it is all sunshine with him. He is a child of nature, and delights in the wild, rugged scenery of his mountain home, and when not at his books, or on his cases, he is as frolicsome as a boy chasing his first butterfly. The elixir of geniality seems ever to course his veins, sweetening his blood with perennial good humor.

HON. JORDAN STOKES.

LEBANON.

THIS cultured gentleman, now in his sixty-ninth year, with the gladness of youth still lingering on his face and abiding in his heart, is rather a child of nature, a plant efflorescent from the vigor of its own tap-root, than the result of early high culture and conventional stimulus. In the midst of grand-children, he still loves the draperies of the seasons, lingers beneath the inspirations of nature, and, above the prattle of his remote little ones, still hears the songs of birds. If he had not been a great lawyer, he might have been a great pastoral poet.

The Hon. Jordan Stokes was born in Chatham county, North Carolina, August 23, 1817, the son of Sylvanus Stokes, a native of that county. His father was a well educated farmer, who combined great force of character with agreeableness of manner, and was readily a favorite among his associates. When Col. Stokes was quite a child the family migrated to Tennessee, and during the journey his father was accidently killed by a team. This occurred in 1818.

Col. Stokes' grandfather, Thomas Stokes, was a Virginian, related to the Stokes family of Richmond, and to Gov. Munford Stokes, quite famous in the annals of North Carolina. His grandmother was the daughter of Rev. Green Hill, who was the treasurer of North Carolina during the Revolutionary war. Col. Stokes still has preserved a continental bill signed by his great-grandfather. The first Methodist conference in North Carolina met in Green Hill's house. The family is of English origin. Col. Stokes' eldest uncle, Dr. William B. Stokes, was a student of medicine under Dr. Benjamin Rush, in Philadelphia, and afterward became prominent in his profession in North Carolina.

Col. Stokes' mother, *nee* Miss Mary Christian, was also a native of Chatham county, North Carolina, daughter of John Christian, who was a drum-major during the Revolutionary war. Her mother, Martha Christian, was likewise a North Carolinian, noted for her kindness of heart and great piety. She and some of her family were Baptists, and their descendants after them.

The mother of Col. Stokes survived her father more than forty years, and died, leaving by him three sons: John T., William B. and Jordan. The eldest son, John T. Stokes, is now a farmer in DeKalb county, Tennessee. The second son, Gen. William B. Stokes, lives in Alexandria, Tennessee, and has for many years been prominent in politics. He represented his district in the United States Congress before the civil war. During the war he was a brigadier-general of cavalry in the United States army, and was brevetted for gallantry.

Jordan Stokes early acquired a great fondness for books, and one of the first to come to his hands was "Hawes' Lectures." This he read assiduously while quite a child, in the midst of the light duties assigned him on the farm, and it exercised a potent influence in the direction of his thoughts and subsequent development. His training in the sciences was thorough, but his opportunity to acquire a knowledge of Greek, Latin and French was not the best. He read law, in 1837-8, in the office of Messrs. Meigs & Rucks (R. J. Meigs and James Rucks), in Nashville, and was licensed to practice, in the summer of 1838, by Judges Maney and Anderson, and began the practice of his profession at Carthage, Smith county, soon thereafter. In 1839, he was elected to the Legislature, as a Whig, from Smith county, over Col. A. W. Overton, the Democratic candidate. At the close of the session he returned to the practice of his profession at Carthage, forming a partnership with William McClain, an old practitioner, father of Hon. Andrew McClain, late United States district attorney for Middle Tennessee.

In the spring of 1840, he married Penelope C., the youngest daughter of Judge Nathaniel Williams. She lived only eleven months after her marriage, and died without children. Shortly after her death Col. Stokes removed to Lebanon and entered into partnership with Samuel Caruthers (afterward a member of Congress from Missouri), succeeding to the law practice of Judge R. L. Caruthers, then recently elected to Congress from the Lebanon district.

On the 11th day of October, 1842, he intermarried with Martha Jane, only daughter of Dr. James and Hannah H. Frazer. Mrs. Stokes had only one brother, the late Henry S. Frazer, of Nashville, and no sister. Her father was a very prominent physician, but equally noted for his high manly character and deep piety. Her mother was the grand-daughter of Rev. Green Hill, spoken of above, and was a woman of far more than ordinary intellect and force of character, and lived to the age of eighty-seven years, having survived her two children and all her brothers and sisters.

Col. Stokes' second wife died at Sunnywild, the residence of her eldest son, James F., in Bolivar county, Mississippi, June 19, 1883, and any sketch of him which did not give prominent and reverential place to her memory would be fatally incomplete. She was a lady of most unusual personal beauty, and a grace of manner equally as rare. Naturally endowed with a scintillating intellect, by early and continuous effort she readily became a mental power in her home and throughout the circle of her acquaintance. Potential as were these attributes, she suffused them with a warmth and wealth of affection which rendered her the sweet inspiration of her husband, as well as the sure sheet-anchor of her sons. Her capacity to adapt herself to all phases of life, without the faintest personal sacrifice, was wonderful, and the humblest marketer left her door genially impressed with her kindly interest in his and his family's weal. The sad tidings of her death brought genuine tears, beyond her own portals, in many an humble home which had glowed with her unostentatious charity and kindness. If the Christian's hope be truth, the great transition to this lady merely involved the assumption of angel wings. Devoutly pious without cant; highly cultured without egotism; beautiful without vanity; a strict disciplinarian without rigor; warmly affectionate without weakness, she was sovereign in her home, with a scepter of love to maintain her sway. Her life was an unmixed blessing, while her death, in its noiseless gentleness, was as the closing of petals at nightime, to open and bloom brighter when the sun reappeared. She bore her husband ten children. The two youngest, Edwin and Arthur, died soon after their birth. William C. and Harry S. each died in early manhood; were both educated at Amherst College, Massachusetts, and Harry S. had graduated in law at Lebanon, and at the Columbia law school, New York city.

Of the six living children, Henrietta H. graduated at the Nashville Female Academy, and married Harry H. Sheets, of Indianapolis. They have three children, William, Harry and James F. James F. Stokes, the oldest now living, was educated at Amherst College, Massachusetts, graduated at the Lebanon law school, and soon after his admission to the bar became attorney-general for the Seventh judicial circuit of Tennessee. In 1876, he was elected to represent Wilson county in the lower house of the Tennessee Legislature. In 1875, he married Miss Blanche McGhee, and in 1877 removed to Bolivar county, Mississippi, where he has since resided, engaged in agricultural pursuits. He has acquired prominence in public matters in his section, having been twice elected president of the levee board, a position which he now fills. He was Democratic elector for the "Shoestring district," in the presidential race of 1880, and recently served as one of the commissioners for Mississippi to the convention held in Washington City for the improvement of western waterways. He has four children, Annie D., Harry S., Miles McGhee and Mary C. The next oldest child living, Mary Ella Stokes, graduated at Mrs. Tevis' school, in Shelbyville, Kentucky, and intermarried with Charles Buford, of Pulaski, Tennessee, January 30, 1884. They have one child, named Martha Stokes. The next oldest son, Jordan Stokes, jr., was educated at Princeton College, New Jersey; graduated at the Lebanon law school, and has since practiced law in partnership with his father. He married Miss Mary Whitworth, the only living daughter of Judge James Whitworth, of Nashville, and now resides near that city. He has three children, Martha K., Anna G. and Jordan. Col. Stokes' youngest daughter, Bettie M. Stokes, graduated

at Ward's Seminary, Nashville, and married George C. Waters, April 9, 1884. Walter Stokes, the youngest living son, has completed the full academic course under Messrs. Webb Bros., at Culleoka, Maury county, Tennessee; has spent two years in the academic department at Vanderbilt University, Nashville, winning, at the commencement in 1885, the founder's medal for oratory, and is now a student in the law department of the university, taking the junior and senior courses of study at the same time.

In religious opinions the family are Methodists, Col. Stokes and nearly all of his descendants being active members of that church. He is a zealous Mason, has risen to the Royal Arch degree, and was for a series of years High Priest of his chapter.

From his earliest manhood he has been an earnest advocate of the political doctrines of the Whig party. During the existence of that party, his whiggery maintained the fervor of religious zeal; he piously clung to it during its stages of decay, and is to-day a loyal mourner about its grave. At no period of his life has he been, in any true sense, an aspirant for political station, though he has often served his people. In 1851-2, he represented Wilson county in the Legislature, and was elected speaker of the house of representatives. In the Scott canvass he was presidential elector for his congressional district, but shortly thereafter declined a nomination for Congress, preferring professional success and the quiet of his home to any inducements offered in the arena of political office-holding. He was elected to the State senate in 1859, and deserved and received the credit of defeating the bill introduced in that Legislature to expel or enslave the free negroes in the State. His speech on this question gave him wide reputation, and indicated a breadth of thought far beyond his time. President Lincoln eagerly sought a copy of the speech; Wendell Phillips expressed the opinion that only a few such men in the South would go far to allay sectional utterances at the North and South. At the called session of 1861, he was, with Whig fervor, the friend of the Union of the States, and opposed secession in all its phases. When the issue finally came, he was consistently a unionist, and accepted the famous Crittenden resolution of July 22, 1861, as a declaration of his political views. It may not be out of place here to exhume this resolution, which passed the house of representatives by a vote of yeas one hundred and nineteen; nays, two; and the senate by yeas, thirty; nays, seven; and of the seven negative votes, six were Democrats: "Resolved, That the present deplorable civil war has been forced upon the country by the disunionists of the southern States now in revolt against the constitutional government, and in arms around the capital; that in this national emergency Congress, banishing all feeling of mere passion or resentment, will recollect only its duty to the whole country; that this war is not waged upon our part in any spirit of oppression, nor for any purpose of conquest or subjugation, nor purpose of overthrowing or interfering with the rights or established institutions of those States; but to defend and maintain the supremacy of the constitution, and to preserve the Union with all the dignity, equality and rights of the several States unimpaired; that as soon as these objects are accomplished, the war ought to cease." Accepting this almost unanimous declaration of Congress, as to the object of the war, Col. Stokes was throughout a consistent, but always conservative, Union man. He held no office, either civil or military, during its continuance, and took no active part in the struggle, save to soften, when possible, its asperities, and ameliorate the condition of his people. As the war progressed, he approved the course of Mr. Lincoln, and though a slave owner, he preferred the preservation of the union of the States to the preservation of the institution of slavery, whenever the sacrifice of one became necessary to the maintenance of the other. When the war was over, and the orgies of reconstruction began, his conservatism forced him into political affiliation with the Democratic party, though never an aspirant for office and little interested in active politics. During the past twenty years, he and men of his school in Tennessee, representing many of her most cultured citizens, have been politically, as it were, between the upper and nether mill-stones of opposing fanaticism, with little opportunity to come to the front or direct the affairs of the State. The subject of this sketch never desired political prominence; has ever shunned the dusty arena, and hence this state of things has given him, personally, neither vexation nor thought.

It is in his profession and kindred pursuits that Col. Stokes has won his laurels, and richly deserves all he wears. From the beginning of his professional life, he has been a patient, tireless, discriminative investigator, even carrying thoroughness to its utmost limit. In his mental make-up there is no place for the superficial, while his powers of memory are remarkable. He is equally at home in all the departments of his profession, though perhaps he has acquired greater reputation in *nisi prius* and criminal cases, owing to his high powers as an advocate. There are few tongues more persuasive or defiant, as the one method or the other best suits the necessities of the particular forensic emergency; while his fiery oratory has often been the lever to hoist a bad case out of court. He accepts without questioning the ethics of the profession, and in its practice allows no trace of casuistry. With the essential merit of the case he has nothing to do—that is the province of court and jury—but through inflexible loyalty to his client, by all the blandishments of oratory and forensic art, he brings these stern umpires to view the evidence and law applicable thereto, favorable to his client's demand or need, as it might be. He has been remarkably successful. In chancery the same energy, tact and learning have secured no less success, and though never the

incumbent of a judicial position, he has delivered, under special appointments, some notable judicial opinions, the most prominent, perhaps, being in the Ducktown mining suit in East Tennessee. He deservedly ranks very high among the many eminent lawyers this State has produced, but while the law has been his mistress, her sway has not been exclusive. His midnight lamp has shed its luster on other pages than those of Chitty, Coke and Story and the like. With a legal erudition which worthily places him at the head of his profession, he has combined an equally extensive knowledge of literature and philosophy, characterized by the same thoroughness. Metaphysical researches have long been his delight, but have been so admirably directed as not to befog common sense. His literary culture and powers of oratory have often brought him forward, on patriotic and festival occasions, and he has responded to such wishes from his friends with an alacrity more common in younger and less prominent men. Recently he delivered at Vanderbilt University an address on The Centenary of American Methodism, which attracted much attention. Its literary attractions were of the highest order, but the most notable feature of the address was the phase or view of Methodism presented. He treated the subject from a secular standpoint, and viewed this great religious sect as an agent of civilization and fashioner of thought in American life and literature. Christianity is no less a political and social than a religious principle, and our government is only a political culmination of the New Testament Scriptures, while Methodism, in its polity, is intensely American. Religion must not only define man's relation to Deity, but comprehend as well his own personality and his relation to his fellow man. The address was in all things worthy of its author.

The inner life of this gentleman is an inviting field. He early determined never to attempt that which did not promise success, but once entered upon, never to abandon the effort while hope remained. To this is largely attributable the success attendant on his efforts wherever directed. His home life has been beautiful. The family fireside has no where radiated greater happiness. The Pythoness who presided is there no longer, but has left imperishable memories. It was her deft hand which governed the little ones. He was only her self-constituted lieutenant, as it always should be. A father ladened with outside care has rarely the poise requisite to wisely judge and properly punish the foibles of children. As the children, however, grew in years they felt more the impress of his direct influence. By nature he was peculiarly fitted to gladden the home of his family, while his pure private life and stern integrity gave to them his hours of leisure. No children have ever left the parental roof to achieve their fortunes elsewhere with sweeter memories. His great and paramount aim ever has been the advancement and happiness of his family.

" To make a happy fireside chime
To weens and wife,
Is the true pathos and sublime
Of human life."

This exquisite quotation was his creed. Now that his children are all grown, and all save one have families of their own, he views the results of his ambition with pardonable complacence. They all inherited or acquired a taste for books, and in their respective spheres of life are useful men and women.

Col. Stokes inherited from his father about ten thousand dollars, and now, after losses by the war, and by security debts, and the expenses of his large family, he is still possessed of ample means. He has as yet none of the usual infirmities of age; his disposition is as sunny and his step as light as a man of forty years. He is in the full active practice of his profession, and can delve over books and papers to the " wee sma' hours " without conscious fatigue. Men of his kind rarely feel age, for there is little that is old in them. The western sky may be as bright and jocund as the east; the length of the reverse shadow is nothing, and only seen when looking backward. Eyes that have ever pursued the path of honest, intelligent conviction pay little attention to shadows, and the heart that is true and pure need not grow old. Earnest in his studies, he is not less so in his sports. The writer has known him to patiently watch his line throughout the day's fishing with never a " nibble," and seen him in inclement weather traverse a half mile of creek bank, in quadruped fashion, to surprise a lot of unsuspecting mallards. It was a wise fish that refused his bait, or mallard that hastened before he came in range, as he is not less skillful with rod and gun than elsewhere. His fondness for these sports amounts to an enthusiasm, though he has ever restricted the indulgence of them to long intervals. Such recreations he has made only aids to his studies, but always enjoys and prosecutes them with zest.

His manly gentleness and modesty, his lofty character, his high attainments, have secured him the enthusiastic devotion of his family, the cordial love of his friends, and the respect and admiration of all. This short memoir of his life richly deserves the perpetuity of print. Tennessee has just cause to be proud of him as one of her citizens, as an expression of her civilization, to bequeath to her youth.

COL. O. C. KING.

MORRISTOWN,

COL. O. C. KING was born in Washington county, Virginia, August 4, 1842, and his father's farm lying partly in Virginia and partly in Tennessee, his father moved across the line into Tennessee when the son was two years old. There he grew up to manhood, doing farm work, attending stock, and going to school. He was educated at different points in Virginia and Tennessee, attending Emory and Henry College one year and Tusculum College three years. He left the latter institution in his junior year, April, 1861, and joined the Confederate army as a private soldier in Capt. Abram Gammon's company, from Sullivan county, which was afterward a part of the Nineteenth Tennessee regiment, Col. Cummings commanding.

Soon after he was transferred from that regiment to a battalion of cavalry under Col. George R. McClelland ; was subsequently promoted to a lieutenancy in an infantry company of Col. Pitts' Sixty-first Tennessee regiment, but became disgusted with infantry service, resigned his position, went back to the cavalry, Col. James Carter's First Tennessee cavalry regiment, and served in that command as a private soldier until he was desperately wounded, in June, 1864, in the valley of Virginia, by a minnie ball, which broke his left thigh and took out about four inches of the bone, which has made that limb some three inches shorter than the other, producing a limp in his walk. He lay seven long, weary months in one position from the effects of that wound, no one supposing he could ever recover. During the war he was in many regular engagements, and in numerous skirmishes while on detached service. During the holidays of 1862–3, he was in the series of engagements around Vicksburg, lasting for seven days. After his return from Vicksburg, and rejoining his command, he was with Col. Carter in all his engagements in upper East Tennessee and southwest Virginia until his command was transferred to the valley of Virginia. He was wounded at the battle of New Hope, June 4, 1864, the first engagement after his command entered the valley. He was in the valley of Virginia when Sheridan made his celebrated raid, in which every barn, mill, granary, haystack and straw pile from Winchester to Staunton were burned or destroyed. From the room where he lay wounded, he counted at one time the light of fourteen barns and mills burning—set on fire by the torches of Sheridan's valiant raiders.

His father having been divested of all his personal property, Col. King (as his friends and admirers love to call him) began school teaching near his father's home. He opened a school in an old store house near his father's dwelling, had to be carried to the school room on a litter, and taught, lying on his back, until he was able to go on crutches and sit upright. Meantime, to show the indomitable pluck and genuine manhood of the gallant young soldier, he read law while teaching, under the nominal tutorship of Beverly R. Johnston and Joseph T. Campbell, of Abingdon, Virginia. When he had accumulated about one hundred dollars, and was thinking of opening a law office, he was indicted for treason in the Federal court at Knoxville. Through the influence of his father, who was an old personal friend of Hon. Connally F. Trigg, the Federal judge presiding, the case was *nolle prosequied* on his paying the costs of the suit—one hundred and fifteen dollars, of which he had to borrow fifteen.

He was licensed to practice law in 1867, at Blountville, by Judge R. R. Butler and Chancellor Seth J. W. Luckey, began practice in the fall of that year, and practiced there till the fall of 1868, when he moved to Mossy Creek, Jefferson county, Tennessee, lived there till 1876, when he removed to Morristown, where he has ever since resided, practicing law, farming, speculating in real estate, and occasionally engaging in other business, such as taking stock in flouring mills, and in railroad and mining enterprises. For ten or twelve years he has devoted much time to investigating the mineral resources of upper East Tennessee, and has invested some money there and in Colorado. He owns now probably more iron ore than any man in East Tennessee, and is interested in zinc and lead mines in that section. He owns lands in Hamblen, Cocke, Sullivan and Jefferson counties, embracing six farms. He began business life very poor, with fifteen dollars borrowed money, a wife, a baby and a pair of crutches.

What is the secret of his business success? The hardest kind of work; though he was not passionately fond of work, still he worked hard because it was a necessity. Moreover, he made it a rule to do whatever he did well, and a little better than some other men would have done it. His law practice was the foundation of his prosperity, and his law practice depended on the faithfulness, diligence and earnestness with which he devoted himself to the interest of his clients. He is by nature an earnest man—a positive, not a negative man. Were he asked to improve upon the definition Demosthenes gave of eloquence, he would substitute " carnestness" for "action." When a case has been entrusted to him, he goes in to win it. From boyhood days he has been a reader of and familiar with the English classics, and he has made a liberal use in his law practice of the advantages derived from them. Of all the instruments a lawyer can use, the Bible is the most potent, and from it Col. King quotes very frequently. He is a very poor collector, can make money faster than he collects it; has never formed habits of economy; is not what is called a frugal man, though by no means improvident, and always manages to keep his expenses within the limits of his purse.

In 1880, he projected the building of a railroad to connect the Kentucky system of railroads with the Carolina system, crossing East Tennessee from north to south through Cumberland Gap. To that end he organized two companies in Tennessee, one in North Carolina, and one in Kentucky, and consolidated them all with two that had been previously organized in South Carolina, under the name and style of the Chicago, Cumberland Gap and Carolina railway company, and perfected a contract with the Atlantic and Northwestern Construction company to build the entire road, about four hundred miles. He was the first vice-president of the company as organized. Soon after making the contract with the construction company, there came a serious disagreement between himself and the construction company, growing out of different interpretations of the terms of the contract, and Col. King resigned his position as director in the railway company, and has since had no connection with the management, though much the largest stockholder in the company.

Col. King may be set down as a Democratic freethinker. Though he has never attended but one political convention, as a rule he acts with the Democratic party. In 1884, he was defeated for Congress in the First congressional district, by Hon. A. H. Pettibone. He was the nominee of the Democratic party, and though the district, which is overwhelmingly Republican, gave Blaine a majority of over five thousand over Cleveland, Maj. Pettibone's majority over King was less than twenty-four hundred. He was made a Master Mason at Bristol, in 1836, and took the Royal Arch and Council degrees in E. H. Guild Chapter, Bristol. He is also an Odd Fellow and a Knight of Honor. His religious views and sympathies are Presbyterian, being of Scotch-Irish descent.

His father, L. M. King, who died at Morristown, in December, 1884, in the sixty-sixth year of his age, was an elder in the Presbyterian church. So also was his grandfather, David King, who died at Lexington, Kentucky, in 1848, an aged man. At the time of his grandfather's death he was on the road from Virginia to Ohio with all of his slaves to liberate them. He came, in 1796, from Lancaster, Pennsylvania, to Washington county, Virginia. The family have all been quiet people, none of them having held official position, but all men of fair means, and good, substantial citizens.

Col. King's mother, Penelope Massengill, was born in Sullivan county, Tennessee, the daughter of Michael Massengill. a farmer. Her mother was Louisa Cobb, the daughter of Caswell Cobb, of Sullivan county. Col. King's mother, now living with him at Morristown, is a member of the Presbyterian church, the mother of four children: (1). Oliver Caswell King, subject of this sketch. (2). Michael Glenn King, who was drowned, when eighteen years old, at Knoxville, in 1862, while attempting to rescue his servant from drowning. He was, at the time of his death, a soldier in McClelland's battalion of Confederate cavalry. (3). Nancy E. King, now wife of Samuel W. Gill, Talbott's, Tennessee. She was educated at Martha Washington College, Abingdon, Virginia, and has two children, Mary Gill, who married, March, 1885, John W. Wooten, of Morristown, and Penelope Gill. (4). Louisa King, educated at Stonewall Jackson Institute, Abingdon, Virginia ; married John W. Donaldson, of Talbott's, Tennessee; has three children, Hugh, Ollie Kate and Leander King.

Col. King married. at Blountville, Tennessee, August 12, 1863, Miss Kate Rutledge, who was born near Blountville in 1844, the daughter of John C. Rutledge, who for twenty years, was clerk of the county court of Sullivan county. He died in 1868, about sixty-five years old. Her grandfather, Robert Rutledge, was a farmer, of a Virginia family, and the youngest brother of Gen. George Rutledge, who figured in the early history of East Tennessee. Her mother was Sallie Cobb, daughter of Caswell Cobb, her mother and Col. King's maternal grandmother being sisters. Mrs. King was educated at the Female Institute at Blountville, is a domestic woman in her tastes, prudent and economical, and to her assistance and good counsel her husband owes much of his success. Five children have been born to them : Michael Caswell; Penelope Louisa; John Rutledge ; Leander Montgomery, "the critical boy of the family "; one unnamed, who died in infancy.

Col. King is something of a diffident man, and on this account does not often seek to be thrown with gentlemen who are prominent. In the work he has to do, he knows no such thing as diffidence, but as a rule makes acquaintances only for business purposes. The ideas of business transform him, come natural to him, and, as it were, take him out of himself, yet under other circumstances he is modest and unpretending almost to a fault.

HON. PETER TURNEY.

WINCHESTER.

A BIG man in every way, in physical proportions, in heart, in brain, in conscience, a man of the highest order of intellectual and legal ability, of lofty courage and unspotted integrity, few public men in Tennessee are so well known as the Hon. Peter Turney, of Winchester, now one of the Supreme judges of the State. Moreover, his square common sense and his great natural ability, as well as his profound legal erudition, enable him, almost without effort, to arrive at conclusions and positions that most other men have to labor to reach. Of warm sympathy, the outgrowth of a gentle heart and a brave, manly and chivalric nature, it has often been said of him that, if his legal decisions ever vary from the strict letter of the law, it is only when the rights of an unfortunate widow or helpless orphan children are involved. *Humanum est errare*—yet if he ever errs it is on the side of humanity.

Judge Peter Turney is a native of Jasper, Marion county, Tennessee, was born September 22, 1827, and is the son of Hon. Hopkins L. Turney, one of Tennessee's most distinguished statesmen of *ante bellum* times, and when "there were giants in those days." Peter Turney received a fair English education at Winchester, Tennessee, and had so advanced in mathematics and kindred studies that, when only seventeen years old, he was a surveyor, on his own account, six months in Franklin county. After this he studied law in his father's office from June 22, 1845, until his father's election to the United States senate the same year. He then studied in the office of Maj. William E. Venable, at Winchester, and September 22, 1848, was licensed to practice by Hon. Andrew J. Marchbanks and Hon. Na-

than Green, sr., the latter then of the Supreme court. After admission to the Winchester bar, he practiced with his father until his father's death, August 1, 1857. He then formed partnership with his brother, Miller F. Turney, and practiced with him until the breaking out of the war, in 1861.

When the war came on, being an ardent southerner and in full sympathy with the secession cause, he entered the Confederate army. He was elected colonel of the First Confederate Tennessee regiment of infantry and on many of the bloody, storm-rent fields of the South he gallantly led "Turney's regiment" to victory. Attached to the brigade of Gen. Robert Hatton (afterward Archer's Tennessee brigade), he fought through the Virginia and Maryland campaigns until the Appomattox surrender. He bore brave and conspicuous part in the battles of Seven Pines, May 31 and June 1, 1862, the second battle at Manassas, Cedar Run, Harper's Ferry, Antietam, Sharpsburg and Fredericksburg, and numerous other engagements of less note.

At Fredericksburg he was wounded in the mouth by a shot which took away all his upper teeth, two of his lower ones, and a part of his tongue, which causes him to this day to lisp a little, makes his articulation a little difficult, but this is only noticeable to those who are aware of the fact. He was also shot in the battles of Seven Pines and Antietam, but not seriously disabled.

He remained colonel of his regiment, but in August, 1863, was assigned to duty in Florida. Later in the same year he was appointed to the command of the eastern district of Florida, and commanded the Confederate forces in a battle on Three Mile creek.

He was recommended by Gens. Robert E. Lee, A. P. Hill and James J. Archer for promotion, but as Col. Turney and President Davis were not on friendly terms he was not raised to a higher rank.

Returning to Winchester, when the war was over, without means, except a house and lot, he resumed his law business and continued in practice there until September 1, 1870, when he went on the Supreme bench of Tennessee, the position he now holds. His first election as Supreme judge was in August, 1870, as the nominee of the State Democratic convention; his re-election occurred in August, 1878, and was without opposition. The salary attached to the Supreme judgeship is four thousand dollars per annum, and, financially, he is now in very comfortable circumstances.

Though not in active politics, Judge Turney is an hereditary Democrat. In 1854, he was a Democratic candidate for attorney-general of his circuit, but was beaten by Gen. George J. Stubblefield, now of Nashville. In 1860, he was alternate elector on the Breckinridge ticket. In 1861, he was elected as a secessionist to represent Franklin county in the State convention, but the convention never met. In 1876, his friends nominated him before the Legislature for United States senator, to fill the unexpired term of Andrew Johnson, deceased, but he was defeated by Hon. James E. Bailey.

He became a Mason in 1857; is also a Knight of Pythias and a Knight of Honor. Both he and his present wife are members of the Protestant Episcopal church.

Judge Turney has been twice married. First, at Winchester, June 10, 1851, to Miss Cassandra Garner, daughter of Thomas H. Garner, of a North Carolina family, a large farmer in Franklin county, Tennessee, and representative of that county in the State Legislature several times. He died in 1881, aged eighty-three years. His father, Thomas Garner, was a pioneer settler in that section and died at the age of ninety-five; a well read man, of strong, quick mind, aspiring to nothing but respectability and industry. Mrs. Turney's mother, was Eliza Wadlington, of a Kentucky family. She died in 1883, at the age of seventy-five. Mrs. Turney (the first) died March 28, 1857, at the age of twenty-one, leaving three children. (1). Thomas Turney, died March 3, 1874. (2). Virginia C. Turney. (3). Hopkins L. Turney.

Judge Turney's next marriage, which occurred in Marion county, Tennessee, April 27, 1858, was with Miss Hannah F. Graham, who was born in Jackson county, Tennessee, daughter of John Graham, a large farmer, a native of Pennsylvania, one of three brothers, one of whom settled in Pennsylvania, one in Virginia and one in North Carolina. Mrs. Turney's mother, nee Miss Aletha Roberts, of Davidson county, Tennessee, was a relative of the Buchanans of Davidson, and of the Ridleys of Rutherford county. By this marriage

Judge Turney has nine children, Teresa, Peter, jr., Aletha, Samuel, Lowndes, James, Woodson, Hannah F. and Miller Francis.

Judge Turney's father, the Hon. Hopkins L. Turney, was one of the ablest and most remarkable men Tennessee ever produced. He was a native of Smith county, born in October, 1797. He never attended school a day in his life, and not until the age of twenty-two could he write his name. But he was of wonderful native ability, vigorous innate talent, and by force of close application and study by what means he could, he conquered obstacles and rose to eminence as a self-made man. He began practicing law at Jasper, Tennessee, in 1825; married in May, 1826; remained at Jasper until February, 1828, when he removed to Winchester, where he practiced law and lived on a farm near town. He represented Marion county in the Tennessee Legislature one term, and Franklin county several terms. From 1837 to 1843 (six years), he was a member of Congress; from 1845 to 1851, he was United States senator from Tennessee. He was a soldier in the war of 1812-14. He was a man of extraordinary natural abilities, a spirited man, a man of leonine courage, "but as gentle as a woman" in the kindliness of his nature. Of great energy, he did with all his might what he had to do, and would never quit until he accomplished it. He was a recognized leader of the Democratic party during his life. He died August 1, 1857.

Judge Turney's grandfather, Peter Turney, came from Germany. He was the son of a German mother but of a French father. He died leaving a large estate, which was wasted by administrators.

The Hon. Samuel Turney, Judge Turney's uncle, was a leading lawyer in Middle Tennessee in his day. He represented White county several times in the Legislature, and was, at one time, speaker of the Tennessee State senate. Judge Turney's oldest uncle, James Turney, had the reputation of being a leading lawyer at Chicago and at Tyler, Texas, at which latter place he died in 1864.

Judge Turney's mother, originally Miss Teresa Francis, was born in Rhea county, Tennessee, December 9, 1809, the daughter of Miller and Hannah Francis. Her mother was the daughter of William Henry, of a Virginia family. Judge Turney's mother died September 5, 1879. She was a woman of great energy and a fine economical manager, and frequently had to manage the farm while her husband was in politics and in Congress.

Sprung from such sturdy ancestry, Judge Turney's early training, as was to be expected, was of the best. It made him a close student in early life, and fastened upon him studious habits that have followed him to maturer manhood. He has stuck close to his profession, kept to his office, and paid but little attention to anything else. Thus inspired by the example of his father, he has made a success.

Physically, Judge Turney is a man who would attract attention in any assembly. He is six feet three inches in height, stands very erect, is portly and stately, and though weighing two hundred and sixty pounds, is a man of fine proportions. His eyes are blue, hair light, voice soft and kindly; his enunciation deliberate. He is a witty, good natured man, loves a good joke and knows how to laugh with his soul.

HON. THOMAS McKISSICK JONES.

PULASKI.

HON. THOMAS M. JONES, one of the most eminent lawyers in Tennessee, and one of the five surviving Tennessee members of the Confederate Congress, was born in Person county, North Carolina, December 16, 1816, but came when an infant with his father's family to Giles county, Tennessee, where he has ever since resided. He was educated at Wirtenburg Academy, Pulaski, until 1831, when he was sent to the University of Alabama, where he remained until 1833. From there he went to the University of Virginia, remaining until 1835. Returning to Pulaski, he read law in the office of Flournoy & Rivers, until the summer of 1836.

About this time the Florida war broke out, and he volunteered for service, raised a large company in Pulaski, called the "Hyenas," which afterward became Company A, of the first regiment of Tennessee mounted men, under Col. Alexander B. Bradford and Lieut.-Col. Terry H. Cahal. Young Jones was made captain of his company, which had among its members a number of young gentlemen who afterward became men of distinction, notably among them being Gov. Neill S. Brown, Supreme Judge Archibald Wright, Hon. Solon E. Rose, Maj. A. F. Goff, Dr. Jesse Mays, J. Nelson Patterson, Daniel V. Wright, and others. He fought through the campaign, the principal battles of which were Lost Creek, Wahoo Swamp and the Withlacoochee.

That war over he returned home, obtained license to practice law from Chancellor Bramlett and Judge Stewart, and at once began practice in partnership with John W. Goode. He practiced steadily until the canvass of 1844, when, being appointed county elector on the Democratic ticket, he stumped Giles county for Polk and Dallas.

In 1845, he was nominated and elected to the Tennessee house of representatives, and served in that body as acting chairman of the committee on the penitentiary and as a member of the judiciary committee. In 1847, he was elected State senator for the counties of Giles and Maury. In 1861, he was elected to the Confederate congress and served in that body with Messrs. Atkins, Caruthers, Currin, DeWitt, and House—all of whose sketches appear elsewhere in this volume. He served till after the fall of Fort Donelson. Having three sons (Calvin, Charles and Thomas) in the Confederate army, two of whom had been taken prisoners at the battle of Fort Donelson, he declined a re-election to Congress, preferring to be with the army. After the fall of Donelson he returned home and remained until the Federal troops invaded Pulaski, took him prisoner and sent him to Nashville to Military Gov. Andrew Johnson, who paroled him on condition that he would not communicate with the Confederate Congress or the Confederate commanders while Pulaski was surrounded by the Federal forces. After their armies had been withdrawn, however, he went south, and, although not a soldier, remained with the army till the close of the war.

After the war he resumed his law practice at Pulaski, which he has steadily followed ever since. He has in the meanwhile held several judiciary appointments: First, as judge of the criminal court, composed of the counties of Giles, Maury, Williamson and Marshall, a position which he filled ten months in 1872-3; next, as judge of the court of commission, with Judges Hickerson and Garner, which he held over twelve months.

He was then, by special appointment of Gov. Marks, made a judge of the Supreme court, was re-appointed by Gov. Hawkins, and again by Gov. Bate. While on the Supreme bench the celebrated case, involving millions of dollars, called "the free territory case," the State of Tennessee ex rel. James L. Gaines, vs. George K. Whitworth, trustee, in which the State, county of Davidson, and city of Nashville claimed the right to tax the real estate granted by the State of North Carolina to the University of Nashville, and exempt from taxation for ninety-nine years, came before that tribunal. Judge Jones delivered the opinion of the court that the property was exempt. (See 8 Lea, p. 594). Under that decision the property rapidly improved and gave Nashville a new start in growth and prosperity.

From his earliest manhood Judge Jones has been a Democrat, true and tried. In all the local campaigns of his county and district his voice was heard resounding from the hustings, rallying the hosts of Democracy in support of the deathless principles of the party of the people. In 1856, he was a delegate to the national Democratic convention at Cincinnati that nominated Buchanan. In 1860, he was a delegate to the national convention at Charleston, which adjourned to Baltimore and nominated Breckinridge, and in the Charleston convention he was a member of the committees on credentials and on permanent organization. In 1880, he was a delegate to the national Democratic convention at Cincinnati, which nominated Gen. Hancock, and he has been a delegate to every State convention held since the war.

In 1870, he was a delegate from Giles county to the State constitutional convention, of which his colleague, Gov. John C. Brown, was president. Judge Jones served on the judiciary committee and advocated the appointment by the governor of the judges of the Supreme court and the chancellors, with a view of keeping the judiciary out of politics, but this the convention overruled. He also favored the insertion of a clause in the constitution forbidding the charge of more than six per cent. interest per annum for money under any circumstances. This also was defeated.

Judge Jones has been a railroad director from 1855 to the present time; was a director in the old Planters Bank eighteen years; director of the National Bank of Pulaski ten or twelve years, and a director of the Columbia, Pulaski and Elkton turnpike company from 1842 to 1855. He has been repeatedly mayor of Pulaski; president of the board of trustees of Giles College from its incorporation till the building was destroyed, and has been for twenty years a vestryman of the Protestant Episcopal church at Pulaski, of which church he is a member.

In 1843, he became a Mason, since which time he has taken all the degrees up to and including that of Knight Templar. The splendid engraving of him accompanying this sketch represents him in his Knight Templar uniform.

Judge Jones first married, in Williamson county, Tennessee, December 25, 1838, Miss Marietta Perkins, a grand-daughter of Col. Nicholas Tate Perkins, and daughter of Dr. Charles Perkins. She was a niece of John Prior Perkins and Constantine Perkins, members of a large family in Williamson county. Her mother, *nee* Harriet Field, was the daughter of Judge Hume Field, of Tuscaloosa, Alabama, formerly judge of the superior court in Virginia. She was a cousin of Col. Hume R. Field, of Confederate war fame, as colonel of the first Tennessee regiment.

By this marriage, Judge Jones had nine children: (1). Calvin Jones, born November 1, 1839; graduated from Nashville University; was adjutant of the Thirty-second regiment, Tennessee volunteers—Col. Cook—was captured at Fort Donelson; was taken sick at Fort Warren, but was nursed to health by the Federal Maj. Dimmick and his daughters; returned home, remained a while and rejoined his regiment, but his health being too feeble for active service, after the battle of Chickamauga, in which he took part, he was assigned to post duty at Macon, Georgia. After the war he practiced

law at Pulaski, but quit law for farm life. He died in 1872. (2). Charles P. Jones, born November 20, 1842; graduated at the Nashville University; served in the army from 1862 to the surrender, most of the time on the staff of Gen. Bushrod R. Johnson with the rank of lieutenant and captain. He was captured at Petersburg and held prisoner till the war closed. He is now law partner with his father. He married Miss Cora Reid, daughter of Rev. Carson P. Reid, a minister of the Cumberland Presbyterian church, and has one child, Cora. (3). Thomas W. Jones, born May 22, 1845; entered the army at sixteen in the Third Tennessee regiment, under Col. John C. Brown; served till the surrender; is now in Colorado in the cattle business, after having practiced law at Pulaski several years. (4). Hume Field Jones, born January 26, 1848; graduated from Giles College; now practicing law at Lewisburg, Tennessee. (5). Harriet Jones, born January 8, 1852; graduated from the Columbia Female Institute; married, in 1871, Hon. Z. W. Ewing, formerly State senator from Giles, Wayne and Lawrence counties; State assessor of railways; visitor to the University of Tennessee, and now chairman of board of education of Pulaski. They have one child, Marietta. (6). Edward S. Jones, born December 29, 1853; graduated at Norwalk, Connecticut; now a professional teacher. He married Miss Anna Bright, daughter of Hon. John M. Bright. They have one child, Mary. (See Judge Bright's sketch elsewhere in this volume). (7). Lucy Anne Jones, born December 25, 1855; graduated at Columbia Female Institute; now wife of James Polk Abernathy, a lawyer at Pulaski, and has two children, Robert Andrew and Thomas Marietta. (8). Lee Walthal Jones, born March, 1857; now connected with the Nashville and Florence railroad. (9). Nicholas Tate Jones, born March 8, 1863; graduated at the Knoxville University, and now a civil engineer on the Nashville and Florence railroad.

The first Mrs. Jones died July 18, 1872. She was a most exemplary Christian woman, a member of the Episcopal church. She was a lady of great firmness and strength of character, of rare intellectual endowments, highly cultured and refined. She shone as a bright light in society and around the fireside. During the war she remained at home and took care of her family, and managed affairs with excellent skill and judgment.

Judge Jones' second marriage occurred at Brownsville, Tennessee, May 9, 1883, to Mrs. Anne G. Wood, an own cousin of his first wife, daughter of Nicholas T. Perkins. Her mother was Lucy P. Turner, daughter of Simon P. Turner, of Raleigh, North Carolina. Mrs. Jones is a graduate of the old Nashville Female Academy. By her first husband, Mr. James Proudfit Wood, a merchant and railroad president, she has one child, Mary, who married J. W. E. Moore, a prominent lawyer of Brownsville, and has three children, Annebel, May and Wood. Mrs. Jones is a member of the Episcopal church, and is a great favorite in society, remarkably kind, gentle and affectionate in her nature, and beloved by the entire community.

Judge Jones' grandfather, Wilson Jones, was born in Brunswick county, Virginia, and was an American officer in the Revolutionary war. The Judge's father, also named Wilson Jones, was likewise a native of Brunswick county, Virginia. He moved to North Carolina, where he married Miss Rebecca McKissick, the Judge's mother, who died in 1826. She was the daughter of Thomas McKissick, who had been a patriot soldier in the Revolution, and was wounded twice. One of his wounds was received at the battle of Brandywine, the ball passing through his chest, entering under the left shoulder and coming out at the right. The old gentleman received a pension until his death, in 1826. The family meanwhile had immigrated to Tennessee, and after the death of his father and mother, Judge Jones lived with his maternal grandparents. The Judge's grandmother, nee Lucy Hudson, was of an English family. She was a member of the Methodist church, and was very strict in raising her grandson. After the death of the grandparents he went to live with his oldest sister, Mrs. Lucy Clack, wife of Spencer Clack, an early settler in Giles county, son of John Clack, author of what is known as the "preference right bill" in the Tennessee Legislature. He lived with this family until he went off to school, as before stated.

Judge Jones had three sisters, Lucy, who married Spencer Clack; Permelia, who married John Walthal, and Susan, who married Gray H. Edwards. He has one brother, Hon. Calvin Jones, now of Somerville, Tennessee, who was educated at Chapel Hill, North Carolina, and was chancellor in West Tennessee for eight years. He married a Miss Williamson, of North Carolina.

Before the war Judge Jones' ambition was to be successful as a lawyer, and he was successful, accumulating a very handsome fortune, consisting of eighty odd negroes and nearly one thousand acres of splendid farming land. He never had any great fondness for politics, and when nominated for office, it was for positions wholly unsought and only accepted as a matter of duty. He was, however, strong and decided in his political views, and his friends pressed him forward, notably Thomas Martin, who was one of his stanchest and truest friends. The key to his success is his rule to do honest labor and to charge moderate and reasonable fees for it, hence his large and lucrative practice. Moreover, he has made it a rule never to engage in speculation, but to invest in productive property. He never charged over six per cent. interest for the use of his money, and was never extravagant. He has lost by security debts fifteen thousand dollars since the war. He is noted for his charity to the poor and his liberality toward all men. The hospitality of the Jones family mansion reminds one of the old times, when men kept open house for the stranger as well as their friends, for under that roof-tree there is an old-fashioned, ante bellum welcome for all.

GEN. MARCUS J. WRIGHT.

MEMPHIS.

THE scion of a sturdy, sterling, and intellectual ancestry, this gentleman has been briefly described as a man "gifted with sound judgment, great executive ability, and a correct literary taste."

Marcus J. Wright was born June 1, 1831, in McNairy county, Tennessee. He was educated at the common schools and at the academy in his native county, and became a fine classical scholar, with a decided penchant for a literary life. He was a hard student, and from his early boyhood manifested the literary bent of his mind. Before the late war he was an able and valued contributor to southern literature, and his essays, sketches, etc., were highly prized in the South.

When he reached his majority he went to Memphis to live, engaged as clerk in a commission house, and afterward spent some time at New Orleans. Returning to Memphis, he studied law, was admitted to the bar, and commenced practice with Col. Leroy Pope. Soon afterward, however, he was elected, as an old line Whig, clerk of the common law and criminal court of Memphis, which position he held up to the war.

When the war came, he espoused the cause of the South, was elected lieutenant-colonel of the One Hundred and Fifty-fourth (senior) Tennessee regiment of infantry, April 4, 1861, and went with that regiment into the Confederate service. His promotion was rapid and brilliant for so young a man. On April 29, 1861, he commanded a battalion of the One Hundred and Fifty-fourth regiment and the Steuben artillery at Randolph, Tennessee, where he built Fort Wright, named by the command in his honor. He commanded his regiment in the battle of Belmont, November 7, 1861, and was military governor of Columbus, Kentucky, from February 3, 1862, to March 8, 1862. He also commanded his regiment at the battle of Shiloh. From June 10 to September 1, 1862, he was a lieutenant-colonel and assistant adjutant-general on the staff of Maj.-Gen. B. F. Cheatham, and as such served with gallantry and distinction at the battle of Perryville. He was commissioned brigadier-general December 13, 1862. He was assigned to the command of Hanson's Kentucky brigade, January 10, 1863, which he relinquished February 1, 1863, to assume command of Donelson's Tennessee brigade, Cheatham's division, to which he was permanently assigned. His brigade was composed of the Eighth, Sixteenth, Twenty-eighth, Thirty-eighth, Fifty-first, and Fifty-second regiments of Tennessee infantry, Murray's 'Tennessee battalion of infantry, and W. W. Carnes' battery of light artillery. He led this brigade into action at Chickamauga and Missionary Ridge, and was twice wounded. He commanded the district and post of Atlanta, Georgia, when it was evacuated by the Confederate armies; also commanded the post at Macon, Georgia. From February 3, 1865, to the end of the war, he commanded the district of North Mississippi and West Tennessee, with headquarters at Grenada, Mississippi.

After the war he returned to Memphis, and shortly after was elected sheriff of Shelby county. At the expiration of his term, he removed to Jackson, Tennessee, and went into the newspaper business, and from Jackson to Columbia, Tennessee, where he became the editor of the Columbia *Journal*. Leaving Columbia, he located in St. Louis, but was only there a short while, when, on July 1, 1878, he was appointed by the secretary of war to collect for the use of the government such records of the late war (on the Confederate side) as could be obtained. This is his present occupation, and the fidelity, zeal, and intelligence he has brought to bear upon his work has not only enriched the war annals of the nation, but added many invaluable volumes to the archives of the government which otherwise might never have been secured.

It is said in Washington, where Gen. Wright now resides, that he is the best known man all over the United States now resident at Washington. His home is the Mecca, not only of Tennesseans and Southerners, but of literary people from the North, and especially those seeking information in regard to the war. His wife, formerly Miss Pauline Womack, of Alabama, enters fully into all of his work, and enchants his visitors by her grace as a hostess.

Gen. Wright is identified with the hardy pioneer settlers of McNairy county, whose efforts have not only made that section one of the most prosperous of our State, but whose lives and characters are ornaments of our common country. His mother was twice married, her first husband being Herbert Harwell, by whom she had five children : Richard S. Harwell, of Purdy, Tennessee ; Dr. Rufus S. Harwell, of Arkansas ; Littleton Harwell, deceased ; Amanda, now widow of Burrell B. Adams, of Corinth, Mississippi ; and Julia Harwell, deceased. By her second marriage, with Maj. Benjamin Wright, she had three children : Hon. John V. Wright, of Nashville, Tennessee ; Mrs. Elizabeth Crump, now

dead ; and Gen. Marcus J. Wright, subject of this sketch. Gen. Wright's mother was born in Dinwiddie county, Virginia, where she lived for more than thirty years. She was sixty-six years of age at the time of her death. She was one of the Old Dominion's most intelligent and cultured daughters, gifted beyond measure with colloquial powers and pleasantry. She always made her visitors feel the charm of her society. She was devotedly attached to her friends, but she had to feel that the persons numbered as such were worthy, and her discrimination was so clear that she was scarcely ever deceived. It is believed that but few mothers ever had more confidence in the integrity and uprightness of their children, or higher hopes of their eminence and prosperity, and it is pleasing to know she had just cause to be proud of them. In her last sickness she expressed her readiness and preparation for death. She was a queenly woman, whose grace, beauty, and intellectual gifts would have adorned any position, and made her the pride of the circle in which she moved.

Gen. Wright's father, Benjamin Wright, was born at or near Savannah, Georgia, on April 2, 1784. By a second marriage of his mother there were three other children, a son and two daughters. The son was appointed a lieutenant in the United States army by President Madison, soon after the declaration of war by the United States against Great Britain, in June, 1812, and was attached to the Thirty-ninth regiment of infantry, commanded by Col. Williams, of Knoxville. He was very soon thereafter detailed for the recruiting service, in which he was very successful, in the country around Nashville, Gallatin, and Lebanon. About this time he was married to Miss Lewis, of Sumner county, Tennessee, a most amiable and accomplished lady, who died soon after the close of that war. Upon the breaking out of the Creek war, in the fall of 1818, the Thirty-ninth regiment was ordered to reinforce Gen. Jackson, who had fought the Indians in several engagements, with Coffee's brigade and other Tennesseans. They were brought into active service at the battle of the Horseshoe, nearly the whole of Jackson's army at the time being from Tennessee. Lieut. Wright here distinguished himself for gallantry, and received several promotions, reaching eventually to that of a field officer. At the battle of the Horseshoe, Lieut.-Col. Samuel P. Montgomery, of the Thirty-ninth regiment, led the charge on the breastworks, and was killed on the ramparts. He was only a few paces in front of Lieut. Wright, who, seeing his leader fall, cried out, "Avenge your leader," and led the charge. The charge was made in gallant style. Gen. Samuel Houston was a lieutenant in the Thirty-ninth regiment, and was wounded in the arm at this battle by a musket ball.

In 1823, Lieut. Wright, who had now been made a major, was married to Mrs. Martha Ann Harwell, at the residence of Col. Stokely Hays, in Jackson, Tennessee, and from that time until his death resided in Purdy, Mc-

Nairy county. Maj. Wright had two children by his first marriage, Frances Wright, who married Elvis Bracken, of Holly Springs, now deceased, and Charles L. B. Wright, who was drowned at Memphis. Maj. Wright volunteered as a private soldier for the Mexican war, and contracted a disease there from which he never recovered. He died in Purdy, January 30, 1860. He was a man of powerful frame, upward of six feet high, straight as an Indian, and as a business man had few equals and no superiors. In his day he was, perhaps, the most popular man in McNairy county, and his popularity with all classes and all parties was due to a personal geniality that never forsook him. It has been said that little children sought his society, and played in trusting fondness at his feet, or "climbed his knees the envied kiss to share." Strong men leaned upon him in hours of adversity, and found an "anchor both sure and steadfast." When the storm came they gathered around his commanding form for protection, as do the beasts of the field 'neath the sheltering oak, when the tempest sweeps the forest and marks its pathway with havoc and destruction. Women, too, were his most ardent admirers, because they knew him to be gallant, truthful, and the soul of honor. No impure word ever soiled his lips, or impure thought ever darkened his counsels. He was a Chesterfield in manners, and belonged to that old school of gentlemen that sprung up immediately subsequent to the Revolutionary period, and of whom it may be truly said, " We shall not look upon their like again." Their devotion to the gentler sex was, perhaps, unsurpassed. He was the embodiment of what the poet calls " social eloquence," and in his conversation there sparkled ever the blaze of wit and flash of bright intelligence. To young men he was especially kind, and they were always his warmest friends and most ardent supporters. Indeed, he exhibited in his daily life a ready sympathy with all classes, and both his right and left hand were devoted to charitable uses. He lived beyond the period allotted by the Psalmist to frail humanity, and at the very threshold of octogenarian manhood, "death touched his tired heart." A polished shaft placed there by filial hands marks the spot where he lies, and on its base, in the chiseled tracery of the sculptor's art, is written in fadeless letters the story of his life. It rises in full view of the small village, and overlooks the little stream whose sunny waves were never brighter than his golden traits of character.

Gen. Marcus J. Wright's half-brother, Richard Harwell, was elegant in person and in dress, and had excellent judgment. He followed mercantile pursuits, and was a prosperous man until the ill fortunes of war ruined his business. Rufus Harwell was a physician, and very popular. He was a remarkably handsome man, and showed by his carriage and his conduct that good and true blood coursed his veins.

Hon. John V. Wright, brother of Gen. Wright, and the eldest son of Benjamin and Martha A. Wright, was born at Purdy, June 28, 1828. He was once a candidate for the lower house of the General Assembly of Tennessee, from McNairy county, but was defeated by one vote —the vote of his opponent. He served three terms in the Congress of the United States, from the (then) Seventh district, in which McNairy county is situated. In 1861, he raised the Thirteenth regiment of Tennessee infantry for the Confederate army, and commanded it as colonel at the battle of Belmont, Missouri, where he was wounded. He was soon afterward elected to the Confederate Congress, where he served until the end of the war. He resided for a number of years at Columbia, Tennessee, but is now living at Nashville. He has held the offices of judge of the circuit, criminal, and chancery courts in his judicial district, and has been several times appointed by the governor as special judge of the Supreme court of the State. He was the candidate of the State-credit Democracy for governor at the election in 1880, but, by reason of the division in the party, was defeated by Gov. Hawkins. He has a leading practice at the bar of Nashville, and has, to a large extent, the confidence and regard of the people. A full sketch of Judge Wright's life appears elsewhere in this volume.

Elizabeth Wright, the only sister of Gen. Wright, married Dr. Charles C. Crump. She was a lady of great elegance and refinement, who, after a few happy years, passed away. After her death her husband removed to Middle Tennessee. Dr. Crump died at his residence in Spring Hill, Tennessee, August 7, 1882. He left three children by his first marriage: Mrs. Alexander, of Spring Hill; Marcus V. Crump, of Brownsville, Tennessee, and Richard O. Crump, of Milan, Tennessee, and one daughter by his last marriage, Lula Crump.

HON. WILLIAM E. B. JONES.

McMINNVILLE.

ALTHOUGH a Marylander by birth, the subject of this sketch has been so long and so prominently identified with Tennessee affairs, he is quite as much a Tennessean as one "native here and to the manner born." The place of his nativity was Annapolis, Maryland, where, on December 21, 1828, he first saw the light. His father, Maj. Richard Ireland Jones, a major in the United States army of 1812, was a native Englishman, born in London, served as a British midshipman, but resigned and came to Maryland when twenty-one years old. He was married three times, and died in Maryland in 1844, at the age of seventy-four, when the son was only fifteen years old.

Mr. Jones' mother, *nee* Lucretia J. Ball, was a native of Kentncky, born the daughter of William and Letitia Ball, of a Virginia family. The grandfather, Edwin Ball, moved from Virginia to Kentucky at an early day. Miss Lucretia Ball was teaching school at Fayetteville, Tennessee, when Maj. Richard Jones met her and there they were married, she being his third wife. She died in 1840, leaving five children, only three of whom survive: (1). Ada, now wife of Dr. Amos Hancock, of Overton county, Tennessee. (2). Emma, now wife of James McMillan, of Monroe county, Kentucky. (3). William Edwin Ball Jones, subject of this sketch. W. E. B. Jones, was educated at St. John's college, Annapolis, Maryland, but he received all of his schooling before the age of fifteen. At about the age of seventeen, he entered the clerk's office of Bracken county, Kentucky, as a deputy clerk, where he remained six months, meantime reading law. Continuing his law studies a year or more after this, he was licensed to practice by Judges Crenshaw and Tompkins, at Glasgow, Kentucky. He began practice at Livingston, Overton county, Tennessee, in September, 1848, and practiced there with considerable success up to the time of the war.

In 1861, he entered the Confederate army, joined Bledsoe's cavalry company, and remained in that company until the latter part of the year, when he was mustered out of service, his time of enlistment having expired. After the war he moved to McMinnville, Tennessee, where he has practiced law ever since, in partnership, two or three years, with W. J. Clift; three years with W. V. Whitson, and ten years with T. C. Lind, his present partner.

A Jeffersonian Democrat in politics, Mr. Jones has never deviated from the principles of that party. In 1860, he was a delegate to the Democratic national conventions at Charleston and Baltimore, at Charleston voting for Johnson, and at Baltimore for Douglas. He was mayor of Livingston one year, and in 1859–60, represented Overton county in the lower house of the Tennessee Legislature, serving on the judiciary and banking committees.

He belongs to no secret society and to no church, though formerly a member of the Christian church, the doctrines of which he still believes.

Mr. Jones first married in Fentress county, Tennessee, December 29, 1850, Miss Vestina Bledsoe, daughter of William Bledsoe. Her mother was, originally, Miss Elizabeth Trosper, of a Kentucky family. Her brothers, Willis S. and Robert H. Bledsoe, were both gallant Confederate officers, the former a major and the latter a captain, in Col. Baxter Smith's Fourth Confederate cavalry regiment. Mrs. Jones was of the same family as the Anthony Bledsoe family, of Sumner county, Tennessee. By his marriage with Miss Bledsoe, Mr. Jones has five children: (1). Emma Jones, educated at Nazareth Academy, Bardstown, Kentucky. (2). Laura J. Jones, educated at the Cumberland Female College, McMinnville. (3). William B. Jones, born February 18, 1857; educated at the East Tennessee University; married Miss Allie, in Dallas, county, Texas, where he now resides. They have one child, Alice Bell. (4). Mary Lucretia Jones, educated at the Cumberland Female College, McMinnville. (5). Minnie Lee Jones, educated at the same school. The first Mrs. Jones, died February 13, 1867, at the age thirty-two; a member of the Christian church.

Mr. Jones' second marriage, which took place in Van Buren county, Tennessee, March 29, 1870, was with Miss Ann L. Page, daughter of Dr. John S. Page. Her mother was Miss Louise Turner. By this marriage, Mr. Jones has four children. (1). Richard Edwin Jones, born April 29, 1872. (2). Idalia Ermine Jones, born February 1, 1875. (3). Annie May Jones, born May 22, 1878. (4). John Meredith Jones, born February 26, 1882.

Mr. Jones has had the experience of beginning life on nothing twice, first when a youth of nineteen, and next after the war. He is now in independent circumstances, owns two valuable farms, and has an interest in two others, besides valuable real estate in McMinnville. He is also a director in the National Bank at McMinnville. He has always made it a rule to be in his office ready for business, and to be prompt and attentive, and has the reputation of being a hard student. He is a man of strong will, and a man of individuality. In manners, he is plain and unassuming, and in address, deliberate and positive. Integrity of character and fixedness of purpose are the factors of his prosperity.

COL. LEONIDAS TROUSDALE.

NASHVILLE.

COL. TROUSDALE was born in Robertson county, Tennessee, February 12, 1823, at his father's farm, near Springfield, the county seat. When he was three years old his father moved to Jackson, in Madison county, of the same State, then a pioneer district, receiving its first generation of white settlers. At the age of seven he commenced attending such schools as were accessible in that half reclaimed country, and at nine commenced the study of Latin. His principal instructor was Samuel McClanahan, a graduate of the South Carolina College, at Columbia, South Carolina. With this gentleman he studied for six successive years, when his teacher was called to the bar, and abandoned the scholastic profession. He very early developed a taste for literary composition, having edited a weekly paper at thirteen, which was circulated among his school-fellows in manuscript. At sixteen he started another journal, also circulated in manuscript. At the age of twelve he returned to his birth-place, Springfield, and attended school at Liberty Academy for two years, under a good classical scholar. In 1837, at the age of fourteen, he entered the University of Nashville, Dr. Philip Lindsley, president. Among his contemporaries there were J. Berrien Lindsley, "Nicaragua" Walker, William T. Haskell (the well-known orator), John M. Lea (afterward judge of the chancery court and mayor of Nashville), Gov. Runnells, of Texas, and Hardy M. Burton, a distinguished lawyer. In the fall of 1839, he entered the East Tennessee University, of which Joseph Estabrook was president, and here he graduated as A.B., in 1841.

Soon after graduation, he emigrated to Carroll county, Mississippi, where he taught school for two years and a half, when he was appointed deputy clerk of the chancery court. In this capacity, however, he served only a few months, when, the war with Mexico having broken out, he enlisted as a volunteer in the First Mississippi regiment, whose colonel was the since renowned Jefferson Davis. The regiment first served under Gen. Taylor, at the mouth of the Rio Grande, where, as always happens with newly recruited soldiers, the troops were almost decimated by diarrhea. The First Mississippi formed part of Gen. John A. Quitman's brigade, which also included the First Tennessee regiment, Col. Campbell; the division commander was Gen. William O. Butler. While in this command he participated in the storming of Monterey, with its succession of sanguinary street fights, and then, after Ampudia had capitulated and marched out of the city, the regiment was ordered to join Scott's army at Vera Cruz. It had, however, only marched as far as Victoria, when it was ordered back to Agua Nueva, and found itself again under Taylor's command, at the battle of Buena Vista, where four thousand five hundred Americans routed

twenty-three thousand Mexicans, under Santa Anna. At this battle the First Mississippi regiment had at one time a very important position, the whole event of the engagement turning upon its maintaining its part against very disproportionate numbers. After this battle he was elected second-lieutenant of his company. At the close of the war he returned to the United States, and was mustered out of the service at New Orleans, where he landed.

In the fall of 1847, he commenced editing a paper called the *Weekly Democrat*, at Carrollton, Mississippi, which he continued till, in the winter of 1849–50, he was elected assistant clerk of the Mississippi senate, and at the adjournment of that body he returned to his native State.

He now took up his residence in Gallatin, where, for a few months, he edited a Democratic paper called the *Tenth Legion*. Moving from thence to Little Rock, Arkansas, he was for twelve months editor of the *Gazette and Democrat*.

After gaining experience and self-confidence, with some reputation, by these fugitive efforts, he moved to Memphis, and there purchased an interest in the Memphis *Appeal*, of which he was co-editor for eight years. In 1860, occurred the great division in the Democratic party, which lost it its power for a quarter of a century, and, together with a parallel split in the Whig party, brought on the civil war. The conflicting claims of Breckinridge and Douglas to the presidential nomination occasioned this division, and also a division between the proprietors of the *Appeal*, and this necessitated the resignation by him of the editorship. At this time the successive deaths of Poindexter and Eastman, of the Nashville *Union and American*, had necessitated an addition to the editorial staff of that paper, and he sold out his interest in the *Appeal* and transferred his services to the other paper, where he had for his colleagues those well-known journalists, John C. Burch, F. C. Dunnington, J. O. Griffith and Thomas S. Marr. The fall of Fort Donelson, in February, 1862, and the consequent occupation of Nashville by the Federal forces, suspended the publication of the paper for some years.

He was now appointed aid-de-camp on the staff of Gov. Isham G. Harris, and, after the transaction of a multiplicity of military business in that capacity, was promoted adjutant-general of brigade on the staff of Gen. Marcus J. Wright and John C. Carter, taking an active part in the Chickamauga campaign of 1863, including the battles of Chickamauga and Missionary Ridge. His health and strength being much impaired by the fatigues and privations of this trying campaign, he now tendered his resignation, which was accepted by President Davis.

He did not long continue idle, however. The Chattanooga *Rebel* was now entrusted to his editorial care. This little journal was one of the most remarkable products of the civil war. Its originator and proprietor was Franc. M. Paul, formerly one of the editors of the Memphis *Bulletin*. Among its editors or contributors were Henry Watterson, of the Louisville *Courier Journal*, Albert Roberts, of the Nashville *American*, Charles Faxon, of the Clarksville *Jeffersonian* (now dead), Leon. Trousdale and others, whose names are well known as writers. It was started by Mr. Paul, at Chattanooga, in 1862, but though it bore the same name throughout, it was published at many different southern towns, migrating from one to another, according to the fluctuations of the war. It remained at Chattanooga till the advance of Rosencrans' army and the bombardment by Wilder's battery made that place a little too hot for typographical proceedings, when it was established at Marietta, Georgia, and after several more removals its publication was finally and forcibly suspended by Gen. Wilson, of the Federal army, at Selma, Alabama, during the celebrated raid he made through that section, just previous to the close of the war. Wilson seemed to have had a special spite against this particular journal, and gave orders, just previous to the evacuation of Selma by his troops, for the burning of a large and valuable building in which the paper was printed. The building was the property of minors, and through the most earnest efforts of their representatives the Federal commander was induced to modify his order so as to spare the building, but directed that the printing material of the *Rebel* office should be effectually wiped out, which order was strictly carried out. Everything that could be destroyed by fire was consumed in the street in front of the office, while the presses, imposing stones and other fixtures that could not be burned were broken into fragments with sledge hammers and axes. In the conflagration were destroyed three complete files of the paper, which contained much matter bearing upon the history of the war in the department in which it had been published that cannot be replaced. The best thoughts and raciest paragraphs ever penned by the able and brilliant writers who filled its columns for three years, perished in that bonfire at Selma; for these same gentlemen, we doubt not, will sustain us in the assertion that they never did better work with their pens than that performed under the inspiration of the stirring times of those years of civil strife.

At the close of the war, Col. Trousdale returned to Memphis and commenced the publication of the Memphis *Commercial*, his colleagues being John M. Keating, John Heart, Rolfe S. Saunders and Capt. W. W. Carnes. The office of this paper, with all its material, was destroyed by fire in the spring of 1867, when he became associated with Albert Pike in the editorial conduct of the Memphis *Appeal*, remaining there one year.

61

It was as a journalist, especially as a leading political writer for the daily press, that Col. Trousdale exhibited his abilities to the best advantage, for in that field he was more at home than in any other. Gifted with a natural aptitude for the profession, and trained in its duties from his earliest youth, he spent the best years of his life on the editorial tripod, and achieved a reputation in that field of labor of which any man might be proud. His editorial career was passed prior to the present era of sensational journalism, but covered a period when the newspaper was, perhaps, more potent in moulding public opinion than it is even in the present day of mammoth sheets, pictorial illustrations and a vaster range of subjects, not to mention the increased facilities afforded for the gathering and dissemination of news from every quarter of the world. His style as a writer is clear, perspicuous and direct, and no one was ever at a loss for the meaning of his sentences, or the drift of his logic. In the discussion of public questions in the days of his literary prime, none of his contemporaries brought to bear on a subject more correct information, deeper thought or sounder logic. Though wielding a trenchant pen, it never shed gall or bitterness in party strife, nor traced a line of personal abuse or villification. The elevated tone of his writings, his strict regard for all the courtesies of the profession, his *esprit de corps*, no less than his ability as an editor, secured the highest consideration and regard of his brethren of the press, and the esteem and confidence of the public.

In 1869, he was elected secretary of the Memphis Chamber of Commerce, to which office he was twice re-elected, being at the same time secretary of the Memphis Agricultural and Mechanical Association, which positions he held for four years. Then he became book-keeper in the county trustee's office, and held that position till he was appointed, in 1875, by Gov. Porter, State superintendent of public instruction. This office he held for six years, being successively reappointed by Gov. Porter, in 1877, and Gov. Marks, in 1879.

During this period his labors were unflagging. The present prosperity and popularity of the public school system are due to those labors. Capt. Thomas H. Paine, his successor, pays the following high tribute to his efforts in behalf of popular education: "To Col. Trousdale more than any other man, are the people of Tennessee indebted for the progress, general development, and present condition of our public school system. Having been State superintendent for six years, he has given the subject much thought, and each term of his service has been characterized by a wise and conservative management of the affairs connected with the work entrusted to his care."

The six years of Col. Trousdale's administration as State superintendent of public instruction, were years of growth and development. During this period, the public school system became rooted in the confidence and affections of the people. Many improvements and agencies were devised to make the system efficient and popular. The counties increased their rates of taxation. An improvement was visible in the *personnel* of the county superintendents and teachers. Many graded schools were established in the cities and towns. Teachers' conventions and institutes were held in various parts of the State. The schools were gradually reduced to system and uniformity. The State Normal College was established to train a corps of teachers. The efficiency of the system of State and county supervision was greatly improved. Col. Trousdale, with native tact, brought on these developments gradually and almost imperceptibly, but the end of his administration showed a far more solid and substantial condition of his department than its beginning. He left the office, upon the incoming of the Republican administration of Gov. Hawkins, beloved by the teachers and people of the State, to whom his faithful discharge of duty and his amiable character had endeared him. A strong pressure was brought to bear on Gov. Hawkins by the educational men, including many Republicans, to retain the faithful officer at his post. The political rule was applied, and Col. Trousdale left the office amid universal regrets. The following extract from one of his circulars to county superintendents in relation to institutes, shows his earnestness, and the breadth of his views: " From such conferences there will almost certainly radiate an enthusiasm and influence which will impel early and active exertions to organize, fraternize and heighten the efforts of all free school teachers throughout the State. Such an inspiration is needed and will be furnished by making these district conferences worthy of the attendance of the best educators of the State. I find, by experience, that the institutes heretofore held have achieved great good, but their diffusion throughout every portion of the State has not been general and systematic enough. I desire that this influence and inspiration, which is great and wonderful, should reach every county, and every school district in the State, however remote and obscure. To this end, I earnestly invoke the active and enthusiastic co-operation of the county superintendents." These institutes were successfully established, and Col. Trousdale brought to bear, in the development of the school interests, an array of talent, such as has never been surpassed in the United States. The ability and eloquence of this noble body of educators deserve to be handed down to posterity. We name a few of these learned and accomplished philanthropists: Supt. S. Y. Caldwell, Drs. E. S. Joynes, N. T. Lupton, W. Leroy Broun, Prof. J. I. D. Hines, Col. S. H. Lockett, Prof. E. Alexander, Rev. W. S. Doak, Capt. Frank M. Smith, Prof. William Carroll, Prof. James E. Scobey, Supt. James T. Leath, Capt. W. R. Garrett, Mrs. Annie Chambers Ketchum, Misses Clara Conway and Jennie Higbee, Profs. J. W. Terrell, S. S. Woolwine, James Dinwiddie and Caskie Harri-

son. There were many others equally deserving and efficient.

In 1881, he was appointed, by Col. Killebrew, assistant superintendent of that department of the National Exposition at Atlanta devoted to the Nashville and Chattanooga and the Louisville and Nashville railroads. For several months he traveled on the Louisville and Nashville railroad and its branches, collecting objects for exhibition.

In March, 1883, he was appointed, by Capt. Paine, clerk and assistant superintendent in the bureau of public instruction, and here he commenced the publication of the *Southwestern Journal of Education*. In this he continues occupied to the present day. In August, 1885, he was appointed surveyor of customs of the port of Nashville.

From this record it appears that Leonidas Trousdale has been what Homer calls Ulysses, πολύτροπος ἀνήρ, a man of many reserves and many resources, often falling, but always falling on his feet, of boundless versatility and indomitable energy. His superhuman activity, under both prosperous and adverse circumstances, has at length told upon his constitution, and he suffers under a distressing nervous malady, which must sadly abridge his enjoyment in life, but which does not prevent him from doing a large amount of work in his office, or from being always prompt to welcome a friend, or do one a service, if it is in his power—and this is no slight undertaking, for of Col. Trousdale's friends the name is legion.

Col. Trousdale's father was Bryson Blackburn Trousdale. He was born in Orange county, North Carolina, about 1793, being brought by his father to Sumner county, Tennessee, in his childhood. His teachers were Gideon Blackman and John Hall, the latter an eminently learned man, whose brother, William Hall, was afterward governor of Tennessee. At about twenty years of age he took a farm near Springfield, in Robertson county, and married Susan, widow of John Harwell, by whom he had four sons and one daughter: (1). Albert Gallatin, died at Corinth, Mississippi. (2). Cincinnatus, a prominent lawyer at Helena, Arkansas; a man of considerable mental 'powers. He was a lieutenant in the Mexican war, and died January 3, 1852. (3). Leonidas, subject of this sketch. (4). Susan, who married, first, Capt. Campbell Allen, who died of consumption, by whom she had two children, both dead; second, in 1855, Gen. S. R. Anderson, who had been colonel of the First Tennessee regiment in the Mexican war, afterward postmaster of Nashville, and general of the First Tennessee brigade, in the Confederate army; he died in 1883. She is now living in Nashville with her daughter, Mai.

Bryson Trousdale was a man of irreproachable character, very temperate when temperance was not in the repute it now holds, and a great friend of education. Though his own education had been limited and his means slender, he spared no expense in the education of his children. A delicate constitution and extreme youth prevented him from participating in Jackson's military exploits. He died at Nashville, in 1878, at the age of eighty-five. His father (grandfather of Leonidas Trousdale) was a Revolutionary soldier of the North Carolina line. He settled, about the close of the last century, in Sumner county, Tennessee, on the spot where now stands the northern part of the town of Gallatin, Tennessee. His father (great-grandfather of Leonidas), was a Scotch-Irishman, who migrated from the north of Ireland to Pennsylvania, and thence to North Carolina. Relatives of the same name may still be found in Ireland.

The mother of Col. Trousdale was born near Petersburg, Virginia, daughter of James and Martha Hicks. She died before her children were grown.

His paternal grandmother was Miss Dobbins, of North Carolina, a relative of Hon. James C. Dobbins, who was secretary of the navy under Mr. Pierce.

His uncle, William Trousdale, was a lawyer in good practice, a soldier in both the Indian and Federal wars of Jackson, and colonel of the Fourteenth United States infantry in the Mexican war. He was wounded at the battle of Chapultepec. Both as a soldier and as a civilian, he was recognized as a man of tried courage and unimpeachable honor. In 1850, he was elected governor of Tennessee. A son of Gov. Trousdale, Julius A. Trousdale, of Gallatin, Tennessee, served under Gen. Bate in the late war, and has been twice elected to the house of representatives and once to the senate of Tennessee. Another son of Gov. Trousdale, the eldest, Charles W. Trousdale, served under Forrest in the late war, and lost a leg at Chickamauga. He resides now at Gallatin, Tennessee. Judge John V. Wright and Gen. Marcus J. Wright are also cousins of

Col. Trousdale, on the maternal side. Memoirs of these gentlemen are given in this volume.

Col. Trousdale married, December 24, 1853, Virginia Frances, daughter of Levi and Martha Joy, of Bolivar, Tennessee, by which marriage he has five children: (1). Lula, a kindergartener at Dyersburg, Tennessee. She studied that system of education at Worthington, Ohio, and is very successful in imparting it in practice. (2). Jennie Joy. (3). Susie, died in infancy. (4). Leon, jr. (5). Levi Joy.

Col. Trousdale attributes his success in life to having striven to do whatever he did well, working systematically and persistently; and, by no means least, to the inspiring enthusiasm, sympathy and assistance of his wife.

He is a Mason of the seventh degree, a member of the Episcopal church, and a conscientious believer in its doctrines; he considers it his highest privilege in life to enjoy a fixed religious faith.

The testimony of all who have been associated with him is, as is expressed by a friend: "He is one of those noble, warm-hearted men, whom it is rare to meet with; a man of unbending integrity, and generous, even to a fault." All concur in placing implicit confidence in his integrity, and in expressing the warmest regard for his social qualities. Especially is the kindliness and urbanity of his disposition manifested toward those who go to his office for information or advice. With an unwearied patience he listens to the most prolix and tedious, as well as the intelligent and considerate, and no expression of impatience or irritation ever clouds his countenance, but the information is always reliable and the advice sound and wise, and given with a cheerful courtesy which makes it doubly acceptable. To have business with Leonidas Trousdale is to be sure of a pleasant interview and profitable counsel.

JAMES MERRILL SAFFORD, A. M., M. D., Ph. D.

NASHVILLE.

PROF. SAFFORD was born August 13th, 1822, in Putnam (now a part of Zanesville), Muskingum county, Ohio. His parents were Harry Safford and Patience Van Horn, the former the son of Dr. Jonas Safford, who was a distinguished physician in Galliopolis, Ohio, the latter a daughter of Gen. Isaac Van Horn, one of the first settlers of Ohio, and an officer in the Revolutionary war. In 1840 he entered the Ohio University, at Athens, when, under the presidency of Dr. William H. McGuffey (afterwards professor of moral and mental science in the University of Virginia), that institution was in its most prosperous condition. From this university he received the degrees of both

Bachelor and Master of Arts. In 1846, he entered Yale College, mostly for the purpose of studying chemistry, natural history and geology. His studies there were pursued with success. During vacations he worked in the field, and traveled much on foot over a large part of the New England States and New York. Some years afterward he received the degree of Doctor of Philosophy, from Yale College. Before leaving the latter college, two professorships were tendered him; one, the chair of mathematics, in the Ohio University, the other, that of chemistry, natural history and geology, in Cumberland University, at Lebanon, Tennessee. He accepted the latter, and entered upon his duties at Lebanon in 1848. He became at once interested in the geology of his adopted State, and soon, through explorations made on his own account, was enabled to publish the first geological map of Middle Tennessee worthy of the name. In 1853, he was joined in marriage to Catharine K. Owen, widow of Dr. B. R. Owen, daughter of Jacob Howard, esq., a native of East Tennessee, and sister of Col. John K. Howard, a well known and prominent politician before the war, who was fatally wounded at the head of his regiment in one of the battles around Richmond, Virginia.

In 1854, Dr. Safford was elected by the Legislature as State geologist of Tennessee. At the expiration of the first term (two years), he was re-elected to the same position, and again in 1858. Short reports of progress were made to the Legislature at the end of each term. In 1860, by the authority of the Legislature, he commenced a full report on the general geology of the State, but the work was stopped by the war. In 1868, the Legislature authorized the completion and publication of the report, which was finished, with a large geological map of the State, in 1869. This work, "The Geology of Tennessee," a large octavo of nearly six hundred pages, is considered by those competent to judge as among the very best reports of the kind and scope so far published. It is a noble monument to the ability, knowledge and untiring industry of the author, and is the great source of all we know on the subject of which it treats.

In 1872, he received the degree of Doctor of Medicine, from the University of Nashville. In 1873, he resigned his professorship in Cumberland University and removed to Nashville. In the same year he was elected to the chair of chemistry in the medical department of the University of Nashville, and in 1874, to the same chair in the medical department of Vanderbilt University, both of which positions he now holds.

He was one of the principal editors of the "Resources of Tennessee," a large work of one thousand two hundred pages, published under the auspices of the Bureau of Agriculture of Tennessee. Without his aid and the information supplied in his "Geology of Tennessee," the "Resources," in its present comprehensive form, would have been impossible. In May, of the same year, 1875, he was elected professor of mineralogy, botany, and economic geology in Vanderbilt University, at Nashville. He has been one of the academic faculty of this noted university from its beginning. His chair is now known as that of natural history and geology. Prof. Safford is one of the old members of the American Association for the Advancement of Science, and is still State geologist of Tennessee. He was appointed State geologist by Govs. Porter, Marks, Hawkins and Bate, and has held the position continuously since the war. In 1876, he was a member of the jury of judges on mines and ores at the Philadelphia Centen-

nial Exposition, also at Atlanta, in 1882, and again at Louisville, in 1883. In 1878, he was appointed by President Hayes one of the United States honorary commissioners to the Exposition Universelle, at Paris. He was one of the editors of the *Rural Sun*, of Nashville, a most valuable agricultural journal, the first two years of its existence.

Prof. Safford was raised a Presbyterian, and has been an elder in the First Presbyterian church at Nashville some eleven years. In 1859, he became a Master Mason, at Lebanon. He has been all of his life a Whig in principles and feelings, and although he loves that old party still, has voted with the Democratic party since the war. He has been a member of the Tennessee State Board of Health ever since its organization. He lost pretty property by the war, but is now in easy circumstances.

The name Safford, originally Stafford, (though some authorities insist *Safe-ford*,) is of English origin. Of Prof. Safford's maternal uncle, Maj. Jefferson Van Horn, was a major in the United States army, and took part in the Mexican war. Prof. Safford's brother, Rev. J. P. Safford, D. D., who died in 1881, was a prominent Presbyterian minister at Zanesville, Ohio. Isaac V. H. Safford, formerly a civil engineer, is now a farmer in California. His sister Annie is the widow of D. L. Triplett, who was a wealthy capitalist of Coshocton, Ohio. His sister Bessie married Frank E. Barney, owner of a large mill property, at the same place.

By his marriage with Mrs. Owen, Prof. Safford has had two children, namely: Annie Safford, born at Lebanon, Tennessee, in 1855, died in 1864; Julia L. Safford, born at Lebanon, Tennessee, October 21, 1860, educated at Ward's Seminary, at Nashville, in which she developed a high order of musical talent. In the beauty of her person, the grace of her manners, the strength of her character, and her varied domestic accomplishments, she is an honor to her distinguished parentage. She married at Nashville, in December, 1881, Mr. D. H. Morrow, an able and prosperous lawyer, of Dallas, Texas, and has one child, Kate Safford Morrow.

By her former marriage with Dr. Benjamin R. Owen, Mrs. Safford has three children, namely: Fannie Owen, now wife of Judge Horace H. Lurton, of Clarksville, Tennessee, has three living children, Leon, Horace and Mary Lurton; Lily Owen, now wife of Richard Morgan, a distinguished lawyer of Dallas, Texas, and has two children, Richard and Owen Morgan; Benjamin H. Owen, a leading druggist of Clarksville, Tennessee, educated at the College of Pharmacy, in Philadelphia, married Miss Mary Kennedy, daughter of Hon. D. N. Kennedy, banker of Clarksville, has three children, Sallie, John and Mary Owen.

Mrs. Safford is a lady distinguished for the force of her character, for her broad, liberal views, womanly dignity, intelligence, sprightliness and industry. In the wide circle of her friends she is frequently spoken of as "a famous housekeeper." She is very fond of literature, music and society, and especially of good company at her own home. Affectionate and kind, noted for charity, she is both a model wife and mother, friend and neighbor.

While Prof. Safford was yet a student at Yale College, his instructor, the celebrated Prof. Silliman, received a letter from Dr. Anderson, president of Cumberland University, at Lebanon, Tennessee, requesting him to recommend some young man qualified to fill the chair of chemistry, natural history and geology, who might be induced to come to Tennessee. In the meantime Prof. Safford had received notice of his election to the chair of mathematics in the Ohio University, at Athens. Prof. Silliman advised him to prefer the call to Tennessee, and there pursue, in a newer field, his favorite geological studies. To this advice Tennessee is indebted for the possession of one of the foremost scientists of the country, and the interests of the State

have been benefited by his intelligent labors beyond calculation. From early boyhood, he was fond of books and mechanical inventions, but his studies of chemistry and geology in college gave the final turn to his mind, and with the zeal of an enthusiast he has devoted his busy life to that which his eminent fitness seems to have foreordained him. As a teacher of geology, he found the geological maps in use in the State very meager and defective, and he soon made a geological map of his own of Middle Tennessee, and, at the urgent solicitation of his friends, applied for and obtained the position of State geologist.

Prof. Safford is a man of great energy and vital force; is determined, and possessed of strong will power and perseverance, yet is modest and retiring, loves study, but is not without ambition. Physically, he is of medium height, stout build, weighs one hundred and sixty pounds; has hazel eyes, silver gray hair and beard, and is the picture of health. His expression is a combination of gravity, severity and contentment.

J. GEORGE HARRIS.

UNITED STATES NAVY.

J. GEORGE HARRIS, a gentleman who first distinguished himself in Tennessee as the brilliant political editor of the old Nashville *Union*, the organ, while in his hands, of Gen. Andrew Jackson and President James K. Polk, and who is now living, a retired pay director of the United States navy, at the home of his daughter, Mrs. Dr. Van S. Lindsley, at Nashville, was born at Groton, Connecticut, a town of Revolutionary historic memories, which Mr. Harris was chiefly instrumental in reviving by a centennial celebration, in 1881, of the battle of Groton Heights, fought September 6, 1771, in which no less than eleven of his ancestors, of the Avery family, were killed and as many wounded. Eight successive generations, moreover, of the Averys lie in the same graveyard, at Pequonnock, a village in the town of Groton.

Up to the time of his mother's death, February 2, 1881, at the great age of ninety-two, Mr. Harris was in the habit of spending part of his time every year at his summer home, at Groton, opposite New London, at the mouth of the Thames. It was on the occasion of his summer visit there, in 1879, that he determined to get up the centennial celebration of the traitor Arnold's assault on the place. A committee was appointed, of which he was made president, and after two years' of preparation—the government contributing ten and the State three thousand dollars—success crowned their efforts with the presence of one hundred thousand people, including the attendance of a large fleet of United States men-of-war, of all the military of Connecticut, with the

governor and staff at the head, of Gen. Sherman and his staff of the United States army, of the chief justice of the United States, and numerous other dignitaries. During the celebration a sham fight occurred, in imitation of the massacre, which engaged all the militia and volunteer corps from abroad, and an attack by the ships from the river gave *eclat* to the scene as one of national importance. There were certain features of the original battle that rendered it peculiarly local. It was fought on Groton soil, and three-fourths of its victims were well-known citizens of the town. Its forty widows in this one town, and the weeping of so many families for the loss of fathers and sons, some falling side by side, made it ever memorable and sorrowful. But the losses in New London, and the desolate homes in other towns, made the calamity more wide-spread. The celebration was distinguished by a parade of Connecticut Knights Templar, by speeches from Gen. Sherman, Gen. Hawley, J. T. Wait, Edward Everett Hale, Dr. Bacon, and the presence of Col. J. W. Barlow, of the United States army, as chief marshal. But to no other man there was that occasion so significant and grateful as to Mr. Harris, whose ancestors, the Averys, were among the earliest settlers of the place. There has been published a large quarto volume on the battle of Groton Heights, containing an account of the centennial celebration; and of the speeches made on the occasion no one surpasses the address of welcome delivered by Mr. Harris, as president of the committee, as follows:

"*Ladies and Gentlemen:* In behalf of the committee

appointed here two years ago by the people and the Groton Monument Association to devise ways and means for repairing and improving the monument, and to make suitable arrangements for celebrating the one hundreth anniversary of the battle of Groton Heights, I extend to this great assembly a most cordial welcome.

"Aided and encouraged in their work by the government, the State, and the people, they have done their duty, and their report is before you in the reconstructed classic shaft that stands here beside us, and in these ample preparations for this centennial celebration.

"We are glad to be instrumental in adding another to the several commemorative centennials that have occurred within the last six years, awakening our entire country to a lively sense of the valor and patriotism of the men of the American Revolution, contributing to heal the wounds occasioned by sectional strife, and renewing the ancient bonds of our common nationality over our widely-extended area of human freedom.

"It has been said, by the greatest of American historians, when referring to the gallant defenders of Fort Griswold, that 'their courage and love of country should be celebrated, not only at the end of a century, but of a thousand years.' And if, in the onward roll of the centuries, their grateful posterity shall assemble here to celebrate the tenth centennial, we may rest assured that the monument we have so handsomely enlarged and so firmly strengthened, according to the admirable plans of a distinguished engineer of the army, will still stand here on this granite hill in its silent but eloquent grandeur, to tell them the same story of the 'times that tried men's souls' that it tells us here to-day.

"We come together, not as did the bereaved kindred of the slain for the first half century after the conflict, to spend the anniversary in mournfully lingering around the broken walls of the old fortification; but rather do we come with hearts full of gratitude for national blessings, and with becoming pride and patriotic exultation, as we reflect on their great and good deeds, study the exemplary lessons they have left us, and teach the rising generations to emulate their examples. Sacred to their memory we bring with us our best offerings, for that they nobly participated in laying the superstructure of our republican government so broad and deep in the cement of perpetual union, that neither foreign invasion nor domestic convulsions can shake it from its solid foundations—

"'They never die who fall in Freedom's cause:
The well-fought field may soak their gore,
Their heads may sodden in the sun,
But still their spirits live and serve
As guides along the pathway of mankind.'

"This is the people's entertainment, to which everybody is respectfully invited, and everybody is more than welcome."

The historian adds: "The stillness of the immense audience during the delivery of these words of welcome was interrupted only by the rustlings of applause at the close of each period."

The original Christopher Avery, and his son James, came from England and settled as farmers near the fishing station, on Cape Ann, where Gloucester now stands, and subsequently moved west, in 1650, to the Pequot country, at the mouth of the Thames, where New London now stands; and from them are descended most of the Avery families of America. The Lindsleys settled about the same time at Branford, adjacent to New London. Two hundred and forty years afterward a young Lindsley (Dr. Van S.) meets and marries a young lady descended from the Averys and Harrises of the early colony, the beautiful and accomplished daughter of Mr. Harris, in a far distant capital of a southern State, thus remodeling family characters on the blended traditions of two ancient parallel ancestries. What is education, civilization, individuality, but the product of centuries, modified from generation to generation? A biographer may detect the differentiation of an individual, but he never can account for it. It is a secret known only to the omniscient Deity. The only real history is biography, but that is only a collection and arrangement of the salient points in a man's outward life, which gives but an approximate idea of his complete character.

A biographical sketch and portrait of Mr. Harris may be found in the "History of Davidson County, Tennessee," and another in the "History of New London County, Connecticut." From these and other sources, more or less authentic, the following sketch is compiled.

As soon as he became of age, he began his career as associate editor of the Political Observer, at New London, in 1830. He afterwards edited the New Bedford Daily Gazette. In February, 1839, he became the editor of the Nashville Union, which he continued to edit, with the exception of one year spent in Europe as the commercial agent of the United States, till 1845, when he was commissioned as a pay officer of the navy. In that capacity he was at the capture of Tuspan, Tabasco and Vera Cruz, on the staff of Commodore Perry, and also with him in his Japan expedition. He afterward spent two years on the west coast of Africa, and for two years was attached to the flag-ship in the Mediterranean squadron. He was fleet paymaster of the Gulf squadron during our civil war, and on duty, afloat and ashore, to the close of the conflict. After sailing entirely around the world, and up and down the ocean, wherever navigable, he was retired under the law at the age of sixty-two, for long and faithful service.

But it is as a writer that Mr. Harris is best known in Tennessee. His fame as a political editor having reached Washington City, the Tennessee politicians at that city invited him, at a critical juncture, to undertake the redemption of Tennessee from under Whig control and make it a Democratic State. In January,

1839, he came to Nashville, and in the month of February following established the Nashville *Union*. The editor of a newspaper in those days was supposed to aim at statesmanship, rather than writing merely as a business profession. The *Union* soon came to be recognized as the home organ of Gen. Jackson and James K. Polk, and its influence under the aggressive policy of Mr. Harris was as extensive in the southwest as that of the Richmond *Enquirer* on the shores of the Atlantic.

His brief editorial career in Tennessee was the turning point in the fortunes of the Democratic party in the State. In 1835, Gen. Jackson had refused to express a preference for a presidential candidate, choosing to abide the decision of the national convention. But the Whig leaders of the State, Bell, Bailie Peyton, Jarnigan, Foster, Fogg, Hall, Barrow, Zollicoffer, and the leading newspapers of the State, persisted in pushing the claims of Hugh L. White, and the electoral vote of the State was cast for him. The only paper that opposed White was the McMinnville *Gazette*, whose editor, Ford, Mr. Harris used to compliment as "among the faithless faithful only he." On the 4th of March, 1839, Mr. Polk left the speaker's chair at Washington and took the stump for governor against the incumbent, Newton Cannon. Mr. Harris had preceded him about three months, and espoused the cause of the future governor, who acknowledged that his triumph was more largely due to Mr. Harris than to any other one of his friends.

The success that crowned the indefatigable labors of young Harris was due, in a great measure, to the constant counsel and advice of Gen. Jackson, then in retirement, who was accustomed to send for him and have him often at the Hermitage, giving him the cue to national and state affairs of the day. Indeed, he at one time strongly recommended Mr. Harris to President Tyler as our minister to Brazil, that our too long delayed claims against that government for spoliations on our commerce in the river La Plata might be promptly settled. Their confidential and cordial relations continued up to the time of the veteran's death, after which, as making record of his gratitude, Mr. Harris delivered Tennessee's eulogy of him at Charlotte, which,

with twenty-five other similar discourses by eminent men in the different States of the Union, was incorporated in a handsome volume that passed through many editions, entitled "A Monument to Jackson."

The history of the newspapers and newspaper editors of Tennessee might justify a separate volume. At the time to which this biography refers, money was not thought of as a means of carrying elections or controlling the press. Mr. Harris, for example, tells his friends that he was never offered and never received a dollar to advocate any measure, or the claims of any political candidate. The press of that day discussed principles, and favored men who represented those principles. The discussion opened on principles, the United States Bank, the tariff, internal improvements by the general government, then dividing the two parties. The contest was the inauguration of what has been aptly styled "hot politics." "Principles, not men," was the cry raised for the first time in the State. Gen. Armstrong ran against Cannon, in 1837, for governor, and was beaten by about twenty thousand majority. In 1839, Mr. Polk overcame Cannon's majority, and was elected by four thousand majority, and a Democratic Legislature was elected which instructed Mr. Foster out of the United States senate and sent Felix Grundy in his stead. Such was the result of Mr. Harris' aggressive political policy as the editor of a leading newspaper of the State.

Mr. Harris married at Nashville, Tennessee, May 5, 1842, Miss Lucinda McGavock, daughter of James McGavock,[*] and granddaughter of David McGavock, of Virginia, who settled at Nashville in 1785–86. Mrs. Harris was born February 18, 1817, and died June 23, 1847. She was educated at the Nashville Female Academy, under Dr. Lapsley, and was in all respects a superior woman, of intellectual culture and great beauty and comeliness of person. The McGavocks are a numerous and prominent family in Davidson and Williamson counties, Tennessee, and are noted—the men for being of sterling character, first-class business men and farmers and fine judges of land, while the women, among their many excellencies, for being model housekeepers and for their whole-souled and unstinted hospitality. By his marriage with Miss McGavock, Mr.

---

[*]The Rev. Robert Gray, of Gallatin, Tennessee, has prepared for publication the genealogy of the McGavock family of Davidson county, entitled "James McGavock and his Descendants," from which it appears that the James here referred to was grandson of the first James, and son of David McGavock, one of the first settlers of Nashville. We are permitted to make the following extract from these very valuable manuscripts : "James McGavock, grandson of the first James, and grandson of David McGavock and Elizabeth (nee McDowell), was born in Virginia, March 28, 1790, and died near Nashville, January 23, 1841. He married Mary Kent, May 12, 1812. Mrs. McGavock, was the eldest child of Col. Joseph Kent, and Margaret (nee McGavock), and also granddaughter of the first James McGavock, was born December 28, 1788, and died April 5, 1827. They settled on the half of a quarter section of land, a part of which is now within the limits of East Nashville, where they had children, as follows : (1). Margaret

K. McGavock, born June 3, 1813 ; married Hardy Bryan, in 1833 ; died, March 21, 1835. (2). Sarah Jane McGavock, born in 1815 ; died an infant. (3). Lucinda McGavock, born February 18, 1817, married Jeremiah George Harris, May 5, 1842 ; died June 23, 1847. (4). Wiley McGavock, born in November, 1818 ; died in 1838, (5). Joseph K. McGavock, born September 27, 1820 ; died (unmarried), September 10, 1845. (6). Mary K. McGavock, born in 1826 ; married Albert G. Wilcox, January 10, 1849 ; died March 9, 1867." The remains of all these, with the exception of those of Mrs. Wilcox, were interred in the little family cemetery near their dwelling, on the spot marked as "Pleasant Mount," upon the old McGavock map of Nashville, reproduced in the "History of Davidson County," but late extension of the city limits rendered it necessary that they should be removed, and in 1883 they were transferred to Lot No. 47, section 5, in Mount Olivet cemetery, at Nashville. Tennessee.

Harris had but two children: Joseph Ewing Harris, educated at Nashville University and Yale College, who died in London, England, August 28, 1865, at the age of 22; and Lucie Harris, educated at Nashville, Philadelphia and Boston, who became the wife of Dr. Van S. Lindsley, lately deceased, whose sketch see elsewhere in this volume.

Mr. Harris is descended from two of the oldest families of America. He is the great-grandson of William Latham, who commanded at Fort Griswold, and also of Parke Avery, his lieutenant. The genealogy of the Avery family is as follows: Christopher Avery was born in England, and died in 1681; James Avery, born 1620, in England, died in 1694; James Avery, 2d, born December 16, 1646, died August 22, 1728; Ebenezer Avery, born May 1, 1678, died July 19, 1752; Elder Parke Avery, born December 9, 1710, died March 14, 1797; Lieut. Parke Avery, born March 22, 1741, died December 20, 1821; Youngs Avery, born April 2, 1767, died May 30, 1837. Mary, eldest daughter of Youngs Avery, born January 19, 1790, married, November 25, 1807, to Richard Harris, of Norwich, Connecticut, by whom she had two children, Jeremiah George Harris and Erastus Richard Harris. She died at Groton, February 2, 1881.

The paternal ancestry of Mr. Harris appears as follows: Walter Harris, born in England in 1600, died at New London, 1654; Gabriel Harris, son of Walter, born in 1630, died in 1684; John Harris, son of Gabriel, born in 1663, died in 1740; Richard Harris, son of John, born in 1700, died in 1751; Jeremiah Harris, son of Richard, born in 1745, died in 1797; Richard Harris, son of Jeremiah, born in 1786, died in 1816; Jeremiah George, son of Richard, born in 1809; Joseph Ewing, son of Jeremiah George, born in 1843, died in 1865.

Mr. Harris' mother was the daughter of Youngs Avery and his wife, Eunice Latham, daughter of Capt. William Latham. These families took an active part in the Indian wars more than two hundred years ago, and were more or less distinguished in the legislature and on the bench, as well as in the field; and their descendants, becoming very numerous, are to be found in almost every State of the Union. True to their patriotic lineage, the immediate ancestors of Mary Avery Harris, her paternal grandfather, Lieut. Parke Avery, and her maternal grandfather, Capt. William Latham, were officers of the Continental army during the American Revolution. They served with Washington at and around Boston before the declaration of independence, continuing in the service up to the close of the war, and were both severely wounded in the battle of Groton Heights, September 6th, 1781. Capt. Latham commanded at Fort Griswold up to the time when Col. Ledyard, as his superior officer, came from New London, and then took command on the morning of the battle.

On the 25th of November, 1807, Mary Avery was married to Richard Harris, of Norwich, by Rev. John Gano Whitman. Her husband was the son of Jeremiah Harris, a descendant of the sixth generation of Walter Harris, from England, who settled in New London in 1650. Richard was born at Norwich, May 25, 1786. Their married life, begun in their youth, was remarkably happy, but brief. He had chosen the sea as a profession, and it became his burial place, on the 21st of September, 1816, while on his passage home from the West Indies.

Left a widow with two children, Mr. Harris' mother taught school twenty consecutive summers near her home. After they were grown, she devoted herself to the filial care of her aged parents. The Rev. Jared R. Avery, to whose church she belonged, and who preached her funeral sermon, at Groton, Connecticut, said of her: "If Mary Avery Harris did not fill the measure of true womanhood to the brim, where will you find a character that has filled it? True to every duty of wife, daughter, mother, friend and neighbor, her pure and active life of faith, hope and charity is left to us an example which, if followed, will surely, through grace, entitle us, as it has entitled her, to 'a mansion not made with hands, eternal in the heavens.'"

HON. JAMES FENTRESS.

BOLIVAR.

THE Fentress family, as far back as the genealogy is traceable, appears to have ever been, as now, a family of strongly-marked characteristics. It is accepted as an early fact in the family history that the great-great-grandfather of the subject of this sketch, being the son of an English 'squire, was the accepted lover of the daughter of aristocratic English parents who resolutely refused their consent to the marriage. The young couple contrived to make their way to Gretna Green, and were married in defiance of parental opposition. The groom, with characteristic pride, refused to claim, nor would he consent that his wife should claim, any part of the estate which was hers in her own right. Actuated by a like motive, his descendants refrained from asserting any claim to the inheritance.

James Fentress, the grandfather of the subject of this sketch, was a conspicuous and influential man in Tennessee, in his day, as the annals of the State abundantly testify. He was speaker of the house of representatives for nineteen years, an occupancy of that chair that has no parallel in our State history.

David Fentress, the father, was a native of Robertson county, though the better part of his life was spent in Hardeman county. He was a lawyer of fine ability, and practiced his profession at Bolivar and in the neighboring courts for twenty-five years with brilliant success. At one time he represented his county (Hardeman) in the Legislature. He was a man of marked literary taste and extensive reading. He was regarded as the best read man in his section, and was invariably appealed to as an authority in all controversies of a literary or historical character. Like Carlyle, he had an irrepressible contempt for shams, and this characteristic imparted a satirical tone to his utterances that was not conducive to personal popularity, though he was universally regarded as the ablest man in his county, and thoroughly honest in all his dealings. He was a man of very strong individuality. He died in 1856, at the age of fifty-six.

Matilda Fentress, the mother, was the daughter of David Wendell, a noted merchant of Murfreesborough, and a man of great moral and Christian influence. She was educated at the Moravian school, in Salem, North Carolina. As illustrating the changes that have taken place in the methods of travel since that day, it may be mentioned that she returned home from Salem on horseback, in company with her father, by way of Philadelphia, he taking that city in the route for the purchase of goods. She first married Evander McIver, of Rutherford county. He dying, she subsequently became the wife of David Fentress, and the mother of five children: Dr. David W. Fentress, now living in

San Saba, Texas, engaged in the raising of cattle; James, the subject of this sketch; Francis, a lawyer, in Bolivar; Kate, the wife of Hon. Albert T. McNeal, a lawyer, in Bolivar; Sallie W., who married Jerome Hill, a leading commission merchant, formerly of Memphis, Tennessee, but now of St. Louis, Missouri. The mother, now past her threescore years and ten, makes her home among her children, chiefly with her son James. Of her five children, all are living. For forty-five years after her marriage, there was not a death among her children or her children's children, who had reached the number of forty-five. She is an orthodox Presbyterian, as are also the children, except the two daughters, who went with their husbands into the Episcopal communion. Her sister Susan married Dr. Lunsford P. Yandell, sr., who was, for many years, the leading professor in the medical university, at Louisville, Kentucky. His sons, Lunsford P. and David W. Yandell are well known surgeons in Louisville. David W. was surgeon-general of the Trans-Mississippi department, in the Confederate service. Lunsford P. Yandell was surgeon of the Fourth Tennessee regiment (Col. Neely). Her brothers, Drs. James E. and Robert S. Wendell, are well-known physicians of Murfreesborough.

Judge Fentress was born, July 27, 1837, at Murfreesborough, while his mother was on a visit to her parents. He grew up at Bolivar, enjoying all the advantages for early instruction which the town afforded. His education was completed at the University of Virginia, in 1856–7. He studied law in the office of his half-uncle, John R. Fentress, at Bolivar, and was licensed to practice by Judges Humphreys and Read, in 1859. He pursued his profession in Bolivar with most flattering prospects until the breaking out of the war, when he at once enlisted in the provisional army of Tennessee for the Confederate service. He was chosen first lieutenant of Company B (Capt. R. P. Neely), Fourth Tennessee infantry, being the first company organized in Hardeman county. The regiment went into service May 14, 1861. Capt. Neely was afterwards made colonel of the regiment, and Lieut. Fentress became captain of the company. The regiment first rendezvoused at Germantown, and then went to Randolph; from Randolph it moved to Fort Pillow, and thence into Missouri, under Gen. Pillow. It returned by way of Hickman, Kentucky, and took possession of Columbus, in that State. From this point it was ordered to Island Number Ten, and thence to the battle of Shiloh, in which it participated. After this, Capt. Fentress, being prostrated by dysentery and pronounced incapacitated for service, was permanently and honorably discharged.

His health rallying, however, he re-entered the service as a private in the Seventh Tennessee cavalry (Col. Duckworth), and served till the close of the war.

The war ended, Judge Fentress, broken in health and fortune, resumed the practice of the law at Bolivar, and soon, by his talents and industry, was rewarded with a lucrative and steadily growing business. In 1870, he was induced to become a candidate for the constitutional convention of Tennessee, and was triumphantly elected over a popular opponent. Although he was one of the younger members, he took a high stand in that body, discussing the leading questions presented with the ability of a matured statesman. It was in this body that he first conspicuously displayed that independence of thought and courage of assertion which themselves proved their legitimacy of inheritance from his father, and which have since been characteristic of the man. He boldly advocated what he believed to be right, without stopping to consider whether he was in the majority or the minority.

Returning from the convention, he resumed the practice of his profession at Bolivar. The election of judicial officers, under the new constitution, soon coming on, he became a candidate for chancellor of the Tenth chancery division and was elected, defeating Chancellor John W. Harris, of Somerville, and Chancellor T. C. Muse, of Jackson. Having served two years with much distinction, and to the great satisfaction of the bar and people of the division, he resigned the chancellorship and resumed his profession, which he found much more remunerative than the office he had vacated. In 1876, he was engaged as the chief attorney of the Tennessee receiver of the Mississippi Central railroad, and after the sale of the New Orleans, Jackson and Great Northern railroad and the Mississippi Central railroad, which were afterward consolidated into the Chicago, St. Louis and New Orleans railroad, he became general solicitor for the consolidated line. This position he held from 1877 to 1882, when the consolidated road was leased for four hundred years to the Illinois Central railroad company. He then became, and is yet, the general solicitor of the Illinois Central and branches, in the States of Tennessee, Mississippi, Kentucky and Louisiana. He is also general solicitor of the Yazoo and Mississippi Valley railroad company, the West and East railroad company, the New Orleans Belt railroad company, and was the first president of the Canton, Aberdeen and Nashville railroad company, of which he is now also general solicitor. These accumulative engagements, involving, as they do, the most delicate, laborious and responsible trusts known to the profession, indicate,

better than any words can do, in what high esteem Judge Fentress is held as a lawyer by the most careful and intelligent business men of the country.

Judge Fentress was happily married in Bolivar, August 24, 1859, to Miss Mary Tate Perkins, daughter of Joseph W. Perkins, formerly a lawyer of Nashville, who was killed in the Mexican war. Her mother was Mary Talbott, of Nashville, a most excellent lady. Mrs. Fentress was educated at Ward's Seminary. Ten children have been born to Judge and Mrs. Fentress: Mary Warren, educated at Miss Baldwin's school, at Staunton, Virginia, and afterward studied two years at the celebrated school of Miss Sarah Porter, at Farmington, Connecticut; Matilda, educated in New York city; Anna Perkins, who died in Chicago, 1878, aged twelve years; Thomas, who died in 1883, in Wyoming territory, on his return with his father from San Francisco; James; David; Frank, who died in 1877, aged three years; Wendell, who died in 1879, aged three years; Calvin; Ethel, a daughter.

The daughters, after receiving their education, went with their mother to Europe, in care of Miss Meta D. Huger, principal of St. Catharine school, at New Orleans, where they spent the summer and fall of 1882, visiting all the capitals of the continent. Judge Fentress, himself, visited Europe, in 1883, to make a personal study of its civilization and form a satisfactory estimate of its people.

As to religion, Judge Fentress, his wife and family are members of the Presbyterian church, of which he has been an elder. In regard to politics, the Fentresses, so far as known, have all been Democrats. The Judge is no exception. He is a decided Democrat, though but little of his time and thought have been devoted to partisan interests. His duties and interests as a lawyer have engrossed his attention for many years. There is not a lawyer in the State who has more exclusively dedicated himself to his profession than he. Nothing has been permitted to divert his mind from the duties he has undertaken, and a most brilliant and gratifying success has been his reward.

Personally, Judge Fentress is most highly esteemed by his immediate fellow-citizens. He has never been a seeker after popularity, and what he enjoys is simply the result of an upright life and a strict attention to his own business. In 1859, he became a Master Mason, and afterwards took the Chapter and Council degrees.

Though Judge Fentress resides, eight months in the year, at No. 207 St. Charles street, New Orleans, he still retains his citizenship in Hardeman county, Tennessee. He clings with affection to his native State.

JOHN R. GODWIN.

MEMPHIS.

THIS eminent merchant, financier and business man, whose career has been so successful, so honorable and so praiseworthy, well deserves a place in this volume as an example for the guidance of the youth of the State. He was born in Cumberland county, North Carolina, November 19, 1830, and nine years later moved, with his father, to Middle Tennessee and settled near Lewisburg. There he lived eight years, on a farm, attending school meantime at Cedar Springs and Rock creek camp-ground, near Farmington. In 1847, the family moved to West Tennessee and settled one mile from Raleigh, then the county seat of Shelby county. Here he worked on a farm and went to school —never attending college, but received a fair English education at the Raleigh Academy, finishing in 1851. That fall he took charge of a country school, three miles north of Raleigh, and taught one session of five months.

In 1852, he started for California with the rush of emigrants for the gold fields, leaving home February 2, in company with five friends—W. B. Reaves, now of Coahoma county, Mississippi, James Allen, Elam Pharr, Edward Parsons, and James Wickham—all young men, about his own age, and from the same neighborhood. Proceeding to New Orleans, they took a steamer for Aspinwall, where they arrived about the middle of February, crossed the Isthmus, twenty-seven miles, on foot, and took passage on a sailing vessel, at Panama, for San Francisco. After being at sea for eighty days, they put into the port of San Blas, on the coast of Mexico, having undergone great hardships on account of the scarcity of provisions and water, and losing thirty of the crew and passengers by death. The vessel had been chartered at Panama, but the captain declined to go further, not having money to reprovision his vessel for the voyage, and most of the passengers were compelled to remain at San Blas for three months. Some of them, among whom were all of Mr. Godwin's friends, except Mr. Wickham. took passage on an American bark, bound for San Francisco, and they parted company with him, never to meet again. Mr. Godwin remained behind with his friend, Mr. Wickham, who had been taken sick. Finally, they took passage on another American bark, together with about two hundred of the three hundred passengers who had first left Panama, and arrived at San Francisco September 11, after a long, hard voyage, during which they again suffered greatly for provisions and water, having been forty days out from San Blas, and eight months on the trip from home.

At San Francisco Messrs. Godwin and Wickham met Col. William Gift, uncle of Mr. Wickham, and an old friend of Mr. Godwin's father, who told them that their friends at home had given them up for lost, and he had also come to the same conclusion. After remaining in San Francisco a few days, Mr. Godwin parted with his friend, Mr. Wickham, whom he has never seen since, and went up the Sacramento river to Tehama, where his brother, Allen Godwin, and two friends, Thomas and Moody C. King, who had gone to California two years before, were living. Arriving there he found them the owners of a hay ranch and running teams to Shasta City, sixty miles away in the mining regions, hauling supplies for the miners. Without a moment's delay he sought employment. A brief greeting, an account of his trip, a square meal eaten on a log, and he was ready for work. In two hours after his arrival he was assisting Mr. Moody King in baling hay. After a short time he engaged in teaming, which was then considered the most profitable and most honorable business that the country afforded. Mr. Godwin's experiences during his residence in California include many interesting incidents. The population on his arrival consisted entirely of eager, bold, adventurous men, there being not a woman or child in all the distance of sixty miles between Tehama and Shasta City. The first woman who went into that region was a Mrs. Read, whose husband is still living, near Red Bluff. On one occasion Mr. Godwin and his brother camped on the site of the present town of Red Bluff, at the head of navigation on the Sacramento river, the very night, in fact, that the town was laid off, there being then no sign of a house there. During the night their commissary department was raided by prairie wolves who left them without supplies for breakfast. In July, 1883, Mr. Godwin revisited the spot, and found one of the most flourishing towns in north California. Upon inquiry he received the sad intelligence that many of the companions of his early days, most of whom had been young men of education and high standing before leaving the east, had turned out badly. Some of them had met violent deaths, while many had contracted evil habits. Those who were still living were scattered over the State. The failure of these friends of his early manhood was, no doubt, due to the absence of moral and religious influence, and the lack of refined female society.

After he had been with his brother and the Messrs. King about three years, they all sold out and returned to Tennessee together. During the three years and nine days that Mr. Godwin was in California, he was not out of employment more than nine days. Though an inexperienced boy when he went out, he had been successful and had accumulated about seven thousand dollars. During all his stay, though away from civilization, and where rough living was prevalent, he had not taken a drink of spirits or played a card, an example which all young men would do well to follow.

On September 20, 1855, he and his companions took passage at San Francisco, on a steamer, for Panama, crossed the Isthmus on the new railroad, which was the first railway that he had seen, and embarked for New York, where they landed October 16, 1855. They then visited Philadelphia and had their savings, which were in gold dust, exchanged for coin at the mint, and proceeded direct to Memphis.

He then went to visit his father at the old homestead, and for the next two years was not engaged in any regular business. In the fall of 1857, he went into merchandising, in partnership with Mr. J. W. A. Jones, at Batesville, Panola county, Mississippi, a new town on the Mississippi and Tennessee railroad, where he helped to build the second house that was erected in that town. At Batesville he remained until the spring of 1860. Having married in the meantime, and desiring to get into a more healthy locality with his family, he closed out his business, which was in a prosperous condition, moved to Drew county, Arkansas, and bought a plantation near Monticello, and there engaged in planting. After the war begun he moved to Ashley county, Arkansas, and bought a plantation on Bayou Bartholomew. He had invested his money in slaves, mules and farming supplies, all of which were swept away by the war. His father having died in 1857, he became the guardian of seven half-sisters and two small half-brothers: these, with the step-mother, had removed and settled in the same neighborhood with him, Drew county, Arkansas, in 1860. The care of this large and helpless family, in a new and strange country, together with his own young wife and two small children, prevented him from going into the war during the first two years.

In the early part of 1863, he entered the First Arkansas regiment of cavalry as a private in company D, commanded by Capt. J. A. Jackson. He was connected with the army of Gen. Price in the division of Fagan and brigade of Slemmons, and served in Missouri, Arkansas and Louisiana. He was with Price in 1864, on his famous raid through north Arkansas, Missouri and into Kansas, returning by way of Fort Scott and crossing the Arkansas river about sixty miles west of Fort Smith. He took part in all the many battles of this raid. After the surrender of most of the other southern troops, his command disbanded on Red river, above Shreveport, and he returned to his home May 5, 1865. Though he had it in his power to obtain promotion, his only ambition was to make a good private soldier, and after the war his commander, Gen. Slemmons, said that he had no superior, as such, in his command.

Reaching home he found his family in very bad health, and as soon as they were able to travel, he removed them to his father-in-law's, in Shelby county, Tennessee, while he continued planting in Arkansas. He also en-

gaged in merchandising, taking the first stock of goods to Ashley county that was carried there after the war. In the spring of 1866, he gave up merchandising, and in the fall of 1867, sold out his planting interests in Arkansas, and settled on a farm which he had bought in Shelby county, Tennessee, in 1866. In September, 1869, he went into business at Memphis, as a cotton factor and commission merchant, at first alone, but after five or six months he associated with him Mr. Robert Spillman, and formed the firm of Godwin & Spillman, which was dissolved after one year on account of the ill health of Mr. Spillman. After this Mr. Godwin continued alone for five years, under the firm name of J. R. Godwin & Co., and then took as partners his brother-in-law, L. D. Mullins, jr., and Mr. S. M. McCallum, and continued under the same firm name till 1882, when Mr. McCallum left the business, which has been conducted by Mr. Godwin and Mr. Mullins till the present time. Mr. Godwin is now the head of a firm which, by careful management, has always been successful, and does now a business of about three quarters of a million dollars a year, while its position among the business houses of Memphis is one of the first.

He has been prominently connected with most of the financial and commercial enterprises of Memphis, and has been identified with various schemes for her material advancement. He has also been the author of numerous articles in the papers of the city, looking to her general welfare. He has been president of the Gayoso oil works since their organization, three years ago; was one of the founders of the Mercantile Bank of Memphis, and has been its president from its organization. This bank has had the remarkable history of having paid a dividend of five per cent. during the first half year of its existence, and when eleven months old its stock was worth from 1.20 to 1.25, with none on the market for sale. He is also a director in the Planters Insurance company, one of the largest in the State. His career as a business man has been one of almost uninterrupted success. Not avaricious, but possessing capacity for accumulating property, he is in possession of a handsome estate, and his fidelity in the positions of trust in the business relations above referred to gives him a reputation second to none among the leading men of the city of Memphis.

Mr. Godwin was married, November 15, 1859, in Shelby county, Tennessee, to Miss Mary F. Mullins. Her father, Rev. Lorenzo Dow Mullins, a Methodist minister, was born in Bedford county, Tennessee, April 6, 1809, and died July 12, 1880. Her mother, Miss Martha Ann McGehee, was born in Louisa county, Virginia, January 28, 1811, and removed to Lawrence county, Alabama, with her parents, in childhood. She was married May 20, 1835, and died April 26, 1876. Mrs. Godwin, who was their third child, was born at Lagrange, Alabama, July 4, 1839. To this union have been born four children, three of whom are now living: (1). Annie May Godwin, born in Shelby county, Tennessee, August 27, 1860; now married to Mr. J. J. Polk, son of Col. Jack Polk, of Bolivar, Tennessee. (2). Lorenzo Russell Godwin, born in Drew county, Arkansas, August 4, 1864; now a student at Vanderbilt University. (3). Robert Allen Godwin, born in Memphis, Tennessee, April 11, 1876. Their eldest son, John Thomas Godwin, who was born in Drew county, Arkansas, March 4, 1862, died January 19, 1875. Mrs. Godwin was educated under Dr. Joseph Douglass, at Marshall Institute, in Marshall county, Mississippi, graduating there in 1858. She is a lady of remarkable piety, has been a consistent member of the Methodist church since her childhood, and now occupies a prominent position among the ladies of her church. Mr. Godwin joined the Methodist church at Monticello, Arkansas, in 1861, and has been an official member from a short time after joining up to the present time. He has represented his church in a number of annual conferences, and was a delegate to the general conference which met at Atlanta, Georgia, in 1878. Mr. Godwin's father, Handy Godwin, who died in 1857, was of English descent, and born in North Carolina. His grandfather, Seth Godwin, was a farmer in North Carolina. His mother, who died in 1832, was Miss Mary McQueen, daughter of Hugh and Effie McQueen, natives of Scotland. They came to Cumberland county, North Carolina, after they were married, and he there engaged in farming. Two of Mr. Godwin's uncles, Norman and John McQueen, went to Wetumpka, Alabama, during early Indian times, and became prominent and successful merchants.

Mr. Godwin was raised an old line Whig, but since the war has been a Democrat. While taking a lively interest in political affairs, he has never consented to become a candidate for office, preferring to devote his time and energy to his business.

His principles have been to act with the strictest integrity in all dealings with all men, and to work with untiring energy upon whatever he had to do, believing that honest, hard work is the shortest road to success. A man is never successful by chance. He has always been very careful about sustaining his credit, and pays his debts dollar for dollar, with interest. He is temperate in his habits, having, in this respect, kept up through life the plan which he pursued while in California. He endeavors to be courteous to all men, and as a result, has never wanted for true friends in any emergency of his life. Integrity, industry and perseverance form the basis of his success. In founding the new government of Memphis, and rescuing the city from the hopeless bankruptcy and ruin which seemed to stare her in the face, Mr. Godwin played an active part. The following account of his connection with these affairs, is from Col. George Gantt, of Memphis, who was an active co-worker in the events narrated:

"The subject of this sketch became prominent in the revolution that overturned the long established form of government in Memphis, and substituted for it the taxing district method of governing. Prior to that, he was chiefly known as a quiet, good citizen, and prominent, as a commercial man, in the specialty of handling cotton among the brainy cotton kings of 'Front Row.' In the dark days of 1878, and near the close of the year, the commanding figure of John R. Godwin was seen in all the meetings on the absorbing topic of abolishing the city government. He was on special and select committees. No man was better equipped for the work. He studied the question with keen interest, and mastered it. He fixed in his mind, that all local government was a mere ruling agency; that it had no element of contract in it; that it was created to serve and promote the welfare of the local territory over which it was set to rule; that when it ceased to do this it was a useless expense; that when, as in the case of the city government of Memphis, it had not only outlived its usefulness, but had become an instrument to oppress and plunder the people for whose welfare it was established, it ought to be cut up by the roots; that the Legislature which made, could destroy, and relief was to be sought and found only in the speedy and complete extinction of the local government by the unconditional repeal of its charter. Few of the masses of the community then understood that the cumbrous machinery, called the city government, was a mere ruling agency, that could be cut up root and branch by a simple abrogation of its charter. To give up its charter and its name was a startling proposition for a city of thirty or forty thousand souls. But the affairs of the community were desperate. The city government was bankrupt, and without credit to buy supplies, even for the hospital. By mismanagement and mal-administration, it had created millions of debt. Whilst it existed, it served no purpose except to enable its hordes of greedy creditors to wring, in the way of taxes, money from a desperate and despairing people, to meet this great debt. In the face of this appalling condition of things, and when just fairly emerged from the great scourge of 1878, which cut down five thousand of the population, and drove thousands away perhaps never to return, the community located on the 'Chickasaw bluffs,' needed leaders and wise counselors. In that exigency, John R. Godwin first appeared as one of the leaders. From the first, he was connected with those who led the movement for disenthrallment and redemption. The remedy proposed was so new as to be startling—it was revolution. The first step was the total abolition of all local government. The timid, the selfish, the creditors, those who had prospered in evil times, and many who acted from honorable convictions, formed a powerful opposition to the new ideas; but Godwin and others cast these ideas as 'seed thoughts' among the people. They took root; everywhere the question was debated the public mind was profoundly agitated; it was the sole topic discussed. In all of this Mr. Godwin bore a conspicuous part. Those who doubted, he sought to convince; the timid, he endeavored to inspire with courage; those who opposed, he boldly met. He was well qualified by nature for the work. Strong and forebearing, courteous and sagacious, well informed and firm as a rock, and enlisted soul and body, he exerted a powerful influence. His purse was open; he gave his time, either in Memphis or at the capital of the State, as duty or necessity required. Wherever there was hard, earnest work to be done, there he was sure to be found. Withal, he was modest and unobtrusive. When the old government disappeared, he was active in the installment of its successor. What is this taxing district? was asked on all hands. Will it stand the ordeal of the courts? Will it work? Who are to fill its offices? He was with the foremost in answering all these questions, and in putting the best men into the offices. He declined all place and preferment himself. He was unselfish and wise, in the important part he bore in filling the official stations with material fit to rule. It was a bold experiment. There were good sense and rare good fortune in the choice of the head of the new government. Wisdom and sagacity, uniting with an unselfish desire to govern well and wisely, filled all the places of official trust with first-class men. The men who first held office under the experiment in government, all deserve the lasting gratitude of the community. In all the struggles in the courts, and in all the elections since the new government began, Mr. Godwin gave valuable aid. His time and his money were freely bestowed. At every session of the General Assembly, since the establishment of the taxing district, there has been more or less important work to do. In all this work Mr. Godwin has borne a prominent part. He resisted, with great force and efficiency, all efforts to impose the debt of the old government upon the new. He faced the persistent effort to do so, and fought it at every step. Powerful interests urged a settlement of the old debt at what he conceived to be a ruinous sum. The Legislature was again and again appealed to on the subject. Many earnest debates arose before the committees appointed by the Legislature to consider the subject. In these debates Mr. Godwin took part. He was encountered by able and earnest men. In these contests he displayed that strong common sense with which he is endowed by nature, and his compact array of facts and figures were hard to resist. Without practice in debate, without eloquence or wit or humor, he was nevertheless very persuasive and forcible. He was strong and logical. Every word stood for an idea; and his ideas were couched in simple and clear terms that went right to the heart of the matter.

" In the final steps which resulted in the settlement of the debt question of the old city government, Mr. Godwin was a conspicuous factor. When the time had ar-

rived for settlement and terms were offered which, in his judgment, the people could bear, he urged their acceptance with all the earnestness and power of his nature. His candor, his well known devotion to the public welfare, his unselfishness and soundness of judgment, gave him great influence in the final and fortunate disposition of this grave and important question to the 'Bluff City.'

" He has, at all times, refused office. He has been earnestly urged to serve as an officer of the local government, as a member of the Legislature, and favorably spoken of for a seat in Congress. But he has declined all these tempting solicitations. In reference to the conspicuous part he bore in the important local affairs of the great and flourishing community in which he lives, he is far from self-asserting, and points with pride and unstinted commendation to others, who were his worthy co-laborers in the good work, as far more deserving than himself. Merit and modesty are often companions. They go well together. Both adorn the character of Mr. Godwin.

" Memphis was visited by a second great epidemic of yellow fever in 1879. It caused profound depression. Great and costly sanitary measures were necessary to save the city. Many thought there was no hope. It was indeed a dark hour. How could a community so stricken and so unfortunate as this was meet the demands necessary for so great and costly a work. No account which omits the part which Mr. Godwin bore in this important affair would be complete. On the 16th of October, 1879, he addressed to the public, through the Memphis Appeal, a letter on this vital question. That letter embodied his own views and those of other leading spirits, whose opinions were in accord with his. It went a long way in shaping and directing public sentiment. The following synopsis will show the scope and spirit of the letter: ' As quite a number of gentlemen have discussed the sanitary needs of Memphis through your paper in connection with what they term the merchants' meeting in St. Louis, and as none of them have given the reasons for the action taken by the Memphis citizens in that meeting, I will endeavor, in the plainest and simplest manner, to do so. This question has been discussed in doors and on the streets almost constantly since I came to St. Louis on the 1st of September. One could scarcely talk five minutes to a Memphis man or woman without hearing this expression: ' What is to be done with Memphis?' Can it be reclaimed? Is there no way of remedying the cause of sickness and making it habitable? If not, then we must look for other quarters, as we are heartily tired of being driven from home and business in this way every year.' This feeling of uncertainty and dread as to the future of Memphis, gave rise to much consultation among those of us here, before the meeting, as to the best method of raising funds for the accomplishment of this work. It was agreed that nothing but a complete sewerage system would give a feeling of security for the future. A stock company was first suggested. It was thought that sufficient capital could be raised in this way, to build main sewers and force property owners to connect with them at a fixed price. This plan was objected to on the ground (1) that it would be a monopoly, and would in some way, manage to be oppressive; and (2) that no legal enactment could compel the lot owners to connect with a corporate sewer any more than he could be compelled to take water or gas from a corporation. This would, of course, defeat the object of sanitation, which to be perfect and effective, must have connection with every lot within reach of a main. The second method—the one adopted in the meeting—was to have the governor call the Legislature and ask them to levy a tax for the purpose of sewering the city and doing such other work as would be needed to put it into first-class condition. The reason for preferring this latter mode of raising the money are (1), free sewers, and every one can be forced to connect with them; and (2), it is the quickest and surest way of getting the means. There are quite a number of large estates which could be reached in no other way, besides a vast amount of corporate property, banks, railroads and insurance companies whose officers have no authority to contribute to this work but will pay the tax cheerfully. The design of this plan is to reach those who are able to pay on an equitable basis. All this talk about selling out the poor man with his little home is mere moonshine. This is a work for those that are able to do it, but we must have unity of action; it is a matter of life and death with us; of half a loaf or no loaf; whether we will live in a pest-house or a clean, beautiful city. The execution of the work we can safely trust to the efficient officers of the taxing district. We hear much said about the government doing the work for us; that the State Legislature would loan us money or donate certain State taxes. These are mere diversions. The expense of our citizens in running away this summer would do the work. Our loss in trade for this and the last month would more than do it over again. We must make up our minds to assist ourselves, or sell our birthright for a mess of pottage to some more resolute people. I learn Gov. Marks declines for the present to call the Legislature together. If nothing can be done earlier, I would suggest that as soon as we return home we come together and agree on what is best to be done; get our representatives in the Legislature to agree with us, and the governor will grant our request. Eight years ago the taxable values in our corporate limits were forty-eight millions, to-day they are sixteen millions, and if the fever remains a few years, they may be sunk much lower. We only ask the State to incur the insignificant amount required to assemble the Legislature. If we take our old place as tax payers, it would be repaid tenfold in a few years.' This letter became a kind of focus around which public sentiment was rallied. Frost came and drove out the

yellow plague. The people returned to their homes. The great question of improving the sanitary condition was never absent from their minds. Around their firesides, at their places of business, everywhere, it was the theme of themes. On the 15th of November, 1879, a great mass meeting was held on the 'bluffs' in front of the city. After many earnest speeches had been delivered, Mr. Godwin offered the following for adoption: 'Resolved by the people in mass meeting assembled, that we respectfully but earnestly appeal to his excellency, to call together at the earliest practicable moment the Legislature of the State, for the purpose of enacting such laws as will enable us to carry into practical operation those measures of sanitary reform which may be practicable and most conducive to the health of our city; and be it resolved further, that we do not regard such legislation as local in its character, but as in the largest sense affecting the property, happiness and lives of all the citizens of the commonwealth; and we therefore appeal to them by every tie of kinship, sentiment of humanity, and feeling of common interest, to join with us in invoking a call of the General Assembly in special session for the purposes aforesaid.' Mr. Godwin spoke briefly in advocacy of the resolution. He spoke with earnestness, with power and force. He spoke to eager ears—to a resolute, sorely tried, but strong audience, ready to meet the exigency, without regard to the sacrifice it involved. The resolutions were unanimously adopted. A committee of fifteen was appointed to carry out the objects contemplated, which they did by preparing suitable measures to be acted on by the Legislature. Gov. Marks (always the stanch friend of Memphis) convened the Legislature in extra session, on the 16th of December, 1879. The necessary legislation was speedily enacted, imposing a tax of two per cent. on all the taxable property of the local territory for the sole purpose of constructing an adequate underground system of drainage. The tax payers responded cheerfully and promptly to this additional burden. The result was the practical realization of what Mr. Godwin urged with so much force and earnestness in his letter of October 16, 1879—the Memphis system of sewerage—the best ever constructed down to that date, and which has probably added more to the present prosperity of Memphis than any thing that was ever done in her history."

These patriotic public scenes are mere episodes in the life of the subject of this sketch. When the public exigencies no longer required his services, he quietly disappeared, sinking himself again into the pursuit of his own private affairs. But it must not be supposed that he has become indifferent to the general welfare of the community in which he resides. It is impossible for such a character to be idle or indifferent, nor would his neighbors allow him to be idle or indifferent, if he felt so inclined. They know his value, and hence he is in demand always when something arises that calls for sound judgment, energy and courageous work.

REV. PETER MASON BARTLETT, A. M., D. D.

MARYVILLE.

THIS gentleman, now the president of Maryville College, Tennessee, was born in Salisbury, Connecticut, February 6, 1820, and there grew up to the thirteenth year of his age, when he went with his parents to Trumbull county, Ohio. In 1839, he entered Oberlin College, where he studied in the preparatory, freshman and sophomore classes two and a half years. He next taught in an academy, in Trumbull county, two years, returned to Oberlin for another year, married in 1845, and the same year took charge of the New Castle, Pennsylvania, Female Seminary, and taught there three years. He then moved to Williamstown, Massachusetts, and entered Williams College, at that place, graduating in August, 1850, with distinguished honors, under the celebrated president, Mark Hopkins. After graduation, he went to New York city, in September, 1850, entered the Union Theological Seminary, and, after completing the three years' course there, graduated in 1853. In the fall of that year, he became general agent of the American Tract Society, with headquarters in Cincinnati, and traveled through the southwestern part of the State, preaching and collecting funds for the society. In the winter of 1854, he went to Circleville, Ohio, took charge of the First Presbyterian church, of which he was the settled pastor for three years, ending July, 1857. His next work was at Lansingburg, New York, as pastor of the Olivet Presbyterian church, at that place. There he remained until 1860, when his wife and child dying, he preached, as a supply, in various places, till 1862, when he entered the Federal army as chaplain of the First New York mounted rifles, Col. C. C. Dodge commanding, and continued in that capacity till August, 1864, when he returned to Massachusetts and supplied a church for the winter, and then settled as pastor of the Congregational church at Windsor Locks, Connecticut, where he remained till March, 1869, when he accepted the presidency of Maryville (Tennessee) College, where he has lived ever since.

He is a man of tall, erect, military figure and carriage, and, it is said, looking not unlike "Stonewall" Jackson; is well preserved and active, with the gray eyes of the Greeks; a man of extensive travel and observation, in peace and war, and under greatly diversified circumstances; a man of books and schools and pastoral experience, of many woes and sorrows, but of great fortitude and cheerful spirits—one of the standard men of East Tennessee.

He was converted at the age of ten, joined the church at fifteen, felt called to the ministry at the age of sixteen, and from the beginning has, in the estimation of the church, lived a life consistent with his profession. He has three times been a delegate to the general assembly of the Presbyterian church of the United States of America. Theology has been his favorite study, and he is a Presbyterian—a Calvanist—a firm believer in man's free agency and in Divine sovereignty, and that all creatures are under God's control and subject to his Divine will. He has risen to distinction, not so much by being ambitious of worldly honor, as by a steady and conscientious discharge of his duties to God and to his fellow men. No friend has ever been solicited to help him forward in getting any prominent position in life. On the contrary, it has all come to him unsought. Thus the degree of D.D. was conferred upon him by Dartmouth College, New Hampshire, without his knowledge. The same is true of his presidency of the Maryville College. He began life without inheritance; his education was obtained mainly by his own efforts, excepting that in his theological studies he was assisted by the American Educational Society. He has taught schools twenty-five years, has preached thirty-three years, the last seventeen years of which he has not received enough money to defray his traveling expenses. In politics, he is a Republican; was for a short time a member of the Good Templars, in Connecticut. He is president of Maryville bank.

Dr. Bartlett's present wife, *nee* Florence M. Alden, whom he married at Cave Spring, Georgia, April 25, 1872, was born at Marietta, Georgia, November 26,1852, daughter of Col. Augustus Alden, a very distinguished educator of that State, who graduated at Yale College in 1817, and spent his time teaching high schools. He was successively president of the Masonic Female College, at Lumpkin, Georgia, and of the Andrews Female College, at Cuthbert, in the same State, and for twenty-five years an elder in the Presbyterian church; always noted for his piety, his handsome figure and profound classical scholarship. He died at Cave Spring, at the age of seventy-two, leaving seven children, of whom Mrs. B. is the youngest.

Mrs. Bartlett comes of an illustrious family. Her mother, Ann L., now living with her at Maryville, is the daughter of Hon. Wilson Lumpkin, the famous governor of Georgia, United States senator from that State, and a leading member of the Baptist church, at Athens, Georgia. He laid out Atlanta, and left a history of Georgia in manuscript, which, it is promised, will soon be published. His daughter, Mrs. Bartlett's mother, was a pupil of Col. Alden, whom she married. Through his father, Rev. Abisha Alden, a Congregational clergyman, at Montville, Connecticut, Col. Alden was a direct descendant of John Alden, of the "Mayflower," who figures as the hero in Longfellow's immortal poem, "Miles Standish's Courtship." On the paternal side, Mrs. Bartlett is the grand-niece of Hon. Joseph H. Lumpkin, an eminent Georgia jurist. Mrs.

Bartlett is a gifted and accomplished lady, distinguished for her strong character and good sense, and was educated in the institution her father taught, and at Columbia, South Carolina. She received her superb musical education in Georgia, New York, London and Dublin. She is a magnificent pianiste, probably without an equal in the South, certainly with few superiors. By his marriage with Miss Alden, Dr. Bartlett has two children: Mason Alden Bartlett, born January 20, 1873; William Thaw Bartlett, born September 20, 1876.

Dr. Bartlett's remote ancestor, Peter Bartlett, an officer in the British army, died near London. His sons, Robert and William Bartlett, came over to Plymouth, Massachusetts, in 1823. Robert Bartlett, the ancestor of Dr. Bartlett, was a prominent man and large property owner in Plymouth, where he died. Dr. Bartlett's grandfather, Sylvanus Bartlett, was a soldier in the Revolutionary war. The father, Isaiah Bartlett, was born in Plympton, Massachusetts, June 12, 1793, went to Connecticut, where he married, at Salisbury; was a wagon and carriage maker and farmer. He died July 17, 1867. He was a deacon of the church, of general reading, and some local prominence.

Dr. Bartlett's mother, Miriam Mason, was daughter of Peter Mason, of Salisbury, Connecticut, where she was born, July 8, 1795. She died September 6, 1879, in Ohio. Her father was a large property owner, and a soldier in the Revolution. Her mother was a Miss Farnham, of a Vermont family.

One of the Bartletts was a signer of the declaration of independence. Samuel Bartlett, president of Dartmouth College, is a descendant of William Bartlett, who came over with Dr. Bartlett's ancestor in 1623. The family is spread over New England and the West, and numbers among its members many professional men, lawyers, clergymen and educators.

Dr. Bartlett was brought up on a farm, worked hard, lived poor while a student, and by his own manual labor and teaching, with the little assistance before alluded to, he got his education. As a teacher, he has his own way, works in his own harness, has always been professionally successful, and is intellectually, physically, religiously, and in business habits, a representative New England man; scholarly, industrious, benevolent, and devoted to the elevation and advancement of the human race. It would be well for Tennessee if she could adopt many more such men as he.

REV. THOMAS W. HUMES, S. T. D.

KNOXVILLE.

REV. THOMAS W. HUMES, S.T.D., of Knoxville, is fairly a representative Tennesssean. He was born in that city, April 22, 1815, and has lived there all of his life. His grandfather, Humes, was an Irishman. His father, Thomas Humes, was also born in Armagh, Ireland, came when a boy to Pennsylvania, to his brother, Samuel, at Lancaster, whose descendants afterward intermarried with the family of Gov. Porter, of Pennsylvania. Very soon thereafter, Thomas Humes came to Tennessee trading. He merchandised at Morristown several years, moved to Knoxville about 1795, where he lived and died a merchant, in September, 1816, at the age of forty-eight. He was an elder in the Presbyterian church, and a man universally loved and trusted for his strict probity and kindly, benevolent disposition. He was one of the first trustees of Hampden-Sidney Academy, of Knoxville, appointed by the Legislature of Tennessee, in 1806. For that day he accumulated a respectable fortune by diligence in business.

Dr. Humes' mother was a woman of remarkable character. Her maiden name was Margaret Russell, daughter of John Russell, of Jefferson county, Tennessee. Her brother, Col. Gilbert Russell, of Mobile, distinguished himself in the war of 1812; was well known in

Washington circles, and left numerous children. Her brother, Andrew Russell, of Abingdon, Virginia, was widely known and highly esteemed in that State. His only child, Elizabeth, married Col. John G. Meem, of Lynchburg, Virginia. Another of her brothers, John Russell, was desperately wounded on the frontier of Canada, in the war of 1812, in the battles of. Bridgewater and Chippewa. Dr. Humes' maternal aunt, Sarah, married Mr. Hugh Martin, a merchant, of Dandridge, Tennessee. Dr. Humes' maternal aunt, Rebecca, married James Craig, a farmer, near Knoxville, an elder in the Presbyterian church, of whom the Hon. Pleasant Miller (son-in-law of old Gov. Blount, territorial governor of Tennessee), said: "James Craig is so honest a man I am willing to swear by him."

Dr. Humes' mother died at Knoxville, in 1854, in her seventy-seventh year, the mother of thirteen children. She was married three times, first to James Cowan, by whom she had four children, Margaret (wife of John C. Greenway, Abingdon, Virginia), Jane (married David Campbell), Mary (who died young) and James Hervey. She next married Thomas Humes, by whom she had eight children: John N., of Abingdon, Virginia, (father of Gen. W. Y. C. Humes, late of Mem-

63

phis), Mary (died the widow of Hon. John White, of Kentucky, formerly speaker of the United States house of representatives), Elizabeth (married Hugh A. M. White, nephew of Hugh Lawson White), Thomas William (subject of this sketch), Andrew Russell (who married the only daughter of John McGhee, was a noted Whig politician, but died at the age of thirty years.) Three other children, Thomas Scott, Sarah and Leah, died in their immaturity. By her last husband, Col. Francis A. Ramsey, a gentleman prominent in public affairs in the early history of Tennessee, she had one child, Dr. Francis A. Ramsey, widely known to the medical profession of Tennessee, notably as medical director of the Confederate army in East Tennessee during the war.

Dr. Humes' mother was a woman of old-fashioned scriptural piety, of great native vigor of mind, strength of will, and of capacity for affairs.

Dr. Humes graduated in his sixteenth year, at East Tennessee College, at Knoxville, under Rev. Charles Coffin, in 1830. His mother having intended that he should be a minister of the gospel, he commenced the study of theology under the direction of Rev. Stephen Foster, of Knoxville, a professor in the college, and became a candidate for orders in the Presbyterian church, in 1833. He afterward went to the Princeton Theological Seminary, where he studied one term. He withdrew his application for orders in the Presbyterian church because he was not able to make the subscription required of him, adopting the Westminister Confession of Faith as containing the system of doctrine taught in the word of God. He then gave his attention to mercantile pursuits.

In 1839, he became editor of the Knoxville *Times*, and afterward of the Knoxville *Register*, and was an active participant in the exciting canvass of 1840. After the successful canvass for Harrison and Tyler, his Whig friends nominated him in convention as a representative to the Legislature, but through their overconfidence of his success and consequent inactivity, he was defeated by a few votes.

This canvass satisfied Dr. Humes' political desires, and he turned his attention again to his relinquished purpose to become a Christian minister, but meeting with the same obstacle which he before encountered to his ordination as a Presbyterian minister, he was driven to sea, at a loss where to find a harbor. After various efforts to that end, he finally applied for orders to the Rt. Rev. James H. Otey, bishop of the Protestant Episcopal church in Tennessee, and was ordained by him a deacon of that church, at Columbia, Tennessee, on the 3d of March, 1845, and in the following August he was ordained a presbyter, by the same bishop, at Knoxville. A year before he had become a lay reader of the Protestant Episcopal church, at Knoxville, and in October, 1846, became the rector of St. John's church, Knoxville, and continued in that rectorship until 1861,

when, because of his sentiments in behalf of the Union of the States, and his unwillingness to offer prayers for the success of the Confederate government and arms, he was compelled to resign. The church, however, requested him to serve them until another minister could be had, which he accordingly did, till he met with the accident of having his leg broken by his horse running away with him, which forced him into inactivity. He remained without ministerial charge for two years, until the United States army, under Gen. Burnside, occupied Knoxville, in September, 1863. At his special request Dr. Humes resumed ministration in the church, there being no other minister at hand. The congregation immediately recalled him to the rectorship, and he continued in that service until the spring of 1869.

In the summer of 1865, he was unanimously elected president of the then East Tennessee University, now University of Tennessee, accepted the office reluctantly, but by urgent persuasion. The grounds and buildings of the institution were almost in a ruined condition, having been occupied during the war by both armies. The United States general in command put Dr. Humes in possession of them, and he set about the work of reinstating the university. With the help of F. D. Allen, now of Harvard University, and John K. Payne, now of Knoxville, a school was begun with crude materials, and in 1871, the first class, numbering four, was graduated. With the assistance of many and warm friends, the school became a success. In 1869, the Legislature of Tennessee was induced, chiefly by Mr. Edward J. Sanford, agent of the trustees, to appropriate the national fund for a college in Tennessee, under the congressional law of July, 1862, to East Tennessee University. Dr. Humes continued in the presidency of the institution until the summer of 1883, when he resigned, and the editor finds him in retirement.

His religion is of a catholic nature, he believing it more important to be a Christian than a Baptist, a Methodist, a Presbyterian, or anything else. He abjures all novel doctrines and usages, and holds that the world is to be regenerated and renewed by the preaching of the simple gospel of the Son of God, as it has been received and held by His universal church from the days of the Apostles, and by obeying His commandments.

In politics he is a Republican, originally a Whig, and has never cast a Democratic vote. When scarcely of age he was made a director in the Great Cincinnati and Charleston railroad company, of which Gen. Robert Y. Hayne was president. He is a Son of Temperance, and is president of the Knoxville Bible Society. At the semi-centennial anniversary of the settlement of Knoxville, held in February, 1842, he delivered the address; also at the dedication of the city cemetery; at the dedication of the State Deaf and Dumb Asylum, at Knoxville; addresses and lectures before various societies, temperance and literary. Some of these have been published in pamphlet form. His life has been one of almost constant activity.

Dr. Humes married, first, at Knoxville, December 4, 1834, Cornelia Williams, daughter of Etheldred Williams and Mary (nee Copeland), of Rocky Springs, Grainger county, Tennessee. His first wife died in 1847, at the age of thirty years, leaving him three children, of whom one, Andrew Russell Humes, survives.

Dr. Humes next married, in Knoxville, April 12, 1849, Anna B. Williams, daughter of William Williams, of New Hartford, Connecticut, a lawyer and member of the Connecticut Legislature, sister of Rev. Robert G. Williams, then principal of Knoxville Female Seminary. She died May 30, 1879. By this marriage, Dr. Humes had five children, three of whom died in infancy. Two daughters survive.

Dr. Humes' usefulness in life has come from swiftness of purpose, trust in God's grace, and loving obedience to His Son, and doing good to his fellow men, without regard to their condition or their relations to himself personally, and by sustained earnestness or enthusiasm. He is largely indebted to his mother for her training of him, and the helpfulness of his wives, both of whom were women of character, and help-meets in the true sense of the word. He has succeeded by sturdy resolution to reject the influence of evil or doubtful directions of personal associates, and to stand aloof from such influences and associations, even if he had to stand alone. He is one of the few men who have been able, when necessary, to say "No," without which his biography might have read very differently. Without being a recluse, he has found companions in books, and pleasure in scientific research. He has always been a public-spirited man.

In 1864, he was president of the East Tennessee society for the relief of suffering people. In this position he was associated with Judge John Baxter, Judge T. A. R. Nelson, Hon. O. P. Temple, William Heiskell, esq., Judge S. R. Rodgers, and others. This society distributed one hundred and fifty thousand dollars among sufferers from the war.

He had a small patrimony to start life on, but has not had money making for his object; yet lives respectably and is in independent circumstances.

HON. JOHN F. HOUSE.

CLAKRSVILLE.

A VOLUME purporting to be composed of biographical sketches of prominent citizens of Tennessee, would be judged incomplete and unfaithful to its task, should it omit to give extended space to the career and character of the distinguished gentleman whose name appears as the title to this article. Though yet at a period of life happily described by Victor Hugo as "the youth of old age," he has been closely identified with the history of public affairs in his native State for the full term of a generation, and in various responsible and exalted trusts has achieved a reputation, within and without her borders, ranking him among the worthiest of her sons whose fame she is proud to cherish. Not unambitious, for generous aspiration is an instinct with those endowed with uncommon talents, it may be truly said of him, that the popular judgment early discerned his intellectual endowments and sterling character, and without effort on his part, dedicated them to the public service. In every sphere in which they have been called into action, he has amply redeemed the auspicious promise of youth, and as the theater for the display of his powers enlarged, his appreciative friends have been more assured of the accuracy of their estimate. Retiring in his nature and deferential to others, and always indisposed to jostle chariot wheels in the race for promotion, he is, without question, accorded a first place—the peer of any man in the State—and adjudged worthy of the first honors her people can bestow.

The territory of Tennessee was ceded to the Federal government by North Carolina, and many of its early settlers were immigrants from that State, and among them were the ancestors of John Ford House. His father, a lad at the time, grew to manhood in Williamson county, Tennessee, and married Margaret S. Warren, a descendant of a prominent family of Virginia—the Dabneys—whose religious faith was Presbyterian, having furnished one or more noted ministers to that church. Mrs. House survives to an octogenarian age, in the immediate neighborhood where her life has been passed, and to the home of this venerable matron on whom, by the death of his father, when he was quite young, the rearing of the subject of this sketch was devolved, her devoted son takes time from his busy life to make frequent dutiful pilgrimages of esteem and affection. At the Williamson county homestead he was born, January 9, 1827. The basis of his education was acquired under the tuition of Edwin Paschall, a man of genuine culture and superior talents, with remarkable aptitude for his profession. He had many pupils who became successful men in various pursuits. He lived to witness such results, and spoke of them with pride, and not least of the success of this pupil, whose distinction entitles him to mention in this work.

Leaving the academy of Paschall, young House entered Transylvania University, near Lexington, Kentucky, but did not complete its curriculum for graduation, his preparatory education terminating at the close of the junior year.

The straitened circumstances which compelled him to leave his college course unfinished, required him also, before the attainment of his majority, to prepare himself for a calling for support, and with this view, he entered the law office of Campbell & McEwen, of Franklin, Tennessee. Here, for a few months, necessarily without much helpful instruction, he plodded his weary way through the intricate pages of Blackstone and Kent, at times quite discouraged. The Lebanon law school, afterward so famous a seat of legal learning, was, at that time, newly opened, and he betook himself thither, and soon, under the systematic and erudite teaching of Profs. Caruthers and Green, he was stimulated with increased zest in his chosen profession, and became a devoted and favorite student, especially of the former. The necessity for immediate exertion for a livelihood, forced him to leave that institution before its entire course of study was completed, but owing to his great proficiency, the faculty awarded him the full honors of a finished course, and conferred its diploma upon him in 1850. An oration, pronounced as a representative of one of the literary societies of that school, was regarded as an extraordinary effort, and laid the foundation of the reputation which has since been so fully sustained at the forum, on the hustings, and in congress. To have endured the critical acumen of Judges Caruthers and Green, by whom it was highly praised, it must have rated far above the pyrotechnic rhetoric customary with undergraduates. Indeed, it became a tradition of the school.

Immediately after leaving the law school, he opened a law office in Franklin, Tennessee, but remained only a few months. In January, 1851, he married Julia F. Beech, a native of the same county with himself—a daughter of Mr. L. B. Beech, a prosperous farmer of that region, whose wife was a Miss Crenshaw, from Virginia. Mrs. House was educated at the Nashville Female Academy, in the palmy days of that renowned school. Their union has been blessed with one child only, which died in infancy. At the time of his marriage, he was newly settled at Clarksville, Tennessee, in the practice of law, and that has since been his home. Clarksville had been long distinguished for the high order of talents and learning possessed by its members of the legal profession, and the young barrister, fresh from his studies, was at once thrown into competition with formidable veterans. An almost immediate success proved the temper of his ability and equipment, and the continued renown of the Clarksville bar is, in a great degree, due to the brilliant addition it then acquired in his person.

By instinct and conviction a Whig, as the country was then politically divided, it was in the following year, memorable for the last national struggle of that party in an organized form, that Mr. House entered the field of political digladiation, as sub-elector for the county of Montgomery, in behalf of the candidacy of Gen. Scott. In the next year—1853—he was sent as the representative of that county in the General Assembly, the first which sat in the present capitol. His talents attracted attention in that body, containing, as it did, more than a usual number of men of ability. A speech in opposition to a measure aiming to institute a radical scheme of law reform, was a conspicuous effort, and illustrated the sound conservation he has always displayed. The term reform was, in that instance, perhaps, as it nearly always is, in matters of public concern, an alluring title to some charlatanical project which usually changes things for the worse. The speech elicited commendation from eminent lawyers of the State. During the session, a *brochure* came from his pen in the form of a report from the committee on Buncombe, which was specially appointed on his motion to consider a proposition to alter the constitution by legislative enactment, reducing the *per diem* of members of the General Assembly. Retrenchment—the twin besetting legislative folly with reform—and its customary motive, was mercilessly caricatured in that humorous paper, which was published at the time. It finely exhibited the power of ridicule which Mr. House frequently uses when the occasion is pertinent.

In a few years, Mr. House had attained a commanding position in his profession, both as counselor and advocate, and was retained in a large number of the important causes arising in the extensive circuit of which Clarksville is the center. In every political contest, however, his eloquent voice was heard, and notably in that of 1856, when the conservatism of the South, under the lead of Fillmore, endeavored to stem the tide of the sectionally aggressive forces which had been set in motion by the repeal of the Missouri compromise two years before. Some of his deliverances of that year were equal to any of his best efforts subsequently, and achieved for him wide fame as a powerful debater. In 1860, he reluctantly left his lucrative business at the call of his party, but the duty was one he would not avoid, and he became the district electoral candidate for Bell and Everett in that decisive contest in which the banner of "the Union, the constitution, and the enforcement of the laws" went down, not to rise again until it emerged, rent and disfigured, from the blood and fire of civil war. In that distempered hour, the utterances of no man in the State were more persuasively eloquent and forcible in the attempt to allay the passions which precipitated that result.

Early in 1861, under the authority of the Legislature, an election was held for delegates to a sovereignty convention to consider the impending crisis in public affairs, and to deliberate on the attitude of the State thereto, and also an election submitting the question of the assembling of such a body. Mr. House was chosen as a delegate, but the popular majority was largely against its assembling, and the proceeding was nugatory. Had the convention been organized, it may well be conjectured that, in some aspects at least, the relationship of Tennessee to subsequent events might have been different, and the fortunes of prominent actors in that era have had another history. A very decided majority of the delegates-elect were devoted to the maintenance of the Union, and representing the latest expression of the popular will, might have organized a preponderating sentiment adverse to an alliance with the Confederate cause, even against the fierce tempest of feeling which swept the State a few months later. Whatever might have happened in such a conjuncture is, however, foreign to this sketch. Mr. House maintained his attachment to the cause of peace, fraternity and union, and would have upheld the Crittenden compromise, or any satisfactory and practicable adjustment, and did not cease to labor and to hope in that behalf, until all efforts and hopes were silenced amid the thunder of guns at Sumter, and the tramp of hosts marching South. Thereupon, he, as did many another true patriot, saw his line of duty in the unification of the people of the State in resistance to coercive measures, and in the rapid progress of events, firmly aligned himself with the southern cause.

When, after the popular vote for "separation," the State formally acceded to the Confederate government, Mr. House was elected a member of the provisional congress, and served in that body until February, 1862, having declined to be a candidate for the permanent congress which superseded the former. He at once sought service in the field, and was assigned to the staff of Gen. George Maney, and participated in the battles of Murfreesborough, Chickamauga, Missionary Ridge and the frequent fierce engagements between the armies of Gens. Johnston and Sherman beyond Dalton, until New Hope Church was reached, in the spring of 1864. At that point he was ordered by the Richmond war office, to report for duty as judge advocate, with the rank of captain of cavalry, of the military court sitting in North Alabama, and was engaged in that service until the termination of hostilities, when he was paroled, at Columbus, Mississippi, in June, 1865. From that point he returned to his home, which, for more than three years, had been within the lines of Federal occupation. Like most, if not all others, who cast their fortunes on the hazard of the losing die in that desperate conflict, he was reduced to the necessity of rebuilding entirely his ruined estate, and to this he set about with characteristic energy, in the practice of the law. As soon as quiet was restored and business resumed, litigation became active, and he was thenceforward constantly engaged in the various courts.

In 1868, he was a delegate to the national Democratic convention, meeting in the city of New York. That was a body not in all respects judiciously constituted, or under the guidance of any well-digested and defined views of public policy, or well in hand in the interest of any leading character as a candidate for the presidency. It was the formative stage of a new political organization in fact, only partly welded then by the fires of the sectional struggle which gave rise to political issues proceeding from it. While Col. House, in common with all conservative men in every section, utterly reprobated the truculent and tyrannical measures of reconstruction which the party in majority were enforcing, with others of the body he did not approve of some extreme utterances put forth in the platform and declarations of its chief spokesmen, which could have no other effect than to bring the disastrous defeat which followed. In 1870, he was a member of the convention called to revise the constitution of the State, and was able and influential in shaping its work. He served as one of the committee on the judicial department. He was the author of a proposition extending the gubernatorial term to four years, and giving the governor the veto power that functionary now possesses, and providing for a lieutenant-governor, who should be ex officio president of the senate. The entire proposition met with the favor of the convention, but was afterward reconsidered and lost by a small majority, except in the feature noted. He was the author also of a wholesome proposition for an amendment remitting the trial, on their merits, of a large and defined class of misdemeanors to justices of the peace, thus superseding the necessity of such culprits being confined in jail awaiting indictment, and being put through the tedious and costly forms of trial in the higher courts. It is the absence of such a provision that so enormously swells the item in the treasury budget under costs of criminal prosecutions. The measure failed by a majority of two votes. In 1872, he supported the forlorn candidacy of Horace Greeley for the presidency, rather as a protest against the Grantism of the period, which seemed to embody all that was politically vicious, whether of principle or practice, than an endorsement of that singular political movement; and at the same election, actively antagonized the return to the public councils of Andrew Johnson, who was a candidate for representative at large for the house of representatives.

In 1874, he was nominated for congress from the Nashville district by acclamation, and took his seat in December, 1875, as a member of the Forty-fourth congress. He received a similar form of nomination in 1876, 1878 and 1880, and voluntarily declined to serve another term. His period of service comprised the last half of Gen. Grant's second term, all of Hayes', and the first half of the Garfield-Arthur administration. His entrance of the national legislature was at the advent of the first Democratic majority in the lower house after the first congress under Buchanan, eighteen years before, and for six years of his service that party was in power in the body. Many important questions were debated, and during the winter of 1876–77, pending the electoral count, the scenes were tempestuous, surpassing in excitement perhaps those of any former time. Col. House was a conspicuous and influential member from the first session. During his congressional career, several Democratic members from his State were his elders in age and of longer service, and their preferment in the organization of the house of representatives, to a degree excluded him from that character of advancement to which his conceded capacity would otherwise have promoted him. But he was at once assigned to leading committees—the judiciary, elections, the Pacific railroad, the Texas Pacific, civil service reform, and the special committee on the laws relating to the election of president and vice-president. He served as chairman of the Democratic congressional caucus, and in 1879 was prominently considered for the speakership of the house, many discreet members of his party urging him as a more judicious choice than either of the recognized aspirants. With characteristic modesty he gave no countenance to the movement. His committee work was promptly and efficiently done in all its stages. While not ambitiously frequent in speech from the floor, from his first effort he always commanded the attention and interest of the body, and his participation in brief current debates was always pointed and forcible. His more formal speeches were always full expositions of the subject, pregnant with thought and suggestion, expressed in vigorous and eloquent diction, and delivered with the animation and fervor of the genuine orator. His first speech in committee of the whole, in 1876, was on a delicate and difficult question at that juncture to a southern representative—the relations of the North and South. It was treated in a considerate and masterly manner, and was pronounced by many of his southern colleagues competent to discriminate, the most statesmenlike utterance drawn forth in the long discussion. It gave great satisfaction to his immediate constituency, and secured his position as a leading exponent of the manliness and conservatism of the southern Democracy. Other notable speeches during his congressional service were those on the Louisiana returning board, whose matchless scoundrelism was vehemently denounced; on the tobacco tax, a subject of great interest to the region he represented; on the state of the Union, involving a discussion of the relations of capital and labor and the burden of the public debt; on the policy of the government toward the Texas Pacific railway; on appropriation measures generally, and equality before the law of the different sections of the country; on civil service reform; on the election of delegate Cannon, of Utah; and on the question of claims against the government. He also delivered eulogies on George S. Houston, of Alabama, and Benjamin H. Hill, of Georgia, who died members of the senate of the United States. Both were models of chaste and tasteful allusion in that most difficult line of oratory, and the latter glowed with admiration of the splendid character it portrayed. His service in Congress was so useful and distinguished, that his retirement was not only cause of regret in Tennessee, but throughout the country. The withdrawal of such men from public employment often gives rise to the reflection that our system should, perhaps, in some manner, offer greater inducements for retaining to the use of the government the superior qualifications they possess, and the valuable experience they have acquired.

In May, 1880, at the centennial celebration of the founding of Nashville, he was selected to deliver the oration at the unveiling of an equestrian statute of Andrew Jackson erected on the grounds of the capitol, and in the presence of the thousands assembled on the occasion, he pronounced an eloquent eulogy on the character of the great soldier and statesman. Since he has been in private life and immersed in professional engagements, he has only appeared in public to serve as a delegate to the national Democratic convention of 1884, and was chairman of the Tennessee delegation in that body. Perfect frankness and unchallenged integrity of motive and conduct have illustrated alike Col. House's public and personal relationships, and no imputation of chicane or demagogy has ever assailed his character. When called upon, he has met every issue at the threshold without equivocal utterance. Educated in the principles and traditions of the Whig party under the tutelage of Clay, Webster, Bell, White and other more or less eminent leaders, which, for more than three decades of the country's history, with varying success impressed the policy of the government, until the era of the civil war, he was its ardent and devoted adherent. Since that period, he has been a not less bold and faithful member of the Democratic party, and in this apparent radical change of political convictions there is no inconsistency. The limit of this sketch affords no proper field for the discussion of the question involved in this statement. Suffice it to say, that the prolonged predominance of a party exercising, during the sectional conflict and for twenty years after, powers of the government far beyond the text and spirit of its constitutional scope, profoundly altered the entire political situation. In resistance to such tendencies and policies, the very essence of the conservatism which was the cardinal characteristic of the Whig party required men who proposed to conform the workings of the government to the intent of the chart of its legitimate functions, to reverse their political attitude. The multifarious mischief of centralization, and the absorption by the general government of all power reserved respectively to the several States and to their peoples, became the paramount evil to be repressed. To this spirit and purpose, is to be attributed Col. House's political views and efforts for twenty years past, and he is but a prominent exemplar and type of a large majority of former southern Whigs. All history teaches true statecraft to be the adoption of principles and the adaptation of measures which may best preserve the proper ends of government and meet current exigencies in public affairs, and that differing periods present different requirements. That is the just and simple solution of the question. To the change in views thus necessitated, Col. House has been inflexibly consistent. He opposes all interposition directly or indirectly by the Federal government with concerns properly within State cognizance and control, and resists the centripetal force in every direction and particular. To this end, he has recently published a letter of great power in opposition to such legislation as presented in the Blair educational bill now pending in congress, and it may be said that no argument delivered against it in the senate of the United States equals that letter in cogency and conclusiveness, either as to the constitutionality or expediency of the measure. He does not hold that the " general welfare " clause in the constitution gives congress general power of legislation on every subject, nor does he on the other hand, assert the qualified sovereignty of the States against the powers delegated to the general government, but he does hold the vast mass of legislation affecting the immediate concerns of the people, to be wholly within the inalienable province of State authority.

Though holding no official connection with the State government since his legislative service more than thirty years ago, he has properly been moved to deep interest in her public affairs, and with customary candor and decision, has expressed his views on questions which have agitated her people. The most distracting of these since the war was the disposition of the State debt. Its final adjustment, determined by the Democratic State convention of 1882, was justified and boldly upheld by Col. House as the wisest practicable settlement of which it was susceptible. Valued friends differed and criticised his course as a departure from the standard by which he had held public and private obligations to be governed. Of course he, with the large majority who coincided with him, knew it was ideally right that the composition of a public debt so contracted should be on terms proposed or agreed to by the creditors, but it was very clear the time when such an adjustment was possible had irrevocably passed, and that in the ferment of popular feeling and the rapid drift of events, repudiation of the entire debt was imminent. The action of the Democratic majority of the State, which alone could effect any permanent settlement acceptable to the people, was timely, and averted a conclusion of the question which might have brought irretrievable ruin and irreparable dishonor. The result, year by year, since

the adjustment, amply vindicates the wisdom and substantial justice of the course pursued by Col. House and those who acted with him.

The biographer's duty would fail in its performance if he did not endeavor to present some of the more personal characteristics of his subject. Col. House is of medium height, compact in figure, and inclining to portliness. He is fully developed in the region of the chest, giving him the powerfully resonant voice he uses with such skill and effect in public speech. His head is large, well set upon its support, and animated by intellectual and expressive features. His carriage and address is one of ease and natural dignity. Neither in the social circle or his daily walk, or before a jury, a deliberative body, or a popular audience, does he present any of the artificial graces of what, for a better word, is usually called style. He is everywhere and in all senses, an earnest man, too deeply interested in whatever is in hand to pause to consider such trivial adjuncts. And yet his deportment is devoid of nothing whose place such things could supply. His forensic and popular addresses, whether the occasion be more or less important, are solid and weighty in matter, and never without point, and clothed in copious and forceful diction, appeal to the reason and judgment of his hearers. Figurative illustration of his line of thought is not wanting, but he uses without distasteful excess, the rare gifts of imagination and fancy natural to him. His temperament is fervid, and breathing through every movement of mind and bodily gesture, there is an intensity of feeling sometimes manifest in vehement delivery. This prompts him, too, at times, to employ invective, and to the display of powers of sarcasm which an antagonist may well apprehend. He easily relaxes from the cares of his office and business, and in the *abandon* of a circle of friends, he is a most entertaining and agreeable companion. For a number of years he has been a communicant of the Methodist church, and has served as a lay representative in its assemblies.

As a public man, he is equally without the art or the inclination to seek popularity by other than legitimate methods—the worthy performance of every duty which may confront him, and the open avowal of his convictions and sentiments. By such means he has maintained a public character than which none is held in higher estimation by his fellow-citizens of all parties, alike for splendid abilities and stern fidelity to every trust. He bids fair to attain a more exalted official station than he has yet held, and in such a sphere he would win the confidence and admiration of the people of Tennessee to an equal degree with any man who has ever served as her representative in the senate of the United States.

COL. WILLIAM SANFORD.

COVINGTON.

THIS gentleman, just turned his fortieth year, is a native of Tipton county, Tennessee, and was born February 15, 1846. His grandfather, Richard Sanford, was a Virginian, who emigrated to Sumner county, Tennessee, in the early part of this century, settled as a farmer, and died soon after arriving in Tennessee. The family is of English origin, and has been many years represented in America. Col. Sanford's father, Robert W. Sanford, was also born in Virginia, and came with his father's family to Sumner county when twelve years of age. In that county he grew to maturity and then went alone to Tipton county, where he was soon afterward elected county court clerk and circuit court clerk—offices which he held for twelve years. He married, in Tipton county, settled as a farmer, and accumulated a large landed estate. His death occurred, in 1861, at the age of fifty-nine. His great good judgment, clear and calm mind, were his leading mental characteristics. He was also a man of impartiality, of singularly benevolent disposition, of abstemious habits and fine business qualifications, particularly in matters of detail. He was a deacon in Mount Carmel Presbyterian church, a Royal Arch Mason, and a Whig.

Col. Sanford's mother, *nee* Miss Frances D. Small, was born in Montgomery county, Tennessee, daughter of Henry Small, a farmer, descendant of one of three brothers who emigrated from Germany to the United States, one settling in Philadelphia, one in the northwest, and one (Col. Sanford's grandfather) in Tennessee. The name was originally Smaltz. Col. Sanford's mother was descended, on her maternal side, from the Bailey family, of Montgomery county, and was of Scotch origin. Her cousin, the late Hon. James E. Bailey, was United States senator from Tennessee, from 1877 to 1881, filling out the unexpired term of ex-President Andrew Johnson. Her brother, Henry D. Small, who died of consumption, in 1863, was a lawyer of prominence and great promise, at Memphis.

The Head family of Sumner county, is a branch of the Sanford family. Col. John W. Head, of Gallatin, was attorney-general of the State of Tennessee, from 1858 to 1861, during which time he became the author of Head's reports, three volumes, Supreme court decisions.

William Sanford's boyhood was a happy, joyous one— living on a farm, going to school, attending church, and with an intense fondness for reading books of every description, and especially, history and books of travel. At the age of thirteen, he read the Book of Revelations at one sitting. At the age of fourteen, he found a copy of Hedge's Logic, and studied it through with

exceptional pleasure as developing his own intellect, while explaining the operations of the mind—sensation, perception, reasoning—then a new world to him, while it also stimulated in him what afterward grew to be a love of the metaphysical. But the epoch of his young life was the study of Milton's matchless and sublime "Paradise Lost," which aroused his fancy, fed his imagination, and gave him a new idea of the dignity and power of language. He was of a delicate constitution and could not attend school regularly, notwithstanding his studious habits, and on his father's advice, to acquire more physical strength, he spent much time in hunting alone, introducing him intimately to the charms of nature—only to be learned in the solitudes of field and forest.

In 1861, the war broke up the schools, and in 1862, the delicate young student enlisted as a private soldier in Company I, Seventh Tennessee cavalry, Col. Duckworth commanding. In this regiment, he fought through the war, served in Tennessee and Mississippi, and participated in the battles of Tishomingo Creek and Harrisburg, and in all the raids and various battles of Forrest's command in 1864. He was twice taken prisoner, first in Tipton county, while at home on leave of absence, and was detained a month; and next, in 1864, during Gen. Hood's retreat from Nashville, and detained two months. At the time of his last capture, he was carrying the flag of his regiment, but his horse being shot from under him, he fell into the hands of the enemy. The title of "Colonel" is purely an honorary one, though if valor and worth be considerations, he certainly deserved it.

The war over, he returned home, went to school a short while, and began the study of law while acting as deputy circuit clerk. He worked out his law course by himself, and, in 1866, was admitted to the bar by Judges Harris and Reeves, and began practice at Covington, where he has always lived. In 1870, he was appointed clerk and master in chancery, and held that position till the spring of 1876, having however, in the meantime, kept up his law practice in all the other courts. From January 1, 1873, until July 1, 1881, he was a law partner with Hon. Holmes Cummins. Since November, 1883, Mr. W. B. Hill, who studied law in his office, has been his partner, the firm now being Sanford & Hill.

Money cannot be taken as the measure of a man's general worth, but it is oftentimes a good test of professional standing and success. From this point of view, if from no other, Col. Sanford is entitled to be classed among prominent and successful attorneys, as he is one of the largest property holders in his town—the result mainly of his professional labors. He has always been a studious man, and a lover and reader of books, and since settled in life, particularly of books of a grave character—historical, scientific, philosophical and the severe theology of the Calvanistic school. These studies, requiring closest attention, critical analysis, and profound application, have trained his mind in the direction of close discrimination, which has been of great service to him professionally. As a lawyer, he has cultivated the habit of consulting the text books for his law first, then writing out for his own eye a clear, precise and definite statement of the question to be investigated, then eliminating the parts he understands, and studying to clear up the difficult points. Another characteristic of his mode of thought and procedure is this: He makes it a rule never to submit to a court an authority that has been modified or questioned without stating the modification or doubt, and not to present a chain of reasoning which does not commend itself to his own mind as well connected and sound. His habit also is, to advise and assist clients to settle controversies without a law suit when possible.

Col. Sanford's manners are easy without being familiar, dignified without being stiff, and stately without the appearance of haughtiness. In the firmness with which he adheres to principle, and in loyalty to his convictions, he is as solid and substantial as a granite column—but a more kindly nature, with more genuine interest in the public welfare, one seldom meets. In politics, he is a Democrat; in religion, an old school Presbyterian, and for five or six years, was an elder in his church, at Covington.

In connection with Dr. Munford, now managing editor of the Kansas City (Missouri) *Times*, Col. Sanford founded the Tipton *Record*, which they both edited a few months. From their hands the paper passed, first, to S. P. Rose, now of Denver, Colorado, but is yet the leading paper of Tipton county.

In 1883, he founded the Tipton County Educational Association, and became its president, the object of the association being to stimulate zeal and interest among the young people in the cause of education. One of its methods is the offering, annually, of free board, books and tuition—*i. e.*, a scholarship—at some college or university, to the student that can stand the best examination in the common school branches—a project which has built twenty school houses in the county and doubled the county tax for education.

Col. Sanford first married, at Covington, in 1867, Miss Bettie Douglas, daughter of Andrew J. Douglas, a farmer, of Tipton county. Her mother, was Miss Laura Smith. Mrs. Sanford died, September 24, 1877, at the age of twenty-eight. She was a lady of quiet, unostentatious benevolence, of great modesty and retiring disposition; with remarkably clear judgment and womanly knowledge of the proprieties of life. By this marriage, five children were born: (1). William, died in 1874, aged six. (2). Allan Douglas, born July 3, 1869. (3). Robert W., born March 28, 1871. (4). Laura K., born July 23, 1873. (5). George A., born November 30, 1875.

Col. Sanford's second marriage, which occurred at Covington, January 30, 1879, was with Miss Wilhelmina Hall, daughter of Dr. William M. Hall, a physician and merchant of Covington, and an elder in the Presbyterian church. Her mother, *nee* Miss Sarah Holmes, is a daughter of Rev. James Holmes, D.D., formerly a missionary to the Choctaw Indians, and a prominent educator in West Tennessee. Mrs. Sanford, through her mother, is descended from the Van Wagenens, an old Dutch family of New Jersey. Mrs. Sanford's maternal uncle, George D. Holmes, is principal of the Tipton Female Seminary, at Covington. Her paternal uncle, John G. Hall, was colonel of the Fifty-first Tennessee regiment in the Confederate service. Mrs. Sanford is a Presbyterian, as was her ancestors for generations back. She is a lady of literary and musical tastes, full of zeal for religion, a Sunday-school teacher, and a good housekeeper. By this marriage Col. Sanford has had two children: (1). Van Wagenen, born February 2, 1880; died January 13, 1882. (2). Rebecca, born January 1, 1885.

HON. DANIEL C. TREWHITT.

CHATTANOOGA.

A S far back as the Trewhitt family can be traced, the great-grandfather of the subject of this sketch came with his brother from England, and settled in Virginia or Maryland.

Judge Trewhitt's grandfather, James Trewhitt, was born in North Carolina, and was a Revolutionary soldier during the entire war. He married Miss Elizabeth Mumford, in North Carolina, in which State he also died. After his death his widow came to Hawkins county, Tennessee, where she married a Mr. James Brown. By her first husband she had two boys, Jesse, a physician, who died in Missouri, in 1865, and Levi; and two daughters, Elizabeth, now wife of John Brown, and Sally, who married Andy McGinnis.

Levi Trewhitt, father of Judge Trewhitt, was a lawyer. He was raised in Roane county. When he was

64

twenty-one, his mother moved to Morgan county, Tennessee, and there he married, in 1819, Miss Harriet Lavender, by whom he had seventeen children, of whom thirteen were raised to maturity. He was county court clerk in Morgan county for many years, including the year 1836. He moved to Cleveland, in Bradley county, in September, 1836, where he practiced law and carried on farming until his death, in 1862, at Mobile, while a political prisoner. Being an ardent Union man and a Whig, and his son having gone to the Federal army the Confederate authorities had arrested him early in the struggle, and held him till his death, as just stated. He began the practice of law in 1833, and during a long and lucrative career, rose to eminence at the bar. He was a man of great firmness, integrity and tenacity of purpose, though without a collegiate education. He espoused the cause of his friends and made his client's cause his cause. As a counselor, he was safe, and as an advocate, without many superiors. He accumulated a handsome property in land and negroes.

Judge Trewhitt's maternal grandfather, Daniel S. Lavender, a noted citizen of Morgan county, held several county offices, from 1818 to 1852. He came from Virginia, and was among the first settlers of Morgan county. His wife was a Kuntz, of Virginia, of German extraction. She died in 1841, at the age of seventy-seven.

Judge Daniel C. Trewhitt, his mother's third son, was born on the waters of Daddy's creek, then in Morgan, now in Cumberland county, Tennessee, and was put to farm work in childhood, going to school in the fall. In 1837-8-9-40, he went to school each fall a session at Oak Grove Academy, in Cleveland. When just turned twenty, he began studying law under his father and his partner, Judge John C. Gaut, now of Nashville; obtained license in 1847, from Judge John O. Cannon, and in 1848, from Chancellor Seth J. W. Luckey, and went to practice in what is now the Fourth judicial circuit of the State, and continued in practice until 1861, residing meanwhile at Harrison, then the county seat of Hamilton county. He practiced away from his father, believing he could, in this way, attain a greater degree of proficiency—forcing himself to rely on his own mental resources.

When the war came on, he made his way across the mountains with about five hundred other unionists and enlisted, at Camp Dick Robinson, in the Federal army. He was first made sergeant-major of the First Tennessee infantry regiment, and in a few weeks afterward was appointed by Gen. Nelson, lieutenant-colonel of the Second Tennessee infantry, which he recruited, filled up and drilled. He commanded that regiment till after the battle of Mill Springs, but becoming sick at Barboursville, Kentucky, he resigned; was afterward appointed by President Lincoln, assistant adjutant-general, with the rank of captain of volunteers, and assigned to duty under Brigadier-Gen. James G. Spears, in April, 1862.

From Barboursville, the brigade marched to Williamsburg, and thence to Camp Pine Knot, whence they were ordered through Big Creek Gap, from which they drove the enemy. Next the command took Cumberland Gap and remained there till November, 1862. Next, the forces moved across the Ohio river and up to the mouth of the Kanawha, and remained there till December, when the army was ordered to Cincinnati, Louisville, Nashville and Murfreesborough; took part in the Stones river battle; remained in camp at Murfreesborough till March, were then ordered to Carthage, and camped there two months, reaching the battle field of Chickamauga on Sunday, too late to be of much service, the troops belonging then to Grainger's reserved corps. The forces were removed to Sale creek and remained there till December. Thence they went to Knoxville, Strawberry Plains and Massengale's Mills.

From the latter place the command was ordered back to Knoxville, where Capt. Trewhitt resigned and returned home to take part in the reorganization of the State under the administration of the civil government, and was commissioned, in 1865, by Gov. Johnson, as chancellor of the then Second, now the Third, chancery division. This position he held till 1870, when the Democrats being enfranchised, he was beaten by Judge D. M. Key for chancellor, under the new constitution. He then resumed practice of law at Chattanooga till 1878, when he was elected judge of the Fourth judicial circuit for eight years, which office he now holds, term expiring September 1, 1886.

He was a member of the Legislature of 1859-60, and served in all the called sessions except the last, which was under Confederate control, voting against every proposition to take the State out of the Union, or having any tendency in that direction.

In 1861, he was elected State senator from the Eighth senatorial district under very singular circumstances. He had entered into an agreement with his opponent, James S. Havron, that if he, Havron, was elected, he should go to Nashville and legislate under the rebel flag; if Trewhitt was elected and a new State was made of East Tennessee, he would go to that, but if not, he would go to the Federal army. Under this compact he was elected by a large majority, and, as East Tennessee was not erected into a State, he went to the army.

In 1861, he was a member of the conventions at Knoxville and Greeneville, convened to consider the best course to pursue in order to sustain the union sentiment, and to preserve the status and relation of the union people of East Tennessee to the federal government.

In 1865, he was a delegate to the convention that amended the State constitution, and since the war has been a steady and unflinching Republican.

He became a Mason in Harrison Lodge, in 1857.

Judge Trewhitt first married in Gwinnett county, Georgia, in 1841, Miss Mary Melissa Winnee, daughter of Thomas Winnee, a merchant in Hall county, Georgia, related to the Lumpkin family of that State. Her mother was an Echols. By this marriage, Judge Trewhitt has two children living: (1). Thomas Trewhitt, born 1842, married Miss Tennessee Hunter, and has four children, Robert, Ernest, Ethel and Beatrice. (2). Mary Jane Trewhitt, now wife of Martin M. Fry, has one child, Daniel Trewhitt. Two children of the first marriage, William and Martha, died, the former ten years old, the latter six. The mother died in 1861.

Judge Trewhitt's next marriage, which took place at Harrison, July 4, 1865, was with Miss Mary Melissa Hunter, daughter of A. P. Hunter, a merchant. Her mother, Paulina Riley, was the daughter of Charles Riley and Peggy Orr. To this marriage with Miss Hunter were born four children, Addison H., Alonzo Sharpe, Paul Woodruff, and Ellen Gahagan Trewhitt.

Judge Trewhitt and wife are both members of the Methodist Episcopal church.

Beginning life with only an academic education, and without money, but with a resolution never to falter,

fall back nor surrender, and with a determination to do no wrong to his fellow man, or if he ever did any wrong to let it be to himself, he has attained to the honors of his profession, and to comfortable financial circumstances. He never sacrifices business to pleasure—attends first to business, seeks pleasure afterwards. He made it a cardinal point to never expose himself of nights at any improper place. It is said of him, he has not will power to resist appeals to his generosity, and that he is liberal to a fault. Another rule with him is, when he has business to transact at any particular point, he transacts it, and at once leaves the point, the place and the people, and never goes anywhere unless he has business there. More than all, he has never been an aspirant for position beyond a laudable ambition to win and hold an honorable reputation in his profession.

He is a man of easy manners, of large, strong build, is five feet ten inches high, and weighs one hundred and seventy-two pounds. While not at all unsocial, he yet loves study and retirement, and is fond of his books and his pen.

GEN. ALFRED E. JACKSON.

JONESBOROUGH.

BEING now the oldest resident of Jonesborough, the oldest town in Tennessee, and among the oldest citizens in Washington county, the oldest county in the State, and having a most interesting family, military and business history, certainly entitles Gen. Alfred E. Jackson to a rank among "Prominent Tennesseans." He was born in Davidson county, Tennessee, January 11, 1807, and for one of his age is remarkably well preserved, only slightly stooped by age, and with a vision so clear he can read printed matter without eye-glasses. He is still engaged in the activities required in attending to large farming and business interests, and can break down almost any young man in Jonesborough in walking. His grandfather, Philip Jackson, came with his wife, Eliza, from Ireland, and settled at Edenton, North Carolina, where both died. Gen. Jackson's father, Samuel D. Jackson, born September 16, 1755, at Carlisle, Pennsylvania, died on his son's farm, on Chucky river, in Washington county, May 7, 1836. He had been a lieutenant in Col. Stark's regiment of Virginia troops, in the Revolutionary war. Before moving to Tennessee, in 1801, he was a wholesale merchant at Philadelphia, and a man of very considerable wealth, but by endorsements for Robert Morris, the celebrated financier, he had to sell out, losing one hundred and nineteen thousand dollars, and had besides to pay thirty thousand dollars for Morris after Morris was put within the prison bounds at Philadelphia. He first settled at Jones-

borough, bought a farm of six hundred and forty acres, on Chucky river, from old Gov. John Sevier and David Ross, father of Rev. Fred. A. Ross, the celebrated Presbyterian clergyman. He had, also, previously bought fifty thousand acres of land from Gov. William Blount, which was the inducement for him to move from Philadelphia to Tennessee. He moved to Jefferson county from Jonesborough, about the year 1804, and settled at a place known as Panther Springs, in the center of his extensive tract of East Tennessee lands, and then in the very midst of the Indian hunting grounds. He spent his life in Tennessee merchandising in Jonesborough, improving his lands, and subsequently in Davidson county, on a farm he bought from Gen. Andrew Jackson. He and Gen. Jackson traced their kinship so closely that he lived three months, about 1805, in Gen. Jackson's house. Some time afterward, Gen. Jackson won ten thousand acres of Samuel Jackson's Harpeth lands from him, which resulted in a street fight, in which Samuel Jackson was run through the body by Gen. Jackson's long cane spear, but not with fatal results. It was a long time after their personal rencounter before the kinsmen made friends, but they finally met on Cumberland mountains, in company with Gen. Coffee and other members of Gen. Jackson's military suite, made up, and, as an evidence of good faith, Gen. Jackson gave his kinsman's son, Henry Jackson, an office in the treasury department, at Washington, which he held until turned out by President Fillmore. Samuel D. Jackson was a very decided man, a successful business man, excitable and passionate in his temperament, and much, in these respects, like the old General, a quality which appears in a milder form in the son, the subject of this sketch. Gen. "Stonewall" Jackson, of Virginia, was a descendant of the same Irish stock. The men of the family are all tall. The subject of this sketch stands six feet three inches in his stocking feet, and is a fair representative of the family.

Gen. Alfred E. Jackson has been more or less intimately associated with the most distinguished men of Tennessee that have lived his contemporaries, among whom he mentions with some pride, Bailie Peyton, Ephraim H. Foster, A. O. P. Nicholson, William Cullom, Robert I. Chester, Chief Justice Deaderick (whom he nursed when a little boy), Neill S. Brown, Aaron V. Brown, Gustavus A. Henry, John Bell, Paul F. Eve, sr., Thomas Menees. Davy Crockett, Meredith P. Gentry, T. Nixon Van Dyke, Robert Hatton and Daniel S. Donelson.

Gen. Jackson's mother, *nee* Eliza Catharine Woodrow, was of a New Jersey Quaker family, but a native of Philadelphia, and a highly educated woman. She was the bridesmaid of Mrs. President Madison, when she first married (to Mr. Todd). She was a member of the Presbyterian church, at Jonesborough and Salem, under old Dr. Samuel Doak, founder of Washington College, and at Jonesborough, under Rev. Charles Coffin, founder of Greeneville College. Of her sisters, Susan Woodrow married Dr. Binney, of Philadelphia, father of Horace Binney, a distinguished lawyer, member of Congress, director in the old United States Bank, and attorney for that bank, under Nick Biddle; Julia Woodrow married James Duncan, of Gettysburg, and another sister married Dr. Spring, of Boston. Gen. Jackson's grandmother, Susan Woodrow, *nee* Firman, was a woman of great business capacity. Benjamin Franklin and William Duncan, of Philadelphia, were her business advisers. She had remarkable economic business talent, and accumulated a handsome property. The mother of Gen. Jackson was a woman of brilliant intellect, had fine conversational powers, was notably intelligent on a wide range of subjects, and able in prayer in church. She was also remarkable for the beauty of her person, a handsome woman, as were her daughters. She mixed in the best society at Philadelphia, and was in the habit of attending the levees of Presidents Washington and Adams, given while that city was the capital of the United States. She was born December 22, 1764, and died, January 8, 1844, at Jonesborough, in the house now occupied by her son. She left six children living of eleven born, namely: Henry, Susan W., Eliza (who, when grown, changed her name to Julia Adelaide), Caroline, Harriet, and Alfred Eugene, the subject of this sketch.

Of these, Henry died at Lynchburg, Virginia, after holding office twenty-four years; Susan W. died the widow of Dr. Thomas G. Watkins, of Jefferson county, Tennessee; Eliza (*alias* Julia Adelaide), married David A. Deaderick, oldest brother of Chief Justice Deaderick, and died in December, 1817, at Cheek's Cross-roads, in Jefferson county; Caroline married John A. Aiken, a brilliant criminal lawyer, of Jonesborough, both of whom died in Rome, Georgia; Harriet married Oliver B. Ross, of Baltimore, and settled at Jonesborough.

Gen. Jackson married in Carter county, Tennessee, June 8, 1826, Miss Seraphina C. Taylor, born June 23, 1808, youngest daughter of Gen. Nathaniel Taylor, a brigadier-general in the war of 1812; sister of James P. Taylor, a distinguished lawyer, and for a time attorney-general of the Eastern judicial district of Tennessee; sister also of Alfred W. Taylor, father of H. T. Taylor, of Knoxville, and of Col. N. M. Taylor, of Bristol, whose sketches appear elsewhere in this volume. Her eldest sister, Anna, married Thomas D. Love, of North Carolina, a lawyer, in Carter county. Her second sister, Lorena, married Gen. Jacob Tipton, removed to Covington, West Tennessee, and there a county was named for him. Her sister Mary married Dr. William R. Dulaney, of Sullivan county. Mrs. Jackson died October 27, 1882. She was a very modest, retiring woman, a member of the Presbyterian church, and was the mother of fourteen children, namely: (1). Samuel Dorsey Jackson, a farmer, at Taylorsville, Tennessee; married Alzinia Wagner, daughter of Matthias M. Wagner, of Johnson county, and has eight living children, Mary, Olive, Sallie, Charles B., Ida, Matthias, Mattie and Lillie. (2). Nathaniel Taylor Jackson, born May 5, 1829; married Lizzie, the only child of Maj. John F. Henry, of Blount county, Tennessee; fell a major (quartermaster) under Zollicoffer, in the Confederate service, leaving one child, Alfred N. Jackson, a lawyer, at Knoxville. (3). Eliza Catherine Jackson, born January 31, 1831; married James E. Murphy, of North Carolina, a lawyer, and has one child, Eugenia. (4). Mary Caroline Jackson, born September 26, 1832; married Gen. James T. Carter, son of Gen. William B. Carter, of Carter county, and has five children, Bettie, Alice, Seraphina (wife of Dr. Burdett, of Nashville), Adelaide (died wife of Edward Koykendoll, of Knoxville) and James T. (5). Henry Woodrow Jackson, born June 29, 1834; died at an early age. (6). Susan Evalina Jackson, born March 3, 1836; married Judge William V. Deaderick, nephew of Chief Justice Deaderick; died, leaving eight children, Alfred Eugene, Cora, John Franklin, Laura (who married John J. Cox, of Sullivan county, and died in 1885, leaving one child, a son), Henry C., Edward, Claude Taylor and Charley Fuller, twins. (7). James Patton Taylor Jackson, born November 6, 1837; named for his uncle, James P. Taylor, a gallant soldier in the Confederate service, from the beginning to the end of the war, was wounded at Shiloh, and died in Mississippi in 1881, unmarried. (8). William Woodrow Jackson, born September 16, 1839; died in infancy. (9). Julia Adelaide Jackson, born April 22, 1841; married Charles L. Fuller, of Nashville, and has four children, Lillie, William, Nellie and Alfred Eugene. (10). Alfred Eugene Jackson, born May 29, 1843; died at Millborough, Tennessee, adjutant of the Twenty-ninth Tennessee regiment, soon after the battle of Mill Spring (Fishing creek). (11). Seraphina Cordelia Jackson, born February 25, 1845; died September 18, 1858. (12). Henry Clay Jackson, born February 2, 1847, is a farmer, in Washington county; for four years was in mercantile business with Hugh Douglas & Co., and three years with Evans, Fite, Porter & Co., of Nashville. (13). Lorena Olivene Jackson, born September 21, 1849; died March 27, 1853. (14). Olivia Lillie Jackson, born May 3, 1852; married Rev. James W. Rogan, now living at Savannah, Georgia, pastor of the First Presbyterian church. Gen. Jackson has about thirty-six grandchildren and ten great-grandchildren.

Gen. Jackson's life has been a very eventful one and full of adventure. He was educated at Washington and Greeneville Colleges, under Rev. Samuel Doak, D.D., who founded the first institution of learning in Tennessee, and Charles Coffin, president of Greeneville College. He maried in his twentieth year, and went to farming on Chucky river, confining his life to farming till 1830, when he commenced boating to North Alabama, which he followed for twenty-three consecutive years, making considerable money by dealing in produce, iron, etc. In 1834, he commenced merchandising, in connection with boating to the south and running wagons to South Carolina, North Carolina and Georgia. He merchandised eighteen years, owning mills and blacksmith shops. In 1843, he moved to Jonesborough, still carrying on the store at his farm. In 1846, he made a contract with Elijah Embree, who had built a rolling-mill and nailery, to take everything he made at a stipulated price, the contract terminating upon the death of Embree, in 1847. By this contract he made a good deal of money. Previous to 1846, he commenced merchandising at Taylorsville, Johnson county. He conducted this business fourteen years, meantime running two stores in North Carolina, one in Watauga county, and one at Burnsville, Yancey county. In 1847, he bought up all the corn in East Tennessee, along the Tennessee river, from the mouth of Clinch to Chattanooga, with a view of supplying the demand in Ireland, during the famine there. He took it to New Orleans in flat boats and sold it to an English purchaser for the Dublin market, and on this venture made one thousand five hundred dollars. On that enterprise he was six months and sixteen days gone, on duty all the time, often working all night on the river himself, steering his boats, which were lashed together. About 1850, he contracted with Bishop Ives, of North Carolina, to

put up a chapel, seminary, boarding house and storehouse at Valle Crucis, in Watauga county, North Carolina. He continued merchandising at Taylorsville, Watauga and Burnsville up to 1861, all at the same time, carrying on, besides, a tannery, a shoe shop and a saddlery shop at Taylorsville.

Not only has his life been very active, but one of much exposure and laboriousness. He has ridden all over East Tennessee and over large portions of Alabama and South Carolina after night, in prosecuting his business—always making personal enjoyment subservient to business duty. He rode from Greeenville, South Carolina, to his home, a distance of one hundred and twenty miles without stopping to rest or to sleep, and twice only to feed his horse. Night after night he has ridden all night in pursuit of business. He once went three hundred miles in a canoe, from Battle Creek to Decatur, Alabama, poling and paddling night and day, sleeping as the canoe floated, rather than be balked in the sale of some West Tennessee lands; then rode forty-six miles at night from Decatur to Tuscumbia, to catch the stage, and got to his destination in time to prevent the loss of his lien and to buy the lands in. In 1840, he walked sixty-three miles in one day, in the month of June, from Asheville, North Carolina, to his farm on Chucky river, to procure a team to lighten a load of five thousand six hundred weight of goods bought in Charleston, and which was being drawn by a team too weak to pull it. A man of wonderful physical endurance, in Alabama he was called "the iron man," partly from his great strength, and partly because of his dealing so extensively in iron, in which he made the bulk of his fortune.

An important part of his life, from 1848 to 1858, in connection with the origin, organization and construction of the East Tennessee and Virginia railroad from Bristol to Knoxville. He became a director of the road in 1850, was the financial agent from 1850 to 1858, and disposed of three hundred thousand dollars of the bonds issued for building the bridges and masonry, besides other contracts, amounting to one hundred and forty thousand dollars. He was author of the bill passed by the Legislature, February 20, 1852, providing for the building of the bridges and masonry, and labored zealously with that body until they passed it. Always a manipulator of men and a marshaler of affairs, during these ten years he neglected his own private business in the interest of the railroad and for the progress of East Tennessee, indirectly thereby enhancing the value of his real estate, some twelve thousand acres. He bought the first locomotives and the first passenger cars on the road, and gave his individual note for one hundred and forty thousand dollars for the iron for thirty miles of the road.

In 1861, he went into the Confederate service as quartermaster on Gen. Felix K. Zollicoffer's staff. As brigade quartermaster he continued up to the death of

Gen. Zollicoffer, January 20, 1862. After that he became paymaster at Knoxville, and disbursed about ten million dollars of Confederate money. He remained in the pay department till February 9, 1863, when he was commissioned a brigadier-general and took the field, assigned to duty with Gen. Daniel S. Donelson, then in command of the department of East Tennessee. He served in Virginia and Tennessee. He fought the battle of Millwood, in September, 1863, and at the battle of Blue Springs, in October, 1863, he captured the One Hundreth regiment of Ohio infantry, for which feat the Yankees gave him the *sombriquet* of "Mudwall" Jackson. He also commanded at the battle of the Watauga, a running fight on the retreat from Blue Springs, with Gen. Foster's brigade, from Henderson to Rheatown; fought three fights at Carter's Depot, two battles at the Saltworks, in Virginia, in one of which, with one thousand eight hundred men, he repulsed Burbridge at the head of six thousand Federal troops, and drove him back with a loss of four hundred men, December 2, 1863. In the last fight in which he took part he engaged, with three hundred men, badly equipped, against Stoneman with six thousand men, and held his position without loss, December 1, 1864. He continued in the service until after the surrender of Lee.

The war over, he remained in Washington county, Virginia. Early in 1869 he went to Knoxville, and did a commisssion business there two years, then returned to Jonesborough, looking after his interests there. Under Brownlow's administration he was sued for an aggregate of three hundred and ninety thousand dollars for imaginary grievances of Union men, all his property being levied upon, and he, besides, indicted for treason in the State and United States courts. It took him ten years to get out of these suits, but he finally did get out without loss, except lawyers' fees and personal expenses. Judge Deaderick was retained as his counsel until he went on the Supreme bench of Tennessee and became chief justice, and it was under his able and skillful management that Gen. Jackson recovered his property. Against the advice of some of his best friends, to give up everything and begin life anew, he was determined to save his property, for which he had labored so hard for forty years. Judge Deaderick stood by him to the last, and finally brought him through, and his estate was saved. His life has been that of a trader, farmer and merchant, all concentrated in one line, and his property now consists of houses and lots and lands in six counties, amounting in all to some ten thousand acres.

In 1872, he had an opportunity to show his gratitude, and he was not slow to do so. In that year he was a member of the judiciary convention that assembled at Nashville to nominate candidates for Supreme judges, and in that convention, and prior to it, he worked zealously to elevate his old friend, Judge Deaderick, to the Supreme bench.

The Bristol (Tenn.), *News,* of July, 1873, contains an interview of its editor with Jefferson Davis, the ex-President of the Confederate States, and, as showing the high appreciation of Mr. Davis for the character and achievements of Gen. Jackson, we copy from it the following: "Mr. Davis enquired particularly as to the health of his old friends, Capt. Sevier and Gen. Alfred E. Jackson, of Jonesborough. To the latter he ascribed in a pre-eminent degree integrity, honesty and valor, adding significantly, 'when we have chopping to do iron is better than gold.' It is with some hesitation that we give publicity to his language touching any gentleman, but his compliment to Gen. Jackson was so generous and so just that we do not feel at liberty to withhold it. It is due to that 'gallant and true man,' as Mr. Davis again spoke of him, and we place it on public record."

Gen. Jackson, previous to the war, was an old line Whig, but since the war he has been a Democrat of the strictest sect. He has never aspired to political life, and the only office he ever held was that of postmaster, at Tempest Valley, on his Chucky river farm. He was appointed by Amos Kendall, under direction of President Jackson, but was not an applicant for the place, though the postoffice was created at his solicitation. President Jackson, in appointing him, said: "You are a sensible man, not to want an office. Every young man that comes here wants an office." Gen. Jackson was formerly a member of the Odd Fellows. In religion, he is an Episcopalian.

It can readily be seen that throughout his life he has had many difficulties to overcome. He had to pay seven thousand dollars for Embree, after his death, and other large sums as security, but he has always made it a point to go through with whatever he undertakes; never became discouraged, but more determined as difficulties multiplied. For kindness shown to Mrs. Johnson and family during the war, President Johnson issued to him a special pardon, and through Gov. William B. Campbell, and other members of Congress, Gen. Fisk gave an order for the restoration of his property, which had been libelled for confiscation.

His life has been a temperate and a regular one: he has never been above doing manual labor. Even after the war, he went to work on rented land, hoed and plowed a mule and a horse and made one thousand five hundred bushels of corn, in 1866, the sale of which brought him his first money after the war. His wife, too, was industrious and economical, and assisted him to retrieve the losses caused by the war. He lost twenty negroes and five thousand bushels of corn at one time, besides cattle, hogs, horses and tobacco to a large amount, during the war, and his cribs and granaries were frequently raided by the Federal foragers. He never gave a mortgage or deed of trust in his life; has the reputation of a man of will power and working force; is a saving man, never tries to make a show, but lives and has always lived the bountifully hospitable life of a genuine Tennessean and a genuine southerner. He has always found it difficult to refuse a favor to a friend. He is remarkably quick, prompt and decided in his conversation and business transactions, is very individual, and of strongly marked personality.

The most popular name in the United States is Jackson; a name that is given to cities and towns and counties in every State in the Union, a synonym for personal courage and iron will, for chivalry, urbanity and success, and the subject of this sketch is a representative of the family in all these respects.

DUDLEY D. SAUNDERS, M. D.

MEMPHIS.

ONE of the best known and most honored names in the medical profession of Tennessee is that of Dr. Dudley D. Saunders, of Memphis. He was born at Rocky Hill, near Courtland, Lawrence county, Alabama, February 26, 1835. He was reared on a plantation, and was afforded all the facilities for acquiring an education by an indulgent and appreciative father, who was a wealthy southern planter.

In 1852, he graduated at LaGrange College, Alabama, but not having decided what profession he would follow he engaged in planting at his old home for two years. He then went to Mobile, Alabama, and studied medicine under the celebrated Dr. J. C. Nott, at Nott and LeVert's infirmary, remaining there twelve months. He then entered the medical department of the University of Pennsylvania, at Philadelphia, took his first course of lectures there, and his second course at the University of New York, receiving diplomas from both institutions. After this he was house physician at Bellevue hospital, New York, for one term. To become even more proficient in his profession, he next went to Europe, traveled over the continent, and pursued his studies at Paris, France, for some time.

Returning to the United States, he settled at Memphis, in the winter of 1859, and was succeeding well in his practice when the civil war broke out. In the early part of the war, he was appointed surgeon in the Confederate army, and soon after was made assistant director of hospitals for the army of Tennessee, a position which he filled with great ability and universal satisfaction until the surrender, when he returned to Memphis and resumed his practice.

Dr. Saunders has twice filled important chairs in the Memphis Medical College—that of surgery previous to the war, and that of anatomy and surgery since. He is a member of the Shelby County Medical Society, the tri-State Medical Association, and the Tennessee State Medical Society. He was president of the latter body in 1885. He is also a member of the American Medical Association. He remained in Memphis at his post of duty through the epidemics of 1867, 1873, 1878 and 1879, and during the 1878 epidemic was stricken down with yellow fever himself. During the epidemic

of 1878 he was president of the board of health, at a time when all of the other members of the board were down with the fever, and at the time that the able secretary of the board, Dr. John H. Erskine, died.

Although not an active politician, Dr. Saunders has always voted the Democratic ticket. In 1860, he was a Douglas man and opposed secession, but when the time came to take sides, he unhesitatingly espoused the cause of the South. He took the degree of Master Mason in Angerona Lodge, No. 168, at Memphis, in 1860. He is also a member of the Knights of Honor.

His father, Hon. James E. Saunders, a lawyer at Courtland, Lawrence county, Alabama, now living, at the age of eighty years, at his residence, Rocky Hill, three miles from Courtland, is a man of wonderful vitality, well preserved in mind and body, active and full of business energy. He is one of the purest of men, of finely organized intellect; modest as a girl, yet courageous as a lion. He is an omniverous reader of books, and a man whose mental digestion of a great variety of subjects is wonderful, as is evidenced by his fund of accurate information on a remarkably wide range of knowledge. He read law with the late Hon. Francis B. Fogg, of Nashville, and practiced until his health began to fail, when he engaged in planting in Alabama. He always endeavored to avoid public life, but was made collector of the port of Mobile during the administration of President Polk, who was his warm personal friend. In 1860, he was elector for the State at large, in Alabama, on the Douglas ticket, conducted a vigorous and spirited campaign in his State, and fought secession on the stump. But when his State severed her connection with the Union, he went with her. He at once volunteered as an aid-de-camp on the staff of Gen. N. B. Forrest, was in the engagement at Murfreesborough, Tennessee, July 13, 1862, when Forrest captured the command of Gen. Crittenden. In this battle Maj. Saunders was shot through and through while storming the court-house. Gen. Forrest said of him, "Though he is one of the most cautious men I ever saw, yet he is fonder of fighting than I am. His caution is only to get accurate information." During the campaign of 1860, the great orator, Hon. William

L. Yancey, said of him, after one of his discussions with ex-Gov. Matthews, of Mississippi, " His political information is as accurate and as general as that of any man I have ever seen on the stump." He was married when eighteen to a lady aged sixteen.

Dr. Saunders' grandfather was Rev. Turner Saunders, a Methodist preacher, who came from Virginia and settled at Franklin, Tennessee. The Saunders family is of English descent.

Dr. Saunders' mother was Miss Mary F. Watkins, daughter of Robert H. Watkins, of Elbert county, Georgia. She is now seventy-eight years of age, is a woman of deep piety, and has been a member of the Methodist church since her childhood. Her father was a planter and owned large landed property in Alabama, to which State he moved from Georgia. Before his death he called his children about him and administered on his own estate, saying he wanted no trouble over his money after he was gone.

Dr. Saunders has been twice married. His first marriage took place at Memphis, February 14, 1860, to Miss Kate Stuart Wheatley, daughter of Seth Wheatley, a lawyer, of Memphis, who died in 1858. Her mother was Miss Cook, daughter of the late Chancellor Cook, one of the old true men of Tennessee. She is descended from the Browns and Littles, of South Carolina, and was a cousin of Morgan L. Brown, of Nashville. The ancestry of the family runs back to the Stuarts—the royal family of England. Mrs. Saunders was educated at Staunton, Virginia, and was a woman remarkable for truthfulness, great vivacity, bright and impulsive disposition, with her impulses generally in the right direction. She died at Marietta, Georgia, in January, 1864, while her husband was post surgeon at that place. To this union were born two children : (1). Mary Lou Saunders, born in April, 1861 ; now wife of Samuel G. Brent, of Alexandria, Virginia, son of Col. George W. Brent, formerly adjutant-general on the staff of Gen. Braxton Bragg, commander of the army of Tennessee. They have one son. (2). Kate Wheatley Saunders, born at Marietta, Georgia, in January, 1864.

In February, 1867, Dr. Saunders was married to his second wife, Miss Mary E. Wheatley, sister of his first wife. By this marriage there are also two children : (1). Dudley D. Saunders, jr., born in March, 1869. (2). Lizzie W. Saunders, born in 1873. The present Mrs. Saunders was educated in Memphis and at a convent in St. Louis. She is a woman of remarkably fine mind, brilliant in conversation, sunny in disposition, with a keen sense of the ludicrous. She is well educated and well informed, with a lofty idea of justice, a great contempt for anything little, and an in-

nate piety which is worn every day, not Sundays alone. Her instruction to her children is to be truthful under all circumstances, and always too proud to do a mean thing. She, as is also her husband, is a member of the Protestant Episcopal church.

In his early life, Dr. Saunders was much given to outdoor sports, hunting and fishing, which were the means of laying the foundation of his strong constitution. He is six feet one inch in height, and weighs two hundred and thirty pounds—a splendid specimen of the physical man, yet also filling the idea Horace had of a perfect man : " *Mens sana in corpore sano.*" His standard of success in a medical man is thorough qualification. The permanent reputation of a medical man, among other things, depends greatly upon the estimate placed upon him by his professional brethren. He has ever cultivated a spirit of frankness and friendship toward them, believing that trickery has never yet accomplished any permanent good. A cheerful, pleasant manner toward the patient, backed by hard work, close attention to business, and an effort to digest thoroughly all knowledge acquired, have characterized his professional life. Good medical books and first-class periodicals have ever been his daily companions and his nightly friends. A thorough knowledge of medicine and the self-reliance necessary to a proper application of it under all circumstances and emergencies, has been his motto. Temperance, morality and purity of character he has ever regarded as essentials of success.

The following is the estimate placed upon Dr. Saunders as a boy, by his father. When seventy-nine years of age, he wrote to his grandson, Dudley D. Saunders, jr., on his fifteenth birthday : " Your father had the endorsement of all his teachers, that he was gentlemanly in his manners, high-minded and fearlessly truthful. He was not remarkable for application to his studies, but when he did study, he concentrated his mind upon his lesson. He managed to get a good education in medicine and literature—I think it was owing to his power of concentration. If he read, he read ; if he played, he played ; if he shot, every nerve was strained for a good aim ; if he fought, it was *manibus pedibusque.*"

A prominent gentleman of Memphis says of Dr. Saunders : " He is a man of great intellect and great force of character. He would have been a success in any line because of his strength of intellect and finished scholarship. In argument he has few superiors. He stands at the head of his profession, and leading physicians all over the country will tell you that Dr. Dudley D. Saunders, of Memphis, is authority on almost all matters pertaining to his profession."

HON. T. W. BROWN.

MEMPHIS.

DISTINGUISHED alike as a lawyer, an orator and a statesman, this gentleman manifestly inherited much of his mental constitution from his parents, both of whom were gifted with exceptional intellectual faculties. Some account, therefore, of his father and mother will properly precede our sketch of the man himself.

Robert Brown, the father, was a merchant from county Antrim, in the north of Ireland, a descendant from the Scotch settlers, who, many generations before, established themselves in a district of the province of Ulster, called the Ulster plantation. He was trained at Belfast, in mercantile pursuits, and was as fine a specimen of that school of commercial men, contributed by the north of Ireland to Boston, New York and Philadelphia, as ever landed upon American soil, notably among them the late A. T. Stewart, of New York. He first emigrated to Philadelphia, a city whose commercial system was first inaugurated by Scotch-Irish colonists and north of Ireland men, and is now controlled by their descendants. Not finding here the opening for his business enterprise which he sought, he moved, successively, to Howard county, Missouri (where he married), thence to Henry county, Kentucky, where he engaged for several years in mercantile pursuits, and finally to Shelby county, in the same State. Here he soon became identified with the works of internal improvement, which, about that time, were inaugurated in Kentucky. In this work at last his excellent administrative talents found an appropriate field for their exercise. Through his skill and experience in such works, he was placed in control of some of the most important enterprises, which gave him congenial employment for the rest of his life. He died, in 1850, in the fifty-sixth year of his life. Intellectually estimated, precision of thought was his leading characteristic, one which constituted him a fine mathematician; morally, he was noted for his strict integrity in all the relations of life.

The wife of the above, Mrs. Matilda Brown, *nee* Matilda Wooldridge, mother of our subject, was a native of Dublin, Ireland, daughter of Richard Wooldridge, a Welshman, and a merchant in Dublin. Her mother was a Miss Mary O'Toole, of a family of historical importance in Ireland. Lawrence O'Toole, a member of the same family, was the first Irishman who wore the cardinal's hat; he was canonized after his death.

The O'Tooles were the leading sept in county Wicklow, and were active for centuries in the struggle against Norman and British supremacy in Ireland; as an inevitable consequence they were always a conspicuous mark for oppression and cruelty on the part of the predominant race, but, so far as history shows, no one of the family ever betrayed the cause of Ireland, or failed to strike a blow for Irish liberty and independence whenever it was practicable to do so.

Mrs. Brown died in Shelby county, Kentucky, at the age of forty-five years. She is remembered as a lady of remarkable beauty, having an entirely Grecian face, and as specially noted for the purity and grace with which she pronounced the English language. She was exceedingly generous, caring nothing for money, except to gratify her liberal impulses. She told her only child that it was disgraceful to hoard money, which made a lasting impression upon him. Exceedingly graceful in person and manner, she attended much to dress, but never sacrificed to her taste in this regard the substantial comforts of her family nor intercepted for it out of her humble means her bounty to the poor. She was a strongly marked character, endowed with remarkable personal courage under circumstances that would have intimidated most women. She did not know what fear was. Proud of her lineage, she delighted to speak of her descent from the O'Tooles, yet never made an indelicate manifestation of hauteur. The poet, Thomas Moore, was frequently a guest at her father's house, in Dublin, and she used to relate many interesting incidents connected with his visits. She often heard him sing his own songs and accompany his voice with some musical instrument. She was, in fact, much cherished in society wherever she lived; delighting in the company of intellectual men and accomplished women, but with all this she was known and beloved for her sympathy with the unfortunate and needy. Such women are rare enough now-a-days.

In the paternal line, Judge Brown is connected with men of eminence in many departments of life. His grandfather, Thomas Brown, was an Irish landholder, a man of education, and of firmness and resolution of character. He lived to the age of ninety years. Not to mention the late Hon. B. Gratz Brown, the St. Louis statesman, ex-governor of Missouri, and vice-presidential candidate on the ticket with Horace Greeley, and his brother, Col. John Mason Brown, the prominent lawyer of Louisville, Kentucky (who married a daughter of Gen. William Preston), the family boasts many eminent personages in Europe. The illustrious Field Marshal Ulysses Maximilian Brown, a favorite officer in the armies of the Empress Maria Theresa, of Austria, and who distinguished himself at the battle of Prague, was a member of this family, as was also the celebrated Scotchman, Thomas Brown, author of "Brown's Mental Philosophy," and recognized as the famous metaphysician, physician, poet and philosopher.

Thomas Wooldridge Brown, the subject of this memoir, was one of several children, all of whom, except himself, died in early childhood. His constitution was

delicate by inheritance, entailing on him a sickly childhood and youth. In spite of this his education commenced early, and he obtained distinction at school.
Born in March, 1828, he entered Centre College, Danville, Kentucky, in 1843. His preliminary examination
was the more searching on account of his youth; it
resulted in his admission to the junior class, in which
his examination at the end of the year placed him second in rank. His father kept him at home the next
year (1844), thinking him too young to graduate; but
for this there is little doubt he would have graduated
at the unprecedentedly early age of sixteen.

He completed his course in 1845, graduating with the
senior class of that year. Centre College was highly
prosperous at this time, and Brown's graduating class
included some of the most brilliant young men of the
southern and western States, among those who have
since become distinguished, being Hon. John M. Har-
lan, of the United States Supreme court; Judge Samuel
Breckinridge, of St. Louis; Rev. Robert Brank, pastor
of the leading Presbyterian church in St. Louis; Hon.
Joseph Lewis, now of the Supreme bench of Kentucky,
distinguished as a brigadier-general of the Confederate
army, and Dr. Robert C. Breckinridge, an officer of the
medical staff on duty at Richmond, Virginia, during
the civil war. Many other class-mates held distinguished positions in after life.

His college course completed, he commenced teaching
school in the Presbyterian Academy at Bardstown,
Kentucky. He was the youngest teacher who ever had
charge of that academy, and had many pupils there
older than himself. His predecessor in charge of the
school was James D. Nourse, a gentleman of considerable literary distinction in those days. He did not
continue long there, but soon commenced the study of
law at Shelbyville, Kentucky, in the office of J. M. and
W. C. Bullock, and after eight months' preparation,
was admitted to the bar by Judges William F. Bullock
and Mason Brown. During the early years of his practice he became acquainted with the celebrated Benjamin Hardin and witnessed some of the brilliant efforts
which adorned the closing years of that eminent lawyer's career. After Hardin's death, Brown was appointed to take charge of two of his most important
cases in Spencer county, which he conducted with
signal ability and won. This was a great triumph for
so young a lawyer, and gave him great eclat in the
courts, establishing him at once among the leading
practitioners therein.

Shortly after this, important constitutional questions
had to be litigated in the Kentucky courts, in consequence of an act of the Legislature suppressing the
State lotteries. This gave to Brown the opportunity
of distinguishing himself in the famous Shelby College lottery case, the decision of which is quoted as
authority in all the lottery cases of the present day.
He advised the institution of the suit and conducted it

to a successful conclusion, against the advice of older
and more distinguished counsel, establishing the le-
gality of the lottery, and saving to Shelby College, his
client, over one hundred thousand dollars. The first
struggle in this case was before the judiciary committee
of the Kentucky Legislature, to which body Shelby
College had applied for relief. The leading adverse
counsel was the Hon. John W. Stevenson, since governor of Kentucky, and United States senator, who was
then already past middle age, and high in authority as
a constitutional lawyer. Brown had already acquired
reputation for judgment and ability in handling constitutional questions, still the contest was regarded as a
very unequal one, especially as all the lotteries in the
United States were arrayed against the college through
their desire to put down a rival competitor. After a
long and heated contest, conducted on his side by
Brown alone, the judiciary committee reported in favor
of the application of Shelby College, much to the
chagrin and disappointment of Mr. Stevenson, which
was aggravated by the compliments paid by the committee to the young lawyer, his antagonist.

After this Brown practiced for several years in the
same place, classed by the consent of all men among
the first lawyers of Kentucky; but about 1860, he determined to remove to Memphis, Tennessee, then
believed to be the best field in the southwest for the
exercise of the talents of a first-class lawyer. It required a year to close up his Kentucky business, and
within that interval the civil war broke out.

This was an era of great surprises. In February, 1861,
the State of Tennessee declared her purpose of abiding
by the Union. In execution of his previously formed
purpose, however, Brown went to Memphis, landing
there just twelve days before the bombardment of
Fort Sumter. This event took place April 12, 1861,
and caused a vast revulsion of feeling throughout the
South. All this is a matter of history, and it need only
be said of Brown that, though opposed to secession on
principle, and believing it to be both unnecessary and
inexpedient, he ranged himself with the southern States
when the first gun announced that war was no longer
avoidable.

He joined the southern army in 1862, after the Federal occupation of Memphis, entering it, as most men did
in those days, as a private in the ranks. He soon, however, received an appointment from President Davis as
judge advocate of Polk's corps of the army of Tennessee,
commanded, after the battle of Mission Ridge, by Gen.
Hardee. He continued on duty in this corps from the
battle of Stones River to the surrender at Greensborough; during this time he only received two leaves of
absence, which occasioned only thirty days' absence
from his command in all. His relations with Gens.
Polk and Hardee were of the most intimate and confidential nature, implying the utmost confidence in his
abilities on the part of those distinguished comman-

lers, by whom efforts were made to have him a command in the line.

The war ended, he resumed the practice of his profession in Memphis, having, like most southern men, lost all of his savings during that great civil struggle. The leading object of his exertions now was to give his children a thoroughly good education, in which he has been entirely successful. His name has been associated with nearly all the remarkable and prominent cases which have been heard in the courts of Memphis, yet, in spite of the arduous duties thus described, he found time to devote his talents to the relief of Tennessee, and, especially, of Memphis, from the corruption and oppression of radical rule, and from the ruin and prostration which it left behind. By tongue and pen, by counsel and active effort, he aided prominently in achieving final success in restoring the State to the control of the people.

In 1868, he was appointed by the Democratic State convention on a committee to present before the national Democratic convention at New York the protests of the State against the iniquities of the "carpet-bag and scallawag government." In this mission he was associated with the Hons. James E. Bailey, John C. Brown, Albert Pike and Gen. A. P. Stewart. The duty of preparing the report was assigned by the committee to Judge Brown, and in less than twenty-four hours it was written, and, on the second day of the convention, was presented and read to thousands in Tammany Hall, and created marked sensation. It was the first effective blow that was struck at the hateful domination of the carpet-bagger. It was printed in all the leading papers North, both Democratic and Republican, the former vigorously endorsing its denunciations, the latter protesting against being held responsible for the iniquities that had so long been sanctioned under the name of reconstruction. This was equivalent to practical unanimity in condemnation of the system, and, in fact, it commenced yielding to the force of public opinion from that time, and, though it died hard, its death had become a foregone conclusion.

This repudiation, by the North, of the radical government in Tennessee, made possible the division in the party between Senter and Stokes, the former representing the sentiment of northern Republicanism, the latter representing that of Tennessee Radicalism. This division resulted in the emancipation of the State and the enfranchisement of the ex-Confederate citizens. But for this report no such happy occurrence would have transpired, in all probability, for many years. The breaking up of radicalism in Tennessee paved the way for the downfall of the radical governments of the other southern States, which followed in rapid succession. The value of this report is difficult to estimate. Its results have been beneficial to the State of Tennessee and to the whole South. All honor, then, to Judge Brown and his noble compatriots. The pen of history

records for them the gratitude of a redeemed State and a disenthralled people.

Judge Brown has occasionally served on the commission authorized by the State Legislature to aid in clearing off the accumulation of business which had completely blocked the proceedings of that court.

He has, also, occasionally, acted as judge in various cases where a special judiciary officer was demanded, and in this capacity he sat upon a case of primary importance and great celebrity—that of Marr v. the Bank of West Tennessee. In this case he first determined the extent of a discharge under the recent bankrupt law, and in his investigation for that purpose, he collected all the bankrupt laws of England and the several States of the Union. At the instance of Judge Hammond, of the United States district court at Memphis, this judgment was forwarded to the judiciary committee of the United States senate, which had then before it a national bankruptcy law, to aid them in the preparation of that measure. It afterward, on an appeal, came before the Supreme court of the United States, and its confirmation stands on the minutes. Moreover, the court did what no Supreme court had ever done before—except as to Judge Reese—paid a special compliment to the judge below for its exactitude and completeness.

Judge Brown married, December 8, 1849, Miss Sarah Ann Craig, daughter of John Craig, of Lincoln county, Kentucky. Her mother was a Miss Ann Gaines, whose father was a Revolutionary soldier. She is of Virginia descent on both sides. She is a lady of very superior mind, finely educated, accomplished and cultured. She exerts a controlling influence in society, and for years has been among the foremost in promoting the active charities of Memphis. Judge and Mrs. Brown have four children living: (1). Emma Wooldridge Brown, graduated at Lausanne, Switzerland; married George B. Morton, of Virginia, now of Allegheny City, Pennsylvania, and has three children, George B., Nellie and Wooldridge. (2). Robert Grattan Brown, after spending two years in Switzerland, graduated at the University of Virginia; studied law, was admitted to the bar at Memphis, after a very satisfactory examination, where he is now practicing law. (3). Thomas Wooldridge Brown, graduated at Davidson College, North Carolina; now engaged in banking at St. Louis. He was for a while editor of the Pine Bluff (Arkansas) *Commercial*. (4). John Henry Brown, educated at Davidson College, North Carolina; now in commercial life in St. Louis.

Judge Brown lost one of his children, William Craig Brown, who died six years old.

In his religious views, Judge Brown is very independent, but was reared in the Presbyterian church. He is a director in the Germania Banking Company at Memphis; was presidential elector for Scott, in Kentucky, in 1852; was elected delegate to two conventions (Douglas, Democratic, and Bell and Everett, Whig), held at Louisville, Kentucky, in 1860, and was on the joint committee appointed to report on the situation. At twenty-two years of age he was offered, by George D. Prentice, a handsome salary to become assistant editor, with him, of the Louisville *Journal*, then the most influential newspaper in the West or South, but this he declined, preferring to devote himself exclusively to his profession.

About this time he also declined a nomination for lieutenant-governor of Kentucky on the Whig ticket, with Judge Loving as nominee for governor. His reason for declining was, that he did not consider the head of the ticket strong enough to win the race, thus throwing upon a very young man, having the second place on the ticket, the burden of the canvass. The Democrats had nominated for governor an exceptionally strong man, Hon. Beverly Clark. The correctness of Brown's judgment was soon evidenced by the withdrawal of Loving and putting in his stead the Hon. Charles F. Morehead, who was well known all over the State and had a large personal following. Notwithstanding his strength in this regard, he beat Clark by only about five thousand votes.

Judge Brown has not been a continuously laborious man, though capable of long and intense labor on special occasions. Yet on the other hand, he has been a constant reader, and his reading has been thoroughly assimilated and incorporated with his naturally powerful mind. Besides, his reading has been of a select character, and he has made it an invariable rule to work whatever material he obtained from standard literature into his mental structure, thus making it his own. He has thought more than he has read, and has no respect whatever for a merely bookish man. At the commencement of his career he was not a fluent speaker, but acquired the faculty of ready speech from the constant habit of composition in writing. For several years he reduced to manuscript every important speech he made, either at the bar or on the stump. He was likewise a constant writer of editorials. Continuing this course, he became by degrees a rapid composer, and at last ceased to need manuscript for any speech, political, forensic or literary, that he was called upon to make. He is generally credited with the ability to make his great efforts with but little labor, but this reputation he disclaims, thinking it more creditable to devote his whole powers to the preparation of the business in hand, giving to his clients and to the public the best of his capabilities.

REV. A. W. JONES, A.M., D.D.

JACKSON.

THE Memphis Conference Female Institute, of which this gentleman has been president since 1853, was founded in 1844, has graduated four hundred and ninety-five alumnæ, and ranks among the most popular colleges in the southern States. In addition to the usual curriculum, it has a commercial department, requiring of its graduates a thorough practice in all the devices of business. It also has an art department, a normal class, a good library, an extensive apparatus, and a cabinet. The prosperity and standing of the school is so largely due to its management under the presidency of Dr. Jones, that a sketch of his life is of more than ordinary interest. History is but the lives of a few individuals who have left their impress on their times and given shape to measures that influenced successive generations.

Dr. Jones was born in Franklin county, North Carolina, December 28, 1815, and spent his youth there on his father's farm, and knew nothing else until he went to Randolph Macon College, Virginia, where he graduated, in 1839, and at once commenced teaching in the same institution as principal of the preparatory department, a position which he filled two and a half years, and then traveled four years in the North Carolina conference as an itinerant preacher. In 1844-5, his health failed, in Newbern, North Carolina, where he was stationed.

In 1845, he came to Jackson, Tennessee, and took the chair of mathematics and languages in the school of which he has been president thirty-one years. After teaching there six years he took a professorship in West Tennessee College, and remained there two and a half years.

In 1853, he was elected president of the Memphis Conference Female Institute, and at once erected, at his own expense, the west wing of the institute, in which the school is conducted, the other buildings being devoted to boarding the pupils.

Dr. Jones was converted in 1829, at thirteen years of age. From boyhood he felt the impression that he was called to the ministry, but decided that point while at college. Indeed, as soon as converted, he commenced praying and exhorting, and was a most zealous Christian from the first. He never sowed " wild oats," never knew what it is to be wicked. The most useful part of his life, he thinks, was while in college, in having a marked religious influence over his fellow students and associates. He has belonged only to two conferences, the North Carolina and the Memphis. Some of his literary addresses have been published, and evince the possession of a high order of literary and scholarly attainments.

In 1855, he became a Mason in Jackson Lodge, No. 45, and since then has taken all the degrees of the Blue Lodge, Chapter, Council and Commandery, and has filled the highest positions in all of them. In 1880, he was Eminent Commander. He was in early times a member of the order of the Sons of Temperance, a cause which he has always favored.

In politics he was never fully identified with any party, though acting always in sympathy with the South, but has been independent in this as in everything else. He has through life been guided by his own convictions. In the conduct of the institute, he has absolute control—is the head, heart and soul of the school. His personality is so marked that he can work only in his own harness, and he impresses his individuality upon everything he engages in. The key to his success is, that he is very individual. He has raised his own children without special regard to anybody's views. What else is there for a man to do, but to see with his own eyes, wear his own head, do his own thinking, act on his own judgment, take the consequences of his own actions and finally give account of himself to God? This rule of conduct is, perhaps, the only true manhood. This independence in the mental make-up of Dr. Jones is evident, even in the tone of his voice, which indicates a man of positive character and decided convictions, and but for the kindness, gentleness and affection equally apparent, he would pass for a stern man and appear abrupt in his manners. In personal appearance, however, he is elegant and dignified; in manners gentle, sympathetic and kind.

Dr. Jones first married, in Warren county, North Carolina, February 12, 1841, Miss Caroline M. Blanch, of a Virginia family, who died the same year of their marriage—December 14, 1841. From this marriage resulted one child, Rev. Amos Blanch Jones, A.M., now president of the Huntsville (Alabama), Female College. He was the captain of a company in the Confederate army, and served through the war, taking a gallant part in the battles of Murfreesborough, Shiloh, Missionary Ridge, and many other minor engagements. He was wounded two or three times. He married Miss Mary Gates, of Egypt, Mississippi, and has two children, Amos Wesley and James Taylor.

Dr. Jones' second marriage, which occurred at Pittsborough, North Carolina, October 4, 1843, was with Miss Mary Eliza Womack, a native of that place, daughter of Green Womack, a merchant. Her mother was a Miss Taylor, of North Carolina. By this marriage, Dr. Jones had six children, four of whom died in infancy. The two surviving are: (1). Dr. J. T. Jones, graduated M.D., at Baltimore; now a practicing physician at Jackson, Tennessee. He married Miss Belle Gates, sister to the wife of his brother, Amos, and has two children, Newton Gates and Mary Eliza. (2). Marianna

Jones, now wife of Dr. W. Bond Dashiell, of Kaufman, Texas; has two children, Bond and Mary Womack.

Dr. Jones' third marriage occurred at Jackson, Tennessee, April 2, 1857, to Miss Amanda Childs Bigelow, who was born in that city, daughter of Elijah Bigelow, of Massachusetts, one of the earliest settlers of Jackson, a teacher and a lawyer. Her mother, also a native of Massachusetts, was originally Miss Maria O. Childs, daughter of Amariah Childs and his wife, Ruth, nee Larkin, of Lynn, Massachusetts. Mrs. Jones' mother taught school in Jackson forty years—teaching three generations. She was a highly educated lady and a devoted Presbyterian. By his marriage with Miss Bigelow, Dr. Jones has had five children: (1). Ida Bigelow Jones, born January 28, 1858; died at Chautauqua, New York, August 16, 1884, twenty-six years of age. She was educated in her father's institute and became a very celebrated elocutionist, and taught in her father's school. She was a controlling spirit, exerting great influence, even over her devoted father, in the management of the school, and had the name of the highest model of woman. She gave great popularity to the elocutionary department of the institute. (2). George C. Jones, born August 29, 1859; graduated at the Southwestern Baptist University, Jackson, Tennessee, at the age of seventeen; graduated at the Vanderbilt University, Nashville, in his twentieth year, in the first graduating class of that institution; taught in his father's school two years; went to Berlin, Germany, spent a year in the Berlin University, studying sciences, and is now professor of natural sciences and languages in the Memphis Conference Female Institute, at Jackson, Tennessee. (3). Eddie Childs Jones, died three and a half years old. (4). Charles Fuller Jones, died in infancy. (5). Ammatelle Jones, born December 8, 1869; now in the senior class in her father's institute.

Dr. Jones' grandfather Jones was a Welshman, came from Wales soon after the Revolutionary war, settled first in Preston, Virginia, and afterward in Franklin county, North Carolina.

The Doctor's father, Rev. Amos Jones, was a magistrate, local preacher, a farmer and "a man of all trades," blacksmith, wheelwright and carpenter, taking up these pursuits as necessity required, but never following either exclusively. He was a very original character; followed his own convictions decidedly and independently; was strong in physical constitution and in mind; a man of positive opinions—there was nothing negative about him. Yet in his nature he was very passionate and sympathetic—weeping often in his preaching. Besides, he was very energetic and industrious. He lived seventy-five years, and died within three feet of the spot where he was born, in Franklin county, North Carolina.

Dr. Jones' mother, nee Mary Myrick, was a very mild, affectionate woman. She raised a large family, six sons and six daughters, all of whom lived to adult age. She died in Milledgeville, Georgia, at her father's, forty-six years old. Of her children, Rev. Turner M. Jones, D.D., is now president of the Greensborough (North Carolina) Female College. Jordan F. Jones is a very prosperous merchant, mechanic and owner of flouring mills in Franklin county, North Carolina. Two of the daughters married Methodist preachers; the others married farmers.

Dr. Jones began life with but little money, gained some by marrying, the balance he has made. When he began studying, he had no confidence in himself, but in a year was ranked among the first, and from that time on was first grade in everything—graduating the vale-

dictorian of his class. His inclination is to be first based upon a conviction of duty to do what he under-takes as a Christian. He is also ambitious to be first in the ministry, first in teaching—to be a leader, disposition that runs through his whole family—to lead to control in what they undertake, not to be followers but managers of affairs. His whole soul has been in the Memphis Conference Female Institute for thirt years, and wherever he goes, his school is on his mind His mind is essentially mathematical, as evidenced b: the system that prevails in his school. His life is rythm, wonderfully regular. He consults friends, bu finally acts on his own judgment.

BENNETT G. HENNING, M.D.

MEMPHIS.

THE subject of this sketch was born in Durham-ville, Lauderdale county, Tennessee, October 16, 1849, and was raised on a farm until twenty years of age. He received his literary education at the Tipton High School, at Covington, one of the oldest schools in West Tennessee, his teacher being Mr. James Byars, who has been principal of the school for more than thirty-five years.

At an early age, young Henning made up his mind to become a physician, and, therefore, after leaving the Covington school, in 1868, went immediately to the Jef-ferson Medical College, at Philadelphia, remained one session and next entered the Bellevue Hospital Medical College, New York, where he graduated in 1870. He was then appointed senior interne at the Jersey City Charity Hospital, and remained in charge of that insti-tution for twelve months. Returning to Tennessee, he located in Memphis, and became connected with the old Memphis Medical College, having charge of the city dispensary from January, 1871, to March, 1872.

In March, 1872, he went to Europe, and pursued his studies in the medical schools of England, France and Germany, and after traveling over Europe, returned to Memphis during the yellow fever epidemic of 1873, and resumed his practice. In 1878–79, he reported the first cases of yellow fever, against the sanction of the board of health, and created considerable excitement thereby. He believed that the best way to fight the fever was to let it be known as soon as possible and get away from it, and this he advised his patrons to do, yet he bravely remained among them and practiced till he had gotten them all out of the city. He was one of the founders of the Memphis Hospital Medical College, and was its professor of the principles and practice of surgery from its foundation up to January, 1884, when he resigned on account of ill health. In order to recuperate his wasted

energies, he gave up his practice and left the city fo fifteen months, returning in the early part of 1886. H health being fully restored, he resumed the duties o his profession and is now in full practice. He has als been re-elected to a professorship in the Memphis Hos pital Medical College, to fill the chair of materia med ica and therapeutics, recently made vacant by the deat of Dr. S. H. Brown. He is a member of the Stat Medical Society of Tennessee, the tri-State Medica Society, the West Tennessee Medical Society, and th Shelby Medical Society. His practice has always bee large, and he stands in the front rank of advancin physicians and surgeons in Tennessee.

Dr. Henning has always been a Democrat, but ha taken no part in politics whatever, except to go to th polls and cast his vote. He became a Master Mason a Memphis, in 1883, and an Odd Fellow at the same plac several years ago. He has never held any office i the lodge or out of it, and has never been a candidat for any office, thinking that to practice medicine a man should follow that and nothing else. He is also a mem ber of the Knights of Honor and of the Ancient Orde of United Workmen. His father, Dr. D. M. Henning whose sketch and family history will be found elsewher in this volume, is a native of Georgia, moved to Wes Tennessee at a very early day, and was one of the pio neers of that country. He, also, is a graduate of Jef ferson Medical College; has always been a temperat and religious man, and has met with marked success not only as a practitioner of medicine, but as a mer chant and real estate dealer, having accumulated one o the largest fortunes in Lauderdale county. He is now seventy-one years of age and resides at Henning, on the Chesapeake and Ohio and Southwestern railroad, a town which was named for him, and the subject of this sketch He has also built up the town of Gates on the same road. He was instrumental in the construction of the road, and was at one time its vice-president. His father was a Methodist minister in Georgia, and his mother was a Miss Meriwether, of an old and distinguished family who figured extensively in Revolutionary times. The mother of the subject of this sketch, was Miss Ann B. Greaves, daughter of Bennett Greaves, of South Carolina, a gentleman of French descent, who moved to West Tennessee at an early day, and was a planter there.

Dr. Henning was married, in 1874, to Miss Cornelia F. Frayser, daughter of Dr. John R. Frayser, whose sketch appears elsewhere in this volume. Mrs. Hen-

ning is a member of the Methodist church, of which church Dr. Henning has also been a member for the past twenty years.

Dr. Henning has been a lover of learning and a hard student from his early boyhood, temperate in his habits and an obedient son. His ambition lies within his profession—a pursuit which he follows with enthusiasm and fidelity, and persistently leaves all other things alone. He early made a resolution never to seek public office, which he regards as one of the worst things a medical man can do. Young in years, but old in observation, the future that spreads out before him is one full of promise, and, without doubt, full of success.

CHRISTOPHER L. HARDWICK.

CLEVELAND.

WITHOUT doubt, one of the best representative business men of Tennessee, one to whom the State can point with pride for his energy, enterprise and integrity, is Mr. Christopher L. Hardwick, the banker and merchant at Cleveland. He was born in Bradley county, Tennessee, February 14, 1827, the son of John W. Hardwick, a native of Georgia, at one time a commissioner for removing the Cherokee Indians from Tennessee, for a long while a planter, and from 1836 to 1844, a hotel keeper at Cleveland. He died in 1853, at the age of fifty-four. Politically, he was a very strong Whig; religiously, a very strong Methodist; a vigorous, independent man—a leader in politics in his town and day. For a considerable time he ran a tannery, and afterward a brickyard, and built some of the first brick houses put up in Cleveland. He owned some fifteen slaves, and was only moderately successful in business, though he always lived well and had plenty.

Mr. Christopher L. Hardwick's grandfather, Garland Hardwick, came from England with two brothers, James and William, and settled in Georgia. Garland Hardwick went to Benton county, Arkansas, where he died, in 1847, about seventy-five years of age. He left six children, George, Garland, John W. (father of the subject of this sketch), Charles, Thomas and Joseph.

Mr. Hardwick's mother was Jane Montgomery, daughter of Hugh L. Montgomery, Indian agent of the general government for the Ocoee purchase. He was a native of Chattooga county, Georgia, settled in Bradley county, Tennessee, about 1834, but went back to Chattooga county, Georgia, in 1840, and there died, about seventy-five years old, a pious Presbyterian. Mrs. Hardwick was educated in Georgia; was a leading Methodist, and never known to be away from the meetings of her church. She died at Dalton, Georgia, March 28, 1879, at the age of seventy-eight, having borne

thirteen children, namely: (1). Caroline, born October 16, 1819; died October 5, 1838. (2). Emily, died the wife of Andrew B. Foster, of Decatur, Texas. (3). Celina, now the wife of William H. Tibbs, a planter, of Dalton, Georgia. (4). Susan, now wife of Milton Holmes, a stock raiser at Decatur, Texas. (5). Huldah, died the wife of Robert Wallace, also of Decatur, Texas. (6). Christopher L., subject of this sketch. (7). Martha, died the wife of William E. Key, in Benton county, Arkansas. (8). Frank E., married, first, Sallie Barksdale, and after her death, Minnie Kelley, and is now living in Benton county, Arkansas. (9). Hugh, now a farmer in Decatur, Texas. (10). Charles, now a farmer in Rush county, Texas. (11). William Henry, died in infancy. (12). Cynthia, died the wife of L. R. Chapman, a farmer in Bradley county, Tennessee. (13). Mary, now the wife of Andrew M. Rogers, at Cleveland, Tennessee.

Christopher L. Hardwick was raised principally at his father's hotel in Cleveland, and was permitted to do pretty much as he pleased, and he pleased to take work wherever he could get it. He worked up to the age of fifteen at twenty-five cents a day in the first brickyard in that place, and helped to build the first brick house in the town. In 1843, he went with his father to Benton county, Arkansas, and remained there farming three years, when he returned, in 1846, to Cleveland, went into a store clerking for his victuals and clothes. He continued in the store till his wages got to be three hundred dollars a year, when he was offered a salary of one thousand five hundred dollars to go to Charleston, South Carolina, as a salesman, but, rather than give him up, his employer, William H. Tibbs, his brother-in-law, offered him one-third interest in the profits of the store if he would continue with him in the management of the business. This proposition he accepted. In 1851, he married, before he had any property. He continued with Mr. Tibbs till 1856, when the firm met with the misfortune of losing fifteen thousand dollars in wheat, which took all the property he had made up to that time, which was some five thousand dollars. He had now left only a wife and three children. From that time, 1857, he commenced merchandising for himself, without any capital except a good credit. He made money fast up to and during the war. From 1862 to 1864, he engaged in farming, in addition to his merchandising. He continued merchandising till 1880, when he quit that business and went into the manufacture of woolen goods at Cleveland.

He was elected superintendent of the Cleveland woolen mills when they were first started. In 1883, he purchased a half interest in the mills; was elected president and superintendent, and in these positions he has continued to the present time. The mills are operated on a capital of one hundred thousand dollars, employing sixty-two hands, at an average weekly salary of five dollars, running nine hundred and twelve spindles, and fifty-four looms. It is what is called a "three set mill," making exclusively jeans. Mr. Hardwick is the principal owner of the mills, his four sons, Frank, John, Oscar and George, being the other owners, and also of the banking institution of C. L. Hardwick & Co., at Dalton, Georgia, a discount and deposit bank, with a capital of fifty thousand dollars, handling annually one hundred and ten thousand dollars, the deposits being about sixty thousand dollars. Mr. Hardwick and his two sons, Frank and Oscar, are owners of the banking institution at Cedartown, Georgia, known as Hardwick & Co., bankers, a new institution, operating on a capital of twenty thousand dollars. Mr. Hardwick is also interested with his son, George, in a spoke and hub factory at Dalton, Georgia, run on a capital of ten thousand dollars, and employing fifteen hands. C. L. Hardwick & Sons are also running the Cleveland stove works on a capital of ten thousand dollars, turning out about twelve stoves a day, and working about fifteen hands. Mr. Hardwick owns also several dwellings and business houses in Cleveland, and is reckoned among the most substantial citizens of East Tennessee.

The secret of his success may be traced back to the fact that when his father let him do as he pleased, he took to work—to hard work—late and early, and this he has kept up to this day, taking care of what he has made, being liberal, giving away large sums to charities, church buildings and schools, to preachers and other worthy purposes. His liberality in these directions has become so well known that the editor makes a record of it here, believing that liberality is an element of success. Another fact in this man's history, that throws light on his success, is that he was always moral, never spent money for whisky, nor gambled, nor dissipated in any way. In business he was always attentive, very polite o customers, and a good manager, loyal to the interests

of his employers when he was a clerk. When he left Mr. Tibbs and put up for himself, in 1856, people flocked to his store and traded with him out of friendship. His manners, solid character, generous spirit, and outflow of sympathy, made him popular with the people, and they liked to trade with him. In these respects he is presented here as a representative Tennessee merchant.

Mr. Hardwick is a Royal Arch and Council Mason, and served a number of years as Master of the lodge and High Priest of the chapter. He is also a Knight of Honor. In politics he is a Democrat, though in Whig days a Whig. He has served as mayor of Cleveland, and is the oldest citizen of the place. He has frequently been delegate to the State conventions of his party, but was never an office seeker. In religion, he followed his mother, and is a Methodist, and has been steward twenty-five years, and Sunday-school superintendent ten years.

Mr. Hardwick married, in Cleveland, March 20, 1850, Miss Isabella M. Tucker, born, February 24, 1835, in Wilkes county, North Carolina, daughter of Joseph Tucker, who moved to Bradley county, Tennessee, in 1838. Her uncles, John and William, were farmers, and her uncle, Joshua, a blacksmith in Bradley county. Her mother was Mary Isbell, of a North Carolina family. Mrs. Hardwick was educated at Cleveland, married at sixteen, and is one of those kind of women who, when their husbands are poor, make money by their needle. A good cook, and skilled in all manner of needle work, she seldom hires help except on extraordinary occasions, and has trained her daughters to lay hold with their hands and let their works praise them. Only a few years ago Mr. Hardwick sold a farm she had made with her needle, but the money she made herself she claims as her own, and has it and its use. They have been married thirty-three years, and have never, up to this time, had a cross word or quarrel with each other. When she wants to buy, she buys without consulting him, and when Mr. Hardwick enters his yard gate, he considers himself within her domain, over which it is her sole prerogative to preside and manage. She never goes in debt. They are both healthy people, of strong make, and have a lively appreciation of getting on in the world by their own energies. Both are members of the Methodist Episcopal church, south.

To his marriage with Miss Tucker were born twelve children: (1). Frank Tucker, born March 23, 1852; educated at Emory and Henry College, Virginia; now a banker at Dalton, Georgia. He married Carrie Belle McCutchen, daughter of Judge C. D. McCutchen, of Dalton, Georgia, and has one child, a son, McCutchen. (2). Joseph Henry, born February 23, 1854; educated at Emory and Henry College, Virginia; married Miss Cooky Harris, of Augusta, Georgia, and has two children, Harrie Belle and George Gray. Joseph Henry is a foundryman, connected with the Cleveland stove works. (3). John Millard, born August 14, 1856; educated at Emory and Henry College, Virginia; now a partner in the Cleveland stove works. (4). James Oscar, born May 3, 1859; graduated at Vanderbilt University, in the literary and law departments; is now banking at Cedartown, Georgia. (5). George Lee, born October 13, 1861; graduated in the literary department of Vanderbilt University, in 1879; now running a spoke factory at Dalton, Georgia. (6). Nora Isbell, born October 23, 1863; graduated at Martha Washington College, Virginia, in 1881; married, March 20, 1883, Mr. John W. Ramsey, a lawyer at Cleveland. (7). Maggie Julia, born May 20, 1866; educated at Martha Washington College, also. (8). French Montgomery, born September 26, 1868, and died, seven months and seven days old. (9). Houston Lafayette, born March 29, 1870. (10). Julius Holmes, born December 4, 1872. (11). Fannie Lucretia, born September 30, 1875, died January 23, 1878, three years, three months and twenty-three days old. (12). Anna Belle, born July 16, 1878. Mr. Hardwick was director in the East Tennessee and

Georgia railroad from 1862 to 1868, and for many years was school director of his town. He appears in these pages as a self-made man, a representative Tennessee business man, and a representative head of a family, his sons being all sober, industrious young men, of good, moral and business habits, and not a stain on the character of any one of the family. They all pay what they promise to pay, all are well educated, and all stout and healthy. Mr. Hardwick has been frequently complimented with the remark that he ought to be proud of his sons, as they are all good business men, making a living for themselves, none of them afraid to work, and all respected. There are none of them hanging round waiting for their parents to die, that they may get the property. Frank T. Hardwick, their oldest son, is said to be the best bank officer in the State of Georgia.

Hardwick is a Norman name and runs through English history, and has for centuries been worn by a noble family in England, but the editor has no reliable data with which to connect the Cleveland family with that of the mother country.

COL. GEORGE GANTT.

MEMPHIS.

H E is philosopher, poet, orator and lawyer. His power of analysis is good, his fund of humor infinite, and his ability to clinch an argument, point a moral, or veil a sarcasm by an illustration or a jest is not surpassed. Thoroughly esthetic in his nature, he shrinks from all that is gross. His food is simple. He shuns stimulants and narcotics, and keeps his blood pure and his body sound. It is thus that he is enabled to perform his enormous professional labor. He is genial but not social, and prefers the seclusion of home or office to any mingling with men. A keen but quiet observer, he knows well the springs of human action, and his judgment of character is almost unerring. No man knows better the current history, and no man has exerted greater influence upon public affairs in his community. His hand is seldom seen, however, except in professional engagements, for he seeks neither place nor notice. On the surface he is ever cheerful, smiling and mirth-making, but there is an undercurrent in his nature of meditative thoughtfulness, not free from melancholy. He ponders much the realities of life, recognizes its sorrows and sympathizes with its sufferers. Against oppression and injustice he is ever in arms, and his instincts always attract him to " the under dog in the fight."

It is, of course, as a lawyer that he is known best,

and he is about equally retained and equally at home in all branches of the profession. It is as an advocate before juries that he is unrivalled, and has won his popular triumphs, but he has no superior in close, clear legal argument before the chancery and Supreme courts.

The one subject he never discusses, and the one person of whom he never speaks, is George Gantt.

His information is large and varied, and he talks well because he thinks much. The 100-3 State debt settlement measure was pushed through by Gantt. He wields a larger influence than any man in Memphis, but works through others in public matters.

Col. Gantt's apprehension of facts, things and men, with common sense to see what they are, is his characteristic. He can paint a man in a sentence better than any other can. His wit and humor give no offense, yet it always conceals a great deal of truth, and carries a moral. He manufactures tales on men that sound characteristic of them. He has a fine fancy and true poetic feeling; loves nature, but is shy of men, and only mingles with them because he has to make a living. The sterling strength of his character is weakened in the public mind by his jokes and lightness in speeches. As a lawyer he ranks with the best at Memphis. He is decidedly the best advocate (i. e., before a jury), in that city. He speaks well anywhere.

HON. JAMES T. SHIELDS.

BEAN'S STATION.

JUDGE JAMES T. SHIELDS, the eminent East Tennessee lawyer, is a native of Grainger county, Tennessee, was born September 1, 1824, and is of Irish descent. His great-great-grandfather was buried in the Atlantic ocean on his passage from Ireland to America. His great-grandfather, William Shields, was one of the first settlers of the old historic town, Frederick City, Maryland, left a large family and, for that day, a very valuable estate, estimated to have been worth five hundred thousand dollars, which, however, went into litigation, and the fund was not distributed until his descendants were so numerous the shares had very greatly dwindled. The old family mansion still stands at Frederick City, but has long since passed out of the family's possession, though many of the Shieldses yet remain in that State.

The Judge's grandfather, James Shields, went from Maryland to South Carolina, and from there to Greene county, Tennessee, at a very early date, where he raised a large family of children and died August 23, 1840, at the age of eighty-three years. He had been a captain in the Revolutionary war, but firmly refused to receive a pension, saying, "I fought for my country and not for money." His widow also refused to receive the pension because her husband would not. He was a farmer, and left a good estate.

The Judge's father, John Shields, was a soldier in the war of 1812, moved to Missouri when quite a young man, returned to Greene county, Tennessee, on a visit, and while there was elected to congress from his district in Missouri, but lost his health, never returned, and never served. He was a merchant, and settled in business at Bean's Station, Grainger county. He married the daughter of Thomas Gill, a wealthy farmer, residing in that neighborhood, and died October 2, 1829, at the age of thirty-seven, leaving two children, viz.: (1) James T. Shields, subject of this sketch. (2). Elizabeth Shields, still unmarried; was educated at the Moravian school at Salem, North Carolina, and is now living with her brother.

Judge Shields' uncles, David, Milton and Samuel Shields, were all successful merchants and manufacturers in Tennessee. They established at Marshall's ferry, in Grainger county, the first paper manufactory in Tennessee, called the "Holston Paper Mills," supplied paper to Cincinnati, Knoxville and Nashville, and did an extensive business of that sort in Tennessee, Alabama and other States. Another uncle, William Shields, became a very wealthy farmer at Springfield, Missouri, and one of his sons, James T. Shields, is now a prominent lawyer in that city. Judge Shields' cousin, Hon. Ebenezer J. Shields, was for a number of years a member of congress from Middle Tennessee. The whole family, indeed, have been, more or less, prominent in business, legal and political circles.

The mother of Judge Shields, *nee* Mary Gill, was the daughter of Thomas Gill, a native of Yorkshire, England, whose father was a prominent land owner in Yorkshire. Thomas Gill was a man of considerable wealth for his day. He emigrated to East Tennessee as early as 1809, coming from North Carolina. The land the Judge now lives upon was purchased by his grandfather, together with other lands, and has been in possession of the family ever since. Thomas Gill married Miss Elizabeth Harrell, daughter of the celebrated Baptist preacher, Harrell, of Bertie county, North Carolina.

After his father's death, Judge Shields' mother went with her two children to her father's, although her husband left a competent fortune. She was a woman of much culture and education, and sent her son to the best schools the country afforded in those days. From early boyhood, he was a great reader, of a studious mind and fond of every branch of English literature. At twenty-two he commenced studying law under the direction of Judge Robert M. Barton and Hon. William H. Sneed; was admitted to the bar in 1852, by Judge Robert J. McKinney, of the Supreme bench, and Judge Robert M. Anderson, and his success at the bar was remarkable from the beginning. He established an office on his farm, near Bean's Station, provided it with a good library, which has been increased from time to time, until now it is the best law library in the State, east of the mountains. From that day to this, here he has lived and practiced, never residing elsewhere, and while engrossed in the cares of a heavy practice, has had the rare felicity of being surrounded by and enjoying with zest the charms of rural delights. He has always commanded a leading practice in East Tennessee from Knoxville east; has always been employed in heavy litigation, many of his fees amounting to thousands of dollars. Among other celebrated cases in which he appeared as counsel may be mentioned the case of C. Amory Stevens and others against the Tennessee railroads. It is a most remarkable history, without a parallel in Tennessee, so far as the writer knows, that a lawyer of Judge Shields' ability should settle down to practice in the country; yet there he has acquired celebrity and gathered around him a clientage of which any lawyer in the State might be proud.

From 1865 to 1873, he was associated in partnership with Hon. John Netherland, himself one of the most eminent and successful advocates that ever practiced in Tennessee. From 1873 to the present time, Judge Shields has been practicing with his son, John K. Shields.

In 1861, Judge Shields was elected to the provisional congress of the Confederate States. He was nominated for the regular congress, but declined serving. He was not in the army on either side. The only part he ever took in politics was while canvassing in connection with those offices. He was a Whig before the war, a rebel during the war, and a Democrat ever since. His grandfather Gill (one of the five men in Grainger county who voted for Adams against Jackson) raised him a Federalist.

In 1870, he was appointed special judge of the Supreme court, by Gov. Senter, and sat through the entire session at Knoxville. For his opinions, see I. Heiskell. Upon the resignation of Hon. T. A. R. Nelson, as one of the Supreme court judges, he was appointed by Gov. John C. Brown to fill the vacancy, accepted, but upon further consideration, declined, and recommended Hon. Robert McFarland, who was appointed. In 1879, when the arbitration court was organized, he was appointed by Gov. A. S. Marks one of the judges of that court, but declined to accept. He was, in 18—, a director in the Cincinnati, Cumberland Gap and Charleston railroad company, and he and his son are now attorneys for the East Tennessee, Virginia and Georgia railroad company.

Since 1869, in connection with his oldest son, William S. Shields, he has been largely engaged in farming, giving that pursuit, however, but little personal attention now, the farm being almost exclusively under the management of the son. The main business on the farm is the growing of grasses, and breeding and selling thoroughbred stock, chiefly short-horn and Jersey cattle and Southdown sheep. The herd of Jerseys on this farm is one of the finest and largest in the South, and from it have been sold stock from Pennsylvania all round the belt of southern States to Texas. In the herd are Jersey cows that have national reputations for their great butter records and individual merits. The name of the farm is Clinchdale. It is a magnificent estate, containing four thousand acres, and is almost as celebrated as Belle Meade, which it much resembles. Although Judge Shields gives but little personal attention to the farm, he takes more pleasure and interest in it than in his law practice, the burden of which now falls upon his son, John K. Shields, who has already won a fine reputation as a chancery and Supreme court lawyer.

Judge Shields married, first, in Tazewell, Tennessee, May 11, 1848, Miss Aurelia Glenn, daughter of Rev. Robert Glenn, pastor of the Presbyterian church at that place at that time. She died in 1849, having borne him one child, a daughter, Mary Aurelia Shields, born April 23, 1849; died March 29, 1876, wife of William D. Gammon, a prominent lawyer at Morristown, leaving three children, Elizabeth, Mary and James Shields.

Judge Shields' next marriage, which transpired December 8, 1852, at Rogersville, Tennessee, was with Miss Elizabeth Simpson, daughter of William Simpson, a native of county Antrim, Ireland, and a prosperous merchant at Rogersville. Her mother, nee Elizabeth Kane, was also of Irish blood. Mrs. Shields was educated at Salem, North Carolina, is a Presbyterian, and a woman of extraordinary good common sense, excellent disposition, fine executive ability, a good and affectionate wife and mother. Her husband, who has always been of feeble health and afflicted with nervous excitability, attributes such success in life as he has attained, in a large degree, to her considerate and affectionate care and support.

By his marriage with Miss Simpson, Judge Shields has been the father of ten children, all sons, three of whom died in infancy, unnamed; one, Robert Gill Shields, died in 1877, at the age of twenty years. The surviving sons are: (1). William S. Shields, born October 13, 1853; educated in Grainger county; now in charge of the Clinchdale home farm, which he has managed with signal ability and pronounced success, and has added much to the reputation of Tennessee as a thoroughbred cattle raising State. In 1879, he was president of the Tennessee Stock Breeders' Association. In 1884, he was elected president of the East Tennessee Jersey Breeders' Association. (2). John K. Shields, born August 13, 1855; educated at home, under private tutors; has been the law partner of his father since the age of twenty-one, and is now doing the larger part of the practice of the firm. He married, in 1881, Miss Mary Fulkerson, daughter of F. M. Fulkerson, of Rogersville. She died in a few months after the marriage. (3). James T. Shields, jr., born May 6, 1852; educated at the University of Tennessee, Knoxville; now a member of the wholesale grocery firm of Coffin, Shields & Co., Knoxville. (1). Samuel G. Shields, born June 19, 1861; educated at the University of Tennessee, Knoxville; now a lawyer at Greeneville, Tennessee. (5). Joseph S. Shields, born May 24, 1863; educated at the University of Tennessee, Knoxville; now engaged in business with Coffin, Shields & Co., Knoxville. (6). Milton L. Shields, born May 10, 1866; now a student in the university at Knoxville.

Judge Shields has many reasons to be proud—of his reputation, rank and success as a lawyer, of his hereditary estate and name, and of his success as a lawyer and stock raiser, but most of all, of his sons, who are all duly impressed with a lively sense of getting along in the world, keeping up the prestige of the family name and adding to its dignity. The family is a remarkable example of "sticking quality," both father and sons remaining, like Macgregor, on their native heath. It is a favorite theory, perhaps a hobby, of the editor, that morality, virtue, intellectual greatness and material prosperity are best fostered in settled families, who thus cultivate a family pride which makes them above doing mean or small things for temporary advantage. This may also be applied to Judge Shields' personal life. He chose the law for his profession because he loved it, has mastered it and devoted himself to it without going into politics, seeking office or any other business, except farming, and this not to an extent to distract his attention from professional requirements. His success has come from closely observing an old saying which he casually heard when a boy: "Play upon one string." Always a close student, he thoroughly investigates his cases. Making a great deal of money, he has lived upon it freely, and has been a very moral man, possessed of the cardinal virtues and free from besetting vices all his life. In his practice he has been bold, but has ever had an unutterable contempt for cunning and petifogging tricks and methods. As a speaker, he is earnest and effective, but his strength and tastes lie chiefly in chancery practice. His speeches, however, are strong and convincing, at times ornate. His main effort in life has been professional success for the benefit of his family. Having inherited a good name from his ancestors, his ambition has been to preserve it untarnished and to perpetuate it. Physically, he looks the lawyer; is six feet high, weighs one hundred and sixty pounds, and has a high forehead. His countenance is open, denoting a kindly nature. His expression is that of a man at home enjoying his *otium cum dignitate*, in a way most satisfactory to himself. He has always been a nervous man and something of a dyspeptic, which has been somewhat against him, and has caused him to decline many offers of preferment in the line of his profession and politically. But his chief characteristic is his devoted attachment to his ancestral home and his family. When offered a Supreme judgeship, he declined, saying, " I cannot give up this home for official honors."

HON. JOHN V. WRIGHT.

NASHVILLE.

THIS big-hearted, big-brained, silver-tongued orator, one of the most distinguished Democratic politicians in the State; one of the most eminent members of the Tennessee bar; renowned likewise as a genial, whole-souled, impulsive and gallant gentleman; who has served three terms in the Federal and two in the Confederate congress; has occupied the bench as judge and as chancellor, and who became still more widely known as a Democratic gubernatorial nominee for Tennessee in 1880, was born in McNairy county, Tennessee, June 28, 1828. Of the older historic statesmen of Tennessee, he most resembles, in personal appearance, Felix Grundy. Of medium height, full build, heavy weight, and symmetrical proportions, his presence in any crowd would attract and please attention. His laughing gray eyes, easy and courteous manners, spirited air, and versatility of talent, mark him as "a man of the world," and especially of the political arena. He is quick-spoken, quick-motioned, alert, agile, and, in business hours, pushing, full of vim and energy. As a conversationalist, he is one of the most genial, charming and companionable of men; quick with repartee, rich in illustration, possessed of a seemingly inexhaustible fund of anecdote and reminiscence, a happy wordchooser, and a most excellent *raconteur*. As a public speaker, his reputation gives him a rank in the galaxy of Tennessee orators whose brightest stars were Jones, Polk, Johnson, Haskell, Gentry, Bell, and Brown. His speeches are less sparkling, perhaps, with wit, humor, and anecdote, but more weighted with fact and "inexorable logic" than were those of the orators in the latter days of the *ante bellum* period. In their day Tennessee eloquence reached its climateric. Its object was amusement and entertainment rather than instruction. Times since the war are more serious, at any rate more practical and matter-of-fact. Men are of graver temperament, and the concerns of business demand of a public speaker facts, figures, and estimated results. In these days, when everybody reads everything in the morning papers, and the reporter forestalls the orator, it requires genius of a high order to make a name as an eloquent speaker, either on the stump or at the bar. But in every age and under all conditions of society, the great orator is "king of men," whether his discourse consists of the logic of business or kaleidoscopic declamation. At the bar of Columbia, where Judge Wright practiced from 1870 to 1883, he made a name for forensic eloquence that is not dimmed by being found on the roll with the names of A. O. P. Nicholson, L. D. Myers, James H. Thomas, I. N. Barnett and W. P. Martin. His speeches in his canvass of the entire State in 1882, in behalf of State credit, and in favor of the payment of the public debt, were pronounced, even by political opponents, as able as were ever delivered by any man in the State on any subject; and it is certain his laborious efforts in that campaign had the final effect of bringing the people to a settlement of the State debt. Even so early as 1855 to 1861, when in the United States congress, in which he took his seat when only twenty-seven years old, and later on, when the Kansas questions were the subject of debate, he made a national reputation as a fluent, forcible, and eloquent speaker.

Judge Wright was raised in a pioneer family, and in boyhood had only the advantages of a common-school education. Later he studied the higher branches—Latin, Greek, mathematics, and law—under David A. Street, a graduate of the University of Virginia, and a fine scholar. His first aspirations were for the law, and this seemed to be the ambition of his parents. He was a wild, frolicsome boy, a leader in most of the boyish sports in his neighborhood, but withal a good student bright minded, quick to learn, and apt to retain. In 1851, he was admitted to the bar at Purdy, after satisfactory examination, by Judges Elijah Walker and A. O. W. Totten, and at once entered upon practice at that place.

It was not long, however, before his brilliant talents were recognized and he was called into public life. His first venture was a failure, but by what manner of means will soon be seen. In 1853 he was called upon by the Democratic party to become its candidate to represent McNairy county in the Legislature. The young barrister consented to make the race, although the Whig majority in the county was nearly four hundred. This majority he cut down, but was defeated by one vote, his opponent voting for himself. The brilliancy of this race, and the fiery eloquence of the youthful politician, stimulated his party, in 1855, to run him for congress, in a district previously represented by a Whig, and he was elected by three thousand majority over his competitor, William P. Kendrick, and had the additional distinction of being the youngest member of that congress. In 1857 he was re-elected to congress, without opposition, and again in 1859, by an overwhelming majority, over T. H. Gibbs.

Then came the war, and in 1861 he raised a company in his native county for the Confederate service, and was elected its captain. This company was merged into the Thirteenth Tennessee infantry regiment at Jackson, and John V. Wright was unanimously elected its colonel, and continued in command of it till after the battle of Belmont, when, on being notified of his election to the Confederate congress, he resigned his military position and took his seat in the congress at Richmond, in which he served till the close of the war. Under Col. Wright, the Thirteenth Tennessee regiment assisted in fortifying Fort Wright, on the Mississippi river, and afterward took part in the operations at New Madrid, Cape Girardeau, Hickman, and Columbus, and was engaged in the hotly contested battle of Belmont, in which he was wounded and had his horse shot under him. Gen. Pillow and Gen. Polk both complimented him highly for gallant conduct in that engagement, and recommended him for promotion. Maj.-Gen. Leonidas Polk, commanding the army, in his report of the battle of Belmont, thus spoke of Col. Wright and his regiment: " The firmness with which Col. John V. Wright and his gallant regiment sustained themselves on the left flank of the first line of battle, as elsewhere, merits strong commendation." Gen. Gideon J. Pillow, in his letter of November 12, 1861, approving the recommenda-

tion of Surgeon John A. Forbes, for leave of absence of Col. Wright, said : " I take great pleasure in testifying to the distinguished gallantry of Col. John V. Wright on the battle-field of Belmont, and though I regret the necessity of temporarily parting with him, yet I am satisfied it is necessary, and therefore I approve of the leave, hoping that in a short time he will join his brave and gallant regiment to lead it to new fields of glory." In his letter transmitting to the authorities at Richmond the resignation of Col. Wright, Gen. Pillow said : " Under the circumstances of the case, I accept the resignation of Col. Wright, deeming his services of higher importance in congress than commanding his regiment in the field. In the battle of Belmont, Col. Wright and his regiment acted with distinguished gallantry. In parting with him, I earnestly ask the president to send Col. Wright back to the field with a brigadier-general's commission."

After the close of the war, Judge Wright, having spent one year in the Confederate army and three years in the Confederate congress, went to Alabama, where he had large property interests before the war, but which were swept away by the tide of conflict. He remained there two years, trying to rebuild the shattered wreck. In 1868, he moved to Winchester, Tennessee, practiced law there two years, and then decided that Columbia, Tennessee, would furnish a better field for his eminent talents, and so took up his residence in that delightful little city, in 1870. In 1876, he was appointed by Gov. James D. Porter judge of the circuit courts of Maury, Williamson, Giles, Marshall, and Lawrence—one of the most important judicial circuits in the State. He filled this position most acceptably to the bar and litigants, for two years. He also served at various times on the bench as special chancellor in the same circuit, and for a short time sat as special judge on the Supreme bench of the State.

In 1880, he was nominated by the State convention of the Democratic party for governor on the State credit ticket, but was defeated by reason of disaffection and division of the party growing out of the State debt question. The canvass he made, however, as has been stated before, was a masterly effort in every particular, and from one end of the State to the other his clarion voice rang out in matchless eloquence, imploring the Democracy to rally around the Jacksonian standard and uphold the honor of the commonwealth.

About the beginning of 1883, Judge Wright removed to Nashville, and began practice of the law in partnership with Hon. Lee Bullock, under the firm name of Wright & Bullock. At present he is the senior member of the firm of Wright & Williams, his partner, Col. Frank E. Williams, being the former law partner of Gov. William B. Bate. The firm enjoys a large and lucrative practice.

Judge Wright belongs to no church, but attends the Protestant Episcopal, of which denomination all his family are members. In 1849, he was made a Master Mason in Purdy Lodge, No. 134. He was very successful, financially, up to the war, and had, by his profession and by marriage, accumulated a large property, consisting of one hundred negroes and several plantations, but by the war he lost the greater part of his fortune. As a business man, his methods are straightforward and prompt. As a lawyer, he is attentive to the interests of his clients. But he is too indulgent a creditor, and withal, his habits and disposition, without being extravagant, are those of the ambitious politician and lawyer, rather than of a man whose object is the accumulation of a fortune. As an illustration, it may be mentioned that he made his first canvass of fifty-five speeches for congress on fifty dollars and a borrowed horse. But men of his caliber do not fail in the long run. Reverses of fortune only develop their manhood, and bring them out stronger and triumphant at last.

Judge Wright comes of military stock. His father, Maj. Benjamin Wright, of Georgia, was an officer in the war of 1812-15, under Gen. Jackson. He was originally commissioned a lieutenant in the regular army, but rose to be captain and major in the Thirty-ninth United States infantry. At the battle of the Horseshoe he was promoted to the rank of major, succeeding Lemuel P. Montgomery, who was killed in that engagement. Late in life he served as a private in the Mexican war, refusing rank offered him, and was said to have been the oldest private in the army. He died at his home in McNairy county, in 1859, at the age of seventy-five, distinguished through all his life for truth, courage, and humanity. Judge Wright's grandfather, John Wright, was a captain in the Revolutionary war. The Wrights are of Scotch-Irish descent. From this ancestry Judge Wright has inherited a courageous, hardy nature, as from his French mother he has derived the grace of manners that distinguish him. His mother, nee Miss Martha Ann Hicks, daughter of Vines Hicks, of Dinwiddie county, Virginia, was of Huguenot extraction. Her mother, Elizabeth Hardaway, of Virginia, was of English parentage. Judge Wright's mother was a very handsome lady, celebrated for her broad good sense, womanly and family pride. She was a devoted member of the Methodist church. She died in 1858, at the age of sixty-five years. Her children by Maj. Benjamin Wright were Judge John V. Wright, subject of this sketch, and Gen. Marcus J. Wright, of Washington City. The latter gentleman was a distinguished brigadier-general in the Confederate army, and now has charge of the collection of Confederate war history and Confederate archives under the United States government. He is a man of broad culture and splendid legal and literary attainments. The only sister of Judge Wright, nee Miss Elizabeth Wright, died the wife of Dr. Charles Crump, of Maury county, Tennessee, leaving three children, to-wit: Marcus V. Crump, now a merchant at Brownsville, Tennessee; Richard O. Crump, and Martha D. Crump, now wife of Joseph Alexander, a merchant of Spring Hill, Tennessee.

Judge Wright's mother, by a former marriage with Herbert Harwell, left several children, among them, Dr. Rufus S. Harwell, of Camden, Arkansas; Richard S. Harwell, a merchant at Purdy, McNairy county, Tennessee; and Amanda F. Harwell, now widow of Burnell B. Adams, of Corinth, Mississippi.

Judge Wright's father, by his former marriage with Miss Mary Lewis, of Gallatin, Tennessee, had two children: Charles L. Wright, deceased; and Fannie Wright, who died at Holly Springs, Mississippi, wife of E. J. Bracken, by whom she had four children: Charles, Ella (now wife of Fielding Lucas, Holly Springs), Fannie, and Ida. John H. Dew, a prominent lawyer at Columbia, Tennessee, was a half-brother of Judge Wright's father.

Judge Wright married in Eutaw, Green county, Alabama, November 23, 1858, Miss Georgia Hays, a native of that county, daughter of George Hays, esq., a large planter, formerly of South Carolina, and of Irish descent—a plain, unostentatious, elegant gentleman. Mrs. Wright's mother was originally Miss Ann M. Beville, of a Virginia family. Mrs. Wright's brother, Hon. Charles Hays was a member of congress from Alabama, six years following the war. Her half-sister, nee Miss Pauline Womack, married Gen. Marcus J. Wright, brother of the subject of this sketch, now living in Washington City. They have three children: John, Casey Young, and Paul Howard.

Gen. Wright, by a former marriage, has two surviving children, Marcus J. Wright, jr., in the signal service of the United States, on duty in the chief office in Washington City, and Benjamin Wright, a cadet in the United States navy, at this writing on the flag-ship Pensacola, in the Mediterranean.

Mrs. Wright was educated at Eutaw, Alabama, and at Charleston, South Carolina. She is a lady of bright, intellectual qualities, and remarkable for good sense, discriminating judgment and taste. In her girlhood she was noted for the beauty of her person, as she remains distinguished for the grace of her manner. By his marriage with Miss Hays, Judge Wright has had eight children, of whom six are living: Annie Wright, born at Eutaw, Alabama, educated at Columbia Female Institute and Ward's Seminary Nashville; Eugenie Wright, died two years old; Pauline Wright; Georgie Wright; John V. Wright; Lily Wright; George Hays Wright, died four years old; and Mary ("Blossom"), Wright.

GEN. CHARLES THURMAN.

NASHVILLE.

ONE of the most prominent and at the same time most favorably known young business men in Tennessee is the subject of this sketch, Gen. Charles Thurman, of Nashville. He was appointed, March 3d, 1883, by Gov. William B. Bate, inspector-general of the State of Tennessee, with the rank and title of brigadier-general, an appointment creditable alike to the judgment of the governor and to the young gentleman upon whom the honor was conferred, in proof of which it was most favorably commented upon by the press throughout Tennessee. An estimate of the mental makeup, the worth and popularity of Gen. Thurman, may therefore be gathered from the comments of the press at the time the appointment was made.

The Nashville *American* of March 4, 1883, said: "His Excellencey, Gov. William B. Bate, on Saturday, appointed Capt. Charles Thurman, of this city, inspector-general of the State of Tennessee. Gen. Thurman is the son of a prominent citizen of Lynchburg, Virginia, Samuel B. Thurman, esq., and is a kinsman of Hon. Allen G. Thurman, of Ohio. He is one of the live and enterprising merchants of the city, and has a legion of friends who rejoice in his promotion to a post he will fill gracefully and worthily. Of fine presence and courtly address, affable manners and a sunny temper, his popularity is a matter of course. He is all enterprise and energy, free handed as a prince, and a hearty supporter of any local movement to promote the commercial advancement of the city of his adoption. The governor could not have made an appointment that will meet with a more general approval."

The Nashville *World*, of the same date, said: "Among the many citizens of the State upon whom the toga of office has fallen, none more worthily deserves the honor nor will wear it more gracefully than Gen. Charles Thurman, who was yesterday appointed inspector-general of the State of Tennessee. Capt. Thurman, as he is familiarly known, has been a citizen of Nashville for comparatively a short time, but in that time no man has won more friends by his princely bearing and strict integrity. He is the son of Mr. Samuel B. Thurman, one of the prominent men of Lynchburg, Virginia, and can proudly boast that the same blue blood which flows in the veins of the illustrious Allen G. Thurman, is part of his inheritance from a common ancestor. Gen. Thurman is well known for his public spirit and knightly bearing, and in all competitive military drills has taken a prominent part. In the summer of 1881, he was chosen captain of the honorary membership of the Porter Rifles. Of well proportioned physique, handsome face, genial manners, and in every respect a gentleman to the manner born, he will perform the duties of the office with credit to the State and to the perfect satisfaction of his many friends."

The *Banner* said: "Capt. Charles Thurman has been appointed inspector-general of the State of Tennessee, by Gov. Bate. Capt. Thurman is one of the livest, and most enterprising men of the city. He is a Virginian by birth, and comes of a good family. He has been engaged in the clothing business here for a number of years. His appointment will give general satisfaction."

The *Evening Journal*: "No act of Gov. Bate, during his official career, has been wiser or more worthily bestowed than the appointment of Capt. Charles Thurman as inspector-general of the State of Tennessee. Capt. Thurman is a courageous, accomplished gentleman, and springs from the best blood of Virginia. He is a near relative of the great and illustrious statesman, Allen G. Thurman, and is recognized by all who know him as one of the most progressive and enterprising citizens of the city. In 1881 he was chosen captain of the honorary membership of the Porter Rifles, and with his splendidly proportioned physique, handsome face and dignified and courtly bearing, has won the admiration and good will of all the military with which he has come in contact. The Captain's promotion is not only warmly endorsed by the general public, but is, indeed, truly gratifying to his best friends."

The *Bristol News*: "The many Bristol and Virginia friends of this gentleman will hail with pleasure the action of Gov. Bate in selecting him for one of the most honorable and conspicuous positions on his staff, having commissioned him as inspector-general of the State of Tennessee. Coming from one of the most distinguished of the soldier governors of the Volunteer State, this is an honor which might swell the pride of men less retiring and modest than Charles Thurman. He is one of the coming men of Nashville, and we confidently predict for him at an early date the mayoralty of that city. He is a man of great liberality, large public spirit and free generosity. He is unquestionably the most popular clothier in Tennessee, and his large house is one of the successes of Nashville. On our fourth page will be found under one heading the comments of the Nashville press on his appointment. His selection by such a soldier and civilian as Gov. Bate, is even more complimentary than a popular election could have been. It speaks more than popularity. It means deliberate appreciation."

Numerous other journals were hearty in their commendation of his appointment, and their spontaneous and unsought compliments, coming from all quarters with one accord, were well merited tributes to Gen. Thurman's sterling business qualifications, his executive ability, and his genial and magnetic personality.

Gen. Thurman was born in Lynchburg, Virginia, April 17, 1854, and grew up in that good old town, attending school until sixteen years old, when he went into the clothing business as a clerk at Lynchburg two years, and at Bristol, Tennessee, three years. At the end of this time he bought the interest of the resident partner and assumed the entire control of the house. He began life on nothing but the capital that strict integrity and industry and an honored ancestral name can give, but during his five years' clerkship so won the confidence of his employers, that he bought his first stock of goods on their endorsement, without a note or security.

In 1875, he became a Mason at Bristol, Tennessee, and is now a Knight Templar, and has held the offices of Senior Warden and Junior Warden, and has been a member of the Grand Lodge. He is also a Knight of Honor. In 1879 he was sent by King Lodge at Bristol, as a representative to the Masonic Grand Lodge of Tennessee, which assembled at Nashville, and while there became so much impressed with Nashville as a great commercial center, that he at once rented a house, one of the largest and best located stores in the city, returned to Bristol and immediately disposed of his stock, and in sixty days was located in Nashville with his family.

It is an interesting and instructive study to trace and observe carefully the lives of such men, and see how true it is that industry and independence are factors of their success. Take, for instance, his appointment as inspector-general by Gov. Bate, which was not of his own seeking, but through the solicitations of his many friends throughout the State, thus showing that people are always ready and anxious to honor and assist those who help themselves.

Gen. Thurman is a man of untiring perseverance, and has ever been sober, industrious and attentive to business, and few men can boast of having lived so temperate a life. He has displayed no ordinary ability as a business man, and has at all times promptly met and fulfilled all business engagements, and this, coupled with his inexhaustible energies and genial temperament, has enabled him to establish one of the largest houses of the kind in the State. His was the first house in the South after the war to uniform and equip a military company out and out, and ever since his first order he has been invariably successful in all competition for the furnishing of uniforms for miliary organizations, as well as for railroad companies and other bodies and corporations having a regulation uniform, and such has been the magnitude and extent of his business in this line that he is to-day one of the most widely known business men in the entire South, and ranks as one of the "solid men" of his adopted city.

Gen. Thurman's father, Samuel B. Thurman, a retired merchant at Lynchburg, now sixty-nine years old, is a native Virginian and a man of remarkable ability and of wide popularity. Truthfulness and punctuality are noted traits of his character. He was educated for a lawyer, and is one of the best read men of his native State. Gen. Thurman's grandfather, Richard Thurman, who was generally spoken of in Lynchburg as "Uncle Thurman" was a well known and prominent character in Virginia. The following sketch of him, taken from the "History of Lynchburg," 1858, pages 131–2, shows that there is good blood in the family, and that they are people of no ordinary merit and ability: "It is proper to mention in this place the name of Mr. Thurman, a devout member of the church, aiding in its extension by his blameless life and example. When very young he had held, during the Revolutionary war, an employment in the army, and to him were accorded the honor and privilege of residing for a length of time with Washington and LaFayette in that small stone building in the city of Richmond, now so reverenced on account of its distinguished inmates at that time. When Gen. LaFayette visited Richmond, in 1825, 'Uncle Thurman' made him a visit at the place, habited in the same clothes which he had worn whilst living in the stone house with himself and Gen. Washington. The interview was extremely interesting and affecting, LaFayette receiving him with open arms, whilst down the manly cheeks of the brave, gallant Frenchman flowed tears of emotion. 'Uncle Thurman,' possessed nearly, or quite as much, influence in his church as a minister of the gospel. He, with the other elders of the Methodist church, sat inside the altar, with their faces turned toward the preacher, and whenever a part of the discourse touched them particularly, they expressed audibly their approbation, in such words as, 'Amen; even so, Lord;' 'God grant it.' These expressions, uttered fervently, so stimulated and animated their preachers, that truly they might have been styled 'Boanerges,' for it was then those burning words were uttered which pierced the consciences and entered the hearts of the hearers, so that multitudes would throng the altar, inquiring with tearful, agonized accents, 'What must we do to be saved?' Mr. Thurman lived to a great age, passing away calmly from earth, and leaving to his numerous descendants the rich inheritance of his blameless, well spent life."

The same "History of Lynchburg" mentions that Gen. Thurman's great uncle, John Thurman, in the year 1817, established the first Sunday-school in the State of Virginia, in the old Methodist church at Lynchburg, and that several members of congress owed their first education to that school.

Gen. Thurman's great-grandfather, Richard Thurman, sr., was a native of Virginia, and of Scotch-Irish descent. He was a soldier in the American Revolution and lived a farmer.

Of the Thurmans who have most illustrated the name in public life, as before mentioned, is that grand old man, Gov. Allen G. Thurman, of Ohio, who for many years was United States senator from that State, and the leader of the Democracy in that august body. No encomia of him are necessary here to freshen the memories of his fellow countrymen as to his exalted character, his eminent abilities, his sterling patriotism, his lofty integrity, so grand, so pure, so noble, he well deserves the pet *soubriquet* of his people, "The noblest Roman of them all."

Gen. Thurman's mother, whose maiden name was Martha Cox, was a daughter of John Cox, of Campbell county, Virginia, descendant of an old English family, who settled in Virginia many years ago, and who, up to the late civil war, ranked as one of the largest land and slave holding families in the Old Dominion. Mrs. Thurman, Gen. Thurman's mother, died in 1861, leaving ten children. One of Gen. Thurman's brothers, Edwin R. Thurman, graduated from Vanderbilt University, Nashville, in 1882, and is now practicing law at Nashville. Three of his brothers, Powhattan, Alexander and Samuel Thurman, served through the entire war in the Confederate army. Powhattan was present at the first battle of Manassas, and did not surrender until Lee sheathed his sword at Appomattox. Gen. Thurman's maternal uncle, Samuel Cox, of New London,

Virginia, is now one of the wealthiest farmers and capitalists in his county.

Gen. Thurman married, at Jonesborough, Tennessee, September 12, 1874, Miss Ollie S. Pepper, of Montgomery county, Virginia, daughter of Paris G. Pepper, who was at one time a large farmer of that county. Her mother, *nee* Miss Ellen Henderson, is a sister of Giles Henderson, a prominent and influential citizen of Montgomery county, Virginia. Mrs. Thurman was educated at Bristol college and at Richmond, Virginia, and is an accomplished lady, noted for the beauty of her person, the grace of her manners, and her high culture. By this marriage there was born to them one child, Alexander Clarence Thurman, who died when less than three years old. Mrs. Thurman is a member of the Presbyterian church at Bristol, but Gen. Thurman, though a believer in the Christian religion, is attached to no communion. In politics he is an ardent Democrat, though his father was a Whig.

COL. DUFF GREEN THORNBURGH.

KNOXVILLE.

MOST of the family retain the *h* at the end of the name, but some of the connexion in America have dropped the final letter; they are all, however, of the same stock. Members of the family first settled in Pennsylvania and Virginia, and are now numerous in Arkansas, Tennessee, Kentucky and North Carolina.

The father of our subject, Ai Thornburgh, died at New Market, Tennessee, at the age of ninety years. He was a native of Jefferson county, Tennessee. His father, Benjamin Thornburgh, was a native of Virginia, from whence he moved to Tennessee, where he was a farmer, and held the office of justice of the peace for about forty years.

There is something singular in the history of the family. Very few of the men have died a natural death, yet those that have been killed lost their lives honorably. Col. D. G. Thornburgh's brother, Montgomery Thornburgh, was arrested by the Confederates, and died in prison at Montgomery, Alabama, in 1862. Lowery Thornburgh, a cousin, was killed in the battle of Sulphur Trestle, near Athens, Alabama, in 1864, while a sergeant in Col. D. G. Thornburgh's command, the Third Tennessee Federal cavalry. Maj. T. T. Thornburgh, Col. D. G. Thornburgh's nephew, lost his life while leading his command in the regular United States cavalry, against the Ute Indians, in 1878. He was a younger brother of Col. J. M. Thornburgh. Two of the Thornburghs, of another branch of the family, lost their lives in the Confederate service. It is a long-lived family.

Of Col. Thornburgh's brothers, Montgomery Thornburgh was attorney-general of the Second judicial circuit for ten years, and was filling that position at the time of his arrest, above referred to. He had also been State senator six years, from 1846 to 1851. Maj. R. Thornburgh, present member of the State Legislature from Jefferson county, is a merchant at New Market, Tennessee. Dr. J. W. Thornburgh, a practicing physician at New Market, represented Grainger county in the Legislature in 1867-8. He was a soldier in the Mexican war, a sergeant in Capt. Reese's company. Benjamin Thornburgh was sheriff of Bolinger county, Missouri, for six years, and is now county trustee of that county.

Of Col. D. G. Thornburgh's sisters, Sarah died the wife of Christie Huffaker, in Knox county, Tennessee; Sophia is the widow of Hamilton Neil, and now lives in Texas; Amelia is the widow of Austin Gooch, Grainger county, Tennessee; Mary Angeline is the wife of James H. Peck, of Rutledge, Grainger county, Tennessee.

Of his nephews, Col. J. M. Thornburgh read law under his father at New Market, Tennessee; commanded the Fourth Tennessee Federal cavalry in the civil war; served as attorney-general of the Knoxville circuit several years; served in congress three terms, and is now a lawyer at Knoxville. Maj. Thomas Tipton Thornburgh served in the Sixth Tennessee infantry regiment of the Federal army during the civil war, and afterward completed his education at West Point, and entered the

67

PROMINENT TENNESSEANS.

regular army with the rank of major. He was killed by the Ute Indians, as before stated.

One of Col. Thornburgh's nieces, Mary Ariana, the daughter of James H. Peck, is the wife of Allen Tate, present attorney-general of the Second judicial circuit.

The great-grandfather of our subject came from England and settled in Virginia. The grandfather, Benjamin Thornburgh, was among the first settlers of Jefferson county, when the country was full of wild Indians; was a justice of the peace for many years, and died at the age of ninety odd years. The father, Ai Thornburgh, was born in Jefferson county; was a merchant and farmer; a justice of the peace for many years, and a member of the Presbyterian church. He was a man of high temper; was a friend of the poor; had the reputation of an honest man, and was a pronounced Union man during the war. In politics he was a Whig, but after the war became a Republican. He died at about the age of ninety years.

Col. Thornburgh's mother, whose maiden name was Mary Lansdown, came from North Carolina, an orphan child; was a devout Christian, and a consistent member of the Methodist Episcopal church for over half a century. She raised all her children to work, regarding labor as honorable and elevating rather than degrading. She also trained them to be self-supporting and self-reliant. She died at the age of eighty-eight years.

The subject of this sketch was born at New Market, Tennessee, February 10, 1832, and there grew up and lived till September, 1883, when he moved to Knoxville, where has resided ever since, engaged in mercantile pursuits. His education was limited to the common schools of the country as they were in his early boyhood. He nor any of his family were ever dissipated or gambled, though full of life and jokes and youthful sports.

His occupation was that of a farmer until the war came on, when he refugeed to the Federal lines in Kentucky, and, with Col. Pickens, raised the Third Tennessee cavalry, and commanded the regiment in 1863. In 1864, he commanded the Fourth brigade of the Cumberland. He continued in service until the latter part of 1864, having served in Tennessee, Kentucky, Alabama and Mississippi, and was in the battles of Stones River (Murfreesborough), and numerous smaller engagements. Near Corinth, he had his shoulder-straps shot off in an engagement on the skirmish line.

In 1865, he was elected from Jefferson county to the Legislature, and served in the sessions of 1865-6-7-8. He was chairman of the committee on elections and of the committee on claims. The newspapers of Nashville were accustomed to speak of him as the "Thad Stevens" of the Legislature, so radical and uncompromising was he as a Republican member. He was afterward special claims commissioner of the general government at New Market.

He married in Nashville, June 26, 1866, Miss Albany Della Rien Samuel. Her grandmother, Belinda Scott, of Virginia, was a relative of Gen. Winfield Scott. Mrs. Thornburgh is a graduate of Ward's seminary, Nashville. She is a member of the Methodist church, is lively in her disposition and diffuses cheerfulness in every circle she enters, and her husband says of her, she is a whole team in the kitchen, a whole team in the garden, a whole team in the parlor, a whole team when it comes to books—i. e., in literature—and is noted for her charity and readiness to help the poor and distressed. By his marriage with Miss Samuel Col. Thornburgh has six children: Charlie, Mary Florence, Ada Dela Rien, Callie Lavinia (died two years old), Blanchie and Frank Pernel.

In politics he was first a Whig and is now a Republican —never having cast a Democratic vote. He was at one time a delegate to the national Republican convention at Chicago.

He was made a Mason in 1852, in New Market Lodge, No. 246, and is now a member of the Royal Arch Chapter at Knoxville; is one of the charter members of Coeur de Lion Commandery, No. 9, Knights Templar, at Knoxville. He served as Worshipful Master of New Market Lodge for three years. He is the senior member of the mercantile firm of Thornburgh & Daniel, Knoxville.

Col. Thornburgh was raised to hard work on a farm. His father never laid a nickel in his hand and said, spend it as you please. What he has he made by hard licks. He says of himself: "I never had any pleasure trips." He made some money on the farm, and by trading in stock; traded in real estate after the war, and made some profit by his speculations. When a boy working for his father, he used to raise potatoes in the missing corn hills, and would buy pigs and calves and fatten them for market, and instead of drinking whisky and living extravagantly, took care of the money he thus made. His rule has been never to take the advantage of a man in a trade or in any other way, but to act honestly and honorably in all his dealings. He never went security, never sued a man, and was never sued; never had a note to go to protest; always kept his business so that he could put it together in twenty-four hours, if it should become necessary. He never went in debt unless he knew he could pay out of it at the appointed time. Above all things he desires to live an honest man, and to leave a record his posterity will have no cause to be ashamed of.

He stands six feet two inches high; weighs two hundred pounds; has an unpretentious air, and looks as much like a well-to-do farmer as a city merchant.

HON. DAVID T. PATTERSON.

HOME.

WHEN Judge Patterson began his career as a lawyer, he attracted marked attention as one of the brightest young men at the bar of East Tennessee. The capacity of his mind was tested by the multitude of cases entrusted to him and the remarkable familiarity which he exhibited in courts with the minutest details of them all. His reliance upon his own judgment through life is illustrated in a casual remark of his to the writer and Mr. A. B. Wilson April 6, 1885. Said he, "When I was on the bench I listened to the evidence, made up my mind from the facts, and never listened to the arguments of the lawyers unless a new point was presented. Then I made it a rule, as the lawyer proceeded, to try to answer him in my own mind; if I could not answer him I thought his case pretty strong. I sometimes made decisions when the subject was under a cloud, but they were seldom reversed."

As a business man his success attests his superior judgment. But his greatest honor is his family; a wife universally admired; a son among the most promising business young men in the country, and a daughter, who is in all her qualities, a splendor.

David T. Patterson was born in Greene county, Tennessee, twelve miles south of Greeneville, February 28, 1819, and there lived until he was fifteen years old, when his father moved to Greeneville district, South Carolina, in 1834. The son, however, after spending two years in the old Greeneville college, returned to Greeneville, Tennessee, January, 1838, for the purpose of reading law, which he did in the office of Hon. Robert J. McKinney, late Supreme judge of the State. After reading with him and also without a preceptor about two years, he was admitted to the bar in February, 1841, his license being signed by Judge Samuel Powell and Hon. Robert M. Anderson, the former of the First circuit, the latter of the Twelfth judicial circuit. He commenced practice in 1841, at Greeneville, including the First judicial circuit, and practiced law there till May, 1854, when he was elected judge of the First judicial circuit, a position which he filled till 1863, being re-elected in 1862. At the first election his opponent was Hon. James W. Deaderick, now chief justice of Tennessee.

In 1863, Gen. Burnside came into East Tennessee with the Federal army and furnished Judge Patterson with two ambulances for the purpose of getting through the lines to Nashville, President Johnson then being military governor of Tennessee, and Judge Patterson's wife, who is a daughter of President Johnson, being anxious to see her father. Judge Patterson took his family, consisting of his wife and two children, Andrew J., and Mary Belle, to Nashville, arriving there in November, 1863, going through by way of Lexington and Louisville, Kentucky, thence by the Louisville and Nashville railroad. He remained at Nashville until June, 1865, when he went to Washington, shortly after the assassination of President Lincoln, and because President Johnson wanted his daughter, Mrs. Patterson, to take charge of the white-house, which her mother, being an invalid, was unable to do.

Judge Patterson is a Democrat, was born a Democrat, but separated from the Democratic party when the question of secession was presented, and co-operated with the Union party. Since the war he has voted with the Democracy. He never held political office nor was a candidate for one, except that of United States senator, to which he was elected in April, 1865, over Hon. Horace Maynard, by a majority of twelve. There was no principle at issue in the contest—the other three candidates, Horace Maynard, N. G. Taylor, and A. A. Kyle, being, like himself, Union men, therefore, it was a personal contest rather than political. In the senate, he was a member of the committee on commerce, and of the committee for the District of Columbia. He was a member of the court on the impeachment trial of Andrew Johnson, voted against the reconstruction measures of congress, and sustained President Johnson's administration.

He was a delegate from the State at large to the Baltimore National Republican convention, in 1864, which nominated President Lincoln for the second term, but did not attend, being absent at West Point Military Academy as a member of the board of visitors that year. In earlier life, he voted for members of the South Carolina Legislature favorable to the election of Martin Van Buren, and voted the Democratic ticket in every presidential election since, except in 1856, when he did not vote for Buchanan, being absent at court, nor did he vote in 1872 for Mr. Greeley, because he thought his nomination a blunder.

During the war, Judge Patterson stood unwaveringly by the Union. He was arrested in November, 1861, by order of Gen. Zollicoffer, under charge of having had something to do with the burning of the bridges in East Tennessee, when the truth was he did all he could to prevent their being burnt, believing it would involve the Union men of East Tennessee in trouble, which it did. After arrest, he was ordered to Tuscaloosa, but was finally released—after going three times to the depot to start for Tuscaloosa—by an order from Richmond; was paroled on honor and liberated, he having made it appear that he had no hand in the bridge burning.

On March 4, 1869, President Johnson's presidential term and Judge Patterson's senatorial term simultaneously expired. He then returned to Greene county, where he has ever since been engaged in the manufacture of woolen goods and flour, and in farming on his estate at Home, formerly Henderson depot, but changed, at his instance, both the post-office and station, to Home, as the residence and estate of Judge Patterson. In the woolen factory the Home Woolen Company employ about twenty hands; on the farm he raises grass and stock, and leads a contented, peaceful and happy life. He was never a member of any secret organization, nor of any church, though a believer in the Christion religion.

Judge Patterson's paternal ancestry were Irish. His great-grandfather emigrated from Ireland and settled in Pennsylvania first, and afterward in Virginia. The judge's grandfather, James Patterson, was born in Virginia; was a soldier in the Revolutionary war, and an elder in the Presbyterian church, of which his wife was also a member. The family on both sides are Presbyterians. James Patterson was a farmer by occupation and a pioneer, having emigrated from Botetourt county, Virginia, in 1783, and settled in Greene county, Tennessee, where the Patterson family has been living for more than one hundred years, though Judge Patterson and his two children are the only lineal descendants of the name now living in that county. James Patterson left four sons, James, Andrew, Nathaniel and William.

Andrew Patterson was the father of Judge Patterson. He was born in Botetourt county, Virginia, in 1777, and came with his father to Tennessee when only seven years old. He was at one time sheriff of Greene county, at another time deputy sheriff, and was clerk of the county court for more than twenty years. He resigned this office in 1834, and immigrated to South Carolina, but left there in 1842, and settled near Independence, Jackson county, Missouri, where he and his wife, Judge Patterson's mother, both died of cholera, in May, 1849, the parents of twelve children, ten sons and two daughters, viz.: James A., William, Joseph T., Benjamin F., David T. (subject of this sketch), Nathaniel G., Andrew Jackson, Martha (married Clarkson), Belle (wife of Tyler Heiskell, of East Tennessee, whom she married in California), Daniel C., Valentine S., and John. William Patterson died in 1845, a member of the Missouri Legislature. He was appointed by President Polk, in 1845, register of the land office, at Clinton, Missouri, but died before assuming the duties of the office.

Judge Patterson's mother, Susan Trotter, was born at Leesburg, Washington county, Tennessee, daughter of Alexander Trotter, a mill-wright, originally from Virginia. Her mother, Isabella Carmichael, was a daughter of James Carmichael, of Virginia. Judge Patterson's mother had two brothers, Joseph and David Trotter, and a half-brother, James G. Guthrie, her mother having married a second time, her last husband being James Guthrie. Judge Patterson's parents were Presbyterians of the blue stocking order; the father was an elder in the church and died in the faith. The

father was a paper manufacturer in Tennessee and South Carolina, and Judge Patterson says. " If I have any trade it is that of being a paper manufacturer, having worked two or three years originally in my father's paper mills."

Judge Patterson married (in the house where the editor wrote this sketch, President Johnson's old homestead), at Greeneville, Tennessee, December 13, 1855, Miss Martha Johnson, who was born October, 1828, daughter of Andrew Johnson; was educated at Miss English's school, Georgetown, District of Columbia; was a frequent guest of Mrs. Polk in the white-house while at school, returned home in 1847, where she has remained ever since, except when with her husband at Nashville and Washington City. She is a lady of energy, of principle, brain and intelligence, and has inherited both the looks and many of the traits of character of her distinguished father, notably his energy, pluck and brain.

By his marriage with Miss Johnson, Judge Patterson has two children, Andrew Patterson, born February 25, 1857; Mary Belle Patterson, born November 11, 1859. Andrew Patterson engaged in the manufacture of cotton yarns at Union, Sullivan county, Tennessee, and is a manufacturer of flour by a patent process at Home depot. He was educated at Morristown. Miss Mary Belle Patterson was educated at the Moravian school, at Salem, North Carolina, and at Binghampton, New York, and is worthy of the blood and name she inherits. There is but one word that can describe her and that is splendor. She married, February 17, 1886, John Landstreet, jr., a prominent merchant of Nashville, and a member of an old and highly respected Baltimore family.

The secret of Judge Patterson's success in life is attributable to two causes—integrity and industry, and his son has inherited these good qualities. When the judge was admitted to the bar he was three hundred dollars in debt, which he paid by hard work. When he was elevated to the bench it was because he had a reputation for integrity and industry, and the people had confidence in his possession of these crowning traits. Is he not a happy man who can say, "I never deceived any man; never defrauded a man out of a cent; never told a man a lie about anything he had a right to inquire of me about?" He is persistent; never yields. If he sets out to accomplish an object, he never gives up his purpose until its impossibility is demonstrated. When he began the practice of law, he determined to be judge of his circuit. In 1849, he was defeated by Judge Luckey, by a very close vote, in the Whig Legislature for the judgeship of the First judicial circuit; but he finally persevered until he accomplished his object.

He has, out of kindness, gone security for several friends, and has suffered heavily by it. He owns valuable lots in Washington City, a large farm in Hawkins county, real estate in Greene county, and an interest in a woolen factory, as before stated.

Mrs. Patterson's father, Andrew Johnson, was born at Raleigh, North Carolina, December 29, 1808; was bound as apprentice to the tailor's trade there; emigrated in early life, a very poor man, bringing his mother with him; established himself in Greeneville, Tennessee, and finally became president of the United States. Mrs. Patterson's mother, formerly Eliza McCardell, was born at Leesburg, Tennessee, but married at Greeneville. She left five children, all now deceased except Mrs. Patterson. The following record, copied from Andrew Johnson's family Bible, has a peculiar and most interesting historical value:

"Andrew Johnson and Eliza McCardell were united in marriage by Mordecai Lincoln, esq., on the 17th day of May, 1827.

"Daniel Stover and Mary Johnson were married April 27, 1852.

"Andrew Johnson, born at Raleigh, North Carolina, December 29, 1808.

"Eliza McCardell, born in Greeneville, Tennessee, October 4, 1810.

"Martha Johnson (Mrs. Patterson), born October 25, 1828, at Greeneville.

"Charles Johnson, born February 19, 1830.

"Mary Johnson, born May 8, 1832.

"Robert Johnson, born February 22, 1834.

"Andrew Johnson, born August 5, 1852."

Of the children of Andrew Johnson it may be said: Martha Johnson is now the wife of Judge Patterson. Charles Johnson was a physician and surgeon of the Tenth Tennessee Federal regiment, and was killed by a fall from his horse at Nashville, April 4, 1863. Mary Johnson married Col. Daniel Stover, of the Fourth Tennessee Federal infantry. He died in December, 1864, the day after the battle of Nashville, leaving three children, Lilly, wife of Thomas Maloney; Sarah, wife of Mr. Bachman, has two children, Johnson and Sam. Col. Robert Johnson, who served in the Tennessee Legislature, commanded the First Tennessee Federal cavalry, and was private secretary of his father while president. He died in April, 1869, unmarried. Andrew Johnson, jr., married Miss Bessie Rumbough, of Warm Springs, North Carolina, and died in 1879.

Mrs. Andrew Johnson, the mother of Mrs. Patterson, was an invalid for ten or fifteen years before her death. On that account Mrs. Patterson presided at the white-house from June, 1865, to March, 1869—her father's presidential term. The mother was a member of the Presbyterian church, modest and retiring in her habits,

universally esteemed, and regarded as a model woman by all who knew her.

In the volume entitled "Ladies of the White-house," by Mrs. Laura Carter Holloway, who, by the way, is herself a Tennessean, Mrs. Patterson is represented as "a firm advocate of those less fortunate than herself;" "with manners free from ostentation;" "an almost sleepless energy;" "a slight, frail form knitted for endurance;" "in her girlhood, never given to light amusement; an earnest, silent working girl; a dutiful daughter;" "a lady of rich simplicity of taste in matters of the toilette;" "of artless, unassuming manners;" "like her father, knowing how to suffer and be strong;" "true to principles; knowing how to wait;" "devoted to her father, his counselor and friend, and from the age of fifteen, his cashier and business manager;" "an early riser; a model house-keeper; always a representative of the middle classes, whose interests her father made the objective point of his statesmanship;" "not disconcerted by her elevation to be, for a time, 'the first lady of the land,' she did the duties of her place with dignity and grace." (See the lengthy sketch of her in Laura Carter Holloway's "Ladies of the White-house," pages 606–650).

By permission of Mrs. Patterson, the editor copied the following autographic memorandum of her father, ex-President Andrew Johnson. The filial piety of the daughter had attached it to the first page of the family record in the family Bible. Its reading reminds one of St. Paul's famous review of his own life—"I have fought a good fight; I have kept the faith; henceforth there is laid up for me a crown." The memorandum is at once characteristic and suggestive, and will pass into history as one of the most remarkable of the crystallized experiences of the world's great men. It is as follows:

"GREENEVILLE, June 29, 1873.

"All seems gloom and despair. I have performed my duty to my God, my country and my family. I have nothing to fear. Approaching death to me is the mere shadow of God's protecting wing. Beneath it I almost feel sacred. Here I know can no evil come. Here I will rest in quiet and peace, beyond the reach of calumny's poisoned shaft, the influence of envy and jealous enemies; where treason and traitors in State and backsliders in church can have no place; where the great fact will be realized that GOD IS TRUTH, and gratitude the highest attribute of man. 'Sic itur ad astra'— such is the way to the stars or immortality. (Written before leaving on Sunday evening while the cholera was raging in its most violent form.)"

GEN. WILLIAM CONNER.

RIPLEY.

GEN. CONNER, like Gen. R. P. Neely and Col. Robert I. Chester, is a landmark in the history of West Tennessee. During his eighty-three years he has been associated with most of the great men of Tennessee, and having made it a rule to be courteous toward his political and religious opponents, men of all creeds and parties are his friends. He has seen twelve presidents, and among the distinguished men of Tennessee, with whom he has been on terms of intimacy and friendship, are the names of Col. John C. McLemore, Col. Robert I. Chester, Charles D. McLean, Gen. R. P. Neely, Gov. William Carroll, Gov. A. V. Brown, Gov. N. S. Brown, Dr. Samuel Oldham, Harrod I. Anderson, Howell Reed, Robert F. Maclin, Gov. Isham G. Harris, Hon. Ephraim H. Foster, Judge A. W. O. Totten, Judge Turley, Judge Archibald Wright, Gen. J. D. C. Atkins, Judge William Fitzgerald and Judge William C. Dunlap. He relates with great glee that he slept with Davy Crockett, knew him well, but never agreed with him in politics, Crockett being an anti-Jackson man.

The name Conner was originally O'Conner, and even as late as the grandfather of our subject the name was so used in the family, but the 'O' was dropped about the end of the American Revolution, the great-grandfather, and seven or eight of his sons in the Revolution, began to be called Conner. The great-grandfather, of Ireland, was of kin to Arthur O'Connor, the old king of Ireland, but he refused to correspond with his family after leaving Ireland, because he was not a Catholic and refused to subscribe to the Catholic creed. The great-grandfather, John O'Conner, a native Irishman, emigrated to Virginia in 1745, settled in Culpepper county, seven miles north of the court-house, and raised eight sons and two daughters, William, John, Lewis, James, Philip, Charles, Timothy and one other. One of the daughters, Gen. Conner's great-aunt, married a Newport, who settled in East Tennessee at a town now called for him. The other daughter married a Taylor, who settled in West Virginia. John O'Conner joined the Baptist church in Virginia, and most of his descendants, who belong to any church at all, are Baptists. He and all his sons were in the Revolutionary war. He died in Virginia, a very old man, about 1780. He was a raw-boned Irishman, out-measuring anybody, almost, from his chin to the top of his head, and a man of very fine sense. His wife was Sarah Kavanaugh, also a native of Ireland. It is doubtless to this Irish ancestry that Gen. Conner is indebted for his pluck, wit, humor, cheerful good nature and contented disposition. Of the children of John O'Conner, William and Sallie Newport settled near Knoxville, East Tennessee; John settled in Kentucky, and afterward moved to a place now known as Connersville, Indiana, and raised a large family there; James went to North Carolina; Charles to Georgia, and his children went to Alabama; Timothy, the youngest, died in Fredericksburg, Virginia, without heirs; Lewis (Gen. Conner's grandfather), remained in Culpepper, afterward Rappahannock county, Virginia, and died there. Sallie Newport's grand children are William Boydston and Benjamin Boydston, of Lauderdale county, Tennessee, Gen. Conner's second cousins, their mother being Sallie Newport's daughter. The grandfather, Lewis Conner, was a Baptist preacher of distinction in Virginia. He died in Rappahannock county, Virginia, in 1832, at the age of eighty-six years, leaving four children, John (Gen. Conner's father), Urial, Mildred, and Sallie. Urial Conner (Gen. Conner's uncle), married Nancy Nalle, in Virginia, and died about 1848, eighty-seven years old, leaving six children, namely: Lewis, John, Zephaniah, Annie, Susan and Ellen. Of these, Lewis settled in Gibson county, Tennessee, married a Miss Withers, and left a large family. Miss Withers' mother was an Ashby, of the celebrated family of Indian fighters, and an own cousin to Gen. Turner Ashby. John Conner married a Miss Terrill, sister of Dr. Urial Terrill, who died August 2, 1885, ninety-four years old, an eloquent orator, a great Whig, and member of the Virginia Legislature. Zephaniah married in Norfolk, Virginia, and moved to Macon, Georgia, and married, a second time, Miss Goodwin. Annie married Judge Henry Tutt, her cousin, now of St. Joseph, Missouri. Urial Conner's daughter, Susan, married James Pendleton, in Culpepper county, Virginia. Ellen married a Tutt, but not of her kin. Gen. Conner's half aunts, daughters of widow Davis, nee Susan Mallory, were three: Molly, wife of Thomas Hughes, of Rappahannock, Virginia; her children were, Berriman, whom Gen. Conner denominates the Napoleon of the fox chase, died a bachelor; Gabriel went to Kentucky, married a Miss Roberts, but had no children; Matthew Hughes, who was said to be the handsomest man of his day, was a lieutenant in the northwestern army in the war of 1812, was at the battle of Lundy's Lane, under Gen. Scott, and died of sickness at Ogdensburg, New York; Thomas Hughes, the youngest child, married a Miss Waldren, of Caroline, county, Virginia, and left a family of three; Lucy Hughes the only daughter, married Thomas Waldren and raised a large family in Rappahannock, Virginia. One of Gen. Conner's half aunts, Fanny, married James Ramey, of Virginia. He moved to Mount Sterling, Kentucky, and raised a large family there. Gen. Conner's half aunt, Sally, married John Lowins, in Culpepper, Virginia. The family mentioned above were mostly farmers; few of them were political aspirants. John and Zephaniah Turner and Henry Tutt were lawyers. Gen. Conner's grandfathers were both surveyors. Mildred (Gen. Conner's aunt), married Richard I. Tutt. Sallie, the other aunt, married Zephaniah Turner, and had six children, John, Lewis, Zephaniah, Urial, Mallory and Henry. John never married; Lewis married Maj. Roberts' daughter, in Virginia; Zephaniah died a bachelor.

During the reign of King George III., before the Revolutionary war, Rev. Lewis Conner, while sick, was summoned to appear before a magistrate to tell by what authority he preached the Gospel. He told the constable who served the writ he would report as soon as he got well, but the constable returned with instructions to bring him sick or well; whereupon the preacher rose from his bed, took the constable by the nape of the neck and the seat of his breeches and pitched him out of his cabin, and that was the last, he said, he ever heard of the writ. For a fuller account of this venerable preacher, see History of Virginia Baptist Ministers. He married a widow, Mrs. Susan Davis, whose maiden name was Mallory, of Irish stock. Her mother was a Street, also Irish. Urial M. Turner, son of Zephaniah and Sallie Turner, nee Sallie Conner, married in Clarksburgh, West Virginia, and had three daughters, Susan, Mildred and Betty. Of these, Susan and Betty married Cumberland George's sons. Susan's husband, John W. George, was a Baptist preacher; Betty's husband was William George. Mildred married Maj. Edward B. Hill, a brother of Gen. A. P. Hill, and now lives in Culpepper county, Virginia.

The father of Gen. Conner, John Conner, was born in April, 1770, in Culpepper county, Virginia, had a limited education, and possessed fine business capacity; acted as sheriff several years in Culpepper, was a major in the war of 1812, and carried a battalion of infantry to Norfolk, and was stationed there nearly two years, until just before the war of 1812 terminated. He died in April, 1815, soon after he came out of the war. He was in command of three hundred infantry and sixty marines stationed on Craney Island, in Hampton Roads, when he was attacked by one thousand five hundred British, in three barges. One of the barges was cut in two by one of his six pounder cannon, which emptied five hundred of the British troops out in Hampton Roads. Another barge got aground and surrendered; the other one retreated. This battle saved Norfolk from capture. The British gave as an excuse for sacking Hampton, that at the battle of Craney Island our men, under Maj. Conner, shot at their men while in the water drowning or struggling for life. He was a successful farmer, and the first man that ever had a cast-iron plow in Culpepper county, or that ever used gypsum or land plaster in that county. He was in politics a Jeffersonian Republican, as was also his father, who was an intimate friend of Jefferson. He was for several years a magistrate, and when he died was State assessor. He belonged to no church, but was always a moral man, and had no use for a man that would not tell the truth and was dishonest. He died in Culpepper county, near Woodville, in April, 1815, aged forty-five years. He was about six feet one inch high, of fine form, active and strong, weighing about one hundred and fifty pounds, had black hair, blue eyes, and a striking countenance; was very social in his disposition, a kind neighbor, a fast friend, full of native Irish wit, apt at story-telling that would set the table in a roar.

Gen. Conner's mother, nee Nancy Wigginton, was born in Culpepper county, Virginia, daughter of John Wigginton, a surveyor, and an associate and intimate friend of Gen. Washington, with whom he surveyed and camped in the woods. Her cousins, Wiggintons, were members of congress, one from Missouri, one from Kentucky, and one from California.

Gen. Conner's maternal grandmother was Elizabeth Botts, a daughter of Seth Botts, an Englishman, who emigrated to Culpepper county, Virginia, about the year 1745, and raised a large family. Seth Botts had a brother named Aaron, and from these two all the American Bottses sprang. Benjamin Botts, a grandson of Seth Botts, was a cousin of Gen. Conner's mother, and the celebrated John M. Botts and Gen. Thomas Botts, of Fredericksburg, Virginia, were his sons.

Gen. Conner's maternal aunt (name forgotten), married William Bell, a hotel-keeper at the Three Forks, near Mammoth Cave, Kentucky. He died over eighty years old, leaving four children: Dr. John Bell, who lived and died at Baton Rouge, Louisiana; Dr. Seth Bell, who lived and died at Huntingdon, Carroll county, Tennessee; Slaughter Bell, of Kentucky, and a daughter, wife of United States Senator Gwynn, of California.

The maternal grandmother of Gen. Conner was Elizabeth Botts, wife of John Wigginton. Their children were Seth, Richard Y., John, Benjamin, Jane, Susan, Nancy (Gen. Conner's mother), and Sally. Of these, Seth Wigginton was captured by the French at sea, in 1802, on a vessel of his own, loaded with tobacco, and he and his ship and cargo were taken to France. He remained a prisoner in France about twelve months, when he escaped to England, in company with an English nobleman, and got back to New York in 1803 or 1804, and died of yellow fever. His papers were never recovered, or the family would have had an immense claim against the French government. He never married. Richard Y. was clerk of Culpepper county for a long time, and died in that office about the year 1809, leaving no children. John Wigginton removed to Kentucky, settled in Christian county, raised a large family, and died there. Benjamin Wiggonton married a Miss Scott, moved to near Lynchburg, Virginia, and died, leaving one son, Frank. Jane Wigginton married Gabriel Jones, of Culpepper county, and after his death she moved to the neighborhood of Bowling Green, Kentucky, and died there, aged ninety-one years, leaving six children, William W., Seth, Gabriel S., John W., Emily and Martha. Emily married George Ronald, a gentleman of fine scholarship, and Martha married a Mr. Perkins. The Ronalds, of Louisville, Kentucky, and W. Ronald, superintendent of the Memphis and Louisville railroad, are descendants of this George Ronald. Susan married William Pendleton, and died childless. Sally married James W. Thornberry, of Louisville, Kentucky, and raised a family there. Her son, Warren Thornberry, recently died at Paducah, Kentucky.

Gen. Conner's mother was raised an Episcopalian, (the Wiggintons were all Episcopalians), but after her marriage she joined the Baptist. She was noted for being systematic and for her success in training her children to attend to business, telling them, at that early day, that slavery would be abolished and then they must necessarily work. She died in January, 1860, in her eighty-fourth year, in Madison county, Virginia, near Locust Dale. She first married John Conner, and afterward Presley N. Smith. She had no children by her last husband. She raised five children of the first marriage, namely: Seth, William (subject of this sketch), Charles, Elizabeth and Champ Carter. Of these, Seth died a bachelor, in Brownsville, Tennessee, aged fifty-two years. Charles married a Miss Colman, and died near Brownsville, Haywood county, Tennessee, in 1863; his only surviving child is Anna W. Conner. Elizabeth married Edward Lightfoot, of Madison county, Virginia, and died in 1838, leaving two children, Ann Virginia, who married Dr. Robert Lake, of Baltimore, then living at White Sulphur Springs, and John Lightfoot, who married, first a Miss Turner, by whom he had two children, John and Elizabeth; John Lightfoot died in 1879. Edward Lightfoot, their father, died in 1883, in Madison county, Virginia. Champ Carter Conner was named for Champ Carter, of Culpepper county, Virginia. He joined the Baptist church at the age of sixteen, and commenced preaching at the age of seventeen. He is said to have been one of the finest of Virginia pulpit orators. When he got through his subject he quit, which is indeed a remarkable record for a speaker. He married Ann Eliza Slaughter, daughter of Col. John Slaughter, of Culpepper county, Virginia, by whom he had five children, Fanny Ball, John Long, Anna Maria, Champ C. and Lizzie. Of these, John Long died in his young manhood; Fanny Ball married E. G. Anderson, and died, leaving one child, Clifford, now at Ashport, Lauderdale county, Tennessee, a farmer; Anna M. is still single, now making her home with Gen. Conner; Champ Carter married Miss Tillie Stephenson, of St. Louis, Missouri, and is now living in Ripley, Lauderdale county, Tennessee. They have three children, Champ Carter, Philip Stephenson and Hallie, a daughter.

Rev. Champ C. Conner, Rev. Peter Gale, and a few others, organized the first Big Hatchie Association, about 1837, which, from a small body, grew so large and unwieldy that it had to be divided. Champ C. Conner, sr., died February 14, 1875, sixty-four years old. He was a man of strong convictions, decided in his likes and dislikes; a man of exceptionally fine mind, highly educated, a captivating orator, a fine parliamentarian, presided with promptness and success, and his decisions as a moderator were almost universally sustained by the assemblies over which he presided. His wife died in August, 1882, sixty years old.

Gen. Conner, who has been a citizen of Lauderdale county, Tennessee, thirty-eight years, was born December 27, 1803, in Culpepper, now Rappahannock county, Virginia, near Woodville, and there grew up. He left there, a married man, in 1828. He was raised to plantation work, but his father having died when the son was not quite twelve years old, he was, in his thirteenth year, put to winding up his father's estate, and so learned business habits very young. He was sickly till ten years old, but afterward was stout and strong, and has seldom been sick since. He went to excellent country schools, was taught English grammar, geography and mathematics, for which latter branch he had a great fondness. He also read a few books in Latin, for which he had not much relish. He attended schools occasionally, till sixteen years of age, and then taught school five years.

He was made deputy county surveyor of Culpepper county at the age of eighteen, and has followed the business of a surveyor and engineer all his life. He has assisted in laying out a railroad, and is a fairly good civil engineer. He left Virginia, first, in 1826, and visited Tennessee, Kentucky and western Virginia, prospecting. In 1828, he moved to Haywood county, Tennessee, near Brownsville, and there lived until 1847, when he moved to Ashport, Lauderdale county, Tennessee, where he remained till 1855, when he moved to the place he now lives at, under whose oaks this biographical sketch was written. Surveying and farming and land agent have been the leading lines of his business. Shortly after coming to Tennessee, he was put into business by Col. John C. McLemore, then the largest land-owner and richest man in the State. This gentleman was, to the day of his death, one of the stanchest friends the General ever had.

In 1873, Gen. Conner was chairman of the committee appointed by Gov. John C. Brown, to select a site for the lunatic asylum for West Tennessee. He was deputy county surveyor in Virginia from 1821 to 1828, and was appointed deputy surveyor by all the surveyors-general, in the different districts in West Tennessee, from 1830 to 1835, when the surveyor-general's districts were abolished and county surveyors established. He was chairman of the county court of Haywood county from 1830 to 1836. He was elected county surveyor of Haywood county, the first surveyor elected in that county. This position he held four years, ending in 1839. He was elected brigadier-general of militia, in 1842, for Haywood, Tipton and Lauderdale counties, and held that position four years. He was well fitted for the brigadier-generalship, having studied military tactics under Maj. Chevis, who taught a military school, in 1813. He was a director of the Mississippi Valley railroad, now the Chesapeake and Ohio, from 1865 to 1868. He was, at one time, a director in the Tennessee Central railroad, a line that has never been built. From 1855 to 1860, he was superintendent of public schools for Lauderdale county, and has always been an ardent advocate of the cause of education. During the civil war the citizens of Lauderdale county, at the suggestion of both Gens. Washburne and Forrest, met together and elected officers for the preservation of the peace, and Gen. Conner was elected judge. As judge of that court of criminal jurisdiction, he succeeded in restoring the reign of law and order in his county.

He was chosen a delegate to the Democratic national convention at Baltimore in 1836, but did not attend. In 1852, he was a member of the Democratic national convention at Baltimore, that nominated Gen. Pierce. In 1860, he represented the Ninth congressional district of Tennessee, in the Democratic national convention at Charleston, and again at New York, in 1868, when Seymour was nominated. He was a member of his congressional convention in 1855, at Trenton. and put Gen. J. D. C. Atkins in nomination. Gen. Atkins is in the habit of telling that it was through the influence and management of his friend, Gen. Conner, that he was first nominated and elected to congress over Hon. Emerson Etheridge.

Gen. Conner was raised by Baptist parents and joined the Baptist church in 1860, in his fifty-sixth year. He was never a profane man, nor guilty of excesses, having led a temperate life from the first. He never gambled, and was never a fighter since his boyhood.

His powers of endurance are something extraordinary. Few young men can keep up with him in walking, and he can ride horseback now all day long. Although eighty-three years old, his natural vigor seems but little impaired.

He became a Master Mason at the age of twenty-one, in Fairfax Lodge, No. 28, and has taken the Chapter and Council degrees. He helped to organize the first Royal Arch Chapters in Brownsville and Ripley, and by special appointment acted as King, when those chapters were organized. He was made a Royal Arch Mason at Culpepper Court-house, Virginia, and though not in a chapter for seventeen years thereafter, worked his way into the chapter at Jackson, Tennessee, about 1844, which was a remarkable feat of memory.

From 1842 to 1847, he merchandised at Brownsville, and at Woodville, in Haywood county, five years.

He went to Brownsville, in 1828, with four hundred

68

dollars and four negro slaves. At one time he owned property in lands and negroes worth some one hundred thousand dollars. He now owns a farm of three hundred acres, the remnant of six thousand and one acres, which he has sold and given to his children. As a business man, he has been quite a success. His method will be read with interest by the children and grandchildren of others besides his own. His principle has ever been to fulfill promptly his appointments, if it were possible. He never tried to cheat a man out of a cent of money he justly owed him. He always tried to keep his credit up in bank and everywhere else, and was careful about contracting small debts, for they are the debts that give most annoyance. His friends have long said of him, "He has the vim of a steam engine, and never says 'tired.'" An energetic man, he has also had great staying power, as this record shows. By nature a high tempered boy, his mother counseled him to curb his temper, and to-day he tells the editor that, acting on her advice, he has succeeded in controlling his temper, until now he does not get angry at all. He has lost many thousand dollars by security debts—a thing of which he is ashamed, but it appears in this sketch as a warning to his posterity that he that striketh hands must smart for it, as Solomon said three thousand years ago.

Gen. Conner first married, in Orange county, Virginia, in 1823, Miss Emily Smith, daughter of John Smith (whose mother, Rebecca Hite, was a German lady). Emily Smith was grand-daughter of Urial Mallory, whose wife's maiden name was Hannah Cave. Mrs. Conner was a second cousin to Richard M. Johnson, vice president of the United States. The Johnsons of Kentucky are of kin to her. Hon. Cave Johnson, of Tennessee, was also of kin to her through the Caves, her grandmother being a Cave, of Virginia. Mrs. Conner's mother, Sallie Mallory, was the daughter of Urial Mallory, of Orange county, Virginia. She died June 18, 1860, while Gen. Conner was attending the Democratic national convention at Baltimore. By this marriage, Gen. Conner had twelve children, three of whom died in infancy, and one, Lewis Alexander, died in 1849, at the age of twenty years. The others are: (1). John, born January 18, 1824; educated at the Nashville University, under President Lindsley. He married Lucy Verser, daughter of Daniel Verser, of Denmark, Tennessee, and has six children, John, Lizzie, Verser, Calvin, Lucy and Robert I. Chester. Of these, John married Kate Commegys, and has two children, Lottie and Emmett. John Conner served in the Mexican war, in Col. Waterhouse's regiment, and was a favorite scout of Gen. Forrest, under whom he was in a number of hard fought battles in the Confederate army. Lizzie, born January 4, 1831, is the wife of William White, and has one child, Mary Elizabeth. They live at Ashport, Tennessee. (2). Sarah Mallory, born September 3, 1825; widow of James

W. Nixon; has six children, James C., George W., Charles P., John Branch, Lida and Linnie. Of these, John Branch Nixon, a druggist at Morrillton, Arkansas, married Miss Mattie J. Williams, and has two children, Sarah Mobley and Joseph Williams. Lida is the wife of Seborn Houton, of Texas. (3). Ann Wigginton, born March 12, 1827, now widow of Austin Mann, married first John H. Tanner, of Brownsville, by whom she had two children, William Henry and Emma. William Henry went into the southern army at the age of fourteen, and has never been heard of since. Emma is the wife of Robert Mann, of Haywood county, Tennessee, and has seven children, Clarence, Thomas Jefferson, Tanner, Robert, Olivia and Ruth. Ann Wigginton next married Austin Mann, who died November 1, 1874. (4). Lizzie Lightfoot, born January 4, 1831; married Judge Edward J. Read, of Crockett county, Tennessee, and has four children, William C., Maud, Lewis Alexander and Laura. Judge Read died October 31, 1884. (5). Susan S. (the fifth child), born April 27, 1834, is the widow of William A. Partee, and has three children living, Lewis C., Algernon Oldham and Emma. Of these, Lewis C. is an engineer in the United States government works, and Algernon is in the United States survey service at Ripley, Tennessee. (6). Emily V., born January 6, 1836; married Dr. John L. Alston, who was chief of Gen. Cheatham's medical staff. He died August 20, 1875. She has one child, a daughter, Annie Laura. Dr. Alston was one of the most eminent surgeons in the United States, and was noted for his compassion for the human race. Among his surgical operations was taking the spleen out of a wounded soldier named Walden, and thereby saving his life. (7). Charles Henry (Gen. Conner's seventh child living), born October 2, 1838, was a West Point cadet, and when the war broke out between the States, he came home, joined the southern army, was made a captain in the First Confederate regiment of cavalry, and when, at Pulaski, Tennessee, Col. H. Clay King and his lieutenant-colonel and major were captured, he took command of that regiment and commanded it during the remainder of the war, mostly under the command of Gen. Wheeler, but was surrendered under Gen. Forrest at the close of the war. He

was wounded at the battle of Paris, Henry county, Tennessee, where he was shot through the thigh. He was the first Confederate wounded soldier brought to Brownsville. He participated in numerous battles, and was in thirty-six engagements in thirty-two days. He was a great favorite with Gen. Wheeler, his commander and old teacher at West Point. After the war he came home, studied law, and acted sometimes as judge *pro tem*. He died, April 13, 1884, leaving two children, William Alva and Fuller Spruill, by his first wife, Laura Spruill, daughter of Dr. Joseph Spruill, late of Oswego, Kansas; and one child, Charles Chesnut, by his last wife, Margaret J., daughter of John Chesnut, a planter, of Kentucky. Her mother was a cousin of Gov. Zeb. Vance, of North Carolina. (8). Presley Nevil, born May 22, 1841; married Ara Botts, daughter of Judge Aaron Botts, a Kentuckian, who died in Memphis. He was a captain in the Confederate army, in the regiment known as the "bloody Ninth," Cheatham's division. He was wounded at Shiloh, in the breast, by a spent ball; at Murfreesborough he was again wounded; at Perryville he was shot around the elbow; and at Chickamauga he was shot in the thigh and carried off the field of battle. From this last wound he has never entirely recovered. He was educated at Oxford, Mississippi, studied law at Lebanon, Tennessee, and now lives near his father, engaged in farming. He has seven children, Presley Nevil, Mary Botts, Rosell, Charles Olive, Aaron Botts, William and Henry Tanner.

Gen. Conner next married Sally J. Terrill, daughter of Edmund Terrill, of Orange county, Virginia, related to the Tolls family and to the celebrated Oliver Cromwell, of English history. Her grandfather was Oliver Terrill. Her grandmother's maiden name was Susan Mallory. Her mother was a Smith. By this marriage Gen. Conner has four children: (1). Seth R., born March 24, 1862. (2). Cornelia Honyman, born April 12, 1864. (3). Robert E. Lee, born December 9, 1868. (4). Willie Terrill, born January 26, 1871.

Thus it will be seen that Gen. Conner has eleven children living of sixteen born; thirty-one grandchildren and eleven great-grandchildren. Twenty-three of his posterity are dead.

HEBER JONES, M.D.

MEMPHIS.

HEBER JONES, M.D., of Memphis, is a gentleman, though of the younger generation, fully entitled to the place which he now occupies among the most eminent and distinguished physicians of Tennessee. Born in Phillips county, Arkansas, September 11,

1848, he left the State while quite young and went to Nashville, Tennessee, where he obtained his preparatory education. Later he entered Nottingham Academy, Somerville, Tennessee, and from thence he went to the University of Virginia, where he graduated in medicine in 1869. His father having offered to give him the best educational advantages procurable, and to allow him to pursue his studies as long as he wished, after graduating he determined to go to Europe, which he did, spending three years in study in the famous hospitals of London, Paris, Vienna and Berlin. During his summer vacations he traveled extensively on the European continent and in the British isles. With a single friend he traversed Switzerland, from Lake Constance to Geneva, on foot, the only satisfactory way to see and appreciate the beautiful scenery of that country. Returning to the United States in the latter part of 1872, he began the practice of medicine at Memphis, and has continued at that place up to the present time.

In 1880, Dr. Jones was elected professor of the theory and practice of medicine in the Memphis Hospital Medical College, resigning the position in 1883. He is a member of the American Public Health Association; of the Tennessee Medical Society; the tri-State Medical Association, and several other similar organizations. He was for two years secretary of the Memphis board of health, and in the midst of the dark days of 1878 he was selected as health officer for that stricken city. He was a member of the Howard medical corps in that and the following year. Throughout the terrible epidemics of yellow fever which scourged his people in the years 1873, 1878 and 1879, he remained at his post and labored unceasingly at the bedside of the sick and dying, with a zeal and energy which taxed to its utmost the great physical strength with which nature has endowed him.

He became a Mason in 1878, and had the honor of being the first to take a degree in the new Masonic Temple at Memphis, upon which occasion he was raised to the sublime degree of Master Mason.

In his political views Dr. Jones adheres to the principles of the old Whig party, and would belong to it to-day if it were in existence, but in its absence he votes with the Democrats—never, however, having taken any very active part in politics, and never having been a candidate for office.

He was married, December 23, 1873, to Miss Valerie Wooten, of Holly Springs, Mississippi, daughter of John W. Wooten, a citizen of that place. Mrs. Jones is of Scotch-English descent. Her family settled first in North Carolina, and moved thence to Mississippi. She is characterized by amiability of disposition and attractiveness of manners. Brilliant in conversation, she is the happy possessor of an easy, genial flow of language,

and meets all persons with a grace and dignity which at once puts them at ease in her presence. When the epidemic of 1878 broke out she was absent from the city, but in spite of her husband's violent protest, returned to join him while it was at its worst, there being a hundred deaths in Memphis the day she arrived there, and in ten days she was stricken with the fever herself.

Dr. Jones' father, Judge John T. Jones, was born in Essex county, Virginia, moved to Arkansas in 1833, and there became prominent as a planter and a lawyer. He has been prominently identified with the agricultural interests of the State, and has served as Master of the National and State Granges. Prior to the war, he served for fifteen years as judge of the circuit court in Arkansas, and then resigned to devote himself to his planting interest. Just after the war he was elected to the United States senate, but did not serve. He is still living in Arkansas, and is a man of strong and decided opinions. He belonged to the old line Whigs, and is still devoted to the principles of that truly grand old party, though he now votes with the Democrats. His father was a farmer in Essex county, Virginia, and a soldier in the war of 1812. His wife, mother of Dr. Jones, was Miss Caroline McEwen, daughter of Col. Robert H. and Hettie McEwen, of Nashville, Tennessee.

Dr. and Mrs. Jones are both members of the Episcopal church.

Stability of character and firmness of purpose are two of Dr. Jones' leading traits. His rule is to decide what to do and then do it with his might. He has adhered closely to medicine since 1866. From the time that he was old enough to know the value of study, he has been a hard student. When at the University of Virginia he would study sixteen or seventeen hours a day, and seldom took a holiday, and this habit he has kept up. He is positive in his nature, and decided in his likes and dislikes; always takes his position on one side of a question, and expresses his opinions freely. He is a clear and vigorous thinker, and the thing which strikes one most on seeing him, is the force and energy of the man; and his conversation, though entirely free from any attempt at display, creates at once the impression of one who knows his subject well. He began life with nothing but his education, his father, though possessing a good property, being an advocate of the theory of educating a young man and then leaving him to make his own way—a course which is sure to make a man of him if he can be made one.

HON. OLIVER P. TEMPLE.

KNOXVILLE.

HON. OLIVER P. TEMPLE has long been a prominent figure among the public men of Tennessee. Among the many distinguished traits of character which have marked him as a man of great force, may be mentioned his keen perception of moral truth, and an exemplification of it in his demeanor as a man, a citizen, a judge, and in whatever sphere of life he has been called to act his part. His personal honesty is proverbial. His bitterest enemy, if he has any, of any sort, will concede this fact. His industry and energy are of the highest order, and only equaled by his fidelity to friends and devotion to principle. The same rule of conduct has always marked his connection with public trust which has been ascribed to his personal character. He is possessed of a large amount of what men call "soul." He is sympathetic and kind, as shown throughout his whole life. He was always popular, as shown in his contest for congress, with Andrew Johnson, in 1847. A young man, and without money or political experience, he entered that struggle in the face of a Democratic majority of two thousand, and reduced it, after a joint canvass with Johnson, then in his prime, to three hundred and thirteen votes! This was a remarkable and certainly a memorable campaign, for although Johnson was considered invincible on the stump, Temple made a reputation possessed by few men in the whole country. His popularity began, or rather grew into magnificent proportions on account of this giant-like contest with Johnson, and it continued to grow up to the late war. In 1860, he was on the Bell and Everett electoral ticket for the Second congressional district of Tennessee, and in that campaign and the discussions which followed, he did as much as any one man to mould the Union sentiment which was so conspicuously displayed by East Tennesseans during the whole war, and which has guided their political action since. This Union sentiment existed in the minds of the people by intuition and education, but it required such courageous men as Mr. Temple to cause it to chrystallize, and lead it to the accomplishment of results. Brave, generous and true, he was accepted as a leader, and the people were quick to seek his counsel and follow his advice.

He was one of the best stump speakers in the State before he was thirty-five years of age. His style was pleasing, his voice good, and his gesticulation and action dramatic, especially when under the full inspiration of his theme. He was not only an orator but a debater as well, and he never failed to impress his hearers, and most generally won his cause before the tribunal of the people. Long before the war he stood among the foremost lawyers at the Knoxville bar, which was always strong, but never stronger than during this period. Subsequent to the war, he became chancellor, first by appointment, and afterward by an overwhelming election by the people. His judicial career of twelve years was admirable and noted, and demonstrated him a wise jurist, with large knowledge of the law as laid down in books, a conscientious, scrupulous and upright judge.

Oliver P. Temple was born in Greene county, Tennessee, near Greeneville, and within one mile of Greeneville College, January 27, 1820. His father was James Temple, a well educated gentleman, of a quiet disposition and high integrity, and greatly respected for his many virtues. He was a farmer and the owner, at his death, of six hundred acres of land, and a few slaves. He was also a surveyor, but this was rather an accomplishment than a profession, and no mean one, nearly a hundred years ago. He died in 1822, at the age of about fifty years.

The mother of Judge Temple was Mary Craig, eldest child of Capt. Craig and Jane Innis Burns. Capt. Craig was born in York, Pennsylvania, served as captain in the Revolutionary war, and at one time commanded the personal guard of Gen. Washington. He was a man of great daring and gallantry, and of a commanding person. He received a bayonet wound in the face, probably at the battle of Brandywine. Six of his brothers were also in the Revolutionary army. After the close of the war, he settled in South Carolina, where he married Jane Innis Burns, of a well known Scotch family. Soon after this he moved to Greene county, Tennessee, where he selected a magnificent farm, on the waters of Richland creek, near Greeneville, which remained in the family until three years ago. Jane Innis Burns was born in South Carolina, daughter of a patriot soldier, who served under Sumter and Marion. Judge Temple's mother was a woman of superior judgment, fine business capacity, strong will, and possessed of great gentleness and amiability. When left a widow in 1822, with seven minor children, she so managed her estate as to nearly double it by the time the youngest reached maturity, and at the same time gave them the advantages of a fair education. She and James Temple were united in the bonds of matrimony in 1810, by Rev. Charles Coffin, D.D., the celebrated president of Greeneville College, who was their neighbor and ever afterward their warm friend. They were both Presbyterians. On the maternal side, all of Judge Temple's ancestors were of Scotch descent, as Craig, Burns and Innis are well known and prominent Scotch family names.

His paternal grandfather was Maj. Temple, of English

descent, and of an old English family. His ancestors probably settled in Ireland as a part of the colonists sent over by one of the English monarchs, to whom were granted large districts of forfeited lands, or they went over with the Puritans to occupy lands confiscated by Cromwell in 1641. Sir William Temple was a privy councilor of Ireland, owned large estates there, and it is possible that some of his poorer relations, who then settled with him in Ireland, were the ancestors of Judge Temple's grandfather. They were all Presbyterians. Maj. Temple was born in Pennsylvania, in 1736, and moved to Mecklenburg county, North Carolina, in 1766. In 1780, he was with the North Carolina forces in the celebrated battle of King's Mountain. In 1785, he moved to Greene county, Tennessee, and selected a farm on Richland creek, adjoining the farm of Rev. Hezekiah Balch, the founder of Greeneville College, and on which farm the college was established. These two persons probably came from North Carolina together, as their farms were entered the same day, and each called for the line of the other. Both were Presbyterians, and both had lived in the same county in the old mother State. This Hezekiah Balch was a cousin of the celebrated Hezekiah J. Balch, who drafted the Mecklenburg declaration of independence. The Temple farm remained in possession of the family until a few years ago, when it was sold for division among the heirs.

Judge Temple's paternal grandmother was Mary Kennedy, a relative of Gen. Daniel Kennedy, well known in the early history of East Tennessee, and was the aunt of Gen. Thomas Kennedy, who was a man of great wealth, and quite distinguished in the early history of Kentucky. The Kennedys were of a leading Scotch family. The Temple family, as far back as it can be traced, has been exceedingly respectable and well connected. As an evidence of this, five female cousins of Judge Temple married five respectable Presbyterian ministers.

The subject of our sketch was raised on the farm, and, like the boys of that day, worked during the summer and went to old field schools in the winter. He has always rejoiced in the fact that he had this early experience in the hardships and toils of farm life, as it has given him a quicker sympathy for, and more liberal views concerning, the great laboring classes. At sixteen, he attended Greeneville College, but was little inclined to regular, hard study. At nineteen this venerable old college having gone down, he attended Tusculum Academy, in Greene county, then under the control of Rev. Samuel W. Doak, a celebrated teacher in his day. Here he applied himself more diligently to his books. In the fall of 1841, he went to Washington College, then just resuscitated under the presidency of that brilliant young scholar, Rev. A. A. Doak. Washington College was founded in 1780, in the wilderness of Washington county, by the justly celebrated Rev.

Samuel Doak, then fresh from the halls of Princeton. This was the first institution of learning west of the Alleghanies, and for a great many years the leading one. It was originally chartered by the Legislature of North Carolina as Martin Academy. In 1795, the territorial Legislature of Tennessee chartered it under the name of Washington College, "in honor of the illustrious president of the United States," as the caption of the act recites. The elder Doak was a remarkable man, as all tradition and authentic history proves. He was distinguished for intellect, learning, and wonderful will power. His grandson, A. A. Doak, was a worthy representative of his celebrated ancestor. In elegant learning, he has, perhaps, never had an equal in the State, and as a chaste and brilliant preacher, he has had but few equals. Unfortunately he died at Clarksville, Tennessee, before he had reached his prime in life, leaving a brilliant son, H. M. Doak (lately editor of the Nashville *American*, and now of the Memphis *Avalanche*), to perpetuate the name of the long line of Doaks.

At Washington College young Temple pursued his studies with great assiduity, graduating in 1844. He was immediately tendered a professorship in the college, which he declined. On leaving college, he at once entered into politics, making speeches for Mr. Clay, in Carter, Washington, Greene, Cocke, Jefferson and Sullivan counties. A few months later he commenced reading law, under the direction of the late Judge Robert J. McKinney. In the same class were F. W. Compton, since one of the Supreme judges of the State of Arkansas, Robert H. Armstrong, of Knoxville, John K. Howard, afterward a well known and brilliant young politician of the State, and John A. McKinney, recently circuit judge of the first judicial circuit.

In 1846, Messrs. Temple, Howard, Armstrong and Compton were all admitted to the bar. Compton and Temple formed a partnership, and located at Greeneville. Messrs. Compton, Howard and Temple all made their *debut* as lawyers in the same case, before Judge Alexander, and were all complimented publicly by him, from the bench, for their efforts.

In July, 1847, Mr. Temple became a candidate for congress against Andrew Johnson, then a candidate for re-election for his third or fourth term. The first suggestion of his candidacy came from Gov. Neill S. Brown, then the Whig candidate for governor of the State. A few others having joined in this suggestion, Mr. Temple took the bold, and to many the astounding step, of contesting the field with the invincible Johnson. It was less than four weeks until the election. Johnson had already been over the district making speeches. He had his followers and friends in every county, who nearly idolized him. He was regarded as the ablest and most adroit debater on the Democratic side in the State. His prestige, too, was great. He had been elected each time he had been a candidate by overwhelming majorities. The district was Democratic at all times by two thousand majority. The announcement that young Temple was a candidate was therefore received, not only by the Democrats, but also by the Whigs, with amazement. In fact, it was the policy of a large number of the Whigs to make no opposition to Johnson in that election, in order to foment the quarrel then brewing between him and the brilliant Landon C. Haynes, and which afterward broke forth with such fury, and lasted during their joint lives. It was this feeling among certain Whig leaders, with perhaps a little jealousy that so young a man as Mr. Temple should suddenly become so conspicuous, that finally defeated him. Mr. Brownlow, who published the only Whig paper in the district, and Dr. Alexander Williams, and a very few others, were the only prominent leaders who really worked earnestly for his election. Mr. Brownlow was enthusiastic, and did splendid work in his paper. The other prominent men were indifferent to the result, or had no confidence in the success of Mr. Temple. Besides this, it was reported at the time that an arrangement had been made, in one or more counties, between certain Whigs, who had purposes to accomplish before the next Legislature, and Johnson or his friends, by which Johnson was to be supported for congress, and Whig candidates for the Legislature elected. The result of the election seemed to give some plausibility to this belief. The result was, Mr. Temple had, within less than four weeks to work, nearly everything to do for himself, with certain undercurrents operating against him. But he entered into the canvass with an energy, and perhaps audacity that, as he looks back at it to-day, astonishes him. He issued a bitter circular, and then went to Johnson's appointments to face him on the stump. While not the equal of his wary antagonist on the stump, he yet possessed a boldness and popular address that were quite taking. Johnson's record was vulnerable, while Mr. Temple had none. Mr. Temple's personal reputation was good, and could not be assailed. All that Mr. Johnson could do was to sneer at him as his "boy competitor," and make disrespectful allusions to his college style of speaking. Mr. Temple on the other hand made a bold, aggressive assault, not always in a very meek spirit, on Mr. Johnson's record. From the start he put him on the defensive, and kept him so until the close of the canvass. Often the debates were bitter and acrimonious, and always spirited. Mr. Johnson was very cunning in conducting his canvass. For example, in Carter county, where the people were nearly all Whigs, his speech was mild and kind in tone, intending to keep down party feeling. The next day, in Jonesborough, in a Democratic county, he was fierce and bitter, in order to arouse the party. Mr. Temple was equally bold and defiant at this point, but for a different reason. This was the home of Landon C. Haynes, and he sought to arouse—and to a certain extent succeeded—the friends of the latter against Mr. Johnson.

The winter before this, Mr. Johnson, anticipating that Mr. Haynes would be his opponent, and not a Whig, had made a bitter speech against Polk's administration, in which he said, among other things, that "it was corrupt from the highest to the lowest." Mr. Temple daily read this speech in a taunting manner, making comments thereon with terrible effect, and appealing to the friends of President Polk to know if they were going to sanction this assault on their president and favorite by voting for Johnson. Johnson's only defense and explanation of this charge were that he was "no grammarian," and that when he used that language he intended to exclude the highest and the lowest; that is, as Mr. Temple retorted, all were corrupt except the president and the servants in his kitchen! Johnson's explanation was always a source of laughter to those who heard it. With this and other charges against him, hurled at him day after day with almost vindictive assurance, Johnson came out of these fierce contests, not with his usual air of a conqueror, but dejected and crestfallen. There was but one way to meet him on the stump, and that was to return boldness for boldness, aggressiveness for aggressiveness. This was the way Landon C. Haynes afterward met him so successfully, in their most memorable contest. It has always been believed by his friends that Meredith P. Gentry would have been successful and more than the equal of Johnson, in their contest for governor, if he had been a little less of the grand and noble gentleman he was, in his treatment of Johnson, and had turned on the latter his own weapons of warfare. But when appealed to by a committee of friends at Clinton to stoop from his lofty position, and meet Johnson on his own ground, Gentry, proudly and nobly, said, he "would see the committee in h—l before he would sacrifice his own self-respect as a gentleman of honor."

The result of the election between Johnson and Temple was a surprise to nearly every man in the district, except the latter. Johnson's majority was three hundred and thirteen! He was amazed and confounded. Temple was not at all surprised. He knew the secret influences which he had put in operation, and confidently expected an election, provided there was a full Whig vote. But in two counties there was not. A full vote in Cocke and Hawkins, would have secured his election. The shortness of the canvass, the belief that Johnson could not be defeated, and the consequent indifference to the result by a majority of the Whigs, prevented Temple from being elected by from five hundred to one thousand majority, or perhaps more. After it was too late, the Whigs all saw what a golden opportunity they had missed. Then, for the first time, when too late, their enthusiasm became aroused. Temple, defeated as he was, felt that he was half conqueror, and Johnson, though elected, was deeply mortified and humiliated. He never quite forgave Temple as long as he lived. This was one of the notable political contests of that day.

It is useless to speculate on the effect the defeat of Johnson in that race might have had on his future political fortunes. He was a man of such ambition, such strong and recuperative powers, and of such infinite resources, that ordinary rules of calculation would fail to give a satisfactory conclusion. But it is almost certain that by a defeat he would have been thrown out of the line of success which he afterward followed up to the very highest positions of honor. It is almost certain that Landon C. Haynes would have been the regular Democratic candidate for congress at the next election, with Johnson probably as an independent candidate. Whether defeated or elected, he would have been somewhat out of line with his party, and the governorship and senatorship would have been postponed, or never attained. That he would have again appeared in politics, and with some success, none will doubt, who knew his great powers and intense ambition. But the probabilities are, that his success and subsequent career would have been greatly modified and changed by a defeat.

This race for congress became the turning point in the life of Temple. A few months after this, receiving an invitation from William H. Sneed, the son-in-law of Dr. Alexander Williams, the large souled and noble friend of Temple from his boyhood, to go to Knoxville to join him and R. H. Armstrong in the practice of law, he at once accepted the flattering offer. His main reason for making this change of residence, was to get out of the First district, and out of politics. He saw clearly, that if he remained in his old district he would be forced to make another race for congress. Young and ambitious as he was, he felt that he was too poor for a political life. And ever since, though active in nearly every political contest from that day to this, except while on the bench, he has constantly resisted the repeated efforts made to induce him to run for congress, several times with a nomination and an election within easy reach. He has always believed a political life most dangerous, and generally fatal to young men. In the month of April, 1848, Temple took up his residence in Knoxville, where he has since resided.

In 1850, at the instance of his friend, Hon. John Bell, then senator in congress, Temple was appointed by President Fillmore, a commissioner, jointly with Col. Charles S. Todd, of Kentucky, late minister to Russia, and Gen. Robert B. Campbell, for many years a distinguished member of congress from South Carolina, to visit the Indian tribes, and conciliate them by presents, in Texas, Arizona and New Mexico. This was done under a special act of congress. The appointment of Temple as the associate of two such aged and distinguished gentlemen as Todd and Campbell, and on so important a mission, was, at the time, justly regarded as a high compliment to him. He spent nearly twelve months on this mission in Texas and on the border of Mexico, at the end of which time it was found that the

special appropriation would soon be exhausted, and thereupon the commission returned home.

In September, 1851, soon after his return home, Judge Temple was united in marriage to Miss Scotia C. Hume. Her father, David Hume, was a Scotchman, of the celebrated Scoth family of that name. He was a remarkable man, both physically and mentally. His wife was Eliza Saunderson, also of Scotch birth, related to many of the best Scotch families, and a woman of conspicuous virtues, intelligence and force of character. The wife of Judge Temple was the youngest of four sisters, all of greatly above average individuality and attractions. Mrs. Temple is a lady of rare graces and personal charms, who, by her warm, genial manners, winning ways, and by the ever present sunshine of overflowing kindliness of spirit, and her striking presence, has always been a great favorite in a large circle of friends, and a leader in society. She has been distinguished for the elegance of her entertainments. She is also equally celebrated for the ease, cordiality and dignity of her manners.

Judge and Mrs. Temple have but one child, Miss Mary B. Temple, who graduated at Vassar College, and whose letters from Europe in 1883, published in the Knoxville *Chronicle*, were received with great favor and admiration throughout this and adjoining States, and for the publication of which, in book form, there has been a general demand by those who read them, and especially by scholars.

Soon after the return of Judge Temple from the frontier, at the solicitation of his noble friend and the able lawyer, William H. Sneed, he again formed a partnership with him for the practice of law, which continued until the latter was elected a member of congress in August, 1855. Temple then formed a partnership for the same purpose with Hon. Conally F. Trigg, late United States district judge of Tennessee, at the instance of the latter and his friends, which partnership lasted until 1859.

In 1860, Judge Temple was a delegate to the Whig national convention at Baltimore, and aided in nominating Bell and Everett for president and vice-president. On his return, against his remonstrance, he was selected as the Bell elector for the Second district. His practice was large and lucrative, and he naturally felt reluctant to abandon it for three months in making the canvass. But kind friends, especially his noble friend, Gen. W. Y. C. Humes, late of Memphis, came forward and agreed to represent him in all his cases. The Breckinridge elector for that district was James D. Thomas, an able lawyer, and a man of much greater ability on the stump than he ever had credit for. Indeed, Judge Temple has often said since, that he found Andrew Johnson nearly as easy to meet on the stump as Thomas. He was adroit, fluent, strong in logic, and powerful in manners. The joint canvass lasted thirty days. It was hot and spirited from the start. After the close of the joint canvass, Judge Temple canvassed several of the adjoining counties, speaking up to the day of the election. He, perhaps more distinctly than any public speaker in the State, in that canvass, presented and pressed on the attention of the people the question of Union or disunion. He was thoroughly and sadly impressed with the danger of civil war. He foretold, almost with the spirit of prophecy, that disunion or secession, and then a conflict of arms, would follow the election of Mr. Lincoln. He charged distinctly, in every speech, that there was a deliberate purpose to break up the Union, in that event, on the part of the southern leaders. He denounced the contemplated purpose in the strongest language he could command, and appealed to the people to rebuke the scheme. He discussed this question, and this one only. He insisted that there was no earthly justification of such a mad act. These speeches, in part, no doubt, helped to fix in the minds of the people in the Second district that sentiment of steadfast loyalty to the Union which has never been shaken, and which has made them the most united and compact body of Unionists in all the land.

In December, following the election of Mr. Lincoln, Mr. Temple addressed a letter to certain gentlemen in Sevier county, which was published in Brownlow's Knoxville *Whig*, in which he reviewed the whole situation, and in which he again denounced secession as a crime, and as a remedy for no existing evil. He insisted that the only safety for slavery was "in the Union, and under the constitution." He insisted that slavery would disappear, sooner or later, under a conflict of arms.

In February, 1861, he was unanimously nominated by the Union men to represent Knox and Sevier counties in the proposed State convention, while John Baxter was nominated as a candidate to represent Knox and Judge Conally F. Trigg to represent Knox and Roane counties. These gentlemen at once entered the canvass, and made speeches all over these counties, calling on the people to vote down the proposed convention as a scheme devised to carry the State out of the Union, and denouncing secession as the worst of all evils. These candidates were all elected, though they had opposition, by overwhelming majorities, while the convention was voted down. Mr. Temple received, in Sevier county, thirteen hundred votes out of thirteen hundred and one.

Again, in May, when the question of secession was a second time presented for the consideration of the people, he took the stump in opposition to it, and made speeches up to the very day of the election. His last speech was at Concord, in a large slaveholding community, where he told the slaveholders that, by his course, he was a better friend of slavery than they were; that they were endangering, and probably destroying, this species of property; that if they went out of the Union they would be whipped back into it again, and that the government was strong enough to do so and would do so. He often declared during this canvass that if compelled to choose between slavery and the Union, he would say, "live the Union; perish slavery."

In June, 1861, after the people of the State had voted in favor of secession, he attended the celebrated Greeneville convention, which had adjourned over from Knoxville to meet in that place. At least five hundred delegates were there from every county in East Tennessee, all excited and infuriated. Messrs. Nelson, Brownlow, Baxter, Maynard, Arnold, Trigg, Netherland, Fleming, Deaderick, Carter, William Heiskell, Senter, Houk, and all the Union leaders, were there. The committee on resolutions reported favorably certain extreme measures, recommended by a distinguished gentleman, providing for the organization and arming of the Union men for armed resistance, and for tearing up the railroads, in the event the Union men were molested by the State or Confederate authorities. Mr. Temple, believing that these measures, if adopted, would only lead to the slaughter of Union men, offered a substitute, providing for the appointment of a committee to memorialize the Legislature for permission to form a separate State out of East Tennessee, with liberty to form their own governmental relations. After an animated, and almost angry debate, lasting nearly a day, this substitute was adopted, thus saving East Tennessee from the most fearful consequences. This substitute was offered to defeat the rash measures proposed, and with little expectation that the Legislature would accede to the prayer of the memorial. The committee to prepare the memorial consisted of Messrs. O. P. Temple, John Netherland and James P. McDowell. This committee soon after performed its duty, but, as was anticipated, the Legislature refused to grant the request.

It has generally been supposed that it was the influence of Andrew Johnson which held the people of East Tennessee so steadfast to the Union in 1861. This is largely a mistake. He did, no doubt, influence many Democrats: but the great body of the Whigs, and many Democrats, had taken their position before his was certainly known by the people. As early as November, 1860, a public meeting was held in Knoxville, during the session of the Federal court, which was gotten up for the purpose of endorsing secession. It was held at night, and a majority of those present favored secession. Messrs. Fleming, J. J. Reese, Temple and others made speeches in opposition, but finding they would be beaten, they succeeded in adjourning the meeting over to the first Saturday in December. That was done to get the country people present. In the meantime, by every means in their power, the people were appealed to to come to the rescue of the Union. When the day came there was an immense crowd of people present, from Knox and adjoining counties. Secession resolutions were introduced, or rather, were pending. Speeches in their favor were made by W. H. Sneed, Judge Bailey, Joseph B. Heiskell, W. W. Wallace, and, perhaps, others, while John Baxter, Fleming, Temple, Reese, and S. K. Rodgers, afterward chancellor, spoke in opposition. The excitement ran high. Late in the afternoon these resolutions were voted down, and substitutes in favor of the Union, adopted overwhelmingly, amid the wildest excitement. The news of this meeting flew all over the country. Brownlow thundered it forth in his paper in exulting tones. Hitherto, since the election in November, everything in the South had seemed to run in favor of secession. Here was a stand made in favor of the Union. The patriotic instincts of the people of East Tennessee were all for the old government. They watched with intense anxiety to ascertain whether those they had trusted as leaders were going to desert them. They also looked with anxious solicitude to the action of the people of the central county of East Tennessee. When they saw that this large meeting of the people had declared for the Union, hope and courage revived, and after that there was never any doubt or faltering on their part. This was the real turning point in the crisis in East Tennessee. It served to give courage, and perhaps fix the position of more than one leader. The people had become their own leaders. This was fifteen days before Andrew Johnson defined his position in the United States senate.

In 1864, Judge Temple resumed the practice of his profession. In 1865, on the opening of the courts, his business was such that he associated with himself Samuel A. Rodgers, then a comparatively young lawyer, but who has since made a fine reputation as circuit judge. In January, 1866, the business of the firm assumed such large proportions that further help was needed, and therefore George Andrews was admitted as a member of the firm. Amid the flood of litigation which followed the close of the war, the business of this firm was immense. In the month of July, 1866, on his return from one of the out county courts, after an absence of nearly two weeks, Judge Temple was surprised to find a commission from Gov. Brownlow appointing him chancellor, in the place of S. K. Rodgers, who had died during his absence. This appointment was not only unsolicited, but absolutely unknown to Judge Temple until receiving his commission. He was exceedingly reluctant to give up his large practice, with the sure prospect of a fortune before him in a few years. He held the question of the acceptance or declension of the office under anxious consideration for three weeks, and at the end of that time, through the persuasion of lawyers and friends, rather than by the assent of his own judgment, he accepted, but not without many anxious, almost sorrowful doubts. He felt then that he was perhaps committing a mistake, and now he looks back on it as the great mistake of his life. Nearly

all the profits of his immense business then on hand were lost to him. He was then in the prime of life. After once getting on the bench, though he frequently thought of resigning, like nearly all judges, he could never quite make up his mind to do so. The result was he remained on the bench until September, 1878, a little over twelve years. By this time the harvest of business caused by the war had been gathered, and new lawyers had come to the front. He had passed out of the profession as a lawyer, and was known only as an ex-chancellor. Judge Temple always thought it extremely unwise for a young lawyer, or one in the prime of life, to accept a judicial position, but that such a position should only be made the means of honorable retirement toward the close of professional life.

At the first judicial election after the war, he was re-elected chancellor without opposition. At the next election, after the amended constitution went into effect, he was a second time elected, over the opposition of a very able lawyer and an ex-judge, by upwards of three thousand six hundred majority. He served out his term, and, in 1878, retired from the bench voluntarily, having the strongest assurance at the time of a renomination and re-election, had he sought the position for another term. He then resumed the practice with all the energy of his younger days, and continued at the bar until November, 1881, when he was appointed postmaster at Knoxville by President Arthur, which position he still holds.

In 1867, on the resignation of Judge Milligan as one of the Supreme judges of the State, in order to accept a position on the court of claims at Washington, Gov. Brownlow immediately offered the vacant position to Chancellor Temple, which the latter at once declined, preferring the chancellorship. He recommended George Andrews, his former partner, for the position, who was thereupon appointed, and who discharged the duties of that high office with signal ability.

In 1874, Judge Temple was appointed, by President Grant, one of the board of visitors to the military academy at West Point, where he served with Senators Hoar and Howe, Francis B. Wayland, Don. Cameron and others. He was appointed chairman of one of the important committees, but declined the position.

He has always taken a deep interest in agricultural development. Some years before the war he was appointed a member of the State Board of Agriculture, and always attended its meetings in Nashville. In 1865, he purchased a small farm in the vicinity of Knoxville, where, while on the bench, he carried on farming until 1876, when he sold the larger part of the farm and returned to the city. His farm was a model of neatness and beauty. In 1872, he was elected president of the Eastern Division fair at Knoxville, and by the aid of his efficient secretary, Mr. C. W. Charlton, and his own efforts, the fair was made the greatest success in every respect of any one ever held there. In the same year,

69

he and Mr. Charlton originated and organized the East Tennessee Farmers' Convention, which has become so celebrated, and which still continues to do so much good for the farming interests. In 1873, he was the president of that convention. He has for many years been a trustee in the University of Tennessee, and is now the chairman of the board of control, which has the oversight of the agricultural farm and the experiment station.

Judge Temple has, at all times, taken a deep interest in all public enterprises calculated to build up the State and his adopted city. He was one of the originators of the Knoxville and Ohio railroad, in 1854, now a part of the Louisville and Knoxville railroad. He was one of the original stockholders of this road, one of the first directors, and the first secretary of the board. He was also a director, soon after the war, for two or three years, in the East Tennessee and Georgia railroad. He was also president of the first macadam turnpike road ever originated in East Tennessee, which position he still holds.

In politics, Judge Temple was a Whig before the war, a Union man during the war, and has been a steadfast Republican since. While on the bench he took no part in politics, except to exercise his right to vote. He constantly refused to make political speeches, or attend political conventions. No judge ever kept clearer of politics.

In 1865, he did all he could, by letter and otherwise, to defeat the plan of Gov. Johnson for reorganizing the State government. He believed that a constitutional convention, composed of delegates duly elected, should have been convened. He did not believe that a mass meeting, composed of everybody who chose to attend, for the most part, if not entirely, self-appointed, with no constituency behind them, competent for the performance of the grave and delicate duty of re-establishing a State and revising a constitution. His sense of propriety was shocked by this bold proceeding, and by the indecent haste with which the work was done. He admitted that there was no absolutely regular mode of calling a convention, all government being broken down; but he insisted that it was competent for the people to again resume their sovereignty and restore the functions of government, and that this should be done in the most solemn and regular way then open to them. The plan adopted he believed to be unprecedented in practice, illegal in principle, and unwise and mischievous in consequences. He still believes that much of the ill feeling which followed might have been avoided, if a wisely chosen constitutional convention had been convened.

Judge Temple was always a busy and hard worker and a good liver. He and his wife have been greatly given to generous hospitality. They have traveled much on this continent. He is fond of books and literature, and occasionally delivers lectures and addresses. A lecture on the "Scotch-Irish of Tennessee" has, by request, been delivered a number of times, and received well. He has always made money, and though, in common with others, he suffered considerably by the disasters of 1873, he is now in reasonably independent circumstances, owning very valuable real estate in Knoxville. Though advanced in life, he is still active, and apparently in his prime, with his hands full of business of nearly all kinds. He and his wife and daughter are all members of the Presbyterian church.

HON. WILLIAM B. STALEY.

KNOXVILLE.

WILLIAM B. STALEY was born at Troy, Obion county, Tennessee, January 8, 1835, the son of Theodore Staley and his wife, nee Miss Nannie Brown, daughter of Peter and Nancy Brown, of that county. His mother died when he was only three years old, and his father moved to Sumner county, Tennessee, where the son grew up, attending the male academy at Gallatin until he was seventeen, when he was sent by his father to Irving College, at which institution he graduated, in 1857. His father was a well-to-do business man of Sumner county, but at the time his son left college had removed to DeKalb county, making his home at Smithville, the county seat. To this village young Staley went after his graduation, and commenced the study of law there in the office of Hon. John H. Savage, who was at the time a member of congress, his brother, A. M. Savage, being in charge of his law business, and it was under this latter gentleman young Staley pursued his legal studies. After reading some time and acquiring sufficient knowledge of the elementary principles of the profession to entitle him to practice, he applied for and obtained license from Judges Robert L. Caruthers and John L. Goodall. Soon after his admission to the bar, he married his excellent wife, who has, through all his years of struggle and success, proven a worthy helpmate in all things. He has ever been a hard student, studying his books and studying his cases thoroughly, and has seldom been beaten in his contests at the bar, and his decisions from the chancery bench have been models of their kind, and have generally stood the severest tests of the higher court when carried up.

In 1859, he left Smithville and settled at Kingston,

in Roane county, where he set resolutely to labor at his chosen life work, and there and then laid the foundation for the brilliant success which he has since achieved. By unflagging industry, strict attention to all business entrusted to him, and loyalty to the interests of his clients, he soon won his way to the honors of his profession. His sterling qualities as a man, no less than his talents and acquirements as a lawyer, made a deep and most favorable impression upon the people throughout the extensive circuit in which he practiced, and he soon built up a reputation for ability, faithfulness and integrity that brought him patronage and fame, and gave him a standing and a name to which any man might be proud to attain.

In 1869, when the question of a convention to form a new constitution for the State, in order to more properly adjust the fundamental law to the changed condition of things brought about by the results of the civil war, was presented to the people of Tennessee, the public mind instinctively turned to the best and purest men in the several counties to represent them in this deeply important undertaking. The people of Roane county, one of the oldest and most intelligent communities in the State, appreciating the high qualifications, patriotism, purity and intelligence of William B. Staley, which so well fitted him to aid in the great work, accredited him as their representative in the convention. The body met in January, 1870, and was composed of the very best and wisest men in Tennessee. In the prosecution of their delicate labors, so full of import to the whole body of the people, no member discharged his duty to the commonwealth more fully, more conscientiously or with more ability than the gentleman who is the subject of this biography. In the convention his course was marked by honesty of purpose, patriotic impulse, and studious, painstaking investigation of all measures presented for the action of the body, leaving it at its dissolution with the sincere respect and friendship of every one of his associates, no matter how widely divergent their views had been upon matters they had been called to pass upon.

So well pleased had been his constituents with the manner in which he had comported himself in the constitutional convention, that in the following year, 1871, they prevailed upon him to accept a seat in the State senate, from the district composed of the counties of Knox and Roane. In the Legislature he displayed the same high order of talent and intelligent appreciation of the best interest of the people that had characterized his labors in the convention. At this session most important legislation was rendered necessary by the adoption of the new constitution, and Mr. Staley took a deep interest in all matters coming up for consideration, and made a fine reputation as a law-maker.

But his tastes did not lie in the line of politics, and he retired from the Legislature with the purpose to devote himself wholly to his profession, which he did

with great success. Seeking a wider field for the display of his fine talents and the utilization of his rare acquirements, he left Kingston early in 1880, and fixed himself at Knoxville, where he has since resided, adding to his fine practice and earning an enviable reputation as a tireless, hardworking and conscientious lawyer and jurist.

He was elected chancellor of the Second chancery division in 1878, his term expiring September, 1, 1886. Since his elevation to the bench, no jurist in the State has made a fairer record, and litigants and bar unite in ascribing to him the high qualities of impartiality, promptness, intelligence and courtesy. In all positions and relations, both public and private, he has done his duty in his own peculiarly indefatigable way, has worn his honors with becoming modesty, and deserves yet higher recognition at the hands of his fellow-citizens. A good judge of men, and one of the ablest members of the Tennessee bench, and, by the way, a political opponent of Judge Staley, says of him: "Judge Staley is rather unprepossessing in appearance to a stranger, but he is an eminent jurist, decidedly the clearest-headed chancellor in the State, and ought to be on the Supreme bench; and he is, withal, emphatically what is termed a self-made man."

Judge Staley married, at Lebanon, Tennessee, October 29, 1857, Miss Mary E. Scantland, who was born in Nashville, Tennessee, October 7, 1837, of English and German blood, daughter of Maj. James M. Scantland, who died when the daughter was only ten years old. He was a native of Virginia, a relative of Chief Justice Marshall. He was the only child of his mother, a Rollins. He was a soldier in the Mexican war and carried the flag of his regiment, and was made a captain at Monterey for distinguished gallantry, and was afterward promoted to the rank of major. He received a wound that caused his death at the storming of the castle of Chapultepec. He was a tall man, six feet two inches high, celebrated in his family for being one of the bravest of the brave. President Polk appointed him to an important position, which he held six months, till his death, in July, 1847, from the effects of the wound received eighteen months before. At one period of his life he was a steamboat captain. He was a member of the old school Presbyterian church, a stanch, aggressive Democrat, fiery, high-tempered, and outspoken. He was too liberal, open-handed and generous, especially in the matter of going security, to accumulate or retain a large fortune, but was in very independent circumstances. His father, James Scantland, of Virginia, was of English blood. Mrs. Staley's mother, Eliza Margaret, nee Halstead, was born and raised in Lexington, Kentucky, daughter of Daniel Halstead, a very wealthy tobacco farmer and slave owner; a soldier in the war of 1812, in which he was captured and held prisoner in England quite a long time. The great-grandfather, Halstead, was a commissioned captain in the Revolutionary war, whose wife escaped from her burning house, set on fire by the tories, with the family Bible under one arm and her first child, an infant (Mrs. Staley's grandfather), under the other. That Bible is now in possession of his daughter, Mrs. Staley's mother, at Covington, Kentucky. Mrs. Staley's maternal grandmother was a Jhans, of the famous German family that first settled Long Island. Her maternal aunt, Sarah Halstead, died the wife of Judge James H. Birch, of Plattsburg, Missouri. Mrs. Staley was educated at the Nashville Female Academy, under Dr. Elliott, and is noted for the energy of her character and her superior domestic management. She is a member of the Protestant Episcopal church.

By his marriage with Miss Scantland, Judge Staley has had thirteen children, five of whom died in infancy. Two sons, Charles and William, studied for the

law, but died when about the age of twenty. These sons were the pride, the hope and love and source of much of the ambition in the hearts of their parents. They inherited the bravery of their grandfather, Maj. Scantland, and it is said of them, "They did not know what fear was."

The surviving children are: (1). Jesse B. Staley, born December 21, 1859; educated at the University of Tennessee; studied law with his father, was admitted to the bar, at Chicago, in 1883, and is practicing law there. He married, in St. Louis, Mrs. Mary Smith, nee Dyer, of New Market, sister of Col. Dyer, of Knoxville. (2). Robert Staley, born May 25, 1867; now a printer. (3, 4). Paul and Guy Staley, twins, born April 19, 1872. (5). Max Staley, born February 21, 1874. (6). Lady Maude Staley, born May 19, 1876.

DANIEL F. WRIGHT, M.D.

CLARKSVILLE.

IN the medical annals of Tennessee and otherwise, the subject of this sketch is widely known in this State, and ranks deservedly high as a ripe and thorough medical scholar, lecturer and writer, and an accomplished litterateur, political editor and devotee of the fine arts.

Dr. Daniel F. Wright was born in the county of Norfolk, England, June 14, 1816, and is the son of Robert Wright, who was a land agent at Norwich. His mother was of the family of Robert Temple, of Weybourne, Norfolk. The family of Robert Wright consisted of four sons and four daughters, and two of each are living. The eldest son succeeded to his father's land agency, and accumulated a large fortune. A daughter married the Marquis Ernesto Pareto of Genoa, Italy, and another was the wife of Rev. Robert Robertson, a missionary of the English church to South Africa. A nephew of Dr. Wright, Dr. Robert Temple Wright, was a professor in a medical college at Lahore, India, and was appointed a government commissioner to report on required improvements in the ambulance system of the British army in India. An uncle, Dr. Warner Wright, was an eminent physician in the east of England, and was joint proprietor with a celebrated surgeon, Mr. Dalrymple, of a private lunatic asylum, near Norwich. It has been customary to say that every generation of the Wright family of which he is a member, has furnished a physician of distinction.

He received the degree of Bachelor of Arts from the University of Cambridge, in 1839, and, for a year or two afterward, taught a few private pupils. In 1841, he emigrated to this country and settled in the State of

Mississippi. At Natchez and Woodville he taught select schools until 1846, when he was employed at St. Thomas' Hall, Holly Springs, where he remained until the autumn of 1849. He then removed to Memphis, Tennessee, and became a student of medicine in the Memphis Medical College, at that time an institution of recognized rank, and having an able faculty, the present Bishop Quintard, of Tennessee, being of the number. He was admitted to the doctorate in 1854, and in the same year he was appointed demonstrator of anatomy in his alma mater. Three years afterward, he succeeded Dr. Quintard as professor of physiology, and in the year following was appointed to the chair of physiology and pathology in the Shelby Medical College, of Nashville, Tennessee, which was the medical department of the Methodist Southern University, and subsequently, under the munificent endowment of Commodore Vanderbilt, of New York, has received his name. He remained in connection with this institution until the suspension of exercises at the outbreak of the civil war. While at Memphis, he was for several years an editor of the Memphis Medical Recorder, and after his removal to Nashville, founded, in connection with Profs. Callender and Maddin, his colleagues, the Nashville Medical Record, whose publication was continued until he entered the Confederate army, in 1861.

In the summer of 1861, he was assigned to duty in charge of the troops at Forts Henry and Donelson; soon after he was, at his own request, transferred to the seat of war in Virginia, where he became surgeon in charge of the great general hospital at Rockbridge

Alum Springs, and on the withdrawal of the Confederate army from that part of Virginia, he was assigned to duty in the Fourteenth Tennessee regiment, Archer's brigade; he soon became brigade surgeon and remained in that capacity until the battle of Sharpsburg, when he was ordered to remain within the Federal lines in charge of the men wounded in that battle. On returning south, under a flag of truce, he proceeded west and was appointed surgeon in charge of the general hospital at Canton, Mississippi, and in the spring of 1863, took the field again as brigade surgeon, in Gregg's brigade, with which he passed through the campaign of Chickamauga and Missionary Ridge. His health being broken down by the rigors of that campaign, he now retired from active duty and spent four months on a trip to his native country. On his return, in July, 1864, he was appointed by the surgeon-general, to the charge of one of the divisions of Winder's Hospital, Richmond, Virginia, and toward the close of the war was relieved from hospital duty and appointed chairman of the examining committee for furloughs and discharges.

As a result of his experience as an army surgeon, shortly after the close of the war he published in the Richmond Journal of Medicine a paper on the effects of ligation of large arteries in the cure of gangrene, erysipelas, etc., which attracted marked attention from the profession in America and England. It was noticed with approbation by Mr. C. F. Maunder, of London, in his Lettsomian Lectures of 1875, and at greater length in his work on the Surgery of the Arteries, in which he quotes from Dr. Wright's original article, and in his comment on the cases there recorded, says the procedure was utterly unknown in England before.

In 1885, he was made a member of the State Board of Health, and in that capacity has made several valuable special reports, notably one on school hygiene, a subject which his experience as a practical educator, his connection with school management, and his extensive professional learning rendered him remarkably competent to present in a strong light. He is now engaged in contributing a series of papers to the Monthly Bulletin, published by the board, on diet and its various articles.

In the standard and current literature of the medical profession in all its branches, perhaps there is no man in Tennessee of superior acquirements and proficiency to Dr. Wright. Though never fond of, or fitted by disposition and habits for, the detail and drudgery of a general practice, his profound knowledge of the great principles of the science and thorough and minute information in all its departments, give his views great weight in the consultation room and as an expert in cases under medico-legal investigation, and in the latter respect his frequent service has given him distinction. At the lecture desk he was always interesting and instructive, and quite popular with his classes. His teachings were weighty of matter, clear and accurate in statement, not too copious in overloading the hearer's attention, and free of all frivolous ornament of style. His medical and other writings are in tasteful, lucid English, scholarly composed, and characteristic of the full mind he brings to every subject treated. His attainments in general literature are varied and extensive, and his scholarship is accurate and ready.

For a number of years since he has resided at Clarksville, and was engaged as editor of the Clarksville Chronicle, a weekly political and general newspaper of long standing and of excellent reputation. Dr. Wright's services with it greatly enhanced its character among similar publications. Its tone was able, and pitched to a region of higher political philosophy than is customary in such journals, and inflexibly maintained sound economic views, especially during the period of agitation of the public mind in regard to the settlement of the State debt. The paper, under Dr. Wright's management, never yielded a jot or tittle to the sentiment of repudiation. At his leisure he continues a contributor to that and other papers, chiefly as a critic in literary, theatrical and operatic matters. In choral and oratorial music he greatly delights, and is a learned and skillful judge of such performances.

He served for a long time as a member of the Clarksville Board of Education, and the schools of that city are largely indebted to his practical knowledge of the proper system of conduct of schools for their reputation for efficiency. He was instrumental in extending their benefits to the colored race, and in successful opposition to the schemes of book publishers for burdening the patrons of schools with the cost of frequent changes in text books.

Dr. Wright preserves the features of his English nativity and education, and they give no little of the finish and force which mark his intellectual organization and individualize his character, yet he is a thoroughly Americanized citizen and identified in thought and sentiment with the country of his adoption. He is a Democrat in politics, and was a sympathizer with the Confederate movement, under firm convictions as to the State-rights theory of the scheme of the government, as given in the history and text of the constitution. His sentiments were fully with the people of the section with whom he had cast his lot, but it was the logic of the situation that chiefly impelled him to maintain their cause in the sectional contest.

He is a baptized child of the Church of England, and a customary attendant on her services, but not a communicant. Though thoroughly imbued with the spirit of modern scientific research, and accepting many of its advanced theories, he does not discard the fundamental doctrines of the Christian religion, nor shout in the train of its scoffers. He is a large-minded and liberally learned man, and that is to say, he can march with science to all its legitimate and tenable conclusions, and yet be an humble, reverent and religious being, and live in awe and worship of the Creator and His precepts.

The record shows him to be verging on threescore and ten of years, and the crown of white hair which surmounts his intellectual head and countenance betokens it, yet he is physically and mentally as alert and vigorous as a man a score of years younger, and is still the methodical student and tireless laborer he has always been, and is in full possession of the faculties and acquirements which have made him, in his profession and whatever field he has entered, the man of mark which entitles him to honorable mention in these pages.

HON. DAVID KING YOUNG.

CLINTON.

THE home of this gentleman, known as "Eagle Bend," is one and one-half miles northeast of Clinton, on the Clinch river, and there the Judge has been living twenty years, engaged in farming, in connection with the practice of law. He was born in Anderson county, five miles west of Clinton, January 1, 1826. His paternal ancestors came from the Highlands of Scotland, and settled in Pittsylvania county, Virginia, before the Revolutionary war. His great-grandfather, Samuel Young, a tobacconist, lived and died in that county. His grandfather, Wiley Young, was also a tobacconist in Virginia, and came to Anderson county, Tennessee, and settled the farm on which the grandson was born. He was a quiet farmer, made some estate, and died May 22, 1853, at the home of his daughter, Mrs. Clarkston, in Scott county, Illinois, at the age of eighty-four. His wife was Miss Nancy Clarkston, whom he married in Virginia, August 3, 1796. He left an only son, Samuel Clarkston Young (who became the father of the subject of this sketch), and four daughters, viz.: Frankie Young, who married a Mr. Clarkston; Annie Young, who married Mr. Frost; Permela Young, who married Mr. Neal, and became the mother of Hon. John R. Neal, speaker of the Tennessee State senate in 1881, and now member of congress from the Third congressional district of Tennessee. The fourth daughter, Elmina Young, married Mr. Hall. All of these daughters, except Mrs. Neal, now living a widow at Philadelphia, Tennessee, after their marriage, moved to western States.

Judge Young's father, Samuel Clarkston Young, was born in Pittsylvania county, Virginia, in 1801, came with his father to Anderson county, Tennessee, in 1810, and there lived and died. In 1830, he was elected by the Tennessee Legislature, county surveyor of Anderson county, and held that office thirty years. He died April 2, 1864, at Clinton. He was an ardent friend and an intense enemy, of strongly marked Scotch character, resolute, of immense will-power, and of strong native intellect, with only moderate scholastic attainments. He was an intense Whig and an uncompromising Union man during the late civil war—a man who would fearlessly proclaim his Union sentiments whenever and wherever they were called in question.

Judge Young's mother, Charlotte Hall, of an English family, was born in South Carolina, in 1797, daughter of David Hall, a Revolutionary soldier, a planter, who moved to Anderson county in the early settlement of the country, kept a wayside tavern when the country was settling up, and died April 22, 1842, at the age of seventy-eight, leaving eleven children, John, Richard, Samuel, David and James, sons; and daughters, Nancy (Mrs. Hobbs), Charlotte (Judge Young's mother), Elmira (Mrs. Yarnell), Obedience (wife of John Young, but not otherwise related), Sarah (wife of Isaac Coward), Matilda (wife of Rev. Sherwood Reese), and Serepta (wife of Edward Prince).

Judge Young's maternal grandmother, formerly Miss Obedience Brazil, was the daughter of James Brazil, who was killed by the Harps, at a point still known as "Brazil's Knob," in Morgan county, Tennessee. See "Life as It Is," a book published by one of the Brazils.

Judge Young's mother, died June 14, 1854, at the age of sixty-four, leaving four children: (1). James H. Young, a local elder for twenty-five years in the Methodist Episcopal church, south; a farmer in Anderson county, on the old homestead, which he inherited from his father. One of his sons, Samuel E. Young, graduated at the University of Tennessee, at Knoxville, in the class of 1878, and is now a prominent lawyer at Sweetwater, Tennessee. (2). Judge David King Young, subject of this sketch. (3). Nancy Ann Young, who died the wife of B. J. Hoskins, in the town and county of Denton, Texas. She left one son, Samuel Houston Hoskins, now a wholesale harness and saddle manufacturer, at Denton. (4). Obedience H. Young, now the wife of Dr. T. J. Coward, Clinton, Tennessee, a prosperous man, and a leading physician of the county. They have one child, David Richard Coward, a scholarly young gentleman, and member of the bar.

The early life of Judge Young, was that of a hard raised mountain country boy—going to school in winter and working on the farm in summer, until he was nineteen years of age, when he went two sessions to Viney Grove High School, in Lincoln county, Tennessee. While there, he taught two public schools at a salary of twenty-five dollars a month. In January, 1847, he returned home and soon after entered Holston College, in

Jefferson county, under Rev. Creed Fulton, and remained there three sessions of five months each. In 1849, he entered the law office of Col. John R. Nelson, of Knoxville, the uncle of the late distinguished Supreme judge, Thomas A. R. Nelson, and read law under his instruction, till November 12, 1849, when he was licensed to practice by Chancellor Thomas L. Williams and Judge Ebenezer Alexander. He at once engaged in the practice of law in Anderson and the surrounding counties, settled at Clinton in December, 1850— practiced in all the courts of that section and in the federal court at Knoxville, until the machinery of justice was disturbed by the presence of hostile soldiery— "*Inter arma silent leges.*".

Judge Young married, in Lee county, Virginia, May 15, 1849, Miss Elizabeth Woodson, who was born in Campbell county, Tennessee, September 2, 1832, daughter of William Woodson, who was born in Richmond, Virginia, in 1801, lived for many years in western Virginia, then settled in Campbell county, Tennessee. About the year 1838, he moved to Lee county, Virginia, where he still resides, a large farmer, in the lower end of the valley of Virginia. A cousin of his, Silas Woodson, was formerly governor of Missouri. Mrs. Young's mother was a Pebley. Her brothers, Andrew and William Woodson, are large real estate owners and farmers in Campbell county, Tennessee. She was educated at Tazewell, Claiborne county, Tennessee; is an ardent Southern Methodist; a remarkable business manager, and with her brains and energy has assisted materially in amassing the handsome property of her husband. By his marriage with Miss Woodson, Judge Young has had ten children: (1). Josephine Young, died at the age of nine, at Clinton. (2). John Young; died two weeks after birth. (3). Horace Woodson Young; was killed by the lever of a cane mill, when ten years old. (4). Charlotte Alice Young, was educated at the Knoxville Female Institute and is a scholarly and accomplished woman. She married John E. Chapman, senior member of Chapman, White, Lyons & Co., wholesale druggists, at Knoxville. She has three children; Maggie, David Carpenter, and Minnette. (5). William Baxter Young, graduated in 1882, with high honor, from the University of Tennessee, at Knoxville. After graduating he went west to see the world, was taken with the typhoid fever at Fort Worth, Texas, and there died, October 14, 1882. His remains were brought home and buried at Clinton. He had the reputation of being one of the most accomplished young men of his age in the university. (6). Minnie O. Young; graduated in the '81 class in Martha Washington College, Virginia, and afterwards took a musical course at Nashville. (7). Samuel Clarkston Young, entered the University of Tennessee in 1881, and died while a student, December 24, 1883. (8). James Walter Young, born July 13, 1868. (9). Etta Iola Young. (10). David K. Young, jr.

In 1863, being an ardent Union man, he went to

Kentucky, organized battery D, of the First Tennessee Federal light artillery, and was assigned to duty with the army of the Cumberland. His command was ordered to Nashville, where, by order of Andrew Johnson, military governor, he was placed in charge of Fort Johnson, which was the capitol building, around which he built fortifications. Early in July, 1864, the military governor determined to have a civil government and reorganize the courts in East Tennessee, and about July 4, 1864, appointed Capt. Young attorney-general for the Third judicial circuit of Tennessee, embracing the city of Knoxville. He resigned his captaincy late in July, 1864, and accepted the attorney-generalship, which position he held about two years. Then, being burthened with a heavy practice in the circuit and chancery courts north and west of Clinton, he resigned the attorney-generalship in 1866. He practiced law in partnership with Col. Henry R. Gibson, under the firm name of Young & Gibson. This firm did a leading law business from January 1, 1868, to March, 1873, when Judge Young went on the bench, by appointment from Gov. John C. Brown. He was afterward elected, in 1874, to fill out an unexpired term of four years. In 1878, he was elected judge of the Sixteenth judicial circuit, comprising the counties of Anderson, Campbell, Scott, Fentress, Pickett, Overton, Cumberland and Morgan, term expiring September 1, 1886. By law, he was made chancellor in five of the counties of his district as well as circuit judge.

As he moved along in the practice of law he invested largely in real estate, purchasing Eagle Bend, one thousand acres, for forty thousand dollars, and real estate in Knoxville valued at twenty thousand dollars. In business relations he is a member of the wholesale drug firm of Chapman, White, Lyons & Co., Knoxville, Tennessee.

In politics, Judge Young is a Democrat; in religion, a member of the Methodist Episcopal church, south; in masonry, a Knight Templar, and has presided over a lodge and over a chapter of Royal Arch Masons. For several years after the war he was a director in the Knoxville and Kentucky railroad, and for two years was railroad attorney on a salary.

Judge Young's success is the result of his energy and go-a-headativeness, and of his rule to do thoroughly and well whatever he undertakes, whether it is building a chicken coop or attending to a big law suit. He made a specialty of the land laws of the State of Tennessee and in land law practice. He has in preparation a volume on the land laws of the State, to be called "The Action of Ejectment in Tennessee." He has attained to the honors of his profession and to financial success by energy, and deferring nothing that should be done now to the next hour. His professional career is a fine illustration of what Shakspeare calls "persistive constancy." His professional career may be well understood from the remark often made of him, that a client never deserts him. Let it not be inferred, however, that Judge Young's self-assertiveness amounts to inordinate vanity. He is at once dignified and familiar; and whatever the degree of his self-esteem, he has never been suspected of setting too low an estimate upon other men. The fine portrait of him accompaning this sketch contains not a trace of what is usually called vanity.

W. H. WOOD.

MEMPHIS.

ONE of the finest types of the successful Tennessee cotton planter, is Mr. W. H. Wood, of Memphis, a record of whose life cannot fail to be instructive as well as interesting.

He is a native of the "Old Dominion," having been born in the good county of Albermarle in that State, November 14, 1814, and lived there on a plantation till he attained his eighteenth year, receiving his education in the common schools of the county, and in a preparatory school at Charlottesville. Like many self-made men, he had but limited opportunities for education. Brought up on a farm, thoroughly in love with a farmer's independent life, he had a decided preference for agricultural pursuits, and it was the wish of his father that he should follow that occupation, but being without capital to engage in that business as largely as he wished, he decided for a time to try another calling.

At the age of eighteen, he removed to Hardeman county, Tennessee, in the then western district, being attracted to that county because four of his older brothers had gone there several years before. During the first two years of his residence in Tennessee he was engaged in merchandising with his brother, David Wood, twelve miles west of the town of Bolivar, and afterward went into business on his own account, opening a store for general merchandise in Bolivar. He continued in this pursuit five years, and then, returning to his first love—agricultural pursuits—began his career as a successful cotton planter, a few miles west of Bolivar. Here he remained until 1863, twenty years in all, and then moved to Memphis, on account of the troubles of the war.

In the meantime, he had purchased a plantation in what was then Phillips, now Lee county, Arkansas, and had acquired considerable planting interests in that State. Not avaricious, but possessing a capacity to accumulate property, when the war began he had amassed a comfortable estate, much of which, being invested in slaves, was swept away in the great conflict between the States.

After reaching Memphis, he engaged in no regular business for several years, but in 1866, resumed planting on his lands in Arkansas, and has continued in that occupation till the present time, residing all the time in the city of Memphis.

One of his objects in engaging in planting after the war was to test the value of free negro labor. He had been a practical, as well as a successful, farmer, and had given his business close attention, so that he knew not only how to have it done, but how to do it. He was sufficiently well posted in the details of his business to know all about its management, and had never failed to make a crop for want of an overseer. Possessing these qualifications, in addition to thirty years' successful experience with slave labor, he was well calculated to make the proposed experiment in labor. Early in January, 1866, he brought three hundred negroes from the State of Georgia to his plantation in Arkansas, and from that time on, has kept employed from one hundred and fifty to two hundred and fifty each year. His experiment has been a decided success, and has amply demonstrated that free labor is more profitable than slave, and he now regards the emancipation of the slaves a most fortunate circumstance for the people of the country, even in a financial sense. His interests were in a remarkably flourishing condition as long as he was able to give them his full attention, and now, when prevented by increasing age from doing so, they are still very prosperous.

Mr. Wood is a stockholder in various banks and insurance companies of the city of Memphis. In the winter of 1866, he was made a director of the De Soto Bank, and served four years. He has declined to serve as an officer in any other corporation, though several times elected.

Mr. Wood has been a Democrat all his life. He took an active part in politics in his county previous to the war, but would never consent to become a candidate for office, preferring to devote his time and his energy to his chosen occupation. The story of his first vote, which was cast before he was nineteen. for Andrew Jackson for president, is very interesting. He had been in Tennessee but a few weeks, but had become acquainted with the sheriff of his county, and was told to cast his vote. Replying that he was not old enough, he was told, "You are as large as any of them," and being introduced by the sheriff to the judge of election, passed in his vote for "Old Hickory." In 1860, he was a Douglas man, and strongly opposed to secession. Since the war he has generally voted with the Democrats, but has not been a party man, and has not taken any active interest in politics.

He became a Mason in Clinton Lodge, No. 54, at Bolivar, Tennessee, nearly fifty years ago, took the degree of Master Mason, and served as secretary of the lodge.

Mr. Wood was married, June 17, 1834, to Miss Benigna Polk, youngest daughter of Col. Ezekiel Polk, of Hardeman county, and a half-sister of Samuel Polk, father of President James K. Polk. Mrs. Wood was born in 1816, and was educated at Bolivar and at Jackson, Tennessee. She has been a member of the Presbyterian church for many years. To this union have been born four children: (1). Mary Morton Wood, born in 1835; now wife of Napoleon Hill, esq., of Memphis. [See sketch of Mr. Hill, elsewhere in this volume.] (2). Sophia Wood, born in August, 1837; died at the age of two years. (3). James Wood, born in 1840; died at the age of one and a half years. (4). Nina Wood, born in November, 1843; now wife of James H. Martin, a merchant, of Memphis, and the mother of seven children.

Mr. Wood's father, Drury Wood, was born in Louisa county, Virginia, and moved to Albemarle county, in the same State, at an early day, and engaged in tobacco planting. He died in 1842, at the age of seventy-five. The Wood family is of Scotch descent, and first settled in Virginia during the seventeenth century, coming over with the Watsons and the Mickeys, descendants of which well known families are living in Virginia at the present time. Drury Wood was the son of David Wood. Thomas and Drury Wood, brothers of the subject of this sketch, are now lawyers at Charlottesville, Virginia. Another brother, Rice W. Wood, who died in 1838, was a prominent lawyer in that town, and served several terms in the Virginia Legislature.

Mr. Wood's mother, Miss Matilda Carr, of Albemarle county, Virginia, was of Scotch-Irish descent, and a daughter of John Carr, a farmer. Her brother, Anderson B. Carr, was one of the early settlers of Memphis, and owned extensive landed interests in that vicinity. He settled at Memphis in 1819, and died about 1846 or 1847. One of his daughters, now living in Memphis, is the wife of Dr. William Hewitt.

Mr. Wood began life with but little and worked his way up. His success is the result of constant, patient effort. In the ordinary pursuits of life, success is not the result of genius or of chance. Mr. Wood's theory is that any man of ordinary capacity, who has energy and directs that energy well, is bound to succeed, while the most brilliant talents, without energy, lead only to failure. In an experience of nearly sixty years, he has come to the conclusion that the opportunities for success in agriculture in the South were never so good as to-day. Lands are cheap, labor is cheap, and all that is necessary to success is intelligence and persistent effort.

GEN. JOHN T. WILDER.

CHATTANOOGA.

THE phrase that best describes and differentiates the personality of the subject of this sketch is the *soubriquet* selected by Gen. Rosencrans, and incorporated in his order issued after the battle of Hoover's Gap and applied to his command, which thenceforward was officially designated and has passed into history as "Wilder's Lightning Brigade."

He is a man of strong will, and a man of thought, or rather a man who thinks and who formulates his thoughts into productive activities. He never cared for money only for its uses—as a tool to work with. He has plenty on which to retire from business and to live a life of ease and comfort to himself and family all of their days, but he would be unhappy if not at work, and at work in new fields of enterprise of his own invention. He is a man who decides and takes hold, never asking any man to lead him. On all subjects that come before him for solution, he deliberates and promptly forms an opinion and acts upon it. He belongs to no church, to no society, being too independent to wear any man's collar or to don the badge

and train in the harness of any organization. In politics, he is a Republican, but not radical. In a word, he is very individual, of strong personality.

Though his father was a man of means, he was too proud to ask him for anything, and left home when a boy, and has made his way by industry and push and vim and snap ever since. His habits were always good. He never drank, never gambled, never used tobacco or dissipated in any way. His rule has been, and is, to find out things difficult to do, and by methods and inventions of his own, work them out and compel success, doing his own thinking; first looking well over the ground to see that he is right, and then going ahead. He is a man of large build, six feet two inches in height, weighing two hundred and ten pounds; is self-collected, always busy, never in a hurry; has an easy, kind-hearted temper, a voice affectionate in tone, never harsh, but vigorous; true to friend and foe; open-eyed, open-hearted, open-handed, and never goes back on his word or his friends. Though essentially a business man, he has scholarly attainments, especially in geology,

70

mining and engineering, studies which he took up and
mastered without a teacher, and on which his advice is
constantly sought by persons interested in the branches
of industry on which those sciences bear. He is the
inventor of Wilder's turbine water wheel, which is
now being manufactured in Wilder's machine shop and
foundry, an engineering business at Chattanooga, employing about seventy-five hands, at an average of two
dollars per day wage, and operated on a capital of about
fifty thousand dollars. To gratify his patriotic spirit, he
has been foremost in the work of developing the mineral
resources and the manufacturing interests of the South,
and especially of Chattanooga, where he settled, in 1870
and over which his cannon had boomed, and of which
he took possession, August 29, 1863, and it is thought
he has done as much to build up the town and to induce immigration and capital into the country as any
man in the State. He has talked, written, worked, traveled, and spent thousands of dollars to make the country known, and has been instrumental in bringing four
million dollars into that section of the State, and the
people who have moved into it upon his representa-
tions are prosperous. He has lived now twenty-one years
among a people whom he once fought with all his dash
and vim, and has not yet received an uncivil or an unkind word from any man in the South, and what is
more, he has hosts of friends among them. He has
never held back from helping to build up the town or
the country, especially in the direction of mining and
manufacturing. His chief ambition is to be the most
useful citizen.

Instinctively despising a man who has no opinions,
and unconsciously disliking to follow anything that
other men begin, even when a soldier, he struck out
for himself, and both as civilian and soldier he has
made for himself a distinguished name without having
reputation for his objective aim. He fought from a
sense of duty, as he works because he wants to do it
The mounted infantry of the armies on both sides in
the late war was first thought of and organized by Gen.
Wilder. While he was at home, in Indiana, on his
first furlough, in 1862, the Confederate cavalryman, Col.
Johnston, made a raid into that State. Col. Wilder,
fertile in resources, at once organized a thirty days regiment, which he mounted, and drove Johnston back.
This was the first appearance of mounted infantry in
the war. The next year they appeared on the southern
side under the leadership of Gen. Forrest.

Gen. Wilder's name and his "lightning brigade" figure prominently in the various histories of the war,
even the most compendious. A portraiture of the man,
rather than his military history, is the object of this
sketch. But a resume of his operations in the war being pertinent to that object, is here given without any
attempt at accuracy of detail. He went out as captain
of company A, Seventeenth Indiana, organized the regiment, was lieutenant-colonel under Col. Milo S. Has-

call, served a year in West Virginia, joined Buell's
army at Louisville, went with the army of the Ohio,
and participated in the battles of Pittsburg Landing
and at and around Corinth. At Nashville, in March,
1862, he was made colonel of a regiment. On his way
back to the army from his furlough home, he met
Bragg's army going into Kentucky, and immediately
stopped, fortified the railroad bridge at Mumfordsville,
held Bragg's army in check five days, and was finally
captured, his ammunition being exhausted, but his
operations saved Louisville. On being exchanged, he
joined his command at Nashville, in November, 1862,
was made commander of a brigade, which he immediately mounted, and the ensuing winter his force was
used as a raiding command, having been furnished with
horses and Spencer rifles. It was this command that
drove Morgan away from the railroad just before the
battle of Murfreesborough. His command was given
the advance, June 24, 1863, of the Tullahoma campaign, forced the passage of Hoover s Gap, held it against
Gen. Bate and a part of Cheatham's division, flanked
Bragg's right center, and got in behind Tullahoma,
which forced that general to withdraw.

Being sent to Chattanooga in advance of the army,
he came upon the town before any one there had an
idea that there was a Federal soldier within one hundred miles of it. He then moved south on the Western
and Atlantic railroad, burning bridges and driving the
enemy's cavalry back to Tunnel Hill. He was then recalled to Thomas' headquarters, at Pond Spring, east
base of Lookout mountain, began the battle of Chickamauga, holding Walker's division a day until Thomas
came twenty miles. This saved Chattanooga. He repulsed five charges at the battle of Chickamauga on
Saturday, keeping his own lines unbroken. He participated in the battles around Chattanooga and all the engagements in Sherman's Atlanta campaign. After the
fall of Atlanta, his health having broken down, in September, 1864, he did no active service, and resigned in
December, 1864. Among his more brilliant achievements was his recapture, at Chickamauga, of the battery Sheridan had lost, a feat which Gen. Thomas acknowledged saved his corps. He was in two hundred
and nineteen fights and skirmishes of all kinds in West
Virginia, Kentucky, Georgia and Alabama, but mostly
in Tennessee. He had thirteen horses shot under him,
and was five times slightly wounded. He was the only
Federal commander that stayed all Sunday night on the
battle-field of Chickamauga; and so thoroughly had he
impressed himself, and infused his own spirit into his
men, he never lost a cannon nor a color during the war,
never assaulted a position he did not carry, never defended one he did not hold, and his flag was never
driven back a rod in any engagement. Such was the
soldier that won for his command the official designation of "Wilder's Lightning Brigade."

Gen. Wilder was born in the village of Hunter,

Greene county, New York, in the heart of the Catskill mountains. January 31, 1830. From the age of fourteen to twenty-one, he served an apprenticeship of seven years as a founder, machinist, mill-wright and pattern-maker, at Columbus, Ohio, and learned it thoroughly. He then started in business at Lawrenceburg, Indiana, but shortly afterward moved to Greensburg, in that State.

After the war, he investigated the iron and coal of the southern mineral belt from Pennsylvania to Tuscaloosa, Alabama, selected Tennessee for his home, bought the ground that Rockwood stands on, in 1865, organized the Roane Iron Company, built a furnace at Rockwood in 1867-8, made the first iron in the South that was made by mineral fuel, and started an industry which has grown to be one of the largest in the country, the Roane Iron Company, one of the strongest in the South, operating on one million dollars paid up capital. His interest in this company he sold out, for he is not a man to float down stream like a knot on a log, but starts an enterprise, gets it under way, sells out and starts a new one to conquer another world. He is now largely interested in the Cranberry iron district, Carter county, Tennessee, and Mitchell county, North Carolina, owns Roan mountain and two hotels on it, and is bringing out that section of country.

The only civil office he ever held was that of postmaster of Chattanooga, under President Hayes' administration.

Gen. Wilder married, in Greensburg, Indiana, May 18, 1858, Miss Martha Stuart, daughter of Silas Stuart, a Pennsylvanian by birth, of Scotch descent, and one of the founders of that town. The family was banished from Scotland, in 1752, for following the fortunes of Charles in the last Scottish rebellion. Mrs. Wilder's mother, nee Miss Rachel Fisher, a native of Ligonier, Pennsylvania, was of Scotch-Irish stock. Mrs. Wilder's brother, John Stuart, is a banker, and her brother, Daniel Stuart, is a wholesale druggist, both at Indianapolis. They are cousins of Hon. Thomas A. Hendricks, late vice-president of the United States. She was educated at Greensburg, Indiana, is a member of the Methodist Episcopal church, and is a plain, straight-forward, sensible, unassuming, charitable Christian mother and wife, and utterly without vanity.

By his marriage with Miss Stuart, Gen. Wilder has six children, the first three born at Greensburg, Indiana: (1). Mary Wilder, born February 18, 1859; graduated from the high school, at Chattanooga, and is one of the best educated women in Tennessee, especially in geology, botany and mineralogy. (2). Annie Wilder, born April 9, 1861; graduated at Chattanooga; married, March, 1883, Mr. F. A. Stratton, now in charge of Roan mountain. (3). Rachel Wilder, born January 1, 1865; graduated at Chattanooga, in 1884. (4). Mattie Wilder, born January 9, 1868, at Rockwood, Tennessee, the first child born there. (5). Stuart Wilder, born at

Rockwood, Tennessee, October 6, 1872. (6). Edith Wilder, born at Chattanooga, July, 1875.

Gen. Wilder comes of a very old family. In 1492, Henry VII. gave Nicholas Wilder the beautiful estate of Purley Hall, on the Thames, in Berkshire, England, just above Reading, for his manly conduct in attacking and carrying the castle in which Richard III. had taken refuge during the battle of Bosworth, and gave him a crest with the motto, "Courage conquers walls." This estate, now owned by Francis Wilder, has been in the family nearly four hundred years. Gen. Wilder's ancestors were Puritans, compelled, by Charles I., to give up their paternal homes in England. They came to America in 1638, and settled near Boston, Martha Wilder, with her two sons, Edward and Thomas, and her two daughters, Mary and Annie. From those two sons have sprung over six thousand Wilders in the United States. One of his ancestors, Ephraim Wilder, was a captain in the French and Indian wars, and helped to capture Louisburg. His grandfathers of the fourth and fifth remove were soldiers in the Revolutionary war, the former losing a leg at Bunker Hill; the latter was bayonetted in the capture of Stony Point, on the Hudson, by "mad Anthony Wayne," and lived till he was one hundred and seven years old. The father, Reuben Wilder, was born at Charlestown, Massachusetts, in 1793, served in the war of 1812, was in the battle of Plattsburg, settled in Greene county, New York, a farmer and miller, and died in Chattanooga, Tennessee, in 1880, eighty-three years old; a man of sturdy self-reliance; a strong man who never used his strength; without ambition beyond living well and educating his children; noted for his broad, practical good sense.

Gen. Wilder's mother, nee Miss Mary Merritt, was of an old Lancashire family in England, who came to New York at an early day. Her father, Samuel Merritt, served, when a boy, sixteen years old, in the patriot army in the Revolutionary war, while his father and brothers supported the crown. Samuel Merritt's father and brothers settled in Canada, but he settled in Hunter, New York, though he subsequently sold out and moved to Huron, Ohio, where he died, in 1850, at the age of ninety-three.

Gen. Wilder has had three sisters: Elizabeth Wilder, who died the wife of William Cure, a farmer, of Rochester county, New York; Clarissa Wilder, now wife of William Markle, of the same county; Mary A. Wilder, now wife of Cyrus Elmendorf, at Chattanooga. He has one brother, Horace M. Wilder, of Chattanooga, retired from business. Very few of the Wilders are in public life, but are noted for being independent, self-reliant, their great hanging-on qualities, and persistency in following out what they undertake. There is not a coward in the family. They have taken a part in every war in America. Many of them are preachers. Marshall P. Wilder is president of the Massachusetts Historical

Society, also of the Horticultural Society, and, although a merchant, was, for many years, president of the American Agricultural Society. Burt G. Wilder is president of Cornell University, New York.

Gen. Wilder is a member of the American Institute of Mining Engineers, of the American Association for the Advancement of Science, and of the Iron and Steel Institute of Great Britain.

As a cavalry commander and raider, as a manufacturer and successful business man, and for the extent and accuracy of his scientific attainments, he is among the most remarkable and interesting men in the State,

and has been long enough identified with its leading industries to justify the editor in giving him a conspicuous place among prominent Tennesseans. In conversation, he is a most rapid, brilliant and animated talker, and so instructive are his utterances and illustrations, that his auditors are charmed, fascinated and spell-bound, not less by the elegant simplicity of his diction than the intense earnestness he manifests to contribute to the general stock of information tending to qualify and stimulate men to enter upon the productive activities to which the wonderful resources of the country and the spirit of the times invite them.

R. W. MITCHELL, M. D.

MEMPHIS.

NATURALLY a physician's life is not noisy, but the career of Dr. Mitchell has been exceptionally quiet. He made his reputation, which was at first local, then State, and lastly national, not by what he has said, but by what he has done. To his biographer he appears most entitled to a page in these honorable records by having gone through five yellow fever epidemics, standing his ground with a noble and lofty heroism, and doing what he could to stay the ravages of remorseless pestilence. To such a one—

"The grateful town with streaming eyes should raise
Historic marble to record his praise."

"The medical hero of the great epidemics," is the noble title nobly won by Dr. Mitchell for his bravery, wisdom and fidelity during the four months of yellow fever scourge at Memphis, in 1878, in which, out of a total population of less than twenty thousand left in the city, five thousand one hundred and fifty persons perished; nine hundred and forty-six negroes and four thousand two hundred and four whites, and in which not more than two hundred white people escaped the fever. Of the one hundred and eleven physicians of the corps under the direction of Dr. Mitchell, forty-five fell a sacrifice to "the long agony and bloody sweat of professional duty before translation." No event in this century so startled and shook the world as this awful epidemic. Nations round the globe sent contributions to the stricken city. It was a touch of sorrow, sadness, suffering and death that made the whole world feel akin. Parties and creeds and nationalities and differences of race were sunk and forgotten, and the brotherhood of man blossomed out into sympathy, as solicitous and tender as that of mother for her child. [For a detailed and thrilling account of this fearful pestilence, see "History of the Yellow Fever Epidemic of 1878," by J. M. Keating, who himself, true to his ancient family motto, "fortis et fidelis," was an eye witness of the scenes

he describes with pathetic eloquence, and assisted in all ways to the relief of his doomed and adopted city. For passages referring to Dr. Mitchell, see pages 365-371. The entire volume is an invaluable contribution to medical literature, and will more than repay a reading.]

Dr. Mitchell was born in Madison county, Tennessee, August 26, 1831, and at the age of five went with his father's family, first to Grenada, Mississippi, where they resided several years, during which time he attended the schools at that place. The family then moved to Jackson, Mississippi, and attended Centenary College several years. When sixteen years old he entered the drug business, as a clerk, and continued in it about three years, when his father removed to Vicksburg. Here he remained with the family about twelve months and then went to Van Buren, Arkansas, and engaged in the drug business two years on his own account. The Arkansas country at that time was rather wild, and satisfied that if he remained there, he too must partake of the habits and vices of the town, he determined to retrace his steps, which he did, going back to a place near Yazoo City, Mississippi, where he studied medicine one year, under his brother-in-law, Dr. A. W. Washburne. He next took a first course in the medical department of the University of Louisiana, at New Orleans, and spent the summer of that year, 1855, as a resident student in the city hospital of Vicksburg. It was here that he had his first experience with yellow fever, having the entire hospital under his control during the absence of the resident physician. This was a fine schooling for Dr. Mitchell, and he turned his experience gained there to great advantage afterward in the epidemics of 1867, 1873, 1878 and 1879, at Memphis, through all of which he stood his ground, while many of his brethren died, thus forever endearing himself to the people of Memphis, and conferring an honor on the name of physician.

In the winter of 1855-6, he took another course in the University of Louisiana, receiving his degree of M.D. in March, 1856, under Profs. James Jones, Cenas, Wedderbum, Riddell, Knott, Hunt and Warren Stone. After graduation, he returned to Vicksburg, and was elected, by popular vote, physician to the city hospital for one year. In 1858, he came to Memphis, as it was a growing place, and under the advice of his friend, Dr. Warren Stone, who had at that day a world-wide reputation as a surgeon. He began the practice of medicine at once, and in 1859, was elected secretary of the Board of Health of the city of Memphis. In 1859-60, he organized the Memphis City Hospital, of which he was placed in charge, in addition to his other position. This position he held until 1861, when he volunteered for the Confederate service with the Tennessee troops, and was appointed assistant surgeon of the Thirteenth Tennessee regiment, Dr. Frank Rice being surgeon-in-chief. He was mustered into the Confederate service with that regiment, and appointed surgeon in the provisional army of the Confederate States of America. He followed the fortunes of the Thirteenth Tennessee through the battles of Belmont and Shiloh, and at the latter engagement was taken prisoner while in charge of a stationary field hospital, carried to Pittsburg landing, detained a prisoner some three weeks, and then sent through the lines to Corinth, arriving there the day of the evacuation of that post by the Confederates. He was then appointed chief-surgeon of Gen. Clark's division. Before breaking camp, however, Clark was ordered to Mississippi, and Dr. Mitchell asked to be allowed to remain with the Tennessee troops. On arriving at Chattanooga he was detained awhile by Gen. Polk, but went on with the main army, and was at the battle of Mumfordsville, in 1863. At Bardstown, Kentucky, he was assigned to duty with Gen. Forrest as chief-surgeon on his staff. A few days after this Gen. Forrest was ordered back to Tennessee, and Dr. Mitchell again asked to be assigned to his old command in the field. He rejoined it (the Thirteenth Tennessee) at Shelbyville, Tennessee, and with them made the hurried march to Perryville, Kentucky, and went through service there, and then in the retreat through Kentucky and East Tennessee. He was at the battle of Stones River with the Thirteenth Tennessee as chief-surgeon on Gen. Preston Smith's staff. Just before the battle of Chattanooga he was taken sick, carried to hospital, where he was prostrated some three weeks; but as soon as able to move about, he rejoined the army against the protest of the hospital surgeon, Dr. Westmoreland. He caught up with the command at Sweetwater; was present at the disaster of Missionary Ridge, then followed the retreat down to Ringgold Gap; was at the battle of Resaca, the battles of Atlanta and Jonesborough, Cave Hill and Franklin. Next he went with Hood's army to Nashville, was on the retreat from Nashville, and then went with the army as far as Au-

gusta, Georgia, where he obtained sick leave and came back as far as Selma, Alabama. Wilson's Federal cavalry entering that town, and the Confederacy collapsing, his military career closed at that place.

Returning home by way of Mobile and New Orleans, he at once went to work, commenced life anew—like many of his comrades—having come out of the war with nothing. From that time he has practiced his profession at Memphis, in partnership, from 1868 to the present time, with Dr. R. B. Maury. Dr. J. Joseph Williams was associated with the firm for a few months in 1873, but he died with yellow fever in that year. Dr. Edward D. Mitchell (his kinsman), a graduate of the Jefferson Medical College, Philadelphia, has been associated with the firm since 1879.

In 1878, Dr. Mitchell was elected president of the Memphis City Board of Health, but shortly afterward resigned. During the epidemic of 1878, he was appointed medical director of the Howard Association of Memphis. The same year he was appointed a member of the board of yellow fever experts, authorized by act of congress, in 1878, to investigate the causes, and the best means of prevention of yellow fever. He is a member of the Shelby County Medical Society, of the State Medical Society, of the American Medical Association, of the American Public Health Association, and of the National Board of Health. In 1870-71, he was professor of materia medica in the Memphis Medical College.

It will thus be seen that Dr. Mitchell has pursued medicine as a profession, faithfully, from boyhood, when he began as a drug clerk. It is a theory all parents should raise their children by, that every child should have one pursuit only, and that they should study that from the beginning, if they would rise to distinction in it. Of the leading traits of Dr. Mitchell's character, one who is entirely competent, and who has had good opportunities for studying him, says : " He is marvelously tender and sympathetic in his feelings. He is very reserved and reticent, but when he does speak he says something. He seems to have been born to command, and ought to be at the head of an army, so great is his power and influence over men. He is a fine disciplinarian, and when he had one hundred and eleven physicians under him as medical director, in 1878, everything went on like clock work. It was a great achievement to go through that epidemic without a jar among all his co-laborers. It was the same when he was brigade-surgeon in the army. He is a generous man, and a remarkable just one, and conscientious in his dealings and professional business. He is a student always, and always considering himself a servant of the people. He has far less of business talent than of professional ability. Let it go down as a part of his history that he is plain, unobtrusive, unpretentious, though a standard man and a standard physician. The prominent feature of Dr. Mitchell's life is that he has been the good and faithful physician always."

Col. J. M. Keating speaks of Dr. Mitchell as "a man of high professional skill, integrity of purpose, courage, coolness and discretion, which made him first among the noble and devoted band of self-sacrificing brothers in the epidemic of 1878," and this seems to be the verdict of all his fellow-citizens.

Dr. Mitchell married, in Memphis, May 7, 1872, Miss Rebecca Park, a native of that city, the daughter of William Park, a native Irishman, who came, when a young man, from the north of Ireland, to Nashville, Tennessee, and first took a clerkship with Crockett & Park, the latter his first cousin, in that city. He afterward settled in Memphis, and was a cotton buyer and commission merchant for forty years. He was a Presbyterian of the north of Ireland Covenanters, and in politics was a Democrat. He died in 1877. He left the reputation of being one of nature's nobleman, generous, open-hearted, full of Irish wit, and a fine business man. His mother was Jane Gibson, of county Tyrone, in Ireland. She came to Memphis a widow, and died eighty-seven years old, a remarkably pious woman, and very conversant with the Bible. Mrs. Mitchell's mother, nee Miss Rebecca Cocke, was born at Strawberry Plains, near Richmond, Virginia, daughter of Bowler Cocke, of a large Virginia family. Her mother was Mary Fox, a near relative of Sir Charles James Fox, the celebrated English orator and statesman. Her grandmother was Mary Carver, daughter of John Carver, who came over in the Mayflower, and was the first governor of Massachusetts. Mrs. Mitchell's sister, nee Miss Mary Park, is now the wife of C. W. Metcalf, a prominent lawyer in Memphis, and has six children, Rebecca, Bessie, William Park, Charles W., Mary and Robert M. Mrs. Mitchell's sister, Miss Lena Park, was educated at Sayre Institute, Lexington, Kentucky, and is now the wife of Judge James F. Read, of Fort Smith, Arkansas. Mrs. Mitchell graduated at Mrs. Knox's private seminary for young ladies, at Nashville. She is remarkably proud of her Irish blood. Her paternal ancestry has had a David Park in it for four hundred years. This lady is noted for her generous hospitality, and is a gleam of sunshine in her family, in her church and in Memphis society. Like her husband, she is of a most unselfish nature.

Dr. Mitchell's father, Gen. G. D. Mitchell, was called the "Chesterfield of Mississippi," the home of his adoption. In ante bellum days he was a general of the State militia; during the late war a quartermaster in the Confederate army. He was a merchant and at one time teacher of a school at Jackson, Mississippi. He died in 1870, at Cooper's Wells, near Vicksburg, at the age of sixty-five. He married, in Madison county, Tennessee, Miss Mary Wood, a native of Tennessee. She died when the subject of this sketch was only twelve years old, and left three children: (1). Martha Mitchell, now wife of N. T. Pugh, clerk of the chancery court at Yazoo City, Mississippi. (2). Almeda Mitchell, now wife of Dr. A. W. Washburne. (3). Dr. R. W. Mitchell, subject of this sketch.

An hereditary Democrat and a Democrat all the way through, Dr. Mitchell has, however, always taken a back seat and a modest position in politics. For six years he was a member of the Memphis board of education, and for five years a member of the Tennessee State board of education. He became a Mason in 1852, at Van Buren, Arkansas, has taken the chapter degrees, and has held all the offices of the lodge, for several years serving as Worshipful Master. In 1857, he became an Odd Fellow. His life has been both a professional and financial success.

The motives acting upon this gentleman may not be fully analyzed, for men often do things from what is called unconscious cerebration. But it is safe to say, that without thinking of the effect his course might have on anybody, he has simply tried to do his duty— and to do it as conscientiously as he could—to his profession, to his friends, to the community and to the State; and this, apparently, without thinking of the effect it might have on people at a distance, or those immediately around him. The following incident will serve to illustrate: While the epidemic was raging in Memphis, in 1878, Mrs. Thompson, a wealthy lady in Washington City, authorized Dr. Woodworth, surgeon of the Marine Hospital, to organize a yellow fever commission, and Woodworth telegraphed Dr. Mitchell, offering him a place on the commission. With a tranquil courage, which belongs only to the highest manhood, Dr. Mitchell wrote on the back of the dispatch, "Thanks for the honor, but I cannot leave my people in their distress," and handed it to the operator. This answer got into the papers, was flashed over the wires in every direction, with the effect of making the Doctor an example of useful and heroic endeavor, and his name henceforth is the influence of a brave conservation of life—not measurable by material, immediate and calculable results—and humanity is the richer for his daring.

HON. THOMAS NIXON VAN DYKE.

ATHENS.

THE Van Dyke family is one of the oldest and most honorable in the State of Tennessee. The genealogy of the family is traced back in unbroken line nearly three centuries, to Thomas Jans Van Dyke, of the Netherlands, whose sons, Jan Thomasse, Hendrick Thomasse and Nicolas Thomasse Van Dyke, emigrated to America, settled on Long Island, New York, in 1652, and took the oath of allegiance in 1687. From these have sprung a numerous progeny, scattered now all over the Union, but recognized as among the most prominent people of the States of New York, New Jersey, Pennsylvania and Delaware.

Thomas James Van Dyke, father of Judge Thomas Nixon Van Dyke, subject of this memoir, was born in Delaware; educated at Lancaster, Pennsylvania; studied medicine with his uncle, Dr. Daniel Robinson, of Baltimore, Maryland, and obtained his diploma in 1791. The same year he was appointed an ensign in the infantry service of the United States, and was afterward promoted to a captaincy in the same service. In 1798, being stationed at the garrison called Belle Canton, near the junction of Tennessee and Holston rivers, then in Roane county, Tennessee, he married Miss Penelope Smith Campbell, oldest daughter of Hon. David Campbell, then living near Belle Canton, where Lenoir's cotton factory now stands. The Hon. David Campbell was then one of the judges of the superior court of the State of Tennessee, and subsequently was appointed judge of the United States court for the then territory of Mississippi. In 1810 or 1811, Thomas James Van Dyke resigned his commission in the United States army, moved to Washington, Rhea county, Tennessee, and engaged in the practice of medicine. Soon after the commencement of the war between the United States and Great Britain, he was appointed a surgeon in the United States army, and died at Fort Claiborne, in what is now the State of Alabama.

After his death his widow, and all her children except Thomas Nixon Van Dyke, our subject, removed to Alabama, and there, in 1822, she married a Mr. Trotter, a cotton planter, living in Washington county, and, at the time of the marriage, representative of his county in the Alabama Legislature. She died soon after her marriage to Mr. Trotter, without any children by him, and was buried on his plantation in Washington county, Alabama.

The children of Thomas James Van Dyke and his wife Penelope Smith Van Dyke were five, three sons and two daughters. The sons were Alexander Outlaw Van Dyke, Jefferson Campbell Van Dyke and Thomas Nixon Van Dyke. Alexander Outlaw Van Dyke was born January 16, 1800, and educated at a grammar school taught by Rev. Mr. Johnson, in Huntingdon, Pennsylvania.

In 1821, he was appointed a midshipman in the United States navy, and when Commodore Porter was appointed to the command of the Mexican navy, in the Gulf of Mexico, in Mexico's revolutionary war with Spain, he took Midshipman Van Dyke with him as a lieutenant in the Mexican navy, and about a year after he died of yellow fever, off Carthagena, and was buried at sea. He was never married. Jefferson Campbell Van Dyke was born January 16, 1801, and died in 1862. He was educated at the common schools of the county; moved with his mother to Alabama, in 1819; studied law, and was admitted to practice in that State. In 1829, he represented the county of Dallas in the Alabama Legislature, and in 1834 or 1835, he was elected by the Legislature comptroller of the State. He married a Miss Cocke, of a Virginia family, and by her had three children, namely, Sarah Gayle Van Dyke, who married Dr. Curry; Vannie R. Van Dyke, who married first a Mr. Horton, second, a Mr. Pegram; Corrie Van Dyke, who married first a Mr. Bohannon, second, a Mr. Ford.

Thomas Nixon Van Dyke, subject of this sketch, was born in South West Point garrison, Roane county, Tennessee, January 22, 1803, and baptized in Huntingdon, Pennsylvania, by Rev. Thomas Breintnall, of the Protestant Episcopal church. He was educated at a classical school at Huntingdon, taught by Rev. Thomas Johnson, a Scotchman and Presbyterian minister. He studied law with his brother-in-law, Gen. William Rudolph Smith, in Huntingdon, and was admitted to the bar in November, 1823; moved to and settled in Mercer, Mercer county, Pennsylvania, in 1826, and in the same year was admitted to practice in the district court of the United States and in the Supreme court of the State of Pennsylvania for the western district of the State.

In the fall of 1828, he removed to Alabama and settled in Tuscaloosa, and the same year was admitted to practice in all the courts of that State. In the fall of 1829, he was elected assistant clerk of the house of representatives of Alabama, to which office he was elected by the three next succeeding Legislatures.

In 1833, he returned to his native State of Tennessee, and settled in Athens, McMinn county. Obtaining license to practice in all the courts of the State, he at once entered upon his long and useful career in this State, always conducting a large and lucrative business.

In 1837, he was appointed a director of the branch Bank of Tennessee, and by the board of directors was elected president of that institution, holding the office for two years, when he declined a re-election, the political party to which he belonged being in the minority—an instance of modesty and unselfishness which would be rare indeed in these days of place-seeking and self-aggrandizement.

He has always been a public-spirited citizen, devoted to the progress and improvement of his State. He was one of the originators of the East Tennessee, Virginia and Georgia railroad, then called the Hiwassee railroad, was elected one of the directors, and subsequently was elected president of the company. On January 10, 1851, he was admitted to practice before the Supreme court of the United States. In 1850, and again in 1851 and 1857, he was appointed a member of the American Legal Association, of New York city. In 1854, he was elected by the people chancellor of the Twelfth chancery division of Tennessee, which division was afterward the Second, and is now the Third. At that time it had eighteen counties in it, ranging round from Blount county, by the lines of North Carolina, Georgia, part of Alabama, and then north across the State to the Kentucky line. His term expired in 1862.

In January, 1864, Judge Van Dyke was arrested, by order of the military authorities of the United States, at his own house, at 2 o'clock A. M., and carried off as a hostage and imprisoned in Camp Chase, near Columbus, Ohio. He remained in prison until the last of March, 1865, when he was released, and then went to his family, in Mineral Point, Wisconsin, his wife, three daughters, a little son, Robert, then three years of age, and a niece of his wife, having been arrested by Federal officers in June, 1864, carried north of the Ohio river, and banished from their home during the war.

In April, 1865, he took his family to Quincy, Illinois. Cut off from home, from his practice and income, with a large family to be supported, and in a country hostile to him, his condition was, to say the least, embarrassing. However, he resolutely accepted the situation, and did what law practice he could get. July 7, 1865, he was licensed to practice in the Supreme court in and for the Western district of Pennsylvania, and September 20, 1865, was licensed to practice in the Supreme court of Illinois. After the war was over he brought his family back, in February, 1866, to his residence, near Athens, McMinn county, Tennessee, and once again resumed the practice of his profession.

On October, 1873, he was commissioned, with J. W. McHenry, of Davidson county, and S. W. Cochrane, of Obion county, to draft a bill according to a joint resolution of the Thirty-eighth General Assembly, for surveying and districting such parts of the State as had not heretofore been surveyed and laid off, in order to perfect titles. In October, 1874, he was a commissioner from the State at large for consideration of the removal of the United States capital. In 1877, and again in 1879, he was appointed a member of the board of trustees of the Tennessee Hospital for the Insane. On December 9, 1875, he was appointed special judge of the Supreme court of Tennessee to try the "Bank of Tennessee new-issue" cases. He was commissioned special chancellor of the Third chancery division four times, from 1878 to 1880.

By a joint resolution of the General Assembly of Tennessee, December 24, 1879, the governor was authorized to appoint a committee of ten, three from each grand division of the State and one from the State at large, to meet similar committees, June 22, 1880, at Charlotte, North Carolina, to make arrangements for celebrating the centennial of the battle of King's Mountain, and Judge Van Dyke was appointed from the State at large.

Judge Van Dyke was married, May 23, 1833, to Miss Eliza Ann Deaderick, who was born May 1, 1814, in Jefferson county, Tennessee, and educated at Greeneville, Tennessee. Mrs. Van Dyke is a lovable lady, a woman of strong sense and excellent judgment, devoted as wife and mother, and a model Christian. Her father was Dr. William H. Deaderick, the half brother of Chief Justice Deaderick. He was born in Virginia, was married in Tennessee, and lived first in Greeneville, next at the Cross-roads, in Jefferson county, and spent the latter part of his life in McMinn county, where he died at the age of seventy-three. He was a practicing physician of decided ability. His wife, nee Penelope Smith Hamilton, was the daughter of Col. Joseph Hamilton, a lawyer of Jefferson county, a native of Rockbridge county, Virginia, one of the first settlers of East Tennessee, and a member of the convention that organized the State. Mrs. Eliza Ann Van Dyke's mother died at Athens at the age of forty-three, the mother of twelve children, namely: George Michael, died in infancy; Penelope Hamilton, who married Victor Moreau Campbell, son of Judge David Campbell; David, who was at the battle of San Jacinto, under Gen. Houston, and died at Athens about 1840; Eliza Ann, Mrs. Van Dyke, wife of the subject of this sketch; William H., died two years old; Joseph, who served in the Confederate army; Margaretta, who married John L. Bridges, of Athens, Tennessee; Frances Nelson, died unmarried; Thomas Scott, a soldier in the Mexican war, and in the Confederate army; Robert H., now living in New York city, a commission merchant; William, a soldier in the Confederate army; Alexander Hamilton, died unmarried, twenty-five years old. Of the twelve, only three are living, Thomas, Robert and Eliza Ann (Mrs. Van Dyke).

By his marriage with Miss Deaderick, Judge Van Dyke has had ten children, namely: (1). Penelope Smith Van Dyke, born August 21, 1834; baptized by Rt. Rev. James H. Otey, bishop of Tennessee; married, September 15, 1856, Thomas Cleage; has nine children, William Deaderick, born September 20, 1857; Thomas Alexander, born June, 25, 1858; Richard Van Dyke, born August 5, 1861; Nellie, born December 21, 1863, died November 23, 1864; Susan Coffin, born at Quincy, Illinois, November 15, 1865; Frances Hamilton, born December 22, 1868; Anna Mary, born March 9, 1871; Letitia, born November 9, 1875, died ——————; Josie Van Dyke, born

July 6, 1877. All these children were baptized by Presbyterian ministers, their parents being members of that church. (2). William Deaderick Van Dyke, born October 20, 1836; baptized by Bishop Otey; educated at Maryville, Blount county, Tennessee; studied law, and became a prominent practitioner at Chattanooga, where he died, in 1883. In 1861, he entered the Confederate army as a private in James B. Cooke's company, but was soon after promoted to the rank of major in the commissary department, and continued in that service until the surrender. He married, June 16, 1859, Miss Anna Mary Deaderick, daughter of Chief Justice James William Deaderick, and by her had four children: Annie Clifton, born in March, 1860; Thomas Nixon, born in 1864; Frances Lavinia, born in 1868; Carrie Shelby, born in ——. (3). Letitia Smith Van Dyke, born October 12, 1838; died, November 7, 1850; baptized by Rev. Mr. Tomes, of the Episcopal church. (4). Richard Smith Van Dyke, born October 14, 1840; died November 14, 1864; was educated at Princeton College, New Jersey, graduated in 1861, and as soon as he returned home that year joined the First regiment of Tennessee cavalry, Confederate States army; went into the army as a private, in Capt. Gouldy's company, and upon the resignation of that officer, was unanimously elected captain of the company, and was soon after promoted to the rank of major of a battalion of cavalry. He was captured at Vicksburg, but as soon as he was exchanged he gathered together his battalion and joined the Confederate army in Virginia. On September 24, 1864, he was wounded in battle near Darksville, in the valley of Virginia, was taken to Lynchburg, and there died from his wounds, November 14, 1864, and was buried in the private vault of William Murrell, in the cemetery of that city. He was baptized in childhood by the Rev. Mr. Tomes, Episcopalian minister. (5). John Montgomery Van Dyke was born October 7, 1842; baptized by Rev. Mr. Tomes; died September 2, 1864. As soon as the war commenced between the United States and the Confederate States of America, he volunteered in the company of Capt. James B. Cooke, Fifty-ninth regiment of mounted Tennessee infantry, Confederate States army, as a private. When Capt. Cooke was elected colonel of the regiment Van Dyke was elected first lieutenant, and soon after was promoted to the captaincy of the company. At the taking of Vicksburg, he was captured and paroled, and as soon as he was exchanged he collected his company together and joined the army again, in Virginia. In one of the battles in the valley of Virginia, near Darksville, he was shot through the bowels, and while being taken off the battle-field, the ambulance and party were captured by a party of Federal soldiers, commanded by an officer. Soon after the Federals were forced to retreat, and having to pass through Darksville, when they reached the village young Van Dyke was discovered to be dead, and was left there. His corpse being

71

recognized by some ladies of Darksville, with whom he had previously formed an acquaintance, his remains were taken charge of by them, and buried in a lot of a gentleman adjoining Darksville, with a head-board, with his name, rank in the army and place of residence put upon it. Since the war, Judge Van Dyke received a letter from a gentleman of that place informing him of these facts, and he at once took steps to have the grave properly cared for and marked by a neat stone monument. John Van Dyke had just left the academy in Athens to go Princeton College, as soon as his brother Richard should graduate there, when the war broke out. (6). Frances Lavinia Van Dyke, was born October 8, 1844; now living at home, unmarried. She was educated at the Female Academy, at Athens; was baptized by Rev. Mr. Tomes. (7). Thomas Nixon Van Dyke, jr., was born November 11, 1846; died February 3, 1863. He was going to school at the academy in Athens, Tennessee, when the war between the United States and the Confederate States broke out. On October 4, 1862, he volunteered for the Confederate service, joined Capt. Blair's company, Sixty-third regiment of Tennessee infantry; was taken sick at Cumberland Gap, Tennessee, from exposure in a Kentucky expedition, was brought home, and died ten days after, and now lies buried by the side of his sister in his father's private graveyard, near Athens, Tennessee. (8). Margaret Josephine Van Dyke, was born August 3, 1849; baptized by Bishop Otey; was educated at the Female Academy, at Athens, Tennessee, and at the Female Academy, in New Albany, Indiana, of both which academies Rev. Mr. Rowley was the principal at the time. She was married, by Rev. Joseph H. Martin, Presbyterian, to Hugh T. Inman, May 23, 1871, and has five children, Annie Martin, Josie, Hugh, Edward and Louisa. (9). Mary Hamilton Van Dyke, was born April 4, 1853; baptized by Rev. Thomas W. Humes, of Knoxville; was educated by Miss Lydia Ann Bridges, in her private school, at Athens, Tennessee; married George M. Battey, October 4, 1881, and has one child, Henry Van Dyke. (10). Robert Deaderick Van Dyke, was born March 17, 1861; baptized by Rev. Joseph H. Martin, a Presbyterian minister, at Athens.

Judge Van Dyke's sister, Mary Hamilton Van Dyke, fourth child of Thomas J. and Penelope S. Van Dyke, was born April 17, 1805; was educated in Nolachucky Academy, in Jefferson county, Tennessee; moved to Alabama, in 1819, with her mother; after the death of her mother, went to live with her aunt, Letitia Nixon Smith, in Huntingdon, Pennsylvania. There she intermarried, in 1824, with Gen. William Rudolph Smith, oldest son of William Moore Smith, and grandson of Rev. William Smith, D.D., provost of the University of Pennsylvania, at Philadelphia. Gen. William R. Smith afterward moved with his family to Mineral Point, Wisconsin, where he died. His widow is still living at Mineral Point with her son, John Montgomery Smith.

Nine children were born to this couple: Rudolph, died unmarried; Richard, married Frances Boyden; Penelope Campbell, married William Henry, a banker, at Mineral Point, who died in 1884; Letitia; John Montgomery, married first Toney Hildebrand, and afterward Jenny Crawford, a widow; Maria; Samuel; Mary; Henry Hobart.

Eliza Rhea Van Dyke, Judge Van Dyke's second sister, was born September 6, 1807; was educated at Nolachucky Academy; moved with her mother to Alabama, in 1819, where she married a Mr. Scott, of Lawrence county, in that State. Afterward, they moved to some place on Red river, in Louisiana, where she died, leaving two or three children.

Judge Van Dyke's paternal grandmother was Letitia, Nixon, daughter of Thomas Nixon. She was three times married; first, to John Rogerson, second, to James Van Dyke, and third, to John Cookley.

Judge Van Dyke's paternal aunt, Letitia Nixon Smith, nee Cookley, married Richard Smith, of Huntingdon, Pennsylvania, son of Rev. William Smith, D.D., provost of the University of Pennsylvania. After the death of her half brother, Thomas James Van Dyke, she sent to Tennessee for two of his sons, Alexander O. and Thomas Nixon, subject of this sketch, whom she raised and had educated. Her husband died in 1822, and in 1843, she came to McMinn county, Tennessee, to live with her nephew, Judge Van Dyke, and died at his house, near Athens, July 10, 1845, and was buried in the private cemetery on his farm. She never had any children.

Gov. Nicholas Van Dyke, of Delaware, who afterward became United States senator from his State, was a cousin of Judge Van Dyke's father.

The boyhood and young manhood of Judge Van Dyke may be regarded as an index to his future life of usefulness, integrity and uprightness. Being the son of a United States army officer, he lived in the garrison till 1810, and was taught to read and write by his father. His father resigned his commission in the army in 1811, moved to Rhea county, and there the son went to an old field school near Washington. After his father's death, when he went to live with his uncle and aunt Smith, in Pennsylvania, he obeyed unquestioning and implicitly whatever they enjoined upon him. When he went to Alabama, in 1828, he had nothing to begin upon except his education, his license to practice law and a fixed moral character, the result of the best of influences and careful training. When assistant clerk of the Alabama Legislature he kept the journal well up and ready, never going to bed until his work was finished and ready to read to the house next morning. Making about five hundred dollars a year, he lived up with the times and managed to spend all his money, but not in dissipation of any kind; never betting, drinking or associating with low company. Afterward, when his law practice enlarged, he made it an invariable rule to attend as faithfully and promptly to a small case for a small fee as he did to a large case for a big fee. Men noticed that he never had to be called in court, and that he was always ready to report promptly, whether he was ready for trial or not, and this drew a large clientele to him. An occurrence in Hamilton county tended to give him a name and make him friends. By showing undaunted pluck and courage, in 1833 (the only fight he ever had with a lawyer), he evinced that high sense of personal honor that is popular in all ages, and unfailingly draws a following. He has always lived an abstemious life, and attended strictly to his duties; has never contracted debt beyond his means of payment, and said with evident pride to the editor, "I do not owe any one a cent." He is an Odd Fellow, a Royal Arch Mason, originally was a Whig, but since the war has voted with the Democrats. In religion, as in politics, he is independent and liberal; agreeing with all in some things, disagreeing with all in some things, but is for sustaining Christianity against all other creeds and modes of worship.

Judge Van Dyke is a man of most venerable appearance; is five feet nine inches high, and weighs one hundred and thirty-five pounds. His flowing hair and beard are white with the frosts of his more than fourscore winters, but the grand old octogenarian bears up well under their weight, and retains a clearness of mind equal to the strongest. His habits are as regular as music. He has never been seriously sick in his life, never had aches or pains, and has never paid out for himself or family as much as one hundred dollars for doctors' bills. His eye is hazel, nose sharp Roman, expression and manner frank, easy, simple and earnest. He is not only a representative Tennessean, but a representative of the highest order of American manhood.

His great personal popularity was shown at the celebration of his golden wedding, May 23, 1883, by the attendance at his residence of a hundred lawyers and judges of East Tennessee, and as many citizens, and the costly presents made by them. The address of the Chattanooga bar on that occasion was a splendid tribute to his "pure and good name, his sound judgment, depth of learning, fidelity of purpose, his enthusiasm for justice, public spirit, private virtue, and to his example as an incentive to high and noble ambition moving in an unsullied sphere." The Chattanooga bar also presented a very fine copy of the Holy Bible, with the family record accurately filled out, with the names and dates of births, marriages and deaths of the family. The address by Rev. E. A. Ramsey, on behalf of the citizens of Athens, and William T. Lane, esq., on behalf of the Athens bar, were also eloquent and beautiful testimonials in recognition of the value of his life, his eminent public services, and his exalted and exemplary character.

HON. ATHA THOMAS.

FRANKLIN.

THE Thomas family came of that hardy race, the Welsh, and the members of the family have preserved their Welsh origin in the peculiar characteristics of sterling integrity and unwearying industry.

Hon. Atha Thomas was born in Williamson county, Tennessee, October 5, 1829, the son of William Thomas, who immigrated to Tennessee from Nottaway county, Virginia, in 1796, the year that Tennessee was admitted into the Union. He settled in the fertile county of Williamson, where he farmed until his death, in 1841, at the age of sixty-three. He was a private soldier in the Creek war under Gen. Jackson. A quiet, plain man, he was quite successful as a money-maker. In politics he was a Whig. He raised nine sons, and none of them ever voted a Democratic ticket until after the late war. He belonged to a family of patriots, and five of his brothers were American soldiers during the Revolutionary war. His brother, Robert Thomas, settled in Davidson county, Tennessee, and there died, leaving one son, Robert H. Thomas.

Atha Thomas' oldest brother, Robert S. Thomas, a mechanic, was chairman of the county court of Haywood county, Tennessee, some thirty years. His brother, Hon. Dorsey B. Thomas, represented in the Tennessee Legislature, first, Haywood county, and in 1869-70, was State senator from Humphreys and Benton counties, was speaker of the senate during that term, and again was a member of the lower house in 1882-83, as the representative from Humphreys county, and also State senator in 1884-85.

Of Mr. Thomas' other brothers, the Rev. Woodlief Thomas, his twin brother, is now a Baptist minister at Tilden, Texas. His brothers, John H., William and Samuel, are dead. R. G. Thomas is a merchant at Brownsville, Tennessee, and Dr. David H. Thomas is a physician at Bell's depot, Crockett county, Tennessee.

The mother of Mr. Thomas, nee Miss Eliza Bass, was a native of Dinwiddie county, Virginia. She came to Tennessee with her brother-in-law, William Beattie, of Rutherford county. She died in 1858, at the age of sixty-five years. Besides her nine sons, mentioned above, she had three daughters, viz.: Sarah W. Thomas, who first married Henry Jamieson, a prominent farmer of Rutherford county, and raised a large family of children. Mr. Jameison died about 1859. She then married John F. Cooper, of Bedford county, where she now lives. Her son, Robert D. Jameison, became quite noted during the civil war for gallantry as a member of Gen. John C. Brown's staff. Her son, Moulton Jameison, a brave, manly young soldier, was a member of the First Tennessee Confederate regiment, and fell in the battle of Perryville, Kentucky. Her third son, Hon. James H. Jameison, represented Rutherford county in

the Tennessee Legislature of 1876, and is now a cotton planter near Columbus, Mississippi. Her oldest daughter, Cornelia Jameison, married John L. Henry, now of Dallas, Texas, one of the most prominent lawyers in that State. Her second daughter, Sallie Jameison, married John F. Carter, a wholesale merchant at St. Louis, afterward at Chicago, where he died, and where she still resides. Eliza B. Thomas, the second daughter, is now the widow of Thomas B. King, and lives in Crockett county, Tennessee. The third daughter, Mary A. Thomas, is now the widow of Opie Pope, and resides in Rutherford county, Tennessee, with her only child, Mrs. Bettie Beasly.

Mr. Thomas was raised to labor on his father's farm, with school advantages in winter seasons, until he was seventeen years of age, when he went to Salem Academy, in Rutherford county, two years, and then attended Wirt College, in Sumner county, from which he graduated in his twentieth year. He next taught school two years, near Franklin, engaged meanwhile in reading law. In 1853, he entered the law school of Cumberland University at Lebanon, where he studied one year, and was admitted to the bar. He next took charge of Thompson Academy, in Williamson county, and taught there until 1861, with fine success, professionally and financially. In 1861, he took charge of the male academy at Franklin, and taught there two and a half years. In 1865, when civil order was restored, he commenced law practice at Franklin, and continued to practice there till January 1, 1883, when, having been elected State Treasurer for two years by the Legislature, he entered upon the duties of the office, retiring in 1885.

He has taught school fifteen years, and practiced law seventeen years. Of too kindly a nature to refuse favors to friends, he has had large sums of security debts to pay, and lost considerably by the war, but is now in comfortable circumstances.

In 1854, he was made a Mason in Hiram Lodge, No. 7, at Franklin, and has taken all the degrees of the York rite, and served as Master, High Priest and Commander.

In the Legislature of 1869-70, when his brother, Dorsey B. Thomas, was speaker of the senate, he represented Williamson county in the lower house, and was chairman of the committee on claims, and a member of the railroad investigating committee. He has generally taken an active part in politics in his county, canvassing it in 1879 in favor of the settlement of the State debt on the 50-4 basis.

Mr. Thomas first married in Williamson county, November 25, 1856, Miss Sarah E. North, a daughter of Rev. Henry B. North, a prominent minister of the Methodist Episcopal church, south, and a Virginian. Her mother was a Virginia lady, who came to Tennessee the widow of a Mr. Bailey. The first Mrs. Thomas was educated at Columbia, Tennessee. She died of consumption in 1858. He next married in Rutherford county, November 30, 1881, Mrs. Bettie M. Sikes, widow of Ambrose T. Sikes, the only daughter and only child of Washington Whittaker, an extensive farmer in Lincoln county, Tennessee. Her mother was a Miss Mosely, of Bedford county, Tennessee. Mrs. Thomas graduated at the Columbia Atheneum. To this marriage have been born two children: Atha Thomas, jr., born August 26, 1882; and Woodlief Thomas, born January 15, 1884.

Mr. Thomas has been a member of the Methodist Episcopal church, south, since 1854; has been repeatedly a lay delegate to the annual conferences, and was a member of the general conference at Louisville, in 1874. His wife comes of a strong Missionary Baptist family, and she is a member of that church.

By being faithful to every trust reposed in him, and by plain, hard toil, Mr. Thomas has achieved his success in life. Throughout his life he has made it a rule to always find something to do, whether the profits were large or small, and he has not allowed himself to know what it is to be idle a day since he first engaged in business for himself. Under the same rule he was raised by his father. When not at school he had to work on the farm. He has been a strictly temperate man. When he came of age he took a pledge of his own accord never to drink at all, and has kept his vow as faithfully as if he had joined the Washingtonians. His father and mother being Primitive Baptists, were opposed to secret societies, and the son, out of respect for them, and as a matter of personal pride, determined to control himself, and since that time has not touched liquor at all, except as a medicine, nor has he spent any time at places of amusement. A handsome, well preserved man, he stands five feet ten and a half inches high, weighs one hundred and ninety-five pounds, and is of large, round make. A good reader of faces would, without doubt, pronounce him a modest, warm-hearted, honest gentleman.

COL. NATHANIEL M. TAYLOR.

BRISTOL.

ONE of the best known and ablest attorneys in East Tennessee is the subject of this sketch, Col. Nathaniel M. Taylor, of Bristol. He was born in Carter county, Tennessee, September 23, 1825, and grew up there on his father's farm. His literary education he received at Washington College. He graduated in the law shool at Lebanon, under Judge Abram Caruthers. His parents were in good circumstances, but the son was raised to work. Says Col. Taylor, "One part of my education, which my father did not neglect, was to make me work." He was a sober sort of boy, but not connected with any church until 1869, when he joined the Presbyterian church at Bristol, and has been an elder in that church for four years. He has been temperate all his life, a teetotaler twelve or fifteen years, and is now an active and public advocate of prohibition.

After his graduation, he began the practice of law at Elizabethton, Tennessee, and practiced there up to the war, when he went into the Confederate service and followed its fortunes to the end, serving in Tennessee and Virginia, most of the time on detached duty.

At the close of the war he moved, August, 1865, to Bristol, where he has resided ever since, engaged exclusively in law practice, steadily refusing to go into politics. His practice from the start was good, and now is as heavy as he can manage. Though his father had considerable property at one time, Col. Taylor began life on nothing, and is now in independent and easy circumstances. For several years he was a director of the Bristol Bank, for some time was county attorney for the East Tennessee, Virginia and Georgia railroad, and is now attorney for the East Tennessee and Western North Carolina railroad.

Up to the war he was a Whig, his ancestors before him, on both sides, were Whigs, but he has been a Democrat from the close of the war to the present. He has never held any civil office. Before the war he was tendered the nomination for State senator, but declined it. He was for years trustee of the Duffield Academy, at Elizabethton. He joined the Masons in 1861, in Desha Lodge, Elizabethton, Carter county, Tennessee, and has served as Senior and Junior Warden.

He married, in Richmond, Virginia, October 26, 1869, Miss Mary K. Jones, who was born in three miles of the "Clay Slashes," in Hanover county, Virginia, daughter of Dr. C. B. Jones, who died in 1885. Her mother was a Miss Wingfield, of Hanover county, Virginia. Mrs. Taylor graduated at Gordonville, Virginia; is a very fine scholar, remarkable for the grace of her person, her strength and pride of character, and skill as a practical domestic manager. She is a member of the Presbyterian church. They have four children: (1). Hugh, born July 2, 1870. (2). Mary, born April 9, 1872. (3, 4). Juanita and Nathaniel M., jr., twins, born October 28, 1876. The latter died November 28, 1876. (5). Bessie, born June 13, 1880.

The Taylors came from Rockbridge county, Virginia, and are of Irish descent. The grandfather, Gen. Nathaniel Taylor, was born in that county, was a soldier and colonel in the war of 1812, and brevetted general at the battle of New Orleans. He was a man of fine property, of fine ability and very popular in his county.

He married Miss Mary Patton, in Rockbridge county, Virginia, and settled among the first pioneers of the country in Carter county, Tennessee, where he engaged in farming. He raised eight children, three sons, James P., Alfred W. and Nathaniel K. Taylor; and five daughters, Anna, who married Col. Thomas Love, of North Carolina; Mary, who married Dr. William R. Dulaney—her son, Dr. N. T. Dulaney, was a member of the Forty-fourth Tennessee General Assembly from Sullivan county; Seraphina, who married Gen. Alfred E. Jackson, of Jonesborough, Tennessee (see his sketch elsewhere in this volume); Elizabeth, who intermarried with Thomas Taylor—both these died in White county, Tennessee; and Lorena, who married Gen. Jacob Tipton, after whom the county of Tipton was named. They moved to West Tennessee and there died.

Alfred W. Taylor, father of the subject of this sketch, was a lawyer; represented Johnson and Carter counties in the Tennessee Legislature; was an elder in the Presbyterian church, at Elizabethton; was a farmer of fine property, and regarded as one of the most upright men in the country. He was called "the honest lawyer." He died October 11, 1856, about fifty-eight years of age.

Col. Taylor's mother, Elizabeth C. Duffield, was born in Carter county, Tennessee, and died April 18, 1881, at about sixty years of age. She was the daughter of Maj. George Duffield, of Philadelphia, Pennsylvania, who was an accomplished scholar. He moved to Carter county at the early settlement of the country, was a lawyer, and at one time was appointed judge of one of the western territories, but in a short time resigned the office and returned home. He was a major in the war of 1812, and took part in the battle of New Orleans. He left three children: Elizabeth C., mother of the subject of this sketch; Samuel L. Duffield; George Duffield, a physician, who died when a young man.

Col. Taylor's maternal grandmother was Sally S. Carter, daughter of Gen. Landon Carter, one of the earliest settlers of Carter county, one of the most prominent men in the settlement, and the father of Hon. William B. Carter, who, for many years, was a member of congress from the First district of Tennessee. The Carter family figured conspicuously in the early history of East Tennessee, and Carter county was named for it. Landon Carter, and the town of Elizabethton was named for his wife, who was originally a Miss Macklin. Col. Taylor's paternal uncle, James P. Taylor, was one of the foremost lawyers in East Tennessee, and attorney-general of the First judicial circuit of Tennessee for a series of years. He married a daughter of Gen. Landon Carter, who was a sister of the congressman, William B. Carter. His son, Rev. N. G. Taylor, of the

Methodist Episcopal church, represented the First Tennessee district in congress of the United States twice. He was also commissioner of Indian affairs under President Johnson. Rev. N. G. Taylor's son, Hon. Robert L. Taylor, represented the First district in congress, was presidential elector on the Cleveland and Hendricks ticket in 1884, and is now United States pension agent at Knoxville. Rev. N. G. Taylor's son, Hon. A. A. Taylor, represented Carter and Johnson counties in the Tennessee Legislature, and was also elector for the State at large on the Republican ticket when Garfield was elected president. Two sons of Rev. N. G. Taylor, David and Hugh, are clerks in government employ at Washington City.

Rhoda Taylor, niece of Gen. Nathaniel Taylor, came from Virginia with him and married David Haynes, of Carter county, Tennessee, and became the mother of the famous Landon C. Haynes, a very prominent lawyer, who moved from East Tennessee to Memphis, and was a member of the Confederate senate from Tennessee. He left a reputation as one of the finest orators in the State. His son, Hon. Robert Haynes, was a member of the Forty-fourth General Assembly of Tennessee, from Madison county.

Gen. Landon Carter, Col. Taylor's maternal great-grandfather, was a member of the first constitutional convention of Tennessee, and his son, William B. Carter, was president of the convention that framed the second constitution of Tennessee. The present William B. Carter, a nephew of Gen. William B. Carter, was a member of the constitutional convention of 1870. Col. Taylor's brothers are, William C. Taylor, a farmer, living on the old homestead in Carter county, went to California—"a Forty-niner"—when the gold fever broke out, remained several years, and returned, but is not married; George D. Taylor, of Carter county, was elected during the war to the Legislature of Tennessee; H. H. Taylor is a prominent lawyer, of Knoxville, Tennessee. Col. Taylor's sister, Mary C., is the wife of Dr. J. H. Pepper, Bristol, Tennessee.

The Carters and Taylors are among the most prominent families of East Tennessee, and have furnished the world a whole host of distinguished, able and brilliant men. Two of the Taylors have been members of congress, N. G. and R. L. Taylor. One of the Carters, Gen. William B., was a member of congress several terms. Three Taylors, A. W., A. A. and G. D., have been members of the Tennessee Legislature. Six of the Taylors have been able lawyers, N. G., R. L., A. A., A. W., N. M. and H. H. Taylor. Admiral S. P. Carter, of the United States navy, is a brother of Rev. William B. Carter, of Elizabethton, son of Alfred Carter.

Col. Taylor's success in life is owing to the fact of his early training by his father and mother. They taught him to be industrious, honest and sober, and that whatever is worth doing at all is worth doing well. They were strict Presbyterians, and taught him to observe the

Sabbath and to avoid bad company, drinking and kindred vices, and especially gambling and swearing. The father was a sort of old Roman in his ideas. He used to say if he was worth a million of dollars, and had one hundred sons, he would teach them all to work. His sons went to college, stayed ten months in the year and returned home, and the father put them to work the other two months. Col. Taylor's efforts to follow out the teachings of his parents are at the bottom of his prosperity.

Of Col. Taylor's Dulaney relatives it may be said here, that Eva Dulaney, daughter of Dr. William R. Dulaney and Mary Dulaney, formerly Mary Taylor, an aunt of Col. Taylor, married Rev. J. W. Bachman, pastor of the Presbyterian church at Chattanooga ; Carrie Dulaney married Hon. John C. St. John, present chancellor of the First chancery division of Tennessee. The three sons of Dr. William R. Dulaney graduated in medicine, to-wit: Dr. Joseph E. Dulaney, deceased, and Drs. Nathaniel T. and William R. Dulaney, now practicing physicians at Blountville, Tennessee.

REV. SAMUEL WATSON.

MEMPHIS.

THIS famous clergyman, teacher, author and editor, who, for thirty-six years, has been a preacher and thirteen years an editor, was born on the eastern shore of Maryland, January 10, 1813, but was brought up mostly in the neighborhood of Nashville, Tennessee, his father having moved there when the son was only six years old. His father being engaged in the cotton factory business, the son worked in that line some four or five years. His education was confined mainly to the English branches. He was never more moral in his preacher life than in his boyhood and young manhood, a result due to the example and precept of his pious father, who was a class-leader for forty years. His father, Levin Watson, was a native of Virginia, of English parents, who were members of the English church. He served in the military service of the United States, in 1812, in Virginia, and died in Woodruff county, Arkansas, seventy-three years old, a naturally good man, universally respected.

Dr. Watson's mother, originally Susannah Smith, a native of Virginia, died when the son was five years old, leaving, beside himself, a daughter, Mary, who married William B. Cook, of Maury county, Tennessee.

Dr. Watson joined the Tennessee conference in 1836, and was stationed the first year on Wayne circuit, the next on Franklin circuit, Alabama, and the next year was stationed at Clarksville. He went to Memphis in 1839, where he has been ever since. He was appointed to the Methodist church at Memphis two years ; next for two years was agent of the American Bible Society, and has filled the appointments of the three principal churches in Memphis ; was elected to edit the Memphis *Christian Advocate* in 1856, and continued to edit it till 1866. He was then on the Memphis district four years, as presiding elder. He was a member of the general conference at Nashville, in 1858, and of the general conference at New Orleans, in 1866. During this time he was editing the Memphis *Christian Advo-cate*. He was president of the State Female College, in the vicinity of Memphis, in 1859. At the general conference of 1870, at Memphis, he was elected to edit the *Christian Index*, which he did three years.

In the latter part of 1872, he withdrew from the Methodist church, from an honest conviction that he was not in harmony with some of the doctrines taught by the church, notably eternal punishment and the resurrection. He has since been lecturing on Christian Spiritualism, in nearly all the States of the Union, taking the ground that primitive Christianity and Christian Spiritualism are identical. He was elected president, first, of the Tennessee State organization of Spiritualists, and in October, 1883, of the Southern Association of Spiritualists. In 1875-6-7, he edited and published the *Spiritual Magazine*, at Memphis. He is the author of a series of books on spiritualism, entitled, "The Clock Struck One," "The Clock Struck Two," and " The Clock Struck Three "—names given to the volumes from the circumstance that an old clock of his that had not run nor struck for years struck *one*, just before each one of four members of his family passed away—his wife and three children. The full titles of the two most famous of these books are as follows: "The Clock Struck One, and Christian Spiritualist. Being a synopsis of the investigations of spirit intercourse by an Episcopal bishop, three ministers, five doctors, and others, at Memphis, Tennessee, in 1856. By the Rev. Samuel Watson." 208 pages; 12mo ; "The Clock Struck Three, being a Review of ' The Clock Struck One,' and reply to it. Part II. Showing the harmony between Christianity, Science and Spiritualism. By Samuel Watson." 352 pages. Chicago: Religio-Philosophical Publishing House, 1874.

Mr. Hudson Tuttle, in a review of the above named works, published in the *Religio-Philosophical Journal*, says: " What is most admirable and charming in these volumes, is the calm spirit of goodness, the depth of fraternal love, the catholicity of thought, which pervades them. Nothing disturbs the serenity of the author. His soul, by the presence and communication of the departed, is entirely uplifted from the pettiness of earth, and he feels that he advocates doctrines too vital to be trifled with and to mention in flippant phrase.

"Mr. Watson is well versed in general science, and his arguments are fortified by its aid, but he evidently feels himself most at home on biblical grounds. For thirty-five years he has taught from its pages, and known no higher court of appeal, and it would be ungenerous to criticise, because he adheres to a method of argument brought into the very constitution of his mind. We may say the Bible has no authority except that of truth, held in common with all books, yet as long as millions accept it as infallible, it becomes an invaluable ally to an unpopular cause. Its texts will be accepted when all other evidence will be rejected with scorn. This line of defense never had an abler defender than Mr. Watson. Every weapon in the vast arsenal is at his command. He leaves not a text idle. All that can be gathered from it is pushed to the front, and on this, his favorite ground, he is invincible. * * Between science and spiritualism there is no conflict, and neither meet opposition in a religion which is another name for moral science—spiritualism.

"Every individual who would understand the truths of the spirit world, must be his or her own medium. God must write his law upon their understanding and put it in their affections. If you want to become mediums for interior communication, you must become absolutely true in every thought, feeling and affection —become absolutely just in all your relations of life, so that morning, noon and night you will be inquiring and thirsting after righteousness." . . . "If spiritualism, in its faith and effects, does not tend to make you better, wiser and purer—holier men and women— as St. Paul says of the Corinthians, it will 'profit you nothing.' That spiritualism which will not redeem you, will not be sufficient to redeem the world.

"These volumes cannot be too highly commended to spiritualists who desire works to give to friends in the churches. They are invaluable as missionary agents. The character of their author, the sincerity, honesty and integrity of his style; the exquisite spirit of goodness and fraternity pervading their every page, will attract and hold the attention, and convince, so far as it is possible for books to convince, of the truth of the sublime doctrines advocated."

Dr. Watson's last book, "The Religion of Spiritualism," was published in 1881, of which two editions have been sold.

Although not an active politician now, Dr. Watson is a Democrat all the way through. In 1881, he was a member from De Soto, Mississippi, of the Union convention that met in Jackson, in that State.

He became a Mason in 1837, at Leighton, Alabama;

took the Chapter degrees at Decatur the same year; took the Council degrees at Nashville in 1839, and became a Knight Templar at Memphis in 1876. He was Grand Chaplain of the State of Tennessee in 1841, and was Chaplain of the Memphis Chapter for many years.

Dr. Watson married, first in De Soto county, Mississippi, in 1842, Miss Mary Dupree, a native of North Alabama, daughter of Allen Dupree, from Virginia. Her mother was Elizabeth Stuart, of Virginia. By this marriage, Dr. Watson had eleven children, all of whom are dead but one, Allena, now wife of Capt. J. W. Fuller, of Augusta, Arkansas. She has two children, Allena and Mary.

His daughter, Ella, married Rolfe Eldridge. She died in 1880, leaving five children, Samuel, Rolfe, John, Robert and Ella. Dr. Watson's first wife died in 1866.

He next married, in Shelby county, Tennessee, June, 1867, Mrs. Ellen Perkins, born the daughter of a Methodist preacher named William T. Anderson. Her mother was Maria Louisa Collins. Mrs. Watson's cousin Ellen, is the wife of Dr. William A. Cantrell, of Little Rock, Arkansas. Through her mother Mrs. Watson is a cousin of Col. John M. Harrell, the brilliant political editor, now of Hot Springs, Arkansas. Mrs. Watson graduated at Tulip Academy, Arkansas, and probably does more public work than any other woman in Tennessee. She is the president of the Woman's Christian Association at Memphis, president of the Woman's Missionary Society of the Memphis annual conference, Methodist Episcopal church, south, president of the Ladies' Aid Society of the Central Methodist church of Memphis, and in point of Christian devotion and to the doing of good, is among the best of women. By this marriage, Dr. Watson has had five children: Lilian, died in infancy; May, now fourteen years old; Samuel, died in his third year; Arthur, now eight years old; Eugene Crowell, now four years old.

Dr. Watson is in independent circumstances, and is indebted to nobody for it but a kind Providence and his own exertions. He began life without inheritance, left his father in his twenty-first year with seven dollars and fifty cents in his pocket, worked eight months for nothing to learn how to work, then began on low wages, which ran up to seventy dollars a month, for superintending a cotton factory. He invested one thousand five hundred dollars, which he made before joining the conference, in the drug business, when he first came to Memphis. He then leased some ground, put up four business houses on it and then bought it. Subsequently, he sold these houses and invested the proceeds in Arkansas lands. He bought seventeen acres in the suburbs of Memphis, improved the property, and after the war sold it at a very considerable advance. His residence on the corner of Union and Wellington streets was built by himself, and is a marvel of good taste. He now owns twelve or fifteen residences in Memphis, and is among the solid men of that city.

HON. JAMES M. MEEK.

KNOXVILLE.

HON. JAMES M. MEEK was born on a farm near Strawberry Plains, Jefferson county, Tennessee, November 21, 1821, and was the oldest of a family of ten children—four sons and six daughters, viz.: (1). James M., subject of this sketch. (2). Adam Alexander, now a farmer on Roseberry creek, Knox county, Tennessee, and has seven children: Mary E., Alice, Adam White, Charles Sheridan, Harriet, Joseph and Florence. (3). Martha J., who died in 1861, the wife of John W. Legg, in Knox county, leaving six children: William, Adam, James, Dan, Kate, and John W.; two died before the mother, John and Della. (4). Louisa, now the wife of Dr. A. A. Caldwell, a member of the Forty-fourth General Assembly of Tennessee, from Jefferson county. She has four children living: Alfred, Addie, Georgie and Sallie. (5). Sallie, unmarried, at home with her parents. (6). Adaline, married Maj. R. Thornburgh, New Market, Jefferson county, Tennessee, and has one child, Mary E. ("Mamie.") (7). Harriet, died single, in 1851, aged eighteen years. (8). Amanda Catharine, married first, Dr. James S. Headrick, and by him had one child, Harriet; by her second husband, R. P. Martin, she has six children: Daniel Robert, Adam Meek, Jennie, Isaac, Mattie and William. (9). John M., born January 2, 1838. In early life he was trained in the common schools of his county, until at the age of seventeen he entered Strawberry Plains College, an institution of merit and character in *ante bellum* times, where he continued until 1859, when he received a certificate entitling him to a diploma, but the war coming on he failed to receive the diploma. He studied law for a time, and after the war, in 1874, procured license to practice, but at this time coming into possession of a splendid farm, the license was laid away and Col. Meek returned to "his first love"—the farm—whereby the legal profession lost one member who could have proven a vigorous and capable advocate, and agriculture received a zealous friend and a progressive votary. He is undoubtedly proud of the profession. His voice and pen sound loud and long the beauties and dignity of farm life, the possibilities and splendid triumphs at the farmer's control, if he will but make an intelligent, energetic effort. He has occupied several positions of public trust creditably. He was first secretary and is now president of the East Tennessee Farmers' Convention. He is capable, serves the organization well, and his many friends hope his sphere of usefulness may be much enlarged, and have urged him as the proper person to be at the head of the State department of agriculture, statistics, mines, etc. As a public speaker, he is bold and vigorous; strikes straight out from the shoulder, and is always listened to with strict attention. He is quick to detect an error, and ready to

expose it in language that is not equivocal. He has pricked the bubble of many an error, common to some people and concerns, and leaves a mark by which all may judge. Col. Meek has been very diligent in his business, and has accumulated a fine property, and appreciates it in a way that comports with the tastes and ideas of an intelligent gentleman. He manages to get an average of twenty bushels of wheat per acre, which is about two and a half times above the general average, and forty bushels of corn. His practice and theme have been the grasses and wheat as standard crops, supplemented by the improved varieties of live stock. He has time and again, through the press of the country, strongly urged these as renovating crops, feasible, practicable, and in themselves most profitable. He is zealous in his advocacy of farmers' associations, contending that it should be a part of every man's creed to belong to and encourage such associations. He is a leading spirit in the East Tennessee Farmers' Convention, an institution in its scope not surpassed in the South. It has attained a wide reputation and commands the respect of all classes, and it has been no child's play to develop its present degree of efficiency and status. Having, however, among its promoters such patrons as Col. Meek, and a few others here and there over East Tennessee, ready and able to maintain its cause, it is no wonder that it has come to be the pride of all, and a leading institution of the country. Col. Meek was married September 28, 1859, to Miss Elizabeth Jane McMillan, daughter of Maj. Gaines McMillan, a farmer of Knox county, Tennessee, and by her has had eleven children: Horace McMillan (died September 8, 1872), Alex. Kennedy, John Lamar, Gaines Monroe, Daniel, White, Mary Elizabeth, Maggie Bennett, Nellie, Bernice, Bertha Cowan, and an infant that died unnamed. (10). Daniel Harrison, the youngest brother of Judge Meek, is now clerk and master of the chancery court at Dandridge, Jefferson county, Tennessee. He married Miss Nettie Jones, and has one child, Lucie E., now the wife of Will M. Fain.

Judge Meek sprung from as good ancestry as the country affords. His grandfather, Adam Meek, emigrated at an early day from the north of Ireland to America, and came of Scotch and English ancestry, which had emigrated to Ireland to escape religious intolerance at home during the reign of James I., and who assisted in the organization of the Irish Presbyterian church at Carrickfugus, in the year 1642. He settled first in Pennsylvania. He served in the continental army during the Revolutionary war, and had his thigh broken at the battle of the Cowpens, and ever afterward used a crutch, but would never take a pension, as he said he was able to support himself. Settling after the war in North Carolina, he soon after emigrated to Tennessee and located in Jefferson county. He was a government surveyor, and entered large tracts of very valuable lands near Strawberry Plains, a part of which still remains in possession of members of the Meek family. He was one of the first justices of the peace of Jefferson county. For a fuller account of this old pioneer, see Ramsey's "History of Tennessee."

Adam K. Meek, Judge Meek's father, a venerable, well preserved and highly respected old gentleman, now in his ninetieth year, having been born July 15, 1796, is still living on a part of the original homestead, where he was born. He was a captain in the Cherokee war, in 1836, and has at times rendered his country efficient service in her armies and in civil positions. The farm on which he now resides at Strawberry Plains, and on which he and all of his children were born, was settled by his father, Adam Meek, when it was a wild Indian country, on the very borders and outskirts of civilization.

It will doubtless be observed by the curious reader of this volume that very few families appear in it who have not moved several times. Migration seems characteristic of the great body of American people. Change of scene, change of location, mark the history of a great majority of our families. The Meek family, however, have demonstrated extraordinary staying power. They are fair representatives of the manners, morals, religion and manhood of the State. Of the first and second generations, all were farmers. Of the present, three are lawyers. The family are all Presbyterians, and all well educated. It is a long-lived people. The grandfather lived to be eighty-seven, the grandmother seventy-five; the father is now ninety, the mother eighty-eight. The men and women are all something above the average of people among whom they live.

Judge Meek's mother, nee Elizabeth Childress, was born in Virginia, December 1, 1798, daughter of John Childress, a Revolutionary soldier. He came to Tennessee and settled in Jefferson county, where he died at an advanced age, leaving a large family, now scattered over the western States, except two daughters: Nancy, the widow of James Hamilton, now ninety-five years old, is living in Jefferson county, and is remarkable for her activity in domestic life. The other daughter, Mary, married Alexander Douglass, and lived to be seventy years of age, and left a large family. Mrs. Meek's praise is that she has raised a strong, industrious family and stood by them in every trial, and that they are all in creditable standing in society.

Judge Meek's early life was spent upon a farm amid the duties and surroundings incident to an industrious and progressive farmer's life. Many of the most distinguished and best men our country affords, have just cause to be proud that they were reared under just such circumstances. The farm and work-shop give us, in most cases, the men that have contributed so much

72

to make our country and its institutions the pride and glory of the world. At the age of eighteen he was sent to school at Maryville, where he graduated in 1850, under Rev. Isaac Anderson, D.D., LL.D., president of Maryville College. After graduation, he read law, at New Market, under Judge Robert Anderson, and was licensed to practice in 1852, by Judges Alexander and Thomas L. Williams.

In 1855, he represented Jefferson county in the Tennessee Legislature. He then practiced law at New Market, and in the surrounding counties until 1862. When the war broke out he took the Union side. In 1861, he was again elected to the Legislature as a Union member.

April 20, 1862, he was arrested at his home by Confederate soldiers, taken to Tuscaloosa, Alabama, confined in a prison there with the Federal troops under Wirtz, and was removed from Tuscaloosa to Montgomery, from Montgomery to Macon, and July 4, 1862, was released and returned home. June 20, 1863, he was arrested again on a charge of high treason, carried to Knoxville and tried by a military commission, of which Isaac Shelby, jr., of Kentucky, was president. Prior to this, in May, 1863, there was a special order from Gov. Isham G. Harris, for the purpose of electing an attorney-general for the State, in the Second judicial district, to fill the place made vacant by the death of attorney-general Thornburgh, and Judge Meek was elected over four competitors, receiving more votes than all of them.

Upon an investigation of the case for treason, the president of the commission ordered his discharge, July 4, 1863. He then left the State and spent most of the time in Kentucky and Ohio, until the summer of 1865. In December of that year, he represented Jefferson county in the constitutional convention at Nashville. In January, 1866, he was commissioned by Gov. Andrew Johnson, attorney-general for the Second judicial circuit, and held that office eight years. In 1866, he was a candidate for judge against James G. Rose (present judge of the Second circuit), and was beaten by one hundred and fifty votes.

February 28, 1883, he was commissioned, by President Arthur, United States district-attorney for the eastern district of Tennessee, the position he now holds, term expiring March 1, 1887.

Politically identified with the Whig party until that party ceased to exist as an organization, he has since that time taken an active interest in, and warmly advocated the principles and measures of, the Republican party.

In 1866, Gov. Brownlow appointed him a director of the East Tennessee, Virginia and Georgia railroad, a position which he filled until 1874. In 1875, he was elected a director by the stockholders of the road, his term expiring in 1879. In that year, he was elected the attorney for the East Tennessee and Georgia railroad, a position which he held until 1883. By election of the bar, he has several times occupied the bench as special judge of the circuit court. He is a director in the East Tennessee National Bank at Knoxville. He became a Mason at New Market, in 1859, and in religion is a Presbyterian.

Judge Meek married, at New Market, November 8, 1859, Miss Elizabeth J. Walker, who was born in Hawkins county, Tennessee, August 5, 1839, daughter of Maj. James H. Walker, a farmer and merchant at New Market. Her mother was Louisa Clarkson. Mrs. Meek's only sister, Mary A., is the wife of Arthur Deaderick, son of chief-justice Deaderick (whose sketch see elsewhere in this volume). Her children are James W., Henry McDowell, Lizzie, Lula and Arthur Monroe Deaderick.

Mrs. Meek graduated at Rogersville Female College, and is a member of the Presbyterian church, and president of the Union Presbytery Home Missionary Society, embracing the counties of Blount, Knox, Jefferson, Sevier and Grainger. To this marriage have been born three children: (1). James K. Meek, born October 23, 1860; graduated in the class of 1881, from the University of Tennessee; now a wholesale merchant at Knoxville. (2). Ada Burnside Meek,

born July 23, 1863; graduated from the Glendale (Ohio) Female College, June 12, 1884. (3). William M. Meek, born August 26, 1866; now a student in the University of Tennessee.

Judge Meek began life on money he made by teaching school for two years after leaving college, and is now one of the wealthiest men of Knoxville. What he has acquired in the way of property has been by industry that never tired, and a resolution that would brook no opposition that a will, determined to succeed, can overcome. He never made a debt he did not pay; never made a promise he did not fulfill, or give a good reason why he did not do it; has a strong, tough constitution and good health; and has outstripped his competitors in the race for success, by having more energy than they. He is a man of fixed religious and political principles, has made friends by showing himself friendly, and is open, frank, liberal and candid to a fault, yet a prudent, economical manager of his affairs. Among the lawyers it was a common remark that he could do more work than any two men in the profession. From 1866 to 1874, he studied and worked, almost as a rule, until twelve o'clock at night. The appreciation in his railroad stock and his judicious speculations in real estate in Knoxville, have also contributed to his financial success.

HON. JERE BAXTER.

NASHVILLE.

HON. JERE BAXTER, the subject of this sketch, was born in Nashville, Tennessee, February 11, 1852. He was educated at the Montgomery Bell Academy in that city, going to school in all only twenty-two months.

At nineteen years of age, much against his father's wishes, he went abroad and spent several years in foreign travel. This trip has a flavor of adventure in it which makes it not uninteresting to relate. He left home on money received from the sale of two mules, and reached Berlin with four dollars in his pocket, all told. Here he obtained employment as a teacher of English, and taught there for two years. His purse thus replenished, he started again for an itinerate over the continent, much of which he accomplished on foot, spending his time in the acquisition of the languages, and in studying the arts of painting and sculpture. During this absence from home, he received in remittances not exceeding eight hundred or nine hundred dollars.

Up to this time of his life his manners were characterized by a quiet and reserve bordering on timidity, in his boyhood even suffering from a terror of the dark, and embarrassment in the presence of strangers, both of

which weaknesses he conquered by pride and a strong will, forcing himself habitually to go into a dark room, and frequently into society.

After Mr. Baxter's return from Europe in 1874, he started an industrial publication in Nashville. It was fairly successful, but he removed it to St. Louis, where it was continued under his management till he sold it out to another publisher. He then applied himself to the study of law, and was soon admitted to the bar. Subsequently he founded the Legal Reporter, which contains the decisions of the State Supreme court, which appointed Mr. Baxter Assistant State Reporter. His publication "supplied a pressing want," and the nine bound volumes of the Reporter are officially recognized authority. At this time Mr. Baxter was but twenty-five years old.

His enterprising spirit was not quite satisfied with the monotony of legal reporting, and he conceived the idea of building what is known as the Baxter Block, on Union between Cherry and Summer streets, in 1879–80 The new Baxter Court, recently erected by him on Church street, is the most admirable office building in the city, and equal to any in the South; with its broad magnificent front, extending far above the adjacent buildings, it attracts the attention of spectators at once. It is six stories high, and contains forty-two rooms which are all leased from three to five years, to first-class occupants.

In the fall of 1879, he engaged in the railroad business, against the advice of his father and brother—who urged him to stick to his profession—and, from November 21, 1880, to November 22, 1882, he was vice-president of the Memphis and Charleston railroad, and from November, 1882, to November, 1883, president of that road, when his term expired. Immediately thereafter, however, he was again elected vice-president of the road, by request of Gen. Hancock.

About this time he began to investigate the coal and iron fields of North Alabama; organized a company composed of George I. Seney, Gen. Samuel Thomas, Calvin S. Brice and others, in the north; J. C. Neely, Napoleon Hill, of Memphis; Samuel Keith, Nat. Baxter, jr., John P. Williams, James C. Warner, and A. M. Shook, Nashville, and others in Atlanta and Montgomery, and was elected president of the company. They purchased two hundred thousand acres of coal and iron lands in that section and are now building a railroad from Tuscumbia to Birmingham to put coal and iron on water transportation—the first time in the history of the South. This road is known, as the Sheffield and Birmingham railroad, and Sheffield, Alabama, on the Tennessee river, is its northern terminus.

Mr. Baxter enjoyed the distinction of being the youngest railroad president in the United States, and is already classed among railroad magnates.

He contributed very greatly to the founding of Sheffield, in Alabama, being largely interested in the stock of the company, and by his push and energy and sublime faith, did probably more than any other one individual towards bringing about the prosperity of that place. He also organized the company to buy South Pittsburg, and is now engaged in building up Arkansas City, which, as president, he is pushing to the front as one of the best commercial points in the South.

While engaged in these multifarious projects, Mr. Baxter bought Maplewood, an extensive farm, settled long ago. He built his present residence, a stately brick, the first two-story brick building in that section of country. The interior furnishings of the beautiful Maplewood residence were selected with the greatest care, and the evidences of wealth and artistic taste are seen on every hand. Rare books, war implements, Revolutionary relics, Grecian statuary, Japanese embroidery, and curiosities in almost every line are to be seen by those who are so fortunate as to visit this delightful home. Maplewood farm is one of the richest and best stocked in the South, and the work under Mr. Baxter's direction is performed in the most systematic and thorough manner. There are twenty-eight hydrants about the place, over two miles of water pipe, and a wind-mill

which does nearly all the pumping from a well eighty feet deep. Five thousand dollars is invested in machinery, and probably half as much more in farm implements. Two hundred horses and fancy thoroughbred cattle wear collars, and at night in the winter or bad weather, each animal is haltered. These facts convey but a poor idea of Mr. Baxter's system and scientific methods in farming.

Mr. Baxter was married at Terre Haute, Indiana, May 24, 1877, to Miss Mattie Mack, daughter of Judge William Mack, of that city. Miss Mack was educated in Cincinnati, and after leaving school traveled extensively in Europe and Egypt. With her brilliant literary attainments and accomplishments in the fine arts, she combines a rare practical judgment and a keen perception of character—qualities which, clad with a queenly presence and graces both of person and manner, mark her as the perfect woman. Of this marriage have been born two sons, Mack and Jere Baxter, jr.

The great success which Mr. Baxter has achieved at so early a period in his life, entitles him to be classed among the most remarkable men which this country has ever produced. His intuition, will power, fertility of resource, strength of constitution, power of endurance and tensity of purpose ensure success in anything he undertakes. By always overcoming difficulties, he has but few difficulties to overcome. What would appear insuperable obstacles to most other men only act as a stimulus to the boldness of his character. He never acknowledges a defeat. When once he fairly enters upon his work all the concentration of his immense energies is directed to its accomplishment. He has been aptly termed a steam engine on legs. Difficulties vanish like bodiless specters at his approach. He is never at a loss to provide a remedy. In this he stands pre-eminent among all his associates. With a sanguine temperament, never giving way to discouraging circumstances, he inspires confidence and wins victories. This peculiarity of temperament would make him a great general. He never knows when he is whipped. When his plans are thwarted in one direction, like a great floodtide, he seeks other outlets, and always comes out conqueror. His mind is severely analytical and at the same time synthetical. He sees at a glance all the weak points in a proposition and provides for them. He combines with the power of a master and brings every agency to work for him. There is no mystery or luck in his success. His powers of intellect, supplemented by a vigorous physical constitution, all bearing in one direction, are simply invincible. He is a good manager of men and always works in the lead. He selects his agents with rare skill and judgment and forms his combinations so as to bear on the strongest points in the accomplishment of his purposes. He is frank and open and keeps nothing in the background, believing that the best way to inspire confidence is to have no secrets. One always knows where Mr. Baxter stands, and he is either an open foe or a sincere friend. His aptitude for acquiring information is very great. He learns in a few days all the salient points in any new field which he may enter. The writer of this sketch has had ample opportunities to admire the readiness with which he familiarizes himself with new subjects, and after a little study he presents them with a perspecuity that is unsurpassed. His liberality is unbounded. No one in distress ever went to Mr. Baxter without having his distress mitigated. He gives largely of his substance. His donations to charitable institutions and churches within the past five years would make a very respectable patrimony. Among his recent gifts is one of ten acres of land for the building of a Widows' and Orphans' Home.

While not regarding Mr. Baxter as faultless, his faults are not so much against society as against himself. With his commanding powers it would be a miracle to have no faults; but these faults are of such a nature that age will cure them. The broad character of Mr. Baxter and his liberal judgment, often too severe on himself, will soon reduce these faults to a minimum. His career thus far is a remarkable one, and life has barely opened to him. He is not yet in his prime, and his friends and country all look forward to the accomplishment of much greater things by him. He has the ability, the courage, the energy, the tenacity of purpose and the power of combination which ought to place him among the great men of the republic.

HON. H. H. INGERSOLL.

KNOXVILLE.

JUDGE INGERSOLL was born in Lorain county, Ohio, in 1844, but has been a resident of Tennessee for more than twenty years, and has taken rank among the State's most prominent and valued adopted citizens. He is a fair representative of that better class of men the tide of war brought to Tennessee, and the State is richer for the fact that when the tide went out, he found permanent lodgment on our shores.

In boyhood Judge Ingersoll worked as a farmer's lad on his father's farm, two miles out from Oberlin, and also worked occasionally in a printing office as a printer's boy. When the late war came on, he was barely turned sixteen, but with boyish enthusiasm, he resolved to enter the Federal army and fight for the preservation of the Union. He enlisted as a private in the Seventh Ohio infantry regiment, Col. Tyler commanding. His regiment went with Gen. George B. McClellan, on his campaign through the wild, rugged region of the West Virginia mountains. Serving that campaign, he returned home to complete his education. In the winter of 1861, he entered Yale College, Connecticut, as a junior. His educational advantages prior to going to college were exceptionally good, as he attended the public schools every winter until fourteen years old, after which he taught school during the winter months, taking charge of his first school when he was only fifteen years old. Being the youngest of a family of six children, four of whom are college graduates, his educational training at home was first-class. As a boy, he was very fond of study and of play; he worked because he was bidden, and because he wanted pocket money. His parents, who were of strict old Presbyterian or Puritanical stock, did not believe in spoiling a boy by giving him money to spend. Taught by them that idleness is a disgrace, and that without industry

and economy one could not expect to succeed in life, his early steps were well directed. His systematic habits, however, are not more the result of study and painstaking than of heredity from his mother, who was a most industrious, busy, excellent housekeeper, ambitious for her children, and systematic in everything, in fact, as regular as the mantel clock in all her household duties. This trait appears to-day in Judge Ingersoll's conduct of his cases in court. Always ready, always prompt, the steps he takes logically follow each other, and are the evidences of carefully studied and prepared plans—always pre-arranged.

A turning point in his young life occurred when about fifteen or sixteen years old, he chanced to meet a traveling phrenologist and physiologist—a superior man in his vocation, big brained, big bodied, big souled. After examining young Ingersoll's head and physique, and learning that he was given too much to study, he told him he would do a great deal better for himself if he would give up his place at the head of his class as a student and scholar, and would never neglect physical exercise, which he advised him to take every day three or four hours; "because," said he, "you have not more than two-thirds as much body as you need; to succeed in life you must have a stouter body to carry your head." He followed the advice, and left Yale College the third strongest man, physically, in a class of one hundred and twenty-five; and from a chest measure of thirty-five inches at sixteen, he has grown to a measure of forty inches. To this is attributable much of Judge Ingersoll's success, as he has always been able to endure the severest mental strain and most exhausting professional labor without breaking down.

His parents assured him when a lad he should have as good an education as the country afforded, but after that he must make his own living. The idea in their minds was that from his boyhood he should be equipped for a start in life, mentally and morally, equal to the best, and that then he must win the race for himself. His life was planned on the idea that success follows a law, and that there is no excellence without labor.

He graduated A.B. at Yale, in the class of 1863, and in 1866, his *alma mater* conferred on him the degree of A.M. He graduated under the learned and celebrated faculty comprising President Woolsey and Profs. Porter, Dana, Whitney, Loomis, Hadley, Thatcher and Dwight. Of his fellow graduates, several have since become prominent men in many stations, among them, William C. Whitney, present secretary of the navy; Bishop Whitehead, of Pennsylvania; Prof. Sumner, of Yale; Judge Vann, of New York ; President Perry, of Drury College in Nebraska; H. L. Terrell, esq., and Dr. Keys, of New York city; Dr. Shepard, of Charleston, South Carolina, and George Sheffield, a capitalist, of New Haven.

At Yale College young Ingersoll devoted himself equally to his studies and to athletic sports, being every day in the gymnasium or boating in the harbor. To this and a similar course of exercise, he owes his strong and compact frame and physique. He chose to content himself with a good or fair scholarship in order to get the very best physical training. As a consequence of this double course of education, he has not suffered serious sickness from the day of his graduation till the present time ; but in the midst of arduous and exacting professional labor, he has always had a sufficient reserve force to bear him through ; and this is to be attributed as much to that excellent physical training as to the good constitution inherited from his mother, a woman of great moral and physical strength and energy. In college he was fondest of mathematics and languages, in which his attainments are about equal.

Immediately after leaving college he went to Kenton, Ohio, and at nineteen, consented to take control of a school of six hundred pupils, in eight departments, studying law at the same time under Col. A. S. Ramsey, of Kenton. In 1864, he read in the office of Mr. William M. Ramsey, of Cincinnati. He was admitted to the bar at Kenton, by Judge Jacob Brinkerhoff, of the Ohio Supreme bench, and Judge J. S. Conkling, of the common pleas bench.

After admission to the bar, he practiced little in Ohio, but studied a good deal. In November, 1865, he came to Greeneville, Tennessee, and practiced law there till 1878, in partnership, first, with James Britton, then attorney-general, and H. L. Terrell, esq., a Yale class-mate, who came with him. The latter is now general counsel of the East Tennessee, Virginia and Georgia railroad, at New York. This firm dissolved in 1869, and Judge Ingersoll associated with himself in practice of law, F. W. Earnest, of Jonesborough, 1871 to 1874. In 1878, he located at Knoxville, where he

has resided ever since, in partnership in law practice, 1878–9, with Col. John M. Fleming, who had been one of the most accomplished newspaper editors in the State. From 1879 to 1885, he has had four concurrent partnerships : Ingersoll & Dosser, Jonesborough ; Ingersoll & Shoun, Greeneville; Ingersoll & Cocke, Knoxville ; Ingersoll & Park, Dandridge.

For the last five years of President Andrew Johnson's life, Judge Ingersoll was his attorney and counsel, and while at Greeneville occupied, by Mr. Johnson's request, an office adjoining his own.

For two years, March, 1879, to December, 1880, he was judge of the Supreme court commission at Knoxville, appointed by Gov. A. S. Marks, with the advice and consent of the senate.

In September, 1878, he was appointed by Gov. Marks special Supreme judge at Knoxville, and under appointment from Gov. Bate, September, 1884, he held the same position for a year in several important cases.

In 1884, he edited " Barton's Suit in Equity," published by Robert Clark & Co., Cincinnati, re-writing a large part of the text so as to conform the book to modern practice, and make a work useful to students and practitioners.

As an advocate, he is best known from his defense of Capt. Johnson, tried in 1885, at Greeneville, for killing Maj. Henry, for the seduction of his wife. It was the most famous of recent criminal trials in the State ; and to his preparation and conduct of the case in successfully introducing evidence of insanity, and his address to the jury upon the law of insanity, seduction and homicide, as well as on the facts of the case, Senator Vorhees, his eloquent associate, attributed the acquittal of their client.

As a judge, he has the true judicial mind—coming to conclusions only after the most careful research. There are two classes of minds in judges—one that decides at first blush and finds reasons afterward; the other that examines the reasons first, and upon that reasoning bases conclusions. The first takes conclusions like a politician, and then hunts up the reason for it afterward. This may be called judge-craft. To the second class Judge Ingersoll belongs.

Judge Ingersoll came to Tennessee at twenty-one, having no kindred or acquaintance in the State. His alarm at the excesses and disorder then prevalent, in 1865, in East Tennessee, and his indignation at the cruelty, injustice and violence then practiced under the Brownlow *regime*, made him, following the bent of his nature, a conservative. There was no Democratic or Republican party there then. All were either radicals or conservatives. He enlisted on the side of the latter with energy and zeal in the contest then going on in Tennessee, and with a resolution never to abandon it till the State was released from the domination of a factious, ignorant and tyrannical minority. At that time all the Confederates in the State were disfranchised. They could neither hold office, vote, or even sit on a jury—and he resolved to give himself no rest in politics until the intelligence, wealth and moral character of the State could take part in its government. He had the pleasure of witnessing and contributing to that result in 1869. With his own hand he signed the papers of enfranchisement for more than a thousand citizens of Greene county. During that period he had a contest also with a tyrannical radical judge, who disbarred lawyers for refusing to take the test oath. Taking up the cudgel in behalf of his brother lawyers, a contest for right ensued, in which he was successful in attaining a judgment of the Supreme court in his favor, and also in securing the passage of an act of the Legislature disestablishing the court that had disbarred him. Judge Ingersoll is a Democrat from sentiment, sympathy and conviction, and has frequently been a delegate to the Democratic State conventions and a regular participant in every political canvass, from 1867 till 1885, except the one of 1882. Besides the judgeships above cited, he has held no offices except that, in 1876 he was the Democratic elector in the First Tennessee district, on the Tilden and Hendricks ticket.

He became a Mason in 1865, in Kenton, Ohio; was made a Knight Templar, at Knoxville, in 1881, and has served as Worshipful Master, High Priest and Captain-General; and has been, for several years, chairman of the committee on appeals and grievances in the Grand Lodge of Tennessee. He is now Senior Grand Warden of that body. He received the 33° of the Scottish Rite in 1884, at Knoxville, and is presiding officer (commander-in chief) of Knoxville Consistory, No. 10. He is also a member of the Grand Army of the Republic. He attends the Protestant Episcopal church, and believes, like Ben Adhem, in religion that ennobles man, lifts him higher and makes him better—that teaches man to love his fellow-man and keep the golden rule; to do right, love the good and speak the truth; that saves man in this world as well as in the next.

Judge Ingersoll married, in Kenton, Ohio, April 11, 1864, Miss Emily G. Rogers, who was born April 18, 1846, daughter of Everett Rogers, a native of Virginia, a contractor and builder. Her mother, nee Catharine Eliza Campbell, was born in Berks county, Pennsylvania, and is a descendant of the clan Campbell, of Scotland. Mrs. Ingersoll was educated at the Wesleyan Female College, Delaware, Ohio, and is a lady of cultivated mind and many graces. She has fine taste as a housekeeper, is very fond of society, excels as a conversationalist, and is noted among her friends and acquaintances for her unstinted hospitality and art of entertaining. She is a woman of decided strength of character, and resolution, and of warm attachments. Her friends and her husband's friends she never forgets.

By his marriage with Miss Rogers, Judge Ingersoll has had two children : (1). Everett Ingersoll, who died in early infancy. (2). Mabel Rogers Ingersoll, born at Greeneville, Tennessee, May 12, 1868; graduated, in 1883, from the Knoxville High School, and in 1886, from the Brooklyn Heights Seminary.

The family name, Ingersoll, derived from the old Danish or Saxon, means "palace in a meadow." The family is Saxon, and appears in English history in the records of the Domesday Book. The ancestral home is in Bedfordshire, England. In 1629, two brothers, Richard and John Ingersoll, emigrated to the American colonies, landed on Massachusetts soil, and settled at Salem. From these two brothers are descended all of the Ingersolls of America. Two have been governors of Connecticut. Five have been members of congress, Charles J., Joseph R., of Philadelphia ; Ralph I., and Colin M., of New Haven, and Ebon C., of Illinois. It was over the remains of the latter that his brother, the celebrated Col. Robert G. Ingersoll, uttered the beautiful sentiments: "This brave and tender man in every storm of life was oak and rock ; but in the sunshine he was vine and flower. He was the friend of all heroic souls. He climbed the heights and left all superstitions far below, while on his forehead fell the golden dawning of a grander day. He added to the sum of human joy, and were every one for whom he did some loving service to bring a blossom to his grave, he would sleep to-night beneath a wilderness of flowers. Life is a narrow vale, between the cold and barren peaks of two eternities; we strive in vain to look beyond the heights ; we cry aloud, and the only answer is the echo of our wailing cry. From the voiceless lips of the unreplying death there comes no word ; but in the night of death hope sees a star and listening love can hear the rustle of a wing."

Among other members of the family who have made the Ingersoll name famous, there was Jared Ingersoll, of Pennsylvania, who was one of the framers of the constitution of the United States in 1787, and Federal candidate for vice-president in 1812; Charles J. Ingersoll was United States minister to the court of St. James, 1850-53; Judge J. E. Ingersoll, of Cleveland, Ohio, and Judge O. M. Ingersoll, of Chicago, and Rev. Dr. E. P. Ingersoll, of Brooklyn, New York, have also added to the reputation of the family; Maj. "Jack" Ingersoll, of Mobile, and William K. Ingersoll, a lawyer, of Vicksburg, are also well known and highly regarded. One of the best known of the family in New York, was Chandler L. Ingersoll, a ship and boat builder, who made a world-wide reputation as a builder of boats and yachts. Of late years Col. Robert. G. Ingersoll, of Washington, the eminent lawyer and the most eloquent lecturer and orator in the United States, has made the name more conspicuous than any other member of the family. Ernest Ingersoll, of New Haven, is also a naturalist and popular author and magazine contributor of high repute.

The father of Judge Ingersoll, Rev. William Ingersoll, was born at Lee, Massachusetts, December 22,

1801; married at Lee; was a farmer, and an evangelist of the Congregational church. He moved to Oberlin, Ohio, as a pioneer of that place, in 1838, and died in May, 1873. He was a man of singular purity, uprightness and piety of character; a man of very decided convictions and positive views, but of great charity and sweetness of temper. He inherited his character, moral and intellectual, from his mother, who was a granddaughter of the Rev. Jonathan Edwards, the distinguished Calvinist divine and author, and president of Princeton College, New Jersey.

The grandfather, David Ingersoll, was also a native of Lee, Massachusetts, born about 1760; married Miss Sarah Parsons, of Stockbridge, Massachusetts, and died at Lee, a farmer, about eighty years of age, leaving thirteen children.

The great-grandfather was known as Esquire William Ingersoll, a native of Springfield, Massachusetts. He was the settler of the town of Lee, founder of the church at that place, and a magistrate of that town for many years. On his gravestone, at Lee, is inscribed: "Satisfied with living and rejoicing in hope of glory, he died August 10, 1815, aged ninety-one years and four months, leaving behind him, in this dying world, one hundred and forty-nine descendants."

Judge Ingersoll's mother, nee Semantha Bassett, was born at Lee, Massachusetts, July 10, 1805, and died at Cincinnati, Ohio, February 12, 1882. Her father, Ansel Bassett, was a native of Massachusetts, a carpenter. Her mother was Mary Dimmock, daughter of old Maj. Dimmock, of Barnstable, Massachusetts, an officer in the Revolutionary war. Judge Ingersoll's brothers are Rev. Edward P. Ingersoll, D.D., pastor of the Church of the Puritans, Brooklyn, New York, and Ansel B. Ingersoll, of Sidney, Ohio. Judge Ingersoll's sisters are, Julia, wife of William B. Wordin, esq., Ridgeville, Ohio; Mary Jane, wife of J. H. Drew, St. Louis, Missouri, and Abbie, wife of W. W. Roberts, Cincinnati, Ohio.

Judge Ingersoll has a good constitution, inherited from his parents, a first-class education, self-reliance, persistent industry, tireless energy, and a devoted application to his profession, together with the use of strong common sense and judgment in the every day affairs of life. Books he has studied very much, men more. Added to these factors of his success, must be mentioned his characteristic honesty of purpose, sincerity and frankness in dealing with men, whereby he has gained and held their confidence. He has always cherished in a high degree a feeling of self-respect, without which no man can maintain a high character. Three writers have most largely influenced his character and conduct in life. After the teachings of Jesus in the four Gospels, he has most read for moral instruction the writings of Carlyle and Emerson.

He recommends to his young friends to study the teachings of the Proverbs of Solomon, the advice which Polonius gives to Laertes in "Hamlet," and Bobby Burns' "Epistle to a Young Friend." These have greatly influenced him. Besides, temperance in habit and in speech, in thought and in conduct, and self-control, have contributed no little to the success he has achieved, the foundation of which has been firmly laid in intelligence, integrity and industry.

As Judge Ingersoll has been frequently in the local lecture field, this sketch of his life may be appropriately concluded with a short extract from his lecture on "Children":

"I think it not strange that the old Persians were sun worshipers. Men must worship something. They always have worshiped Power. And what form of force so potent, what energy so persistent, as the blessed sunbeam, dispensing its gracious light and heat?

"It sprouts the seed, swells the bud, bursts the blossom, and ripens the fruit. It gilds the dawn and gladdens the day, which, even dying, rejoices in its Hesperian beams. It paints with beauteous tints the sweet cheek of the ripening fruit, and the sweeter face of the laughing girl. It gives the gaudy, leonine beauty to the sunflower, and the perfect loveliness to the lily. It clothes the meadow in a richer green than Lyons factor or Brussels weaver can give his fabric, and spreads upon the flower garden a robe of more gorgeous variety than was ever seen in far-famed Gobelin tapestry.

"It wakens alike the melody of the song-bird, and the chorus of the chanticleers, the joyous prattle of the babe and the lusty call of the herdsman. It dances in the sparkling rivulet, and shimmers in the smooth surface of the lake. It startles you in

the Borealis race
That flit ere you can point their place.

It gladdens you in

the rainbow's lovely form,
Evanishing amid the storm.

"It hath separated the light from the darkness, and the water from the dry land; and in the ages gone it hath prepared the coal and the diamond, and stored them away in mountain and river for the use of men and women to-day. It shines upon the mountain, and it crumbles; upon the blade of grass, and it grows. It gives health to the sick and strength to the weak, courage to the timid and hope to the despairing. It vivifies all nature, and maketh glad the heart of man.

"Love is the sunlight of society. Open the windows of the soul, and it cheers and gladdens all within. This sunlight of love I bespeak for the children. It is their birth-right—their heavenly heritage."

D. M. HENNING, M.D.

HENNING.

DR. HENNING was born in Clarke county, Georgia, August 24, 1813, and was brought up there, doing work on his father's farm and going to school at intervals until grown to manhood, when his father moved to Madison county, Tennessee, in 1833, and there he worked three years more on the farm. Among his classmates in Franklin College, Athens, Georgia, which he attended about two years, were Hon. Alexander H. Stephens, Gov. Howell Cobb, Gen. Robert Toombs and Bishop Pierce—a quartette of Georgia's ablest and most distinguished sons.

After coming to Tennessee, young Henning took charge of his father's farm three years, and then began the study of medicine in the office of Drs. John and Thomas Ingram, at Denmark, Madison county, Tennessee. In 1835–6, he took a course of lectures in Jefferson Medical College, Philadelphia, and in 1836–7, a second course, graduating, in 1837, under Profs. Robert Dunglison, Patterson, McClellan (father of Gen. George B. McClellan), Sam McClellan, Green and Revere.

When he went to Philadelphia to study medicine, upon his arrival there, he opened his trunk and found a small Bible, in which was placed a piece of paper, containing advice in his mother's handwriting, requesting him to meet her at the throne of grace, at an hour named, and if he would not do that, to at least remember that at that hour—at the hour he had left—his mother was praying for her son. This incident led to the conversion of the son, and shaped his entire future life. The editor deems a record of this fact as of more importance as an incentive to mothers who would influence their children for good and for all time, than would be a story of battles, sieges, and " hair-breadth escapes in the imminent deadly breach."

After graduating, he returned home and practiced physic in Haywood county two years, in partnership with Dr. Allen J. Barbee, but not making much money for some years. Indeed, his beginning was not promising in a financial point of view. In 1838, he moved to Lauderdale county, purchased some town property in Durhamville, and has been a citizen of that county ever since, accumulating property year by year by his practice, but mostly by buying and selling lands in that county, and now owns five thousand five hundred and thirty-seven acres in ten separate tracts, on two tracts of which are towns, Gates on one tract, and Henning, named by the railroad company for himself, on another, and on eight others he has farms in cultivation. He practiced medicine from the time of his graduation up to the war, since when he has not been in the regular practice. During his practice, which extended from Brownsville to the Mississippi river, it took four horses

to supply him, and he had often to stay in negro cabins at night, the country then being new and thinly settled. He never had a spell of sickness that amounted to anything, except an occasional chill, and still looks the picture of health, at the age of seventy-one. His habits have not been irregular except what was open to his profession, but he has never been intoxicated, and has lived in all respects a prudent life.

He belongs to only one secret institution, to-wit, Masonry, with which he has been connected from his young manhood, and which he served as Master of the lodge, at Durhamville, for several years. He was an old line Whig until the war, but since that time has voted the Democratic ticket, but never held an office or asked for one. In 1838, he joined the Methodist church, and has served as financial officer of that denomination.

Dr. Henning married, in Haywood county, Tennessee, December —, 1839, Miss Ann Balloune Greaves, who was born in South Carolina, the daughter of Bennett Greaves, a rice planter in that State, but a cotton planter in Tennessee after 1833, when he moved to Haywood county, where he died. Her mother was a Miss Rachel Davis, also of South Carolina, of Scotch descent. Her sister, Addie, is the wife of William Shaw, formerly sheriff of Haywood county. Mrs. Henning was educated at Lagrange, Fayette county, and Brownsville, Haywood county, Tennessee. She lived a modest, retired, religious life, without attempt at show or desire to make herself prominent in any way, except by her Christian principles of virtue and fidelity, and in all the relations of life was devoted to her God and her family. Her peculiar character was so excellent in all directions, and made so deep an impression on her surviving husband, that he has not contemplated a second marriage. She died in September, 1878, at the age of sixty.

By his marriage with Miss Greaves, Dr. Henning has three children living: (1). Frances A. Henning, educated at Lauderdale Female Institute, at Durhamville; married William H. Moorer, a farmer, who had served as a soldier in the Confederate army, under Gen. Forrest. She has six children living, Willie, Charles, " Tee," Annie, Frances and " Judge." (2). Bennett G. Henning, a physician at Memphis, whose sketch appears in another part of this volume. He married a daughter of Dr. Frayser, of Memphis, whose sketch also appears in another part of this book, and by her has three children living, David M., Emma and Bennett. (3). Ella Henning, educated at Jackson (Tennessee) Female College, and married Dr. Henry B. Moorer, brother of William H. Moorer, above mentioned, and has one child living, Henry B.

Dr. Henning has had nine children, six of whom are dead; five of them died in infancy. One, Addie Henning, married Dr. James Hall, of Clinton, Mississippi, and died suddenly, two years after her marriage, leaving one child, David Meriwether, now being raised by his grandfather, Dr. Henning, who makes his home with his daughter, Mrs. Frances Moorer, at Henning, Tennessee.

Dr. Henning's father, John Henning, was born in South Carolina. In that State he married a Miss Greene, who died, leaving him two children, both of whom are now dead. His second wife, Judith Burnley Meriwether (mother of Dr. Henning), was the daughter of Gen. David Meriwether, of Georgia, of Revolutionary fame. By this lady he had nine children, five sons, Joseph, David, (subject of this sketch), James, William and Francis, and four daughters, Eliza Jane, Frances Ann, Sarah Thomas, and Henrietta. Of the sons, all are dead except Dr. Henning. Of the daughters, only two survive.

Dr. Henning's father, Rev. John Henning, was a farmer and a Methodist preacher, belonging to the South Carolina conference, and afterward to the Georgia conference. He died in Haywood county, Tennessee, sixty-seven years old, leaving a spotless reputation as an heirloom to his church and family. He was married three times, his last wife being Mrs. Loftin, who still survives him. He was a Welshman by birth, and came to America from Wales, with his brother, Thomas, and settled in South Carolina. Thomas Henning married and settled in that State.

For five years Dr. Henning was a director, and two years of that time was vice-president, of the Mississippi Valley railroad, afterward called the Paducah and Memphis railroad, and now the Chesapeake, Ohio and Southwestern railroad—an important link in the great "Huntingdon system." He has been a stern, fixed and undeviating friend of the Chesapeake, Ohio and Southwestern road from its inception, and paid the first dollar that was advanced to mark out its line. In 1873, he resigned his position as vice-president of the Paducah and Memphis railroad, since which time he has held no official position with the road. But in 1883, the county court of Lauderdale county appointed him and Dr. Wardlow to adjust the indebtedness of the county to the railroad, amounting to two hundred and twenty-five thousand dollars, which they did to the satisfaction of the tax-payers of the county, and of the railroad company.

When Dr. Henning came to Tennessee to practice physic, he settled on the borders of emigration, without money, and his success is attributable to the fact that, in all his speculations in life he adhered to this principle: That if he borrowed money, he would pay it back on the exact day promised. On this rule, his veracity being at stake, his character as a gentleman being at stake, he has often borrowed money at twenty-five per

73

cent. to pay a debt drawing six per cent. This method of his becoming known, he won the unlimited confidence of the people, and his promise circulated as current money with the merchant. Of old time it was said, "A good name is rather to be preferred than great riches." And certainly a good name is a power. It opens all the avenues to men's hearts, and to all departments of trade and business. It is worth more than ready money in hand, for it represents values, and when transmitted, it is a letter of introduction and credit to sons and grandchildren, opening to them the doors into society and into the great commercial centers and circles which control the markets of the world. This gentleman, having from the start set a value on his good name, has won a reputation for honor, truth and conscience that has given him a place among the standard men of the country, such that men speak of it as an honor that he is among their friends and they among his associates.

Dr. Henning stands five feet eleven inches in height; weighs one hundred and ninety pounds; has blue eyes, fair complexion, and an expression of kindliness and benignity. His conversation is a continuous flow of animated narrative, abounding in anecdote and personal mention of characters who have figured in the history of the country, and with whom he has been more or less connected. For instance, he voted for the celebrated Davy Crockett for congress, and delights to tell of the peculiarities of that uncouth, yet able and celebrated backwoods statesman. In his manners Dr. Henning is very plain and unpretentious, and without the appearance of that pride which is akin to arrogance. Yet he is a man of positive character and influences, such as attach strong friendships and tend to build up communities in material and moral prosperity.

___

Since the above sketch was prepared, Dr. D. M. Henning has passed away, having died at the residence of his son-in-law, Henry B. Moorer, in Henning, on Friday, May 21, 1886, in the seventy-third year of his age. The following obituary is taken from the columns of a local newspaper:

"The lives of but few men have been more intimately associated with the growth and prosperity of this section than the one whose name heads this notice. He was born in Georgia, in 1813, and his parents removed to Madison county, Tennessee, at a very early day, where Mr. Henning resided until after he graduated as a physician. He then settled near Durhamville, in 1839, and practiced his profession there for many years.

"Of strong common sense and excellent judgment, he early saw the advantages which this section naturally possessed, and his life was spent in efforts to increase its material wealth. A brusque and apparently austere manner covered the kindest of hearts, and no one ever appealed to him for aid in vain. Without ostentation he gave liberally to every charity. A shrewd business man, his simple word was a guarantee, binding as any bond.

"Since the death of his wife, which occurred in 1878, Dr. Henning resided with his children, and at the time of his death was living with his daughter. Mrs. Henry Moorer. He sat down to the dinner table on Friday last in apparently good health, but became unconscious and died in a few moments after sitting down. He was a member of the Methodist church, and was buried a Trinity church, in Haywood county, where rest his wife and several children. He leaves a son and daughter— Dr. B. G. Henning, of Memphis, and Mrs. Moorer."

ETHELBERT BARKSDALE WADE.

MURFREESBOROUGH.

ALTHOUGH comparatively a young man, the subject of this sketch will be recognized as a conspicuous personage, oftentimes seen in the capital building at Nashville during legislative sessions, while his face has been a familiar one in nearly all the State Democratic conventions covered by *post bellum* politics.

It does not often happen that a teacher lives to become the biographer of one of his pupils, as in the present instance, and those of Hon. James D. Richardson and Dr. John H. White, whose sketches will ‚be found elsewhere in this volume. The first two of these gentlemen, when mere lads, were for a time under the editor of this volume, while he had charge of Central Academy, in their fathers' neighborhood, and it is with the greater pleasure that he writes their sketches, because of their personal merit and the excellence of their respective families. Both had a good send-off, their fathers being wealthy, distinguished and representative men, and each son having inherited the leading and peculiar traits of his father. Some one has wittily said that if he were called on to advise a boy how to succeed in life, he would tell him first to select a good father and mother to be born of. In the case of Mr. Wade, as also of Maj. Richardson, they had a good induction, their respective parents ranking among the very first people of their county. Their fathers have passed away, but live again and are worthily represented in the sons.

The subject of this sketch was born in Rutherford county, Tennessee, where he still resides, September 24, 1843. Ethelbert was educated at the "old brick academy" (Central Academy), in Rutherford county, under several teachers, but the war coming on when he was seventeen, his education was cut short, and he has never been to school since.

In August, 1861, he enlisted in the Eighteenth Tennessee Confederate infantry regiment, under Col. (afterward Gen.) Joseph B. Palmer, a soldier and officer of distinction, and served with that regiment in Tennessee and Kentucky as a private. He was captured at Fort Donelson in February, 1862, taken to Springfield, Illinois, and imprisoned in Camp Butler till the following summer, when he made his escape and joined Bragg's army at Sparta, Tennessee, on its way into Kentucky. He served through the Kentucky campaign in the Fifth Arkansas regiment (Col. Featherston), and was in the battle of Perryville. When the army returned to Tennessee, his old regiment (Eighteenth Tennessee), which had been exchanged, participated in the battle of Murfreesborough, and when the army retreated to Tullahoma, January, 1863, he received an appointment in the regular army of the Confederate States, and was assigned to duty on Gen. John B. Hood's staff, as an aid-de-camp, and served in that capacity with that distinguished soldier in all his victories and defeats, till the end of the war, surrendering at Albany, Georgia, where he was on leave of absence awaiting orders, after Gen. Hood was relieved of the command of the army of Tennessee.

After the war he returned to Rutherford county, and has been engaged in farming ever since. In the meantime he has been elected assistant clerk of the Tennessee house of representatives two terms, and principal clerk four terms. From January to December, 1884, he was clerk to the committee on mines and mining of the United States house of representatives, resigned that position to accept the chief clerkship of the Tennessee house of representatives, session of 1885. In 1885–6, he received an appointment in the lower house of congress, and also acted as Washington correspondent of the Nashville *Daily American*.

In politics he is a thorough Democrat. Besides the offices above named he has served two terms (three years a term) as school director of his home district. In 1884, he was alternate delegate from the Fifth congressional district to the national Democratic convention at Chicago that nominated Cleveland and Hendricks. He belongs to no secret society, but is a member of the Presbyterian church. ,

Mr. Wade married, in Forsyth, Georgia, September 24, 1864, Miss Dora L. Cochran, who was born August 20, 1845, daughter of Hon. Allen Cochran, for several terms a member of the Georgia Legislature, a leading citizen of Monroe county, Georgia, and a large planter.

Her mother was a Miss West, of a family of large connection and influence in Georgia. Mrs. Wade was educated at Lucy Cobb Institute, Athens, Georgia, where she graduated in 1863. She was raised in affluence, but since the war she has entered the industries of life with a spirit and energy charactefistic of southern women, and her husband having a similar history and experience, she joined him in trying to keep up the prestige of their inherited names, and recover the fortunes swept away by the war. She is a lady of great energy, industry and perseverance, and is a member of the Baptist church.

The Wades came to Tennessee from Maryland. The grandfather Wade settled in Rutherford county about the year 1810. Ethelbert's father, Levi Wade, was born in Maryland, July 8, 1797, and came with his father to Tennessee while he was quite a youth ; began life with very little property, and just before the war owned two thousand acres of land in Rutherford county and one hundred and twenty-five slaves, besides railroad and bank stocks—property which he accumulated by farming, and buying cotton in the seed and ginning and shipping it to the cotton markets. He was a pushing man—very systematic in his business habits—a man of fine administrative ability—a splendid manager and universally respected for his integrity. In 1837, he represented Rutherford county in the Tennessee Legislature. He was a representative man, but very individual. Eminently social and friendly as a neighbor, and liberal in his sentiments, yet he wore his own head, held himself responsible to himself, managed his own affairs in his own way, worked in his own harness, and was never one of any man's following. His business he mastered in its minutest details and planned over night what each of eighty field hands must do the next day. He was always on time with his engagements. An ardent Whig, his ideal politician, next to Henry Clay, was his neighbor and friend, Dr. John W. Richardson, who for many years represented Rutherford county in the State Legislature. He (Wade) was a warm friend of education, and probably no father ever gave greater indulgence to his children. He gave them every advantage, with the largest freedom, to develop their distinctive personalities. He recognized their separate right to life, liberty, and the pursuit of happiness, and thus made them self-reliant, self-helpful, and, at the same time, self-controlling. In these respects he was himself their example. He was in later life known as " Esquire Wade," having at one time been a justice of the peace.

Ambitious to do the best he could, Ethelbert Wade, although he had no capital left him to start on, has fairly succeeded in life. He has filled the positions to which he has been called with marked ability and credit. His manners are pleasant, and he has a happy faculty of mixing with people and making friends. His habits are good, his morals conservative ; he never uses tobacco in any form, is temperate, and with a reputation above reproach. He is a tireless worker, a good manager, and faithful and impartial in his conduct as an officer.